1 MONTH OF
FREE
READING
at
www.ForgottenBooks.com

ISBN 978-0-483-50296-3
PIBN 10785110

THE AMERICAN JOURNAL

OF

SOCIOLOGY

Volume 4

1898-1899

Reprinted with the permission of the original publishers

JOHNSON REPRINT CORPORATION

NEW YORK, NEW YORK

THE AMERICAN JOURNAL

OF

SOCIOLOGY

EDITOR

ALBION W. SMALL

ASSOCIATE EDITORS

CHARLES R. HENDERSON   MARION TALBOT

FREDERICK STARR   CHARLES ZUEBLIN

GEORGE E. VINCENT   WILLIAM I. THOMAS

VOL. 4

BI-MONTHLY

JULY, 1898—MAY, 1899

CHICAGO

The University of Chicago Press

1899

First reprinting, 1959, Johnson Reprint Corporation

CONTENTS.

ARTICLES.

iii

REVIEWS.

CONTENTS

THE AMERICAN

JOURNAL OF SOCIOLOGY

VOLUME IV   JULY, 1898   NUMBER 1

A RETARDED FRONTIER.

AMERICAN history has been described as very largely a record of the westward movement of a frontier ; not a geographical boundary, but a type of social life which has reacted upon and modified the ideals and political institutions of the nation. Beginning in earnest after the Revolution, and getting a further impetus with the close of the war of 1812, this frontier swept on like a wave seeking channels of least resistance. It followed water courses—the Hudson, the Mohawk, and the Ohio ; it penetrated mountain passes, pouring through Cumberland and Big Stone gaps into Tennessee and Kentucky, and sweeping around the foothills of the Blue Ridge into Alabama. Having passed the Appalachian barrier, it spread over the prairies of the Mississippi basin until it broke against the Rockies. But this on-rushing tide left quiet pools in the mountains of Virginia, North Carolina, Kentucky, and Tennessee. There the frontier has survived in practical isolation until this very day. Only recently have we fully realized this fact, made vivid by the stories of Miss Murfree, Mr. John Fox, Jr., and other writers.

It was from a desire to see something of this old frontier life that I recently undertook a very short journey in the mountains of eastern Kentucky. In this descriptive article I shall simply jot down certain impressions and indicate a few lines of investigation which this interesting social survival suggests. It is hardly necessary to say that I have attempted no sweeping generalizations on the basis of a four-days' ride through parts of three counties.

Kentucky is divided into " Pennyroyal," " Bluegrass," and " Mountain." The boundaries of these popular provinces are somewhat vague ; but in general it is a division into western, central, and eastern sections. The mountain region is bounded on the east by the Big Sandy river and the Cumberland mountains, from which the hills, gradually descending, die away westward into the rolling Bluegrass country. This district of eastern Kentucky is drained by the Kentucky and Licking rivers and by tributary streams of the Big Sandy. The structure of the country is such as to form many narrow, isolated valleys, communicating with each other only by means of wide detours along the water courses, or by sharp and difficult ascents of the steep divides. The drainage system, therefore, as in most hilly country sides, creates social groupings, determines lines of travel, fixes the location of little settlements and county seats, and furnishes a means of local designation. There is an odd analogy between the address of the Londoner and that of the Kentucky mountaineer. Instead of the main thoroughfare, side street, and lane of the complex English description, we have the " fork," " creek," and " branch " of the Kentucky direction.

The region, originally well wooded, has in many places lost the most valuable of its trees, among which are poplar, oak, elm, ash, hickory, and walnut. Lumber companies and individuals are cutting timber rapidly and floating the logs down to the mills along the rivers. In many valleys whole mountain sides have been desolated by " girdling " the trees and leaving them to die and fall. Such areas are appropriately called " deadening." But in spite of all this, there are large districts of beautiful forest land, made more delightful still by a dense undergrowth of laurel and rhododendron. Throughout the western counties of the region there is abundance of bituminous coal and considerable deposits of excellent cannel. On many of the farms in Breathitt, Perry, and Knott counties it is not an unusual thing to find family coal pits from which fuel is dug as it is needed.

There are three general types of farms in this region: the valley farm, with its fields spread out along the bottom lands; the cove farm in the cove or hollow at the mouth of a "branch;" and the hill farm, pushing its corn fields up the steep slopes, sometimes to the very top.

MOUNTAIN GIRLS ON THE HIGHWAY

It was a hill farmer who, according to mountain tradition, fell out of his corn field and broke his neck. These three types are by no means clearly defined. Oftentimes the valley farm creeps up the mountain side, for the valleys at best are very narrow, and only where the stream has swept round the long curves and deposited a generous "bottom" is there chance for level tillage on a considerable scale.

The highways oftentimes set out pretentiously from the county seats, but when they leave the main streams and turn up the creeks there is rapid degeneration. The bed of the stream becomes the roadway for much of the distance, and in many valleys the fording is so frequent as to seem well-nigh continuous. Riding is almost the only means of travel. Saddle-bags are as commonly used as they were by circuit riders and other travelers in Indiana and Illinois fifty years ago. Wagons are relied upon only for transporting farm products and store goods. Oxen are generally the chief draught animals in the more remote regions. In the springtime a heavy rain of a few hours will cause "a tide" which for a day or more effectually puts a

stop to travel. In the summer the creeks are very low, and offer no obstacles save the loose stones which cover their beds. The population of this region is singularly free from what we are wont to call "foreign" elements. The mountaineers are predominantly, if not exclusively, of English, Irish, and Scotch origin. They came in the westward movement from Virginia and North

AN "UPRIGHT" CORN FIELD

Carolina. Such names as Noble, Allen, South, Strong, Combs, Sewell, Hargis, Stacy, and Mullins tell of British stock.[1]

By intermarriage for three or more generations the ties of kinship have been extended along the forks and creeks, until one is struck by the frequent recurrence of the same name. The family ties seem very strong and arouse, perhaps, the keenest sense of social solidarity to which the mountaineer responds. This tribal spirit has been a powerful factor in the feuds and

[1] Professor William I. Thomas, who spent several summers in the Cumberlands, gathered from the daily speech of the mountaineers a list of three hundred words obsolete since about the sixteenth century or surviving only in the dialects of England.

"wars" that have played so striking a part in mountain life during the last thirty years.

The typical mountain family very considerably must exceed the numerical average for the country as a whole. It is by no

A TYPICAL CABIN

means an unusual thing to find a family in which ten children have been born, while the number rarely falls below five or six. The general health, so far as one gets impressions from casual inquiry, seems to be exceptionally good. One mother asserted with pride that she had raised twelve children without losing one, and without so much as having a doctor in the house. She spoke learnedly of certain potent herbs, but she summed up her medical theory and practice by saying that when the children were sick she kept them in bed until they got well.

The houses of the mountains, outside of the county towns, are almost without exception built of hewn oak logs, dovetailed securely at the corners. The crevices are filled with mud, and generally a split oak strip is spiked between the logs. The pitched roofs are covered with long, hand-made shingles, irregular and curled. The chimney, except in the case of the poorer cabins, is made of stone, frequently carefully cut and fitted. The crudest form of chimney is built cob-house wise of small sticks, smeared inside and out with clay. Along the front of many cabins there is a covered "gallery" or porch. In the older houses there are no windows, all light and air being admitted through the door, or through the chinks between the logs. A "double" cabin is really a combination of two cabins under the same roof. Sometimes there -is an open space or hall between them. Again they are simply built end to end, the doors of both opening on the same gallery. In the latter case, although there seems no real separation, each room, from the standpoint of the other, is spoken of as " t'other house." Families of social pretension have, in addition to the two rooms of the main cabin, a cook-house at the rear, and in one establishment we found a dining-room beside. In a vague way, so far as there is any social stratification, it is reflected in the number of rooms of the family domicile. The one-room cabin represents the lowest stage, while the possession of four or five rooms confers real distinction.

The furniture of the cabins is primitive and simple. A sufficient number of bedsteads, sometimes of the old-fashioned four-poster type, often rough home-made products; a few hickory splint-bottom chairs, a table or two, and shelves for blankets or "kivers," complete the average equipment. In many houses there are old Connecticut clocks. In one cabin we saw two clocks side by side, keeping time exactly together. The old man pointed with pride to them and to the shadow of the sun upon the floor as it approached the noon mark.

Agricultural and industrial processes are relatively crude. The chief crops are corn, a little oats, potatoes, tobacco, and sugar cane. These supply all the staple products necessary to the family life. The list of domestic animals includes horses, cows, mules, sheep, pigs, geese, and chickens. The sheep and geese are kept for their wool and feathers, and are rarely killed for food.

The mill is the only mountain industry which has been specialized in any marked way. At intervals of a few miles along the streams there are log dams and small grist-mills, which look more like rustic summer houses than places of manufacture. Although the family ordinarily depends upon the water-mill, now and then there is a hand-mill near the cabin door, as a last resort in case the domestic economy, never very carefully organized, has failed to maintain its supply of corn meal. Iron working is largely given over to log blacksmith shops in the small settlements and at the crossroads. But on many of the isolated farms there are forges for domestic use. Tanning seems to be a rare industry among the mountaineers, who have come to depend for saddle and harness upon the storekeepers. Portable steam saw-mills have almost wholly superseded the old-time saw pit, with its "top-sawyer."

A HOME-MADE COTTON GIN

By far the most interesting industry is the making of textile fabrics. The men are now more rarely clad in home-made jeans, which they have exchanged for "store clothes." But the women still wear very generally, and always for common use, "linsey" gowns of their own weaving and making. Almost every cabin among the older mountaineers has its spinning-wheel and hand-loom. Many of the younger generation show a disposition either to buy store goods or to depend upon older and more skillful neighbors for the weaving of their cloth, if not for the carding and spinning of their wool.

The linsey is not, as we had fancied, a plain dull brown or gray. The yarns are dyed brilliant red, green, yellow, and blue, and are oftentimes woven in really complex patterns of checks and stripes. The rather brilliant, crude colors of the new material yield gradually to water and sun, softening frequently into pleasant and subdued tones. The mountaineers also raise small quantities of cotton and flax for muslin and linen. The coarse muslins of the stores, however, are too cheap to permit this industry greatly to enlarge. The mountain product of woolen dress goods, on the other hand, is held in high esteem,

SPINNING FLAX

and nothing could be more contemptuous than the references of the Kentucky housewives to the machine-made cloth of the storekeepers.

But linsey forms only a part of the mountain weaving. Blankets and coverlets, known as " kivers," come in considerable numbers from the household looms. The wealth of the housewife is reckoned in " kivers." The mountain bride brings as her dowery a collection of these treasures, to which she adds as many as she can to pass on to her own daughters. In several families we were shown thick, well-woven quilts which had come down from a great-grandmother, and were cherished with something like Roman awe for household gods. We heard much complaint of the modern dyes sold in the stores. They were compared disparagingly with the more permanent colors given by the bark and berry dyes of the earlier days. Yet, so far as we could discover, the analine products are very generally used.

The art impulse of the women seems to find its chief expression in these textile fabrics. The patterns are spread by imitation up and down the valleys, the old traditions being constantly modified by suggestions from the mill goods of the towns.

WEAVING ON A HAND-LOOM

There are, besides, inventors and authorities who make innovations and set fashions going. In one cabin, among a dozen brilliant linsey " kivers," we found one with yellow, white, and red stripes — a veritable Roman blanket. It was quite unlike anything we had seen on our journey. The only suggestion as to the origin of the idea was the simple statement of the maker that she thought the colors " would look pretty." In another case a woman spread out for our admiration a quilted coverlet of store cotton. On a ground of blue she had sewed large conventional red figures. It was so utterly different from the other things we had been shown that we expressed surprise and curiosity. With a smile of triumph she let us into the secret. She had copied the jig-saw scroll work on one of the more pretentious houses in the nearest county seat.

The whole subject of domestic industry, especially the textile side of it, can just now be studied to great advantage in eastern Kentucky, and it seems unfortunate that someone is not taking advantage of this opportunity. Every year, with the modernizing of the region, the conditions become less primitive and simple.

The food of eastern Kentucky ought not to be confused with that of the Bluegrass and Pennyroyal regions. Corn pone, bacon, and fried chicken are appetizing enough in print, but they vary in attractiveness with different parts of the South. The mountaineers have preserved all the primitive processes of the real frontier. Their cooking is correlated with all the other elements of their life, and they seem to thrive upon a diet which to the stranger from without makes the call to meals the gloomiest of summons. We were too early for chickens, which were served only two or three times during the trip. But, so far as we could learn, the rest of the *menu* was thoroughly typical. The staple article is corn bread. It is made by mixing coarse corn meal and a dash of salt with cold water, until the whole is a pasty mass. This is pressed into a frying pan, or skillet, three or four inches deep. The pan is then covered with an iron lid and thrust into the open fire, where glowing embers are piled upon it. It is left only long enough to form a crust or skin upon the surface of the bread. The center of the loaf is never cooked. After the allotted time the bread is turned out upon the table, sometimes broken into pieces on a plate, sometimes left whole to be plucked away as needed by the hungry family. Biscuits of wheat flour and soda or baking powder are sometimes served. They are usually heavy and yellow, and exhale an unpleasant odor. Potatoes are usually boiled or baked. Sometimes they are mashed and given a brown color by the liberal use of ham fat. "Ham meat" is for the most part fried in irregular pieces, which float about in a flood tide of grease. Occasionally the meat diet is varied by roast spare ribs, and, in the season, it is, of course, relieved by "chicken fixings." The butter is a white cottage cheese, very much like the butter made by the Bedouin goatskin churns in Palestine. The coffee is ordinarily a black, uninviting liquor, boiled for a long time in a large pot. This pot is a type of perpetuity. It seems never to be cleaned. Before each meal a little more ground coffee is added and the same amount is drained away into the cups.

Thus there is a constant, slowly changing sum of coffee grounds which lives on year after year. Milk is rarely used by mountaineers for their coffee. In the remote districts only "long sweetenin'" is to be had, *i. e.*, molasses made from sugar cane

THREE PATTERNS OF "LINSEY"

raised on the farm. "Short sweetenin'," a cheap grade of brown sugar, is found on the tables of the well-to-do who live nearer to the county seats. Eggs, usually fried in the ham fat, are looked upon as something of a luxury. Sweets and preserves have a place upon most of the tables. Apple-butter and various preparations of dried fruits are common ; and sometimes a pudding of dumplings and fruit is attempted. It would be hard to imagine anything more unattractive than either the food itself or the way of serving it. The table is sometimes covered with brown oil-cloth, and frequently with a piece of cotton spotted with coffee and grease stains. Two-tined steel forks, steel knives, and pewter spoons are, of course, the rule. One of the most pressing needs of this region seems to be education in the simplest domestic economy — and yet the people are healthy in spite of "hog and hominy."

The hospitality of the mountains is proverbial, and, what is more to the purpose, seems still to be offered with genuine good will. To be sure, in the county towns and along the more frequented highways there are signs of commercialism and traces

A GRIST-MILL

of cautious suspicion. But in the more remote valleys the traveler is received with a welcome in which the "quarter" he pays for his meal and his horse's corn seems to be a small factor. Yet we heard from one or two cynical old people that the times have changed, and that it is no longer an unusual thing to be refused a night's lodging, or even a meal. One of these praisers of the past told of a whole afternoon spent in one valley in a vain attempt to find a place of shelter for the night. Finally, he said, he just stopped asking and got down and went in and stayed. He knew they wouldn't put him out if he once got in.

But we met with almost no rebuffs. Our own sense of delicacy prevented our spending one night in a single-roomed cabin where three persons were down with the fever. On another occasion we were refused a meal for what seemed a very urban reason. The cook had gone away. With these exceptions we were welcomed quietly, not effusively, at every house where we dismounted. We would ride up to the fence of the yard about

MILL WITH OVERSHOT WHEEL

the cabin, tether our horses, climb over the rails — there was rarely a gate — make our way to the "gallery," and ask for a meal. The request was readily granted, with conventionally diffident remarks about the larder. Boys unsaddled our horses and took them to the rambling log barn for their meal of corn. After dipping into the wash-basin, we sat talking with our host, while the women of the household prepared the meal which we needed and at the same time dreaded.

The decorations of the cabin were confined ordinarily to cut-paper fringes on the shelf above the fireplace, or on corner brackets nailed to the logs. In several cases the inner walls were covered with pages from illustrated magazines and papers, and with advertising posters in brilliant colors. It was a rare thing to find pictures of any other kind, and photographs and tintypes seemed almost unknown. In many of the cabins there was a small shelf of books, chiefly school texts, owned by the younger people, and it was not uncommon for the host or hostess to point with half-apologetic pride to the decorations of the room as the work of the "gals." The interiors of the cabins, especially the sleeping rooms, were given an odd look by the lines of garments hung along the rafters above the beds. There

WHIP-SAWING

were no chests of drawers, or boxes for clothes, but simply ropes stretched from one side of the cabin to the other, and nails driven into the beams above. From these hung linsey dresses and store clothes, and now and then a bright "kiver," a pair of winter boots, strings of dried apples, bunches of yellowish green tobacco, and other odd-looking articles. The general effect of the room was a little that of a pawnshop in Petticoat Lane.

The conversation turned, for the most part, upon personal topics, and we felt it necessary to give a fairly detailed account

A SCHOOLHOUSE

of ourselves. No one ever seemed surprised at our desire to see the mountains, and we tried not to betray any consciousness of the unusual conditions in which we were placed. Whenever the talk turned from personal matters, it easily worked around to theological discussions, in which most of our entertainers seemed to take keen pleasure. One man said that he was regarded as a dangerous character in his valley, a sort of freethinker, a mountain Ingersoll perhaps, because he had avowed his doubts about predestination. Another was an orthodox member of the Baptist church, and took strong ground against "fiddling" and "frolics."

We had heard so many stories of the ignorance of the mountaineers that we were somewhat disappointed by their familiarity with a good many things we had expected them not to know. We did not, for example, find a person who had not heard of the explosion of the "Maine." There was a good deal of desultory interest in the possibilities of a war with Spain. But the whole question seemed remote, and was so thought of by the

A "MOONSHINE" STILL

people themselves. As one old man said: "I reckon we mountaineers wouldn't know much about a war if there was one."

The chief contact with the outside world is through the lumbermen who go down the river on their rafts as far as Frankfort, or even to the Ohio, or through the merchants who make periodical trips to the "settlements," as the towns and cities of the Bluegrass region are called.   In one or two places we heard of sons who were in the army or navy, and of their letters which were handed around from house to house, or reported by friendly gossip. A few papers, chiefly agricultural journals and religious weeklies, are to be found in the more accessible cabins.   But we spent the night with one family that had not seen a paper for months. They were ten miles from the nearest post-office.

The mountaineers in the county towns are fond of telling anecdotes to illustrate the ignorance of the backwoods-men. Many of these have been embodied in the stories of mountain life. The jests are passed about with great glee by the storekeepers and petty lawyers of the little towns. The tale that had greatest vogue at the time of our visit was of the mountaineer who complained that he could not sleep because of the electric light in his hotel room at Lexington. When he was asked why he didn't blow it out, he replied that he couldn't, "because they had the blamed thing in a bottle." Most of the stories have about them a suggestion of newspaper origin.

It is perfectly obvious that these mountain folk must have only the most shadowy ideas about the world outside. We found middle-aged and old women who had never been outside the valley in which they lived, and had not so much as visited the little town at the lower end of it. One boy knew of Chicago only as the source of an arnica tooth soap which he highly prized and imported into his valley. A woman whom we met on the outskirts of Jackson replied, to our eager inquiry for war news, that her old man had heard somebody say, who had read it in a paper, "that England and France were goin' to begin a war tomorrow morning." And she added, with apprehensive uncertainty: "There be a France, ain't there?"

The young people, however, are clearly gaining in general information from attending the district schools established throughout the region, and the public schools and academies in the county seats. The district school is "kept" in the typical log-cabin schoolhouse, with rough benches, an open fireplace or a huge iron stove, and oftentimes with plain planks for a blackboard. The efficiency of the teachers has steadily improved, and although the schools are in session for only a short period, the character of the work has advanced in a marked way. It is through the school system and the young that connections between the national life and this partially isolated region are being more intimately established. The most influential single agency which is attempting this task is the college at Berea, Ky. Here is the point of contact between the great social tradition of the wider world and the narrow life of the Kentucky uplands. The young mountaineers resort in increasing numbers to this college, where manual dexterity, intellectual training, æsthetic standards, ethical and religious ideals are communicated by earnest and devoted teachers. The plans of Berea, so far as one may judge from its publications, are based upon a careful study of the peculiar conditions and needs of the region, and have already resulted in setting at work refining and elevating influences in many a mountain cabin.[1]

[1] The college has published a number of pamphlets and reports, which may be obtained upon application to President Frost, Berea, Ky. Several illustrations for this article have been furnished through the kindness of the Berea authorities.

The æsthetic impulses of the mountaineers have already been hinted at. The dress of the men has almost no suggestion of tidiness, to say nothing of taste. It was not unusual to find relatively well-to-do citizens going about in worn or tattered garments. The storekeepers, lawyers, and doctors were the only exception, and many of them had a shabby look. The women, on the other hand, especially the younger of them, show an art feeling in their linsey dresses of bright patterns, their ruffled white and pink sun bonnets, and bits of bright ribbon at their throats. Their shoes, however, are in many cases very large and coarse, and obtruded themselves painfully from beneath the linsey gowns. The older women seem to care much less for appearances. They have a worn and faded look, the inevitable result of years of child-bearing and unremitting work over the blazing fire, at the loom, and, it may be, in the field.

The interest of these people in theology and church organization is keen. The "meeting" offers an opportunity for sociability hardly second to the singing school and the frolic. One Sunday evening, in the courthouse of a small town, we heard a traveling evangelist, at the close of an earnest sermon, beg the people to go quietly to their homes and not to stop and "visit" as they usually did. We could infer from this how important a function of sociability the church renders among these folk.

Theological discussion satisfies the appetite for metaphysics, and offers opportunity for intellectual exercise and discipline. Along with this fondness for theological dogma, we found traces of a tradition of folk-lore and superstition which seemed to offer an inviting field of study to the student of folk-psychology.

The moral standards of the mountaineers have been modified in a marked way of late. Probably in popular thought the chief associations with the mountains are "moonshine" and feuds. It was something of a surprise to us to learn that all three of the counties through which we rode had adopted a no-license policy, and that for a considerable period a regular feud or "war" had not been known. Nor was this change chiefly the result of outside pressure. It grew out of a popular reaction against the uncertain, lawless, terrifying régime of whisky and bloodshed. The conviction gradually gained ground that liquor was the source of the evil. In creating this feeling missionaries and temperance workers took an important part. So far as we could learn from conversations with all kinds of people, the prohibition sentiment is wide-spread and vigorous. Several old men discoursed very rationally about the dangers to life and property, and the disgrace to the mountains, which the old system involved. The sending of state troops a few years ago seems to have made a perceptible impression upon the people. They realized then as never before the existence of an external authority which cannot be ignored.

To be sure, whisky is still made in violation of the revenue laws, but the traffic is now doubly under ban. In our four-days' ride we saw "moonshine" only once, and then in such circumstances as testified to the reality of the sentiment against its use.

The "feud," which Mr. Fox has described so vividly in his story, *A Cumberland Vendetta*, seems to be typical of mountain "wars." In the little county town of Hazard we heard details of the famous Franche-Eversole feud, which was suppressed only a few years ago, after sixty or more lives had been sacrificed. The account was full of ambuscades, of firing from the cover of cabins, of besieging the courthouse and stores, of pitched battles in the streets. One story was of a woman who, learning that her husband had been surprised by his foes, filled her apron with cartridges, seized a Winchester, and rushed through the fight to her "old man." Once armed he fought his way out in safety.

Although these tales are related with great gusto, there is no expression of regret that the times have changed. We were impressed everywhere with the popular dislike of the old order of things and a sense of relief from the dread and uncertainty of other years.

Public opinion in the mountains often finds expression in a rude fashion. Night riders or Kuklux constitute themselves arbiters of conduct and visit the cabins of real or supposed offenders. We heard frequently of these parties, several of which seemed very active at about the time of our visit. Whatever of good the system may involve theoretically seems more than counterbalanced by the opportunity which it affords for irresponsible persecution and private revenge. We heard murmurings against the practice, and the hope was more than once expressed that the law would be invoked to stop it.

Somewhat akin to " Kukluxing" is the plan of leaving letters of warning at the doors of idle or vicious persons. The community tries to protect itself in this way against imposition or moral contagion. So long as a family is in real need, neighborly aid is never withheld ; but once let the suspicion get abroad that a lazy husband is trying to shirk his share of work and depend upon his neighbors, and he will find a letter some morning under his door giving him a week in which to show signs of industry. Failing in this, he will have his choice of a flogging or of being driven out of the valley. There are no poorhouses in the mountains. The worthy poor are cheerfully aided ; the idle are compelled to work or to go away.

I hope I have succeeded in giving at least a general idea of the interesting field for social study which this retarded frontier affords. Here the economist, the anthropologist, the linguist, the historian, and the sociologist may find materials for special studies which would be of great value. A series of monographs on the chief aspects of this curious social survival ought to be written before the life, now being modified so rapidly, has lost its comparatively primitive character. Let students of sociology leave their books and at first hand in the Cumberlands deal with the phenomena of a social order arrested at a relatively early stage of evolution.

GEORGE E. VINCENT.
THE UNIVERSITY OF CHICAGO.

THE UNITED STATES SUPREME COURT AND THE UTAH EIGHT-HOURS' LAW.

ALTHOUGH it has passed almost as unheralded by the serious journals devoted to sociology as by the daily press, the recent decision of the supreme court of the United States sustaining the constitutionality of the Utah statute which constitutes eight hours a legal working day in mines and smelters may, without exaggeration, be compared with the Dred Scott case as a decision of the highest national importance. For while that decision fomented rebellion and contributed mightily to the forced reconstruction of the southern states, this decision averts a danger no less actual, though more insidious and slow to be perceived; while that decision worked destructively, this one works constructively; while the Dred Scott decision destroyed the hope that chattel slavery could be restricted by constitutional methods, this decision confirms the hope that industrial freedom may be established and extended by these methods, legislatures and courts working harmoniously to promote the health and welfare of the wage-earners. By its reasonable and affirmative construction and definition of the intent and scope of the fourteenth amendment to the constitution of the United States, this decision opens the way for a long and peaceful evolution of the beneficent powers of the states, and for reasonable and equitable conditions of work. The fact that it immediately secures for the employés in certain industries in Utah the benefits of the legal working day, while of great importance, is not the vital point in this decision. Far more important to the nation and the future is the fact that it rehabilitates the states in the performance of some of their most weighty functions, and reaffirms principles which, formerly regarded as self-evident, have in recent years been not only disputed but abrogated by state supreme courts in a long series of decisions.

In all great industrial countries it has long been recognized that manufacture and commerce need equitable conditions; that legislative requirements of whatever kind, if imposed upon one, must be imposed upon all alike; that discrimination must be avoided, not alone because it is unjust, but because it is fatal. Hence legislation regulating the conditions of employment is usually embodied in national measures, the execution alone being left to the local authorities, while broad, fundamental provisions are uniform for one industry throughout an empire, a republic, or a kingdom. In America alone the constitution leaves in effect to the states the regulation of the relations of employés to their work, and of the conditions surrounding and attending that work (except that employés who come under the interstate commerce act receive the benefit of certain safeguards precribed under that act).

When, therefore, state supreme courts take the position held by the Illinois court in its decision (Ritchie *vs.* the People) of March 15, 1895, annulling the Illinois eight-hours' law, viz.: that, in consequence of the fourteenth amendment to the constitution of the United States, the individual states also are prohibited from interfering with these relations and conditions, commerce and manufacture in states affected by such decisions are, *pro tanto*, worse off than in other states and countries; for they are thus left without either state or national provision for that uniformity of relations which is one of their most vital interests. This construction of the fourteenth amendment, adopted and disastrously applied in recent years by the supreme courts of Illinois and several other states, has exercised a doubly injurious influence: it has minimized the power and efficiency of the states, and it has thereby deprived employés of a protection which they could derive from no other source. Incalculable national importance attaches to this decision of the federal supreme court, because it checks that blighting tendency of the state supreme courts.

But for the unwholesome decisions of state courts arbitrarily placing limitations upon the powers of the states and reducing to lawlessness (for lack of any legislative body recognized by the state courts as competent to deal with them) the relations of employés to their work, much of the present epoch-making federal decision might seem to be mere truism. Under existing decisions, however, it offers the curious and instructive spectacle of the federal supreme court assigning to the states duties and powers which the supreme courts of those states have declared not to be theirs.

In 1895 the supreme court of Illinois decided that the state cannot restrict by legislation the hours of labor of any adult. About the same time the legislature of Colorado inquired of the Colorado supreme court whether a proposed statute limiting to eight hours the working day of laborers and mechanics would be constitutional ; or whether it could be rendered constitutional by an amendment providing that it should apply only to mines and factories. The supreme court of Colorado replied that both proposals "would be unconstitutional, because they violate the rights of parties to make their own contracts—a right guaranteed by our bill of rights and protected by the fourteenth amendment to the constitution of the United States." In 1894 the Nebraska supreme court had decided that "an act of the legislature of that state providing that eight hours should constitute a legal day's work for all classes of mechanics, servants, and laborers throughout the state, excepting those engaged in farm and domestic labor, and making violation of its provisions a misdemeanor, was unconstitutional and, therefore, void, both as special legislation and as attempting to prevent persons, legally competent to enter into contracts, from making their own contracts." Of these decisions and opinions so careful a writer as Mr. F. J. Stimson said, no longer ago than the September issue of the *Atlantic Monthly:* " These decisions have undoubtedly given the quietus in t he United States to any attempt to limit generally the time that a grown man may labor."

In our report as factory inspectors, for 1895, we referred to the Illinois decision in the following terms : " The new feature introduced into the body of American legislative precedent by this decision is the court's assumption that it is not exclusively a matter of the constitution of Illinois. The state constitution could be altered, by a constitutional convention, so that the hours of labor could be regulated by legislative enactment, as they are in the older industrial communities. The court, however, makes the fourteenth amendment to the constitution of the United States the basis of its decision. If this position were sound, all efforts for legislative restriction of the working day would be wasted, since there is no prospect of any immediate change in the constitution of the United States.

" Happily the weight of precedent is not on the side of the Illinois court ; the precedents of the courts of Massachusetts and New York are in the other direction. In Massachusetts, for twenty years past, it has been an established principle of the supreme court that the hours of work of women and children may be regulated by statute. The Massachusetts precedent has had such weight in New York that no case has been carried to the supreme court or to the court of appeals. The constitutionality of the ten-hours' law, though suits have been brought under it repeatedly, has never been disputed. It remained for the supreme court of Illinois to discover that the amendment to the constitution of the United States, passed to guarantee the negro from oppression, has become an insuperable obstacle to the protection of women and children. Nor is it reasonable to suppose that this unique interpretation of the fourteenth amendment will be permanently maintained even in Illinois. When the observation of a few more years shall have convinced the medical profession, the philanthropists, and the educators, as experience has already convinced the factory employés, that it is a life-and-death matter to have the working day of reasonable length guaranteed by law, it will be found possible to rescue the fourteenth amendment from the perverted application upon which this decision rests. We may hope that Ritchie *vs.* the People will then be added to the reversed decisions in which the supreme court of Illinois is so rich." At that time no one could foresee that the Illinois decision would be overruled so promptly or so authoritatively as the event has proved.

Undeterred by the three recent and discouraging decisions of western courts, the people of Utah fell back upon the precedent of Massachusetts, whose supreme court had decided in 1876

(People *vs.* the Hamilton Manufacturing Company) that the Massachusetts legislature had the power to restrict by statute the hours of labor of adult women employed in factories. The Illinois supreme court, in its decision annulling the Illinois eight-hours' law, had taken occasion to refer to the Massachusetts decision, stating that "it is not in line with the current of authority," and explaining that it could be arrived at only by reason of the "large discretion vested in the legislative branch of the government." The "large discretion" referred to is contained in the following words of chap. ii, sec. 4, of the constitution of Massachusetts: "Full power and authority are hereby given and granted to the said general court, from time to time, to make, ordain, and establish all manner of wholesome and reasonable laws, ordinances, statutes, directions, and instructions, either with penalties or without: so as the same be not repugnant to this constitution, as they shall judge to be for the good and welfare of this commonwealth, and for the governing thereof."

From the days of this sweeping Massachusetts provision, which took effect October 1, 1780, and has remained in force in Massachusetts unchanged to the present day, the tendency has been to reduce the powers of legislatures, both by restrictions inserted in state constitutions and by the interpretation placed upon those constitutions by state supreme courts. Strongest of all has been the use of the fourteenth amendment by the state courts. This tendency to reduce legislative power in the states to zero (degrading the state government to a mere mechanism for laying and collecting taxes for the maintenance of the judiciary, the militia, and the state charities) reached its culminating point in the Illinois decision of 1895 (Ritchie *vs.* the People). How far the pendulum has already swung back toward the position of Massachusetts in 1780 is shown in the action of the people of Utah, in the decision of their supreme court, and in the present decision of the supreme court of the United States.

The people of Utah, instructed by the supreme court of Illinois in 1895, showed by their action in 1896 that they had learned their lesson. For, not content with such sweeping generalities as those of the Massachusetts state constitution, they incorporated in their own constitution of 1896 an article dealing explicitly with the rights of labor, as follows:

ARTICLE XVI, SECTION 1. The rights of labor shall have just protection through laws calculated to promote the industrial welfare of the state.

SEC. 2. The legislature shall provide by law for a board of labor conciliation and arbitration, which shall fairly represent the interests of both capital and labor. The board shall perform duties and receive compensation as prescribed by law.

SEC. 3. The legislature shall prohibit:

(1) The employment of women, or of children under the age of fourteen years, in underground mines.

(2) The contracting of convict labor.

(3) The labor of convicts outside of prison grounds, except on public works under the direct control of the state.

(4) The political and commercial control of employés.

SEC. 4. The exchange of blacklists by railroad companies or other corporations, associations, or persons is prohibited.

SEC. 5. The right of action to recover damages for injuries resulting in death shall never be abrogated, and the amount recoverable shall not be subject to any statutory limitation.

SEC. 6. Eight hours shall constitute a day's work on all works or undertakings carried on or aided by the state, county, or municipal governments; and the legislature shall pass laws to provide for the health and safety of employés in factories, smelters, and mines.

SEC. 7. The legislature, by appropriate legislation, shall provide for the enforcement of the provisions of this article.

In accordance with the provision of sec. 7 of this article, the Utah legislature proceeded to enact a statute, of which the essential features are as follows:

SECTION 1. The period of employment of workingmen in all underground mines or workings shall be eight hours per day, except in cases of emergency where life or property is in imminent danger.

SEC. 2. The period of employment of workingmen in smelters and all other institutions for the reduction or refining of ores or metals shall be eight hours per day, except in cases of emergency where life or property is in imminent danger.

On June 26, 1896, one Holden was arrested under a warrant charging him with employing a man to work in a mine ten hours in one day. The court, having heard the evidence in the case, imposed a fine of $50 (fifty dollars) and costs, and ordered the defendant to be imprisoned in the county jail for a term of fifty-seven days, or until the fine and costs were paid. The case was immediately appealed, under habeas corpus proceedings, to the supreme court of Utah, and the law was sustained. The case was then carried to the federal supreme court, which handed down its decision on February 28, Justices Peckham and Brewer dissenting. The law was again sustained. The position of the supreme court of the United States was defined as to the constitutionality of statutory restrictions upon the hours of labor of adults ; and as to the powers and duties, in general, of the states with regard to the health and welfare of employés as such. Although the decisions of the supreme courts of Nebraska, Illinois, and Colorado are referred to indirectly only, they are all comprehensively overruled. But the great, the incalculable service which is rendered by this decision is its rout and destruction of the bogy-man with which state supreme courts have for years been terrifying themselves, and each other, and timorous legislatures, under the name of the fourteenth amendment to the constitution of the United States. Once for all, it is convincingly laid down by this decision that state legislation restricting the hours of labor of employés in occupations injurious to the health will not be annulled by the federal supreme court on grounds of conflict with the fourteenth amendment to the constitution of the United States.

The decision is so coherent, so closely knit, that injustice to it is done by quoting isolated parts of it by way of illustrating the position taken by the court. Yet, in default of space for reproducing the whole of this humane and enlightened utterance, it must suffice to give some of the characteristic dicta. Says the court: "The constitution of the United States, which is necessarily and to a large extent inflexible, and exceedingly difficult of amendment, *should not be so construed as to deprive the states of the power to so amend their laws as to make them conform to the wishes of the citizens as they may deem best for the public welfare, without bringing them into conflict with the supreme law of the land.*" And again the court says: "An examination of the classes of cases arising under the fourteenth amendment will demonstrate that, in passing upon the validity of state legislation under that amendment, this court has not failed to recognize the fact that the law is, to a certain extent, a progressive science; that in some of the states, methods of procedure which, at the time the constitution was adopted, were deemed essential to the protection and safety of the people, or to the liberty of the citizen, have been found no longer necessary; that restrictions which had formerly been laid upon the conduct of individuals, or of classes of individuals, had proved detrimental to their interests, while, on the other hand, *certain other classes of persons (particularly those engaged in dangerous or unhealthy occupations) have been found to be in need of aaditional protection.*' "Of course it is impossible to forecast the character or extent of these changes; but in view of the fact that, from the day Magna Charta was signed to the present moment, amendments to the structure of the law have been made with increasing frequency, it is impossible to suppose that they will not continue, *and the law be forced to adapt itself to new conditions of society, and particularly to the new relations between employers and employés as they arise.*" And again the court says: "While this court has held that the police powers cannot be put forward as an excuse for oppressive and unjust legislation, it may be resorted to for the purpose of preserving the health, public safety, or morals, or the abatement of public nuisances, *and a large discretion is necessarily vested in the legislature to determine, not only what the interests of the public require, but what measures are necessary for the protection of those interests.*" Finally the court quotes with approval the most advanced position taken by the supreme court of Utah, as follows: "*Though reasonable doubts may exist as to the power of the legislature to pass a law, or as to whether the law is calculated or adapted to promote the health, safety, or comfort of the people, or to secure good order or promote the general welfare, we must resolve them in favor of that branch of the government.*"

Having thus come to the rescue of the state legislatures and their powers in general, the court deals with their duties in regard to the health of employés as such. It sets forth the general proposition that " It is as much in the interest of the state that the public health should be preserved as that life should be made secure. With this in view, quarantine laws have been enacted in most, if not all, of the states ; insane asylums, public hospitals, and institutions for the care and instruction of the blind established ; and especial measures taken for the exclusion of infected cattle, rags, and decayed fruit. In other states, laws have been enacted limiting the hours during which women and children shall be employed in factories ; and while their constitutionality, at least as applied to women, has been doubted in some of the states, they have been generally upheld. Thus in the case of the Hamilton Manufacturing Company (120 Mass., 283) it was held that a statute prohibiting the employment.of all persons under eighteen, and of all women, in any manufacturing establishment more than sixty hours per week violates no contract of the commonwealth implied in the granting of a charter to a manufacturing company, nor any right reserved under the constitution to any individual citizen, and may be maintained as a health or police regulation."

It is refreshing to find the valuable Massachusetts decision thus authoritatively brought back into the " current of authority " from which it was, as we have seen, thrust forth by the Illincis court in its now overruled decision of 1895 in the case of Ritchie *vs.* the People.

The court also settled the vital question : Who shall decide which occupations are sufficiently injurious to justify the restriction of the hours of daily labor of persons employed in them ? On no point have state courts been more arrogant, the Illinois court taking, perhaps, the most extreme position of all in the following passage of its decision (Ritchie *vs.* the People): " It (the eight-hour section of the factory law) does not inhibit their (women's) employment in factories or workshops. On the contrary, it recognizes such places as proper for them to work in by permitting their labor therein during eight hours of each day. The question here is not whether a particular employment is a proper one for the use of female labor, but the question is whether, in an employment which is conceded to be lawful in itself and suitable for woman to be engaged in, she shall be deprived of the right to determine for herself how many hours she can and will work each day. *There is no ground—at least none which has been made manifest to us in arguments of counsel—for fixing upon eight hours in one day as the limit within which woman can work without injury to her physique, and beyond which, if she work, injury will necessarily follow.*" The court was naturally not in a position to investigate the conditions of work in the factories and workshops of Illinois. That is not its function. But the legislature of 1893 had been in a position to investigate the whole condition of manufacture in the state; it had, indeed, appointed a joint committee of the house and senate to investigate the factories and workshops in operation; this committee had visited a large number of establishments, and had taken a large amount of testimony from employers and employés, physicians, visiting nurses, inspectors, and other witnesses, and had decided that, in view of the intensity of work and the rate of speed required in virtually all occupations, eight hours did constitute a limit of hours beyond which women could not work without injury. All this no court can do; it has no apparatus for such investigations; but that did not prevent the Illinois court from usurping the right of decision which the present decision of the federal supreme court happily reassigns to the legislature. On the powers of the legislature in the matter of health and hours of labor, the federal supreme court says: "These employments, when too long pursued, the legislature has judged to be detrimental to the health of the employés; and, so long as there are reasonable grounds for believing that this is so, its decision upon this subject cannot be reviewed by the federal courts." And elsewhere the court quotes with approval the words of the Utah court: "It may be said that labor in such conditions must be performed. Granting that the period of labor each day should be of reasonable length, twelve hours per day would be less injurious than fourteen, ten than twelve, and eight than ten. The legislature has named eight. Such a period was deemed reasonable."

The Illinois court (Ritchie *vs.* the People) said: "The police powers of the state can only be permitted to limit or abridge such a fundamental right as the right to make contracts, when the exercise of such power is necessary to promote the health, comfort, welfare, or safety of society or the public ; *it is doubtful whether it can be exercised to prevent injury to the individual engaged in a particular calling.*" In beneficent contrast with this sinister dictum is the following from the United States supreme court : " The legislature has also recognized the fact, which the experience of legislators in many states has corroborated, that the proprietors of these establishments and their operatives do not stand upon an equality, and that their interests are, to a certain extent, conflicting. The former naturally desire to obtain as much labor as possible from their employés, while the latter are often induced by the fear of discharge to conform to regulations which their judgment, fairly exercised, would pronounce to be detrimental to their health and strength. In other words, the proprietors lay down the rules, and the laborers are practically constrained to obey them. In such cases self-interest is often an unsafe guide, and the legislature may properly interpose its authority.

" It may not be improper to suggest in this connection that, although the prosecution in this case was against the employer of labor, who apparently, under the statute, is the only one liable, his defense is not so much that his right to contract has been infringed upon, but that the act works a peculiar hardship to his employés, whose right to labor as long as they please is alleged to be thereby violated. The argument would certainly come with better grace and greater cogency from the latter class. *But the fact that both parties are of full age, and competent to contract, does not necessarily deprive the state of the power to interfere, where the parties do not stand upon an equality, or where the public health demands that one party to the contract should be protected against himself. The state still retains an interest in his welfare, however reckless he may be. The whole is no greater than the sum of all the parts, and when the individual health, safety, and welfare are sacrificed or neglected, the state must suffer.*"

This decision is, of course, not retroactive, and therefore does not revive the Illinois statute restricting to eight hours per day the work of female employés engaged in manufacture, which was enacted in 1893 and annulled by the state supreme court in 1895. It does, however, by overruling virtually every proposition laid down by the Illinois court in that decision, give satisfactory assurance that the next eight-hours' law enacted in Illinois, if restricted in its terms to occupations dangerous to the health of the employés, must stand as good law, and cannot be annulled. This decision also renders it probable that legislation in regard to the hours of labor will, henceforth, deal not especially with women or children, but with all the employés in occupations injurious to the human organism. Thus the miners in Illinois may obtain statutory confirmation of the eight-hours' day which they now enjoy only by means of contracts enforced by the dread of renewed strikes. And the women in the Massachusetts cotton mills who tend ever-increasing numbers of machines, at ever-increasing rates of speed, will be entitled to claim legislative restriction of the hours of labor on their behalf, on the ground of the exhausting nature of their occupation. The same reasoning applies to all the women driving foot-power sewing machines in sweatshops and to numerous other employments.

The logical result of this decision should be renewed activity on behalf of the statutory eight-hours' working day for all young people, on grounds of health; and for all adults in occupations injurious to the health. While it seems reasonable to suppose that, in view of this federal precedent, state supreme courts would not annul such statutes, it would be safer to embody in state constitutions provisions similar to those already embodied in the state constitutions of Massachusetts and Utah. Effort for legislative restriction of the work day need not, however, be deferred to await such action; for this precedent is of such weight, and so explicit that, after it, state courts will have either to ignore it willfully, or to change the lines of reasoning which they have followed hitherto.

The immediate practical lesson of this decision for the advocates of social amelioration by constitutional methods seems to be briefly as follows :

1. Legislation limiting the hours of labor of employés in occupations injurious to the health will not be annulled by the federal supreme court on the ground of conflict with the fourteenth amendment to the constitution of the United States.

. 2. The short working day may be established by statute in the various states for all those occupations which are, in themselves, injurious to the health of the employés; *and it rests with the state legislature to decide which are such occupations.*

3. Legislation limiting the hours of labor of employés need not be restricted to women and minors, as has been the usage hitherto; the question being, henceforth, not as to the age or sex of the employés, but as to the nature of the occupation.

4. It is desirable to provide for such legislation by inserting in the state constitution (wherever there is not already such an enabling article) a provision similar, either to the general article of the Massachusetts constitution, or the special article providing for the rights of labor which forms the distinguishing characteristic of the new Utah state constitution.

It is also to be remembered that these things do not occur spontaneously; they are the fruits of long and patient labor. Adverse decisions in many states have cumbered the earth with error, discouragement, apathy, if not actual antagonism, to this sane and hopeful, though slow and difficult, method of social amelioration. And the present decision does but open the way, by sustaining a statute affecting a few hundred men in a state not highly developed industrially, and by affording a precedent, national in its scope, for doing over again successfully work which, in many states, has once been done in vain by the patient effort of the labor organizations. A long campaign lies before these organizations before the older states can be brought to the point thus early reached by Utah. State constitutional conventions must be held ; state constitutions must be amended ; legislatures must be induced to act; state supreme courts must be brought to follow this decision of the federal supreme court ;

years must be consumed in education and agitation before the fruits of this harvest of enlightened judicial interpretation can be fully reaped and enjoyed by the toilers throughout the United States. No time should be lost; the work should begin at once.

FLORENCE KELLEY.

HULL HOUSE,
Chicago.

NOTE.—Cases to which reference is made in the foregoing: Ritchie *vs.* the People, Illinois, March 15, 1898; Law *vs.* Rees Publishing Company, Nebraska, June 6, 1894; People *vs.* Hamilton Manufacturing Company, 120 Massachusetts, 383, 1876; Holden *vs.* Hardy, United States supreme court, February 28, 1896.

THE PERSISTENCE OF SOCIAL GROUPS. III.[1]

THE precisely contrary picture, namely, the most extreme ductility and exchangeability of the sociological forms as a condition of self-preservation, is shown for example by groups that maintain their existence within larger groups either by tolerance or it may be purely *par nefas*. Only by means of the most complete elasticity can such a society combine firmness of coherence with the constant necessity of defense or with the necessity of rapid shifting from defense to offense. Such a group must be able, so to speak, to crawl into every hole. It must be able, according to circumstances, to expand or to contract. Like a fluid body it must be able to take on any form that offers itself. Thus bands of rogues and conspirators must acquire capacity to divide instantly and to act in separate groups; to follow without restriction now this and now that leader; whether in direct or indirect contact, to preserve the same group spirit; after each disruption to reorganize themselves at once in any form that is possible at the moment, etc. They arrive in this way at that power of self-maintenance in consequence of which the Gipsies are wont to say of themselves: "It would be useless to hang us, for we never die." Similar assertions have been made about the Jews. The force of their social coherence, the sense of solidarity which is practically so influential among them, the actual, although often relaxed, exclusiveness toward all but Jews—this sociological bond, it is said, may have lost some of its confessional coloring since the emancipation, but it has only exchanged it for the capitalistic. For that very reason, it is said, "the invisible organization of the Jews is unconquerable, for so soon as hatred of Judaism robs it first of the power of the press, then of the power of capital, finally of equal civic rights, the Jewish societary unit does not forthwith disappear. It is only robbed of its socio-political organization. It is once more con-

[1] Translated by ALBION W. SMALL.

35

firmed in its original confessional coherence. This socio-political play has repeatedly occurred locally, and may be repeated universally." Indeed, when we observe the versatility of the individual Jew, his wonderful facility in adjusting himself to the most manifold tasks, and in adapting his personality to the shifting conditions of life, we might characterize this as a reflection of the sociological group form in the form of the individual. Whether this assertion about the history of the Jews is correct in substance or not, its presumption is equally instructive for us, viz., that the self-preservation of a social unit may be directly realized through change of its form of manifestation, or of its material basis ; that its power of persistence resides in this very capacity to undergo outward change.

Through their relations to further sociological concepts of more capital rank these two ways of social persistence come into especially characteristic antithesis. When, for instance, the preservation of a group is very closely bound up with maintenance of a particular stratum in its existence and peculiarities—for example, the highest, the broadest, or the middle stratum—the first two cases demand more rigidity of the social-life form, the last more elasticity. Aristocracies are in general conservative. If they are in reality what the name asserts, they are the most adequate expression of the actual inequality between men. In this case—with reference to which I do not here inquire whether the presumed condition is ever more than partially realized—the spur is lacking for revolutionary movements, viz., non-correspondence between the inherent qualifications of the people and their social situation. Such lack of correspondence is the point of departure both for the most important and heroic of human deeds and for the most senseless undertakings. Given then this most favorable case of an aristocracy, the whole aristocratic class is bound to punctilious insistence upon the conditions which are essential to its preservation; for every experimental disturbance might threaten that fine and rare proportion between qualification and position, either in reality or in the feelings of the persons concerned, and thus might furnish an impulse for radical transformation.

The real occasion for such change of an aristocracy, however, will be that such absolute justification of the regulating system scarcely ever exists. The lordship of the few over the many is likely to rest rather on a totally different basis, and not on the ideal appropriateness of this relation. Under these circumstances the ruling class will have the utmost interest in affording the least occasion for movements toward disturbance and innovation, for every movement of that sort would stimulate the rightful or supposed claims of the ruled. There is danger in this case that not the persons merely, but the whole constitution, might be changed, and this is the decisive period for our course of thought. The very fact that violent changes in the personnel of the ruling class have often been brought about with the assistance of the masses calls attention to the possibility, which has not seldom become a reality, that on such an occasion the whole aristocratic principle may be overturned. Because of this connection the aristocratic form of constitution will maintain itself best through the utmost immobility of its status. This by no means holds good for political purposes alone. It is true also for ecclesiastical, family, and social groupings into which the aristocratic form may enter. In general, so soon as this form has once established itself, a severe conservatism will be most favorable, not merely for the momentary personal standing of the regulating system, but also for its preservation in form and principle.

This often appears clearly enough in the history of reformatory movements in aristocratic constitutions. That adaptation to newly emerging social forces or ideals, such as takes place through diminution of exploitation and subjection, through legal definition of rights in place of arbitrary interpretation, through increase of the rights and of the shares of goods assigned to the lower classes—such adaptation is not wont, so far as it is a voluntary concession, to find its ultimate purpose in that which is changed by the concession, but rather in that which may be preserved by means of such concession. The limitation of the aristocratic prerogative is only the *conditio sine qua non* of saving the aristocratic régime at all. If the movement is allowed to go so far, however, these concessions no longer suffice. Each reform is likely to uncover new points demanding reform, and the movement which was inaugurated for the confirmation of the existing order leads, as though on an inclined plane, either to the overthrow of that order or, if the new demands cannot prevail, to a radical reaction which may reverse the changes already made. This danger which threatens at every modification and compliance of an aristocratic constitution, viz., that the concession made for the sake of self-preservation may by sheer force of its own specific gravity lead to a complete overthrow, exhibits conservatism, at the start, and the form of defense which is invariably rigid and unyielding, as most favorable for the aristocratic social form.

In case the form of the group is determined, not by the eminence of a numerically small stratum, but by the most extensive stratum and its autonomy, the self-preservation of the group will likewise be promoted by stability and unshaken firmness. An immediate influence in this direction is the fact that the great mass, in so far as it functions as the permanent vehicle of a social unity, is very rigid and immovable in its temper. The mass is in this respect very sharply distinguished from any multitude that may actually assemble. The latter is highly variable in its moods and acts, and may change its attitude from one extreme to another upon the most casual impulse. In case the mass is not roused by direct physical excitement and in consequence of stimulations and suggestions from opposite sides, nervous vacillation begins in place of firm direction, thus putting the mass at the mercy of every actual impulse; in case its deep and permanent character operates rather, the mass follows the law of inertia. It does not change its condition from rest *or movement* by its own initiative, but only as a result of the coöperation of new positive forces. Hence it is equally the case that movements which are carried on by great masses, and are left to themselves, move on consistently to their extreme, and on the other hand a once attained equilibrium of conditions is not easily abandoned, so far as the change depends on the mass. It corresponds better with the healthy instinct of the mass to guard itself against change of circumstances and agitations by substantial firmness and rigidity of form rather than by pliable adaptation and quickly effected alteration of attitudes.

In the case of political constitutions, an additional element of essential importance is that the foundation of their social form upon that stratum which is most extensive and in which rights are most equal occurs chiefly among agricultural peoples — the old Roman peasant class and the old German community of free men are cases in point. Here the action of the social form is prejudiced by content of social interests. The cultivator of the soil is *a priori* conservative. His occupation requires long terms, abiding arrangements, resolute persistency. The uncertainties of the weather, upon which his fortunes hang, incline him to a certain fatalism, which shows itself, with respect to external powers, rather in enduring than in evading. His processes cannot be made to confront changes of conjunctions with such quick qualitative modifications as those of manufacturer or merchant. The technical conditions, therefore, create for groups whose form-maintenance is identical with that of a chiefly agricultural mass the disposition to procure this maintenance by firmness and persistence, not by variability of their life processes.

It is quite otherwise in case the middle class has undertaken leadership and the social form of the group stands or falls with the predominance of this middle class. This middle class alone has both an upper and a lower boundary. This is of such a sort that individuals are constantly brought within it both from the higher and from the lower class, and other individuals go from the middle class in either direction. The character of fluctuation is impressed on this stratum, therefore, and the appropriateness of its attitude will, therefore, be in large measure an appropriateness of adaptations, variations, concessions, through which the inevitable movement of the whole may be at least so guided or opposed that the essential form and force of the group may remain throughout all change of conditions. We may designate the sociological form of a group which is characterized by the extension and prevalence of a middle class as that of *continuity*.

Such a form coexists neither with an actual ungraded equality of individuals throughout the group, nor if the group consists of an upper and a lower class separated from each other by no intervening medium. The middle class, in fact, adds an entirely new sociological element. It is not only a third in addition to the two. It does not merely have somewhat the same, that is, quantitative, relation to each of these that they have to each other. The new element is rather that this third stratum itself has an upper and a lower boundary, that upon these boundaries an exchange with the other two strata is constantly taking place, and that through this continual fluctuation effacement of boundaries and continual transitions are produced.

An actual continuity of social life does not arise from the fact that individuals are built into positions one above another, with never so slight gradations. This would still produce discontinuous structure. Continuity exists only when single individuals circulate through higher and lower positions. Only thus is the separateness of strata changed over into an actually uninterrupted structure. In the fortune of the individuals the upper and the lower situation must first meet, in order that the sociological picture may show an actual mediation between the upper and the lower. Precisely this, and not a simple intermediate position, is secured by a middle class. It requires little reflection to discern that this closeness of gradation must characterize also the grades within the middle class. The continuity of stations with reference to repute, possessions, activity, culture, etc., rests not merely in the minuteness of the differences which are coördinated in an objective scale, but rather in the frequency of the change which leads one and the same person through a number of such situations, and thus produces at the same time perpetual and varying personal unions of objectively different situations. Under these circumstances the social aspect, as a whole, will be that of *elasticity*. The dominant middle class affords the medium of easy interchangeability of the elements, so that the self-preservation of the group throughout the change of external or internal circumstances and assaults is accomplished not so much because of fixity and rigidity in the cohesion of its elements as because of facile yielding and quick transformation.

In the same way it may be shown, in the opposite direction, that a group with very many positions, built the one above another in close gradation, must have the character of decided fluidity and variability, if the greatest perplexities and disturbances are to be avoided. When a great multiplicity of situations is possible, it is from the outset less probable that each will at once fall into the right position than in the case of a fixed social system which assigns each a place within the great group comprehending many forms of action. Where a group contains only a few sharply distinguished stations, the individuals are there, as a rule, from the beginning carefully trained for their sphere. Such constitutions may secure harmony between the dispositions and the station of individuals through the fact that the separate life spheres are relatively broad, and their demands and opportunities are extensive enough to offer appropriate places for the individuals, diverse as they may be from variations of heredity, education, and example. A class constitution, consequently, provides for a preëstablished harmony between the qualities or dispositions of the individual and his position in the social whole. In case, however, on account of the existence of an extensive middle class, the clearly defined classes have given place to a great number of graduated stations, the forces named cannot with certainty predispose the individual to the situation to which he belongs. What was in the other case preëstablished harmony must in this case be reached *a posteriori*, empirically; the individual must have the possibility of passing from an inappropriate to an appropriate position. In this case, therefore, the self-preservation of the group form demands that there shall be easy shifting of boundaries, constant correction and interchangeability of situations, and likewise a ready constructibility of the latter, so that special individuals may find special positions. Thus, in order to maintain its integrity, a group with a predominant middle class needs a policy quite different from that of a group under aristocratic leadership, or one entirely without class divisions.

The following, however, is to be added : What instability and variability of the group form are in succession, that the division of labor is in coexistence. In the former case the group has to adapt itself by various modifications of its form to the different life conditions which emerge one after another. In the latter case the problem of the group is to adjust its varying individual members to satisfaction of the diverse coexisting demands. The whole diversity and gradation in callings and positions to which we have referred is evidently possible only through division of labor. Consequently this division of labor, like its counterpart, variability of social life form, is a characteristic of the middle class and of its predominance. Neither the aristocracy nor the class of free peasant citizens tends to any large degree of division of labor. The aristocracy has no such tendency, because every division of labor brings with it gradation of rank, and this is repugnant to the class consciousness and inimical to its unity. The peasant class does not have it, because it is not required or per-. mitted by its technique. It is peculiar, however, that variability and division of labor, much as they essentially and in their personal agents depend on each other, with respect to the self-maintenance of the group, often work in direct opposition to each other. This results, on the one hand, from the fact, emphasized above, that multiplicity and easy gradation of positions which arise from division of labor lead to all sorts of difficulties and perplexities, unless there be added easy mobility and transferability of the social elements. These tend to offset the dangers that come from extreme division of labor, viz., disintegration (*Zersplitterung*), one-sidedness, discrepancy between the talent and the station of individuals. On the other hand, the complementary relation of division of labor and variability in respect to maintenance of the group is manifest in the following manner. There will be many cases in which the inconstancy of the middle station produces uncertainty, indefiniteness, and uprooting. This is prevented by division of labor, since it binds the elements of the group wonderfully close together. Petty groups of nature peoples, however centralized their organization may be, are easily disrupted, because each little component of the group is equally capable of separate existence. Each can do just what the other can. Owing to the hardships of their lot in external relations they are thrown upon each other. No particular qualifications of these instinctive allies are involved, however. They can associate quite at will.

The cohesion of a great civilized group, on the other hand, rests on its division of labor. The one is absolutely dependent on the others. The disruption of the group would leave each individual quite helpless. Thus division of labor, with its linking of individuals to each other, works against variability in case this would harmfully affect the maintenance of the group. This will be observable even in small groups. A band of settlers will be on the whole very pliable and variable. It will dispose itself now in centralized form, now in very free fashion, according as it is under pressure from without or has plenty of scope for action. It will confide leadership according to changing interests to frequently changing persons. It will seek prosperity now in attachment to other groups, now in exercise of the largest autonomy. These variations of their sociological form will be sure in certain cases to promote self-preservation. On the whole, however, they will give occasion for conflicts, uncertainties, and divisions; all this is energetically counterbalanced by developed division of labor. On the one hand, this puts the individual into dependence upon the group; on the other hand, it gives the group a lively interest in holding fast to the individual.

In all the cases considered thus far, the easy changeability of group life, its inclination to transfers of both formal and personal sorts, has been an adaptation to the necessities of life ; a bending necessary to avoid breaking, whenever there is a lack of that substantial firmness which, in any event, would defeat every exertion of destructive force. By its variability the group responds to the change of circumstances, and accommodates it so that the result is its own confirmation. But it may now be asked whether such changeability, such persistence through changing and often contradictory conditions, actually promotes the maintenance of the group merely as a reaction against the change of external conditions, or whether the most immanent principle of the group existence may not urge the same demand. Quite apart from the question, what external or internal occasions call forth the variations of its attitude, may not the force and health of the life process of the group, as development of purely inherent energies, be bound up with a certain change of its poise, a shifting of its interests, a somewhat frequent reconstruction of its form? Of the individual we know that varying stimulations are necessary for maintenance. The force and unity of his existence are not preserved by unbroken mechanical sameness of external and internal condition and action. On the contrary, the individual is likewise naturally adapted to preservation of his unity in change, not merely of what he does and endures, but also in change within each of these factors of his experience. It is consequently not impossible that the bond which holds the group together needs varying stimulation in order to remain in consciousness and force. A hint of such relation of things is contained in certain phenomena which manifest an intimate mixture (*Verschmelzung*) between social unity in general and a definite content or equipment of the unity. A case in point occurs, as may easily be understood, when a condition that is definite either in content or otherwise remains long unchanged, and there is danger that the condition disturbed presently by some outward circumstance may drag down the social unity itself in its fall. Just as religious conceptions are often, by long reciprocal relationship, closely interwoven with moral feelings, and by virtue of this association the removal of the feeling by enlightenment results in uprooting the ethical norms at the same time, so a formerly rich family often goes to pieces on losing its property, and likewise many a poor family when it suddenly becomes rich. In a similar way a state that has always been free may be torn by factions and dissensions after it loses its freedom (I call to mind Athens after the Macedonian period), and likewise a state formerly under despotic rule so soon as it suddenly becomes free. The history of revolutions presents the latter case often enough. It appears, therefore, as though a certain changeability in the conditions and formations of the group protects it against too rigid combination of the essential unity of the group with a particular form of the unity. In case this close combination exists in a group, the occurrence of a change, in spite of the rigid form, threatens the very life principle of the group. Against this danger fre· quent change seems to act like a sort of inoculation. The bond between the most essential and the less vital relationships remains looser, and a disturbance of the latter opposes less danger to the preservation of the group in its essential unity.

We are easily inclined to regard peace, harmony of interests, concord, as the essence of social self-preservation; all antagonism, on the other hand, as destructive of the unity which it is the essential aim to preserve, and as the fruitless consumption of force which might be used for the positive up-building of the group organism. Yet it seems more correct to interpret a certain rhythm between peace and strife as the preservative life form. This interpretation may be applied equally in two directions. It is true both of struggle between the group as a whole and external foes, in alternation with peaceful epochs, and also of the strife of competitors, parties, opposing tendencies of every sort, by the side of the facts of community and of harmony. The one is an alternative between harmonious and discordant phenomena in a series, the latter in coexistence. The motive of both is in the last analysis one and the same. It realizes itself in different ways. The struggle against a power standing outside the group brings the unity of the group and the necessity of maintaining it unshaken to most lively consciousness. It is a fact of the greatest social significance, one of the few which are true almost without exception of group formations· of every sort, that common antagonism against a third party under all circumstances tends to consolidate the combining group, and with much greater certainty than community in friendly relationships toward a third party. There is scarcely a group — domestic, ecclesiastic, economic, political, or whatever — that can dispense entirely with this cement. In the purest reciprocity there develops here the consciousness of existing unity and practical reinforcement of it, each growing and working on the basis of the other.

It appears to be necessary for us human beings, whose whole psychical nature is built upon our sensitiveness of difference, that a feeling of separateness should always exist alongside of the feeling of unity to make this latter perceptible and tangible. Now this process may, as suggested, proceed within the group itself. Aversions and antagonism between group elements may bring the actual unity of the whole, existing in spite of them, to keener effectiveness. Since these oppositions shorten the social binding cords, they tighten them at the same time and thus make them more perceptible. This is also the way to snap them, to be sure. But before that occurs, these counter-movements, which are possible only on the basis of fundamental coherence and closeness of relationship, will have brought these oppositions into more and more energetic functioning. Nor is it essential whether the adjustment is accompanied by correspondingly sharpened consciousness of the adaptation or not. Thus attacks and violence among the members of a community have had as a consequence the enactment of laws in defense against such assaults. Although these laws were measures in opposition to the hostile egoism of individuals, yet they brought the community as a whole to consciousness and expression of its totality, its coherence, its solidarity, and its unity of interest. In like manner economic competition is a highly intimate reciprocal relationship which brings the competitors and their customers closer together. It makes the former more dependent upon the latter and upon each other than they would be if it had not existed. ·Accordingly, this wish to anticipate hostilities and to minimize their consequences has led to unifications (for example, industrial and political compacts), to all sorts of usages in economic and other transactions, which, although they grew up solely on the ground of actual or possible antagonism, nevertheless have resulted in positive promotion of the coherence of the whole.

This double rôle of opposition as related to social self-preservation — with reference to external and to internal relations, as antithesis between the whole group and an external power, and as antithesis between the elements of the group among themselves —is reproduced as genuine sociological life form in the narrower relationships between individual people. These also plainly need the stimulus of difference in order to retain and protect their unity. Now this difference may reside either within the relationship itself, in the different characteristics of its temporal divisions, or in the difference which appears between the relationship as a whole and, on the other hand, experiences and emotions quite outside of it. Thus it is often remarked that friendship, love, and marriage need occasional interruptions in order to get a true realization of their meaning and intimacy (*Festigkeit*), after reconciliation. Similar relationships are to be distinguished which do not require this internal difference, but rather, along with more even internal character, become conscious of their own weal through the difference from that which the world otherwise affords, and that which is otherwise known of it. The last form surely stands higher in the scale, and gives evidence of stronger, positive motives of coherence. The first form, in its turn, stands lower, according to the degree of frequency in the alternation between the divergent and the convergent periods. The lowest grade is represented by the formula : "One minute blows, the next agreement (*Pack schlägt sich, Pack verträgt sich*)." This marks a condition in which the essential and permanent relationships have only a slight value in consciousness ; the disposition being rather determined at each moment by external stimuli, which work in accidental alternation, now in attraction, now in repulsion. For that very reason, however, there is in all this a deep utility in connection with the promotion of coherence. For wherever the occasion to be conscious of precisely this coherence is in itself slight, and the capability of appreciating it is itself not particularly developed, there will be needed, in order to arouse it, constantly renewed psychological impulses and rude stimulation from contrasts. These cannot be furnished better than in the form of constantly renewed agreements after constantly repeated disagreements. This at the same time affords the background from which unity at last appears.

I come back, herewith, to the starting point of this discussion. Enmities and strifes are, in their significance for the self-preservation of the group, the characteristic examples for the value which variability of group life, change of its forms of activity, possess for this purpose. For, although antagonism, in general, never entirely and universally dies out, yet it accords with its nature to build only a spatially and temporally limited section between the operations of the forces that make for coherence and unified harmony. In its peculiar nature, antagonism presents one of those contrast-stimuli, evidently demanded by the innermost needs of the unifying social bond, because there, as elsewhere, the permanent can emerge and come to conscious force only as a function of the changeable. Social unity is the abiding form, or element, or whatever we may call it, which asserts itself as the substantial in all changes of its peculiar, special shape, its content, its relations to the social interests and destinies; and asserts itself the more, the livelier the change of these factors. The depth (*Vertiefung*), intensiveness (*Festigkeit*), and unity of the marriage relationship, for example, is surely, *ceteris paribus*, a function of the manifoldness and changeableness of the destinies, the experience of which stands out in distinction from the unchangeability of the matrimonial communion.

It is the essence of the human that the condition of the existence of its separate factors is the existence of their opposites. The manifoldness of formations, of changes, of contents, is so essential for the self-preservation of the group, not only because in each limited period the unity of the group stands out in contrast with the passing variations, but especially because the unity always recurs as the same, while the formations, the changes, the contents, from which it is distinguished are each time different. It therefore gains thereby, as against all interruptions, those chances of confirmation and effectiveness which truth possesses over error. Little as the truth, in and of itself, in the isolated case, possesses an advantage, or a mystic power of prevalence, over error, yet its ultimate victory is probable for the reason that truth is only one, while errors about the same subject are countless. It is therefore to be assumed from the start that the truth will more frequently reappear in the see-saw of opinions, *not than error in general, to be sure, but than any given error.* So the unity of the social group has the chance to preserve, to strengthen, and to deepen itself against all interruptions and fluctuations, because these are always of different sorts, while the group unity at each reappearance is the same. By virtue of this fact, the above discussed favorable consequences of social variability for the maintenance of the group may exist without the necessity that the fact of change in general shall enter into serious competition with the principle of unity.

I close these criticisms herewith. In the nature of the case they do not attempt completeness in any direction. They rather serve to exemplify the principle which alone, in my opinion, can found an independent science of sociology, viz., the abstraction of socialization, as a form of existence with and for others, from the concrete conditions, interests, emotions, which make up the content of that form. Neither hunger nor love, neither labor nor the religious sentiment, neither technique nor the contents of intelligence, are in and of themselves alone social in character; but the coexistence and reciprocal influence of human beings make them factors actual and effectual. Although reciprocity, unity, contrasted station of human beings emerge always merely as the form of some concrete content, yet upon abstracting isolation of that form from the content rests the possibility of a science of society in the exact sense. This, as a matter of course, is not affected by the circumstance that the content of socialization, its material purpose and interest, often, if not always, decides upon its special formation. Thus the geometrical description of a crystalline form is a problem the independence of which is absolutely unaffected by the fact that its realization in the case of a single body depends upon the chemical constitution of the same. The enormous wealth of problems which this point of view makes visible within the field of historical reality seems to be beyond doubt. In view of the fact, however, that this point of view has not yet been used to differentiate a special province of research, it is first of all in order to train the vision to discern in the case of separate phenomena what is sociological and what belongs in the domain of other sciences, in order that sociology may at last stop plowing in already cultivated fields. This study is dedicated to that propædeutical purpose.

GEORG SIMMEL.

UNIVERSITY OF BERLIN.

THE LAW RELATING TO THE RELIEF AND CARE OF DEPENDENTS. V.

THE LAW RELATING TO THE CARE AND TREATMENT OF THE DEFECTIVE.[1]

THE public makes special provision for the education of the deaf and dumb and the blind, and for the care and treatment of the insane, the idiotic and feeble-minded, the epileptic and the inebriate, as well as for the care of paupers and dependent children. The laws concerning the dependent have been discussed in previous papers ; those concerning the defective classes will be discussed in this. The justification for discussing the laws relating to defectives in a study of the poor laws is found in the facts that (1) special provision is made by the public for them, and (2) historically, as the result of classification, the defective classes have largely been taken from the dependent class and methods of treatment more appropriate to them adopted.

I. THE DEAF-MUTES AND THE BLIND.

As it is impossible to educate the deaf-mutes and the blind in our non-specialized public schools, special institutions have been established for that purpose. The fact that there are relatively few of this class necessitates that they should be brought together in a central institution and that the state should provide for the extraordinary expense involved in thus educating them away from home. Such provision has, with a few exceptions, been made by all our commonwealths.[2]

In a number of the eastern states, where private institutions are well developed, the pupils are sent to private schools at public expense. In a number of western states, yet too sparsely set-

---

[1] The authorities to which references are made in this paper, when not stated, are those cited in a previous paper, pp. 632, 633, JOURNAL OF SOCIOLOGY, March, 1898.

[2] Only in Oklahoma and New Mexico has no provision for the education of the blind been found. All provide for the education of deaf-mutes.

tled to afford institutions of their own, they are sent to those of the neighboring states.[1] The great majority of the states have, however, one or more public institutions to which all may be sent. In some cases both classes are educated in different departments of one institution, in others in separate schools.[2] These educational facilities are usually offered to children of "school age." Sometimes the term of instruction is fixed, and in many cases is very short.[3] In most of the states, however, this entire matter is left with the board of directors of the institution. Usually maintenance and tuition are provided for all by the state free of charge. In some sixteen states, however, a distinction is made between indigents and those able to pay, the latter being compelled to pay their expenses.[4] In Missouri the

[1] In the following states both the blind and the deaf and dumb are sent to private institutions or to the institutions of neighboring states: Massachusetts, New Hampshire, Vermont, Maine, Connecticut, Delaware, Pennsylvania, Wyoming, Idaho, Nevada, and Arizona. The same is true of the blind in Rhode Island and New Jersey, and of the deaf and dumb in Oklahoma and New York.

[2] In Virginia, West Virginia, Maryland, North Carolina, South Carolina, Florida, Louisiana, Minnesota, Montana, Colorado, Washington, and California one institution serves for the education of both the deaf and dumb and the blind. In Mississippi, Georgia, Tennessee, Texas, Arkansas, Michigan, Indiana, Ohio, Illinois, Wisconsin, North Dakota, South Dakota, Iowa, Nebraska, Kansas, Missouri, and Oregon they are educated in separate institutions, each state having two. Kentucky has three, one for the blind and one for white and one for colored deaf-mutes. Alabama has two institutions, a second one having been established for the colored blind and mute. New York has a school for the blind, while Rhode Island, New Jersey, and New Mexico have institutions for the deaf and dumb.

[3] The term of instruction is fixed in Texas and Oregon at two; in Georgia, four; in Kentucky and West Virginia, five, and in Alabama, six years.

[4] In the following states all are maintained and educated free of charge, the county, as a rule, paying the cost of clothing and transporting the indigent: Massachusetts (ch. 329, Supplement), Maine (126, 206, ch. 11), Connecticut (Act of May 23, 1893), Rhode Island (23, ch. 85; 4, ch. 86), New York (8, p. 284), West Virginia (ch. 45, as amended in 1895), North Carolina (2230, 2238), Georgia (1215, 1235), Texas (121-136), Arkansas (4039-4044), Louisiana (No. 49, Acts of 1888), Michigan (1851-1853, 1871), Indiana (2807-2809), Ohio (665-668), Illinois (97, ch. 23), Minnesota (3442-3443), North Dakota (960-963), South Dakota (261, 269, 271), Iowa (2762-2765, 2776-2779), Nebraska (2513⁸⁻⁹), Kansas (6153-6154), Montana (3442-3443), Wyoming (Act of 1890), Utah (2102, 2116), Colorado (3253, Mills' Supplement), Washington (1981, 2010), and California (2238-2240). In Massachusetts, Rhode Island, and Minnesota the pupils may reimburse the state. In New Hampshire (1, ch. 86), Vermont (684, 687), Maryland (1-5, art. 30), New Jersey (1-12, p. 1179), Pennsylvania

county, which is responsible for the indigent as paupers, must bear the expense.[1] In Delaware the expense of educating the deaf-mutes and the blind is deducted from the school fund drawn by the counties.[2]

While, for reasons of economy, most of the blind and the mutes are educated in state institutions, the larger cities have in a few instances provided facilities for them as a part of their public-school systems. In Pennsylvania school districts of more than 20,000, having eight or more deaf-mutes, may, as a part of the public-school system, provide schools for them.[3] In Wisconsin cities and villages may establish schools for the deaf and dumb and the blind. If approved by the state board of control, the state pays them $100 for each child educated during the school year. The local governments not having such provision send their defectives to the state institutions, paying $100 per year toward their support.[4]

While most of the states have provided special schools for the education of these defectives, this does not solve the problem of support in adult life, particularly for the blind. Most of this class cannot become self-supporting, and many are necessarily supported at public expense. A few states have made special provision for them, usually with the idea of making them self-supporting. In 1886 Ohio enacted a law providing for the establishment of a state institution where the able-bodied, dependent blind of the state might be brought together and given opportunities for work. This institution met with poor success, however, and was discontinued in 1896. In 1885 California made institutional provision for the indigent blind of both sexes. Work was to be required of the able-bodied. In 1890 Iowa established "The Industrial Home for the Adult Blind," the object of which was "to provide a working home and means

(1, p. 705), Virginia (1658), South Carolina (1060, 1061), Florida (274, as amended in 1895), Mississippi (2316), Alabama (1095, 1096), Kentucky (284, 289, 299), Idaho (Act of March 14, 1891), Nevada (1498–1500), Arizona (Act of March 4, 1895), New Mexico (Act of February 24, 1887), and Oregon (2714) tuition and maintenance are furnished free of charge to indigents only, others being compelled to pay.

[1] 5712, 5729.
[2] Act of March 23, 1875.
[3] 6, p. 706.
[4] 573, 579*a*.

for the blind to earn and provide their own subsistence." They are taught a trade and then may, if they care to, remain and ply it in the institution. The statutes of Maryland (8, art. 30) authorize the directors of the institute for the blind youth to use a part of the endowment fund for the erection of workshops and a store, for the manufacture and sale of articles; the indigent adult blind of the state being permitted to enjoy the opportunities afforded by the institution. Finally, the statutes of New York provide that the directors of the institution for the blind at Batavia may, upon his graduation, set an indigent pupil up in business, the expense involved being charged to the county responsible for him as a dependent.

II. THE INSANE.

Every commonwealth, with the exception of Oklahoma Territory, has provided one or more hospitals for the custody and treatment of the "acute," "violently," and "dangerously insane."[1] With a few exceptions, the idiotic, the harmless insane, and cases of delirium tremens are explicitly excluded. The provision for the violent cases of insanity is, however, in many states very inadequate, and many are confined in the almshouses and jails.[2]

Historically the insane have been treated first as possessed, then as vagrant, and finally as diseased. In 1744 all the insane

[1] For the acute insane New York has eleven hospitals; Ohio (including the Long-view Asylum) six; Illinois, Indiana, Iowa, Massachusetts, and Virginia, four; California, Michigan, Minnesota, Missouri, North Carolina, and Tennessee, three; Maryland, Mississippi, New Jersey, Pennsylvania, South Dakota, Nebraska, Texas, Vermont, Washington, West Virginia, and Wisconsin, two; while each of the remaining states and the District of Columbia have one. Oklahoma sends her insane to the hospitals of the adjoining states.

[2] By an act of June 29, 1895, Connecticut prohibits the retention of the insane in the county jails. In Michigan (1902) they are not to be kept in the jail longer than ten days. In a number of states it is provided that the insane are not to be retained in the almshouses when there is sufficient room for them at the hospital. In Massachusetts (ch. 319, Supplement) cases of insanity of less than twelve months' duration must be treated when retained in the almshouse. In most of the states the hospital facilities are inadequate, and many of them expressly provide that the dangerously and the indigent insane shall be confined in the almshouse or the county jail until room may be had for them in the hospitals.

of England were ordered to be confined as a dangerous class of vagrants. This legislation was copied by the colonies, and even now, when insanity is recognized and dealt with as a disease, traces of the old treatment are found. These are to be seen in the commitment laws of several of the states.

The states may be thrown into four groups, according as the insane (1) are arraigned or tried in the county or the justice court, and committed to the hospital without a medical examination or the testimony of a medical authority; or (2) are tried in the county or justice court and committed, an examination and certificate of insanity by one or more physicians being required; or (3) are examined by, and committed upon the certificate of, one or more physicians, the function of the court being reduced to registering their finding; or (4) are arraigned, and an inquisition made, by a regularly constituted commission.[1]

In the first group are Colorado, Louisiana, Maryland, New Mexico, Texas, Virginia, and Wyoming. In Virginia a person suspected of being insane is ordered by a justice to be brought before him and two other justices for examination. Witnesses (including a physician, if one is attending the case) are subpœnaed to appear. If committed, the patient is reëxamined and received or dismissed by the board of trustees of the asylum.[2] Upon petition to the effect that a person is insane and dangerous to the community, the county or probate judge in Colorado, Maryland, Texas, and Wyoming impanels a jury (in Colorado and Texas of six, in the others of twelve), which decides as to the insanity of the person in question.[3] However, in Texas trial by jury applies only to the pauper insane. Other patients are committed by the court upon the certificate of insanity made, upon examination, by a physician. In Louisiana and New

[1] The commitment laws of the several commonwealths were treated at length in a committee report, made by Stephen Smith at the National Conference of Charities and Corrections in 1892. The report was based upon MR. HARRISON'S *A Collection of the Lunacy Laws of the United States*, compiled in 1884. While a few states have amended their law for the better since this report was made, its statements in most cases still hold true. The report referred to will be found in the *Report of the N. C. C. C.* for 1892, pp. 94–124.

[2] 1669.   [3] 2935; I, art. 59; 96; 2391.

Mexico the insane are examined and committed by the court.[1] In Kentucky, also, a lunatic may be examined by a jury of six, or, if he is not brought into court, by two physicians appointed by the court to visit and examine him in his home. The judge commits or dismisses the "lunatic" upon the finding of the jury or the committee of physicians.[2] In Rhode Island an insane person may be committed by the justice of the peace, or, upon petition, a justice of the supreme court may appoint a committee of three to make an examination of the lunatic, he then deciding the case in accordance with the evidence secured. In neither case is medical testimony necessary.[3] In Mississippi the board of trustees for the hospital may admit patients upon the certificate of two physicians, or the case may be adjudicated, the person being tried by jury in the chancery court.[4] In Wisconsin and Vermont a trial by jury may be demanded after an examination has been made by physicians appointed by the court.[5]

The second group, in which the decision as to insanity and the power of commitment rests with the court, jury, or justice, but in which a medical examination by one or more competent physicians must be made, includes the great majority of the commonwealths. The court hears the case, taking the testimony of at least one physician, in Arizona, Arkansas, Idaho, Missouri, Nevada, New Jersey, Ohio, and Oregon.[6] The same provision, except that the testimony of at least two physicians must be taken, obtains in California, Connecticut, Massachusetts, Michigan, Minnesota, Montana, South Carolina, Utah, and Washington.[7] In Montana the relatives of the person whose sanity is questioned may demand a trial by jury. In Wisconsin commitment is made by the court upon an examination by two physicians appointed by him for that purpose, or a trial by jury may be demanded. In New York the court commits upon the finding of two

[1] 1768; 52.
[2] 2156–2157.
[3] 6–11, ch. 82.
[4] 2835, 2843.
[5] 592, 593; Shumway *vs.* Shumway, 2 Vt. 339.
[6] 2156; 3991–3992; 769–776; 491–496; 1457; 26, p. 1984; 703–706; 3557.
[7] 2210–2217; Act of June 13, 1895; 11–13, ch. 87; 1901; 3462–3465; 2300–2305; 1588; 2171–2177; 1544.

"examiners in lunacy," or he may institute further inquiry into the case, or an appeal may be taken and the case tried by jury. The " examiners in lunacy" are physicians of three years' experience who are registered with and certified to by the Commission in Lunacy.[1] Minnesota also provided for " examiners in lunacy,'' but that part of the statute has been declared unconstitutional. In Florida the court orders commitment upon the basis of the evidence taken by a committee of three, one of whom must be a physician, appointed by him to make an examination of the lunatic.[2] In Alabama the case is heard by the court with or without a jury, the testimony of at least one physician being taken.[3] In Georgia, Illinois, Kansas, and Oklahoma trial is by a jury, one of whom must be a physician.[4] In Indiana, North Carolina, Tennessee, and West Virginia the case is tried before the justice, or justices, of the peace instead of the court, the testimony of at least one physician being required.[5] In Indiana the inquest is before two, in North Carolina before two or more justices.

In the third group, where the insane are admitted to the hospital upon the certificate of physicians, the court recording the finding in the case without having power to revise the decision, are Delaware, Mississippi, New Hampshire, Pennsylvania, Vermont, and the District of Columbia. Patients are admitted to the hospital in Delaware upon the certificate of two physicans with five years' experience, whose ability and integrity are certified to by someone capable of administering oaths.[6] A like provision is found in Vermont, New Hampshire, and the District of Columbia.[7] In New Hampshire, however, the court has held that a certificate " to the genuineness of the signatures of the physicians and to their respectability is not essential to a legal commitment."[8] In Pennsylvania the friends of a lunatic may secure his admission to the hospital by filing with the court

[1] 60–63 ch. 545, Acts of 1896.   [3] 1241.
[2] Act of May 29, 1895.
[4] Acts of November 11, 1889, and December 17, 1894 ; 5–10, ch. 85 ; 3677–3681 ; Act of 1895.
[5] 2843–2851 ; 2256–2257 ; 2579 ; 9, ch. 558.   [7] 3239–3240 ; 18, ch. 10 ; 4845–4846.
[6] Act of April 12, 1893.   [8] Howe *vs.* Bancroft, 62 N. H., 362.

the certificates of two physicians to the effect that he is insane. In other cases the court appoints a committee of three (a physician, a lawyer, and a third) to visit and examine the afflicted person. Their finding is recorded with the court, and this certificate commits the insane person to the hospital.[1] The law in Mississippi has been referred to above. In addition to these cases, the friends of an insane person may in several states, upon the presentation of a certificate of insanity signed by two or more competent physicians, secure his admission to the hospital as a "pay patient."

Iowa, Maine, Nebraska, North Dakota, and South Dakota form the last group, those having regularly constituted commissions for the examination and commitment of the insane. In Maine the commission is composed of certain municipal or town officers. The evidence and certificates of at least two physicians are required.[2] In Iowa and Nebraska each county has three commissioners of insanity, one of whom is the clerk of the court, one a physician, and one a lawyer, the latter two being appointed by the court and serving for two years. The commissioners appoint a physician to examine the insane person, and the decision as to insanity and the commitment are made by them.[3] In Iowa an appeal may be taken within ten days to the circuit court. The commissions in the two Dakotas are quite similar to these, consisting of the judge of probate and a physician and a lawyer appointed by the board of county commissioners and serving for two years.[4] Their powers and duties are the same as those of the Iowa and Nebraska commissions.

The indigent insane are usually maintained and treated in the hospitals at state expense, the costs of transporting and clothing them being at the expense of the county or political division responsible for them as paupers. In a few states all are cared for free of charge, regardless of their ability to pay.[5] In a few other states the whole expense is borne by the county or

[1] 1–7, p. 1252.
[2] 13, ch. 143.
[3] 2189–2198; 3336–3342.
[4] 1513, 1530 (N. D.); 2179–2185 (S. D.).
[5] This is the case in Illinois (44, ch. 23, and 15, ch. 58), Indiana (2763–2765), Minnesota (3461), North Dakota (998), and Ohio (631).

other unit responsible for the indigent cases as dependents,[1] and, finally, in five states the expense is shared between the state and the county or town.[2]

Few states have made any adequate provision for the care of those cases proving to be chronic. While a few states have special wards or special asylums for this class, they are usually discharged from the hospitals in order to obtain room for the more recent and the more violent cases. Six states (California, Illinois, Massachusetts, Nebraska, New York, and Pennsylvania) have established state asylums, and transfer their chronic patients to them.[3] Some few of the harmless class are boarded with families. In Massachusetts the State Board of Lunacy and Charity is authorized to board out the harmless insane who are state dependents. The overseers of the poor are likewise authorized to board out those who are dependent upon the towns. The expense of boarding these with families is not to exceed the

[1] The indigent insane are a county expense in Alabama (1245, 1255), Maryland (2, art. 59), Michigan (1904, 1912, 1914), Missouri (484, 5556, 5558), South Carolina (1585, 1601), South Dakota (Act of March 27, 1891), and Tennessee (2619, 2623–2627). In Michigan the insane after two years' confinement become state charges. The counties bear the expense of those indigents in Iowa (2218–2226, 2236) and Nebraska (3365–3366) who have, the state of those who have not, county settlements. So, too, in Massachusetts (31, 34, ch. 87) the state or the town bears the expense according as the indigent is a state or a town charge, and in New Hampshire (20–26, ch. 10) the state, the county, or the town bears the expense according as the person is a criminal, or as he has only a county settlement, or as he has a town settlement.

[2] In Connecticut (Act of June 13, 1895) the relatives, or, if indigent, the county, must pay $2 per week for the patient, the state bearing the additional expense. The state of Maine (14, ch. 143) pays $1.50 per week for each indigent inmate of the asylum, the towns bearing the remaining expense. The counties of Pennsylvania (52, p. 1258, and 162, p. 1268) pay $1.75 per week toward the support of their indigent acute insane, the state not more than $2 to cover the additional cost. In the case of the chronic insane, the counties pay $1 per week, the state not more than $1.50. The counties of New Jersey (29, 30, 36, p. 1985) pay $3 per week toward the support of their indigents in the state hospital, the state, as will be seen later, subsidizing in turn the counties caring for the insane. Finally, the state of Wisconsin (595, 604 *k and n*) pays the counties $2.75 per week for the acute, and $1.50 per week for the chronic insane, cared for by them, the counties in turn paying $1.50 per week for the indigent patients cared for by the state.

[3] MR. WARNER, in his *American Charities*, states that the popular clamor against adjudging anyone incurably insane has been sufficient in California to defeat the purpose of the law providing a hospital for chronic cases, and that the new hospital and the old ones alike are used for both the curable and the chronic insane.

expense of caring for them in the hospital. The state board is to visit all persons so boarded out at least once in three months, and to remove them if not well cared for.[1] In 1889 Michigan authorized the overseers and the superintendents of the poor to board out idiots and the harmless insane. Minnesota has made provision for boarding those who cannot be cared for in their homes, with families, the expense of so doing not to exceed $3 per week.[2]

Insane criminals are sometimes cared for in the prisons, sometimes in the hospitals for the insane. When transferred to the hospitals, they are usually confined in a special ward. Four states (Massachusetts, New York, Michigan, and Illinois) have established special hospitals for them. When cured, they are transferred to the prison, or, if the sentence has expired, discharged.

From the condition of the inmates more abuses are likely to arise in connection with the hospitals for the insane than in connection with other institutions. To prevent these abuses many of the states have made it incumbent upon the boards of directors to visit and inspect their hospitals frequently. As will be seen in a subsequent paper, where state boards of charities have been created, the hospitals for the insane are to receive their special attention.

We have thus far been concerned almost exclusively with the state hospitals. The state system of care has prevailed. Yet a word should be said concerning the "Wisconsin plan," a compromise between the state and the county systems.

In Wisconsin the counties are authorized, with the consent of the State Board of Control, to establish county asylums for the insane. These are designed primarily for the care of the chronic cases, yet they are also used to some extent for the treatment of the acute insane. When approved by the state board, the state pays them $1.50 per week for each chronic, and $2.75 per week for each acute case, cared for. When the county does not care for its own insane, but sends them to the state hospital, it must pay the state $1.50 per week for each indigent so sent.[3]

[1] Ch. 385, Supplement.   [2] 3489.   [3] 604 *k-n*.

New Jersey has provision for something not dissimilar to the "Wisconsin plan." The counties are authorized to erect hospitals for the insane. These are subsidized, the state paying $2 per week for each indigent patient treated. As the counties must pay not to exceed $3 per week for the indigents sent to the state hospital, it seems that inducement is given for the development of local care.x Missouri has authorized all counties having a population of more than a hundred thousand (the city of St. Louis) to establish asylums for the insane and to withdraw their patients from the state hospitals, the state paying the counties so doing $1 per week for each indigent patient treated.[2] And, lastly, Kansas has adopted the policy of paying the counties for caring for those insane who, because of insufficient room, cannot gain admission to the public hospital.[3]

The last point of which we wish to speak is the lunacy commissions of a number of states, and the supervision and regulation of private asylums and retreats for the insane.

In Massachusetts the law relating to the commitment and discharge of the insane applies as well to the private as to the public hospitals, and no one may be admitted except upon the certificate of two physicians. All private asylums must be licensed by the governor and his council, and are subject to visitation by them. The State Board of Lunacy and Charity may visit and inspect both public and private hospitals and discharge patients at its will.[4] Similarly, in Connecticut all private asylums must be licensed by the governor. All superintendents of asylums must have had three years' experience in the treatment of the insane. A license may be revoked for failure to comply with the conditions upon which it was granted.[5]

The Commission of Lunacy of New York visits all institutions caring for the insane, whether public or private, at least twice each year; all cases received at the hospitals must be reported to it within ten days and all cases discharged within three days; all "examiners in lunacy" must be registered with it; and all private asylums must be licensed by it. License may be

[1] Act of February 14, 1888.   [3] 3734-3736.   [5] Act of June 9, 1879.
[2] 517-520.   [4] 1, 12, 13, 53, 54, ch. 87.

granted only after an examination of the plan of the premises and of the number of patients to be received by the institution, etc., and may be revoked by the commission at any time. This commission consists of three men, one of whom (the chairman) must be a physician, with ten years' experience in the practice of medicine and five years' experience in the treatment of the insane, and another a lawyer, with ten years' experience in the practice of his profession. The chairman receives an annual salary of $5,000, the lawyer $3,000, and the third member of the commission $10 per day for the time actually spent in the performance of his duties. The members are appointed by the governor and serve for a term of six years.[1] Private asylums are similarly licensed in New Jersey by the board of managers for the public hospitals, and are visited and inspected by it at least once each year.[2]

Maryland has a lunacy commission consisting of the attorney-general and four other members, two of whom must be physicians, appointed by the governor and serving for four years. The commission has supervision over all institutions caring for the insane, and all private asylums must be licensed by it. However, this does not apply to incorporated institutions and to county asylums not receiving "pay patients" from other counties.[3] In Pennsylvania all private asylums must be licensed by the lunacy commission and must report all cases admitted to it. The commission may fix the conditions of reception and discharge of patients, etc. All hospitals, private and public, are to be visited by it annually and a report made to the State Board of Public Charities. The commission consists of five members, appointed by the state board.[4]

Vermont has three supervisors of the insane, appointed by the governor and serving for six years. All private asylums must be licensed, and may be visited and inspected by them. They form a board of appeal in cases of commitment.[5] Similarly, in Illinois all private asylums are to be licensed by the State Board of Commissioners of Charities and Corrections.[6] In

[1] 1-14, 47, ch. 545, Acts of 1896.   [3] 12-27, art. 59.   [5] 2898-2905; 3274-3279.
[2] Act of February 26, 1895.   [4] 18-23, 26, 27, p. 1254.   [6] 33, ch. 85.

Minnesota all private asylums must be licensed by the board of managers of the public hospitals. And, lastly, the State Board of Health of New Hampshire serves as a lunacy commission in that state. It must, through a representative, visit all institutions caring for the insane at least once each four months, and records of all patients received at hospitals must be filed with it within three days.[1]

III. THE IDIOTIC AND FEEBLE-MINDED.

The third class of defectives to receive special attention was the idiotic and feeble-minded youth. Like the blind and the deaf and dumb, such persons require special institutions for their education and treatment. Twenty-three states now provide special facilities for their education and treatment, nineteen in state institutions, four in private institutions or in the public institutions of the neighboring states. Where special provision has not been made for this class, large numbers of them are found in the almshouses. Where special provision has been made, it is, as a rule, very inadequate for the care of all.[2]

Although the curative and custodial element has constantly become more prominent, historically the primary purpose of the organization of the institutions for the feeble-minded was that of affording educational facilities for them. The four states of Delaware, New Hampshire, Rhode Island, and Vermont now make provision for the education of the feeble-minded and the imbecile, as well as the blind, in private institutions or in the public institutions of the neighboring states.[3] In Minnesota,

[1] 32–36, ch. 10.

[2] For an excellent article, giving the statistics of the public institutions for the feeble-minded in the nineteen states, see F. M. POWELL's paper on the "Care of the Feeble-minded," *Report of the N. C. C. C.*, 1897, pp. 287–302.

The twenty-four institutions of these nineteen states care for 8,492 feeble-minded persons. The census of 1890 reports 95,609 such persons in the United States. This shows that the great majority of this class of defectives is, as yet, unprovided for.

DR. FERNALD, in the *Report of the N. C. C. C.* for 1893, gives a detailed history up to that time of the institutions for the feeble-minded in the several states. A table taken from that paper, giving the location, date of organization, and capacity of the several institutions, may be found on p. 278 of WARNER'S *American Charities.* The table given by Mr. Powell, however, gives more complete and more recent data.

[3] The statutes of Delaware (by an act of February 22, 1861) provide that indigent,

Montana, and Washington the blind, the deaf and dumb, and the feeble-minded are all educated in separate departments of the same institutions.[1]   The remaining sixteen states have one or more independent institutions for this class.[2]

Usually two departments, the one educational, the other custodial, are organized.   Admission is usually limited to children of school age.[3]   After the course of instruction has been completed, the board of trustees may discharge the person or may retain him in the custodial department of the institution. Usually none are excluded because of a special kind of mental deficiency.   New York, however, has special institutions for unteachable idiots and epileptics, and so excludes them from the school for the feeble-minded.   Massachusetts has also made special provision for epileptics, and likewise excludes them from the institution for feeble-minded youth.   In Washington only those capable of instruction are admitted.

As with the blind and the deaf-mutes, some states educate all the feeble-minded free of charge, regardless of their ability to pay, while others educate only the indigent at public expense.[4]

idiotic, and feeble-minded children may be sent to the Pennsylvania Training School for the Feeble-minded, the expense not to exceed $1,600 in any one year, and no county being entitled to send more than two such indigents at one time.   New Hampshire (1, ch. 86) makes an annual appropriation of $1,000 for the education of the indigent feeble-minded of the state.   Vermont (682) makes a similar appropriation of $2,000.   Rhode Island (ch. 85) makes provision for the education of imbeciles, as well as of the blind, in institutions within or without the state.

We have been unable to find whether any imbecile youths are really educated in accordance with these provisions.

[1] 3437-3446; 2300-2307; 1997-2011.   Each of the three departments of the Minnesota school has its own superintendent.

[2] The sixteen states are California, Connecticut, Illinois, Indiana, Iowa, Kansas, Kentucky, Maryland, Massachusetts, Michigan, Nebraska, New Jersey, New York, Ohio, Pennsylvania, and Wisconsin.   Of these (see *Report of the N. C. C. C.*, 1897, p. 290) New York has three institutions, and Pennsylvania and New Jersey two each. In addition to this Dr. Powell reports North Dakota as caring for forty-five feeble-minded persons in the hospital for the insane at Jamestown.

[3] In a few states the ages are limited as follows: California (Act of 1885), Iowa (2714), and Nebraska (3080), from five to eighteen; Kentucky (617), from six to eighteen; Michigan (20, Act of June 2, 1893), from six to twenty-one; Kansas (6175), and Ohio (671), under fifteen; Indiana (2834), under sixteen; and Pennsylvania (19, p. 707), under twenty.

[4] In the following states all are maintained and educated at state expense, the

Special provision has been made for the adult feeble-minded in New York, New Jersey, and Iowa. New York has a custodial asylum at Rome for adult unteachable idiots. New York and New Jersey have state homes for the detention and care of feeble-minded women. In 1892 Iowa provided for the erection of cottages for feeble-minded adults in connection with its school for feeble-minded youths.

IV. THE EPILEPTIC.

Little has been done to remove the epileptic from contact with the insane and the feeble-minded. In a few instances, as in Virginia, they are placed in a separate ward of the insane asylum. Only three states, Ohio, New York, and Massachusetts, have established institutions designed solely for their care and treatment.[1]

A measure providing for a hospital for the epileptic was passed by the Ohio legislature in 1890. Patients are committed by the probate judge upon the certificate of a practicing physician. The patients are apportioned among the several counties of the state in proportion to population, and are a state expense. New York established Craig Colony, a similar institution, in 1894. In the following year Massachusetts also established a hospital for epileptics. It is designed for the care of those adult epileptics who are not idiotic, inebriate, or violently insane. The laws relating to the commitment and support of the insane apply to the commitment and support of the epileptic.

V. THE INEBRIATE.

With the recognition of inebriety as a disease and not as a crime, a few states have made public provision for its treatment. In a few states the law provides that the inebriate may be com-

county (or town) bearing the expenses of clothing and transporting the indigent: Illinois, Iowa, Kansas, Michigan, Minnesota, Montana, Nebraska, Ohio, and Washington. In the other states only the indigent pupils are a public expense.

[1] For an account of the work done by the Ohio Hospital for Epileptics, see a paper by H. C. RUTTER, "Colony Care of the Epileptic," *Report of N. C. C. C.*, 1897, p. 63. Something in regard to Craig Colony may also be found in the same report, p. 69, in a paper by WILLIAM P. SPRATLING on "Industrial Education for Epileptics."

mitted to the hospitals along with the insane. In Vermont they may be committed like the insane to the hospital or to private institutions for the cure of drunkenness.[1] Massachusetts has established a state institution for the treatment of such cases, the laws relating to the commitment and support of the insane applying.[2] Pennsylvania authorizes the counties to establish hospitals in connection with the workhouses, and to commit all inebriates for a course of treatment of from six months to two years, the indigents to be committed at the expense of the county.[3] In Michigan and Wisconsin they are to be committed to some private asylum, if indigent at public expense.[4] The commitment in the former state is to be for not longer than thirty days ; the cost of treatment in the latter, not greater than $130. In Louisiana the judge of the district court may, upon the application of the relatives of an indigent drunkard, who has lost the power of "reasonable self-control," commit him at the expense of the parish to some institution for treatment, provided, however, that the institution will agree to cure the inebriate at a cost not to exceed $100.[5] Minnesota has provided for the commitment of drunkards to a special department of the state hospital for the insane.[6] She also authorizes the county judge to commit drunkards to some institution to take the "gold cure, " the cost of treatment not to exceed $100.[7] And, lastly, California has authorized certain counties holding lands reserved for that purpose to erect hospitals for the inebriate.[8]

VI. CONSUMPTIVES AND TUBERCULAR PATIENTS.

Massachusetts, always leading in providing for the care of the indigent and for the treatment of the defective, has established a state hospital for consumptives and tubercular patients. The laws (except as to commitment) relating to the insane apply here also.[9]

Good management of state institutions is necessary for effi-

[1] 4557-4558.
[2] Act of June 5, 1889.
[3] Act of June 26, 1896.
[4] Act of June 2, 1893 ; Act of April 19, 1895.
[5] Act of July 12, 1894.
[6] Act of April 25, 1895.
[7] Act of April 22, 1895.
[8] Act of March 27, 1895.
[9] Act of June 5, 1895.

cient service. The selection of directors is the thing cf most vital importance in the creation of an institution. The selection must be removed from politics, and be such as to secure intelligent men. To remove the selection from politics, all opportunity for financial gain, either by salary or in awarding contracts, must be removed. To secure intelligent service, appointments must be for long terms, and the board must be a continuous body. A brief notice of the appointment of boards of directors, their salaries, if any, and the appointment of officers for the several state institutions has been reserved for this place.

The boards of directors for the several state institutions are usually appointed by the governor, with the advice and consent of the senate. In a few of the southern states, however, the (nominal) consent of the senate is not required. In Nebraska the members of the boards are elected by the general assembly. In a few of the western states certain of the state officers serve in the capacity of a board of control. The boards of directors are, with two exceptions (not including the salaried state boards of control, which will be discussed in a subsequent paper), unsalaried, or have salary only sufficient to cover expenses.[1]   In Georgia the trustees for the asylum for the insane receive $300 per year, but this is in lieu of all expenses.[2]   In Colorado the trustees for the school for the blind and the deaf and dumb receive annual salaries of $150, while the trustees for the hospital for the insane receive salaries of $600.[3]   Fortunately no such flagrant case of salaried boards, such as Indiana formerly had, now exists. The provision that members of boards shall not be interested in any contracts awarded is almost universal, and in many cases penalties are attached for its violation, but it is doubtful whether such legislation is, or can be made, effective. Continuous boards have become quite the rule.[4]

[1] In the following states the boards of the several institutions receive payment for the time spent in the performance of their duties (ranging from $2 to $10 per day, the time being limited to a few days per year), and mileage : California, Arizona, Iowa, Michigan, Nebraska, North Dakota, Vermont, Maine, Texas, Washington, and Idaho.

[2] 1343.   [3] 2970.

[4] The boards of some, or all, of the institutions of the following states are so

With few exceptions, the states have a distinct board for each institution. A few states have, however, sought to secure more efficient service by centralizing the direction of the several institutions in the hands of a single board. In some instances the several state hospitals for the insane have been placed under the direction of a single board.[1] Seven states (Kansas, Rhode Island, Arkansas, South Dakota, Wyoming, Iowa, and Wisconsin) have created state boards of control, and vested the management of all the state institutions for defectives in them.

Usually the legislatures have left the boards of directors free in the management of their respective institutions. They usually have power to appoint all necessary officers (or to appoint a superintendent and to confirm his appointments), and to fix their salaries. But two or three instances remain where, as in Mississippi and Nebraska, the governor appoints the superintendents of the several institutions.[2] The legislature has, however, in a number of instances fixed the salaries of some, or all, of the officers of the institutions.[3] In New York the salaries of the officers and employés connected with the hospitals for the insane are fixed by the Commission in Lunacy.[4]

H. A. MILLIS.

THE UNIVERSITY OF CHICAGO.

arranged as to be continuous bodies : Arizona, Connecticut, California, Colorado, Illinois, Indiana, Kentucky, Louisiana, Maryland, Massachusetts, Michigan, New Hampshire, New Jersey, New Mexico, New York, North Carolina, North Dakota, Ohio, Pennsylvania, Tennessee, Texas, Utah, Vermont, Virginia, Washington, and West Virginia.

[1] This is the case in New Jersey, Minnesota, and Texas.

[2] 2816; 3330.

[3] The salaries of some, or all, of the officers in the institutions of the following states are fixed by statute : Colorado, California, Florida, Illinois, Kentucky, Maine, Ohio, North Dakota, Nevada, and Washington. In a few instances, as in Indiana and Michigan, maximum salaries are fixed.

[4] 38, ch. 545, Acts of 1896.

SOME DEMANDS OF EDUCATION UPON ANTHROPOLOGY.

The current emphasis upon the genetic method of study has focused attention upon many subjects that would otherwise have but a limited interest. As an end in itself, anthropology is of interest to the few; as a means of interpreting other sciences an acquaintance with its leading facts and principles is indispensable to the many. But even from the standpoint of means the circle of interest is widening. Heretofore the genesis of industries or institutions has been studied mainly for the purpose of gaining an insight into the product of development; with the progress of analytical thought the emphasis of interest is placed upon the process, as a means of gaining principles of interpretation. As a result, anthropology has come to have a significance for lines of thought upon which it was formerly thought to have but little bearing.

Until recently, education has run in the grooves of tradition, but the past twenty-five years have seen the breaking up of old ideals and methods, and an attempt to reconstruct both anew, not only on the basis of psychology and ethics, but on that of the social sciences as well. The emphasis on the social aspects of education is a marked feature of the present time. But the consideration of education from this broader standpoint demands a broader basis of tributary sciences, both for the building up of scientific pedagogy, and for the practical administration of educational affairs. As a social institution, the school cannot be efficiently directed without a knowledge of social agencies in general, nor can education as a social process be effectively furthered without an insight into the nature of the general processes of development. Hence sociology has become a necessary factor in the teacher's equipment.

But if education thus looks to sociology for insight, it recogizes that sociology itself finds that insight in no small degree in anthropology, and that many questions of both practical and theoretical import can only be solved, if solved at all, by the help of that science. The question of parallelism between the development of the individual and that of the race, with the consequences assumed by the culture-epoch theory that such a parallelism must determine the sequence of thought in the school curriculum; the extent and character of the recapitulation of race experiences and interests in the individual; the relation of motor activity to intellectual development in the individual and in the race, with its consequences for education; the function of play in development, and its bearing upon the educational process — all these must be considered from the anthropological standpoint as well as from the psychological, as has been the case hitherto. From the practical side, also, anthropology is coming to have an increasing significance for education, both directly and indirectly.

That the present status of anthropological science is such as to furnish pedagogy the needed assistance will hardly be claimed. Pedagogy needs many anthropological data not yet obtained; it needs also principles of interpretation which must be derived from those facts organized in such way as to yield their pedagogical significance. It may be claimed that the science itself is not yet sufficiently organized to furnish interpretive principles, but as long as the interest is focused on facts only, this will remain so. It is true that interpretation must be based on a broad foundation of facts, but the mere accumulation of data is insufficient. That observation and interpretation are mutually interpretive is a recognized principle in modern psychology. Its application to anthropological investigation has not been sufficiently recognized. Are the anthropological data insufficient to give an insight into the different phases of human development? The organization of those thus far obtained into a working body of knowledge will hasten their accumulation.

It is evident that the value of anthropological data to any science seeking the aid that anthropology can give, will depend on the organization of the data from the standpoint of the science that seeks it. The facts of anthropology have received synthetic treatment from many standpoints, those of social and industrial development in particular. The syntheses made by Morgan, Spencer, Ward, Giddings, and others, are of great value to all, but to sociology in particular, because written on the basis of a sociological interest. But while such a synthesis is fundamental, and hence of general value to education, a further synthesis is needed, within the organization already effected, of such data as have a direct bearing upon education. What has been done meets a general need ; the specific need remains to be met by a synthesis of anthropological data from the educational standpoint so arranged as to show their educational significance. To indicate what these specific needs are, with some suggestions as to how they may be met, as a result of personal experience in directing elementary school work, is the purpose of this paper.

Thus far, anthropological investigation has been confined almost wholly to the phenomena of adult life, the child in race history being left practically out of consideration. Where child life has received any attention it has been in connection with some phase of adult life, such as the status of woman, or tribal customs, and but seldom from an interest in the facts of child life in themselves. Since the adult in the early stages of race development is in many respects comparable to a child, and the general progress from savagery to civilization has been a progress from mental and moral infancy to maturity, the facts of adult life among the people in the different ethnic stages are of great value to the educator, as a means of giving an insight both into the nature of developmental processes, and into the natural sequence of interests and intellectual and emotional attitudes. A brief but reliable history of race development from the educational standpoint is greatly needed.

But this is not enough for educational purposes. Childhood has usually been considered as something static—the same in savagery and in civilization. But a little reflection will show that the activities and psychical processes of the primitive child must have been as much simpler than those of the child of modern culture as the activities and processes of the adult in savagery were simpler than those of a Gladstone or an Edison, the product of modern civilization. If there is any reason, then, for studying the psychical evolution of man from the standpoint of anthropological data, there is as good a reason for studying the evolution of childhood. This is true on the external as well as on the internal side. A study of the characteristics, the status, and the conditions of child life, in its relations to the sum of the life activities, during the successive stages of race development — an anthropological history of childhood, in short, would be an invaluable contribution to modern educational literature, giving an insight into the principles underlying the educational process, and throwing light on development in general. If the prolongation of the period of infancy has been the means of raising man from the infancy of primitive life to the maturity of civilization, is not such a study of childhood during the steps in the process worthy of the study of mankind? Chamberlin says: "The position of the child in the march of civilization, and the influence of the child idea upon sociology, mythology, language, and religion, would be a valuable contribution to modern thought, for the touch of the child is upon them all, and the debt of humanity to little children has not yet been told."

This need from the side of theoretical pedagogy suggests the practical necessities of the schoolroom along similar lines. Every teacher knows that the interest of children is in no way so effectively aroused as through the consideration of other children. Does it seem difficult to teach the geography of South America, or China, or Africa in a vital way? Approach these countries through the avenue of their child life, and a live interest will not be lacking. This shows why such books as *Seven Little Sisters*, *Children of the Cold*, *Ten Boys from Long Ago to Now*, and *Hiawatha's Childhood* are educational classics, and perennially interesting, though the correctness of the data may be questioned in some instances. But what applies to geography applies equally to other lines. Many schools have adopted the culture-epoch theory in a modified form, as a basis of the curriculum, emphasizing the industrial and artistic activities in the race epochs instead of confining the attention to the literary products of the epochs only. The teachers who are working out these new and original methods are greatly handicapped by the lack of available data concerning the periods in question, even from the standpoint of adult activities. To such, an anthropological history of childhood, or a series of type studies of child life among representative peoples in the different stages of race development, would be a veritable boon. At present the teacher who is trying to work on such original lines must either be a specialist in anthropology, which is hardly likely, or she must manufacture facts in the absence of reliable data.

But the organization of anthropological material would have a value more far-reaching still. Sociology and economics, until recently confined to the college or the university, are claiming a place in the curriculum of the secondary schools. But there is no reason whatever why a foundation of the most practical character for both sociology and economics should not be laid in the elementary school, by means of the lines of work suggested. Type studies of race development at its different stages, with emphasis on the social and industrial activities, would furnish the best possible means of interpreting modern conditions, and of appreciating the elements of value in social and industrial relations. With the teacher properly equipped, much could be done in the grammar schools, with but little additional effort, that must at present remain undone. Were the facts so organized as to be accessible to the pupils through reading and reference work, even more could be accomplished. The needs may thus be grouped under three heads — those of the educational specialist who needs a scientific treatment from the standpoint of principles; those of the intelligent teacher who needs reliable and available data; and those of the pupil who needs suggestive and interesting reading matter that will have a permanent value.

Several attempts to collect anthropological material relating to child life have been made within the last few years, those of Ploss and Chamberlin being best known. Many isolated facts could also be collected from the general literature of the subject. The material already collected needs reorganization, however, before it can yield its highest value for educational purposes. The usual method of investigation has been to select some one phase of the life process, some one activity or relation, and trace it from its genesis in race history to its maturity at the present time. This method has its value from the standpoint of results and is a necessary stage in the evolution of a completed method. The life process is a unity, which, like any other, must be analyzed, the attention being focused successively upon its different elements, in order that the significance of the whole may be realized. But unless the unity as such be kept in mind, with the purpose it is to serve as a means to further insight, there is danger of getting lost in the analysis. Thus far the emphasis in anthropological investigation has been placed on tracing the different elements in the life process one by one, from their genesis to their present state, to the neglect of the return move-ment, the placing these elements in their true relation to each other and to the ethnic periods. Hence the elements in question have been suspended in a vacuum, and have not been serviceable, since they lacked relations. For educational purposes a cross section of any one ethnic period showing all the life activities in their relations would serve a better purpose than a longitudinal section showing one activity during many. The plan pursued isolates the facts by separating them from their many relations, and thus destroys their value. The method suggested would group the available facts of a given period and, by placing them in their natural setting, would give them a double significance. The work done thus far has been the first stage in a complete method, but the second must follow closely upon the first, both for the sake of the science itself as well as for those to which it is tributary. The same criticism may be made on much of the work in child-study. The study of many children with reference to a single characteristic, isolated from its setting in heredity and environment, is the first stage in a complete method. The study of all the characteristics of one period in child life, in their natural relations, is its necessary completion. The child-study movement is doing much to make a future history of childhood from the anthropological standpoint possible, but, like anthropology itself, it needs to work from the synthetic standpoint if its results are to be of the highest value for educational purposes. As a possible basis for the organization needed, the accompanying chart of anthropological development is suggested, as a framework in which to place material already available. To the writer its value is twofold. It gives the general facts of race development in a convenient form, and in so doing it affords a basis for comparing the development of the race with that of the child at the present time, from the standpoint of activities and processes. It thus meets, in a slight degree, one of the needs of the present. The ultimate purpose of its construction, however, was to suggest a principle on the basis of which the facts of child life might be organized, and thus become available for educational purposes. With the general view which the chart affords continually in mind, the facts of child life will be constantly seen in their true relation to the social and industrial conditions of the period in which they occur. Their true setting in the activities and interests of the period being obtained, as well as their sequence in culture history, true interpretation becomes possible.

Since the framework is of some importance if the results are to have validity, it demands further consideration. No credit for originality is claimed either as to form or organization. The general form was suggested by the chart of social organization in Small and Vincent's *Introduction to the Study of Society*. The division into stages is that adopted by Morgan, and that of masculine and feminine activities that suggested by Mason. It is a graphic representation, for convenient reference, of data already collected and in the relations they occupy in the works of the authors mentioned.

Any schematic representation of this character is open to criticism on the basis of inadequacy. The difficulty of representing the facts of geological, palæontological, or anthropological development progressively is that the successive stages are seldom if ever found in nature in their true relations, that many gaps occur for which the missing links cannot be found, and hence the whole is but a skillful piece of patchwork which may mislead instead of instruct.   This is particularly true of anthropological data, since customs and institutions may disappear as the result of conquest or imitation of other forms.   Visualization has a value, however, in spite of the possibilities or error, and such value is relied upon in the construction here presented.

Objections are usually made to the drawing of distinct dividing lines between the periods of development, but such lines must be understood as indicating general transitions only. Development has not been uniform, and while certain activities, modes of life and materials may have predominated in one period, these either persisted with diminished emphasis into the next, or they were gradually transformed into related ones, continuing in connection with the new forms upon which the emphasis is placed.

A similar criticism is likely to be made on the division of labor on the basis of sex.   This division holds in general for the prehistoric period, though there were many lines in which both sexes shared, the predominance being, however, on the one side or the other.   Thus, while man was the main food producer, woman shared in this to some degree, her activities being especially connected with the vegetable kingdom.   Since man's activities along this line were connected mainly with the animal kingdom, the particular habitat, as predominantly animal or vegetable, determined largely the male or female preponderance in procuring the food supply.   So, too, man shared in the feminine activities of preparing food and providing shelter, and in the education of the boys when the proper age was reached.   It is worthy of note that the feminine activities passed over into the hands of men as they became organized, in the later stages of development.   The arts, language, and religion, on the other hand, had a social, not a sex origin.

In addition to the points mentioned it must be kept in mind that race development has not been uniform and homogeneous, and that progress from cultural infancy to the maturity of civilization cannot be traced in any one people.   Many peoples are still in their earliest or savage state ; others have progressed into some phase of barbarism, while relatively few have attained cultural maturity. Hence, at any historic period peoples could have been found in any or all of these stages, with infinite grada-tions between. Thus the North American Indians, when dis-covered, represented in different localities the status of savagery, and two distinct subdivisions of the state of barbarism. It must also be remembered that, while there has been a general similar-ity in the modes of life and the development of institutions among the peoples that have passed through the stages in ques-tion, there has by no means been uniformity. Thus the hunt-ing, the pastoral, and the agricultural stages are generally con-sidered as necessarily successive with all peoples that have passed beyond them. But the North American Indians who reached the borderland of civilization passed immediately from the hunting to the agricultural stage, since the American continent contained no animals suited to domestication. In Europe and Asia, on the contrary, where all the animals that have been domesticated were found, the pastoral period was prolonged and continued in connection with the agricultural until civilization was attained. Hence, if a view of the whole process of devel-opment is desired, representative peoples from the different ethnic periods must be selected for purposes of study.

It may be claimed that on this basis no ultimate principles of interpretation can be derived, since it is impossible to deter-mine what is due to the peculiar genius of a people, and what to universal characteristics. Thus the development of the Hebrews throws but little light on that of the Greeks, and that of the American races has undoubtedly as little in common with that of European stocks as have the first mentioned races. The force of this argument is not denied, but the value of accurate data concerning the life activities of each is not thereby les-sened. It must be remembered that no ultimate value is claimed for the synthesis suggested by the authors who furnish the data. The urgency of present needs is sufficient to make the attempt at placing available data in better working form of some value, while something more fundamental is being worked out.

While the purpose in making the chart was that above men-tioned, the mere arrangement of the facts of anthropological development has suggested a new interpretation of the culture-epoch theory, the correspondence between the stages in the development of the individual and the three great stages in the development of the race being too significant to escape attention. The fundamental interests in both the individual and the race grow out of the food process; hence the fundamental activities are determined by these fundamental needs. The intellectual and moral life assumes organized form on the basis of the activities in question, both in the individual and in the race. A comparison between the individual and the race from the intellectual side only, a passing from sense perception to reason, lacks foundation without a consideration of the social and industrial life of which it is the outgrowth. The parallelism frequently traced on the moral side, from blind impulse to moral freedom, is likewise of little value when taken out of its setting in the whole life process. It is because the culture-epoch theory in its current form is confined to the historic peoples only, neglecting the ages of accomplishment that lay back of these, and in whose light the historic peoples must be interpreted, and because the whole industrial and, to a great extent, the social development is ignored, that the theory is inadequate to the purposes it should serve. By the adoption of the theory from the anthropological standpoint both objections would be met. The working out of the theory on the anthropological basis will be given in a future paper.

The services that anthropology can render the educational cause are thus many and varied. Education can no longer be isolated; it is identifying itself more and more closely with the general movements of the time. In this movement anthropology is destined to play an increasingly important part. If the peculiar character of the present educational need will in any degree stimulate anthropological research; if it can give it a new direction and focus; if it can create a wider interest in it on the part of the general public, it can in part repay the services it hopes to receive at the hands of that science.

NINA C. VANDEWALKER.
MILWAUKEE STATE NORMAL SCHOOL.

: the culture-
stages in the
stages in the
escape atten-
...tual and the
: fundamental
: needs. The
... of the basis
... and in the
the race from
perception to
... of the social
The parallel-
...d impulse to
...en out of its
.... the culture-
... historic peo-
... that lay back
.. must be inter-
a great extent,
... is inadequate
... of the theory
...ions would be
...thropological

... educational
... no longer be
...sely with the
... anthropology
... If the pecu-
... in any degree
... it a new direc-
... it on the part
...ces it hopes to

VANDEWALKER.

		BARBARISM ACTIV		
		STATUS	UPPER STATUS	
	4. Shelter.	dobe and dwellings.	Houses of durable material. Cities, with gates and battle / Temple architecture.	
			with shuttle.	
Organization of Domestic, Economic, Educational, and Religious Activities.	3. Clothing.	cotton, linen.		
		ganization of schools. ith rites and ceremonies.		
	2. Care of Chil			
		es made. other neces	sary articles.	
Feminine Activities.	1. Preparation			
			ing, cooking, etc.	
			etc.	
			hood.	
Social Organization requiring both sexes.	Form of Fa		language. Monogamic family.	
			Property organiza	
	1. Getting of			
Masculine Activities.				
			Iron implements. sword of iron.	
Organization of Military, Judicial, Political, and Commercial Activities.	3. Trade and		Ships, wagons, chariots. cattle, etc.	
	Representat	xico, itons emi-	Grecian tribes of the Homeric Age; Italian tribes before the founding of Rome; Germanic tribes of the time of Cæsar.	Invention of

ECCENTRIC OFFICIAL STATISTICS. IV.

THOUGH in his contribution to the March number of the JOURNAL OF SOCIOLOGY Mr. William M. Steuart sedulously avoids direct reference to the writer and his contributions to this Journal, his misquotations, as well as his quotations, betray his evident purpose to discredit the writer and his criticisms of official statistics and Colonel Wright's use of the same. Notwithstanding this evident purpose, this eminent census official, so far as his statements are true, strongly confirms these criticisms, while by his misstatements he incidentally illustrates the unreliability of the officials responsible for the statistics criticised.

In his first contribution to this Journal (January, 1897) the writer criticised an article by Mr. Steuart published in the January, 1896, Bulletin of the Department of Labor, presenting the same as a fair specimen of the contributions of the United States government to social science. In this article, intended for the information of a class having little knowledge of statistics, Mr. Steuart not only compares incomparable estimates of value, but states: "The total value of the products of productive industry, which include manufactures and farm, fishery, and mineral products, for the same year (1890) amounted to $12,148,380,626." This statement the writer contrasted with statistics presented by an able and seemingly conscientious census official, Mr. George K. Holmes, published in the November, 1895, Labor Bulletin, in which, the value of material consumed being deducted, the total value of the products of productive industry was given as $7,302,854,-901. Regarding these widely differing statements the writer remarked: "The value of the products of industry, as stated by Mr. Steuart, is thus 66 per cent. greater than the value as stated by Mr. Holmes. As both statements are 'official' and have the indorsement of the highest statistical authority, Colonel Wright, we must accept both statements as undoubtedly correct, and as equally illustrating the value of the contributions of the United States government to social science."

Mr. Steuart seeks to evade the force of this criticism by presenting a fallacious and totally different statement, attributed by implication to the writer. Mr. Steuart says (p. 630): "The census office has published the total annual value of the products of establishments engaged in the manufacturing and mechanical industries as $9,372,-

79

437,283. It is asserted that this is wrong, and that it should be reduced by $5,162,044,076, the cost of materials, and the difference $4,210,393,207 given as the true value of products. This latter sum comes nearer representing the enhanced value of the raw materials, or the value added by the expenditure of capital, labor, and other manufacturing processes. It is the amount added to the wealth of the country by manufacturing processes, but it is not the true value of the products of the manufacturing establishments of the country. One writer criticising these totals even went so far as to say that the two values had been published in official reports as the value of the products of industry, yet one was 66 per cent. greater than the other, and that the public was expected to accept both as showing the same thing. The public will accept nothing of the kind, though the writer referred to may."

So far from asserting that $4,210,393,207, or any other amount, represents the true value of manufactured products, the writer stated in a footnote (p. 526): "The census furnishes no data from which may be ascertained the value of manufactured products, which, besides the value added in manufacturing, would include the value of products of the mine, field, forest, and fisheries, consumed in manufacturing industry." It would seem that the value of manufactured products can be ascertained only by aggregating the values of finished products; yet Mr. Steuart would include also the value of manufactured products consumed in the manufacture of other products, though these values, having been destroyed, have no existence save in the minds of eminent census officials. To these Mr. Steuart also adds the value of mineral, farm, and fisheries products, which have likewise been consumed, and thus would discover the value of the products of productive industry.

It may be noticed that Mr. Steuart does not deny the authenticity of the writer's quotation of Colonel Wright's letter to the chairman of the Senate Committee on Census, in which that gentleman declares the incomparability of census wage statistics, which, in his *Atlantic Monthly* article, he compares as demonstrating the greatly improved condition of wage-earners. Mr. Steuart, nevertheless, labors to prove the comparability of these statistics. For this purpose he quotes remarks of the census of which, as chief of division, he is himself the author, as follows: "The tendency of the questions used in 1880 was to obtain a number in excess of the average number of employés, while it is believed the questions used in 1890 obtained the average number. The questions in 1890 also tended to increase the amount of wages as compared with 1880, and secured a more complete return of the officers, firm members, and clerks and their salaries." For some reason about which we will venture no surmise, Mr. Steuart ends the citation in the middle. He does not quote the rest of his own sentence, which establishes the writer's contention and disproves his own, viz.: "than was reported at previous censuses; therefore the average annual wages per employé, as obtained from the reports of the two censuses, are not comparable, nor should the amounts be used to ascertain the percentage of increase" (see *Compendium, Eleventh Census*, Pt III, p. 668).

Mr. Steuart says also : "It is asserted that the presentation of $484.49 as the average per capita wages for all classes of employés, or $444.83 as the average for the employés exclusive of officers, firm members, and clerks, in comparison with $346.91 for all classes in 1880, is erroneous ; also that the division of the total wages by the average number employed is not the correct method of obtaining the average wages." This seems another palpable misrepresentation and evasion. What the writer contended, as will be seen by reference to his article, was that average annual earnings (not rates of wages) could be obtained only by dividing the total wages by the total number of employés. This Mr. Steuart admits farther along in his article, saying: "But it must be remembered that the wages reported were paid to have certain positions of employment filled, and the number of those positions is probably the true divisor for the total wages; the average comes nearer this number than the total or greatest number. But as carefully explained by the census reports, the average given for wages is not the true average yearly earnings per workman " (p. 628).

How carefully this is explained in the census reports may be seen by reference to the same, or to p. 527 of the writer's first article, in which the remarks of the census are more fully quoted than space will here permit. In the census are given tables purporting to show "average annual earnings," which Mr. Steuart admits the figures given do not represent. Mr. Steuart also acknowledges that the only true way to find average annual earnings is to ascertain the total wages and the total number of workers and divide the one by the other. This has been precisely the writer's contention in his criticism of Colonel Wright's contribution to the *Atlantic Monthly*. In that article, after quoting the fallacious statistics of the Aldrich report, Colonel Wright says : " It is often contended that the increase in rates of wages does not indicate the true social condition of the wage-earner; that rates of wages belong to economics, and that earnings themselves are the surest indication of social progress. This is quite true. . . . . But fortunately we are not obliged to depend upon the increase of rates of wages to show that the ordinary man is better off than at any former time in our history, because our censuses report aggregate earnings and also the number of persons among whom the earnings are divided." After quoting census wage statistics for 1850 and the decades following, Colonel Wright says: "Here is a steady, positive increase in the average annual earnings of the employés in our great industrial pursuits." Yet, according to Mr. Steuart, this is not true, the figures quoted representing practically rates of wages, that which would be earned by an employé who had full employment. If there was little lost time, there would be but little difference. That there was but 5.01 per cent. of lost time during the census year, Colonel Wright attempts to demonstrate in the *Forum* (February, 1898). The absurdity of Colonel Wright's conclusions was shown by the writer in the *Journal of Political Economy* (March, 1898), and need not be considered here, except as these conclusions illustrate the utter worthlessness of the statistics on which they are based. While the writer has maintained that the figures quoted by Colonel Wright do not represent average annual earnings, he has not, as intimated by Mr. Steuart, maintained that they were too high as representing rates of wages, though that is probably the fact; nor is it true, as Mr. Steuart declares, that the criticism of the totals of the Eleventh Census has invariably been that they are too large. The writer has made no such criticism. He has, however, maintained that the more complete returns of the last census are not comparable with those of 1880, and still less with those of the earlier censuses. The incompleteness of the earlier censuses was recognized by General Francis A. Walker, superintendent of both the Ninth and Tenth Censuses, who, possessing a comprehension of the proper use of statistics which seems lacking in officials of the last census, was careful to caution the public against comparisons of incomparable statistics. While the earlier bulletins of the last census were grossly misleading, the final reports, published after the retirement of Mr. Porter, contain explanations and cautions that might, in a measure, have prevented the prevailing misunderstanding as to the facts, were it not that prominent census officials, in contributions to the magazines, persistently misrepresent them. Mr. Steuart admits that it is possible that the method adopted in 1890 did result in a fuller report of certain industries, especially the hand trades, but he seems not quite certain of this, nor in fact of anything else save that a less complete return of the rural districts in 1880, and the omission of certain large establishments in 1890, in which it is notorious that the lowest wages are paid, offset the fuller enumeration of the higher-paid hand trades, and in no wise affected the comparability of the wage statistics.[1]

Colonel Wright seems to have been possessed with the same idea that out of this comedy of errors the truth might be evolved ; for in a letter to the writer dated May 3, 1894, he says: "The canvass of the principal cities was undoubtedly more thorough than at 1880, but, on the other hand, it is believed the canvass of the rural districts was more complete at 1880 than at 1890. It, therefore, cannot be said that the entire canvass of 1890 was more complete than at 1880. The change in the form of inquiry, considered by itself, cannot be considered as abnormally increasing the product. The product reported for 1890 is comparable with an exactly similar amount for 1880." Regarding this idea of balancing one error with another, General Walker remarks on p. xxiii of the *Ninth Census :* "Every error that occurs in the census of a country, or in any statistical result whatever, is to be regretted as an independent evil, hardly less when it balances another error than when it exaggerates the amount of error already existing. Two wrongs no more make a right in mathematics than in morals, and a falsehood in figures is none the more to be tolerated or excused because it may serve to conceal another falsehood."

It seems never to have occurred to our astute census officials that if the enumeration of the rural districts in 1890 was so deficient as to offset the more complete enumeration of the cities and make the total

---

[1] As to the comparability of the data, Mr. Steuart remarks in the *Census (Compendium,* Pt. II, p. 704) : "No previous census of the United States obtained so complete reports regarding such trades as masonry, carpentering, blacksmithing, cooperage, painting, plumbing, and similar trades using machinery to a limited extent.

"Previous census inquiries omitted the following industries : Bottling ; cars and general shop construction and repairs by steam railroad companies ; china decorating ; clothing, women's dress-making ; coffins and burial cases, trimming and finishing ; cotton, cleaning and rehandling ; cotton ginning ; cotton waste ; drug grinding ; druggists' preparations, not including prescriptions ; gas, illuminating and heating ; hay and straw, baling ; millinery, custom work ; petroleum refining (petroleum refining formed part of a separate report at the census of 1880, and the statistics were not included in the report on manufactures). *The inclusion of these industries in the Eleventh Census, together with the changes referred to, renders it impracticable to use the data for 1880 as a basis for comparison without carefully taking these facts into consideration.*"

product comparable, this fact alone would destroy the comparability of the wage statistics. In the one census we thus have a larger proportion of the lower-paid operatives who work in the country where the cost of living, and as a consequence wages, are less, and in the other census a diminished proportion of this class of workers and a largely increased proportion of the higher-paid wage-earners of our cities. As previously shown, there was from 1880 to 1890 an increase of 267 per cent. in the number of those reported in the manufacturing statistics as engaged in five of the building trades.

The manufacturing schedule of 1890 called specifically for a report of the salaries of clerks and of officers of corporations, and the estimated value of the services of the employer, and only for the average number of employés, while the schedule of 1880 called for the greatest as well as the average number of employés and for the amount paid as wages. As to the result of this change in methods we have presented the statement of a former census official quoted and not disputed by Colonel Wright.

Considering Mr. Steuart's tergiversations, we can do no otherwise than accept this statement, which Mr. Steuart does not directly dispute, not only because Mr. Waite appears the more credible witness, but because we find him corroborated in part by so respectable an authority as General Walker, who, on p. 381, " Volume of Industry and Wealth," *Ninth Census*, remarks :

" In reference to certain of the common trades, it needs to be stated, in explanation, that the apparently inadequate amount of wages reported is due to the fact that a very large body of labor is included which is not represented in the wage column. Thus the statistics of carpentering show that for a total production of $132,901,432 (the value of materials being $65,943,115) the amount of wages paid was only $29,169,588. The consideration above noted is sufficient to account for the seeming deficiency, inasmuch as the labor of proprietors of establishments in this line (certainly not less than 17,142, and probably rising to 20,000) was compensated, not out of the wages paid, but out of the profits of the business. In some branches of industry the number of ' hired hands ' is even less than the number of artisans working in their own shops, and hence receiving no wages, but living off the profits of manufacture."

Mr. Waite's statement seems also corroborated by Mr. Steuart, who says : " An examination of the original report of 1880 reveals the fact that, to some extent at least, officers, firm members, and clerks, as well as other employés, were reported indiscriminately and one lump sum given as wages for all." While this does not show that even in these exceptional cases the value of the services of employers and salaries of officers and clerks were included in the lump sum reported as wages, it is an admission that in the more numerous instances only wages proper were included. Yet we find accompanying census tables, and referring to the wages of officers, firm members, and clerks, the footnote, " Not reported separately in 1880." The inference from this has been that, though not reported separately, they were included in the aggregate. This we see by Mr. Steuart's own admission is not true to any considerable extent. For this misleading footnote Mr. Steuart, as the author of the text accompanying these tables, appears to be responsible.

It would seem that even an eminent census official should understand that average wages obtained by dividing the earnings of operatives proper by the number of operatives plus employers and clerks would give an average below the true average, and not comparable either with the average for all classes or for operatives proper, as obtained at the last census.

While championing the Eleventh Census, Mr. Steuart unwittingly testifies to the worthlessness of the original data. As to this he is corroborated by Colonel Wright. The manufacturing enumeration of the principal cities was at the last census taken from the enumerators of population and intrusted to special agents, while this enumeration for the rural districts was, as formerly, made by the enumerators of population. The better facilities enjoyed by the special agents, who had no other duties to engage their attention, account for the more thorough enumeration of the cities, but as the enumeration of the rural districts in 1890 was made by the same class of officers and in a manner similar to that of 1880, there seems no way to account for the less thorough enumeration of the rural districts at the last census, unless we conclude that these officials were less competent and efficient than the same class of officials at the census of 1880.

This is undoubtedly the case, and may be accounted for by the fact that in 1890 the census office was made part of the political machine, and that appointments were made as rewards for political services. As is invariably the case with the spoils system, this resulted in the appointment of the most unfit class of officials that could possibly be selected.

Regarding this system and its results, General Walker remarked :

"As assistant marshals are appointed under the American system, nice discriminations in respect to industrial relations can hardly be maintained in a sufficient proportion of cases to give value to the aggregate results." General Walker, being eminent as an economist, and not as a politician, may be supposed to have used his utmost endeavor to discourage the appointment of officials for political reasons. That he was, in a measure at least, successful is shown by the fact, testified to by Mr. Steuart and by Colonel Wright, that the enumeration of the rural districts was more thorough in 1880 than in 1890. As showing the manner in which appointments of enumerators were made at the last census it may be proper to relate incidents that fell under the writer's observation.

In that ward of Chicago in which he resided a Mr. W. kept a restaurant, at which the writer was in the habit of taking his meals. This restaurant keeper, it seems, had been of service to the alderman of this ward by activity at the primaries. As related to the writer by Mr. W., this alderman came to the latter and asked him if he would not like a job where he could make some money, and, on his assenting, obtained for him an appointment as assistant marshal or enumerator. On obtaining his commission and schedules, Mr. W. came to the writer to ask information as to his duties, and finally became convinced that he would be unable to do the work. Finding that he could not himself employ someone to do the work for him, he went to the alderman, who at his request had the appointment given to a person keeping a barber shop adjoining his restaurant, who, while undoubtedly more competent than the restaurant keeper, had no especial fitness for the work. In neither case does there seem to have been, by the appointing power, any questions asked as to the fitness of the appointees.

The enumerator in the district in which the writer resided was a superannuated clergyman who had been active as a stump speaker for the party in power. Calling at the writer's place of residence, he was unable to obtain the proper information because the person with whom he roomed was unable to furnish it. Meeting the enumerator on the street, the writer volunteered to furnish the information, and was met by the reply: "Oh! I've got past that."

The writer knows from experience on the Chicago school census that in a large proportion of cases a number of calls at the same place are necessary to obtain such information as was called for by the census schedule. Paid by the number of names returned, and inadequately for a thorough and correct canvass, it is not to be supposed that a lot of political heelers who considered their jobs rewards for other services would in many instances do otherwise than fill out their schedules with very little regard to facts. The writer cannot, of course, say that these instances are fair illustrations of the manner in which appointments were made and the work done at the last census, but an examination of the returns made by this class of officials, and a comparison with the work of special agents, indicate that these cases are not exceptional. Taking, for example, the returns of occupation from which Colonel Wright has sought to demonstrate that there was during the census year practically no unemployment, we find them simply absurd. For instance, of 12,369 paper hangers we find it reported that but 3,452 were unemployed for a month or more at their principal occupation. Nearly everyone knows that paper hanging is done almost exclusively at house-cleaning time, and it is impossible that this class of workmen could have averaged more than six months' employment.[1]

It may be said for the enumerators that as the schedules called for information which it would be utterly impossible for them to obtain with

[1] The following is a statement of the percentage of the total sales for the last year in each month furnished by the business manager of the wall paper firm of Alfred Peats & Co., 143 and 145 Wabash avenue. This firm is undoubtedly the most extensive retail dealer in this line of goods in the West, and claims to have larger sales than any other retail firm in the United States. As wall paper is retailed for immediate use, these figures may be taken as a fair indication of the proportion of work done by paper hangers in each month of the year:

	Per cent.
January,	2.80
February,	4.94
March,	14.76
April,	22.87
May,	20.55
June,	9.67
July,	4.73
August,	3.61
September,	3.86
October,	5.39
November,	4.05
December,	2.27

Taking April and May as months in which paper hangers were fully employed, it appears that for one-half the year five-sixths of the workers were unemployed at their principal occupation. The census statistics of unemployment for this class are as follows:

Total number employés	Total number unemployed	1 to 3 months	4 to 6 months	7 to 12 months
12,369	3,452	1,550	1,525	377

any degree of accuracy, they were in a measure excusable for filling out their schedules as they might think the case to have been. If, as the returns show, the workers were at work, there would be but few instances in which they would be found at their place of residence, and even where they were found, cases where the information could be given offhand must have been exceedingly rare. Yet from these necessarily unreliable returns we find the most eminent of our statisticians endeavoring to demonstrate that which common observation shows is not true.

Comparing the returns made by the enumerators as to the numbers engaged in manufacturing industry with the returns made by special agents, we find that the former are, in many instances, grossly inadequate, especially as relates to females and children; and, comparing both classes of returns with the reports of factory inspectors, we find that the reports of special agents also fall far short of showing the fact.

In a former paper attention was called to the fact that, among other omissions, the manufacturing tables report no females and but three children employed in the cigar and tobacco industry in Jersey City, while the state factory inspector reported 2,500 females and 260 children in the single establishment of Lorillard & Co. In the occupation tables we find 723 females reported in this industry and city. Mr. Steuart asserts that some of the largest sugar refineries, paper mills, cigar factories, and establishments engaged in other industries absolutely refused or willfully neglected to furnish the information required for the census, and expresses the opinion that they undoubtedly offset the inclusion of the minor industries referred to and tended to counterbalance the results of the more thorough canvass.[1] That is, the omission of the poorly paid workers in tobacco factories tends to offset the largely increased enumeration of the higher-paid wage-earners in the building trades and makes the wage statistics comparable. Mr. Steuart's statement of the refusal of the manufacturers to furnish the information required by the census confirms the truth of the assertion of Edward Atkinson, quoted in the writer's second article (July, 1897), regarding the census of 1880: "If the questions had been put in such a way that the profits of the different arts investigated would have been disclosed, manufacturers would have returned no answer

---

[1] Regarding the omissions referred to, Mr. Steuart remarks in the *Census* (*Compendium*, Pt. II, p. 704): "The establishments thus neglecting to comply with the requirements of the law are, with but few exceptions, unimportant, and their omission from the tables can have but slight effect upon the totals."

whatever, or would not have given correct and complete answers." The attempt being made at the Eleventh Census to obtain this information, a number of establishments, it appears, refused to make return. What assurance have we that the remainder have given correct answers? In many industries the manufacturers have asked protection from foreign competition, on the ground of the high wages paid their labor. What reason have we to suppose, if this be the case, that they would make return showing that they were paying low wages?

Mr. Steuart does not state that the Lorillard establishment was one of those refusing to make return. This is a matter of interest, because from such a statement we might judge whether or not this establishment was omitted from the census because of the large number of females and children employed and the small wages paid, as indicated by the small wage loss from the strike of June 14 to 27, 1887, reported by Colonel Wright in his report on strikes and lockouts. That there is ground for this ungracious suspicion is shown by the returns of other localities. In Chicago, for instance, we find in the same industry the returns, as made by enumerators of population, special agents, and the state factory inspector, to be as follows:

	Males	Females	Children
Census tables of occupation, - -	2,434	456	—
Census tables of manufacturers, -	2,176[1]	781[2]	58
State factory inspector's report, 1894,	2,613[1]	1,136[1]	568

As state factory inspection in Illinois was organized in 1893, we give the figures for the first year in which there was a fairly complete report. As, according to the returns of factory inspectors of other states, there was after the panic of 1893 a large falling off in the number of employés in this industry, particularly of children, it is almost certain that the number of children employed in 1890 was greater than in 1894. We are unable to give the number of children returned by the enumerators of population, because the lowest age classification as published for the cities is from ten to twenty-four. By this method embarrassing comparisons are avoided. This method of tabulation, the change in age classification, particularly the change in the question from age last birthday to age nearest birthday, all tend to confirm the suspicion of a purpose on the part of eminent census officials to mislead the public.

Of this change in the question from age last birthday to age nearest birthday, which has the effect of excluding a very large proportion

[1] Over sixteen.   [2] Over fifteen.

of those who would otherwise have been included in the number of child workers, no note is made in the remarks of the census. The writer having called attention to this change, and that Colonel Wright, in his report on the employment of women and children, to discredit the investigation of his own department, quoted the tables of occupation in utter disregard of this important change, Mr. Steuart, in his reply, endeavors to mislead the public by quoting from the writer's criticism of Colonel Wright's *Record* article, and declaring : " Colonel Wright had reference entirely to statistics as reported by manufacturing establishments, and in them the question as to 'age nearest birthday' òr at 'last birthday' did not appear at either census." As to his *Record* article this is true, and the writer is perhaps in error in supposing that this change affected the manufacturing statistics; that, in ascertaining the number of workers below fifteen and sixteen years of age, the enumerators who returned a large proportion of manufacturing establishments took any notice of the words which they found on their instructions, repeated from the population schedule in bold-face type, " age nearest birthday." Not being an eminent census official, the writer makes no claim to infallibility, and should feel obliged to Mr. Steuart for pointing out this error, had he not in doing so endeavored to lead the public to infer that he was also in error in his more important criticism of Colonel Wright's quotation of the returns of occupation, in which Mr. Steuart does not deny that the change from age last birthday to age nearest birthday was made. A comparison of manufacturing and occupation statistics necessarily fails to fully indicate their unreliability, because the deficiencies in one class of returns must to a large extent offset and conceal those of the other. The deficiency of both of these classes of census statistics is shown where comparison is possible with factory inspectors' reports. These latter are admittedly incomplete, save as to establishments employing a considerable number of females or children. The following comparisons of statistics of the tables of occupation returned by the enumerators of population and those of the manufacturing reports are given as illustrations of the unreliability of one or both classes of statistics.

Taking the state of Nebraska, in which a large proportion of the manufacturing returns must have been made by the same officials who made the returns of occupation and of unemployment, we find the occupation returns of the number of persons ten years of age and over engaged in manufacturing and mechanical industry, and the manufacturing returns, to be as follows :

	Aggregate	Males	Females	Children[1]
Occupation tables, -	- 55,792	47,905	7,887	279
Manufacturing tables, -	23,876	21,447	1,715	714

The manufacturing statistics representing the average number of employés and the occupation statistics the total number, if we accept them as at all accurate, we must conclude that employés of manufacturing establishments in this state were unemployed considerably more than one-half the time. Yet the statistics of unemployment show an almost insignificant amount of lost time, being for the manufacturing and mechanical industries as follows:

	1 to 3 months	4 to 6 months	7 to 12 months
Males, - - -	5,371	4,820	1,099
Females, - -	355	264	141

If we adopt the method of Colonel Wright in the *Forum* and take the mean of each period as representing the average, this unemployment would be an equivalent of not more than 3,600 males and less than 270 females unemployed for twelve months.

For the state of Kansas the returns are as follows:

	Aggregate	Males	Females	Children
Occupation tables,	- 54,674	46,103	8,571	138
Manufacturing tables,	- 32,843	29,157	2,805	881

The report of unemployment for this state shows also an insignificant amount of lost time, being as follows:

	1 to 3 months	4 to 6 months	7 to 12 months
Males, - - -	4,874	5,893	1,816
Females - - -	366	494	207

In New York state, where the returns of manufactures are principally those of special agents, we have a reverse of this showing, except as to children, the manufacturing statistics indicating a larger number of employés than the tables of occupation. The returns for New York state are as follows:

	Aggregate	Males	Females	Children
Occupation tables, -	828,216	634,430	193,786	13,739
Manufacturing tables,	850,084	633,389	204,432	12,263

It should be remembered that children in the occupation tables include those from ten to fourteen years of age, while the figures of the manufacturing tables represent the number of children, boys under

[1] Children in the occupation tables include those from ten to fourteen years of age nearest birthday; in the manufacturing tables males to sixteen and females to fifteen years of age.

sixteen, girls under fourteen. Thus one table reports a greater number of children under fourteen than the other under fifteen and sixteen. The statistics of unemployment are as follows :

	1 to 3 months	4 to 6 months	7 to 12 months
Males, - - -	65,677	47,454	12,664
Females, - -	18,827	9,891	3,546

The number engaged in manufactures as returned by enumerators of population is not published for cities, but we find for each city a table of selected industries, with a footnote stating that the aggregate given includes the number in all industries, whether specified or not. Taking the city of Troy, N. Y., we find thus reported 8,451 females engaged in all industries, including 1,654 servants, besides not a few teachers, saleswomen, boarding-house keepers, etc. In the manufacturing tables we find reported for this city 13,953 females above the age of fifteen engaged in manufacturing industry alone. Though the manufacturing returns for New York are evidently more complete than those for Nebraska, a comparison with the New York factory inspector's report shows them deficient as to the number of females and children, especially the latter. According to the census there were but 2,063 children employed in the 25,403 establishments in the city of New York for which return was made.

According to the factory inspector's report, which gives the name of each establishment and the average number of employés therein, there were in the 2,147 establishments visited in the second district, which includes only that part of New York city south of Twenty-third street, 1,108 boys and 1,951 girls under sixteen years of age. For this year (1890) the inspection was declared by the chief inspector incomplete because of an insufficient number of deputies. In 1891 there was a fuller, but still very incomplete inspection, but 3,891 establishments in the second district being visited. In these, however, the average number was reported as, boys, 1,735; girls, 2,353. Thus, in that part of the city there are reported, in but a small proportion of the manufacturing establishments included in the census, double the number of children found by census enumerators in the whole city. In the cigar and tobacco industry in this city, the tables of occupation report 9,910 males and 4,975 females, while the manufacturing census shows 10,500 males, 6,772 females, and 164 children in 1,295 establishments. The New York factory inspection in 1890 extended to but 128 establishments in this industry, in which were reported 5,143 males, 6,757 females, and 469 children. In two establishments as many children are reported as are returned in the census for all establishments. As shown in a preceding article, Colonel Wright's report on strikes and lockouts shows 13,500 females on a strike in this city and industry in 1886.

These are but a few of the very many instances of glaring discrepancies between census and factory inspectors' reports that might be added to those cited in the writer's preceding article. Of these and other seeming defects in census statistics to which attention has been called Mr. Steuart takes no notice, but declares that they are the only data that can be relied on as showing the actual facts. This statement, being "official," and doubtless inspired by our most eminent statistical authority, may be accepted by those who accept authority as truth. It is to be regretted that Mr. Steuart fails to indicate which class of statistics — the tables of occupation, or those of manufactures — shows "the actual facts." H. L. BLISS.

CHICAGO.

REVIEWS.

L'Ouvrier Américain. Par E. LEVASSEUR. Paris: L. Larose, 1898.
2 vols. Pp. 634, 516.

IT is a great advantage to have our institutions and social conditions, as well as our literature, studied and presented to us by the
French mind. Professor Levasseur must be heard with respect and
attention. He has prepared himself for this investigation by valuable
previous studies, by a large collection of documents and authorities,
and by travel in this country. In these two volumes he has brought
together a vast amount of information on a subject of transcendent
importance.

The entire work is divided into three principal parts, which are
designated: "The Workman at Work," "The Workman at Home,"
and "The Labor Questions." The method is to assemble significant
data on each topic, and then to treat them critically, with a view to
estimate the worth of various opinions, practical measures, and of
legislation.

In the first part, "The Workman at Work," the author discusses,
with ample fullness of details, the progress of American industry
during the past fifty years, the productive force of machinery and
labor, labor laws and the discipline of the factory, trade unions, wages
of men, women, and children ; the sweating system, competition of
immigrants, negroes, and prisoners ; strikes, boycotts, lockouts, blacklists, crises, and the causes which regulate nominal wages. In the
second part, "The Workman at Home," we have discussions of the
budgets of households, food, clothing, housing, building and loan
associations, saving, and real wages. In the third part, "Labor
Questions," there is a treatment of fortune-making and democracy in
America, the protective system, public relief of the indigent, patronage
and profit-sharing, workingmen's associations and coöperation, conciliation and arbitration, and socialism. Finally, the author presents
his own point of view, and ventures on a modest prophecy of the next
twenty or thirty years. It will be convenient to use the author's own
summary of the argument which runs through the work.

American industry has had, during the past century, and especially during the last fifty years, an ample and magnificent development. Production has increased nearly fivefold during the last thirty years (1860–90). None of the great nations of the world have equaled the United States in this respect. This industry shows a marked tendency to concentration. Production increases, but the number of establishments diminishes. For example, the manufacturers of agricultural machinery numbered 2,076 in 1870 and produced a value of $52,000,-000; and in 1890 the number of factories had fallen to 910, but these produced $82,000,000. The small industry retires. The "trusts" are inevitable; they are the result of liberty, and they are also a menace to liberty.

The American is an inventor; the number of patents issued after examination is a proof of it. The American is quick to use improved methods, and competition and high wages compel him to adopt the best appliances. When wages rise, managers are prompted to substitute machinery for hand work; and with larger production wages tend to rise. Managers cannot afford to tolerate indolent workmen at high wages; thus workmen become more alert and energetic. Will the machine drive out the workman? The workman is tempted to think machines are his enemy, especially at the time of change. All economic evolution occasions loss of capital, displacement of men, individual cases of suffering, which social sympathy seeks to mitigate. It is unfair to judge the general tendency from short views. From the dawn of civilization improved tools have caused occasional pain, but, on the whole, steady improvement for the race. Census returns show an absolute and relative increase in the number of workmen, and consumption absorbs the products of industry. The working class, in compensation for passing crises, enjoys a triple advantage — a larger demand for labor, wages higher on account of increased productivity, and commodities at a lower price. All society participates in the last source of gain.

Demand and supply react upon each other. Americans boast of the largest consumption to each inhabitant, and many of their economists consider this intensity of consumption as the stimulant of their industry, and as the cause of their high wages. There is never too much wealth, although it may be improperly distributed. The American business manager goes straight forward, seeing gain and desirous of securing it quickly. Therefore he uses machinery, and requires of his workmen all they can do. He has himself arisen from the working class, and has not always the polish of education.   He calculates closely.   He is occupied with his own business and not with that of others, and thus becomes profoundly *individualistic*, often egoistic and harsh with his fellow-citizens.   When work is done and wages paid, manager and workmen think they are no further bound to each other—a right judgment from a legal point of view.   From the social point of view this individualism is seen to exclude schemes of patronage.   The American workman wishes to be independent, and recognizes no obligation of gratitude to his employer.   He is in the shop on a bargain and not as a child.   He goes where he thinks he can do best for himself.

Immigration is offensive to the working class, because it intensifies competition for wages.   But, since America owes its industrial advance to immigration, it cannot be entirely suppressed.   The mold of character is an Anglo-Saxon type.   The English, Scotch, and Germans have furnished the most highly esteemed element, and the Scandinavians only a little less.   The Irish, spite of being less acceptable, are numerous enough to be politically strong; the Italians and the Slavs in a lower degree.   The Canadians form a group suspected on account of their clannish ways, but are prized by employers because they will work for low wages.   The French are too few to influence politics.   The party of the workingmen has demanded and secured laws restrictive of immigration.   The Chinese are entirely excluded.   Contract labor, in spite of the employers, has been prohibited.   Defectives are excluded on grounds of general welfare.

Nominal wages have, perhaps, doubled in fifty years.   It is impossible, on account of the variety of conditions, to state an average.   Perhaps $1.75 to $2 represents nearly the average in the United States, about double that in France.   The wages of women are almost half those of men.   Children under sixteen receive less than women.   There are fewer married women in factories than are seen in Europe, a sign of better conditions.   The number of women employed in industry has relatively diminished ; that of children has decreased still more.

In America, as in Europe, there are *famine* wages, that is, wages which do not afford the income of married laborers.   These are found chiefly in the sweated industries of clothing, and, while difficult to improve, affect comparatively few workmen.   Real wages have increased even more than nominal wages, because the prices of most commodities have fallen, while wages were rising.   The American workman dresses well, enjoys good food, and has many amusements. His standard of life is highest of all workmen. There are very great differences of income, but the workmen have had a good share of all gains, and the improvements in transportation, schools, lighting, streets, and other public wealth are shared by them. This progress is due to science, invention, management, and labor, and each has reaped a benefit.

In order to meet the power of employers on better terms, the workmen have formed trade unions, and, in order to provide for emergencies, they have associated themselves in mutual-benefit societies. There are advantages and disadvantages in unions, but they cannot be repressed; they must be recognized, and they should be made legally responsible for their use of power. The outlook for schemes of arbitration and conciliation is not altogether hopeful, but they are worthy of consideration.

The "protective system" of tariffs is not regarded by the author as helpful to wage-earners. Charity and public relief are treated as palliatives, not as remedies. Patronage is not congenial to the American spirit. Profit-sharing has not been very successful. Coöperation has been carried forward chiefly in building and loan associations, while in societies for consumers or producers comparatively little progress has been made.

Socialism is defined and condemned. The author believes that the teachings by which it is propagated in America are dangerous and should be met by argument. The rapid rise of great fortunes, and the isolation of industrial classes in two hostile camps, tend to endanger social order. The problem of state intervention is pressing and difficult. Socialists urge extension of state functions as a stage in the way to final absorption of all business by government. The degree of intervention must be determined by convenience, not by general theory. Factory legislation is needed to protect the health of workmen, but it should not interfere with the liberty of capitalist managers. The hours of labor should not be fixed by law, but by free agreements, and trade unions may help to secure shorter hours. It is entirely legitimate to regulate the housing of the people by law.

Professor Levasseur criticises Professor Ely for confusing morals with political economy. They are separate sciences, but do not conflict. "It is an error, propagated in America as in Europe by reformers, that political economy is a science without compassion, because it studies economic facts and laws, and does not construct seductive

Utopias." The wage system is permanent, and the wisest friends of workingmen will seek to amend its operations, rather than invent some totally new method.

We shall not advance suddenly from egoism to altruism, from antagonism to solidarity, from wages system to coöperation, from capitalism to collectivism, from misery to happiness. Progress is slow. The dreams of Fourier in 1803 were not realized, and the dreams of socialists will fail. Yet there will be important changes and improvements. The general direction of the near future is indicated by what we see before us: an enlargement of industry, an extension of markets, a higher standard of living, urban congestion, a larger proportion of the population living upon wages and salaries, a wider field for the negroes in industries, a restriction of immigration, probably further rise in wages, an improved type of workingmen, increased and dangerous interference with industry by government as workingmen gain political control, more power for trade unions. Trusts will compete with trusts and be regulated by law, and each decade will present new problems.

It will be seen that the standpoint of the author is that of an economist who inclines to liberalism and individualism, rather than to socialism. He is a friendly critic of American character and methods. He has taken great pains to secure correct and adequate data from the best sources. The style is clear and interesting, and the matter of supreme importance. On some of the most critical points the statistical material is too scant and doubtful for absolute conclusions, and men will continue to interpret the tables by "estimates" in order to attain to peace of mind or vantage ground for controversy. This large and serious effort to reach a satisfactory view of the actual condition and prospects of American workmen leads us to a new appeal to the government to secure and furnish more reliable information. The book is an argument in favor of a permanent and richly equipped census bureau in the United States, and adequate labor bureaus in the various states.   C. R. HENDERSON.

France. By JOHN EDWARD COURTENAY BODLEY. The Macmillan
    Co., 1898. Two volumes. Pp. vi+346 and vi+504. $4.

THE author is in love with his subject, he has had remarkable facilities for knowing it, he writes with combined dignity and raciness, he interests the reader from the first word of the preface, and does not allow interest to droop until he closes his second volume with the opinion of socialist doctrines in the French parliament : "One may indeed read them for instruction in manners, but it is vain to apply them to establish any doctrine."

The work has been so advertised that many will be disappointed by their first reference to the table of contents. It does not, and does not profess to, undertake for France all that Bryce has done for the United States. It may well be compared with that portion of Bryce which treats of the American constitution. The author's own statement is : "The capital subject of these volumes is 'Political France after a Century of Revolution.'" An introductory chapter of sixty-two pages presents social and industrial France in bird's-eye view. This ground has been more fully, if not so philosophically, covered in the two series of essays of Miss Betham-Edwards: "France of Today" (1892 and 1894). No book has done for English readers what Mr. Bodley has accomplished in the succeeding chapters. His main topics are : Book I, "The Revolution and Modern France ;" Book II, "The Constitution and the Chief of the State ;" Book III, "The Parliamentary System ;" Book IV, "Political Parties." A. W. S.

The Social Mind and Education. By GEORGE EDGAR VINCENT, Assistant Professor of Sociology in the University of Chicago. New York : The Macmillan Co., 1897. Pp. ix + 152. $1.25.

THIS book is a clear and firm presentation of educational doctrine under the conception of the social mind. It shows how the individual "writ large" in social progress finds the aim and method of his development in that progress. "The thought of social philosophy which sees in the development of society the growth of a vast psychic organism, to which individuals are intrinsically related, in which alone they find self-realization, is of the highest significance for the teacher, to whom it suggests both aim and method." The whole exposition rises out of, and has its validity in, the intrinsic relation of the individual to the social whole. The book is, therefore, a contribution to educational philosophy from the standpoint of social philosophy.

There are three distinct points of value in the treatment: one of method and two of result. Teachers are not accustomed to approach educational problems from the sociological point of view; yet such method of study is absolutely essential to a comprehensive grasp of educational problems. Whether a conception of the social mind, which the author develops in the first chapter, is adequate to a complete theory of education or not, no complete theory of education is possible without the application of such a conception. The value of the treatment to the reader does not depend on his full agreement with the author in viewing "social philosophy as a *scientia scientiarum*," as presented in the second chapter, and that social philosophy is, therefore, a science of education, but in having explained and emphasized a new category of educational thought.

The only difficulty in trying to explain the education of the individual by the conception of the social mind is in the constant effort required to think of two things as one which are constantly spoken of as if they were two. The author guards this point with great care, illustrating again and again that there is no such thing as a social mind apart from the individual mind. He shows that the social mind is only the individual mind in a condition which "results from the interaction of communicating minds." All this effort to guard the location of the social mind in the individual mind raises the question as to whether the most advantageous starting point for educational philosophy is not the individual mind rather than the social mind. From this point the individual mind would be traced in its development into and through the social mind. Then social philosophy would appear as a phase of educational philosophy. Then pedagogy would be the *scientia scientiarum*. This movement, rather than the other, is supported by the fact that there is other mind than social mind, in and through which the individual develops. The social environment is not the individual's only environment, and the question arises as to the complete adequacy of a principle of education which pertains only to one aspect of the pupil's life. Be this as it may, the author shows clearly what he attempts to show, namely, the working value of a social conception as applied to education.

The first fruit of the method is brought out in chaps. 3 and 4, under the titles: "The Development of Social and Individual Thought" and "The Social Mind and Education." In these we have a clear statement of the doctrine of the parallel development of the individual and the race. The author guards well against the danger of making the parallel into definite stages and fixed products; and thus disarms the criticisms invited by the "culture-epoch" theory as it is usually presented.

Since the pupil passes through the same stages of development as the race, the same phases and modes of life and thought, the method of the race's development becomes a guide to the general development of the individual. The pupil must repeat the experience of the race; but he must do this by "short cuts," as clearly brought out. The author defines education to be a "purposeful social effort to effect 'short cuts' in the mental development of the individual." The problem of teaching, then, is to produce the race experience in the individual in the shortest possible amount of time.

There is one point implied in this theory that should not be overlooked, namely, that the pupil cannot inherit race experience and culture as one inherits property and the advantages of material civilization; but he must attain to it through experience; must earn it. The "short cut" must not cut short the legitimate experience in the process of attaining knowledge. The memory process of book learning is a desperate effort to make unearned appropriation of race experience. But in this the pupil does not repeat the experience of the race, for the race did not advance by that process. Hence, in this race development theory for the individual there is not only marked out the general stages of the process, but, what is of more vital consequence, the essential nature of the process. Let it then be said with emphasis that the pupil must repeat the *experience* of the race; and, being an individual, must make the shortest cut possible consistent with repeating the essential elements of the race experience. Straight and narrow is the way.

The book culminates in a strong and much needed emphasis of unity of thought in a curriculum of studies. This is done in the last two chapters of the book: "Integration of Studies" and "A Tentative Curriculum." The author seems to feel strongly the need of a reform in college courses, to the effect that there should be courses given which will unify and systematize the various subjects studied. This need is certainly imperative. The college student usually has no organizing principle for his life and thought. While this might be supplied, more or less, in the various lines of study, it can be effectively done only by a systematic effort and course of work. The author presents a "tentative curriculum" in order to suggest the method of carrying out the general thought of unification.

The book moves wholly in the thought of giving the individual to be educated his intrinsic unity with the race, and since the race experience is integrated, organized experience, either unconscious or conscious, the student, to realize in himself the social mind, must integrate the experience of the race. Unity with the race through the unity of the race's experience is the fundamental doctrine of the book. And this to the end of the self-realization of the individual. It is worth while to read the book if one should receive only the deepened impression that the individual can realize himself only through social life; and therefore the problem of education is to relate him intrinsically to that life. The whole educational scheme diverges from this point.

ARNOLD TOMPKINS.

UNIVERSITY OF ILLINOIS,
Champaign, Ill

Cases on American Constitutional Law. Edited by CARL EVANS BOYD, PH.D. Chicago: Callaghan & Co., 1898. Pp. 11 + 678, 8vo. Cloth, $3.

THE scope of this work is briefly and, as it seems to me, fairly expressed in the preface: "In making this collection of cases, it was not my purpose to attempt to rival the notable collection of Professor Thayer. I have had the more modest design of bringing together within the compass of a single volume a sufficient number of the leading decisions of the supreme court of the United States on constitutional law to form the basis of a university course in that subject . . . . A work of this kind is necessarily a compromise between the desirable and the attainable. The exigencies of space have compelled me to exclude numerous and instructive decisions which many persons may expect to find and which I would have been glad to print. For the further economy of space, arguments have been omitted and the notes are few."

Such a frank statement in the preface puts the reader at once on good terms with the editor and leads him to expect to find in the book just what it contains, namely, a selection of cases which have been notably influential in determining the course of the development of the constitutional law in the United States.

The cases selected are arranged under the following heads: (1) "Validity of Legislation," (2) "Taxation," (3) "Money," (4) "Commerce," (5) "Police Power," (6) "General (Implied) Powers," (7) "Executive Powers," (8) "War—Martial Law," (9) "*Ex post facto* Laws and Bills of Attainder," (10) "Impairment of Contracts," (11) "Civil and Political Rights," (12) "The Federal Government and the

States," (13) "International Relations — Indian Affairs," (14) "Jurisdiction of the Federal Courts," (15) "Political Questions," (16)
"Enforcement of Executive Power by Judical Process."

The book is equipped with table of contents, table of cases, and
index. The helpful character of the notes appended to the cases,
especially the longer ones, such as that which accompanies the Dred
Scott case, leads one to wish that the author had added fifty pages or
more to the book, filled with matter of this kind.

A comparison of Mr. Boyd's compilation with that of Professor
Thayer shows that, while the latter has incorporated a great many of
the decisions of the supreme courts of the states, the former, as he
states in his preface, has limited his work to the decisions of the United
States supreme court. The limited scope of Mr. Boyd's work has
also obliged him to select what he considers the most important case
in establishing a constitutional principle, while Professor Thayer has
often been able to include several of the more important.

The bulk of the work under review is, of course, occupied with
cases which time has demonstrated to be turning points in the development of our constitutional law, but later cases, such as the income tax
cases and the Debs case, are also represented.

With Mr. Boyd's compilation as a text-book, Thayer's cases as a
reference book, and the decisions themselves as sources, the study of
constitutional law ought to become popular in our colleges and
universities.   C. H. Hastings.

Les Bases Sociologiques du Droit et de l'État. Par Michel-Ange
Vaccaro, Membre de l'Institut International de Sociologie,
Directeur de la Rivista Scientifica del Diritto. Ouvrage
traduit sur l'édition italienne, par J. Gaure, Avocat, et com-
plètement refondu. Bibliothèque Sociologique Internationale, No. XI. Paris: V. Giard et E. Brière. Pp. lxi+480.

So far as form goes, Signor Vaccaro's thesis belongs side by side
with Tarde's *Imitation*, viz.: "The ultimate law to which all others are
subordinate is *adaptation*." The content of this thesis, as it appears
in the present volume, is less positive and complete than Tarde's conception of what is involved in imitation. The thesis rather serves
Vaccaro as a principle of discovery and a norm of classification. In
those characters it is serviceable, but it has no *a priori* value as a constructive rule. I do not discover that the author attaches to it any

such value, and he thus keeps within the lines of inductive method instead of attempting to derive objective knowledge from metaphysical presumptions. It is not a "principle" to be used as the major premise of syllogisms. In other words, to say that the law of life is "adaptation" amounts to the assertion that the history of the world records progress toward *correlation* of the elements concerned. "Adaptation" is therefore in Vaccaro's usage a formal concept, with no means of valuing this term in the series to which it applies, except by comparison with the less complex correlations that have gone before. I cannot discover that the author has anything in mind in connection with this concept that is not more than covered by the Spencerian formula of evolution. It is a term for the world's habitual behavior. It does not tell us anything about what will be done the next time a variant enters. I confess, however, that it seems to me worth while to follow this author in rummaging among human experiences with his dark lantern, "adaptation." After an introductory chapter of sixty pages, his chief divisions are these: I, Adaptation as the Law of Life; II, The Biological Function of Pleasure and Pain; III, Human Adaptation and its Particular Characteristics; IV, Struggle and Adaptation between Man and the Cosmic Forces; V, External Struggle between Human Groups; Elimination; VI, Causes which Directly Mitigate the External Struggle; Beginnings of Adaptation; VII, Causes which Indirectly Mitigate the External Struggle; Ulterior Adaptation between Human Groups; VIII, The Past and the Future of this Struggle and of Adaptation between Human Groups; IX, Internal Struggle and Adaptation in Simple Human Groups; X, Internal Struggle in Composite Groups; Adaptation between Conquerors and Conquered; XI, Internal Struggle in Composite Groups; Adaptation among Conquerors; XII, The Past and the Future of Struggle and Adaptation in Human Groups.   A. W. S.

Alien Immigrants in England. By W. CUNNINGHAM, D.D. With three maps and seven illustrations. Social England Series. Swan Sonnenschein & Co. and The Macmillan Co., 1897. Pp. xxiii + 286. $1.25.

"THE 'Social England' series rests upon the conviction that it is possible to make a successful attempt to give an account, not merely of politics and wars, but also of religion, commerce, art, literature, law, science, agriculture, and all that follows from their inclusion, and that, without a clear knowledge of the last, we have no real explanation of any of the number."

The series is wisely planned, and the present volume places an important section of knowledge about England within easy reach. The main divisions of the material are the following: I, "The Norman Invasion," the foreign element which it brought, their distribution and influence. II, "The Latter Middle Ages": (*a*) Finance: Jews, Templars and Lombards, English factors and staples, English financiers; (*b*) Commerce: the Gascony merchants, hostmen, restrictions and grievances in connection with trade, the alien subsidies; (*c*) Industry: showing the influence of Flemish weavers, Italian artisans, and of aliens in general; (*d*) corresponding period of Scottish history. III, "The Reformation Period and Religious Refugees." IV, "Intercourse with the Dutch." V, "Latin Immigrations": (*a*) the Huguenots; (*b*) the Palatines; (*c*) the Émigrés. VI, "Conclusion: the Influence of Aliens in England.'   A. W. S.

_____

Sociologie et Politique. Par Louis Gumplowicz, Professeur de sciences politiques à l'Université de Graz, Membre de l'Institut International de Sociologie. Avec préface de René Worms. Bibliothèque Sociologique Internationale, No. XII. Paris: V. Giard et E. Brière. Pp. 300.

The original from which this volume is translated was published in German in 1892 under the title *Sociologie und Politik.* The very apologetic introduction by M. Worms does not render a sufficient reason for republishing the book in a French version. A properly descriptive title would be "Professor Gumplowicz's opinions about politics, not hazarded upon their own merits, but tacked as riders upon an assumed science of sociology." The argument of the book would furnish suggestions toward a method of solving the problem: "If A had a son and B a daughter, and the two were married, and the union produced children, would Gymnasium or Realschule better fit their talents?"

Neither sociology nor politics is yet a "science" in such a sense that it can furnish a definite foundation for the other. By yoking the names together in this fashion, Gumplowicz has encouraged incredulity about possible scientific treatment of either. It is true, as the editor claims, that this book, and we may add *Der Rassenkampf* as well, is "suggestive." So is Jules Verne. It is more to the point that Professor Gumplowicz is unfortunate in his excursions outside the field of Austrian jurisprudence and legal history. On that territory he is a master. In sociology—and possibly in politics—he is an amusing amateur.   A. W. S.

Reflections on the Formation and the Distribution of Riches. By TURGOT. Economic Classics Series. Edited by PROFESSOR W. J. ASHLEY. The Macmillan Co. Pp. xxii+112. $0.75.

THIS series is wisely planned, and furnishes easily accessible means of studying important chapters in the history of economic theory from the sources. The execution of the plan on the part of both editor and publisher leaves nothing to be desired, unless we demand that the series be indefinitely extended.   A. W. S.

Students' Edition of a Standard Dictionary of the English Language. JAMES C. FERNALD, Editor; FRANCIS A. MARCH, LL.D., Consulting Editor; Associate Editors: JOHN W. PALMER, M.D; FRANCIS A. MARCH, JR., PH.D.; WILLIAM R. COCHRANE; EMMA FISKE ROBERTS, M.A.; FRANK H. VIZETELLY. Funk & Wagnalls Co. Pp. 915, 8vo. $2.

THE title page states the aim of the volume as follows: "Designed to give the orthography, pronunciation, meaning, and etymology of over 60,000 words and phrases in the speech and literature of the English-speaking peoples, with synonyms and antonyms, containing, also, an appendix of proper names, foreign phrases, faulty diction, disputed pronunciations, abbreviations, etc., etc., and 1,225 pictorial illustrations."

This is a busy man's compend of the complete "Standard." For all but the one scholar in ten thousand it contains enough.

The Twentieth Century City. By REV. JOSIAH STRONG, D.D. The Baker & Taylor Co. Pp. ix + 186. Paper, $0.25; cloth, $0.50.

THIS little book would be rated higher if *Our Country* and *The New Era*, by the same author, had not already made a stronger impression in the same cause which the present essays serve. Practically no new facts are presented in this argument. The variations and additions are with the aim of persuasion rather than of instruction. The whole plea is sane, and it deserves the attention of all who propose to take the social situation seriously. A. W. S.

Le Décalogue Agricole. Un esquisse d'un Programme d'action catholique dans les campagnes. Par le P. HENRI WATRIGANT, de la Compagnie de Jésus. Abbeville: C. Paillart, 1896. Pp. 60. Fr. 0.50

THIS interesting syllabus of lectures is typical of the social activities of the French Catholic clergy. The subjects touched are religious instruction and worship, Sunday rest, problems of domestic, economic, and civic interest, morality, recreations, and social intercourse. The appendix furnishes a very full bibliography. The purpose of the pamphlet is to furnish topics for conferences rather than to offer a discussion of the problems named. It is highly instructive as showing what the rural clergy of France are thinking about in connection with the life of their parishes. C. R. HENDERSON.

Die Armenpflege. Einführung in die praktische Pflegethätigkeit. Von DR. JUR. E. MÜNSTERBERG. Berlin: Verlag von Otto Liebmann, 1897. Pp. 213.

IN a series of semi-popular lectures the well-known author of *Die Armengesetzgebung* has produced in excellent form a small handbook for practical workers. It is an admirable sketch of the field, with particular reference to German conditions. The references to the literature of the subject are carefully selected and would be a good guide for the purchase of a new library. The principal topics are public poor relief, private charity, the connection between public and private relief, the means of help, special branches of relief, and the principles of administration. The author shows familiarity with English and American methods, as well as with those of the continent. He was formerly head of the relief system of Hamburg, and is recognized as one of the first authorities in the world in this field. Readers of this Journal will recall his valuable articles on German poor relief.

C. R. HENDERSON.

NOTES AND ABSTRACTS.

Some Aspects of the Labor Problem.—The labor question is one of ethical principles and ideals, as well as of economic facts. It must be considered in its relation to the organization, tendencies, and ideals of human society as a whole. (1) "The *laissez-faire* spirit, which during a considerable part of this century has prevailed in economic discussion, and which has so strong an affinity for an essentially materialistic philosophy, is selfish and heartless." (2) "The indolent, optimistic spirit is as foolish as the *laissez-faire* spirit is heartless." The evolution of society is a process wrought out through the intelligent endeavors of men. Along with the present process of industrial organization, two ideas are becoming fixed convictions in the popular mind. "One is the right of wage-earners to organize for the protection and advancement of their interests; the other is the necessity that wage-earners shall organize for their own protection as long as competition between capital and labor remains the controlling principle in economic life." The labor question is not (1) a question merely of more or less wages. (2) It is not a question merely of the more equal division of wealth. (3) It is not merely a question of the control of industry by the workingmen. (1) "There is a very deep feeling, which many employers share, that the relation between employer and employé ought not to be a mere cash relation." The workman's labor is not merely a commodity, it is at once his capital and his life. (2) "There is also among laboring men a feeling that labor is inequitably divided." "A more equitable division of labor in producing material values would leave breathing space and leisure for the increased production of other and higher values." (3) "There is a conviction also, which grows deeper and more widely extended every day, that a vast amount of unpaid labor is exacted from the working class." This evil is traceable partly to the present economic organization in connection with the instinct of human selfishness. "The labor question is thus a question of a great social and industrial readjustment. Its solution is looked for in a social order that shall modify, by political as well as moral forces, the pitiless operation of so-called 'natural laws' of trade; that shall reduce selfish competition to the minimum; that shall allow no man, or group of men, artificial and exceptional advantages in the race of life; that shall compel idlers to become beneficent producers of values, or lose means of wasteful and debauching self-indulgence; that shall make it possible for every man who will work, not only to work, but also to receive his full share of the product of his labor by a more equitable division both of labor itself and of the fruits of labor; and that shall make life richer and sweeter for all the people, so that the privileges of intelligence and culture shall not depend solely or chiefly on the individual possession of wealth."—Rev. Philip S. Moxom. *Publications of the Christian Social Union*, No. 47.

Consumers' Leagues.—While direct employers are often helpless, consumers have the power to secure just and humane conditions of labor, if they would only use it. The great difficulty for conscientious purchasers is that of learning what fair conditions are. and where they do and do not exist. To meet this difficulty consumers' leagues have been established, first in England in 1890, in New York in 1891. "Recognizing the fact that the majority of employers are virtually helpless to improve conditions as to hours and wages, unless sustained by public opinion. by law, and by the action of consumers. the Consumers' League declares its object to be to ameliorate the condition of the women and children employed in the retail mercantile houses of New York city, by patronizing, so far as practicable, only such houses as approach in their conditions to the 'standard of a fair house,' as adopted by the league, and by other methods." The advisory board is required to prepare and publish a "white list" of retail mercantile houses which should be patronized by members. The league has a definite standard of wages, hours, and conditions of a "fair house." This standard has not been altered, but the number of names on the list has increased from eight in 1891 to forty in 1898. The work has been taken up by many other cities in New York. In 1897 consumers' leagues began work in Philadelphia, Brooklyn, and Chicago, and in January, 1898, the Massachusetts League was established. Although consumers' leagues are necessary, yet improvements in the conditions of wage-earners should, where possible, be secured by their own associated action, "because such action develops the moral and intellectual nature of those who take part in it, and because advantages gained by self-effort are better appreciated and more lasting than those conferred in consequence of the exertions of others." The Retail Clerks' Protective Association attempts this, and should therefore be encouraged.— MRS. CHARLES RUSSELL LOWELL, *Publications of the Christian Social Union*, No. 46.

The Real Causes of the Industrial and Colonial Development of England.—At the beginning of the last century Latin peoples exhibited more enterprise than the Anglo-Saxon. The supremacy of the Anglo-Saxon today is not to be exclusively explained by the constitution of society, particularly that of the family. The beginnings of England's greatness are to be traced in the rapid series of mechanical inventions of the last century in textile and iron industries. England's geographical position, moreover, protected her from continental troubles; her coal mines furnished magnificent forces to work the steam engine, newly invented, and her situation forced her attention upon ocean commerce. Most of all, the principle of private initiative, "self-help," has made England great. The meddling of government and over-centralization, the refusal of proper authority to local colonial representatives, have ruined France's imperial ambitions. She must follow the principles that have made England great, including the right of free testamentary bequest.— URBAIN GUERIN, "Des causes réelles du développement industriel," *La Réforme sociale*, May 28, 1898.

Anglo-Saxon Methods à propos of the Spanish-American War.—It is too often assumed that the Anglo-Saxons are a superior race. Latin peoples, however, discovered, or first explored, America, India, Australia, and the Cape of Good Hope. The Anglo-Saxons have won their way by a continuous course of perfidy, greed, and rapine; violating treaties, and imposing upon weaker nations. America has done the same in her actions toward the Indians and Mexico, and now toward Spain. The Latin peoples are a brave and energetic people; but there is an element of nobility and generosity in their natures that prevents the highest success. We must acknowledge the energy, perseverance, and practical sense of the Anglo-Saxons. We admire their spirit of self-reliance and the greatness of their success; but we must not forget that, in spite of the grandeur of the spectacle, their successes have been obtained by means which a just and Christian people cannot approve, far less follow as an example.— HUBERT-VALLEROUX, "Procédés anglo-saxons à propos de la guerre hispano-américaine."

Oversaving and the Unemployed.—Underconsumption is not the only cause of unemployment. Sometimes it is the absence of one requisite of production, as a result of war or drought, for example, which causes a cessation of industry. Moreover, any catastrophe which affects the prosperity and the purchasing power of a foreign country may render useless some part of the producing power. "No doubt the evil effects of unemployment may be intensified by bad social arrangements, but unemployment is not necessarily a mark of disease in a community. And, on the other hand, though full employment may be an index of full consumption, that consumption may be badly distributed." A community in which one class were slaves, or had only their labor, "might be in a thoroughly unsatisfactory condition, and yet there might be in it full employment, and full, though badly distributed, consumption." Though inequalities of wealth are not necessarily a direct cause of under-consumption, they are likely to bring about unemployment indirectly by facilitating saving. If the requirements of consumption are satisfied and consumption stands still, it is useless to save in order to increase production. Moreover, the attempt to make useless savings is not only futile, but positively injurious in causing congestion in the market for the saved goods and consequent unemployment, except in the case of the saved goods being wholly useless, in which case they are practically only a mode of consumption. "If, then, the amount of useful employment depends upon and is limited by the requirements of the community for consumption, for the community permanently to reduce its consumption in order to permanently increase its power of production is a process of self-stultification certainly useless and probably harmful. The use of saving is to increase production; the object of increasing production is to supply an increased consumption." In a country where production tends to outstrip consumption, and where there is a danger that oversaving may cause unemployment, the wasteful consumption of the rich may really benefit the poor — not because it is wasteful, but because it is consumption. Wasteful consumption is, however, not the rich man's only alternative to useless saving. Surplus wealth could be largely drawn upon for public purposes without much danger of checking production by trenching on the capital needed for the assistance of labor, by expenditure in improving the dwellings of the poor, in the provision of public baths and libraries, in the maintenance of an efficient system of public education, and in the erection of public buildings.— F. C. Channing, *Économic Review*, April, 1898.

A Summary of the Treaties, Laws, and Ordinances of the Year 1897.—A few of the acts cited are as follows: Of treaties by Germany with other nations: A treaty with Italy for the establishment of accredited bills of exchange in their mutual commerce. With Russia, freeing the citizens of each nation from the obligation of paying taxes or serving in the national defense in the land of the other nation. With France, recognizing French authority in Tunis, and receiving the same commercial and other rights in Tunis as at present in France proper under existing treaties. With Holland, an extradition treaty concerning offenders of the respective nations, in the country and colonies of the other. With Japan, a commercial and juridical treaty, giving each in the matter of tariffs the "right of the most favored nation." Citizens of each nation have full right to travel and settle in any part of the territory of the other, with full protection of life and property assured. In Japan, however, foreigners must obtain consular passes good for a year, in order to travel or reside outside of incorporated municipalities. The extra-territorial jurisdiction of consuls over citizens of their nationality in Japan is abolished. Foreigners are now under the jurisdiction of the local Japanese courts.

Between Prussia and Hesse an agreement was reached uniting the state railroads of Prussia and Hesse in operation and finances.—"Uebersicht über die Verträge, Gesetze u. Verordnungen des Jahres 1897," *Zeitschrift für die gesammte Staatswissenschaft*.

Conclusions from a Study of Profit-Sharing.—(1) The name must be reserved for those contracts by which the workman receives, above his salary, a share in the profits of the enterprise. This definition excludes mere gratuities, also agreements by which the workman receives a supplement to his salary other than a share of the profits, such as a premium for sales, assiduity, long service, etc. It excludes cases in which this share is not an addition to the salary, but is the sole pay, as in farming on shares. (2) Profit-sharing is an agreement. Without this agreement the workman has no right, no claim to such a share of the profits. He has no right, because by his salary he has had in advance his share. If he has preferred security of the present to uncertainty of the future, how can he claim a share in profits? He has had his share, a share fixed in advance and often consumed before the profits exist. Besides, in most cases, it is not the workmen who make the profits, any more than it is an editor's cook who makes his articles. They merely contribute to bring them about. (3) Profit-sharing is really a favor granted by the employer, and not always advisable. For instance, to use extraordinary profits to secure wholesome dwellings and permanent institutions for the workingman's benefit is often wiser and kinder. Profit-sharing can give good results only when the profits to be distributed are considerable, and when the workmen are intelligent enough to comprehend it. (4) It can thrive only in an atmosphere of liberty. If a workman prefers a salary pure and simple, the state has no right to impose on him a different form of pay. Besides, if imposed on employers, unless the laws at the same time fix an obligatory tariff of wages, the unwilling employer would recoup himself by lowering wages. Profit-sharing, made compulsory, would lose its supplementary character and become an integral part of the principal remuneration. As the congress of 1889 recognized, "profit-sharing cannot be imposed by the state, it must result solely, according to circumstances, from the initiative of the employer or from the request of workmen, agreed to by him, like any other agreement relative to the remuneration of labor."— MAURICE VANLAER, "Les conclusions d'une Étude sur la participation aux bénéfices," *La Réforme sociale*, April 1, 1898.

·**Definition and Classification of Sociology and the Social Sciences.**— Socia sciences refer not only to man, but to other beings. When two beings join each other and create voluntary or necessary relationships between them, there exists a society. The study of such a society constitutes a social science, which takes different names according to the facts examined. It is called sociology when it studies society as a whole and seeks general laws. Perhaps the relationships between inanimate things, between planets and even molecules, constitute a sociology in the widest sense of the word. Concrete sciences do not all fall into a linear order, but rather into a group of superimposed planes, thus : Concrete sciences : (1) study of real beings considered in their parts and in the functions of their parts — biology, geology, botany, mineralogy, geology, astronomy ; (2) study of the unity of an individual being — psychology and psychological sciences ; (3) study of the union of several individuals — sociology and social sciences ; (4) study of the union of all societies — cosmology, theodicy, and cosmological sciences. Social sciences, like others, are pure or applied. The first establish facts, compare them, and seek their causality. Social sciences and sociology then form a whole of graded sections, thus : Social sciences : (1) establishment of facts — sciences of religion, history, geography, law, economy, philology, ethnology, etc.; (2) comparison, and study of succession in time, place, and cause — comparative religion, comparative history, etc. Sociology : (3) investigation of special laws — sociology of religions, of history, etc.; (4) general laws — general sociology. Sociology may then be defined as the philosophy of the social sciences. Applied science has two peculiarities — it looks at the present and the future, and it bears the personal active stamp of man, whose office in pure science is passive. Thus special sociology is : (1) pure — religion, history, geography, law, economy, linguistics ; (2) applied — special laws of religion, history, etc., directed toward future improvement ; (3) contingent — religion, etc., applied according to circumstances to obtain improvement. General sociology is, in a similar way, pure, applied, and contingent. From this scheme results the complete definition of sociology as "the science of the laws of society (pure sociology), of the application of these laws (applied sociology), and of the contingent application of the absolute application (contingent sociology)." The social sciences may be distinguished as : (1) qualitative — history, economics, law, etc. ; (2) quantitative — historical statistics, economic statistics, etc. Sociology itself is neither qualitative nor quantitative, but looks now from one point of view, now from the other, now from both.—RAOUL DE LA GRASSERIE, "Definizione e classificazione della sociologia e delle scienze sociali," *Rivista Italiana di Sociologia*, March, 1898.

Man's Dependence on the Earth.—The different regions of the earth are of two classes—those which repel and those which attract man. The reason for the contrast is to be found in the complex relation between the land and man. This relation is constantly varying, and man changes his place according as he finds a fuller satisfaction of his desires and wants. "The study of the relations between man and the earth comprehends three parts : the determination of the factors on which the value of the relation depends ; the variations of the relation, and the inquiry whether it tends toward a limit, and, if so, toward what limit." Three series of conditions determine the existence and development of man in general, "for living, the realization of a certain minimum of indispensable natural requisites ; for the creation of a particular civilization, a certain material abundance, which can be obtained only by utilizing the resources of the planet ; and for the transformation of this local civilization into a general civilization, facilities for outside contact and mutual exchange." While the laws of human development remain the same everywhere, necessarily very unequal values attach to different regions in their relations to man. Four factors — relief, climate, geological structure, and situation — and their infinite combinations, furnish the reasons for the contrasts in the various regions of the earth and the human communities developed in them. Both earth and man are constantly undergoing changes, but there is no correspondence either in the rate or the nature of the changes. "The rational study of the soil as related to the successive scientific, historical, and social conditions of man gives the key to the local shiftings of civilization through the ages." Evolution of the earth is going on slowly, and it has its limitations. The earth will reach a condition in which it will not furnish even the minimum necessary to existence. Exploitation of the earth's resources is pursued too recklessly. The remedy is to be found in applying rational and scientific methods of exploitation.— M. L. GALLOUÈDEC, *Appleton's Popular Science Monthly*, May, 1898.

The International Coöperative Congress at Delft.—From the papers presented and the reports given, it would seem that in Russia, Roumania, Switzerland, Italy, Servia, the Netherlands, Belgium, Germany, and Great Britain coöperation everywhere seems spreading and progressing. From the United States alone coöperation is reported as not progressing — perhaps due to general trade depression. There were no reports from France, Denmark, or Austria. In Russia coöperation has been much hindered by government protection and interference. In Roumania coöperation is propagated largely by national exhibitions. Servia is multiplying its banks. In Switzerland there are said to be 2,223 coöperative concerns registered, of which 1,191 are dairies and cheeseries. There are also in addition 491 more or less coöperative societies. Coöperation in Italy is represented chiefly by banks. The pope's encyclical approved village banks — Roman Catholic, of course. The papers and discussions at the congress were not of very high value and were not well managed, but the alliance undoubtedly exhibits an increasing strength with each passing year.— HENRY W. WOLFF, *Economic Review*, January, 1898.

An Italian Sociologist in Northern Countries : A Review of Ferrero's "L'Europa Giovani : Studi e viaggi vei poesi del Nord."—The foreigner who possesses a scientific interest is especially qualified in many ways for the study of a given people on account of his personal indifference.

In Germany today, according to Ferrero, two great political forces confront each other, militarism, or Bismarckism, and socialism. Both are alien to the German character, which tends to a peaceful, constructive life. Militarism is due to one man, Bismarck, whose power is to be explained by the "law of singularity," that by which a leader exercises sway by means of qualities alien to his people ; instance Napoleon, Cavour, Parnell. The results of the supremacy of these alien political principles are disastrous. Widespread discontent exists. Socialism, the foe of militarism, is making wonderful progress. Its party organization is so finely administered that the Italian government might be happy to possess an equal one. But neither of these forces are final; Cæsarism and socialism will die together.

English socialism is not like German socialism, a creed, an ideal, an end in itself, but rather a political engine for securing certain practical advantages, as shorter hours, higher wages, or increasing political power.

Russia is a land of religious quiet compared with German discontent and London noise. Moscow is the one holy city left in Europe. The Slav characteristics of resignation and patience, contempt of pain and death, find themselves expressed in social conditions. In the factory, whose workers lead the shut-off life of a monastery, every detail of life, working, eating, sleeping, is regulated by the employer. The voluntary "Avtel," or club, plays a great part in all industries, but especially in agriculture. It contracts with the employer, and the members live together during the completion of the work, obviating the necessity of an entrepreneur. It will scarcely suffice in the more complicated system which will come with greater capitalism and machinery.

Ferrero says that the prevailing motive of the Latin race is passion, of the Germanic "the sentiment of duty and chastity;" therefore the former is a decaying race compared with the latter.—BERNHARD W. HENDERSON, *Economic Review*, January, 1898.

SEMINAR NOTES.

THE METHODOLOGY OF THE SOCIAL PROBLEM. DIVISION I. THE SOURCES AND USES OF MATERIAL.

PART I. GENERAL METHODOLOGY.

CHAPTER I.

INTRODUCTION.

RADICAL error and persistent confusion would be forestalled, if students could be familiar from the start with the fact that sociology is not, first and foremost, a set of schemes to reform the world. To deserve respect sociology must become an accredited section of general philosophy. Sociological methodology has the task of arranging all the kinds and sources of knowledge which have a bearing upon the relations of men to each other.

In order to show that the new order of knowledge called sociology is not Quixotic in calling for an organization of kinds of knowledge that are known by name only to exceptional people, it should be said that sociology is a pursuit which may be undertaken successfully only by persons whose philosophical talents and training are of the first order. Tom, Dick, and Harry may and must have opinions about the social relations with which they are most intimately concerned, but only one man in ten thousand is likely to engage profitably in an attempt to organize all the facts about society into a system. This is only parallel with the facts about division of labor in all other human pursuits. Out of ten thousand good machinists there would probably not be more than one fitted by nature and by training to pursue the science of physics. Sooner or later, to be sure, all physical science enlarges the possible knowledge of all men. Progress in sociological science should have similar results. It remains true, nevertheless, that the most generalized knowledge, whether physical or social, is beyond the present reach of all but a relatively small number. Less general ized knowledge, special phases of knowledge, special applications of knowledge, will and must suffice for the majority.

It must accordingly be understood that this outline is not a programme which the author would advise all members of society to adopt as their introduction to right thinking about society. It is not presumed that citizens in general must do without the kinds of opinions which they require for practical purposes, unless they consent to plod through the following survey of social science and its divisions of labor. That is no more the case than mastery of the science of astrophysics is necessary before one can become an able-bodied seaman. The method to be outlined is rather the programme which must be followed in order to make the most comprehensive organization of knowledge about society that our present insight permits. Such a method is to be judged on its merits as an *organization of knowledge and of research*, not by the criterion of its immediate availability for popular programme making.

The "social problem" is, first and foremost, the problem of knowing society, both actually and potentially. What to do about improving society at any particular point depends upon assumed knowledge about the facts of social structure and social forces. To a certain extent we have such knowledge. We want and need more. To get it is the most difficult task that science has yet proposed. It involves organization and adaptation of all extant knowledge about people, and of all known methods of getting more knowledge. The "social problem" is not an abstract problem. *It is the problem of thinking the whole human reality as a whole.* It demands such correlations of all special inquiries into human facts that each will complete and be completed by the rest.

This contribution to the methodology of the social problem begins with certain elements of general methodology as represented by Wundt's *Methodenlehre*. That work is used, however, very much as the Roman nobles of the Middle Ages used the Colosseum; viz., as a quarry for material which is put to uses quite different from those that the author intended. At the same time, the attempt is made to interpret Wundt and to advertise the desirability of much more extended use of his work than can be made in this course. This intention is more fully carried out in the lectures upon the syllabus than in the printed notes themselves. These latter contain careful translations of considerable portions of the *Methodenlehre*. They include free translations, paraphrases, and adaptations of other portions. They depart from Wundt's programme very early, however, and attack the problem of sociological method from a direction quite different from his angle of approach. Although the organization here attempted, if successful, will entirely displace Wundt's correlation of problems after those of psychology, yet the freest use is made throughout of everything in his work that will serve the present purpose.

These notes contain no definition of sociology. The plan is to make plain, if possible, what sort of knowledge about society is yet lacking, and to find in that hiatus the problem of sociology. If we are successful in making out that there is an order of social problem not only unsolved, but unformulated elsewhere, the discovery may indicate where there is room for sociology.

The logic of method is this: Given, *first*, a reality of which the mind is conscious, and about which the mind proposes questions; to discover, *second*, what elements are involved in answers to the questions, and to discover, *third*, by what means the implicit requirements of the questions may be satisfied.

To mark the most general bearings of the social problem, we may begin with the observation that we have before us the task of *investigating reality*. There are but two sides of reality to be studied. We cannot completely separate them if we will. It is impossible to know much about either without learning much about the other. Unless the mind turns from reality to fantasy, it has but this single choice, viz., between studying chiefly the world of things, on the one hand, or chiefly the world of people, on the other. Besides these there is no reality open to our research. To our minds, things have, and always must have, their meaning from their relations to persons. The physical universe may have a quite different meaning to an infinite intelligence, but men have to estimate it in its relation to human conditions. Human wants decide for human minds what is worth knowing about the world of things. A well-balanced conception of the world of people is a necessary condition of the broadest and deepest knowledge of the world of things. The converse of this is also true, viz., a well-balanced conception of the world of things is a necessary condition of the broadest and deepest knowledge of the world of people. All students of men should qualify themselves by much schooling in the sciences of things. But men cannot successfully take a standpoint outside of humanity. Our outlook is the human outlook. Until a very recent date most students of social facts went gaily at their work without thought of a social standpoint. If it were wise to tell the whole truth, I should add that ninety-nine in every hundred students of social facts still cheerfully continue the same unconscious programme. I refrain from the assertion, and simply say that we dissipate our energies if we fail to recognize the unity of our subject-matter. The object of human knowledge is not many "subjects," but one cosmos. That cosmos, as I have said, is composed of a world of things and a world of people. This world of people is in turn a unit. For convenience we divide it into parts, but we delude ourselves unless we keep ourselves conscious that those parts are all actual members of the social whole. All observable reality that does not belong to the world of things belongs to the social realm. It is either men, or men's groupings, or men's workings. Whether we study men's bodies, or their tools, or trades, or arts, or foods, or clothes, or houses, or wars, or games, or words, or prayers, or oaths, or songs, or books, or laws, we are studying phases of the one social fact. We are all studying one thing, whether we call ourselves students of language, or literature, or ethnology, or history, or psychology, or philosophy, or æsthetics, or theology, or economics, or civics, or sociology. Our subject-matter is the world of people, its conditions, its elements, its forms, its processes, its products. We falsify this world at the start, unless we study our portion of it in conscious recognition of its place in the unity.

The number of facts observable in the world of people is so enormous that, from the beginning until now, the rule has been for students of human facts to get so overwhelmed by the mass of facts within some one section of the world of people that they have never developed a sense of the proportions and unity of human society. They have been like Yankee Doodle. They could not see the town for the houses. Consequently, the world of people has been to them either a vast, senseless confusion, or it has been a little oasis of order surrounded by a wilderness of chaos. For illustration of the latter case I would cite those expounders of religions or literatures who have supposed themselves to understand their abstraction of social facts, while they were ignorant as babes about all the rest of the civilization in which the religion or the literature had its setting; within which alone either can be seen in its real meaning. I would cite those expounders of economics or politics who imagine that either of these groups of abstractions from the facts that make up a society can be known as they are without relating each objectively, not only to the other, but to the natural environment, the domestic institutions, the æsthetic standards, the social traditions, the intellectual attainments, the religious beliefs, and the moral codes of the society concerned. Above all I would cite every version of history which professes to report the life of any society, without placing in due proportion and perspective each of the great groups of human workings. These together, not in abstraction, fashion both the individual units and the social combinations of the period described. Whatever phase of human fact we choose to learn most intimately, we distort and mangle and pervert it, unless we first get such an outlook over the whole range of human facts that we can see our particular department of men's life in its actual working relations with all the rest.

I regret that the man whom I rate as the most acute social philosopher in Europe has a radically different view from my own about the scope of sociology. A short time ago we were discussing our differences, and I tried in vain to argue him into acceptance of my position. Presently I said: "However we may define our territory, the sociologists, at all events, are fighting for the perception that every point in every man's life is related to every point in every other man's life." Like a flash he answered: "There I agree with you; and when we have made everybody see that, the social problem is solved.'

This outline is an argument for synthesis of knowledge and organization of study. Every person who attempts to form opinions about society ought to do enough study of formal social science, as contrasted with study of concrete social facts and abstracted groups of social relations, to get a good working comprehension of the proposition that in the world of people everything is related to everything. Let us not imagine that we are equipped for sane judgment of human relations until we are thoroughly aware that, whatever be our particular field of knowledge, our neighbors, studying other phases of human fact in all directions around our own field, are really completing our imperfect knowledge. Let us be specialists if we may. Let us concentrate our original research upon one of the great phases of human fact. But let us avoid being partialists, by learning how that phase must be coördinated with all the other phases in a true report of the world of people.'

This syllabus of method has been prepared to meet the wants of students who are ambitious to investigate society in the most comprehensive way. It must be said at the outset that scientific method is not absolute but relative. The procedure that is valid at one stage of knowledge is not the appropriate process at another stage. The things that we want to know vary with the progress of general knowl-

' *Cf.* University of Chicago *Record*, February 4, 1898.

edge, as well as with the mental development of the individual. Neither general nor individual knowledge advances in a straight line. A slight revision of a single portion of knowledge has often compelled reconsideration and readjustment of the whole body of scientific beliefs then prevalent. The purpose of this syllabus is to explain the correlation of scientific research which is "indicated" by our present insight into social relationships.

The reality which our minds encounter is the *world of people*, inseparable in fact from the world of things. Men have investigated this dual reality sufficiently to have furnished a somewhat circumstantial answer to the questions: What do we know about the world of people? What do we *need* to know about the world of people? How must we go to work to get the lacking knowledge?[1] In order to get the benefit of accumulated knowledge about the world of people, and in order to control the mental processes that are involved in making our knowledge more precise, we must master—both theoretically and practically—certain methodological elements. Those in most constant demand, for the purposes here in view, are characterized in the next chapter.

CHAPTER II.

ESSENTIAL METHODOLOGICAL PROCESSES.[2]

I. ANALYSIS.

The objects which we encounter in experience are complex. Every object or event represents either many permanent and coexistent aspects, or many conditions following each other in time. Frequently these two sorts of marks form combinations with each other. Analysis is consequently that form of methodical thinking which is, as a rule, set in motion by the natural qualities of the object of thought. A clear and definite conception of objects is the fundamental condition of scientific research, and at the same time the most obvious mark of distinction between scientific scrutiny and ordinary observation. The first step of investigation must consequently be definite

[1] *Vide* "The Sociologists' Point of View," AMERICAN JOURNAL OF SOCIOLOGY, September, 1897, pp. 145-55.

[2] Following WUNDT, *Methodenlehre*, 2. Band, 1. Abtheil., pp. 1-17. To make assurance doubly sure it may be worth while to state explicitly that these citations from general logic do not amount to a claim that these fundamentals belong within the field of sociology. The sociologist must go to school under many teachers. Because he has not learned, as well as he should, some of these elementary lessons in logic, it is necessary to review these portions of antecedent methodology, and to insist that sociologists need to pay more heed to their requirements.

representation of the different elements, which must be simultaneously or successively perceived, of which the fact consists. This analysis of facts takes place, however, in a definite order of succession, within which in general three stages may be distinguished. Of these only the first is the necessary preparation for all the rest in the sense just indicated. The others may combine with synthetic methods. In this combination they form parts of induction and deduction.

The first of these steps or stages is **elementary analysis**. It consists of separating a phenomenon into the visible parts composing it, without any concern about the relation of these parts to each other— *e. g.*, the movement of a tree in a gale, into the fluttering of the leaves, the bending of the limbs, and the swaying of the trunk. Such is the analysis which furnishes the uncriticised, or partially organized, raw material of social knowledge which I call descriptive sociology. To be sure, this material is accumulated partly by means of scientific processes in which there is a high degree of refinement beyond the primary processes to which I am referring. Relatively, however, accounts of the component activities of associated men, even when they are descriptions in turn of industries, of politics, of domestic, artistic, intellectual, social, religious institutions, are merely elementary analyses. Examinations of the relations between the distinguished parts are not properly begun. This elementary analysis, of whatever degree its precision, serves in the first place merely descriptive purposes. Description consists essentially in pointing out things that exist side by side, and one after the other. Such description prepares the way for search into causal relations, although when the subject-matter is very complicated we have to be a long time content with description alone. Causes are too obscure for immediate detection within the described facts. Moreover, this elementary analysis may make use of various sorts of aids. Thus the different senses may in turn be brought to bear on the thing observed. The ears may report the sounds made by the tree and the wind. The nose may report the odors pressed from the leaves, etc. Or the subjective feelings created—fear, awe, pleasure—may be made parts of the analysis and description. All the time the logical character of the process remains one, and even when artificial helps are brought to bear on the facts—field glasses, instruments for measuring the velocity of the wind, etc.—the analysis is still the same. So is it when the description is made up from the testimony of many witnesses, from various historical documents, from statistical tables, etc. Even when the ultimate purpose of analysis is the discovery of causes, so long as causes are not discovered, and the search merely succeeds in making the details of the facts more clear, the process is, after all, only elementary analysis—as I remarked in the case of descriptive sociology.

A case in point is chemical analysis, although it is a process so much more complex psychologically than the process of describing the movements of a tree. The result of qualitative chemical analysis is merely a knowledge of the component elements of the substance examined, without reference to the more precise conditions of their combination. In these complicated cases, however, elementary analysis tends irresistibly to pass over into the more advanced stages of the analytical method.

The second stage of analysis is **causal analysis**. It consists in the separation of a fact into its component parts with reference to the causal relations of the same. Thus tree, swaying motion, sound, may he analyzed as above in a merely descriptive or elementary fashion ; but when there is advance to a different logical plane the process changes. Or I may say, when the process changes, the analysis is evidently proceeding on a different logical plane. Thus, "the god in the tree and the god in the air are angry with each other, and, wrestling together, they make what we see," viz., the details analyzed into the other terms above. Here the components of the distinguished parts are gods, passions, contest — in turn causes and effects. This analysis for purposes of explanation presupposes elementary descriptive analysis. Yet the descriptive analysis may be very summarily performed or combined with explanation, so that investigation really begins at once with the latter. Instances are physics, psychology, and history; while, on the other hand, chemistry, physiology, political and social science are parts of knowledge in which descriptive analysis is a stadium of intelligence with a distinct importance of its own.

The ground of this difference lies in the different tasks of these sciences. Physics and psychology concern themselves with the explanation of general phenomena, the one of objective, the other of subjective, occurrences. To this end, each begins analysis with the simplest facts, in which, without any descriptive preparation, a consideration of causes becomes at once necessary. The investigation of more complicated phenomena may then follow close upon that of these simpler causal analyses, and there is at once connected with these simple analyses an attempt to test the causal principles, analytically reached, by seeing whether they are applicable as explanations in a synthesis. Such simple points of departure are wanting in history. As a compensation, and logically a similar affair, history employs a comprehensive process of abstraction, which permits seizure upon certain chief factors of historical events, which may be easily referred back to certain psychical motives.

Quite in contrast with this is the situation of the other group of sciences. In their case the simple facts are for a long time beyond reach — thus the facts which qualitative and quantitative analysis must discover in chemistry, the morphological and chemical qualities of an organ in physiology, the facts about occupations and customs in sociology. Hence the initial necessity of independent descriptive analysis.

I speak of this at length, because in the social sciences, with the single exception of political economy, men have hardly begun the necessary process of descriptive analysis, at the basis of all credible science or philosophy or theory of society. That is, they have hardly begun to propose the necessary question: What are the different processes that combine to make up the life of men in society?

Causal analysis is distinguished particularly by its arbitrary isolation of specific elements from the whole complex mass of facts under investigation. This isolation is with the aim of discovering the causal relations of the elements thus separately considered. Elementary analysis goes no farther in changing the object of contemplation than to separate its component parts successively from each other (thus doing in thought what is done literally when the different parts of a manikin are in turn removed and laid aside in the process of illustrative dissection).

To return to the case of our tree in the gale: descriptive analysis does not furnish an instantaneous photograph, nor even a kinetoscopic view, but something midway between the two, *i. e.*, a *naming* of leaf, branch, trunk, with the conditions of each, as though for the moment the remainder did not exist.

Causal analysis goes beyond this in misrepresenting its object, *i. e.*, it ignores altogether the existence of certain parts. It does not then confine itself to demonstration of the remaining parts. On the contrary, it makes every possible attempt to change the conditions of their coexistence or sequence. Thus the device of isolation is reinforced by arbitrary variation of the elements. (For example, in the familiar case of iron filings agitated upon the surface of a glass disk, and the variation of introducing a bar of magnetized steel beneath the disk, with resulting arrangement of the iron filings into the so-called magnetic curves.) This reinforcement of causal analysis by arbitrary variation of the constituent elements may take place whenever the nature of the object permits either the total removal of certain elements or an alteration in their proportions. The analytic form of experimentation consists of such arbitrary variation. Whenever experiment can be used, it deserves preference above every other kind of causal analyis. It is the most direct way of determining the causal relation of the parts of a phenomenon. In certain subjects experiment is out of the question (as, *e. g.*, in the case of certain questions of human physiology, and of the most general cosmological, biological, and historical and social problems). In this case the closest approach to experiment, or the best alternative, is observation of the variations among the elements of phenomena of like general nature. (Thus we cannot produce murderers for scientific purposes, nor may we produce the conditions which incite to murder. We must resort, in the study of homicidal tendencies, to comparison of the conditions under which homicides have occurred.) In other words, we must observe variations that take place, without the assistance of the observer, instead of making variations. The more closely these collected variations resemble the constructed variations, the more nearly will they approach experimentation in value as the source of causal conclusions.

It must be observed in passing that the discovery of appropriate facts, such as parallel variations, is very largely a matter of accident, especially in the earlier stages of any causal analysis. · In the most favorable cases, therefore, much time must elapse in research. Moreover, there must be an extensive collection of material upon which observations can be made. (For instance, Darwin's labors for thirty years in collecting observations before he ventured his generalizations on the variations of species.)

It not seldom happens that approximation to the experimental method is estopped by the fact that the objects observable are too individual in their character, so that even the somewhat like phenomena are still too different for precise comparison. This is the case, for example, with those incidents of evolution in which periodical repetition is out of the question, at least in any period which we can observe. This is true of the origins of cosmic and organic structures, and of historical occurrences. In such instances comparative causal analysis must be content in part with remote analogies, in part it must be guided by presumptions from a more general range of facts, from which application is possible to the object under investigation. Thus, for example, analysis of the origin of species falls back on observation of individual development and upon the demonstrable variations of artificially produced types.

In a different field, historical analysis follows generally recognized psychological principles in place of experimentation, and so reaches tentative conclusions.

The third stage is **logical analysis.** It consists in the separation of a complex fact into its component parts, with reference to the logical relations of the same. The presupposition of the process is that ideas have been formed of the qualities of the (distinguishable) elements which make up the whole under investigation. If this condition is fulfilled, logical analysis then undertakes to follow out the separate consequences which result from these qualities.

For example, legal conceptions may be cited. It is presumed that primary descriptive analysis has proceeded far enough to put the thinker into possession of the separate notions involved in jural society. Logical analysis then undertakes to arrange these distinct notions in rational relations to each other, thus forming a philosophy of legal society.

II. SYNTHESIS.[1]

Synthethic procedure may consist in the simple reversal of a preceding analysis. In that case the synthesis is of a reproductive character. It has a relatively limited value, since it serves practically as a corroboration — or, as we say in arithmetic, a " proof " — of the analytic results. The synthetic process may, however, be so used that only certain results of the previous analytical investigations are employed, or, perhaps, only the elementary conceptions,

[1] *Vide* SMALL, " Sociology and Economics," *Journal of Political Economy*, March, 1895, pp. 179 *seq.*

while the synthesis itself binds together the elements in new and independent fashion. An example of this sort is social philosophy, as understood by the present writer. We posit the necessity, first of collecting social facts, then of analyzing social facts. As the product of analysis we have the groups of ideas peculiar to vital science, to mental science, to economic science, to political science, to ethical science, and the various subdivisions of each. The first process of social philosophy is a bringing together of these analyzed groups in such fashion as to present a conception of the whole, *i. e.*, human association, a fact having a past, a present, and a future. In this synthetic process we reach the concept social organism, a concept not given by the antecedent analytic process.

Between the two sorts of synthesis, the reproductive and productive, there are many intermediate sorts. These are reinforced especially by the synthetic form of experimental processes. A common illustration of reproductive synthesis is the fusion of H and O into water, by the passage of the electric spark. The result is a synthetic and experimental demonstration of the chemical composition of water.

Again, after analysis of sound has distinguished component sounds, experimental synthesis produces those sounds simultaneously, in order to see whether they actually compose themselves into the complex sound first analyzed. So of light, etc. But the more creative process of experimental productive synthesis is suggested by these primary processes. *E. g.*, instead of taking all the components found by analysis to be in sunlight, the investigator puts two or more colors together to determine the product of them by synthesis. A special form of synthesis is that which selects from the data of antecedent analysis merely the elements, with which the process of building up is maintained. Geometry is the best illustration. The elements with which it is concerned are the point, the line, and the plane. With these construction is carried on, and this term is best for the process. The productive character of construction in this sense is evident. The analysis which reached these simple elements was of a very primary order. It by no means gave, *prima facie*, as its correlates, the numberless forms and relations in two or three dimensions in which these elements may be combined. The analysis, in other words, does not of itself foreshadow what will be constructed by subsequent synthesis.

The sociologist is consequently bound to understand the traps and snares for the mind throughout its process of building up ideas. We are not only in a world of composite realities, but all our thoughts about the world are composite. They are syntheses of syntheses of syntheses, up to the *n*th power. These thoughts, however, form the material upon which the sociologist is employed, the tools with which he works. He is at the mercy of any false synthesis that may have occurred anywhere in the long process of building up current social ideas. Thus the elementary ideas of the sociologist, *e. g.*, rights, duties, obligations, liberty, individuality, equality, society, nation, sovereignty, government, property, etc., are constructions of many past minds. They are not necessarily coherent constructions. We might throw into the air pieces of material which might for a moment assume shapes conformed to geometric definition. It would by no means follow that these fantastic shapes are permanent and useful correlations of that material. The like is true of social concepts. They may be merely the product of a series of psychological accidents. They may thus be very monstrosities of thought. It is impossible to tell how far back in the process of building up concepts out of concepts the vitiating false synthesis may have occurred. Hence the fully equipped sociologist must be able to criticise the synthetic process from the beginning. It is to be noticed, further, that synthesis may be of threefold stages, corresponding to those of analysis.

1. **Elementary synthesis.** This stage, to be sure, is usually taken for granted in elementary analytical synthesis.

To go back to our tree swaying in the gale, there has been a synthetic process which results in the judgment: "Tree is not man, nor mountain, nor horse." This elementary synthesis is taken for granted when analysis begins to separate the attributes in tree, so that there can be discrimination of oak, elm, maple tree, etc.

2. **Causal synthesis**, on the contrary, is a highly important stage of critical knowledge. It is a serious component of experimental processes. It has its place not merely in confirming the results of analysis by reversing the method of approach; it brings new things to light.

3. **Logical synthesis** operates in all mathematical or other thought construction. These constructions are sometimes facilitated by concrete observation (*Anschauung*), as in synthetic geometry, or in mechanical invention, when deliberately studied out, or in improvement of a social combination, like a railroad association, or a mutual benefit order. In other cases these constructions follow out purely conceptual associations of ideas, as in the case of the demonstrations of Euclid or Hegel's dialectics.

While the method of Euclid is the least objectionable of these different processes (of logical synthesis), it still shows plainly that it is really a process of reproductive synthesis. This does not always come to light in other applications. In fact, the method of Euclid simply recasts analytical results in the synthetic form. When this is not the case, as in the synthetic (constructive) attempts of philosophical dialectics, it is all too easy for arbitrary combinations of ideas to insinuate themselves into the place of valid logical constructions.[1]

In general, the synthetic method is of less wide application than the analytic. Facts defy synthetic construction after they have attained a certain degree of complexity. For example, physics and chemistry analyze the

[1] An illustration is the vagary of Novicow in deriving institutionalized aristocracy from the organic concept. In the same logical category is Bellamy's nationalism, George's single tax, Tolstoi's non-resistance, etc.

most complex substances and processes. They can reproduce only those that are comparatively simple. The chemist may easily separate water into its component gases. He reunites them only with the greatest difficulty, but he cannot at all produce artificially some of the most common natural compounds of several chemical elements.

For similar reasons, synthesis is of limited availability in the psychical sciences. Most psychological, social, and historical facts are of too complicated nature to permit any other than analytical investigation of any great scope and precision. In psychology synthetical experiment is possible to a limited extent. In like manner economic science has arrived at certain synthetic constructions. These, however, have only a hypothetical value. They rest on the assumption that certain conditions exist. This assumption may never quite correspond with the facts.

In all this there is caution and instruction for the sociologist. We are at once put on our guard against the expectation that a way may be quickly found to reconstruct our forms of thought about life. Still less may we anticipate the invention of ways to reconstruct the forms of life itself. In reducing life to systematic formulation we are shut up very closely to reporting, with necessary analytical precision, facts as they are. The moment we venture upon construction of the elements of life into new combinations, we run the risk of falsifying some of the essential elements of the combination.

III. ABSTRACTION.

Abstraction means eliminating certain elements from a complex conception or group of conceptions and retaining the remaining elements as components of a concept.

E. g., we will take the concept "plant," understanding by it a member of the vegetable kingdom in the widest sense, as distinguished from an animal. If, now, we throw out notion after notion, belonging within this general conception, we shall have an *abstraction* left. Thus, plants live different periods, from a few moments to centuries. We will throw out all but ability to live a long term of years. Plants grow in the water, from the air, on other plants, and on animals. We will throw out all but the idea of growth from the ground. Plants are of one stem or many stems. We leave out all but the one. They creep along the ground, or climb upon walls, or other supports, or stretch upright into the air without support. We will throw out all but the last idea. Plants are of all sizes, from microscopic littleness to the height of hillocks. We will exclude all but the height of twenty feet or more. We have now an abstraction from the plant kingdom. We have singled out a subject of that kingdom. Its description is (its individuality, that in which all the other subjects of the kingdom are not precisely like it), "a perennial plant which grows from the ground, with a single, permanent, woody, self-supporting trunk or stem, ordinarily to a height of at least twenty-five or thirty feet" (*Century Dictionary*). But this individual of the plant kingdom needs a name. We therefore call it "tree." When we say "tree," we connote the complicated process of elimination, of which the above is merely a hint. Each of the words descriptive of tree, as distinguished from other subjects of the plant kingdom, is a word that stands for an exclusion of some plant trait which does not belong to the plant tree.

Scientific judgments are comparisons of abstractions. Errors of judgment are very largely the result of thinking about "plant" what is true only of "tree" and of assuming for "tree" whatever is the case with "plant." As we rise from relatively simple to more and more complex concepts, this liability is increased. In social science the danger is seldom absent, and few are the reasoning processes which entirely escape it. That old scapegoat, "the economic man," has borne ten thousand sins of this class.[1]

Accordingly, abstraction is the chief working means for the construction of general ideas. Abstraction rests, however, upon analysis. The facts with reference to which general ideas are to be derived must first be separated into distinct components, before the process of elimination can begin. The scientific significance of abstraction rests partly on its own inherent value, and partly and chiefly upon its importance as component and assistant of other logical processes. One of the most important achievements of the analytical method is success in bringing out into distinct relief, above the mass of details that make up a complex fact, certain elements, to be held isolated for a while, in order that they may be subjected to close examination.

There is another decided advantage possible in combining analysis and abstraction, viz., following the analysis many sorts of abstractions may be made by the free choice of the investigator, and the one abstraction may be made to complement the others. (This is illustrated in the case of "health, wealth, sociability, knowledge, beauty, righteousness.")

Abstraction is of two primary sorts, viz.: (1) isolating (abstraction), (2) generalizing (abstraction).[2] The former of these is the more primary. To it the analytic method always leads in the first place. It is also presupposed in every generalizing abstraction. It does not follow, however, that the two are regularly consecutive gradations of development. On the contrary, isolating abstraction has its own independent value. In many cases it is impossible to advance beyond this form of abstraction. In others, generalizing abstraction, so far as it is possible, adds relatively little of importance. The essence of isolating abstraction consists in arbitrarily contemplating certain components of a complex object of knowledge as though they were entirely separated from other components.[3]

The crusades, e. g., manifested economic, ethnic, social, æsthetic, intellec-

---

[1] Vide AMERICAN JOURNAL OF SOCIOLOGY, March, 1897, pp. 744-5; review of Godkin.

[2] An illustration of (1) is Spencer's (a) sustaining system, (b) transporting system, (c) regulating system; of (2) Giddings' "consciousness of kind"

[3] E. g., General Walker's abstraction of economics from ethics, etc., i. e., contem-

tual, and ethical elements. Now I may properly set myself to study the economic sequences betrayed during the crusades. I may set myself to abstract these altogether from political, intellectual, æsthetic, and ethical developments. I will start with the fact of overcrowding, say, in France. Some of the incidents of overcrowding are sanitary, but I do not enter into these realities. I am tracing only economic causes and effects. Some of the influences are on family relationships. They are material for me, though not as domestic matters, but as industrial matters. Some of the incidents are criminal, such as bodily violence, robbery, etc. I might turn away from my proposed abstraction to weigh the ethical quality of these, but that is none of my business now. Some of the incidents are those of mob violence under the guise of military conquest: murder, rapine, outrage. These again are stuff for the moralist, but in a quite different way stuff for me. Other incidents are those of superstition and sacrilege and profanation under the guise of religion. Whatever is of economic impulse and for economic interest in all this is my material. I am to trace, if possible, how the mind of man is acted upon, and how it reacts, so far as its economic interests are concerned, by all the circumstances in which economic interests are seen to be a factor in this period. If I ask how the same minds *ought to have been affected* by giving just weight to all the considerations involved, I am simply quitting my proposed task, and taking up another. My proposed object was to get together certain series of facts about the play of mind under given conditions with reference to economic interest. Economic science has for its ideal this same thing, not for one period, but for all periods; and the gathering of all these facts so abstracted into generalizations about the actual reactions of mind upon the economic motive. When we take up the question, "What ought to be our attitude toward certain economic relations," we enter upon a distinct inquiry, as different as diagnosis of a disease is from discovery of ways to treat the disease. We cannot call the two things by the same name, without creating hopeless confusion from the start. The former inquiry is what the economists mean by economics, when they say it has nothing to do with ethics. This is not to say that economics may, can, or must ignore actions that are ethical in quality. It is to say that economics may, can, and must ignore the ethical aspects of those actions, and calculate them simply as factors of such and such force, to be determined by any available means of measurement. To say that economics has nothing to do with ethics is not to say that economics is simply a calculation of forces into which the intellectual and moral character of men does not enter. It is to say that economics is a calculation of all the forces, physical, mental, and moral, that enter into reaction with self-interest in the pursuit of wealth; but solely, in the first instance, with a view to clear knowledge of their actual action; not at all, in the first place, with reference to an estimate of the moral quality of the action. When

plating the activities directed to the production of wealth entirely apart from the other activities which compose the whole of human pursuits.

we undertake to organize and *direct* economic action, to say what the policy of a community should be about a given subject — currency, taxation, hours of labor, etc.—we at once presuppose this economic abstraction, and a series of other abstractions synthesized into a social philosophy. The "great bad" of recent social theory has been the assumption that a working social philosophy is furnished by the economic abstraction alone.

(The process, just illustrated, is logically the same which the physicist, performs when he studies the breaking up of a pencil of light by passage through a prism. He watches the course of the different resulting rays, the angles of refraction, the distribution of the colors. He shuts out of view, *e. g.*, all phenomena of heat, produced in the prism. Or he might reverse the abstraction, ignoring the optical and abstracting only the thermic phenomena.)

Generalizing abstraction consists in ignoring all the qualities of the phenomena under consideration which are liable to variation, from case to case; and in emphasizing certain properties remaining common to the whole group of phenomena under discussion, and treating them as marks of a general concept. Thus the abstraction "solid" has no reference to special forms of solids, as cube, sphere, cone, etc., nor to particular substances that may be found in these forms. It abstracts the one trait of having the three dimensions, length, breadth, and height, in relatively permanent form. Or again, the abstraction "charity" does not take into account the diversified types of charity — hospitals, lodging houses, soup kitchens, bureaus of justice, etc.; it abstracts the single trait of *voluntary effort for the welfare of others*.

Generalizing abstraction falls into two subdivisions: (1) In case the subject-matter of analysis is *actual objects of observation or thought*. In this case concepts of *species* result from the analysis, as in zoölogy, or in political science when governments are classified, and traits common to some or all are, in turn, abstracted. (2) In case the subject-matter of analysis is *propositions* which formulate certain *relations* of objects. Here a process of isolating abstraction is presupposed, and the product of this form of generalizing abstraction is abstract rules or laws. An instance is the physical law that "action and reaction are equal;" the psychical law that "as the twig is bent the tree's inclined;" or the social law that "individual interest yields to common weal."

Ordinary mental processes which precede scientific processes prepare in some measure both forms of abstraction. These uncritical processes have comparatively little effect upon isolating abstraction. On the other hand, they lend themselves far too readily to generalizing abstraction. Concepts which have been formed by uncritical generalization are caught up into learned tradition without being made to furnish scientific credentials, and henceforth they introduce confusion, fallacy, and contradiction. Yet the source of the trouble remains long undetected. A familiar form of the involved fallacy is the tacit assumption that concepts formed by elementary generalization of the unintelligent sort are actual elements of knowledge given in positive experience, *i. e.*, elementary data. Thus in zoölogy the notion prevailed for a long time that each organic species is a primitive organic form. The *canis familiaris* and the *felis domestica* were held to be actual objects, but no one thought of admitting that the *ruminants* or the *vertebrates* as such have or ever had existence (*i. e.*, the easy common abstraction was made into a concrete reality, while the more remote abstraction of really the same nature was devoid of reality).

I must again call attention in this connection to the abstraction "sovereignty," to which, in the same way, real existence has been attributed by the process of crystallization of abstractions into concrete existences. In close relation to above, logically, is our treatment of the concept "law;" *i. e.*, we conceive of law as metaphysical necessity or as physical necessity, perhaps in the latter case deriving the attribute from law as *generalized physical order*. But we forthwith treat the concept "law" as though it actually carried its attribute of necessity into its workings, when its essential nature is only that of *human command*. As a result we have the whole brood of impotent social philosophizings which posit law as a self-enforcing potency. The methodological fault goes back to the rudimentary generalizing abstraction.

In close interdependence with abstraction is the *naming* of phenomena. Nomination is a product of isolation. The name of an object, whether produced in the ordinary course of language development or invented for scientific purposes, always stands for a single, though composite peculiarity (as in the case of "tree" above). A generalization is now closely associated with the naming. The name, originated in connection with a single object, is forthwith carried over to all the objects having the same peculiarity, and the name thus binds those objects together in a genus or species. It comes to pass, then, that nomination, besides being the product of isolating abstraction, is in consequence of that fact the most important coadjutor of generalizing abstraction. The natural sequence or correlation of isolation and generalization appears in the natural history of names as just sketched. It must be noticed here that names are accordingly both friends and foes of science. They bring advantages. They contain almost equal disadvantages. A name which has come into such common use that all traces of its original arbitrary assignment to objects are lost carries with it enormous authority; *e. g.*, the name "virtue." We accept it as though it were the name of a concrete entity, whose attributes have been accurately ascertained. We forget that it was once the name of one kind of action, as for instance, among the Romans, "valor." That action had a certain evident utility. All actions believed to have a similar utility came to have the same name. But in scientifically appraising the concept "virtue" we have to ask, "Is that judgment of utility valid? Is that utility general or special? Do all the acts now subsumed under the term 'virtue' actually serve that utility?" Unless we get clear answers to these questions, it is quite possible that we are permitting the snap judgments of former men to be substitutes for processes which we would feel bound to perform before forming judgments of our own. So much for the disadvantage of names. The advantages do not require emphasis here.[1]

CHAPTER III.

LIGHT ON THE SOCIOLOGICAL PROBLEM FROM THE FOREGOING DISCUSSION.

These distinctions enable us to see certain facts best expressed in very simple form. Men have looked out upon the world of reality and have instinctively begun the process of descriptive analysis. That process has very early resulted in a discrimination of the world of things from the world of people. So soon as that distinction was made, analysis pressed on further within each division. Men have tried to analyze both the world of things and the world of people. They have arrived, in the former case, at a descriptive analysis so minute that the world of things is parceled out among a large number of sciences, each devoted to certain groups of things, or to certain properties of things. These sciences have minutely described their several parts of the world of things, and they have, moreover, done much to make out the causal relations both within the things which they study, and between these things and the rest of things. In attempting to analyze the world of people, other men have separated that human world into parts, and have organized divisions of research devoted to groups of people or to certain phases of fact about people. All this we now see is the result of more or less successful efforts to analyze and describe the world of people. Men have gone farther, and have tried to make *causal* analyses of the world of people. These have taken the various forms of social theories, of varying degrees of generality. The credibility of this causal analysis depends in the first instance, of course, upon the exactness and thoroughness of the previous descriptive analysis. The present task of the social sciences in general is to review the accepted analysis of the world of people, to criticise the same, and so to reorganize descriptive analysis that the facts shall more precisely appear, and that causal analysis may proceed upon a

[1] We depart from Wundt's order to take it up again in Part II. Wundt's treatment of (a) determination, (b) induction, (c) deduction, deserves equal consideration. It is passed over in this syllabus, because the elements just analyzed have received relatively less attention, and there are among the sociologists more obvious examples of fallacy from ignorance of them.

body of more precisely ascertained facts. It will help us in working for such reorganization of social analysis distinctly to define the purpose which the analysis is to serve. Why do we want to analyze the world of people ? My answer is that we want to know:

1. *How does it come about that men's efforts take the turn they do, when many of them live in company?* (This question calls for (*a*) knowledge of the facts of human experience, (*b*) interpretation of these facts so that both static and dynamic laws appear.)

2. *What sort of goal is indicated as the rational social aim by the facts discovered in the world of people?* (This question constitutes a demand for social teleology.)

3. *To what use may we put the answers to 1 and 2 in making our efforts go straighter toward the social goal in the future?* (This question calls for social technology.)

In other words, we want so to know the world of people that we shall understand it profoundly for the most practical purposes. This being the criterion, we have to examine the so-called social sciences to see if they furnish the knowledge needed. Do they between them successfully analyze the world of people ? Do they furnish the descriptive facts needed for the causal analysis which shall answer the question : How do social facts come about ? or, Why are the facts of human association as they are ?

Proceeding in this way we may take fair account of what the social sciences have tried to do. In this review we shall discover that between them there has been failure to detect and describe facts and relations which seem to be the hyphens and the cement and the cohesive force of the whole. Thus we may make a catalogue of what the social sciences have done, and are trying to do, but this will serve to demonstrate a need of reorganizing social science in general, rather than a satisfactory present organization of the social sciences, capable of serving as a sufficient foundation for a constructive system of social aims.

It must be remembered, too, that the division between the world of things and the world of people is not a mathematical line. To know the world of people we must first know that world of things on which the world of people rests, and by which it is constantly influenced. Especially must we know those biological relationships in which the world of things shades off imperceptibly into the world of people. We must know those phases of the whole world which can with the least certainty be wholly assigned to the world of things on the one hand, or to the world of people on the other. This is the realm of biology and psychology. The sociologist must depend upon the biologist for instruction about the borderland between the world of things and the world of people. The sociologist must begin to know how to discover for himself among the phases of reality which appear to belong distinctly in the world of people. Hence he must be at least an initiate, if not an expert, in the methods of psychological analysis.

Now, in order to give another indication that all this very remote preliminary discussion has direct bearings upon every general and special problem of social science, the whole course, from this point, will be made to rally around a single question. It includes innumerable lesser questions that might be proposed in making a catalogue of unexplored social relationships. Let us suppose, for the sake of simplicity, that the social problem is concerned with this one question only, instead of with the thousand and one which are involved, viz.: *What factors prevent, permit, or promote variations in types of correlation among people, and what are the formulas of these influences?*

It will be seen that this question calls for research among social correlations of all orders. What influences preserve or destroy the correlation which any *family* type presents? Or we may propose the same form of question with respect to international alliances or to the present social equilibrium in any country.

It will be obvious, too, that we must have a working concept corresponding with the expression "*variation in types of correlation among people.*" I mean by this phrase *any change which results in a new ratio of valuation or in a new form of functional importance among the individuals affected.*

The question proposed is a concrete expression of the proposition that, in presuming to study "the social problem," we come under the necessity of finding out what are *the most general influences* that operate in the world of people. It may be worth while to point out that the terms of the question suggest at once the categories which will be needed later; viz., the category of *social order*, in which the statical laws prevail ("prevent"); and the category of *social progress*, in which the dynamic laws prevail ("permit or promote").

It is clear, too, that the answer to our question must involve at last a synthesis of answers to the same question in its application to different life spheres. For instance, comparative constitutional history collects cases of variations in structure of the governmental system, economic history cases of variations in structure of the industrial system, etc.; but no special search-science generalizes these results so as to answer our question.[1]

Whether students of society like it or not, all researches about society actually converge toward answer to this question; and, conversely, there can be no answer to the question unless it is constructed by combining and generalizing the fragments of the answers which are furnished by the special social sciences. Thus ethnography is either a collection of curios, good for nothing but amusement, or it is the raw material of ethnology, which tries to answer more or less of our general question. The same is true of history, economics, etc.

I get my own view of the tasks of social science in the largest sense (1) by keeping the fact constantly in mind that we must be able to answer questions like the above, before social science will amount to anything; (2) by remembering that our only means of answering these questions is such investigation of the inside facts of society as will reveal the workings of all the influences concerned in social reactions; (3) by submitting to the necessity of following discovered principles of research, from the foundation up through the whole mass of evidence in which truth about social influence is contained. In other words, if we are to prepare ourselves either to discover truth about such questions as the above, or even to pass judgment upon statements on the subject made by others, we must learn the methods of knowledge throughout the whole region of facts in which knowledge is contained. Hence we have to be sure of the rudiments of *psychical science*, because it deals with those forces which are elementary among the factors of social reactions.

The departments of knowledge which must somehow be controlled before we shall be in a position to answer questions of the order of generality just proposed may be indicated in various ways.

In the first place, a scientific order may be considered, as it appears in the table of contents of Wundt's *Methodenlehre*.[2]

CONTENTS OF WUNDT'S " METHODENLEHRE."

FIRST VOLUME.   FIRST DIVISION.   GENERAL METHODOLOGY.

Chap.   I. *The Methods of Investigation.*
          1. Analysis and synthesis.
             (*a*) General significance of the analytical and of the synthetic method.

[1] *Cf.* AMERICAN JOURNAL OF SOCIOLOGY, September, 1897, pp. 161–3.
[2] *Vide* WARD, " The Place of Sociology among the Sciences," AMERICAN JOURNAL

(*b*) Analysis.
(*c*) Synthesis.
2. Abstraction and determination.
3. Induction and deduction.
Chap. II. *The Forms of Systematic Exposition.*
    1. Definition.
    2. Classification.
       (*a*) General characteristics of classification, and development of forms of classification.
       (*b*) Descriptive classification.
       (*c*) Genetic classification.
       (*d*) Analytic classification.
       (*e*) Double, triple, and quadruple division.
    3. Proof.
       (*a*) General tasks of processes of proof.
       (*b*) Direct forms of proof.
       (*c*) Indirect forms of proof.

SECOND DIVISION. THE LOGIC OF MATHEMATICS.

Chap. I. *The General Logical Methods of Mathematics.*
Chap. II. *Arithmetical Methods.*
Chap. III. *Geometric Methods.*
Chap. IV. *The Idea of Functions and the Infinitesimal Method.*

THIRD DIVISION. THE LOGIC OF THE NATURAL SCIENCES.

Chap. I. *The General Foundations of Natural Sciences.*
    1. The development and division of the natural sciences.
       (*a*) The development of the natural sciences.
       (*b*) The system of the natural sciences.
    2. Principles of interpretation in the natural sciences.
       (*a*) Causal and teleological aspects of nature.
       (*b*) The postulate of observability.
       (*c*) Critical doubt.
       (*d*) The principle of simplicity.
    3. The principles of mechanics and the causal idea in mechanical theory.
       (*a*) The development of the fundamental idea of mechanics.
       (*b*) Formulation of the mechanical axioms of Newton.
       (*c*) Fundamental teleological theorems of mechanics.
       (*d*) Fundamental causal theorems of mechanics.

OF SOCIOLOGY, July, 1895, and *Outlines of Sociology*, chap. 1. This chapter is cited here, not because it throws special light on this stage of our argument, but because it sums up analyses of the subject-matter of the social sciences, in a way to which it will be useful to refer back presently.

(*e*) Phoronomic (kinetic) and dynamic assumptions of mechanics.

(*f*) The causal idea of mechanical theory, and the postulate of restricted natural causality.

4. The general methods and means of investigating nature.

(*a*) General character of the methods of natural science.

(*b*) The experimental method.

(*c*) The comparative method.

(*d*) Description and explanation of nature.

Chap. II. *The Logic of Physics.*

1. The physical methods.

(*a*) Analysis of natural phenomena.

(*b*) Synthetic production of natural phenomena.

(*c*) Physical induction.

(*d*) Physical abstraction.

(*e*) Physical deduction.

2. Aids to physical investigation.

(*a*) Physical observation.

(*b*) Measurement of natural phenomena.

(*c*) Mathematical auxiliaries of physical investigation.

(*d*) Determination of physical constants.

3. The substructure of physical phenomena.

(*a*) The hypothesis of continuity and of atoms.

(*b*) Dynamic atomic theory.

(*c*) Kinetic atomic theory.

(*d*) Reversion to conceptions of continuity.

(*e*) Logical test of hypotheses.

4. General natural laws.

(*a*) Laws and functions of force.

(*b*) Laws of energy.

(*c*) Ideas of physical limitations.

Chap. III. *The Logic of Chemistry.*

1. Chemical methods.

(*a*) General tasks of chemical research.

(*b*) Chemical analysis.

(*c*) Chemical synthesis.

(*d*) Chemical induction.

(*e*) Chemical abstraction and deduction.

2. Chemical statics and dynamics.

(*a*) The principles of chemical statics.

(*b*) The principles of chemical dynamics.

3. The chemical conception of atoms.

Chap. IV. *The Logic of Biology.*

1. Biological methods.

(*a*) General tasks of biological research.
(*b*) Morphological analysis.
(*c*) Researches in physiological chemistry
(*d*) Researches in physiological physics.
(*e*) Physiological and pathological analysis.
2. The general laws of vital phenomena.
   (*a*) Biological tendencies.
   (*b*) Teleological principles of biology.
   (*c*) Causal principles of biology.
3. Fundamental biological ideas, and hypotheses about the general coherence of vital phenomena.
   (*a*) The organic individual and the elementary organism.
   (*b*) The systematic ideas of biology.
   (*c*) The causes of life.
   (*d*) The concept "disease."

SECOND VOLUME. FOURTH DIVISION. THE LOGIC OF THE PSYCHICAL
SCIENCES.

Chap.   I. *The General Foundations of the Psychical Sciences.*
1. Development and articulation of the psychical sciences.
   (*a*) Development of the psychical sciences.
   (*b*) The system of psychical sciences.
   (*c*) Relation of psychical sciences to philosophy.
2. Principles of discovery in the *psychical sciences.*
   (*a*) The principle of subjective judgment.
   (*b*) The principle of dependence upon psychical environment
   (*c*) The principle of natural determination of psychical occurrences.
   (*d*) Causal and teleological conceptions within the psychical sciences.
3. The general methods and auxiliaries of the psychical sciences
   (*a*) Relation to the methods of natural science.
   (*b*) Psychological analysis and abstraction.
   (*c*) The comparative method.
   (*d*) Interpretation.
   (*e*) Criticism.
   (*f*) The idea of law in the psychical sciences.
Chap. II. *The Logic of Psychology.*
1. The general types (*Richtungen*) of psychology.
   (*a*) Materialistic psychology.
   (*b*) Intellectualistic psychology.
   (*c*) Voluntaristic psychology.
2. Individual psychology.
   (*a*) The tasks of individual psychology.

2. Economics.
   (*a*) Tasks and types of economic theory.
   (*b*) Abstract economic theory.
   (*c*) Concrete economic doctrine.
   (*d*) Theoretical and practical political economy.
3. The science of law.
   (*a*) The development of law.
   (*b*) The idea of law and the tasks of the juridical sciences.
   (*c*) The "civilistic" and the "publicistic" method.
   (*d*) Norms and definitions of law.
   (*e*) Legal deduction and juristical proof.
4. The principles of sociology.
   (*a*) Society and community.
   (*b*) The organization of society.
   (*c*) The social laws.
   (*d*) The social norms.

Chap. V. *The Methods of Philosophy.*
   1. The methodological tendencies of philosophy.
   2. The empirical method.
   3. The dialectic methods.
      (*a*) The antithetic method.
      (*b*) The ontological method.
      (*c*) The method of development of immanent ideas.
   4. Philosophy as theory of the sciences.

The different kinds of knowledge needed about the world of people and their relations to the world of things appear in better correlation in a modification of De Greef's scheme (p. 139).

The point to be emphasized here is not the finality of De Greef's classifications, but that it is necessary to learn about all the subjects charted by De Greef, and to study them according to plans which we shall go on to outline. No individual student is sure of ever reaching the point at which he is conscious of a need of going outside of one or other of the divisions of fact about the world of people, in order to organize that division into relationship with other divisions. Much less is any single student sure to reach a conscious need of more abstract generalizations of the facts contained in these divisions than summary formulas of the laws of sequence which operate there. Those needs exist, however, in the nature of the world of people and in the corresponding requirements of thought. That world will not be understood unless the needs are recognized. In outlining the elements of the social problem, then, I shall trace the steps by which,

REORGANIZATION OF DE GREEF'S CLASSIFICATION OF SOCIAL PHENOMENA.

Base

1 (g) ECONOMIC PHENOMENA	2 (h) GENETIC PHENOMENA	3 (i) ARTISTIC PHENOMENA	4 (j) PHENOMENA PERTAINING TO BELIEFS	5 (k) MORAL PHENOMENA	6 (l) JURIDICAL PHENOMENA	7 (m) POLITICAL PHENOMENA

A. Production
  Agricultural
  Industrial
	(Concerned with the reproduction of producers)
	A. The family
		A. Fine arts	A. Positive
			  Political
			  Juridical
				A. Ethics
				  Political
				  Juridical
					A. Public law	A. Internal
						  Politics
						  1. Juridical
						  2. Moral
						  3. Philosophical
						  4. Artistic
						  5. Civil
						  6. Economic

B. Consumption
  Reproductive
  Non-productive
	B. Marriage	B. Industrial arts	B. Metaphysical
			  Moral
			  Artistic
				B. Customs (coutumes)
				  Religious or scientific
				  Artistic
					B. Administration	B. External
						  Politics
						  1. Juridical
						  2. Moral
						  3. Philosophical
						  4. Artistic
						  5. Civil
						  6. Economic

C. Circulation
  Of fiduciary signs representing products
  Of supply and demand for products
  Of products and producers separately
  Of products with producers
	C. Sexual affinity	C. Religious	C. Religious
			  Genetic and pertaining to family relations
				C. Morals (mœurs)
				  Civil
				  Economic
					C. Penal and moral law
					D. Law of thought
					E. Artistic law
					F. Civil law
					G. Economic
					  Agricultural
					  Industrial
					  Commercial	

Individuals : the elementary psychic factors ; the psychic substratum and environment.

The physical substratum and environment.

in actual experience, we pass from one stage of comprehension to another, and discover interrelationships among various departments of fact in the world of people.[1]

PART II. THE LOGIC OF THE PSYCHICAL SCIENCES.[2]
CHAPTER I.
SPECIAL INTRODUCTION.

These notes proceed upon the assumption that the student intending to enter the field of the social sciences has prepared himself by mastering the methodology of the physical sciences, at least in its rudiments. He is supposed to understand the general correlations of the different aspects of the world of things, which concern, in turn, physics, chemistry, and biology. It is presumed that the student is sufficiently intelligent about the problems presented by the phenomena on the borderland between the world of things and the world of people to make logical use of knowledge that may be gained by special investigations within that territory, at least so far as the knowledge affects the conditions of the world of people. In other words, familiarity with the discussions cited at the head of this section is, from this point, taken for granted. Otherwise expressed, it is assumed that the phenomena represented by the lower section of the "base" in De Greef's chart (above, p. 139) are understood in their most general relations to all else represented by the chart. The foregoing presumptions lead to the further presumption that the student is prepared to take cognizance of what is represented by the upper section of the "base" in De Greef's chart. He must have differentiated the world of things from the world of people, and must have perceived that *the world of people is composed of people.* To get ahead in answering the comprehensive question which makes our problem (above, p. 132), we are obliged to take due account of the fact that people are members of the animal kingdom. The laws of life reign among them before the laws of mind get control. Hence we cannot adjourn

[1] *Vide* SMALL, "The Sociologists' Point of View," AMERICAN JOURNAL OF SOCIOLOGY, September, 1897, pp. 155-70.

[2] *Vide* SPENCER, *The Study of Sociology ;* WARD, "The Relation of Sociology to Cosmology, Anthropology, Psychology," AMERICAN JOURNAL OF SOCIOLOGY, September, 1895 — March, 1896, and *Outlines of Sociology,* chaps. 2-5; HYSLOP, *The Science of Sociology ;* WUNDT, 2. Bd., 1. Abtheil., *passim,* particularly pp. 514-80, "Die Logik der Biologie."

biological study the moment we pass to the world of people. To know all about the forces at work in the world of people we must know how to detect and formulate the biological forces. Man is first an animal. The elementary study of man falls within "the highest section of zoölogy."[1] Hence the study of man is a biological rather than a sociological pursuit.[2]

But man is an animal *plus* something. This *plus* is not present in the other animals in sufficient force to be a distinguishing trait. Man is a *psychic animal.* While we assume for the present, therefore, that the study of man as an animal has been provided for in planning study of the world of things, we shall see later that complete investigation of man as a psychic animal will send us back for instruction to the science of anthropology. That is, we are dependent upon anthropology, not only for knowledge of man as part of the world of things, but also for some of our knowledge of man as the primary element of the world of people. We must consult anthropology for part of our knowledge about the physical conditions of psychic action.

So far as we know, there are but two elementary factors at work in the world of people. These we term, in general, the *physical* and the *psychical.* Considering the world of things the realm of the physical, we have to do, not wholly, but by way of difference, with the action of the psychical element, when we abstract the world of people from the whole reality. The problem presented by our guiding question (above, p. 132) amounts to this: *In what way does the psychical factor work in the world of people?* From the standpoint thus determined, each of the "sciences" that have grown up in connection with the facts about the world of people must be appraised by the answer to this question: *How much of the necessary work of collecting and sifting the evidence about the workings of the psychic factor in the world of people has the science in question done, and how much has it left undone; how much has it the means of doing, and how much is beyond its means?*

We must here anticipate a conclusion that will be forced upon us when we come to investigate the above question in its application to the various sciences about humanity. We must be forewarned that it is almost impossible to find a spokesman for one of the divisions of human science who makes approximately just claims for the service rendered by his own science. The anthropologist, the ethnologist, the philologist, the historian, etc., etc., each may be found maintaining that

[1] *Vide* SMALL and VINCENT, *Introduction to the Study of Society*, p. 56.
[2] *Vide* WARD, *Sociology and Anthropology.*

his science has to do with the "total output of the human mind." We are accordingly not only confronted with the task of investigating the workings of the human mind, in all its essential operations, but the difficulty of that task is enormously increased by the embarrassments introduced through the conflicting claims of people who have attempted to discharge the task. Our efforts to arrange objectively correct categories for the different kinds of products of psychic action are obstructed at every turn by the arbitrary divisions of human "science." We insensibly yield more or less to the impression that facts, as such, must be assignable to groups corresponding with divisions of sciences dealing with the facts. Then we find that a given phenomenon is part of the material of half a dozen or more "sciences." Let us take the present situation of the Austro-Hungarian parliament for example. It may be used as material by ethnologist, psychologist, philologist, historian, economist, political scientist, moralist, and sociologist. What becomes of the "boundaries of the sciences" in view of their thus foraging in the same field ?

The clue to the solution of the puzzle has already been given in Part I. It is, more definitely, that, in general, *the sciences dealing with the world of people are either concerned with certain abstractions from the whole sum of facts*, or *they deal with the facts in so far as they are accessible through certain restricted sorts of evidence, or so far as they can be discovered by application of certain peculiar processes of investigation.* The phenomena themselves form one whole, appearing to us in countless manifestations. That complex aggregate is represented by the De Greef chart (above, p. 139). No portion of that chart represents the preserve of any single science. The sciences, physical and psychical, are merely good or bad divisions of labor, for the purpose of acquiring such knowledge of the things represented by the chart as will tend to answer the most general questions about the coöperation of physical and psychical factors in the world of people ; such questions, for example, as the one we have formulated as the inclusive question of sociology ; representing an order of generality to which no single division of labor upon human facts corresponds (above, p. 132). In view of the foregoing, it is in order to consider the relations of psychical science in general to the large problems presented by concrete social conditions.

Before entering upon this part of the discussion it is pertinent to correct an error which has been spread of late by numerous writers on both sides of the Atlantic. The error consists, first, in assuming that certain crude mechanical conceptions of social forces, or certain interpretations of society as material for zoölogical classification and clinical dissection, have not merely persisted, but have monopolized sociological theory until less than half a dozen years ago. The error consists, second, in claiming for certain very recent and quite commonplace assertions of psychic force in society the merit of originality; and in crediting them accordingly with the service of rescuing sociology from barren materialism. This is as if Rip Van Winkle should be regarded as author of all the changes that were going forward while he was asleep.

It is true that there remain even now a few sociological theorists who are trying to breathe the breath of life into mechanical or biological literalism proposed as a version of society. It is also true that these conceptions lost their prestige more than twenty years ago. Many sociologists still use biological metaphors as tools of investigation and as means of expression. Other writers have been unable to understand that most of the men who employ this biological language long ago eliminated from their own use of the terms all mechanical and biological literalism. This obtuseness has produced persistent confusion of figurative language with ideas foreign to the users of the language. The fact is that almost invariably, during the last two decades at least, the men who have employed these physiological terms have been perfectly clear in their own minds about the subordination of these physical terms to the service of expressing chiefly psychical relations. They have not thought it worth while to guard themselves enough to make misinterpretation impossible on the part of critics predisposed to misconception. Consequently there has been a chance to win victories over straw men by correcting alleged errors which had real existence only in the case of rare and unimportant theorists. In making the most of this opportunity, men who seem sincere in the belief that they are communicating to the world the boon of a fresh discovery, have, over and over again, within the past two or three years announced, with most Quixotic gravity, that psychical factors are the determining elements in social reactions!

All this might be passed over without comment if it did not imply misinterpretation of nearly all (and surely of the best) that has been written on sociology for the last twenty years, together with much that is still older. It is hard to see how this misinterpretation can be other than conscious falsification in some instances. Nobody who presumes to write about sociology deserves forgiveness if he is so ignorant of what other men have thought and said as to suppose that the assumption of the psychical as the determining factor in social movements marks a recent change of front in sociology. Since Schäffle and De Greef in Europe, and Ward in this country, the assumption has been decisive and all but universal. With every recent investigator worth consideration, the sociological problem has been some part of the problem of discovering the ways in which psychic factors work in society. The sociologist who does not know this must have followed Comte's programme of refusing to consult the writings of others. In calling attention to the relations of psychic facts and of psychological science to the social and the sociological, we are not exploiting a novelty. We are still within the limits of the familiar and the practically undisputed. The doubt is about the *formulas* of psychical force, not about its presence nor its prevalence.

ALBION W. SMALL.

THE UNIVERSITY OF CHICAGO.

WALSH SCHOOL YARD — SCENES IN WALSH PLAYGROUND

THE AMERICAN

JOURNAL OF SOCIOLOGY

VOLUME IV   SEPTEMBER, 1898   NUMBER 2

MUNICIPAL PLAYGROUNDS IN CHICAGO.

A "return to nature" is as necessary a demand for the modern city as it was for the romanticists of the eighteenth century. There can be no successful life which ignores nature. This is as true of the city or the nation as it is of the country or the individual. The cities of the world which are today beginning to realize their possibilities are trying to conform to nature. One promise for the future of Chicago is that she, too, has begun to realize her natural advantages.

Chicago enjoys two great natural advantages — the lake and the river. The lake is appreciated for its shipping facilities, its abundant supply of fresh water for the use of the municipality, and it is beginning to be appreciated for its beauty. Since the world's fair and the expansion of the park and boulevard system, one can readily anticipate a future in which full use will be made of the lake front of Chicago.

The mention of the river usually provokes a smile. Its possible beauty is forgotten in the recognition of its value to commerce, to manufactures, and to the sewage system. The commerce will probably, in large measure, pass away, and with it many of the manufactures, as the development of the South Chicago district takes place. The river will then remain only a great sewer, unless the original ideal of the ship canal is realized, and a modern and scientific method of sewage disposal is introduced. Should this be done, there will again arise the possibility of the enjoyment of the river for the sake of its beauty. At present the tendency of most well intentioned efforts for municipal improvement is to expropriate the river districts for the benefit of the lake region. One of these forms of expropriation is the unique park and boulevard system of Chicago, admirable in conception, but imperfect in realization. A complete chain of parks and boulevards encircling the city, it was thought originally, would satisfy every need of the growing population. This supposition was based on the following assumptions: the streets connecting with the boulevards will be available for private vehicles; the street railway systems will be adequate; every man, woman, and child possesses ten cents. None of these assumptions being true, the park system is in so far imperfect. The inevitable misfortune was that no city large enough to need and support such a system of encircling boulevards and parks could afford to dispense with a central boulevard system and numerous small parks. Even if the streets were all good and the transportation arrangements adequate, a city of a million and a half of inhabitants, under present conditions, always contains a large mass of overworked, underpaid, and densely crowded people. This class can rarely, if ever, visit the distant parks. Another very large class can go but seldom, and needs, for hygienic reasons, space for recreation within easy access of their homes. These classes in Chicago are found chiefly in the river districts. If one traces the two branches of the river on the map, from the northwest and southwest to the point at which the river enters the lake, it will be seen that they pass through a parkless region.

Between six and seven hundred thousand people live more than a mile from any large park. The most serious aspect of this is that those wards which are so deficient in park space are also those in which the houses are most crowded. The way in which one part of the city is favored at the expense of another may be best indicated by observing that the eleven wards which contain the bulk of the park and boulevard system include 1,814 acres of park space, the population being about 425,000; this means 234 people to each acre of park space. The remaining twenty-three wards of the city, with a population of over a

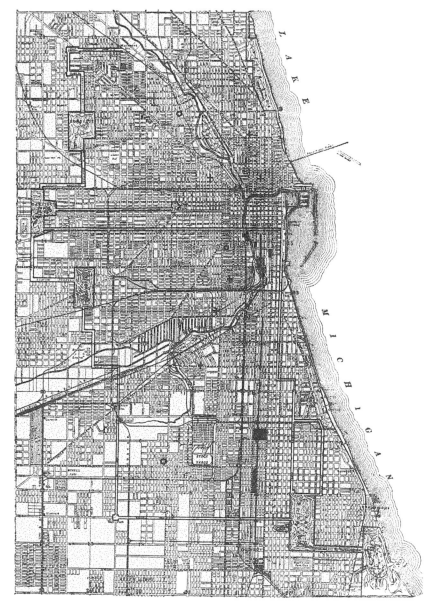

0 SOCIAL SETTLEMENT PLAYGROUNDS
X MUNICIPAL PLAYGROUNDS

million, contain 228 acres of park, or 4,720 people to each acre of park space. This second division includes, of course, some sparsely settled districts, where the need for parks is not so great; if we were to compare, however, the eleven favored wards with eleven wards along the river, we should find the proportion even more startling.

It is in this large, neglected area that the municipal playgrounds have been established,[1] which it is hoped are but the beginning of an extended movement in favor of small parks and, possibly, a central boulevard system connecting the river districts with the outer zone of boulevards and parks. By consulting the map it will be seen that the playgrounds established by social settlements (indicated by circles) are, roughly speaking, in the river region, and that this is, if possible, more true of the municipal playgrounds (indicated by crosses). The municipal grant of a thousand dollars provided that these playgrounds should be placed in school yards, and the schools were selected partly by reason of their location in crowded districts, and partly on account of the character of their yards. Some of the neediest districts, such as that immediately north of the river (Hoyne School), the Harrison street region of vice and poverty (Jones School), and the Fifteenth street and Wabash avenue section had to be neglected because the school yards were inadequate. The six schools chosen had, with one exception, satisfactory yards for playground purposes, although the schools were all located in portions of the city deficient in open spaces.

The least satisfactory school yard, that of the Washburne School, near Halsted and Fourteenth streets, is in the midst of a crowded Russian-Jewish quarter, notable for its rear tenements, ill-paved, unclean, and ill-smelling streets; and the next nearest school had no yard whatever. This has been the most frequented playground and the most difficult to manage, two attendants proving quite inadequate, several hundred children crowding into the small yard daily. Something of the need of this section and the way it has been met by the playground is seen

[1] For an account of the origin of the playgrounds in Chicago see the succeeding article by Miss American.

in the transfer of the boys from the narrow alley to the more attractive, if not spacious, playground.

The Walsh School, Twentieth street, near Halsted, furnished

BARBER STREET — WASHBURNE SCHOOL IN DISTANCE

a good double yard, rectangular on one side and triangular on the other, thus enabling the younger and older children easily to be separated. The attendant at this playground was a skilled turner, and won the affection and admiration of the boys by the feats he taught them on the buck. Although the Turn-gemeinden had kindly offered a variety of equipment, this was the only yard in which the committee felt justified in using leather apparatus. The result, however, showed a keen appreciation by the boys of the privilege. Considerable gymnastic work was also done by the girls here.

A CORNER OF THE WASHBURNE SCHOOL

At the Washington School, on the northwest side of the city, a playground had been conducted the previous season under the patronage of a west side woman's club. The familiarity with the object of the playground thus simplified the work at this place. At the two north side grounds and at the Bridgeport ground on the south side the attendance was rather disappointing. In each case, as will be seen in the photographs, there was a fairly spacious yard, and the schools were in the midst of populous regions—the Holden School in Bridgeport has a school population of over two thousand. Various explanations may be given, as will be noted later, there appearing to be no question as to the need of playgrounds in these sections of the city.

Each of the playgrounds was supplied with a sand bin, wood paving blocks for building, swings, see-saws, and parallel bars. In addition, some of them had ladders, climbing ropes, ring-

WASHBURNE PLAYGROUND

toss, and other games and apparatus, in accordance with the needs of the children and the capacities of the attendants. Various organized games were introduced by both the men and the women, the various helpers being able to suggest, in addition to well-known American and English games, some of the national sports of the Germans, Russians, Scandinavians, and Japanese. No pains were spared to interest the children and educate them in rational play. Every fortnight a meeting was held of the playground committee and all the attendants, so that each yard had the benefit of the experience of every other.

In addition to the playgrounds; there was opened at the Foster School in the Jewish quarter a playroom with a trained kindergartner in charge. This proved to be altogether too popular. It was continually taxed beyond the capacity of the young woman, several, rather than one, being necessary. However, various indoor games were used, and, if the janitor of the building had done his duty, the room would have been a great success, even with inadequate equipment. This experiment was financed by a small private gift and indicated a most urgent need, but to meet which both funds and skill are necessary.

The experience of these two months in municipal playgrounds suggests three questions: (1) What have been the difficulties? (2) What has been the success? (3) What of the future?

1. *Difficulties.*—In the seven school buildings used five janitors were most obliging, exhibiting sympathetic interest in the work, but two seriously hindered the success of the playgrounds by their antagonism. The discipline of the school system is rather lax in the summer time, and the official in charge was deaf to all the appeals of the committee. Although the school board and Superintendent Lane were most courteous and granted all the necessary privileges, it is apparent that the use of the school yards as playgrounds implies the education of school officials and a reorganization of the janitor service. The only duties of the janitor were the usual care of the buildings and grounds and the extra duty of general superintendence of the property, and the cleaning of the room used in rainy weather, and the toilet rooms. For this he received, in addition to his salary, a considerable fee from the playground committee, but—to mention only one grievance—always in the case of one ground, and sometimes in others, it was impossible to have the use of the yards Saturday afternoons, a serious inconvenience, as can readily be imagined. A fundamental difficulty, of course, is the total lack of yards in connection with some schools and inadequate space in other yards. It is still possible in Chicago to provide all schools with adequate

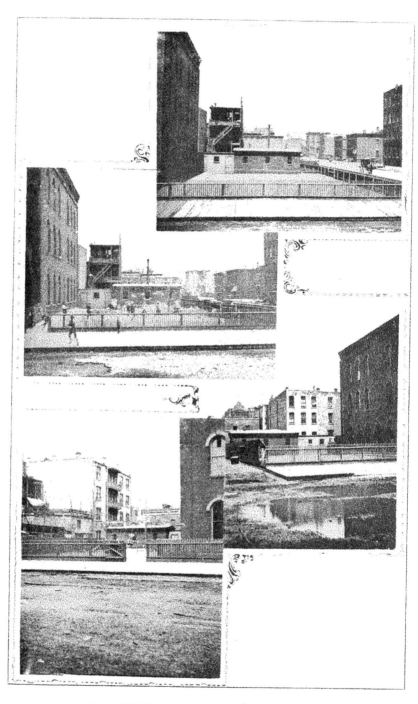

KINZIE SHCOOL YARD — UNEQUIPPED AND EQUIPPED

yards without resorting to the pitiful expedient of using the roofs as in New York.

A great difficulty came from the mixed nationalities and the separative influence of parochial schools. At the Holden playground in Bridgeport it was discovered, after a fortnight or more, that many children were kept away by the supposition that the privileges of the yard were available only for children in attendance regularly at the school, and this misapprehension was strengthened by boasting assertions of boys who were enrolled on the school register. At this same yard it was found extremely difficult to engage the young Polish children of the parochial schools in organized play. They seemed utterly unused to organization. It must be noted, though, that ignorance of play and lack of initiative on the part of nearly all the children in the playgrounds was marked. Some explanation of this fact will be found in the character of the constituencies of the playgrounds. The Holden School population is largely German and Polish; that of the Washington School, Scandinavian; of the Walsh School, Bohemian; the Washburne, Jewish and Irish; the Kinzie, Italian and Irish; the Lyman Trumbull, Scandinavian and German. These forces could be overcome if children had adequate opportunity for play, but the limitations of the streets and alleys as recreation grounds all operate to the destruction of initiative and organization.

Failure of the children to appreciate their privileges, due evidently to the old-fashioned prison idea of school, hindered the work of the attendants. The swings were the most popular form of amusement, doubtless because the most individualistic, and at first there was little consideration of others, but a constant improvement was noted as the attendants became personally acquainted with the children, and the idea gained ground that mutual consideration was necessary even for one's own enjoyment. The lack of experience and want of personal acquaintance with the children presented a difficulty which was gradually removed. These attendants should know the children and their needs at least as well as the school-teachers do.

The committee experienced great difficulty in getting the use of the municipal appropriation, owing to the irregularity of its disbursements. Serious problems would be solved if these playgrounds were made permanent and put under the control of the school board or the park commissioners.

2. *Success.*—The need, which had been seen and met in other cities and which all students recognized, of systematic play was manifest from the beginning and has been met in the case of hundreds of children through these six playgrounds and the playroom. Not all the attendants were skilled gymnasts, and the kindergartners were not specialists in play; yet a new world of pleasure and profit must have been opened to most of these children by the coöperative activities of the playground. No visitor could doubt that instruction in play is quite as essential to the child's welfare as the other instruction he receives. Even in the most difficult cases—the older boys without initiative—there was diversion for a time and at least a momentary interruption to cigaret smoking—itself probably a contributory cause to lack of initiative.

The amount of juvenile criminality prevented it would be difficult to state even approximately, the proportion of the population reached being so small, but it is generally thought to be considerable. In spite of the occasional accidents in the playground, none of them serious, there was unquestionably a contribution made to the health of the community by these oases in the midst of arid streets. While the playgrounds seemed not to be so much used by mothers with babies as is reported from other cities, a great relief came to the mothers by the occupation of so many children during the much-dreaded vacation time.

The greatest success was perhaps in the demonstration of how much can be done for little money. A thousand dollars from the Chicago city council provided for the equipment of the grounds and the salaries of the men custodians. Considerably less than that amount from the vacation-school board furnished remuneration for the janitors and kindergartners. It is not invidious to mention here that the success of the playgrounds is largely due to the initiation of the movement by Miss Sadie American, the sympathy of Mayor Harrison, and the invaluable services of Mr. J. P. Gavit, of the Commons, chairman of the playground committee, and Mr. W. H. Noyes, of the Henry Booth House. This does no injustice to the thirteen faithful attendants and the other members of the committee.

3. *Future.*—This short experiment will indicate both nega-

LYMAN TRUMBULL SCHOOL YARD

tively and positively the methods to be pursued. It must not be supposed that we are limited for suggestions to the experience of this two-months' attempt in six playgrounds. The three settlement playgrounds in Chicago and the accomplishments of other cities will also guide us.[1] The most evident need of the future is that all schools shall be provided with yards. They are fairly well supplied already, but those schools which are deficient are often in the most needy districts. The yards should be open after school hours during the school year and all day in vacation, preferably under the direction of the school

[1] See the succeeding article by Miss American.

board. The number of attendants should be proportioned to
the number of children, but relatively fewer will be necessary
when the children become accustomed to the use of the yards.
The necessity will be rather to provide more skilled attendants
or introduce play into the educational system.

LYMAN TRUMBULL PLAYGROUND

Some of the school yards, as can be seen in the illustrations,
are already well provided with trees. It would not be difficult
to beautify all the yards in this simple way. In at least one
case in Chicago, that of the Hyde Park High School, an attractive flower bed adorns the front yard. Window boxes in the
school buildings, after the manner of the vacation schools,
would furnish a great attraction.

The great *raison d'être* for playgrounds in connection with
school buildings is because they are always accessible, being
near the homes of the children. An additional reason of importance is that of making the school as attractive as possible. There

is another need of the little children, however, which can best be met by providing playgrounds in the parks, as has already been done in Douglas park and as is frequently done in Great Britain and Germany. The school yards, however, do not furnish adequate open space in their respective districts, and their use as playgrounds only indicates the need of the whole population for further provision for recreation grounds near their homes. The school playgrounds may be looked upon as a continuation of the educational system. There is also need of public places for recreation, where the family may be united in its pleasures. These the small parks would supply, without necessitating in them such provision for play as would annoy older people. Work is a cardinal principle of American life. To this must be added play.

CHARLES ZUEBLIN.

THE UNIVERSITY OF CHICAGO.

HOLDEN PLAYGROUND

THE MOVEMENT FOR SMALL PLAYGROUNDS.

WITH children as with adults character more clearly reveals itself in leisure moments than in busy ones. Watch men at their pleasures, at cards ; watch children when they do not think themselves observed, and selfishness and greed and disregard of rights manifest themselves.

In a playground with proper supervision children for their own good soon recognize that they must regard others' rights, and that in order to enjoy themselves they must permit others to do so ; that they must respect property which they have in common as well as that of one another ; and these habits help to build up men who make good citizens, carrying the same principles into adult life.

While this has been called the children's age, they have not yet been accorded their full rights. Place to play is one of these. Teams and traffic and the hungry builder have claimed all open spaces for their own. Property is more considered by the law than person, and even an empty lot which tempts the boys to use it as a ball ground at the same time invites the interference of the police, lest windows be broken or passers-by be struck. The school yards and basements offer excellent space for play. It would seem to be an extremely poor financial policy which has millions invested in buildings that are idle one-quarter of the time; yet this is the short-sighted policy of the majority of our school boards. It is questionable whether any private enterprise outside the church would be content with such management.

In several cities, under private management, school yards have been opened to the children during the mornings of July and August. Boston was the pioneer, and the Massachusetts Emergency and Hygienic Association has for two years maintained playgrounds, each of which is under the supervision of one or more kindergartners, according to the number of children frequenting it, and is equipped with sand gardens, swings, picture books, small blackboards, small toys and games. These play-grounds are designed especially for young children, and, while not regular kindergartens, the children are occupied by kinder-

SAND BIN

garten games, songs, etc., and hundreds avail themselves of the privileges thus afforded.

Another method of entertaining and occupying children is followed by the Episcopal city mission, which is unique in its way, I believe, except for one similar room maintained in the Foster School in Chicago this year. There are a number of playrooms kept open during July and August, in the Sunday-school rooms of churches or halls. Here there are morning sessions of one and three-fourths hours each, with an average attendance of fifty children. "Everything" says Mr. Allen, under whose care they are, "depends upon the personality of the teachers, of whom each room has two, one playing the piano, while the other guides the children, whose ages average from five to fifteen, to say nothing of the babies they bring under their care. We prefer girls, as boys can go off for long strolls. We have limited classes and sessions, as we deem these necessary to the best results. We teach seven hundred children each day, and then *they play our games on the street* all day. We have little equipment: flags for patriotic purposes, perforated cards, colored paper for folding, and books to paste in, and a few toys." For details see *Our Neighbors*, August, October, and November, 1897.

The good example of Boston has been followed in Providence, R. I., Philadelphia, and Baltimore, Md., where in 1897 the United Women of Maryland maintained several playgrounds in school yards.

In Philadelphia one playground was kept open in 1894 by the City Parks Association. During 1895 various organizations held meetings agitating the subject, then petitioned the board of education; until finally the use of four school yards was granted. Councils appropriated $1,000 for their maintenance, and in each "one kindergartner was appointed by the city director of kindergartens as care-taker and the janitor as assistant to protect property and keep order." The plan followed is practically the same as that in Boston. This year twenty-seven such playgrounds are maintained by the board of education — the grounds being open in the afternoon, under the supervision of the janitor only.

Said one kindergartner in a yard where several hundred children were seated in a ring on benches and chairs supplied in plenty, singing songs together: "I get along beautifully when there are not more than two hundred or three hundred children! But sometimes, when there are more, I have all I can do just to keep order. But they are so happy to come and are so good I have little difficulty." All about were baby carriages with babies fast asleep in all the din. "The mothers leave them," said the matron, "and I make them the center of my work. I tell the children they must be careful not to disturb the babies, not to bump up against them; and you would be surprised at their care and thoughtfulness. It keeps them from getting too wild.'

Jumping ropes, jackstones, faba-gaba, ringtoss were games supplied, beside blocks, etc., for the youngest tots. And this matron advocated slate and colored chalk as an infinite source of amusement and a saving of fences and steps from decoration more appropriate to the slate.

When I was leaving the yard I saw a tot of perhaps three and a half years carrying a child about two inches smaller than herself. As I looked at the matron, she said: " Yes, many such come, and for them it means so much. They sit with the babies in their arms and watch others play. Occasionally I take the child for a while when I can, and they are so grateful ; they play a while, and I never have to call them back — they come of their own accord." Can we do enough for such as these ? The playground committee of the Civic Club, of which Mrs. Lundy is chairman, has done much to further and perfect these grounds and constantly visits them, suggesting, aiding, cheering on the children and matrons.

In addition the Culture Extension League has opened a playground in Dickenson square, the equipment of which cost about $12,000. It has separate shelters for boys and girls, with shower baths ; has running track, swings, sand bins ; but a lack of grass and shade which certainly impairs its usefulness. Another playground is maintained by them on ground recently condemned and cleared by the city and immediately adjoining the college settlement. This has the supervision of the settlement workers and one or two paid assistants, and is open from 8 A. M. to 6 P. M., and is used by children of all ages.

Chicago, in 1897, had one such playground in the Washington School yard, maintained by the West End District of the Associated Charities, and in addition has had for five years, supported by Hull House, a large playground in an empty lot, equipped with swings, see-saws, giant stride, and sand bins, where older children, too, were allowed to play. In 1896, under the auspices of the university settlement of the Northwestern University, a large and splendidly equipped playground was opened, which will accommodate 3,000 or 4,000 children, the necessary funds being contributed by several gentlemen desirous of furnishing an object-lesson to the city. Numerous swings, large and small, giant stride, see-saws, sand piles, etc., afford ample amusement for the children, who fairly swarm there. There is also a large shelter, provided with plenty of benches and with retiring rooms. A police officer, who is a father to the boys, and a matron have charge of the grounds. The police in the neighborhood are much interested in this venture. In the spring they planted six trees in the grounds.

Lieutenant Kroll, of the neighboring precinct, says:

We're going to make this a fine place! Not less than fifteen lives have been saved from the electric car since the establishment of the playground, and juvenile arrests have decreased fully 33⅓ per cent.

Asked for an explanation of this assertion, he said:

The young boys between thirteen and sixteen who are not at work loaf around street corners; they have no place to go; they get into the saloons, they annoy the passers-by, or they form in crowds. They resent the interference of the police, and finally they are arrested. We hate to do this, as it is the first step pushing a boy downward into the criminal class. Since the playground has been opened and they are permitted to come in here, they give us no trouble whatever.

They are able to take their fun in an orderly way, instead of in a way which leads to the habit of disrespect for the law and the breaking of regulations, and character is, after all, merely a bundle of habits. Few will question that disrespect for the law is one of the evils of the day in our country.

In the spring of 1898 an appropriation of $1,000 was obtained from the Chicago city council for "temporary small parks," the administration of which was turned over to the vacation-school committee of the women's clubs. The use of six school yards, basements, and one room to be used on hot and rainy days was asked of the board of education, and, being granted, the yards were equipped with swings, see-saws, sand bins, and cedar building blocks. The Turnverein was greatly interested, and loaned portable apparatus for each school, such as parallel bars, horizontal bars, horse, ladders, etc., which are taken into the building at night.

The playgrounds chosen were all in densely populated districts and among various nationalities, and were the Washington School, corner of Morgan and Ohio streets; the Kinzie School, Ohio street and La Salle avenue; the Walsh, Twentieth and Johnson streets; the Holden, Deering and Thirty-first streets, and the Lyman Trumbull, Division and Sedgwick streets. For each there were engaged a kindergartner and a man who should be a "big brother to the boys," for the older boys were considered equally or more than the younger ones, the committee believing that they run the most danger, and older boys will not be constantly under the supervision of a woman. There is too much of sentimentalism over the influence of the kindergarten and kindergartner—they have their great use and value, but also their decided limitations, and it is time we recognize this. Boys want a man to guide and imitate, an athletic young fellow whom they will respect, admire, and love. And such the committee tried to provide. The men were inexperienced, but entered into the spirit of the work with enthusiasm, and from week to week rose in efficiency on the mistakes of the foregoing days. Mayor Harrison greatly favors this work, and it is to be hoped it may be extended another year. Seven hundred and fifty dollars additional were contributed by persons interested in securing the greatest efficiency possible in these grounds.

In Worcester, Mass., one playground has been opened.

In New York, for several years, a playground has been maintained by the Nurses' Settlement, at 265 Henry street, where uninviting back yards have been transformed into a very bower of delight, showing what can be done in restricted spaces. Sand bins canvas-covered, a large tent, hammocks, awnings, parallel bars,.and toys daily afford delight to the ninety children who are admitted, and whom a kindergartner entertains. In the afternoon a privileged few are permitted to come in. A few fine trees left from ancient days help to add to the beauty of this oasis in the wilderness.

The Union Settlement, at 237 South One Hundred and Fourth street, maintains a larger playground, similarly equipped; like which there is also one on West Thirty-seventh street, and one on West Sixty-eighth street, the latter open all day.

The many forces working to establish playgrounds combined and organized this year what is known as the Outdoor Recreation League, the objects of which are declared to be:

1. To obtain recognition of the necessity for recreation and physical exercise as fundamental to the moral and physical welfare of the people.

2. To secure the establishment in the city of New York of proper and sufficient recreation places, playgrounds, and open-air gymnasiums for the people.

The league has opened open-air gymnasiums in West Sixty-ninth and West Ninety-fourth streets, is about to do so in Division and Hester street parks, and maintains a boys' camp at Pelham Bay park. Through its influence $15,000 was appropriated for school playgrounds by the school board, and twenty schools were opened. The New York schools have no yards, but large basements, and in some schools roof spaces, which have been equipped fully, and a magnificent work is under way. The equipment consists in sand piles, parallel bars, horizontal bars, hitch and kick standards, see-saws, swinging ladders, overhead ladders, and basketball. Small blocks for building are furnished and the spaces arranged for shuffleboard, handball, hop scotch, ringtoss, prisoners' base, hand tennis, etc. Six custodians, usually two men and four women, are assigned to each school — a director and two assistants in the morning from 8 to 1 o'clock, and the same in the afternoon from 1 to 6 o'clock.. From one to five hundred frequent the grounds at one time. The custodians are working out the problem of their own particular group of children, who must be differently handled according to their nationality and surroundings.

There is a small circulating library in each of fourteen playgrounds, and on each of the three recreation piers maintained by the city kindergartners, bringing joy to the little ones who formerly listlessly sat about.

Where permission has been granted in the parks, large tents have been set up, in which, too, a care-taker helps to amuse and occupy the children.

This work is under the same management as the vacation schools — that of Superintendent Seth T. Stewart, to whom each day the custodians send a report of numbers attending and games played, with such suggestions as they will give. He has three assistants, supervising kindergartens, games, and use of physical apparatus, respectively. The custodians are variously drawn from kindergartners, teachers, college men, and graduates of Posse Gymnasium, Boston.

This step is certainly the most advanced of any yet taken toward the more complete and fuller use of our schools, and, if properly carried out in New York and other cities, will be the little shining jewel in the crown of our system of education, sending forth a dancing, joyful gleam to brighten the dullness of young lives.

The establishment of the small parks in New York, at the cost of millions of dollars, was perhaps the first step toward the solution of this great problem. The Outdoor Recreation League has brought about a tremendous advance through its influence, and is making another great stride in establishing gymnasiums in these small parks. For the open space does much; but since it seems to be true that our young people are forgetting how to play and exercise, it is needful to have them taught and guided once again.

That this question is not a simple one, to be lightly passed over, but is far reaching and has to do with the underlying principles of good citizenship, perhaps no higher authority could be quoted to prove than the report of the Committee on Small Parks in the city of New York, of which Abram S. Hewitt was chairman. It says:

Improvements of property have left to the children no other opportunity for play than such as can be found in the streets. It is impossible for the children to use them for games of any kind without incurring the interference of the police. A sense of hostility between the children and the guardian of public order is thus engendered, leading to the education of citizens who become enemies of law and order. The outlay for police, courts, reformatories, hospitals, almshouses, and prisons is thus largely increased."[1]

Play is the natural expression of the physical energies, the animal spirits. It is nature's way of toning up life. Dam up

[1] See Report of the Committee on Small Parks, New York, 1897.

the legitimate outlet, and the forces will break forth in other and illegitimate directions.   Again, quoting from the above report, we find :

> With a common accord the precinct captains attribute the existence of juvenile rowdyism and turbulence to the lack of a better playground than the street . . . . Children use the middle of the street, and a great many accidents are caused thereby.   They break lamps and windows, because they have no other provision made for them.   Loudon, after an experience of forty years battling with the slums, says, tersely : "Crime in our large cities is to a great extent simply a question of athletics."

Europe is far ahead of us in the treatment of the problem, and in providing spaces for and supervisors of sports for children, which we would do well to copy.   In England, Scotland, Holland, France, and Germany very much has been done during the past decade.

Where small parks have been made, the verdict of the police is unanimous that they have changed the character of the neighborhood.   Give the children adequate playgrounds, and the same spirit and imagination which form rowdy gangs form baseball clubs and companies for plays and games and drills of various kinds.   Children's imagination is vivid and must be satisfied.   It will satisfy itself, whether we wish it or not.   Feed it properly, and it will blossom into beautiful fruitage ; starve it and throw it back upon itself, and we have all the ugly excrescences, deformities, and depravities of crowded-city life.

The majority of our city parks have no special arrangements for children, although in many parts of the parks the children are unrestricted, but it is a question whether the best interests of the city would not be served by copying the European method, *i. e.*, by having a supervisor of sports and regular places in the parks given over to the exclusive use of the children as their right ; for, though not restricted in their play, it naturally happens that the little ones are crowded out by the bigger ones, and that when grown folk wish the place the children have to give way.   Not all persons realize the child's need for space to run around, for a place to make a noise, for a place for the larger play of his imagination in concrete form.

To Boston we must return for the model as well as the earliest playgrounds, and for a large and liberal provision for needs greater in New York and Chicago than in Boston itself.

In the Charles Bank outdoor gymnasiums we have such a model gymnasium and playground. The cost of maintenance is about $5,000 a year for the men's gymnasium and somewhat less for the women's. I quote from the report of the superintendent, who is a "practical instructor in gymnastics and athletic exercises":

The gymnasium, 450 × 150 feet, is inclosed by an iron fence, on the inside of which is a strip of green five feet wide, studded here and there with bushes and trees; inside of this is a running track, five laps to the mile. Within this the ground is fitted with gymnastic apparatus and places for high jumping, running, broad jumping, pole-vaulting, putting the shot, throwing fifty-six pound weight, etc. The apparatus consists of swings, single and double, breast bars, climbing ropes and poles, one rope ladder, one inclined ladder, one iron Jacob's ladder, one perpendicular ladder, four pairs of flying rings, four single trapeze, inclined and perpendicular poles. This apparatus is suspended from two iron frames, each 160 feet long. We have also two sheds with twelve sets of chest weights, several horizontal bars, eight sets of parallel bars, two giant strides, two sets of quoits, two Swedish vaulting boxes, a bed of tan bark 45 × 20 for tumbling and various other exercises, and a large platform for class work, which I hold at 4:30 and 8 P. M. daily, Saturdays excepted, when one class is held at 10:30 A. M.

Individual instruction is given at all times except class hours. From early spring till late fall the average daily attendance is 1,500. The gymnasium is open from 6:30 A. M. to 9 P. M. daily, except Sunday. About 200 attend the classes, and 125 young men receive athletic training daily. I give all the instruction myself, having no assistant. I have two men to look after the building, which contains 196 lockers, a general shower-bath room with five rain showers and nine sprays, hot and cold water. About 10 per cent. of those attending use the lockers and bath.

Boys over nine years old may enter and use the apparatus, and great care is taken that none shall use it to his harm. None under fourteen are allowed in during school hours. It is truly a cosmopolitan attendance; college students, sons of the wealthiest and most aristocratic families, and the poorest meet here on common ground and practice together in the most friendly spirit; they learn to respect each other, and the influence which the institution has on the young men who frequent it is very great, not only physically, but mentally and morally.

The gymnasium is open from April till about Christmas time, when the apparatus is dismantled and the grounds flooded for skating. At night they are lighted by thirteen arc lights.

The apparatus cost about $1,800; the men's and women's buildings about $18,000. In the women's division the gymnasium is covered with an awning, has a high board fence, and is equipped similarly to the men's division, with sand piles and provision for small children. The building here has a playroom which, with the grounds, is open Sundays after 1 o'clock, as well as the rest of the week, although the gymnasium is closed. The hours are from 8 A. M. till a half hour after sunset. Boys under nine are admitted into this ground, which has a superintendent and two assistants, beside the force caring for the building. The success of this division is equally great with that of the men's.

In Wood Island park there is a similar gymnasium, in which the building cost $21,000, and the gymnasium apparatus about $3,500.

Boston is striding ahead in providing thus for the good of its people; ten tracts of land have already been secured under the "Park Act" as recreation spaces, and she contemplates placing gymnasia in all of them, while House Bill No. 1149, reported to the Massachusetts legislature March 29, 1898, provides for a "comprehensive system of playgrounds for Boston," permitting an expenditure not to exceed $200,000 in any one year. Says Mayor Josiah Quincy: "We hope within a year or two to have Boston in the lead in this respect;" and in his address for 1897:

I know of no direction in which the expenditure of a few hundred thousand dollars will do more for this community through the healthful development of its children than by the judicious provision of properly located and equipped playgrounds. So much public attention has been given to the advantages of extensive park areas that the equally great need of comparatively small open spaces, particularly in thickly settled districts, for use as playgrounds, has been overlooked. If one-twentieth of the sum expended for park systems could be devoted to playgrounds, in my opinion there would be a still larger percentage of return in healthful physical development and social well-being.

It would, therefore, appear in the interest of good citizenship and of economy in morals, and even — what seems of greater importance to many — of economy in money, that one of the most necessary steps to be taken in our commonwealths is to establish such playgrounds and outdoor gymnasiums, with proper provision for their use in winter, where the pleasant surroundings would prove a powerful competitor for the saloon — another phase of their usefulness for children of a larger growth.

When we realize, in acts as well as in words, that an ounce of prevention is worth a pound of cure; when we see that construction from the foundation up is more profitable than destruction and the almost hopeless effort to build strong and well on rotten foundations; when we care as much for character-producing investments as for those bringing large and immediate money returns, and often entailing larger expenditure in time and effort and means; when we are content to trust in the promise of the future, measured by a normal growth and not by the magic maturity bearing in its heart the seed of its sure decay — then we will know that to provide proper playgrounds for children of a larger as well as smaller growth is to insure such men and citizens as go to make a republic of men fitted to govern themselves and to lead the world in the onward march against all that cramps man's development and prevents his becoming free in the fullest sense of the word.

The child is father to the man, and the street is no place of rest or refuge for one or the other in his leisure moments. May the wise see to it that resorts for upbuilding recreation insure such occupation of leisure hours as shall be indeed a recreation for body and spirit, and give us a generation strong and joyous and fortified to resist and repel with a happy laugh every deteriorating temptation and tendency.

SADIE AMERICAN.

CHICAGO, August, 1898.

THE DELUSIONS OF DURKHEIM'S SOCIOLOGICAL OBJECTIVISM.

I CANNOT leave without reply a letter from Professor Durkheim to the editor of the AMERICAN JOURNAL OF SOCIOLOGY, published in the May number of that review, and purporting to be an exhaustive refutation of my criticism of Durkheim's book on *Suicide*. The French professor accuses me of superficiality and carelessness, claiming that the whole of my argument is based on the *erreur matérielle* of discussing, under his name, ideas entirely foreign to him. But it will prove an easy, though not agreeable, task to show the fallacy of Durkheim's alleged refutation.

I.

The debated point in my article is a statement bearing upon the logical defectiveness of Durkheim's theory of the social phenomenon. I wrote:

Durkheim's error consists . . . . in having misinterpreted the true relationship of the "element" to the "whole" in all combinations. Social fact exhibits properties of its own, but what is its point of departure, if not the combination of individuals? These latter, undoubtedly, are an essential factor of the social phenomenon, for the same reason that the elements of a chemical combination are essential factors of the chemical compound. Durkheim completely overlooks the fact that *a compound is explained both by the character of its elements and by the law of their interaction.* He tries to explain the "product" by the "product," thus overthrowing the scientific conception of cause.

Durkheim declares this statement to be entirely erroneous, and claims to have unmistakably admitted that "individual" factors must be taken into account in order to explain the "social" compound. In proof of this assertion he quotes two passages from his book. The first (p. 363) is as follows: [1]

---

[1] To avoid misunderstandings, all quotations from D.'s books will be given in the original text in preference to a translation.

L'intensité (des courants suicidogènes) ne peut dépendre que des trois sortes de causes suivantes : (1) *la nature des individus qui composent la société ;* (2) la manière dont ils sont associés, c'est-à-dire la nature de l'organisation sociale ; (3) les évènements passagers qui troublent le fonctionnement de la vie collective sans en altérer la constitution anatomique.

The intelligent reader will soon notice that this passage, intended to be a death-blow to the unfortunate critic, falls short of the mark, as it by no means includes the assumption of the efficacy of "individual" causes on the *production* of the "courant suicidogène," the passage only referring to the *intensity* of the "courant," leaving unsolved the question of its origin. But there is more. In giving the foregoing quotation from his book, Durkheim omits to reproduce the important qualifying propositions immediately following on the same p. 363 :

Pour ce qui est des propriétés individuelles, celles-là seules peuvent jouer un rôle qui se retrouvent chez tous, car celles qui sont strictement personnelles ou qui n'appartiennent qu'à de petites minorités sont noyées dans la masse des autres ; de plus, comme elles diffèrent entre elles, elles se neutralisent et s'effacent mutuellement au cours de l'élaboration d'où résulte le phénomène collectif. Il n'y a donc que les caractères généraux de l'humanité qui peuvent être de quelque effet. Or, ils sont à-peu-près immuables, du moins, pour qu'ils puissent changer ce n'est pas assez des quelques siècles que peut durer une nation. Par conséquent, les conditions *sociales* dont dépend le nombre des suicides sont les *seules* en fonction desquelles ils puissent varier, car ce sont les seules qui soient variables.

Thus, when given in its logical integrity, the very passage which Durkheim triumphantly opposes to my argument clearly goes to show that he never meant to acknowledge the influence of the individual conditions upon the intensity of the "courant suicidogène." When, on p. 363, he mentions the "nature of the individuals" in connection with the causes determining the intensity of the "courant," he does so merely for the purpose of enumerating all the possibilities of explanation, proceeding later on to eliminate those alleged causes shown by further analysis to be entirely ineffectual. The correctness of this interpretation of Durkheim's passage is confirmed by the following quotation from p. 366 of his book, in which he sums up his view of the action of "individual" factors on the genesis of suicide :

> Si, dans un même milieu moral . . . . tels individus sont atteints et non tels autres, c'est sans doute, au moins en général, parceque la constitution mentale des premiers, telle que l'ont faite la nature et les événements, offre moins de résistance au courant suicidogène. Mais si ces conditions peuvent contribuer à déterminer les sujets particuliers en qui ce courant s'incarne, ce n'est pas d'elles que dépendent *ses caractères distinctifs ni son intensité.*

Now, if we were to admit, as Durkheim would have us believe, that, on p. 363 of his book, he distinctly acknowledges that "individual" factors act upon the "courant suicidogène," it would be impossible to conciliate this view with the passage quoted from p. 366, in which any influence of "individual" factors upon the "distinctive character and intensity" of the "courant" is positively denied. Nor would it be possible to harmonize that famous passage with the following ones, selected at random among many others in the book on *Suicide* :

> (P. 336) Le taux social des suicides ne s'explique que *sociologiquement.* C'est la constitution morale de la société qui fixe, à chaque instant, le contingent des morts volontaires. Il existe . . . . pour chaque peuple une force *collective* d'une énergie déterminée qui pousse les hommes à se tuer.

> (P. 336) Chaque groupe social a réellement pour cet acte (le suicide) un penchant collectif qui lui est propre *et dont les penchants individuels dérivent,* loin qu'ils procèdent de ces derniers.

> (P. 346) Les causes qui fixent . . . . le contingent des morts volontaires pour une société ou une partie de société déterminée doivent être indépendantes des individus, puisq'elles gardent la même intensité quels que soient les sujets particuliers sur lesquels s'éxerce leur action.

> (P. 366) La cause productrice du phenomène (suicide) échappe nécessairement à qui n'observe que des individus, *car elle est en dehors des individus.*

I need draw no conclusions. These quotations speak for themselves. That Durkheim should make an attempt to delude the reader by only partially citing from his book is unpleasantly suggestive of pettifoggery. His course in this matter, all the more astonishing in a scholar of Professor Durkheim's standing, proves that my thrust went home, and I struck at the very root of the subtle and misleading error which so profoundly contaminates Durkheim's sociological speculations.

II.

The second passage quoted by Durkheim in his alleged refutation of my criticism is the following (p. 350):

Il est bien vrai que la société ne comprend pas d'autres forces agissantes que celles des individus, seulement les individus, en s'unissant, forment un être psychique d'une espèce nouvelle . . . . *Sans doute, les propriétés élémentaires, d'où résulte le fait social, sont contenues en germe dans les esprits particuliers.* Mais le fait social n'en sort que quand elles ont été transformées par l'association. L'association est, elle, aussi, un facteur qui produit des effets spéciaux.

This passage is only a paraphrase of another one from the essay on the *Méthode sociologique*, where, on p. 127, Durkheim writes :

En s'agrégeant, en se pénétrant, en se fusionnant, les âmes individuelles donnent naissance à un être, psychique si l'on veut, mais qui constitue une individualité psychique d'un genre nouveau. C'est donc dans la nature de cette individualité, *non dans celle des unités composantes*, qu'il faut aller chercher les causes prochaines et déterminantes des faits qui s'y produisent.

By this quotation Durkheim endeavors to prove that he in no way denies that the germs of social fact are to be sought for in the individual, but only emphasizes the fact that society, like a chemical compound, possesses characters dissimilar to those of the constituent elements in isolation. All this, however, was by no means new to me, and I had perfectly understood that Durkheim's conception of the social phenomenon does not include the absurd hypothesis of a society without individuals. In my article I wrote :

We do not believe Tarde's interpretation of Durkheim's theory to be entirely correct, although it might apparently be justified by some obscure passages of Durkheim's essay on the *Méthode*. When Durkheim emphasizes the antagonism between the concept of the individúal and that of society, he does not, of course, suppose the possibility of a society without individuals, but only means that the aggregation of human beings termed "society" represents a reality of a different order from that represented by every individual, separately and singly considered. Nothing is more scientific than such a position. The process of cosmical evolution would be really inexplicable if we should fail to find in a complex fact new properties, new qualifications, widely differing from those of its single elements. Social fact has undoubtedly properties of its own that make it quite dissimilar to the individuals producing it by their aggregation, just in the same way as the biological phenomenon shows peculiarities unknown to its vital elements. In other words, we find in collective or social life the production of forces or powers not given in the individual organism.

If Durkheim has read and understood the foregoing, how is it that he should accuse me of ignoring the question whether the synthesis realized in social phenomenon be of a purely mechanical or of a chemical character? But this is not the question at issue in my criticism of Durkheim's theory. We both admit that society is a "compound" wholly different in character from its constituents. What I contest is the possibility of explaining the "compound" without analysis, *i. e.*, without its reduction to elements, a possibility logically presupposed by Durkheim when he lays down the fundamental law of sociological research:

(P. 135, *Méthode*.) La cause déterminante d'un fait social doit être cherchée parmi les faits sociaux antécédents, et non parmi les états de la conscience individuelle. (P. 128) . . . . toutes les fois qu'un phénomène social est directement expliqué par un phénomène psychique, on peut être assuré que l'explication est fausse.

According to this view, a "compound" (social fact) must be explained by tracing back the action which another "compound" (social fact) exerts on it. But how can a "compound" act upon another without giving birth to a new combination in which both disappear? And how can this combination take place without a molecular arrangement, *i. e.*, without a new arrangement of its constituent elements? Here again the "element appears to

be the first cause of every combination of a "chemical" character. To adopt the old Aristotelian distinction, the "elements"
furnish the *matter*, while the law of their mutual action determines the *form* of the combination. The cause of variation
lies in the "element," while the law of interaction represents
the repetition, the rhythm. A helpful analogy is supplied by
the loom, which, although working in the same way, brings about
different results according to the different material which it is
called upon to weave.

III.

But there is another point. A theory which, like Durkheim's
theory, postulates (1) the combination of individuals as the
fundamental condition of society, and (2) the coalescence of
these units or elements into a "compound" wholly different in
character from the isolated constituents, must not only take into
account the character of the elements, but also the way in which
the elements react upon each other, *i. e.*, what I have called the
law of their interaction. How can we explain the wonderful
result of association, the forming of "un être psychique d'une
espèce nouvelle" (p. 350), an entirely new being in whom many
individual minds appear to be, as Durkheim says, "pénétrées et
fusionnées" (p. 127, *Méthode*), without presupposing the working of a law of inter-cerebral or inter-elementary action, operating whenever two minds at least (the elementary society) are
brought into contact?[1] If it be true that association is, as
Durkheim claims, a "facteur actif" (p. 350), a tremendous
agency of transformation of the individual mind, this cannot
become intelligible unless we admit the fundamental fact of the
action of one brain upon another brain, of one upon many, of
many upon one; in short, the law of imitation. This law is
strongly denied by Durkheim. But if we have to interpret his
conception of the social phenomenon without the help of the imitation theory, the cyclopic scaffolding of a so-called "objective"
sociology falls into ruins, and nothing is left of it but a certain

[1] I have also brought out the importance of this point in a review of Durkheim's
book published in the July number of the *Psychological Review*.

number of vague and empty formulas, like " collective currents," "collective forces," etc. Durkheim refuses to admit the action of one brain upon another as the fundamental and really elementary fact of sociology; consequently the very fact which he establishes as the most important in his explanation of the social phenomenon, *i. e.*, combination, remains an unsolved enigma. When Durkheim attempts to demolish Tarde's theory by proving the inadequacy of the word "imitation" instead of demonstrating the non-existence of the fact, we must rather pity the speculative intoxication which prevents him from seeing that, by denying the law of inter-cerebral action, imbedded in the imitation theory, he nullifies his own theory of social forces, and reduces it to a mere verbal construction.

IV.

In conclusion: Durkheim's theory presupposes (1) the presence and contact of individuals, (2) their combination. But he denies (1) the necessity of inquiring into the character of the "elements" to be combined, and (2) the law of inter-cerebral action, *i. e.*, the only intelligible process of combination or organization. Thus we are brought to the question: How are the "collective forces" or *courants* originated, and how do they invest and penetrate the individual after having been produced through social or "collective" elaboration? For us all, I believe, these are puzzling enigmas, and we should like to have, on these very points, a precise, definite, and conclusive answer from the *Maître* of the University of Bordeaux.

GUSTAVO TOSTI.

NEW YORK CITY,
July, 1898.

THE LAW RELATING TO THE RELIEF AND CARE OF DEPENDENTS. VI.

THE STATE ORGANIZATION AND SUPERVISION OF CHARITIES.

THE preceding papers of this series have dealt with the laws relating to the care and treatment of the dependent and defective classes. The present paper deals with the provisions made for the supervision of the public (and to some extent the private) charitable institutions of the several states and their organization into state systems.

The poor law is usually administered by civil or judicial officers as one of their many duties. As a rule, each of the several public institutions of the state has a distinct board of directors. Under such circumstances it is not to be expected that each officer administering poor relief, or that each director or officer of an institution, should always know the best thing to be done, or, knowing the best thing, should always do it. Much less is it to be expected that the various local and state institutions should all work together as a system, so that the greatest good might be accomplished by the charitable effort of the state. Consequently, a public agency has been created to advise where needful, to secure the enforcement of the law where necessary, and to organize the state's charities. This agency is the "state board of charities."

The state organization of charities began soon after the close of the Civil War. This movement has continued until now twenty-four of the forty-eight commonwealths have a "state board of charities," bearing this or a similar title.[1] Each board

---

[1] The dates of the organization of the boards in the several states, together with the references to them, are as follows: Massachusetts (ch. 79, R. S., 1882), 1863; New York (ch. 545, Acts of 1896), and Ohio (655–659, Gaique's R. S., as amended in 1892), 1867; North Carolina, discontinued and reorganized in 1889 (2331–2339, Code of 1883), 1869; Illinois (ch. 85, Hurd's R. S.), Pennsylvania (1–20, pp. 295–8 Brightly Purdon's Digest), and Rhode Island (ch. 291, Gen. Laws, 1896), 1869; Wisconsin (Act of April 17, 1891, as amended in 1895 (ch. 202)), and Michigan (9882–

has functions peculiar to itself, just in so far as each state has had conditions peculiar to itself. They have been organized to promote the efficiency of penal institutions and of the provisions for the dependent and defective classes, but emphasis is, in the one instance, placed upon one thing, in the other upon another.

But while the state boards differ greatly, they readily fall into two classes—the *advisory* and the *administrative*. Those of the former class have advisory powers only, while those of the latter have immediate control of the several state institutions. The advisory boards visit and investigate the charitable and penal institutions, counsel with their boards of directors and employés, and make public the results of their investigations together with their recommendations. The administrative boards differ from the ordinary boards of directors chiefly in that the control of all the state charitable institutions is vested in them. They have the same powers and duties in connection with the several institutions that the ordinary board of directors has in connection with its particular institution.

Of the twenty-four states, seven have the administrative boards.x The most noted one of these is that of Wisconsin. For many years that state had both advisory and administrative boards. The "State Board of Supervisors" formed a board of control for all the state charitable and reformatory institutions. The "State Board of Charities and Reform" was an advisory body with one or two executive functions. In 1891 both these boards were abolished and the present "State Board of Control"

9888, Annot. Stat., 1882), 1871; Connecticut (1884-8, Gen. Stat., 1888, as amended in 1895), and Kansas (ch. 131, Webb's Gen. Stat., 1897), 1873; New Jersey (Act of March 23, 1883), and Minnesota (459-463, R. S., 1894), 1883; Indiana (3239-3243, Thornton's Ind. Stat., 1897), 1889; South Dakota (Act of March 6, 1890), and Wyoming (Act of January 8, 1891, as amended in 1895), 1890; Oregon (Act of 1891), and Colorado (384ᵃ⁻ᵇ, Mill's Supplement), 1891; Montana (Act of March 3, 1893), and Arkansas (3929-3931, Sandels and Hill's Digest), 1893; New Hampshire (ch. 116, Acts of 1895, and ch. 91, Acts of 1897), and Tennessee (2672-2677, Supplement of 1895), 1895; Missouri (Acts of March 19 and March 23, 1897), 1897; and Iowa (Act of ——— 1898), 1898.

ᵃ They are Arkansas, Iowa, Kansas, Rhode Island, South Dakota, Wisconsin, and Wyoming.

created to exercise the functions formerly exercised by the two. It controls the several state institutions and inspects annually all county insane asylums, almshouses, jails, and police stations. The board is a salaried, continuous body, consisting of five members, one appointed by the governor each year, serving for five years. The salary of members is $2,000 per year. The board has also an annual appropriation of $3,000 to defray the salary of a secretary and other expenses.

The Rhode Island State Board of Charities and Corrections has control of all the institutions on the State Farm. It consists of nine members (and a salaried secretary), appointed by the governor and confirmed by the senate, serving for six years. It is an unsalaried board, only the actual expenses incurred being defrayed by the state.

South Dakota, Kansas, Iowa, and Arkansas have placed all their state institutions for defectives under state boards of control. South Dakota's board is a continuous body, consisting of five members, appointed by the governor and confirmed by the senate, and serving for six years. They receive $3 per day for the time spent (not more than one hundred days per year) in the performance of their duties. The board of trustees of the Kansas state institutions for defectives is very similar to that of Dakota. The Arkansas board has control over the schools for the blind, and the deaf and dumb, and the hospital for the insane. It consists of six members, one from each congressional district, appointed by the governor and serving for two years. The Iowa legislature, at its last session (1898), placed all the state institutions under the control of a board of three.

The State Board of Charities and Reform of Wyoming, created in 1891, was in 1895 given full control of all the state institutions. It combines the functions of an administrative and of an advisory board. Besides directing the several institutions, one of its members must visit all county jails at least once each year. Unlike the other state boards, it consists of certain state officers, viz., the state treasurer, the state auditor, and the state superintendent of public instruction.

Seventeen states have advisory boards. These are usually

unsalaried, continuous bodies, consisting of five, six, or nine members appointed by the governor, with the advice and consent of the senate, and serving for long terms.[1] The boards of Indiana, Ohio, Oregon, and Tennessee are bipartisan, and their appointment is vested in the governor alone. In North Carolina the members are chosen by the general assembly. In Minnesota, Missouri, New Jersey, Ohio, Tennessee, and Indiana the governor is *ex officio* a member and the chairman of the board. In Pennsylvania the secretary, and in New Hampshire the secretary of the State Board of Health, are *ex-officio* members of the boards of charities of their respective states.

The greater part of the work of the advisory boards is done by a paid secretary, who is appointed and usually has his salary fixed by the board. We find no provision for a paid secretary in Montana, North Carolina, and Tennessee. In a few instances his salary is fixed by statute, and is in such cases almost invariably low.[2]

The duties of the advisory state boards may be divided into those of visitation and inspection of state institutions, visitation and inspection of local institutions, visitation and inspection of private institutions, general investigations into the questions of pauperism, insanity, and crime, and reporting their action and recommendations to the governor or the legislature.

[1] All the advisory state boards are continuous bodies, the terms of only a part of the members expiring at a time. With the exception of New York's board, they are all unsalaried. The members of that board receive their expenses and $10 per day for the time spent in the performance of their duties.

The boards consist of three (appointed) members in Montana; four in Michigan; five in Connecticut, Illinois, New Hampshire, North Carolina, and Pennsylvania; six in Colorado, Indiana, Minnesota, Missouri, New Jersey, Ohio, Oregon, and Tennessee; nine in Massachusetts; and of eleven in New York. They serve for three years in Indiana, Minnesota, Ohio, and Tennessee; four years in Connecticut; five years in Illinois, Massachusetts, New Hampshire, North Carolina, and Pennsylvania; six years in Colorado, Missouri, Montana, New Jersey, and Oregon; and eight years in Michigan and New York.

[2] The salary of the secretary is fixed in the following states: Connecticut, $1,500; Missouri, $1,000; Ohio, $1,200; and Pennsylvania, $3,000.

The annual appropriation made for carrying on the work (including clerk hire, traveling expenses, stationery, etc.) in some of the states is as follows: Colorado, $3,000; Indiana, $4,000; Michigan, Minnesota, and Oregon, $5,000; Missouri, $1,500; and Montana, $1,000.

Usually all institutions for the dependent, defective, and delinquent classes, wholly or partially supported by the state, are supervised by the state boards. These include the prisons, reformatories, and industrial schools, hospitals for the insane, institutions for the blind, deaf and dumb, feeble-minded and epileptic, and state schools for dependent children. The prisons are excepted in New York, Massachusetts, and New Hampshire. So, too, are the institutions for the education of the blind and the deaf-mutes in a few of the eastern states. In New York the Commission on Lunacy has supervision over the hospitals for the insane. The state board of New Hampshire was created to secure the enforcement of the law relating to the care of dependent children, and so has supervision over none of the state institutions. The Lunacy Commission (the State Board of Health), however, performs the functions of a supervisory body for the hospitals and retreats for the insane.

The institutions are usually visited regularly by a committee delegated by the board. The committee has power to enter and inspect all parts of the institutions, to examine the records and all contracts, to hear complaints, and in such cases to take the testimony of the inmates. The boards are usually left free to make their own rules in regard to all these matters.

This same power is usually extended over local institutions. In Ohio, however, this is not the case. In Massachusetts and Michigan all almshouses are to be visited annually; in New York and Pennsylvania, biennially. But usually the power of visiting local institutions is permissive, and the frequency of inspections is left to the discretion of the board. Reports of the work of the local institutions may be required, and are usually made annually. The state boards of New York and Pennsylvania are to prescribe a uniform system of records to be kept by the administrators of the poor law throughout their respective states. The boards of some other states may require such records to be kept as they deem desirable. In Michigan the duty of providing blanks for keeping uniform records devolves upon a committee consisting of the secretary of state, the attorney-general, and the secretary of the State Board of Charities.

The state boards of Colorado, Connecticut, Illinois, and Massachusetts have the same power of inspection of private asylums and retreats for the insane as of public hospitals. In Illinois the state board has the power of licensing them. The power of the state boards of New York, Pennsylvania, Missouri, and Montana extends to institutions receiving aid from the public as well as to those wholly supported by it.

One of the most important duties of the boards and their secretaries is that of collecting statistics concerning the various questions with which they have to deal. In some of the laws great emphasis is placed upon this. In North Carolina the board is to examine the "general condition of the state as affected by crime, vagrancy, and pauperism," and it is to "give special attention to the causes of insanity, defect or loss of the several senses, idiocy, and the deformity and infirmity of the physical organization." The county commissioners are to make an annual report to it on the question of pauperism. In Connecticut the board is to collect statistics in regard to pauperism and poor-law administration and to publish them in its annual report. This will suffice as illustration. Similar provisions are found in nearly all the acts creating the several state boards.

The boards are to report annually or biennially to the governor or to the legislature, showing the conditions of the various institutions and recommending needful changes in the law or its administration. Each board is expected to plan a system for the legislature to attempt to arrive at, and to map out a policy to be pursued by it, in its legislation.

This is the constitution and these are the powers and duties common to the advisory state boards. Their functions have been determined by the conditions existing in the several states. As the charitable work of the states has extended, new powers have been conferred upon the boards and new duties have been added. Nearly all the state boards were organized as purely advisory bodies, but, owing to the exigencies of the situation, few remain so now. The executive powers conferred upon them are varied and many.

In Massachusetts and New York, where there is a distinction

between "town" and "state paupers," the latter class are under the direction of the state board. In the former state they are cared for in state institutions, or, if harmless insane, or dependent minors, may be cared for in families. The representative of the board must find families with which to place persons of these classes and visit them when so placed. In New York institutions organized for the care of dependent minors are incorporated only with the consent of the state board. The New Hampshire state board was expressly created to secure the enforcement of the law relating to finding family homes for dependent children. It is to see that such children are removed from the almshouses, placed with families, and are then well cared for. On January 1, 1898, it became the duty of the Indiana State Board of Charities to secure the enforcement of the law relating to the dependent children of that state. The board is to appoint one or more agents to coöperate with the local authorities in finding homes for dependent minors and in visiting them when placed in them. In Connecticut one member of the board is to serve on the board of directors of each county children's home.

In Minnesota, Oregon, Pennsylvania, Tennessee, and Indiana the plans for all jails, almshouses, hospitals, reformatories, and homes of various kinds must be submitted to the state boards for their approval. The Board of State Commissioners in Illinois must audit the accounts of all the state charitable institutions before the warrants are issued by the state treasurer.x   The board also licenses and visits private institutions for the insane.

Lunacy commissions have been created in a few states to supervise the treatment of the insane. As they were noticed in the preceding paper on "Defectives," it will not be necessary at this time to do more than call attention to them.

In a number of instances the appointment of local commissions or agents to help the state boards in their inspection of

---

¹ Dr. Wines has claimed that the power to audit the accounts of the several state institutions of Illinois, and to recommend the granting or refusal of appropriations asked for by them, has given the state board much more influence than it would otherwise have had. He recommends it to the other state boards.

institutions has been authorized. The state boards of New York and Pennsylvania are authorized to appoint a committee of three in each county for the visitation of the local public institutions, the jail, and the almshouse.[1] In Pennsylvania the power of visi- tation also extends to public and private asylums and retreats for the insane. In Illinois it is incumbent upon the state board to appoint such a committee of three.[2] The state board of New Jersey may appoint two representatives in each county.[3] The county agents serve in a somewhat similar capacity in Michigan.[4] The state board of Tennessee, organized in 1895, has appointed a committee of six, three men and three women, in each county to aid it in its work. Perhaps other state boards have done likewise.

Ohio and Colorado provide for the appointment of county boards by the probate court. In Ohio the boards consist of five members (three of whom are women), whose duty it is to visit the local institutions and to make an annual report to the clerk of the court and the State Board of Charities. In Colorado the boards consist of six members, two being appointed each year and serving for three years. They visit and inspect all local institutions quarterly, and make an annual report to the State Board of Charities and Corrections. As is the duty of the county agent in Michigan, someone appointed by the board in each county must appear in court in the interest of a minor when arraigned. In both Ohio and Colorado the appointment of these boards is mandatory.

The state charities aid associations of New York and New Jersey are of much importance in the supervision of the charities of those states, and should receive attention here. They are voluntary organizations, having committees in most of the counties of both states. Permission is secured from the courts to visit and inspect the local institutions. The organiza- tions are of such repute that their investigations and reports

[1] Ch. 546, Acts of 1896 ; 20, p. 298.
[2] 34, ch. 85.
[3] 6, Act of March 23, 1883.
[4] Ch. 346.

have been a great factor in the advancement of the charities of those two states.[1]

H. A. MILLIS.

UNIVERSITY OF CHICAGO.

[1] See Art. ii, ch. 546, Acts of New York, 1896, and Acts of April 16, 1886, and March 23, 1892, of the legislature of New Jersey.

For an account of the work done in New York, see MR. HOMER FOLKS' paper on "The Work of the State Charities Aid Association of New York," *Report of the N. C. C. C.*, 1897, p. 278.

New Jersey subsidizes the association in that state.

THE INSTINCT OF WORKMANSHIP AND THE IRKSOMENESS OF LABOR.

It is one of the commonplaces of the received economic theory that work is irksome. Many a discussion proceeds on this axiom that, so far as regards economic matters, men desire above all things to get the goods produced by labor and to avoid the labor by which the goods are produced. In a general way the common-sense opinion is well in accord with current theory on this head. According to the common-sense ideal, the economic beatitude lies in an unrestrained consumption of goods, without work ; whereas the perfect economic affliction is unremunerated labor. Man instinctively revolts at effort that goes to supply the means of life.

No one will accept the proposition when stated in this bald fashion, but even as it stands it is scarcely an overstatement of what is implied in the writings of eminent economists. If such an aversion to useful effort is an integral part of human nature, then the trail of the Edenic serpent should be plain to all men, for this is a unique distinction of the human species. A consistent aversion to whatever activity goes to maintain the life of the species is assuredly found in no other species of animal. Under the selective process through which species are held to have emerged and gained their stability there is no chance for the survival of a species gifted with such an aversion to the furtherance of its own life process. If man alone is an exception from the selective norm, then the alien propensity in question must have been intruded into his make-up by some malevolent *deus ex machina*.

Yet, for all the apparent absurdity of the thing, there is the fact. With more or less sincerity, people currently avow an aversion to useful effort. The avowal does not cover all effort, but only such as is of some use ; it is, more particularly, such effort as is vulgarly recognized to be useful labor. Less repugnance is expressed as regards effort which brings gain without giving a product that is of human use, as, for example, the effort that goes into war, politics, or other employments of a similar nature. And there is commonly no avowed aversion to sports or other similar employments that yield neither a pecuniary gain nor a useful product. Still, the fact that a given line of effort is useless does not of itself save it from being odious, as is shown by the case of menial service ; much of this work serves no useful end, but it is none the less repugnant to all people of sensibility.

"The economic man," whose lineaments were traced in outline by the classical economists and filled in by their caricaturists, is an anomaly in the animal word ; and yet, to judge by everyday popular expressions of inclination, the portrait is not seriously overdrawn. But if this economic man is to serve as a lay figure upon which to fit the garment of economic doctrines, it is incumbent upon the science to explain what are his limitations and how he has achieved his emancipation from the law of natural selection. His emancipation from the law is, indeed, more apparent than substantial. The difference in this respect between man and his sometime competitors in the struggle for survival lies not in a slighter but in a fuller adjustment of his propensities to the purposes of the life of the species. He distanced them all in this respect long ago, and by so wide an interval that he is now able, without jeopardy to the life of the species, to play fast and loose with the spiritual basis of its survival

Like other animals, man is an agent that acts in response to stimuli afforded by the environment in which he lives. Like other species, he is a creature of habit and propensity. But in a higher degree than other species, man mentally digests the content of the habits under whose guidance he acts, and appreciates the trend of these habits and propensities. He is in an eminent sense an intelligent agent. By selective necessity he is endowed with a proclivity for purposeful action. He is possessed of a discriminating sense of purpose, by force of which all futility of life or of action is distasteful to him. There may be a wide divergence between individuals as regards the form and the direction in which this impulse expresses itself, but the impulse itself is not a matter of idiosyncrasy, it is a generic feature of human nature. It is not a trait that occurs sporadically in a few individuals. Cases occur in which this proclivity for purposeful action is wanting or is present in obviously scant measure, but persons endowed in this stepmotherly fashion are classed as " defective subjects." Lines of descent which carry this defective human nature dwindle and decay even under the propitious circumstances of modern life. The history of hereditarily dependent or defective families is evidence to this effect.

Man's great advantage over other species in the struggle for survival has been his superior facility in turning the forces of the environment to account. It is to his proclivity for turning the material means of life to account that he owes his position as lord of creation. It is not a proclivity to effort, but to achievement — to the compassing of an end. His primacy is in the last resort an industrial or economic primacy. In his economic life man is an agent, not an absorbent; he is an agent seeking in every act the accomplishment of some concrete, objective, impersonal end. As this pervading norm of action guides the life of men in all the use they make of material things, so it must also serve as the point of departure and afford the guiding principle for any science that aims to be a theory of the economic life process. Within the purview of economic theory, the last analysis of any given phenomenon must run back to this ubiquitous human impulse to do the next thing.

All this seems to contradict what has just been said of the conventional aversion to labor. But the contradiction is not so sheer in fact as it appears to be at first sight. Its solution lies in the fact that the aversion to labor is in great part a conventional aversion only. In the intervals of sober reflection, when not harassed with the strain of overwork, men's common sense speaks unequivocally under the guidance of the instinct of workmanship. They like to see others spend their life to some purpose, and they like to reflect that their own life is of some use. All men have this quasi-æsthetic sense of economic or industrial merit, and to this sense of economic merit futility and inefficiency are distasteful. In its positive expression it is an impulse or instinct of workmanship; negatively it expresses itself in a deprecation of waste. This sense of merit and demerit with respect to the material furtherance or hindrance of life approves the economically effective act and deprecates economic futility. It is needless to point out in detail the close relation between this norm of economic merit and the ethical norm of conduct, on the one hand, and the æsthetic norm of taste, on the other. It is very closely related to both of these, both as regards its biological ground and as regards the scope and method of its award.

This instinct of workmanship apparently stands in sheer conflict with the conventional antipathy to useful effort. The two are found together in full discord in the common run of men ; but whenever a deliberate judgment is passed on conduct or on events, the former asserts its primacy in a pervasive way which suggests that it is altogether the more generic, more abiding trait of human nature. There can scarcely be a serious question of precedence between the two. The former is a human trait necessary to the survival of the species ; the latter is a habit of thought possible only in a species which has distanced all competitors, and then it prevails only by sufferance and within limits set by the former. The question between them is, Is the aversion to labor a derivative of the instinct of workmanship ? and, How has it arisen and gained consistency in spite of its being at variance with that instinct ?

Until recently there has been something of a consensus among those who have written on early culture, to the effect that man, as he first emerged upon the properly human plane, was of a contentious disposition, inclined to isolate his own interest and purposes from those of his fellows, and with a penchant for feuds and brawls. Accordingly, even where the view is met with that men are by native proclivity inclined to action, there is still evident a presumption that this native proclivity to action is a proclivity to action of a destructive kind. It is held that men are inclined to fight, not to work—that the end of action in the normal case is damage rather than repair. This view would make the proclivity to purposeful action an impulse to sportsmanship rather than to workmanship. In any attempt to fit this view into an evolutionary scheme of culture it would carry the implication that in the prehuman or proto-anthropoid phase of its life the race was a predaceous species, and that the initial phase of human culture, as well as the later cultural development, has been substantially of a predatory kind.

There is much to be said for this view. If mankind is by derivation a race not of workmen but of sportsmen, then there is no need of explaining the conventional aversion to work. Work is unsportsmanlike and therefore distasteful, and perplexity then arises in explaining how men have in any degree become reconciled to any but a predaceous life. Apart from the immediate convenience of this view, it is also enforced by much evidence. Most peoples at a lower stage of culture than our own are of a more predatory habit than our people. The history of mankind, as conventionally written, has been a narrative of predatory exploits, and this history is not commonly felt to be one-sided or misinformed. And a sportsmanlike inclination to warfare is also to be found in nearly all modern communities. Similarly, the sense of honor, so-called, whether it is individual or national honor, is also an expression of sportsmanship. The prevalence of notions of honor may, therefore, be taken as evidence going in the same direction. And as if to further fortify the claim of sportsmanship to antiquity and prescriptive standing, the sense of honor is also noticeably more vivid in communities of a somewhat more archaic culture than our own.

Yet there is a considerable body of evidence, both from cultural history and from the present-day phenomena of human life, which traverses this conventionally accepted view that makes man generically a sportsman. Obscurely but persistently, throughout the history of human culture, the great body of the people have almost everywhere, in their everyday life, been at work to turn things to human use. The proximate aim of all industrial improvement has been the better performance of some workmanlike task. Necessarily this work has, on the one hand, proceeded on the basis of an appreciative interest in the work to be done; for there is no other ground on which to obtain anything better than the aimless performance of a task. And necessarily also, on the other hand, the discipline of work has acted to develop a workmanlike attitude. It will not do to say that the work accomplished is entirely due to compulsion under a predatory régime, for the most striking advances in this respect have been wrought where the coercive force of a sportsmanlike exploitation has been least.

The same view is borne out by the expressions of common sense. As has already been remarked, whenever they dispassionately take thought and pass a judgment on the value of human conduct, the common run of mature men approve workmanship rather than sportsmanship. At the best, they take an apologetic attitude toward the latter. This is well seen in the present (May, 1898) disturbance of the popular temper. While it may well be granted that the warlike raid upon which this community is entering is substantially an access of sportsmanlike exaltation, it is to be noticed that nearly all those who speak for war are at pains to find some colorable motive of another kind. Predatory exploit, simply as such, is not felt to carry its own legitimation, as it should in the apprehension of any species that is primarily of a predaceous character. What meets unreserved approval is such conduct as furthers human life on the whole, rather than such as furthers the invidious or predatory interest of one as against another.

The most ancient and most consistent habits of the race will best assert themselves when men are not speaking under the stress of instant irritation. Under such circumstances the ancient bent may even bear down the immediate conventional canons of conduct. The archaic turn of mind that inclines men to commend workmanlike serviceability is the outcome of long and consistent habituation to a course of life of such a character as is reflected by this inclination.

Man's life is activity; and as he acts, so he thinks and feels. This is necessarily so, since it is the agent man that does the thinking and feeling. Like other species, man is a creature of habits and propensities. He acts under the guidance of propensities which have been imposed upon him by the process of selection to which he owes his differentiation from other species. He is a social animal ; and the selective process whereby he has acquired the spiritual make-up of a social animal has at the same time made him substantially a peaceful animal. The race may have wandered far from the ancient position of peacefulness, but even now the traces of a peaceful trend in men's everyday habits of thought and feeling are plain enough. The sight of blood and the presence of death, even of the blood or death of the lower animals, commonly strike inexperienced persons with a sickening revulsion. In the common run of cases, the habit of complacency with slaughter comes only as the result of discipline. In this respect man differs from the beasts of prey. He differs, of course, most widely in this respect from the solitary beasts, but even among the gregarious animals his nearest spiritual relatives are not found among the carnivora. In his unarmed frame and in the slight degree to which his muscular force is specialized for fighting, as well as in his instinctive aversion to hostile contact with the ferocious beasts, man is to be classed with those animals that owe their survival to an aptitude for avoiding direct conflict with their competitors, rather than with those which survive by virtue of overcoming and eating their rivals.

" Man is the weakest and most defenseless of all living things," and, according to the Law of the Jungle, it is his part to take advice and contrive and turn divers things to account in ways that are incomprehensible to the rest. Without tools he is not a dangerous animal, as animals go. And he did not become a formidable animal until he had made some considerable advance in the contrivance of implements for combat. In the days before tools had been brought into effective use — that is to say, during by far the greater part of the period of human evolution — man could not be primarily an agent of destruction or a disturber of the peace. He was of a peaceable and retiring disposition by force of circumstances. With the use of tools the possibility of his acquiring a different disposition gradually began, but even then the circumstances favoring the growth of a contentious disposition supervened only gradually and partially. The habits of life of the race were still perforce of a peaceful and industrial character, rather than contentious and destructive. Tools and implements, in the early days, must have served chiefly to shape facts and objects for human use, rather than for inflicting damage and discomfort. Industry would have to develop far before it became possible for one group of men to live at the cost of another ; and during the protracted evolution of industry before this point had been reached the discipline of associated life still consistently ran in the direction of industrial efficiency, both as regards men's physical and mental traits and as regards their spiritual attitude.

By selection and by training, the life of man, before a predaceous life became possible, would act to develop and to conserve in him instinct for workmanship. The adaptation to the environment which the situation enforced was of an industrial kind ; it required men to acquire facility in shaping things and situations for human use. This does not mean the shaping of things by the individual to his own individual use simply; for archaic man was necessarily a member of a group, and during this early stage, when industrial efficiency was still inconsiderable, no group could have survived except on the basis of a sense of solidarity strong enough to throw self-interest into the background. Self-interest, as an accepted guide of action, is possible only as the concomitant of a predatory life, and a predatory life is possible only after the use of tools has developed so far as to leave a large surplus of product over what is required for the sustenance of the producers. Subsistence by predation implies something substantial to prey upon.

Early man was a member of a group which depended for its survival on the industrial efficiency of its members and on their singleness of purpose in making use of the material means at hand. Some competition between groups for the possession of the fruits of the earth and for advantageous locations there would be even at a relatively early stage, but much hostile contact between groups there could not be ; not enough to shape the dominant habits of thought.

What men can do easily is what they do habitually, and this decides what they can think and know easily. They feel at home in the range of ideas which is familiar through their everyday line of action. A habitual line of action constitutes a habitual line of thought, and gives the point of view from which facts and events are apprehended and reduced to a body of knowledge. What is consistent with the habitual course of action is consistent with the habitual line of thought, and gives the definitive ground of knowledge as well as the conventional standard of complacency or approval in any community. Conversely, a process or method of life, once understood, assimilated in thought works into the scheme of life and becomes a norm of conduct, simply because the thinking, knowing agent is also the acting agent. What is apprehended with facility and is consistent with the process of life and knowledge is thereby apprehended as right and good. All this applies with added force where the habituation is not simply individual and sporadic, but is enforced upon the group or the race by a selective elimination of those individuals and lines of descent that do not conform to the required canon of knowledge and conduct. Where this takes place, the acquired proclivity passes from the status of habit to that of aptitude or propensity. It becomes a transmissible trait, and action under its guidance becomes right and good, and the longer and more consistent the selective adaptation through which the aptitude arises, the more firmly is the resulting aptitude settled upon the race, and the more unquestioned becomes the sanction of the resulting canon of conduct.

So far as regards his relation to the material means of life, the canon of thought and of conduct which was in this way enforced upon early man was what is here called the instinct of workmanship. The interest which men took in economic facts on the basis of this propensity, in the days before spoliation came into vogue, was not primarily of a self-regarding character. The necessary dominance of a sense of group solidarity would preclude that. The selective process must eliminate lines of descent unduly gifted with a self-regarding bias. Still, there was some emulation between individuals, even in the most indigent and most peaceable groups. From the readiness with which a scheme of emulation is entered upon 'where late circumstances favor its development, it seems probable that the proclivity to emulation must have been present also in the earlier days in sufficient force to assert itself to the extent to which the exigencies of the earlier life of the group would permit. But this emulation could not run in the direction of an individual acquisition or accumulation of goods, or of a life consistently given to raids and tumults. It would be emulation such as is found among the peaceable gregarious animals generally; that is to say, it was primarily and chiefly sexual emulation, recurring with more or less regularity. Beyond this there must also have been some wrangling in the distribution of goods on hand, but neither this nor the rivalry for subsistence could have been the dominant note of life.

Under the canon of conduct imposed by the instinct of workmanship, efficiency, serviceability, commends itself, and inefficiency or futility is odious. Man contemplates his own conduct and that of his neighbors, and passes a judgment of complacency or of dispraise. The degree of effectiveness with which he lives up to the accepted standard of efficiency in great measure determines his contentment with himself and his situation. A wide or persistent discrepancy in this respect is a source of abounding spiritual discomfort.

Judgment may in this way be passed on the intention of the agent or on the serviceability of the act. In the former case the award of merit or demerit is to be classed as moral; and with award of merit of this kind this paper is not concerned. As regards serviceability or efficiency, men do not only take thought at first hand of the facts of their own conduct; they are also sensitive to rebuke or approval from others. Not only is the immediate consciousness of the achievement of a purpose gratifying and stimulating, but the imputation of efficiency by one's fellows is perhaps no less gratifying or stimulating.

Sensitiveness to rebuke or approval is a matter of selective necessity under the circumstances of associated life. Without it no group of men could carry on a collective life in a material environment that requires shaping to the ends of man. In this respect, again, man shows a spiritual relationship with the gregarious animals rather than with the solitary beasts of prey.

Under the guidance of this taste for good work, men are compared with one another and with the accepted ideals of efficiency, and are rated and graded by the common sense of their fellows according to a conventional scheme of merit and demerit. The imputation of efficiency necessarily proceeds on evidence of efficiency. The visible achievement of one man is, therefore, compared with that of another, and the award of esteem comes habitually to rest on an invidious comparison of persons instead of on the immediate bearing of the given line of conduct upon the approved end of action. The ground of esteem in this way shifts from a direct appreciation of the expediency of conduct to a comparison of the abilities of different agents. Instead of a valuation of serviceability, there is a gauging of capability on the ground of visible success. And what comes to be compared in an invidious comparison of this kind between agents is the force which the agent is able to put forth, rather than the serviceability of the agent's conduct. So soon, therefore, and in so far, as the esteem awarded to serviceability passes into an invidious esteem of one agent as compared with another, the end sought in action will tend to change from naïve expediency to the manifestation of capacity or force. It becomes the proximate end of effort to put forth evidence of power, rather than to achieve an impersonal end for its own sake, simply as an item of human use. So that, while in its more immediate expression the norm of economic taste stands out as an impulse to workmanship or a taste for serviceability and a distaste for futility, under given circumstances of associated life it comes in some degree to take on the character of an emulative demonstration of force.

Since the imputation of efficiency and of invidious merit goes on the evidence afforded by visible success, the appearance of evil must be avoided in order to escape dispraise. In the early savage culture, while the group is small and while the conditions favorable to a predatory life are still wanting, the resulting emulation between the members of the group runs chiefly to industrial efficiency. It comes to be the appearance of industrial incapacity that is to be avoided. It is in this direction that force or capacity can be put in evidence most consistently and with the best effect for the good name of the individual. It is, therefore, in this direction that a standard of merit and a canon of meritorious conduct will develop. But even for a growth of emulation in the productive use of brain and muscle, the small, rude, peaceable group of savages is not fertile ground. The situation does not favor a vigorous emulative spirit. The conditions favorable to the growth of a habit of emulative demonstration of force are (1) the frequent recurrence of conjunctures that call for a great and sudden strain, and (2) exposure of the individual to a large, and especially to a shifting, human environment whose approval is sought. These conditions are not effectually met on the lower levels of savagery, such as human culture must have been during the early days of the use of tools. Accordingly, relatively little of the emulative spirit is seen in communities that have retained the archaic, peaceable constitution, or that have reverted to it from a higher culture. In such communities a low standard of culture and comfort goes along with an absence of strenuous application to the work in hand, as well as a relative absence of jealousy and gradations of rank. Notions of economic rank and discrimination between persons, whether in point of possessions or in point of comfort, are almost, if not altogether, in abeyance.

With a further development of the use of tools and of human command over the forces of the environment, the habits of life of the savage group change. There is likely to be more of aggression, both in the way of a pursuit of large game and in the way of conflict between groups. As the industrial efficiency of the group increases, and as weapons are brought to greater perfection, the incentives to aggression and the opportunities for achievement along this line increase. The conditions favorable to emulation are more fully met. With the increasing density of population that follows from a heightened industrial efficiency, the group passes, by force of circumstances, from the archaic condition of poverty-stricken peace to a stage of predatory life. This fighting stage—the beginning of barbarism—may involve aggressive predation, or the group may simply be placed on the defensive. One or the other, or both the lines of activity—and commonly both, no doubt—will be forced upon the group, on pain of extermination. This has apparently been the usual course of early social evolution.

When a group emerges into this predatory phase of its development, the employments which most occupy men's attention are employments that involve exploit. The most serious concern of the group, and at the same time the direction in which the most spectacular effect may be achieved by the individual, is conflict with men and beasts. It becomes easy to make a telling comparison between men when their work is a series of exploits carried out against these difficult adversaries or against the formidable movements of the elements. The assertion of the strong hand, successful aggression, usually of a destructive character, becomes the accepted basis of repute. The dominant life interest of the group throws its strong light upon this creditable employment of force and sagacity, and the other, obscurer ways of serving the group's life fall into the background. The guiding animus of the group becomes a militant one, and men's actions are judged from the standpoint of the fighting man. What is recognized, without reflection and without misgiving, as serviceable and effective in such a group is fighting capacity. Exploit becomes the conventional ground of invidious comparison between individuals, and repute comes to rest on prowess.

As the predatory culture reaches a fuller development, there comes a distinction between employments. The tradition of prowess, as the virtue *par excellence*, gains in scope and consistency until prowess comes near being recognized as the sole virtue. Those employments alone are then worthy and reputable which involve the exercise of this virtue. Other employments, in which men are occupied with tamely shaping inert materials to human use, become unworthy and end with becoming debasing. The honorable man must not only show capacity for predatory exploit, but he must also avoid entanglement with the occupations that do not involve exploit. The tame employments, those that involve no obvious destruction of life and no spectacular coercion of refractory antagonists, fall into disrepute and are relegated to those members of the community who are defective in predatory capacity; that is to say, those who are lacking in massiveness, agility, or ferocity. Occupation in these employments argues that the person so occupied falls short of that decent modicum of prowess which would entitle him to be graded as a man in good standing. In order to an unsullied reputation, the appearance of evil must be avoided. Therefore the able-bodied barbarian of the predatory culture, who is at all mindful of his good name, severely leaves all uneventful drudgery to the women and minors of the group. He puts in his time in the manly arts of war and devotes his talents to devising ways and means of disturbing the peace. That way lies honor.

In the barbarian scheme of life the peaceable, industrial employments are women's work. They imply defective force, incapacity for aggression or devastation, and are therefore not of good report. But whatever is accepted as a conventional mark of a shortcoming or a vice comes presently to be accounted intrinsically base. In this way industrial occupations fall under a polite odium and are apprehended to be substantially ignoble. They are unsportsmanlike. Labor carries a taint, and all contamination from vulgar employments must be shunned by self-respecting men.

Where the predatory culture has developed in full consistency, the common-sense apprehension that labor is ignoble has developed into the further refinement that labor is wrong—for those who are not already beneath reproach. Hence certain well-known features of caste and tabu. In the further cultural development, when some wealth has been accumulated and the members of the community fall into a servile class on the one hand

and a leisure class on the other, the tradition that labor is ignoble gains an added significance. It is not only a mark of
inferior force, but it is also a perquisite of the poor. This is the
situation today. Labor is morally impossible by force of the
ancient tradition that has come down from early barbarism, and
it is shameful by force of its evil association with poverty. It is
indecorous.

The irksomeness of labor is a spiritual fact; it lies in the
indignity of the thing. The fact of its irksomeness is, of course,
none the less real and cogent for its being of a spiritual kind.
Indeed, it is all the more substantial and irremediable on that
account. Physical irksomeness and distastefulness can be borne,
if only the spiritual incentive is present. Witness the attractiveness of warfare, both to the barbarian and to the civilized youth.
The most common-place recital of a campaigner's experience
carries a sweeping suggestion of privation, exposure, fatigue,
vermin, squalor, sickness, and loathsome death; the incidents and
accessories of war are said to be unsavory, unsightly, unwholesome beyond the power of words; yet warfare is an attractive
employment if one only is gifted with a suitable habit of mind.
Most sports, and many other polite employments that are distressing but creditable, are evidence to the same effect.

Physical irksomeness is an incommodity which men habitually
make light of if it is not reinforced by the sanction of decorum;
but it is otherwise with the spiritual irksomeness of such labor
as is condemned by polite usage. That is a cultural fact. There
is no remedy for this kind of irksomeness, short of a subversion
of that cultural structure on which our canons of decency rest.
Appeal may of course be made to taste and conscience to set
aside the conventional aversion to labor; such an appeal is made
from time to time by well-meaning and sanguine persons, and
some fitful results have been achieved in that way. But the
commonplace, common-sense man is bound by the deliverances
of common-sense decorum on this head—the heritage of an
unbroken cultural line of descent that runs back to the beginning.

THORSTEIN VEBLEN.

THE UNIVERSITY OF CHICAGO.

POLITICS IN PUBLIC INSTITUTIONS OF CHARITY AND CORRECTION.

DURING the discussions conducted by the National Civil-Service Reform League, one important field has been greatly neglected — that indicated in the title of this article. It was natural and proper that the reform should aim to correct abuses in the postal department, in all branches of the general government, and in municipal administration; but the treatment of the helpless poor should not be forgotten. In 1896 the National Conference of Charities and Corrections discussed a report on the spoils system, and the writer presented another report in May, 1898.

The laws of the several states relating to such appointments and the tenure of office have been summarized in the AMERICAN JOURNAL OF SOCIOLOGY, November, 1897, and January, 1898, by Mr. H. A. Millis. But are these laws properly administered, and how do they work? Schedules of questions were sent out to well-informed persons in all parts of the country, and many replies were received which throw interesting light on the subject.

The testimony before the committee seemed to justify certain conclusions which are briefly stated in their report. The "merit system" seems to be making progress in state institutions, especially those for the insane, for the deaf-mutes, and the blind. Less rapidly the better principles are accepted in state correctional institutions, as prisons and reformatories. It is in local institutions, such as city hospitals, jails, and in county charities, that we find the worst forms of neglect and incompetence, often of positive corruption.

Of course, partisan appointments are not often as bad as it is possible for them to be, owing to the presence of an enlightened public sentiment which makes it good policy even for partisans to appoint capable administrators. But the spoils system only too often works its natural and inevitable consequences, and the charitable purpose of the community is thwarted by dishonest or inefficient agents.

It is the purpose of this article to present, as far as possible in the very language of competent informants, some of the illustrations of the actual working of the spoils system in the designated field of inquiry.[1]

[1] Through the kindness of Mrs. Josephine Shaw Lowell, Mr. J. G. Thorp,

EASTERN STATES.

A general view, based on long personal observation and experience, and on wide correspondence, is presented in this statement:

The general conclusions concerning New England are, I think, that there is very little serious attempt to make these positions the award of party service, largely because the New England states are and have been for so long a time under the control of one party; and of course also, and perhaps chiefly, because the local public sentiment, generally speaking, will not suffer removals to get men in for party reasons. On the other hand, I think it pretty apparent that when appointments are to be made, they are almost universally made from the party which happens for the time being to be in control; and if good men are appointed, as they generally are, such a result does not offend the public sentiment. Certainly nowhere in New England do we find wholesale removals on any change of party administration, but where vacancies occur after a change of party control, those vacancies are filled from the controlling party; though in Massachusetts, while the above is practically the rule, in recent years we have had plenty of cases where not only members of the minority party have been reappointed, but new men belonging to that party have been put in to fill vacancies which have occurred. The public sentiment in this state will not permit the use of these offices for partisan purposes.

CONNECTICUT.

More particular illustration may be found in a discriminating letter from Connecticut:

The requirement of non-political appointments to the board of direction of the state prison and to the boys' school has not been interpreted to mean appointment on merit alone, for it has, I think, been the invariable custom to give the party for the time being in the majority, *i. e.*, the party of the appointing power (the governor), the majority of the board.

The present warden of the state prison is a Democrat, though the board is Republican; and his being left in is the more striking because he took the place of a Republican ousted under a Democratic administration. The idea of other than political fitness in appointment seems here to have scored a success; and, indeed, it is my impression that the general drift is that way; though such a thing as examination, or even formally requiring previous experience in the sort of work required, has not yet begun to dawn. . . . .

Speaking of a certain board, this competent informant adds:

Appointments have been made to it in some instances for which the only obvious explanation was that the governor wanted to compliment somebody

Professor Frank A. Fetter, and others, we are permitted to use the materials here arranged. Some correspondents request that their names be withheld.

or to gratify some personal friend. I suppose that it is much the same everywhere—and will be to the end of the chapter. And, indeed, it is marvelous
how well, on the whole, boards appointed in this fashion do their work — men
chosen frequently who have never shown the slightest spark of interest,
not to say·special knowledge, in the kind of institutions they are called upon
to manage. It is a compliment to the latent intelligence and conscientious-
ness of the average citizen, even if it does look a trifle hazardous. In the
appointments of city charity commissioners there is a distinct tendency to
ignore politics. How long it will last is a question.

In the election of town officers one correspondent says:

Politics enters into the choice of these officials in a good many cases,
leading to frequent changes and consequent confusion in the administration.

Another letter from Connecticut says of the insane asylum of the
state :

The appointment of trustees may have something of a political flavor, but
that of the superintendent has been given for merit only, although no examination or competitive tests have been employed. The local sentiment in
regard to this institution favors the appointment on grounds of professional
fitness rather than by political favor . . . .

The office of county commissioner is a political one, and in some cases
there may have been a political element in the appointment of superintendents, but as a rule, I should say, they were chosen on account of their general
fitness for the position. No examination or competitive tests are held. Local
sentiment in regard to the county homes (for dependent and neglected children) favors the appointment of officers for merit.

The office of selectman is a political one, and in some cases politics
influences the appointment or removal of the superintendent of the almshouse, although in other cases superintendents who have shown themselves
especially fitted for the position have been retained throughout a long term
of years. I fear there is a considerable local sentiment in favor of considering the position of superintendent of the town almshouse as a political prize,
although I do not think that this sentiment obtains largely among the best
class of citizens.

In respect to the state prisons:

The board is largely filled by political appointments. Politics is doubtless an influence in the appointment of the warden, and no competitive examination is held for any of the positions. There is reason to believe that local
sentiment is not averse to this political element, if the matter is not abused.

There is no competitive examination for positions in the state school for
boys, and no evidence of local sentiment requiring it. The offices of sheriff
and jailer are elective and political. It would be difficult to alter the system

in this state, although I think better results would be obtained if the county prisons were controlled by the state under a board of prison commissioners.

RHODE ISLAND.

There are thirty-eight cities and towns in Rhode Island. In the cities the office of overseer of the poor is distinct from any care of institutions; in the towns the overseer is generally superintendent of the poor-farm also. The present incumbents have held office from one year to twenty-four years; twenty-three having served more than three years. The longer terms are about equally divided between those elected by the people and those chosen by councils. The long term seems to mean the continuance of one party in control and that the party to which the overseer belongs. Fifteen overseers had retained their office after a change in political administration and thirteen had not. The office is not much sought in country places.

NEW HAMPSHIRE.

The correspondent from New Hampshire speaks of the changes in county officers, superintendents of poor farms, and others whose "retention in the employ of the county institution depends upon their political influence with the county commissioners." In respect to the state board of charities he incidentally reveals a weak point in the system of appointments: "The board has been continually changing in its make-up, so that at this day we are just beginning to get 'the hang of the schoolhouse,' and hope soon to accomplish the end for which the board was created."

MASSACHUSETTS.

Our correspondent believes that political (partisan) considerations do not affect the appointments in the case of superintendents of hospitals for the insane and their subordinates; that city and town relief officers and superintendents of almshouses are selected for fitness; that wardens of the state penitentiary have sometimes been chosen on partisan grounds, but that the present incumbent is retained because he is satisfactory; that the reformatories for men, women, and youth are relatively free from partisan influence, and their superintendents, chaplains, and physicians are chosen on the ground of merit. Subordinate officers in the penitentiary and men's reformatory are under civil-service rules. Political interference seems to have touched the management of the houses of correction in Suffolk county, but the direct masters are retained through political changes. The trustees of Boston institutions for children and for the insane seem to be free from partisan interference. Political influences do not prevail in state institutions for delinquent children. County jails and sheriffs are somewhat affected by political considerations. The police and lock-ups in cities are protected by civil-service rules.

NEW YORK.

The information collected by Mrs. Josephine Shaw Lowell comes from superintendents of institutions, managers, superintendents of the poor, and from other persons in a favorable position to know the facts. The mode of working under the civil-service rules is of interest.

State institutions. — The answers from half the superintendents of state institutions heard from state that appointments and removals are made under the civil-service law and rules, and that political and personal favor is not considered. Extracts from less general replies reveal something of the old leaven working beneath the surface. "A" says :

I do not think that there is any "spoils system" in our school at the present time. Whatever may have been the custom in the past, I feel that our present board of management has an earnest desire to promote the best interests of the school. Of course, there may be a case now and then where some pressure may be exerted in behalf of a personal friend seeking appointment, or something of that kind, but it is never pushed to extremity ; and the civil service and the views of the superintendent rule in the matter. Local sentiment in this community, as in all communities, doubtless is apt to be selfish and to consider its own interests first. This must be taken, as we take human nature, I suppose, with some amount of allowance. I feel that we have no special reason here for complaint.

"B":

I think, if the selection of men and women to fill public offices were based upon *fitness* and *ability* alone, every department would be better served.

The board of directors of this institution having changed in its political character has made some little difference in the positions filled. I can see, however, no detriment in these new appointments, and in many cases they are distinct improvements over the officers occupying positions under the old régime.

The sentiment throughout the county in regard to this institution is that it has been, since its inception, distinctly Democratic in its officers and management. This is not untrue to fact.

"C":

I believe in civil service in institutions of this character. I must decline to express my views on the subject at length, as, in all probability, I shall shortly be a victim to the spoils system, as you term it, and, consequently, it would be indelicate for me to protest against it at this time, for fear of being charged with selfish motives.

"D":

First, under the laws of the state of New York, the managers of state hospitals appoint the treasurer from an unclassified list, and he can only be removed by the managers after charges have been filed in writing and an opportunity to be heard is given. The managers also appoint the superintendent from the merit list, as submitted by the State Civil-Service Commission. Formerly they were compelled by the law to select from the first three names of the eligible list certified by the commission, but under the present civil-service law they hold a fitness examination of all those who are on the eligible merit list and select the one whose combined standing for merit and fitness is highest. The superintendent, like the treasurer, can only be removed by the managers upon charges preferred in writing, and an opportunity to be heard being granted.

Second, all other appointments in state hospitals are made by the superintendent, certain positions being in the classified list of the civil service, while others are exempted.

First assistant physicians, second assistant physicians, assistant physicians, junior assistant physicians, and internes all have to undergo a competitive examination for merit, which is conducted by the State Civil-Service Commission. In addition, the same regulation in regard to an examination for fitness prevails as in the case of the superintendent, with the exception that the superintendent appoints, instead of the board of managers.

I might say here that the civil-service regulations provide certain qualifications for these positions as well as that of the superintendent. The superintendent must be at least thirty years of age, and have had not less than five years' experience in the care and treatment of the insane. First assistant physicians must have had three years' experience in the care and treatment of the insane and must be at least twenty-five years of age. Second assistant physicians are promoted without examination from either the list of assistant or junior assistant physicians. Assistant and junior assistant physicians must take a competitive examination, and must have had an experience of at least one year in hospital work. Internes pass an examination without having had any previous hospital or other experience. Their salaries are lower than the junior assistant physicians', and the intent is that they should be drilled in hospital work and thus become trained for the higher places.

Stewards are appointed by the superintendent from an unclassified list, and can only be removed by the superintendent upon charges preferred in writing and an opportunity to be heard being granted. This same regulation applies to the various positions in the medical service.

Skilled mechanics (positions paying more than $720 a year), clerical positions, and a few others are governed by the same general civil-service regulations as obtain in the positions mentioned above, but those who occupy them can be removed at any time by the superintendent when in his opinion their services are not satisfactory.

The other positions in the service are non-competitive, but the applicants have to take a civil-service examination to test their qualifications for the work ; this examination being conducted by the local civil-service board, appointed by the State Civil-Service Commission and selected from the list of officers of the institution. This local board submits at stated intervals a report showing the appointments, resignations, discharges, and promotions. In the case of original appointments, the examination papers are forwarded to the State Civil-Service Commission for inspection and filing.

In an experience of many years in public hospitals for the insane, party politics have not controlled ; in fact, so far as my personal knowledge goes, applicants are not appointed with regard to their political or religious belief, but simply and solely for fitness.

" E " has a less optimistic outlook :

At present party service solely governs the appointment of men in all the grades, with a strong tendency toward making the appointment of women a personal favor to political friends. In the subordinate places : firemen, engineers, gardeners, watchmen, etc., etc., when the place is wanted the incumbent goes, regardless of civil-service certificate. Local sentiment is summed up on the one hand in the old war cry, " To the victors belong the spoils," modified by the "Thief! Thief!" of the vanquished. Even our bread and butter carries the taint of politics, especially the egg part of it. The steward is beset by dealers in every kind of commodity, and all with a backing not to be despised, if his goods are.

" F ":

It was the design of the framers of our prison law to take the prisons out of politics, as is evidenced by chap. 382, Laws of 1889, sec. 30, which says that the superintendent of prisons shall appoint certain officers, "and he may remove them from office when in his judgment the public interests shall so require." Also subdivision 3 of the same section says : " No appointments shall be made in any of the state prisons of this state on the grounds of political partisanship, but honesty, capacity, and adaptation shall constitute the rule for appointment, and any violation of this rule shall be sufficient cause for the removal from office of the officer committing such violation."

There is scarcely a state in the union which permits politics to interfere with its prison management, and up to the present time New York state has not attempted to run its prisons as a part of any political machine. As instance of the truth of this, Warden Brush was appointed at Sing Sing by the first superintendent of prisons, Louis D. Pillsbury, and served successively under Superintendent I. V. Baker and Superintendent Austin Lathrop, until he was forced, by ill health, to resign and shortly afterward died.

Isaiah Fuller was appointed at Clinton by Superintendent Pillsbury, and served during Mr. Baker's term and five years under Superintendent Lathrop, when he was removed as a result of an investigation on charges of cruelty toward prisoners.

There are officers today in the prisons of this state that have served thirty years, and during my connection with the prisons there have never been any removals on account of politics or partisanship.

Very few men are adapted to prison work, and every change of prison officials has a detrimental effect on prison discipline. The changes in prison work entailed by the constitution which went into effect one year ago makes changes in prison management at the present time a very hazardous experiment, as the prisons were never in such a critical condition as at the present time. Established industries, which were all wiped out by the new constitution, are being replaced by other industries, and this change would seem to require persons with prison experience.

The following are the only interesting statements from managers of institutions:

"AB":

I resigned because it was evident to me that the spirit of the civil-service law (if not the letter of the law) was seriously violated.

The removal of the steward was the most flagrant act of injustice. One of the board of trustees was quite frank in saying to me that he wanted the spoils and did not wish to conceal his desire.

"CD":

Inasmuch as I am a manager of the state hospital, I think it would be indelicate in me to furnish the information you seek in your communication of the twenty-fourth instant. Therefore I hope you will excuse me in declining to do so.

Mrs. Lowell's judgment is:

It would seem to be the fact, judging from most of the replies received, that usually the state institutions of New York (by which is meant the institutions supported by state appropriations and managed by local, unpaid boards appointed by the governor) have been free to a great degree, and many of them entirely, from political influence, but that it has existed in some few of these institutions in the past, and that it is a growing evil.

In considering the references to the civil-service law in the replies received, it is also necessary to remember the following facts:

1. That under the present civil-service law of the state of New York ("the Black Law") there is no position which is not in reality

removed from the test of competitive examination. for the appointing power can choose, and is intended by the law to choose, any person who has been able to get upon an eligible list, even at the very bottom. In a report of the Civil-Service Reform Association, published March 21, it is shown that, in one case at least, a man standing 200th on the merit eligible list of the State Civil-Service Board was appointed to an office. The governor of New York, in preparing the law which bears his name, intended to give to the appointing power liberty of selection, and he has accomplished his purpose.

2. That the stewards of the state hospitals, asylums, and houses of refuge were in 1897 removed by the State Civil-Service Board, necessarily with the governor's approval, from Class II, in which competitive examinations are required, to Class I, in which no examinations are required. As the stewards of the state institutions àre the persons who have the control of the purchase of supplies and who, therefore, are the most liable to be assailed by improper local influences, placing this office entirely at the mercy of personal and political pressure is an ominous step, and one which bodes ill for the comfort of the inmates of state institutions and for the economy of state funds.

In this connection the following extract from the letter of a disinterested citizen in regard to one important state institution probably points to a greater evil than is suggested even, for if one institution is so threatened, it is probable that all are alike exposed to it :

The largest charitable institution in our neighborhood, the asylum for the insane, has never been run on the spoils system, and has always been successfully managed. Now, however, an attempt is being made to turn the asylum into a political machine, and the friends of the institution view the threatened change with alarm.

The following extract from the letter of a state commissioner is disheartening, for it is undoubtedly true :

It is my experience that well-meaning men, who are in favor of the merit system in the abstract, are perverted when they become public officials, and are easily persuaded in their own minds that they know personally someone who could better fill any position under them than anyone else in the state.

City and county institutions.—In respect to local institutions Mrs. Lowell writes :

The replies in regard to city and county institutions have been extremely meager. The nine replies received from superintendents of the poor contain but little that bears upon the subject of the inquiry, and although a special inquiry as to poorhouses, jails, and penitentiaries was addressed to the secretaries of the thirty-seven civil-service boards of the cities of the state, the only information received was the following reply from an inland city :

" Our local city and state institutions are well under the control of the civil-service system, but in our county institutions it is ignored entirely."

The only replies from the superintendents themselves which are to the point are the following :

From a superintendent of the poor :

Appointments in the poor office, and the almshouse, are made by the superintendent of the poor, solely, and are invariably on the ground of fitness for the work required, and politics has nothing whatever to do with it.

As a matter of curiosity, the undersigned made an investigation, and found that there were about as many employés in the almshouse of the opposite political party as of the party to which he belonged. I do not inquire as to an applicant's politics, only as to his experience.

In the city poor office all the employés are of the dominant political party. The Civil-Service Commission here never included the city poor office in its examinations, until two years ago. At that time all the incumbents were obliged to take the examination, and, being thoroughly familiar with all the duties of the place, of course they stood highest. Since that time there have been no changes in the department.

The appointments are made by a committee of the common council. At the last general election there was a complete reversal of parties in power, here, and it is a matter of considerable speculation what the Democratic party will be able to do, in the matter of rating their friends high enough on "fitness" to land them, to the exclusion of Republicans.

I think party leaders would think that employés should be of the dominant political party ; however, they do not try to influence the subscriber to make an appointment solely on political grounds.

From a city commissioner :

In the hospital the superintendent appoints all nurses, attendants, and orderlies, fixes their salaries and prescribes their duties, subject to my approval ; likewise all promotions and removals are made by him. All appointments are determined by fitness. Inasmuch as civil-service rules apply, appointments are made accordingly, everything else being equal, and where civil-service rules do not conflict, party service and personal favor have their influence here as elsewhere.

Many facts are cited from a report of the New York County Visiting Committee, October, 1897, from which it is evident that the "spoils system," during the years 1896 and 1897 at least, was responsible in the Department of Charities of New York city for cruelty of various kinds to helpless babies and to the aged sick, causing much suffering and in many cases death.

That this state of things existed under an administration which in some other departments was really a "reform administration" makes the facts even more disgraceful than they otherwise would be.

The following is an extract from a letter, dated March, 1898, from an ex-official (a Republican) of New York city, turned out of office by the present administration:

The customs governing appointments and removal of officials are for the most part, or at least at present, strictly partisan in character. The district leaders of Tammany Hall have promised positions to so many and the pressure is so great that it is proposed to wipe out the entire eligible list in the civil service and at once have examinations, which will relieve the pressure by making appointments as fast as they can be classified. It is proposed to take every position of importance off the classified service, leaving only clerkships and other minor positions. It is also proposed that if the new regulations had to be submitted to the State Civil-Service Board, the leaders of Tammany Hall would be compelled to confer with Senator Platt, who is supposed to control the state board, to arrange that by their approving the new rules a division of the offices would be made in the proportion of 70 per cent. to the Democrats and 30 per cent. for the Republicans. The Democrats propose to discharge every man who was appointed during the "Strong" administration.

The local sentiment on the subject of appointments and removals by citizens generally is that the law in all cases should be observed, where now it is violated or evaded every day.

Among political leaders the civil-service law is looked upon as a good thing to stop pressure for place, as all the leaders have to do to get rid of a persistent office seeker is to tell him he can do nothing for him until he gets on the "list," and then, if he has the right "pull," he will be appointed.

The following extract from a letter of an ex-civil-service commissioner of New York city confirms the previous testimony as to the administration of 1895–6 and 1897 in the Department of Charities of that city:

. . . . The Civil-Service Commission kept close watch to prevent evasions of the rules, but on more than one occasion was estopped by the asseverations of the charities department. Although the Civil-Service Commission, with the evidence before it, had every reason to doubt the statements of the department, and no reason to change its opinion because of them, it can be understood that the position was a delicate one. My opinion is that the Board of Charities, under the presidency of Mr. ——, was most inefficiently administered, and that the reason for said inefficiency was the political activity of Mr. —— and his continuous effort to appoint for political reasons alone. . . . . I have had evidence that even the better-paid employés, who

could only be taken from an eligible list, were induced to join political associations and become more or less active political workers, under threat, I
suppose, of removal. . . . .

County jails and penitentiaries.—Mrs. Lowell writes:

In regard to the jails of the state I have received no response to my
inquiries, but it is well known that they are generally in a deplorable condition, owing to the fact that the sheriffs, who have charge of them, are elected
as members of one or other of the political parties, and that they have no
salaries, but make their money out of the board of the prisoners.

Attempts have been made from time to time to change the system and
place the jails under the charge of salaried keepers, but in vain. The sheriffs
have a single term of three years, and are, of course, nominated without
regard to their qualifications for managing a prison.

I have been equally unfortunate in obtaining information in regard to the
county penitentiaries.

The failure to show an interest in this important subject on the part of
officials and members of reform organizations of all kinds has been very discouraging, and has convinced me that the people of the state of New York
are far from understanding the tremendous evils that grow out of politics in
public institutions.

From the manager of a state insane hospital, May 3, 1898:

The party machines, both Democratic and Republican, in the counties of
the state are, I am assured, as corrupt and as fully charged with the purposes of rule or ruin as were ever the corresponding machines in New York
city. The demagogues in the rural districts are very apt and ready scholars,
and quickly fall in line with the plans and methods of the political bosses
in your city. There is the same method of packing conventions with delegates chosen by a self-styled caucus of three or four men seated at a table
in a drinking saloon; the same sort of control is exercised over the organization by the district or county chairman, who appoints the temporary
chairman, who appoints the committee on credentials, who names the members of the convention, regardless of any regularity or irregularity in the
choice made by their constituents. So that the county or district boss
controls the organization of the party, and thus attains despotic power in the
councils thereof.

He describes an attempt to place certain hospitals in the hands of
incompetent and subservient managers:

With four Republicans and three Democrats in the board, the Republican
machine thought they had control, and laid down and openly announced their
programme. The treasurer was to be forced to resign, and in his place was to
be put a man who would by intimidation bulldoze about one hundred employés

at the hospital into voting the Republican ticket. The superintendent of the hospital, by arts familiar to political "heelers," was to be browbeaten, nagged, and worried and insulted until his sense of self-respect should compel him to resign; with him would also go the steward, his appointee. The board would then put in as superintendent a country doctor, already selected, who had no more qualifications for the position than any other crossroads doctor; he would be merely a manikin; he would appoint a steward, also already selected, who would make purchases in those mysterious ways unknown to outsiders, but perfectly familiar to political thieves of every grade; and *commissions*, small but frequently recurring, would be the order of the day. "Tips" would be privately conveyed to dealers in groceries, provisions, clothing, etc., and those too honest to take such hints would find very soon that their goods were not wanted at any price. Now, all this I find to have been the subject of conversation among those quiet men, silent listeners, but quick to learn, who in every party are always keeping themselves well informed of the "true inwardness" of affairs.

Of course, such things could never be established by any evidence admissible only in a court at law, but it is none the less tangible and well founded.

The local sentiment regarding all this sort of proceeding is, with the better part of the community, wholly opposed to it at every stage, for these machine men obtain their most numerous supporters among the corrupt classes, the vicious and saloon element, and all others of the degraded sort, with no conscience and no sense of responsibility as citizens. The Republicans in —— county, for instance, are in revolt against their machine, and its power is likely to be overthrown in the next campaign. I need not say, for you will readily infer it as true, that the county bosses are always in close affiliation and in cordial coöperation with the two head bosses in New York, Croker and Platt. . . . .

From a private individual, May 2, 1898 :

. . . . . The almshouse is the only institution that I have any positive knowledge of. All I can say of this institution is that each keeper, on entering office, removes such of the attendants and superintendents of departments as he may wish to, and gives the places to relatives and friends. Further than this I am unable to make a statement. I suppose this is one of the desirable attainments of this office. As to whether these removals and new appointments are detrimental to county interests, I cannot say. One keeper who, a few years ago, was in office as superintendent, had his wife as matron (which was quite proper), two sons had good-paying positions, daughter was superintendent of sewing department, son-in-law house physician, other relatives having good-paying positions. When time came for reëlection, a superintendent of road work was boarded, with a number of his assistants, at the expense of the county (the object, to secure political influence, as all the men, amounting, perhaps, to several hundred, were voters). . . . .

From the secretary of a local civil-service reform association, April 30, 1898:

. . . . The county offices are not even yet under the civil-service laws, and I could get no clear information. I knew at the outset, however, in a general way, what has since been confirmed by the managing editors, city editors, and some of the reporters of several of the papers here, that in both the jail and penitentiary the administration is bad, and the offices are given through favoritism and not for fitness. I was told at more than one newspaper office that in both these places there is some abuse to write up every few months, and that the management is wasteful, inefficient, and incompetent. I could not get details from them. About two years ago there was a rather elaborate writing up of the penitentiary. . . . .

From an ex-civil-service commissioner of New York city, April 30, 1898:

. . . . One of the most plausible sources of evasion of the requirements of the civil-service statute is the change in classification of the different positions. This has not only been used as a means of transferring persons to the exempt schedule, so that no examination whatever should be required upon their admission to the public service, but offices have sometimes been created for the purpose of compelling the creation of a new eligible list, and the consequent filing of new applications, under circumstances when very few persons would know of the intended examination. The Civil-Service Commission undertook to guard against this method of evasion by establishing the practice that a mere change of name of a position should not be considered as a change of classification, and that, if an eligible list existed for a given position, it should be used for all similar positions. This was a fruitful source of controversy with the departments, but we adhered to it rigidly, and with very good results.

In short, my experience as civil-service commissioner convinced me that the true conception of a civil-service office has not yet found a home in the minds of most public officials. This conception is that the true function of the office is to do for the heads of departments what in a small office, and with ample leisure, they might do for themselves, but what, under existing conditions, it is impracticable for them to do properly, that is to say, to absolutely undertake to furnish them with the most competent persons for any particular employment. I am convinced that where the examiners are competent, and where they have proper information in regard to the duties of the office, they can determine the fitness of candidates to the best advantage, and that by experience they come to be better qualified to do this than most public officials. I do not say this because I think they are by nature any wiser or better than other people, but because they make a specialty of examinations, and, if intelligent, learn by experience the fittest method of examination.

I often hear the argument from educated and intelligent people that the civil-service system is an evil. They admit it to be a necessary one to prevent greater abuses, but they think that the system of examinations is scholastic, and ill-adapted to attain the objects of the statute. In this I am convinced they are mistaken. I do not mean to say that civil-service examinations have always been of the most appropriate character. There has been a great deal learned in the administration of the system. Undoubtedly in December last it was much better administered in the city of New York than it was when the system was first introduced. I believe the same to be true of the administration of the federal service. I do, however, recognize the danger that examiners will fall into ruts, and that heads of departments will fail to give them the proper information as to the duties of the office for which a complete examination is to be had. It is to avoid these evils that the interest and coöperation of all intelligent students of social science are of the greatest value. . . . .

CENTRAL STATES.

MICHIGAN.

Michigan may be taken as an example of states where, in a very high degree, worthy traditions have strong influence on appointments. The prisons are managed by boards appointed by the governor, with the consent of the senate. Both political parties must be represented in these boards. These boards appoint wardens and have power to remove for cause, after an opportunity of hearing upon written charges. Subordinates are appointed by the wardens, subject to approval of the boards.

Iu the hospitals for the insane the boards appoint the superintendents, and they appoint their subordinates.

It is claimed in all the state institutions that promotions are "based on merit." Nothing like a civil-service examination is required, except in the case of attendants, where graduation from the training school is requisite for future promotions. Of course a "merit system" without initial free competitive examination is not the genuine article. The jails and other local institutions are largely under control of party leaders, but the visitations of the agents of the state board and public opinion mitigate the evils of this system. Complaints in relation to the jails, the police courts, and the sheriffs are very frequent, and the evils are charged to "politics."

OHIO.

An administrative officer of a state institution writes:

There are no rules governing promotions, but it has been the aim of the present management to advance in position those whose services have been highly satisfactory in lower positions, when opportunity offers. Teachers, matrons, and attendants are selected from a list of applicants without regard to party affiliations. But I can easily see how a board of trustees can be so constituted as to make these intentions of a superintendent, who is responsible for an institution, null and void, and I can also easily understand how the service in an institution could be greatly impaired by an organization made up independent of the wishes of the superintendent. No examinations or tests have ever been held as a basis of selecting persons to serve in the institution. . . . . It is my opinion that the theory of party leaders and societies is to the effect that the institution should be managed independent of party politics, ... but when a party is once in power, the pressure for place becomes so great that this theory is often thwarted and the practical spoils system instituted in its place.

The following letter from an experienced superintendent of a county infirmary throws strong light on the forces at work:

The laws of Ohio relating to infirmaries provide for the election of three directors, one being elected each year, and each serving a term of three years. These directors have charge of the county infirmary, and, in certain cases, dispense relief to persons outside of the infirmary. They also appoint a superintendent of the infirmary.

Their authority in these matters is absolute, and unconditional; they are responsible to no one, and not subject to censure or removal, public opinion and their own sense of duty being the only restraining influence over them. They adopt no rules of administration.

Custom grants to each infirmary director at least one reëlection, provided he has not done something to incur the displeasure of the public.

No one at all conversant with American politics need be told that, under these circumstances, the party having a majority controls the election of infirmary directors, that party fealty is the first condition of success, and that their official acts must be in conformity with the wishes of their party. In granting relief to the poor, however, party lines are entirely ignored, the poor are all treated alike, regardless of their party affiliations. So far as I know, the infirmary directors never inquire, nor do they know, what the party preferences of those who receive relief at their hands are. It is only in dispensing the patronage of the infirmary, which includes purchasing supplies therefor, that favoritism appears, and it is not party favoritism so much as the personal favor of the directors that is manifested.

The management of the infirmary is mainly through a superintendent who, by a well-established custom, is appointed for one year only; if his administration is satisfactory to the directors, he is reappointed each year. The superintendent's duties are defined by law as follows: "He shall perform such duties as they (the directors) impose upon him, be governed in all respects by their rules and regulations, and may be removed by them at pleasure." With this law the reason for the custom of appointing a superintendent for one year only is plain; it places the superintendent completely and absolutely under the control of the directors; if the personnel of the board is changed, he can be removed; their wishes and pleasure are the rules of his action, whether it be in appointing his subordinates, purchasing the supplies, or managing the infirmary. The good-will of the directors is the one essential condition necessary to the success of a superintendent; without this good-will neither party service, personal merit, nor fitness for the place avails a superintendent anything. Through this control the directors or any one of them can wield all the influence and patronage of the infirmary in his own behalf, and keep himself in the background; if anything be wrong, the superintendent is censured; the director reaps the benefit.

It is this fact, and not party discipline or party fealty, which impels a superintendent to take an active part in party politics, and use the influence and patronage at his disposal to further the interests of his party's candidate for infirmary director, that prompts him to seek influence in the party councils, so that the right man (to him) is nominated. These are facts, indisputable facts. It does not necessarily follow, however, that because of these facts either infirmary directors or superintendents are mercenary, or corrupt; as a rule they are all honorable and upright men, who do their duty conscientiously. They are politicians from necessity and not from choice. The conditions surrounding them require them to be active in politics, so as to maintain their position and influence.

Local sentiment in this county is very strongly in favor of this state of affairs. Recently an influential party leader was appointed a director of the workhouse; in this capacity he voted for a member of the opposite party for superintendent. He was promptly denounced as a traitor to his party; his motives were impugned; his removal was demanded from all parts of the county; the central committee of his party passed strong resolutions to that effect; his influence is gone, for the time being at least; petitions are now being circulated and extensively signed to have his office legislated out of existence, and not a single voice is raised in his behalf, not even among the opposing parties.

While public opinion here concedes partisan influence in the control of penal and charitable institutions, it does not tolerate extravagant, corrupt, or dishonest management thereof. The party in control is held responsible as strictly as the officers. Corrupt or dishonest practices on the part of an officer will, in this county, insure the defeat of his party as surely as it will insure his own defeat.

INDIANA.

Professor Frank A. Fetter gives a summary of the course of legislation governing administration :

Almost every possible method of appointment of boards of trustees and directors seems to have been tried. It is probable, almost certain, that political management was the unquestioned rule from the beginning until little more than a decade ago. We surmise, therefore, that many of the changes of directing boards were caused by the desire to get the control of the patronage away from the other party. But the power would be again vested in the governor when he was politically in accord with the legislature.

The first board of managers of the state prison was elected by the legislature in 1821. In 1824, however, the governor was given the power to appoint or select the managing officers of the prison, there being no board of control ; this policy continuing for eighteen years. From 1842 to 1855 the warden or superintendent was elected on joint ballot of general assembly. From 1855 to 1893 the board of directors appears to have been elected by joint ballot of the general assembly, and it appointed the superintendent and determined the political complexion of the staff. In 1893 the appointment of this board was vested in the governor. In 1895 a special election board, consisting of the leading state officers, was given the power of selecting the board. In 1897 the appointment of the managers of the new reformatory (old prison south) and of the state prison (old prison north) was given to the governor, and it was made the duty of these boards to manage the prisons without regard to politics. The former board is now equally divided as to political views ; the latter is all of the party of the governor.

The woman's prison has never been politically managed. An effort was made to drag it into politics in the early days, we are informed, but this was unsuccessful. Since 1877 it has been managed entirely by women, and it is their pride that efficiency and character are the only tests for service there.

In the institutions for the blind, deaf, and insane, respectively, it was successively provided between 1844 and 1853 that trustees should be annually elected by the legislature by ballot, appointed by the governor alone, by the governor with the consent of the senate, by the legislature first, but vacancies as they occur to be filled by the governor, and finally by a *viva voce* vote of the legislature. It is impossible without further evidence to detect any reason or regularity in these changes. In 1853 trustees of the three institutions were made elective by joint ballot of the general assembly. The number of he members of the board changed, but the method of selection remained the same for twenty-six years. In 1879 the appointing power was given to the governor, the consent of the senate being necessary. The two branches of government were then politically in accord. In 1883 the appointing power was reclaimed by the assembly, the bill being passed over the veto of the governor, who was of opposite politics. He emphasizes in his veto the hindrance to efficient work by the legislature that was caused by the selection of these boards and the fostering of partisan spirit; but makes no mention of its effect on the administration of the institutions. Under this law a part of the directors went out of office each two years, and succeeding legislatures being Republican, a goodly proportion, perhaps all, of the members were Republicans by 1889. The newly elected Democratic legislature then, desiring to make a clean sweep, held a party caucus, nominated candidates, repealed the old law, and enacted another, almost the same, over the veto of the governor, who was of opposite politics.

In 1893, aften ten years of legislative election, the governor was again given the appointing power, both executive and legislative branches being Democratic. The greatest of all forward steps was taken in 1895, the legislature being Republican and the governor a Democrat, when non-political management was enjoined on the boards of these institutions by the law, and it was further provided that not more than nine of the total of eighteen members composing the six boards should be of one political party. In 1897 a slight backward step was taken by the victorious Republicans in permitting as many as twelve of the eighteen to be of one party. A much more radical change by political leaders was only prevented by a most earnest protest from all the friends of non-partisan management throughout the state.

The School for Feeble-Minded Children, the Soldiers' Orphans' Home, were at the first under non-partisan control, both being under one board. As with the other state institutions, their trustees were elected in 1883 by the legislature. In 1885 this was changed, and politics have since not been in the boards. The Reform School for Boys has from the beginning been managed in a non-partisan manner.

Rules of administration adopted by boards of directors. Extracts from regulations for the Northern Indiana Hospital for Insane, at Longcliff, near Logansport.

Non-partisan employment.

The board shall not consider political belief in the employment or dismissal of the superintendent, nor in the confirmation or non-confirmation of the employment of others by the superintendent. In the engagement of all officers and employés only merit, fitness, and character shall be considered. (See Acts 1895, p. 302, sec. 7.)

Selection of officers and employés.

It shall be the duty of the medical superintendent to select and employ any such assistant physicians, clerks, attendants, skilled workers, and servants as may be, in his judgment, necessary to enable him to properly perform the work with which he is charged, subject to the confirmation of the board. A refusal of confirmation, however, on the part of the board of any such selection shall constitute a vacancy, and thereupon the superintendent shall make other selections until such consent be secured.

An officer of the Southern Hospital for the Insane, at Evansville, states :

No formal rules adopted by the board of trustees in regard to appointments, except that no more than one member of a family may have employment in the institution at the same time. This is an excellent aid to discipline.

The Institution for the Education of the Deaf has, by its board of trustees, adopted a very complete set of rules, an extract from which is as follows :

The appointing power.

The superintendent shall be the executive head of the institution, and the organ of communication with subordinate departments. Into his hands is committed the management of the institution in all its departments; and the subordinate officers, teachers, and employés are to adhere to the plans of operation which he may mark out, and promptly and cheerfully comply with all his directions, not only in the performance of the duties as may be by him specified in " rules of the superintendent," but also in such others as it may be deemed just and proper to assign them.

By statutory enactment he has powers concerning operatives, as follows : (1) He shall appoint all officers, teachers, secretaries, assistants, physicians, attendants, and employés as may be necessary, but the board of trustees shall prescribe the number thereof, confirm or reject the appointments, and fix the amount of compensation. (2) He shall take personal charge and supervision of the institution and of the pupils thereof, and have the direction of all persons connected therewith, subject to the order and control of said board. (3) He may, for good cause, discharge any of said persons and appoint other competent persons in their places. He shall report such changes, and the causes therefor, to the said board at the next meeting thereof ; and also the appointments made, because of such changes, for confirmation or rejection. If rejected, he shall make other suitable appointments.

He shall frequently inspect all parts of the establishment, and take the most efficient, or even stringent, measures for enforcing neatness, order, and regularity in all departments. And it shall be his duty to discharge immediately any person employed who shall appear inefficient, neglect allotted duties, or manifest a spirit of insubordination.

The following reply was received from the School for Feeble-minded Youth, at Fort Wayne :

There have been no rules adopted. The law is so plain and straightforward that it is not susceptible of misunderstanding. It has been lived up to in letter and spirit. The theory upon which the trustees act is that the superintendent shall be held to the strictest account, not only for his own behavior and successful work, but for the character, fitness, and success of every subordinate. Hence, they have nothing whatever to do with appointments or removals.

In the Indiana Reform School for Boys, at Plainfield, "all rules are made by the superintendent and approved by the board of control, leaving these matters entirely with the superintendent."

Customs governing appointments, etc.—The president of the Indiana Reform School for Girls and Woman's Prison, Mrs. Claire A. Walker, writes :

During the fifteen years that I have been connected with this institution, appointments, removals, and promotions of officers and employés have always been made irrespective of politics. Perhaps this is largely due to the fact that, as women, we have no politics. That factor has never entered into the management of the institution, and no doubt this has been greatly to the benefit of the institution.

It is to be noted that for twenty years the board of managers has been composed of women, and that every person connected with the institution, excepting the engineer, has been a woman.

The blank form of application used by the Southern Indiana Hospital for Insane contains the question : "What is your politics ?" An officer explains to us that this "is asked merely that we may keep the appointments equally divided between the parties." This would appear, therefore, to be rather a *bipartisan* than a *non-partisan* method of appointment, such as is contemplated in the law which says that only qualification, merit, and fitness shall be considered, and political beliefs or affiliations shall not be taken account of. At any rate, this is the view of another superintendent, Dr. S. E. Smith, of the Eastern Hospital, who, writing of his own institution, says :

A bipartisan management, applying other than to the organization of the board, is only one step in advance of the partisan plan. No recognition of political faith should be made by the appointing power, and the superintendent should never know the poll of his institution. It is my custom to furnish the leading political parties with the names of the legal voters and give them opportunities to make a poll of the voters on the condition that under no circumstances must the result be revealed to me, directly or indirectly.

The blank used by the Institution for the Education of the Deaf for applications contains a long list of questions, but no reference whatever to political affiliations.

The reply to this question by Alexander Johnson, superintendent of the School for Feeble-Minded Youth, is as follows :

The custom governing appointments has been to consider solely personal merit and fitness for the place. The judge of this merit and fitness has been the superintendent. Having complete authority gives him so deep a sense of responsibility that it is extremely unlikely any consideration but the good of the state, as represented by the best possible conduct of the institution, should govern him.

While fully believing in the method of competitive examination, wherever possible, so far this has not seemed practicable in this institution. In the peculiar work which we have to do, the personal equation is of so much value that it seems difficult to devise a theory of examination which would result in giving us the help we need. Practically, we employ our help in extremely subordinate positions to begin with, and promote those who prove themselves fit in the most severe of competitive examinations, namely, that of a close oversight of their daily work and conduct.

In the Reform School for Boys "merit alone is the basis of appointment to positions, and merit alone as to the tenure of such employment."

The practice in these matters at the Eastern Hospital for the Insane is admirably described as follows, by the superintendent :

The medical superintendent appoints all subordinates, assigns them to duty, and reports his action at the next regular meeting of the board of trustees for confirmation. An applicant applies to the medical superintendent and is furnished with a form of application, which must be filled in his own handwriting. From the references furnished, *confidential* inquiries are made concerning the applicant's character, habits, and qualifications. General letters of recommendation or petitions are not considered. Personal interviews are requested and usually obtained. When a vacancy occurs, if it cannot be filled by a promotion, the applications are examined and the applicant appearing best qualified for the position is selected. This selection is made without regard to the time of filing the application and without any limitation whatever, except a preference for residents of the state. If, however, a non-resident has the highest qualifications, he is appointed.

A member of the board of trustees under no circumstances indorses an application for employment.

Promotions are made whenever practicable. It is always preferred to fill the higher positions from members of the service, and thereby recognize faithfulness and efficiency.

Nepotism and favoritism are forbidden.

The power of discharge belongs to and is exercised by the medical superintendent, and his action is reported to the board of trustees. From the action of the medical superintendent there is no appeal. Violation of regulations, use of intoxicants, immoral conduct, incompetency, and neglect of duty are causes for removal.

These replies doubtless represent fairly the conditions existing in the institutions of the state, though there may be some variation in the practical execution of the rules. We were personally informed by the assistant superintendent of one institution that political influence had "everything to do with appointments" to subordinate places. We can hardly believe that these words mean all that they appear to, but when the trustees and superintendents are not sincere believers in non-partisan management, they will, of course, fail to execute it in an ideal manner.

Local sentiment on the subject.—The sentiment in favor of non-partisan management of these institutions has undoubtedly advanced greatly in Indiana within the past decade. It is nothing short of remarkable. Those now in control of the state institutions are, in the main, in thorough sympathy with the movement. The effort of some political leaders to restore the old conditions met with vigorous protests two years ago, from so numerous and from such influential quarters that the effort was quickly abandoned. Dr. Jos. D. Rogers, superintendent of the Northern Indiana Hospital for Insane, who has been for nearly twenty years continuously connected with some one of the hospitals of the state, and who therefore has been the witness of the change that has occurred, writes:

The policy above referred to has very general indorsement in all classes of society, and the more influential party leaders uniformly express satisfaction in being exempt from the responsibility of partisan management of such institutions.

The *Indianapolis News* of September 6, 1897, in commenting on the rules adopted by the Institution for the Deaf to insure and promote the merit system, said: "In a word, the institute is conducted on purely business principles, without any relation whatever to politics. It has taken many years and many bitter experiences to bring the state institutions up to this high level. Ten years ago the partisan system was in full tide . . . . It will be impossible ever to revert to the old system . . . . The people, too, have got hold of the principle that these institutions should be managed for the sole benefit of the inmates . . . . It is a step that will not be retraced. The progress is both real and permanent."

The superintendent of the Eastern Hospital writes: "The local press and influential citizens, without regard to party, support the non-partisan management of this hospital." And all the replies received from those connected with the state institutions agree in saying that the prevailing sentiment and influence now support the merit system. Yet it must be remembered that it was only by the most vigorous efforts on the part of the friends of the merit system that some of the leaders of the dominant party in the last legislature (1897) were dissuaded from taking a long backward step in this regard. This possibility still exists, and to ignore it is to incur a danger. ·The vigilance of the friends of non-partisan control cannot be relaxed.

The following suggestive statement by Mr. Alexander Johnson of the way the merit system should be administered is of value, as calling attention to a possible danger.

It is possible to carry out some details of the merit system in a way to make the management of an institution extremely difficult. For instance, when a board of complaint can exist in an institution, composed of *three subordinate employés*, to whom other subordinates, who may be discharged for incompetence, may make their complaint, and to whom the head of the department must give reasons which are satisfactory for discharging an insubordinate or incompetent official, it is evident that discipline cannot be maintained as it must be in an institution where large numbers of feeble and helpless inmates are cared for. I have been informed that such a board of complaint or supervision exists in the post-office department of this city. I can only say that it would be impossible to conduct an institution for feeble-minded, a hospital for the insane, or a state's prison upon any such basis. Nothing is more necessary than that the superintendent shall have the peremptory power of removal of any of his subordinates, although it is also necessary that the reasons for the exercise of such power shall be stated in writing to a board of trustees, or some other body which is superior to him.

Miss Mary T. Wilson, president of the Indiana State Conference of Charities, writes:

I believe I have seen more harm come from personal favoritism and nepotism during the years of my connection with public institutions than from political preferences. This phase of the matter might be considered with great profit. Nothing so destroys the discipline of an institution as these two causes. Politicians have put no more incompetent persons on our pay-rolls than have clergymen and other good citizens who push an applicant through sympathy or other sentimental reasons. The merit system, honestly and conscientiously carried out, is the best safeguard against political influence and the no less harmful one of personal favoritism.

Our conclusion must be that of one of the superintendents: "I know no instance of the failure of a careful and painstaking management under the merit system."

County and municipal charities and corrections.—The conditions of management in the local charitable and correctional institutions are very different. The chief exception to the general rule of political management is the case of the orphans' homes, of which there are about forty in the state. Some of these are conducted by societies, some by church organizations, but most of them are owned and controlled by the counties. The secretary of the Board of State Charities says: "It seems that generally, even where the homes are owned by the counties, the matrons are not selected on account of political considerations."

Boards of children's guardians exist in at least two of the large cities of the state. They were evidently intended to be non-partisan, and have been so managed. Inaugurated largely through the efforts of Oscar McCulloch, it could hardly have been otherwise. From a report sent us by N. A. Hyde, president of the board of Marion county (Indianapolis), we take the following:

The board is appointed by the judge of the circuit court and reports to him. The board appoints the matron and assistants, who hold office while performing satisfactory service. There are no written rules of administration. Appointments are made solely on grounds of personal fitness. No influence of party nor favoritism is known in the administration. No trace of partisan spirit has ever appeared in the board.

In these cases the merit system may have been easier to apply, both because the officers are generally not voters, and because the boards are mainly under the control of women. In all other kinds of local public charities the election is along political lines. The 1,016 township trustees, who act as outdoor relief officers, are thus chosen. It is frequently charged that party advantage determines some of the relief. A prominent politician informs us that control of the office of trustee is looked upon by party leaders as being of the highest political importance. He suggested that a comparison of the relief granted in election and non-election years would show that politics is a large factor. There are no statistics as yet available over a series of years making the comparison possible. Over a third of a million dollars are annually distributed through the agency of the trustees for outdoor relief; nearly half as much additional is expended for this purpose by the county commissioners. Fortunately a number of these officials are men of high integrity. For men who fall below that standard the pressure of political influence to use the opportunities of the position for party advantage must be tremendous. The law of the state does not make the receipt of outdoor relief a bar to the suffrage, and the twenty thousand adult male paupers are thus in many ways a source of political corruption.

Every one of the ninety-two counties of the state has a poor-farm, or county asylum. The superintendent is, so far as our pretty extensive information indicates, always selected from the dominant party, that is, by the majority of the county commissioners. It is considered a part of the duties of the superintendent to see that the inmates vote for his party. There are nearly two thousand such voters in the state. In those counties where the political parties are of nearly equal strength the change of superintendents is frequent. Many county asylums have undoubtedly been very badly managed, but it is conceded that on the whole some improvement has been made in this respect. Some of the present incumbents have taken a most commendable interest in the work, both of the National Conference of Charities and Correction and of the Indiana State Conference of Charities. Vast room for improvement remains, however, in most of the counties, and the merit system in these institutions seems yet a long way off.

There are but few public hospitals in the state. The City Hospital at Indianapolis is the most prominent, and it is under political management and control.

With reference to county and municipal institutions of correction and restraint the tale is soon told. They are all under political management. The work of the Board of State Charities in visiting and inspecting them has had a helpful influence, but there are the usual and universal marks of political control. The complaints are not of political favoritism in the treatment of prisoners, though such cases may occur. The faults are frequent changes, inexperience, unfitness of attendants, general laxness. It is, perhaps, inevitable that small institutions, not justifying the employment of specialists, should continue to have many of the faults here found. At present, however, the difference is slight between the smaller and larger cities, in this regard.

We will conclude the consideration of the whole subject with the words of Mr. Alexander Johnson. He says in a letter to the committee:

I believe that without an enlightened and vigorous public sentiment the very best scheme will go astray. It is a commonplace that the stream cannot rise higher than its source, and I do not believe any adroit machinery will secure good and honest government for a nation of tricksters and thieves. Hence, I believe that every effort should be made to enlighten the public mind, and especially should faithful service of the state command public approval from the reformers.

THE NORTHWEST.

From the great Northwest no details of value have come. A witness from Nebraska testifies that civil-service reform has yet work to do in those new lands. "The customs governing appointments, removals, and promotions in these state institutions are, unfortunately, under the principle that 'to the victors belong the spoils,' and not in accordance with the fitness and qualification of the party. When there is a change in the politics of the administration, there is a complete change in all these places of public trust." Another writes of state institutions: "The test for appointments is somewhat political. There is no competitive examination. It is thought best by those most interested in these institutions that they should be removed from political influences as far as possible."

THE PACIFIC COAST.

CALIFORNIA.

The only state on the Pacific coast for which our correspondence furnishes evidence is California.

Professor Carl C. Plehn expresses the judgment :

Almost all appointments in California outside of the university and the Deaf, Dumb, and Blind Institution are made for political reasons. It is, however, not often that this method of appointment is so abused as to result in serious harm. . . . . No local sentiment on the subject of appointments has ever been given expression to my knowledge during the last five years.

Another person in good position to know the facts speaks very strongly of the unfit appointments in several of the state institutions, and declares that the partisan politicians have prevented the organization of a state board of charities, lest it might uncover the abuses. "As for town and county jails, and lock-ups, they are very, very bad, and contrast unfavorably with those of eastern states."

A correspondent says of a city and county hospital :

Since the members of the board . . . . owe their positions to one or the other of the political parties, they are expected to consult the wishes of the political managers in making all appointments. . . . . In case a political appointee is flagrantly unfit for the position given him (which not unfrequently happens), he may be removed, and his placed filled by an appointee chosen by the board with reference to his professional fitness and not his political influence. While the present board may have backbone enough to thus ignore the politicians, previous boards have not had such independence, and consequently the hospital was under the complete sway of the spoilsmen. Disputes between the administration and impertinent, often ignorant, politicians seriously interfere with the discipline and effectiveness of the staff. The patients must suffer.

In a reform school for boys the radical and irrational changes seemed to destroy the contentment and order of the community. Ninety-five boys out of 365 escaped in less than a year. The present board is not necessarily inferior to the former, but the partisan interference has crippled their usefulness and undermined discipline.

The same correspondent cites evidence that in the asylum for the insane the attendants were assessed 3 per cent. of their salaries for election expenses.

The last legislature of California brought the hospitals for the insane under the merit system. In other state charitable institutions there is no scheme of examinations, though they are generally non-partisan in management.

The penitentiaries are non-partisan in their wardens and most of the subordinate officials; but still, I believe, there is no regular civil-service administration. The same wardens have been in charge, regardless of the politics of the state, for many years. The reformatories are somewhat partisan. The jails and houses of correction are, as far as I have observed, strictly partisan. The sentiment of intelligent and responsible people generally is that in all these institutions appointments should be made for merit only; but there has been no public expression, as far as I can recall, in regard to the city and county jails. It is a sad fact that they are generally considered as very proper and necessary spoils for the political victor.

THE SOUTH.

The following information may be taken to represent a very general condition of administration and the current of opinion favorable to civil-service reform.

KENTUCKY.

Few reports were received from Kentucky, but few were needed to answer the main inquiries. Political management appears to be the practically general rule. The penitentiary is under the direction of the Sinking Fund Commissioners, who are *ex officio* the governor, attorney-general, auditor, and treasurer. The wardens and deputy wardens are appointed by the governor; guards by the commissioners. For the Lunatic Asylum and the Feeble-Minded Institute the superintendents are appointed by the governor; employés and attendants by the superintendents, in conjunction with the board of commissioners. Schools for the blind, and deaf and dumb are officered by boards of directors, who are appointed by the governor. Evidently here the evil lies not in the method of appointment so much as in the custom of treating the institutions as political spoils.

The message of Governor William O. Bradley to the general assembly in 1898 compliments the condition of all the state institutions. A general reduction of their expenses took place in 1896, as compared with 1895. He states that they "are well officered, and are moving along harmoniously and successfully, the management comparing favorably with any period in the past" (for the first time the Republican party, that of the governor, is in control of the state). Further on in his message, however, the governor implies that under no management as yet have the administrations of these institutions been as efficient as they should be. He says:

The charitable and penal institutions of the state should be placed on a thoroughly non-partisan basis, and officers appointed on account of their especial fitness and experience. Such a system prevails in many states of the union, and in every instance has proven most beneficial. Charities should not be used to promote political ends.

No particular party is responsible for the prevalence of the rule in Kentucky, but each and all are to blame for it. By reason of this system, at the end of every four years, the successful candidates, desirous to reward their friends, turn out of office those who have acquired experience and substitute others to whom the duties are entirely novel. . . . .

For years there has been no complaint in this state concerning the management of charitable and penal institutions. How could it be expected that these great interests should thrive as they deserve when inexperienced men are so frequently in control? If a change is to be effected, someone must inaugurate the movement; and, with the interest of the state far above party ties, I earnestly call your attention to this great wrong, and recommend its discontinuance.

He then suggests the appointment of three non-partisan commissioners on the Board of Charities and Corrections — experienced men, to be selected, if necessary, from any state in the union — whose business it should be to look after the selection of officials and to care for the financial and other interests of the institutions.

Commenting further on the present *ex officio* political commissions directing the institutions, he says that their other duties are onerous—

and their proper discharge demands their whole time and attention. The consequence is that, in attempting to discharge the duties of the two positions, they will necessarily neglect the duties of one of them. Besides, they have so many friends to reward that, in the exuberance of their gratitude, infirmities of applicants are overlooked at the expense of the state.

We will add the following opinion from P. Caldwell, superintendent of the Industrial School of Reform at Louisville :

The sooner all of these public institutions are taken out of politics, the better. General fitness should alone be considered in selecting men or women for this work. The spoils system in state institutions should be relegated as a thing of the past. It will take time and hard knocks to change this villainous custom, but at least it is a service to get people to think about it.

TENNESSEE.

Political appointments are also the rule in Tennessee. Directors, trustees, etc., are appointed by the governor and confirmed by the senate. "Appointees are generally (we surmise that it is uniformly) of the same political faith. Politics enters into a great majority of appointments. A competent observer says that politics or favoritism, seldom merit or fitness for the place, determines the selections. There are no tests or examinations in competition. The sentiment of political leaders favors the existing conditions."

There is one hopeful feature in the situation. In 1895 a Board of State Charities was established, and is composed of representative men. Not more than four of the six shall be of one political party. The influence of such a board will be wholesome toward the formation of a sound sentiment on the subject of the management of the state institutions.

NORTH CAROLINA.

There is no civil-service system in the state. Very little influence has been exerted by politicians in partisan appointments heretofore, except as regards the offices of steward and engineer. A strong public opinion has insisted upon the retention of superintendents and assistant physicians who had shown themselves effective and trustworthy. Recently an attempt was made to displace occupants of offices in state institutions, but the court decided cases against the legislature.

In regard to the state penitentiary, the system of appointment as a reward for political services has gradually gained entire control, with the exception of the position of architect and warden.

County officers and employés under control of the commissioners are invariably elected for political reasons, but there is a reasonable attention paid to qualifications and general character.

The State Board of Public Charities reports defects in management to the governor, and if admonitions are not heeded by county officials, they are handed over to the solicitor and judge of the district for prosecution. This promotes improvement.

It must be acknowledged that, while appreciating certain points of advantage in the system of civil service and appointment by competitive examination, public opinion favors appointment for political reasons. But when technical fitness is especially required, it is generally recognized, and position conceded upon grounds of qualification.

SOUTH CAROLINA.

Our correspondent believes that in case of poorhouses, state asylums, and prisons, "the best men obtainable are appointed to these positions. In this part of the South there is virtually only one political party, the Democratic; sometimes we are divided into different factions, but even then I do not think appointments are made in penal and charitable institutions solely upon factional grounds." He does not mention any civil-service rules or methods of selection and promotion.

VIRGINIA.

As a usual thing, appointments are confined to persons members of the political party in power, but personal merit and fitness for the place usually have the desired weight. There are no examinations and tests in competition. Local sentiment is not sufficiently crystallized to be of definite weight.

LOUISIANA.

Dr. Searcy said before the New Orleans Conference in 1897 :

By far the most objectionable and baneful influence that injures state care of the insane comes through politics. This is the same old hydra-headed specter that has impaired city and county care, only it is in a broader, higher field, where it has not quite the same advantage. "To the victors belong the spoils" is never so baneful a political maxim as where the spoiling affects as sacred institutions as insane hospitals.

In the southern states there has been considerable political constancy in the state governments for a number of years, or until quite recently. Whatever objection has been found to hospital management in this section, it has not had its origin in frequent political changes, and, as a rule, the stability of control has, that far, had a salutary effect.

In the past two or three years, in the state governments of some of the southern states, this baneful principle has shown itself. In one or two states clean sweeps of the insane hospitals have been made, along with everything else, for political reasons only, and the thing is partially accomplished, or threatened, in other states. This practice is growing and has a most ominous future.

This meeting could not exert a more salutary influence than in the direction of a protest against the plunder of such institutions for political purposes.

Dr. Searcy quotes the following sayings of General Brinkerhoff:

As a hospital flag on every battlefield of civilized warfare is an emblem of neutrality and a sacred guarantee of protection to sick or wounded men, so, and more so, in political warfare the asylums for our dependent and defective classes should be sacred from the attacks of contending parties.

Generally the appointment of the members of the boards of control of state hospitals for the insane, and other state beneficiary institutions, is made by the governor. Sometimes, if not often, he is influenced by previous political obligations, necessitated in his election, so that he is unduly constrained to appoint persons who are not acquainted with or interested in the duties of the place or are inclined to control such places, not for the good of the *patients*, but for selfish or political purposes.

CONCLUSION.

There is a very general conviction among superintendents that an examination is superfluous. A very capable manager of a boys' reform school in Pennsylvania writes:

Appointments are made on the ground of efficiency, not by written examination, but after personal interview and careful investigation of the antecedents of the applicants by those who are responsible for their conduct. No political or other influence seems to be exercised in this matter.

Another able superintendent (of Wisconsin) states that four of the five members of the board must be of the same political faith as the executive.

The board never experiences any trouble in finding competent men *of its own political faith* (*!*) to fill these positions.

These replies show how far our most intelligent men are from appreciating the elementary principles of a permanent and professional service.

Another says:

I do not agree with Hon. Philip Garrett in the idea of any fixed rule for appointing subordinates in the public service. I believe in selecting competent and conscientious superintendents, hold them accountable for results, and give them the helm. An excellent cook may not know the multiplication table, and I have one now who writes her name "X."

But this excellent gentleman proves in the very next sentence of his letter that his principle breaks down, and that to "give the superintendent the helm" is really to make him a slave of his political masters.

When leaving ———— I appealed to the president of the board of trustees to disregard clamor and keep good people at work without regard to political convictions. I argued at some length about the duty involved; but the gentleman looked up after I had finished and said: "Mr. ————, I quite agree with all you have said. It is beautiful in theory, but the fact is, we Pops are hungry. I believe in the doctrine that 'to the victors belong the spoils,' and we will gather them as fast as possible."

In his further disclosures of experience in a western state, he shows that so long as a superintendent has the power to select subordinates without examination or legal rules of promotion, he at once is liable to attack from members of the board on behalf of personal or political friends. The preliminary free competitive examination is the only device ever invented to protect the responsible administrator from his friends and relations. It brings conduct under the reign of law and eliminates caprice and private interest.

It is apparent that the fundamental principles of the civil-service reform are but dimly apprehended even among honest and capable officials educated under the spoils system. The ideas which have become familiar as the alphabet in English and German administration seem to us foreign. This is entirely clear from the cloudy definitions given to the "merit system" by many upright officers who really imagine they have adopted and are living up to the most modern ideals of appointments.

C. R. HENDERSON.

THE UNIVERSITY OF CHICAGO.

SEMINAR NOTES.

THE METHODOLOGY OF THE SOCIAL PROBLEM. DIVISION I. THE SOURCES AND USES OF MATERIAL.

PART II. THE LOGIC OF THE PSYCHICAL SCIENCES.

CHAPTER II.

DEVELOPMENT OF THE PSYCHICAL SCIENCES.[1]

Like mathematics and natural science, the psychical sciences have developed out of philosophy. Ethical rules which, derived from observation of human conduct and its motives, were deposited in ancient proverbial popular wisdom, together with a body of naïve reflection about the general correlations of natural phenomena, constitute everywhere the beginnings of scientific thought. At the outset, science is dominated by interest in the cosmological problems. The consequence was that for a long time the science of the psychical nature of *man* — psychology — which, we would say, should have been posited as the basis of all other psychical sciences, was entirely neglected. That is, psychology was not made into a distinct and independent realm of research. Meanwhile it was treated either as a branch of natural philosophy or as an appendix of metaphysics. It has followed, in fact, that the development of the psychical sciences has not proceeded from psychology, but from the cultivation of special fields of research, whose coherence in a totality analogous with that of the natural sciences has but just been apprehended. Accordingly the phrase "psychical sciences" (*Geisteswissenschaften*) is of recent origin. It seems to have occurred for the first time in the attempts, in the early decades of this century, to find a comprehensive classification of the sciences.[2]

[1] The remainder of Part II, *i. e.*, chaps. 2–5, is an epitome of Wundt, 2. Bd., 2. Abth., pp. 1–51. *Cf.* WARD, *The Psychic Factors of Civilization.*

[2] Thus BENTHAM (*Chrestomathia*, 1829 (?)) divides all sciences into *somatology* and *pneumatology;* AMPÈRE, *Essai sur la Philosophie des sciences*, Paris, 1834, into *cosmology* and *noology.*

Hegel designates as *Geisteslehre* — theory of spirit — the whole body of philosophy which corresponds with the *Geisteswissenschaften* — psychical sciences — (*Encyclopädie*, III, § 386).

John Stuart Mill seems to have been the first to put alongside of the logic of the natural sciences a logic of psychical sciences.

The first phenomena of psychical life to arrest attention were the reflex actions of consciousness upon the conduct of peoples. Yet the early historians were in bonds to that cosmological conception which traced psychical facts to an external order of nature that manifested itself in the acts of avenging and rewarding divinities. The stories told by Herodotus are in this vein. Thucydides began to set an example of positive criticism of tradition for the sifting out of fact from fiction.

Side by side with historical investigation, *political philosophy* (*Staatslehre*) developed. Though necessarily a branch of psychical science, it long remained, and is still, in close union with general philosophy. In the ethical precepts which tradition ascribes to the earliest sages of Greece, there is a combination of practical wisdom with the stern political consciousness which dictated the law-giving of the time. Neither here nor in the Pythagorean school, in spite of the profound philosophical discernment, is there any profound scientific reflection upon ethical and political tasks. In the fifth century B. C. the Sophists assumed the functions of public political teachers. They brushed aside as useless all speculations about the connections of natural phenomena. They devoted themselves to the service of training individuals for the needs of practical, and especially political, careers. Herewith was aroused an interest in the theoretical problems connected with rhetoric and politics. In the question whether the chief products of associated life, language, morals, state, are derived from *nature* or from *statute*, the antithesis for the first time appears which up to the present moment has divided thinkers about society. The foundation of the Platonic *academy* marks a turning point in the development of psychical science. In it—probably from Pythagorean influence—there was, for the first time, an attempt at scientific organization of research, of which our modern academies are in some sense copies. Even Plato, however, was too much influenced by the Socratic impulse for reform to perform the proposed task with empirical precision and patience. Not how things *are*, but how they *should be*, was the thought of his *Politics*. Hence, with Plato, politics, like physics, had not so much the task of comprehending the *real* world as of constructing an *ideal* one.

Aristotle was really the first to demand in all fields of research comprehensive collection of empirical *facts* as a preparation for general philosophical reflection. His doctrine of the state, in common with that of Plato, was accordingly his abstraction from the circumstances of his time and environment, based, at the same time, on comparatively thorough knowledge of the past. In the Platonic academy the principle of the division and correlation of labor in the sciences seems to have been carried into effect only in mathematics and astronomy. In the Aristotelian school, *per contra*, the plan of minute investigation was applied to all branches of natural and psychical science. The teacher of Alexander the Great not only had animals from all zones for his zoölogical study; he was the first scientist who could command a great collection of books, from which he and his pupils could extract deep knowledge of the literature and philosophy of earlier times. From these sources, too, came his *Politics*, the ripest of his works.

New light has been thrown upon the method of Aristotle's researches by the latest discovered of his writings, the fragment upon the *State of the Athenians*. This is evidently only a section of a collection of studies, and possibly a study for the *Politics*. It shows how influential Aristotle's work has been to observe that, with modifications needed after the Greek city states had passed into national states, and after representative systems were developed, Aristotle's classification of the forms of states is still more generally accepted than any other.

At the same time, the Greek philosophers had failed to give profound study to *law*—that system of standards which is a most important factor in associated life. We owe the development of this branch of psychical science to Roman genius. The Romans entered upon this work virtually without reference to *philosophy*, but solely from utilitarian motives of the most practical order. Yet Greek philosophy, and particularly that of the Stoics and of Aristotle, has left evident traces of mighty influence even on this matter-of-fact work that began deliberately in the first century before Christ, and ended in the codification of Justinian, in the sixth century after Christ.

The development of another branch of psychical science falls in the same period of Græco-Roman culture, viz., *philology*. This division of knowledge has had most important influence upon the progress of all the other psychical sciences. The Sophists had developed interest not only in eloquence, and so necessarily in language, but also in grammatical and even etymological questions. All this was without signs of scientific method, however.

Aristotle and his school planned, and to some extent executed, systematic studies in literary history. Then the method developed in the Græco-Roman era. The chief motive of this study was the desire to carry over into the life of the time the spiritual products of a past that had become strange. Such a motive is especially potent in a time of conscious transition, and accounts for the further pursuit of these researches during the Renaissance. At this time philology stood at the summit of its influence. It roused even philosophy and natural science to new life.

All other psychical sciences have had their origin in comparatively recent times, as particular branches of history, politics, jurisprudence, or philology. Then gradually, in the course of the seventeenth and eighteenth centuries, a separate field of investigations was set off from political philosophy, viz., the *philosophy of industry*, or, as we now say, *economics* (*Wirtschaftslehre*). This pursuit stood toward politics in much the same relation of philology to history. It dealt with relations that political philosophy had ignored, viz., the production of goods, and traffic in commodities and in money. But as this field was restricted, and yet evidently related to another territory that had not been explored, its cultivation necessarily soon led to examination of contiguous ground, viz., wherever the relations of life are susceptible of numerical expression, a method called statistics began to be applied. Thus there began to be tabulated facts about the ages of the population, marriages, births, deaths, occupations, crimes, arrests, punishments, conditions of dwellings, and so forth. All this is intended to be material for a science of population (demography), which some of its representatives regard as the inclusive science of society. This science again stands in close relationship with history, since the mental traits of peoples and the conditions of society rest on historical development, and at the same time are determining factors in this development. Consequently *history* and *social science* came to assume the form of parallel, closely related general sciences, each of which includes a number of minor special sciences, the separation of which has been dictated by considerations of practical convenience. Among these the clearest are philology, as distinct from history, and economics and jurisprudence, as distinguished from general social philosophy.

An analogous process of division occurred in philology. In the Alexandrian period its interest was wholly in the literary monuments of ancient Greece. During the Renaissance the view was broadened to include not merely the Roman literature of earlier times, but, through the influence of the Old Testament, Semitic culture in general began to be taken into account. At the same time the *art* of antiquity began to be studied by the side of its languages and literature. There consequently begins an extension of philological pursuits in two directions: first, the philology of separate languages and literatures; second, comparative philology, which has given the impulse to a number of related sciences — comparative mythology, jurisprudence religion, etc. In all these there is, of course, inevitable reciprocal reference between each and history. It is to be remarked in this connection that the *comparative* element has relatively larger scope in those cases in which the psychical products concerned are most spontaneous and unreflected, *i. e.*, in a certain sense *natural* products, *e. g.*, in the case of language, myths, customs, and, to a certain extent, *law*.

On the other hand, the more distinctly historical (genetic) treatment prevails in proportion as the objects concerned are of arbitrary and even individual origin — as in the case of art and works of literature. Hence, we have history of art and of literature, but no science of *comparative* art or *comparative* literature. In the former cases we have comparative philology and the history of language, comparative mythology and the history of mythology, etc.

The nature of the researches involves, moreover, the more general character of the comparative sciences, since they concern themselves with a wide territory, if not with *all* the psychical products of their class, while the historical sciences may confine themselves to the narrower examination of a *series*, or even a series within a series. For instance, the history of the Indo-Germanic languages is one of the widest fields that can be covered by a historical language science. On the other hand, we have the history of the

German language ; or, narrower still, the history of low German, or of the high German, or even of the dialect of a given region. While, then, the subdivisions so derived may be regarded as parts of philology in the broadest sense, they are, of course, not less special fields of *history*. Besides these historical species, there are other kinds of historical science with more direct historical pedigree ; thus, derived from political philosophy and jurisprudence, we have *constitutional* history, history of law, economic history, and history of economic theory. These divisions, which are concerned rather with the *conditions* out of which historical occurrences were derived than with the events themselves, have been subsumed in recent usage, with history of art and literature, under the still more comprehensive term *Culturgeschichte*, history of civilization, and this has been put over against *political* history.

In this way our own century, particularly, has developed a host of special psychical sciences. To such an extent is this true that our age perhaps ought to be known, not as the era of *physical* science, but as the era of *psychical* science. In general the physical sciences are pursuing the paths marked out for them in the seventeenth century. The *psychical* sciences, on the other hand, since the comparative method has been adopted, and since the historical treatment of problems has been applied to all sorts of material of psychical interest, have undergone such thorough renovation that its present import is measureless (*i. e.*, the significance of the changes which these psychical sciences have undergone is too great to be comprehended).

This mushroom growth of the psychical sciences has made it virtually inevitable that the logical organization and coördination of their multiplying disciplines should be far behind that of the natural sciences. The chief responsibility for this condition of affairs — besides the relatively recent development of the last mentioned comparative and historical specialties — must be borne by two circumstances.

First, the interlacing of these different subjects is vastly more manifold than in the case of the natural sciences. To such an extent is this the case that there is little agreement in any of these departments as to where the one science ends and the other begins. More than this, it is doubted if fixed boundaries can ever be drawn between many of the chief of these sciences — *e. g.*, philology and history, political and cultus-history, or even between social philosophy and history.

Second, there is up to date, for the psychical sciences, no such fundamental discipline as *mechanics* for the natural sciences. Mechanics is fundamental *not merely* in furnishing the universally applicable presuppositions by means of which all physical, chemical, and biological problems are to be solved, for there is still room for differences of conception and opinion about some of these fundamental notions ; but, still more, mechanics furnishes the *method* by means of which the special problems had to be treated.

Within the psychical sciences we are far from recognition of a fundamental science of a parallel sort. If we were to collect opinions today among workers in this field, about the sciences which they are disposed to put in this fundamental position, we should get the most incongruous and contradictory testimony. Some would say philology, some history, some anthropology, some sociology. Not less irreconcilable are present opinions about the relation of psychical sciences to philosophy. We all know — or ought to — that both natural and psychical sciences had their origin in philosophy. Since history, philology, jurisprudence, and social science have, in part, branched off from philosophy, in part have come into existence by combining philosophical doctrines with certain rules of practical life, has not philosophy served its purpose, and must it not now retire from influence? Or, has philosophy, in contrast with the psychical disciplines, a new aim, and is its mission under the changed circumstances as important as it was in the beginning?

There is no sign of agreement about this question. Even among those who do not wish to do without philosophy in connection with the psychical sciences there is uncertainty and disagreement about the rôle that philosophy should assume — whether *within* or outside of the psychical sciences, whether in superiority or subordination to them. Hence we shall examine more closely the relations of some of the psychical sciences to each other, and then their relations to philosophy.

CHAPTER III.

THE SYSTEM OF PSYCHICAL SCIENCES.

Without doubt the system of psychical sciences has its most evident sanction in the fact that the individual members which we reckon in the system actually exist, viz., history, philology, economics, jurisprudence, etc., and that from the beginning they have been in close relationship with each other. Although the comprehensive term "psychical sciences" is of recent origin, it is a fact that the sciences so designated constitute a combination of related provinces, like the combination composing the natural sciences, or like the various branches of mathematics. Such a combination does not exclude relations between the members and other sciences lying outside the combination, just as such relations exist between mathematics and natural science. The closer relationship *within* the combination will manifest itself in the fact that between the coherent but independent sciences of the combination there will appear intermediate territories, about the precise assignment of which there will remain uncertainty ; and, further, that for one of these provinces sometimes the methods and sometimes the results of the related provinces are indispensable.

At the same time, the fact of the actual existence and intimate interrelationships of the psychical sciences does not suspend the necessity of investigating the *reasons* for their inclusion in the systematic unity, and also the reasons which made them actually branches of the same genealogical tree. This obligation is the more imperative, because, in spite of the actual intimacy of relationship, it has been long in storming the perceptions of persons most concerned, and, furthermore, doubts still exist as to whether more effective combination is possible through the mediation of a fundamental science, and, if so, which of the existing sciences may best serve that fundamental purpose.

Since now the actual historical development of the sciences is subject to disturbance from numerous accidental influences which obscure the logical coherence, it is desirable to pursue investigation of the profounder grounds of this coherence, without reference to the historical limitations. In other words, it is best to keep in view merely the actual problems of the separate disciplines and to find, if possible, the trait that is common to them all, in consequence of which they have instinctively, rather than deliberately, manifested unity.

The peculiar difficulty of this question evidently consists in the fact that we cannot deal with concrete phenomena, like the objects studied by natural science. We cannot point to objective space-relations which demonstrate unity of basis. On the contrary, psychical phenomena, or rather phenomena which cause us to conclude that psychical processes have occurred, are presented to us in connection with objects which belong to the material world, and so far fall within the competence of the physical sciences. No analogous difficulty exists in the natural sciences, because in their realm phenomena are endless, in the study of which we have no occasion to assume any coöperation of psychical factors. In consequence of this we are in a position to abstract the psychical element from the whole, for the purposes of natural science, in the relatively few cases in which there is coöperation of psychical facts. This abstraction is justified by resigning the study of these coöperating psychical elements to disciplines lying outside the natural sciences.

The things studied by the psychical sciences, on the other hand, are always at the same time natural objects. The abstraction permissible to the natural sciences, and even necessary to them within the limits which they set to themselves, is neither permissible nor possible for the psychical sciences. If man and the other beings endowed with some measure of mentality were the only objects in nature, natural science would then be in a situation like the actual status of psychical science, *i. e.*, natural science might begin with animal physiology instead of with the mechanics of ponderable bodies. Under that supposition it is more than doubtful if the separation of natural and psychical science could have occurred. At all events, the division would have been different from that which actually exists. We avoid this difficulty, if we start with the supposition at the basis of the pretentious classifications of Bentham and Ampère, viz., that there are (*a*) corporeal and (*b*) psychical objects, constituting contrasted material for scientific division, like the plants and the animals, or like vertebrate and invertebrate animals. But *there are no psychical objects*, in the same sense in which we speak of *natural* objects. There are only objects which present phenomena that lead us to posit psychical antecedents.

At this point Comte lost his bearings. He made the psychical sciences coördinate with the special natural sciences. His thesis was *that the psychical sciences differ from physiology only in the fact that the latter studies the living organism as an individual, while the former, viz., history, economics, jurisprudence, etc., deal with a multitude of similar human organisms.*[1] This view makes sociology merely the highest member in the scale of natural sciences.[2] It makes sociology differ from the natural sciences, not in principle, but only in consequence of the greater complexity of the phenomena with which it is concerned.

This contention of Comte is a negative variation of the same philosophy that divided things into bodies *corporeal* and bodies *psychical*. Since there is no such thing known to our experience as independent spirits, separate from bodies, Comte denies the possibility of relatively independent psychical sciences. The denial would be pertinent if it were necessary for psychical sciences to have for their subject-matter objects absolutely distinct from natural objects. Since such objects do not exist, while, on the other hand, the separate psychical sciences do exist, the valid conclusion is rather that this whole division of the sciences, in correspondence with a supposed separateness of *objects*, is untenable. It is as though we should say that we cannot have a science of geometry separate from crystallography.

The one motive which, from the beginning, has determined the division of scientific labor has been the discrimination of the different classes of *occurrences* given in our experience. In some cases the reference has been to *objective* traits of those occurrences, in others to *subjective* valuations of those occurrences. Only after the discrimination of specific occurrences had been followed by a grouping of certain important classes of occurrences, was the attempt to distinguish definite *objects* made into a subsidiary principle for the determination of scientific territories, *e. g.*, in natural science, and in the shape of subordination in mathematics and the psychical sciences. In the latter stage, particularly, the increasing importance attributed to the *derivation* of the objects is really another manifestation of the tendency to make occurrences, rather than physically separate entities, the basis of distinction.

Let us take the point of view that the original distinction of division in the subject-matter of experience must have its ground in *differences between classes of occurrences*. If we try to account for the cleavages between sciences from this point of view, it is entirely intelligible that one and the same entity may be subject-matter for quite different sciences. Each grand division of scientific labor, *i. e.*, each "science," rests on an obvious abstraction from the material given in experience. This abstraction is then exploited to the utmost extent of logical elaboration. In this logical process we dis-

---

[1] *Positive Philosophy*, I, secs. 1–3 and sec. 46.
[2] Spencer has been charged by De Greef with coming to this result.

sect the actual unity of the given facts, in a more or less artificial way, in order to arrive at determination of the abstract conceptions involved in the facts. These abstract conceptions are then combined as nearly as possible into a report of reality.

By this sort of isolating abstraction, *mathematics* — *e. g.*, as a system of conceptions and operations which have their basis in the *formal* qualities of real things — has separated itself from the "*real sciences*" (*reale Wissenschaften*) or "natural sciences," which deal less with the *form* and more with the *content* of observed reality.

Within the circuit of research about the actual, the so-called *natural sciences* have reserved a field for themselves, consisting of those facts which may be reported by the senses, *in so far as they may be reported by the senses.* This limitation of territory is tenable if we keep in mind that the restriction relates, not merely to the *objects* themselves with which natural science deals, but also to the *aim* of natural science.

This aim is reached when it has answered the questions : *How do given data of sense perception arrange themselves in harmony with the entire collection of our sense perceptions ?* Hence natural science, when legitimately acting, calls to its assistance only natural phenomena in explaining other natural phenomena. When natural science is compelled to use hypotheses of natural objects or occurrences which are not discoverable by the senses, the device is still with the intention of bringing objectively sensible phenomena into logical arrangement.

We may accordingly define natural science briefly as *an arrangement of sense perceptions so that they do not contradict each other.* We might then describe the psychical sciences in parallel fashion, as *an attempt to arrange psychical manifestations so they do not contradict each other.* But it is not difficult to see that this description and this antithesis are inadequate and inexact. They rest on a false analogy. The old psychology used to speak of "the objective and the subjective sense," "*das äussere and das innere Sinn.*" There are no "objects of the subjective sense," as the concept was used in the old psychology, but only objects of the objective sense.

Accordingly, the events which are assigned to the "spiritual world" are events which are contained in the physical, sensible world. Even for psychology, therefore, the notion of a pure psychical science, devoted solely to so-called *subjective* experience, is not exact, for no psychology can entirely ignore the physical conditions and manifestations of psychical life. How much less completely may such abstraction be carried out with problems of history, philology, economics, jurisprudence, etc.! All of these get their peculiar reality by virtue of the existence of the physical world, and of the conditions which it establishes for human life.

In other words, here is the evidence in support of the assertion that there are for our experience no psychical objects, as such, but only occurrences which we refer to psychical *factors*. With these psychical factors, so far as our experience goes, the physical factors are indissolubly bound. Even the assumption of psychical *occurrences* is, therefore, an *abstraction*, in which we disregard the accompanying *physical* occurrences. To be sure, the assumption of purely *physical* occurrences is a similar abstraction, made easy for us by the limitations of sense perception. In our *own selves*, however, this fictitious antithesis of the physical and the psychical *meets* in a reality which is wholly neither. In man physical and psychical occurrences shade off into each other in ways which defy abrupt separation. The suspicion is, therefore, well grounded that neither a purely physical nor a purely psychical world has anywhere a real existence.[1]

It remains, then, to discover whether there are qualities inherent in some parts of observable experience which make them distinguishable, though not distinctly separate, from the so-called natural phenomena. It is evident, from the foregoing that discrimination from the physical is not an affair of direct perception, through the use of one set of perceptive organs for the one kind of object, and of another set of perceptive organs for the other kind of object. That was the fiction behind the alleged antithesis of "subjective and objective perception." The distinction is reached rather by *reflection* upon the *content* of experience. Clear realization of the logical elements of this reflection may arise very late. Hence, science instinctively presses on in advance of consciously organized method, and, in a measure, anticipates results which must be verified and justified later. It is to be further said that we have no right to expect discovery of an exact balance of contrasted traits between the physical facts on the one hand, and psychical facts on the other ; *i. e.*, we are not to expect that physical facts will possess a certain number of traits not found in the psychical, and psychical facts a corresponding number of traits not found in the physical. It will be enough if we find, *on one side*, traits which do not appear on the other. This is the actual situation. Moreover, it is the situation that should be expected, for the very reason that the psychical world is not in external antithesis with the physical world, but the psychical is everywhere a something added to the physical, and we cannot *think* it sundered from the physical.

Here, then, appears the best division line between the realms of the physical and of the psychical. In fact, there are *three* marks which we always refer to the psychical working in the physical. These three traits always work together. The one which is foremost in a given case joins presently with the others. The three traits are (*a*) *valuation*, (*b*) *design*, (*c*) *volition*.

(*a*) The element of *valuation* is the most primary mark of the psychical in contrast with the physical. Natural science deliberately ignores valuations. Wherever they emerge in connection with natural science they are extraneous and gratuitous ; phenomena regarded as phenomena are neither good nor bad, neither beautiful nor ugly. Even their utility, outside of their own process, is

[1] *Cf.* MÜNSTERBERG, "Psychology and the Real Life," *Atlantic Monthly*, May, 1898, p. 608.

not called in question by theoretical physical science. On the other hand, *the psychical world is the world of values.*

These may occur in the most multiform qualitative modifications, and in the most various degrees. Sensuous, æsthetic, ethical, and intellectual values are merely the most evident groups, between which there occur innumerable transitions and combinations. A common feature, however, is that they move between contrasted extremes. They thus point to *feeling* as the subjective condition of their existence. In a judgment of values the action of the *feelings* comes first as a rule, and combines presently with intellectual weighing of *quality* and *degree* of value. In the psychical world, everything has its positive or negative, its greater or lesser, value. Apparent exceptions mean only temporary suspension of motives or of judgment.

(*b*) Every valuation rests implicitly, however, upon the positing of a *purpose*. *The psychical world is the realm of purposes.* Hence, natural science is obliged to reckon with the notion of purpose, as a phase of causality, wherever psychical facts coöperate in the production of physical objects or processes. (Thus, mechanics in the case of machines, and biology in the case of propagation among the higher order of animals. For what is the machine designed? What are the elements of human sexual selection?)

(*c*) Formation of purpose is finally the outcome of *volition*. Not mere presentation of a conception to the mind makes it into a purpose, but *volition*, which is in closest connection with valuation. Feeling, from which valuation springs, may be described as incipient volition. Physical nature is without volition in its units. *The psychical is the realm of will.* This proposition requires more emphasis than the preceding.

Conception (*Vorstellung*), thought apart from will and the adjunct purpose and valuation, is simply a phenomenon of natural science. Intelligence is the unification of volition and conception in knowledge and in self-control of action. Intelligence is, accordingly, a mark of the psychical, in so far as it organizes the elementary traits of *volition*, *purpose*, and *valuation*. The further consideration must here be added that the objects of scientific attention gain in importance in proportion as these purposes become more *significant*, and the valuations connected with these purposes become more *comprehensive*. In the light of this consideration, it is plain that the deliberative action of the will is the final criterion of those phenomena which are the peculiar subject-matter of the psychical sciences. Hence, *man* is the wellnigh exclusive subject-matter of these sciences — not man in abstract isolation from surrounding nature, but actual human beings.

In short, the division line between the psychical and the natural sciences must be drawn *where man, as a willing and reflecting agent, begins to be an essential factor in phenomena.* All phenomena in which this factor may be disregarded fall within the territory of the natural sciences. It need hardly be repeated that even the objects in which the psychical sciences find these phenomena become material for the natural sciences when the non-psychical factors of these phenomena are the questions at issue.[1]

Individual man as thinking and willing agent is the first datum of psychical science. Without knowledge of man, the individual, problems presented by combinations of men would be forever insoluble. Knowledge of the individual must, moreover, begin with concrete and individual experiences. For general application, however, only so much of these is pertinent as has its source in universal human qualities and impulses. The individual, not *as* individual, but as *genus*, is the first matter of interest in psychical science. The scientific discipline whose part it is to consider man in this universal form is psychology. In this view, psychology must have the importance of a fundamental science. More than this, *individual* psychology, as above described, is at the same time *general* psychology.[2]

This position is by no means universally accepted among the workers in psychical sciences. A chief reason lies in the fact that, up to date, official psychology has rendered but slight aid to the sciences of humanity. Meanwhile scholars have not tried to get along without knowledge of *man*. Instead of waiting for the psychologists to furnish it, however, they have foraged for it themselves. As in politics, so in the psychical sciences, everybody has supposed himself to be familiar with the fundamental principles concerned. It has also come about that men who did not call themselves psychologists have been collecting psychological material, and have stored it in their museums and libraries under all sorts of labels, from anthropology to philosophy and religion.

It is further true that many of the professional psychologists have not yet freed themselves from the channels of a *priori* philosophy, and have consequently offered speculation in the place of science. These facts explain why psychology is not accorded the place in science which belongs to it. They do not justify further uncertainty about the order of dependence among the materials out of which a system of psychical sciences must be constructed. With philosophy of any a *priori* sort, psychology has no more and no less to do than *physics* or *history*. The composition of our *conceptions*, the develop-

[1] The foregoing distinctions come to have most radical importance whenever we take up questions which have both physical and psychical relations. For instance, in my seminar course upon *social teleology*, or the systematization of judgments about the *value of conduct*, we have to start with a review of so-called *evolutionary ethics*. We find that most of the men who have been dealing with what they call evolutionary ethics have not been in the ethical field at all. They have been studying problems of animal *instinct* or of reflex actions in animals and man; *i. e.*, matters of physiological psychology; immensely important in themselves, but not having the ethical bearings that have been supposed. This supposition has been possible because there has been no such precise limitation and definition of ideas as the foregoing.

[2] Here we sharpen the perception that not only the physical base of De Greef's chart, but the psychical base, in the personal units, must be understood as introduction to social action.

ment of the will, the constitution of the *feelings*, the connection between them and other facts of consciousness — all these are separate problems of experience, not less than the phenomena of heat and light or groups of historical events. Metaphysics is no more and no less demanded in systematizing the one sort of phenomena than the other.

It must not be forgotten, however, that, for reasons already noted, psychology must necessarily form a sort of intermediate territory between the natural and the psychical sciences. In much of its work the methods of natural science will be applicable. In other parts the view points of psychical science will fix the fundamental rules. In consequence of this close relationship to both natural science and psychical science, special psychological sciences have already developed as mediators on the one side or the other. Thus, *psycho-physics* or *physiological psychology* is concerned with the reciprocal relations of corporeal and psychical processes, while *folk-psychology* deals with such facts as language, customs, etc., which grow out of the association of many individuals in closer or more comprehensive unities. In this connection *pedagogy* must be named. Its basis is almost entirely psychological. Its aims, however, are ethical, and its material is found in every science.

We have, then, these general psychical sciences which we may properly call the psychological sciences. Then the special psychical sciences so often mentioned, viz., history, philosophy, jurisprudence, economics, etc. The latter are concerned with certain phases of psychical development, or with certain psychical products. They consider these either in their general relations or in particular historical or ethnological isolation. There inevitably arises between them meanwhile a reciprocal relationship, which as yet is barely recognized, between these special researches and general psychological disciplines, notably folk-psychology. The more special researches bring material for the more general, while the latter help to make interpretation of the former possible.

In classifying the special psychical sciences we may adopt either of two points of view. *First*, we may follow the example of natural science in distinguishing and separating processes from objects. Natural sciences are accordingly (*a*) *explanatory* (physics) or (*b*) *descriptive* (zoölogy). We should have, then, among the psychical sciences (*a*) the *historical*, or narrative, and (*b*) the *systematic*, or those that attempt to interpret. Or, *second*, we may start with the view that the subject-matter of the psychical sciences is partly *fugitive phenomena*, in the shape of passing incidents, partly correlations that are relatively *permanent*, and may thus be regarded as components of a general societary condition. The former of these modes of division may be the more logical. The latter is closer to practical requirements. Existing sciences easily conform to it. Each systematic discipline has its historical parts.

Accordingly, it is best at present to divide the special psychical sciences into two great classes of (*a*) *historical* (genetic) sciences and (*b*) *societary* (structural) sciences.[1]   In the former group belongs, with the historical disciplines in the narrower sense, *philology;* in the second group, *ethnology, economics, jurisprudence,* and *sociology,* in various of the senses in which the latter term is today used to mean something less comprehensive than social philosophy.

Here it may be noted that at present sociology, when understood in the larger sense contrasted with the above, seems to occupy a place in the second group corresponding with that of universal history in the first group. Sociology depends for material upon the special investigations of the other members of the group. Sociology, in turn, must organize those materials. Hence sociology is today, in fact, scarcely distinguishable from the history of civilization, on the one side, or, on the other side, from special attempts to organize interpretation of social relationships, such as general economics.

Since all societary conditions are products of historical development, we must advance the next step by treating of the logic of the historical sciences, as introductory to the logic of the social sciences. The close connection of the territories expresses itself in the fact that each social science includes one or more historical disciplines, *e. g., economics,* the *history of economics,* and *economic history.*

CHAPTER IV.

RELATION OF PSYCHICAL SCIENCES TO PHILOSOPHY.

Since the psychical sciences are coördinate with and supplementary to the natural sciences as organizations of experience; since psychology is the most general member of the class of psychical sciences, it goes without saying that the relation of psychical sciences to philosophy will be *like* that in the case of psychology and the natural sciences. No scientific philosophy can do without these divisions of experience. They, however, may address their own proper tasks, without any further philosophical assistance than the assumed veracity of the general system of perceptive agencies through which reality is reported in consciousness.[2]

The more they do this, the better it will be for their proper offices. This freedom from all sorts of metaphysical anticipation in dealing with the data of experience by no means involves perpetual prohibition of scientific thought upon relations transcending experience, particularly teleological foresight. (*a*) To demand that science shall *begin* without philosophy is not to demand that it shall end without philosophy. On the contrary, (*b*) *positive treatment of reality always sooner or later begets a philosophy from within, if it is not suppressed by arbitrary imposition of a philosophy from without.* In the last two remarks (*a*) and (*b*) is a clue to the radical difference between the obsolescent and the adolescent philosophy. The old philosophy was a Noah's

[1] This is a variation of COMTE'S *Descriptive and Statical Sociology* and WARD'S *Statical and Dynamic Sociology.*

[2] *Vide* contents of WUNDT, *Logic of Physics and Chemistry*, chaps. 2 and 3.

ark, in which all the knowledges that were to be saved must be able to find a place. The new philosophy is a growing city, which enlarges its borders and increases its means of sheltering the people who demand accommodation. Or, more literally, philosophy is today not a dictator of science, but a collector and organizer of science. Philosophy has to do with the proximate results of sciences what each science has to do with the proximate results of its own kind of observations, viz., get them so clear that they do not contradict each other, but rather complement each other.

In accordance with the remark above to the effect that science is *endogenous* philosophy, we find that all sciences which have become somewhat mature have preserved and sharpened the distinction between their strictly positive elements and the *hypothetical* elements, which also have a place in the final form of the science. Thus in physics we have the more *positive* elements summed up in the formulæ of *inertia* and *energy*, united with the more *hypothetical* elements summed up in the theorems about the general properties of matter (indestructibility, transference of energy, etc.).[1]

While the parallel between natural and psychical sciences in their actual development is not absolute, it is obvious, *first*, that philosophical theses up to date play an important rôle. The historians cherish the fond illusion that with them the dominance of *a priori* philosophy is ended. But if we look closely at the present discussions about such subjects as the nature of *law, state, industry, society*, we soon find that most of the disputants are following the tactics of mediæval philosophy, while armed with the verbal weapons of modern knowledge. When the historians declare that the philosophy of history is a humbug, they mean that they do not accept some other man's philosophy of history. They do not mean that they themselves have no philosophy of history. Every modern historian who is large-minded enough to advance from facts to the *relations* of facts has his own philosophy of history, whether he has formulated it or not. The difference between natural science and historical science, in this respect, is simply that in the former a certain minimum of fundamental philosophy is agreed upon and accepted. In the historical sciences men are all at sea, but each historian supposes himself to be in the path of the trade winds. The present situation among the historians is precisely like that among the scientists at the beginning of the modern era. We may, therefore, anticipate like approach to common fundamental philosophy of history and of society.

Elements of such common philosophy will be discussed later. At present we are concerned with the kinds of philosophical presuppositions with which the psychical sciences start. They are a sort of guiding maxims. They must everywhere be brought to bear on the special problems of psychical science. They are drawn from the arsenal of philosophy, because they anticipate every analysis of individual cases. They have consequently occupied the skirmish line of positive science in its war of liberation against speculative philosophy.

[1] *Vide Logic of Physics and Chemistry.*

We call these maxims *principles* of *discovery*. They are of pre-scientific origin, as above noted. They are nevertheless indispensable to science. No one of them alone is sufficient for the valuation of psychical facts. Together they constitute an indispensable machinery of reflection upon reality. They serve their purpose by setting research in motion.

In a similar way sociology, in its most general and formal shape, as we are now getting it organized, will be virtually a set of guiding principles for each social science.

CHAPTER V.

PRINCIPLES OF DISCOVERY IN THE PSYCHICAL SCIENCES.

A. THE PRINCIPLE OF SUBJECTIVE JUDGMENT.

The guiding principles of psychical science are, in one respect, different from the analogous presuppositions of physical science, viz., the former are much more evidently true within their own field. Such controversy as has been waged in physical science about the presence or absence of certain fundamental relations has in psychical science never occurred; *e. g.*, *mechanical* causation *vs.* *purpose* in nature. There has been practically no dispute about the validity of judging others and their actions by ourselves; or about the supposition that the events of the psychical world are not merely performances of individuals, but that the latter are themselves, in part at least, products of the psychical environment in which they appear; or, finally, that individuals, like communities, are determined in some degree by nature. All these positions have been so generally accepted that they may almost pass as self-evident truths.

This situation is in close connection with the character of immediate reality which belongs to psychical knowledge, in contrast with our knowledge of nature. All the above mentioned heuristic principles of the psychical sciences are essentially psychological maxims, since they are fundamental to all psychological judgments, particularly those of practical life. Nevertheless, even here, controversy over ways of looking at the material is not wholly wanting. This contest refers, however, not to the applicability of these maxims, but to the *extent* of their application. Over the question of the weight to be allowed to each principle in proportion to the rest there are views so extreme that the one or the other of these principles is treated sometimes as of no consequence whatever, and, on the other hand, as the determining factor. Instead of tending toward settlement, this difference seems to be growing more pronounced than ever, perhaps because men are just becoming distinctly aware of the points of difference. This appears most clearly in the case of the first principle to be considered, viz., that of *subjective judgment*. In spite of its self-evidence, it is capable of most divergent interpretation, so far as the kind and degree of its application are concerned.

Wherever we are conscious of phenomena outside of ourselves, which we can associate with remembered psychical experiences of our own, that subjective experience of ours is the most obvious measure of the observed phenomena. The primary discrimination of the psychical is always instinctive rather than deliberate (*planmässig*). It is judgment from a *total impression*, not from clearly conceived special marks. It may, therefore, err in many ways by making the boundaries either too broad or too narrow. For the first rough impression, however, our own subjective experience is a measure. In case the objective circumstances only partially coincide with the subjective experience, we are at once ready to coördinate them with subjective experiences none the less, since these are most familiar to us, and the easiest to posit. (So early men interpreted natural phenomena as acts of will.) Hence the most natural of the two errors just mentioned is that of too generously extending the realm of the psychical. This error made mythology, etc. (Giddings' "consciousness of kind" is an example of excessive assumption of similarity to our own processes in primitive processes.)

Hence, progressive scientific reflection is the more inclined to err in the other direction by requiring as credentials of the psychical an amount of intellectual performance which is possible only at a high stage of psychical development. To find the mean between these extremes is a task requiring patient and judicial research, or long social development.

After such progress, naïve and instinctive assumption of the psychical in objects passes into conscious and systematic interpretation of the subject into the object. This first in psychology itself, by taking past states of the subject's consciousness as objects of contemplation, and later by extending the same observation to other persons. The other psychical sciences use this process in three forms : *First*, they judge persons acting with reference to the historical and social influences which they set in motion. *Second*, they judge by the subjective standard collective occurrences, which must be referred to the coöperation of several persons. Here the search is for the psychical influences which acted on the individuals, and for the causal relations of the same to the total occurrence in question. *Third*, psychical products of every sort — literary, artistic, historical monuments, etc. — are subject to judgment by the same measure. Whether the authors are otherwise known or not, the manner of men that they must have been is conjectured by reflecting what states of consciousness in ourselves would have been potent to produce such results.

Problems of this sort, in which the psychical character of a creator must be construed from his works, are evidently the most difficult. This appears in notable controversies over the question, which of certain otherwise known persons were the authors of certain works — the Junius letters, the Shakespearean plays, the Psalms, and many paintings and sculptures. Also in the questions about the individual or plural authorship of many works — the biblical writings, the Homeric poems, the Indian epics, and many modern inventions, *e. g.*, the sewing machine. This form of judgment is of the most frequent application in criminal prosecutions.

Errors in the application of the principle of subjective judgment are easy and obvious. To guard the use of the principle, these errors must be made conspicuous—a sort of logical rogues' gallery. They are in principle chiefly two:

First, assigning the activity of mind concerned in judging to the objects judged. Thus is produced a tendency to one-sided intellectual explanation of psychical facts.

Second, attributing the individual traits of the *person judging* to the object judged. Hence follows the tendency to refer objective psychical facts entirely to given individuals, and further the tendency to a one-sided individualistic conception, and, furthermore, negligence of the variability of men along with changing circumstances — *i. e.,*‚the *un*historical judgment of times and persons.

Of these errors, the *first* — one-sided intellectualism — is perhaps most common. It appears in the attempt to account for everything — the most important developments of psychical life — morality, law, religion — as exclusively the products of conscious calculation of utility. In explanation of historical events the attempt is frequent to make them appear as products of deliberate intention. In reality, logical reflection had little to do with them, but they came from the most confused mass of *feelings*. Or, how often, when there was evident intention, an entirely different end was reached, on account of the intervention of secondary motives ; and from the outcome we reason back to the existence of primary motives which were in reality not present. This is illustrated by a passage in Tolstoi's *War and Peace*. He argues that history has imported intentions into the minds of both French and Russians that never existed. He shows how all the events of the year 1812, up to the burning of Moscow, might have occurred of necessity, without any of the systematic planning on the part of any of the actors which has been attributed to them. He declares that the Russians had no sort of desire, as has been supposed, to lure the French into the depths of Russia. They rather did all they could to stop them on the borders. The Russians charge the French, and the French the Russians, with the burning of Moscow. The city was burned, says Tolstoi, because, abandoned by its inhabitants, occupied by soldiers who were heedless in handling fire, it was in a situation in which any wooden city must burn.

Frequent as these errors are, it is usually not observed in connection with them that *they often spring from the very condition in the interpreter which is essential to calm and judicial judgment.* The calmer and cooler the interpreter is in his estimate of events, the more inclined he is, unless fortified by previous training in overcoming the tendency, to imagine that the actors whom he is judging were in the same deliberate mood. He consequently attributes to definite and clear-cut aims and intentions what was due to a multitude of previous incongruous impulses.

The *second* — the *individualistic*— conception is so clearly connected with the subjective criterion that it inevitably colors first judgments of objective psychical events. To unsophisticated reflection the circumstances and destinies of peoples always seem to be the immediate outcome of the acts of a few eminent men, and this impression is confirmed by all success in putting such acts of individuals in a connected historical series. This impulse holds its sway even in advanced stages of reflection. It is much easier to grasp certain relations of an individual to events than to bind together the innumerable influences that make a historical incident. Hence the reduction of the individual element in any historical reaction to its actual proportions is one of the most tremendous tasks presented to the investigator, and it demands the most mature self-restraint against inveterate psychical habit.

But the principle of subjective judgment impels not merely to the subjectivizing and individualizing of objective events, but further to the projection of the *observer's own* subjective state into these interpretations. That is, the tendency is to constant anachronism in judgment, against the fact that the person judging is a *later* product than the people observed, and to a considerable extent, therefore, a *variation* from their type. Men of past times are, in general qualities, like ourselves, but not in those minor modes of thinking and feeling which make the final arbiters of acts. It is, therefore, a matter of long training and experience to learn how to judge the content of minds distant from us by the lapse of time.

The one-sidedness and the errors thus pointed out constitute a large part of what we mean by the *unhistorical* view of things. Every judgment is unhistorical which uses the standard of one age as the interpreter of another.[1] Yet not history alone, but ethnology, economics, jurisprudence, and æsthetics, suffer from the same fault of trying to make our own time a sufficient measure of all times. The fault of *un*historical judgment is, consequently, only a special case under the more general error of *defective objectivity*. Hence the principle of subjective judgment implies as correlates and correctives other principles of discovery. In fact, the principle of demand for objectivity, particularly that historical facts shall be seen in the light of their own time and culture, involves the following principle, viz.:

B. THE PRINCIPLE OF DEPENDENCE UPON THE PSYCHICAL ENVIRONMENT.

This principle seems to be the direct antithesis of the preceding. The former principle called for translation of the observer and interpreter into the consciousness of actors to be judged, in order to trace events from those actors' states of consciousness. This principle calls for attention to the psychical *medium* in which these actors moved, in order, so far as possible, to trace influences upon events from this medium. This apparent antithesis, however, is only in appearance (*i. e.*, between principles A and B).

The psychical medium itself is made by the combined minds of many individuals. To understand it and them, we have to use the process of subjective judgment. Hence, this principle, after all, means only a change of focus for

[1] A capital instance is pointed out by JHERING, *Der Zweck im Recht*, I, 246.

the first — an extension of its scope, so that it shall try to take in not merely a few individuals, but all the psychical factors that contribute to the influences of the times under investigation.

Thus the individualizing tendency finds the very widest field in attempting to solve the problem of the spirit of a given time by the biographical method. This method is adopted by historians who believe in the "great man" theory. Nevertheless, even such historians emphasize, and perhaps unduly, the psychical *medium* which cannot be traced to distinct individuals.[1]

This characteristic of the biographers is closely connected with their attention to the *individual*. Every attempt to realize the course of the individual's development tends to call up the external conditions under which this development occurred. The closer we get to the personality of people in the past, the more we must come in contact with the outward circumstances which are the mold as well as the product of their personality. Hence it comes about that the one-sidedness which at first springs from the principle of subjective judgment presently finds its corrective in *complete* study of the most *appropriate* object for the application of the principle, viz, the *individual*.

Since the principle of dependence upon the psychical environment leads to extension of subjective judgment so as to cover many individuals who are in relations of psychical reciprocity, we reach judgments about many psychical influences which are not individual in their nature, or at least cannot be traced to definite persons. Language, customs, beliefs, constitute a psychical atmosphere around every man. Without these, no man would exist in his own peculiarity. These may not be precisely estimated, yet they may weigh more in determining each individual character than any of the special influences. Besides these there are many circumstances, which are, in the last analysis, of an individual sort, but their individual source cannot be traced ; so that they are parts of the general medium which surrounds the individual. Such, in a measure, is, *e. g.*, in America, the *Monroe doctrine*. Such was the *Washingtonian temperance movement*, which has become a permanent factor in American thought. Such was the *Channing* influence, which has affected all *American theology*, etc. In each of these instances, and in connection with everything that has occurred within the scope of these influences, an explanation of events must of necessity involve some sort of appraisal of the relative effect of the universal and of the particular factor. The true explanation will exclude neither of these influences, but will find

[1] For example, Lehmann's biography of Scharnhorst enters into an extensive description of the martial spirit of the time, which, according to the author, surrounded his hero with molding impressions *from the cradle.* Hayms (*Hegel und seine Zeit*) traces the scholastic, and at the same time *streng architektonische Darstellungsform* of the Hegelian logic to Hegel's early occupation as a teacher in the *Gymnasium* and to his life in Nürnberg—"*eine Stadt, wo er von Bau- und Skulpturwerken deutscher Kunst umgeben war*" ! !

actual proportions. Corresponding with these two elements of reality there has arisen a division in psychical science, viz., into individual psychology, dealing with individual psychical facts, and folk-psychology, dealing with psychical manifestations pertaining to associated life. As the former is the general basis for psychical sciences, the latter is the special preparation for those studies which deal with the phenomena of associated life.[1]

The demand for the reduction of psychical facts to individual causes is, therefore, even in the case of the special social sciences, only in so far capable of fulfillment as it is in folk-psychology, in the case of the general products of associated life which it treats, viz., language, morals, etc. The psychical forces which work in the community must conform to the occurrences in the consciousness of individuals, and no psychical potency can operate in the community which does not first have its seat in the individuals composing the community. The community, nevertheless, brings into existence new conditions for the operation of these forces. There result peculiar phenomena. To understand them, both the individual and the general factors must be considered.

This brings us to definition of the *relation* of the two principles of *subjective judgment*, and *regard for environment*. The former is the more fundamental. It is presupposed in the application of the second. The latter is not less essential, and it may not be omitted even from interpretation of the individual, because human *community* is a fact as primary as the existence of individuals.

The principle of dependence on the psychical environment, in attempting to supplement knowledge of the conditions immanent in the individual by knowledge of the influences that work upon the individual from without, leads further to a *third* principle, which must be applied along with the foregoing in order to exhaust the empirical conditions under which psychical events occur. In extending the principle of subjective judgment to examination of the environment, we necessarily emphasize the physical phase of the environment. But observation of the environment involves further discrimination of a psychical and a material external world. These two are in reality as inseparable as are the psychical and the physical nature of the individual. In both cases marks of difference are so obvious that the necessary distinction, once made, is too useful to be rejected. Hence we find the concluding principle of discovery in the psychical sciences in the principle of the *natural limitation* of psychical occurrences.

C. THE PRINCIPLE OF THE NATURAL DETERMINATION OF PSYCHICAL OCCURRENCES.

Since man is a part of nature, he is subject to the influence of physical nature in all that he thinks, feels, and does. This is none the less true of

[1] Hence the courses given in the University of Chicago by Professor Thomas (folk-psychology) and Professor Vincent (mass-psychology).

human association. The organization of human groups rests on psychical conditions. Social organizations are, accordingly, never merely psychical, but always at the same time physical.

As psychical influences may be divided into the internal and external, so, also, may the physical. In the case of psychical influences we have found that it would be partial and unscientific to consider the one side without the other. In the case of physical influences the internal may often be viewed separately from the external. In psychology, for example, the physical element to be considered is almost exclusively that of the individual. So, also, in the sciences which deal chiefly with the performances of individuals, such as pedagogy, and the investigation of æsthetic, ethical, and intellectual productions, in which studies the psychological standpoint is decisive. The principle of the *influence of external nature* is effective, on the contrary, in study of *common* achievements and *societary* conditions and occurrences, *i. e.*, in history proper as well as in the social sciences. The former of these principles, severely followed, leads to a materialistic psychology, the second to a materialistic theory of history and society.

It is to be noted, however, that the two forms of materialism are not necessarily inseparable. The second does not bear the name with full justice. We may believe in a domination of human culture by external material facts without on that account going over to materialism, in the psychological sense. On the other hand, we must not overlook the fact that between the two conceptions, and in proportion as they are one-sidedly held, there is a strong affinity. The psychological materialist is always inclined toward social materialism. The social materialist is less certainly, but still generally, predisposed to psychological materialism.

The natural environment has first an *æsthetic*, second a *teleological* influence. The æsthetic effect is through the conceptions and feelings, and then the qualities of character produced by constant and repeated contact with natural objects. In the last century this influence was credited with exaggerated importance by many philosophers (*e. g.*, Herder, *Ideen zur Philosophie der Geschichte der Menschheit*, Buch VIII., 11). Doubtless this influence, though always real, has *a kind* of diminuendo value, from the stages of culture that produced mythologies and folk-lore to the more matter-of-fact and unsentimental present. The case is different with the *telic* influence of the environment. Nature is always a positive factor in men's plans, fixing certain tasks — like preserving the dykes in Holland, or the levees of the Mississippi, or the clearing of snow from the roads in our own latitude in winter — and challenging to certain kinds of endeavor for improvement of the conditions of existence. The most systematic and objective study of man in relation to the task of adapting himself to natural conditions has been made in various forms by the *economic* sciences.

ALBION W. SMALL.

THE UNIVERSITY OF CHICAGO.

REVIEWS.

The Logical Process of Social Development. A Theoretical Foundation for Educational Policy from the Standpoint of Sociology. By JOHN FRANKLIN CROWELL. Henry Holt & Co. Pp. ix+358.

THE author aims to solve a double problem, viz.: "First, to determine in a theoretical outline the nature and logical method of the social process; second, on the foundation of these results to determine the normal educational policy for the community" (Preface, p. vi). The present volume is devoted to the first part of this task, viz., "that of arriving at such an interpretation of the logical process of social development as will serve for a conceptual outline of social policy in which education may take its normal part in national progress." A second volume is promised, applying the results presented in this book to actual conditions. The author's presentation of "the sociological basis" is in the following form:

Dr. Crowell's work deserves very much more attention than it is likely to get. His powers of analysis and abstraction are evidently of high order, but nothing less than overpowering sense of professional duty will induce anybody to attempt playing the Bowditch to his Laplace to the extent of puzzling out the meaning to the end. This is unfortunate, for the author uses some of the most timely conceptions in sociological theory, and there is hidden away in the excessively obscure form of the book some extremely useful discrimination.

To begin with the least essential fault, it is to be regretted that the author has not been more precise, or at least more perspicuous, in the use of terms. He uses many familiar words in more than one sense, and just when it is necessary to be sure of their exact force they apparently mean something to the author which they do not suggest to the reader; or they stand for one of several concepts, and the reader cannot tell which of them to select. If I am not mistaken, this is true of the very important term "type." It sometimes means a real correlation of persons. Again it means a subjective construction of represented persons into conceptual relations. Still again it means a potential, but unimagined, arrangement of persons. Possibly it has other shades of meaning. At all events, I fail to see how either of above senses fits in certain cases.

The same might be illustrated in the case of the term "social." It is so liberally used that I find myself unable to associate distinct notions with it in a particular case. For example, on p. 14, the word is used as substantive or adjective eight times, and I find it impossible to frame a theory that will give to the term the same force in each instance. In connection with the first line of p. 19, the query arises, "Would the phrase 'social man' mean the same thing if the attributive were omitted?" If not, where have we a specimen of "man" not "social," and are there enough of him to form a class which we must exclude from sociological consideration? The next sentence seems to imply that "social man" and "man" are interchangeable terms for the *genus* that sociology studies. This conclusion is reinforced by the assertion (p. 49):

Sociology has nothing to do with any human being except as he is or has been a member of a collective kind, and being or having been such, it has everything to do with him that in any way gives him a social value.

Not least among the difficulties of the reader, therefore, is his perplexity about when to interpret the term "social" as adding something to a proposition, and when to treat it as dead wood. What precise content the term has when it is a meaning factor, is a question that few readers will be able to answer.

Trouble of similar sort is found with the terms "sociology" and "sociological." They have been used so liberally that clearness has been sacrificed. For instance, on p. iv, the author proposes his general question in the words : " . . . . By what *sociological* methods must we proceed, etc.?" But on p. 58 he begins to discuss "*sociological* types," and describes a *sociological* type as one of four species of "types of personality," or of "social organization." Evidently the term "sociological" has distinct intention and extension for the two uses. "Sociological" apparently means something like "progressive" in some cases; in others, "superior" (*vide* pp. 58, 62, 84, etc.).

Again, the terms "social" and "sociological" are made antithetical in some parts of the discussion (*vide* table of contents and p. 16), while they appear to have no antithetical force in other passages. This still further confuses concepts. Besides this, the terms "social" and "sociological" are sometimes used as formal and sometimes as qualitative categories. Uncertainty about the content of propositions is inevitable, and the reader's patience is correspondingly overtaxed. If the thought is precise, justice both to author and reader demands more precise expression.

There is, also, a lack of traceable coherence between propositions, in the earlier chapters particularly; and this makes it impossible, in many cases, to decide just what idea the author intends to convey. An occasional illustration would have enabled the reader to settle upon that one of alternative interpretations of abstract statements which was in the writer's mind. In the absence of such clues the meaning is doubtful. A paragraph, and then a chapter, and then another, made up of these vague and unintegrated propositions presents a problem too intricate for solution.

Perhaps the most obvious case of inexact and inconsistent use of terms is the following. The first sentence of the preface declares :

The social process in its logical character is here regarded as the process of the selective survival of *types of personality*.

The first sentence of chap. I reads :

This book is a theoretical attempt to introduce orderly arrangement into the study of the phenomena of social life by the rigid application of a single logical hypothesis — the selective survival of *sociological types*.

As a matter of course, we assume, then, that "types of personality" and "sociological types" are equivalent and interchangeable. On any other hypothesis the propositions quoted would be at variance with each other. They would be of different degrees of exactness, though not necessarily irreconcilable. It is most natural to understand them as identical. Attempting to get exact conceptions from these terms upon this assumption, we read on until, at p. 58, the author deliberately tells us that:

A *sociological type* is either a potentially normal type of personality or a theoretically superior type of social organization. . . . . It is one of four terms in the typological series.

That is, "sociological type," instead of being equivalent to "type of personality," stands for a species, while the supposed equivalent stands for the genus containing the species. No wonder that our attempt to get precise notions from the author's language has given us the impression of a wild-goose chase. After we have detected this variability of terms in a few instances, the temptation is strong to charge all further vagueness to similar shiftings of verbal usage which have escaped detection.

But the faults of style are of less importance than the faults of method. The former are individual. The latter are common to a considerable number of sociologists. Some of them, too, are making important contributions to sociology, in spite of the faulty method. I believe the present author is entitled to some of this credit, in spite of the vagaries to be noted.

For illustration of the tendency which the author exemplifies I select the following (pp. 59–60):

By whatever name it be known, this *constructive anticipation of the normally potential type*[1] is real to both logic and to life which science observes; . . . . because the process of scientific thinking is none other than this process — the application of past experience to the new conditions that arise by the projection of the observed order of events into the future. The social spirit speculates on what had better be done next. The social process answers this question by giving, in the sociological type, the next term potentially normal enough to meet the anticipated requisites of survival. Development arises from this very act of realization.

Thus the author confidently and dogmatically propounds a theory in serene disregard of the most obvious facts which confront anyone who approaches social changes from the other point of view, viz., first, observation and grouping of phenomena; second, inquiry as to what

[1] The italics in this case are the author's.

influences appear in the group or series of facts under observation. The generalization would be upset instantly by the course of English history, for example. Everybody knows that, so far as conscious and avowed aims are concerned, the look of English leaders from time immemorial has been, *in form*, backward, not forward. They have demanded "the ancient rights of Englishmen," not "the normally potential type." What wonder that "sociology" is ridiculous, not merely in the eyes of business men, but to historians and other nearly related investigators, when sociologists persist in forcing fanciful interpretations upon facts which have been more truly explained by less pretentious students?

The mistake in all this is, first, in crediting men in the past with a kind and degree of reflection upon social changes that they never bestowed; and, second, in assuming that a factor (*e. g.*, "speculative sense of the socially superior as a realizable social end," p. 60), which may, by a stretch of imagination, be traced in some past changes, is the significant and dominant influence in all changes. The credulity necessary for either assumption would be capable of taking *Alice in Wonderland* literally. Not one person in a thousand in the United States today knows what a "social type" means. Possibly one hundred in a thousand would be able to entertain the notion if it were sufficiently explained. Possibly ten out of the hundred more abstract thinkers might be capable of aiming their action toward an abstractly conceived social type. That this mental process is now or ever has been the typical, regular, usual determining influence in changing the forms of society is a supposition so extravagant that no student of history would feel safe in predicating it in full force of any single social change on a large scale. If there is a better *prima facie* case than the doctrinaire factor in the French Revolution, it does not occur to me, and I should like to see Dr. Crowell pick his way through even the more familiar records of that period, and bring his theory out intact.

When the author asserts (p. 63) that "no parliamentary discussion ever takes place without taking into account the effect of any measure on the type that normally tends to prevail," he is as near and as far from the truth as though he should say : "No fire department ever answers an alarm without taking into account the chemical relations of oxygen to the properties of other substances." The things taken account of in either instance may be translated by philosophers into terms of the relations alleged ; but to assert that they are in that form in the minds of the actors, or that the efficient motives in the minds of the actors are considerations of that order of generality, is arrant nonsense. Congressmen voted for or against forcible dealings with Spain because they wanted to avenge the "Maine," or to stop cruelty, or to remove obstacles to trade, or to secure their own reëlection. Their votes will affect future types of correlation in the United States, in Cuba, in Spain, and perhaps in the rest of the world; but that consideration of social types as types ever entered the thoughts of 5 per cent. of them is too absurd for second mention by anybody but a speculative sociologist. How can we expect to win the respect of sane men for sociology if we persist in making it a farrago of conceits that vaporize at the first contact with reality?

The method is still more radically at fault in selecting for examination purely conjectural conditions, as though they were real reactions encountered in the course of observation. The first step is, therefore, to beg the question of fact. Thus (p. 65):

> The problem then is to find, for the right grasp of the societary processes, a guiding standard or progressive point of view going before and giving precision of aim to the tendential forces, so that these various type-developing tendencies may find the forces to which they are capable of converging, etc.

Everything that the author has said up to this point makes it necessary to understand the above as though he had said expressly that the desired standard is *consciously* in the minds of effective members of society. It is, however, a plain begging of the question to proceed upon the assumption that there is any such conscious standard. The hypothesis of a "tendency-controlling criterion" is perfectly legitimate, if used as a pointer in the collection of evidence. It is entirely illegitimate when taken as an established position from which argument may proceed. Nobody has proved that such a conscious criterion exists. On the contrary, everybody who has given much attention to the facts, including the present author when in a realistic temper, doubts the wide prevalence of such a state of consciousness. A bigger book than the volume in hand could be filled with evidence against the hypothesis easier than the author could convince a jury of historians that any single case of social modification may be accounted for by the assumption. It is pure illusion to suppose, therefore, that a principle so utterly supposititious can be made a scientific basis for pedagogy or anything else. It has no feet for its own support.

It is difficult to understand how a writer so intelligent as the present author can have come to maturity in this half of the nineteenth century with so little respect for the requirements of exact science. It would seem as though he would find it occasionally necessary to drop down into the concrete long enough to find a point or two of correspondence between his generalizations and reality. It would seem likely *a priori* that he would try to discover in the course of human experience at least one specific "sociological type" for example, the use of which he might demonstrate in a single instance. If the architect of human fortunes has always been the "sociological type," it would seem as though a solitary instance at least might be specified. To inductive thinkers the name and address of a thousand such would have to be assured in order to give the hypothesis credit. The method of the author is not inductive, however, and it apparently does not acknowledge the necessity of evidence. There are hints at supposed cases in point (*vide* pp. 74, 109, 111, 154, etc.), but these are merely dogmatic illustrations, not cases critically examined in test of the thesis. Accordingly the book is full of generalizations that are true of nothing in particular.

This disregard of the canons of inductive science does injustice to the elements of truth which might be discovered by critical use of the author's postulate. "Selective transition" (p. 84) is not a factor utterly unknown in social changes. It is not present in these changes in the form and force which the author presumes. Accordingly such a writer as von Jhering has detected much more than the present author about the facts of individual contribution to social changes. Even in case of conscious societary action, the thing willed is only rarely change of type—as when a state adopts a new constitution—and in those rare instances the change is thought of as a change of type by a rare few only. The conscious end in most cases is a specific good of situation or possession. This good, when realized, may be a factor making for change of type, but this latter fact does not help the author's thesis.

Several traits of Dr. Crowell's style are exemplified in the following sentence (p. 100; *cf.* pp. 117, 154, etc.):

Personality has become what *he* is by conformity to traditional type: this factor, plus *his* impelling desires, are the two forms indicating to us what *he* tends to become.

I do not understand these liberties with the personal pronouns. To my mind no end justifies the means. The solecisms throw no light on the thought. There is a still more radical fault involved, viz., that of dealing with the abstraction, *personality*, when we ought to be studying the concrete qualities of *persons*. It crops out again in this form (p. 128):

The traditional and the adoptive types of personality . . . . become more and more complemental . . . . as the societary *process* becomes more fully aware of the potential aims comprising the social policy.

Again (p. 140):

The consciousness, among the ruling *tendencies*, of active or latent qualities or conditions incompatible with the potential type . . . . is the characteristic antinomy of this aspect of social evolution.

Again, on p. 163, "personality" and "the social tendencies" are referred to in company with, and apparently in distinction from, "the community," as being guided by synthetic *judgments* in the selection of the means of social realization, and (p. 241) we read: "Social selection may be defined as the preference of the *social process* for the type that normally tends to prevail."[1]

All this personification of an abstraction is more than a figure of speech. It may lead the persons who practice the corresponding habit of thought to ignore concrete realities and to put in their place arbitrary mental constructions. The present author has succumbed to this temptation. I might accordingly state my case against the whole method illustrated by this book by charging that it tends to substitute conventional, arbitrary, unreal concepts, as subject-matter and material for conclusion, for the real concepts that must be the subject-matter of objective science. The method is then not objective science. It is the systematization of fictions. For instance, "the type of person recognized as entitled to control in the family, the class, the community, and the nation" (p. 103). This is a philosopher's conceit. It plays absolutely no rôle in the real world. No flesh-and-blood man ever wrestles with such a concept in the business of life. We deal with individuals and concrete things and conditions. We must "keep off the grass," if the city ordinance says so; we must "move on" in the crowded street, if the policeman has orders to make us; we must pay an income tax, if it gets to be the law of the land; but it is the rare specialist only who ever thinks to generalize these incidents of life, or who discerns in them any relation to "types" of any sort. The illusion to which such writers as the present author yield is that the real world has conducted its affairs after philosophers' fashion. It is the illusion that men have had in mind, before action, the same estimate of their acts which philosophers pass after the event! It seems hardly possible that any man in his right mind could deliberately maintain that this is the case. Yet Dr. Crowell's main thesis amounts to this. Unless he holds to it in this

[1] *Cf.* use of terms "social spirit" and "social process" in quotation above from p. 59.

sense, his "logical process of social development" ceases entirely to be an attempt at genetic explanation.[1] It does not offer a clue to the actual motivation of social development. It simply shows how the course of human actions might have been recommended to the reflective in advance, if anybody had been able to see future events in the same light in which they present themselves to Dr. Crowell now that they are past.

Perhaps the thoroughly artificial character of the whole discussion is still more evident in connection with the following passage (p. 155):

The four typal principles are: *typal integration, typal differentiation, typal assimilation,* and *typal solidarity.* . . . . These principles are, therefore, the *causal relations* which sociology, like every other body of knowledge, finds it necessary to formulate.

That is, the author is not content to treat the most abstract general concepts as concrete realities. He posits them as efficient causes! Scientific examination of facts cannot, of course, come within the scope of such a method. It reduces to dialectics pure and simple. Its naïve assumption is that the categories which the mind must use in order to think the actual over again must be the factors which produced these realities (*cf.* pp. 172–3).

It may seem strange that so much space is given to a book that must be so seriously arraigned. The explanation is that the subject is important; it has received comparatively little treatment; and in spite of all that has been said, the author has made a certain contribution to the machinery of sociological investigation. If he had undertaken much less, his contribution might have been clear and available. His constant straining after expression of universalities impresses the reader as a symptom of incomplete acquaintance both with life and with science. Intimate knowledge of the relations generalized would keep most scholars from multiplying propositions that purport to epitomize all human experience. Dr. Crowell has floundered through a quicksand of speculation which he might have avoided by sharply distinguishing between a genetic explanation of society and the concepts which we find it useful to employ when we set in order and try to explain what we have learned about society. The book is the mouthpiece of "two voices;" the one trying to formulate the law of societary evolution, the other explaining "the logical processes especially appropriate for the investigation of social phenomena" (p. 5).

[1] This applies with equal force to the substance of Book III, *The Sociological Axioms.*

Most of the time the author vainly attempts to tell the two stories at once, with the result that he expresses neither correctly. If he would shake off the incubus of his genetic hypothesis, and give us separately his account of the categories necessary in critical study of social relations, the service would be considerable. He has done very nearly this in the final chapter, "The Theoretical Method of Types." It is the most straightforward analysis in the whole book. It is a pity that the entire discussion is not equally lucid.

ALBION W. SMALL.

American Contributions to Civilization, and Other Essays and Addresses. By CHARLES WILLIAM ELIOT, LL.D., President of Harvard University. New York: The Century Co.

SUCH force, ripeness, strength, and sanity as America has developed must be sought in the thinking of the class to which President Eliot belongs. He is the busy man of leisure, the practical theorist, the cosmopolitan frontiersman, the cultured man of affairs of our American élite. The type is too little known abroad, and more rare than we could wish at home. Yet, where there is one American who writes on the plane which President Eliot occupies, a thousand think or at least feel there, and his book will help them frame their thought. His chapters are entitled: "Five American Contributions to Civilization;" "Some Reasons why the American Republic May Endure;" "The Working of the American Democracy;" "The Forgotten Millions;" "Family Stocks in a Democracy;" "Equality in a Republic;" "One Remedy for Municipal Misgovernment;" "Wherein Popular Education has Failed;" "Three Results of the Scientific Study of Nature;" "The Happy Life;" "A Republican Gentleman;" "Present Disadvantages of Rich Men;" "The Exemption from Taxation;" "The Future of the New England Churches;" "Why We Honor the Puritans;" "Heroes of the Civil War;" "International Arbitration;" "Inscriptions."

A. W. S.

Unforeseen Tendencies of Democracy. By E. L. GODKIN. Houghton, Mifflin & Co., 1898. Pp. vii + 265.

"I HAVE endeavored in the following pages, not to describe democracy—something which has been done by abler hands than mine—but to describe some of the departures it has made from the ways which its earlier promoters expected it to follow. It has done a great many things which they never thought it could do. Not nearly all the deductions from the principles of equality have been correct. The growth of democracy has dissipated a good many fears about the 'mob;' but on the other hand it has failed to realize a good many expectations about its conduct of government." In pursuit of the purpose thus indicated, Mr. Godkin devotes chapters to "Former Democracies;" "Equality;" "The Nominating System;" "The Decline of Legislatures;" "Peculiarities of American Municipal Government;" "The Growth and Expression of Public Opinion;" "The Australian Democracy."

The tone of the book has not quite the quality which has come to be expected of the author. There is much less of his own opinion, and much more analysis of objective conditions, than we are familiar with in Mr. Godkin. The consequence is that many readers who are forearmed with prejudice against the author's beliefs about policies will find themselves accepting his diagnosis of conditions. In fact, the book contains analysis and interpretation which equals the keenest and strongest in Montesquieu, Tocqueville, Bagehot, and Bryce. There are passages which suggest these writers in turn. Until the temper of American democracy so changes as to make Mr. Godkin's diagnosis obsolete, his book will have an educational value not exceeded in their time by that of the *Spirit of the Laws*, and *Democracy in America*. If I were to name the books which best deserve study by American citizens, this latest volume by Mr. Godkin would be placed high in the list.   A. W. S.

_____

Principes Sociologiques. Par CHARLES MISMER. Deuxième édition, revue et augmentée. One volume. Paris: Félix Alcan. Pp. 287, 8vo. F. 5.

MORE sociological "principles"! We must take them as they come, and perhaps their very futility and fatality will convince us at last that it were better to settle upon a method. Let the author speak for himself: "The conception which dominates this work has its point of departure in gravitation, unique first cause, generative principle of all forces and all laws. The general movement which draws the universe along subjects all the elements which compose it to a law of solidarity and to a law of perfectibility. Man being part of nature, solidarity and perfectibility are necessarily applicable to the social order. But that which applies to the social order applies equally to the moral order. Solidarity and perfectibility offer the best criterion of morality and find their sanction, like all other causes, in their effects. Finally they dictate the *credo* of the future religion, if it is true, as seems to be the result of historical experience, that the religious form is indispensable to constitute the unity of the human race. Such are the principal features of this conception long held and reflected upon by the author." We must have recourse to colloquial wisdom for a fair estimate of this reasoning: "If anybody likes that sort of thing, it is just the sort of thing he likes."   A. W. S.

The State and Charity. By THOMAS MACKAY. New York: The Macmillan Co., 1898. Pp. 200.

THE author is strongly "individualistic." He regards poor relief as a means of prolonging the economic dependence of a class, a way of hiring people to incapacitate themselves for labor. Public relief obstructs the progressive forces of society and hinders the mobility of labor. All would be employed if the mechanism of exchange were perfect, and poor relief injures this mechanism. The better instincts of the modern mind are against all forms of dependence. A Jewish prayer is quoted as a sign of this feeling: "O release us speedily from all our anxieties, and suffer us not, O Lord our God, to stand in need of the gifts of mankind nor of their loans; but let our dependence be solely on Thy hand, which is full, open, and ample, so that we may not be put to shame, nor ever be confounded."

True charity is free, and is not to be identified with poor law which is compulsory.

An interesting sketch of English charitable endowments and systems of public relief is given; the investigations of commissions; the vacillating and contradictory forms of public opinion. While the author is strongly opposed to outdoor relief, he admits that some form of public care is still necessary, and he gives as an objective test that of the workhouse. "An applicant for relief is *destitute* when he is willing to surrender the maintenance which he derives from his own resources in exchange for an adequate but carefully regulated maintenance within the walls of some poor-law institution. No body of men is able to tell a destitute person at sight, and if the relief of destitution is the province of the guardians, the destitute must be marked out by an automatic test. An adoption of this rule would, of course, put an end to three-fourths of the pauperism of this country."

The Charity Organization Society was founded to represent this view, that individual, domestic relief should be left to private benevolence, and that all paupers dependent on rates should be cared for in institutions. It is interesting to see the nature of the opposition to this movement on the part of politicians and the representatives of the ancient and traditional relief agencies. The belief that pauperism, social dependence, is the permanent fate of an entire class in the community is at the bottom of this antagonism, both in England and in America. Many later economists and socialists believe that this tendency is fostered by capitalist managers in order to have a large "reserve army" of the unemployed to lower wages by competition with the more competent. Loria goes so far as to teach that the charity fund is a regular part of modern investment, and that capitalists think it pays to expend a good deal in this direction. Of this Mr. Mackay says nothing. He thinks that with a perfect mechanism for exchange there would be no unemployed class, and that outdoor relief is an obstruction to freedom of labor movement.

The discussion of "voting charities" (p. 154) deserves especial attention. In London men subscribe to certain hospital and other funds on the distinct agreement that they can send any (poor) friend on their card. So it comes about that a man in need of such help must search all over the West End for some rich patron in order to gain the benefits. In America the same abuse is growing up under cover. We may not have any avowedly "voting charities," but it is pretty well understood that a patron of certain eleemosynary institutions has a" pull " with the almoners or superintendents which will not be disregarded. The demoralizing effects are beginning to appear in this country, and they are inevitable.

The Charity Organization Society was forced to add a department of relief, against its own desires, because of the refusal of parish authorities and private relief societies to coöperate with it in division of labor. In a rational and consistent system the poor law would be confined to relief of paupers in institutions; endowed charities would concentrate their miserable doles in pensions, education, and provident schemes. The experience with chaotic relief ought to teach us something in America — but will it ?

This little volume has much in it worth the attention of American students of social economics and charity. Those who favor an extension of old-age pensions, compulsory sickness insurance by the state, and other "socialistic" measures, will find in these chapters something for reflection, and something which will stir their antagonism.

C. R. HENDERSON.

NOTES AND ABSTRACTS.

Capacity and Calling.— It is important for sociology to investigate how far capacity conditions calling. Socialists claim that in the lower occupations are many men of great but unutilized capacity. "The stupid rich" keep down "the intelligent poor" in order to prey upon them. All socialistic teaching is based upon the assertion that private ownership is a holding, through accident or robbery, of the common property, and is not a consequence of greater intellectual and moral efforts. Professor Herkner writes: "Hardly a fifth of the common people can enter a learned profession. Many, called by nature to intellectual pursuits, remain far from higher education, while many without such calling, but favored by society, take academic courses." "Only a fifth" is debatable. At any rate it is well known that the learned professions are overcrowded, and that there is therefore an educated proletariat which causes serious difficulties. Statistics for 1882–96 from two common schools of a south German city lead to a less optimistic conclusion about this intelligence "lying fallow." The first school was attended by the children of workmen, day laborers, and petty tradesmen. The school had seven divisions, covering the age from seven to fourteen. Work was marked as "very good," "good," "fair," "sufficient," "unsatisfactory." Not one pupil received the mark "very good." The group "fair" was largest. "Fair" and "sufficient" included the great mass. In the other school, attended by children of better-paid workmen, low officials, and petty tradesmen, the results are about the same, except that in the sixth division two pupils were marked "very good." In the next division under the same teacher they received only "good." The marks for diligence were higher than those for mental gifts. With higher work the proportion of "good" and "fair" would doubtless lessen, as statistics of the gymnasium show that when a kind of work comes that requires less memory and more independent intelligence the well-marked groups shrink rapidly. Of course, if their parents had money and time enough, some of these moderately gifted pupils might rise into the higher professions. But what would be gained? A greater overcrowding. It is far better that those marked "fair" to "good," which, considering the elementary nature of the work, means only relatively good, should remain in their own circles to give them intellectual guidance, development, and union with other circles. Genius and really great endowments are not suppressed by social conditions. Society in its own interest is bound to summon undoubted talent, but not moderate ability, to the higher professions.—ADAM RÖDER, " Capacität und Beruf," *Zeitschrift für Socialwissenschaft,* April, 1898.

Improved Tenement Homes for American Cities.— "There is no agency in the world that has a greater influence upon the welfare of the people than one which directly affects their health and social environment." Experience shows that improvements in the dwellings of the poor have had a decided influence upon the character of the inmates. Under existing conditions providing better habitations for the poorer working classes seems to be a proper subject for the consideration of state and municipal governments. "The first and most important step is the enactment of proper sanitary and building laws and the inauguration of a thorough system of tenement-house inspection. Second in importance is the expropriation of property in the crowded districts. Another step, which is common in European countries, is the encouragement of model tenement enterprises by granting them special favors, such as reducing the tax rates, ceding land, granting subsidies, making loans at a low rate of interest, etc. Lastly, when private and philanthropic enterprises refuse to provide proper housing facilities, it becomes the duty of the local authorities to do so." New York has the best sanitary code and the best organized corps of sanitary inspectors of any American or European city. Philadelphia and Chicago have in recent years made improvements in their sanitary laws and ordinances relating to tenement houses. Existing regulations in Boston and Brooklyn are fairly comprehensive, and their health departments are well equipped. New York is the only large American city that has done anything toward the expropriation of crowded and unsanitary districts for park purposes, and that only since 1895. For many years European cities have turned their attention in the direction of making parks, playgrounds, and other breathing spaces where they are most needed. This is especially true of the large cities of Great Britain — London, Edinburgh, Glasgow, Liverpool, Manchester, Birmingham, Newcastle-upon-Tyne, and Dundee. Nothing has been done by public authorities in American cities in the way of encouraging model tenement enterprises, except negatively by the enactment of sanitary and building regulations. In England the public authorities have gone much farther. In the United States no steps have been taken to erect municipal tenements. On the other hand, in London, Manchester, Liverpool, Glasgow, Birmingham, and Huddersfield dwelling houses have been constructed and are being managed by the municipal corporations. " While in exceptional instances municipalities may be justified in providing healthy homes for the poorer working classes, the great work of furnishing homes for these people devolves upon commercial and philanthropic enterprises. Philanthropy has done much in European cities toward accomplishing this end, but it alone can do but a very small proportion of the work needed in all large cities. The great problem with respect to model tenement houses is how to secure the investment of capital on a paying basis in such enterprises." During the last twenty years large tenement enterprises have been successfully organized and operated in many cities in America, Great Britain, France, Germany, Holland, and Sweden. Some of these institutions are organized on a purely commercial basis and distribute all their net earnings as dividends to the shareholders. Others are semi-philanthropic, the dividends being limited usually to 4 or 5 per cent. of the actual invested capital, and the balance of the net income being devoted to improvements, extension, etc. Still others are purely philanthropic, the entire profits being applied to the extension of the enterprise. In a few German cities working people have created coöperative building funds for the construction of model tenements, shareholders being, as a rule, the occupants. The success of a model tenement enterprise is dependent upon the efficiency of the management and upon its adaptation to the requirements of desired tenements in respect to location, privacy, health, safety, and comfort. While such enterprises do not usually realize immense profits to the investors, it has been established beyond a doubt, both in America and in Europe, that they insure a safe and fair return on the money invested.— G. A. WEBER, *Municipal Affairs*, December, 1897.

Prison Reform. (1) Prisons and prisoners; (2) our female criminals; (3) juvenile reformatories in France.

(1) *Prisons and Prisoners*, by W. D. Morrison.—The author's experience supports the conclusion of Lord Kimberley's Convict Prison Commission of 1879, and of Mr. Herbert Gladstone's commission of 1894, viz., that, owing to the conditions of English prison life, " imprisonment not only fails to reform offenders, but, in the case of the less hardened criminals, especially first offenders, it produces a deteriorating effect." The first and most pernicious result of this deteriorating process is that it turns the casual offender into a habitual criminal. Imprisonment as now exercised does not protect society, but breeds worse criminals to prey upon society. Of the 18,000 prisoners at present in the prisons of England and Wales, more than one-half will return again after liberation. Mr. Gladstone's report ascribes the failure of the prisons in reforming their occupants to the excessive centralization. Among the good features of the bill now before Parliament may be mentioned the granting of the right to a prisoner unable to pay a fine of paying so much of the fine as possible and shortening the sentence proportionately; also the right of a prisoner sentenced for more than nine months to work out one-fourth of the time gives hope in place of degeneracy. The bill's defects are the failure to make the inspectorships independent of prison commission and the keeping secret of the "special rules," resulting in a nullification of the "general rules" for prison management. Provision is needed to prevent the punishments of food deprival and close cells for those likely to be mentally affected.

2. *Our Female Prisoners*, by Eliza Orme.—The whole system of prison administration, so far as it affects female prisoners, requires overhauling. The inebriate should be separated from others and be kept in healthy districts, under care of a

physician, until cured. The employments of women should be chosen particularly with reference to their being enabled to earn their livelihood upon liberation. Prisons should be smaller and staffed by competent, trained women, who should not have their energies or capacities injured by overwork. Prisoners must be treated as individuals. Economy is to be obtained, not by saving in the case of present prisoners, but in reforming them so that their numbers, and the consequent expenditures, shall decrease.

3. *Juvenile Reformatories in France,* by E. Spearman.—The necessity of separating juvenile from old offenders is everywhere recognized today. In France both governmental and private reformatories are well developed. An offender under sixteen, if acting without "guilty knowledge," may, at the discretion of the judge, be sent to his parents again, or to certain governmental or private colonies, generally in the country, where they are taught trades and agricultural pursuits. Girls and boys under twelve years are placed under the influence of women almost entirely; and even in the case of older boys the value of women's influence is recognized. Many of the private reformatories are church institutions managed by "sisters." All external signs of restraint, except in colonies of the worst boys, are absent, and the surroundings are beautiful in every way. The desertions are few. Colonies are now usually divided, according to age, in small groups ; in the future they will probably be divided more and more carefully, according to moral character.— *Fortnightly Review,* April and May, 1898.

BIBLIOGRAPHY.

September—for May-August.

CONDUCTED BY C. H. HASTINGS

NEW BOOKS AND NOTICES OF BOOKS REVIEWED.

Explanation. *Titles not starred* represent new publications announced in the standard publishers' lists since the last issue of the bibliography. A *star prefixed* to a title indicates that it was taken from a review of the work in the periodical cited after the title. It may or may not be a new announcement. The *arithmetical signs* following the citation to a review indicate the tenor of the review: X uncertain ; +, favorable ; —, unfavorable; + —, favorable, but with reservations ; — +, unfavorable, but with commendation ; + +, very favorable ; — — very unfavorable ; + + —, very favorable, but with reservations ; — — +, very unfavorable, but with commendation. Absence of any sign indicates that review has not been read. The *publication date* when not given is understood to be the current year. *Prices quoted* are usually for volumes bound in cloth in the case of American and English books, in paper in the case of all others. *New editions, translations*, and *new periodicals* are placed at end of classes.

Abbreviations. *See* at end of Bibliography.

SUBJECT INDEX.

[The *figures* refer to the number of the class ; *each* of the *letters* following the figures refers to initial of author's surname, or to entering word of title.]

AUTHOR INDEX TO BOOKS REVIEWED.

1. Anthropology.

Florke, Gust. Der Einfluss der Kiefer u. Zahne auf den menschlichen Gesichtausdruck. Ein anthropologisch-ethnograph. Studie. Bremen. W. B. Hollmann. 96 pp. 8vo. M. 1.50.

Robin, Paul. Dégénérescence de l'espèce humaine, causes et remèdes. communication à la Société d'anthropologie de Paris. P., libr. Stock. 8 pp. 8vo. f. 0.25.

Thomas, Cyrus. Introduction to the study of Amer. archaeology. Cin., Robert Clark Co. 391 pp. 8vo. $2.

2. Biology, Evolution, Science.

Blackwell, Elizabeth. Scientific method in biology. L., Elliot Stock. 84 pp. 12mo. 2s.

Le Dantec, Félix. Evolution individuelle et hérédité. Théorie de la variation quantitative. P., F. Alcan. 512 pp. 8vo.

Rawitz, Bernh. Für die Vivisection. Eine Streitschrift. Greifswald, J. Abel. 45 pp. 8vo. M. 1.

3. Charities.

Burdett, H. Burdett's hospitals & charities, 1898 ; being the yearbook of philanthropy & the hospital annual. L., Scientific Press. 970 pp. 8vo. 5s.

Chilcott, T. B. The law relating to the administration of charities under the charitable trusts act, 1853, 1894, etc. L., Stevens & Hall. 8vo.

Fürth, Henriette. Das Ziehkinderwesen in Frankfurt am Main u. Umgebung . . . . Frankfurt a. M., Mahlau & Waldschmidt. 23 pp. 8vo. M. 1.20.

Gaillard, Henri. Le troisième congrès International des sourds-muets (Genève, 1896). P., 35 rue du Faubourg Saint-Jacques. 96 pp. 8vo. f. 1.

Great Britain—Parliament. Endowed charities (County of London). Tooting, Graveney & Lower Tooting. L., Eyre & Spottiswoode. 3d.

Koch, E. Les invalides du travail et de la guerre. Historique et organisation générale de l'œuvre nationale des maisons de retraite régionales et départementales. P., impr. Hennuyer. 67 pp. 8vo.

*Mackay, Thomas. The state & charity. L., Macmillan & Co. 201 pp. 12mo. $1. (JPE., Je. +)

*Münsterberg, E. Die Armenpflege. Einführung in die praktische Pflegethätigkeit. B., Otto Liebmann, 1897. 213 pp. M. 3. (AJS., Jl. + +)

Poor law conferences. Proceedings of the various conferences, 1897-8, with papers read at each conference . . . . L., P. S. King. 755 pp. 8vo. 12s.

Tuetey, Alex. L'assistance publique à Paris pendant la Révolution. Documents inédits . . . . 3 Hopitaux et hospices. 4 Hospices et atéliers. P., Impr. nationale. 821 & 933 pp. 8vo.

Wichern, J. Die Brüderschaft des Rauhen Hauses. Eine Jubelgabe. Hamburg, Agentur des Rauhen Hauses. 131 pp. 8vo. M. 1.

4. Cities.

Artigues, Geo. Du régime municipal de Paris (thèse). P., libr. Arthur Rousseau. 193 pp. 8vo.

Baddeley, J. J. Guide to the Guildhall of the city of London . . . . and the municipal work carried on therein. L., Simpkin, Marshall, etc. 206 pp. 8vo. 6d.

Great Britain—Parliament. Water supply of the metropolis; report . . . . 1898. L., Eyre & Spottiswoode. 6d.

Harris, Mary Dormer. Life in an old English town: a history of Coventry from the earliest times, comp. from original records. L., Swan Sonnenschein. 416 pp. 8vo. 4s. 6d. (Social England series.)

Histoire générale de Paris. Topographie historique du vieux Paris. Ouvrage commencé par A. Berty, continué par S. M. Tisserand. T. 6. Région centrale de l'Université. P., Impr. nationale. 597 pp. 4to. f. 30.

London Manual, for 1898-9, ed. by Robert Donald . . . . L., Lloyd. 330 pp. 8vo. 1s. 6d.

Mandat-Grancey, E. de. Chicago. P., Plon, Nourrit & Cie. 32 pp. 8vo. f. 0.15. (Bibliothèque illustrée des voyages . . . .)

Mauri, Aug. Le finanze di Milano nel medio evo: noto di conferenza. Monza, tip. Artigianelli-orfani. 27 pp. 8vo.

Meiklejon, M. J. C, London; a short history. With maps and illustrations. L., Holden. 262 pp. 8vo. 1s. 6d.

New Jersey—An act relating to boroughs (revision of 1897) in the state; with notes . . . compiled by A. F. Skinner. Newark, Loney & Sage. 94 pp. 8vo. paper. $1.50.

New York City—The law and practice of the municipal court under "The Greater New York Charter," with the boundaries of boroughs, districts, and wards; with forms and exhaustive index, by G. F. & J. C. L. Langbein; 4th ed. N. Y., Banks & Bros. 609 pp. 8vo. $5.

Pennsylvania.—The law of boroughs, including the rights and duties of borough officers, by W. Trickett, V. 2, 1893-8. Phil., T. & J. W. Johnson Co. 381 pp. 8vo. $4.

Sparling, S. E. Municipal history and present organization of the city of Chicago; thesis . . . . Madison, Wis., the University of Wisconsin. 188 pp. 8vo. $0.75. (Bulletin of the University of Wisconsin.)

Strassenhygiene in europäischen Städten. Sammelbericht der aus Anlass des 9. internationalen Kongresses f. Hygiene u. Demographie in Madrid . . . 1898. B., A. Hirschwald. 83 pp. 8vo. M. 2.40.

*Strong, Josiah. Twentieth century city. N. Y., Baker & Taylor Co. 186 pp. $0.50. (AJS., Jl. +)

Boulnois, H. P. The municipal & sanitary engineer's handbook. Ed. 3. N. Y., Spon & Chamberlain. 474 pp. 8vo. $6.

Gregorovius, Ferdinand. Hist. of the city of Rome in the middle ages, from the 4th German ed. by Annie Hamilton. In 5 vols. Vols. 1 & 2. N. Y., Macmillan Co. 12mo. Each $2.

5. Criminology and Penology.

Bianchi, G. L. Intorno al fondamento dell' imputabilità penale; teorica del libero arbitrio; critica della scuola positiva: dissertazione di laurea. Torino, tip, Pietro Gerbone. 58 pp. 8vo.

Cosentino, Pa. I delinquenti: note di antropologia criminale. Palermo, tip. Matteo Verso. 135 pp. 8vo. L. p.

Great Britain—Parliament. Judicial statistics, England & Wales, 1896. Pt. 1, Criminal Statistics; statistics relating to criminal proceedings, police, coroners, prisons, reformatory & industrial schools, & criminal lunatics, for 1896. L., Eyre & Spottiswoode. 1s. 7d.

Jaeger, Johs. Zunahme der Verbrechen u. Abhilfe. Ein Beitrag zur Lösg. der sozialen Frage. Lp., A. Deichert Nachf. 131 pp. 8vo. M. 1.80.

Minovici, Prof, L'anthropologie criminelle et la résponsabilité. P., impr. A. Lévy. 15 pp. 8vo.

Proal, L. Political crimes, with an introd. by F. H. Giddings. N. Y., D. Appleton & Co. 355 pp. 12mo. $1.50. (Criminology ser.)

Sammlung ausserdeutscher Strafgesetzbücher in deutscher Uebersetzung. Hrsg. v. der Red. der Zeits. f. die gesamte Strafrechtswissenschaft. 11. Entwurf e. allgemeinen bürgerlichen Strafgesetzbuchs f. das Königr. Norwegen . . . . B., J. Guttentag. 126 pp. 8vo. M. 4.

Statistik der zum Ressort des königl. preussischen Ministeriums des Innern gehörenden Strafanstalten u. Gefängnisse f. den 1. IV. 1896-7. B., R. v. Decker. 221 pp. 8vo. M. 10.

Untersuchungen zur deutschen Staats- und Rechtsgeschichte, hrsg. v. Otto Gierke. 55. Friese, Vict, Das Strafrecht des Sachsenspiegels. Breslau, M & H. Marcus. 206 pp. 8vo. M. 9.

Weismann, Jak. Ein Vierteljahrhundert deutscher Strafgesetzgebung. Rektorsrede. 25 pp. 8vo. M. 2.40.

6. Education.

Binet, A., & V. Henri. La fatigue intellectuelle. P., libr. Scheicher frères. 342 pp. 8vo. 90 fig. & 3 planches.

Crowell, J. F. Logical process . . . . educational policy; see 18.

Davidson, Thomas. Rousseau & education according to nature. N. Y., C. Scribner's Sons. 253 pp. 12mo. $1. (Great educators series.)

France—Ministère de l'instruction publique . . . . Annuaire, 1898. P., libr. Delalain frères. f. 5.

France—Ministère de l'instruction publique . . . . Enquêtes et documents relatifs à l'enseignement superieux. 69. Rapports des conseils des universités pour l'année scolaire 1896-7. P., Impr. nationale. 257 pp. 8vo.

France—Ministère de l'instruction publique . . . . Services de l'instruction publique et des beaux-arts. P., Impr. nationale. 224 pp. 4to.

Friedburg, Emil. Die Universität Leipzig in Vergenheit u. Gegenwart . . . . Lp., West & Co. 160 pp. 8vo. M. 3.50.

Great Britain—Parliament. National education in Ireland. Appendix to the report of the commissioners for 1896–7. L., Eyre & Spottis-woode. 8vo. 1s. 4½ d.

Holman, H. English national education ; a sketch of the rise of public elementary schools in England. L., Blackie & Son. 255 pp. 8vo. 2s. 6d.

Italy — Ministero della publica instruzione. Annuario, 1898. Roma, tip. Ludovico Cecchini. 682 pp. 8vo.

Jahrbuch des Vereins f. wissenschaftliche Pädagogik. Begründet v. P. T. Ziller. Hrsg. Thdr. Vogt. 30. Jahrg., 1898. Dresden, Bleyl & Kaemmerer. 286 pp. 8vo. M. 5.

Jahres-Verzeichniss der an den deutschen Schulanstalten erschienenen Abhandlungen, IX, 1897. Br., A. Asher & Co. 80 pp. 8vo. M. 2.40.

Laurie, André. La vie de college dans tous les temps et dans tous les pays. L'écolier d'Athènes. P., impr. Chamerot. 334 pp. il. 18mo. f. 3.

Letourneau, Ch. L'évolution de l'éducation dans les diverses races humaines. P., libr. Vigot frères. 625 pp. 8vo. f. 9.

Lexis, W. Die Besoldungsverhältnisse der Lehrer an den höheren Unterrichtsanstalten Preussens. Jena, G. Fischer. 100 pp. 8vo. M. 1.80.

Pestalozzi, J. H. Letters on early education addressed to J. P. Greaves, Esq., tr. from the German MSS. Syracuse, N. Y., C. W Bardeen. 180 pp. 16mo. $1. (Standard teachers' libr.)

Picks, G. Manual training: woodwork, a handbook for teachers. . . . . 275 ill. L., Macmillan & Co. 196 pp. 4to. 7s. 6d.

Secondary Education: Essays by various writers, ed. by Christopher Cookson. L., Henry Frowde. 314 pp. 8vo. 4s. 6d.

Vincent, G. E. Social mind and education: *see* 18.

7. Ethics, Philosophy, and Psychology.

Ambrosi, Lu. La psicologia del l'immaginazione nella storia della filosofia: esposizione e critica. Roma, soc. edit. Dante Alighieri. 562 pp. L. 6.

Baumann, Jul. Realwissenschaftliche Begründung der Moral, des Rechts u. der Gotteslehre. Lp., Dietrich. 295 pp. 8vo. M. 7.

Fouillée, Alfred. Psychologie du peuple française. P., F. Alcan, 395 pp. 8vo. f. 7.50.

Fulliquet, Georges. Essai sur l'obligation morale. P., F. Alcan. 458 pp. 8vo. f. 7.50.

Guastella, Cosmo. Saggi sulla teoria della conoscenza: saggio I. Sui limiti e l'oggeto della conoscenza a priori. Palermo, Remo Sandron edit. 571 pp. 16mo.

Lehmann, Alfr. Aberglaube u. Zauberei von den ältesten Zeiten bis in die Gegenwart. Deutsch v. Dr. Petersen. (In 6 Lfgn.) 1. Lfg. Stuttgart, F. Enke. 96 pp. 8vo. M. 2.

Lotz, Rud. Die Philosophie u. der Zweck des Lebens. Athen, Barth & v. Hirst in:Komm. 73 pp. 8vo. M. 1.60.

Marchesini, G. La crisi del positivismo e il problema filosofico. Torino, fratelli Bocca. 192 pp. 8vo. L. 3.

Mills, W. Nature and development of animal intelligence. L., Fisher Unwin. 320 pp. 8vo. 10s. 6d.

Morgan, C. L. Psychology for teachers. . . . . N. Y., C. Scribner's Sons. 240 pp. 12mo. $1.

Monrad, M. J. Die menschliche Willensfreiheit u. das Böse. Aus dem Norweg. . . . . Lp., A. Janssen. 64 pp. 8vo. M. 1.20.

Müller, Jos. System der Philosophie. Enth.: Erkenntnistheorie, Logik u. Metaphysik, Psychologie, Moral u. Religionsphilos. Mainz, F. Kirchheim. 372 pp. 8vo. M. 5.

Philosoph. Studien, hrsg v. W. Wundt, 14. Bd. 1. u. 2. Hft. Lp., E. Engelmann. M. 4.

Royce, Joseph. Studies of good & evil: A series

of essays upon problems of philosophy & of life. N. Y., D. Appleton & Co. 384 pp. 12mo. $1.50.

Sutherland, Alex. Origin & growth of the moral instinct. N. Y., Longmans, Green & Co. 2 v. 8vo. $8.

_____

Guyau, M. Sketch of morality, independent o f obligation or sanction, trans. from the 2d French ed. by Gertrude Kapeteyn. L., Watts. 228 pp. 3s. 6d.

8. Family.

Durkheim, E. Prohibition de l'inceste . . . . *see* Année, 18.

Fédération abolitionniste internationale contre la prostitution réglementée . . . . par G. de M. P., Giard & Brière. 79 pp. 16mo. f. 1.

Great Britain — Parliament. Births, deaths & marriages. 43d annual report. 1897. L., Eyre & Spottiswoode. 8vo. 5d.

Jacob, G. Die Prostitution u. ihre polizeiliche Bekämpfung. Lp., W. Friedrich. 24 pp. 8vo. M. 0.60.

Laupts, Dr. Tares et poisons. Perversions et perversité séxuelle. Une enquête médicale sur l'inversion. Préfacé par Emile Zola Paris, libr. Carré. 328 pp. 8vo.

Meynial, E. Le mariage après les invasions. 1er fasc.: Origines romaines et germainiques. P., libr. Larose. 107 pp. 8vo.

Prostituées (les) à Paris. Notes et souvenirs d'un ancien agent des moeurs. P., bib. du journal Fin-de-Siècle. 270 pp. 18mo. f. 3.50.

Virmaitre, Ch. Paris impur. Les maisons de rendez-vous. P., libr. Alfred Charles. 292 pp. 18mo. f. 3.50.

Sanger, W. W. History of prostitution: its extent, causes & effects throughout the world. New ed. N. Y. Medical Pub. Co. 709 pp. 8vo. $2.

9. Finance and Taxation.

Austria — K. k. Finanz-Ministerium. Mitteilungen. 4. Jahrg. 1. u. 2. Hft. Wien, Hof-u. Staatsdruckerei. pp. 1-160, 161-429. 8vo. M. 4 u. 5.

Austria — K. k. statist. Central-Com. Statistik der Sparcassen . . 1895. 105 + 59 pp. 4to. M. 3. (Oesterreich. Statistik, 49. Bd., 3. Hft.: *see* 19.)

Bachmann, H. Die Effektenspekulation unter besond. Berücksicht. der deutschen Börsenen-quete [aus Zeitschr. f. schweiz. Statistik]. Zürich, A. Müller's Verl. 132 pp. 8vo. M.3.20.

Banca popolare agricola commerciale di Pavia (società anonima cooperativa) resoconto dell' esercizio 1897 . . . . Pavia, fratelli Fusi. 46 pp. 4to.

Blanc, Joseph. Histoire des principes de la répartition et de la quotité dans l'impôt direct (thèse). Toulouse, libr. Rivière.

Böhmert, Wilh. Die Verteilung des Einkommens in Preussen u. Sachsen m. besond. Berücksicht. der Grossstädte u. des Landes . . . . Dresden, O. V. Böhmert.

Brown, John. Parasitic wealth ; or, money reform: a manifesto to the people of the U. S. & to the workers of the whole world. C., H. Kerr & Co. 169 pp. 8vo. $1.

Calmon, A. Histoire parlementaire des finances à la monarchie de Juillet. T. 3. P., C. Lévy. 448 pp.-8vo. f. 7.50.

Camera di commercio ed arti di Roma. Atti e documenti relativi all' ispezione ministeriale. Roma, tip. Innocenzo Artero, 1897. 252 pp. 8vo.

Carver, T. N. The Ohio tax inquisitor law. N. Y., Macmillan Co. [for Am. Economic

assoc.].   pp. 167-212. 12mo.   Pap. $0.50.
(Economic studies.)

Chesnelong, Ch. Le régime fiscal des successions et l'impôt progressif. P., impr. de Soye et fils. 35 pp. 8vo.

Conigliani, C. A.   La riforma delle leggi sui tributi locali: studi e proposte. Modena, tip. della Società tip.-antica tip. Soliani. 751 pp. 8vo. L. 10.

Cotton, W. Everybody's guide to money matters (English); with a description of the various investments chiefly dealt in on the exchange, also some account of the pitfalls prepared for the unwary. . . . . N. Y., F. Warne & Co. 150 pp. 12mo. $1.

Dubois, Paul. Essai sur les finances communales. P., Perrin & Cie. 313 pp. 16mo.

Farrer, Lord. Studies in currency 1898: or, enquiries into certain modern problems connected with the standard of value & the media of exchange. N. Y., Macmillan. 440 pp. 8vo. 12s.

France — Ministère des finances. Budget des dépenses. Exercice 1898. Budget annexe de l'administration des monnaies et médailles. P., Impr. nationale. 128 pp. 4to.

George, Henry. Writings. Memorial ed. In 10 vols. Vols. 5-8. N. Y., Doubleday & McClure Co. Per set $25.

(The) Gold standard: a series of papers issued by the Gold Standard Defence Association, 1895-8. L.: Cassell & Co. 8vo. 2s. 6d.

Great Britain — India. Financial statement & proceedings of the legislative council of the governor general thereon. L., Eyre & Spottiswoode. 1s. 6d.

Great Britain — Parliament. East India (income & expenditure). Return for the 11 years 1886-7—1896-7. L., Eyre & Spottiswoode. 7d.

Great Britain — Parliament. Local taxation returns (England) 1895-6. Pt. 7. Summary with appendix. L., Eyre & Spottiswoode. 1s. 1½ d.

Great Britain — Parliament. Revenue departments for 1898-9. Estimates, customs, inland revenue, post-office, post-office packet service, post-office telegraphs, with index. L., Eyre & Spottiswoode. 1s. 3½d.

Great Britain — Royal commission on local taxation. Minutes of evidence. L., Eyre & Spottiswoode. 4s. 2d.

Grossi, Nic. Nuovo progretto per le finanze dello stato e comuni italiani. Napoli, tip. di Gennaro Errico e figlio. 30 pp. 8vo.

Hand- u. Lehrbuch . . . . Finanzwissenschaft: see 13.

Hoyle (pseud.). The game in Wall street & how to play it successfully. N. Y., J. S. Olgive Pub. Co. 80 pp. $1.

Italy — Direzione generale delle imposte dirette. Legge, decreto, regolamento, capitoli normali e tabella dei compensi per gli atti esecutivi per la riscossione delle imposte dirette. Roma, tip. Nazionale di G. Bertero, 1897. 122 pp. 8vo.

Italy — Ministero delle finanze. Relazione della direzione generale delle imposte dirette e del catasto per l'esercizio finanziario 1896-7. Roma, tip. Elzeviriana. 97 pp. 4to

Justice, A. R. An equitable exchange systsm. Ph., A. J. Ferriss. 141 pp. 16mo. $0.50.

Kappelmann, H. Handbuch f. preussische Sparkassen. Lp., Duncker & Humblot. 144 pp. 8vo. M. 3.60.

Kiebel, Herm. Die Steuerpolitik der Besitzenlosen. Wien, M. Breitenstein. 50 pp. 8vo. M. 0.70.

Ridley, W. Interest or usury: thoughts on modern methods of finance & their effect on national life. L., Simpkin, Marshall, etc. 104 pp. 8vo. 1s.

*Rostand, Eugène. Le concours des caisses

d'épargne au crédit agricole. Applications à l'étranger et modes pratiques de réalisation en France . . . P., Guillaumin & Cie., 1897. 278 pp. 8vo. f. 6. (J Ec., D.+ +)

Say, Léon. Les finances de la France sous la troisième République. T. 1er (1871-5). P., libr. C. Lévy. 509 pp. 8vo.

Steiger, J. Die Silberentwertung u. ihre Bedeutung f. die Volkswirthschaft der Gegenwart, zumal f. die Schweiz. [Aus Ztschr. f. schweiz. Statistik.] Basel, R. Reich. 47 pp. 4to. M. 1.60,

Straulino, Giov. Le instituzioni di credito e la circolazione monetaria nello stato; studio di economia politica. Firenze, fratelli Bocca. 236 pp. 8vo. L. 2.50.

Supino, Cam. La borsa e il capitale improduttivo. Milano, Ulrico Hoepli edit. 180 pp. L. 3.

Tenerelli, F. G. L'azione delle imposte indirette sui consumi, com particolare riguardo alla legislazione italiana. Torino, fratelli Bocca. 287 pp. 8vo. L. 3.

U. S. bankruptcy law of 1898, uniform system, with marginal notes & index. Wash., Wash. Law-Book Co. 30 pp. 8vo. paper. $0.50.

War revenue law of 1898, with index. Wash., Wash. Law-Book Co. 40 pp. 8vo. paper. $0.25.

10. History.

Davitt, Michael. Life & progress in Australasia. N. Y., New Amsterdam Book Co. 500 pp. $2.50.

[*Bibliography of History will be brought to date in next issue.*]

11. International Law.

Bares, C. Le blocus pacifique. Toulouse, impr. Berthoumieur. 160 pp. 8vo.

Nouveau recueil général de traites et autres actes relatifs aux rapports de droit international. Continuation du grand recueil de G. F. de Martens par Felix Stoerk. 2. serie. T. 23. 1 livr. Lp., Dieterich's Verl. pp. 1-292. M. 13.60.

Recueil des traités et conventions, conclus par la Russie avec les puissances étrangères. Publié . . . . par. F. de Martens. T. 12. St. Petersburg, A. Zinserling. 504 pp. 8vo. M. 12.

Reddaway, W. F. Monroe doctrine. N. Y., Macmillan Co. 162 pp. 12mo. $1.25. (Cambridge Univ. Press.)

Ullman, E. Völkerrecht. Freiburg i. B., J. C. B. Mohr. 376 pp. 8vo. M. 9. [Aus Handbuch des öffentl. Recht.]

12. Labor.

Arbeitsvermittelung & Arbeitseinstellung: see Austria—Statist. Dept., Handelsministerium, 19.

Bender, Emile. Le salaire effectif; sa protection par la loi (thèse). Lyon, impr. Legendre & Cie. 182 pp.

Centralstelle f. Arbeiter-Wohlfahrtseinrichtungen. Schriften, Nr. 14. Br., C. Heymann's Verl. 53 pp. 8vo. M. 1.20.

Great Britain — Labour Department. Report by Miss Collet on changes in the employment of women & girls in industrial centers. Pt. 1, Flax & jute centers. L., Eyre & Spottiswoode. 8vo. 6d.

*Great Britain — Labour Department. Strikes & lockouts: report of the chief labor correspondent. L., Eyre & Spottiswoode. 209 pp. 8vo. (JPE, Je.X)

Internationale (der) Kongress f. Arbeiterschutz in Zürich . . . . 1897. Amtlicher Bericht des Organizationskomitees. Zürich, Buchh. des schweiz. Grütlivereins in Komm. 280 pp. 8vo. M. 2.

Jurnitschek, Osc. Ueber den Strike der englischen Maschinenbauarbeiter in den J. 1897-8.

Nach persönl. Beobachtgn. Vortrag. Wien,
Mainz. 56 pp. 8vo. M. 1.20.
*Levasseur, E. L'ouvrier américain. P., Larose.
2 v. 634 & 516 pp. 8vo. (AJS., Jl.+ + —)
(JPE., Je.)
Ranelletti, Oresto. Sulla responsabilità degli luti
pubblici per gli atti illeciti da loro commessi.
Città di Castello, tip S. Lapi. 25 pp. 8vo.
Rist, C. Réglementation légale de la journée de
travail de l'ouvrier adulte en France (thèse).
P., libr. Larose. 369 pp. 8vo.
Scalori, Ugo. Cl' infortunati del lavoro nella
teoria e nella legge. Mantova, tip A. Mon-
dori e figlio. 140 pp. 8vo.
Thurow, Herm. Die praktischen Erfolge der
Achtstunden-Agitation. B., Buchh. Vor-
wärts. 32 pp. 8vo. M. 0.20.
Webb, Sidney & Beatrice. Problems of modern
industry. L., Longmans, Green & Co. 294
pp. 8vo. 7s. 6d.
*Willey, F. O. The laborer & the capitalist. N.
Y., Equitable Pub. Co., 1897. 311 pp. 12mo.
(JPE., Je. — —)

13. Political Economy.

Biblioteca dell' economista : scelta collezione delle
piu importanti produzioni di economia politica,
antiche e moderne, italiane e straniere, diretta
dal S. Cognetti de Martiis. 4 serie. disp. 89–
91. Torino, Unione tip.-edit. L. 1.50 la disp.
Cohn, Gust. System der Nationalökonomie. Ein
Lesebuch f. Studirende. 3. Bd. Nationalökonomie des Handels- u. des Verkehrswesens.
Stuttgart, F. Enke. 1030 pp. 8vo. M. 24.
Cossa, Em. Del consumo delle ricchezze: saggio
di economia sociale. Parto 1. Letteratura
economica dei fenomeni del consumo. Bologna,
libr. Treves. 278 pp. 8vo. L. 5.
Crook, J. W. German wage theories: a history of
their development. N. Y., Macmillan Co. 113
pp. 8vo. $1. (Columbia Univ. studies.)
Jane, F. T. All the world's fighting ships: illustrated portrait details of over one thousand
war ships. with notes & other statistics. B.,
Little, Brown & Co. 218 pp. 4to. $3.50.
Mill, J. S. Correspondance inédite avec Gustave
d'Eichthal (1828–42, 1864–71). Avant-propos
et traduction . . . P., libr. F. Alcan. 238 pp.
18vo. f. 2.50.
Pantaleoni, Maffeo. Pure economics, tr. by T. B.
Bruce. N. Y., Macmillan Co. 315 pp. 8vo.
$3.50.
Reinhold, K. T. Die bewegenden Kräfte der
Volkswirthschaft. Lp., C. L. Hirschfeld. 632
pp. 8vo. M. 10.
Sammlung nationalökonomischer u. statistischer
Abhandlungen des staatswissenschaftlichen
Seminars zu Halle. Hrsg. v. Joh. Conrad.
16. u. 17. Bd. 16. Dodd, Arth. Die Wirkung
der Schutzbestimmungen f. die jugendlichen
u. weiblichen Fabrikarbeiter . . . 17. Frey-
mark, Herm. Die Reform der preussischen
Handels- u. Zollpolitik von 1800–1821 . . . 236
u. 103 pp. à M. 4.50.
Savatier, Henri. La théorie moderne du capital et
la justice. P., libr. Rondelet & Cie. f. 5.
*Schmoller, Gustav. Ueber einige Grundfrage der
Socialpolitik und der Volkswirthschaftslehre.
Lp., Duncker & Humblot. 143 pp. 8vo.
(JPE., Je. X)
Turgot, A. R. J. Reflections on the formation &
distribution of riches, 1770. L., Macmillan
& Co. 8vo. 3s. (Economic classics.)
Volkswirtschaftliche Zeitfragen. Vorträge u. Ab-
handlgn., hrsg. v. der volkswirthschaftl.
Gesellschaft zu Berlin. 156. Hft. (20. Jahrg.
4. Hft.) Brentano, Lujo. Die Entwickelung
des englischen Erbrechts in das Grundeigen-
thum. Br., L. Simion. 31 pp. M. 1.
Wörterbuch des Volkswirthschaft in 2 Bdn. Hrsg.

Ludw. Elster. 1. Bd. Jena, G. Fischer. 1092
pp. 8vo. M. 20; bd. M. 25.

14. Political Science.

Barassi, Ludovico. Teoria della ratifica del con-
tratto annullabile. Milano, Ulrico Hoepli
edit. 437 pp. 8vo. L. 6.50.
Bertha, A. de. La constitution hongroise. Précis
historique, d'après le docteur Samuel Rado.
P., impr. Plon, Nourrit & Cie. 183 pp. f.
2.50.
Biblioteca di scienze politiche e amministrative. 2.
serie: Scelta collezione delle piu importanti
apere moderne italiane e straniere di dritto amministrativo e constituzionale, diretta da
Attilio Brunialti. Fasc 89. Torino, Unione
tip.-edit. Pp. 401–80. L. 1.50 il fasc.
Botsford, G. W. Development of the Athenian
constitution. N. Y., Macmillan Co. 249 pp.
8vo. $1.50. (Cornell studies in classical philol-
ogy.)
*Boyd, C. E., ed. Cases on American constitu-
tional law. C., Callaghan & Co. 678 pp. 8vo.
$3. (AJS., Jl.++) (ALR., Je.++) (ALRe.,
Ap. —) (JPE., Je.+)
Brassey, T. A. Naval annual for 1898. N. Y.,
imported by C. Scribner's Sons. 468 pp. 8vo.
$5.
Castiglioni, Lu. Le presinti reforme dell' ordi-
namento amministrativo in Italia. Milano,
tip. Sonzogno. 239 pp. 16mo. L. 2.50.
Chadman, C. E. Direct legislation by the initiative & referendum; a summary of the history
of the Swiss cantons & the Swiss confederation. C., Home Study Pub. Co.
Clarke, R. F. Science of law & lawmaking,
being an introduction to law, a general view
of its forms & substance, & a discussion of the
question of codification. N. Y., Macmillan &
Co. 473 pp. 8vo. $4.
Coutant, Paul. Le vote obligatoire (thèse). P.,
Chevalier-Marescq & Cie.
Duguit, Léon, & Monnier, Henry. Les constitutions et les principales lois politiques de la
France depuis 1789. . . . Précédées de notices
historiques et suivis d'une table analytique dé-
tailée. P., libr. Pichon. 424 pp. 12mo. f. 6.
Elliott, C. B. Principles of the law of public
corporations. C., Callaghan & Co. 83 + 364
pp. 8vo. Shp. $6.
Entscheidungen des königl. preussischen Oberverwaltungsgerichts. Hrsg. v. Oberverwaltungs-
ger.-Räthen Freytag, Techow, etc. 23. Bd.
Br., C. Heyman's Verl. M. 7.
Farlie, J. A. Centralization of administration in
N. Y. state. N. Y., Macmillan Co. 207 pp.
8vo. (Columbia Univ. studies.)
France—Sénat. Annals du Sénat. Débats parlementaires. Ses. extra. de 1897. T. 50. . . . 19
oct. au 23 déc. 1897. P., Impr. des journaux
officiels. 308 pp. 4to.
France—Ministère des colonies. Annuaire . . .
1898. P., Charles Lavauzelle. 733 pp. 8vo.
f. 6.
Godkin, E. L. Unforeseen tendencies of democ-
racy. Bo., Houghton, Mifflin & Co. 265 pp.
12mo. $2.
Gooch, G. P. History of English democratic
ideas in the seventeenth century. Cambridge,
Univ. Press. 372 pp. 8vo. 5s. (Cambridge
historical essays.)
Görne, George v. Das Repräsentativsystem der
Zukunft. Lp., M. Sängewald. 80 pp. 8vo.
M. 1.
Great Britain—Parliament. Correspondence re-
specting the affairs of China, 1898. L., Eyre
& Spottiswoode. 7½d.
Hamilton, Alex., Madison, James, and Jay, John.
The Federalist: A commentary on the
const. of the U. S., ed. with notes, illustrative

documents, and a copious index, by Paul Leicester Ford. N. Y., H. Holt & Co. 793 pp. 12mo. $2.50.

Hand- u. Lehrbuch der Staatswissenschaften in selbständigen Bänden. Begründet v. Kuno Frankenstein, fortgesetz von Max v. Heckel. 1. Abtlg. 6. Bd. Fircks, Arthur. Bevölkerungslehre . . . 492 pp. 8vo. M. 13.30. 2. Abtlg. Finanzwissenschaft. 4. Bd. Lp., C. L. Hirschfeld. 354 pp. 16mo. M. 10.

Handbook of Jamaica for 1898. Compiled by J. L. Roxburgh & J. C. Ford. L., Stanford. 577 pp. 12mo. 7s. 6d.

Ilbert, C. The government of India : being a digest of the statute law relating thereto. Hist. iutro. & ill. docs. L., Henry Frowde. 648 pp. 8vo. 21s.

Jahrbuch der internationalen Vereinigung f. vergleichende Rechtswissenschaft u. Volkswirthschaftslehre zu Berlin, hrsg. v. Dr. Bernhöft u. Dr. Meyer. 3. Jahrg. 1897, 2. Abtlg. B., K. Hoffmann. pp. 273-934 M. 16.80.

Keltie, J. S., ed. Statesman's yearbook ; statistical & historical annual of the states of the world for 1898. Thirty-sixth year. N. Y., Macmillan Co. 1166 pp. 12mo. $3.

Maitland, F. W. Township & borough, being the Ford lectures. . . . N. Y., Macmillan Co. 220 pp. 8vo. $2.75. (Cambridge Univ. Press ser.)

McConachie, L. G. Congressional committees: A study of the origin & development of our national & local legislative methods. N. Y., T. Y. Crowell & Co. 441 pp. 12mo. (Library of economics & politics.)

Moses, Bernard. Democracy & social growth in America: four lectures. N. Y., G. P. Putnams. 129 pp. $1.

Naval Annual, 1898, ed. by T. A. Brassey. L., Simpkin, Marshall, etc. 476 pp. 8vo. 12s. 6d.

New York—Primary legislation in the state. N. Y., published by the author, L. Starckie. 116 pp. 12mo. $0.50.

Notiz-Buch f. Reichstags-Wähler. Statistik der Wahlen zum deut. Reichstag in den J. 1871-97. . . . Dresden, H. Schoenfeld. 404 pp. 12mo. M. 1.

Primo Trattato completo di diritto amministrativo italiano a cura del prof. V. E. Orlando. Fasc. 19-29, 23-26. Milano, tip. della Società edit. libraria. pp. 481-576, 577-768. L. 1 il fasc.

Richter, Eug. Politiches A-B-C Buch. Ein Lexikon parlementar. Zeit- u. Streitfragen, 9. Jahrg. B., Verlag Fortschritt. 490 pp. 8vo. M. 3.

Sagnac, Ph. La législation civile de la Révolution française (1789-1804). P., Hachette et Cie. 453 pp. 8vo.

Specht, Fritz. Die Reichstags-Wahlen von 1867 bis 1897. Eine Statistik der Reichstagswahlen, nebst den Programm der Parteien u. dem Verzeichniss der gewählten Kandidaten. B., C. Heymann's Verl. M. 5.

Staats-, Hof- u. Kommunal-Handbuch des Reichs u. der Einzelstaaten (zugleich statist. Jahrbuch). Hrsg. von Jos. Kürschner, 1898. 13. Ausg. Eisenach, Verlag v. Kürschner's Staatshandbuch. 136 pp. 8vo. M. 6.50.

Year-book for Australia for 1898. L., Kegan Paul. 8vo. 10s. 6d.

Year-book of British Columbia & manual of provincial information, . . . by R. E. Gasnell. L., Kegan Paul. 8vo. 12s. 6d.

15. Religion and the Churches.

Allen, W. O. B., & McClure, E. Two hundred years: the history of the Society for Promoting Christian Knowledge, 1698-1898. L., S. P. C. K. 560 pp. 10s. 6d.

[*Bibliography of Religion will be brought to date in next issue.*]

16. Sanitary and Domestic Science.

Buckton, Mrs. C. W. Comfort & cleanliness: the servant & the mistress question. N. Y., Longmans, Green & Co. 96 pp. 16mo. $0.75.

Domestic economy for teachers, revised by J. C. Horobin. L., Nelson. 464 pp. 8vo. 2s. 6d.

Handhabungen (Die) der Gesundheitsgesetze in Preussen . . . . in einzelnen Abhandlungen erläutert. Hrsg v. Dr. Springfeld, F. Siber & B. R. Schoetz. 1. Bd. B., R. Schoetz. 156 pp. 8vo. M. 3.

Lush, Ethel R. Lessons in domestic economy. Pt. 1. L., Macmillan & Co. 8vo. 6d.

Morton, Honner, ed. Complete system of nursing; written by medical men & nurses. N. Y., imported by C. Scribner's Sons. 403 pp. 12mo. $3.

17. Socialism.

Bebel, Aug. Akademiker u. Sozialismus. Vortrag. B., Verlag der Sozialist. Monatshefte. 14 pp. 8vo. M. 0.50,

Blum, Hans. Die Heiligen unserer Sozialdemokratie u. die Pariser Commune v. 1871 in ihrer wahren Gestalt. . . . Wurzen, C. Kiesler. 79 pp. 8vo. M. 0.80,

Bohm-Bawerk, E. v. Karl Marx & the close of his system: a criticism, trans. by Alice M. Macdonald. L., Fisher Unwin. 222 pp. 8vo. 6d.

Delville, G. Socialisme et propriété : discours prononcé à la Chambre des députés. . . . . 1897. P., à la Petite République, 12, rue Paul-Lelong. f. o.20,

Handbuch f. sozialdemokratische Wähler. Der Reichstag, 1893-8. Hrsg. vom sozialdemokrat. Parteivorstand. B., Buchh. Vorwärts, 399 pp. 8vo. M. 3.

Jentsch, Carl. Socialauslese. Kritische Glossen. Lp., F. W. Grunow. 236 pp. 8vo. M. 2.80.

Lichtenberger, A. Le socialisme utopique. Etudes sur quelques précurseurs inconnus du socialisme. P., F. Alcan. 277 pp. 18mo.

Mehring, F. Gesch. d. deutschen Sozialdemokratie. 27.-33. Hft. Stuttgart, Dietz Nachf. à M. 0.20.

Sanders, George. A reality; or, law & order vs. anarchy & socialism: a reply to Ed. Bellamy's "Looking backward" & "Equality." Cleveland, O., Burrows Book Co. 239 pp. 8vo. $2.

Schmöle, Jos. Die sozialdemokratischen Gewerkschaften in Deutschland seit dem Erlasse des Sozialisten-Gesetzes. 2. Tl. Einzelne Organisationen. 1. Abtlg. Der Zimmerverband. Jena, G. Fischer. 300 pp. 8vo. M. 6.

Scotsburn (pseudonym). What is socialism? N. Y., imported by C. Scribner's Sons. 430 pp. 12mo. $3.

Sombart, Werner. Le socialisme et le mouvement social au 19e siècle. P., Giard & Brière. 195 pp. 18mo. f. 2. (Bibliothèque socialiste internationale.)

Verly, H. Les socialistes au pouvoir, simple histoire à la portée de tout le monde. . . . . P., libr. Le Soudier. 168 pp. 18mo.

Rivista popolare di socialismo. Anno 1, no. 1 (15 marzo, 1898). Milano, tip. Marco Polo. 12 pp. 4to. L. o.15 il no.

18. Sociology (General).

Abramowski, Ed. Le materialisme historique et le principe du phénomène social. P., Giard & Brière. 41 pp. 8vo.

Annals de l'Institute international de sociologie. Publiées sous la direction de René Worms, sécretaire général. T. 4, concernant les travaux du troisième congrès, tenu à Paris. . . . . 1898. P., Giard & Brière. 589 pp. 8vo. f. 10.

*Année (l') sociologique, publiée sous la direction d'Emile Durkheim et collaborateurs (1re

année, 1896-7). I. Mémoirs originaux : Durkheim, E., La prohibition de l'inceste et ses origines ; Simmel, G., Comment les forms sociales
se maintiennent. II. Analyses des travaux
du 1er juillet 1896 au 30 juin 1897. P., F. Alcan. 563 pp. 8vo. f. 10. (JPE., Je. + +)
Biederlack, Jos. Die sociale Frage. Ein Beitrag
zur Orientierg. üb. ihr. Wesen u. ihre Lösg. 2.
Aufl. Innsbruck, F. Rauch. 220 pp. 8vo. M.
1.80.
Comité des travaux historiques et scientifiques—
Section des sciences économiques et sociales.
Bulletin. P., Impr. nationale. 110 pp. 8vo.
Crowell, J. F. Logical process of social develop-
ment : a theoretical foundation for educational
policy from the standpoint of sociology. N.Y.,
H. Holt & Co. 358 pp. 12mo. $1.75.
Deschanel, Paul. La question sociale. P., libr.
C. Lévy. 369 pp. 18mo. f. 3.50.
Devaux, R. L. Partageons. De l'égalité des con-
ditions. Petite étude sur la question sociale.
P., libr. Chamul. 36 pp. 18mo. f. o.40.
Espinas, Alfred. Etude sociologique. Les ori-
gines de la technologie. P., F. Alcan. 295 pp.
8vo. f. 5.
Gasparotto, Lu. Il principio di nazionalita nella
sociologia e nel diritto internazionale. Torino,
fratelli Bocca. 149 pp. 8vo.
Grenier, A. S. Répertoire des faits politiques,
sociaux, économiques (2e année, 1897). P.,
Berger-Levrault & Cie. 485 pp. 8vo.
*Gumplowicz, Louis. Sociologie et politique. P.,
Giard & Brière. 300 pp. 8vo. (Bibliothèque
sociologique internationale) (AJS., Jl. — —).
Henderson, C. R. Social elements, institutions,
character, progress. N. Y., C. Scribner's Sons.
405 pp. 8vo. $1.50.
Jacquinet. Des problèmes de la vie et de la mort et
de quelques puestions sociales qui s'y rat-
tachent. P., Perrin & Cie. 131 pp. 18mo.
Lilienfeld, Paul. Zur Vertheidigung der orga-
nischen Methode in der Sociologie. Br., G.
Reimer. 76 pp. 8vo. M. 1.20.
*Mallock, W. B. Aristocracy & evolution : a study
of the rights, the origin & the social functions
of the wealthier classes. N. Y., Macmillan
Co. 385 pp. 8vo. $3. (JPE., Je. —+)
Mikhailowsky, N. Qu'est-ce que le progrès?
Examen des idées de M. Herbert Spencer ; tr.
du russe. P., F. Alcan. 204 pp. 16mo. f.
2.50.
Oppenheimer, Frz. Grossgrundeigentum u. soziale
Frage. Versuch e. neuen Grundlegg. der
Gesellschaftswissenschaft. B., "Vita," Deut-
sches Verlagshaus. 504 pp. 8vo. M. 5.
Sansoni, Eug. La libertà pratica: saggio. Firenze,
fratelli Bocca edit. 426 pp. 8vo. L. 7.
Sherard, R. H. White slaves of England : being
true pictures of certain social conditions. . . .
1897. Ed. 2. L., James Bowden. 320 pp.
8vo. 1s. 6d.
Sigel, F. Sociology applied to politics : social
theories & Russian conditions. Ph., Am.
Acad. of Pol. & Soc. Science. 37 pp. 8vo.
(Publications of the society, No. 226.) Paper,
$0.35.
Staats- u. socialwissenschaftliche Forschungen.
Hrsg. v. Gust. Schmoller. 16. Bd. 1. Hft.
(Der ganzen Reihe 68. Hft.) Lp., Duncker
& Humblot. 86 pp. M. 2.20.
Stein, Ludw. Wesen u. Aufgaben der Sociologie.
Eine Kritik der organ. Methode in der Socio-
logie. B., G. Reimer. 38 pp. 8vo. M. o.60.
[Aus " Archiv f. system. Philos."]
Tarde, G. Les lois sociales. Esquisse d'une socio-
logie. P., F. Alcan. 167 pp. 18mo.
*Vaccario, Michel-Ange. Les bases sociologiques
du droit et de l'État, tr. sur l'éd. italienne. . . .
P., Giard & Brière. 480 pp. (AJS., Jl. +)
Vincent, G. E. Social mind & education. N. Y.,

Macmillan Co., 1897. 152 pp. 8vo. $1.25.
(AJS., Jl. + +)
Wallace, A. R. The wonderful century : its successes & its failures. L., Swan Sonnenschein.
412 pp. 8vo. 7s. 6d.
Watrigant, Henri. Le décalogue agricole. Un
esquisse d'un programme d'action catholique
dans les campagnes. Abbeville, C. Pillart,
1896. 60 pp. f. o.50. (AJS., Jl. +)

Kidd, Benjamin. Social evolution. New ed., revised, with additions. N. Y., Macmillan Co.
404 pp. 12mo. $1.50; paper, $0.25.
Tarde, G. La logique sociale. 2e éd. revue et
augmentée. P., F. Alcan. 468 pp. 8vo.

19. Statistics.

Algiers — Statistique générale de l'Algérie 1894-6.
Alger-Mustapha, impr. Giralt.
Arbeits-Statistik der deutschen Gewerkvereine
(Hirsch-Duncker) f. d. J. 1897. . . . . B., C.
Haase. 123 pp. 8vo. M. 3.
Austria — K. k. Ackerbau-Ministerium. Stati-
stisches Jahrbuch für 1896. 2. Hft. 1. & 2. Lfg.
Wien, Hof- u. Staatsdruckerei. 173 u. 248 pp.
8vo. M. 2.
Austria — Ackerbau - Ministerium. Statistisches
Jahrbuch für 1896. 2. Hft. 2. Lfg. Wien, Hof-
u. Staatsdruckerei. 248 pp. 8vo. M. 4.
Austria — K. k. statist. Central - Commission.
Oesterreichische Statistik. 46. Bd., 4. Hft., 2.
Abtg.; 47. Bd., 1. & 2. Hft.; 49. Bd., 1. u. 2.
Hft., 4. Abtg., 3. Hft. Wien, C. Gerold's Sohn.
Austria—Statist. Depart. im k. k. Handelsministe-
rium. Statistik des auswärtigen Handels des
österreichisch-ungarischen Zollgebiets. . . . .
1896. 3. Bd. Wien, Hof- u. Staatsdruckerei.
243 u. 199 pp. 8vo. M. 6.
Austria—Statist. Departem im k. k. Handels-
ministerium. Nachrichten üb. Industrie,
Handel & Verkehr. 66. Bd. 1. u. 2. Hft.
Statistik des österreichischen Post- u. Telegra-
phenwesens im J. 1896. Mit e. statist. Uebersicht
. . . . Europa. 67. Bd., 2.-4. Hft. Wien, Hof-
u. Staatsdruckerei. 328 pp. 8vo. M. 5.
Austria—Statist. Depart. im k. k. Handelsministerium. Die Arbeitsvermittlung in Oesterreich.
Wien, A. Holder, 304 u. 217 pp. 4to. M. 4.80.
Austria—Statist. Depart. im k. k. Handelsmini-
sterium. Die Arbeitseinstellungen u. Aus-
sperrungen im Gewerbebetriebe in Qesterreich
während des J. 1896. Wien, A. Holder. 127
u. 333 pp. 8vo. M. 2.40.
Bavaria—Zeitschrift des königl. bayerischen stati-
tischen Bureau. 30. Jahrg. 1898. 4 Nrn. 4to.
(Nr. 1, 98 pp.) München, J. Lindauer in Komm.
M. 6.
Bern—Mitteilungen des bernischen statistischen
Bureaus. Jahrg. 1898. 1. Lfg. Muhlemann,
C. Geschichte in Thätigkeit des bernischen
Bureaus des Kantons Bern von 1848-98. Bern,
Schmid & Francke in Komm. 132 pp. 8vo.
M. 1.60.
Bremen—Bureau f. Brem. Statistik. Jahrbuch.
1892. 2. Hft. Zur allgemeinen Statistik d. J.
1895 u. 1896. Bremen, G. H. v. Halem in
Komm. 553 pp. 8vo. M. 7.50.
Bremen — Bureau f. Brem. Statistik. Schiff- u.
Waarenverkehrs im J. 1897. Bremen, G. A. v.
Halem in Komm. 280 pp. 8vo. M. 7.50.
Breslau—Statist. Amt. Breslauer Statistik. 17.
Bd. 3. Hft. Breslau, E. Morgenstern Verl.
306 pp. 8vo. M. 6.
France—Ministère de l'agriculture. Statistique
agricole de la France. Résultats généraux de
l'enquête décennale de 1892. P., Impr. nationale, 1897. 816 pp. 8vo.
France—Ministère de l'agriculture. Statistique
agricole annuelle pour 1896. P., Impr. na-
tionale. 261 pp. 8vo.

Gemeindelexikon f. das Königr. Preussen auf Grund der Materialien der Volkszählg . . . 1895 . . . vom königl. statist. Bureau. 7. Prov. Sachsen. B., Verl. des k. statist. Bureau. 291 pp. 8vo. M. 4.

Germany— Kaiserl. statist. Amt. Statistik des Deutschen Reichs. B., Puttkammer & Mühlbrecht. Neue Folge. 92., 93: 1, 106., 110. u. 112. Bd. 306, 157, 696, 574 u. 500 pp. 4to. M. 1, 6 u. 5.

Germany—Kaiserl. statist. Amt. Statistisches Jahrbuch f. das Deutsche Reich. 19. Jahrg, 1898. B., Puttkammer & Mühlbrecht, 222 pp. 8vo. M. 2.

Germany—Kaiserl. statist. Amt. Vierteljahrshefte zur Statistik des Deutschen Reichs . . . B., Puttkammer & Mühlbrecht. 75 pp. 4to. M. 1.

Germany—Kaiserl. statist. Amt. Vierteljahrshefte zur Statistik des deutschen Reichs. Jahrg. 1898. Ergänzung zum 1. Hft. Hauptergebnisse der gewerbl. Betriebszählg, 14. VI. 1895. B., Puttkammer & Mühlbrecht. 124 pp. 4to. M. 2.

Hartleben's statistische Tabelle über alle Staaten der Erde. 5. Jahrg. 1898 . . . Wien, A. Hartleben. 98 pp. 16mo M. 1.50.

Hungary — Kön. ung. statist. Bureau. Ungarisches statistisches Jahrbuch. Neue Folge, IV, 1896. Amtliche Uebersetz . . . . Budapest, F. Kilian. 500 pp. 8vo. M. 10.

Italy — Direzione generale della statistica. Elenco delle società di M. S. Roma, tip. Italiana. 215 pp. 8vo, L. 1.50.

Italy — Direzione generale della statistica, Cause di morte: statistica dell' anno 1896. Roma, tip. Nazionale di G. Bertero, 1897. 36 pp. 8vo.

*London—Statistical officer of the County Council. Statistical abstract for London, 1897. Vol. 1. 75 pp. 8vo. (MA., Mr.+)

*Mayr, Georg von. Bevölkerungstatistik. Freiburg, J. C. B. Mohr, 1897. 486 pp. 8vo. M. 12. (Handbuch des öffentlichen Rechts. Einleitungsband, hrsg. von Max v. Seydel. 6. Abthg.) (DL., Jan. 22 + +) (PSQ., Mr.+ +) (AAP., Mr. + +) (JPE., Je. + +)

Munich — Statistisches Amt. Mitteilungen. 16. Bd. 1. Hft. Münchener Jahresübersichten f. 1896. München, J. Lindauer. 106 pp. 4to. M. 2.

Prussia—Königl. statist. Bureau. Gemeindelexikon f. das Königr. Preussen. Auf Grund der Materialien der Volkszählg. von 1895 u. anderer amtl. Quellen. 10.-12. Hft. Br., Verlag des k. statist. Bureaus. 180 u. 191 pp. 8vo. M. 2.60 u. 4.60.

Prussia — Königl. statist. Bureau. Preussische Statistik . . . . 142. Hft., 1 Thl., 146. Hft., 2 Thle., 148. Hft., 2 Thle., 149. Hft., 152. Hft.

Romero, Matias. Geographical & statistical notes on Mexico. N. Y., G. P. Putnam's Sons. 286 pp. 8vo. $2.

Statistisches Jahrbuch der Stadt Berlin. 22. Jahrg. Statistik des J. 1895. Im Auftrage des Magistrats hrsg. von R. Bäckh. Br., P. Stankiewicz. 595 pp. 8vo. M. 10.

Strassburg i. E. — Beiträge zur Statistik der Stadt. Hrsg. vom statist. Amt der Stadt. IV. Hft. Geissenberger, N. Die Personal- u. Gewerbebesteuerung in Strassburg . . . . 100 pp. 8vo. M. 2.

Switzerland — Schweizerische Statistik. Hrsg. vom statist. Bureau des eidgen. Departementes des Innern. 115. Lfg. Die Bewegung der Bevölkerung in der Schweiz im J. 1896. Bern, Schmid & Francke in Komm. 33 pp. M. 3.

Switzerland—Statistisches Bureau des eidg. Departement des Innern. Schweizerische Statistik. 112. Lfg. Zürich, Art. Institut Orell Füssli in Komm. 137 pp. 4to. M. 9.

Württemberg — K. statist. Landesamt. Statistisches Handbuch f. das Königr. Württemberg. Jahrg. 1897. Stuttgart, W. Kohlhammer. 256 pp. 8vo. M. 2. (Aus Württ. Jahrb. f. Statistik u. Landeskde.)

20. Unclassified.

Alkohol, der Mörder, im J. 1897. Dresden, O. V. Bohmert. 39 pp. 8vo M. 0.60.

Anzoletti, Luisa. L^a donna nuova. Milano, tip. L. Cogliati. 48 pp. 16mo. L, 0.60.

Austria— K. k. Eisenbahn-Ministerium. Hauptergebnisse der österreichischen Eisenbahn-Statistik im J. 1896 . . . Wien, Hof- u. Staatsdruckerei. 651 pp. 8vo. M. 6.

Austria—Ministerium des Innern. Stenographisches Protokoll in der . . . 1897 Enquête über die Reform des Krankenversicherungsgesetzes. Wien, Hof- u. Staatsdruckerei. 477 pp. 8vo. M. 5.

Baronchelli, Donato. Esposizione ed esame critico del collettivismo pratico. Bergamo, tip. di Maggioni e Secomandi. 85 pp. 16mo.

Beaune, H. La participation aux bénéfices dans l'industrie et le commerce. Lyon, libr. Cato [1893]. 32 pp. 8vo.

Bennett, R., & Elton, J. History of corn-milling. V. 1. Handstones, slave & cattle mills. L., Simpkin, Marshall, etc. 266 pp. 10s.

Bensing, Frz. Der Einfluss der landwirthschaftlichen Maschinen auf Volks- u. Privatwirthschaft. Breslau, Schletter. 205 pp. 8vo. M. 4.60.

Bryce, James. William Ewart Gladstone; his characteristics as man & statesman. N. Y., Century Co., 1898. 104 pp. 16mo. $1.

Coal Tables. Statement showing the production & consumption of coal & the number of persons employed in coal production in the principal countries of the world, 1883–96. . . . L., Eyre & Spottiswoode. 5½d.

Colleville, Docteur. A travers le sixième congrès international de Bruxelles contre l'abus des poisons alcooliques. Reims, impr. Monce, 1897. 61 pp. 8vo.

Congrès international d'agriculture, tenu à Budapest . . . 1896. Comptes rendus. (Ungarisch, deutsch, französisch u. englisch.) Wien, W. Frick. 2 v. 536 & 686 pp. 8vo. M. 4.

Congrès (neuvième) du crédit populaire (assoc. cooperatives de crédit) tenu à Lille . . . . 1897. Actes du Congrès. P., Guillaumin & Cie (1897). 404 pp. 8vo.

Cooke, S. The foundations of scientific agriculture. N. Y., Longmans, Green & Co., 1897. 268 pp. 12mo. $1.50.

Coöperative societies, Statistics of, in various countries. Prepared by the statistical committee of the Internat. Cooperative Alliance. L., P. S. King & Co. 330 pp. 4to. 10s.

Coste, Adolphe. Alcoolisme ou épargne. Le dilemme social. Ed. 5. P., F. Alcan. 192 pp. 16mo. f. 0.60.

*Cunningham, W. Alien immigrants in England. L., Macmillan & Co., 1897. 286 pp. 12mo. $1.25. (AJS., Jl. +)

Daum, Adolph. Die Bekämpfung der Trinksitten durch die Gesetzgebung. Wien, Manz. 20 pp. 8vo. M. 0.40.

Documents relatifs à l'histoire de l'industrie et du commerce en France. I. Depuis le 1er siècle avant Jésus-Christ jusqu'à la fin du 13e siècle . . . par Gustave Fagniez. P., Picard et fils. 349 pp. 8vo.

Dunkelberg, F. W. Die landwirthschaftliche Betriebslehre in ihren naturgesetzlichen, volkswirthschaftlichen u. culturethischen Grundlagen. 3. Thl. A. u. d. T. Die landwirthschaftl. Taxationslehre . . . Braunschweig, F. Vieweg & Sohn. M. 6.

Field, H. M. The life of David Dudley Field.
N. Y., C. Scribner's Sons. 361 pp. 8vo. $3.
Fiorentino, Pietro. Le associazioni e le società
in genere e quelle di mutuo soccorso in specie,
studiate nella odierna evoluzione sociale in
rapporto al diritto civile italiano. Cantania,
tip.-edit. dell' Etna, 1897. 245 pp. 8vo.
France—Ministère de l'agriculture. Annuaire
. . . 1898. P., Impr. nationale. 470 pp. 8vo.
France—Ministère des travaux publics. Statistique
des chemins de fer français au décembre 1896.
Documents principaux. P., Impr. nationale,
1897. 541 pp. 4to. f. 5.
Gand, M. La propriété collective en Suisse.
L'Allemand dans le canton d'Obwalden. P.,
libr. Sueur-Charruey. 40 pp. 8vo. (Extrait de la
Revue de Lille.)
Gladstone, W. E. Statesman & scholar; ed. by
David Williamson; many por. & ill. L.,
Ward & Lock. 450 pp. 8vo. 5s.
Great Britain—Customs tariffs of the United
Kingdom from 1800 to 1897. L., Eyre &
Spottiswoode. 7s. 6d.
Great Britain—Board of Trade. Accounts relat-
ing to trade & navigation . . . 1898. L., Eyre
& Spottiswoode. 8d.
Great Britain—Board of Trade. Emigration &
immigration. Statistical tables . . . 1897. L.,
Eyre & Spottiswoode. 6d.
Great Britain—Board of Trade. Report on all
the railway, etc., bills . . . 1898. L., Eyre &
Spottiswoode. 8d.
Great Britain—Parliament. Agricultural returns
for Great Britain, showing acreage and pro-
duce of crops, prices of corn, number of live
stock, etc. L., Eyre & Spottiswoode. 8vo.
1s. 6d.
Great Britain—Parliament. Friendly societies:
industrial & provident societies & trade
unions; reports for 1896. Part. B. Appendix L.
L., Eyre & Spottiswoode. 10½ d.
Great Britain—Parliament. Irish agricultural
statistics fro 1879. Produce prices, 1881-7. L.,
Eyre & Spottiswoode. 3s.
Great Britain—Trade of the United Kingdom
with foreign countries & British possessions,
1897, comp. with four preceding years. L.,
Eyre & Spottiswoode. 7s. 7d.
Grimaldi, Onofrio. Manuale di estetica. Brin-
disi, tip. D. Mealli. 160 pp. 8vo. L. 2.
*Grinling, C. H. History of the Great Northern
railway, 1845-95. N. Y., New Amsterdam
Book Co. 429 pp. 8vo. $5. (Athenæum, Mr.
12. p. 340) (Academy, Mr. 26 ×)
Handbibliothek f. das deutsche Genossenschafts
wesen. Hrsg. v. Hans Crüger. 3. Bd. Breslau, E. Morgenstern. 350 pp. M. 5, geb. 6.
Handwörterbuch d. Versicherungswesen. 2. & 3.
Lfg. Strassburg, Baumgartner. à M. 1.50.
Holland, L. Suggestions for a scheme of old-
age pensions. Intro. chap. on report of Com-
mittee on O. A. P. L., Arnold.
Kataster der im Königr. Preussen vorhandenen
eingetragenen Genossenschaften. Bearb. v.
der preuss. Central-Genossenschafts-Kasse.
B., C. Haymans' Verlag. 649 pp. Fol. M. 45.
Kunstedt, Jul. Wie muss das deutsche Volk die
gesammelten 600,000,000 Mark der Alters-,
Invaliditäts- u. Unfall-Versicherungsgenos-
senschafts-Fonds zum Besten des Vaterlandes
anlegen? Ein Vorschlag friedl. Socialreform.
. . . Zürich, C. Schmidt. 54 pp. 8vo. M. 1.
Lewinstein, Gust. Der Tabakkonsum in den
einzelnen Staaten der Erde u. die Einnahmen
der Staaten aus dem Tabak. Nach amtl.
Quellen zusammengestellt. B., W. Peiser.
80 pp. 12mo. M. 0.80.
Mase-Dari, E. La rendita e la proprieta del suolo
nella crisi agraria attuale. Torino, Roux,
Frassati & C. 79 pp. 8vo. L. 1.50.

McCarthy, Justin. Story of Gladstone's life; ed.
2; rev. & enlarged. L., Black. 466 pp. 8vo.
7s. 6d.
McConnell, F. Note-book of agricultural facts &
figures for farmers & farm students. Ed. 6.
L., Lockwood. 468 pp. 12mo. 6s.
Molinari, G. de. Grandeur et décadence de la
guerre. P., libr. Guillaumin & Cie. 314 pp.
18mo. f. 3.50.
Mongredin, A. Hist. of the free-trade movement
in England. New ed. Intro. & supp. chapters
by H. de B. Gibbens. L., Cassell & Co. 200
pp. 8vo. 1s.
Mucke, R. Urgeschichte des Ackerbaues u.
der Viehzucht. Eine neue Theorie m. e.
Einleitung üb. die Behandlg. urgeschicht.
Probleme auf statist. Grundlage. Greifswald,
J. Abel. 404 pp. 8vo. M. 9.60.
Mühlbrecht, Otto. Bibliographie des bürglichen
Gesetzbuches f. das deutsche Reich. . . . . B.,
Puttkammer & Mühlbrecht. 44 pp. 8vo. M. 1.
Nansouty, M. de. L'année industrielle. Décou-
vertes scientifiques et inventions nouvelles en
1897. P., libr. Juven & Cie. 334 pp. f. 3.50,
Ritchie, J. E. The real Gladstone: an anecdotal
biography. L., Fisher Unwin. 296 pp. 8vo.
5s.
*Robinson, H. P. Year-book of railway literature.
C., The Railway Age, 1897. 427 pp. $1.
(AAP., Mr. + +)
Rodiet, Antony. L'alcoolisme chez l'enfant: ses
causes et ses effets en pathologie mentale
(thèse). P., libr. Carré & Naud, 1897. 99 pp.
8vo.
Schevichaven, J. van. Vom Leben u. Sterben.
Das Gestern u. Heute der Lebensversicherg.
Aus dem Holl. übers . . . Wien, F. Deuticke.
395 pp. 8vo. M. 9.
Shaler, N. S. Outlines of the earth's history:
a popular study in physiography. N. Y., D.
Appleton & Co. 417 pp. ill. 12mo. $1.75.
Smith, G. A. Free trade movement & its results.
244 pp. 8vo. 2s. 6d. (Victorian era series.)
Sohni, Arrigo. Le associazioni in Italia avanti e
origini del comune . . . . Modena, tip. della
Società tip. antica. 140 pp. 8vo. L. 4.
Stead, W. T. Gladstone, 1809-98: a character
sketch, with portraits & ill. L., Review of
Reviews Office. 84 pp. 8vo. 1s.
Stetson, Charlotte Perkins. Woman & econom-
ics: a study of the economic relations between
men & women as a factor in social evolution.
Bo., Small, Maynard & Co. 340 pp. 12mo.
$1.50.
Swan, H. H. Economic aspects of railroad re-
ceiverships. N. Y., Macmillan Co. [for Am.
Economic Assoc.]. 161 pp. 12mo. $0.50.
(Economic studies.)
Systematische Zusammenstellung der Zolltarife des
Inu- u. Auslandes. Hrsg. v. Reichsamt des
Innern. Br., E. S. Mittler & Sohn. A. Tex-
tilindustrie. 226 pp. 8vo. B. Landwirt-
schaft. Nahrungs- u. Genussmittel. 307 pp.
4to. M. 3.
Testa, Lu. L'ultimo quarto di secolo dell' in-
dustria italiana. Miliano, tip. Angelo Matelli.
424 pp. 4to. L. 15.
Thiers, A. De la propriété. Nouvelle éd. P., lib.
Hachette & Cie. 443 pp. 8vo. f. 6.
Tischert, Geo. Fünf Jahre deutscher Handels-
politik (1890-94). Lp., F. W. Grunow. 371 pp.
8vo. M. 3.60.
Tolstoy, Leo. What is art? Chaps. 1-9. Trans.
L., Brotherhood Pub. Co. 24 pp. 4to. S. 1.
("The New Order" extra, Jan., '98)
Trénedy, J. L'alcoolisme et ses remèdes (thèse).
Rennes, impr. Oberthür. 24 pp. 8vo.
Valenti. Ghino. Il dazio sul frumento e l'agri-
coltura italiana; prolusione al corso di econo-
mia dell' agricoltura e di politica agraria nella

r. universita di Bologna. . . . Bologna. Nicola Zanichelli. 56 pp. 8vo. L. 1.
Volksunterhaltung (Die). Vorträge u. Berichte v. F. S. Archenhold u. a. . . . . Bericht üb. den 1, Kongress f. Volksunterhaltg . . . , 1897 zu Berlin . . . . B., F. Dümmler's Verl. 136 pp. 8vo. M. 1.50.
Walcker, Karl. Die Kompetenz der Religion, der Ethik, des Patriotismus, der Verfassung, Gesetzgebung, Justiz, Presse, der Vereine u. der öffentlichen, nationalen u. internationalen Meinung m. besond. Berücksicht. der Frage der Beleidigungen u. der Pressfreiheit. Lp., A. Strauch. 76 pp. M. 2.
Willoughby, W. F. Workingmen's insurance. N. Y., T. Y. Crowell & Co. 386 pp. 12mo. $1.75. (Library of economics & politics.)
Wokurek, Ludwig. Die österreichische Unfall-

versicherung. Eine krit. Studie. Wien, F. Deuticke. 109 pp. 8vo. M. 2.
Wolff, H. W. Coöperative credit banks: a help alike economic & educational for the laboring & cultivating classes. L., P. S. King. 58 pp. 8vo. 6d.
Young, Arthur. Autobiography, with selections from his correspondence; ed. by M. B. Edwards. N. Y., imported by C. Scribner's Sons. 480 pp, il. 12mo. $4.80.
Zacher, Dr. Die Arbeiter-Versicherung im Auslande. 2. u. 3. Hft. 2. Die Arbeiter-Versicherung in Schweden. 3. Die Arbeiter-Versicherung in Norwegen. B., Verlag der Arbeiter-Versorgung. M. 2.
Zenker, E. V. Anarchism: a criticism & history of the anarchist theory. N. Y., imported by C. Scribner's Sons. 266 pp. 8vo, $3.

ARTICLES IN PERIODICALS.

[Articles preceded by stars and followed by a reference to a number of the JO RNAL will be found in abstract under the head "Notes and Abstracts" in that number of the JOURNAL.] U

Æsthetics: Doumic, René. Les idées du comte Tolstoi sur l'art, RDM, My. 15.
Dubufe, M. G. Art et métier. II. L'architecture, RDM., My. 15.
Finck, H. T. Utility of music, F., My.
Agriculture: Ballod, Carl. Die Bedeutung der Landwirthschaft u. der Industrie in Deutschland, JGV., 22: 3.
Deherain, P. P. La science et l'agriculture: la terre arable, RDM., Je. 1.
Anarchism: Lum, D. D. Bases d'une morale anarchiste, HN., Ap.
Anglo-Saxon Alliance: Bryce, J. A. Essential unity of England and America, Atlantic, Jl.
Flower, B. O. Proposed federation of the Anglo-Saxon nations, A., Ag.
Greenwood, Fred. Anglo-American future, NC., Jl.
*Vallerou, Hubert. Procédés Anglo-Saxons, à propos de la guerre Hispano-Américaine, RéfS., My. 16. (AJS., Jl.)
Anthropology: Ammon, O. Histoire d'une idée. L'anthroposociologie, RIS., My.
Fouillée, Alfred. L'anthroposociologie, RIS., My.
Peet, S. D. Caves and cliff-dwellings compared, Am. Antiquarian, Ag.
Pulle, F. L. Profilo antropologico dell' Italia, AAE., 5: 1.
Thieullen, Ad. Les véritables instruments usuels de l'âge de la pierre, Bulletins de la Société de l'anthropologie, 1898: 1.
See also Education.
Architecture: Middleton, G. A. T. Fire resisting construction, EM.. Ag.
Associations: Banneaux, L. La Ligue du coin de terre et du foyer insaisissable, RSC., Je.
Brown, M. W. Evening Press newsboys' assoc., Ch.R., Jl.
Austria: Benoist, Charles. L'Autriche future et la future Europe, RDM.
Hirst, F. W. A dissolving empire, FR., Jl.
Schäffle, Albert von. Austria-Hungary under the reign of Francis Joseph, F., Jl.-Ag.
Baths: Van Alstine, Mayor. Don't need public baths, S., Jl.
Biography: Gladstone, Atlantic, Jl.
Gladstone. Leroy-Beaulieu, AEL., Jl.
Gladstone. Theodor Barth, Cos., Ag.
Gladstone. Norman Hapgood, CoR., Jl.
Gladstone. F. de Pressensé, Cos., Jl.
Gladstone. Lord Stanmore, FR., Jl.
Gladstone. A. de Malarce, JEc., Jl.
Gladstone. Justin McCarthy, F., Jl.

Gladstone & the Roman Catholic church. Wilfred Meynell, NC., Jl.
Gladstone. Francis de Pressensé, RDM., Jl. 1.
Gladstone & the nonconformists. Guinness Rogers, NC., Jl.
Gladstone. Paul de Ronsiers, SS., 25: 6.
Gladstone's theology. G. W. E. Russell, CoR., Je.
Gladstone. W. T. Stead, RRN., Jl.
Malthus, Centenary of. J. Bonar, EcJ., Jl.
Pobedonostzeff. Constantine, a statesman of Russia. A. D. White, Century, My.
Wilhelm, Kaiser. Poultney Bigelow, Century, J.
Wiseman, Cardinal. St. George Mivart, ACQ., Ap.
Biology: Dastre, A. Théorie de l'énergie et le monde vivant, RDM., My. 1.
Oswald, F. L. Secret of atavism, PSM., Je.
Boys: Brown, M. W. Evening Press newsboys' assoc., Ch.R., Jl.
Sanborn, A. F. Boys & boys' clubs, NAR., Ag.
Building: see Architecture.
Canada: Benzon, Th. Au Canada: l'éducation de la société, RDM., Jl. 15.
Burinot, J. G. Canada's relations with the U. S. & her influence in imperial councils, F., My.
Farrer, Edward. Anglo-American commission, F., Ag.
Canals: Haupt, L. M. National influence & the isthmian canal, EM., Jl.
Ludlow, Wm. Trans-isthmian canal problem, Harper's, My.
Nimmo, Joseph. Nicaragua canal in its commercial & military aspects, EM., Ag.
Central America: Curtis, W. E. Central America: its resources & commerce, F., My.
Charities: Bentzon, Th. Les femmes du Canada français. I. Etablissements de charité, RDM., My. 15.
Charities of Bristol, ChOR., My.
Hayter, Richard. Army & navy aid: relief of dependent families, CR., Jl.-Ag.
Lallemand, Léon. Le associazioni di beneficenza nella provincia di Quebec, RBP., Ap.
(La) Mendicita in Piemonte e il regio recovero di Torino, RBP., My.
Millis, H. A. Relief & care of dependents, AJS., Jl.
Münsterberg, Emil. Bericht über die 17. Jahresversammlung des deutschen Vereins für Armenpflege u. Wohlthätigkeit, JGV., 22: 3.
National conference of charities & corrections, report of meeting, 1898, ChR., Je.

New York state custodial asylum for feeble-minded women, ChR., Ag.
Parry, Judge. The insolvent poor, FR., My.
Pecker, Dr. L'association des dames Mauloises: secours aux femmes en couches, RP., My.
Wines, F. H. Flood at Shawneetown, ChR., Je.
See also each number of ChOR.. ChR., RBP., RP.
Chemistry: Berthelot, M. E. Genealogy of chemistry, PSM., Ag.
Child-Saving: *see* Boys.
Children: Adler, Felix. Punishment of children, Ethical Addresses, My.
Barr, M. W. Defective children, their needs & their rights, IJE., Jl.
Barr, M. W. Training of mentally deficient children, PSM., Ag.
Burk, Frederick. Growth of children in height, & weight, AJP., Ap.
Matiegka, Heinrich. Die Beziehungen zwischen Körperbeschaffenheit u. geistiger Thätigkeit bei Schulkindern, Mittheilungen der anthro. Gesellschaft in Wien, 28:3.
Thulié, H. Premières mésures à prendre contre le développement de la criminalité infantile, RPh., Jl.
See also Girls.
China: Brandt, M. von. Germany & China, F., My.
Christianity: *see* Religion.
Christian Socialism: *see* each number of Revue du Christianisme sociale.
Churches: Beyschlag, Willard. Origin & development of the Old Catholic movement, AJT., J.
Buckley, G. W., & others. Churches & the social question, A., Ag.
DeWitt, John. Place of the Westminster assembly in modern history, Presbyterian & Reformed Review, Jl.
Cities: Barnett, S. A. Twenty-five years of East London, CoR., Ag.
Bertolini, A. Gli Italiani a Chicago, GEc., Je.
Estabrook, H. K. Slums in Boston, ChR., Jl.
Harrison, Frederic. Ideal London, CoR., Jl.
Maltbie, M. R. Recent municipal progress in London, MA., Je.
Martin, E. S. East side considerations, Harper's, My.
Prienne, H. Villes, marches et marchands au moyen âge, RH., Je.
Tooke, C. W. Uniformity in municipal finance, MA., Je.
White, Henry & others. The city's health, MA., Je.
Wilcox, D. F. First municipal campaign of Greater New York, MA., Je.
See also Criminology & Penalogy, Socialism, Water.
Coal: Taylor, Benjamin. Coal supplies of the world, NC., Jl.
Collectivism: *see* Individualism, Coöperation.
Colonies: Collier, James. Evolution of colonies, PSM., Jl.-Ag.
Constitution: Whitney, E. B. Cuban revolt & the constitution, YR., My.
Consumption: *see* Sanitary Science.
Continental System: Sloane, W. M. Continental system, PSQ., Je.
Co-operation: Brelay, Ernst. Les sociétés ouvrières de production, RéfS.. My. 1.
Coöperation in practice, EcR., Jl.
Lambrechts, H. Le crédit rural. RSC., My.
McVey, F. L. Coöperation by farmers, JPE., Je.
Muller, Victor. Le Vooruit: un type de société coopérative, SS., 25:6.
(Les) sociétés de crédit en 1897, JEc., Jl.
Wolff, H. W. Eine Internationale genossenschaftliche Statistik, JNS., My.

Credit: *see* Coöperation.
Criminology and Penalogy: Amos, Sheldon. The prison treatment of women, CoR., Je.
Bonsal, Stephen. Convict system of Siberia, Harper's, Ag.
Bromby, C. H. Judicial sentences and the habitual criminal, LQR., Ap.
Howard John. Elisabeth Gilman, ChR., Jl.
Mailly, Caignart de. L'évolution de l'idée criminaliste au 19e siècle et ses conséquences, RéfS., Je. 16.
Makarewicz, J. Evolution de la peine, AAC,. Mr.
Morrison, W. D. Prisons & prisoners, FR., My.
Orme, Eliza. Our female criminals, FR., My.
Pottet, E. Les bibliothèques dans les prisons, RPe, Je.
Saccozzi, Augusto. L'idea della pena nei pazzi criminali, RDC.
Sighele, Scipio. La delinquenza delle grande citta, RDC., Je.
Soloviefĭ, Wladimir. De la peine de mort, RIS., Mr.
Tarde, G. Problems de criminalité, AAP., Jl.
Vence, C. de. Les criminels dans l'art et la littérature, RPe., Je.
See also Children and each number of BG., ChOR., ChR., RDC., RPe.
Cuba: Chamberlain, J. E. War for Cuba. F., Je.
Davery, Richard. Glimpses of Havana & the Havanese, FR., My.
Foraker, J. B. Our war with Spain: its justice & necessity, F. Je.
Gossip, I. H. D. The mournful case of Cuba. FR., My.
Gunton, Georg. Spain & Cuba: a few facts, GM., My.
Hershey, A. S. Intervention & the recognition of Cuban independence, AAP., My.
Hull, R. T. Cuba & its value as a colony, F., Je.
Lee. Fitzhugh. Cuba & her struggle for freedom, FR., My.
Musgrave, G. C. The Cuban insurrection, CoR., Jl.
Democracy: Alix, Gabriel. Les lois de la démocratie, RéfS., My. 1.
Demography: *see* Population, Statistics.
Dependents: *see* Charities.
Direct Legislation: *see* each number of New Time.
District of Columbia: West, H. L. Little kingdom of the President, F., Je.
Domestic: Smith, Mary Roberts. Education for domestic life, PSM., Ag.
Education: Bezold, Fr. v. Die ältesten deutschen Universitäten in ihrem Verhältnis zum Staat, HZ., 80:3.
Burnham, W. H. Some aspects of the teaching profession, F., Je.
Dewey, John. Harris's psychologic foundation of education, EdR,. Je.
Dewey, John. Primary-education fetich, F.. My.
L'évolution politique de l'école primaire, RDM, Je.15.
Fouillée, A. Les réformes universitaires, RPP., Jl.
Henderson, C. H. The philosophy of manual training, PSM., Je.-Ag.
Lévy, R. G. Les universitées et l'économie politique aux États-Unis, AEL., Jl.
Mackenzie, J. S. Bearings of philsoophy on education, IJE., Jl.
Medd. J. C. State in relation to education. EcR., Ap.
Schiedt, R. C. Rational training of children a problem in pedagogical psychology, S., Ag.
Vanderwalker, N. C. Some demands of education upon anthropology, AJS., Jl.

Hungary: Bernát, St. Die Agrarbewegung in Ungarn, Leben, Jl.
(La) Constitution hungroise, RPP., Jl.
Immigration: MacDonald, William. French Canadians in New England, QJE., Ap.
Indians: Powell, J. W. How a savage tribe is governed, F., Ag.
Individualism: Darin, A. De M. Brunetière et de l'individualisme, RMM., My.
Kohler, J. Collectivismus u. Individualismus in der Geschichte, ZS., Ap.
Infanticide: Matignon, J. J. Note complémentaire sur l'infanticide en Chine, AAC., My. 15.
Injunction: Rogers, J. T. The injunction, NT., My.
Stillman, J. W. Misuse of injunction, A., Ag.
Innere Mission: *see* each number of MIM. and Fliegende Blätter aus dem Rauhen Hause.
Insane: Daniel F. E. Criminal responsibility of the insane, A., Ag.
Institutional Church: *see* each number of Open Church.
Insurance: Friendly societies & the poor law, ChOR., Je.
Rauchberg, Heinrich. Die Statistik der Unfall- u. Krankenversicherung der Arbeiter in Oesterreich 1890-5, ASG., 12:6.
Ueber Privatversicherungswesen, JGV., 22:3.
Interest: *see* Finance.
International Law: Desjardins, Arthur. La guerre hispano-américaine et le droit des gens.
Ireland: O'Shea, J. J. Ireland looking back, ACQ., Ap.
Russell, T. W. What the unionists have done for Ireland, NAR., Ag.
Irrigation: Palmer, George. Tank irrigation in India, EM., My.
Italy: Calajarmi, N. La dernière crise italienne, RPP., Jl.
Ferrero, G. Le condizioni dell Italia, GEc., Je.
Fioretti, Giulio. La disette en Italie, SS., 25:6.
Misgovernment of Italy, FR., Je.
Vecchia, G. D. Revolt in Italy, CoR., Jl.
Zerboglio, Adolfo. Les révoltes et la réaction en Italie, DS., Je.
Japan: *see* Family.
Joint Stock Companies: Kuefstein, Franz. Das Actienwesen u. seine Bedeutung im heute herrschenden Wirtschaftssystem, Leben, Jl.
Labor: Avenel, George. Paysans et ouvriers depuis sept siècles, RDM., Je. 15-Ag. 1.
Bosanquet, Helen. Industrial democracy [Review of Webb's book]. ChOR., Jl.
Clement, Henri. La vie ouvrière aux États-Unis, RéfS., Je. 16.
Felton, Katherine. Rousier's theory of the evolution of the laborer, JPE., Je.
Grätzer, Rudolf. Die Lage des deutschen Handwerks u. seine Organisation, ZS., Ap.-My.
Kelley, Florence. United States court & the Utah eight hours' law, AJS., Jl.
Kelley, Florence. Drei Entscheidungen Oberster Gerichte über den gesetzl. Arbeitstag in den Vereinigten Staaten, ASG., 12:6.
North, S. N. D. Levasseur's American workingmen, PSQ, Je.
Rousiers, Paul de. L'ouvrier américain et l'évolution industrielle, SS., 25:4.
Smith, E. J. New trades combination movement, EcR., Ap.
Stanton, Theodore. French view of the American workingman, F., Je.
Stevens, Alzina P. Die Gewerkvereine der Vereinigten Staaten, ASG., 12:6.
Stimson, F. J. National arbitration law, IJE., Jl.
Willoughby, W. F. French workingman's compensation act, QJE., Jl.

See also Coöperation, Machinery, Strikes, Unemployed, Wages.
Labor Colonies: Buxton, Noel. Labor homes, EcR., Jl.
See also each number of Der Wanderer.
Land: Gallouédec, M. L. Man's dependence on the earth, PSM., My.
Vallée-Poussin, J. de la. La propriété paysanne en Belgique, RSC., Ap.
Language: Vidmar, Const. Die Weltsprache-Idee u. das Volapük, Das Leben, Jl.
Law: Barclay, Shepard. The danger line, ALR., Jl.
Lewis, W. D. Study of the common law, ALR., Ag.
Pollock, Frederick. English law before the Norman conquest, LQR., Jl.
See also each number of ALR., ALRR., LQR., ZPO.
Legislation: Vergilii, Filippo. Législation ouvrière, DS., My.
See also each number of ASG., EcR., JNS., RPP.
Liquor Question: Denis, Jules. Conséquences sociales de l'abus des boissons, Revue du Christianisme social, My.
Lippert, G. Die Frage des Alkoholmonopoles, ZVS., 7:2.
Rouby, Dr. Les crimes de l'alcoolisme, AAP., My.
Vincelles, Comte de. Une tentative de lutte locale contre l'alcoolisme, RéfS., Je. 1.
Literature: Faguet, Emile. The influence of Balzac, FR., My.
Thomas, Calvin. Have we still need of poetry? F., Je.
Wildenbruch, Ernst von. Evolution of the German drama, F., My., Jl.
Manual Training: *see* Education.
Manufactures: McKinney, L. F. Depression in the cotton industry, F., Jl.
Dowd, Jerome. Textile war between the North and South, F., Je.
Machinery: Davis, C. W. Does machinery displace labor? F., Jl.
Monopolies: *see* Trusts.
Music: *see* Æsthetics.
Navies: Clowes, W. L. Sea power at the end of the 19th century, EM., Jl.
Wilson, H. W. Navies & naval construction programme of 1898, EM., Ag.
Oklahoma: Candee, Helen C. Social conditions in our newest territory, F., Je.
Peace: Smith, F. Peace as a factor in social & political reform, PSM., Je.
People's Palace: Pyfferoen, Oscar. Le peuple's palace et les polytechnics de Londres, RéfS., Je. 1.
Philippines: Gunton, George. The Philippines, an unknown empire, GM., Je.
Hilder, F. F. Philippine islands, F., Jl.
Vanderlip, F. A. Facts about the Philippines, Century, Ag.
Philosophy: Brunschvieg, L. De quelques préjugés contre la philosophie, RMM., Jl.
Espinas, Alfred. Babeuf et le Babouvisme, RIS., My.
See also History.
Political Economy: Green, H. S. S. Mr. Godkin & the new political economy, A., Jl.
Marx, Karl. Salaire, prix et profits, DS., My.
Pantaleoni, M. Attempt to analyse the concepts of strong & weak in their economic connection, EcJ., Je.
Sorel, G. Nuovi contributi alla teoria marxistica del valore, GEc., Jl.
Veblen, Thorstein. Why is economics not an evolutionary science, QJE., Jl.
Wolf, Julius. Illusionisten u. Realisten in der Nationalökonomie, ZS., Ap.-My.

Pomeroy, Eltweld. Law of averages, NT., My.
Posada, Adolfo. Le droit et la question sociale, RIS., Ap.
Ratzel, F. Il suolo e la popolazione, RItS., Mr.
Roberty, E. de. L'élite et la foule, HN., Jl.
Simmel, Georg. Persistence of social groups, AJS., Jl.
Sociale Reformbestrebungen, Das Leben, Ap.
Solvay, Ernest. Principes de politique sociale, AIS, 4 : 1.
Steinmetz, S. R. Le cours d'ethnologie et de sociologie à l'Université d'Utrecht, RIS., Mr.
Tarde, G. Les lois sociales, RMM., My.
Tosti, Gustavo. Social psychology & sociology, PsR., Jl.
Wines, F. H. Sociology & philanthropy, AAP., Jl.
Worms, René. L'économie sociale, RIS., Je.
See also Population, United States.
Speculation: see Exchanges.
Stocks: see Exchanges.
Statistics: Baines, J. H. Census matters discussed at statistical institute, 1897, RJS., Je.
Bliss, H. L. Eccentric official statistics, AJS., Jl.
Cannan, Edward. Demographic statistics of the United Kingdom, JRS., Mr.
Collet, Clara E. Collection & use of statistics on industrial employment of women, JRS., Je.
Hauptergebnisse der Gewerbezählung im deutschen Reich, JNS., My.
Kiaer, A. N. Die repräsentative Untersuchungsmethode, ASAr., 5: 1.
Meinzingen, Fr. von. Die Reorganization der Statistik der Bevölkerungsbewegung in Oesterreich, ASAr., 5: 1.
Salvioni, G. B. Statistik der Haushaltung, ASAr., 5: 1.
Street Railways: Rowe, L. S. Relation of cities & towns to street railway companies, AAP., Jl.
Streets: Waring, G. E. Street cleaning methods in European cities (and other articles on street cleaning), MA., Je., Supplement.
Strikes: George, J. E. Settlement in the coal-mining industry, QJE., Jl.
Suffrage: see Elections.
Sugar: Zolla, D. La question des sucres, AEL., Jl.
Superstition: Evans, E. P. Witchcraft in Bavaria, PSM., My.
Pokagon, Simon. Indian superstitions & legends, F., Jl.
Suicide: Proal, Louis. Les suicides par misère à Paris, RDM., My. 1,
Sweating System: Richter, G. E. Sweaters of New York, New Time, Je.
Syndicates: Sorel, G. L'avenir socialiste des syndicats, HN., Mr.
Tariff: Ford, W. C. Official tariff comparisons, PSQ., Je.
Hobson, J. A. Free trade & foreign policy, CoR., Ag.
Taxation: Myrbach, Franz von. Die Reform der direkten Steuern in Oesterreich, JGV., 22 : 3.
Sieghart, R. Reform of direct taxation in Austria, EcJ., Je.
Wells, D. A. Principles of taxation, XIX., PSM., Ag.

Zeumer, Karl. Zur Geschichte der Reichssteuern im früheren Mittelalter, HZ., 81: 1.
Trusts: Donald, R. Defeat of the oil kings, CoR., Ag.
Edgeworth, F. Y. Prof. Graziani on the mathematical theory of monopoly. EcJ., Je.
Jenks, J. W. Recent legislation & adjudication on trusts. QJE., Jl.
Rousiers, Paul de. Les industries monopolisées aux États-Unis, " Le Trust " de l'acier, SS., Jl.
Unemployed: Channing, F. C. Oversaving & the unemployed, EcR., Ap.
United States: Adams, Brooks. Spanish war & the equilibrium of the world, F., My.
Adams, C. K. Neglected aspects of the Revolution, Atlantic, Ag.
Anglo-American Joint High Commission, NAR., Ag.
Carnegie, Andrew. Distant possessions, NAR., Ag.
Collision of the old world & the new, CoR., My.
Coubertin, Pierre de. Die Beziehungen zwischen Europa u. den Vereinigten Staaten im zwanzigsten Jahrhundert, DR., My.
Hasse, A. R. Our national records, F., Jl.
Herbert, H. A. The fifty-million appropriation & its lessons, F., My.
Hull, J. A. T. Hull army bill, F., Je.
Lieber, G. N. Independence of the military system, F., My.
Nelson, H. L. The people & their government, Harper's, Jl.
Olney, Richard. International isolation of the United States, Atlantic, My.
Peffer, W. A. United States Senate, NAR., Ag.
Ridpath, J. C. United States & the concert of Europe, Ar., Ag.
Rives, G. L. Need of a permanent diplomatic service, F., Ag.
Schouler, James. New constitutional amendments, F., Ag.
Thurlow, S. L. Repetition of our history in our war with Spain, F., Ag.
Urdahl, T. R. Relation of the colonial fee system to political liberty, AAP., Jl.
Vincent, J. A retarded frontier, AJS., Jl.
White, S. M. Our inadequate consular service, F., Jl.
See also Canada, Cuba.
Utopias: Adler, Georg. Plato's Idealstaat, ZS., My.
Vacant-Lot Cultivation: Potato patches in the South, ChR., Je.
Rivière, Louis. Les jardins ouvriers aux États-Unis, RéfS., Je. 15.
Voting: see Elections.
Wages: Gunton, George. Are wages really falling? GM., Ag.
Marx, Karl. Quelques questions relatives aux dettes publiques, DS., Je.
War: Barrows, S. J. Ethics of modern warfare, F., Jl.
Water: Hazen, Allen. Purification of river water supplies, EM., My.
Philadelphia's filthy water, S., Jl.
Weather: Moore, W. J. Weather forecasting, F., My.
Wheat: see Food.
Women: Niemann, Sup. Die moderne Frauenbewegung in Deutschland, MIM., Je.

ABBREVIATIONS USED IN BIBLIOGRAPHY.

A.	Arena.	JHS.	Johns Hopkins University Studies in History and Political Science.
AA.	American Anthropologist.		
AAC.	Archives d'Anthropologie Criminelle.	JPE.	Journal of Political Economy.
AAE.	Archivo per l'Antropologia e la Etnologia.	JNS.	Jahrbücher für National-Oekonomie und Statistik.
AAP.	Annals of the American Academy of Political and Social Science.	LC.	Literarisches Centralblatt.
AC.	L'Association Catholique.	LG.	Labor Gazette.
ACQ.	American Catholic Quarterly Review.	LoQR.	London Quarterly Review.
AEL.	Annals d'École Libre des sciences politiques.	LQR.	Law Quarterly Review.
		MHM.	Mansfield House Magazine.
AGP.	Archiv für Geschichte der Philosophie.	MIM.	Monatsschrift für innere Mission.
AHR.	American Historical Review.	MA.	Municipal Affairs.
AIS.	Annals de l'Institute de Science Sociale.	NA.	Nuova Antologia.
AJP.	American Journal of Psychology.	NAR.	North American Review.
AJS.	American Journal of Sociology.	NC.	Nineteenth Century.
AJT.	American Journal of Theology.	NS.	Natural Science.
ALR.	American Law Register.	NT.	New Time.
ALRv.	American Law Review.	NW.	New World.
AMP.	Académie des Sciences Morales et Politiques, Séances.	NZ.	Neue Zeit.
		PhR.	Philosophical Review.
AOR.	Archiv für öffentliches Recht.	PSM.	Popular Science Monthly.
ASA.	American Statistical Association, Publications.	PSQ.	Political Science Quarterly.
		PsR.	Psychological Review.
ASAr.	Allgemeine statistisches Archiv.	QJE.	Quarterly Journal of Economics.
ASG.	Archive für sociale Gesetzgebung und Statistik.	QR.	Quarterly Review.
		RBP.	Rivista Benificenza Publica.
ASP.	Archiv für systematische Philosophie.	RCS.	Revue de Christianisme sociale.
BDL.	Bulletin of the Department of Labor.	RDC.	Rivista di discipline carcerarie.
BG.	Blätter für Gefängnisskunde.	RDI.	Revue de Droit internationale.
BML.	Banker's Magazine, London.	RDM.	Revue des deux Mondes.
BMN.	Banker's Magazine, New York.	REA.	Revue mensuelle de l'École d'Anthropologie de Paris.
BOT.	Bulletin de l'Office du Travail.		
BS.	Bibliotheca Sacra.	RéfS.	Réforme sociale.
BSt.	Bulletin de Statistique et de Legislation Comparée.	ReS.	Revue Socialiste.
		RH.	Revue historique.
BUI.	Bulletin de l'Union Internationale de Droit Pénale.	RHD.	Revue d'Histoire diplomatique.
		RIF.	Rivista italiana di Filosofia.
		RIS.	Revue internationale de Sociologie.
C.	Cosmopolis.	RiIS.	Rivista italia na di Sociologia.
ChOR.	Charity Organisation Review.	RISS.	Rivista internazionale di Scienze Sociali
ChR.	Charities Review.	RMM.	Revue Metaphysique et de Morale.
CoR.	Contemporary Review.	RP.	Revue philanthropique.
DL.	Deutsche Litteraturzeitung.	RPe.	Revue pénitentiaire.
DR.	Deutsche Revue.	RPh.	Revue philosophique.
DRu.	Deutsche Rundschau.	RPP.	Revue politique et parliamentaire.
DS.	Devenir Social.	RRL.	Review of Reviews, London.
DZG.	Deutsche Zeitschrift für Geschichtswissenschaft.	RRN.	Review of Reviews, New York.
		RSC.	Revue sociale catholique.
EcJ.	Economic Journal.	RSI.	Revista Storica italiana.
EcR.	Economic Review.	RSP.	Revue sociale et politique.
EdR.	Educational Review.	RT.	Revue du Travail.
EHR.	English Historical Review.	S.	Sanitarian.
EM.	Engineering Magazine.	SR.	School Review.
F.	Forum.	SS.	Science Sociale.
FR.	Fortnightly Review.	VWP.	Vierteljahrschrift für wissenschaftliche Philosophie.
GEc.	Giornale degli Economisti.		
GM.	Gunton's Magazine.	YR.	Yale Review.
HLR.	Harvard Law Review.	ZE.	Zeitschrift für Ethnologie.
HN.	Humanité Nouvelle.	ZGS.	Zeitschrift für die gesammte Staatswissenschaften.
HR.	Hygienische Rundschau.		
HZ.	Historische Zeitschrift.	ZPK.	Zeitschrift für Philosophie und philosophische Kritik.
IAE.	Internationales Archiv für Ethnographie.		
IJE.	International Journal of Ethics.	ZPO.	Zeitschrift für das private und öffentliche Recht.
JAI.	Journal of the Anthropological Institute of Great Britain and Ireland.	ZPP.	Zeitschrift für Psychologie und Physiologie der Sinnesorgane.
JCB.	Journal of the Canadian Bankers' Association.	ZS.	Zeitschrift für Socialwissenschaft.
		ZVR.	Zeitschrift für vergleichende Rechtswissenschaft.
JEc.	Journal des Economistes.		
JFI.	Journal of the Franklin Institute.	ZVS.	Zeitschrift für Volkswirthschaft, Socialpolitik und Verwaltung.
JGV.	Jahrbuch für Gesetzgebung, Verwaltung und Volkswirthschaft.		

[The titles of articles selected from periodicals not in this list will be followed by name of periodical in full.]

THE AMERICAN

JOURNAL OF SOCIOLOGY

VOLUME IV   NOVEMBER, 1898   NUMBER 3

CHICAGO VACATION SCHOOLS.

"CHICAGO, ILL., August 12, 1898.

"*VACATION-SCHOOL TEACHERS:*
Just a few lines to let you know that I am one of the many mothers in this district who think that the vacation school has been a wonderful success. It has taught morals and manners to our children. We never could afford to take our children into the country, and we can't be thankful enough for the good you teachers have done to our children. They have been kept off the streets, and we don't have to drive them to school. The teachers have treated the children as though they were their own. The children never get tired tell-ing us what they saw on the excursions.

MARCHING TO THE WOODS

It was just grand. Hoping that a vacation school will be in every school next year, I am

' Yours, respectfully,

"ONE OF THE MOTHERS."

The above letter, taken from among two hundred commenda-tory letters from parents relative to the vacation-school move-ment, tells the whole story. What further evidence is needed to convince those who gave service or money to the cause that their labors were appreciated and their money well spent!

"What shall we do with our children during the long summer vacation?" is the problem that confronts all parents who live in the densely populated districts of large cities. Any movement that tends to care for the children and keep them from the dangers and debasing influences of the streets is heralded with delight. If they are interested but a few hours per day, it has a softening and directing influence upon the plays and manners of the children for the remaining portion of the time, gives the child something to think about, and temporarily closes the devil's workshop.

It was in the attempted solution of the vacation problem that the vacation-school movement originated. Within the last five years all of the large cities have been grappling with the situation, but the experimenting has been entirely along industrial lines of education. The children have been taught to cobble shoes, recane chairs, mend old clothes, etc.; each good in itself, but not especially conducive to the highest development of that power within a child which makes for individuality and character building. It was left to the women's clubs of Chicago and vicinity to attempt a solution through purely educational methods, and for this purpose sufficient funds were raised to establish and maintain five schools. The committee selected the Jones, Seward, Montefiore, Adams, and Polk Street schools, where the greatest need of vacation schools was apparent—schools where there is so little that is natural and so much that is artificial, among people that have formed the bases of nearly all sociological theories, people upon whom innumerable volumes have been written and many experiments tried.

Cards of admission had been distributed among the principals of surrounding public, private, and parochial schools, with instructions to give them to those children who in their judgment would be most benefited by attending a vacation school. The truant officers of these districts were also used to ferret out the worthy ones.

The principal of each vacation school was told to accept the first four hundred children that presented admission cards. The number by necessity was limited to four hundred, as it was intended to have but forty pupils to each teacher. On the morning of July 5 nearly one thousand children came to each school, except at the Jones, and clamored for admission. At one of the schools it was found necessary to call in the police to remove the parents who crowded the halls of the building, insisting that their children must be accepted.

At the Polk Street School about fifty of the children were "held up" on their way to school and their cards of admission taken from them. It took some time to detect the thieves and give the cards to their rightful owners. If a child was absent from school two

A GROUP OF VACATION-SCHOOL GIRLS

days in succession, his place was given to one on the waiting list. From twenty-five to fifty presented themselves each morning to see if there were any vacant places.

In the above an exception is made in the case of the Jones School, on account of its isolation. At this school none were turned away. Four hundred and thirty-six were enrolled, fifteen of whom came from the Holden School and fifteen from St. Peter's School. The remaining 406 lived within three blocks of the Jones. This membership is very large, when we consider that there is an enrollment of only 550 in the regular school. Two hundred and sixty that came the first day remained during the entire six weeks.

Each school was equipped with a kindergarten and two manual-training outfits, eight aquariums, about forty window boxes twelve ant nests and six insect holders, colored chalk and water colors. The aquariums, window boxes, ant nests, and insect holders were to receive the material gathered on excursions, for use in the schools. The regular sessions were from 9 to 12. The subjects taught, for which no books were allowed, were nature study, drawing and painting from nature, music, gymnastics and games, sewing and manual training. In each

A CLASS IN NATURE STUDY

school two teachers were employed for nature study, two for drawing, one for music, one for gymnastics, two for sewing, two for manual training, and two for the kindergarten. Besides these teachers there were 150 of last year's normal-school graduates, each of whom donated a week of service to the vacation schools, and to their efficient help much of the success of the schools is due. Their training at the normal school not only fitted them to lead the children, but often they were a source of inspiration to the regular teachers.

Of the seventy teachers and directors twenty-nine were from the Chicago public schools, five from outside public schools, twenty-one from private schools, four from social settlements, and eleven without previous experience in teaching. The average amount paid each teacher for six weeks' service was $50.60. No amount of praise can do justice to the untiring efforts of these teachers, who for so slight a money consideration devoted their summer vacation to education and the betterment of the children under their charge.

A PAINTING CLASS

In determining the nationality of the children who attend the vacation schools we characterized those whose parents were born in the United States as Americans. We experienced some difficulty in classifying some, especially those at the Jones School. For instance, we ran across this combination: A boy's parents were born in Germany; after coming to this country, the father died and the mother married a negro. The boy had a negro brother in the kindergarten. To further complicate matters, the boy's elder sister married a Chinaman. So the white German boy had a colored brother and a Chinese brother-in-law. Fortunately for us the family was small.

In the Jones School we found 46 per cent. Russian Jews, 20 per cent. Italians, 12 per cent. German Jews, 7 per cent. Irish,

5 per cent. colored, 5 per cent. Americans, 2 per cent. Chinese, 3 per cent. miscellaneous. Polk Street School: 35 per cent. Jewish, 30 per cent. Italian, 10 per cent. German, 7 per cent. Irish, 7 per cent. Bohemian, 4 per cent. American, and 7 per cent. composed of all other nationalities. At the Adams School: 40 per cent. Swedish, 20 per cent. Irish, 14 per cent. German, 14 per cent. American, and 12 per cent. mixed. Montefiore: 40 per cent. Italian, 20 per cent. German, 11 per cent. Swedish and Norwegian, 10 per cent. Irish, 5 per cent. American, 4 per cent. Polish, and 10 per cent. mixed. Seward: 32 per cent. German, 22 per cent. Bohemian, 15 per cent. Irish, 8 per cent. English, 6 per cent. American, 4 per cent. Polish, and 13 per cent. miscellaneous. Summarizing, we find that in the vacation schools we had 20 per cent. Italian, 18 per cent. Jewish, 18 per cent. German, 12 per cent. Irish, 11 per cent. Swedish, 6 per cent. Bohemian, 6 per cent. American, 2 per cent. Polish, and 1 per cent. colored.

The discipline in the schools was something remarkable. No children were sent away permanently for bad conduct, and there was but little need of reprimands. This becomes more wonderful when we consider the mixture of nationalities and number of schools represented. Each of the five schools, excepting the Jones, had a fair representation from at least eight surrounding schools, public, private, and parochial, none of the four schools having over 60 per cent. of its pupils who lived in the boundaries of the district within which the school was located.

In many cases we succeeded in keeping children in school that could not be kept in regular schools, but the reformatory effect as regards "bumming" from school was not as prominent as we had hoped. A boy who has the habit of running away from school will do the same in vacation schools, and take the risk of giving sufficiently valid excuses to enable him to hold a place in his class excursions. The effect, however, of bringing such a boy under the influence of a tactful teacher and into contact with nature cannot in six weeks be determined. We know, however, of individual cases where boys would not attend the regular school, who never missed a day in the vacation school, and these same boys have been of great assistance in bringing others into the school. Some have attended on condition that their chums would be admitted. Many children who received no admission cards presented the flag pins, claiming that they were entitled to school privileges because they had bought flags, which had been sold throughout the schools. About twenty parents took their children out of school because they said they supposed that regular school instruction would be given in all branches. Their

MARCHING FROM POLK STREET SCHOOL

children had failed to make the grade, and they thought they might make up the work in the summer. A school without books was an unheard-of departure, and many parents as well as visitors were curious to know what was going to be done. When it developed that the book of nature was to be opened, and that the summer would be spent in reading headlines and noting some of the contents of the book, some became so interested that they were desirous of reading a few chapters.

As outlined in the curriculum, all work was correlated with excursions. The children were taken into the country or to the city parks. Variety of scenery and productions were carefully considered, a typical farm visited, and the children were brought into close contact with the beauties and harmonies of nature. On these excursions we sought for impressions rather than expressions. The expressions were cultivated during the four days of the week the children were kept in school, through the mediums of oral speech, drawing, painting, singing, and manual training.

Every school was taken from its environment once every week. At first we went to city parks for the purpose of familiarizing ourselves with the handling of children, but even these trips were productive of much good. A little girl seven years of age informed us that she had never been to the park before. I asked her if she had ever ridden on the street car. She replied: "Yes, I've hitched, but I never sat up straight like this before."

STREET IN FRONT OF JONES SCHOOL

On these trips we observed the natural instincts of the children, and we learned more of their characteristics and inner lives than we could learn in a year of regular school work.

On one of the farms we visited the children were given all the milk they could drink and all the berries they could eat. But they drank and ate sparingly until we had wandered away, when they returned and hurriedly feasted, filling their pockets with berries and bottles with milk. A description of one of these excursions, as reported by one of the teachers, is so vivid that I quote it in full: "Our second excursion was auspiciously started by a softly cloudy day, which promised shelter from the hot sun's rays, with little danger of rain. The children marched in good and regular order to the station, bearing greasy bags, newspaper bundles, and dirty boxes of watermelon slices, hard-boiled eggs, sausage, bakery cakes, well crushed, and pop galore. Many whose delectable lunches were in the least accessible had them eaten before we reached our destination—Thornton, Ill. It was pathetic to see the children rush for the ill-smelling and dusty chickweed of the roadside. One of their chief questions, iterated and reiterated at the park last week, had been: 'Can't we pick the flowers?' And this time, when we started, I said, 'We may pick whatever we choose, boys and girls, when we get into the real country;' and verily they did; and what is more, many clung to the poor, faded, smelly things all day and carried them home, along with the fresher and daintier flowers picked later. After a tramp through the woods, one little girl looked up into my face and said: 'Teacher, is this the woods?' And such wondrous things as they did find! 'Teacher, we found an apple tree and a banana tree by the river.' I told them more about the banana trees, one of which they had seen at the park conservatory last week, and helped to satisfy them that it could scarcely grow here; but alas! the crab-apple tree was there, and

JUST LEAVING THE CARS

how they did pick the little green apples! And the wonder was that so few offered to eat them. One boy said, as he poured a capful into my basket: 'I am going to take these home, so I can remember the trip.' Some of the children who had wandered away from us came wildly and excitedly back, tumbling over each other and calling: 'We've seen a bear! we've seen a bear!' From their description it must have been a large and timid dog, though they did insist that it was a bear: 'Because we ought to know; didn't we see one in Lincoln Park?' Such a happy day, chock-full of experiences of beautiful things and wondrous things! It seemed almost like fairyland, and I wondered, as the train pulled out, how they could bear to think of returning to their dirty, cramped homes, and odorous streets."

For the purpose of answering the oft-repeated questions, "How did your excursions differ from a picnic?" and, "What did you do on these excursions?" I will say that each teacher was held responsible for the instruction and discipline of a certain number of children, usually about fifteen, and she was directed to keep them with her at least one-half of the time we were to remain. During this time the drawing teachers taught

ON THE BEACH AT EDGEBROOK

drawing and painting, the others taught nature study; some following the course of an old river bed, some observing animal life, while others directed their energies toward plant life. On the farms the farmer hitched his horses to the mower and cut grass, and went through much of the machinery work that is done on the farm. About an hour before we were to return the children were turned loose to do as they wished. This time was usually spent in games and songs under the direction of the gymnastic and music teachers.

The most pleasurable and profitable excursion of the summer was taken on the "Whaleback" to Milwaukee. About fifteen hundred children, 70 per cent. of whom were never on a boat before, enjoyed this ride. The boat ran near the shore, which gave an excellent opportunity to study local geography, and with memory, pencil, and brush the incidents of the trip were well preserved for expression in the schoolroom.

The knowledge gained in the parks gave great pleasure to

IN THE RIVER AT MOMENCE

the children, as they rolled along the railways on the following excursions, in the recognition and naming of the trees near the tracks and in the forests beyond. It was a matter of surprise that, if a name was given at all to a tree seen from the car window, it was almost always correct, leading one to wonder what might possibly be accomplished for the children of the city of Chicago if our park commissioners would set apart a certain small portion of land in each park in which might be cultivated, not only familiar trees, but also the common grains and vegetables. If the children had seen such beds of plants, they would not have called a potato patch a corn field, nor a hornet's nest in a large tree a cabbage, nor would they have expected to pick potatoes from vines in the same manner as grapes are gathered.

In the excursions to the country the good accomplished

cannot be estimated, and to attempt to make a complete report of it in its bearings upon the character of the children is a task, it seems to me, impossible. It is not sentiment to say that in the lives of these children the report will finally be written.

I am not bold enough to sit down and with the scalpel and microscope seek to analyze and place the impressions made upon the character of the little fellow whom I found sitting alone upon a high bank, beneath the shadow of a great oak; he was looking across the valley at the fresh, green fields on the plain, fringed by the growth of timber beyond, over which the shadows of the summer clouds were chasing each other, emphasizing the freshness and beauty of the scene. I sat down beside him. He turned his face, made radiant with the joy of a new possession, and said : " Is dis purty ting ours, is dis all in de United States?" And yet there are those who say that we should teach more facts to cultivate the love of country. At a cost of less than $1,400 two thousand children per week for six weeks were carried into the country, in view of beautiful landscapes, among myriads of birds and flowers, to "a world unknown." Over 70 per cent. of the children had never been two miles from their own doorstep. These excursions were made possible by the helpful attitude of the transportation companies. They did everything in their power to make the excursions a success. Twelve thousand children on over thirty excursions without an accident!

SPECIAL WORK.

Credit is due Professor William P. Beeching, supervisor of nature study, for much of the report on special work that follows.

NATURE STUDY.

I believe that the most efficient work in this department can be accomplished by teachers who are fitted by training and experience to be what are called "all-around teachers," that is, teachers who can give fair lessons in painting or drawing and good lessons in language, or an interesting exercise in nature study. They accomplish very much more with the children we have in the vacation schools than the teacher who is merely an expert in a special department. If specialists are to be employed as nature-study teachers, such persons should be selected as have been fairly well trained for the work in a training school or in the school of experi-ence. No person who simply likes nature for the sake of nature alone should be chosen as an instructor in this depart-ment. Such people are almost certainly lectur-ers and not teachers. They are impatient to have the children see at once the thing in which they themselves

CLASS WORK IN THE FIELD

are interested, thus robbing the pupil of the great pleasure of dis-covery and the valuable discipline coming from real investigation. In such schools as these there is not time to train teachers in methods of work, no matter how good material they may be made of, nor how well "educated" they may be.

The study of nature in the vacation schools may be char-acterized as a study of life. Great care was exercised to pre-serve all forms. The boy who caught the bumblebee in his hand, and christened it a Spanish bug on account of its yellow back, was taught that peace with Spain was about to be declared, and he should release the bug, though the Spaniard did strike him with his stiletto.

MANUAL TRAINING.

In this department the teachers attempted to utilize material gathered during their trips to the woods. The outcome of their efforts was most satisfactory in the construction of easels, pic-ture frames, flower-pot holders, etc., showing much ingenuity and taste. Children of all grades took this work, and the results plainly showed that our present plan of beginning manual training in the seventh and eighth grades is "hitching the horse to the wrong end of the wagon."

DRAWING AND PAINTING.

The drawing teachers all sought to coöperate with the nature-study teachers in their work, and the result was very

ON MR. SWEET'S FARM AT GLENWOOD

satisfactory. I am convinced that for field work all attempts to represent nature in any of its forms should be by means of water colors, and not by crayons or pencils. Some advocate the crayon at first, but, judging from the summer's work, the handling of the brush is freer, and certainly the color of the paint is softer, much more pleasing, and more truthful than the crayon.

MUSIC AND GAMES.

The music as taught in the vacation schools was recreative in its nature, the emphasis being put upon the interpretation of songs and vocal cultivation. A carefully selected programme of typical songs, correlating with the work of the school, introduced the children at once to good music and real experiences. Songs of industry, nature, and patriotism not only furnished themes for vocal activity, but, when the children were vitalized and aroused through the moods of the songs, dramatic expression in rhythms and games followed naturally, the children reveling in freedom

A TYPICAL GROUP FROM THE JONES

of motion and spontaneous exercise. Vocal technique was controlled by idea, and the children were led to artistic song through interpretation. Stories served as connecting links here and there, emphasizing points. The military moods made for good order, self-control, and discipline, and a strong reaction upon bearing and physical conditions was observed. The industrial themes gave opportunity for reviving the traditions of the trades and guild life, while nature songs brought the life of bird and bee and visions of green fields within dingy city walls. Enthusiasm remained unabated during the term. Each school had a very successful kindergarten, and three of the schools had a deaf class, under the direction of Miss McGowan, that did remarkable work in so short a time.

Two bathrooms—one at the Jones School and one at the Montefiore—were maintained during the six weeks. There

was an attendant at each bath, who on an average bathed about twenty children per day, and washed and combed as many more. One of the agreeable features of the baths, which goes to prove that soap is a wonderful civilizer, is the disgust that the children show when they put on their filthy clothes after a bath. They at once see that their clean bodies and soiled clothes do not harmonize.

The Public-School Art Society and some of the regular schools loaned their fine collections of pictures to the various schools, which gave beauty to the decorations and helped to enhance the artistic taste of the children. The total expense of the five schools, including the excursions and pay of teachers, was less than $6,000.

JIM

SEWING.

All the girls took this work, and the sewing was probably more reluctantly missed than any other subject. It was really surprising to observe the interest and faithfulness in this department. Parents as well as children sought the work in these classes.

SUGGESTIONS FOR THE FUTURE.

In reviewing the work of the vacation schools and weighing carefully the many difficulties encountered, some of which may be avoided in the future, I present the following suggestions: The superintendent should be appointed not later than February, so that he may have time carefully to arrange a curriculum and outline the work to be accomplished. He should have the power to select the teachers, thus making him directly responsible for the educational work. Each school must be provided with a strong principal, whose duty shall be to carry out the work outlined by the superintendent. He will have no time to do class work.

There should be no "head teachers" in the various schools, but all should receive the same pay for the same amount of work. There should be directors for each department, who, if appointed in time, could plan the work and each take charge of a class in some one of the schools. An exception to the above should be made in the case of directors of nature study and excursions. The teachers should receive more money for their services. Only teachers of similar educational ideas should be placed in the same school, but individual schools should attempt the solution of the various problems that present themselves. Sloyd might be taught in one school and manual training in another; fancy work in one and plain sewing in another. As long as the schools are experimental, why not attempt something that would benefit all who are trying to discover what is best for the American child?

A TYPICAL POLK STREET GIRL

The teachers should be appointed in time, so that they may make the necessary preparation for the work. They should visit all of the excursion grounds before the beginning of school at least twice with the director of nature study, who should have plainly outlined what is to be seen and how to see it. Frequent teachers' meetings should be held before and during the term, for the purpose of comparing notes and receiving suggestions. At least three parents' meetings should be held at each school during the season, and teachers of one school should have a kindly interest in all, feeling that their school is only a part of a system. At least two cadets should be assigned to each school for the entire term at a small salary, say 50 cents per day.

Everything considered, the most successful excursions were where the schools were divided into two divisions — grammar and primary — each going at different times.

A TYPICAL PROGRAMME OF WORK.

Class	Time, 9–9:40	Time, 9:45–10:25	Time, 10:30–11:10	Time, 11:15–11:55
	Subject	Subject	Subject	Subject
A^1	Nature study	Drawing	Music or gymnastics	Boys, manual training Girls, sewing
A^2	Nature study	Drawing	Music or gymnastics	Boys, manual training Girls, sewing
B^1	Drawing	Music or gymnastics	Boys, manual training Girls, sewing	Nature study
B^2	Drawing	Music or gymnastics	Boys, manual training Girls, sewing	Nature study
C^1	Music or gymnastics	Boys, manual training Girls, sewing	Nature study	Drawing
C^2	Music or gymnastics	Boys, manual training Girls, sewing	Nature study	Drawing
D^1	Boys, manual training Girls, sewing	Nature study	Drawing	Music or gymnastics
D^2	Boys, manual training Girls, sewing	Nature study	Drawing	Music or gymnastics

The one great lesson that the vacation schools teach is that this class of children can be reached only through personal contact with the teacher. Advice, direction, and admonition mean nothing to them. A teacher must come down to the children, play their games, think their thoughts, and gradually lead them to understand the natural laws of the Creator. In the regular school work the average teacher begins her cut-and-dried programme at 9 o'clock and finishes it promptly at 3:30. In six weeks she knows the names of the children of her room, and possibly can tell whether John is bright or dull, mischievous or angelic. She has learned that, since the child was branded by the previous teacher; but as to his tastes, delights, occupation out of school hours, the games he likes to play, the places he haunts, or the hovel he calls home — all these concern her not. In the vacation schools the teacher has to know her pupils at once. She goes with them

A PUPIL FROM THE JONES

to the woods, walks with them by the brook, hears the same birds, beholds the same landscape; and in the shade of some friendly oak she listens to the sad or happy tales told by the children of their home life; she hears how the mother depends upon John's selling papers for the support of the family; she sings songs of nature, patriotism, and love. The teacher thus gives her pupils the attention and the affection which the children crave. Many children have we heard say: "Oh, if our regular school was like this!" The secret of successful work in vacation schools, as well as in other schools, lies in the spirit with which the teachers enter the work. With a corps of natural teachers, having the spirit, with sufficient money to carry on the work as it should be done, the vacation schools of Chicago would be one of the greatest of factors in training children for citizenship. I believe the time is not far distant when the people will awaken to the fact that in congested and poverty-stricken districts vacations are the devil's seed time, and that the schools should be kept open the year round, with a change in the course of study to meet the demands of the seasons—the year divided into four periods and teachers receiving their vacations as do the professors in the University of Chicago. With the period of idleness cared for, we shall be a long step toward the solution of the social problem which confronts us today.

O. J. MILLIKEN.

THE LAST DROP OF MILK

THE MOVEMENT FOR VACATION SCHOOLS.

MARCHING TO THE FARM

THERE is an old-fashioned notion that pictures vacation as a period of relaxing all the restraining discipline of the school year — a time when the whole being can stretch itself, as it were, and attain fuller proportions by doing as it listeth, running about in green fields, chasing butterfly, or bird, or bumblebee, climbing trees and wading brooks, or browsing in pure animal enjoyment.

The growth of our large cities, with the consequent crowding of population, has changed all this, and what grass there is no longer invites the tripping feet, but sternly warns "keep off!" Birds and butterflies have fled to the parks, too distant for the child to follow; and the buzz of bees is replaced by the gong of the electric-car Moloch, claiming the street for his own, and sacrificing all who may dispute his sovereignty.

So vacation now brings with it something of worry and trouble, even to the well-to-do who make every provision to occupy and safeguard their children — plan country visits or excursions, picnics and parties, supply toys and games and books, and, when the vacation is over, send the children back to school with a sigh of satisfaction that nothing has happened, and that eternal question, "Mamma, what shall I do next?" will not now be heard.

But for the children of the poor the close of the school year opens a period fraught with special danger and difficulty. Living in crowded tenements, where often kitchen and living room and sleeping chamber are all within the same four walls, they have no space in which their natural activity may spend itself. It is "Johnny, don't do this," and "Johnny, don't do that," until in sheer despair Johnny must flee to the street for such diversion as he would have. The dust and dirt are better than the "don'ts" dinning in his ears. Toys he has none; even the garbage box or ash pile may furnish a temporary plaything. His greatest danger, however, lies in the enforced idleness and the company in which it is apt to push him. That this is no idle fear for our children is sufficiently attested by the history of our street gangs, with their boys from nine years up, and the number of juvenile arrests. An investigation of one district in Chicago proved that juvenile arrests increased 60 per cent. in July and August, and the inference seems justified that the closing of school and the enforced idle street life of the boys were its cause.

The recognition of the necessity of doing something to overcome the evil of these conditions has led to what may now, since it has become so widespread, be called the vacation-school movement and the movement for playgrounds, both having as motive the desire to take the children from the streets, the latter wishing to provide place in which the children may work at their pleasures, the former·wishing to provide and prove work itself pleasure.

The vacation school seeks to teach resourcefulness, that element in which our common schools seem lacking, by giving the hands something to do. Many toys are given to children for which they care little; but who ever heard of any child that would not be interested in a tool box? And tools, in one way and another, are the sources of attraction in vacation schools.

So long ago as 1872 the school committee of Cambridge, Mass., urged "the need of providing occupation for those children whose natural guardians are unable to do so. For two months in the summer the schools are closed . . . . the scholars who can be taken into the country profit by the vacation. But it is a time of idleness, often of crime, with many who are left to roam the streets, with no friendly hand to guide them, save

that of the police.   Our system seems to need vacation schools
. . . . in which the hours and methods of study should be
adapted to the season." (See Annual Report for 1897, Cambridge, Mass.) But, in spite of the wisdom of the committee

SINGING IN THE WOODS

and repeated mooting of the subject, with requests for an appropriation, the Cambridge council has not yet seen fit to provide
the necessary funds.   But there, as in other cities, it has remained
for women to be sufficiently far-sighted and sympathetic to find
the ways and means to satisfy the growing need of the children,
and to avert the threatening evils of the street.   The first vacation
school was established in Boston in 1885, and since then New
York, Chicago, Cambridge, Cleveland, Brooklyn, Philadelphia,
Indianapolis, and New Haven have organized vacation schools.
All alike hope that before long the boards of education in their
respective cities will undertake their management.   New York
has already done so, after an object-lesson of four years conducted by the Association for the Improvement of the Poor,

while the Philadelphia board this year opened three schools on petition from the Civic Club.

One of the most significant statements is that of Superintendent Cogswell, of Cambridge, Mass., in his report for 1897.

He says: "The value of these schools consists not so much in what shall be learned during the few weeks they are in session, as in the fact that no boy or girl shall be left with unoccupied time. Idleness is an opportunity for evil-doing. . . . . . These schools will cost money. Reform schools also cost money. . . . . It is by no means certain that, considered in the light of dollars and cents only, it is not true economy for the city to spend money for vacation schools."

A LUNCH ON THE FARM

In 1896 Mr. Daniel Cameron, president of the Chicago board of education, in his outgoing address said, in effect, that "the problem of the children in crowded districts in the summer was one which the board would find it must very soon face; that there seemed pressing necessity to cope with the growing evil conditions; and that the vacation school, as conducted that year in Chicago, seemed to offer a solution of the difficulty."

A great number of teachers and principals testify to the demoralizing effect of the long weeks of idleness and the necessity of spending the greater part of the early fall months in overcoming the summer deterioration.

In the following pages the attempt is made to give some account of the vacation schools in regard to which any information has been obtainable. If the list is incomplete, it is because no record of other schools has been found.   No attempt, however, is made to include the many summer classes of one kind and another which have for years been maintained by individuals and societies, with the same motive, perhaps, but less consciously understood, and which have done good service in combating the weariness, or worse, of the many idle hours.

Boston, 1885. — Though from Cambridge comes the first mention of vacation schools, to Boston belongs the honor of being the pioneer actually to realize them.   In 1885 Mrs. Quincey Shaw opened the North Bennett Street Industrial School classes during the mornings of six weeks in July and August. Five hundred children between the ages of three and eighteen were enrolled, while the daily attendance averaged 250.   The attendance has varied from year to year, and new classes have been added to those first opened.   The expense has run from $700 to $1,500, approximately.   It, however, appeared to me, from a visit in 1896, that this was a place in which a variety of classes was offered to attract the children, and entire latitude of choice allowed them, rather than that it was an organized school in the general acceptation of the term, with only such work as seemed fitted to produce the best results in the children.   The following extract from the report of 1896–7 perhaps expresses the motive and success of these classes :

"Ten large, airy rooms are filled daily by children from the streets.   The occupations provided for them are all manual, and every effort is made to arouse and maintain a lively interest and regularity of attendance by means of thoroughly good teaching, by abundant variety of work, and by the attractive and (wherever possible) useful character of the occupations.   Among these are sloyd, leather work, typesetting, chair-seating, basket weaving, cooking, plain sewing, fancy work, paper folding, drawing, clay modeling, color work, and kindergartens of two grades. One of the results of last summer's work which gave most evident delight to the children was the reseating of sixty-six shabby chairs, most of which were brought from the houses of the little boys, who carried them back, almost as good as new, with boisterous satisfaction, thanks to their own skill."

The Tyler Street Vacation School, carried on by Denison House and Ward XII Conference of Associated Charities (see reports of College Association 1894 to 1897), was opened July 8, 1895, and continued during the mornings of six weeks, the school committee granting the use of the building. A superintendent, nine teachers, and several volunteers cared for the 137 children who attended daily — about 50 per cent. of those enrolled, the cost being about $650. In 1897 the best work seems to have been done ; 222 registered on the opening day. I quote from the report : "The daily attendance, owing to more cautious methods of admission, persistent calling at the homes, and prompt dismissal of pupils absent without excuse on two successive days, was this year nearly two-thirds of the members registered, as contrasted with last year's proportion of one-half."

The children were classified in three distinct departments : the kindergarten, primary, and advanced class. In the primary department "the work, largely manual, was grouped about one strong central idea. 'Our country' was the principle chosen, and the children worked out their own ideas in painting, wood work, sewing, and singing. The result was shown on closing day in painted flags and strips, and pictured stories of Columbus, Miles Standish, and Hiawatha. The industrial work of the advanced class consisted in sewing and carpentry for girls and boys respectively. A new feature of the sewing room was 'mending day,' Friday, when busy groups were seen darning, patching, or replacing buttons on clothing brought from the family mending basket. On other days the girls did 'practice work' on sample strips until promoted to work on useful articles. A few advanced pupils learned something of cutting, fitting, and embroidery. The carpentry class comprised two divisions, with work similar in character, but adapted to individual ability."

But the striking success of the year was the science course by Miss Roberta Reynolds, of Radcliffe. Three mornings a week lessons were given on animal life, beginning with the monkey (illustrated by a living specimen), and continuing through the higher forms to the lower, in the following order :

Elephant, camel, cat (with comparison with larger members of the same order), rabbit (with a general talk about squirrels), rats, and mice. Other forms specified were as follows :

Birds : Specimen, thirty skins of New England birds (which the children learned to recognize). Superficial classification based upon bills and toes.

Reptiles : Specimen, a horned toad.

Amphibians : Specimen, tadpoles, frog, toad.

Fishes : Specimen, gold fishes.

Crustaceans : Specimen, live crabs, and many dried and alcoholic specimens, given by a friend.

Mollusks : Specimen, clams furnished by pupils.

Insects : Specimen, mounted specimens lent by a friend.

Echinoderms : Specimen, star fishes, sea urchins, sand dollars.

A large cage proved useful for the various animals lent by the Court Street Bird Store. Two hours a week were devoted to the study of *plant life*. There were afternoon excursions to seashore and parks, where specimens for class work were collected, and also to museums and library.

The mothers' teas, three in number, were informal afternoon meetings at the school of superintendent, teachers, and specified divisions of children, with their mothers. The practical use of such meetings in establishing confidence, interest, and coöperation is self-evident. At the close of the term all the parents were invited, and typical work of every department was on exhibition. Tea and music entertained the guests. The work shown, and the behavior of the children on that occasion, proved the value of the school to be fully what it had cost. The total expenditure was about $650.

New York city.— The most important and best organized effort to maintain vacation schools, and the most far-reaching in its effect, was that of the Association for the Improvement of the Poor, in 1894. Impressed with the immediate need that something radical be done to combat the evils of the coming summer, they accepted a plan presented by Mr. William W. Locke, and asked for and were granted the use of four public-school buildings in the poorest neighborhoods. Their appeal for funds brought $5,000 to their treasury to maintain vacation schools. Many more children applied than could be admitted, and some came long distances to the school. The age limit was from five to fifteen, corresponding to the grades from kinderten to first grammar. No text-books were used. From the beginning the A. I. C. P. had felt it was the duty of the board of education to maintain these schools, and it conducted them under its auspices only as an object-lesson to prove their need and usefulness. In 1897 the school board, after careful consideration, adopted vacation schools as a part of the public-school system of New York city, and appropriated $10,000 for their maintenance this summer, estimating $1,000 as the cost of each school.

This year ten schools have been opened by the board of edu· cation and are under the supervision of Superintendent Stewart. In each school there are a few expert teachers, but the majority are normal-school students, quite inexperienced, and the work naturally shows the result of their well-meant, but not always successful, efforts. The superintendent expressed himself as satisfied that it would be unwise another year to have so many inexperienced teachers.

In one school which I visited the principal was laying most stress on organized play, and was training the boys in companies for a tournament in hand-tennis, endeavoring to rouse their ambition to attain the highest degree of skill. The girls were having games and dances, and were utilizing the small space allotted to them in a really remarkable way. It struck me as an excellent training to teach them how to use the small spaces in their home and the street. At the same time they were learning beautiful poems, and training their voices to pleasant, modulated tones. Singing was incidental and scarcely emphasized sufficiently to be called a study.

In another school a skillful teacher, who had filled the room with interesting objects from nature, was conducting a nature-study lesson, in which the children were thoroughly interested. They had planted peanuts, and were watching the growth and development, while all their other work—clay modeling, drawing, painting, and study—centered around the familiar carrot which they had never suspected of such interesting possibilities. Material for nature study is sent in from the country by one engaged especially for the purpose, but this seems scarcely adequate to the need.

Cleveland.— As an outgrowth of a summer sewing class there was established in Cleveland, in 1897, under the auspices of " The Old Stone Church " and in one of the public schools (the Rockwell), a small vacation school, which was fortunate in having the advice and superintendence of Miss Emma Davis, one of the school supervisors. It consisted of only two classes — kindergarten, and one for children from seven to ten years old — with about fifty in each class. This year Goodrich House will coöperate with the school, and thus make it possible to have some older children. There has been a greater demand for admission than it was possible to satisfy.

It is, perhaps, a sad commentary on our popular education that one sees in a report such a sentence as : " Our school is planned rather for character than knowledge — our aim being to give the children active employment in which they could be happy, with as little of the ordinary school routine as possible."

In the nature work special attention was given to a pair of canaries, and the sparrow and robin, birds constantly about, while an aquarium stocked with fish, and bugs and beetles brought into the room, furnished further material for study. In history interest was centered in Ohio and special emphasis laid on the lives of the great men she has given to the nation. Manual training consisted in form study, color lessons, clay modeling, cardboard, paper folding and cutting, outline sewing, drawing and designing, and sewing for both boys and girls — the Pratt system being followed in the last.

Brooklyn.—The Brooklyn Vacation School owes its existence directly to the inspiration of Mr. John Graham Brookes. It was opened in July, 1897, and continued like the others for a period of six weeks. The board of education allowed the use of its buildings, and loaned the manual-training and kindergarten equipment necessary. The motive of the school seems to be industrial rather than purely educative, as will be seen from the course of study, which includes carpentry, chair caning, basket weaving, cobbling, sewing, drawing, modeling, water colors, and kindergarten. So far as I can gather from the reports, the children were allowed to choose that which they desired to do, and to spend the greater part of the time in that work, and little attempt was made to interest them in things of which they knew nothing, and which make for a broader view of life. Nature study seems not to have been included, and the " useful " seems to have been the ideal throughout. Toys and games exercising muscles of the body were a part of the course. The police in the neighborhood testify that the school has done much good.

Cambridge, Mass.— Although the first to see and express the need, it was not until 1897 that Cambridge really had a vacation school, and this it owed to a committee of women. For several years three summer kindergartens had been maintained by Grace Episcopal Church and the Cantabrigia Club. Out of these, perhaps, grew the vacation school held in the manual-training school in 1896, having sixty boys, and growing in 1897 to include 120 boys and sixty girls, the latter in a separate building—the Holmes School—where the board of education furnished the sloyd equipment, but popular subscription supplied the funds for maintenance. Mr. A. L. Ware was in charge of both schools, while Mr. A. L. Morse, head of the manual-training school, gave most valuable aid and advice. The attendance for boys averaged 96.3 per cent., for girls 90.7 per cent. The cost of maintenance was about $1,300.

The pupils were chosen by the committee obtaining lists of names from the Associated Charities and the superintendent of schools, visiting the parents when the object of the school was explained, and inviting mother or father to enroll the child.

An admission card must be presented each day. In 1897, of the 120 boys sixty-one had attended in 1896, and the same proportion of the girls. There is a waiting list, and it seems to be the policy of the committee to impress upon all that it is a privilege to be allowed to come to the classes. The school is continued with the same numbers this year. Instruction is given in carpentry, sloyd, drawing, natural science, and singing, the girls having two lessons a week in cooking and practical home talks. Differing from other vacation schools, this has two sessions a day, of three hours each, one set of children attending in the morning, and another in the afternoon. The children are allowed to choose when they will come. Thirty children at a time are assigned to each of three teachers in wood work, while the other thirty pursue some study together. Each session is divided into two periods of one and one-half hours each.

There is no classification as to ability, the effort being made to give individual instruction as far as possible.

Philadelphia.—This summer of 1898, as the result of a petition from the Civic Club, the Philadelphia board of education determined to open three vacation schools as an experiment, with a principal and three assistants in each. They doubted whether the schools would be filled, but so great was the pressure that in one school twelve teachers were necessary to care for the pupils demanding admittance and filling the school to its utmost capacity. The policy of the committee was an exceptionally enlightened and generous one. The teachers were the best obtainable. Aquaria, palms, and other plants were supplied, and modeling tables which the teachers transformed into miniature landscapes, giving the rooms a delightful appearance. Nature study and manual training were laid down as essential studies, and each principal was allowed to adapt the course to the children under her charge. Each school was working out its own plan, and all seemed good. The one visited, the Beck School, seemed to me almost ideal in its spirit and work. The boys were learning Swedish sloyd, taught by an expert, and gymnastics were an important part of the work. Another class was engaged in simple wood carving, and interested to a degree. Sewing, clay modeling, and drawing; nature study, literature, and civics, with physical culture, completed the course. A happier company of children I have never seen. This district was almost entirely Russian and Jewish, while the other schools drew from an American population. One school in a manufacturing district had had a loom given to it, and weaving was being taught by the janitor, a practical weaver, while cooking was added to the course of study. The principal of this school was the principal of the winter school, and had asked for the position, as she was so keenly anxious for the benefit of a vacation school for her children, to prevent the general demoralization which caused her so much trouble each fall.

In the third school the department idea was followed, each teacher having charge of one subject instead of one class. The report of the schools in Philadelphia will undoubtedly contribute much to the future development of the best work in vacation schools. The liberal and enlightened policy of the school board in adopting them as a part of the regular system, without first compelling their maintenance by private citizens and awaiting strong popular pressure, cannot be too highly commended, nor can the helpful and broad-minded attitude of the chairman of the committee, Mr. Kavanaugh.

Baltimore.— Mr. William W. Locke, who had charge of the New York schools, has this year gone to Baltimore to organize vacation schools there, but any further information has not been obtainable.

Chicago.— In March of 1896, at a conference of the Associated Charities, after a report on vacation schools, a committee was appointed to see what might be done to establish them in Chicago. This committee raised the first $200 toward the maintenance of a school and ascertained that the board of education would favor the project. Through the chairman the matter was presented before the educational committee of the Civic Federation, of which President Harper of the University of Chicago was then chairman, and this committee was asked to undertake to conduct vacation schools, which it consented to do. Eight hundred dollars was raised, and it was determined to open one school which should be a model so far as possible. The Joseph Medill School was chosen, situated in a workingmen's district, and drawing from a mixed population.

The course of study was arranged with the advice of President Harper, Professor John Dewey, of the University of Chicago; Colonel Francis Parker, of the Chicago Normal School, and Professor Gabriel Bamberger, of the Jewish Training School. No text-books were used. Manual training, including sloyd, paper folding, drawing, clay modeling, and sewing for the girls, was given to all classes from the kindergarten up; singing and gymnasium work were important features, but, above all, a weekly excursion to the country was the center around which all study in the school revolved. The exursions were made possible through the generosity of the Chicago *Record*.

Cards were distributed through the neighborhood of the school, and before long the throng asking admission was so great it was necessary to ask police aid to keep order. Three hundred and sixty children were finally admitted; during the term over 4,000 applied. The teachers engaged were the best obtainable, it being felt that in a school of this kind, where everything depended upon the personality of the teacher, excellent results could be obtained only by experienced teachers. The excursions were not conducted as picnics, but each class in care of its teacher used eye and ear and hand to gather all the information possible, to see the life under stone or in flower, to know the country as a place of beauty and productiveness both. Throughout the term the course of work was guided by the advice of Professor Bamberger, who was chairman of the educational committee. The school commissioner of the district, who was at first doubtful as to the success of the venture, testified that nothing that had occurred in the district had been of so much benefit as had the vacation school. The most pathetic as well as lamentable ignorance of the country and country life was discovered, proving that from books alone, without actual sight of the objects studied, comparatively little is learned by the children, as is illustrated by the child who pictured a cow as big as a dog, who was shocked that milk should come from the cow; by the one to whom a puddle was a lake, and by the numbers who had never seen a group of trees, nor a field of clover or wild flowers, when these *seemed* so easy of reach.

In 1897 circumstances rendered it impossible for the Civic Federation to conduct a school. The settlement of the University of Chicago was, however, fortunate enough to have money given to it for this especial purpose, and a school was conducted in the Seward School in the Stockyards district, under the management of Miss Mary McDowell, head worker of the settlement.   The principal chosen had been secretary of the educational committee of the Civic Federation the previous year, and was familiar with the Medill School; the course of study pursued was much the same, with the addition of housework, and of a Clean City League, meeting after school hours.   Nature was not the central thought, as only occasional excursions were taken by the classes.   One of the direct and excellent results of the school was the introduction of manual training into the regular school curriculum in response to a petition from the parents in the districts, to whom its value had been demonstrated during the summer session.

Those interested in vacation schools during previous years felt that to bring them to the notice of the general public an organized effort must be made to establish them.   Therefore, in December, 1897, a vacation-school committee was appointed in the Chicago Woman's Club, which asked and obtained the aid of forty-three city and suburban women's clubs.   These formed a joint committee which raised $9,600.   Five schools were opened on July 5 with 2,000 pupils.   At the same time a permanent committee was appointed, "whose special business it shall be to carry the work to a successful issue, *i. e.*, until vacation schools have been incorporated as an organic part of the public-school system."   The press generously kept the project before the public.   The joint committee worked hard and faithfully, dispelling the ignorance as to what these schools really are.   Appeals for money were at first met with the reply, "We have too much school already;" but the argument, "There will be no books, only manual training and visits to the country," almost invariably quieted all objections, and the necessary funds were cheerfully given.   The statement of the danger of learning vice and evil in the street was the most potent argument in favor of the work.

The members of the joint committee, all women, felt they

were able to raise the necessary funds, but, realizing how many excellent projects are wrecked by "'prentice hands," and understanding fully the responsibility resting on them in this important matter, determined to get the best advice possible in the conduct of the schools. They, therefore, extended an invitation to the following educators to take full charge of the educational side of the schools. Not one refused, and the generosity, sympathy, and enthusiasm with which these men and women gave an afternoon fortnightly of their valuable and busy time to consider the best course to pursue cannot be sufficiently appreciated, and to say that their advice was invaluable to the whole movement is to express little of the debt we owe them. They are: Professor G. Bamberger, superintendent Jewish Training School; Professor Charles Thurber, dean Morgan Park Academy; Dr. J. M. Coulter, University of Chicago; Colonel F. W. Parker, superintendent Chicago Normal School; Professor W. S. Jackman, Chicago Normal School; Miss Jane Addams, Hull House; Professor Charles Zueblin, University of Chicago; Dr. H. H. Belfield, superintendent Chicago Manual Training School; Miss Maud Summers, principal Kinzie School; Mrs. H. F. Hegner, Kindergarten Training School, Chicago Commons; Mr. John P. Gavit, Chicago Commons; Miss Anna Bryan, Kindergarten Training School, Armour Institute; Professor G. N. Carman, superintendent Lewis Institute. To these was added the chairman of the committee of women's clubs, Miss Sadie American. They at once organized themselves into a "board of education," with the following committees:

Teachers and janitors.
Curriculum and excursions.
Rules and regulations.
Buildings and grounds.
Supplies.
Finance.

The child himself, and how to expand and develop the good and beauty in him, was the central thought influencing the "board" in arranging the curriculum. As the pivot of the work, weekly excursions into the parks and surrounding country, under such guidance as should make him open his eyes in wonder indeed at the marvelous things he constantly passed by; nature study, music, and manual training in that sense of the term which makes it systematic, educative discipline, were felt to be the best means to accomplish this object.[1] Special provision was also made for teaching in each of four schools a small class of deaf children, who are usually completely overlooked.

At once a superintendent was engaged, that he might advise with the board, which was fortunate in securing the services of a school principal whose whole-hearted and enthusiastic devotion to his profession, and whose sympathy for the children, insured success in his part of the work—Mr. O. J. Milliken, principal of the Fallon School. At the same time the following assistants were engaged : Mr. W. P. Beeching, supervisor of nature study; Mrs. Frances E. Raymond, director of excursions ; Miss Mari R. Hofer, supervisor of music, and Miss Louise Heller, for sewing.

For each school were engaged a kindergartner and assistant, teacher in music and accompanist, sewing teacher with assistant, two teachers each in manual training, drawing, and nature study, and one in gymnastics. Of the seventy teachers, twenty-nine were from the Chicago public schools, five from outside public schools, eleven from private schools, eight from the Jewish Training School, two from the Chicago Manual Training School, four from social settlements, and eleven had held no positions, but came highly recommended. Fifteen teachers were men. The proof of the practicability and value of excursions as an organic part of school work is the notable contribution of these schools to "the cause of education."

The students of the normal school offered their services as assistants, and ten were assigned to each school each week for one week's service. They were most helpful in schoolroom and excursion, and at the same time gained valuable experience for themselves.

The pedagogical and sociological clubs of the University of Chicago and the students of pedagogy and sociology, many of

[1] For details see superintendent's report, foregoing.

whom are themselves teachers, from all parts of the country, have been most interested observers of the work, and have expressed themselves as convinced of the importance and value of this movement to convert the vacation from a time of demoralization to one of recreation in the best sense of the word.

SADIE AMERICAN.

CHICAGO.

NOTE.—An additional detailed report of the Chicago schools will be published. It may be had on application, accompanied by five cents for postage, to Vacation School Committee, Chicago Woman's Club, Fine Arts Building.

Justice to Boston demands correction of an error in the September number of this JOURNAL, p. 159, third line from the bottom: For "two" read "ten."

CONCERNING A FORM OF DEGENERACY.

I.

THE CONDITION AND INCREASE OF THE FEEBLE-MINDED.

THE fact that degeneracy is the source of some of the most serious of the evils which afflict society, and that many of these evils are clearly preventible, has not, hitherto, received much public attention. It is true that a few among the more advanced students of penology have suggested that many of the habitual criminals, who display evil mental or physical traits which apparently cannot be corrected, are degenerates; that, hence, they are unfit for free, social life, and should be debarred from pleasures and opportunities which they cannot or will not enjoy without injury to themselves and others; and that they should, by all means, be prevented leaving offspring who would probably inherit the evil tendencies of their parents. But the general public, even many educated and thoughtful citizens, do not know these facts, and look upon those who would apply the results of scientific reasoning to the control of the lives of even the lowest members of society as enthusiasts or worse. Yet a comparatively brief consideration of those whose needs or misdeeds furnish philanthropists and penologists with their reason for existence, and give the tax assessor his chief claim upon our property, will convince a candid student that many of them may be clearly differentiated as degenerates; that some of them are so far below the normal that their unhindered increase is a serious menace to the well-being of the race; that their number tends to increase more rapidly than that of normal citizens, since they are infinitely less prudent; that they cause an increasing drain upon the resources of the tax-payer; and, most serious of all, that, unless the tendencies they disclose shall be checked or offset, the average standard of manhood and womanhood, both physical and mental, must inevitably be lowered.

Unfortunately we have no trustworthy national statistics

regarding the increase or decrease of dependency, defectiveness, or other marked form of degeneracy. The increase, serious though it be, is not quite so alarming as would appear from the often quoted figures of the United States census, with the conclusion drawn from their casual inspection by some students of sociology.[1] Until the census shall have been taken a number of times upon a uniform system and by trustworthy officers, who shall have been selected for competence alone, we shall be unable to prove by official figures some conclusions which otherwise seem certain.

The object of the present and a succeeding paper is to set forth some facts regarding one of the most dangerous of the degenerate classes, to tell what measures have been taken in various states to remedy or avert the evils they threaten, and to suggest a possible and hopeful method with regard to them; a method which if it shall be successful, may possibly indicate for us a course to pursue with regard to other classes of degenerates.

There are few persons who do not exhibit some of the so-called stigmata of degeneracy. A desire to forestall criticism makes it needful to say here that only those who are so degenerate as to be a source of marked danger to the community are the subjects of this essay.

THE FEEBLE-MINDED.

The phrase " feeble-minded," for some years past, and especially in the United States, has been adopted as a useful generic term. Excluding insanity, it includes all other grades of mental defectiveness, from that of the hopeless and abject idiot, incapable of any purposive action, up to the high-grade imbecile, who would be classed as normal but that he occasionally betrays his feebleness by conspicuously foolish errors of judgment, or lack of common sense, or weakness of will, or failure to comprehend common proprieties; and the so-called moral imbecile who only shows mental abnormality by a total lack of moral perception.

[1] Census of 1850 showed 15,787 idiots, or 681 in each million of total population; census of 1890, 95,609 idiots, or 1,527 in each million — a total increase of 505 per cent., or, per million, 124 per cent., in forty years.

Besides its usefulness as a generic term, the phrase " feeble-minded " is more acceptable to the relatives and friends of those so called than the terms idiot and imbecile.   It meets the incessant public demand for euphemisms which shall seem to soften the harsh facts of existence.   The term has been accepted by the legislatures of many states, and their institutions for the care of idiots and imbeciles are frequently designated " schools for feeble-minded youth."x

An elaborate definition of the difference between idiocy and insanity would occupy too much space for this essay.   Briefly, idiocy is a condition of arrested psychical development.   It may occur at any mental stage of infancy, childhood, or youth.   It is often caused, or accompanied, by coarse brain-disease, but more frequently presents no discoverable, pathological evidence of its existence.   It is, however, impossible to doubt that it is always the product of abnormal conditions of the brain or other nerve tissue, although we may not be able to recognize them under the microscope.

To the average citizen the word idiocy denotes a condition by itself, unconnected with other abnormalities.   Only within recent years have students begun to notice that the idiot is one of the many varieties of neuropathics.   Recent studies have disclosed how intimate are the relations between these varieties and how extensive is the connection.

Differing in externals and agreeing chiefly in that all are alike degenerates, we find in the neuropathic family[2] the insane, the epileptic, the hysterical, the paralytic, the imbecile and idiotic of various grades, the moral imbecile, the sexual pervert, the kleptomaniac; many, if not most, of the chronic inebriates; many of the prostitutes, tramps, and minor criminals; many habitual paupers, especially the ignorant and irresponsible

[1] It is worth noting, as soon as these "schools" are mentioned, that, although most of them began as schools proper, and discharged their pupils when of age, they are now becoming permanent asylums for the great majority of their inmates, and only hope to discharge to a life of free, self-directing activity a small minority of those they teach.   Those most recently created — as, for instance, that of Wisconsin — have begun as asylums for permanent care, as well as training schools for the improvables, from the outset.

[2] See La famille neuropathique, by DR. CHARLES FÉRÉ.

mothers of illegitimate children, so common in our poorhouses; many of the shiftless poor, ever on the verge of pauperism and often stepping over into it; some of the blind, some deaf-mutes, some consumptives. All these classes in varying degree, with others not mentioned, are related as being effects of the one cause—which itself is the summing up of many causes—degeneracy.

Carefully excepting those imbeciles and idiots whose defect has some traumatic origin, is the result of disease, or has some other accidental cause—and these are by no means few—we find that the idiots of various types with whom we have to deal in this paper not only sustain a general relation to the other classes enumerated above as degenerates, but very close relations of blood are often found between them and individuals of other types of degeneracy. They themselves often belong to two classes, as idiotic and paralytic, idiotic and mute, or epileptic, or hysterical. Especially close and frequent are the relations between idiocy, epilepsy, insanity, and paralysis, and between all these and tuberculosis. The classification of a mentally defective person as a terminal dement, or a low-grade idiot, is often impossible without knowing the history of the case. Hysteria and paranoia present some identical symptoms. Epilepsy may coexist with idiocy or result in insanity. The dividing line between imbecility and criminality is often indistinguishable. Several of these types frequently coexist in the same family, the hereditary taint taking one form or the other, as circumstances may determine.

Here are a number of instances taken from the records of one state school for the feeble-minded illustrating the class of relationships referred to above:

A. and O. C——. Brothers, middle-grade imbeciles. Father a feeble-minded drunkard. Mother said to be feeble-minded. The boys came from the poorhouse.

E. B——. Low-grade idiot girl. A mingled family history, on both parental sides, of insanity, epilepsy, consumption, neuralgia, scrofula, and deaf-mutism.

L. T——. A cretinoid, dwarf, mute idiot. One sister also cretinoid and mute, and one brother mute, but intelligent, who afterward died of consumption, were inmates of the state school for the deaf. Her oldest brother, a laborer of the lowest class, has served a term in state's prison for incest. Her father was a habitual drinker, although not a drunkard. Her mother is an overworked, underfed woman of the lowest type of German immigrants, who, as well as an older sister, has somewhat cretinoid features.

L. and L. N——. Twin girls, low-grade imbeciles. One sister is an inmate of a hospital for insane. Their father was feeble-minded. They have two brothers, also twins, both of whom are left-handed.[1]

E. I——. A high-grade imbecile girl, is dying of consumption. Her father, mother, and four sisters have died of the same disease. One other sister is also consumptive.

J., J., J., and E. X——. Three brothers and a sister, high- and middle-grade imbeciles. Their mother, who is feeble-minded, lives in a poorhouse with three younger children, the fruit of a second marriage.

M., R., and A. D——. Two brothers and a sister, high-grade imbeciles, have two first cousins, also high-grade imbeciles, in the same institution. This family has a mingled history of pauperism, imbecility, inebriety, and crime on both parental sides for several generations back.

J. B——. Middle-grade imbecile boy ; has a brother of low order of intellect, who is a habitual criminal. His mother and grandmother were feeble-minded. His mother had five illegitimate children, all born in the county poorhouse, concerning whose paternity nothing is known.

K., S., and B. S——. Two sisters and a brother, middle- and high-grade imbeciles, are the illegitimate offspring of an imbecile woman who has spent most of her life in the county poorhouse. She has twice been married, each time to a feeble-minded man, by whom she has had other children. Her father and grandmother are known to have been inmates of the same poorhouse, the defective records of which omit other members of the family who are supposed to have been inmates also. Most of the family are feeble-minded ; all are either indoor or outdoor paupers.

R. C——. A high-grade idiot boy ; has one feeble-minded sister. One uncle on maternal and one on paternal side were feeble-minded. His father is a paralytic. His mother had a numerous family, most of whom died in infancy. He is a psychopathic sexual pervert.

J., J., and E. C——. Three brothers, middle- and high-grade imbeciles. Father was a weak-minded drunkard. One uncle was a low-grade idiot.

G. C——. A high-grade imbecile girl ; was the fruit of incestuous intercourse between her mother and her mother's grandfather.

M. B——. A high-grade imbecile ; epileptic and paralytic. Her mother died of consumption one week after the birth of M.

B. I——. A high-grade imbecile ; epileptic and paralytic. Father very nervous. Several deaf-mute relatives. Two epileptic aunts.

[1] The proportion of left-handedness observed in pupils of institutions for feeble-minded is many times greater than in normal children.

L. B——. A high-grade imbecile consumptive. Her mother was a prostitute. Her grandmother died of consumption. L. has a mulatto half-brother, she being white.

J. and M. D——. Brother and sister, middle-grade imbeciles; are hairless. One imbecile brother, also hairless, lives in a county poorhouse. Another brother and sister are also feeble-minded.

J. and L. I——. Brother and sister. Girl a high-grade imbecile of good disposition. Boy a typical moral imbecile, his special form of depravity being to wound the feelings of those who have been most kind to him, especially the lady teachers, for whom he plans ingenious and elaborately worked out schemes of outrage. Their mother was feeble-minded.

K. D——. High-grade imbecile; a family history of consumption, inebriety, and feeble-mindedness.

R. D——. High-grade imbecile. Her grandmother died of epilepsy. She has three aunts who are congenital deaf-mutes.

J. and J. F——. Brothers; middle-grade imbeciles. Father and mother both died of consumption.

R. G——. High-grade idiot, mute, but hearing. His grandfather is insane. Three uncles are mute and insane.

E. T——. A low-grade epileptic, imbecile girl; has the following among her relatives in the past two generations: Her grandfather, J. T., who was a patient in an insane hospital for twenty years, had six sons, uncles of E. Two were patients in the same hospital, one of whom committed suicide ; two other sons, not classed as insane, committed suicide, and one other committed murder. E. had a grand-uncle, also insane, who had a son who committed a very atrocious murder.

F. and M. B——. Brother and sister; boy an epileptic, low-grade imbecile ; girl a middle-grade imbecile. Their mother is insane; father and paternal grandfather were drunkards.

M. L——. A low-grade imbecile. Father a drunkard ; mother intemperate and consumptive ; one sister a deaf-mute.

S., L., and B. N——. Two sisters and a brother ; middle- and high-grade imbeciles. Their mother is insane; father somewhat weak-minded. There are eight children in the family, not one of whom is quite sound in both mind and body.

M. N——. Low-grade imbecile. Father and mother both demented. One brother is feeble-minded. A pauper family.

E. and J. P——. High-grade imbecile brother and sister. Both parents were feeble-minded. Paternal grandfather feeble-minded and paralytic.

J. Q——. High-grade imbecile girl. Her mother was feeble-minded and cancerous. Her maternal grandmother feeble-minded, epileptic, and paralytic.

M. R——. Low-grade imbecile. On mother's side three uncles and two aunts died of consumption. On father's side a great-aunt was insane, an aunt eccentric, an uncle deaf-mute.

M. and E. X——. Brother and sister. Boy high-grade idiot; paralytic. Girl a moral imbecile. Father a congenital deaf-mute and a drunkard. Mother was a prostitute and female tramp.

Such examples might be multiplied indefinitely. They are the commonplaces of the institutions for the feeble-minded.

The cases above adduced illustrate the hereditariness of imbecility. Few who have had experience in dealing with this class of neuropathics doubt that their defects are chiefly due to that cause. The degree to which this is true has been noticed but recently,[1] and the induction is still too narrow for accurate conclusions. Enough cases, however, have been observed to show that the defects classed under this head are probably more certainly hereditary than any other traits, either mental or physical. It also seems true that those children of a feeble-minded parent who escape idiocy or imbecility will probably exhibit some other type of defectiveness, either bodily or mental, or both.[2]

The degree of heredity is, in some cases, clouded by the effects of infantile environment or pseudo-heredity, which are often similar to those of heredity proper. For sociological, if not for physiological, purposes, it may be permitted to class as hereditary influences those exerted on the child during infancy. The contact between mother and child during nursing is only less close than it was during pregnancy, and pre-natal influences, producing traits of character resembling acquired traits of the parent, are frequently, although perhaps inaccurately, classed as hereditary influences. Data on this subject are rare. Those we have point to the conclusion that infantile environment has little to do with feeble-mindedness, which is either sporadic, caused by accident, or truly hereditary.

[1] See "Feeble-mindedness as an Inheritance," by ERNEST BICKNELL, secretary of Indiana state board of charities, in *Proceedings of Twenty-third National Conference of Charities and Correction*, Grand Rapids, 1896.

[2] "Of all classes of degenerates none transmit their infirmities in greater degree than the imbeciles. When the ancestral stock is properly classed under this head, they must transmit in every case some form of degeneracy to offspring, the majority of whom are noticeably mentally feeble, while many are criminals, inebriates, or prostitutes." (From "Care of the Feeble-minded," by DR. F. M. POWELL, in *Proceedings of Twenty-fourth National Conference of Charities and Correction*, Toronto, 1897.)

Recent tabulations of pauper records show, what might have been expected *a priori*, that the relations between that form of dependence and mental defectiveness are very close.[1] The result of hundreds of experiments with children of paupers is conclusive that the alleged hereditariness of pauperism is rather the result of infantile environment than a true taint of blood. From which we may safely conclude that, in the relation between pauperism and feeble-mindedness, the latter is the cause of the former, rather than *vice versa*.

The feeble-minded and idiotic of the United States now number about one hundred thousand,[2] less than ten thousand of whom are under adequate care and guardianship, in the schools and asylums provided by the states, or in private institutions of the same kind.[3] Most of the other 90,000 are suffering various degrees of neglect. Some are in town or county poorhouses, or other unfit institutions, where a small per cent. are usefully employed; the others, at the best, are harmless; most of them are mischievous. Some are in private homes, a burden almost heart-breaking where they are kindly cared for, suffering unspeakable cruelty and degradation where they are abused or neglected. Some are wandering about, debased and debasing. Few are in anything but unfit surroundings. Many are reproducing their kind, with little or no hindrance. Few poorhouses of the land are without one or more families of imbeciles among their inmates. Still more numerous are the cases of idiotic

---

[1] See "Feeble-mindedness as an Inheritance," by E. BICKNELL, quoted above.

[2] The following figures from the United States census may be useful for reference:

	1850	1860	1870	1880	1890
Feeble-minded and idiotic	15,787	18,930	24,527	76,895	95,609
Insane	15,610	24,042	37,432	91,997	106,254
Deaf-mutes	9,803	12,821	16,205	33,878	41,283
Blind	9,794	12,658	20,320	49,928	50,411

[3] There are about thirty-four such institutions now in this country, twenty-four supported by nineteen states, the remainder controlled by private enterprise and supported by tuition payments. For recent statistics see "The Care of the Feeble-minded," by DR. F. M. POWELL, in *Proceedings of the Twenty-fourth National Conference of Charities and Correction*, Toronto, 1897.

women, the mothers of defective illegitimate children, often begotten as well as born in the poorhouse. Under present conditions few of these unhappy creatures will escape repeated motherhood until past the reproductive age. From these 90,000 neglected or abused feeble-minded persons have come, or will come, most of the next generation of idiots, imbeciles, and epileptics, and a vast number of the prostitutes, tramps, petty criminals, and paupers.

Of all the dangerous and defective classes this is the most defective, and the most dangerous to the commonwealth, the most to be pitied in themselves, and the most costly to the taxpayer.

After what has been said above there would seem to be no need of argument to convince anyone who accepts these premises that the care and control of the feeble-minded should be undertaken by the state; that the increase or the continuance of a class so defective, so injurious, and so certain to transmit its defects to posterity should be checked.

The history of what the states have done and are doing, and a suggestion of what should now be done, will be the subjects of a subsequent paper.

ALEXANDER JOHNSON.

FT. WAYNE, IND.

SANITY IN SOCIAL AGITATION.[1]

NEVER was the air so full as now of social agitations. On the whole, this is a healthy sign. I sympathize with the mighty social movement of which these agitations are incidents. I cannot sympathize with the methods which some of the most conscientious and high-minded agitators adopt. I am aware that my relation to the different parties concerned with these social questions is very much like that of the Girondists at the beginning of the French Revolution. They deplored the selfishness and obstructiveness of the privileged classes on the one hand, but they equally disapproved the extravagant theories of the popular leaders on the other hand. They were consequently despised by the court party on the one side, and by the revolutionists on the other. They were presently ground between the upper and nether millstone of this double hate.

Modern business is a sensitive plant. Some of the men who have the heaviest responsibilities for its cultivation would suppress every implication that there is anything to improve in business practices. They would have all criticisms of present social order sternly ignored, except within the inner councils of the managing few. On the other hand there is persistent popular clamor for wholesale and radical reform in the present ways of doing business. Between these two extremes it is not a pleasant nor a popular rôle to search for the golden mean. Nevertheless, the scholar's ambition is to find and tell the truth, not merely to repeat the things that people want to hear.

I have in mind the sort of agitation which holds before our imagination the prospect of accomplishing some wide-reaching changes in the world's ways of doing things, in the hope of

[1] The substance of this paper was read in April, 1898, at a conference called by the National Christian Citizenship League, to consider the general topic "Present-Day Social Problems *in the Light of the Teachings of Jesus.*" The heat with which the paper was denounced by leading members of the league afforded new evidence that the message was timely.

getting people to decide on some new programme which will mark a distinct era in progress.

Now, there is this to be said at the outset: The bulk of human progress thus far has been achieved, not by design, but by accident. I mean by this that individual men have not been wise enough to understand all the consequences of their acts, and that bigger and better things have resulted than the persons tributary to them could foresee or foreordain. Men have started to do one thing, like ending England's oppression of her American colonies. They have ended by accomplishing a very different thing, namely, the independence of the colonies.

From this many men argue that agitation and foresight and planning about social improvement are useless altogether. This is not true. Social conditions may be improved by bringing our thought and work to bear on them. I therefore speak of social agitation, not as something to be discouraged in itself, but as something from which we may expect beneficent results; as something, however, which may bring direful consequences, unless it is temperate. I shall try to point out some of the facts which wise agitation will respect.

Social progress involves four elements, viz., (1) discovery, (2) persuasion, (3) individual adjustment, (4) social adaptation. In order to make my discussion bear as distinctly as possible upon this general statement, I will confine myself for illustration throughout this paper to the labor question. What is true of the labor question, in the particulars to which I refer, is true of all desired social progress.

The terms of the labor problem, as I see it, are these : (1) It is said that labor is not free, but that capital tyrannizes over labor. It may be that this statement sums up the whole matter in the minds of those who think it is true. In that case the items that follow are merely details under that general formula, viz.: (2) the conditions of labor are said to be unfair in respect of (*a*) sanitation, (*b*) hours, (*c*) wages, (*d*) chance for advancement, (*e*) opportunity to get returns for inventive ideas, (*f*) security of employment; (3) there is a permanent percentage of unemployed labor ; (4) politics adds to the hardships of labor; (5) all these hardships together prevent the laborer from giving his children a start in the world that will enable them to escape their father's lot.

Let us suppose that nobody questions the truth of these statements in the abstract. The labor problem then is : How may we change this state of things? How may all the unemployed have a paying job? How may the mischiefs of political meddling be stopped? How may an equal start in life be assured to all the children in each generation? How may workers secure altogether satisfactory conditions under which to work? How may the advantage of the capitalist over the laborer be removed? This is the labor problem. I repeat, then, my first statement : Progress in solving such a problem involves four elements, at least : (1) discovery, (2) persuasion, (3) individual adjustment, (4) social adaptation. I will try to show clearly what this means.

First, as to the primary necessity of discovery. We have assumed that everybody pleads guilty to the charges, or, at least, "guilty with extenuating circumstances," or "guilty on some of the counts." If we try to find out what any particular man means when he admits, for example, that capital tyrannizes over labor, we shall discover that, although he may be sincere in saying it, yet, if he is a capitalist himself, he means it somewhat as many good people mean the confessions they make in prayer meeting that they are "miserable sinners." If anyone should take them at their word, and point out any particular instance in which they had sinned, confession would very likely turn into denial, and even to counter-charges against the accuser. Everybody that stops to think about it has some sort of an idea that things are not right in the labor world. They are not as they are going to stay. They are not settled. The question is : Just where is the spot at which things begin to get out of gear, and how shall we go to work to put them to rights?

This shows what I mean when I say that progress in solving the labor problem involves, first, discovery. It may be that every voter in Chicago has an opinion of his own on this matter; but, at all events, there may be as many different shades of opinion as there are voting precincts in the city. Of course, all these opinions cannot be correct. How shall we find out who is right? Some discoveries must evidently be made. I have no doubt there are several thousand people in Chicago who would undertake to settle the labor problem in the United States tomorrow, if they could be made Czar of the United States for that purpose. One of them might then silence all the other opinions, and make everybody else act according to the Czar's opinion. Whether right or not, his plan would control the country, till it convinced everybody or until it collapsed from structural weakness. But, fortunately or unfortunately, no one of us can be a czar, and the next best thing is to get the necessary multitudes to think the same way about a great many complicated matters of fact and of judgment. All this calls for the same sort of discovery that is necessary in science or in the mechanic arts. For instance, it is a commonplace idea that we are not using our coal in the best way to produce power. A fortune is all ready for the man who shall discover a better way. Meanwhile, nobody thinks of damning "society" for not developing power direct from the coal. We want to do it, but how? Again, everybody knows that a considerable part of our fuel goes up the chimney. It is easy enough to say, " That fuel ought not to be wasted," but I have heard no social agitators declaim against !'society" because the fuel still is wasted. We have yet to discover how to prevent the waste. Until we make the discovery, it is useless to call each other names for not saving the loss.

Once more, I have heard chemists express the opinion that the time will come when we shall be able to get food enough to feed the human race directly from the air, without resort to the soil. They say it is possible, only chemistry has not yet discovered ways of doing it profitably on a large scale. Meanwhile, there are people on the verge of starvation. Do I hear somebody say that we "ought" to get the use of the food carried in the air? I agree with him, but I hope I shall not hear him denounce anybody, and especially not the government, or the church, for not giving us the neglected means of subsistence.

It would really be rather hard if the politicians and the church members had to bear, not only their own share of human blame, but also responsibility for not making chemistry yield up the secrets of nature faster.

This may seem to be making light of the subject, but I am serious and earnest when I say that the need of discovery about social facts, before we can solve the labor problem, is precisely parallel with that in the cases I have cited. There ought not to be any unemployed or underpaid men in the world, just as there ought not to be any unappropriated food in the air, or fugitive fuel sneaking out of our chimneys, or power lost in generation. But who has discovered what is to be done in either case? Until the discovery is made, that "ought" has to be understood in a Pickwickian sense. It expresses our common ignorance and helplessness, not our refusal to do something which is perfectly plain.

Now, let us apply these illustrations a little more closely to the labor problem. Suppose we adopt the general statement that "*fair distribution*" *would solve the labor problem.* This sounds very clear and definite. In fact, however, to ninety-nine persons in a hundred it is merely a new way of stating the old puzzle, viz., What *is* "fair distribution"?

So far as I know, there is only one body of men in the world that can make a perfectly distinct statement of what, in their opinion, would be absolutely fair distribution. That is the group for which Edward Bellamy speaks.x His idea of fair distribution is "always and absolutely equal" distribution. The only thorough-going method proposed for making this distribution is the programme of those disciples of Marx who insist upon the time standard of wages, *i. e.*, whatever the occupation, an hour's wage for an hour's work. If we suppose that these two views always go together, which is not invariably the case, then we may say that the world is now divided into two parts : first, those who believe that every man in the world can earn in an hour the same amount that any other man can earn ; second, those who believe that work varies in value. It is not my purpose to discuss these

---

[1] See *Fabian Essays*, American edition, introduction, p. xvi.

beliefs, but simply to state the facts.   It may be that one man
in a thousand in the United States believes that the day's work
of any man, selected at random, is worth as much as the day's
work of any other man in the nation.   I should be very much surprised, however, at proof that one person in ten thousand believes
it.   Yet, for the sake of argument, I will assume the possibility
that the time unit will prove to be the proper unit of labor value.
I will assume that the man who ties corn fibers together to make
brooms earns as much as the man who engraves designs on
cylinders for printing cloth.   I will assume that the man who
weaves chair bottoms earns as much as a patternmaker in a
machine shop.   I will assume that the hod-carrier earns as much
as the locomotive engineer, and that the press-feeder earns
as much as the managing editor.   It is within the bounds of
credibility that a numerical majority of men may some day think
these things are true.   The hard fact remains at present, however, that the vast majority of men do not believe they are true.
We do not believe that the time standard of wages is the fair
standard, any more than we believe that the earth's surface is
the inside of a ball, or that there is no such thing as sickness or
pain.   We do not belong to this majority because we are less
honest, or less just, than men of Mr. Bellamy's sort, but we see
things from another point of view.

    In this situation, what is sanity ?   Why, it is perfectly sane
for Mr. Bellamy and his fellow-believers to do their best to convince the rest of the world that they have made a discovery.
Indeed, the only sanity, from their point of view, is to preach their
doctrine, and to make converts to it as fast as possible.   If they
should ever bring a working majority over to their view, in any
country, it would then be in order for them to propose changes
accordingly.   Meanwhile, it is thoroughly insane for men of that
belief to agitate for revolutionizing the industrial system to match
that belief ; for the same reason that it would be insane for the
Mormon hierarchy to demand that the United States should make
itself over according to the Mormon model. But such insanity
would be mild and hopeful compared with that of the men who
have not even defined to themselves what fair distribution would

be, and yet turn themselves into detonators of all sorts of social explosives, in the interest of they know not what.

As I have said, there are simply two parties of us in the world on this question, viz., first, the small contingent who believe there should be one rate of wages for an hour's work, for all sorts, conditions, and occupations of men ; and, second, the great mass of us, who for our lives can arrive at no common belief about an artificial scheme of distribution that would be absolutely fair to all, or even in the end more fair than the system which is evolving along with all other human institutions. Whatever our shade of opinion about possible checks and balances, in some way or other the law of supply and demand seems to us a factor that neither can nor ought to be thrown out of the calculation. Our suspicion is that this factor alone is bound to upset every theoretical scheme of equal distribution that will ever be invented.

For the great majority of men, therefore, who are in this state of disagreement about the fundamental conception of fairness in distribution, sanity in social agitation would not indulge in wholesale dogmatism, much less in wholesale denunciation. It would rather choose retail experiment with practical checks and balances. It would attempt to discover by experience what serves to secure more stable equilibrium among workers, and it would make this discovery a basis for further experience and experiment. It is quite possible for men who are as wide apart as the poles in philosophical theory to agree that a given wage scale is inhuman, and that pressure of some sort should be exerted to raise it. Adam Smith and Karl Marx and Herbert Spencer would probably all agree that Mayor Harrison ought to be supported in representing the taxpayers against the franchise-grabbers. Orthodox political economists and radical socialists might easily stand shoulder to shoulder in an attack on sweat-shops, or in a fight against truck payments. We have discovered chances for some steps ahead in these directions, and we may rationally move on accordingly. But where we are not sure of the direction to take, discovery and not dogmatism is social sanity. For this reason I would say that the trade-union principle is thoroughly sound and sane. Such men as our friend, Mr. Nelson, too, are object-lessons in social sanity. I have not heard him telling how to organize Kingdom Come out of people of doubtful qualifications for free citizenship anywhere. He can tell us, however, how he made discoveries about his own business, that have helped his own policies, and have tended to raise the general level of business morality. I would name the firm of Procter & Gamble and the National Cash Register Co. as good examples of social sanity. Such concerns as these have tried thoroughly commendable experiments within the range of possibility in their own business. They have contributed more to a final solution of the labor problem than all the visionaries who offer sentiment as equivalent for discovery, and rhetoric as substitute for experience.

The obstinate fact is that nobody in the world is wise enough to convince a majority in any nation today that he has a workable solution of the labor problem. Sanity in social agitation will accordingly tone down its style of assertion in candid recognition of this fact. It is either insane or dishonest to talk as though wide-reaching social reforms, such as a permanent solution of the labor problem, have been thought through, and could be brought about forthwith, if we would only say so. No well-informed and well-balanced person will assert or imply that the way to accomplish such a reform has been discovered.

On the other hand, a hundred minor plans and policies have been discovered, which make for *partial* solution of the labor problem. A hundred means are known, applicable at different points of the industrial system, under different circumstances, in different conditions. For instance, no one can read the two latest books of Sidney and Beatrice Webb without the conviction that the possibilities of labor organization are hardly yet imagined. In America we are at least a generation behind England in the maturity of trade-unionism. Again, the insurance principle, as a factor of mighty possibilities in future developments of the problem, has hardly yet touched the imagination of reformers. I do not mean mere life insurance, or old-age, or accident, or loss-of-employment insurance alone. I mean the extension of the insurance principle as widely as the organization of labor can extend. I mean the insurance of laborers by laborers, and of labor organizations by labor organizations, just as fire- and life-insurance companies underwrite each other, and just as corporations in a trust secure each other.

A few days ago an invitation to buy a life-insurance policy came to me on a letter-head bearing the legend "Scientific Socialism." The solicitor represented one of the best-known old-line companies. I am surprised, not that a wide-awake insurance agent at last has the wit to call the business " scientific socialism," but that all the companies have not long ago exploited this idea for what it is worth. The explanation probably is that the old-line insurance companies have been doing business chiefly with the conservative element of our population, at any rate with those who could command a surplus, and among these people panic is likely at the bare mention of socialism. The fact is, however, that insurance is thoroughly scientific socialism, and, conversely, all the feasible socialism that I know anything about is at bottom scientific insurance.

Still further, coöperation, profit-sharing, and other forms of industrial partnership may not have satisfied their most sanguine friends, but they have not yet been worked to the limit. The claims of the laborer to a share of proprietorship in the business are by no means settled. We have not heard the last of income tax, and inheritance tax, and we might indefinitely extend the list with specifications which have been found available in the interest of fairer distribution.

In view of these facts, my second main proposition is this, viz., so much discovery having been made, reform is nevertheless not at once and directly feasible. There must in most cases be a long, hard, intermediate process of *persuasion*. In any case where a way of carrying on business more justly has been discovered the lesson has to be taught to other people in like lines of business. The news has to be carried. People have to be told that something has been tried in a business like theirs, and that it has worked. Then they have to be persuaded to try it themselves.

Just after the Pullman strike in 1893, I was a member of a

committee appointed by the Civic Federation to consult with leading employers and capitalists in Chicago about calling a conference on the subject of arbitration. One of the most astonishing discoveries made by the committee was that a large number of prominent business men had not so much as heard that arbitration had ever been tried. They had never heard of the Massachusetts or the Pennsylvania experiment, still less of English, French, and Swiss plans. They thought arbitration was an offhand invention of some Chicago enthusiasts, or at best a theory concocted by a few irresponsible college professors. These men were open to argument, they were willing to hear facts, and they finally furnished the money for the conference ; but if this process of education and persuasion had been omitted, they might have considered "arbitration" a pure theory to this day.

A well-known eastern expert in economics has long contended that the labor problem might be settled in the United States if we would reduce ourselves to the corn standard of food, at the same time holding on to the wheat standard of wages. As a mere proposition in arithmetic, that. is a perfectly clear solution. The margin between the wheat and the corn standard of diet would save to the workers of the country enough for luxuries to absorb all the idle labor. No politics, no legislation, no revolution is called for in the programme. Why not solve the social problem by this easy device ? Simply because the stupid facts of human inertia and incredulity are in the way. A fact may come to light and be accepted by a few. It is quite another matter to persuade the multitude that it is a fact. Until they are persuaded, to all practical intents and purposes the fact might as well not exist. No matter what we may discover about better ways of living, until enough individuals accept the discovery as fact, agitations for action on the lines of the discovery are simply putting the cart before the horse. Next to discovery must come education. We must spread the news. We must make known the better ways of doing things. We must show that they have worked, and therefore will work in like circumstances again. Any social agitation which does not conform to this programme is bound to run amuck. The reason is that men's minds work this way, and social progress must, sooner or later, reckon with the mental make-up of the people concerned.

Then, third, as to the need of individual adjustment. Suppose we have discovered some facts which make for the solution of the social problem. Suppose enough people are convinced that these methods are in the line of progress to make the change practicable, if the convinced people say so. Is progress then to be expected at once? If men were built on the automatic, self-winding, time-lock, hair-trigger plan, yes. But they are not. Some people will jump at a new scheme, simply because it is new, if nobody can get ahead of their impulsiveness and point out objections. But, on the whole, it is decidedly human to let some time pass between our admission that a thing is useful and our decision to use it.

For instance, Tolstoi and Wallace have described the hostility of Russian peasants to modern farming implements. They tell us that, over and over again, after the reaping and threshing machines had proved their capacity, the peasants have waited until the proprietor was out of sight, and then have smashed the innovations. When I was a student in Berlin, sixteen years ago, I got a large amount of free instruction in German by arguing with the barbers about the "clipper." Whenever I seated myself in the barber's chair, I would start the question: "Why do you not use the clipper, as the barbers do in America?" The reply would always be: "O, they are very good things, but —," and then each would have a different reason for not adopting them. One would say, "It isn't professional;" another, "They are too expensive;" another, "Our customers wouldn't like them," etc., etc. It was only the usual pause before adopting improvements.' Last autumn I went to the same shop in the Kaiserhof, and each of the twenty barbers employed had a box that reminded me of a surgeon's case, containing four clippers, besides all the other tools of a barber's outfit. There had to be a gradual personal adjustment, but it came at last and made a reform.

The New England town of 8,000 inhabitants in which I lived for eleven years did not contain a sewer when I first became a taxpayer. For a long time nobody could be made to admit that sewers were needed. Gradually a few people took advantage of natural water courses, and turned their sewage adrift for the benefit of the people down stream. Then a beginning of public sewerage was made as an experiment, and later an extensive system was carried out by the town. Up to the date of my removal, however, all the wisdom of the town had failed to make the citizens generally take advantage of this new means of sanitation. There were many householders who still endangered the health of their neighbors by lazily assenting to the abstract proposition that "drainage is a good thing for the town," while they refused to connect their own premises with the sewers. Discovery, persuasion, and, after that, individual adjustment are steps in the social process for each of which time has to be allowed; and a sane social leader will discount this necessity and govern his programme accordingly.

Fourth, in case of any extensive reform, all these elements have to be subordinated to a process of social adaptation. This may not always come last in actual order, but it always has its turn and its influence somewhere in the series. For brevity I illustrate merely by reference to recent legislation in Illinois. We long ago discovered our need of reform in various directions. A certain percentage of our citizens had reached conclusions about better ways of conducting our affairs. It was necessary to change our public organization more or less. We had to get new statutes enacted. In that way we adapted our state and municipal institutions to a better order of things in connection with our revenue system, our primary elections, the merit system in the civil service, registration of land titles, etc., etc.; but meanwhile we dropped a cog in social adaptation by losing our grip on control of city franchises.

The point which I am urging is that all the other stages in social reform are abortive until this stage of social adaptation, in some form or other, supplies its share in the conditions of social progress. All the clear ideas in the minds of individuals, all the fervent exhortations to act in accordance with the ideas, may be so much waste material and misdirected energy. This is the case if there exists a veto upon the application of the ideas, in the shape of social arrangements with which the ideas cannot coöperate. It is the case if the champions of the ideas fail to direct their energies to the reconstruction of those traditional social arrangements. For example, we may say that the marriage and divorce laws of the United States ought to be uniform ; and it is true. We may, accordingly, draft a law as we think it ought to be, and we may present it to Congress and demand its adoption. We might as well ask for a law requiring the sun to rise in San Francisco. Our constitution is such that Congress has no power in the premises, and our efforts must follow another line—*i. e.*, either amendments to the constitution or uniform state legislation—or they will be futile.

Having thus indicated some of the limits which social sanity must recognize, I must call special attention, further, to the fact that these barriers do not miraculously disappear from our path when we claim to approach social problems "in the light of the teachings of Jesus."[1] For my part, I have no doubt that all genuine social progress fits with the spirit of Christian teaching. More than that, I believe that the New Testament leads in the direction of the best social progress. But this does not tell the whole story. The Christian revelation means that right is sovereign and will prevail, but Jesus did not profess to furnish specifications that would inform us in advance what the specific right is in all the changing complexities of life. The teaching of Jesus is that, if anything turns out to be unfair, God is against it, and Christians must quit it and fight it. If anything turns out to be fair, God is for it, and Christians must adopt and defend it. Our opinion about a disputed question of fairness does not deserve another feather's weight of influence simply because we label it "the teaching of Jesus." On the contrary, so many addle-brains have tried to get an influence upon social problems by claiming the indorsement of Jesus for their foolish frothings that any social doctrine which claims the sanction of Jesus encounters the *prima facie* suspicion of being a fraud. Men who have been unwilling to study either the teachings of Jesus or the conditions of social problems scientifically have persistently

[1] *Vide* note, p. 335.

demanded a hearing, as specially accredited apostles of social righteousness. Christian sanity, in dealing with social questions, involves, on the one hand, the most patient study of the fundamental ethics disclosed in the New Testament, and, on the other hand, thorough analytical study of the complexities of our modern social conditions. To revert to the main illustration of this paper, no man has a right to say what Jesus would call "fair distribution" among modern men, till our knowledge of cause and effect in our present industrial system reveals to us clearer theorems of fairness and unfairness under present relations.

But the zealots say : "This gives no chance for social ideals ! This does not allow us to exhort men to do the better things that they know !" Men of the impetuous type that I have in mind demand: "Is the 'law of love' no index of social duty? May we not exhort men, 'Do to others as you would have them do to you'?" I answer, yes, of course, and no one will denounce more stoutly than I any violation of these laws. No one will exhort more loyally than I for obedience to these social principles. But let us not throw dust in each other's eyes, while we are professing to show what these laws reveal.

An illustration occurs to me from Dr. Mitchell's *Hugh Wynne, Quaker*. The father, the mother, and the rich aunt each sincerely loved Hugh, the hero of the story. The father's love followed one set of judgments, and he did what he could to spoil his son by over-severity. The aunt's love obeyed another set of judgments, and she did what she could to spoil the boy by over-indulgence. The mother's love listened to a third system of judgments, and she was in a fair way to make both evil influences effective by irresolute and inconsistent mediation. What was the trouble? Love was the law of each. Why did not love direct the three persons alike and rightly? Because there is a difference between the *feeling* of love and the *principle* of love and the *programme* of love. This difference is what our zealous agitators in the name of Christian righteousness do not understand.

The *feeling* of love may be described as the sentiment of devotion to the good of its object. This feeling alone is literally blind, whether its object is son or lover or neighbor or humanity or God.

The *principle* of love, among those who accept Christian standards, is: "Whatsoever ye would that men should do to you, do ye even so to them." This principle is also blind as a direct guide to details of action in a new case. For example, it does not tell us what sort of a constitution should be given to "free Cuba," or what plan of currency reform would accomplish most, or what is the best method of preventing juvenile crime. Having the feeling of love and the formal principle, we must have an enlightened *programme* of love.

The programme corresponding with the feeling and the principle of love must be discovered at every new turn of circumstances. We need to find out what we would want others to do to us if we were in the new circumstances and fully understood them. Until that discovery is made, the man who wants to obey the Christian law of love, without being willing to investigate the circumstances, may stumble on the right thing to do, but he runs a hundred risks of doing the wrong thing. By virtue of this sentiment of love, he is not infallible by any means. He must make up his judgments about the application of his feeling of love, just as the churches of the United States are today[1] forming their opinions about the duty of our government toward the Philippines. We cannot claim to utter any Christian dictum upon details until we are better instructed about all the facts.

What conclusions are to be drawn from the foregoing considerations? I will mention four: First, we may do incalculable damage by agitation that disregards these principles. If we agitate for social adaptation before there is persuasion and education, or for individual adjustment before there is discovery, we assume, and we teach others to assume, that there is ripeness for social change, when we are really accountable for knowing and for showing that the fullness of the times is not yet come.

Second: The men who declaim against "society," and especially against "the church," for not ushering in Kingdom Come

[1] September, 1898.

at once are incurring grave responsibility for reckless use of half-truths.

Third: The professional champions of the poor, who cater to the impression that slow pace in social progress is due to the faults of the rich, are robbing Peter of precious reputation to pay Paul with irredeemable expectations. While I have never had a relative, so far as I know, who could be classified as rich, I have from boyhood been on terms of intimacy with rich men and their families, from those called rich in a country town to some so rated in Chicago. I have not known a very large proportion of the rich people in the United States, to be sure, any more than I have known a large proportion of the poor. So far as my acquaintance with rich men has gone, however, it has brought me into personal contact with just two individuals to whom I would be willing to apply any of the terms of opprobrium which so many social agitators feel at liberty to fling freely at rich men in general. My own observation leads me to the conclusion that rich men, as a rule, have a conscience that is quite as active as the conscience of the poor. Rich men, as I have known them, feel their social responsibilities, and are as genuine as their poorer neighbors in desire to discharge them. Indeed, my own personal complaint against rich men, as a class, is that they feel *too much* responsibility, and often stand in the way of progress by assuming that they are the only capable judges and executors of what is good for the people, while the people cannot be trusted to decide what is good for themselves. Ill-balanced social agitators confirm this tendency in rich men when they rouse the masses to chimerical sentiments.

It is a false analysis which divides men, in connection with social progress, into the rich and the poor. That is not the real line of cleavage. Men are sagacious and foolish. Men are unselfish and selfish. My acquaintance with rich men makes me believe that the unselfish among them are in the vast majority. There should be, not suspicion, but mutual understanding and sympathy between the wise and generous rich and the wise and generous poor.

Fourth: I am perfectly aware that certain of those who are

looking to this conference for light will be highly displeased with what I have said, and will be ready to impute a total and final conclusion entirely foreign to the spirit of my argument. They will say: "He means, then, that we should never agitate at all, and indeed never try to do anything. Let things go. Every man for himself. Don't try to make any improvement." I will not say that I do not care for the criticisms of men who will draw this inference. I do care for it. They are the very men whom I have had in mind in preparing this paper. I wish I could persuade them that I want to do more and better than they can ever accomplish by any programme which does not pay due regard to the principles here set forth.

My own conclusion is that, because there is so much to be done, no prudent man will jeopardize any part of it, even temporarily, by tolerating a false method. "If the blind lead the blind, both shall fall into the ditch." Wise and sane sympathizers with the social movement may and will share, at a thousand points, in promoting splendid social progress.

ALBION W. SMALL.

THE UNIVERSITY OF CHICAGO.

THE BEGINNINGS OF OWNERSHIP.

In the accepted economic theories the ground of ownership is commonly conceived to be the productive labor of the owner. This is taken, without reflection or question, to be the legitimate basis of property; he who has produced a useful thing should possess and enjoy it. On this head the socialists and the economists of the classical line—the two extremes of economic speculation—are substantially at one. The point is not in controversy, or at least it has not been until recently; it has been accepted as an axiomatic premise. With the socialists it has served as the ground of their demand that the laborer should receive the full product of his labor. To classical economists the axiom has, perhaps, been as much trouble as it has been worth. It has given them no end of bother to explain how the capitalist is the "producer" of the goods that pass into his possession, and how it is true that the laborer gets what he produces. Sporadic instances of ownership quite dissociated from creative industry are recognized and taken account of as departures from the normal; they are due to disturbing causes. The main position is scarcely questioned, that in the normal case wealth is distributed in proportion to—and in some cogent sense because of—the recipient's contribution to the product.

Not only is the productive labor of the owner the definitive ground of his ownership today, but the derivation of the institution of property is similarly traced to the productive labor of that putative savage hunter who produced two deer or one beaver or twelve fish. The conjectural history of the origin of property, so far as it has been written by the economists, has been constructed out of conjecture proceeding on the preconceptions of Natural Rights and a coercive Order of Nature. To anyone who approaches the question of ownership with only an incidental interest in its solution (as is true of the classical, preevolutionary economists), and fortified with the preconceptions of natural rights, all this seems plain. It sufficiently accounts for the institution, both in point of logical derivation and in point of historical development. The "natural" owner is the person who has "produced" an article, or who, by a constructively equivalent expenditure of productive force, has found and appropriated an object. It is conceived that such a person becomes the owner of the article by virtue of the immediate logical inclusion of the idea of ownership under the idea of creative industry.

This natural-rights theory of property makes the creative effort of an isolated, self-sufficing individual the basis of the ownership vested in him. In so doing it overlooks the fact that there is no isolated, self-sufficing individual. All production is, in fact, a production in and by the help of the community, and all wealth is such only in society. Within the human period of the race development, it is safe to say, no individual has fallen into industrial isolation, so as to produce any one useful article by his own independent effort alone. Even where there is no mechanical coöperation, men are always guided by the experience of others. The only possible exceptions to this rule are those instances of lost or cast-off children nourished by wild beasts, of which half-authenticated accounts have gained currency from time to time. But the anomalous, half-hypothetical life of these waifs can scarcely have affected social development to the extent of originating the institution of ownership.

Production takes place only in society—only through the coöperation of an industrial community. This industrial community may be large or small; its limits are commonly somewhat vaguely defined; but it always comprises a group large enough to contain and transmit the traditions, tools, technical knowledge, and usages without which there can be no industrial organization and no economic relation of individuals to one another or to their environment. The isolated individual is not a productive agent. What he can do at best is to live from season to season, as the non-gregarious animals do. There can be no production without technical knowledge; hence no accumulation and no wealth to be owned, in severalty or otherwise.

And there is no technical knowledge apart from an industrial community. Since there is no individual production and no individual productivity, the natural-rights preconception that ownership rests on the individually productive labor of the owner reduces itself to absurdity, even under the logic of its own assumptions.

Some writers who have taken up the question from the ethnological side hold that the institution is to be traced to the customary use of weapons and ornaments by individuals. Others have found its origin in the social group's occupation of a given piece of land, which it held forcibly against intruders, and which it came in this way to "own." The latter hypothesis bases the collective ownership of land on a collective act of seizure, or tenure by prowess, so that it differs fundamentally from the view which bases ownership on productive labor.

The view that ownership is an outgrowth of the customary consumption of such things as weapons and ornaments by individuals is well supported by appearances and has also the qualified sanction of the natural-rights preconception. The usages of all known primitive tribes seem at first sight to bear out this view. In all communities the individual members exercise a more or less unrestrained right of use and abuse over their weapons, if they have any, as well as over many articles of ornament, clothing, and the toilet. In the eyes of the modern economist this usage would count as ownership. So that, if the question is construed to be simply a question of material fact, as to the earliest emergence of usages which would in the latterday classification be brought under the head of ownership, then it would have to be said that ownership must have begun with the conversion of these articles to individual use. But the question will have to be answered in the contrary sense if we shift our ground to the point of view of the primitive men whose institutions are under review. The point in question is the origin of the institution of ownership, as it first takes shape in the habits of thought of the early barbarian. The question concerns the derivation of the idea of ownership or property. What is of interest for the present purpose is not whether we,

with our preconceptions, would look upon the relation of the
primitive savage or barbarian to his slight personal effects as a
relation of ownership, but whether that is his own apprehension
of the matter. It is a question as to the light in which the savage himself habitually views these objects that pertain immediately to his person and are set apart for his habitual use. Like
all questions of the derivation of institutions, it is essentially a
question of folk-psychology, not of mechanical fact; and, when
so conceived, it must be answered in the negative.

The unsophisticated man, whether savage or civilized, is
prone to conceive phenomena in terms of personality; these
being terms with which he has a first-hand acquaintance. This
habit is more unbroken in the savage than in civilized men. All
obvious manifestations of force are apprehended as expressions
of conation — effort put forth for a purpose by some agency
similar to the human will. The point of view of the archaic
culture is that of forceful, pervading personality, whose unfold-
ing life is the substantial fact held in view in every relation into
which men or things enter. This point of view in large measure
shapes and colors all the institutions of the early culture — and
in a less degree the later phases of culture. Under the guidance
of this habit of thought, the relation of any individual to his
personal effects is conceived to be of a more intimate kind than
that of ownership simply. Ownership is too external and colorless a term to describe the fact.

In the apprehension of the savage and the barbarian the
limits of his person do not coincide with the limits which modern biological science would recognize. His individuality is
conceived to cover, somewhat vaguely and uncertainly, a pretty
wide fringe of facts and objects that pertain to him more or less
immediately. To our sense of the matter these items lie outside
the limits of his person, and to many of them we would conceive him to stand in an economic rather than in an organic
relation. This quasi-personal fringe of facts and objects commonly comprises the man's shadow; the reflection of his image
in water or any similar surface; his name; his peculiar tattoo

marks; his totem, if he has one; his glance; his breath, especially when it is visible; the print of his hand and foot; the sound of his voice; any image or representation of his person; any excretions or exhalations from his person; parings of his nails; cuttings of his hair; his ornaments and amulets; clothing that is in daily use, especially what has been shaped to his person, and more particularly if there is wrought into it any totemic or other design peculiar to him; his weapons, especially his favorite weapons and those which he habitually carries. Beyond these there is a great number of other, remoter things which may or may not be included in the quasi-personal fringe.

As regards this entire range of facts and objects, it is to be said that the "zone of influence" of the individual's personality is not conceived to cover them all with the same degree of potency; his individuality shades off by insensible, penumbral gradations into the external world. The objects and facts that fall within the quasi-personal fringe figure in the habits of thought of the savage as personal to him in a vital sense. They are not a congeries of things to which he stands in an economic relation and to which he has an equitable, legal claim. These articles are conceived to be his in much the same sense as his hands and feet are his, or his pulse-beat, or his digestion, or the heat of his body, or the motions of his limbs or brain.

For the satisfaction of any who may be inclined to question this view, appeal may be taken to the usages of almost any people. Some such notion of a pervasive personality, or a penumbra of personality, is implied, for instance, in the giving and keeping of presents and mementos. It is more indubitably present in the working of charms; in all sorcery; in the sacraments and similar devout observances; in such practices as the Tibetan prayer-wheel; in the adoration of relics, images, and symbols; in the almost universal veneration of consecrated places and structures; in astrology; in divination by means of hair-cuttings, nail-parings, photographs, etc. Perhaps the least debatable evidence of belief in such a quasi-personal fringe is afforded by the practices of sympathetic magic; and the practices are strikingly similar in substance the world over—from the love-charm to the sacrament. Their substantial ground is the belief that a desired effect can be wrought upon a given person through the means of some object lying within his quasi-personal fringe. The person who is approached in this way may be a fellow-mortal, or it may be some potent spiritual agent whose intercession is sought for good or ill. If the sorcerer or anyone who works a charm can in any way get at the "penumbra" of a person's individuality, as embodied in his fringe of quasi-personal facts, he will be able to work good or ill to the person to whom the fact or object pertains ; and the magic rites performed to this end will work their effect with greater force and precision in proportion as the object which affords the point of attack is more intimately related to the person upon whom the effect is to be wrought. An economic relation, simply, does not afford a handle for sorcery. It may be set down that whenever the relation of a person to a given object is made use of for the purposes of sympathetic magic, the relation is conceived to be something more vital than simple legal ownership.

Such meager belongings of the primitive savage as would under the nomenclature of a later day be classed as personal property are not thought of by him as his property at all ; they pertain organically to his person. Of the things comprised in his quasi-personal fringe all do not pertain to him with the same degree of intimacy or persistency ; but those articles which are more remotely or more doubtfully included under his individuality are not therefore conceived to be partly organic to him and partly his property simply. The alternative does not lie between this organic relation and ownership. It may easily happen that a given article lying along the margin of the quasi-personal fringe is eliminated from it and is alienated, either by default through lapse of time or by voluntary severance of the relation. But when this happens the article is not conceived to escape from the organic relation into a remoter category of things that are owned by and external to the person in question. If an object escapes in this way from the organic sphere of one person, it may pass into the sphere of another ; or, if it is an article that lends itself to common use, it may pass into the common stock of the community.

As regards this common stock, no concept of ownership, either communal or individual, applies in the primitive community. The idea of a communal ownership is of relatively late growth, and must by psychological necessity have been preceded by the idea of individual ownership. Ownership is an accredited discretionary power over an object on the ground of a conventional claim; it implies that the owner is a personal agent who takes thought for the disposal of the object owned. A personal agent is an individual, and it is only by an eventual refinement—of the nature of a legal fiction—that any group of men is conceived to exercise a corporate discretion over objects. Ownership implies an individual owner. It is only by reflection, and by extending the scope of a concept which is already familiar, that a quasi-personal corporate discretion and control of this kind comes to be imputed to a group of persons. Corporate ownership is quasi-ownership only; it is therefore necessarily a derivative concept, and cannot have preceded the concept of individual ownership of which it is a counterfeit.

After the idea of ownership has been elaborated and has gained some consistency, it is not unusual to find the notion of pervasion by the user's personality applied to articles owned by him. At the same time a given article may also be recognized as lying within the quasi-personal fringe of one person while it is owned by another—as, for instance, ornaments and other articles of daily use which in a personal sense belong to a slave or to an inferior member of a patriarchal household, but which as property belong to the master or head of the household. The two categories, (*a*) things to which one's personality extends by way of pervasion and (*b*) things owned, by no means coincide; nor does the one supplant the other. The two ideas are so far from identical that the same object may belong to one person under the one concept and to another person under the other; and, on the other hand, the same person may stand in both relations to a given object without the one concept being lost in the other. A given article may change owners without passing out of the quasi-personal fringe of the person under whose "self" it has belonged, as, for instance, a photograph or any other memento. A familiar instance is the mundane ownership of any consecrated place or structure which in the personal sense belongs to the saint or deity to whom it is sacred.

The two concepts are so far distinct, or even disparate, as to make it extremely improbable that the one has been developed out of the other by a process of growth. A transition involving such a substitution of ideas could scarcely take place except on some notable impulse from without. Such a step would amount to the construction of a new category and a reclassification of certain selected facts under the new head. The impulse to reclassify the facts and things that are comprised in the quasi-personal fringe, so as to place some of them, together with certain other things, under the new category of ownership, must come from some constraining exigency of later growth than the concept whose province it invades. The new category is not simply an amplified form of the old. Not every item that was originally conceived to belong to an individual by way of pervasion comes to be counted as an item of his wealth after the idea of wealth has come into vogue. Such items, for instance, as a person's footprint, or his image or effigy, or his name, are very tardily included under the head of articles owned by him, if they are eventually included at all. It is a fortuitous circumstance if they come to be owned by him, but they long continue to hold their place in his quasi-personal fringe. The disparity of the two concepts is well brought out by the case of the domestic animals. These non-human individuals are incapable of ownership, but there is imputed to them the attribute of a pervasive individuality, which extends to such items as their footprints, their stalls, clippings of hair, and the like. These items are made use of for the purposes of sympathetic magic even in modern civilized communities. An illustration that may show this disparity between ownership and pervasion in a still stronger light is afforded by the vulgar belief that the moon's phases may have a propitious or sinister effect on human affairs. The inconstant moon is conceived to work good or ill through a sympathetic influence or spiritual infection which suggests a quasi-personal fringe, but which assuredly does not imply ownership on her part.

Ownership is not a simple and instinctive notion that is naïvely included under the notion of productive effort on the one hand, nor under that of habitual use on the other. It is not something given to begin with, as an item of the isolated individual's mental furniture; something which has to be unlearned in part when men come to coöperate in production and make working arrangements and mutual renunciations under the stress of associated life—after the manner imputed by the social-contract theory. It is a conventional fact and has to be learned; it is a cultural fact which has grown into an institution in the past through a long course of habituation, and which is transmitted from generation to generation as all cultural facts are.

On going back a little way into the cultural history of our own past, we come upon a situation which says that the fact of a person's being engaged in industry was *prima facie* evidence that he could own nothing. Under serfdom and slavery those who work cannot own, and those who own cannot work. Even very recently—culturally speaking—there was no suspicion that a woman's work, in the patriarchal household, should entitle her to own the products of her work. Farther back in the barbarian culture, while the patriarchal household was in better preservation than it is now, this position was accepted with more unquestioning faith. The head of the household alone could hold property; and even the scope of his ownership was greatly qualified if he had a feudal superior. The tenure of property is a tenure by prowess, on the one hand, and a tenure by sufferance at the hands of a superior, on the other hand. The recourse to prowess as the definitive basis of tenure becomes more immediate and more habitual the farther the development is traced back into the early barbarian culture; until, on the lower levels of barbarism or the upper levels of savagery, "the good old plan" prevails with but little mitigation. There are always certain conventions, a certain understanding as to what are the legitimate conditions and circumstances that surround ownership and its transmission, chief among which is the fact of habitual acceptance. What has been currently accepted as the *status quo*—vested interest—is right and good so long as it does not meet a challenge backed by irresistible force. Property rights sanctioned by immemorial usage are inviolable, as all immemorial usage is, except in the face of forcible dispossession. But seizure and forcible retention very shortly gain the legitimation of usage, and the resulting tenure becomes inviolable through habituation. *Beati possidentes.*

Throughout the barbarian culture, where this tenure by prowess prevails, the population falls into two economic classes: those engaged in industrial employments, and those engaged in such non-industrial pursuits as war, government, sports, and religious observances. In the earlier and more naïve stages of barbarism the former, in the normal case, own nothing; the latter own such property as they have seized, or such as has, under the sanction of usage, descended upon them from their forebears who seized and held it. At a still lower level of culture, in the primitive savage horde, the population is not similarly divided into economic classes. There is no leisure class resting its prerogative on coercion, prowess, and immemorial status; and there is also no ownership.

It will hold as a rough generalization that in communities where there is no invidious distinction between employments, as exploit, on the one hand, and drudgery, on the other, there is also no tenure of property. In the cultural sequence, ownership does not begin before the rise of a canon of exploit; but it is to be added that it also does not seem to begin with the first beginning of exploit as a manly occupation. In these very rude early communities, especially in the unpropertied hordes of peaceable savages, the rule is that the product of any member's effort is consumed by the group to which he belongs; and it is consumed collectively or indiscriminately, without question of individual right or ownership. The question of ownership is not brought up by the fact that an article has been produced or is at hand in finished form for consumption.

The earliest occurrence of ownership seems to fall in the early stages of barbarism, and the emergence of the institution of ownership is apparently a concomitant of the transition from a peaceable to a predatory habit of life. It is a prerogative of that class in the barbarian culture which leads a life of exploit rather than of industry. The pervading characteristic of the barbarian culture, as distinguished from the peaceable phase of life that precedes it, is the element of exploit, coercion, and seizure. In its earlier phases ownership is this habit of coercion and seizure reduced to system and consistency under the surveillance of usage.

The practice of seizing and accumulating goods on individual account could not have come into vogue to the extent of founding a new institution under the peaceable communistic régime of primitive savagery; for the dissensions arising from any such resort to mutual force and fraud among its members would have been fatal to the group. For a similar reason individual ownership of consumable goods could not come in with the first beginnings of predatory life; for the primitive fighting horde still needs to consume its scanty means of subsistence in common, in order to give the collective horde its full fighting efficiency. Otherwise it would succumb before any rival horde that had not yet given up collective consumption.

With the advent of predatory life comes the practice of plundering—of seizing goods from the enemy. But in order that the plundering habit should give rise to individual ownership of the things seized, these things must be goods of a somewhat lasting kind, and not immediately consumable means of subsistence. Under the primitive culture the means of subsistence are habitually consumed in common by the group, and the manner in which such goods are consumed is fixed according to an elaborate system of usage. This usage is not readily broken over, for it is a substantial part of the habits of life of every individual member. The practice of collective consumption is at the same time necessary to the survival of the group, and this necessity is present in men's minds and exercises a surveillance over the formation of habits of thought as to what is right and seemly. Any propensity to aggression at this early stage will, therefore, not assert itself in the seizure and retention of consumable goods; nor does the temptation to do so readily present itself, since the idea of individual appropriation of a store of goods is alien to the archaic man's general habits of thought.

The idea of property is not readily attached to anything but tangible and lasting articles. It is only where commercial development is well advanced — where bargain and sale is a large feature in the community's life — that the more perishable articles of consumption are thought of as items of wealth at all. The still more evanescent results of personal service are still more difficult to bring in under the idea of wealth. So much so that the attempt to classify services as wealth is meaningless to laymen, and even the adept economists hold a divided opinion as to the intelligibility of such a classification. In the common-sense apprehension the idea of property is not currently attached to any but tangible, vendible goods of some durability. This is true even in modern civilized communities, where pecuniary ideas and the pecuniary point of view prevail. In a like manner and for a like reason, in an earlier, non-commercial phase of culture there is less occasion for and greater difficulty in applying the concept of ownership to anything but obviously durable articles.

But durable articles of use and consumption which are seized in the raids of a predatory horde are either articles of general use or they are articles of immediate and continued personal use to the person who has seized them. In the former case the goods are consumed in common by the group, without giving rise to a notion of ownership; in the latter case they fall into the class of things that pertain organically to the person of their user, and they would, therefore, not figure as items of property or make up a store of wealth.

It is difficult to see how an institution of ownership could have arisen in the early days of predatory life through the seizure of goods, but the case is different with the seizure of persons. Captives are items that do not fit into the scheme of communal consumption, and their appropriation by their individual captor works no manifest detriment to the group. At the same time these captives continue to be obviously distinct from their captor in point of individuality, and so are not readily brought in under the quasi-personal fringe. The captives taken under rude conditions are chiefly women. There are good reasons for this. Except where there is a slave class of men, the women are more useful, as well as more easily controlled, in the primitive group. Their labor is worth more to the group than their maintenance, and as they do not carry weapons, they are less formidable than men captives would be. They serve the purpose of trophies very effectually, and it is therefore worth while for their captor to trace and keep in evidence his relation to them as their captor. To this end he maintains an attitude of dominance and coercion toward women captured by him; and, as being the insignia of his prowess, he does not suffer them to stand at the beck and call of rival warriors. They are fit subjects for command and constraint; it ministers to both his honor and his vanity to domineer over them, and their utility in this respect is very great. But his domineering over them is the evidence of his prowess, and it is incompatible with their utility as trophies that other men should take the liberties with his women which serve as evidence of the coercive relation of captor.

When the practice hardens into custom, the captor comes to exercise a customary right to exclusive use and abuse over the women he has seized; and this customary right of use and abuse over an object which is obviously not an organic part of his person constitutes the relation of ownership, as naïvely apprehended. After this usage of capture has found its way into the habits of the community, the women so held in constraint and in evidence will commonly fall into a conventionally recognized marriage relation with their captor. The result is a new form of marriage, in which the man is master. This ownership-marriage seems to be the original both of private property and of the patriarchal household. Both of these great institutions are, accordingly, of an emulative origin.

The varying details of the development whereby ownership extends to other persons than captured women cannot be taken up here; neither can the further growth of the marriage institution that came into vogue at the same time with ownership. Probably at a point in the economic evolution not far subsequent to the definitive installation of the institution of ownership-marriage comes, as its consequence, the ownership of consumable goods. The women held in servile marriage not only render personal service to their master, but they are also employed in the production of articles of use. All the noncombatant or ignoble members of the community are habitually so employed. And when the habit of looking upon and claiming the persons identified with my invidious interest, or subservient to me. as " mine " has become an accepted and integral part of men's habits of thought, it becomes a relatively easy matter to extend this newly achieved concept of ownership to the products of the labor performed by the persons so held in ownership. And the same propensity for emulation which bears so great a part in shaping the original institution of ownership extends its action to the new category of things owned. Not only are the products of the women's labor claimed and valued for their serviceability in furthering the comfort and fullness of life of the master, but they are valuable also as a conspicuous evidence of his possessing many and efficient servants, and they are therefore useful as an evidence of his superior force. The appropriation and accumulation of consumable goods could scarcely have come into vogue as a direct outgrowth of the primitive horde-communism, but it comes in as an easy and unobtrusive consequence of the ownership of persons.

THORSTEIN VEBLEN.

THE UNIVERSITY OF CHICAGO.

STUDIES IN POLITICAL AREAS. III.

THE SMALL POLITICAL AREA.

THE smaller the area, the more rapid is the progress of its
history. A limited territory is more easily mastered ; it develops industrially and politically at an earlier period. The high
degree of exploitation practiced in it produces for a time more
of the various elements of power—men and wealth—than a
large area does. Individuals, classes, parties, races, are brought
nearer together ; the adjustment of differences is often hastened
by force, and the development of the whole thereby promoted.
The history of the small area is, therefore, that of a country in
the lead, with a capacity to impart a powerful stimulus to
others. Thus it happens that limited regions have, for short
periods, been more influential historically than large ones. This
is the meaning of Johann von Müller's saying : "Most great
things have been accomplished by small nations or by men of
little strength and great mind." The districts limited by nature
assume the leadership for a large region ; this function then
gradually passes over to states of larger extent, with slower but
more lasting progress, in proportion as their greater resources
are developed. Thus we see the general advance of mankind
from smaller to larger areas repeating itself, and consequently
the types peculiar to restriction and expansion regularly following one another. After Greece came Italy ; after Denmark,
the German coast, with the Hanse towns and the Prussian colonies of the Teutonic knights ; after Portugal, Spain ; after the
Netherlands, England ; after Brandenburg, Prussia ; after the
West Indies, North America ; after New England, the United
States ; after Bengal, India ; and after Cape Colony, English
South Africa, reaching to the Zambezi. We speak of the great
political influence which it has fallen to the lot of small states to
wield, and we overlook the fact that this has often become
prominent just in the transition from the narrow area of prepa-

ration to the broader one of expansion. From the time there has been a history telling about different tribes and nations on terms of rivalry or acting and reacting upon one another, one has always had the lead. It opens the way, sets the example, and exercises thereby a powerful influence in political, intellectual, or economic matters, the first two more often from an economic basis. Such a people always operates with concentrated strength from a small territory upon outside aims. England offers in the present the most stupendous example of the kind, and that with results which cannot yet be measured.

The progress of historical events enacted within close, confined limits gives the impression of something finished, which even appeals to the æsthetic sense in comparison with movements losing themselves in the vast perspective. The more thorough comprehension and utilization of natural conditions here necessary cause the historical individuality to mature earlier and to reveal more sharply drawn features. In a restricted environment, moreover, man himself appears great as a molder of history. There is a certain attractive definiteness in the great history of little states, from Greece and Rome to Great Britain. This is undoubtedly what Spörer meant when he said that "the process of development of the ancient mind had something of the clearness and distinctness of an artistic composition."[x] This is particularly true of the history of the city-states; they, indeed, are the greatest examples of historical greatness in ancient times. Their importance, as well as the interest which they arouse in us, is altogether out of proportion to their area, but not to the closeness of the connection existing between the land and its people participating as one body in all the move ments of its history.

The very thing which limits and hems in a region often affords to the life forcing its way upward in narrow confinement the possibility of expansion and a field of activity in distant parts. It is true that in the Mediterranean countries the limited character of the area, determined by land and climate, tended to

---

[x] SPÖRER'S notice of C. CURTIUS' "Topographie von Athen," *Geographische Mitteilungen*, 1869, p. 46.

concentrate and intensify everything. This was the case in Egypt and Mesopotamia, just as in Greece and Rome; but the latter stood in connection with a broad sphere of action in the numerous seas to which they had access through their thousand bays, and on which they first secured proper play for their concentrated energies. We find the same two conditions and the same result in Carthage as in Lübeck, Genoa, and Venice. Denmark also, the Netherlands, and Portugal show this same combination of complete isolation in their older, internal development, with all the advantages of transoceanic expansion. In the continuous union of the two, in consequence of which the widest spreading of the people could not break the wholesome bonds of an intense political personality, lies the unrivaled greatness of the British empire. Small inland states, also, press toward these fields of greater activity, which, however, are open to them only through some connection with maritime powers, as in the Hanse towns and in Augsburg's relation with Spain in Venezuela, or by a non-political participation in the competition of foreign trade, such as Switzerland has assumed with great success. The fact that Switzerland and Belgium afford the most fruitful soil in Europe today for international dreams and plans, not seldom Utopian in their character, reminds us of the saying: "The Swiss must have a loophole."[x]

A number of the effects of these naturally isolated regions result simply from their limited area, and therefore characterize islands also, inasmuch as in them the limitation of the territory is absolute. While the population of a small country can spread beyond its boundaries as far as the habitable land extends, in islands all habitation ceases at their shores. This condition makes for that rapidly increasing density of population which we have characterized in our *Anthropogeographie* as their "early statistic maturity," with the immediate consequences, emigration, colonization, and commerce. Upon islands, therefore, the question of space acquires particular importance[2] as an element in economic and political affairs; their nature and form lead

---

[1] HILTY, *Vorlesungen über die Politik der Eidgenossenschaft,* 1875, p. 69.

[2] See *Anthropogeographie,* II, pp. 237 *et seq.*

islands to a careful use of their scant territory, their position to the enjoyment of unlimited space, and out of the combination of these two impulses issue the greatest historical results.

The other great European powers which aim at the same goal as England have been very slow, in the course of their development, to make the most of their greater area—the one advantage which the little island country could never contest with them. Meantime, the latter has continued to exercise the influence which emanates from a more mature, advanced people. A great part of the development of Europe has consisted in the assimilation of English ideas and institutions, and by reason of the immense start which this small land has in the race, this process will continue to endure for a long time yet, especially since English influence is already beginning to make itself felt by way of North America, for example, from non-European countries also. Even yet, one-half the total merchant fleet of all maritime states carries the English flag, and England's exports are equal to those of Germany and France together, although its area is only one-third as large. For all the other European states, naturally, one of the most important questions is, how far they may follow the course of this progressive country, which is by its geographical character so much more free and independent, without disregarding their own peculiar conditions. Consider how far Japan has outstripped China and Corea; and this has happened not merely since the invasion of European and American influence, which could penetrate the smaller country more easily and pervade it quickly, whereas in the tenfold population of China it could not reach beyond the borders: even before, Japan had of herself modified and further developed the elements of Chinese civilization which had come over to her chiefly by way of Corea, and since the seventeenth century she had already adopted very gradually the acquisitions of European culture, mainly under the guidance of Holland. In consequence, she was far ahead of China even before the great turning-point of 1853. San Domingo and Cuba successively progressed, not only beyond the other West India islands, but all Central America. On the eve of the French Revolution, San

Domingo's flourishing condition stood without a parallel in colonial history. The leading position then assumed in turn by Cuba would have been more lasting, had it not been for the competition offered by the immense area of the United States, upon which Cuba is becoming more and more dependent.

The wholesome limitation of a country in the first stages of its growth need not be caused necessarily by the sea. In the New England states this function was performed by mountains and forests, which were inhabited by hostile Indian tribes. Only a hundred years ago there lay in Vermont and Maine a "young" West and North for the old New England states—Massachusetts, Connecticut, Rhode Island, and New Hampshire. They too, therefore, had the advantage of developing inside narrow boundaries and with a broad horizon. In the same way the mountains of Spain forced the Moors into a few favored regions, and in consequence gave rise to dense populations, large cities, and lasting traces. In Russia, where Islam was spread out over a territory three times as big, a sparse population, small towns, and no monument of any significance are the result.

There are political aims which require only a minimum of space for their achievement. Rome proved that a great empire could grow out of the district of a city, and that it would, therefore, be idle to designate a minimum area for a state. A coaling station can be very important, and yet it is always very small. St. Helena is only forty-seven square miles in area, but has great political importance in consequence of its position in the south Atlantic, which is so poor in islands, twelve hundred miles from the African and twenty-two hundred from the South American coast. This importance has belonged to it from the seventeenth century, when it was the main stopping point for the Dutch between Holland and Java, and has only been diminished by the transfer of the East India route to the Suez canal. A trading people, in founding cities and colonies, does not in the beginning aim at territorial possession, but it only wants a base here and there for maritime commerce and the control of the sea. Even the greatest colonies of the present time have developed out of narrow strips of shore, like the half mile along the rivers and coasts in Sierra Leone to which England, in the absence of rivalry, has limited her expansion only since 1883. The Phœnician and Greek colonial cities sought the spring of political power, not in territory, but in wealth. Founded as they were by emigration, further migration beyond the seas was to them more natural as the last political resource in case of increase of population than expansion over the land. How slight was the bond that held them to the soil is shown by the vast scheme of Bias of Priene to transplant the Greek settlements of Asia Minor to Sardinia in the western Mediterranean. There lies a contrast found throughout universal history in this rapid expansion over a thousand limited areas, all of which taken together could not make one large, enduring state, and the slow, onward, swelling inner colonization of the great powers in the neighboring continents of Africa and Asia.

The matter of area grows still more limited in the case of political possessions which have, as it were, only a symbolic value, and in many cases are no longer to be regarded as political realities. The *loges* or factories which the French have retained according to the treaty of 1787 upon English soil in India, in addition to the five acknowledged remnants of their empire, at Jugdia, Patna, Dakka, Cossimbasar, and elsewhere, have never been made use of by the French in the sense in which the treaty intended—that is, for trade under the French flag; and nevertheless, in spite of all offers on the part of the English, they have never been relinquished. The small islands of St. Pierre and Miquelon (area, ninety-one square miles) off the coast of New Foundland hold a similar position, although they are of considerable commercial value.

Phases of development which according to their nature are limited find the most favorable environment in contracted areas. For that primitive stage of political development in which one clan holds itself apart from another and each forms a small community for itself, mountains and forests encourage the inclination toward restriction of territory. But from the open plains, which do not favor this tendency, state-making on a larger scale penetrates into these retreats. The family element in the feeling of nationality is from its nature limited in point of extent, and its development is, therefore, promoted by an isolated environment. The Denmark of the thirteenth century, the Swiss Federation of the fourteenth, and the Netherlands of the sixteenth were far ahead of their great neighbors in point of national self-consciousness. A small people preserves its peculiar character in isolation. The Jews were influenced, to be sure, by the people of Egypt, Syria, and Mesopotamia; but they were few enough in number to retain their distinguishing stamp. Too small to be politically eradicated, they grew up from political weakness to intellectual and spiritual independence. The fate of the Saxons in Siebenbürgen is in its fundamental features and conditions similar.

Even when a tribe has gained possession of a much broader region, still it always tends to restrain efforts directed at more extensive absorption of territory. The growth of the state always becomes in time a struggle with the tendency toward tribal segregation, and the conflicts between national and economic interests are the most unavoidable of all. In this century, notable for the formation of great states, even in western and eastern Europe we have seen states splitting up for reasons of nationality or national religion, but without doubt only temporarily. Higher civilization, to be sure, through the cultivation of the traditions and intellectual treasures stored up in language, causes a sharper separation of peoples, each of which tries to develop that which is most peculiar to itself; but at the same time, civilization creates for them a broader field through commerce and political expansion. Herein lies an antagonistic principle which is working disruptions in every civilized people of the present time, but which seems to be allayed everywhere by the superior influence of greater space, and to this result again trades more than anything else has contributed. The language of a people which enjoys political and economic supremacy forces itself not simply on subjected races. We see this process going on in all directions and on the largest scale in North America, where English has attained a universal sway in intellectual, economic, and political matters. This has been promoted, to be sure, by political conditions, but in general it has developed independently by reason of the superiority of English civilization. The result is the wholesome condition of parallel growth in expansion of nationality and extension of political sway.

The rapid course of the active life of a people dwelling in a small territory, with its often brilliant features, early leads to old age, and very often to a complete decay of its political importance, ending in a historical disappearance, as in the case of Macedon after its third Roman war, or in that of the Greek states when they were absorbed by Rome. In a narrow area the people become too numerous ; they interfere with one another, they irritate, fight, and wear out one another, unless colonization makes more room for them. The city-states are the classic ground of civil strife, which ended in emigration or expulsion. Without imports from other regions, they grow poor from an increase of population out of proportion to their area; with it, they easily grow dependent upon outside countries, and not unfrequently is this the case when, through supplies from subject colonies, their own freshness and energy are paralyzed, as a national life, at any rate, is prone to become without the new tasks which belong to large territories. An intellectual impoverishment becomes unavoidable in a contracted mental horizon, even in the midst of apparently inexhaustible wealth. We find this even in the classical literatures which " knew and recognized only themselves " (Saint-Beuve), where the limited range of their imaginations is reflected in the use of the same ever-recurring figures from nature, history, and mythology, and in their adherence to a few models.

In a limited area rulers and peoples change rapidly, early finish the course of their lives. Consider in how many hands Sicily has been, and how the different nationalities have stamped upon it the mark of their presence and deeper influence. In Greece, the way the most widely different tribes crowded in and over one another confuses our understanding of its history, which, also, suffers from an excess of independent phases of development, in part brilliant, but always entirely too limited in point of territorial extent. Everything, on the other hand, which retards the quick rate of these life-processes of nations keeps a state young. From their very nature the Mediterranean countries had to grow old earlier, just as they were earlier to be settled and to reach their zenith. The damp swamp and forest regions of the North, on the contrary, remained younger so long as they could offer to their inhabitants new fields for expansion.

The purely political effects of a narrow territorial environment long continued are embraced in the term "political provincialism" (*Kleinstaaterei*). No one has analyzed this quality more clearly than Niebuhr where he gives the history of the fall of Achaia: in substance he says that the nation enjoyed prosperity without opportunity for exercising its powers, and that this prosperity gave rise to moral degeneration. Such a condition finds a corrective when smaller states stand in intimate relations with large ones of the same nationality ; but when they continue their isolated existences, independent of one another, and have no activity within themselves, all virility and worth necessarily die out, and a wretched local vanity appears. Great states call forth stirring emotions, peculiarly their own, which keep our feelings alive and ourselves busied, while in small states passion wastes itself upon paltry interests.[1]

As a concomitant of this dull uniformity of interests among the inhabitants of a confined area we would mention, also, the monotony of aims and activities which tends to drag down to the common level everything preëminent, and wherever possible to obliterate it. The smaller a political territory is, so much the more monotonous is its physical character. Varied land forms, classes of vegetable life, and climatic conditions involve, as a rule, wide areas. In a mountain range, therefore, or a plain, or a forest or prairie region, or in one climatic zone, there are several, or, in the beginning, even numerous political districts which are naturally of the same or like character ; just for that reason they have little to exchange with one another, and are not in a position to exert reciprocally much influence. Moreover, the similarity in the resources and employments of the people works toward the same result.

[1] *Vorlesungen über ältere Geschichte*, edited by M. NIEBUHR, 1851, III, p. 523.

From numerous small circles of existence, therefore, there would always result a monotonous totality, capable of only slight variations, even if the social, economic, and political inertia did not become more pronounced with the narrowness of the horizon and their attachment to a soil so limited that it even fails to provide sufficiently for the simplest conditions of an independent life. The success of the Greek colonies in Asia Minor was only passing, because they ignored the smallness of its basis. With the slight exception of Chios and Lesbos, they took no permanent hold upon the mainland, suffered the interior of Asia Minor to loom up before them as a distant world, and in time of political danger sought protection from the mother country; hence their almost quite passive attitude in the midst of great historical events. The principality of Liechtenstein in 1866 fell, so to speak, out of the hands of Germany into those of Austria, without being able to have any voice in the matter one way or the other. Moreover, no necessity was once felt of making her any explanation of this change. Hermann Wagner wrote in 1869 : " The principality of Liechtenstein can properly no longer have a place in the group of German states. It is a sort of appendix of the Austrian monarchy, in the dominion of which it lies."[1] The history of the German imperial cities, nay more, of the whole of the old empire, affords similar examples in abundance. Their want of capacity for independence leaves its stamp in these same uncertain relations peculiar to little countries which are under two masters. This passive attitude comes from the consciousness of insufficient means; we find it, also, in medium powers. The neutrality of Switzerland, Belgium, and Luxemburg can be traced back to this cause, as also the withdrawal of many powers from great colonial undertakings. In 1871 the Netherlands gave up their possessions on the coast of Guinea because the unhealthy climate cost them too many men ; and they feared the difficulties of wars with the natives, for which they would have had to use the troops intended for the Indies. This resignation forms a marked contrast to the

---

[1] HERMANN WAGNER, *Der deutsche Zollverein und die Freihafengebiete Deutschlands,* 1869.

contemporaneous tendency toward expansion which is making itself felt on the part of all the larger states of Europe.

The greatest concentration of political forces is reached in cities, for in them space is eliminated out of the list of political obstructions ; hence they show, with stormy adjustment of internal differences, the most rapid development to centers of power, towering far above the wide domain beneath them. The phases of intellectual progress which find their best conditions in the closely associated activities of many people are characteristic of such foci in particular. The transition from the mythological to the scientific age — an epoch in the history of mankind — was accomplished first in small Greek colonial towns, thriving by their trade on new soil, and with limited space. Commerce, which, according to its nature, promotes the development of such places of preëminence or seeks its support in them, favors this early maturity, depositing in it at the same time the never-failing seeds of decay. So long as there have been great cities, they have outstripped their countries in good and evil. The rôle of Paris in the history of revolutions is nothing new. To be sure, the quick tempo of political changes in France was due in part to the national character, but also in part to the lack of the obstructions afforded by mere distance in the twenty-nine square miles of the capital, Paris. A great number of the famous Italian and German trading towns of the Middle Ages, with the expansion of their commerce, rapidly attained the size and population at which they then remained for five hundred years. Lübeck grew with the rapidity of a New York or Chicago. After Henry the Lion had changed it from a provincial town of Holstein to the chief port of his duchy, it stood for a hundred years at the top of the North German cities, and only all-powerful Cologne could be compared with it. In regard to the Hanse towns, Dietrich Schäfer advances the supposition that, in the first century after they were founded, in most cases they already embraced the area which they then retained, till in the present time the totally different phenomenon of the universal growth of population brought to them also an increase. We can, therefore, speak of a development centuries ahead of its time. And what is particularly noteworthy in the matter, the towns of the Baltic most favored in geographical position, Stettin, Danzig, and Königsberg, advanced in that first growth more slowly; only, however, to stop the process later and to resume it again earlier. In the first half of the fourteenth century the largest cities of the Baltic at that time, Lübeck and Danzig, may be estimated to have had forty thousand inhabitants each.x We must imagine the rapid development of the great cities of antiquity on this order. Australia affords the best examples of the kind in present times, for there the peripheral character of all colonial development is accentuated by the nature of the country, which concentrates all the productive industries on anything like a large scale, especially the cultivation of wheat and sugar cane, also sheep raising and gold mining, in effect upon a narrow strip of coast averaging about one hundred and eighty-five miles in breadth. Hence we find cities like Sydney, with 383,000, and Melbourne, with 491,000 inhabitants (1891), whose magnificence forms a sharp contrast to the barrenness and monotony of the rural districts, with their mere beginnings of civilization. The hypertrophic development of the young city of Brisbane (1891, population 94,000) makes itself felt in the separatist tendency of North Queenland, as in the influence of social parties upon the course of politics in New South Wales and Victoria.

The concentration of all political organization in the city arose first out of a matter of space, namely, out of the difficulty of exercising control over wide areas. It is to be found in the Mediterranean more than anywhere else — among Phœnicians, Greeks, Romans, and later among the Italians, for, as Freeman says, mediæval Italy with its city-states is "a living repetition of the political history of ancient Greece." This fact is intimately connected with the character of the country, where the moisture and fertile soil are scattered, often only oasis-like here and there, so that the settlements in general are less numerous than elsewhere, less evenly distributed, though in individual cases larger and more like cities. In consequence, the cities attach them-

---

¹ See the criticism of these figures in SCHÄFER's *Die Hansestädte*, pp. 219 *et seq.*

selves more closely to one another, and also to the soil and the coast, and then only upon the sea do they find the expansion and increase of wealth which the nature of the land denied them.

Narrow territories bring into the foreground the question of land, or, in other words, the question of space, in consequence of attention's being unavoidably directed to the relation of area to population. The question arises early, therefore, on islands and in other confined regions. They soon lead either to emigration — voluntary or compulsory—and colonization, for which little Thera, as founder of Cyrene, is typical ; or to resistance to unfair division of the land, as in the case of England, where, as early as the sixteenth century, protest was made against the conversion of the commons into inclosed pastures ; or finally to the restriction of the natural increase of population. Malthus, in his *Essay on Population*, calls attention to the prevalence among island peoples of customs designed to act as a check to such increase. Moreover, it is not an accident that the book which treated this phenomenon as a scientific problem appeared in an island country; there even today we meet such facts as that the Scotch islands all taken together constitute the single larger region in Scotland where the number of the inhabitants has diminished. All the evils of a redundant population appear in accentuated form in contracted areas, and especially the fundamental evil, the low value put upon human life, which leads to all kinds of desolation; for this the islands of Polynesia and Melanesia afford numerous examples. While in big countries, and particularly in colonies, the increased value of every human being promotes political freedom, there it is hampered by the depreciated value of the masses. All checks to increase of population have an incalculably far-reaching effect ; they prevent any influx of men and capital, and, by invading the natural course of increase, injure the health and morality of the community, and, in general, place the future of the people on too narrow a basis. This isolation, however, from the nature of things, cannot be lasting, and as soon as it is broken through, the people, whose progress has been arrested, are exposed in consequence to the greatest, oftentimes most violent, changes. The rapid disappearance of the Guiana Indians, Caribs, and Tasmanians illustrates the extreme effect of this. The population of the Libyan oases$_x$ is on the road to the same end; as the increase is artificially checked, the negro threatens to become the dominant element, causing a substitution of race such as has already taken place in Jamaica and other small islands of the West Indies, or, in times for us prehistoric, upon the islands of Melanesla form the spread of settlers from Polynesia and Micronesia.[2]

FRIEDRICH RATZEL.

(Translated by Ellen C. Semple.)

[1] G. ROHLFS, in the *Geographische Mitteilungen*, p. 447, 1860: "The importation of negroes goes on continually; and since neither the Berbers nor Arabs receive new white elements, as was formerly the case, through Christian slaves, it can easily be foreseen that in a given time, conditions remaining the same, Berbers and Arabs will be absorbed by the black population."

[2] Chapters I and II in this series appeared in this JOURNAL, November, 1897 and January, 1898.

SEMINAR NOTES.

THE METHODOLOGY OF THE SOCIAL PROBLEM
DIVISION I. THE SOURCES AND USES OF
MATERIAL.

PART IV. THE LOGIC OF THE SYSTEMATIZING SOCIAL
SCIENCES.

CHAPTER V.[1]

FURTHER FORMULATION OF ELEMENTS OF THE SOCIAL PROBLEM.

The social problem involves —

(*a*) *Discovery of the general laws of interrelationship between human individuals and human institutions.* The same conception may be put in alternative form thus: The social problem involves —

(*b*) *Generalization of the conditions of social order and social progress ;* or, once more, the social problem involves —

(*c*) *Formulation of the reactions of social forces in their most general forms.* In order to solve the social problem we must be able —

(*d*) *To describe and classify and formulate the changes wrought in persons and in societies by the different elements of human experience.* The ultimate aim of this search is knowledge about social relations which will guide effort toward the further changes which civilized men may desire to effect.[2] To indicate the presumptions, or rather the conclu-

[1] The subjects omitted for the present are : Part III, *The Logic of the Genetic Sciences of Society:* chap. 1, "Philology;" chap. 2, "History;" chap. 3, "The Relation of the Social Problem to the Philosophy of History;" chap. 4, "Anthropology;" chap. 5, "Ethnology;" chap. 6, "Folk-Psychology;" chap. 7, "Demography;" chap. 8, "Statistics;" chap. 9, "Analysis of Contemporary Institutions and Conditions." Part IV, *The Logic of the Systematizing Social Sciences:* chap. 1, "Philosophy of History;" chap. 2, "Political Economy;" chap. 3, "Political Science;" chap. 4, "Ethics;" chap. 5, above.

[2] *Vide* VINCENT, "Province of Sociology," AMERICAN JOURNAL OF SOCIOLOGY, January, 1896 ; SPENCER, *Study of Sociology,* chap. 3 ; BERNÉS, *Revue internationale de sociologie,* December, 1895.

sions, from which the sociologists proceed, it is necessary to refer again, in brief, to the different lines of investigation which have for their subject-matter —

(*a*) The physical environment of society.

(*b*) The human individual.

In the first place, this organization of social research presupposes the accumulated results of the physical and biological sciences, so far as these interpret the objective world in which men have to work out their destiny.

In the second place, the sociologist presupposes the physiological, anthropological, and psychological research which analyzes human characteristics as exhibited in the individual. In addition to these, or perhaps properly as a subdivision of the psychological analysis, the sociologists must derive their immediate data with reference to the individual from psycho-ethical generalizations of motives betrayed in human actions. By this I mean that before science that is properly *social* begins, as distinct from science that is concerned solely with the individual, analysis of individual traits must have taken into account all the peculiarities of individual action which betra the individual impulses or springs of individual action, which are the units of force with which social science must deal. The most useful generalization of individual characteristics that can be cited in this connection is suggested in Small and Vincent, *Introduction to the Study of Society*, pp. 173, 177. In a word, the human individual is a center of energy to which we give the general name of *desire*. Individual desire, at a given moment, is compounded of the following elements: desire for (*a*) *health*, (*b*) *wealth*, (*c*) *sociability*, (*d*) *knowledge*, (*e*) *beauty*, (*f*) *righteousness*.

For the purposes of the sociologist, the human individual may be considered (1) as having his habitat in the environment which the physical sciences define; (2) as exerting his peculiar reaction upon the environment, physical and human, through the operation of these desires. It need only be noticed in passing that the total of these elements of energy, in individuals, may vary greatly from time to time, and that the ratios of the different forms of the energy (*a*)–(*f*) may be incalculably diverse. The direction and force of the reaction of the individual upon his surroundings depend both upon the total energy of combined desires and upon the assortment of desires comprising the total.

On the other hand, the interpretation of our general formula ((*a*),

p. 380) depends upon our view of "institutions." The term "institutions" covers *recognized and sanctioned forms of human conduct.* Thus institutions include —

1. *Forms of thought* (mythology, folk-lore, superstitions).

2. *Forms of expression* (gesture, language, ceremonial, art).

3. *Forms of personal action* (methods of hunting, fishing, tillage, neighborhood intercourse).

4. *Forms of coöperation* (in worship, war, industry, government).

Institutions are, therefore, as concerns the nature of their sanctions, (*a*) *customary*, (*b*) *contractual*, (*c*) *prescriptive.* There is no single classification of institutions which will serve as a constantly satisfactory analysis. For our present purpose we may adopt, by way of illustration, De Greef's classification of *phenomena* as a tentative classification of *institutions.*

Let us represent institutions in general by the letters *g, h, i, j, k, l, m*, denoting the several columns in the De Greef chart (above, p. 139), starting on the left. Now we may repeat in more specific terms our original thesis about the implications of the social problem, viz.: The social problem involves the task :

(*e*) *Of discovering the general laws of interrelationship between the individual element in society, represented in terms of desire by the product a b c d e f, and the institutional element, represented collectively by the product g h i j k l m.*

This general task of sociology may be represented graphically as follows (see opposite page).

That is, we may suppose the cube whose base is *A B C D* to represent the total experience of the human race. The base represents contemporary human activities at the initial period of their existence. Each plane parallel with the base represents a " civilization," *i. e.*, the plexus of human activities filling up a period. The irregular lines traversing these planes (from each of the letters *g, h, i, j, k, l, m*) denote departments of activity. Each activity (as symbolized by the line *g*) becomes more involved in successive planes up to that which represents the latest stage of civilization (*F G H I*). The points which constitute these lines make parts of several of the lines at more than one point. These points may symbolize the individuals carrying on the activities. Having this figure in mind, we may further vary the first formula of this chapter thus :

(*f*) *The social problem is the problem of knowing the laws of the forces whose resultants appear both in the plexus of motions represented in the*

h^n i^n I

j^n k^n l^n m

B^V ---- III ---- C^V

B^{IV} ---- C^{IV}

B^{III} ---- D^I ---- C^{III}

a^{II} h i C^{II}

C^I

c

j k l m

lines of a given plane, and also in the variations that ensue in the passage from plane to plane.

The social problem is, accordingly, the problem of knowledge which all the social sciences must together collect and organize. The social sciences have for their common task, then —

(*g*) *Discovery of the laws of reciprocal influence between individuals and institutions.* This discovery must be sought through investigations of such reactions both in selected eras — prehistoric, ancient, mediæval, modern, contemporary — and in *successive* civilizations; *i. e.*, it must be both statical and dynamical. No single section of this study can be complete in itself. In order to justify generalizations, there is need of a distinct department of social investigation whose function shall be to combine the results of all related investigations.

Throughout men's study of human association, distinguished from all the studies of individual characteristics, men have been pursuing the quest of relationships between the individual and institutions within the conditioning environment. This generalized statement of the object of search may or may not have been adopted in any particular instance. Species or specimens alone of these reactions may have absorbed attention at particular times. Comparatively restricted groups only may have been carefully investigated. All the study that men have given to phenomena of association falls partly, however, under this description. We have at length developed a distinct consciousness that this knowledge of the relations of the individual to institutions is a scientific desideratum. With this consciousness we are aware that there has been a vast amount of study of portions of the phenomena included under this general formula. We see that this study has been pursued with the use of categories differing widely in their appropriateness and precision. (*E. g.*, we use the unequally precise terms "economic," "social," "political," "ethical," "historic," phenomena.)

We are thus sharpening the scientific perception that we now need, first of all, adequate objective description and classification of reactions between individuals and institutions. Such descriptions and classifications we have, to a certain amount and extent, with partial interpretation, as, *e. g.*, in the case of large sections of industrial phenomena. Here cause and effect in the play of the wealth desire are made to do most of the interpreting. Whether the interpretations are final, remains to be seen. We are discovering further, however, that most of the reactions between individuals and institutions have been very imperfectly observed ; that there are important phases of phenomena which have been virtually overlooked; and, consequently, that the interpretations derived from partial observation and imperfect coördination of facts must be considered as, at best, provisional, until there has been further investigation and correlation of reciprocally modifying social reactions. In view of all this, progressive solution of the present social problem clearly requires—

1. Extension of the method of positive observation to all classes of societary phenomena which have not been adequately observed.

2. Discovery of the relations between such of these phenomena as have been abstractly interpreted, *i. e.*, in abstraction from the containing reality.

3. Extension of the method of abstract interpretation to other homogeneous groups and other series of phenomena.

4. The highest possible generalizations of societary facts, by qualitative or quantitative explanation of all reactions between individuals and groups, which can be seen to fix or to modify either individual or social types.

This study of reactions in general, between individuals and institutions, has never been distinctly proposed till the sociologists began to organize the study. Certain aspects of it have been studied ever since men began to think; *e. g.*, the reactions between rulers and ruled. Other aspects or abstractions have been made the subject-matter of very advanced and developed sciences (*e. g.*, economics), but, as we see if we use the figure (opposite p. 382) in connection with the De Greef chart (p. 139), these are but fragments of the whole subject, and until they are thought in connection with the whole, they must necessarily be very incomplete. As a challenge for criticism I offer, therefore, this thesis :

History, up to date, has not so much as intelligently attempted to map out the field of investigation in which we must discover the classes of knowledge that above diagram shows to be needed as a condition of understanding the experience of men in society.

During the last century the historians have learned wonderfully *how to do it*, but they have incidentally unlearned *what to do*. They have found a *method*, but meanwhile have lost their *problem*. That is to say, if we let fall a line from the plane $F\ G\ H\ I$ to the plane $A\ B\ C\ D$—say from M^n to M (political institutions)—we shall have a relatively fair indication of the breadth of view which certain groups of historians have taken. If we draw similar lines connecting other phenomena or institutions in the different strata of human experience, as from G^n to G, etc., they will fairly indicate the breadth of view taken by other historians. There has thus far been no adequate programme for covering the ground of human experience in such a way that knowledge necessary for large generalizations is accessible.[1] A substantially similar claim is to be made with reference to each of the other search-sciences of society.

This claim must be tested in the case of history by critical analyses of the tasks which representative historians propose, and by classification of the results which they obtain. This test should answer the following questions :

1. Does the author make distinct provision for treating all the institutions shown by the De Greef schedule to be concerned ?

2. In so far as the author contemplates treatment of all, or any, of these divisions of activity, does he apparently give them proportional attention ?

3. Does the author give evidence of such exhaustive examination of these institutions separately that his conclusions are credible about the actual balance of influence that shaped events in the period treated ?

4. What *explanations* apparently account for deficiencies under above heads ?

5. What further discrepancies between historical programmes and the demands of sociological method does the author illustrate ?

PART V. THE LOGIC OF SOCIOLOGY.

CHAPTER I.

THE SCOPE OF SOCIOLOGY.

It is not the present purpose to make a definition of sociology that shall precisely differentiate it from the other kinds of dealing with the social problem which we have discussed. Nor are we now concerned with the chronological relations of the sociologists' invasion of the field of social inquiry, but rather with its logical significance.

[1] On the function of history from the psychologists' point of view, *vide* MÜN-STERBERG, in *Atlantic Monthly*, May, 1898, pp. 605 and 611.

While researches of the orders already discussed were becoming more and more scientific, men who called themselves sociologists (after the time of Comte) began to make themselves heard. To this day they have not agreed among themselves as to their mission, and, naturally enough, they have not succeeded in convincing other scholars that they have a mission. They have nevertheless persisted in declaring that the older sciences do not take up all the unknown factors of the problem of knowledge about society. Their insistence has been very much like a groping in the dark to get hold of a body whose presence is felt, which, however, can be neither described nor located. Sometimes the sociologists have declared that their subject-matter is entirely distinct from that of the other investigators of society; sometimes they have said that it is the same subject-matter viewed in other lights; sometimes they have said that their quest is for "principles" antecedent to the things observed by the traditional social sciences; sometimes they have protested that their vocation is in generalizing the conclusions of the older forms of research. Through all this vagueness and uncertainty, definiteness and precision have been emerging.

On the one hand, it is becoming evident that there are no primary facts about human beings, whether in their individuality or in association, certain aspects of which may not fall within the claim staked out by one or more of the social sciences. On the other hand, it is evident, *first*, that the social sciences, previous to the advent of the sociologists, had not given due attention to the primary facts of certain kinds, *e. g.*, those now gathered by demography, folk-psychology, and mass-psychology. It is evident, *second*, that the social sciences, before the time of the sociologists, had either generalized relationships among associated people from very insufficient evidence, as in the traditional philosophies of history; or they had narrowed their generalizations to formulas of relationships within an abstracted stratum of social activity, as in pure economics. Accordingly, it is obvious to men who have kept informed about the methodology of social inquiry that new processes must be invented to work these neglected fields. Such processes are, in fact, rapidly developing; and it is plain, too, that the knowledge already acquired about the habits of men in association is capable of generalization in more meaning terms than the special sciences of humanity have learned how to use. In other words, we have learned and are still learning, for example:

(*a*) Laws of purely *personal* association.

(*b*) Laws of tribal or *racial* association.

(*c*) Laws of *industrial* association.

(*d*) Laws of *political* association.

(*e*) Laws of *confessional* association.

(*f*) Laws of *fortuitous* association (crowds), etc., etc.

All these are probably parts of more inclusive laws of *association*. The sociologists are gradually tending to the perception that here is a problem near at hand, viz., *to make out the most general laws of human association*.

The discovery of this problem at once settles some of the previous controversies. It is clear to all sociologists who understand the requirements of positive science that the general must be found in the special. It is not something that exists outside of the particulars. In other words, the search-sciences about society are the immediate sources from which material for generalization of the laws of association must be drawn. If those search-sciences have not yet done their work well, they must be called upon for better work ; but their primary function is obvious, viz., discovery and preliminary arrangement of the data. The task of finding larger truths than the search-sciences have reached about the laws of association requires the construction of new categories, and such arrangement of knowledge brought in and primarily organized by the search-sciences that the categories will be properly filled out.

Instead of arguing from *a priori* principles how these categories shall be arranged, it will serve the immediate purpose better to cite tentative categories that have been proposed, and to point out that they have served to clarify sociologists' conceptions of the task to be undertaken. We may pass directly to Herbert Spencer. Without criticising the process by which Spencer reached his categories, and without attempting to decide how much of his whole system is speculative and how much genuinely inductive, we may start with the fact that, as the case lies in Mr. Spencer's own mind, he has taken into view, by title at least, all the elementary facts that occur in human life. He has a place for each of these facts, in his scheme of sociological classification, regardless of whether they are originally discovered by anthropology, or history, or philology, or economics, or whatever.

In *Principles of Sociology*, Mr. Spencer distinguishes certain great groups, in which he marshals these facts from all sources. These groups of evidence are :

Part   I. The *Data* of Sociology (which prove to be no more and no less *data* than the evidence in the following groups) :

Part III. Domestic Institutions.
Part IV. Ceremonial Institutions.
Part V. Political Institutions.
Part VI. Ecclesiastical Institutions.
Part VII. Professional Institutions.
Part VIII. Industrial Institutions.
(*Cf.* De Greef's groups in the chart, p. 139.)

In the above groups, Mr. Spencer supposes himself to have included, in form, all the essential evidence about human reactions. This is the evidence out of which sociological formulas must be constructed. Whether Spencer worked inductively is not worth inquiring at this point. At all events he concludes, whether before or after hearing the evidence we will not ask, that the same general law of evolution which he finds in the sphere of physics and biology persists in human association.

This general formula of evolution is in the now famous proposition :

"*Evolution is an integration of matter and concomitant dissipation of motion; during which the matter passes from an indefinite, incoherent homogeneity to a definite, coherent heterogeneity; and during which the retained motion undergoes a parallel transformation.*" (*First Principles,* § 145.)

Mr. Spencer believes that the variations in types of correlation among human beings are in accordance with this formula. The kinds of evidence classified in above groups, or completing such a schedule as that of De Greef, must test the belief. Mr. Spencer's fundamental organization of the evidence is contained in part in *The Principles of Sociology*, Vol. I, Part II, entitled, "The Inductions of Sociology." Whether we attach great value to these inductions or not, they at least serve to illustrate the perception that there are *general forms of relationship between persons* which other researches have dealt with in particular manifestations; which, however, have never been thoroughly examined, either analytically or comparatively. These inductions are scheduled under the titles :

I. What is a Society ?
II. A Society is an Organism.
III. Social Growth.
IV. Social Structures.
V. Social Functions.
VI. Systems of Organs.

VII. The Sustaining System.
VIII. The Distributing System.
IX. The Regulating System.
X. Social Types and Constitutions.
XI. Social Metamorphoses.
XII. Qualifications and Summary.

In all this, conceptions are exploited which call for a different order of generalization from that which is peculiar to any search-science about society. The idea of social "*type*," for example, refers not merely to a *political* type, nor to an *ecclesiastical* type, but to a *correlation of persons*, for whatever chief purpose ; *i. e.*, to *type generally*, not specifically. It leads to the perception that there are forms of correlations of persons, produced by large varieties of motive, yet manifesting similarities and possibly samenesses of structure and process. The biological coloring in Spencer's terms may be a mere accident of immature thought. It is not essential. It marks a stage in the endeavor to express the problems of social correlation which the sociologists are trying to define. Since Spencer wrote, the sociologists have made their expressions of their problem still more definite.

In general, we may conclude about the present outlook of the sociologists as follows :

All the kinds of knowledge which have been discussed thus far in this course may be considered as one body of facts, discovered by different processes, and analyzed and classified so as to keep its distinct phases as clear as possible. When knowledge about people is considered thus as a whole—these facts set in order by ethnology, history, philology, and the other "sciences" of human products—it constitutes a stage of knowledge which I prefer to designate collectively by the term **descriptive sociology**. Without making definitions, I offer the following outline of different stages in the process of organizing and interpreting the raw material of knowledge about society. This outline will help to distinguish subsequent stages of interpretation.

1. **Descriptive sociology**[1] sets in order the *forms* in which societary contacts occur. Descriptive sociology has to recast, if necessary, and so far as necessary, the material which is collected at first hand by other stages of the scientific process (history, ethnology, etc.), so that these common forms will appear in the discrete facts. The antecedent social

---

[1] Against the use of this term *vide* WARD, "Static and Dynamic Sociology," *Political Science Quarterly*, Vol. X, No. 2; and in favor of it, SMALL, same title, AMERICAN JOURNAL OF SOCIOLOGY, September, 1895, and May, 1898, p. 857.

sciences are thus, so to speak, partial products, or trial divisors, to be calculated into the more general formulas of descriptive sociology.

The still unfamiliar concept "*social forms*" may become clearer by reflection on an unclassified and uncriticised *list* of the most obvious of them. This list has no reference to the relative importance or generality of the forms named. Regardless of the relationships which may be made out between these forms (as of genus and species), they are named as illustrations. Most of them are suggested by Simmel (*Annals of the American Academy*, December, 1895, pp. 57, 62, etc.):

(1) Secrecy (secret societies); (2) authority; (3) subordination (personal); (4) equality; (5) control (by the group), and (6) conformity (on the part of individuals, without subordination to other persons individually); (7) competition; (8) imitation; (9) opposition; (10) division of labor; (11) hierarchies; (12) parties; (13) interaction and stratification of groups; (14) manifold reactions against external influences; (15) agency and clientage; (16) dealer and customer; (17) spokesman and constituent (not involving authority); (18) representation (with authority); (19) *primus inter pares* (perhaps resolvable into (17)); (20) *tertius gaudens* (the non-partisan, sometimes).[1]

The best of Herbert Spencer's work consists in making out social types, though he would not say so. One of Dr. Simmel's pupils (Thon) defines sociology thus: "Sociology is the science of (*a*) the *forms* and (*b*) the *psychical motivation* of human association."[2]

This necessitates study of the *psychical forces*, working through the forms. Even Dr. Simmel, who emphasizes (*a*) as the sole province of sociology, sees more to reward research in (*b*). He simply does not want the name "sociology" to cover more than (*a*). Without taking up the question of nomenclature, we may be certain that the social problem involves study of (*b*). It has been pursued under two categories, "static" and "dynamic," as follows:

2. **Statical** (sociology) **interpretation** deals with the laws of coexistence among social forces.[3]

3. **Dynamic** (sociology) **interpretation** deals with the laws of serial relationships among social forces.[4]   Quite likely we shall presently

---

[1] The most elaborate treatment of a typical form is SIMMEL, "Superiority and Subordination as Subject-Matter of Sociology," AMERICAN JOURNAL OF SOCIOLOGY, September and November, 1896.

[2] AMERICAN JOURNAL OF SOCIOLOGY, January, 1897, p. 570.

[3] *Vide* WARD, *Dynamic Sociology*, first edition, I, pp. 81 and 127-8.

[4] *Vide* WARD and SMALL on "Static and Dynamic Sociology," *loc. cit.*

agree that the real problems in this department of knowledge concern the laws of variants only; the law of constants emerging in the previous inquiry.

The present condition of systematic thinking upon the social problem is this:

A. We have so clearly discerned the need of more detailed and more authentic knowledge that enormous demands are made upon the search-sciences for more of the sort of evidence which their processes must supply.

B. The thesis of *Simmel*, that sociology must be the science of social *forms*, has at least this effect upon the present stage of correlation, viz., it makes us conscious that we have no adequate schedule of the "forms" of social life.[1]

C. That being the case, we obviously cannot have adequate analyses of the *laws* of those forms.

D. The perception is spreading that the study of society up to date has accumulated merely an unclassified catalogue of social influences; that our knowledge of these influences is, at the most, only qualitative, not quantitative; that we have tentatively generalized many of these influences, both statically and dynamically; but that our formulations of them must be highly questionable until our schedules and classifications of social forms are more complete and critical.

E. There are, therefore, the following kinds of work to be done upon the fundamental social problem :

1. Further collection and primary analyses of elementary material.

2. Generalization of this material into a hierarchy of the *forms of associated life*. If Simmel has not been the path-breaker in this part of the work, he has surely given precision to the formulation of the task, and has offered the most exact specimens of work upon it. His sort of criticism may give value to Spencer's material (*vide* pp. 388–9, above), which it does not at present possess.

3. Extension and criticism of the catalogue of *qualitative* social forces, both static and dynamic. Here are to be tested all the special and general hypotheses in social psychology (Durkheim, Giddings, Jhering, Ross, Tarde, Vaccaro, Ward, *et al.*).

4. Teleological construction, on the basis of our inevitable valuations, and such tentative generalizations as may from time to time be adopted.

[1] *Vide* THON, AMERICAN JOURNAL OF SOCIOLOGY, January, 1897, pp. 568, 570.

5. Technological invention and adaptation, *i. e.*, applied sociology, or social economics in the largest sense; social control on the basis of systematized knowledge of social elements.

Before passing to more special divisions of methodology, it may be well to notice a frequent objection to this whole plan of investigation. Self-confident critics affect to dispose of the sociological programme which we have outlined (especially pp. 114, 132, 167–9) with the summary judgment that the problem is preposterous, the solution impossible, and the method useless.

In reply we modestly insist that, if the verdict holds, it necessarily condemns all study of society that tries to reach valid generalizations, and it consequently dooms us to choose between wholesale credulity and utter agnosticism about efficient social forces. We cannot argue with the man who declares that social forces are beyond human formulation. On the other hand, no man who assumes that social forces may sometime be formulated can justify a less comprehensive survey of their operation than this syllabus proposes. Anything less inclusive is an abstraction. It is not the whole, but a selected part. Formulation of the facts about the part cannot be complete and conclusive. They must be placed in their relations with the whole.

Proposal of such a general plan of social research is sometimes characterized as over-ambitious and chimerical. It should rather be said that general propositions about social laws, if not authorized by such survey as we have indicated, are merely irresponsible guesses. If we are confined to them for social guidance, our wisdom is sententious ignorance. Instead of over-ambition, insistence that there can be no credible generalizations of social laws until they are derived from comprehensive criticism of social relations is rather the humility of intelligent scholarship.

The world will be full of glib social doctrinaires so long as partialists can get credit for wisdom about society. The pedantry that prefers to be satisfied with a narrow generalization, rather than risk testing it by reference to a wider range of relations, affects lofty disapproval of the larger inquiries which genuine scientific curiosity pursues. These extensions of search forthwith discredit previous formulas. They rouse suspicion that accepted versions of special relations are provincial and premature. They impeach dogmatic authority. They concede that prevalent notions covering the questions to be investigated are unsanctioned and unreliable. They advertise the purpose of holding all judgments about partially known relations as provisional until all the available evidence is collected and weighed, and until the relations in question can be correlated with all the coöperating factors. This admission that we are at the beginning of accurate knowledge about society rebukes the self-esteem of men who have made no close investigation of any portion of social reality, but who wish to be heard as social oracles. It tends to set a just appraisal upon men who have worked out minute fragments of knowledge and want these parts to be accepted as final for the whole. In other words, calm analysis of the processes involved in acquiring authentic and coherent knowledge of the essentials of human association exposes, on the one hand, popular ignorance jealous of implications that knowledge is lacking, and, on the other hand, pedantry and sciolism posing as scholarship. Every person with an *a priori* theory or programme about society; every person who wants to divide up the facts of human experience into convenient little blocks of toy knowledge with which he may play science; every person who wants to pretend that he·understands the laws of influences in society, resents the connotations of our method. It means that we know comparatively little about society as yet, and that it will take long, hard, combined labor, by many searchers and organizers working within sight of each other, to get social facts into such shape that they will tell us much general truth.

The most energetic and contemptuous criticisms of the methodology we are developing come from men who want to preach social doctrines, and who instinctively know that doctrines of the degree of generality which they wish to promulgate have no present sanction but dogmatism. Hence they wish to be at liberty to dogmatize, and are jealous of methodology that exposes the poverty of evidence behind their dogmatizings. Every man who wants to pretend that we know more about society than we do, objects to the exhibit which our analysis makes of the considerations involved in knowledge of society.

On the other hand, the men who yield to the discipline of a genuinely scientific method frankly admit that we have as yet relatively little sociological knowledge which deserves to be dignified as "science." We have a vast range of unsolved problems, all visibly composing a comprehensive social and sociological problem. The perception that these problems exist, and that they demand solution, need not make Hamlets of the sociologists while solutions are in abeyance. On the contrary, clear perception of the intricacies and difficulties of the social problem prompts sociologists to do the best they know in the way of immediate social action; if for no other reason, because it is the best available substitute for scientific experiment.[1]

Meanwhile it is puerile to reject a method indicated by the implications of a complex problem on the ground that it is complex. If it were less complex it would not satisfy the conditions of the problem. We cannot teach a boy in the grammar school to calculate the next eclipse with nothing but the rule of three. No more can we work out real formulas of social forces in terms less complex than the factors actually involved. Hence the alternative, either persistent parade of mock knowledge, or consent to go about the quest of real knowledge in the only way in which it can be found.

ALBION W. SMALL.

THE UNIVERSITY OF CHICAGO.

[1] "The Sociologists' Point of View," AMERICAN JOURNAL OF SOCIOLOGY, September, 1897, pp. 153-5.

REVIEWS.

Les Lois Sociales. Esquisse d'une sociologie. Par G. TARDE.
Paris : Félix Alcan, 1898. Pp. 172.

M. TARDE has presented in this little volume the substance of a
course of lectures delivered at the Collège Libre des Sciences Sociales,
October, 1897. The book is an epitome of the three principal books on
sociology previously published by the same author, viz.: *Les Lois de
l'imitation, L'Opposition universelle,* and *La Logique sociale.* It is
also an attempt to show the relation which, in the author's own view,
exists between the three books.

Whatever may be M. Tarde's permanent place in sociological
theory, he is certainly a very prominent, perhaps the most prominent,
figure just at present among the founders of the new science. All
sociologists will accordingly welcome this brief résumé of his views.

The fundamental methodological conception of Tarde's system is
that science is consideration of reality under three aspects, *i. e.*, the
repetitions, the *oppositions*, and the *adaptations* with which the given
portion of reality is concerned. Scientific discovery involves detection of these *repetitions, oppositions*, and *adaptations* in spite of the variations, "dissymmetries," and "disharmonies" by which they are con-
cealed (p. 10). Tracing out cause and effect is not the whole of
science. If it were, pragmatic history would be the most perfect
specimen of science. In addition to *causes*, we need to know the *laws*
of phenomena. Hence science has to use the three keys named, to
discover the laws of repetition, of opposition, of adaptation (p. 11).

These considerations indicate what sociology must do in order to
deserve the name "science" (p. 13). Hence M. Tarde entitles the
three chapters which make up the body of the book : chap. 1, "The
Repetition of Phenomena;" chap. 2, "The Opposition of Phenomena;"
chap. 3, "The Adaptation of Phenomena." Starting with astronomy
as an illustration, the author reaffirms (p. 18) that science always deals
with similarities and repetitions, and that its progress is always an
advance from obvious and extensive manifestations of these aspects to
their hidden and microscopic forms. Passing from illustrations to

the science of society, Tarde declares (p. 24) that, if we consider a town, a crowd, an army, instead of the objects studied by astronomy or biology, the same scientific relations will appear, *i. e.*, our knowledge passes from premature generalities, founded on vain and illusory analogies, to generalizations based on a mass of minute facts relatively precise and similar.

Sociology has been struggling long toward possession of such material in its own sphere. Tarde asserts that the vain efforts of Plato, Aristotle, Vico, Montesquieu, Chateaubriand, Hegel, and the recent evolutionists failed because they could not get their vision trained on sufficiently minute facts. A change promising better results came in with the attempts of the philologists, the philosophers of religion, and especially the economists, to perform the more modest task of identifying minute facts and of formulating their laws. In perfect accord with the view which this JOURNAL has editorially maintained, Tarde speaks of "these specialists in sociology" (p. 26). It is these searchers among the constituent facts of human activity who get out the raw material of sociology. No sociological generalizations can be worth considering, unless they are generalizations of the data furnished by these "specialists in sociology." Tarde next attends to the claim that the explanation of all the facts brought to notice by the "specialists in sociology" must be *applied psychology*. Referring to the argument to this effect at the close of Mill's *Logic*, he points out that the psychology to which Mill looked for the key to social phenomena was merely individual psychology; "a sort of English associationalism, magnified and exteriorized." On the contrary, says Tarde, our explanations of social facts will come, not from *intra*-cerebral, but from *inter*-cerebral psychology (p. 28). "The contact of one mind with another is an event entirely distinct in the life of each. It is sharply separated from the totality of their contacts with the rest of the universe, and it produces the most unforeseen states of consciousness, states inexplicable by physiological psychology."

Tarde finds in the facts of association this initial problem: "Many minds, impelled each by its own desires, fix upon the same objects, affirm the same idea, try to bring to pass the same thing. In other words, they act as though they were moved by a common impulse. They become practically a unified force producing types and qualities of associated activity. How is this convergence to be explained?" In a word, says Tarde (p. 35), not by heredity, nor by identity of geographical environment, but by "*suggestion-imitation*." "Organic needs, spiritual tendencies, exist in us at first only as realizable virtualities under the most diverse forms, in spite of their vague primordial similarity. Among these possible realizations it is the imitated indication of a first initiator which determines the choice of one rather than another." Accordingly Tarde holds (p. 41) that this fact of imitation is the pass-key to the social mystery. It will furnish the formulas which will reduce the apparent chaos of history and of human life to orderly expression.

Tarde's weakness is just at this point. The play of imitation in human affairs is beyond question. But that imitation tells the whole story is preposterous. Tarde's theory claims to account for the incessant appearance of variation in men's ideas, feelings, and actions; but the claim is unfounded. He assumes "élite initiators" at the beginning of the social process, but he asserts that after this initial moment all the members of society are mere imitators. I suppose he would say that the first soldiers who used powder and shot, instead of pikes and arrows, simply imitated former soldiers in using *weapons;* the increased effectiveness of the weapons does not count. The inventors of armor-clad vessels imitated all the sea fighters in *protecting themselves* against other sea fighters. The means employed are merely imitative combinations of previous elements, etc., etc.[1] No one will be satisfied a great while with this stretching of the truth.

The effect of M. Tarde's second chapter, " Opposition of Phenomena," upon my mind, is to impeach, rather than to confirm, his main thesis. Tarde divides oppositions in human societies into the three chief forms of war, competition, and disputation. His contention is, first, that each of two opposing social factors is itself the terminus of a "radius of imitation ; " second, that the opposition between these factors is merely a mediary affair, destined to disappear in the eventual adaptation (p. 104). The former of these propositions is the original thesis to be proved, and the chapter on " opposition " certainly makes the thesis no more probable. As I understand Tarde's claim,

[1] This seems to be the import of a passage on p. 134, the implications of which are utterly arbitrary, viz.: " We must avoid confounding, as is so often done, the *progress of instruction,* a simple fact of imitation, with the *progress of science,* a fact of adaptation ; or the progress of industrialism with the progress of industry itself; or the progress of morality with the progress of moral theory; or the progress of militarism with progress of the military art ; or the progress of language — i. e., its territorial spread — with the progress of language in the sense of refinement of its grammar and the enrichment of its dictionary." This passage will be referred to below.

it would be expressed in the concrete: " Charles the First was the latest term of one series of imitations ; Cromwell the latest term of another series; the Restoration, or the Act of Settlement, the accommodation or ' adaptation ' of the two." Or " Bourbonism was the end term of one series of imitations ; Jacobinism of another ; Bonapartism their ' adaptation.' " Of the claim thus expressed, we may say, without much risk: first, if any historian believes that either the Stuarts, or the Puritans, or the Bourbons, or the Jacobins can be disposed of in terms of " imitation," he would confer a favor upon the sociologists by making himself known ; second, even assuming that the primary thesis were established, the formulation thus far does more to raise the hypothesis of an undetected factor in the process of " adaptation " than to satisfy the mind with the simple factor " imitation." In other words, to recur to the last illustration, Tarde's own argument has the effect of provoking the presumption that a something, which we may call Napoleonism, was a real coördinating factor in the reaction between Bourbonism and Jacobinism. Tarde's own argument seems, therefore, to make rather toward a conclusion more like Baldwin's, viz., a " dialectic of social growth " (Social and Ethical Interpretations, p. 543). He has not yet made it credible either that " imitation " is the sum and substance of both thesis and antithesis, or that " imitation " is the combining agency by force of which the synthesis, or equilibrated social status, results.

In chap. 3, "The Adaptation of Phenomena," the author describes adaptation as a condition of the elements composing an aggregate. It is of two degrees: first, that presented by the relations of the component elements of an aggregate to each other ; second, that which unites these elements to the systems in which they are contained, or, in a word, to the environment (p. 117). "Adjustment within itself differs very greatly in every order of facts, from adjustment to external conditions; just as repetition of self (habit) differs from repetition of others (heredity or imitation), as opposition within the self (hesitation, doubt) differs from opposition to others (conflict, competition.)" All science is progressive endeavor to think the adjustment actually given in the portion of reality contemplated (p. 118). This is true of sociology, from its first forms in theology (p. 123), through its forms as philosophy of history, down to the evolutionary sociologists (p. 124). At this point Tarde brings the following indictment against the evolutionists: " The same error always reappears in their method, viz., they believe that in order to discover regularity, order, logical progress, in the facts of society, the details must be left behind, because they are essentially irregular. A very high point of outlook must be taken so as to bring vast wholes within a panoramic view. It is assumed at the same time that the principle and source of all social coördination resides in some very general fact, whence it percolates by degrees and in progressive dilutions down into particular facts. In a word, man is carried along by a law of evolution within the action of which his initiative is only apparent" (p. 125). Tarde declares, on the contrary, that close adaptations are to be found only in the details of human facts; that the farther we go from the small and closely knit social group — from the family, school, workshop, congregation, convent, regiment — to city, province, nation, the less perfect and striking is the solidarity. At this point, again (p. 127), it seems to me that in recording a correct observation — viz., "civilization is characterized by the facilities which it offers for the realization of an individual programme of social reorganization "—Tarde points toward the very facts which will presently compel radical restatement of his hypothesis. This is still more evident a little later, when he says (p. 129): "We must look for elementary social adaptation in the brain itself, in the individual genius of the inventor. Invention — I mean that which is destined to be imitated, for that which remains shut up in the mind of its author does not count socially — invention is a harmony of ideas which is the mother of all the harmonies of men." In all this Tarde is dealing with factors in the situation with which his own thesis in its present form is irreconcilable. He is refuting himself. Tarde has done most notable service in calling attention to the function of imitation. His service ends when he attempts to make us believe that imitation is the social *factotum*. We may admit that "at each cerebral alliance of two inventions in a third, imitation is involved " (p. 133), but it is equally clear — or more so — that, as Tarde declares on the following page, "these two progressions — the imitative and the inventive — are continually interlaced." The logical categories, "repetition," "opposition," "adaptation," give no license to assign rank and importance to one of these factors to the prejudice of the other. It is sheer dogmatism to imply (as in the passage quoted above from p. 134) that invention is simply and solely a function of imitation. The presumption is decidedly against it. Imitation is evidently a factor in the social reaction, and we must assign it due value. But variation, as Tarde himself is compelled to advertise, is a constant social phenomenon. Masking it under the term adaptation does not change the reality, nor diminish the probability that something quite as radical as imitation gets in its work when a variation is produced. What that something is need not now be asked. In trying to show that imitation is the one essential social process, Tarde has, in spite of himself, made it more evident that imitation is not the only essential social factor.

It ought to be evident by this time to every intelligent sociologist that "imitation" is but one among the unnumbered terms of the multiple working hypothesis which is marking out promising lines of social research.

In spite of M. Tarde's earnest harking back to the minute realities, his reasoning seems to be based at last on a realism that attributes efficient functioning force to abstract ideas. This appears in the closing sentence of the book: "The mutual harmonies of our three terms, repetition, opposition, adaptation, are easily intelligible when we consider progressive repetition as functioning in the service of the adaptation which it extends and develops, in favor sometimes of the opposition which it also conditions. We may also believe that all three labor together for the extension of universal variation under individual and personal forms of the highest order."

Albion W. Small.

Manuel de bibliographie générale (Bibliotheca bibliographica nova). Par Henri Stein. Paris: Alphonse Picard et fils, 1898. Pp. 20 + 895, large 8vo. (Manuels de bibliographie historique, II.)

This book comes of good antecedents. Its author, M. Henri Stein, is editor of *Le bibliographie moderne*, the French organ for the advancement of the science of bibliography, and of *Polybiblion*, which is doing more than any other periodical in France, or in the world, probably, to exploit the whole field of current bibliography. M. Stein was coeditor with M. C. V. Langlois of *Les archives de l'histoire de France*, published in 1891–3, which forms the first volume in the series of "Manuels de bibliographie historique," and which has been highly commended. M. Langlois, the coworker of M. Stein, published in 1896 *Manuel de bibliographie historique*, which, though a small book, is packed with valuable information well digested, arranged, and indexed as to general bibliographical works and the bibliography of European history. M. Stein in his introduction claims to have profited by the mistakes of his immediate predecessor in the field of the bibliography of bibliographies, M. Léon Vallée, whose *Bibliographie des bibliographies*, in spite of its omissions and questionable arrangement, has continued to be of great assistance to workers in libraries. Lastly and most important of all, the author claims that the manual under review is a continuation and revision to date of Petzholdt's *Bibliotheca bibliographica*, which has been generally admitted by bibliographers to be the most profound work yet published on the bibliography of bibliographies. We have a right, then, to expect much from M. Stein.

The title is somewhat misleading. The book contains titles not only of general bibliographical works, but also of special bibliographies which deal with the literature pertaining to all the arts and sciences. Moreover, it lists, in addition to bibliographies proper, books which contain valuable bibliographical matter in any quantity from two pages up.

The matter contained in the body of the work is divided by M. Stein into the following main divisions, with as many subdivisions as occasion requires : (1) bibliographies universelles, (2) bibliographies nationales, (3) sciences religieuses, (4) sciences philosophiques, (5) sciences juridiques, (6) sciences économiques et sociales, (7) sciences pédagogiques, (8) sciences pures, (9) sciences appliquées, (10) sciences médicales, (11) philologie et belles-lettres, (12) sciences géographiques, (13) sciences historiques, (14) sciences auxiliaires de l'histoire, (15) archéologie et beaux-arts, (16) musique, (17) biographie. This classification of the field of literature agrees in the main with the classifications current in French bibliographical publications. It differs a great deal from Petzholdt's classification, and seems to be no better and no worse than a dozen other schemes of division which one might name.

Following these seventeen main divisions, which constitute the body of the work, we find three long appendices, a supplement, and an index.

The supplement contains a list of such bibliographical books as have appeared while the manual was passing through the press, and also such of an earlier date as were omitted by accident. The introduction to the book is dated December 31, 1896, but a great many works published in 1896 appear in the supplement. It also contains all books listed of date 1897 and a few of date 1898. It is unfortunate that the main lists were closed so long before the work was finally issued. The titles of many works are to be found in the appendix, the most recent, of course, and the most valuable in other respects. For example: Sabatier's *Esquisse d'une philosophie de la religion*, with its valuable bibliographies; *L'année philosophique*, Stammhammer's *Bibliographie der Social-Politik*, Monroe's *Bibliography of Education*, Poole's *Index*, Campbell's *Index Catalogue of Works Relating to India*, Brook's *Bibliography of Municipal Government*, Galey and Scott's *Guide to the Literature of Æsthetics*, Henshaw's *Bibliography of American Economic Entomology*, etc. Users of the index will do well to refer to the supplement in nearly every case. Such reference is facilitated by numbering each entry in the index with the page on which the item would have occurred if included in the body of the work.

The first appendix is devoted to a "Systematic list of all the localities in the world which possessed a printing establishment before the nineteenth century;" the second to a "List of the general indexes to periodicals in every language;" the third to a "List of the catalogues of printed books in the principal libraries of the world."

Unquestionably these supplements contain valuable matter. I do not remember to have seen anywhere lists of places of publication, periodical indexes, or library catalogues which can approach them in completeness. The antiquarian bookseller, librarian, and cataloguer will make full use of these appendices and thank M. Stein most heartily. But, for all that, the worker in practical bibliography, for whom the book is, according to the introduction, more especially intended, will regret that so much space was used for these appendices, occupying, as they do, about one-quarter of the book.

Inasmuch as the book is not so large as Petzholdt's *Bibliotheca bibliographica*, and not nearly so compactly printed, one's curiosity is properly aroused to know how the author manages to add the bibliographies that have appeared since Petzholdt published his work in 1866, and still have room to spare for appendices. The author's policy is clearly stated in the introduction. "Every bibliography which has become old and useless has been systematically discarded. What good can come of swelling the size of a book with references which only lead the reader astray and cause him to lose time that might be employed to much better advantage? . . . . All the explanatory notes in the text have been reduced to the lowest terms, and their brevity contrasts singularly with the long dissertations of Petzholdt which have appeared to me useless and, in general, little read. . . . . The remarkable publications are always indicated by detailed and favorable notice ; as for the *publications détestables*, they have been purely and simply passed by in silence."

The policy announced in the introduction seems to have been in general carried out through the book. No one would ever suspect, from consulting the lists, that such persons as Power, Sabine, Petzholdt, Vallée, Ottino, and Fumagali had lived and had written bibliographies of bibliographies. This policy must be responsible for the omission from the lists of bio-bibliographical works of Michaud's *Biographie universel* and the inclusion of Hoefer's *Nouvelle biographie générale*. Can it also be responsible for the omission of Sabine's *Bibliotheca Americana*, of Lalor's *Cyclopædia of Political Science*, of McCulloch's *Literature of Political Economy*, and many other useful works that might be mentioned ?

This policy of throwing out books because later books have appeared in the same general field I maintain is all wrong. In the libraries of Paris, with its Bibliothèque Nationale of two million volumes, and its secondary libraries aggregating two million more, it may be proper to help the reader by putting only the latest bibliographies within his reach ; but Paris is not the world, and probably not France, in this respect. Most of us are troubled with too few bibliographies, rather than too many. Not all libraries can afford to buy all the bibliographical works they would like. If they cannot have the latest, is this any reason why their readers ought not to be referred to one that is nearly as late and nearly as good ? Besides, it requires the most careful comparison of two works to be able to decide with justice that one work does entirely replace another. Take the case of Hoefer and Michaud, mentioned above. Granted that Hoefer is a little later than the second edition of Michaud, and that the concise bibliographical references appended to the articles in Hoefer do contain substantially all the references mentioned in Michaud, can M. Stein deny that the running comments which accompany the references in Michaud are in many cases very suggestive ? He surely would be one of the last to admit that bibliography stops with a mere listing of the title, else he ought in strict logic to suspend further publication of the "Partie littéraire," of *Polybiblion*.

It also appears from the passage quoted, and the lists confirm it, that the manual is not Petzholdt brought to date. To me it seems that the best part of Petzholdt is left out. M. Stein has doubtless lived in an atmosphere saturated with bibliographical information for so long that he has little use for the long characterizations of Petzholdt. But if he were compelled to acquire a rational knowledge of bibliography at short notice, and often to bridge over gaps in the field caused by inability to get and become familiar with certain books, I am sure he would appreciate Petzholdt's long and careful discussions. No one would be able to learn from Stein's manual what the London catalogue is, which is liable to be met with in half a dozen different forms in as many different libraries, all of different appearance and covering different periods. Petzholdt uses a page for it, but he sets the tangle straight.

As to the last point of policy stated in the passage quoted, I cannot believe that the author is consistent. Hoefer gets no word of commendation, and surely he is not "detestable." The same is true of Winsor's *Reader's Handbook of the American Revolution*, Channing and Hart's *Guide to the Study of American History*, and any number of bibliographies which appear in the lists without characterization.

Considering the influence that the policy above discussed might have in limiting the number of bibliographies listed, I do not find many omissions which would be called serious in a library which had nearly all those included, but in case a library has but two or three in a certain field, if one or two of those are omitted it becomes a serious matter. I believe that at least nine out of ten libraries will fall in the latter class.

In the list of national bibliographies I am surprised to find Hinrich's *Halbjahrskatalog* missing. It is included in Petzholdt's and Langlois's lists, and is generally regarded as one of the most useful tools of the trade. How does M. Stein manage to get along without it ? The London catalogue is omitted entirely, leaving no regular list to cover the years 1824–35. True, it is a poor catalogue, but it does cover the ground after a fashion. The American catalogue edited by Leypoldt and his successors should count five volumes all told, and not four; while Kelly is credited with six volumes instead of two, the proper number. The list of national bibliographies is, on the whole, however, very satisfactory and the number of countries covered surprisingly large.

In the social sciences I notice various omissions which might certainly as well be included as many that are included. Examples are : Rand's *Bibliography of Political Economy;* Tolman's *Handbook of Sociological Information ;* Bowker and Iles' *Reader's Guide in Economic,*

Social, and Political Science; Charlemagne Tower, *Collection of American Colonial Laws; Catalogue of the Hopkins Railway Library;* Gross' *Bibliography of British Municipal History.*

Numerous real or apparent oddities of classification appear. Westermarck's *History of Human Marriage* under " sciences philosophiques" is an example.

Typographical errors and minor errors of fact are quite common; *e. g.*, Palsgrave for Palgrave, p. 114; Strikles for Strikes, p. 126; Baltimore, 1890, for Chicago, 1895, in date and place of publication of the AMERICAN JOURNAL OF SOCIOLOGY, p. 116.

The index which concludes the work is very full, occupying ninety pages. That is, it is full as to subject entries, but author and title entries are entirely wanting. What led the author to omit these is more than I can imagine. Petzholdt and Langlois have author entries in the index, and Vallée's main arrangement is by authors. All users of these books will, I am sure, agree that the ability to refer at once to a certain bibliography is very desirable. Granted that the book will be referred to nine times out of ten by subject, what is the harm of providing for the tenth time? Lack of space would be the natural excuse. But how can this be put forward consistently when the space that might have been used for author and title entries has been used for indexing names of places having printing establishments, which were already alphabetically arranged in one list and are of use only to specialists?

The author, I claim, is guilty of another minor sin in neglecting to provide for a short symmetrical table of contents. He does, indeed, give us an outline of main divisions and subdivisions in the middle of the introduction, but many will never find it, and when found it is of not much use, for there are no page references.

It seems to me a great pity that M. Stein did not conclude to take all the space that was necessary to really bring Petzholdt down to date, to include all the bibliographies, full characterizations of them, and the valuable appendices as well. Two volumes would probably have sufficed, and few who really appreciate such work would have begrudged him three. For, after enumerating the serious faults in the work, I am in justice compelled to say that the work is today, for the bibliographer and reference librarian, the most valuable single-volume reference book in existence.

C. H. HASTINGS.

Social Elements, Institutions, Character, Progress. By CHARLES
RICHMOND HENDERSON. New York: Charles Scribner's
Sons. Pp. vi + 405.

THIS book is divided into several parts, each part being, in some
sense, introductory to the next following part:

Part I, "Basis of Society in Nature."
Part II, "The Social Person."
Part III, "Social Institutions."
Part IV, "Social Psychology, Order, and Progress." An appendix
gives directions for local studies, maps, and topics for discussion.

Those who had read carefully the works previously published by
Dr. Henderson were prepared, when the present volume was announced,
to expect a book of great interest and value. In this expectation they
will not be disappointed, even though they should be constrained occasionally to place an interrogation point after some statement of the
author, for the purpose of giving it further consideration. The work,
as the writer says, has been prepared both for ordinary readers, many
of whom care for little more than a surface knowledge of a subject, and
also for students, including teachers, who are, as a rule, seeking to get at
the real truth. The adoption of the book by the *Indiana Teachers'
Reading Circle* indicates that it is intended to meet the wants of teachers
of common schools, a class of persons who, more than any others,
excepting possibly parents, have occasion to make use, in their daily
labors, of practical facts such as are discussed in this treatise. The
book will, consequently, be especially valued on account of its adaptation to educational purposes. The introduction states very clearly the
field of study and the means of learning the facts to which attention is
to be directed. The order and arrangement of the matter conform
admirably to the principles of pedagogy and the general laws of teaching. Any intelligent instructor will be able to follow readily the steps
and progress of the discussion. The purpose of this article is chiefly
to notice the happy application of some of these principles.

It is agreed by all experienced students of pedagogy that the child,
and indeed the more advanced learner, must begin, in the investigation
of any complex subject, with the near-at-hand and with the concrete.
If the world is to be studied, one should commence with his own
home, his neighborhood, his immediate surroundings. If a principle
is to be easily and thoroughly comprehended, it must be seen embodied
in some institution or some mode of living. Dr. Henderson well says:

"All journeys and all voyages must start from home. "The right method is to proceed from the present to the past." Not only is the past to be learned by starting from the present, but the future must be predicted in the same way. "The order we know must have in itself the germs of the coming order, since life cannot arise out of nothing."

In treating of the physical basis of society, the author has avoided the error of making nature everything. The child becomes acquainted with humanity before he becomes acquainted with what we call nature. Nature has value and meaning only as it comes into contact with humanity. In the discussion of the social person, an important truth is well stated : "There is no social mental experience outside of individuals. There is no social brain or consciousness apart from the separate brains and inner lives of the millions of individuals who compose the race." The social institutions are presented in the natural order—the home, the family, and later the auxiliary institutions. The discussion of the social arts, both the useful and the fine, and the treatment of industrial organizations have especial practical value, not only for teachers, but for all workers in the social field.

The chapter on the tendency toward "Economic Betterment" gives a mass of most interesting matter, which appears to justify the position of Dr. Henderson, although he evidently anticipates a questioning of the correctness of his assumptions. It is true, or seems to be, that "The great majority of the population of civilized lands have made progress in the possession and enjoyment of the resources of the best existence." To teachers the discussions of topics relating to "Economical Betterment" are of the very highest value. The extent of meaning attached to the idea of "social movement" will naturally incite careful thinking. It is doubtless true, though not generally accepted, that "It is not increasing poverty and depressing pauperism and desperate misery which incite social unrest and discontent, so much as it is the taste of better means of living. The poor are not growing poorer, but richer," etc. To both the parent and the teacher the following conclusion in the chapter on social misery presents food for thought : "The most encouraging and necessary effort is that directed to the proper education of wayward youth. Prevention is the true policy of nations. . . . . Education, mental, moral, and spiritual, is the chief means of restoring the wanderer, and it is the only way of turning childhood and youth from the downward path to ruin."

Space permits only a brief reference to the chapters on "The

School" and its social service, and on "Religion and the Church."
They are both particularly valuable to teachers and managers of schools,
as is also the discussion of the "Problems of Social Psychology," and
the succeeding chapters. It is a matter of congratulation that a book
of this kind has been written by a man who believes in the existence
and importance of the spiritual element in human nature, and is not
afraid to speak of the church and religion ; and to say, after treating
nature studies most generously, "But the environment in which the
citizens are living is not merely the physical world about us. Physical
science is not the only science which deals with reality. Unless we
actually identify physiology and psychology, matter and mind, and beg
the whole question of materialism, there is still nearer to us than nature
a world of spirit, of thinking beings."

The teachers of Indiana are very fortunate in having this book
upon their reading list. The suggestions, in the preface, to students
as to the manner of using the work, and the directions, in the appendix,
for local studies, are of great practical value. Readers cannot do
better than to adopt and follow the order of "topics for papers and
discussions" given for the successive chapters, making use of maps and
charts of their own immediate neighborhood, prepared by themselves.

DANIEL PUTNAM.

STATE NORMAL SCHOOL,
Ypsilanti, Mich.

La guerre et ses prétendus bienfaits. Par J. NOVICOW. Paris:
Armand Colin et Cⁱᵉ, 1898. Pp. 198.

THIS work has a double claim to attention : in the first place,
because the writer is already well known as the author of *La politique
internationale, Les luttes entre les sociétés humaines,* and *Conscience et
volonté sociales;* secondly, because the book covers, in brief compass,
practically the entire field of discussion as to the causes and results of
war. This will appear most clearly from an inspection of the table of
contents, which is here transcribed :

    I. "La guerre considerée comme fin."
    II. "Le raisonnement unilatéral."
    III. "La guerre est une solution."
    IV. "Résultats physiologiques."
    V. "Résultats économiques."
    VI. "Résultats politiques."

VII. "Résultats intellectuels."
VIII. "Résultats moraux."
IX. "Survivances, routines et sophismes."
X. "La psychologie de la guerre."
XI. "La guerre considerée comme forme unique de la lutte."
XII. "Les théoriciens de la force brutale."
XIII. "Synthèses de l'antagonisme et de la solidarité."

The author is an impassioned advocate of universal peace, and in this work vigorously attacks the arguments advanced by those who believe war beneficial, or at any rate unavoidable, paying special attention to the book entitled *Ueber Krieg, Frieden und Cultur*, by Max Jahns.[1] In spite of the brevity caused by the treatment of so many topics, the book is very clear and vigorous in style, entertaining, full of keen observation and persuasive argumentation. The criticism is particularly sharp and telling when directed against what M. Novicow calls the "raisonnement unilatéral" of his opponents. For example, nothing could be better than his exposure of the logical error committed by those who defend war as an end in itself, whereas it has never been more than a means; or extol the virtues produced by successful warfare, but are silent concerning the vices engendered by servitude; or laud the glory of a war in defense of country, but say nothing of the dishonor involved in wanton aggression: forgetting that a conqueror implies a conquered, and that a defender presupposes an aggressor.

But in spite of these merits, the reader is at times conscious of a feeling of disappointment, not because he has received little, but because he had expected more. Slips in historical statements are rather frequent: *e. g.*, on p. 146 occurs this statement, "Auguste ferma le *premier* le temple de Janus." The argument is not strengthened by the frequent use of strong language: *e. g.*, Bismarck is *ce hobereau;* Roon, Moltke, and Bismarck are *les trois copains;* war is always murder, massacre, or collective assassination; force is always brutal, etc., etc. Consistency is sometimes cast to the winds, as on p. 94, where we read: " . . . . Si la France renonçait à l'Alsace-Lorraine, elle aurait bientôt le sort de la Pologne. Les Français (et tous les autres peuples) doivent revendiquer leurs droits jusqu'à la dernière goutte de leur sang." Inasmuch as opinions differ, radically and permanently, as to the rights of the several nations, this declaration would appear to make an end of the argument for universal peace. There is frequently

[1] Berlin, 1893.

an air of artificiality about the treatment of political affairs which reminds one irresistibly of Rousseau and the atomistic social philosophy of the eighteenth century: *e. g.*, "Le bien-être des hommes n'est pas en fonction des divisions politiques. Que l'Europe soit partagée en dix états ou en cinquante, elle ne sera pour cela ni plus civilisée, ni plus barbare " (p. 71). And, finally, there are not wanting examples of the "one-sided reasoning" with which M. Novicow charges his opponents.   Thus he argues that because questions still remain which threaten war, therefore the eight thousand wars of the past have all settled nothing; and also that because the smaller states have opposed political consolidation by war, therefore war has never consolidated great states.   Such arguments are surely rather ingenious than convincing.

After proving, to his own satisfaction, that war is, and always has been, an unmitigated evil, in every respect, M. Novicow finds himself confronted with this question : Why is it, then, that war still continues, and that men are still found to defend it ?   His answer is brief and to the point: War continues from force of habit (*routine*), and men defend it because they have confused it with competition in general (*la lutte*).   The discussion of this proposition is one of the most original and suggestive parts of the book.

The last two chapters contain a polemic against the theories advanced by Gumplowicz in *Der Rassenkampf*, and, at the end, an eloquent plea for peace.   But unfortunately, the "Synthèse de l'antagonisme et de la solidarité" proves to be metaphysical to a degree, and we are left in the dark as to the means by which peace is to be obtained and maintained.

EDWARD VAN DYKE ROBINSON.

ROCK ISLAND, ILL.

Socialism and the Social Movement in the Nineteenth Century.   By WERNER LOMBART, Professor in the University of Breslau. Translated by Anson P. Atterbury; introduction by Professor John B. Clark.   New York: G. P. Putnam's Sons, 1898. Pp. xvii + 199.

THIS volume of public addresses gives the most significant elements of socialism without burdening the page with minor details.   The author regards socialism as the most significant form of prolitariat struggle for recognition, power, and material well-being.   The class is itself the product of the capitalistic system of industry; and the attempt of this class to maintain its place and advance its interests is not the result of agitation, but of inherited social conditions. No ruling class ever made concessions to the lower classes out of philanthropy, but only when urged by powerful pressure. The economic doctrines of Karl Marx, in relation to "surplus value," are abandoned; but · his claim to recognition rests on his exposition of the historic conception of the social movement, and the inner relationship of the economic, social, and political manifestations and precedents. He showed most clearly that the social movement is toward the communization of the means of production, and its way is the struggle between classes. The author is in manifest sympathy with these views of history; only he urges legal methods and freedom from vindictiveness in the combats of classes. The synchronistic table of events in the movement from 1750 to 1896 is a valuable feature of the work.

C. R. H.

Annual Report (*31st*) *of the State Board of Charities for the Year 1897.* Two volumes. New York and Albany: Wynkoop Hallenbeck Crawford Co. Pp. 1190 + 926.

THESE two volumes are for the student of public charities a genuine contribution to knowledge. They deal with the complex system of relief in a great and highly developed state. The facts are presented in a clear order, and the discussions are written by persons of experience and ability. The articles on civil-service examination, placing-out bills, dispensaries, custody of the feeble-minded, and the various reports on particular institutions constitute a mine of information. It is worth while for a rich state to publish this material for practical and theoretical students and workers. C. R. H.

Annales de l'Institut International de Sociologie. Tome IV. Contenant les travaux du troisième congrès tenu à Paris en juillet 1897. Paris: V. Giard & E. Brière, 1898. Pp. 589. F. 10.

THE general secretary of the "Institute," the editor of this volume, evidently thinks that the session of which it is a report was the most successful of the three thus far held. It does not strike me that the intrinsic weight of the papers and discussions justifies this estimate. It is quite credible, however, that the discussions were "more animated" than at the previous sessions. The chief interest centered about "the organic theory of societies." Our French friends — including all the gentlemen who took part in the debate — are passing through a stage of thinking on this subject which Americans interested in the matter emerged from two or three years ago. It would hardly be possible to arouse American sociologists to very lively controversy over what remains in dispute. The men among us who make most use of the organic concept are satisfied that their opponents disagree with them only verbally, so far as the essential idea is concerned. Beyond that there remain merely differences of judgment about details in employing the concept. Since these differences relate to details and not to essentials, even the most zealous friends of the organic concept are satisfied that it can now take care of itself. They are content to assume that it is taken for granted, and their interest is transferred to other fields. They will hardly care to join the members of the "Institute" in threshing the old straw.

The remarks upon the principal papers are epitomized in the report. The leading contents are as follows:

"La définition de la sociologie," L. Stein.
"Le cerveau individuel et le cerveau social," R. Garofalo.
"L'économie de la douleur et l'économie du plaisir," Lester F. Ward.
"L'importance sociologique des études économiques sur les colonies," Achille Loria.
"La théorie organique des sociétés," J. Novicow, P. de Lilienfeld, G. Tarde, C. de Kranz, L. Stein, René Worms, S. R. Steinmetz, C. N. Starcke, R. Garofalo, Ch. Limousin, N. Karéiev, A. Espinas.
"Les lois de l'évolution politique," C. N. Starcke.
"Les sélections corollaires," S. R. Steinmetz.
"L'évolution de l'idée de monarchie," Raoul de la Grasserie.
"La mission de la justice criminelle dans l'avenir," Pedro Dorado.
"L'obligation sociale de l'assistance," Alfred Lambert.
"L'expérimentation en sociologie," René Worms.
"La science comme fonction de la société," Fr. Giner de los Rios.

                                                            A. W. S.

Congressional Committees. By LAUROS G. MCCONACHIE, PH.D. (Library of Economics and Politics.) New York: Thomas Y. Crowell & Co., 1898. Pp. xiv+441, 12mo.

THIS is a painstaking and exhaustive treatise introductory to the general thesis. Dr. McConachie has traced the evolution of the committee system in the colonies and provisional governments prior to the establishment of the federal constitution. After showing the relation of the congressional committee to the government and to the interests of the people, he takes up its development in the house and senate separately. While the author has not given special emphasis to the economic importance of such study, his standpoint being one of political science, the investigation may well be utilized by the student of economics. Government today, more than at any other time in the development of political institutions, has taken on an industrial and economic aspect. Its basis, the conservation of the general welfare, is economic. Every new decree is inaugurated, every modification is made, with this in view. The gradual development of new industrial functions, managed or controlled by the political organization, has brought the institutions of government more forcibly within the notice of the economist. The economic interest of the individual members of society is being worked out in the political organization. A study of the economic institutions of today must of necessity include government. The thesis of the author may be regarded as being the adaptation of the committee system to the economic interests of the people organized in the state. F. A. C.

The Study of Man. By ALFRED C. HADDON. New York: G. P. Putnam's Sons; London: Bliss, Sands & Co., 1898. The Science Series, Vol. I. Pp. xxv + 410, 8vo. $2.

KEEPING strictly within the limits which the author himself marks out, this little book — *The Study of Man* — is a success. It is not intended for the specialist, not even for the student, but for the amateur and "the intelligent reader." It is a series of popular discussions of some of the subjects studied by the anthropologist, intended to show their importance and treatment. The work naturally presents chiefly the work of other students, but in the latter half Professor Haddon presents considerable of his own investigations into the meaning of children's games and toys. This part of the book appears to be a series of popular lectures and presents a fair degree of connectedness in developing a single line of research. Mr. Haddon's book may be expected to give "outsiders" an interest in and appreciation of the work of the anthropologist which may prove helpful. F. S.

NOTES AND ABSTRACTS.

Very instructive notices of the family care of certain classes of the harmless insane are given by Dr. J. A. Peeters, medical director of the Colony of Gheel, Belgium, in two papers: "La situation actuelle de la Colonie de Gheel" (1895), and "L'assistance et le classement des aliénés dans d'autres pays" (1898).

The Unit of Investigation in Sociology.— Apart from difficulties due to inadequate and inaccurate terminology, sociology suffers most at the present time from lack of unity in its subject-matter. Sociologists could much better risk the dangers of dissensions among themselves by coming closer together and dealing with the same subject-matter than they can afford the consequences of the present isolated efforts in building up corners of a far-too-greatly-generalized science. The adoption of the cell in biology and of the sensation in psychology as the definitely recognized unit of consideration has resulted in more systematic and better coördinated knowledge in those sciences. Is it possible to find in the data of sociology any constantly recurring factor in the socializing process which is fundamental to the concept of society in all stages of development, and which therefore can be regarded as a unit of investigation, consideration, and reference for all truly sociological data? I propose to examine briefly one such unit, which I will call *the social imperative*, and to contrast it from the point of view of its utility in sociology with three other concepts, which are commonly used in the same way: viz., (1) the family; (2) the social man; (3) the social type. The social imperative is the modifying influence which makes the individual act differently in the presence of his fellow-man from the way in which he would probably act under the same circumstances if he were alone. It is the sum of the animate influences which modify individual action in the direction of social ends, though these influences in complex societies may be crystallized for the most part in institutions, customs, and laws. It is, in brief, the social "ought." Many sociologists have adopted the family as the unit of consideration in studying society. But this is an essentially mechanical concept. The concept of the social man is too vague to adopt as the unit of investigation, as the qualities which under all conditions and all forms of society would characterize the truly social individual cannot be determined. The social type as a unit of investigation may be objected to on similar grounds. In contrast with these three concepts the social imperative is a concept that brings us at once to the vital point in the examination of any group of social phenomena. To view the facts of social life as they relate to some social imperative, to measure the reactions of individuals both quantitatively and qualitatively in past and present history, and to study the nature of social imperatives through their analysis and classification, should be a chief aim of sociology.— SAMUEL MCCUNE LINDSAY, *Annals of the American Academy*, September, 1898.

The Socialistic Party of France in 1898.—The year 1898 marks an important step in the history of international socialism. In this year important elections were held in France, Belgium, and Germany. It is the aim of the socialistic party in all these countries to fight for modern political liberty denied and abandoned by the bourgeois party, which is reconciled with the reactionary party in the common hatred of socialism. While the socialistic parties of Germany and Belgium are compact blocks, that of France is split up into numerous organizations which not long ago were fighting among themselves. Besides these organizations are many propagandists of socialistic ideas, and a crowd of discontents and sentimentalists, often confounding agitation with fruitful action and demagogy with democracy, who are called socialists, but are not such. Here are included the former followers of General Boulanger. This regretable confusion and the division of the party had a sad influence on the deputies of the legislature of 1893-8 : out of forty-seven deputies a dozen were always ready to scatter their vote. For the last two years dissensions have multiplied. They were due especially to the foreign question and the military question. Thus some of these so-called socialists vilified the government for the lukewarmness of its attitude toward Russia. Others claimed that to attack the army would arouse suspicion as to our patriotism. Finally the Dreyfus affair seemed about to lead to the full development of these useless disputes. The last campaign was remarkable for the spirit of solidarity and fraternal courtesy which reigned among the organizations formerly at rivalry. In 1898 French socialism made a most important advance: it attained unity. The number of votes for socialistic candidates as determined by the socialists themselves has almost doubled throughout the whole country since 1893, and the representation has been considerably increased. They had before them, too, a government ready to fight them by any means from calumny to physical violence, driving the electors from the polls. The most shameful electoral frauds were perpetrated in many provinces. Only when the socialistic candidate attained an overwhelming majority was he proclaimed elected. Universal suffrage is profoundly vitiated by the intervention of agents of the administration in the elections. It carries with it a load of interests which form a block in favor of the official candidate. It is especially in the country that its influence is great. The formidable administrative centralization of the country places immense influence in the hands of those in power. A man is easily frightened and menaced in his own security and that of his family. This year the government did its best to suppress socialism. The progress made by the socialists among the stubborn rural population is what is most remarkable about the general elections of 1898. Socialism this year has also overcome the capitalistic forces which were united for the assault.

The situation of the party was a delicate one : by uniting with the radicals it risked losing its identity; by fighting alone it risked losing the elections. These and many other difficulties were heroically overcome.— GUSTAVE ROUANE, *La Revue socialiste,* July, 1898.

Observations on the Problem of the Man of Genius and the Mass in History. — A reaction is taking place from the doctrines of Spencer, Lombroso, etc., toward those of Emerson and Carlyle. The truth is, as I hope to have demonstrated in my book, *De Historia y Arte* (on history and art), Madrid, 1898, that the case in favor of genius is not so absolute as was once erroneously supposed. The inquiry that ought to be made is not with the hope of systematically affirming or denying the influence of genius ; but of examining the degree of influence of both the masses and the man of genius, and the law which governs the mutual influence and reaction between them. Almost all authors of our day who have treated the problem apparently agree in recognizing that there is a double force in history — genius and the mass. When one tries to determine the elements which genius furnishes, and which the crowd furnishes, the difficulty arises. Really thinkers are divided into two distinct schools : the first reduces the function of the mass to that of a simple executor of the orders of a man of genius ; the second holds that genius is begot by the spirit of the times, which, being its original cause, even though genius is not entirely contained within the spirit of the times, supposes a certain intellectual collaboration on the part of the masses, which, though they do not at first receive the teaching of the great man, encourage his advance and are ready to second his efforts — the impulse which comes from its own representative ideal. The question is really a complex one. There is, first, the question, which is strictly the psychology of genius, which seeks to determine *what are the essential characteristics of genius itself*—a problem attempted by Lombroso and Nordau. Secondly, there is the study of the *genesis of the elements, intellectual or otherwise, which constitute genius,* embracing such questions as whether they are completely original or a synthesis of past or present thought. Thirdly, there is the question which seeks to determine *how genius acts upon the masses.* The confusion of the second and third questions accounts for most of the differences between writers on the subject. But it is at once clear that, whatever solution is given to the second, the third remains absolutely intact. Furthermore, the imperfect manner of stating the problem, and the lack of precision in the use of essential terms, are another source of confusion. The mass is not the same thing for all authors. Spencer means by it the entire nation, or all humanity for a given epoch. Kidd, on the contrary,' means a group of specialists. All authors, in reality, admit a mass of some kind. whatever they may call it, upon which genius depends. Another question has pro duced the greatest confusion. This is the value of the acts of single individuals. Daily experience shows that every social work is realized by the initiative of one or more individuals ; and when this individual is absent, though the mass represented continues to exist, the work falls and dies. But the necessity of representation for the mass, it must be remembered, tells us nothing of the autonomy of the individual, of his originality and independence of the mass. Upon all the questions we have con- sidered depends another of immense practical value : Given a man of genius, who exercises a special function in history and an undeniable influence, what is the cause of the efficiency of his action ? Is it the energy of his personality which acts irre- sistibly on the mass ? Is it a certain preparation which the mass has acquired for his efforts, which enables it to second his efforts, without which support his action would be unstable ? The importance of such a question is enormous for practical life, and especially for law, for it involves the question : " Can one impose any idea, any action, upon a mass, holding it as amorphous, indifferent ; or must one continually count on its psychological condition ? "

If we proceed seriously, as science demands, we must believe that neither the state of social psychology nor of history permits us to give a definite answer. The question will be cleared up only after a minute and absolutely rigorous historical study. The problem is purely one of observation. Each people and each individual must be carefully studied. — RAFAEL ALTAMIRA, *Revue internationale de sociologie*, June.

The Recent History of the Living-Wage Movement.—In the early eighties the working classes were divided into three groups : (1) those whose wages were governed entirely by the law of supply and demand applied to the labor market ; (2) those whose wages were determined in some fixed ratio to the price of the product ; (3) an aristocracy of labor whose organization was so powerful, and whose strategic position in the labor market, owing to the possession of special skill, was so strong, that it was able to command a high rate of wages and to utilize the fluctuations of trade to its advantage. The great depression of 1886–87 coincided with an out- burst of enthusiasm for social reform and economic inquiry, and the first great achieve- ment of the new spirit was to determine that wages should be independent of competition in the labor market. The next point fought for was the principle that wages should not depend upon prices. As competition among workmen had been set aside, so competition among employers has ceased to be recognized as a reason for réduction of wages. Public opinion now concedes that wages should be a first charge on production.

The question of a living wage does not appeal directly to those workmen whose remuneration is high enough to enable them to dispense with care for the minimum limit of comfort. Their principal aim is to bring the backward districts up to the same wage level as the better-organized centers, and to protect the standard of life from attacks by machinery and from the pressure of the unemployed. The regula- tion of overtime and of machine labor are their burning questions, and the method of settlement will be found in the establishment of joint committees of employers and employés, with independent umpires. The minimum living wage must in any case be fixed by the workmen, and experience shows that public opinion will back up the workers. The claim constantly put forward by employers, that they have the right to manage their own businesses without outside interference, has been in every case set at naught ; and the contrary principle has been established, that the community has the right to intervene in any dispute between capital and labor.—HENRY W. MACROSTY, *Political Science Quarterly*, September, 1898.

The Relation between Parents and Children among the Nature Peoples. —Unfortunately the relation of facts is always less simple than we think ; the demand of our intellect for unity is often a little too strong. Especially in the realm of social science hasty conclusions are still the order of the day. One assumes something, not because it is so, because one has actually so observed it, but because it would agree so finely with something else. This is all very unscientific, but it suits our best thinkers not seldom. Really we proceed still from the theory and seek facts merely for illustration. If one does otherwise, starts from the facts and goes no farther than they permit, then people are astonished that his result is not so beautifully rounded off, not so faultless, as their own fancies. That the latter, even if ever so consistent, harmonious, complete, are yet absolutely worthless, that does not appear to such people.

Bücher, for example, in his suggestive book *Die Entstehung der Volkswirthschaft* makes the following statement : " The psychical bond which binds children and parents to one another is but a fruit of civilization, and among the lower races the mere anxiety for self-existence outweighs all other emotions. Boundless selfishness is characteristic of the savage." I have undertaken a special investigation of this question of the relations of parent and children among the lower races, using a collection of notes made absolutely without regard to this question. I have divided my material into four groups. The first contains the cases of the absolute spoiling of children without any education at all; the second, those of rudimentary education without discipline ; the third, those of harsh treatment with strict education ; the fourth, the cases of neglect. Class I I found to contain 48 out of the 104 instances investigated; Class II, 31 ; Class III, 13 ; Class IV, 12. It is a very noteworthy result that the two first groups, characterized by great parental love, with little or no disciplining of the children, are by far the most numerous. These two groups have not been formed out of the higher nature peoples, but, on the contrary, contain all the unsettled tribes. Besides, the disciplining and neglecting classes belong to the lowest and the developed agriculturists and also to the nomads. I believe, therefore, to have established that the lowest peoples in the majority of cases, and certainly the unsettled peoples, love tenderly their little children, spoil, and do not discipline them.

I should not like to enter too deeply into the explanation of the established facts. On general biological grounds one might hold it probable that primitive men must love their children to whom they grant life, because otherwise the chances against the child's life would be too unfavorable. Confessedly the love of apes for their young is great, and a similar tenderness and care are necessary to men as long as they are in a hard and continual struggle with nature. Selectively this primitive child-love was unavoidable because necessary as instinct. This given instinct was strengthened through various circumstances. The long-continued nursing of the child among low peoples must have deepened the tenderness of the mother, while the very close living-together of primitive peoples worked in the same direction. Discipline was unnecessary, education superfluous, through the great simplicity of the conditions in which these children grew up. There was no priesthood as an organized corporation, with peculiar views, outside of the people. There were few rules, and hence few transgressions possible. In advanced conditions the number of rules increases, the organization of society becomes stricter, the economic and moral relations more complicated. Adaptation through education becomes indispensable, and at the same time, because the father must support the child out of his means, the child becomes much more dependent on the father. Education and discipline come in with the half-culture (*Halbkultur*) stage. Our riper culture is alarmed again at over-education and demands the free evolution of the childish nature, while the spoiling of children is again becoming customary in the higher circles. Thus is evident the incorrectness of the proposition that education proceeds with the growth of culture from original harshness to ever greater mildness. On the contrary, it began mild and has only now again become mild. — S. R. STEINMETZ, " Das Verhältniss zwischen Eltern und Kindern bei den Naturvölkern," *Zeitschrift für Socialwissenschaft*, August, 1898.

The Present Condition of Social Democracy in Germany.—Germany has become the classic land of modern socialism. The number of votes cast by the socialistic party has increased irresistibly, hand in hand with the industrial development of Germany. The party polled in the year 1871 124,700 votes ; in 1874, 352,000 ; in 1877, 493,000 ; in 1884, 550,000 ; in 1887, 763,100 ; in 1890, 1,427,000 ; in 1893, 1,786,700. At the last election, that of June 16, 1898, the social democrats polled 2,120,000 votes. Thus they constitute by far the largest of the parties, having secured as much as one-fifth to one-third of all the votes polled in the election of 1893, and having increased this again by some 19 per cent. in the election of 1898. With proportional representation in Parliament the social democrats would have more than one hundred out of the present 397 members elected. The center (the Catholic party) counts 102 of the 397 members of the Parliament; the two conservative parties have 74; the national liberals 50; and 56 belong to the social democrats; the remainder belong to the small parties. The existing wide discrepancy between the popular strength of the social democracy and its representation in Parliament is in great part due to the fact that no redistribution of representatives has taken place since the foundation of the empire. Along with the rapid industrial development of Germany, the urban population, especially of the large cities, has increased out of all proportion to the rural population, and consequently the parliamentary representation of the urban population has constantly lost ground as compared with that of the rural districts. The bourgeois parties also combined against the social democrats in the by-elections, in more than 100 of which the party was interested. The watchword of the social democrats during the last campaign was dictated by the actions of the government and of the agrarian conservative parties. The social democrats made their strongest fight in defense of the electoral franchise, which was attacked more openly and ruthlessly than ever before during the last Parliament by the conservatives and national liberals. Another, more threatening, danger the social democratic platform calls attention to. The government is devising ways and means still further to abridge the right of combination, already hemmed in by all sorts of governmental and legal ordinances. The platform then turns against the colonial and naval policy, and finally defines the position of the party in regard to the commercial treaties. Nothing is included in this platform which could have been omitted from the platform of any middle-class democratic party. Social democracy stands at the head of every serious opposition to the feudal squirearchy, to absolutism, militarism, and to the rule of the police in Germany. Thus it shows, without prejudice to its proletarian socialistic aims, the tendency to develop into a universal people's party in Germany, which will be joined by all those liberal elements that are disgusted with the weakness and barrenness of middle-class liberalism. What stamps this party more properly as a social democratic party is its critical attitude toward the entire capitalistic order of society. An excellent and comprehensive picture of the whole past development of the socialistic party in Germany is offered in the now completed *History of the German Social Democracy*, by Dr. Franz Mehring.—CONRAD SCHMIDT, *Journal of Political Economy*, September, 1898.

Labor Crises and their Periods in the United States.—The quantitative study of the labor problem is a comparatively new department of economic science. It would be desirable to extend our investigation to other countries besides the United States, but a brief survey of what has been done abroad shows at once the insufficiency of our data. Labor disturbances occasion a very serious loss even compared with commercial failures. The employer agrees to pay a certain wage on the expectation that after selling his goods he will have left a profit. If he is disappointed he must either stop producing or reduce expenses by introducing new methods, increasing hours, cutting wages, or finding some other expedient. This process almost always involves injury to the wage receivers. If they refuse to accept his efforts, they strike. If strikes become general, we have a condition of things similar to commercial crises, viz., a group of people anxious to render services in return for wages and another group anxious to obtain those services and pay for them, but a failure to make the exchange on account of the difficulty of agreeing upon the terms. The immediate cause of strikes is not as a rule the break-down of credit, though it is often a remote cause. The best way to estimate the severity of strikes would be by the number of days' labor lost. The reports do not give this, so it is necessary to estimate it by multiplying the number of men striking by the average duration of strikes for the year. The labor crisis is not the result of a single cause, but depends for its recurrence and its character upon three main forces, two of which may be considered to be cyclical and the third constant. The two former are the commercial crisis and the labor movement. The constant force is the general economic condition of the country. Of these three the commercial crisis is probably the most important.— HENRY W. FARNAM, *Yale Review*, August, 1898.

BIBLIOGRAPHY.

November—for September–October.

CONDUCTED BY C. H. HASTINGS.

NEW BOOKS AND NOTICES OF BOOKS REVIEWED.

Explanation. *Titles not starred* represent new publications announced in the standard publishers' lists since the last issue of the bibliography. A *star prefixed* to a title indicates that it was taken rom a review of the work in the periodical cited after the title. It may or may not be a new announcement. The *arithmetical signs* following the citation to a review indicate the tenor of the review: × uncertain ; +, favorable ; —, unfavorable ; + —, favorable, but with reservations ; — +, unfavorable, but with commendation ; + +, very favorable ; — — very unfavorable ; + + —, very favorable, but with reservations ; — — +, very unfavorable, but with commendation. Absence of any sign indicates that review has not been read. The *publication date* when not given is understood to be the current year. *Prices quoted* are usually for volumes bound in cloth in the case of American and English books, in paper in the case of all others. *New editions, translations,* and *new periodicals* are bracketed. Abbreviations. *See* at end of Bibliography.

SUBJECT INDEX.

[The *figures* refer to the number of the class ; *each* of the *letters* following the figures refers to initial of author's surname, or to entering word of title.]

AUTHOR INDEX TO BOOKS REVIEWED.

NEW BOOKS.

1. Anthropology, Ethnology.

*Espinas. Alfred. Les origines de la technologie. P., F. Alcan, 1897. 300 pp. 8vo. (RIS., Ap. + +)

*Haberlandt, Michael Völkerkunde. (Sammlung Goschen. 73. Bd.) Lp., Goschen. 200 pp. 8vo. M. 0.80. (LC., Jl. 30 + +)

*International folk-lore congress of the World's Columbian Exposition. V. 1. C., Chas. H. Sergel Co. (Dial, S. 6 +)

Lehmann, Alfr. Aberglaube u. Zauberei von den ältesten Zeiten an bis in die Gegenwart. Deutsch v. Dr. Petersen. Stuttgart, F. Enke. 6, Lfg. pp. 481–556. 8vo. M. 2. (Complete, cloth, M. 13.)

*Mortillet, Gabriel. Formation de la nation française. P., F. Alcan. 336 pp. 8vo. (RIS,. S. + + —)

Pothier, General. Les populations primitives. Essai d'interprétation de documents archéologiques par la géologie et les textes. P., libr. Champion. 329 pp. 8vo.

Teit, James. Traditions of the Thompson River Indians of British Columbia. . . . B., Houghton, Mifflin & Co. 8vo. $3.50.

2. Biology, Evolution, Science.

Année (l') biologique. Comptes rendus annuels des travaux de biologie générale (2e année 1897), publiés sous la direction d'Yves Delage . . . . Georges Poirialt, secrétaire de la redaction. P., Sleicher frères. 808 pp. 8vo.

Darwin, Charles. Journal of researches into the natural history of the countries visited during the voyage round the world of H. M. S. "Beagle" . . . . (Sea library.) L., W. H. White. 538 pp 8vo. 3s. 6d.

Foster, Michael, & Lankaster, E. R., eds. Scientific memoirs of Thomas Henry Huxley. In 4 v. V. 1. N. Y., D. Appleton & Co. 32 plates, por. 8vo. $7.50. [Edition limited to 100 sets.]

Lair, A. E. La vie et la mort: synthèse des principes découvertes modernes. P., libr. Tignol. 250 pp. 16mo.

*Mivart, St. G. Groundwork of science: a study of epistemology. N. Y., G. P. Putnam's Sons. 328 pp. 8vo. $1.75. (Science ser., no. 2.) (Outlook, O. 1 + +)

3. Charities.

(Das) Armenwesen: öffentliche Armenpflege in Wien u. deren geschichl. Entwicklg. . . . vom Armen-Departement des Wiener Magistrats. Wien, W. Braumüller in Komm. 121 pp. 8vo. M. 4.

Aus der Arbeit der freien kirchlich-sozialen Konferenz. Red. Ernst Böhme 1898. 12 Nrn. (Nr. 1–6, 60 pp.) 4to. B., Buchh. der Berliner Stadtmission. M. 1.50.

(Die) Berliner Unfallstationen. Bericht üb. die Organisation des Rettungs- u. Krankentranspertwesens der Reichshauptstadt. B., C. Heymann's Verl. 50 pp. 8vo. M. 0.60.

Coerper, Fr. 50 Jahre der Evangelischen Gesellschaft f. Deutschland in Elberfeld-Barmen. Eine Festschrift . . . . Elberfeld, Buchh. der Evangel. Gesellschaft. 223 pp. 8vo. M. 1.

Congresso (Primo) di beneficenza dei sordomuti in Milano, 1898 [resoconto]. Milano, tip. Pulazato e Giana. 188 pp. 8vo.

Deglin, H. L'organisation et les organisateurs de la charité. Nancy, Berger-Levrault & Cie. 35 pp. 8vo.

Evangelisch-sozialer Kongress. Verhandlungen, 1898. Göttingen, Vandenhoeck & Ruprecht. 165 pp. 8vo. M. 2.

Für Feste u. Freunde der innern Mission. Bilder u. Bildnisse aus der christl. Liebesthätigkeit. Gesammelt u. hrsg. v. M. Hennig. 11.–20. Hft. 8vo. (à 16 pp.) B., Buchh. des ostdeutschen Jünglingsbundes. à M. 0.10. (2 Bd. kplt. M. 1.50.)

Glen, W. C. & R. C. General orders of the poor law commissioners, poor law board, etc. Ed. 11. L., Knight.

Gohre, P. Evangelical-social movement in Germany, its history & aims. Abridged trans. . . . L., Ideal Pub. Union. 236 pp. 8vo. 2s.

Great Britain — Endowed charities (administrative county of Glamorgan & county boroughs of Cardiff & Swansea). Return comprising the reports made to the charity commissioners . . . . 1818–37. L., Eyre & Spottiswoode. 3s. 6d. County of Anglesey, 3s. 10d.

Hennig, M. Festbüchlein der inneren Mission. . . . B., Buchh. des ostdeut. Jünglingsbundes. 30 pp. 8vo. M. 0.15.

*Mackay, Thomas. State and charity. (AJS., S., p. 274; 268 +)

Oubert, Adolphe. Des moyens de prévenir et de réprimer le vagabondage et la mendicité: étude de législation comparée. i on, Barbier-Marilier. 8vo. (RIS., S.) D[.]

Schultz, Otto. Innere Mission auf dem Lande. Aus der Geschichte e. armen Rhongemeinde. Ein Denkstein zum Jubelfest der inneren Mission. B., Buchh. des ostdeutschen Jünglingsbundes. 80 pp. 8vo. M. 1.

Vitzthum v. Eckstadt, Otto. · J. H. Wichern's Aufruf zur inneren Mission, seine Denkschrift v. 1849 u. der gegenwärtige Stand der inneren Mission der ev.-luth. Kirche im Königr. Sachsen: Vortrag. (Kleine Bibliothek f. innere Mission.) Dresden, Niederlage zur Verbreitg. christl. Schriften in Komm.

[Wichern, J.] Marksteine. Neues Festbüchlein des Rauhen Hauses, 1833–98. 2. Aufl. Hamburg, Agentur des Rauhen Hauses. 159 pp. 8vo. M. 1.]

4. Cities.

Appleton's dictionary of Greater New York & its vicinity. N. Y., Appleton. 12mo. $0.30.

Cornil, Georges. L'assurance municipale contre le chomage involontaire. Bruxelles, J. H. Moreau. 191 pp. 8vo. (ZS., Jl.)

*Edwards, P. J. History of London street improvements, 1855–97. L., P. S. King & Son. 416 pp. 8vo. 4s. 6d. (Academy, Ag. 13 + + —)

*Harris, Mary Dormer. Life in an old English town: a history of Coventry, from the earliest times, compiled from official records. (Social England series.) N. Y., Macmillan Co. 307 pp. 8vo. 17s. 6d. (Nation, Jl. 14)

*Hegel, Karl. Die Entstehung des deutschen Stadtwesens. Lp , S. Hirzel. 192 pp. 8vo. M. 4. (ZS., Ag.)

*Kuczynski, R. Der Zug nach der Stadt. Statistische Studien über Vorgänge der Bevölkerungsbewegung im Deutschen Reiche (München: chener volkswirtschaftliche Studien. 24 Stücke). Stuttgart, J. G. Cotta. 284 pp. 8vo. (JGV., 22:3) (LC., My. 28)

*Maltbie, M. R. English local government of today: a study of the relations of central & local government. N. Y., Macmillan Co., 1897. 296 pp. 8vo. (RIS.. Jl. + + —)

Quellen zur Geschichte der Stadt Wien. Hrsg. vom Alterthums-Vereine zu Wien. Red. v. Ant. Mayer. 3. Abth. 1. Bd. 3. Grundbücher der Stadt Wien. 1. Bd. Die ältesten Kaufbücher (1368–88). Bearb. v. Frz. Staub. Wien, C. Konegen in Komm. 458 pp. 4to. M. 24.

*Records of the borough of Northampton. V. 1 ed.

by C. A. Markham; V. 2 ed. by J. C. Cox.
Published by order of the corporation of North-
ampton. (Athenæum, Ag. 13 — +)
Statistische Daten über die Stadt Wien f. d. J. 1896.
Wien, W. Braumüller in Komm. 38 pp. 16mo.
M, 0.40.
Statistisches Jahrbuch der Stadt Wien. 1896. 14.
Jahrg. . . . . (Mittheilungen des statist. De-
partements des Wiener Magistrats.) Wien,
W. Braumüller in Komm. 891 pp. 8vo. M. 10.

5. Criminology and Penology.

Ferri, Enrico. Difese penali e studi di giurispru-
denza. Torino, fratelli Bocca. 469 pp. 8vo.
L. 9.
[Garraud, R. Traité théorique et pratique du
droit pénal français. 2e éd. T. 2. P., libr.
Larose. 752 pp. 8vo. Complete, f. 60.]
Gross, Hanns. Criminalpsychologie. Graz,
Leuschner & Lubensky. 721 pp. 8vo. M. 10.
Harpner, Gust. Das österreichische Strafverfahren.
Rechte u. Pflichten der Behörden u. Staats-
bürger. Leichtfasslich dargestellt. Wien,
Wiener Volksbuchh. 152 pp. 16mo. M. 1
Leloir, G. Code d'instruction criminelle avec
l'indication sommaire de la doctrine et de la
jurisprudence. P., libr. Pédone. 582 pp. 8vo.
f. 18.
Marzo, Salvatore. Storia della procedura crimi-
nale romana: la giurisdizione dalle origini
alle 12 tavole. Palermo, Alberto Reber edit.
164 pp. 8vo. L. 4.
*Proal, Louis. Political crime, tr. fr. the French.
D. Appleton & Co. 355 pp. 8vo. $1.50.
(Criminology series.) (Academy, S. 10 — —)

6. Education.

*Butler, N. M. Meaning of education. N. Y.,
Macmillan Co. 230 pp. D. $1. (Academy,
S. 17 — —) (Dial, O. 16 +)
*Davidson, Thomas. Rousseau as an educator.
(Great Educators.) N. Y., Chas. Scribner's
Sons. 253 pp. 8vo. $1. (Critic, Ag. + +)
(Academy, S. 17 + +) (Dial, O. 16 + + —)
(EdR., S. + + —)
*Eliot, C. W. Educational reform: essays & ad-
dresses. N. Y., Century Co. 418 pp. 8vo. $2.
(Dial., O. 16 + +) (Outlook, O. 8 + +)
France — Ministère de l'instruction publique et des
beaux-arts. Rapport sur l'éducation popu-
laire en 1897-8 adressé à M. Alfred Ram-
baud, ministre . . . . par M. Edouard Petit.
P., impr. nationale. 90 pp. 8vo.
*Harris, W. T. Psychologic foundations of edu-
cation. N. Y., Appleton. 400 pp. 8vo. $1.50.
(International education series, V. 37.) (Dial,
O. 16 + + —) (Nation, Ag. 18 X) (EdR.,
Je.)
*Herbart, J. F. Application of psychology to the
science of education, trans. . . . . . N. Y.,
Chas. Scribner's Sons. 231 pp. 8vo. $1.50.
(Nation, Ag. 18 X)
Hogan, Louise E. A study of a child; il. with
over 500 original drawings by the child. N. Y.,
Harper Bros. 220 pp. 8vo. $2.50.
Holman, H. English national education. (Acad-
emy, S. 17 + —)
Lois et règlements organiques de l'enseignement
primaire en France (1881-99). . . . . P., libr.
Delalain frères. f. 2.50.
Müller Joh. Pädagogik u. Didaktik auf modern-
wissenschaftlicher Grundlage. Mainz, F.
Kirchheim. 192 pp. 8vo. M. 3.
Nisio, G. La instruzione primaria e la normale
nella esposizione nazionale svizera del 1896 in
Genevra ; notizie, giudizi, parazioni e pro-
poste. Torino, G. B. Paravia e C. 363 pp.
8vo. L. 3.
Pädagogische Zeit- u. Streitfragen. 54. Hft.
8vo. Wiesbaden, E. Behrend. 54. Bergmann,

Paul. Die Sittlichkeitsfrage u. die Schule.
Vortrag. 35 pp. M. O.80.
*Petersilie, A. Das öffentliche Unterrichtswesen
im Deutschen Reich u. die übrigen euro-
päischen Culturländern. 2 Bde. Lp., Hirsch-
feld, 1897. 448 pp. u. 608 pp. 8vo. M. 28
(Hand- u. Lehrbuch der Staatswiss. 3. Abth.
2. Bd.) (LC., Je. 4)
Pratesi Plinio. Questioni pedagogiche e di am-
ministrazione scholastica. Torino, G. B.
Paravia e C. 142 pp. 8vo. L. 2.50.
*Rein, W. Encyclopädisches Handbuch der
Pädagogik. 3. Bd. 4. Bd., 1. Hft. Langen-
salza, Beyer & Söhne, 1897. 968 pp. u. pp.
1-480. 8vo. M. 22.50. (LC., S. 10)
*Rouse, W. H. D. History of Rugby school.
(English public schools.) L., Duckworth.
436 pp. 8vo. 5s. (Academy, S. 17 +)
(Athenæum, O. 8. +)
[Rivista di filosofia e pedagogia: pereodico
mensile diretto dai Pietro Romano e Angelo
Valdarnini. Anno I, fasc 1 (luglio 1898).
Asti, tip. G. Brignolo. 64 pp. 8vo. L. 1 il
fasc.]
Schmid, K. A. Geschichte der Erziehung vom
Anfang an bis auf unsere Zeit, bearb. in
Gemeinschaft m. e. Anzahl v. Gelehrten u.
Schulmännern. Fortgeführt v. Geo. Schmid.
4. Bd. 2. Abtlg. 2. (Schluss-) Lfg. St., J. G.
Cotta. pp. 317-881. 8vo. M. 18.

7. Ethics, Philosophy, and Psychology.

Alexander, Archibald. Theories of the will in the
history of philosophy. N. Y., Chas. Scribner's
Sons. 357 pp. 12mo. $1.50.
Année (l') psychologique, publiée par Alfred
Binet [and others]. P., libr. Schleicher frères.
853 pp. 8vo.
*Baldwin, J. M. Story of the mind. (Library of
Useful Stories.) N. Y., D. Appleton & Co.
236 pp. 16mo. (Nation, O. 13 + + —)
Brockdorff, Baron Cay v. Kants Teleologie (Diss.).
Kiel, Gnevkow & v. Gellhorn. 60 pp. 8vo.
M. 1.20.
Dagneaux, H. Histoire de la philosophie. P.,
libr. Retaux. 524 pp. f. 5.
*Groos. Play of animals. N. Y., Appleton.
341 pp. D. $1.25. (Dial, S. 16 +)
*Hartmann, Eduard von. Ethische Studien. Lp.,
Haacke. 241 pp. 8vo. M. 5. (LC., S. 24)
Kowalewski, Arnold. Ueber das Kasualitätspro-
blem. Eine philosoph. Studie. Lp., O. Mutze.
121 pp. 8vo. M. 2.60.
*Lipps, Theodor. Zur Psychologie der Sugges-
tion. Vortrag. . . . . Lp., J. A. Barth, 1897.
45 pp. 8vo. M. 1.20. (DL., S. 24)
Mantegazza, Paul. Rätsel der Liebe. Aus dem
Ital. . . . . Jena, H. Costenoble. 301 pp.
8vo. M. 3.
*Mills, Wesley. Nature & development of ani-
mal intelligence. N. Y., Macmillan Co.
307 pp. 8vo. $2. (Dial, O. 16 X)
[Revue du monde invisible, paraissant le 15 de
chaque mois. 1re année. No. 1, 15 juin 1898.
64 pp. 8vo. P., impr. Téque, 29 rue de
Tournon. France, f. 10; étranger, f. 12.]
Scherer, K. C. Das Tier in der Philosophie des
H. S. Reimarus. Ein Beitrag zur Geschichte
der vergleich. Psychologie. Würzburg, A.
Göbel. 183 pp. 8vo. M.
*Stern, Paul. Einfühlung u. Association in der
neueren Aesthetik. Ein Beitrag zur psy-
chologischen Analyse der aesthetischen Anschauung. Hamburg, Voss. 82 pp. 8vo. M.
2. (LC., S. 17)
*Sutherland, Alexander. Origin & growth of the
moral instinct. N. Y., Longmans, Green &
Co. (Nation, S, 15 — +)
Tufts, J. H., & Helen B. Thompson. The individual & his relation to society as reflected in

British ethics. Pt. 1. Individual in relation to law and institutions. C., Univ. of Chicago Press. 53 pp. 8vo. $0.35. (Univer. of Chicago contributions to philosophy, No. 5.)

*Wundt, Wilhelm. Ethics: an investigation into the facts and laws of the moral life, trans. V. 1 & 2. N. Y., Macmillan Co. $2.25 & $1.75. (Outlook, S. 24 + + —)

8. Family.

Deshayes, F. Questions pratiques de droit et de morale sur le mariage (clandestinité). P., libr. Lethielleux. 455 pp. 8vo.

Goldstein, J. Die vermeintlichen u. die wirklichen Ursachen des Bevölkerungsstillstandes in Frankreich. (Aus "Bayer. Handels-Zeitg.") München, Piloty & Loehle. M. 1.

Juvara, Alfred. Les enfants naturels, en droit international privé (thèse). P., libr. Pédone. 211 pp. 8vo.

Morsier, A. de. Rapport au congrès de Londres (1898) sur la lutte contre la prostitution réglementée en France. Alençon, impr. Guy.

Rohleder, H. Die Masturbation. B., Fischer's medicin. Buchh. M. 6.

Vernet, Honoré. De l'incapacité de la femme mariée, en droit français (thèse). P., libr. Pédone. 157 pp. 8vo.

9. Finance, Taxation.

Banca cooperativa popolare di Padova alla esposizione generale italiana in Torino. Padova, tip. fratelli Salmin. 127 pp. 4to.

*Carver, T. N. Ohio tax inquisitor law. N. Y., Macmillan Co. [for the Am. Econ. Assoc.]. 45 pp. 8vo. (Economic studies.) (RIS., S. X)

Codice finanziario del regno d'Italia, raccolta sistematica di tutte le leggi, regolamenti, decreti e circolari sulle imposte dirette e indirette e sulle tasse (diretti) . . . . per cura degli Sebastiano Gianzana, Francesco Bo e Pietro Tappari. V. 9. Torino, Unione tip. edit. 684 pp. 8vo. L. 2.25.

*Dannenberg. Hermann. Die deutschen Münzen der sächsischen u. frankischen Kaiserzeit. 3. Bd. B., Weidmann. pp. 759-874. 8vo. M. 12. (LC., Jl. 2)

Finances (les) de la Russie; dette publique, commerce extérieur, chemins de fer, d'après les documents officiels. P., libr. Chaix. 296 pp. 4to.

Foretti, Giulio. Pane, governo e tasse in Italia: considerazioni impopolari. Napoli, Luigi Pierro. 167 pp. 8vo. L. 2.50.

Heilfferich, Karl. Deutschlands Münzreform u. die Silberentwertung. . . . . St., A. Bonz & Co. in Komm. 60 pp. 8vo. M. 0.60.

Luzzatti, Giac. Debiti e crediti: prolusione ad un corso libero di scinza monetaria nella r. universita di Padova. Padova, fratelli Drucker edit. 50 pp. 8vo.

Luzzatti, Giac. Della moneta ideale ne' suoi rapporti colla moneta reale in circolazione in un paese. Verona, fratelli Drucker edit. 60 pp. 8vo.

Macleod, H. D. Indian currency. L., Longmans, Green & Co. 8vo. 2s. 6d.

Mitteilungen aus der Verwaltung der direkten Steuern im preussischen Staate. Nr. 35. R. v. Decker. 83 pp. 8vo. M. 0.90.

Montanari, Lu. I dazi interni di consumo nella storia e nella scienza delle finanze: note di studio. Castrocaro, tip. Amilcare Barboni. 81 pp. 8vo.

[Moxom, T. B. English practical banking. Ed. 9. L., J. Heywood. 120 pp. 8vo. 4s. 6d.]

Norman, J. H. British India's future standard currency. L., Gee. 36 pp. 8vo. 6d.

*Prager, Max. Die Währungsfrage in den Vereinigten Staaten von Nordamerika. . . . .

Stuttgart, J. G. Cotta, 1897. 476 pp. 8vo. M. 10. (Münchener volkswirths. Studien, 23.) (LC., Ap. 2)

*Russell, H. B. International monetary conferences: their purposes, character, & results. N. Y., Harper & Bros. 477 pp. 8vo. $2.50. (Athenæum, Ag. 13 + +)

*Schurtz, H. Grundriss einer Enstehungsgeschichte des Geldes. Weimar, Emil Felber. (ZS., Je.)

Trasi, Ant. Proposita di una tassa unica in surrogazione del dazio consumo. Milano, tip. Nazionale di V. Ramperti. 14 pp. 8vo.

Wolfrum, Max. Die Währungsreform u. die Notenbanken in Deutschland. Gablonz, H. Rössler in Komm. 18 pp. 8vo. M. 0.50.

10. History.

*Andrews, C. M. Historical development of modern Europe from the Congress of Vienna to the present time. In 2 v. V. 2, 1850-97. N. Y., G. P. Putnam's Sons. 467 pp. 8vo. $2.50. (Outlook, S. 17 + +) (Nation, O. 20+)

*Aubrey. John. Brief lives, chiefly of contemporaries, set down between 1669 and 1696, ed. by Andrew Clark. 2 v. L., Henry Frowde. 25s. (Critic, O. X) (Nation, S. 1 X)

Beer, Adf. Die österreichische Handelspolitik unter Maria Theresia u. Josef II. (Aus "Archiv. f. österr. Gesch.") Wien, C. Gerold's Sohn. 204 pp. 8vo. M. 3.40.

Beiträge zur alten Geschichte u. Geographie. Festschrift f. Heinrich Kiepert. B., D. Reimer. 355 pp. 8vo. M. 28.

Bonnaffé, Edmond. Études sur la vie privée de la renaissance. P., libr. May. 196 pp. 16mo.

*Colquhoun, A. R. China in transformation. N. Y., Harper Bros. 397 pp. maps. 8vo. $3. (Athenæum, Jl. 30 + +) (Dial, S. 16 + + —) (Outlook, O. 1 + + —)

Connelly, W. E. Provisional govt. of the Nebraska territory. Kansas City, Mo., G. D. Fearey, secretary Western Hist. Soc. 400 pp. 8vo. $4.

*Dunning, W. A. Essays on the Civil War & reconstruction. N. Y., Macmillan Co. (Critic, S. + +) (Nation, Jl. 21 + +)

Egerton, H. E. A history of British colonial policy. N. Y., New Amsterdam Book Co. $4. (PSQ., S. + + —)

Escott, T. H. S. Personal forces of the period. L., Hurst & Blackett. 366 pp. 8vo. 6s.

*Ferryman, A. F. M. Imperial Africa: the rise, progress & future of the British possessions in Africa. V. 1. British West Africa. L., Imperial Press. 528 pp. 8vo. 12s. 6d. (Athenæum, S. 17 — — +)

*Forbes, Archibald. Life of Napoleon the Third. N. Y., Dodd, Mead & Co. (Dial, O. 1 + —) (Outlook, O. 1 +) (Nation, O. 6 + —)

Gairdner, James. Life & reign of Richard the Third. (Academy, S. 3 + —)

Garland, Hamlin. Ulysses S. Grant, his life & character. N. Y., Doubleday & McClure Co. 524 pp., il. 8vo. $2.50.

Gibbins, H. de B. The English people in the nineteenth century: a short history. L., Black. 180 pp. 12mo.

*Harrisse, Henry. Diplomatic history of America: its first chapter. 1452-1493-1494. L., B. F. Steven. (Nation, S. 8 X)

*Hartmann, L. M. Das italienische Königreich. Lp., G. Wigand, 1897. 368 pp. 8vo. M. 12.50. (Geschichte Italiens im Mittelalter. 1. Bd.) (LC., Ap. 30)

Heco, J. Erinnerungen e. Japaners Schilderung der Entwicklg. Japans vor u. seit der Eröffng. bis auf die Neuzeit . . . übersetz. . . . Stuttgart, Strecker & Moser. 364 pp. 8vo. M. 3.50, geb. 4.50.

*Holm, Adolf. Geschichte Siciliens im Alterthum. 3. (Schluss·) Bd. Lp., Engelmann. 787 pp. 8vo. M. 18. (LC., Jl. 23 + +) (Nation, S. 1 + +).

Jesuit relations. V. 21, 25, 26. Cleveland, Burrows Brothers Co. $3.50 each.

*Krout, Mary H. Hawaii & a revolution: personal experiences of a correspondent. . . . . N. Y., Dodd, Mead & Co. 330 pp. 12mo. $2. (Dial, O. 1 +) (Outlook, O. 1 + —)

Lacombe, P. Introduction à l'histoire littéraire. P., libr. Hachette & Cie. 420 pp. 8vo. f. 7.50. (De l'histoire, considérée comme science.)

*[Langlois, C. V., & Charles Seignobos. Introduction to the study of history, trans. by G. G. Berry. Pref. by F. York Powell. L., Duckworth. 378 pp. 8vo. 7s. 6d. (Academy, S. 24 + —)]

Lord, E. L. Industrial experiments in the British colonies of North America. Balt., Johns Hopkins Press. 154 pp. 8vo. $1.25. (Johns Hopkins Univ. studies.)

*Maclay, E. S. History of the United States navy from 1775 to 1898. N. Y., D. Appleton & Co. 2 v. (Critic, Ag. + +—)

Meikeljohn, M. J. C. The United States: their geography, resources, commerce, and history. . . . L., Holden. 24 pp. 8vo. 6d.

*Moses, Bernard. Democracy & social growth in America. (AJS., S., p. 278) (JPE., S. + —)

Moses, Bernard. Establishment of Spanish rule in America: an introduction to the history & politics of Spanish America. N. Y., G. P. Putnam's Sons. 328 pp. 12mo. $1.25.

Mosnier, Louis. Origines & développements de la grande industrie en France du 15e siècle à la Révolution (thèse). P., libr. Fontemoing. 183 pp. 8vo.

Olivetti, Aug. Per la interpretazione economica della storia: alcune note sull' assegnazione colonaria nel dritto e nella nita romana. Bologna, libr. fratelli Treves. 103 pp. 8vo.

*Oman, Charles. History of the art of war. N. Y., G. P. Putnam's Sons. (Athenæum, Je. 11 + + —) (Critic, S. + +)

Roberts, Sir R. H. Forty-one years in India from subaltern to commander-in-chief. N. Y., Longmans, Green & Co. 507 pp. $2.50.

[Rogers, J. E. T. Industrial & commercial history of England: lectures delivered to the University of Oxford, ed. by his son, A. G. L. Rogers. Impr. 3. L., Fisher Unwin. 488 pp. 8vo. Each 3s. 6d.]

Rowland, Kate Mason. Life & correspondence of Charles Carroll of Carrollton. N. Y., G. P. Putnam's Sons. 2 v. (Nation, S. 1 — +)

Schwill, Ferdinand. History of modern Europe, with maps & genealogical tables. N. Y., C. Scribner's Sons. 434 pp. 12mo. $1.50.

Sidel, Geo. Die Königin Marie Antoinette, e. Heldin im Kampfe m. der Revolution u. Gegenrevolution. Weisenburg, R. Ackermann. 532 pp. 8vo. M. 3.50.

*Sorel, Albert. Eastern question in the eighteenth century. 292 pp. 8vo. 3s. 6d. (Academy, S. 3 + +) (Nation, O. 20 +)

*Statham, F. R. Paul Krüger & his times. L., Unwin. 320 pp. 8vo. 7s. 6d. (Academy. Je. 18 — +) (Athenæum, Ag. 6 +) (L C., My. 14)

*Steevens, G. W. Egypt in 1898. N. Y., Dodd, Mead & Co. (Academy, Je. 11 +) (Outlook, S. 17 +)

*Stevens, B. F., ed. Facsimiles of manuscripts in European archives relating to America 1773-83. V. 25. Index. L., B. F. Stevens. (Nation, Ag. 11 + +) (Athenæum, Jl. 16 + +)

*Story, A. T. Building of the British empire. N. Y., G. P. Putnam's Sons. 2 v. $3. (Outlook, S. 17 + +)

*Stutzer, Emil. Deutsche Socialgeschichte, vornehmlich der neuesten Zeit. Halle, Buchh. des Waisenhauses in Halle a. S. 272 pp. (ZS., My.)

*Thorpe, F. N. Constitutional history of the American people, 1776-1850. N. Y., Harper Bros. 2 v. 8vo. $2.50 each. (Dial, O. 1 + —)

*Tout, T. F. Empire & the papacy, 918-1273. N. Y., Macmillan Co. (Periods of European history, 2.) 534 pp. 8vo. $2. (Nation, S. 29 + + —)

*Younghusband, Francis. South Africa of today. L., Macmillan & Co. 177 pp. 8vo. (LC., Je. 18)

11. International Law.

Kobler, G. Die Quarantine-Frage in der internationalen Sanitäts-Gesetzgebung. Wien, A. Holder. 96 pp. 8vo. M. 1.50.

Liszt, Frz. v. Das Völkerrecht, systematisch dargestellt. B., O. Haering. 254 pp. 8vo. M. 6.

Nouveau recueil général de traités et autres actes relatifs aux rapports de droit international. Continuation du grand recueil de G. F. de Martens par Félix Stoerk. 2e série. T. 23. 2e livr. Lp., Dietrich. M. 16.

[Rivista di diritto internazionali e di legislazione commerciale. Anno 1, fasc. 1 (giugno, 1898). Napoli, Detken e Rocholl edit. 48 pp. 8vo. L. 1 il fasc.]

12. Labor.

Aftalion, Albert. Les lois relatives à l'épargne de la femme mariée; leur importance pratique pour la protection de l'épouse dans les classes laborieuses (thèse). P., libr. Pédone. 212 pp., 8vo.

Aldrich, M. A. American federation of labor. N. Y., Macmillan Co. (for Am. Econ. Assoc.) pp. 219-66. 12mo. $0.50. (Economic Studies, V. 3, no. 4.)

Brooke, Emma. Tabulation of the factory laws of European countries in so far as they relate to the hours of labor & to special legislation for women, young persons & children. L., Richards.

Cruchon, Joseph. Etude sur la réglementation de la durée du travail industriel (thèse). Avranches, impr. Jeanne. 180 pp. 8vo.

*Deutsche Arbeitsnachweis-Konferenz (Erste). . . . Verhandlungen . . . . 1897, hrsg. v. J. Jastrow. B., H. S. Hermann. 165 pp. (ZS., Je.)

Drucksachen der Kommission f. Arbeiterstatistik. Verhandlungen. Nr. 15. 2do. B., C. Heymann's Verl. M. 0.60.

Dyhrenfurth, Gertrud. Die hausindustriellen Arbeiterinnen der Berliner Blusen-, Unterrock-, Schürzen- u. Trikotkonfektion. Lp., Duncker & Humblot. 141 pp. 8vo. (Staats- u. socialwiss. Forschungen, hrs. Schmoller.) (ZS., Ag.)

Hird, Frank. The cry of the children: an exposure of certain British industries in which children are iniquitously employed. N. Y., M. F. Mansfield & Co. 96 pp. 12mo. $0.75.

Jourdain, Victor. La législation française sur les coalitions ouvrières; son évolution au 19e siècle. Lille. libr. Le Bigot frères. 180 pp. 8vo.

*Levasseur, Emile. L'ouvrier américain. (AJS., S., p. 277.) (ZS., Ag.)

*Lloyd, H. D. Labor copartnership: notes of a visit to co-operative workshops, factories, and farms in Great Britain & Ireland. . . . . N.Y., Harper Bros. 351 pp. 12mo. $1. (Nation O. 13 + +)

Reichenbach, A. Die Arbeit in ihrem Wesen, ihrer Entwicklung u. kulturgeschichtlichen Bedeutung. Zürich, Buchh. des schweiz. Grutlivereins. 160 pp. 8vo. M. 1.25.

Robinson, Harriet H. Loom & spindle; or, life among the early mill girls; with a sketch of the "Lowell Offering" & some of its contributors; introd. by C. D. Wright. N.Y., T. Y. Crowell & Co. 216 pp. 16mo. $1.25.

Rohrscheidt, Kurt. Vom Zunftzwange zur Gewerbefreiheit. Eine Studie nach den Quellen. B., C. Heymann's Verl. 668 pp. 8vo. M. 12.

*Schmöle, Josef. Die socialdemokratischen Gewerkschaften. (AJS., S., p. 278) (ZS., Ap.) Schriften der Centralstelle f. Abeiter-Wohlfahrtseinrichtungen. Nr. 15. B., C. Heymann's Verl. M. 1.20.

[Slater, J. Law of arbitration & awards. Ed. 3. L., Stevens & Haynes. 6s. 6d.]

*Webb, Sidney & Beatrice. Problems of modern industry. N. Y., Longmans, Green & Co. 386 pp. 8vo. $2.50. (Outlook, S. 17 + + —)

*Willey, F. O. The laborer and the capitalist. (AJS., S., p. 277) (Nation, Ag. 18 + +)

13. Political Economy.

Berner Beiträge zur Geschichte der Nationalökonomie, hrsg. v. Aug. Oucken. Nr. 11. Stockhausen, Vikt. v. Die Wertlehre Proudhons in neuer Darstellung. 126 pp. 8vo. M. 1.60. Bern, K. J. Myss.

*Kovalewsky, Maxime. Le régime économique de la Russie. P., Giard & Brière. 367 pp. 8vo. f. 7. (Bibliothèque sociologique internationale.) (RIS., Jl. + +)

Marx, Karl. Value, price & profit. Addressed to working men, ed by . . . . Eleanor Marx Aveling. L., Swan Sonnenschein. 94 pp. 12mo.

Münchener volkswirthschaftliche Studien. Hrsg. v. Lujo Brentano u. Walth. Lotz. 26. Stück. 8vo. St., J. G. Cotta. 26. Böhm, Otto. Die Kornhäuser. Eine Studie üb. die Organisation des Getreideverkaufes in Amerika, Indien u. Russland, sowie in einigen deutschen Staaten. 96 pp. M. 2.40.

*[Pantaleoni, Matteo. Pure economics. (AJS., S., p. 277) (JPE., S. + +—)]

Souchon, Aug. Théorie économique dans la Grèce antique. P., libr. Larose. 205 pp. 12mo. (ZS., My.) (RIS., S.)

Volkswirthschaftliche Zeitfragen. Vorträge u. Abhandlgn., hrsg. v. der volkswirthschaftl. Gesellschaft in Berlin. 158. Hft. (20. Jahrg. 6. Hft.) 8vo. B., L. Simion. 158. Lewinstein, Gust. Einige Betrachtungen üb. die aktiven u. passive Handelsbalanze der Staaten. 32 pp. M. 1.

*Wörterbuch der Volkswirtschaft, unter Mitwirkung einer grossen Anzahl Fachgenossen hrsg. v. Ludwig Elster. 1. Bd. Abbauhypotheken- u. Grundbuchwesen. Nachträge. Jena, G. Fischer. 1092 pp. 8vo. M. 20. (LC., S. 3 + +)

14. Political Science.

(L') Année politique (24e année, 1807), avec un index raisonné, une table chronologique. . . . P., libr. Fasquelle. f. 3.50.

Arzens, J. L'échec du gouvernement parlementaire et la réforme de notre régime constitutionnel. P., libr. Chevalier-Marescq. 239 pp. 8vo. f. 3.50.

[Beaumarchais, M. D. de. La doctrine de Monroë. L'évolution de la politique des États-Unis au 19e siècle. 2e éd. P., libr. Larose. 238 pp. 8vo. f. 6.]

Beiträge zur Geschichte des römischen Rechts in Deutschland. In Verbindg. m. anderen Gelehrten bearb. v. J. Kohler. 3. Hft. 8vo. St., F. Enke. M. 5. 2. Kohler, J., u. Erich Liesegang. Das römische Recht am Niederrhein. 156 pp.

Bismarckreden 1847–95. Hrsg. v. Horst Kohl. 1. u. 2. Aufl. Lp., G. J. Goschen. M. 6.75.

*Bismarck-Portefeuille, hrsg. v. Heinrich von

Poschinger. 1. u. 2. Bd. St., Deutsche Verlagsanstalt. 197 u. 198 pp. (ZS., Je.)

*Busch, Moritz. Bismarck: some secret pages of his history, being a diary kept during 25 years of official & private intercourse. . . . . . 2 v. 8vo. N. Y., Macmillan & Co. $10. (Athenæum, S. 24 + + —) (Academy, S. 24 — +) (Dial, O 16 + + —)

*Clarke, R. F. Science of law & law-making. L., Macmillan & Co. 473 pp. 8vo. $4. (Athenæum, Ag. 20 — —) (Nation + —)

Cleiftie, E. Les conseils de prud'hommes; leur organisation et leur fonctionnement au point de vue économique et social (thèse) P., libr. Pédone. 145 pp., 8vo.

*Cosack, Konrad. Lehrbuch des deutschen bürgerlichen Rechts auf der Grundlage des bürgerlichen Gesetzbuches für das Deutsche Reich. 1. Bd. 1. Abth. Die allg. Lehren u. das Recht der Förderungen. 1. u. 2. Abschn. Jena, G. Fischer, 1897-8. 387 u. 615 pp, 8vo. (LC., Ag. 6 + —)

Dernburg, Heinr. Das bürgerliche Recht des deutschen Reichs u. Preussens. 3. Bd. Das Sachenrecht. Halle, Buchh. des Waisenhauses. 792 pp. 8vo. M. 11.

Dritto (Il) civile italiano secundo la dottrina e la giurisprudenza esposito dai proff. Bianchi, Caporali & others) per cura di Pasquale Fiore, Disp. 259-264. Napoli, Eugenio Marghieri edit. L. 1 la dispensa.

*Fleischmann, Max. Der Weg der Gesetzgebung in Preussen. Abhandlungen aus dem Staats- u. Verwaltungsrecht, hrsg. von Prof. Siegfried Brie. Heft 1. Breslau, M. u. H. Marcus. 128 pp. 8vo. (JGV. 22:3)

Gaullieur, H. The paternal state in France & Germany. N. Y., Harper Bros. 255 pp. 12mo. $1.25.

Geffcken, Heinr. Lex Salica. Zum akadem. Gebrauche hrsg. u. erläutert. Lp., Veit & Co. 332 pp. 8vo. M. 7.

*Gooch, G. P. History of English democratic ideas in the seventeenth century. Cambridge, Camb. Univ. Press. 372 pp. 8vo. 5s. (Athenæum, Jl. 9 + +—)

Heymann, P. A. de. La guerre: son importance dans la vie du peuple et de l'état. P., libr. Charles Lavauzelle. 43 pp. 8vo. f. 1.

*Hilty, Carl. Politisches Jahrbuch der Schweizerischen Eidgenossenschaft. 11. Jahrg. 1897. Bern, K. J. Wyss. 790 pp. (ZS., Jl.)

[Illing, R. Handbuch f. preussische Verwaltungsbeamte, im Dienste des Staates, der Kommunalverbände, der Korporationen u. f. Geschäftsleute. 7. Aufl. 2 Bde B., A. Haack. 1542 u. 1639 pp. 8vo. M. 38.50.]

Jellinck, Geo. Das Recht der Minoritäten. Vorträge. Wien, A. Holder. 43 pp. 8vo. M. 1.

*Jenks, Edward. Law & politics in the middle ages. N. Y., Henry Holt & Co. 352 pp. 8vo. (JPE., S. +)

*Kent, William. Memoirs & letters of James Kent, late chancellor of the state of New York. Bo., Little, Brown & Co. (Nation, Ag. 4 ×)

[Kosmodike. Zeitung f. den internationale Rechtsverkehr. (In französ., deutscher u. engl. Sprache.) Hrsg. v. Alex. v. Harder. 1. Jahrg. 2. Sem. Juli-Decbr. 1898. 6 Nrn. 4to. (Nr. 7, 24 pp.) f. P., Verlag der Kosmodike. Vierteljährlich, M. 3.]

Kürschner, Jos. Der neue Reichstag, 1898-1903. X. Legislaturperiode. 80 u. 415 pp. 64mo. Lp., G J. Göschen. M. 1.

*Lafitte. J. P. La représentation proportionnelle. P. C. Levy, 1897. f. 1. (RIS., Ap.)

Leroy, Maxime. L'esprit de la législation napoléonienne (thèse). Nancy, libr. Crepin-Seblond. 264 pp. 8vo.

Lippmann, Karl. Die Konsularjurisdiktion im

Orient. Ihre histor. Entwicklg. von den frühesten Zeiten bis zur Gegenwart. Lp., Veit & Co. 192 pp. 8vo. M. 5.60.

Lowe, Charles. Prince Bismarck(Statesmen series). L., W. H. Allen. 244 pp. 12mo. 2s. 6d.

Lowe, Charles. Prince Bismarck: an historical biography. L., W. Heinemann & Sons. 360 pp. 12mo. 2s. 6d.

*Maitland, F. W. Township & borough. (AJS., S., p. 278) (JPE., S. + +)

Matter, P. La dissolution des assemblées parlementaires . . . . P., Alcan. 288 pp. 8vo. f. 5.

*McConachie, L. G. Congressional committees. N. Y., T. Y. Crowell. 441 pp. 12mo. $2. (Nation, S. 15 + —) (PSQ., S. + +)

Miles, N. A. Military Europe. N. Y., Doubleday & McClure Co. 112 pp. 8vo. $1.50. (Outlook, S. 17 + +)

Penzler, Johs. Fürst Bismarck nach seiner Entlassung. Leben u. Politik des Fürsten seit seinem Scheiden aus dem Amte . . . . 6. Bd. 1894-5. Lp., W. Fiedler. 409 pp. 8vo. M. 8.

Pobyedonostseff, K. B. Reflections of a Russian statesman. Trans. from the Russian. . . . L., Richards. 284 pp. 8vo. 6s.

Renard, Georges. Contribution à l'histoire de l'autorité législative du sénat romain. Le sénatus-consulte sur le quasi-usufruit (thèse). P., Berger-Levrautl & Cie.

Sammlung nationalökonomischer u. statistischer Abhandlungen des staatswissenschaftlichen Seminars zu Halle . . . . hrsg. v. Joh. Conrad. 20. Bd. Festgabe für Johannes Conrad. Zur Feier des 25-jähr, Bestehens des staatswiss. Seminars zu Halle. . . . Jena, G. Fischer. M. 9.

Schvarcz, Jul. Die Demokratie. 2. Bd. 2. Abth. L., W. Friedrich. pp. 145-647. 8vo. M. 13.

*Taylor, Hannis. Origin & growth of the English constitution. . . . In 2 pts. Pt. 2. The aftergrowth of the constitution. B., Houghton, Mifflin & Co. 645 pp. 8vo. $4.50. (Outlook, O. 8 + + —)

*Zimmermann, Alfred. Die Colonialpolitik Grossbritanniens. 1. Tl. Von den Anfängen bis zum Abfall der Vereinigten Staaten. B., Mittler & Sohn. 870 pp. 8vo. M. 10. (LC., Jl. 9)

15. Religion, Churches.

*Allen, W. O. B., & McClure, Edmund. History of the Society for Promoting Christian Knowledge, 1698-1898. L., S. P. C. K. (Athenæum, S. 3 + —)

Böhmer, Jul. Brennende Zeit- u. Streitfragen der Kirche. Gesammelte Abhandlgn. 3. u. 4. Giessen, J. Ricker. 108 u. 96 pp. à. M. 1.75. (Kplt. in 1 Bd. M. 7.50.)

Cole, L. T. Basis of early Christian theism. N. Y., Macmillan Co. 60 pp. 8vo. paper. $0.50. (Columbia Univ. contributions to philosophy.)

Corpus scriptorum ecclesiasticorum latinorum, editum consilio et impensis academiæ litterarum cæsareæ Vindobonensis. V. 35, pars 2. Lp., G. Freytag. M. 14.20.

Dahlmann, J. Buddha. Ein Culturbild des Ostens. B., F. L. Dames. 223 pp. 8vo. M. 6.

Debidour, A. Histoire des rapports de l'église et de l'état en France de 1789 a 1870. P., F. Alcan.

*Dictionary of the Bible, ed. by James Hastings. In 4 v. V. 1, A-Feasts. N. Y., Charles Scribner's Sons. 8vo. $6. (Critic, S. X) (NW., S. + +)

Fonsegrive, George. Catholicisme et démocratie. P., libr. Lecoffre. 283 pp. 18mo.

Geden, A. S. Studies in comparative religion. L., C. H. Kelly. 328 pp. 12mo. 2s. 6d. (Books for Bible students.)

George, C. Unity in religion: an inquiry into the teachings of great religious systems of the world. L., Swan Sonnenschein. 8vo. 1s.

Gladden, Washington. The Christian pastor & the working church. N. Y., C. Scribner's Sons. 485 pp. 8vo. $2.50. (International theological libr.)

Graetz, H. History of the Jews. In 6 v. V. 6. Index vol., with a memoir of the author & a chronological table of Jewish history. Phil., Jewish Pub. Soc. of Amer. 644 pp. 8vo. $3.

Harnack, A. History of dogma, trans. from 3d German ed. . . . . V. 4. L., Williams & Norgate. 366 pp. 8vo. 10s. 6d. (Theol. trans. libr.)

*Jackobs, H. E. Martin Luther, the hero of the Reformation. N. Y., C. P. Putnam's Sons. (Critic, S. + +)

Jalaguier, Ferdinand. La doctrine de l'infallibilité: son origine, son histoire (thèse). Montauban, impr. Granie.

*Jastrow, Morris, Jr. Religion of Babylonia & Assyria. Bo., Ginn & Co. 780 pp. 8vo. $3.25. (Handbooks on the history of religions, no. 2.) (Outlook, O. 15 + +)

[Knox, John. History of the reformation of religion within the realm of Scotland. Ed. for popular use by C. J. Guthrie. . . . . L., William Black & Sons. 392 pp. 8vo. 7s. 6d. (Academy, S. 17 X)]

Lane, C. A. Illustrated notes on English church history. V. 1. From the earliest times to the dawn of the Reformation. Rev. ed. comp. 200,000 vols. 304 pp. 12mo. 1s.

Lang, Andrew. The making of religion. L., Longmans, Green & Co. 390 pp. 8vo. 12s.

Lilley, J. P. Principles of Protestantism: an examination of the doctrinal differences between the Protestant churches & the Church of Rome. L., T. & T. Clarke. 262 pp. 8vo. 2s. 6d. (Handbooks for Bible classes.)

*Luthardt, C. E. Die christliche Glaubenslehre. Ip., Dörffling & Francke. 633 pp. 8vo. M. 11. (LC., S. 24)

Mason, A. J. Thomas Cranmer. Bo., Houghton, Mifflin & Co. 12mo. $1.25. (English leaders of religion ser.)

Miles, G. The bishops of Lindisfarne, Hexham, Chester-le-Street & Durham, 635-1020 A. D., being an introduction to the ecclesiastical history of Northumbria. L., W. Gardner. 328 pp. 8vo. 10s. 6d.

Most, J. La peste religieuse, tr. de l'allemand. Wattrelos, impr. Deryckere. 16 pp. 16mo.

Müller, F. M. Sacred books of the east, tr. by various oriental scholars. Amer. ed in 12 v. V. 2. N. Y., Christian Literature Co. 62+360 pp. 8vo. $3.

Müller, Hermann. Les origines de la compagnie de Jésus Ignace et Lainez. P., Fischbacher. 329 pp. 8vo. (JI. 9)

Pastor, L. History of the popes from the close of the middle ages, drawn from the secret archives of the Vatican & other original sources, from the German, ed. by F. I. Antrobus. V. 5. L., Kegan Paul, Treuch, Trubner & Co. 616 pp. 8vo. 12s.

Petrie, W. M. Flanders. Syria & Egypt, from the "Tell el-Amarna letters." N. Y., imp. by C. Scribner's Sons. 187 pp. 12mo, $1.

Piepenbring, C. Histoire du peuple d'Israel. Strassburg, J. Noiriel. 730 pp. 8vo. M. 6.40.

Rauschenbusch, A. Die Entstehung der Kindertaufe im 3. Jahrh. n. Chr. u. die Wiedereinführung der biblischen Taufe im 17. Jahrh. n. Chr. . . . . 2. Aufl. Hamburg, J. G. Oucken Nachf. 138 pp. 8vo. M. 0.75.

*Rawlinson, George. Memoir of Major-General Sir Henry Creswicke Rawlinson, Bart. N. Y., Longmans, Green & Co. (Dial, O. 16 X) (Nation, Jl. 7 X)

Riordan, M. O. Draper's conflict between religion & science. 47 pp. 8vo. 2d.

Rome—Le chef suprême: l'organisation et l'administration centrale de l'Eglise. Publiée par Mgr. Charles Daniel [& others]. P., Plon, Nourrit & Cie. 1er fasc. pp. 1–28.

Sacred books of the Old and New Testaments: a new English translation [printed in colors, exhibiting the composite character.of the books], with explanatory notes & pictorial ill.; prepared by eminent biblical scholars of Europe & America & ed. with the assistance of H. H. Furness, by Paul Haupt. Old Testament in 20 pts. N. Y., Dodd, Mead & Co. Pts. 3, 10, 14. 107, 216, 237 pp. $1.25, $2.50, $2.50.

St. Clair, G. Creation records discovered in Egypt. L., David Nutt. 504 pp. 8vo. 10s. 6d. (Studies in the Book of the Dead.)

*Scherer, Rudolf v. Handbuch des Kirchenrechtes. 2. Bd., 2. Abtlg. Graz, Moser. pp. 257–880. 8vo. M. 14. (LC., Jl. 30 + +)

Spence, H. D. M. Church of England: a history for the people. V. 3. The English Reformation. 476 pp. 8vo. 6s.

Stave, Erik. Ueber den Einfluss des Parsismus auf dem Judenthum. Ein Versuch. Lp., O. Harrassowitz. 380 pp. 8vo. M. 6.

*Tiele, C. P. Elements of the science of religion. Pt. 1. Morphological, being the Gifford lectures . . . . 1896. Edin., Wm. Blackwood & Sons, 1897. 302 pp. 7s. 6d. (NW., Je. + +)

Workman, H. B. Church of the West in the middle ages. Vol. 1. From Gregory the Great to St. Bernard (books for Bible students). 328 pp. 12mo. 2s. 6d.

16. Sanitary and Domestic Science.

Dibdin, W. J. Purification of sewage & water. L., Sanitary Pub. Co. 8vo. 21s.

[Dodd, C. I. Domestic economy for scholarship students. Ed. 2. L., Hughes. 178 pp. 8vo. 2s.]

Millas, P. H. Des droits de l'hygiène vis-à-vis de la propriété bâtie, et législation en vigueur en France et à l'étranger (thèse). Toulouse, impr. Cléder.

Thudichum, J. L. W. Briefe üb. öffentliche Gesundheitspflege, ihre bisherigen Leistungen u. heutigen Aufgaben. Tübingen, F. Pietzcker. M. 3.60.

17. Socialism.

Bassi, Ercole. Socialismo e cooperazione; questioni sociali; dialoghi popolari. Milano, Giacomo Agnelli. 154 pp. 16mo. L. 1.25.

*Sombart, Werner. Socialism. (AJS., S., p. 278) (Outlook, S. 10 + +)

[*Bibliography of Socialism will be brought to date in next issue.*]

18. Sociology (General).

*l'Année sociologique. (AJS., S., p. 278) (JGV., 22: 3) (ZS., Je. X)

[Biederlack, Joseph. Die sociale Frage. Ein Beitrag zur Orientierg. üb. ihr Wesen u. ihre Lösg. 3. Aufl. Innsbruck, J. Rauch. 238 pp. 8vo. M. 1.80.]

Blaviel, Abbé de. Questions philosophiques, politiques, sociales. Cahors, libr. Delsaud. 383 pp. 16mo. f. 2.50.

Bosanquet, Mrs. Bernard. The standard of life & other studies. L., Macmillan Co. 228 pp. 8vo. 3s. 6d.

Bova, Gaspare. La questione sociale: pensieri. Palermo, tip. Ponteficia. 13 pp. 16mo.

Chaplet, F. Essai sur la question sociale. Laval, Barneoud & Cie. 29 pp. 8vo.

Cornelius, Bodo. Schafft bessere Generation! Ein Beitrag zur Lösg. der socialen Frage. Lp., A. Strauch. 40 pp. 8vo. M. 1.

Cornero, Charles. Idée sur la civilisation au XXe siècle; inventions et propositions inhérentes;

progrès de civilisation italienne. Torino, impr. Vaccariano. 51 pp. 8vo.

Cosentini, F. La sociologie et G. B. Vico; tr. de l'italien. P., Giard & Brière. 27 pp. 8vo.

*Crowell, J. F. Logical process of social development. (AJS., S., p. 279; 257 + —)

*Demolins, Edmond. Anglo-Saxon superiority: to what it is due; tr. from 10th French ed. N. Y., imported by Chas. Scribner's Sons. 427 pp. 12mo. $1.50. (Academy, S. 24 + + —)

*Eliot, C. W. Amer. contributions to civilization. N. Y., Century Co. (AJS., S +)

*Fouillée, Alfred. Psychologie du peuple français. P., F. Alcan. 391 pp. 8vo. (RIS., + + —)

*Goblot, E. Essai sur la classification des sciences. P., F. Alcan. 8vo. (RIS., S.)

Lewetzki, G. Willensbildung. Ein Beitrag zur Lösg. der socialen Frage. B., Selbstverlag (S. W. Kommandantenstr. 5a). 24 pp. 8vo. M. 0.60.

*Lilienfeld, Paul de. La méthode graphique en sociologie. P., Giard & Brière. 136 pp. (ZS., Ap. +)

*Mismer, Charles. Principes sociologiques. P., F. Alcan. 8vo. (RIS., Mr. + +) (AJS., S. X)

*Naudet, Abbé. Le christianisme social (propriété, capital et travail). P., Bloud et Barral. 416 pp. 18mo.

Olly, E. N. Limitations of wealth; or, how to secure prosperity for all. N. Y., Lewis Weed Co. 31 pp. 12mo. $0.50.

Ostrander, Dempster. The social crisis, the duty of the government. N. Y., F. T. Neely. 270 pp. 12mo. $0.50.

Paultre, P. Etudes sociales: socialism, collectivisme, anarchie. Chateaudun, impr. Prud'homme. 77 pp.

*Perris, G. H. Count Leo Tolstoy. N. Y., New Amsterdam Book Co. (Critic, S. X)

[Platter, Jul. Kritische Beiträge zur Erkenntnis unserer socialen Zustände u. Theorien. 2. Aufl. Bern, Steiger & Co. 558 pp. 8vo. M. 5.]

*Ratzenhofer, Gustav. Die sociologische Erkenntnis. Lp., Brockhaus. 372 pp. 8vo. (RIS., Jl. X)

*Rigolage, Émile. La sociologie d'Auguste Comte. Résumé. P., F. Alcan. 472 pp. 8vo. f. 7.50. (LC., Je. 4) (ZS., My.)

*Soulier, H. Des origines et de l'état social de la nation française. P., Giard & Brière. 520 pp. 8vo. (JPE., S. X)

*Stein, Ludwig. Die sociale Frage in Lichte der Philosophie. Vorlesung über Socialphilosophie u. ihre Geschichte. St., F. Enke, 1897. 719 pp. 8vo. M. 16. (RIS., My. + + —)

*Stuckenberg, J. H. W. Introduction to the study of sociology. N. Y., A. C. Armstrong. $1.50. (Nation, S. 8 X) (NW., S, + —)

*Tarde, G. Etudes de psychologie sociale. P., libr. Giard & Brière. 333 pp. 8vo. f. 7. (Bibliothèque sociol. internat.) (RIS., Jl. + + —)

Tiger, J. Platon et la question sociale. P., libr. Roger & Chernoviz. 15 pp. 8vo.

Vanderwotte, Paul. De l'organisation des sociétés civiles dans leur rapports avec les tiers (thèse). P., libr. A. Rousseau. 197 pp. 8vo.

*Wallace, A. R. The wonderful century. N. Y., S., p. 279) (Outlook, S. 17 + +) (Nation, S. 22 — — +)

*Walrus, Léon. Études d'économie sociale (Théorie de la répartition de la richesse sociale). P., F. Alcan. 496. 462 pp. (JGV., 22: 3)

Wines, F. H. Sociology & philanthropy. Ph., Amer. Acad. of Pol. & Soc. Sci., pp. 49–57. 8vo. $0.15. (Publications of the society, no. 232.)

19. Statistics.

[Bibliography of Statistics will be brought to date in next issue.]

20. Unclassified.

Béchade, F. Le régime fiscal et économique de l'alcool en France (thèse). Bordeaux, impr. Gounouillhou.

*Blondel, Georges. L'essoir industriel et commercial du peuple allemand. P., libr. Larose. 220 pp. 8vo. (JGV., 22: 3) (RIS., My + +)

Bordiga, Oreste. Economia rurale. Parte I. (I fattori della produzione agraria). Milano, tip. Francesco Vallardi. 251 pp. 16mo. L. 2.50.

Borght, R. van der. Die soziale Bedeutung der deutschen Arbeiterversicherung . . . . Jena, G. Fischer. 84 pp. 8vo. M. 2.

Brooke, C. P. Cotton: its uses, varieties, fiber, structure, cultivation & preparation for market . . . . also the manufacture of cotton seed oil. N. Y., Spon & Chamberlain. 362 pp. $3.

*Coutarel, A. Le participationnisme, ou la justice dans l'organisation du travail. P., libr. Giard et Brière. 379 pp. 8vo. f. 6. (RJS., S. X)

*Edwards, Clement. Railway nationalization. . . . L., Methuen & Co. 233 pp. (ZS., My.)

Eymard, L. Économie politique. Les syndicats agricoles (thèse). Carpentras, libr. Seguin. 185 pp. 8vo.

Germany — Reichsversicherungsamt. Amtliche Nachrichten. Beiheft. Statistik der Ursachen der Erwerbsunfähigkeit (Invalidität) nach dem Invaliditäts- u. Altersversicherungsgesetz. 227 pp. 4to. M. 5.

Germany — Reichs-Versicherungsamt. Amtliche Nachrichten. Gesammt-Register f. die Jahrgange 1885-97. B., A. Asher & Co. 340 pp. 4to. M. 6.

Great Britain — Old age pension committee. Report with . . . . evidence and appendices. L., Eyre & Spottiswoode. 1s. 9d.

Handwörterbuch d. Versicherungswesens. 4. u. 5. Lfg. S., Baumgartner. à M. 1.50.

*Jastrow, Hermann. Das Recht der Frau nach dem bürgerlichen Gesetzbuch. B., Otto Liebmann. 213 pp. (ZS., Jl. + +)

Jones, W. H. Practical guide to the liquor licensing acts. L., E. Wilson. 134 pp. 12mo. 2s. 6d.

Kropotkine, Pierre. La morale anarchiste. P., impr. Blot. 32 pp. 16mo.

Müller, Josef. Eine Philosophie des Schönen in Natur u. Kunst. Mainz, Kirchheim, 1897. 271 pp. 8vo. M. 5. (LC., Jl. 16)

*Müller, Max. Landwirtschaftslehrer: die Getreidepolitik, der Getreideverkehr u. die Getreidepreise in Schlesien während des 18. Jahrh. Weimar, E. Felber, 1897. 129 pp. (JGV., 22: 3)

Schriften der Centralstelle f. Vorbereitung v. Handelsverträgen. 2. Hft. 8vo. B., Siemenroth & Troschel. 2. Sartorius v. Walterhausen, A. Deutschland u. die Handelspolitik der Vereinigten Staaten v. Amerika. 84 pp. M. 2.

Stelz, Johs. Die Lebensversicherung in ihrer Bedeutung f. das sociale u. Familienleben. Karlsruhe, F. Metzler. 35 pp. 8vo. M. 0.60.

*Tolstoy, Leo. What is art? Trans. from the Russian by Aylmer Maude. N. Y., T. Y. Crowell & Co. (Nation, S. 22 ——)

*Tunnell, G. G. Transportation on the Great Lakes of North America. Wash., Govt. Print. Office. 107 pp. 8vo. (House Doc. no. 277, 55th Cong., 2d Sess.) (JPE., S. + +)

*Ulrich, Franz. Staatseisenbahnen, Staatswasserstrassen u. die deutsche Wirhschaftspolitik. Lp., Duncker & Humblot, 1898. 48 pp. 8vo. M. 1. (LC., S. 17) (JGV., 22: 3).

Wagner, Karl. Das Problem vom Risiko in der Lebensversicherung. . . . Jena, G. Fischer. 160 pp. 8vo. M. 3.60.

Weichs-Glon, Frdr. Die Brotfrage u. ihre Lösung. Lp., Duncker & Humblot. 110 pp. 8vo. M. 2.20.

*Willoughby, W. F. Workingman's insurance. N. Y., T. Y. Crowell & Co. 386 pp. 12mo. $1.75. (JPE., S. + +)

*Zacher, F. Die Arbeiter-Versicherung im Auslande. 4. Hft. Die Arbeiter-Versicherung in Frankreich. B., Verlag der Arbeiter-Versorgg. 85 pp. 8vo. M. 2. (ZS., My.)

ARTICLES IN PERIODICALS.

[Articles preceded by stars and followed by a reference to a number of the JOURNAL will be found in abstract under the head "Notes and Abstracts" in that number of the JOURNAL. Articles dealing with *Biography, Associations, Cities,* and *Towns* will be found grouped under those heads.]

Accidents: *see* Labor.

Africa: Bourne, H. R. F. Sierra Leone troubles, FR., Ag.

Cust, R. N. Africa in 1897, Asiatic Quarterly Review, O.

Griffiths, A. Kitchener & Khartoum, FR., S.

Agriculture: Bourguin, Maurice. L'intensité de la crise agricole d'après la statistique décennale de 1892. RPP., S.

Crawford, Virginia M. Englishwomen & agriculture, CoR., S.

Dehérain, P. P. L'enseignement agricole, RDM., S. 15.

Grandeau, L. Mouvement agricole, JEc., Ag.

Anarchism: Andrews, J. A. L'anarchisme et le mouvement social en Australie, HN., Ag.

Anglo-Saxon Alliance: Barnaby, Nathaniel. Rational basis for Anglo-American co-operation, EM., O.

Dicey, A. V. England & America, Atlantic, O.

Schurz, Carl. Anglo-American friendship, Atlantic, O.

Anthropology: Andree, Richard. Anfänge der Weberei, Globus, S. 10.

Bissing, F. de. Les origines de l'Égypte, L'Anthropologie, Je.

Henning, C. L. Die neuesten Forschungen über die Steinzeit und die Zeit der Metalle in Aegypten, Globus, Jl. 30.

Livi, R. La distribuzione geografica dei caratteri antropologici in Italia, RiIS., Jl.

McGee, W. J. Course of human development, F.S

Myres, J. L. Prehistoric man in the eastern Mediterraneum, Science Progress, Jl.

Taylor, William. Pueblos & ancient mines near Allison, N. M., American Antiquarian, O.

See also Art, Labor.

Anthropometry: Grannelli, A., & G. Pardo. I sistemi di segnalazione antropomet., RDC., O.

Arbitration, International: Besson, Emmanuel. L'arbitrage international et la codification du droit des gens (à propos du rescrit du Tsar). RPP., S.

Woodruff, C. R. Fourth international arbitration conference, AAP., S.

Army: *see* United States.

Art: Friederici. Die darstellende Kunst der Eskimos, Globus, Ag. 27.

Galabert, Ed. Le rôle social de l'art, RIS., S.

Lehr, Henry. Qu'est-ce que l'art? Revue chrétienne, S. 1.

Sharp, Wm. Art Treasures of America, NC., S

Burton, Rich. Literature for children, NAR., S.
Castagnol, T. Une réforme à l'université américaine d'Harvard, SS., S.
Chaboseau, Augustin. L'extension universitaire, ReS., S.
Compayré, Gabriel. Contemporary education in France, EdR., S.
Compayré, G. L'enseignement intégral d'après un livre récent, RPh., Jl.
Demolins, Edmond. L'école nouvelle, SS., S.
Green, J. M. New Jersey system of public instruction, EdR., O.
Harris, W. T. The older & the newer education, EdR., S.
Hervey, W. L. Study of education at the German universities, EdR., O.
Martin, C. D., Mrs. Education in Hawaii, Education, S.
Mayo, A. D. Significance of illiteracy in the U. S., Education, S.
Menos, J. H. Nouvelle éthique sociale dans l'éducation, HN., Ag.
Mill, T. E. Higher educa. & the state, NT., O.
Münsterberg, Hugo. Psychology & education, EdR., S.
Parodi, D. La question de l'enseignement secondaire, RMM., S.
Paulsen, Friedrich. Examinations, EdR., S.
Politics & education in Chicago, EdR., S.
Rousiers, Paul de. Problèmes d'éduca., SS., Ag.
Stanley, H. M. The teaching of psychology, EdR., S.
Tompkins, Arnold. Herbart's philosophy & his educational theory, EdR., O.
Vidari, G. Le scuole secondarie e la società presente, RIF., Je.
See also Agriculture, Associations, Colonies, Ethics, Manual Training, Sanitary Science.
Egypt: see Anthropology.
Eight-Hour Day: see Labor.
Elections: see France.
England: see Great Britain.
Environment: see Heredity.
Ethics: Everett, W. G. The concept of the good, PhR., S.
Smith, Goldwin. Origin of morality, NAR., O.
See also Religion, Socialism, Sociology.
Ethnology: Steinmetz, S. R. Das Verhältnis zwischen Eltern u. Kindern bei den Naturvölkern, ZS., Ag.
See also Anthropology.
Evolution: Fages, C. L'évolution du darwinisme biologique, RIS., Jl.
Jones, Henry. Social & individual evolution, NW., S.
Pfleiderer, Otto. Evolution & theology, NW., S.
Exchanges: François, G. The Paris bourse, JPE., S.
Expansion: see United States.
Exports: see United States.
Factory Inspection: Furth, Henriette. Berichte der preussischen Fabrik-Inspektoren für 1897, Deutsche Worte, S.
Finance: Bericht über die Finanzverwaltung Preussens, Annalen des deutschen Reich, 31:11.
Bunzel, Gustav. Das moderne Geld- u. Creditwesen, ZVS., 7:3.
Ghidiglia, C. La pubblicazione dei documenti finanziari dell' antica repubblica di Venezia, GEc., S.
Lévy, R. G. La dette anglaise, RDM., S. 15.
Louis, Paul. La réforme fiscale, ReS., S.
McLeod, F. F. Fiat money & currency inflation in New England, AAP., S.
Morrill, J. S. Populist conceit, F., O.
Outerbridge, A. E. Curiosities of American coinage, PSN., S.
Samson, John. Truth about Chili's financial position, Journal of Finance, S.

Sternes, W. P. A new standard & a new currency, JPE., S.
Vanderlip, F. A. Lessons of our war loan, F., S.
Vinck, Émile. La réforme monétaire aux États-Unis, AIS.
Walras. Le comptabilisme social: l'unité fixe de la valeur, AIS., Ag.
France: Scaife, W. B. Legislative elections in France, NAR., O.
See also Children, Education, Insurance.
Germany: Poinsard, Léon. L'Allemagne contemporaine, SS., S.
Guilds: Hopkins, E. W. Ancient & modern Hindu gilds, YR., Ag.
God: Howison, G. H. The real issue in the conception of God, PhR., S.
Great Britain: Bright, Charles. An all-British, or Anglo-American, Pacific cable, FR., S.
Drage, Geoffrey. England & Russia in the far East, F., O.
Vambéry, H. Englands gefahrdete Machtstellung in Asien, Cosmopolis, Ag.
Wilson, H. W. Anglo-Russian understanding, National Review, S.
See also Africa, China, Finance, India, Legislation, Postal, Property, Railroads, United States.
Greece: Miller, W. Regulation of Greece, Cosmopolis, Ag.
Hawaii: Beardslee, L. A. Difficulties in assimilating Hawaii, NAR., O.
Foster, B. Leprosy & the Hawaiian annexation, NAR., S.
See also Education.
Heredity: Brinton, D. G. The factors of heredity & environment in man, AA., S.
History: Hart, A. B. The historical opportunity in America, AHR., O.
Harrison, Fred. Historical method of J. A. Froude, NC., S.
Puywode, Gustave du. Des lois de l'histoire, JEc., Ag.
Imperialism: see United States.
India: Elements of unrest in India, Asiatic Quarterly Review, O.
Leitner, G. W. The Amir, the frontier tribes, & the sultan, Asiatic Quarterly Review, O.
Individualism: Moore, Wentworth. The individualist, FR., Ag. & S.
Industry: Schäffle, A. Zum Kartellwesen u. zur Kartell-Politik, ZGS., 54:4.
Schoenhof, Jacob. Industrial investigations, F., O.
Inheritance: La Grasserie, Raoul de. De l'indisponibilité et de l'inivisibilité totales et partielles du patrimoine, RéfS., S. 16.
Innere Mission: see each number of MIM.
Insane: Channing, Walter. New Massachusetts board of insanity, ChR., O.
Sanborn, F. B. Curability of the insane. ChR., S.
Insurance: Australian life insurance societies, Journal of Finance, S.
Hofmann, F. Arbeitslosenversicherung in St. Gallen u. Bern, ASG., 13:1.
Kirchenberg, Ernst. Die Invaliditäts- u. Altersversicherung der Hausweber, JNS., 16:2.
Salmon-Legagneur, Paul. La caisse des incendiés du département de la Meuse, et les récents projets de création de caisses départementales d'assurance, RéfS., S. 16.
See also Salvation Army, Labor.
Intemperance: see Liquor Question.
International Law: Racioppi, F. Lo stato d'assedio e i tribunali di guerra, GEc., Ag.
See also Arbitration.
Italy: Ebray, A. La défense sociale en Italie, RPP., Ag.
Samaja, Nino. Les émeutes de la faim en Italie, HN., Ag.-S.
See also Children.

Settlements: *see* each number of Commons.
Sex : Block, Maurice. Un problème de statistique humaine et sa solution, JEc., Ag.
See also Biology.
Slavery : Bugbee, L. G. Slavery in early Texas, PSQ., S.
Social Movements : *see* each number of AAP., HN., ReS., RIS., SS.; *also* Anarchism.
Social Question: *see* Sociology.
Socialism : Adler, Georg. Zur Geschichte der deutschen Socialdemokratie. ZS., Ag.
Application du système collectiviste, ReS., Ag.
Fournière, Eugène. La cité idéale, ReS., Ag.
Gide, Charles. Les théories économiques de Karl Marx, RCS., S.
Masaryk, T. G. La crise scientifique et philosophique du marxisme contemporain, RIS., Jl.
Merlino, S. La morale et le socialisme, HN., Ag.
Ni dieu ni maitre, RSC., Ag.
Schmidt, Conrad. Present condition of social democracy in Germany, JPE., S.
Sencer, G. M. Le socialisme en Espagne, RPP., Ag.
See also each number of Amer. Fabian, DS., & ReS.
Sociology: Berry, L. F. Social teachings of Jesus, BS, Q.
Caldwell. Philosophy & the newer sociology, CoR., S.
Cavaglieri, G. Svolgimento e forme dell' azione collettiva, RilS., Jl.
Dewey, John. Social & ethical interpretations in mental development, NW., S.
Lindsay, S. M. Unit of investigation in sociology, AAP.
Mallock, W. B. Herbert Spencer in self defence, NC., Ag.
Reich, E. Schubert-Soldern über die soziale Frage, VWP., Jl.
Roberty, E. de. L'idée d'évolution et l'hypothèse du psychisme social, RPh., Jl.
Schitlowsky, Ch. Ludwig Steins Socialphilosophie, Deutsche Worte, S.
Simiand, F. L'année sociolog. 1897. RMM., S.
Spencer, Herb. What is social evolution? NC., S.
Successful mediocrity, EdR., Jl.
Topinard. The social problem, Monist, O.
Tosti, Gustavo. Delusions of Durkheim's sociological objectivism, AJS., S.
Tugan-Baranowsky, M. Die sozialen Wirkungen der Handelskrisen in England, ASG., 13 : 1.
Valbert, G. Etudes d'un homme d'état russe sur la société moderne, RDM., S.
Villa, G. L'odeierno sviluppo delle scieuze storiche e sociali, RilS., Jl.
Worms, René. L'économie sociale, RIS., Jl.
See also Art, Education, History, Theaters.
Spain: Dillion, E. J. Coming Carlism, CoR., S.
Dynastic crisis in Spain, FR., Ag.
Ruvigny, Marquis de, & Metcalfe, Cranstoun. Carlist policy in Spain, FR., S.
Spanish-American War: *see* United States.
Speculation: *see* Exchanges.
Statistics: *see* Agriculture, Cuba, Industry, Sex.
Street Railways: Knox, E. F. V. Legal aspects of electric street traction in England, EM., O.
See also Railroads, and each number of Street Railway Review.
Suffrage: *see* Voting.
Sugar: Oudin, P. La question des sucres, SS., Ag.
Tammany: Cary, Edward. Tammany past & present, F., O.
Tariff: Giretti, E. Le illusioni ed i danni del protezionismo, GEc., S.
Taxation: Bullock, C. J. Direct & indirect taxes, PSQ., S.
Cassel, G. Volksrepräsentation u. Besteuerung, ZGS., 54 : 4.

Lucay, Comte de. L'impôt général sur le revenu dans le passé et le présent, RéfS., S. 16.
Mensi, Franz von. Die Revision des Grundsteuerkatasters in Oesterreich, ZVS., 7 : 3.
Ortlof, Herm. Neuere Entwickelung der Einkommensteuer-Gesetzgebung im Grossherzogtum Sachsen-Weimar, JNS., 16 : 2-3.
Tuttle, Leonard. Social option in taxation, MA., S.
Veber, Adrien. La suppresion des octrois, ReS., Ag.-S.
West, Max. Recent inheritance-tax statutes & decisions, JPE., S.
Theaters: Twain, Mark. About play acting, F., O.
Trade Unions: *see* Coöperation.
United States: Army mismanagement, ChR., O.
Barker, Wharton. Industrial interests of the U. S. in the far East, EM., O.
Breckinridge, J. C. Our national folly & its victims. NAR., O.
Colomb, P. H. U. S. navy under the new conditions, NAR., O.
Conant, C. A. Cost & finances of the Spanish war, RRN., S.
Conant, C. A. Economic basis of imperialism, NAR., S.
Diezmann, M. Der Aussenhandel der Vereinigten Staaten im Rechnungsjahre 1897, JNS., 16 : 2.
Devine, E. T. A week at Montauk, ChR., O.
Dicey, Ed. New American imperialism, NC., S.
Dunham, Carroll. Medical & sanitary aspects of the war. RRN., O.
Fisher, H. N. Development of our foreign policy, Atlantic, O.
Ford, W. C. New opportunities for American commerce, Atlantic, S.
Harisse, Henry. Outcome of the Cabot quarter-centenary, AHR., O,
Imperialism, true & false, YR., Ag.
Low, A. M. Amateurs in war, F., O.
MacDonald, William. Dangers of imperialism, F., O.
Parker, J. H. Some lessons of the war from an officer's standpoint, RRN., O.
Powers, H. H. The war as a suggestion of manifest destiny, AAP., S.
Procter, J. R. Isolation or imperialism, F., S.
Rives, G. L. Spain & the United States in 1795, AHR., S.
See also Anglo-Saxon Alliance, Art, China, Cuba, Education, Finance, Great Britain, Hawaii, Industry, Labor, Literature, Monroe Doctrine, Philippines, Women.
University Extension: *see* Education.
Vacation Schools: *see* Education.
Utopias: Kirchenheim, A. von. Die neuesten Utopien, ZG., Ag.
Voting: Haynes, G. H. Qualifications for the suffrage, PSQ., S.
Wages: Atkinson, E. Evolution of high wages from low cost of labor, PSM., O.
Macrosty, H. W. Living wage movement, PSQ., S.
Schmid, Hans. Der Minimallohn, Deutsche Worte, S.
War: *see* United States.
Water: Bashore, H. B. Mistakes of small towns, S., O.
Women: Braun, Lily. Die Frauenfrage im Alterthum, ASG., 13 : 1.
Holmes, Lizzie M. Woman's future position in the world. Arena, S.
Robinson, Miss H. H. Le mouvement féministe aux États-Unis, RPP., Ag.
Trautman, Mary E, [& 13 others]. Woman's work on city problems, MA., S.
See also Agriculture.

ABBREVIATIONS USED IN BIBLIOGRAPHY.

Places of Publication: B., Berlin; Bo., Boston; C., Chicago; Cin., Cincinnati; F., Frankfurt a. M.; Fr., Freiburg i. B.; L., London; Lp.. Leipzig; M., Milan; N. Y., New York; P., Paris; Ph., Philadelphia; S., Strassburg; St.. Stuttgart; T., Turin; W., Washington. *Prices:* d., pence; f., franc; L., lira; M., mark; s., shilling. *Months:* Ja. F. Mr. Ap. My. Je. Jl. Ag. S. O. N. D. *Periodicals:*

A.	Arena.	JHS.	Johns Hopkins University Studies in History and Political Science.
AA.	American Anthropologist.		
AAC.	Archives d'anthropologie criminelle.	JPE.	Journal of Political Economy.
AAE.	Archivo per l'antropologia e la etnologia.	JNS.	Jahrbücher für National-Oekonomie und Statistik.
AAP.	Annals of the American Academy of Political and Social Science.	LC.	Literarisches Centralblatt.
		LG.	Labor Gazette.
AC.	L'Association catholique.	LoQR.	London Quarterly Review.
ACQ.	American Catholic Quarterly Review.	LQR.	Law Quarterly Review.
AEL.	Annals d'École libre des sciences politiques.	MHM.	Mansfield House Magazine.
		MIM.	Monatsschrift für innere Mission.
AGP.	Archiv für Geschichte der Philosophie.	MA.	Municipal Affairs.
AHR.	American Historical Review.	NA.	Nuova antologia.
AIS.	Annals de l'Institute de science sociale.	NAR.	North American Review.
AJP.	American Journal of Psychology.	NC.	Nineteenth Century.
AJS.	American Journal of Sociology.	NS.	Natural Science.
AJT.	American Journal of Theology.	NT.	New Time.
ALR.	American Law Register.	NW.	New World.
ALRv.	American Law Review.	NZ.	Neue Zeit.
AMP.	Académie des sciences morales et politiques, Séances.	PhR.	Philosophical Review.
		PSM.	Popular Science Monthly.
AOR.	Archiv für öffentliches Recht.	PSQ.	Political Science Quarterly.
ASA.	American Statistical Association, Publications.	PsR.	Psychological Review.
		QJE.	Quarterly Journal of Economics.
ASAr.	Allgemeine statistisches Archiv.	QR.	Quarterly Review.
ASG.	Archive für sociale Gesetzgebung und Statistik.	RBP.	Rivista benificenza publica.
		RCS.	Revue de christianisme sociale.
ASP.	Archiv für systematische Philosophie.	RDC.	Rivista di discipline carcerarie.
BDL.	Bulletin of the Department of Labor.	RDI.	Revue de droit internationale.
BG.	Blätter für Gefängnisskunde.	RDM.	Revue des deux mondes.
BML.	Banker's Magazine, London.	REA.	Revue mensuelle de l'École d'anthropologie de Paris.
BMN.	Banker's Magazine, New York.		
BOT.	Bulletin de l'Office du Travail.	RéIS.	Réforme sociale.
BS.	Bibliotheca Sacra.	ReS.	Revue socialiste.
BSt.	Bulletin de statistique et de legislation comparée.	RH.	Revue historique.
		RHD.	Revue d'histoire diplomatique.
BUI.	Bulletin de l'Union internationale de droit pénale.	RIF.	Rivista italiana di filosofia.
		RIS.	Revue internationale de sociologie.
C.	Cosmopolis.	RilS.	Rivista italia na di sociologia.
ChOR.	Charity Organisation Review.	RISS.	Rivista internazionale 'di scienze sociali
ChR.	Charities Review.	RMM.	Revue metaphysique et de morale.
CoR.	Contemporary Review.	RP.	Revue philanthropique.
DL.	Deutsche Litteraturzeitung.	RPe.	Revue pénitentiaire.
DR.	Deutsche Revue.	RPh.	Revue philosophique.
DRu.	Deutsche Rundschau.	RPP.	Revue politique et parliamentaire.
DS.	Devenir social.	RRL.	Review of Reviews, London.
DZG.	Deutsche Zeitschrift für Geschichtswissenschaft.	RRN.	Review of Reviews, New York.
		RSC.	Revue sociale catholique.
EcJ.	Economic Journal.	RSI.	Revisita storica italiana.
EcR.	Economic Review.	RSP.	Revue sociale et politique.
EdR.	Educational Review.	RT.	Revue du travail.
EHR.	English Historical Review.	S.	Sanitarian.
EM.	Engineering Magazine.	SR.	School Review.
F.	Forum.	SS.	Science sociale.
FR.	Fortnightly Review.	VWP.	Vierteljahrschrift für wissenschaftliche Philosophie.
GEc.	Giornale degli economisti.		
GM.	Gunton's Magazine.	YR.	Yale Review.
HLR.	Harvard Law Review.	ZE.	Zeitschrift für Ethnologie.
HN.	Humanité nouvelle.	ZGS.	Zeitschrift für die gesammte Staatswissenschaften.
HR.	Hygienische Rundschau.		
HZ.	Historische Zeitschrift.	ZPK.	Zeitschrift für Philosophie und philosophische Kritik.
IAE.	Internationales Archiv für Ethnographie.		
IJE.	International Journal of Ethics.	ZPO.	Zeitschrift für das private und öffentliche Recht.
JAI.	Journal of the Anthropological Institute of Great Britain and Ireland.		
		ZPP.	Zeitschrift für Psychologie und Physiologie der Sinnesorgane.
JCB.	Journal of the Canadian Bankers' Association.		
		ZS.	Zeitschrift für Socialwissenschaft.
JEc.	Journal des économistes.	ZVR.	Zeitschrift für vergleichende Rechtswissenschaft.
JFI.	Journal of the Franklin Institute.		
JGV.	Jahrbuch für Gesetzgebung, Verwaltung und Volkswirthschaft.	ZVS.	Zeitschrift für Volkswirthschaft, Socialpolitik und Verwaltung.

[The titles of articles selected from periodicals not in this list will be followed by name of periodical in full.]

THE AMERICAN

JOURNAL OF SOCIOLOGY

VOLUME IV   JANUARY, 1899   NUMBER 4

SOCIETY'S NEED OF EFFECTIVE ETHICAL INSTRUCTION IN SCHOOL AND CHURCH, AND THE SUGGESTION OF AN AVAILABLE METHOD.

As THE practical portion of an article on the "Function of the Church," in the September, 1896, issue of this JOURNAL, a discipline was outlined that seems to me likely to prove effective for the development of the ethical and religious life. Mrs. Fairchild's article, "The Scientific Study of Philanthropy" (this JOURNAL, January, 1897), furnishes the method for the class in philanthropy provided for in the original article, and this is an attempt to supplement still farther by supplying the needed method of ethical education.[1]

In this article a consideration of a desirable result will lead to a statement of a method of its attainment. One of the necessary conditions of a peaceful and joyful world-progress in civilization is a *world-homogeneity of the ethical ideals* in which peoples believe. The cause of the war with Spain was a sentiment in the United States in favor of freedom. Spain seemed to us to hinder, for the sake of her national greed, the development of Cuba. Had Spain's ethical development kept pace with ours, Spain's service to Cuba would have become what ours will be, and resentment against oppression would not have arisen among us, because there would have been no oppression.

[1] This method, worked out to supplement the present work of the church, is also available for the public schools. It is hoped that the school superintendents and

433

And what is true in this single affair is true in general. If Russia's national ethical ideal is so selfish as to allow her to attempt at all hazards to monopolize the working power of China, and to get industrial control of the rest of the world by manufacturing in China for half cost to producers of England, United States, France, Germany, and the rest, then war, born of the instinct for self-preservation, is inevitable. If in this case a world-homogeneity is gained on a level of willingness to industrially enslave other nations whenever opportunity offers, there can be no peaceful development of civilization; but if by some ethical education there can be a world-homogeneity of opinion in favor of equal opportunity for the adjustment of the civilization of each nation to that of every other, then progress can be made in peace.

National homogeneity of ethical ideals is a desirable condition, providing for national strength and progress without internal strife. What we want to avoid is not simply sectional war, such as the rebellion, but internal disputings that arouse enmities and destroy the sympathies that make a united nation. And a republic is especially subject to weakenings caused by differences of ethical ideals. An anti-war party can make a much more effective resistance to the leadership of Congress here in the United States than it could in Russia to the resolves of the Czar. Facilities for social control are developed in Russia, and obedience to government is a habit of the people, but our republic stimulates individuality, diversity of opinion, unwillingness to follow leaders. Our national activities need the backing of unanimity of public opinion, and at the foundation of individual

---

principals, and the professors of pedagogy, will take the suggested method seriously. Dr. G. Stanley Hall gives me permission to quote him as considering this matter "worthy of most serious attention." Dr. W. J. Milne, of the New York State Normal College, Albany, N. Y., sympathizes with the fundamental idea, and arranged for a presentation of the method on October 27, before an audience of about five hundred of Albany's thoughtful people, and on the afternoon of that same day Professor Charles W. Cole, superintendent of schools in Albany, with the assistance of Principal John Howe, made a trial with 200 children in School No. 4, which they consider successful. Dr. Wallace Buttrick, of the Emmanuel Baptist Church, Albany, N. Y., Dr. T. P. Sawin, of the First Presbyterian Church, Troy, N. Y., and Mrs. Fairchild, of the New York State Library School, heartily approve this suggested method.

opinion, and therefore of public opinion, is the sense of the right and wrong, the fine and the ignoble.

The present educational disciplines of our schools provide for the development of intellectual strength; strength that, uncontrolled by ethical convictions, makes likely the more serious personal and party conflicts. A trained leader can create a party on a platform inimical to national well-being. Incidentally our schools tend to create an ethical homogeneity, because the teachers are personally exemplars of common ideals, and the schools are, from necessity, miniature communities. But the national need justifies a thorough ethical discipline in the public schools.

Individuals relinquish a purely self-centered life-struggle, and group into nations, and sacrifice for national existence, because by means of a group-centered struggle many goods are obtainable for the individuals which could not be secured by purely individual effort. The nation, our nation, a republic, by adding an ethical discipline to the public schools, and producing a greater degree of homogeneity of ethical ideals, could *strengthen itself to increase the chances of popular contentment and happiness.* Individuals would gain in two ways by this ethical homogeneity.

(1) Personal worth is a large factor in securing happiness for the individual. This factor would be influenced by an efficient ethical discipline. A street car contained a company of ladies and gentlemen whose sense of the obligations of cleanliness prescribed that their bodies should emit no offensive odors. A laborer right from his work, a gentleman at heart, took a seat, and was disgusted and hurt by having the gentleman sitting next to him move out of smell. The conductor and laborer exchanged glances of sympathy: they did not understand that the laborer was at fault, but considered the gentleman a snob. In any community there are hundreds of men and women who fail to gain desired recognition and attention from their neighbors, and fail because of personal unworthiness. They are intellectually worthy, but have not the conduct that makes them attractive, interesting, respected, and loved. In an essential they are below the group into which they want to socialize, and in marriage,

business, and social relations they have continual unpleasantnesses.

(2) The immediate source of most of our minor sorrows is unkind and unfair treatment from others. We are cheated, and our money does not go as far as wanted. Our interests clash with a neighbor's, and we find ourselves losing reputation through false witness. Our motives are proved low, our personal character shady, our business practices dishonest, our credit a bluff. If weak, guilty or not, we are downed, and our neighbor profits. The period of the struggle is painful, even if we win. The ethical boss is frequent. He decides our affairs of home and heart, and is pleasant or lowering according as we fulfill or not his judgments of what we ought to have done. Impoliteness, intended or ignorant or careless, causes many a pang and anger. We cease to be useful to old friends, and find ourselves neglected. All these incidents show that the self-interest of our associates needs to be held in check by respect for ideals of justice, courtesy, and love. What causes sorrow when administered by a neighbor is much more destructive of happiness when coming from a wife, husband, or child. Many a hair grows gray and face care-worn because someone from whom we do not want to be free is not controlled by ethical ideals to act and speak in love.

And we discover people with a genius for friendship, whose souls understand our sorrows and ambitions, and who would not do us wrong. Life is at its best when we are associated with these, and although other elements enter to make them what they are to us, we recognize that they could not be to us what they are, were not their understanding and practice of fine conduct so perfect. If the public schools administered an effective ethical discipline, they would tend to produce a community ethical homogeneity that would make it easier for the child to grow into perfect socialization with his environment, and many a life otherwise criminal or malcontent might become a success. The number of unpleasantnesses arising from misconduct would surely be reduced—a gain for us all in city and in home.

Granted that religion does most to temper the soul to kindness, and would that this article offered some suggestion as to how the church might win people to fuller understanding of the love of God; it is wisdom, however, to strengthen the church at any point, whenever possible. The church needs some method of revealing the *application of the love of God to human conduct.* The child comes and asks, "Who is my neighbor?" Two girls were picking coal from a dump, and doing it for the sake of mother. They espied two girl schoolmates, dressed in stunning style, carrying a parasol, and soon to pass by the dump. I saw them skulk away and hide behind the fence until the Misses Style had passed. A boy explained this hiding by saying: "Aw! Those girls would say, 'You have to work on the dump.'" The Golden Rule and Prayer are familiar, but the interpretation thereof is vague. The church should educate into an understanding of what Christianity applied to everday life really is, and should sanction these definite interpretations as the will and love of God. And the church needs a method of doing this effectively.

The position of this article is the same as that of the original article,[1] *i. e.*, that the church and school are distinct and coördinate and coöperating educational institutions, and that the church is assigned the leadership in the task of educating the ethical as well as the religious life. But the schools should supplement the ethical education of the churches. And there is a natural division of labor. Professor James Baldwin states strongly, in his *Mental Development, Social and Ethical Interpretations*, what seems to me the justification of the method which is suggested in this paper, and his classification of the sanctions for conduct suggests the following, suited to this discussion:

1. *The conscious, personal desires* of physique, intellect, and soul of the subject. Under this head will come desire for food, for the fulfillment of ideals and tastes, for honor and esteem.

2. *The conscious, social desires* of the society in which the subject lives, *i. e.*, the established ideals and tastes of family,

---

[1] Reprints of this and of Mrs. Fairchild's article can be had of E. C. B. at 25 cents a copy.

community, and nation, general customs, civic ordinances, state and national laws.

3. *The unconscious impulses* of personal and social life, and the influences of impersonal nature. Under this head will come the influences that create moods, that furnish conditions favorable to mob stampedes, and that throw a schoolroom into unaccountable disorder.

4. *Theistic*, the influence of the " Not Ourselves " that seems to permeate all being with motive-full, organized personality.

What we wish to educate is the conscious personal desires, the first class: the third class, unconscious impulses, are indirectly effective on conduct, and therefore in no way available for purposes of education. We have left, therefore, the second and the fourth, viz., conscious social desires, and whatever of knowledge we receive of the love and will of God. The school can reveal to the child the social desires, and the church the love and will of God. It is education of her people into homogeneity of social desires that concerns the nation, because unity and strength are attainable when such a condition exists: the church is interested in bringing into effective social control ethical ideals established by the Christ. The division of labor is not strained, but provides a definite basis for coöperation in accord with natural relations and involving no organic connection. The school should educate into an understanding of the dominant ethical ideals of the environing life of the child, and needs a method of doing this. The same method will serve both institutions, because the discipline required is the same in kind.

I leave for later discussion questions involved in the application to the church of the method suggested in this article, and confine the discussion from this point strictly to the public schools. Since it is an education in ethics that we seek, there must be an *explanation of the psychology* of this new method. Baldwin cannot be far wrong when he divides the self of the child into (1) the ego-self and (2) the alter-self. The mother, father, nurse, other children of the household, and their friends and neighbors, constitute the child's alter-self, and throughout its entire life there is a dialectic, an interdiscussion, between the ego- and the alter-self. And one of the ways by which the child comes to its thought of self is by discovering what other people are, and applying his discoveries to himself. The child has at hand a developed intelligence — his parents, teachers, preachers, and friends; and they, if they educate him ethically, make easier this discovery of the common ideals and customs, and the conditions into which he has been born. The school should help him to understand the ethical alter-self in order that his ego-self may develop into harmony with this socius, and become intelligent and self-controlled to coöperate with those around him.

The pedagogy of this ethical discipline will conform to that of all educative disciplines, so far as general pedagogy is concerned. It will differ from the regular school pedagogy in that the *chief concern is the production of an emotional effect.* There must be produced in the child more than an intellectual understanding of ethical theory. The child must resolve to fulfill ethical ideals. To illustrate, scholarship demands that the scholar's ideal shall be understood by the children, but the more serious task is to win their hearts to its fulfillment. Our discipline must reveal the true scholar's emotional apprehension of this ideal, awaken the children to an appreciation of the fact that devotion to this ideal seems admirable in the eyes of all educated people. The ethical lectures must interpret to the children the *adult feeling* about their quarrels and fights, their school failures and successes, the boy at work and at play, the sneak, the thief, the bully, the cry-baby, and the general good-for-nothing; and reveal adequately the adult admiration, even passionate delight, in the large-hearted, earnest, all-alive boy and girl.

We must deal, not with abstract, but with *concrete questions,* because the child mind has not begun to deal with abstractions. A child is sailing his boat in a park pond, and some tease comes by. A stone pitched into the water a foot from the boat swells the water, and over goes the boat. The child cries out: "You stop; it is not fair for you to sink my boat." It does not say:

"It is not right for one boy to spoil the property of another.'
Our pedagogy will compel us, therefore, to gather the concrete
ethical problems of the children, and to discuss with them the
definite questions of right and wrong involved in their everyday experiences. And we shall expect the child to develop
into devotion to general ethical ideals through becoming
enthusiastic over definite conduct solutions of its own daily
difficulties. Our discipline will be a progressive one, because
we shall discuss the questions involved in each episode with the
children of about the age of the participants. We shall
recapitulate the culture development of the race just in so far
as this is actually done by the child born into the socius of
these later times, because our discussions are led by the questions arising out of the experiences of the children.

Thus far this article has outlined the thought process by which
the main features of this new method have been determined.
The point of peculiar interest, and which leads me to hope
seriously that an effective method has been devised, is that,
when we have thus determined the main features of the desirable method, in essentials it is a *method that has been continually
in operation in the homes.* The school simply needs to artificialize
a method that is natural, followed without special thoughtfulness by parents. Parents naturally give ethical instruction to
children at the time of some episode. John comes home with a
black eye, and the fact is apparent that he has had a fight.
The father inquires what it was all about. The causes are given :
"Jack hit me. We were in swimming, and I was going to dive
in backwards. Jack gave me a shove sideways, and I hit my
head against a stake. I asked him if he meant anything by it,
and he said he did. I dared him to come out onto the bank,
and the other boys said he dasent, so he came out, and, well!
he reached me once in the eye, but he couldn't adone it if I
hadn't aslipped in the mud." The father follows this recital
of the fight with his most effective ethical instruction. Acting in accordance with the sentiments which his ethical education has created in him, he doles out to the boy in emphatic
and mandatory words the answer which the developed intelli-

gence of the father gives to the concrete ethical problem of the boy.

The method which I suggest, and have tested to the point of willingness to state it, simply artificializes this natural method.

THE GIRLS

I take my camera, and hunt for important episodes of child life in homes and schools and streets and playgrounds. If fighting is to be discussed, I must be on hand when some fight takes place, and I must press the bulb of my camera just at the time when the fight is significant. If a girl goes to help an old lady replace parcels which the wind has scattered from her market basket, I must catch her in the act of doing this kindness. If two girls are quarreling over a skipping rope, I must catch them at the critical moment of the quarrel. The disappointments of my hunt are as keen as those of the Adirondack deer hunter, and my successes are of permanent value.

From these negatives are made slides, and thus is provided *visual instruction in ethics.* By means of these slides, and a recital of the incident involved, I can throw a hundred or more boys and girls into a realization of the episode of the photograph. If I show a picture of a fight, they realize approximately the experiences of those watching or participating in the fight. The questions of right and wrong that were uppermost in the minds of those in the picture can be made uppermost in the minds of the boys and girls within sight of the picture. And I thus gain the vantage ground that comes naturally to the father when he discusses with his son a fight from which the son is smarting in body and in soul. I give them, while thus appreciative of a difficulty into which many a boy comes, emphatic and specific directions as to what the finest conduct under these circumstances is, in my judgment, considered to be by the developed intelligence of their community, and express the sentiments of respect and contempt that attach to the various participants. I furnish them illustrations and thus interpret to them impressively the application of the ethical standards of their socius, and by *"suggestion-imitation"* they tend to habituate themselves to the fulfillment of these standards, a full understanding of which can come to them only in their adult mind.

The children have a right to better than the personal judgments of any one man, and if I submit for criticism to quite a circle of good judges of fine conduct these ethical lectures, then they can give to the children a consensus of adult opinion, and there need be no serious mistakes in doctrine, because we are not trying to give absolute ethical truth, but simply the judgments of the many who have good judgment in these matters. Someone may defend the boy's right to fight at every insult, but it is certainly true that the boy who does this will get himself disliked by his socius, juvenile and adult.

Extemporaneous ethical lectures are entirely unsatisfactory except to the egotism of the lecturer, because the pedagogy of the education of the emotions requires an artistic presentation of the thought which cannot be gained except by laborious composition; the lecture must have literary qualities, and bear rehearing, and the pictures must be set at the effective place in the text. Further, it is desirable, in order to produce the degree of homogeneity needed, that the same ethical ideals be given the entire child life of city and nation. Effective lectures can be belivered from manuscript, since they are given in the dark, and any good teacher can easily prepare to deliver them. In the country schools where a stereopticon is not available an oil lantern will serve. The University of the State of New York rents stereopticons to country schools in the state.

If these lectures be printed and these slides duplicated, and the schools of the United States incorporate this discipline into their curricula, then approximately every child of our nation is brought under the same ethical ideals. At present the child of the home of culture and the child of the slums get very different training. The fruits of this thorough ethical education would be — the churches being also at work to relate the gospel of love to practical life — an approach to that needed higher degree of community and national ethical homogeneity.

A little more definiteness as to manner of handling these episodes will give a better ground for discussion. The group on the dump containing the girls who hid behind the fence was photographed before I interrupted the industry. If I take proper precautions to avoid any recognition of the children, I can show this picture on the screen, and tell the incident. I have also a picture of two girls who might have been their snobbish persecutors. And I have a picture of children gathering wood in a snowstorm, and of hovels where they live. A combination of these pictures and others, and an earnest expression of the sympathy for the girls that work on the dump for their mother that burns in every true woman's heart, and of contempt for the idle, parasoled stuckups who sneered at them, will tend to change the youthful snobs into loving women, and arouse self-respect in those who do their share of the world's work even while they are children. Another series of pictures and an explanation will impress the idea that cleanliness is demanded of the gentleman, and slovenliness is punished by social ostracism. The lecture which I have used to test the method in the public schools deals with fighting, and is now a combination of forty pictures and six transparencies. Twenty-four children of the seventh grade made a report in writing without knowledge at the time of the lecture that this would be required. The Albany *Argus* gives the following boy's report of the lecture.

THE FIGHT BETWEEN JOHN AND JACK.

Once upon a time two boys had a fight. The fight began in this way : One day a group of boys was playing pitch. They were using celluloid buttons, and the game was exciting. Jack was not playing, but John was. Now Jack, to be funny, picked up John's button, which was close to the goal, and started on a run. Now this made John angry, and he started after the joker on the run. He took the button away from him and returned to the game. Jack again picked up the button and ran away with it. This time John caught Jack and punched him in the back, whereupon Jack turned around and punched John in the face. Now I think a better way to settle the affair would be to tell Jack to keep away and leave the buttons alone ; and if he did not, the best thing to do would be to catch Jack and all the boys hold him, while one could give him a good spanking. But suppose the other boys would not spank the joker Jack ? Why, if I were John, I would pick up my button and walk away. Boys over ten years old are too old to fight. Some boys love to fight simply because they do not know any better. Those kind of fellows are to be pitied. Mr. Fairchild made other very interesting remarks, of which I have not time to write. He was well applauded when the lecture closed.

WILLIAM McCORMICK.

The applause indicated that the interest of the children was reached, and that they did not feel as if I had been scolding them. I condemned Jack, and I proved to them that he deserved it, and that the fine fellows have good times and no fuss. Their hands said : "That's so ; you're right."

A tabulation of these returns from twenty-four children of the seventh grade — eight boys and sixteen girls — gives the following results :

Boys	Girls	Total	Idea expressed
8	16	24	Disapproval of the fight and of Jack.
4	4	8	Boys over ten are too old to fight:
4	4	8	Toughs fight ; gentlemen do not.
2	3	5	Do as the gentlemen do — walk off.
3	1	4	Boys have the most fun when there is no fuss.
1	3	4	Right to fight for a good cause, but not for a trifle.
2	1	3	Do your best to give the rest a jolly good time.

This table of ideas is quite complete, and makes one point clear. The children grasp the concrete disapproval of this fight, but are slow to fix in memory the generalizations of the lecture ; "Do your best to give the rest a jolly good time," is given by only two boys and one girl. These generalizations have been made more striking by introducing transparencies. If the wording of the lecture were changed to make these more emphatic, probably we should bore the children. The children will willingly listen more than once to the lecture, and will discover the generalizations.

To complete the statement of this suggested method I have but to include one of the shorter discussions of an episode. The test of this method is its availability for the younger grades. I therefore give the story " Six Boys and a Cart." For use in the schools this lecture ought to be enlarged to include about twenty pictures illustrative of its various points.

SIX BOYS AND A CART.

I was walking one day on the sidewalk of a street in Boston, that famous city by the sea, where the colonists under Governor Winthrop settled in 1630, and now one of the largest cities in the United States. My camera was under my arm, and I was looking for boys. The boys have just as fine a time where there are no elegant houses and the people are not rich, and there may be a splendid playmate under some poor clothes. My eyes were wandering all around ; not a boy escaped me. I want to show you the boys that were having the most fun. They are just boys with ordinary clothes, and they know how to have a good time. See this picture.

Here is a strong-wheeled cart just large enough to hold the driver. If I were driver, I would not ask a better team than these four stout boys. One of them has his hat off, and the driver has it on his cart. When the word comes, " Get up there," this boy-horse ducks his head, and off they all go like the wind. You cannot break the cart, and it would take a long drive to tire the team.

This picture shows them halted at the street corner ; you can imagine how they looked when they came dashing along the sidewalk. What would have happened if the team had not stopped when the driver said " Whoa ! " ? There is a sudden drop from the sidewalk to the driveway, and this would have given the driver a hard jolt, had the team kept its break-neck pace. I saw them come prancing up to the jolting place, and heard the driver call out, " Whoa ! " These boys stopped.

But I know some two-legged horses that would not have stopped. I know some big boys that would have invited this little fellow with the round cap, who seems to be watching the fun, to have a fine ride, and then, when he accepted the invitation, supposing that he was dealing with gentlemen, they would have turned and dashed up to the jolting place, given the cart a jerk and a twist just at the jolt, and then laughed and sneered when the cart bounded into the air, turned half over, and dropped the little boy on his head on the hard stones. This meanness they call fun, and I despise this fun that makes another cry.

If I were by and saw some bullies, some mean ones, trying this trick, do you know what I would do? If I were big enough, or could get enough boys to help me, I would take their cart and give the little fellow the finest ride he ever had.

Perhaps it would be only fair, if there were a machine that would catch the bullies one by one, and gently knock their heads against the stones of the driveway just a little harder than gravity did the head of the little boy who took them for gentlemen. Thus they might learn how hard the stones are and how mean they are.

There is not a bully in this group — not a mean one. I am not sure that the boys take turns riding, but I think they do. At least I did not see anyone crying because he could not ride.

If I were a boy, do you know what I would do? I would get a strong cart, and then I would be a fine enough fellow to have some splendid friends, and I would not have a fuss with any one of them. I would try never to get mad myself, and we should have the best of rides and take turns.

Get a cart,	Down the bully,
Have some fun ;	Run like mad ;
Be a boy,	Keep your temper,
Learn to run.	You're my lad.

The handling of these episodes is a delicate matter. How shall we treat the evil of life? The hothouse boy, reared in ignorance, is blighted by the first hot breath upon his cheek, and it is far better that the evils that are common and sure to be understood some time should be explained, when the children become curious, by those who hate evil rather than by those who like it. These lectures must show the ugliness of the evil they discuss, and they must avoid being a revelation of evil that is unknown and would prove strange and fascinating. The final impressions of each lecture must be of the positive beauties of life and of definite directions as to fine conduct.

There is nothing strikingly new in the positions of this article. In 1882, *Princeton Review*, article on the "Moral and Religious Training of Children," Dr. G. Stanley Hall said:

During the first four or five years of school life the point of prime importance in ethico-religious training is the education of conscience. A system of carefully arranged talks, with copious illustrations from history and literature, about such topics as fair play, slang, cronies, dress, teasing, getting mad, prompting in class, white lies, affectation, cleanliness, order, honor, taste, self-respect, treatment of animals, reading, vacation pursuits, etc., can be brought quite within the range of boy and girl interest.

And Dr. Charles De Garmo, in annual report of the American Academy of Political and Social Science, 1892, discussing " Ethical Training in the Public Schools," said :

We must impart to the child those ethical ideals that form the content of the highest morality. Besides ethical content in dramatic literature we have in the bustling daily life about us a perpetual illustration of ethical and unethical principles reduced to concrete practice. The thoughtful teacher needs to induce the pupils to look about them,

It is the effort of this article to provide an effective method of accomplishing what many great educators have recognized as desirable. If visual instruction in ethics is successful and finally incorporated in our public schools, the children, their parents, and the nation are gainers to no slight degree. The importance of the matter to those whom the public schools and the churches are designed to serve will justify investigation and experiment on the part of superintendents and pastors. Correspondence and coöperation in practical experiments with this method are invited. Reprints of this article will be offered as a bulletin of the Educational Church Board, 29 South Pine avenue, Albany, N. Y. E. M. FAIRCHILD,

Lecturer for E. C. B.

SIX BOYS AND A CART

TRADES UNIONS AND PUBLIC DUTY.

The habitual use of "the people" as a phrase practically equivalent to
the "working classes" is a constant admission of the fact that the proletariat
is not, properly speaking, a "class" at all, but the body of society itself.
                                                        —*Auguste Com*

In this paper I have assumed that the general organization
of trades unions and their ultimate purposes are understood, and
also that we recognize that the public has a duty toward the
weak and defenseless members of the community. With these
assumptions granted, two propositions are really amazing: first,
that we have turned over to those men who work with their
hands the fulfillment of certain obligations which we must
acknowledge belong to all of us, such as protecting little children from premature labor, and obtaining shorter hours for the
overworked; and, second, that while the trades unions, more
than any other body, have secured orderly legislation for the
defense of the feeblest, they are persistently misunderstood and
harshly criticised by many people who are themselves working
for the same ends.

The first proposition may be illustrated by various instances
in which measures introduced by trades unions have first been
opposed by the public, and later have been considered praiseworthy and valuable, when the public as a whole has undertaken
to establish and enforce them.

For years trades unions have endeavored to secure laws
regulating the occupations in which children may be allowed to
work, the hours of labor permitted in those occupations, and
the minimum age below which children may not be employed.
Workingmen have accepted women into their trades unions, as
an inevitable development of industrial conditions, but they
resent the entrance of children into their trades, not only because
children bring down wages, for women do that as well, but because
children are injured by premature labor. The regulation of child

labor is one of the few points in which society as a whole has made common cause with the voluntary efforts of trades unions, but the movement was initiated and is still largely carried forward by them. It is quite possible to understand the reasons for this.

We may imagine a row of people seated in a moving street car, into which darts a boy of eight, calling out the details of the last murder in the hope of selling an evening newspaper. A comfortable-looking man buys a paper from him, with no sense of moral shock; he may even be a trifle complacent that he has helped along the little fellow who is making his way in the world. The philanthropic lady sitting next to him may perhaps reflect that it is a pity that such a bright boy is not in school. She may make up her mind in a moment of compunction to redouble her efforts for various newsboys' missions and homes, that this poor child may have better teaching and perhaps a chance of manual training. She probably is convinced that he alone, by his unaided efforts, is supporting a widowed mother, and her heart is moved to do all she can for him. Let us imagine that next to her sits a workingman trained in trades-union methods. He will probably view with indignation the spectacle of a heedless child jumping on moving cars at the risk of his limbs, shouting out facts and reports that should be unknown to him for many years, and he may wonder for the hundredth time why it is that society allows this utter waste of its immature members. He knows that the boy's natural development is arrested, and that the abnormal activity of his body and mind uses up the force which should go into growth. He is forced to these conclusions because he has seen many a man enter the factory at eighteen and twenty so worn out by premature work that he is laid on the shelf within ten or fifteen years. He knows very well that he can do nothing in the way of ameliorating the lot of this particular boy; that his only possible chance is to agitate for proper child-labor laws in order to regulate, and, if possible, prohibit, street vending by children, so that the child of the poorest may have his school time secured to him, and may have at least his short chance for growth.

These three people sitting in the street car are all honest and upright, and recognize a certain duty toward the forlorn children of the community. The self-made man is encouraging one boy's own efforts. The philanthropic lady is helping on a few boys. The workingman alone is obliged to include all the boys of his class. Workingmen, in their feebleness in all but numbers, have been forced to the state to secure protection for themselves and for their children. They cannot all rise out of their class, as the occasionally successful man has done ; some of them must be left to do the work in the factories and mines, and they have no money to spend in ameliorating philanthropy.

In order to secure help from the state they have been obliged to agitate, and to make a moral appeal to the community as a whole — that most successful appeal which has ever distinguished great popular movements, but which we seem to distrust, and do not ordinarily use so often as the appeals to self-interest, national tradition, or class prejudice. Almost all the labor legislation which has been secured in this country to protect the workman against the harshest conditions of industry has been secured through the efforts of trades unions, the training in which naturally leads men to appeal to the state, and to use those tools which democracy affords.

Child-labor laws once enacted and enforced are a matter of pride to the entire community, and they even come to be regarded as a register of the community's humanity and enlightenment.

To consider the second proposition: For many years I have been impressed with the noble purposes of trades unions, and the desirability of the ends which they seek ; and at the same time I have been amazed at the harshness with which their failures are judged by the public, and the undue stress which is laid upon the violence and disorder which sometimes accompany their efforts.

How far is this violence and the consequent condemnation of the public the result of ignoble purposes on the part of the trades unions, and how far is it the result of the partial effort and failure which we thrust upon them, when the trades unions alone are obliged to do what the community as a whole should undertake ? Scenes of disorder and violence are enacted because trades unions are not equipped to accomplish what they are undertaking. The state alone could accomplish it without disorder. The public shirks its duty, and then holds a grievance toward the men who undertake the performance of that duty. It blames the union men for the disaster which arises from the fact that the movement is a partial one.

The public is forced to one of two alternatives: that the state should not attempt to ameliorate the lot of workingmen by regulating hours, etc.—and this in spite of the recent decision of the United States Supreme Court in sustaining the eight-hour law—or that the trades unions, unassisted, are doing that for which we are all responsible, and which we all ought to undertake.

What, then, is this labor movement, which, when it incorporates its doctrine into legal measures, becomes orderly and smooth-working, and, when it undertakes to enforce them, itself becomes violent and difficult ?

We are prone to interpret the significance of any living institution, not by its creed and its declaration of principles, which we seldom read, but by its actual manifestations when it attempts to make over the truth thus stated into direct expressions of free living. We judge it by its blundering efforts to apply its principles to actual conditions ; by the oft-time failure of its representatives, when the individual finds himself too weak to become the organ of corporate action. To judge an organization fairly by these blundering manifestations requires care, and cannot be done easily.

The very existence of failure and blunder may only confuse us as to the moral significance we are striving to apprehend. If we may use a historic instance, we shall doubtless find that two bodies of men developed the doctrine of the Christian church. On one side were the scholars, the bishops, and dignitaries who met in ecumenical councils and determined creeds and definitions. On the other side were the great body of Christians who had to do with the world, who were grappling with the conditions in German forests and on the plains of Spain and Lombardy, and from these the outside peoples made up their minds what they had a right to expect from Christians. These outside people doubtless often misunderstood, not only the spiritual significance as expounded by the councils, but even the stunted beliefs which filled the cloudy minds of the worshipers. The Moslems who drove them from Spain believe, to this day, that the Christians cannibalistically ate little children at their baptismal ceremonies and became drunk with wine at the holy altar. These false ideas had much to do with the zeal and animosity with which the Mohammedans drove them beyond the Pyrenees. The Moslems retained the field, conquerors who had totally misunderstood the principles and faith of those whom they had conquered. They supposed that they had driven forth monsters, and they swept and garnished the country, and established a national life upon narrower precepts than those which had prevailed before.

It is easy to misjudge from the outside act. The man who reads the newspapers, and has no other acquaintance with labor organizations than the record of their outside and often unofficial acts, is almost sure to be confused in regard to their ultimate objects. It is also difficult for the victorious side to see fairly. There is no doubt that the employer, the man who represents vested interests, often routs and defeats labor organizations, drives them from the field with an honest misunderstanding of what they are trying to do, and of the principles which they represent. He is flushed with triumph and imagines a victory which he has never achieved.

We may consider half a dozen measures which trades unions have urged, and concerning which the community has often been stirred by indignation, and find that, when the public undertakes to enforce identical, or similar, measures, they are regarded with great complacency. The disapproval may be merely the result of the fact that the trades unions alone are doing that which belongs to the entire public.

The following six measures may be thus considered : *first*, the harsh treatment of a non-union laborer during a strike ; *second*, the dictatorship of the walking delegate ; *third*, the use of the boycott ; *fourth*, the insistence upon shorter hours of labor ; *fifth*, the limitation of apprentices ; *sixth*, the sympathetic strike. It is quite possible to compare all of these to national measures of which we approve and concerning which we are a part, but which the community as a whole undertakes to enforce. Reasoning by analogy is always dangerous, and its conclusions may well be questioned, but to find that we can parallel these six efforts of trades unions with six others undertaken by the government is certainly suggestive.

1. We hear from time to time of a strike in which men are prevented from taking the places of the strikers, and in the ensuing struggle are beaten and injured. We call the whole affair brutal and unjustifiable, and our sympathies are aroused for the men whom the strikers drive away from the chance to work. We make no sincere effort to find out what principle it is that justifies the strikers to themselves in their action. It is hardly possible that large bodies of men, all over the country, should repeat this course of action, over and over again, without an underlying motive which seems right to them, even if they are mistaken. An attempt to take a scholarly and fair view of life is bound to find out what this motive is. To condemn without a hearing, to correct without an understanding, has always been the mark of the narrow and uneducated person. It is not difficult to see the significance of a fine action ; the test of our insight comes in interpreting aright an action such as this.

Let us put ourselves in the position of the striking men who have fallen upon workmen who have taken their places. The strikers have for years belonged to an organization devoted to securing better wages and a higher standard of living, not only for themselves, but for all the men in that trade. To this end they have steadily contributed from their wages. They have given their time to the study of trade conditions, and enthusiastic and unceasing service to bettering those conditions in the only way that seems to them possible. They have thus worked, not only for themselves and their children, but for all their class. Every gain they have made, every advance they have secured, has been shared with the very men who now, when these gains are at stake, range themselves on the other side. They honestly believe, whether they are right or wrong, that their position is exactly the same which a nation, in time of war, takes toward a traitor who has deserted his country's camp for that of the enemy. It is possible that the deserter from the army has become convinced that his country's cause is not a just one; or that his personal interests are best served on the other side, or that he earns food for his wife and children, but his course is never justified on these grounds. The country which has nourished and sustained him has a claim upon his services in this time of war. When he is punished, society justifies it, even when we may not agree with the principles for which his country is at that moment fighting.

These, of course, are the ethics of warfare, and only on this ground can be defended; but do we realize that the workman considers the entire industrial struggle one of war, and that all the animosity on the part of the community but intensifies this position, and prolongs these ethics? We regard the treatment accorded to the deserter with much less horror than the same treatment when it is accorded to the "scab," largely because in one instance we as citizens are participants, and in the other we allow ourselves to stand aside.

2. We hear contemptuous references to the walking delegate and agitator, without stopping to ask ourselves why the workingman is not entitled to his advocate, paid to represent his legal and industrial rights, quite as much as the manager of the corporation is entitled to his lawyer. We ignorantly allow ourselves to believe that a walking delegate may declare a strike at his own pleasure, without taking the pains to discover that the organization of a trades union is so democratic that no one man, even in exceptional crises, can set aside the constitution of his union. Indeed, the walking delegate is almost the only professional man whose fees are set by those employing him. He is paid the standard wage received in his trade, and no more, and holds office subject to the vote of his union, which may fail to reëlect him at any annual meeting. In case of his failure of reëlection, his chances for obtaining work at his trade are much lessened by the fact that he has held this office. At any moment in his

career he is far from possessing that plentitude of power with which the popular mind has clothed him.

In spite of all these facts, the community continues to dogmatize concerning the dictatorial action of the walking delegate, whose every executive act has been authorized by his constituency. An ignorant person might easily consider a peace commissioner sent by the United States to Paris as a raging dictator. That is quite possible if one looks at his outside acts alone, but we are accustomed to consider a minister plenipotentiary in relation to government, and do not misunderstand his power, but we are slower to realize that it is only as a commissioner that the business agent of the union orders strikes and arranges terms of settlement.

3. We condemn the boycott, and say that the trades unions are bigoted in their allegiance to each other, and harsh to those outside their membership. Within a few years circles of women in several great cities have formed themselves into a "consumers' league," because they have become uncomfortable concerning the conditions under which clothing is manufactured and sold. The members of these little circles, because of a stirring of conscience in regard to social wrongs, exert themselves to buy goods only from houses which conform to a certain required standard of sanitation, wages, and hours of work. They are willing to submit to a certain inconvenience and to a possible loss of opportunity for "bargains." They naturally regard themselves as an advance guard, and if given to self-congratulation would perhaps claim that they were recognizing a social duty which the community as a whole ignores.

The members of these consumers' leagues are beginning to hold conventions to discuss the propriety of a label which shall mean that those houses to which it is given provide seats for their saleswomen, summer vacations, and so on. All this is a valuable effort in the right direction, but it has already been initiated and sustained for many years by trades unions. So early as 1885, in New York a blue label was put upon cigars made by union men, and loyal trade-unionists were supposed to smoke no others. The label claimed to guarantee not only the payment of union wages, but fair conditions of manufacture. Many a workingman has spent his Saturday evening going from one store to another, until he found a hat with the trade-union label in its lining. He might, possibly, have bought cheaper and better-looking hats elsewhere, and it would have been easy to urge the smallness of the purchase as an excuse from the search. In short, the advanced woman is only now reaching the point held by the trade-unionist for years. The consumers' league carefully avoids the boycott, as does, indeed, the trade-unionist when he purchases only labeled goods. He is again using the method in his organization that the nation has long used when it prohibits by high tariff the importation of certain goods in order that home products may be purchased, which have been manufactured under better conditions. Who cannot recall the political speech urging high tariff for the protection of the American workingmen, in their wages and standard of living? It is singularly like the argument used by the workingman when he urges the boycott, or the more peaceful method of purchasing labeled goods made by union workmen who have been paid union wages. Here, again, as in the case of industrial warfare, I do not wish to commit myself to the ethics involved, but merely to point the analogy, and call attention to the fact that the public is apt to consider the government righteous and the trades unions unjustifiable.

4. For years trades unions in every country have steadily bent their efforts toward securing a shorter working day. In many unions these persistent efforts have been crowned with success, but many others are still making the attempt to secure the eight-hour day, and have before them a long and troublous undertaking. Here, again, trades unions are trying to do for themselves what the government should secure for all its citizens; has, in fact, secured in many instances. Almost all the large cities of the United States employ men upon municipal works for only eight hours a day, and the federal government has established eight hours as the normal working day in several departments. In England eight hours is the established working day for work undertaken by the national government as well as by the muni-

cipal governments. Parliament has also passed acts regulating the number of hours a man may work in the manufacture of white lead and other deleterious materials. The factory inspectors of Germany have recently recommended to the government that imperial laws should regulate the hours of work in manufacture, according to the danger involved in the manufacturing process; that the legal hours of work in the manufacture of India rubber, for instance, be limited to an hour and a half per day. The German government is seriously considering these propositions, but we may easily imagine the derision with which an American manufacturer would greet such a proposal if it were advanced by a trade union. A law passed in Illinois in 1893 regulating the working hours of women who were employed in manufacture to eight hours a day, or forty-eight hours a week, was successfully resisted by the manufacturers, and declared unconstitutional by the Illinois supreme court. The argument urged by the manufacturers against its enforcement was that the Illinois employers could not sustain the competition of their rivals in other states, who were not restricted by the same law. The difficulty of limiting the hours of labor in some states and leaving them unlimited in others shows most clearly the magnitude of the undertaking assumed by the trades unions, and the unfairness of leaving the task to them.

5. The limitation of the number of apprentices is a position which the skilled trades-unionists have long held, but which is gradually being given up as indefensible. Still there have been reasons in the minds of trades-unionists, ethical concepts which did once induce them to undertake this line of action; just as governments may give up certain ethical standards which they formerly acted upon with a good conscience. The limitation of number of apprentices was instituted in those trades which required a long apprenticeship before a man became a journeyman or a master workman. The man who had submitted to this long course of training, from one to eight years, during which time he had earned but little, held that he had a right to secure to himself reasonable expectation that this trade would be valuable to him after it was once acquired; he

demanded a guarantee that he should not be obliged to throw away all those years of training, simply because too many men were allowed to enter the trade and reduce its wages.

All this was nearly analogous to the plea of the inventor when he applies to the government to protect his invention, which has cost him years of work and study, from the unlimited competition of others; and possibly even more analogous to the position of the author who wishes to be secured by a copyright. Only the federal government can undertake to perform either of these functions. The disorder again arises from the fact that the trades unions undertake to do for themselves what they are not authorized by society to do, rather than from the purpose and end to be attained. If all the living inventors formed a voluntary organization, and declined to allow more than a limited number of new inventors to enter it, we should doubtless have scenes of violence. It required a discussion of many years by the most learned men in the nation to discover the ethical basis of the author's copyright.

6. We see a great sympathetic strike ramifying throughout the entire unions of a trade and its allied trades; we suddenly hear of men all over the country leaving their work, places which they may have held for years, which they know that it may be difficult, and perhaps impossible, again to secure. They certainly do this under some dictate of conscience, and under some ethical concept that stands to them as a duty. Later many of them see their wives and children suffer, and yet they hold out, for the sake of securing better wages for workmen whom they have never seen, for men who are living in another part of the country, and who are often of another race and religion. We see this manifestation, and read about it, and do not make a really intelligent effort to discover its ethical significance. We say the men are foolish and doomed to fail; we allow our minds to become confused between the motives of the strike, and the riots and militia which often become associated with it. We are lost in its manifestation, and do not even comprehend that at such a time a great accumulation of moral force has overmastered hundreds of our fellow-citizens. They are, for

the time being, in the grasp of a great social passion, which is making for the emancipation of the wage-earner, as, in another time, a great social passion insisted upon the emancipation of the slave. We study other great movements toward human freedom, and fail to comprehend that the consciences of our contemporaries are aroused to a participation in the same great struggle.

We condemn in trades unions what we praise when undertaken by the state, when it enters into a prolonged civil war to rid itself of slavery, or finds itself involved in international complications and expensive warfare for the sake of securing political freedom for the Cubans. If the United States undertook the war with Spain for the reasons alleged, the government has certainly taken part in a great sympathetic strike. Concerning the action of the state, we have all been educated by years of discussion and a sense of participation and responsibility. Concerning the action of the trades unions, we allow ourselves to remain singularly ignorant, and insist that they shall bear forward a great movement toward social amelioration, not only without our sympathetic understanding, but with the added burden of public disapproval.

After all, the state, the nation, as Mazzini pointed out, represents no more than a mass of principles in which the universality of its citizens were agreed at the time of its foundation. But we would not have the state remain motionless and chained to the degree of civilization attained at the moment the state was founded. We would have a rational development of the truths and principles which gave vitality to the state at first. If the' objects of trades unions could find quiet and orderly expression in legislative enactment, and if their measures could be submitted to the examination and judgment of the whole without a sense of division or of warfare, we should have the ideal development of the democratic state.

Probably the labor organizations come nearer to expressing moral striving in political action than any other portion of the community, for their political efforts in most instances have been stimulated by a desire to secure some degree of improvement in the material condition of working people. As a whole they still expect legal enactment to satisfy the desire, not only for social order, but for social righteousness, and they are only slowly losing their habit of turning to the law for moral support. They are still endeavoring to secure each advance in ethics by a step taken in politics, and this endeavor is the one safeguard of democracy.

The well-to-do portions of the community are prone to think of politics as something off by itself. They may conscientiously recognize a political duty as part of good citizenship, but political effort is not the natural expression of their moral striving. A contempt for law is almost certain to follow, when we lose our habit of turning toward it for moral support. There is little doubt that appeals through corporation attorneys are often made to legislative bodies solely with the view of protecting vested interests and property rights. In their preoccupation there is no time to consider morals or the rights of the community as a whole. This non-moral attitude, as well as the immoral one of open corruption of legislators, does much toward destroying the foundations of democratic government.

The body of trades-unionists in America are becoming discouraged from the fact that moral appeal and open agitation do not have fair play, because the "interests of capital" are not confined to these, but have methods of securing legislation which are perforce denied to the workingmen. Such scenes as were enacted in the Illinois house and senate in the winter of 1897 do much toward loosening faith in legislatures and turning into cynics men who before believed in legislation. The confidence of workingmen in the courts has been shaken by the fact that the judges have so often been trained as corporation attorneys, and it is a common assertion which may often be heard in workingmen's meetings that the militia and United States troops are almost invariably used to protect the interests of the employer in times of strike. How deep-seated this conviction has become, and how rapidly it has grown, may be illustrated by a little history from the International Cigarmakers' Union, one of the most peaceful and highly organized trades unions in America. This union, which dates from 1864, sent its first president into the Civil War, where he was killed in battle. His portrait is often found in the local head-quarters of the union; his history and character are familiar to many of the members of the organization, and his name has become surrounded by a genuine hero-worship. Yet this same union has now a clause in its constitution providing that no benefits can be paid to any member whose illness results from "the performance of military service," on the ground that his service would only be required to put down his brother-work-man when striking for his rights. So thoroughly has a large body of intelligent workingmen become convinced that the country's troops are on the side of capital, and instances may easily be adduced showing a like distrust of the courts and legis-latures.

Any sense of division and suspicion is fatal in a democratic form of government, for although each side may seem to secure most for itself, when consulting only its own interests, the final test must be the good of the community as a whole.

One might almost generalize that the trades-union movement, as such, secures its lower objects best where there is a well-defined class feeling among the proletarians of its country, but that it accomplishes its highest objects in proportion as it is able to break into all classes and seize upon legislative enactment. A man who is born into his father's trade, and who has no hope of ever entering into another, as under the caste system of India or the guilds of Germany, is naturally most easily appealed to by the interests within his trade life. A workingman in America who may become a carpenter only as a stepping-stone toward becoming a contractor and capitalist, as any ambitious scholar may teach a country school until he shall be fitted for a college professorship, does not respond so easily to measures intended to benefit the carpenter's trade as he does to measures intended to benefit society as a whole; and it is quite as important that the appeal should be made to him in his capacity of citizen as that it should be large enough to include men outside his class.

That all its citizens may be responsible is, then, perhaps

the final reason why it should be the mission of the state to regulate the conditions of industry. The only danger in the movement, as at present conducted, lies in the fact that it is a partial movement, and antagonizes those whom it does not include. It may certainly be regarded as the duty of the whole to readjust the social machinery in such a way that the issue shall be a higher type of character, and that there shall be a moral continuity to society answering to its industrial development. This is the attempt of factory legislation. It is concerned in the maintenance of a certain standard of life, and would exercise such social control over the conditions of industry as to prevent the lowering of that standard. After all, society as society is interested in this, and there is no more obligation upon workingmen to maintain a standard of living than there is upon the rest of us. It is well, sometimes, to remind ourselves that, after all, the mass of mankind work with their hands.

Is it too much to hope that in time other citizens, as well as trade-unionists, may be educated to ask themselves: " Does our industrial machinery, or does it not, make for the greatest amount and the highest quality of character ? " And that when it is answered, as it must be at the present moment, that the state does not concern itself with the character of the producer, but only with the commercial aspects of the product, is it again too optimistic to predict that those other citizens will feel a certain sense of shame and recognize the fact that the trades unions have undertaken a duty which the public has ignored ?

JANE ADDAMS.

HULL-HOUSE.

CONCERNING A FORM OF DEGENERACY.

II.

THE EDUCATION AND CARE OF THE FEEBLE-MINDED.

THE history of the education of the feeble-minded begins with the present century.[1] The early recorded cases were in connection with schools for deaf-mutes, the first being a single case in Paris, France, in 1800. Later several cases are reported in Hartford, Conn., about 1818, and in Paris from 1828 to 1833. The true method of education for this class of defectives had not been found, and the early attempts were not successful enough to justify continuance.

In 1837 the apostle to the idiot appeared in the person of Dr. Edouard Seguin, who began a work in Paris which continued until he came to America eleven years later, and opened the first school for idiots in New York. In 1842 a school for cretins was established in Switzerland, and one for idiots in Berlin. The first school in England began in 1846. It was private, but was soon followed by fine public institutions.

Dr. Seguin's efforts met with such remarkable success that his method was plainly indicated as the correct one. His *Treatise on Idiocy*, published in 1846, continues to be the text-book of the profession. The book was specially attractive to advanced educators and to alienists. The physiological method of education which Dr. Seguin taught has had a profound effect, not only on the methods of training defectives, but on the science of education in general.

Public attention to the needs of the idiot began in New York and Massachusetts in 1845, in which year superintendents of hospitals for insane in both states made the necessity of some action in the matter a part of their public reports. The next

[1] See "The History of the Treatment of the Feeble-minded," by WALTER C. FERNALD, M.D., in proceedings of the Twentieth National Conference of Charities and Correction, Chicago, 1893.

year, 1846, the legislatures of both these states began consideration of the question.   In 1848 the General Court of Massachusetts
made its first appropriation for an experimental school in connection with the Institution for the Blind.   This was begun in
October, 1848.   A few months earlier in the same year, and
almost simultaneously with Dr. Seguin's school in New York, the
first private school for the feeble-minded in America was opened
at Barre, Mass.

Agitation of the question was kept up in New York until, in
1851, an appropriation was made by the legislature, and in
October of that year an experimental school near Albany com-
menced a work for the state of New York which has resulted
in the present splendid training school at Syracuse, and the
three custodial asylums for adult idiots and imbeciles in other
parts of the state.

In Pennsylvania a private school at Germantown, organized
in 1852 by Mr. J. B. Richards, who was the first teacher of the
Boston school, developed the next year into an incorporated
institution, supported partly by private subscriptions and partly
by public funds.   Removed, two years later, to a site near Medea,
Pa,. the school has grown into the present beautiful institution
village of Elwyn, with more than a thousand inhabitants, including those of all grades of idiocy and imbecility.

The institution in Ohio was established in 1857, and the
state, which is famous for its liberality to its benevolent institutions, has not been niggardly to the feeble-minded.

Schools were established in Connecticut in 1858; Kentucky,
1860; Illinois, 1865.   Other states soon followed the example
of their more progressive sisters, and there are at present in the
United States twenty-four institutions supported wholly or in
greater part by public funds, and about nine private institutions
of a similar kind supported by tuition payments.[1]

In four institutions which were organized for the custodial
care of adult idiots, and in, perhaps, three of the more recent of

[1] For recent statistics see "Care of the Feeble-minded," by F. M. POWELL, M.D.,
in the proceedings of the Twenty-fourth National Conference of Charities and Cor
rection, Toronto, 1897.

the general state institutions, permanent or asylum care has been the main purpose from their inception. In these the education of the feeble-minded has been understood to mean education for life in the institution. All the other institutions were established in the hope of training the feeble-minded, as most deaf-mutes and many of the blind may be trained, so as to fit them for self-directing activity in the common walks of life.

The early teachers of the feeble-minded jealously guarded their schools from the danger of becoming asylums. Admission was restricted to those classed as improvables, which term meant such as it was thought could be graduated from the school with a mental equipment equal to or not much below that of the average citizen. Epileptics and the so-called custodial cases were refused admission. The school for the feeble-minded was held to be "a link in the chain of common schools — the last, indeed, but still a necessary link in order to embrace all the children of the state." "The institution, being intended for a school, should not be converted into a hospital for incurables."[1] "The training of the feeble-minded does not belong to therapeutics. It is an educational work, governed by psychology and physiology, the former reached through and founded on the latter."

Notwithstanding such strong statements as those quoted above, the fact that the early superintendents were nearly all physicians gave undue emphasis to the medical side of the work, and helped to confuse that easily muddled thing, the public mind, which, in this country at least, associates with the word "doctor" the work of healing, not of educating. Even to the present day, many persons whose positions and general knowledge ought to make them qualified to pronounce a trustworthy opinion, imagine that the possession of a diploma of medicine is a prerequisite to the proper executive and educational management of a training school for the feeble-minded, while they would not dream of requiring such a qualification, in addition to educational and executive ability, from the superintendent of a school for the deaf or blind.

[1] Dr. Howe, Massachusetts, in early reports of the school.

The early institutions began in a small and tentative way, and with much public criticism and suspicion. Their promoters hoped to win favor by success, which should be demonstrated by graduating their pupils fit for the activities and responsibilities of citizenship. For many years it was not assumed that, in any cases, the institution care should be permanent. Inmates were not (and still in most states are not) *committed* to the institution, but were *admitted* under certain rules as to age, residence, etc., much as they are to the common schools. It was long the belief of the managers (as it is today contended by the proprietors of some small private institutions) that, to achieve good results, the number in any one school should be very small. An inevitable and striking result of this theory was a ratio of cost so high that only remarkable results in the improvement of the pupils could justify its being defrayed from public funds.[1]

As the years went by, pupils, admitted as children, reached the age limit of the institutions, and were discharged from their watchful and kindly care. Among these, instances became known of imbeciles who, having been under training for years and having greatly improved, were returned to their old wretched surroundings, where they speedily lapsed to their former degraded condition, made all the worse for them by the contrast with their cleanly and orderly life in the institution. Others of a higher grade, discharged as capable of self-support, missing the gentle but firm control to which they had been accustomed, showed traits of character that had seemed eradicated, wandered off and became criminals, tramps, or drunkards. Others settled down to ordinary life, but seized the first opportunity to marry. Some of these became paupers, their children inheriting their defective traits. In every institution there began to be an accumulation of inmates at or past the legal age limit, who yet were so manifestly unfit for self-control that the managers felt it a wrong both to them and to the community to dismiss them.

[1] The ratio of expense is still excessive in many institutions. This fact, next to public ignorance and indifference, is the greatest obstacle in the way of that complete provision by the state for all the feeble-minded which is the necessary first step toward diminishing their number.

Such facts as the above, the apparent constant increase of the defective classes, and the attention so largely given to social problems by educated people, have radically changed the theories of the leaders in the care of the defectives. Slowly but surely the conviction has become general, especially among the trustees and officers of institutions, that admission as a pupil of the training school should be but the first step to permanent care ; that, with a few exceptions, so few that they may be disregarded in establishing a policy, all the pupils of the school, from the lowest to the highest grade, ought to be permanently retained in the safe, kindly, maternal care of the state. The above conviction is now held by all who have expressed themselves publicly within the last few years in this country, excepting a few persons whose pecuniary interests seem in conflict with such a theory. It has been acted upon by the legislatures of many states, whose laws have been changed by removing from the institution code the age limit of retention, and in some cases of acceptance. In at least one western state the doors of the institution have been opened so wide as to admit an imbecile mother with a large family of idiotic children. Other states have provided separate custodial asylums, especially for adult females. While it is generally accepted that the imbeciles of all classes should be segregated, the special importance of not only admitting, but of committing and retaining in permanent care, all idiotic women of child-bearing age is appreciated by every intelligent person as soon as the proposition is made in his hearing. In the annual reports of institutions this principle is often mentioned as the improvement in law and practice that is now most necessary. A belief in the necessity of permanent care for all this defective class is professed by the superintendent of every state school for the feeble-minded in the United States today.

It is a startling fact, and one that needs explanation, that the present special public provision, in the United States, for the feeble-minded is only sufficient for about 10 per cent. of the whole number. This is in marked contrast with the provision for the insane, which in most states is rapidly approaching adequacy for all, both acute and chronic cases, and in the whole country is probably within 25 per cent. of being adequate. And yet, if the facts set forth in the former paper are actual, the idiotic present a more serious menace to the commonwealth than do the insane. The cause of this anomalous condition is not hard to find. The average citizen is afraid of the insane. A few among them are so dangerous that the whole class is feared. People knowing an insane man to be at large in the streets would dread personal violence. The dangers from the idiotic are less obvious. The evils that they cause are chiefly economic evils. True, there are some thieves, fire-bugs, rapists, and murderers among them, but these are the small minority. So the average citizen looks upon the feeble-minded with contempt or indifference, and is careless whether they are cared for by the state, at a high standard of care and cost, and with almost perfect protection to themselves and the community; or by the town or county, at a low standard of care and cost, and with little or no protection; or whether they have no care and no protection, and therefore cause no public cost which is apparent at the first glance. The average citizen only sees things that are very prominent, and only dreads consequences that are immediate. The man of large means, whose annual tax bill is a heavy one, looks with much questioning upon public expenditures for measures of prevention. He feels the cost at once; the advantages, to be gained in a few years or, perhaps, in the next generation, he does not appreciate. The members of our legislatures are mostly ordinary citizens, upon whom receiving the majority of the votes cast in their district has conferred no genius for statesmanship; they must be chiefly reached through their feelings. They are willing to relieve the distress and suffering of the poor, neglected idiot, when it is made clear to them; but few of them entertain the statesmanlike view of averting dreadful, remote consequences, by action involving immediate and, perhaps, unpopular appropriations.

In other words, let us say, the public conscience is not yet awake to the claims of the feeble-minded. The dangers they threaten are not known, their distress is not understood or felt by citizens at large. It is part of the purpose of this essay to help awaken a public interest that is so sorely needed.

It has been intimated above that the early hopes of the first promoters of the training of the feeble-minded were not realized. It has not been found practicable to discharge large numbers of the educated imbeciles to care for themselves and direct their own course of life. But it by no means follows that it is not possible to train large numbers of them so that they may earn their own livelihood. It is necessary here carefully to discriminate between self-support and self-direction. The fact is that, given the right training, followed by favorable opportunity under wise and kindly guardianship, large numbers of the feeble-minded may be rendered entirely self-supporting. Another large proportion may be taught to do some work. Only a small minority is incapable of any useful labor.

The proportion of the feeble-minded who may be made to earn their own living, under control, is variously estimated. The superintendents of at least two of the large training schools, both men of practical common sense, place the estimate as high as 50 per cent. of the whole number admitted. It is instructive to notice that estimates of this kind tend to become larger, especially as made by the managers of institutions which have a large acreage of farming and fruit-growing lands.

In considering such estimates as the foregoing, we must remember that an able-bodied laborer, with steady employment, can provide for himself, a wife, and several children ; the product of his labor should be equal, at least, to the support of three adults. If, therefore, an imbecile laborer perform one-third of a man's full work, or just as much more than that as will pay for the extra supervision required because he is feeble-minded, he is entitled to be classed as self-supporting.

It is possible that the time may come when there will be so large a number of adult imbeciles, gathered into the institutions, who have received all the advantages that the training school can give them, that it may be difficult to provide them with profitable labor. But that time appears to be far distant in most places of the kind. Few or none of them are yet doing all that they believe to be possible of the work of the intitution, by the labor of their trained inmates. Farming, gardening, laundering, cooking, the domestic work of the house, the manufacture of clothing and shoes, carpentering, road-making and grading, lumbering, quarrying, brick-making, building, the care of the lower-grade and the younger inmates—these and kindred occupations absorb, as yet, all the available trained labor, and, in fact, there is not nearly as much of such labor available, in most institutions as now organized, as could be profitably utilized.

The education given in the schools is usually of a very practical nature. For many of the pupils it begins with the simplest habits of life; it goes on through the kindergarten, the primary school, and manual training of all kinds, until it ends in the workshop, the farm, or the domestic department. Since the general acceptance of the theory of permanent care the training school has taken on a new meaning. Just as the normal child is, or should be, trained in the common school for the duties and responsibilities of citizenship in the great world, so the abnormal or feeble-minded child is trained in this special school for the duties and the pleasures of life in the little world to which he belongs. The training involves the whole being to a much greater extent than does that of the common school. The physical, mental, and emotional natures must be cultured simultaneously. The base of the educative work is physiological. The education is by doing. Dormant capacities must be wakened. Weak faculties of all kinds, not only the mental faculties of memory, judgment, and will, but sight, smell and taste, hearing and feeling, must be developed and strengthened by systematic exercise.

The institution inmates are usually divided into educables, industrials, and custodials. The two former differ chiefly in age, and the classes grade into each other as the child grows into the stature of the man. The custodial class includes all who are not susceptible of the higher training. These again are divided from the others by grades that are sometimes almost imperceptible. Being natural divisions, they have no hard and fast lines between them, and inmates classed as custodials often improve until they are fit for transfer to a higher grade.

What has been said above plainly indicates the future of the work of caring for the feeble-minded, at least for many years to come. The institutions can take these undesirable and hurtful citizens and make of them, or of many of them, self-supporting members of a separate community, and at the same time avert the dangers of reproduction and increase. In this work the training school is the nucleus; around it, and subsidiary to it, the whole institution should cluster.

It is true that the cost of these schools has been great in the past, and when we consider the number to be provided for—at least ten times as many as are now in the institutions—the total cost would appear prohibitory of this plan.[1] But just as soon as it is demonstrated that a large proportion is self-supporting; that the improvables can be cared for, with decency and humanity, at a very moderate ratio of expense, by utilizing the labor of the trained higher grades; that only the younger ones, who belong to the educable grade, and a few of the lowest grade, violent and dangerous idiots, require a high per capita cost—it seems probable that the means to gather in and care for the whole class will be forthcoming. When that period arrives, the number of idiots and imbeciles in the nation will cease to increase, and, if other classes of degenerates can also be brought under control, the number may diminish very rapidly. It is too much to claim that idiocy and imbecility can be stamped out, even by the most vigorous segregation of the present generation. Sporadic cases continually occur from apparently inscrutable causes. Accident and disease will have their victims; but these are few, indeed, compared with those whose mental weakness is the result of evil heredity.

The method suggested for carrying out the theory above stated is known as the colony plan. Although not in full operation anywhere, yet beginnings have been made which have abundantly justified the expectations of their promoters. The plan in its fullness is somewhat as follows:

[1] These considerations of cost have reference rather to present public opinion and possibility of immediate action than to the real interests of the commonwealth. It would be far cheaper to segregate the entire class of the imbeciles and idiots, were the cost five times greater than that of the most expensive training school, than to neglect them as we are now doing.

With the training school as a nucleus, the chief executive department, the hospital for the sick, the industrial building, and the departments for the very lowest custodial grades being closely connected with it, let there be attached to each institution one or more large tracts of land, in, or near, a state of nature, and containing as many of the natural opportunities of wood, stone, brick-clay, coal, etc., as possible. Especially let there be a soil that is, or may be made, highly fertile. Upon such a tract let there be erected a few simple, substantial buildings, sufficient, to begin with, for a colony of two hundred trained male imbeciles, graduates of the training school, who have been taught to labor. At least one-fourth of these should be of the brightest class of high-grade imbeciles ; the remainder may be of the middle and lower grades, of whom a fair proportion may be of the custodial class. Let all the male employés be mechanics or practical farmers. Let the colonists build houses, to receive from time to time all the graduates of the training school whose labor can be spared from the mother house, and all the middle-grade non-improvable idiots who may be received by the institution after the colony begins. Let the houses be plain, substantial buildings, constructed of the available material on the land, whether that be stone quarried, or bricks made, on the premises. Along with the erection of the cottages should go the building of halls, gymnasiums, and chapels, as may be desired. Let the method of life be simple and plain, as near the normal life of the farmer and the gardener as possible. Let the lands be cleared, ditched, and brought to the highest possible state of cultivation ; the grounds around the buildings adorned with shrubbery, lawns, and flower gardens. Let the whole colony become a "village of the simple," its inhabitants an industrious, celibate community, having all that other villagers enjoy, except the excitement of popular elections, and the pleasures, trials, and anxieties of married life.

Such a colony, having the mother house as its market for the produce of its farm, dairy, orchards, and gardens, could, when completed, be made to pay much of its maintenance cost by its products. The cost of its buildings and equipment, on the plan outlined, would be surprisingly low. The colony should be allowed to increase in number until the land is fully occupied. It should include groups of able-bodied, but feeble-minded, laborers, and of lower- and middle-grade idiots, in caring for whom the higher-grade imbeciles can be usefully employed.

On a tract of one thousand acres there would be room for, perhaps, three hundred adult trained imbeciles and twice as many more of the lower grades. For many years, if the land were wisely selected, all the available labor could be usefully employed in clearing, building, fencing, draining, farming, gardening, and stock raising. If ever the crops became more than the colony and the mother house could use, a good market for the finished products—butter, cheese, canned goods, dried fruits, jams, jellies and pickles, dressed meat, bacon, hams and lard, and, possibly, clothing, shoes, brushes, etc.—could be found in the state institutions for the insane, the blind, and the deaf without invading the ordinary avenues of commerce.

In such a colony the trained imbeciles, both the higher- and the middle-grade, would be entirely self-supporting, and the burden of the others, with adequate care and protection, would be much less in first cost than that of their present neglect, or semi-neglect; while the results in economy of every kind in the future would give the state an enormous return on its investment.

No completed colony of the kind exists today, but in Ohio, Massachusetts, Illinois, Wisconsin, Indiana, California, and other states beginnings have been made, and some of them have advanced far enough to demonstrate that the plan is entirely practicable. If this plan should be found successful as applied to the feeble-minded, why should it not, with modifications, apply to other classes of degenerates?

ALEXANDER JOHNSON.

FT. WAYNE, IND.

SEX IN PRIMITIVE INDUSTRY.

LABOR represents the expenditure of energy in securing food, and in making the food process constant and sure; and we may well expect to find that the somatological differences shown to exist between man and woman[1] will be found reflected in the labors of primitive society. An examination of the ethnological facts shows that among the primitive races men are engaged in activities requiring strength, violence, speed, and the craft and foresight which follow from the contacts and strains of their more motor life; and the slow, unspasmodic, routine, stationary occupations are the part of woman. Animal life is itself motor, elusive, and violent, and both by disposition and of necessity man's attention and activities are devoted first of all to the animal process. It is the most stimulating and dangerous portion of his environment, and affords the most immediate and concrete reward. And contrasted with this violent and intermittent activity of man we find with equal uniformity that the attention of woman is directed principally to the vegetable environment. Man's attention to hunting and fighting, and woman's attention to agriculture and attendant stationary industries, is so generally a practice of primitive society that we may well infer that the habit is based on a physiological difference. An explanation of exceptions to the rule, and the departure from it in the later life of the race, we shall have to seek in changes in the social habits of the race.

The labors of woman in early society were exacting, incessant, varied, and hard. The remark of Letourneau that woman was first a beast of burden, then a domestic animal, then a slave, then a servant, and last of all a minor, is a fair conclusion from the reports of early missionaries and travelers. And, indeed, there is not doubt that if a catalogue of primitive forms of labor

[1] See " On a Difference in the Metabolism of the Sexes," AMERICAN JOURNAL OF SOCIOLOGY, July, 1897.

were made, woman would be found doing five things while man does one. An Australian of the Kurnai tribe once said to Fison: "A man hunts, spears fish, fights, and sits about;"[1] and this is a very good general statement of the male activities of primitive society the world over, if we add one other activity—the manufacture of weapons. On the other hand, Bonwick's statement of the labors of Tasmanian women is a typical one:

"In addition to the necessary duty of looking after the children, they had to provide all the food for the household, excepting that derived from the chase of the kangaroo. They climbed up trees for the opossum, delved in the ground with their sticks for yams, native bread, and nutritive roots, groped about the rocks for shellfish, dived beneath the sea surface for oysters, and fished for the finny tribe. In addition to this, they carried, on their frequent tramps, the household stuff in native baskets of their own manufacture. Their affectionate partners would even pile upon their burdens sundry spears and waddies not required for present service, and would command their help to rear the breakwind, and to raise the fire. They acted, moreover, as cooks to the establishment, and were occasionally regaled, at the termination of a feast, with the leavings of their gorged masters."[2] Among the Andamanese, while the men go into the jungle to hunt pigs, the women fetch drinking water and firewood, catch shellfish, make fishing nets and baskets, spin thread, and cook the food ready for the return of the men.[3] In New Caledonia "girls work in the plantations, boys learn to fight."[4] In Africa the case is similar. Among the Bushmen (to take only one example from this continent) the woman "weaves the frail mats and rushes under which her family finds a little shelter from the wind and from the heat of the sun," constructs a fireplace of three round stones, fashions and bakes a few earthenware pots. When her household labors are done, she gathers roots, locusts, etc., from the fields. On the march she frequently carries a child, a mat, an earthen pot, some ostrich eggshells, and "a few ragged

[1] FISON AND HOWETT, *Kamilaroi and Kurnai*, p. 206.
[2] BONWICK, *Daily Life of the Tasmanians*, p. 55.
[3] OWEN, *Transactions of the Ethnological Society*, New Series, Vol. II, p. 36.
[4] TURNER, *Nineteen Years in Polynesia*, p. 424.

skins bundled on her head or shoulder," while the man carries only his spear, bow, and quiver.x The conditions among the American Indians were practically the same. Cotton Mather said of the Indians of Massachusetts : "The men are most abominably slothful, making their poor squaws or wives to plant, and dress, and barn, and beat their corn, and build their wigwams for them ;"² and Jones, referring to the women of southern tribes, says : "Doomed to perpetual drudgery and to that subordinate position to which woman is always consigned where civilization and religion are not, she was little less than a beast of burden, busy with cooking, the manufacture of pottery, mats, baskets, moccasins, etc., a tiller of the ground, a nurse for her own children, and at all times a servant to the commands and passions of the stronger sex."³

Primitive woman was certainly very busy, but I have seen no reason to believe that she considered her condition unfortunate. Our great-grandmothers were also very busy, but they were apparently not discontented. There was no reason why woman should not labor in primitive society. The forces which withdrew her from labor were expressions of later social conditions. Speaking largely, these considerations were the desire of men to preserve the beauty of women, and their desire to withdraw them from association with other men. It is the connection in thought and fact between idle and beautiful women and wealth, indeed, which has frequently led to the keeping of a superfluous number of such women as a sign of wealth. The exemption of women from labor, in short, implied an economic surplus which early society did not possess. The lower classes of modern society do not possess it either, and there the women are still "drudges," if we want to use that word about a situation which is normal, in view of the economic condition of the men and women concerned It was necessary that primitive society, in the absence of elaborate machinery for doing things, in unstable and precari-

---

¹ ARBOUSSET AND DAUMAS, *Voyage of Exploration*, p. 249 ; MOFFAT, *Missionary Labors and Scenes in Southern Africa*, p. 53.

² SCHOOLCRAFT, *History, Condition, and Prospects of the Indian Tribes of the United States*, Part I, p. 285.

³ JONES, *Antiquities of the Southern Indians*, p. 70.

ous food conditions, and without resources accumulated from preceding generations, should utilize *all* its forces. The struggle for existence, in its harshest sense, was but little mitigated, and no group could have spared at all the industry of women. The best returns from activity will of course follow when each individual is doing something he is specially well fitted to do, and natural selection seems to have seen to it that primitive society should so divide the labor as best to utilize social energy by assigning to men the tasks requiring violent exertion, and to women those requiring constant attention.

But was not primitive man very lazy, and did he not do fewer things than he reasonably could have done ? If we mean by lazy an aversion to certain types of action, primitive man was doubtless lazy ; but if we mean an aversion to all kinds of exertion, he certainly was not lazy. He was so thoroughly aroused by certain kinds of stimuli, and so exhausted by the expenditure of energy in reacting to these stimuli, that periods of recuperation, or "sitting about," were necessary. Heckenwelder's remarks on the labor of men and women among the Indians of Pennsylvania are very instructive, although they relate to tribes which had come under white influences to some extent : "The work of the women is not hard or difficult. They are both able and willing to do it, and always perform it with cheerfulness. Mothers teach their daughters those duties which common sense would otherwise point out to them when grown up. Within doors their labor is very trifling ; there is seldom more than one pot or kettle to attend to. There is no scrubbing of the house, and but little to wash, and that not often. Their principal occupations are to cut and fetch in the firewood, till the ground, sow and reap the grain, and pound the corn in mortars for their pottage, and to make bread which they bake in the ashes. When going on a journey or to hunting camps with their husbands, if they have no horses, they carry a pack on their backs which often appears heavier than it really is ; it generally consists of a blanket, a dressed deer skin for moccasins, a few articles of kitchen furniture, as a kettle, bowl, or dish, with spoons, and some bread, corn, salt, etc., for their nourishment. I have never known an Indian woman complain of the hardship of carrying this burden, which serves for their own comfort and support as well as of their husbands. The tilling of the ground at home, getting of firewood, and pounding of corn in mortars, is frequently done by female parties, much in the manner of those husking, quilting, and other *frolics* (as they are called) in some parts of the United States . . . . [When accompanying her husband on the hunt the woman] takes pains to dry as much meat as she can, that none may be lost ; she carefully puts the tallow up, assists in drying the skins, gathers as much wild hemp as possible for the purpose of making strings, carrying bands, bags, and other necessary articles; collects roots for dyeing; in short, does everything in her power to leave no care to her husband but the important one of providing meat fo. the family. After all, the fatigue of the women is by no means to be compared to that of the men. Their hard and difficult employments are periodical and of short duration, while their husbands' labors are constant and severe in the extreme. Were a man do take upon himself a part of his wife's duty, in addition to his own, he must necessarily sink under the load, and of course his family must suffer with him. On his exertions as a hunter their existence depends ; in order to be able to follow that rough employment with success, he must keep his limbs as supple as he can, he must avoid hard labor as much as possible, that his joints may not become stiffened, and that he may preserve the necessary strength and agility of body to enable him to pursue the chase, and bear the unavoidable hardships attendant on it ; for the fatigues of hunting wear out the body and constitution far more than manual labor. Neither creeks nor rivers, whether shallow or deep, frozen or free from ice, must be an obstacle to the hunter when in pursuit of a wounded deer, bear, or other animal, as is often the case. Nor has he then leisure to think on the state of his body, and to consider whether his blood is not too much heated to plunge without danger into the cold stream, since the game he is in pursuit of is running off from him with full speed. Many dangerous accidents often befall him both as a hunter and a varrior (for he is both), and are seldom unattended with painful consequences, such as rheumatism or consumption of the lungs, for which the sweat-house, on which they so much depend, and to which they often resort for relief, especially after a fatiguing hunt or warlike excursion, is not always a sure preservative or effectual remedy."ₓ

The male and female come together by sexual attraction, and the chances of life are increased through association which permits each to do that class of things which by reason of its somatic habit it can do most effectively. Man's exploits were, however, of a more striking and sensational character, appealed to the emotions more, and secured the attention and the admiration of the public more, than the "drudgery" of the woman. The unusual esteem given by society to the destructive activities of the male can be very well understood in connection with a reference to the emotions. The emotions of anger, fear, and joy, to take only these examples, represent a physiological change in the organism in the presence of dangerous situations. Anger is a physiological preparation to resist, to crush a dangerous object; fear is an organic expression of inadequacy to avert the danger; and joy, in one of its aspects, is an organic revulsion answering to the recognition of the fact that the danger is safely passed. The same type of situation incessantly recurring in the life of the race, and constantly met by the same organic changes, has resulted in a fixed relation of certain types of situation to certain types of emotion. The forms of activity recognized first of all in the consciousness of the race as virtuous are simply those which successfully avert danger and secure safety. Courage, intrepidity, endurance, skill, sagacity, an indomitable spirit, and a willingness to die in fight, are virtues of the first importance, vitally indispensable to the society in conflict with man and beast, and they are virtues of which man is by his organic constitution, by the very fact of his capacity for the rapid destruction of energy, particularly capable. Man's exploits, therefore, first of all had social attention. Even if primitive life had been as hard as

---

¹ John Heckenwelder, *History, Manners and Customs of the Indian Nations,* pp. 155-8.

Hobbes would have it, "solitary, poor, nasty, brutish, and short," mere negative, habitual hardness, and miserableness of condition, did not get the attention of primitive society particularly. Their life was hard, as we look at it, not as they looked at it. They could not compare themselves with the future, and comparisons with the past were doubtless in their favor. The occupations of women were not of an emotional type, and, apart from sexual life, they got their excitements as spectators and approvers of the motor activities of the men. The Hebrew girls who went out with harps and timbrils to meet a victorious army, and sang that Saul had slain his thousands, but David his ten thousands, represent the relation between mighty deeds and social attention and approval. Thus the attention which the organism gives to situations of danger, through violent physiological readjustments fitted to meet the situation, has a parallel in the attention given by society to social means of meeting situations dangerous to the common life and welfare. We have a very plain continuance of the primitive appreciation of the virtues of violence in the worship of military men nowadays, and it is significant, also, that the appreciation of the fighting quality still reaches its most animated expression in women— the sex constitutionally most in need of social protection. It can hardly be denied, therefore, that man both enjoyed this exciting kind of performance more than the labors which women were connected with, and that the women justified him (if we assume that they passed any judgment on his conduct at all) in refraining from doing many things which he could have done perfectly well without constitutional hurt.

The abundance of the labors of primitive woman seems to be accounted for further by the fact that a stationary life is the condition of a greater variety of industrial expressions than a life inclined to motor expressions. It is notorious that a wandering life is not favorable to the development of industries. Industries, in their very nature, handle and shape stationary stuffs, for the most part, and woman developed the constructive or industrial activities as a simple consequence of her more stationary condition of life. The formation of habit is largely a matter of attention, and the attention of woman being limited by her bodily habit and the presence of children to objects lying closer at hand, her energies found expression in connection with these objects. First of all, the house was identified with woman. The home was, in its simplest terms, the place where the wandering male rejoined the female. It was a cave, or a hollow tree, or a frail structure. It was sought or made with reference to safety and comfort, particularly with reference to the comfort of the young. Recognizing the greater interest of the woman in the child, it is evident that shelter was a more important consideration to her than to the man. The house is, indeed, a very fit accompaniment of the stationary habit of woman, and usually we find the most primitive tribes recognizing her greater interest in it. Even when the houses are built by men, they are generally owned by the women. Man as a solitary animal might, of course, make himself a shelter, but he had a particular interest in being about the shelter of woman, and it was under her shelter, after all, that children were born and that society accumulated numbers. This resulted, as I have shown, in the maternal system[1] or the recognition of woman as the head of the household, and implicitly the recognition of woman as the owner of the house. So, when the Indian squaw carries the wigwam on the march, she is carrying her private property and one of her own particular appurtenances. Contrary to the witty phrase of Letourneau which I have quoted above, man is rather, in the sense in which I am now speaking, the domesticated animal. He has been inducted into the family. The estufas of the Pueblo Indians and the men's club houses in Africa represent the failure of men to assimilate completely in a society which was essentially female in its genius, and the club still stands for a difference in interest between the male and the female.

From the house, or shelter, as a base woman got such connections with food as she might. For it is an error to suppose that she was in the most primitive times entirely dependent on man for food. She appears to have been quite as active in developing food surroundings in her way as man was in his.

[1] AMERICAN JOURNAL OF SOCIOLOGY, March, 1898.

The plant world gave her the best returns for the effort which she could make. She beat out the seeds of plants, digged out the roots and tubers which the monkeys and pigs were seen to grub for most eagerly,[1] strained the poisonous juices from the cassava and made bread of the residue, and it was under her attention that a southern grass was developed into what we know as Indian corn. Looking back on this process we call it the domestication of plants, and we are likely to regard it as a more conscious process than it really was. It was the result of her conversion to her own uses of the most available portion of her environment. In view of her physiological habit, the animal environment was, for the most part, out of the question, and her attention was of necessity directed to the plant side. While less remunerative in its beginnings than the animal side of the process, it was, perhaps, at all times less precarious and uncertain, and we find in consequence that the economic dependence of man on woman is as evident as her dependence on him. A dinner of herbs is a humbler resort than a roast of antelope, but there was less doubt that it would be forthcoming, and primitive man was often, when in hard luck, dependent on the activities of his wife, or the females of the group. The domestication of animals appears similarly to be the following up by man of his connections with animal life, when this life began to be less abundant. It is probable that the practice originated in the habit of taking the young of animals home as pets, and there is apparently a point of difference between the attention of the men and the women given to animals once taken into the household. The men were interested in these animals as reviving in memory the emotional situations of hunting life, and also in the clever and imitable accuracy of coördination and superhuman development of sense-perceptions, while there was always in the attitude of woman toward these animals a touch of maternal feeling, such as is still expended on the "harmless, necessary cat." And, in a small way, woman also contributed to the domestication of animals by giving them suck, partly from a physiological pleasure in having

[1] RATZEL, *History of Mankind*, Vol. II, p. 289.

the breasts drawn, and partly as an economic investment. In Tahiti and New Britain, for example, the women suckle the pigs, and the old women feed them.[1] Aside from this, the connections which primitive woman has with animal life is very slight. Worms and insects, shellfish, and even fish she may capture, but after this her relation to animal life is in caring for the flesh and skins turned over to her by the man.

It was a very general early practice that, when man had killed his game and brought it home, he was not concerned in the further handling of it. He did not, indeed, in all cases bring it home, but sent his wife after it. The Indïans killed buffalo only as fast as the squaws could cut them up and care for the meat, and the men of the Eskimos would not draw the seal from the water after spearing it. Exhausted by extraordinary efforts, the man may well have left the dressing of the animal upon occasion to his wife, and, exhausted or not, he soon fell into the habit of doing so. It thus turns out that all labors relating to the preparation of food, and to the utilizations of the side products of food stuffs, are apt to be found in the hands of the women. Vessels are necessary in cooking, both to carry and hold water, and to store the surplus of food, both vegetable and animal, and the woman, feeling the need of these in connection with what she has set about doing, weaves baskets and makes pottery. Fetching wood, grinding corn, tanning the hides, and in the main the preparation of clothing, follow rather necessarily from her relation to the raw products. Spinning and weaving and dyeing are related closely to the vegetable world to begin with, and it is to be expected that they would be developed by the women. But man is very deeply interested in clothing on the ornamental side, and the farther back we go in society, the more this holds, and sometimes, particularly in Africa, since the domestication of oxen there, the men prepare the leather and do the sewing, even for the women. There is, indeed, nothing in the nature of sewing to make it a woman's occupation. It involves a relation of the hand to the eye— similar to that which the man is always practicing and using

[1] RATZEL, *ibid.*, Vol. I, p. 253.

i. e., reaching a given point, perhaps with mechanical aids, through the mediation of these two organs. It is a motor matter, therefore, and one of the first industries undertaken by men. There are many exceptions to the general statement that early manufacture (weapons excepted) was in the hands of women, but the exceptions may be regarded as variations due to the fixation of habit through single and peculiar incidents, or they are the beginning of the later period when man begins to practice woman's activities.

The primitive division of labor among the sexes was not in any sense an arrangement dictated by the men, but a habit into which both men and women fell, to begin with, through their difference of organization—a socially useful habit whose rightness no one questioned and whose origin no one thought of looking into. There is, moreover, a tendency in habits to become more fixed than is inherently necessary. The man who does any woman's work is held in contempt not only by men, but by women. "As to the Indian women, tney are far from complaining of their lot. On the contrary, they would despise their husbands could they stoop to any menial office, and would think it conveyed an imputation upon their own conduct. It is the worst insult one virago can cast upon another in a moment of altercation. 'Infamous woman,' will she cry, 'I have seen your husband carrying wood into the lodge to make the fire. Where was his squaw, that he should be obliged to make a woman of himself!'"[1] That men are similarly prejudiced against women's taking up male occupations we know from modern industrial history, without looking to ethnological evidence. Habit was, however, in another regard favorable to woman, since what she was constantly associated with and expended her activities upon was looked upon as hers. Through her identification with the industrial process she became, in fact, a property owner. This result did not spring from the maternal system; but both this and the maternal system were the results of her bodily habit, and the social habits flowing from this. "When the woman as cultivator was almost the sole creator of property in land, she

[1] Irving, "Astoria," *Works*, Vol. VIII, p. 134.

held in respect of this also a position of advantage. In the transactions of North American tribes with the colonial governments many deeds of assignment bear female signatures, which doubtless must also be referred to inheritance through the mother."x Among the Spokanes "all household goods are considered as the wife's property."² The stores of roots and berries laid up by the Salish women for a time of scarcity "are looked upon as belonging to them personally, and their husbands will not touch them without having previously obtained their permission."³ Among the Menomini a woman in good circumstances would possess as many as from 1,200 to 1,500 birch-bark vessels, and all of these would be in use during the season of sugar-making.⁴ In the New Mexican pueblo, "what comes from outside the house, as soon as it is inside is put under the immediate control of the woman. My host at Cochiti, New Mexico, could not sell an ear of corn or a string of *chile* without the consent of his thirteen-year-old daughter, Ignacia, who kept house for her widowed father. In Cholula district (and probably all over Mexico) the man has acquired more power, and the storehouse is no longer controlled by the wife. But the kitchen remains her domain; and its aboriginal designation, *tezcalli* (place, or house, of her who grinds), is still perfectly justified."⁵ "A plurality of wives is required by a good hunter, since in the labors of the chase women are of great service to their husbands. An Indian with one wife cannot amass property, as she is constantly occupied in household labors, and has not time for preparing skins for trading."⁶ The outcome of this closer attention of the woman to the industrial life is well seen among the ancient Hebrews: "A virtuous woman . . . . seeketh wool and flax, and worketh willingly with her hands. She is

[1] RATZEL, *ibid.*, Vol. II, p. 130.

[2] BANCROFT, *Native Races of the Pacific States*, Vol. I, p. 277.

[3] FEATHERMAN, *Social History of Mankind: Aoneo-Maranonians*, p. 364.

[4] W. J. HOFFMAN, "The Menomini Indians," *Fourteenth Report of the Bureau of American Ethnology*, p. 288.

[5] A. F. BANDELIER, "Report of an Archæological Tour in Mexico," *Papers of the Archæological Institute of America*, Vol. II, p. 138.

[6] DORSEY, "Siouxan Sociology," *Fifteenth Report of the Bureau of American Ethnology*, p. 225.

like the merchant ships: she bringeth her food from afar. She riseth also while it is yet night, and giveth meat to her household, and their task to her maidens. She considereth a field and buyeth it; with the fruit of her hands she planteth a vineyard. . . . . She perceiveth that her merchandise is profitable: her lamp goeth not out by night. She layeth her hands to the distaff, and her hands hold the spindle. She spreadeth out her hand to the poor; yea, she reacheth forth her hands to the needy. She is not afraid of the snow for her household; for all her household are clothed with scarlet. She maketh for herself carpets of tapestry; her clothing is fine linen and purple. Her husband is known in the gates, when he sitteth among the elders of the land. She maketh linen garments and selleth them; and delivereth girdles unto the merchant."[x]

There must come a time in the history of every group when wild game becomes scarce. This time is put off by successive migrations to wilder regions; but the rapid increase of population makes any continent inadequate to the supply of food through the chase indefinitely. Morgan estimates that the state of New York, with its 47,000 square miles, never contained at any one time more than 25,000 Indians.[2] Sooner or later the man must either fall back on the process represented by the woman, taking up and developing her industries, or he must change his attitude toward animal life. In fact, he generally does both. He enters into a sort of alliance with animal life, or with certain of its forms, feeding them, and tending them, and breeding them; and he applies his katabolic energies to the pursuits of woman, organizing and advancing them. Whether the animal or the plant life receives in the end more attention is a matter turning on environment and other circumstances. When the destructive male propensities have exhausted or diminished the food stores on the animal side, and man is forced to fall back on the constructive female process, we find that he brings greater and better organizing force to bear on the industries. Male enterprises have demanded concerted action. In order to surround a buffalo herd, or to make a successful assault, or even to row a large boat, organization and leadership are necessary. To attack under

[1] Prov. 31: 10–24.　　　　　　[2] MORGAN, *Ancient Society*, p. 111.

leaders, give signal cries, station sentinels, punish offenders, is, indeed, a part of the discipline even of animal groups. The organizing capacity developed by the male in human society in connection with violent ways of life is transferred to labor. The preparation of land for agriculture was undertaken by the men on a large scale. The jungle was cleared, water courses were diverted, and highways prepared for the transportation of the products of labor. But more than this, perhaps, man brought with him to the industrial occupations all the skill in fashioning force-appliances acquired through his intense, constant, and long-continued attention to the devising and manufacture of weapons. "Unaccommodated man" is a very feeble thing in nature, but he made various and ingenious cutting, jabbing, and bruising appliances. His life was a life of strains, both giving and taking, and under the stress he developed offensive and defensive weapons. But there is no radical difference, simply a difference in object and intensity of stimulus, between handling and making weapons and handling and making tools. So, when man was obliged to turn his attention to the agriculture and industries practiced by primitive woman, he brought all his technological skill and a part of his technological interest to bear on the new problems. Women had been able to thrust a stick into the earth and drop the seed and await a meager harvest. When man turned his attention to this matter, his ingenuity eventually worked out a remarkable combination of the animal, mineral, and vegetable kingdoms: with the iron plow, drawn by the ox, he upturned the face of the earth, and produced food stuffs in excess of immediate demands, thus creating the condition of culture. The destructive habits of the katabolic nature were thus converted under the stress of diminishing nutrition to the constructive habits represented primarily by the anabolic nature, and the inventive faculty developed through attention to destructive mechanical aids was now applied equally to the invention of constructive mechanical aids.

Primitive life was rich in emotional incidents and interests, and types of pleasure and pain became fixed in connection with activities vitally good and vitally bad. When society is compelled to substitute more and more the routine, dead, mechanical, recurrent, and re-recurrent performances which we call labor for the uncertain, perilous, and vicissitudinous relations and activities of primitive life, the ends become less fascinating, the stimuli less intense, the reactions less pleasurable and painful. The organism functions without interest, and the performance is irksome. This principle applies to both sexes, for the females participate socially in the activities of the males; and exhibit, indeed, more vivid emotion than the men. In social and sexual rivalry, also, the women participate without hindrance. The root of the irksomeness of labor is, therefore, the fact that the race was used to habitually more exciting performances, and got its type of pleasurable reactions fixed by these. Play reproduces in principle and often in very faithful detail the situations and the movements which meant life or death to primitive man: and we are not so completely weaned from the old ways but that in intervals of the routine of a work-a-day world we turn for pleasure and recreation to hide and seek, football, golf, or cards, seeking reinstatement of the situations with which emotional reactions have been historically associated, or an imitation of such situations. Or we resort to the theater, where others imitate and reproduce emotional situations in imagination instead of action. Mr. Veblen has traced the irksomeness of labor[1] to the recognition by the laboring classes that the non-laboring classes do not work, the distastefulness lying in the comparison. No doubt the comparison may make the labor more disagreeable, but there is an aversion to routine performances in children before they recognize that labor has any caste meaning. If you take children from their animal play and propose some form of work as a new game, they will enter it eagerly, but very shortly they are pitiably bored, unless an element of rivalry is skillfully introduced. Different forms of labor retain in varying degrees the conflict element, and where doubt, rivalry, risk, judgment, reward, or disaster is involved, the labor is still as fascinating as a fight or a game.   W. I. THOMAS.

THE UNIVERSITY OF CHICAGO.

[1] AMERICAN JOURNAL OF SOCIOLOGY, September, 1898.

SOME INEQUALITIES IN LAND TAXATION.

THE RESULTS OF AN INVESTIGATION BY THE MINNESOTA BUREAU OF LABOR.

THE Minnesota Bureau of Labor has just completed a study of land taxation in that state. The statistical force of the bureau has been engaged upon this investigation the greater portion of the time for the past three years. The data employed are the sales of realty by warranty deeds and by mortgage foreclosures. A comparison is made between the amounts stated in these instruments of sales as the consideration for transfer and the equalized assessed value of the lands sold. The report includes the tabulation of 26,881 sales of realty by warranty deed in the eighty-one counties of the state in 1895, and 8,216 in fifteen counties in 1896. The amount of these sales, as stated in the deeds, was, for 1895, $50,380,017, and for 1896, $16,791,715. There were also tabulated in the same investigation 5,518 sales of realty by mortgage foreclosures in the eighty-one counties of the state in 1895, and 2,534 foreclosures in three counties in 1896. The amount of these sheriff certificates, in 1895, was $10,951,-080, and for 1896, $7,731,476. The investigation thus tabulated 43,049 distinct sales of realty of a recorded consideration of transfer of $85,854,288.

The instruments tabulated constituted, however, only about two-thirds of those of record which were examined with a view of tabulation. The other third were rejected because, for one reason or other, they showed on their face that the stated consideration was probably not the true value of the land sold. The investigation, therefore, involved a consideration of over 60,000 recorded sales of realty.

The bureau investigated the subject of the reliability of such data as a measure of the relative taxation of different classes of property and of the different sections of the state. It points out in its forthcoming report the limitations that surround the use of such data, and calls attention to a large number of interesting phases of the tax question, as well as to the purely statistical elements presented in the tables.   A discussion of all, or even a few, of these subjects is impossible in an article such as the present. Attention is called to only two of the leading facts brought out by this investigation.   They are the greater relative taxation of the acre or farm property owned by the poor, and the reason for the same.   The report includes the tabulation of many thousands of sales of city or town lots.   Those sales are tabulated by themselves, as are the sales of acre or farm property.   No detailed reference will here be given to the relative taxation of city lots.   Only the sales of acres by warranty deed and by mortgage foreclosures will here be passed in review.   At the close of the article are to be found brief summary tables of all the facts to which reference is here made.   The percentages of those tables are the only portions thereof which are given in tabular form in connection with the reading matter here presented.

Minnesota has three quite important cities within its borders. They are Minneapolis, St. Paul, and Duluth.   The counties containing them are Hennepin, Ramsey, and St. Louis.   In the report these counties are referred to as the city counties.   The balance of the state, including seventy-eight counties, is spoken of as the rural counties.   As the character of the real property sold in the last few years and the condition of sale under which land is transferred are, and have been, quite different in the city and rural sections, the data of land values and of actual and relative assessment for the two sections have been tabulated apart.   There are here given only the data for acre property in the rural counties. Those data amply suffice to set forth the character of the assessment of farm property in the state, and the circumstances under which a faulty system of assessment has grown up in most of the western states, and the causes and cure for the same.   Attention is now called to those data.   The following is a condensed exhibit from the accompanying tables of the relative assessment of the acre or farm property in the seventy-eight rural counties of Minnesota, sold by warranty deed and mortgage foreclosures.   The exhibit presents separately the percentages for improved and unimproved acres. These percentages express the parts which the assessed value of the lands sold bears to the recorded selling value of the same. Some of the lands classed as unimproved on the book of the assessors and so tabulated here had houses and other buildings upon them, but these were so poor that they were not taken into account by the assessors in their appraisement.

Classification by amounts of sales	Improved acres		Unimproved acres	
	Warranty deeds	Mortgage foreclosures	Warranty deeds	Mortgage foreclosures
$ 500 and less	65.91	228.34	57.60	148.95
501 to $ 1,000	58.51	93.18	51.53	84.02
1,001 to 2,000	47.19	72.90	44.51	65.31
2,001 to 3,000	40.60	66.12	39.14	50.74
3,001 to 5,000	36.39	61.39	35.88	54.52
5,001 to 10,000	34.40	47.95	36.58	45.82
Over 10,000	29.66	64.91	37.82	64.04
Total,	39.40	84.29	42.37	74.65
Below average amt.	47.87	127.87	51.00	103.82
Above average amt.	35.64	65.81	38.55	59.05

The improved acres sold by warranty deeds in those seventy-eight counties, and here tabulated, numbered 655,974. The consideration for the sales stated in the deeds was $13,640,879. The average sale was approximately $2,500. There were 3,138 sales for amounts below the average and 2,020 for amounts above it. The sales by mortgage foreclosures of the same class of property conveyed title to 142,969 acres. The amount of sheriff certificates was $1,007,620. The average foreclosure was approximately $1,000. There were 572 foreclosures for amounts below this sum and 337 for amounts above it. Both series of percentages exhibit a regular gradation from the sales with the smallest amounts up to those for the largest. There is but one exception, and that is found in the group for foreclosures in amounts over $10,000. This contained only two sales, which were plainly of land that differed from the body of acres sold by foreclosures. They should, therefore, be disregarded in any consideration of relative taxation of the more, and of the less, valuable tracts of land. Disregarding them, it can be said that the percentages for sales of improved acres by warranty deeds and those for mortgage foreclosures agree in this respect. They show a much higher relative assessment for the lands sold for small amounts than for those disposed of for larger ones. The different classes, or groups, from the least valuable to the most valuable, form a more or less regular series. The tracts of land sold by warranty deeds for amounts less than $500 were assessed for 65.91 per cent. of the selling value, while those for amounts over $10,000 were assessed relatively only 45 per cent. as much, or for 29.66 per cent. The average assessment of all lands sold by warranty deeds was 39.40 per cent. of the selling price. The tracts selling for less than $500 were, therefore, forced to pay relatively 1.67 for every 75 cents paid by the owners of the land sold in amounts over $10,000, and where each should pay one dollar. The lands selling for less than the average amount of all sales were assessed at 47.87 per cent. of the selling price, while those selling for amounts above the average were assessed only 35.64 per cent. The former were assessed relatively 34 per cent. more than the latter. Here is a greater relative over-assessment of the poorer and a more unjust under-assessment of the richer owners of realty than has been disclosed by any similar tax study in the United States. Before explaining the origin of the vicious system of assessment which works this practical injustice, the reader's attention is first directed to the figures showing the relative assessment of unimproved lands, or lands having upon them no valuable buildings to attract the notice of the assessors.

Of sales by warranty deeds of unimproved acres in the rural counties there were tabulated in the report 8,200, conveying 796,591 acres, for a stated consideration of $11,377,525. The average consideration was approximately $1,500. There were 5,693 sales for sums below this average and 2,507 for amounts above it. Of corresponding sales by mortgage foreclosures there were 644, conveying 90,984 acres, with amounts of sheriff's certificates making a total of $651,857. The average for each sale was about $1,000. There were 452 sales for amounts below this average and 182 for amounts above it.

The percentages for assessment for the sales by warranty deeds of unimproved acres make a series, the highest being for the group for the smallest amounts and the lowest for the group with the amounts between $3,000 and $5,000. After this group is reached, the percentage materially rises to the group for the largest sales, those for amounts over $10,000. The figures for mortgage foreclosures show the same regularity for the groups from $500 to $3,000, but a slight irregularity in the series for amounts above $3,000. But there were only ten sales in the larger two of these groups, and the variation noticed between the two series of percentages is, under these circumstances, nothing strange. The lands conveyed by warranty deeds for amounts below the average were assessed 51 per cent. of the selling value, while those for amounts above that average were assessed 38.55 per cent. The less valuable tracts were assessed relatively 32 per cent. more than the more valuable. This quite closely agrees with the corresponding variation noted for the improved acres of 34 per cent.

Noting the series of percentages presented in the foregoing table, the economic student will want to know how far this apparent variation in relative assessment is expressive of an actual discrimination by the Minnesota assessors, and how much of it is due to sacrifice sales and sales with unreal considerations stated in the deeds of transfer. The officers of the Minnesota bureau gave much consideration to this subject. Its agents expended much time and labor in a special investigation into the same. The results of that investigation are given at length in the published report both for city lots and rural acres or farm property. For farm property the conclusion reached was that the percentages fairly represented the relative assessment of the different classes of property. Attention is here called to one fact of the many presented in proof of that belief.

It is well known that the maximum credit usually allowed on farm lands in Minnesota is from 60 to 66 per cent. of the selling value of the land mortgaged. Land thus mortgaged for the maximum of credit that may be secured upon the same should, when sold by foreclosure, show an amount of sheriff certificate approximately equal to from 60 to 66 per cent. of the true selling value of the land when disposed of by private sale. The percentages of assessment of such land should bear to that of similar lands sold by warranty deed a ratio of 100 to from 60 to 66. This would be the case, providing the lands sold by warranty deeds do not have fictitious considerations stated in the same. The following exhibit presents for the seventy-eight rural counties the percentages of all acres sold by warranty deeds, and also of those sold by foreclosures, and the percentage which the former constitute of the latter. The groups over $5,000 are here consolidated into one, since there were only five sales by foreclosures over $10,000.

Classification by amounts of sales	Percentages of assessed value to stated selling price		Percentages which the former are of the latter
	Deeds	Foreclosures	
$ 500 and less	59.04	190.78	30.95
501 to $1,000	53.65	89.39	60.02
1,001 to 2,000	45.68	70.00	65.26
2,001 to 3,000	39.92	62.08	64.30
3,001 to 5,000	36.22	58.59	61.82
Over 5,000	34.36	53.51	64.62
Total,	40.75	80.50	50.62

The percentages of the last column are obtained by dividing those of the first by those of the second. On the assumption that the lands sold by foreclosures are, by groups of sale, assessed relatively the same as the lands sold by warranty deeds, the percentages in the last column show the relative credit secured by the loans which led to the foreclosures here tabulated. The percentages in the last column, with the exception of that for sales in amounts less than $500, are such as would occur on the conditions of assessment above stated, where there was no material number of deeds tabulated with sacrifice sales, or with fictitious stated considerations, or other factors creating large apparent variations in relative assessment. For all excepting the first group the table leaves but little room for doubt that most, if not all, of the variation shown in the percentages of assessment records discriminations by the assessors against the poor man, or at least against the owner of cheap, or little improved, land.

The figures for the first group measure quite accurately the loss by mortgage foreclosures of the poor men who secure credit in small amounts and are unable to meet their obligations. Where the average man, with a fair amount of resources, obtains a credit on real estate security of from 60 to 66 per cent. of its selling value, the poorer man obtains such credit only on the average of 33.95 per cent. By inability to meet his obligation he loses the balance of his possessions, or substantially 70 per cent. of his prior savings. This sacrifice throws the loss of the poor man by inequitable assessment into the shadow and proves conclusively how much worse as a taskmaster are debts assumed under conditions that prevent their payment than is the vicious assessment of Minnesota acre realty.

The various tables of the report throw much light upon the character and origin of the discrimination of assessors, above noted, by which the poor man, or the owner of cheap land, is made to pay relatively a higher taxation than the richer land-owner, or the valuable lands. One series of tables which throws much light upon the question contains the data for forty-one rural counties, in all of which improved acres were assessed relatively considerably less than were the unimproved. The following table presents for those counties the average selling and assessed value of the acres conveyed by warranty deeds, and the percentage which the latter value was of the former.

Classification by amounts of sale	Improved acres			Unimproved acres		
	Average per acre		Percentage assessed to selling value	Average per acre		Percentage assessed to selling value
	Selling value	Assessed value		Selling value	Assessed value	
$ 500 and less	$ 6.85	$ 4.53	66.22	$ 6.75	$4.01	59.34
501 to $ 1,000	9.26	5.27	56.90	9.98	5.20	52.09
1,001 to 2,000	14.61	6.54	44.77	13.34	6.00	44.94
2,001 to 3,000	19.85	7.66	38.60	16.53	6.76	40.87
3,001 to 5,000	24.14	8.14	33.71	17.57	6.55	37.26
5,001 to 10,000	26.85	8.53	31.76	15.35	6.13	39.93
Over 10,000	48.76	10.95	22.45	10.37	4.59	44.25
Total,	19.88	7.34	36.95	12.64	5.61	44.40

A glance at the foregoing exhibit discloses this fact: the average selling price per acre of improved lands in this group of counties increased from the first subgroup up to that for amounts over $10,000. The average assessed value also increased, but not to the same extent. As a result, the percentages of assessment for improved acres decreased without a break from the sales for the smallest amounts to those for the largest.

The unimproved acres in this group of counties had a low average selling price for the tracts sold in amounts less than $500. That average increased until sales are reached with amounts for from $2,000 to $3,000. Afterward that average decreases. The percentages of relative assessment move in lines the very converse of the averages for the selling price of the land. The sales of improved and unimproved acre property agree in these particulars: they record the highest percentage of assessment for the lands worth the least per acre; that percentage decreases until the highest average selling price per acre is reached; the percentages of relative assessment make a series more or less regular and proportional to the changes in the average values per acre. The discrimination here shown is one primarily between the owners of land with a high value per acre and that with a low value, and not between the rich and the poor; but this discrimination works to the detriment of the poor and to the advantage of the rich as classes.

The beginnings of this system of unjust assessment are found in the condition of affairs that once existed in all parts of the state, and of the Northwest, but which has now been superseded in most of the older counties. In the first settlement of any agricultural county of the western prairie states the land taken up was all of nearly, if not quite, the same value per acre. It had about the same natural resources and no artificial ones. It was all without improvements, or additions made by man. Under these circumstances an honest and equitable assessment would be one that appraised all acre property at substantially the same rate per acre. This was the first assessment in all the counties of Minnesota and of the western states. But with the fuller settlement and more complete development of any section there has come a great variety in the buildings erected and in the changes and improvements in or upon the several tracts of land in any township or county. For a time no attention is paid by the assessors to these improvements. The original flat or level assessment—so much per acre—would, with few exceptions, prevail. Such a condition leads, first, to assessing the vacant or unimproved acres at a higher relative amount than the improved. It gives to the most improved land the greatest degree of tax exemption. Later, when the assessors begin to take notice of buildings and improvements, they lay less stress upon them than upon the land. As a result, a portion of the earlier injustice caused by the bad assessment still remains in most counties of Minnesota. The report of the Minnesota bureau calls special attention to the statistics of a few counties which exhibit the worst phases of this faulty method of assessment. In Cottonwood county the average selling price per acre varied from $10.25 to $35.80, while the average assessment for unimproved acres varied between $6.41 and $6.90, and that for improved from $6.99 to $7.48.

As a result of this faulty system of taxation, in the group of seventy-eight rural counties for which the figures were presented in the first exhibit, the poor owner of a small tract of improved land is assessed $1.62; the rich owner of a large tract of vacant land, 90 cents; and the rich owner of improved land only 70 cents, where all should pay one dollar. The system works to the benefit of all classes excepting the poor man. The rich resident farmer is satisfied because he receives the most benefit. He is specially satisfied because he is taxed relatively less than the owner of non-resident vacant acres. But the system of assessing vacant lands more than improved actually exempts the rich owner of such land from a part of his true burden of taxation and secures his exemption at the expense of the very poorest resident owner.

Incidental to the foregoing analysis of the facts disclosed by this investigation of land taxation in Minnesota, attention is here called to the 1898 report of the Kansas Bureau of Labor. This work, just out of press, contains the summary of an investigation similar to the one made in Minnesota. The same general principles of investigation were followed, although the Kansas report, in its tabulation, presents its figures in a way which shows even better than that of the Minnesota the principle which lies at the basis of this unjust assessment of acre property. A number of the newer counties, notably Ford, furnish illustration of almost perfectly level assessment. Improved and unimproved acres, though selling for widely differing prices, were assessed at practically the same amount per acre. The discrimination thus affected in Ford county, Kansas, between the poor owner of cheap land and the rich owner of highly improved land is greater than was found in any Minnesota county. Wyandotte county in Kansas, like the older counties in Minnesota, furnishes an illustration of a practically just assessment of land, since there are in it no wide disparity in the relative taxes paid by the cheaper and the dearer lands.

The level assessment of acre property, which has its fullest application in such counties as those of Cottonwood and Otter Tail in Minnesota, is a practical exemplification of the results that would everywhere follow the general introduction of that first step toward single tax which has been advocated by some of Henry George's disciples. It raises the present tax upon real property by an assessment primarily upon land in the state of nature, and takes but a small and incidental notice of the improvements made thereupon by man. Its practical results, as has been pointed out above, is to lay additional and seemingly unjust burdens upon the poor landowner to the benefit of the richer. This is all wrong, unless there is, incidental to this seeming injustice, some benefit gained for the poor which more than balances this loss by over-assessment.

In this connection it may be said that no one has stated the principles in accordance with which all systems of raising public revenue must finally be judged better than Mr. Henry George. He tells us very forcibly and correctly that systems of taxation should be fostered which lay the lightest relative burden upon the man struggling on a basis of slender resources to win an industrial and economic independence. Applying this principle to the situation which exists today among Minnesota farm owners, this question arises: Is this level assessment which disregards, in part or wholly, the values of buildings and improvements the best and most equitable method of levying taxes on realty owned and controlled under existing circumstances? In answering this question no one should fail to distinguish the import of the condition above set forth. The complete theories of Mr. George call for a social order quite at variance with the one which now exists. Under it land would be held and transferred under conditions very different from anything of which we have practical experience today. The question is not, then: Would a level assessment under the conditions described by Mr. George be the best one? It is: Is the level assessment—an assessment that regards land values and disregards the values of improvements—the best under existing conditions? If it is, it must lay the fewest obstacles in the way of the poor man striving to gain the ownership of a farm or home, or to create such a farm out of the wilderness. But to levy on a farm of 160 acres, with few improvements and worth in the markets of the day only $750, as heavy taxes as on a farm of the same size and selling for $3,000, as is done in numberless cases in Minnesota, is to lay, under existing social and economic conditions, unjust as well as heavy burdens upon the poor owner of poor land. It places the heaviest load of taxes upon the man starting out in the struggle for industrial progress, and relieves the man who by his accumulation has won a certain degree of financial independence. It makes it more difficult for the poor man in debt for his farm to pay for the same. The facts collected by the Minnesota Bureau of Labor, while they do not in the least throw light upon the relative benefits for the toiler, under the existing social system, and under such a system as Mr. George has pictured, do demonstrate this truth: they prove that with land ownership, under the existing social order, an assessment which considers land values, and not the value of improvements, is the worst possible method of raising public revenues. It doubles the share of tax to be paid by the poor man starting in life, and brings to him no corresponding or compensating benefit. The

AN EXHIBIT OF THE RELATIVE TAXATION OF ACRE PROPERTY IN
MINNESOTA IN 1895.

Classification by amounts of sales	Number of instruments	Number of lots	Number of acres	Consideration	Assessed value	Percentage assessed value of stated value

A. Rural Counties, Sales of Improved Acres by Warranty Deeds.

Classification by amounts of sales	Number of instruments	Number of lots	Number of acres	Consideration	Assessed value	Percentage
$ 500 and less.....	434	26	20,195	$ 156,737	$ 103,309	65.91
501 to $1,000....	789	22	63,332	627,862	367,350	58.51
1,001 to 2,000....	1,424	51	152,826	2,260,639	1,066,834	47.19
2,001 to 3,000....	962	22	119,999	2,489,849	1,010,809	40.60
3,001 to 5,000....	1,041	5	164,944	4,106,851	1,494,396	36.39
5,001 to 10,000....	457	15	107,326	3,065,451	1,054,478	34.40
Over 10,000....	51	19	27,352	933,490	276,919	29.66
Total........	5,158	160	655,974	$13,640,879	$5,374,095	39.40
2,500 and less.....	3,138	108	293,851	$4,193,327	$2,007,378	47.87
Over 2,500.....	2,020	52	362,123	9,447,552	3,366,717	35.64

B. Rural Counties, Sales of Unimproved Acres by Warranty Deeds.

Classification by amounts of sales	Number of instruments	Number of lots	Number of acres	Consideration	Assessed value	Percentage
$ 500 and less.....	2,836	54	98,093	$ 744,998	$ 429,092	57.60
501 to $1,000....	1,842	17	137,665	1,441,384	742,726	51.53
1,001 to 2,000....	1,927	7	206,203	2,945,936	1,311,305	44.51
2,001 to 3,000....	860	18	119,408	2,176,166	851,819	39.14
3,001 to 5,000....	545	365	103,956	2,090,449	749,995	35.88
5,001 to 10,000....	145	33	53,948	1,003,294	366,989	36.58
Over 10,000....	45	24	77,318	975,298	368,827	37.82
Total........	8,200	518	796,591	$11,377,525	$4,820,753	42.37
1,500 and less.....	5,693	78	334,927	$3,489,703	$1,779,842	51.00
Over 1,500.....	2,507	440	461,664	7,887,822	3,040,911	38.55

C. Rural Counties, Sales of Improved Acres by Sheriff's Certificates.

Classification by amounts of sales	Number of instruments	Number of lots	Number of acres	Consideration	Assessed value	Percentage
$ 500 and less.....	272	1	35,325	$ 77,007	$175,837	228.34
501 to $1,000....	300	3	40,345	223,027	207,821	93.18
1,001 to 2,000....	229	...	35,549	311,863	227,359	72.90
2,001 to 3,000....	60	...	13,615	145,552	96,245	66.12
3,001 to 5,000....	32	3	9,228	120,662	74,073	61.39
5,001 to 10,000....	14	59	5,547	94,838	45,472	47.95
Over 10,000....	2	...	3,360	34,671	22,506	64.91
Total........	909	66	142,969	$1,007,620	$849,313	84.29
1,000 and less.....	572	4	75,670	$300,034	$383,658	127.87
Over 1,000....	337	62	67,299	707,586	465,655	65.81

AN EXHIBIT OF THE RELATIVE TAXATION OF ACRE PROPERTY IN
MINNESOTA IN 1895—*continued.*

Classification by amounts of sales	Number of instruments	Number of lots	Number of acres	Consideration	Assessed value	Percentage assessed value of stated value

D. Rural Counties, Sales of Unimproved Acres by Sheriff's Certificates.

Classification by amounts of sales	Number of instruments	Number of lots	Number of acres	Consideration	Assessed value	Percentage assessed value of stated value
$ 500 and less.....	235	...	21,360	$ 69,256	$103,157	148.95
501 to $1,000....	217	8	27,004	157,905	132,679	84.02
1,001 to 2,000....	138	145	23,844	193,334	126,276	65.31
2,001 to 3,000....	22	...	4,631	51,902	26,337	50.74
3,001 to 5,000....	22	...	6,744	83,142	45,328	54.52
5,001 to 10,000....	7	...	3,880	48,446	22,196	45.82
Over 10,000....	3	149	3,521	47,872	30,657	64.04
Total........	644	302	90,984	$651,857	$486,630	74.65
1,000 and less.....	452	8	48,364	$227,161	$235,836	103.82
Over 1,000....	192	294	42,620	424,696	250,794	59.05

E. Forty-one Special Counties, Sales of Improved Acres by Warranty Deeds.

Classification by amounts of sales	Number of instruments	Number of lots	Number of acres	Consideration	Assessed value	Percentage assessed value of stated value
$ 500 and less.....	264	11	13,640	$ 93,385	$ 61,844	66.22
501 to $1,000....	387	...	33,301	308,517	175,532	56.90
1,001 to 2,000....	689	9	74,459	1,087,680	487,005	44.77
2,001 to 3,000....	482	19	62,258	1,235,659	476,923	38.60
3,001 to 5,000....	464	...	75,992	1,834,394	618,329	33.71
5,001 to 10,000....	161	...	39,855	1,069,970	339,787	31.76
Over 10,000....	27	14	11,200	546,089	122,604	22.45
Total........	2,474	53	310,705	$6,175,694	$2,282,024	36.95
2,500 and less.....	1,599	28	152,675	$2,089,829	$855,467	40.93
Over 2,500....	875	25	158,030	4,085,865	1,426,557	34.91

F. Forty-one Special Counties, Sales of Unimproved Acres by Warranty Deeds

Classification by amounts of sales	Number of instruments	Number of lots	Number of acres	Consideration	Assessed value	Percentage assessed value of stated value
$ 500 and less.....	1,449	8	57,586	$ 388,968	$230,833	59.34
501 to $1,000....	1,040	9	81,285	810,858	422,394	52.09
1,001 to 2,000....	1,030	7	117,372	1 566,131	703,806	44.94
2,001 to 3,000....	423	16	64,724	1 070,173	437,369	40.87
3,001 to 5,000....	254	5	55,139	968,524	360,914	37.26
5,001 to 10,000....	67	21	30,506	468,365	187,033	39.93
Over 10,000....	26	8	59,763	619,702	274,201	44.25
Total........	4,289	74	466,375	$5,892,721	$2,616,550	44.40
1,500 and less.....	3,036	24	195,154	$1,899,888	$983,970	51.79
Over 1,500....	1,253	50	271,221	3,992,833	1,632,580	40.89

selling value of realty is the only true and honest measure of its proper share of public taxation.   To assess any class of realty more than another, on any speculative theory, is to wrong someone.   To assess vacant or unimproved farm property more, relatively, than the improved is to lay specially onerous burdens on the poor, to cripple the man with limited resources, and to destroy some of the motives on the part of the poor for saving, and some of the opportunities for this saving which exists when all classes of property bear each its proportional share of public expenditure.

It is possible that in a later number of this JOURNAL attention will be called to some of the other inequalities of taxation discovered in Minnesota by the investigation of its labor bureau, and also to the lessons to be deduced therefrom.

L. G. POWERS,

ST. PAUL, MINN.   *Commissioner of Labor.*

THE BARBARIAN STATUS OF WOMEN.

It seems altogether probable that in the primitive groups of mankind, when the race first took to a systematic use of tools and so emerged upon the properly human plane of life, there was but the very slightest beginning of a system of status, with little of invidious distinction between classes and little of a corresponding division of employments. In an earlier paper, published in this JOURNAL,[1] it has been argued that the early division of labor between classes comes in as the result of an increasing efficiency of labor, due to a growing effectiveness in the use of tools. When, in the early cultural development, the use of tools and the technical command of material forces had reached a certain degree of effectiveness, the employments which occupy the primitive community would fall into two distinct groups — (a) the honorific employments, which involve a large element of prowess, and (b) the humiliating employments, which call for diligence and into which the sturdier virtues do not enter. An appreciable advance in the use of tools must precede this differentiation of employments, because (1) without effective tools (including weapons) men are not sufficiently formidable in conflict with the ferocious beasts to devote themselves so exclusively to the hunting of large game as to develop that occupation into a conventional mode of life reserved for a distinct class ; (2) without tools of some efficiency, industry is not productive enough to support a dense population, and therefore the groups into which the population gathers will not come into such a habitual hostile contact with one another as would give rise to a life of warlike prowess ; (3) until industrial methods and knowledge have made some advance, the work of getting a livelihood is too exacting to admit of the consistent exemption of any portion of the community from vulgar labor ;

[1] "The Instinct of Workmanship and the Irksomeness of Labor," September, 1898, pp. 187–201.

(4) the inefficient primitive industry yields no such disposable surplus of accumulated goods as would be worth fighting for, or would tempt an intruder, and therefore there is little provocation to warlike prowess.

With the growth of industry comes the possibility of a predatory life ; and if the groups of savages crowd one another in the struggle for subsistence, there is a provocation to hostilities, and a predatory habit of life ensues. There is a consequent growth of a predatory culture, which may for the present purpose be treated as the beginning of the barbarian culture. This predatory culture shows itself in a growth of suitable institutions. The group divides itself conventionally into a fighting and a peace-keeping class, with a corresponding division of labor. Fighting, together with other work that involves a serious element of exploit, becomes the employment of the able-bodied men ; the uneventful everyday work of the group falls to the women and the infirm.

In such a community the standards of merit and propriety rest on an invidious distinction between those who are capable fighters and those who are not. Infirmity, that is to say incapacity for exploit, is looked down upon. One of the early consequences of this deprecation of infirmity is a tabu on women and on women's employments. In the apprehension of the archaic, animistic barbarian, infirmity is infectious. The infection may work its mischievous effect both by sympathetic influence and by transfusion. Therefore it is well for the able-bodied man who is mindful of his virility to shun all undue contact and conversation with the weaker sex and to avoid all contamination with the employments that are characteristic of the sex. Even the habitual food of women should not be eaten by men, lest their force be thereby impaired. The injunction against womanly employments and foods and against intercourse with women applies with especial rigor during the season of preparation for any work of manly exploit, such as a great hunt or a warlike raid, or induction into some manly dignity or society or mystery. Illustrations of this seasonal tabu abound in the early history of all peoples that have had a warlike or barbarian past.

The women, their occupations, their food and clothing, their habitual place in the house or village, and in extreme cases even their speech, become ceremonially unclean to the men. This imputation of ceremonial uncleanness on the ground of their infirmity has lasted on in the later culture as a sense of the unworthiness or Levitical inadequacy of women ; so that even now we feel the impropriety of women taking rank with men, or representing the community in any relation that calls for dignity and ritual competency ; as for instance, in priestly or dipplomatic offices, or even in representative civil offices, and likewise, and for a like reason, in such offices of domestic and body servants as are of a seriously ceremonial character — footmen, butlers, etc.

The changes that take place in the everyday experiences of a group or horde when it passes from a peaceable to a predatory habit of life have their effect on the habits of thought prevalent in the group. As the hostile contact of one group with another becomes closer and more habitual, the predatory activity and the bellicose animus become more habitual to the members of the group. Fighting comes more and more to occupy men's everyday thoughts, and the other activities of the group fall into the background and become subsidiary to the fighting activity. In the popular apprehension the substantial core of such a group — that on which men's thoughts run when the community and the community's life is thought of — is the body of fighting men. The collective fighting capacity becomes the most serious question that occupies men's minds, and gives the point of view from which persons and conduct are rated. The scheme of life of such a group is substantially a scheme of exploit. There is much of this point of view to be found even in the common-sense views held by modern populations. The inclination to identify the community with its fighting men comes into evidence today whenever warlike interests occupy the popular attention in an appreciable degree.

The work of the predatory barbarian group is gradually specialized and differentiated under the dominance of this ideal of prowess, so as to give rise to a system of status in which the non-fighters fall into a position of subservience to the fighters. The accepted scheme of life or consensus of opinions which guides the conduct of men in such a predatory group and decides what may properly be done, of course comprises a great variety of details; but it is, after all, a single scheme — a more or less organic whole — so that the life carried on under its guidance in any case makes up a somewhat consistent and characteristic body of culture. This is necessarily the case, because of the simple fact that the individuals between whom the consensus holds are individuals. The thinking of each one is the thinking of the same individual, on whatever head and in whatever direction his thinking may run. Whatever may be the immediate point or object of his thinking, the frame of mind which governs his aim and manner of reasoning in passing on any given point of conduct is, on the whole, the habitual frame of mind which experience and tradition have enforced upon him. Individuals whose sense of what is right and good departs widely from the accepted views suffer some repression, and in case of an extreme divergence they are eliminated from the effective life of the group through ostracism. Where the fighting class is in the position of dominance and prescriptive legitimacy, the canons of conduct are shaped chiefly by the common sense of the body of fighting men. Whatever conduct and whatever code of proprieties has the authentication of this common sense is definitively right and good, for the time being, and the deliverances of this common sense are, in their turn, shaped by the habits of life of the able-bodied men. Habitual conflict acts, by selection and by habituation, to make these male members tolerant of any infliction of damage and suffering. Habituation to the sight and infliction of suffering, and to the emotions that go with fights and brawls, may even end in making the spectacle of misery a pleasing diversion to them. The result is in any case a more or less consistent attitude of plundering and coercion on the part of the fighting body, and this animus is incorporated into the scheme of life of the community. The discipline of predatory life makes for an attitude of mastery on the part of the able-bodied men in all their relations with the weaker members of the group, and especially in their relations with the women. Men who are trained in predatory ways of life and modes of thinking come by habituation to apprehend this form of the relation between the sexes as good and beautiful.

All the women in the group will share in the class repression and depreciation that belongs to them as women, but the status of women taken from hostile groups has an additional feature. Such a woman not only belongs to a subservient and low class, but she also stands in a special relation to her captor. She is a trophy of the raid, and therefore an evidence of exploit, and on this ground it is to her captor's interest to maintain a peculiarly obvious relation of mastery toward her. And since, in the early culture, it does not detract from her subservience to the life of the group, this peculiar relation of the captive to her captor will meet but slight, if any, objection from the other members of the group. At the same time, since his peculiar coercive relation to the woman serves to mark her as a trophy of his exploit, he will somewhat jealously resent any similar freedom taken by other men, or any attempt on their part to parade a similar coercive authority over her, and so usurp the laurels of his prowess, very much as a warrior would under like circumstances resent a usurpation or an abuse of the scalps or skulls which he had taken from the enemy.

After the habit of appropriating captured women has hardened into custom, and so given rise on the one hand to a form of marriage resting on coercion, and on the other hand to a concept of ownership,[1] a development of certain secondary features of the institution so inaugurated is to be looked for. In time this coercive ownership-marriage receives the sanction of the popular taste and morality. It comes to rest in men's habits of thought as the right form of marriage relation, and it comes at the same time to be gratifying to men's sense of beauty and of honor. The growing predilection for mastery and coercion, as a manly trait, together with the growing moral and æsthetic approbation of marriage on a basis of coercion and ownership,

[1] For a more detailed discussion on this point see a paper on "The Beginnings of Ownership" in this JOURNAL for November, 1898.

will affect the tastes of the men most immediately and most strongly; but since the men are the superior class, whose views determine the current views of the community, their common sense in the matter will shape the current canons of taste in its own image. The tastes of the women also, in point of morality and of propriety alike, will presently be affected in the same way. Through the precept and example of those who make the vogue, and through selective repression of those who are unable to accept it, the institution of ownership-marriage makes its way into definitive acceptance as the only beautiful and virtuous form of the relation. As the conviction of its legitimacy grows stronger in each succeeding generation, it comes to be appreciated unreflectingly as a deliverance of common sense and enlightened reason that the good and beautiful attitude of the man toward the woman is an attitude of coercion. "None but the brave deserve the fair."

As the predatory habit of life gains a more unquestioned and undivided sway, other forms of the marriage relation fall under a polite odium. The masterless, unattached woman consequently loses caste. It becomes imperative for all men who would stand well in the eyes of their fellows to attach some woman or women to themselves by the honorable bonds of seizure. In order to a decent standing in the community a man is required to enter into this virtuous and honorific relation of ownership-marriage, and a publicly acknowledged marriage relation which has not the sanction of capture becomes unworthy of able-bodied men. But as the group increases in size, the difficulty of providing wives by capture becomes very great, and it becomes necessary to find a remedy that shall save the requirements of decency and at the same time permit the marriage of women from within the group. To this end the status of women married from within the group is sought to be mended by a mimic or ceremonial capture. The ceremonial capture effects an assimilation of the free woman into the more acceptable class of women who are attached by bonds of coercion to some master, and so gives a ceremonial legitimacy and decency to the resulting marriage relation. The probable motive for adopting the free women into the honorable class of bond women in this way is not primarily a wish to improve their standing or their lot, but rather a wish to keep those good men in countenance who, for dearth of captives, are constrained to seek a substitute from among the home-bred women of the group. The inclinations of men in high standing who are possessed of marriageable daughters would run in the same direction. It would not seem right that a woman of high birth should irretrievably be outclassed by any chance-comer from outside.

According to this view, marriage by feigned capture within the tribe is a case of mimicry—"protective mimicry," to borrow a phrase from the naturalists. It is substantially a case of adoption. As is the case in all human relations where adoption is practiced, this adoption of the free women into the class of the unfree proceeds by as close an imitation as may be of the original fact for which it is a substitute. And as in other cases of adoption, the ceremonial performance is by no means looked upon as a fatuous make-believe. The barbarian has implicit faith in the efficiency of imitation and ceremonial execution as a means of compassing a desired end. The entire range of magic and religious rites is testimony to that effect. He looks upon external objects and sequences naïvely, as organic and individual things, and as expressions of a propensity working toward an end. The unsophisticated common sense of the primitive barbarian apprehends sequences and events in terms of will-power or inclination. As seen in the light of this animistic preconception, any process is substantially teleological, and the propensity imputed to it will not be thwarted of its legitimate end after the course of events in which it expresses itself has once fallen into shape or got under way. It follows logically, as a matter of course, that if once the motions leading to a desired consummation have been rehearsed in the accredited form and sequence, the same substantial result will be attained as that produced by the process imitated. This is the ground of whatever efficiency is imputed to ceremonial observances on all planes of culture, and it is especially the chief element in formal adoption and initiation. Hence, probably, the practice of mock-seizure or

mock-capture, and hence the formal profession of fealty and submission on the part of the woman in the marriage rites of peoples
among whom the household with a male head prevails. This
form of the household is almost always associated with some
survival or reminiscence of wife-capture. In all such cases,
marriage is, by derivation, a ritual of initiation into servitude.
In the words of the formula, even after it has been appreciably
softened under the latter-day decay of the sense of status, it is
the woman's place to love, honor, and obey.

According to this view, the patriarchal household, or, in other
words, the household with a male head, is an outgrowth af emulation between the members of a warlike community. It is,
therefore, in point of derivation, a predatory institution. The
ownership and control of women is a gratifying evidence of
prowess and high standing. In logical consistency, therefore,
the greater the number of women so held, the greater the
distinction which their possession confers upon their master.
Hence the prevalence of polygamy, which occurs almost universally at one stage of culture among peoples which have the male
household. There may, of course, be other reasons for polygamy, but the ideal development of polygamy which is met with
in the harems of very powerful patriarchal despots and chieftains
can scarcely be explained on other grounds. But whether it
works out in a system of polygamy or not, the male household
is in any case a detail of a system of status under which the
women are included in the class of unfree subjects. The dominant feature in the institutional structure of these communities
is that of status, and the groundwork of their economic life is a
rigorous system of ownership.

The institution is found at its best, or in its most effectual
development, in the communities in which status and ownership
prevail with the least mitigation; and with the decline of the
sense of status and of the extreme pretensions of ownership,
such as has been going on for some time past in the communities of the western culture, the institution of the patriarchal
household has also suffered something of a disintegration. There
has been some weakening and slackening of the bonds, and this

deterioration is most visible in the communities which have departed farthest from the ancient system of status, and have gone farthest in reorganizing their economic life on the lines of industrial freedom. And the deference for an indissoluble tie of ownership-marriage, as well as the sense of its definitive virtuousness, has suffered the greatest decline among the classes immediately engaged in the modern industries. So that there seems to be fair ground for saying that the habits of thought fostered by modern industrial life are, on the whole, not favorable to the maintenance of this institution or to that status of women which the institution in its best development implies. The days of its best development are in the past, and the discipline of modern life—if not supplemented by a prudent inculcation of conservative ideals—will scarcely afford the psychological basis for its rehabilitation.

This form of marriage, or of ownership, by which the man becomes the head of the household, the owner of the woman, and the owner and discretionary consumer of the household's output of consumable goods, does not of necessity imply a patriarchal system of consanguinity. The presence or absence of maternal relationship should, therefore, not be given definite weight in this connection. The male household, in some degree of elaboration, may well coexist with a counting of relationship in the female line, as, for instance, among many North American tribes. But where this is the case it seems probable that the ownership of women, together with the invidious distinctions of status from which the practice of such an ownership springs, has come into vogue at so late a stage of the cultural development that the maternal system of relationship had already been thoroughly incorporated into the tribe's scheme of life. The male household in such cases is ordinarily not developed in good form or entirely free from traces of a maternal household. The traces of a maternal household which are found in these cases commonly point to a form of marriage which disregards the man rather than places him under the surveillance of the woman. It may well be named the household of the unattached woman. This condition of things argues that the tribe or race in question has entered upon a predatory life only after a considerable period of peaceable industrial life, and after having achieved a considerable development of social structure under the régime of peace and industry, whereas the unqualified prevalence of the patriarchate, together with the male household, may be taken to indicate that the predatory phase was entered early, culturally speaking.

Where the patriarchal system is in force in fully developed form, including the paternal household, and hampered with no indubitable survivals of a maternal household or a maternal system of relationship, the presumption would be that the people in question has entered upon the predatory culture early, and has adopted the institutions of private property and class prerogative at an early stage of its economic development. On the other hand, where there are well-preserved traces of a maternal household, the presumption is that the predatory phase has been entered by the community in question at a relatively late point in its life history, even if the patriarchal system is, and long has been, the prevalent system of relationship. In the latter case the community, or the group of tribes, may, perhaps for geographical reasons, not have independently attained the predatory culture in accentuated form, but may at a relatively late date have contracted the agnatic system and the paternal household through contact with another, higher, or characteristically different, culture, which has included these institutions among its cultural furniture. The required contact would take place most effectually by way of invasion and conquest by an alien race occupying the higher plane or divergent line of culture. Something of this kind is the probable explanation, for instance, of the equivocal character of the household and relationship system in the early Germanic culture, especially as it is seen in such outlying regions as Scandinavia. The evidence, in this latter case, as in some other communities lying farther south, is somewhat obscure, but it points to a long-continued coexistence of the two forms of the household; of which the maternal seems to have held its place most tenaciously among the subject or lower classes of the population, while the paternal was the honorable form of marriage in vogue among the superior class. In the earliest traceable situation of these tribes there appears to have been a relatively feeble, but growing, preponderance of the male household throughout the community. This mixture of marriage institutions, as well as the correlative mixture or ambiguity of property institutions associated with it in the Germanic culture, seems most easily explicable as being due to the mingling of two distinct racial stocks, whose institutions differed in these respects. The race or tribe which had the maternal household and common property would probably have been the more numerous and the more peaceable at the time the mixing process began, and would fall into some degree of subjection to its more warlike consort race.

No attempt is hereby made to account for the various forms of human marriage, or to show how the institution varies in detail from place to place and from time to time, but only to indicate what seems to have been the range of motives and of exigencies that have given rise to the paternal household, as it has been handed down from the barbarian past of the peoples of the western culture. To this end, nothing but the most general features of the life history of the institution have been touched upon, and even the evidence on which this much of generalization is based is, per force, omitted. The purpose of the argument is to point out that there is a close connection, particularly in point of psychological derivation, between individual ownership, the system of status, and the paternal household, as they appear in this culture.

This view of the derivation of private property and of the male household, as already suggested, does not imply the prior existence of a maternal household of the kind in which the woman is the head and master of a household group and exercises a discretionary control over her husband or husbands and over the household effects. Still less does it imply a prior state of promiscuity. What is implied by the hypothesis and by the scant evidence at hand is rather the form of the marriage relation above characterized as the household of the unattached woman. The characteristic feature of this marriage seems to have been an absence of coercion or control in the relation between the sexes. The union (probably monogamic and more or less enduring) seems to have been terminable at will by either party, under the constraint of some slight conventional limitations. The substantial difference introduced into the marriage relation on the adoption of ownership-marriage is the exercise of coercion by the man and the loss on the part of the woman of the power to terminate the relation at will. Evidence running in this direction, and in part hitherto unpublished, is to be found both in the modern and in the earlier culture of Germanic communities.

It is only in cases where circumstances have, in an exceptional degree, favored the development of ownership-marriage that we should expect to find the institution worked out to its logical consequences. Wherever the predatory phase of social life has not come in early and has not prevailed in unqualified form for a long time, or wherever a social group or race with this form of the household has received a strong admixture of another race not possessed of the institution, there the prevalent form of marriage should show something of a departure from this paternal type. And even where neither of these two conditions is present, this type of the marriage relation might be expected in the course of time to break down with the change of circumstances, since it is an institution that has grown up as a detail of a system of status, and, therefore, presumably fits into such a social system, but does not fit into a system of a different kind. It is at present visibly breaking down in modern civilized communities, apparently because it is at variance with the most ancient habits of thought of the race, as well as with the exigencies of a peaceful, industrial mode of life. There may seem some ground for holding that the same reassertion of ancient habits of thought which is now apparently at work to disintegrate the institution of ownership-marriage may be expected also to work a disintegration of the correlative institution of private property; but that is perhaps a question of speculative curiosity rather than of urgent theoretical interest.

THE UNIVERSITY OF CHICAGO.   THORSTEIN VEBLEN.

CRIMINAL ANTHROPOLOGY IN ITS RELATION TO CRIMINAL JURISPRUDENCE.

CRIMINAL anthropology, or criminology, is a science, if one may call it such, of but recent development. Considering its subject-matter, and the number and prominence of its advocates, it is perhaps more intimately connected with criminal jurisprudence than with any other science. Although criminal anthropology is closely related to many other fields and lines of thought and work, the object here is to show its relation to jurisprudence only; and as a consequence other of its important lines of work are omitted in this discussion.

While criminal anthropology pursues its distinct method of investigation, and adopts an entirely different basis from that of jurisprudence, it is wholly dependent upon the latter, and can be of but minor practical service, except through the channels of legislation and the courts of justice. Law determines who shall constitute the criminal class upon the theory of the protection of society, and criminal anthropology, accepting this definition, attempts to determine the causes of crime, and the methods best adapted for its repression and prevention. It will be seen from its object that, if this science can be placed upon a sound foundation and some of the nonsense eliminated which characterizes it, as all new sciences, its service, in relation to the administration of justice, will be inestimable. In order to show the relation in which the two now stand it will be necessary to sketch the origin and development of each.

Criminal anthropology is a branch of sociology, and its purpose[1] is to investigate crime scientifically: to study its origin and causes, and to determine, if possible, what proportion of responsibility belongs to society and what to the criminal. The remedies are to be examined as well as the causes, and also the effect of punishment as a means of reformation and prevention. From the nature and extent of its work, criminal anthropology may be said to comprehend three parts — general, special, and practical. The first consists in a summary and classification of all the facts known, and is used as the basis for further work; the second includes the investigation of individual criminals,

[1] *Cf.* MACDONALD, *Abnormal Man;* WILSON, report on "Criminal Anthropology" (*Smithsonian Report,* 1890).

historically, physically, psychically, and socially, with a view to their analysis and the determination of the causes of crime ; while the third embraces a consideration of methods and institutions for the repression and prevention of crime. Criminologists thus become those who study crime with reference to its origin, propagation, prevention, and punishment.

The origin of criminal anthropology[1] under this title may be said to have been in 1885, when the First International Congress of Criminal Anthropology was held at Rome. Its antecedents were the investigations of and published results in Morel's *Traité des dégénérescences physiques, intellectuelles, et morales de l'espèce humaine, et des causes qui produisent ces variétés maladives*, in 1857; Darwin's *Origin of Species*, in 1859; Spencer's *First Principles*, in 1862; Despine's *Psychologie naturelle*, in 1868; Maudsley's *Responsibility in Mental Disease*, in 1872. The precursor in associations was the establishment by Broca in Paris, in 1859, of an anthropological society having a branch of criminal anthropology. The needed impulse for a centralization of these studies was given by the publishing of Lombroso's works, the first, *L'Uomo Delinquente*, appearing in 1876. Lombroso and his associated school of criminal anthropologists, including Italian scientists and jurists, may thus be called the innovators of the science, although it existed in fragments previous to their work.

It is, perhaps, unfortunate that at the beginning of the science two opposing schools should have arisen, Lombroso and the Italians leading the one, the French the other. It will be necessary to examine the beliefs and methods of each, for the lines of reform suggested are different, and if either predominates, the recommended changes in law and procedure will vary, and the future of the science accordingly change.

The Italian school emphasizes the biological, pathological, and atavistic side, and would account for the presence of crime and distinguishing characteristics of criminals upon these bases. In this belief, the investigations have been principally along anatomic lines,[2] the

[1] *Cf.* FERRI, *Criminal Sociology; Smithsonian Report*, 1893 (section on "Criminal Anthropology"); MACDONALD, *Criminology*.

[2] This in itself has induced much hostile criticism of the Italian school, by the general public, and it has been charged by those who would consider only more conspicuous data that criminal anthropology narrows crime down to the mere results of conformation of skull and convolutions of the brain. These in themselves are merely morphological observations and but preliminary steps, although not generally so regarded by critics of the school.

assigned reason being that the organ must be studied before the function and the physical before the moral. It has continually sought to ally the criminal with animals and barbaric peoples. One of its principal assertions is that the criminal is a man of arrested development, and harmonizes with the civilization of previous decades rather than with the present one ; that modern civilization has so rapidly advanced that it exceeds the natural capacity of many individuals who live in its midst. With this anatomical or biological basis in view, an extended series of anthropometrical measurements and psychological experiments,[1] *e. g.*, of hearing, sight, touch, smell, sensibility to locality, pain, pressure, etc., have been taken, and a comparison has been made with similar measurements of and experiments upon normal persons. From the results of this laboratory work the school has announced what it defines as a criminal type, and asserts that all born criminals have characteristic anomalies either physical or mental. The former most frequently refer to the cranium and face, the latter to defective intelligence and absence of moral sensibilities. Criminals are divided into the two categories of "born" and "occasional," although the more accurate division into born, insane, occasional, and habitual criminals, and criminals by passion, is used by some criminal anthropologists.

The born criminal is asserted to possess the criminal type, or at least some of the specified anomalies. There is a tendency to allege that the occasional criminal may also possess them, although not to so great a degree. The effect of environment is not absolutely excluded, but is considered as of minor importance. Atavism is one of the pivots of the thought of this school. So strongly is the biological side emphasized that it is asserted that " the great under-class of criminals have defective organisms, especially in relation to the brain and nervous systems, and that they are all more or less deficient in moral sense. They are perversely wicked, ignorant, and have a bad heredity." Consequently not much stress is placed upon reform, but primarily upon prevention. These conclusions of the school are the result of the most elaborate and assiduous investigation, and are supported by the prestige of prominent scientific names.[2]

The French school is the result of a dissent from the Italian. While admitting the importance of the anatomical and physiological

[1] *Cf.* LOMBROSO, *Female Offender; L'Uomo Delinquente.*

[2] The prominence given by this school to anatomy, physiognomy, etc., has been the cause of much misapprehension and misunderstanding, and has induced a belief in the existence of no small degree of nonsense in the new science. Many rash state-

study of the criminal, they deny its precedence. Instead, they emphasize the psychological and sociological, and hold that the criminal should be studied as a member of the social organism; that he is equally the product of heredity and environment. Lacassagne, a prominent exponent of this school, has said: "Every society has the criminals that it deserves, and there is something radically wrong in the organization of the state." They deny that a criminal presents any peculiar anatomical characteristics, or that there exists a criminal type. They have less sympathy with the study of the body, physiognomy, speech, handwriting, sensibilities, etc., than with the study of social institutions and the environment and heredity. They believe the great causes of crime are to be found not so much in an innate tendency to commit crime as in a lack of resistance to the pressure of social and physical life. They assert that three-fourths of the criminals are such by occasion, and are not so born, and deny that crime is a disease, or is due to disease. In support of this denial they rely upon prison statistics, which show that 82. per cent. of the prisoners incarcerated are in good health. They hold that the criminal is only *slightly* abnormal, and show that of those who are guilty of crimes as many are at large in society and are classed as normal as are incarcerated in penal institutions, the ratio of convictions to crimes committed being less than one-half. The French faction characterizes Lombroso's theory as "a revival of the empiric science of phrenology," and the Italian results are deemed inconclusive because "the series of observations is limited, processes defective, methods dissimilar, and the observers inexperienced." Little importance is attached to the theory of atavism or regression. Love of pleasure, aversion to labor, defective social institutions, bad financial administration, are among the alleged causes of crime. Consistent with these views is the fact that all socialists interested in the work are adherents of the French school. No laboratory work has been done by this faction, as the causes are not

ments have been made, similar to Lombroso's recent one in a work upon *Chirography*, where he said it is possible to distinguish a criminal by his handwriting; and also in a recent meeting, where it was declared that at no distant day a criminal might be recognized and convicted by his physiognomy and the shape of his cranium. Whatever may be the possibilities, science as such is not concerned with them, and the public is not prepared for the unauthenticated statements which in many instances are based upon meager observations of normal persons with which comparisons have been made. The hasty and extreme conclusions formed by this school have done much to bring the science into the disfavor which to some extent it possesses, and to characterize its members as inaccurate in their work.

sought in the individual alone. Manouvrier and Lacassagne may be said to be the present leaders of this school.

While the two factions are thus radically opposed in both methods and conclusions, the tendency during the past five years has been to coördinate all theories,[1] and to consider crime as the result of multifarious causes — anthropological, physiological, and sociological; and in this union and harmonizing of the work of criminal anthropology lies its main advantage and possible assistance in criminal-law reform. The great progress of the work, as conducted by both schools, and the intercourse and discussion afforded by the meetings of the Congress of Criminal Anthropology, have been very influential in producing this result.

Having outlined the origin and development of criminal anthropology, it will be necessary to glance hastily at the other important element of the discussion — criminal jurisprudence. The purpose of the following outline is not to give a historical survey of the development of the system, but to show the *idea* of crime, its origin, and the methods employed for its repression; to show the various stages through which crime has passed and the beliefs held, according to the degree of knowledge incident to the period. For this purpose a division is made into four stages — that of revenge or retribution, repression, reformation, and prevention.

Criminal law had its origin[2] in the necessity for preserving peace and harmony as civilization progressed and social life became complicated. It is that branch of jurisprudence which relates to the definition and punishment of acts or omissions which are attacks upon public order; abuses or obstructions of public authority; actions injurious to the public generally; attacks upon the persons and property of individuals, or rights connected with them.

In all the primitive relations of mankind revenge was one of the predominating principles, and was executed first by the individual, then by the clan or family, and finally delegated to the community and to the state. Crime was undefined or uncodified. The rule of procedure was the simple one that whatever injury was done by one individual to another, or by one clan to another, could be expiated by similar injuries or by warfare. The early penalties, if they may be called such,

[1] *Cf. Report of Criminal Anthropological Meeting*, 1897; *Report of United States Commissioner of Education*, 1893-4, chaps. 14, 15; 1889-90, chap. 18.

[2] *Cf.* CHERRY, *Growth of Criminal Law ;* STEPHENS, *History of Criminal Law in England*, Vols. I, II ; WINES, *Punishment and Reformation ;* MAINE, *Ancient Law*.

were death and mutilation, and a gradual substitution of a system of fines for the less serious offenses. Private warfare and blood feuds were the rule, and organized revenge[1] was the principle predominating in primitive justice. Moral rights were unrecognized, and force was the only method of offense or defense. With the development of community life it was found impracticable and inexpedient for every injured individual or family to pursue, capture, and wreak vengeance upon the perpetrator of an injury, and the gradual delegation of the right to the chief or sovereign was substituted. Specific crimes were declared, and certain chosen representatives administered, not justice in the modern sense, but vengeance, which was the prevailing sentiment of the one injured. Many of the crimes and punishments of primitive law exist today almost unchanged, but are administered with a different knowledge and purpose. The rule then, as now, was, " the greater the crime, the greater the penalty."

The procedure corresponded to the *idea* of crime, and consisted primarily in nothing more than private warfare. From this it developed into the law of infangthef, which was a recognition of the *right* of the injured party to exterminate the offender or receive compensation for the act. Sir Francis Palgrave observes upon this point: "Perhaps the name legal procedure can scarcely be given with propriety to these plain and speedy modes of administering justice; they are acts deduced from the mere exercise of the passions natural to man, and the law consists only in the restrictions by which the power of self-protection was prevented from degenerating into wanton and unprovoked cruelty." Following infangthef came the development of police organization, purgation, ordeal, and trial by combat. The last three were characteristic of the early courts or tribunals where the trial was conducted. These latter were at first only public meetings for the adjustment of personal difficulties. Accusation by either a committee appointed for that purpose or a private accuser was the method of indictment, and the receiving of testimony was common in these primitive courts. The idea of revenge as the permanent factor in early punishment of crime is clearly brought out by a study of the methods of trial and punishment.

The second period is dominated by the idea of repression, not unmixed, however, with that of vengeance. The repressive theory in existence at this period differs from the present one in the idea of

---

[1] This is not unknown today, as is illustrated by the Mafia of Italy and the well-known "vendetta."

intimidation which was so prominent during the Middle Ages. The characteristic feature of this period may be said to differ from the retributive one in that the former consists in the desire for retributory punishment—the desire for indemnity for the past—while the purpose of the latter is to gain security for the future. This is the *idea* which divides the first period from the second.

This second period is characterized by a rapid growth of institutions and a marvelous development of community life. Crime became specifically defined in decrees and laws, and sovereignty attained its greatest height, while with it grew much of the oppression and unfairness which distinguished the administration of justice. In the first place, the state or sovereign had gained absolute control of the punishment of the criminal as a natural consequence of the solidarity of families and communities, and this exclusive right, theoretically at least, was administered in the interest of peace. From the keeping of the king's peace, therefore, grew the modern theory of the protection of society.

The procedure was distinguished by the most unjust proceedings, and the barbarous punishments and the cruelty of this period far exceed that of any other in the history of law. The sovereign or state was everywhere paramount, and individual rights, when in opposition to the sovereign, were not recognized. Death, torture, and mutilation were the penalties, and bills of attainder and numerous ingenious forms of summary proceedings existed. The union of church and state brought within the law a vast number of crimes, and persecution was a dominant feature of the legal system. The idea of reforming or "curing" the criminal was just dawning, and the belief was that it could be done by terrorizing or through intimidation. The extortion of confessions by means of torture, the ingenuity of which has never been surpassed, condemnation without trial, rules of evidence enabling convictions and making them possible without arraigning the accused, severe penalties for misdemeanors, and unrestrained capital punishment, were among the characteristics of this period. Crime was the *willful* act of the individual, environment and heredity as factors in producing crime being unrecognized. The only question was as to the guilt of or the utility of removing the accused for political or personal reasons. No mitigating circumstances were possible. Insanity was confounded with religious beliefs, and made its possessors objects of persecution rather than furnished a defense. The number of capital offenses, including religious crimes, at one time in England exceeded 160, and all punishments were enforced where the ecclesiastical courts had jurisdiction. As a result, revolutions, revolts, fanaticism, and suppressions of all kinds existed, and it was this condition which furnished the reaction of the reformative period.

In the injustice of the laws of the Middle Ages is found the root of the development of trial by jury, the present system of appeals, appearance by counsel, right to a speedy and public trial, right of being confronted by the accuser, rules relating to incriminating evidence and conviction upon one's own confession, or that of accomplices, and many other rules of law and evidence. To this source may be traced, also, the abolition of crimes of religion, the abatement of the severity of punishment, and the separation of church and state which are found in the present century. The reformative tendency became well defined about the middle of the eighteenth century. Contemporaneous with, and incident to, it was the development of the prison system. Previous to this time prisons existed, but not as places of detention for punishment or reform. They were used merely as temporary places of detention for those awaiting sentence to execution, exile, transportation, or release. Imprisonment was not in itself a punishment. Together with the prison system came the establishment of asylums, workhouses, and reformatories. Insanity was recognized as a defense, and the study of the causes of crime and the nature of the criminal was entered upon. For the first time the idea of vengeance seemed disappearing in the background of history, and science and knowledge were supplanting fanaticism, superstition, and persecution. Education, moral training, discipline, were being introduced where only punishment and extermination had hitherto existed.

In contrasting this period of reform with that of repression, we find in the former the most absolute safeguards thrown up about the criminal, the state handicapped, and the most liberal rules applying to the defense. Nearly all of the present rules of evidence, which are so obnoxious to criminal anthropologists, can be traced to the reaction against the atrocities of the Middle Ages and to the determination to prevent a continuance of the "star chamber" methods. There remain, however, to a great degree, the same system of punishment, somewhat humanized, and the same disregard of the criminal and his surroundings which existed in the previous stages of the development of criminal law.

We have designated three periods of criminal law, using the idea of crime in punishment rather than giving a historical survey. The fourth period — that of prevention — is just dawning, and it is not safe to say that it is well out of the meshes of the idea of reformation. The idea of reform is still the dominant one, and is but slowly developing into reform as a means of prevention. To prevent the commission of crime is novel, and is very far removed from our hasty survey of vengeance. Prevention differs from reformation in this: the object is the good of society, the individual being but slightly considered in the former. In the latter society is considered, but the individual also is an important element. If society is best benefited by reforming the criminal, this is the better method; but if incapable of reform, then permanent incarceration or extermination — which is prevention. In preventing crime, the criminal and causes of crime are studied, and an attempt made to remove the latter; if this is not possible, then of necessity the criminal must be removed. Whatever the causes, *he* must not be permitted to continue a *probable* career of crime or beget a family of paupers, idiots, or criminals. . Criminal anthropology may be said to be the herald of this idea of preventing crime, but it is certain that the idea is becoming a firmly rooted one. Reformatories and prisons are necessary elements of this system, but they are places for discipline and education, not for punishment. A system of scientific jurisprudence is essential to any prevention of crime, and all of the reforms proposed by criminal anthropologists are characteristic of this period. All the suggested changes in criminal law are based upon this idea of prevention.

Criminal-law legislation, as enacted at present, is upon the basis of reform, and remains upon the same foundation as was primitive law — that in its application the act and not the individual should be the object to which attention was directed. The idea dominating the repressive system has been outlined in the discussion of the work of the criminal anthropologists. It is not a mere revision of the system of criminal law and procedure, but that legislation may be influenced in many other lines. It is necessary that the great causes of crime should be reached, and until then the criminal must be kept from them. The basis of the preventive system is a consideration of the individual rather than of his act, and of his relation to the social whole. This is a radical departure from the dominant idea in criminal-law legislation during the previous three periods. The ideas of vengeance, repression, and reform have been logical developments into each other, and have been upon the common legal theory. They are closely related, and have been so intermingled that it is impossible to distinguish the exact period when each began.   With the preventive system there can be no such harmonious development; for, while it is the logical result of the increasing knowledge and development of social and political life. it requires a change of the fundamental principles governing the system of criminal law.

In this outline of crime and punishment the attempt has been to outline the development of the idea of crime and punishment, and to show the position of criminal anthropology as being the summit in the evolution of the thought regarding it.

We have outlined the two systems so as to see the different theories, the origin of each, and their mutual relation.   Before passing to a consideration of the reforms demanded, it will be necessary to glance more specifically at the doctrines of criminal anthropology which are the basis for reform.   These doctrines are founded upon the researches into history, the study of the individual in the laboratory and in society, and of social and legal institutions.   As a result of this study, in which almost every known science has been utilized, the necessity has been perceived of working through the channels of legislation and the courts of justice, in order to remedy certain existing evils, and to this end certain defects are pointed out and substitutions recommended, in accord with modern thought and knowledge.   The knowledge of man and society which forms the present basis of the law's operation should be superseded by the modern enlightened ideas, for the faulty systems of criminal jurisprudence are the greatest detriment in the way of decreasing the amount and causes of crime, and are to a great extent responsible for the increased amount of litigation between the state and the criminal.

In reflecting upon the right of the criminal anthropologists to claim these reforms (which right may be questioned, by reason of the comparatively short time that the science has been in existence, and because of the limited amount of work performed), it must be remembered that in America the work is less strongly organized and has not attained the prominence or commanded the attention that it has in Europe.   The workers are, for the greater part, mere names to most Americans, while in Europe they are in the closest relation with the people and with the government.   The interest there is incessant, and does not depend upon reports and occasional congresses, but upon constant research and experiments.   By reason of the few translations of reports and publications of the students and investigators in criminal anthropology, there is not the interest and coöperation in America which would otherwise obtain. Americans, as a rule, are familiar only with the Italian school, the study and theories of the sociologists and psychologists being unknown. The "criminal type" is considered here as the pith of the whole science, and its establishment as a fact is regarded as the object of all investigation, whereas it is only one of the most debatable theories, is only inconclusively proved, and is so recog-- nized in Europe. The increased amount of English writing and translation is tending to remove these erroneous, narrow views, and thus to establish a less critical and more scientific attitude.

The following is a brief résumé of the conclusions of the criminal anthropologists :[1]

1. Criminal anthropology renounces entirely the law of retaliation as the end, principle, or basis of judicial punishment.

2. The purpose of punishment is the necessity of protecting society against the consequences of crime, either by moral reclamation of the criminal or by his removal from society. Punishment is not for the purpose of satisfying vengeance.

3. Society should have legal rights and privileges equal to those of the criminal, and systems and institutions should be modified to conform to this view. An absolute equality for each should be maintained.

4. In criminal anthropology it is not sufficient to study the fact of crime. The criminal must also be considered. It has become necessary to define the causes which produce crime, to study the sphere of action of the criminal, as well as to give attention to measures for the safety of society against his acts. Criminal anthropology does not study him in the abstract and speculate over his guilt and responsibility, but it analyzes him according to results of purely scientific investigation and with the aid of exact methods.

5. In crime the results of two factors are seen reciprocally reacting : (1) the individual peculiarities in the nature of the criminal, or his psychophysical organization ; (2) the peculiarities of external influences, such as climate, country, social surroundings, etc.

6. Relying upon exact methods, criminal anthropology reveals the criminal as possessing an organization more or less unfortunate, vicious, impoverished, ill-balanced, defective, and not adapted to struggle with surrounding conditions, and, consequently, incapable of maintaining the struggle in legally established ways. This defect of adaptation varies with conditions.

7. The causes of crime are three: immediate, which arise from the character of the individual ; remote, which are found in his unfavorable surroundings, under the influence of which organic peculiarities are developed into

[1] *Cf. Report of United States Commissioner of Education*, 1893-4, p. 1684.

more or less constant criminal agents; predisposing, which push these ill-proportioned and viciously developed organizations toward crime.[1]

8. Basing crime on scientific grounds, criminal anthropology has for its purpose a fundamental study of the actual criminal and his crimes as ordinary phenomena, which it must investigate throughout their whole extent, from their genesis to their free growth and development; and thus the phenomenon of crime is united with great social questions and legal systems. Based upon these principles, criminal anthropology logically recognizes an absence of reason in the repressive measures determined in advance, as to their duration and specific character. On the contrary, it affirms the necessity of studying individual characteristics before rendering decisions. The terms of punishment should endure so long as the causes exist which necessitate them, but they should cease with the causes.

9. Biological and anthropological studies are indispensable for placing penal legislation upon a solid foundation.

10. The certainty, not the severity, of punishment operates as a deterrent in crime, prevention being the object of punitive measures.

Upon theories and conclusions so radically different as those of criminal jurisprudence and criminal anthropology it is difficult to see a means of reconciliation. The hope lies in the fact that the theories are more diverse than the methods of practical work, since jurists are to some extent recognizing the same evils and recommending similar remedies. In theory the one system is scientific, the other legal; one considers the individual and his environment, the other considers only the act; one is the result of a comparatively modern study of man and institutions, the other is based upon necessity and relies on the precedent of centuries and on rules venerable for their antiquity; the one is revolutionary, the other conservative; one is the result of the study of society and individuals, and consists largely of theories or propositions, the value of which is unknown, as they are mainly untested, while the other arises from the necessity of protecting society, and has already demonstrated its priority and efficiency in the matter of protection.

[1] In his admirable work upon *Punishment and Reformation*, Mr. F. H. Wines, among many other classifications, divides the causes of crime into individual, social, and cosmical. In enumerating the causes, he adopts an excellent method by using first those relating to the individual, as physical and mental desires; then broadening into those relating to the family, as education, discipline, etc. Following this are those of the community, as poverty, wealth, density of population, employment, rural or urban life, etc.; and from this into the social and political whole, which includes legislation, government, war, etc.

In nearly all of the reforms suggested and enumerated hereafter some legislative action has been taken, varying in the different countries, but jurisprudence has made the attempt alone, and not by indorsing the theories of criminal anthropology. The tendency is, however, for jurists and scientists to unite in the effort for reform, and at the Third International Congress of Criminal Anthropology, held at Brussels, one of the distinctive features was the prominent part that jurists took in the deliberations and debates.

In dealing with the specific reforms advocated, it has been thought advisable to use the United States as illustrative, by reason of the increased facility for study, and because the majority of the rules of procedure and laws in force reflect the attitude and progress of other civilized countries. Although there is a greater diversity of law and decisions, owing to the prevailing systems of state government, the purpose is to show the extreme limit to which legislation has gone in advancing the work of criminal anthropologists, and the main obstacles which arise and prevent its further progress. In matters of advanced penology the United States ranks among the first. It must be remembered that these reforms are not urged each by itself, but as parts of a system ; that, while one country may represent a more advanced condition in one reform, as France does in her system of identification of criminals, and England in her provisions for the incarceration of acquitted, although guilty, insane criminals, no one of them has a *system* founded upon the recent developments in science and upon modern knowledge, or possesses more than a fraction of the proposed system. While the legal attitude in European countries has been obtained, I do not know that any similar results have been secured as to the relation of the legal system of the United States to criminal anthropology.

FRANCES ALICE KELLOR.

THE UNIVERSITY OF CHICAGO.

(To be continued.)

REVIEWS.

Die soziologische Erkenntnis. Positive Philosophie des sozialen Lebens. Von GUSTAV RATZENHOFER. Leipzig: F. A. Brockhaus, 1898.[1]

IN a magazine review it is difficult to do justice to a work like Ratzenhofer's. Ratzenhofer resembles that other equally important sociologist of German Austria, Gumplowicz: he is not merely a fully independent thinker, who understands how to concentrate philosophically and cast into a unified form the most comprehensive physical, psychological, and sociological science; he is also very peculiar in regard to the systematic formation of his thought, and employs necessarily a terminology at variance with scholastic language. This work, written for professional colleagues, with whom it avoids every explanation, even for the sake of the coherence of its thought, is therefore a very difficult work to arrange in an assenting and dissenting criticism. Instead of such a notice, therefore, we shall best do justice to the work before us by an analysis, with occasional digression for comment. We may preface this analysis by a single general objection. Ratzenhofer himself maintains that the present work, together with his other, entitled *Wesen und Zweck der Politik*, which appeared in 1893, form "the doctrinal structure [*Lehrgebäude*] of sociology." They might be the beginning, perhaps, of "a doctrinal structure" or "system." The work is, indeed, a compendium of signal importance and of enduring value, pregnant with thought and suggestive; it is so systematically put together that every stone is indispensable and none superfluous. But are these two treatises, after all, "the" system or even the "doctrinal structure" of sociology? This the reviewer cannot concede. The book under discussion, *Soziologische Erkenntnis*, fully deserves its alternative title whereby it claims to be "a positive philosophy of the social life." It is undoubtedly the most significant of recent attempts at philosophical concentration of sociological knowledge; it is, further, a vigorous attempt at the dovetailing of a "posi-

[1] Translated from *Zeitschrift für die gesammte Staatswissenschaft*, Viertes Heft, 1898 (pp. 733 ff.), by MR. and MRS. CHARLES A. ELLWOOD.

528

tive philosophy of the social life" into a unitary philosophy of the universe. The reviewer is acquainted with no other such attempt more significant in content, or in style more perfect. But "the doctrinal structure of sociology" is not yet to be regarded as effected by it. I expressed my opinion concerning this recently in the introduction to the second edition of my *Bau und Leben;* namely, that "the doctrinal structure" of sociology cannot from the outset be finally constructed, because all the special disciplines of social science are not yet even combined for a sociologically unified presentation, to say nothing of being combined in proportional measure for the above purpose. The reviewer, who cannot be reproached with being an enthusiast for the continuation of the traditional parceling out of social investigation, is still unable at present to give up the opinion that the possibility of a definitive "positive philosophy of the social life" is not yet given; that the time is not yet come — a fact, moreover, which Ratzenhofer himself opportunely emphasizes on p. 4 and elsewhere. If the reviewer could subscribe to all the rest of the work — which, moreover, is not the case — he could not indorse the first two lines of the preface, according to which the two works "form the doctrinal structure of sociology," either in respect to the words "the" or "doctrinal structure." Having prefaced the review with this single general remark, we shall now proceed to our analysis.

Ratzenhofer's *Sociologische Erkenntnis* treats of its subject-matter under seven principal divisions, viz.: I, " The Nature of Sociological Knowledge;" II, "The Psychological Basis of Sociology;" III, "The Physical-Science Basis of Sociology;" IV, "The Social Process of the Human Race;" V, "The Basis of Sociology;" VI, "The Social Forces;" VII, "Social Development in the Light of Social Knowledge."

For the present review the first division, which treats of the nature of sociological knowledge, is of special significance. This is not to say that the other divisions are only a supplement of significant ideas; the remainder of the work is rather throughout a suggestive sample of inquiry in respect to the " nature of sociological knowledge." For a review in a journal of social science, however, this first division has an especial significance for the purpose of indicating what the author wishes, and what I might in sincerest acknowledgment say he *is*. The reviewer is able in many respects to indorse unreservedly its content, in spite of holding another professional view as to the nature and conception of politics.

The contents of the first division regarding the nature of politics are further divided into three subdivisions : (1) "The Task of Sociology," (2) "The Method of Sociological Investigation," (3) "The Positivism of All Knowledge and Science."

In the portion upon the "task of sociology" Ratzenhofer devotes a few pages to a survey of the consideration and investigation thus far of the reciprocal relationships among men — a survey which could scarcely be more simply and correctly given. He remarks (p. 2) : "Without being reasonably conscious of the connection with one tendency or another, men have always given much attention to social relationships, because they recognized that they dominate the most essential part of their life interests. The state, law, and industry were investigated without succeeding in obtaining a scientific basis for these branches of knowledge. Mind remained yet as something independent of material conceptions, and the destiny of men seemed to be an arbitrary work of divinity or chance. With such opinions it was difficult to believe in a scientific content of the reciprocal relationships of men. The psychical sciences remained far behind securely advancing physical science, until at the end of the nineteenth century they are forced by the latter to recognize as undeniable the conformity of everything in existence to law. The researches which concerned themselves with the reciprocal relationships of men were, from the writings of Aristotle down to modern times, of a predominantly descriptive and only incidentally investigating character. Attaching itself to Galileo and Bacon's conception of the world, the endeavor to find out the causes of historical effects progressed slowly ; and the historical school began with Machiavelli and Montesquieu to acquire influence over political science. The development of humanity and of its culture was judged by Herder, for example, by means of the natural sciences ; especially the investigation of the economic life of peoples made advancement by virtue of the energy peculiar to its interests. Malthus and Smith really began the scientific treatment of human relationships. But these doctrines concerning the economic relationships of men could not be verified, and are coming to be more and more contested, because they lack the basis of a doctrine of human reciprocal relationships, and because they were conceived at a time when natural science had not yet demonstrated convincingly that conformity to law upon which they necessarily rest. Attempts, on the contrary, to found a sociology — the most famous of which was Herbert Spencer's — were not able to dispel the doubts in respect to it, because this meritorious fault is (to such a degree) inherent in these attempts : viz., they seek to explain society merely from the nature of the individual, while the real question pertains to society itself. Therefore the purpose of Quetelet, and of all statistics, to comprehend society in 'human averages' has failed. Society is no phenomenon of averages, but an effect of all individual phenomena in which the conformity to law of the reciprocal relationships of men is fulfilled. So the result was that sociology in general did not meet with that belief in its scientific mission which acts as a spur to all investigation. It was denied with especial vehemence that sociological knowledge is possible as a part of philosophy. People believed that they could exhaust the subject-matter of sociology with the descriptive special sciences, like ethnology or demography. Without connection, full of contradiction, and unconscious of purpose, a series of special sciences now concerned themselves with the reciprocal relationships of men. Jurisprudence, upon a historic foundation, stands impotent in the face of social needs ; the political sciences, which never had a sure foundation, lose their authority; the special sciences, like ethnology, culture-history, and others, dispense with all guidance and put forth wild sprigs on the tree of science. Statistics believes that it can derive the conformity of social affairs to law from inadequate numerical material, and overlooks the fact that the most essential qualities in the social life are practically intangible. History does homage to a fantastic view of the reciprocal relationships among men ; sciences like medical jurisprudence, criminal anthropology, psychiatry, which ought to proceed purely experimentally, become whole schools (Lombroso, Benedikt, etc., etc.), with corrupting theorems concerning the moral nature of men ; for even ethics can find in philosophy hitherto no reliable foundation. So the development of all the special sciences which discuss the reciprocal relationships of men is just at present in a crisis. This crisis rests chiefly upon the circumstance that natural science has thrust back speculative philosophy in every direction, while the judgment of social relationships cannot dispense with philosophical discussion. However, all the adversities which sociological thinkers like Schäffle, Gumplowicz, and others have experienced cannot check the human endeavor to bring the great world process of social evolution under universally valid propositions. And so will these attempts necessarily lead to sociology becoming a science so soon as the necessary preliminary conditions for it are found."

It is notorious that those who decades ago claimed for sociology an independent place as a science, alongside of the psychical sciences, have experienced severe rebuffs from the latter. While consistently validating the above historico-scientific conception as to the "denial on the part of the psychical sciences" of an independent sociology, Ratzenhofer flings the gauntlet in the face when he remarks (p. 5): "While philosophy has in the main hitherto recognized only two principal territories, psychical life and the phenomena of the material world, there has remained a third territory, by it too little considered, which has a psychical life, as well as, also, the phenomena of the material world—the societary life. In the fathoming of the same philosophy must find its reawakening. The societary life points to the innermost instincts of man as the explanation of the position of every individual as distinct from the generality. It opens for us the outlook upon a gigantic field of science which we, in the dimness of our discernment, hitherto have regarded as belonging partly to the science of individual consciousness and partly to the sciences of the material world. It devolves upon sociology as a part of philosophy, of course with psychology, to disclose the fundamental principles of this domain of science and to command it. As the latter (psychology), upon the basis of physiology, investigates the inner nature of man, the former (sociology), upon the basis of history and ethnology, discloses the external relationships of man. But both disclose the physical life of men only in conjunction with natural science, whereby the comprehension of all knowledge appertaining thereto devolves upon sociology. A philosophy without sociology is like a psychology without physiology: it is a speculation given over to subjective fallacies. Along with cosmological, psychological, and ontological problems belong also the sociological; for our thinking is not fully circumscribed until to the ideas of the world, I, and eternity are added those of human reciprocal relationships. Because this problem has not hitherto been fundamentally considered, the moral ideal of philosophers (humanity, virtue, happiness, etc.) has remained a phantasma; we comprehend it only when we fully understand psychological knowledge concerning the individual will through sociological knowledge concerning the social will. Sociology is the philosophical basis for the sciences of human relationships and their most essential manifestation, politics. What physics and chemistry are to natural science, such is sociology to the sciences concerned with human relationships; what mechanics is to material forces, such is a doctrine of politics to social forces. Sociology purposes, therefore, not the concrete investigation of single social phenomena—that is the task of the special sciences related to it — but it purposes rather the investigation of the conformity to law of the societary life. Indeed, sociology is the result of those single inquiries which have concerned themselves with social relationships from time immemorial, just as natural science is the result of experiences and observations which have through all time been accumulated. It is manifest that such a sociology cannot be a complete structure of knowledge, because only upon its foundation will regulated investigation of social relationships arise; but thereby sociology is only following the same course of development which is common to all the sciences. For the auxiliary sciences advance hand in hand with the fundamental science, and the corresponding systems of the same do not arise until general investigation has reached considerable proportions. Only from a philosophy widened through sociological knowledge can ethics and æsthetics, free from objection, arise, and the philosophy of law, political science, and political economy be able really to become sciences."

The second subdivision of the first part is devoted to the method of sociological investigation. In it Ratzenhofer points out that the independence of sociology is not to be denied on the ground that it has not from the beginning had a perfect method, and, at present, has not yet such a method; even the exact science of astronomy has had the same fate. Sociology must endeavor to get nearer the truth, while it more and more excludes the errors (of speculative construction). Natural science, which points out with its method the way of empirical investigation, may at present not yet exempt sociology from further using to a certain degree the crutches of speculative knowledge. "Since the natural sciences"— Ratzenhofer remarks (p. 10)— "at least in regard to their relation to social phenomena, proceed utterly unconscious of purpose, speculative knowledge must for a long time yet be the touchstone for the validity of many mediated facts. We meet here the old experience that the psychical sciences can only thrive when induction and deduction supplement each other, and when a judicious use of speculation is not denied them. It would be easy to show that at present many sciences, or special branches of knowledge demeaning themselves as science, prolong their life through the denial of this mixed method, that they go astray into fields of investigation which are without interest through overvaluation of induction, or have fallen into trivial hair-splitting through overvaluation of deduction. To the natural sciences there remains always with their investigations an indissoluble residue which is reserved to speculation; but every speculation is worthless which loses sight of 'the realistic background."

The third subdivision of the first part treats of the "positivism of all knowledge and science." The author here adopts the most rigorous standpoint of Comtean positivity (*Positivität*); but in spite of it, or just on account of it, he rejects the haughty and sterile conception of the "purposelessness" or, more plainly speaking, "disinterestedness" of all science. He remarks (p. 17): "Science is no longer satisfied with an insight into things, with investigation of the existent and the past ; it wants rather to put insight and retrospection at the service of prevision." According to Huxley, every science whose future application deeply concerns it, must take care "that it be possible for it to divine from the existing state the past and the future.' Only through such knowledge does science preserve its proper position in the life of man. " If we consider the task of science to be the seeking of laws for all phenomena, we find that a multitude of endeavors which are but distantly related to science sail under its flag ; for the search for laws in phenomena is not the gratification of mere desire of knowledge, but the effort even in itself is purposeful, because only from conformity to law can conclusive inferences regarding the past and future arise. That, in this case, the past, whether it be investigated or ascertained through deduction, will be put at the service of prevision lies in the nature of purposeful science." Nägeli says rightly : "If causal knowledge succeeds in foretelling future events with the same certainty and precision as astronomy, it will stand the test." With the demonstration of laws in human relationships we enter the path in which prevision into events is to be found—a path which has long since been trod experimentally by the science of medicine and with full certainty by all exact sciences.

This review can only consider much more briefly the remaining six divisions of Ratzenhofer's *Soziologische Erkenntnis*.

The second division treats of the "psychological" basis of sociology in four subdivisions : (1) "The Place of Man in the Universe," (2) " The Biological Origin of Consciousness," (3) " The Innate Content of Consciousness," (4) " Consciousness as Distinct from the Outer World." The third division, which is devoted to the "natural-science basis of sociology," treats the subject under four subdivisions : (1) " The Relation of Natural Law to Sociological Knowledge," (2) "The Doctrines of Universal Evolution," (3) " The Redistribution of Matter and Its Consequences," (4) " The Doctrines of Biological Phenomena." Both the second and third divisions are teeming with intellectual power and knowledge, especially with unerringly applied knowledge of the natural sciences. The latter, especially in regard to Weismann's theory of heredity, will be very suggestively turned to account in the founding of a sociology.

Ratzenhofer's ontological digressions, based upon his pantheistic world-philosophy, we pass without comment. They are, and perhaps will always remain, speculative postulates of the same doubtful value as those of a theistic world-philosophy. Besides, Ratzenhofer's ontological speculation remains no capstone on the sociological structure, but is followed out in its consequences. It has certainly neither convinced us in its major proposition of the primitive force, and of its differentiation in creation, even up to social creation, nor has it convinced us with its wealth of deduction derived for special "sociological knowledge." However, let the reader here judge for himself.

A presentation of the author's view of the "unity of biological and sociological evolution"—a unity toward which the whole discussion of the first and second divisions is aimed—will be most objectively given, if we quote the following passages from the concluding remarks of the third division (p. 117): "An essential reason why sociological intelligence has so long delayed to recognize a unity of law for biology and sociology has its roots in the apparent freedom of movement of social elements in comparison with cells (*biophores*) in the organism. The cell apparently belongs permanently to the organism; it comes, it goes, with the individual, and is not, like the elements of society, able to change its association, or to belong to several structures. This possibility, despite the concession of unity of law, lies, above all, in the fact that a unitary origin from primitive force belongs to both organic and social structures. If an organism evolves itself from the germ, in accordance with its innate interest, it stands forthwith, in relation to the outer world, individualized and isolated. In this condition of life it is able neither to fulfill the destiny of its species nor to preserve itself. Since propagation is, as it were, an extension of the individual beyond his own bodily substance, innate interest forces the individual to enter into relationships beyond his sphere of bodily sensibility, and thus to form social ties in association with individuals having related interests; this is likewise an extension of the individual beyond the limit of his bodily interests. The same interest which evolves a creature somatically, and then mentally, renders social relations also necessary to it; for, otherwise, the creature leaves its narrow life-purpose unfulfilled and exposes this to infractions. Social relationships, hence social structures, are a consequence of our biological evolution, of the primitive force working therein, and of differentiating individuation. Self-preservation, physiological interest, the effort to perfect our individual and social interest, the effort to propagate our racial interests, force us to social relationships. Thus we can impute to social evolution as a more remote effect of causes active in the evolution of the creature no other laws than those which are peculiar to biological occurrences—just as the laws of chemistry, physics, mechanics, geology, and, lastly, cosmology were fundamentally established by recourse to earlier evolutionary processes. So the unity of law in the world spontaneously presents itself. The difficulty in discerning this unity disappears before a knowledge of the decisive significance of inherent 'interest' for all individuation of primitive force. Just as, in the order of evolution of conscious creatures, we observe a growth of the faculties of consciousness whereby the individual seeks more and more to guard his interest through extensive thought-combinations, so the changes accompanying social phenomena grow more and more out of the immediate realm of physiological interest, and gain a psychical content. But in this connection we may not forget that this content has the nucleus of its being always in that physiological interest. The lower the organism stands, the simpler is the dependence of the social structure to which it belongs upon the material concerns of the species. The social structures of the plant world are but the product of its propagating increase ; those of the animal world are a product of this increase, and also a product of natural selection, of union for predatory purposes, and for protection against other species. For men also the same motives for social union originally existed ; but with increasing civilization the mediate gratification of wants becomes the motive for social union, whose coherence with the material interest of the individual or the species can be recognized only through combinations of ideas. Through elevation of the social world into the world of psychical relationships the validity of biological laws is not, on that account, annulled, because everything psychical has its roots in the reality of facts and phenomena. We must only know how to apprehend these biological conditions intelligently. The nearer the motive to a social union stands to physiological interest, the less easily can a societary element withdraw from its association ; it will arise and perish in its association like the cell in the organism. This is met with in most associations based upon descent. If the motive of association arises among those of transient relationships, the maintenance of which can have a proportional significance for the fate of the individual, indeed, but does not absolutely decide it, then the individual can also change his association. This social mobility is related to the transitoriness of the thoughts of our conscious organism. But this mobility is limited through the individual's innate interest; for, if he undervalues any material part of this latter, he perishes through the biological law according to which the dependent cell dies, if it leaves that organic complex which has developed it..... Because man, in his highly developed conscious state, recognizes that the social development is able to guard his individual interest, even in political struggle, the social part of his innate interest is strengthened more and more. Thus individualistic differentiation loses, in the natural course of evolution, a part of its anti-social effect. In its stead social evolution appears with a growing perfection of the conscious organism. A systematic penetration into the social nature of men will increase insight into the unity of law of all phenomena; and, with constant reliance on the assured teachings of the natural sciences, we shall obtain the certainty of the genetic agreement of social with all other phenomena of life."

In order to characterize completely Ratzenhofer's conception of the relation of social to physiological phenomena, it seems fitting to present further from Division V the following passage. This passage seems to us to be, in another relation also, one of the most significant and pregnant which the book contains, particularly as it presents more clearly Ratzenhofer's peculiar theory of interest. The author remarks (p. 221): "The agreement of the organic life-process with the social process is no figurative comparison, but it is causal. That hitherto the science of society has not been able to demonstrate this connection through-natural law is the essential cause of its poor success. The older method of biological analogy ought, moreover, to have set the critique of former sociological speculation on its guard, because every science works with comparison, and even astronomy bases its most important discoveries upon geometrical similarity. When, for example, a well-known scholar (Wundt, *Logik*, II, 576) says: 'Presumptively the method of biological analysis will find application also in the future as a means of exposition, where it is suitable to give expression to that view which places value upon the connection of societary systems united in the state; on the other hand, those views which give preference in politics and economics to individual interest will intentionally avoid such comparisons'—it calls attention, in the first place, to the already mentioned animosity toward sociology, and, secondly, it suggests how alien the individualistic knowledge of the acutest thinkers was only a short time ago to the real nature of social occurrences; otherwise it must even at that time have struck the author of the above lines that 'societary systems' and 'individual interest' have the relation of cause and effect, and this results directly from biological occurrences. Since the organism is morphologically developed through the innate interest of the germ, and since in this development of the nervous system conformably to its germ is pre-patterned also the psychical life of the creature, man moves in conformity to interest in the presence of the social world, and conducts himself in it in accordance with his germ capacities, and according as his innate interest and the interest later necessitated (acquired) through life-conditions prescribe for him. All life springs from the unsearchable primitive force; the differentiation of this life follows through adaptations to life-conditions for creatures with an innate interest, which really comes to expression in the germ capacities. Without differentiating causes the cosmic world would remain an infinite extension of original matter and the organic world the repetition of homogeneous cells. Through the differentiating change of conditions of life physiological interest awakes with life, and individual interest with consciousness. These are but the differentiated individualization of the interest of the species. The physiological interest, which, confronting the various life-conditions, impels to varied organic evolution, forces also the individual to an adaptive behavior, whereby, however, he is brought into opposition with his fellow-creatures; the adaptive behavior finds expression partly through natural selection, partly through the survival of the fit, partly through the change of location of those who have been disadvantaged— the opposition manifests itself in the struggle for existence. As long as only the interest of the species dominated, the social interest was the same to all. But as soon as individual interests arise, social interest also differentiates itself at once; for every individuality, be it a species under organisms or a community, has its special social interest. The differentiation of the organic world into different species is, strictly considered, a social differentitation of all creatures. In the social process of mankind, as well as of single animal species, this differentiation is continued upon the basis of different graded characteristics of the morphological and intellectual variety. And in this continuation of differentiation and of all development into the territory of intellectual manifestations of life, which, however, can be nothing else than the product of morphological facts in the organism, the undeniable connecting link between the organic and the social world is found— a transitionary stage which we by no means merely hypothetically assume, but which we see unmistakably proven every hour in ourselves and our environment. That among all creatures differentiation in the case of mankind is so much more manifold and complicated is due to the fact that man is himself the paramount product of differentiation of the organic world. We may not compare man with the animal species somatically nearest him. For he has, even in the lowest races, passed through such a differentiation of his consciousness, that is, of his intellect, that between him and the most highly developed animal world there exists an unbridgeable chasm. Man has been differentiated from the animal world through certain capabilities. Therefore the social differentiation of men happens in great part in the territory of interests which stand in a very mediate, even if fundamental, connection with physiological interest. The social activities of animals, on the other hand, rest merely upon immediately operating physiological impulses. To this circumstance is to be ascribed also the fact that the differentiation of human communities is not merely the resultant of active physiological interests. Already to individual interests belong thought-associations, built upon ideas, whereby man subjects his choice of comrades to cautious, or at least instinctive, reflections. In so far as such spring merely from individual interest, they lead the man back to the demands of his physiological interest. He who belongs to his social group only conditionally and unreliably becomes an egoist. But in so far as such reflections spring from the interest of the species, or finally from social interest, they guide the man to moral renunciation of self, whereby he receives impetus to coördinate or even subordinate his individual weal to that of his community. This is an evolutionary phenomenon, which points to the underlying principle of all creation. In the interest of the species is shown the effort of primitive force to resist the degeneration caused through differentiation and variation—a phenomenon which is determinative for the question as to the inheritance of acquired characteristics. The production of unifying mutual relationships manifests itself in the face of the individualistic atomizing impetus as indispensable for the natural development of society, just as the biological degenerations caused through variation are brought back to the normal of the species through the continuity of the germ plasm—unless compelling causes exist in the conditions of life for that variation. The degenerations caused through individualization lead partly to voluntary, partly to forced, subordination of individuals in a social union. The more life incites individual interests, the more important is social constraint to limit the degenerating differentiation, in order not to endanger the species and its social structures through war of all against all. Since, however, all interests are ever firmly anchored in the physiological interest, nature always brings back with its conditions of life all extravagances of individual and social development, whether they be the product of excessive differentiation or of inexpedient socialization, to the paths of social necessity founded in the needs of nourishment and propagation. The first sure concept which we have of the nature of our being is *interest*, and this is also the guiding principle in the biological as well as in the social process. Since inherent interest is modified in creatures through the change of life-conditions, the causes of social structures becoming differentiated are given. We must recognize clearly the fact that variation of interests goes in advance of the phenomena of the social process ; just as the natural change of life-conditions goes in advance of this differentiation of interest. The cause of this differentiation lies in the needs of men, and that of change of life-conditions in universal, natural occurrences with their consequences for organic and social life. The innate and acquired interest is the source of all human needs, and, in its changeable manifold forms, the guiding motive of all movements in the biological, psychical, and social process of the individual and of humanity. 'Interest,' therefore, in positive philosophy takes the place of the contradictory concept 'purpose,' which gave the widest opportunity for every erroneous presupposition and every vagueness concerning the relation of mind and nature. Indeed, the vanishing of this concept is alone a far-reaching step for the furtherance of metaphysical knowledge."

The fourth division is entitled : "The Social Process of the Human Race." It discusses successively : (1) "Primitive Social Structures ;" (2) "The Evolution of Higher Social Structures," which through a blending of militant with industrial tribes is claimed to have produced the state and the people (*das Volk*) ; (3) "Social Differentiation within the State," which, according to Ratzenhofer's view, produced the nation (*die Nation*) ; (4) "Social Differentiation of the Sphere of Civilization" (*Kulturkreis*) ; (5) "The Extension of a Dominating Social Process over Humanity" (commerce, colonization, migration, etc.). All these chapters contain thoughts which are worth reading, but which for a later "doctrinal structure of sociology" will scarcely be authoritative. However, we would not fail to bring to notice two single conceptions, with one of which we disagree, with the other we agree. I refer to Ratzenhofer's "nation" and "sphere of civilization." Concerning the origin of the nation, Ratzenhofer's opinion is: "While a people, conceived as a mass of subjecting and subjected tribes, is effectuating differentiation, the blending of tribal oppositions advances, and there is developed an organization of guiding, operating, and administered social structures, which finally, despite inner struggles, become a social unity called a nation. The nation is the completion of the process which was introduced through the founding of the conquering state." That is not the whole truth, however, about the origin and nature of the "nation." On the other hand, noteworthy suggestions are found in Ratzenhofer's chapter on the "Sphere of Civilization" (*Kulturkreis*) as the "territory of coöperative social evolution." Political science, perhaps, has occasion to consider more important than hitherto Ratzenhofer's "sphere of civilization" as the material foundation of consonant and dissonant political organization. Ratzenhofer remarks: "All the phenomena of interest, which with differentiation become effective within the state, spread beyond the state to seek within kindred civilization support and satisfaction. On this account many social structures will have adherents also beyond the limits of the state, and there will result, notwithstanding the state, a social differentiation of the sphere of civilization. The social differentiation of the sphere of civilization has always been dangerous to the state as an organization of power. It dissolves the inner necessity of its exclusiveness, and points through social relations to the widening of political barriers and relations of authority. Even if the instinct of conquest was generally the visible motive for widening the domain of the state and for creating great empires, nevertheless the fact of a homogeneous civilization, and even more the fact of social relationships with outside territories, has been the inner cause of the expansion of state domain. To this effort is to be ascribed the fact that a state should attain the leadership inside a sphere of civilization, through political superiority — as Athens or Sparta in the Greek sphere of civilization — or that a state should extend its sovereignty over the whole respective sphere of civilization — as Rome, the Frankish empire, or the empire of the Caliphs. In order to escape the menace of peoples of kindred civilization, states have endeavored to shut off also socially their political individuality, or at least to prevent the loosening of their social condition through the spread of social relationships with foreign countries, which develop all too easily into political intermingling."

The fifth division is entitled: "The Fundamental Doctrines of Sociology." It discusses successively: (1) "Individualization and Socialization" (authority and partisanship, order and freedom); (2) "Social Differentiation and the Leading Principle in the Social Process; (3) "Social Individualities" (forms of association); (4) "The Conditional Tendency to Perfection in the Social Process;" (5) "The Fundamental Phenomena of the Social Process." As such are treated: nutrition and reproduction; the act of perfecting (*Vervollkommung*); variation; the struggle for existence; absolute hostility; differentiation; the relation of authority; individualization and socialization; variation of interests; association; social necessity; the state, society. At the conclusion of this division an epitome of Ratzenhofer's sociology in eighteen propositions is given upon seven pages (pp. 244–50). In this appears, with the concluding thesis, a second state, the later state of equality(*Gleichheitsstaat*), in opposition to Ratzenhofer's above emphasized state of inequality. "In proportion as the civilized state takes the place of the conquering state, the differences in the satisfaction of interest among individual men are again equalized. The political, social, and economic inequality among men is transformed to the equality in participation of enjoyment which exists in primitive social conditions. The all-sided socialization of humanity complicates social structures, but it approaches to harmony of interest, through a growing perfection of the social organization, without, however, being able, with the existing diversity of life-conditions, to remove all motives for social conflict. The social order is an organization of the struggle for existence for the purpose of assured nutrition and propagation of healthy generations. It is therefore justifiable to assume, as the concluding stage of social evolution, a condition in which, despite manifoldness of professional individualities, a cultural, political, and social equality of men appears under the guidance of individuals who are intellectually and morally most perfect. Under this domination of moral and intellectual authority, social evolution, without degeneration of innate and acquired interests, would, perhaps, be possible; but this equality would remain immeasurably modified through the inequality and change of life-conditions."

The sixth division treats of "The Social Forces" in four subdivisions: (1) "Social Impulses," (2) "Individual Will," (3) "The Development of Individual Will," (4) "The Social Will." The seventh division, finally, discusses in detail (1) "The Activity of the Individual Will in Itself" (*an sich*) (the problem of the freedom of the will herein discussed); (2) "The Activity of the Social Will in Itself and in Its Relation to the Individual Will," (3) "The Modalities of the Evolution of the Will," (4) "The Principal Phenomena of Human Evolution which Comprehend all Manifestations of the Will" (culture, politics, civilization). The general value of these last divisions consists in the counter-application (*Rückanwendung*) of sociology to psychology, ethics, and æsthetics. Especially are the discussions of "social regeneration" (upon the basis of Weismann's theory of heredity) of great interest (pp. 271–84).

The whole work closes with the propositions: "The theological phase of intellectual evolution socialized society upon the basis of an absolute subjection of the individual. The metaphysical phase raised the individual at the expense of his necessary socialization. On the other hand, it devolves upon the positivistic phase to obtain again the full significance of socialization, in order that individuals may be able to perfect themselves physically, intellectually, and morally. Theological knowledge started from God and ended in uncertainty or in doubt. Metaphysical knowledge started from belief in the infallibility of our reason and ended with pessimism and materialism. Positivistic knowledge starts from the natural facts of our ethically demonstrable evolution, and ends with the certainty of our perfection in the system of mutual dependence of all things, which points the way to rise inwardly to a belief in God."

Dr. A. Schäffle.

_____

Elements of Sociology. (A Text-Book for Colleges and Schools.) By F. H. Giddings, M.A., Ph.D., Professor of Sociology in Columbia University. The Macmillan Co., 1898. Pp. x + 353. $1.10.

Whatever the sociologists may think of Professor Giddings' viewpoint or method or conclusions, they cannot afford to neglect anything that he writes. They are alike following the true, even if vague, instinct that the rest of social science fails to provide sufficiently for investigation of all the relations which must be explained before the conditions of the conduct of life can be completely understood. If others are closer than Professor Giddings to adequate perception of what sociology involves, none deserve more generous recognition for helping to spread the conviction that it has a province, and none are working more earnestly to discover and define that province. While I am obliged to differ with him fundamentally, I cannot guard myself too carefully against seeming to imply that it is easy to demonstrate a better way. Whatever he publishes contains evidence of wide information, of force and massiveness of thought, of independence and vigor of judgment, which entitle him to the most respectful hearing. His conception of sociology, however, seems to make it responsible for wider and deeper wisdom about society than available knowledge can at present authorize. To justify its existence, sociology is accordingly called upon for deliverances far in excess of visible scientific sanction. To one who holds, in contrast with Professor Giddings, that sociology is today less a scheme of knowledge than a scheme of problems, these deliverances necessarily seem premature. They compromise sociology in the eyes of men who respect the proprieties of science in other departments. They place it outside the scientific pale, in a series with astrology and alchemy and phrenology.

Sociology is an empty pretense if it in any way sets up a rivalry or competition with any other division of human knowledge. Sociology has no reason for existence except as a complementary division of knowledge about humanity. Sociology cannot be extemporized. It cannot be created in isolation from the researches that are prying into the elements of human conduct. It cannot be respectable if it undertakes to dogmatize about the constitution, processes, and results of human conduct ahead of authentic results from scientific research.

The present book is written for use in schools and colleges. To those who are familiar with Professor Giddings' previous work it goes without saying that the thought is presented with rare skill. The doctrines could scarcely be rendered in more appropriate and persuasive manner in text-book form. If Professor Giddings is right that the contents of the book are sanctioned by the present state of science, and if he is right that these phases of doctrine about society are good for college undergraduates, and even younger pupils, the author is certainly to be congratulated upon having organized a most attractive body of instruction, and pupils might be assured that they would look in vain for stronger guidance through the difficulties of this type of social philosophy. Without claiming any other sanction for my dissent than the authority of facts open to all, which must at last reconcile differences of opinion, I venture to express a very decided judgment in the negative upon both points. While I can offer no important suggestions toward the improvement of the book for its purpose, if its doctrine is scientifically tenable, and if it belongs in the undergraduate stage of study, my belief is very firm that neither supposition is correct. In the author's judgment it would be wise to devote a large part of the time available for the social sciences to study under guidance of this text-book (p. vi). My dissent from this judgment is a consequence of my belief that the subjects to which the book is devoted are not yet under control of the human mind as ascertained knowledge. The contents of the book are, therefore, hypotheses in didactic form.

So long as any subject-matter is in the hypothetical stage, it is bad pedagogy to give it dogmatic expression in the undergraduate course. Professor Giddings has given to his doctrine as authoritative expression as though it had passed out of the region of uncertainty, and had established itself as unquestionable reality. This is simply not the case. The subject-matter is for that reason not suitable, in this form at least, for the undergraduate curriculum. As between this book and courses appropriate to undergraduate stages of maturity in anthropology, ethnology, history, economics, civics, psychology, logic, and ethics, I would go beyond Professor Patten's somewhat startling statement before the American Economic Association several years ago: "No sociologist ought to be admitted to any college faculty without the consent of the economists." I would amend by substituting for "the economists" "all the members of the faculty who believe that there is such a thing as a rational correlation of sciences and a necessary integrity of science." Sociology has no competence to speak in advance of these sciences, except as to the *forms* of knowledge about society. It were vastly better for teachers with the sociological point of view to fill up the undergraduate time with either or all of the studies named, than for anyone, under supposed license of sociology, to lead undergraduates into such a very largely speculative "study of the nature and laws of human society" as this book contains. The form in which theorizing about society is put in this book must inevitably tend to create in the minds of immature students the impression that there is a sociological system of doctrine about "the nature and laws of human society," not composed out of the specific truths discovered by ethnology and history and comparative politics and psychology, but outside of, in addition to, and partly in antithesis with, the concrete or less generalized truths ascertained by these sciences.

Rather than leave that impression, exclude "sociology" from under-graduate curricula altogether. Students will get a more sane view of human relationships as a whole from wise instruction in the special social sciences than from unauthorized generalization under the title of sociology.

In other words, the book contains nothing which deserves to be accepted as established truth, that might not be better presented to undergraduates in courses upon the special branch of social science to which it primarily belongs. The book contains, and is controlled by, a speculative element which would make it more difficult than ever for the rest of the college course to develop power of cor-relating truth in a consistent and balanced system corresponding with reality. There is no sociology yet which can speak with authority upon the whole range of subjects that the book covers. It is vastly better for undergraduates to study where the ground is more secure, than to learn a system of doctrine about so many things that nobody knows. Some parts of sociology may be taught to undergraduates in such a way as to reinforce and be reinforced by everything else taught in college. The subject ought never to be introduced in col-leges if it must be presented as ideology, not coherent with knowledge ascertained by other branches of research.

It would obviously be unfair to require of a text-book the proofs and the elaborations that would be demanded in a complete treatise. The remarks that follow have reference less to the elementary form of the theory and method than to the more complete system which this form necessarily suggests to Professor Giddings' fellow-workers.

The table of contents indicates Professor Giddings' view of the scope of sociology more conclusively than any formula could define it. The titles of chapters are as follows: I, "Population and Society;" II, "Where Aggregations of People are Formed;" III, "How Aggre-gations of People are Formed;" IV, "The Composition and the Unity of a Social Population;" V, "The Practical Activities of Socii;" VI, "Socialization;" VII, "Coöperation;" VIII, "Social Pleasure;" IX, "The Social Nature;" X, "The Classes of Socii;" XI, "The Preëminent Social Class;" XII, "The Social Mind: Modes of Like-mindedness;" XIII, "Sympathetic Like-mindedness and Impulsive Social Actions;" XIV, "Formal Like-mindedness: Tradition and Conformity;" XV, "Rational Like-mindedness: Public Opinion and Social Values;" XVI, "Social Organization;" XVII, "Component Societies;" XVIII, "Constituent Societies;" XIX, "The Character and Efficiency of Organization;" XX, "The Early History of Society;" XXI, "Tribal Society;" XXII, "Civilization;" XXIII, "Progress;" XXIV, "Democracy;" XXV, "The Theory of Society."

I share Professor Giddings' belief that sociology is destined to have something to say, and something worth saying, about the whole range of subjects above indicated. At present, however, the sociologist who claims to speak as a specialist upon all that is here involved must choose between two decidedly different alternatives. He must either pose as the high priest of a very naïve opinionolatry, or he must consent to speak cautiously, tentatively, and for the most part formally about relations which, in the greater number of instances, cannot be generalized with authority until special investigators have put much more information at the disposal of the generalizer than anybody possesses today.

The book before us shows distinctly what that "subjective interpretation," of which so much was said in the *Principles of Sociology*,[1] amounts to in practice. Judged by its works, it may be called *impressionistic conceptualism*. The thing which we want philosophy to furnish is a report of reality that might be called *objectivistic conceptualism*. The difference between the two is measured by the different ratios in which the personal equation of the formulator enters into his report of the object. The worth or worthlessness of a conception depends upon whether it reproduces the actual properties of the object or forces into the object accidental peculiarities of the subject. The most ardent adherent of the Berkeleyan idealism would hardly maintain that the doctrine authorizes the individual consciousness to prescribe to all consciousnesses the form and content of mental images. There is no more sanction in pure idealism than in gross materialism for an infallible individual subjectivity.

Entirely apart, therefore, from the question of content, the form of Professor Giddings' doctrine is not the scientific form, and it is, therefore, not in place as an introduction to study of real things. In contrast with the sort of study of society which students, young and old, need most to pursue, Professor Giddings' method may be compared with that of Dr. Mulford in *The Nation*, as contrasted with Professor Woodrow Wilson's method in *The State*. Each book displays genius of a high order. Each, doubtless, has a mission. For a beginner in political science, Professor Giddings should in consistency prefer Mulford, while all but a small minority of political scientists would prefer

[1] *Principles of Sociology*, pp. 10, 22, 36, etc.

Wilson. For scientific purposes, the difference is like that between one of Turner's suggestions on canvas of a stormy day on the English coast and an admiralty chart of the same spot. In the National Gallery the impressionist's work would be most admired. In the wheelhouse of the skipper feeling his way into port the work of the realist and the literalist would be of most use.

Professor Giddings does not make his readers confront the thing that is, but he shows very early that his doctrines deal with something possibly quite different, viz., those impressions and conceptions which things, or their symbols, have deposited in his mind. He imagines that he is describing when he is only interpreting in advance of description. What he believes to be objectivity of the most penetrating order is extremely defective objectivity. It promotes a factor of reality to supremacy, if not to monopoly, in the object characterized. For instance, he does not show his readers how to find out for themselves what "society" is. Instead of that he asks us to think about society in terms of an abstracted phase of societary reality, thus: "Society, then, as a mode of activity of intelligent individuals is *the cultivation of acquaintance and like-mindedness*" (p. 5); and again: "A society is a number of like-minded individuals — socii — *who know and enjoy their like-mindedness*, and are therefore able to work together for common ends" (p. 6). These definitions compel us either to rule out of consideration many, and perhaps all, of the associations of people which would best reward study, or to credit them in advance by definition with a character which is certainly not correctly expressed in these formulas. No fair and natural interpretation of these definitions could be made to admit the following into the category "societies": the English during the Wars of the Roses; the Germans during the Thirty Years' War; the Italians from Odoacer to Garibaldi; the French most of the time from Philip I to President Faure; the Americans from Jamestown and Plymouth to the Cuban war.

If we could agree in advance that any selected national, not to say international, groups are "societies," it would be play for a student of history to make out from the evidence a strong case for the generalization: "A society is a number of *un*like-minded individuals who know and enjoy their unlike-mindedness." Nobody would concede that this thesis tells the whole story, but it formulates so important an element in the case that no one not mortgaged to a prejudice would be satisfied with Professor Giddings' thesis after considering other aspects of the facts.

Professor Giddings would say that the traits of recognized likeness are so fundamental that they include all the accidents of opposition. This is not true, however, when stated in terms of consciousness. It is true if stated in terms of attributes the most decisive of which are not conscious at all. They are rather common susceptibilities, and consequently common relationships to certain telic economies. The author seems to encounter this fact at times, and he varies his formula accordingly.[1] An ingenious conceptualist may plausibly interpret like irritability as "like-mindedness." This interpretation can stand, however, only as an impressionist's representation, not as a realist's report of reality.

My meaning will be evident, then, when I say that the first fifteen chapters of the book contain Professor Giddings' account of what he finds when he consults his own consciousness as to the traits which society would exhibit if it conducted itself in accordance with his conceptions. I do not mean to imply that he thinks the social reality incorrectly at all points, by any means. I mean to say that his rendering is somewhat analogous with a photograph of an engraving from a portrait. Neither that nor a photograph from nature is perfect, but we have no doubt, on general principles, which is likely to be the closest likeness. Chaps. XVI–XXII, inclusive, traverse much of the same ground that is covered by the previous chapters. They seem, however, to have been written from a more objective standpoint. They try to give an account of the structure and partially of the development of actual primitive society, in accordance with the conceptions of society worked out in the previous division. The remaining chapters, on "Progress," "Democracy," and "The Theory of Society," are conceptual again rather than objective.

Along with surrender to this subjectivistic conceptualism Professor Giddings' method is seduced by his unquestioning faith in the finality of phrases as an equivalent for scientific discovery. It leads him to overestimate what he has accomplished, when he has merely grouped a lot of familiar things and put a label of his own on them, even though this label takes the place of more specific and scientific designations and classifications. To illustrate, we may take the schedule in chap. V of "the simple modes of all the practical activities known to a population." These are said to be (1) "appreciation," (2) "utilization," (3) "characterization," and (4) "socialization." Nothing indicates that Professor Giddings is conscious of any anomaly in making

[1] *E. g.*, on p. 82. Further reference to this passage follows on p. 552.

(4) coördinate with the other three, as a simple process proceeding from the individual alone. But passing this, and referring to the "complex activities" in the same chapter, we find that the author has created an order of sequence in the development of social activities which bids defiance to facts in most wholesale fashion. The alleged order of activities is (1) economic, (2) legal, (3) political, (4)—"which presupposes all the others that have been described"—"cultural" (p. 45). Whether the four categories are the most discriminating in this connection is a question by itself. That there is any such lineal uniformity as Professor Giddings asserts in the emergence of these activities is contrary to all the evidence.

But the fatality of phrases appears when the attempt is made a few pages later (45–7) to use the first four categories as clues to "motives of activity.' The author could hardly have gone about the work more sagaciously, if he had been deliberately bent upon creating such confusion in students' minds that they could never again use any of the psychological analyses which have organized this chaos into approximate order. I do not recall a more fantastic substitution of phrases for precision than in the next following passage (pp. 47–52) on "The Methods of Activity." The arbitrary use of the terms "attack" and "impression" betrays an irresponsibility to accredited usage which is neither serviceable nor excusable. I have seldom experienced a more definite shock than when I turned the leaf and read, at the top of p. 50, that "all these methods . . . . are so many modes of one universal method . . . . called *conflict"!* If Professor Giddings had promulgated a theory of optics in terms of the thesis, "all optical phenomena are consequences of a particular physical property, viz., *white;*" and if in an elementary text-book he had concluded his analysis of optical phenomena with the assertion, "all these methods of action are so many modes of one universal method, viz., *black,*" he could not have been more mystifying than in his manipulation of phrases to make "consciousness of kind" as the principle fit with "conflict" as the method of all social activities.

Other illustrations of the same futility of phrases are apparent in the whole discussion of the "unit of investigation" (pp. 9–11). It is a profitless magnification of the commonplace. Of course we are dealing with "human individuals in conscious combination." At least they are conscious, though not necessarily conscious that they are in combination. It may impress some imaginations as a very considerable advance in knowledge to be able to vary the verbal symbol for

these familiar individuals, and to call them "the units of investigation" or "socii." To others it is nothing but very wasteful marking
time. When we call John Smith a *socius*, he remains the same John
Smith. When he enlists in the army, and tires of camp life, and fights
with Tom Brown, and we call it "consciousness of kind," instead of
conquering new territory for science, we are simply betaking ourselves
to pitiful logomachy in default of science.

The speculative temper is so dominant in Professor Giddings' work
that there are few important passages in the book which critical readers
will accept without challenge. In many of these cases, to be sure, the
author may prove to be right, or nearer right than his critics, but he
will have some very difficult tasks to sustain himself in his positions.

For instance, the chapter on "Coöperation" (p. 76) fortifies very
precise dogma with very inexact dialectics. Instead of examining the
different discoverable genera and species of coöperation, and generalizing their conditions and characteristics, the author incontinently con-
ceptualizes it, and then offers explanations for the alleged traits. Thus:
"Nearly every kind of activity in society is a form of coöperation"
(p. 76). "Coöperation can be established only in a population which
in a measure has become socialized. There must be a consciousness of
kind, communication, habits of imitation ; or, if these fail, where the
population contains elements not yet assimilated and too unlike for harmonious combination, there must at least be an established toleration"
(p. 77). Professor Giddings does not realize that his own qualification
in this last clause makes his use of his conception fallacious. But
he continues : "Obviously there can be no coöperation unless there is
among the individuals who are to combine their efforts a common
interest in some object or end which they wish to attain." The truth
of this proposition depends, of course, upon previous agreement about
the content of the concept "coöperation." I have no desire to quib-
ble about terms, but the fact is that people who have had a very small
modicum of common interest, and would not have understood it
if they were told that they were working to a common end, have '
been coworkers toward a common achievement. They have been
enticed by certain interests which appealed to them in severalty or in
minor groups, while the accomplishment of their discrete purposes
tended, without their thought or ken, to bring about a composite result.
Much more of this than the chapter allows has occupied human history. Accordingly it is not difficult to see that an inductive study of
"mutual aid" would have to begin far back of Professor Giddings'

starting-point. It would soon sweep aside his dogmas about "consciousness of kind." It would generalize *coördinations* rather than arbitrarily conceived coöperation.

In the same chapter that versatile factor "consciousness of kind" appears as "similar response to the same stimulus" and "perception by each that all have the same interest" (p. 78). But a moment later (p. 82) there is another lightning change, and "like-mindedness" or "consciousness of kind" reduces itself to its lowest terms, viz., "responsiveness of the like nervous organizations of the coöperating animals or men to the same stimulus." If Professor Giddings means by this formula what it means to the physiologist, he has no right to insist that it is identical with any formula whatever in which consciousness is a term. In the examples that follow, however, it appears more plainly than ever that "consciousness of kind," which Professor Baldwin has referred to as "the climax of descriptive vagueness,"[1] is merely a prospector's claim to anything that may hereafter be discovered in the unexplored territory to which it asserts a title.[2]

But there is another element in the book, of which a very different estimate is necessary. It is not so matured as to be suitable for use with undergraduates, but it suggests abundant problems for the research work of older students. It becomes prominent from the eighth chapter, where there is a beginning of analytical examination of concrete phenomena. It is never free from the glossing conceptualism above described, but it may well provoke to further analysis, and exclusion of the unwarranted assumptions. Beyond this incipient description there is a series of formulations,[3] which I frankly admire, although I am more than doubtful about their content. As mere speculations they are brilliant. If they are actual generalizations of pertinent data, they are masterly in form, whether they will stand the test of larger induction or not. In these formulas Professor Giddings boldly but correctly illustrates the order of generality to which sociologists aspire to carry knowledge of society. In order to establish generalizations of that order, however, we must win the coöperation of the historians. They, with the ethnologists, must gather and arrange suitable data for generalization. We are but little better furnished with competent evidence as yet than most of the philosophers of history have been. However brilliant our hypotheses, therefore, they must remain under suspicion until they can

[1] *Social and Ethical Interpretations*, p. 483.

[2] This is most curiously confirmed by the assertion (p. 341) that "the law of least effort" merely furnishes terms for "ultimate explanation" of consciousness of kind!

[3] Pp. 137, 139, 140, 154, 168, 171, 192, 215, 219, 221, 230.

be inductively verified. Professor Giddings' formulas might well serve as theorems for doctors' dissertations.

The faults of method which make Professor Giddings' system so assailable are, therefore, the weaknesses of a strong thinker. Being so fast in a race, he will not drag the plow. The consequences may be emphasized in one more radical criticism of his work.

The "note to reviewer" sent by the publishers calls special attention to the last half of the last chapter, among other passages. It is "believed to be a new contribution to psychology, no less than to sociology." In the proposition, "the ultimate psychologcial motive is the persistent desire of consciousness to be clear and painless, and, if possible, pleasurable" (340), I find nothing that Patten and Ward have left unsaid, and I wonder that the chapter makes no specific reference to their discussions of the "pain and pleasure economy." More significant, however, is the treatment of "ejective interpretation" (pp. 341–3). I will not try to speak for Professor Baldwin, but it is not difficult to imagine what his estimate will be of a "contribution to psychology" which consists of applying a slightly varied phrase to one of his perceptions isolated from its counterpoising perceptions. The "ejective stage," according to Baldwin, is only one side of the "dialectic of personal growth" (*Mental Development*, pp. 8–9). Professor Giddings seems to imply that "ejective interpretation ' is not merely one factor in " the give-and-take between the individual and his fellows " (Baldwin), but that interpretation of one's fellows and of the social whole in terms of the interpreter's inner self is standard and authoritative. Here seems to be an avowal of methodological principle which I have supposed Professor Giddings to follow unintentionally. If he actually means to assert a right to make his own consciousness the scientific measure of objective reality, he virtually declares that to be the primary methodological virtue which I have heretofore assumed to be an unacknowledged and unconscious vice. The trouble with "ejective interpretation," as a scientific norm, is that in our interpretation of ourselves we are prone to set a value on ourselves which at once disarranges objective valuation. Just before Dewey appeared at Manila Admiral Montojo issued to his command a memorable specimen of interpretation in this form. It was an appraisal of American character. It was "subjective" and "ejective," but it promoted the gaiety of nations because it was defectively objective. In other words, the Spanish admiral thought, but he did not know. The subjective process in science may be likened to the physical process of adjusting a field glass when examining a distant object. The observer may first place the big end of the instrument to his eye, with the result that he dwarfs the object. After reversing the instrument, further adjustment is necessary to make the focus exact. The eye, which for this purpose is analogous with subjectivity, is the medium of interpretation of course, but the object is the fixed quantity, and in the last analysis it is the object, not the eye, which determines the correctness of the report. Science is not made by subjectivity. Science is the output of subjectivity applying itself to the objective and correcting itself by progressive apprehension of the objective. If we attempt to make a science upon the contrary hypothesis, it reports reality, not in terms of itself, but in the form and moving imposed upon it by our subjectivity. It would require the courage of one's convictions thus to propose oneself as the norm of all external reality. It is too late in the history of science, however, for even such self-confidence to be taken at its own appraisal by cautious seekers after knowledge. Science is interpretation of reality by itself, not by that fraction of reality which comes to consciousness in myself.

Sociology has nothing to gain, but everything to lose, by ignoring the conclusions of the centuries about the limitations and restraints which must be enforced upon speculation, if it is to be kept serviceable. Speculation does not alter its character when we entitle it "subjective interpretation" or "ejective interpretation." It is the same anticipatory surmising, which may or may not prove to be in accordance with the facts. It should be added that many of Professor Giddings' propositions doubtless appear more dogmatic in cold type than they would seem in connection with his verbal explanations. I do not wish to exaggerate that element in his method, nor to depreciate the helpfulness of his fertility in speculation. My main contentions are, first, that the larger generalizations of sociology are not yet ripe for undergraduate consumption ; second, that among investigators in sociology speculation should be welcome as a handmaid, but intolerable as a dictator.   ALBION W. SMALL.

The Psychology of Peoples. Its Influence on Their Evolution. By GUSTAVE LE BON. New York: The Macmillan Co., 1898. Pp. xx + 236.

THIS translation of Le Bon's *Lois psychologiques de l'évolution des peuples* (Paris, 1895) forms a sort of companion volume to the same writer's *Psychologie des foules* (Paris, 1896), which a year or so ago appeared in English under the title of *The Crowd*. M. Le Bon may be described as an intellectual kodak fiend. His books are filled with snapshots at truth, interesting in themselves, but sadly unconnected, and out of focus. The volume under consideration purports to be merely a summary of conclusions reached in rather exhaustive special studies. It would be unfair, therefore, to criticise too harshly the apparently unsupported dogmatism and finality of judgment which pervade the book.

The argument is briefly this: Each people has a soul, not a mystical entity, but a community of sentiments and beliefs which are transmitted by physical and social heredity. These elements, predominantly emotional, constitute the popular character, which determines its political institutions, its arts, its religion. The intellectual life of a people is to be distinguished from its character. The former is easily modified; the latter relatively permanent. Indeed, the most striking thing about a psychological race is its fixity of character, which remains practically unchanged beneath what seem to be radical modifications of thought, dress, manners, speech, art forms, etc. Intellectual changes are, however, very gradually transformed into emotional beliefs, which thus slowly become a part of a people's character. There is progress in spite of apparent fixity, but this advance is only achieved by gradual accumulations of minute changes. The decadence of a people is due, not to loss of intellectual power, but to a disaggregation of collective character.

It is further asserted that races may be profitably classified only by their psychological character, *i. e.*, into (1) the primitive, (2) the inferior, (3) the average, (4) the superior. The delightful relativity of these categories is obvious. Again, the superiority of a race depends ess upon the average it attains than upon the wideness of variation of individuals within it. The progressive races, therefore, are not approaching a Utopian equality, but are being constantly differentiated, and throughout the book M. Le Bon shows the antipathy to democratic institutions and the dread of socialism which are so conspicuous in *The Crowd*.

It may be said that this little work recasts into a sort of coherent system a great many opinions which have become commonplaces with philosophical students of history and politics. It says, cleverly enough, that governmental institutions are effects rather than causes; hat prejudices and emotional beliefs are more potent than rational arguments; that institutions cannot be transplanted from one people to another without undergoing radical changes. All these and many other things are restated in a somewhat new terminology, which gives them, perhaps, a touch of novelty, but they are interspersed with so many unwarranted generalizations that the book, as a whole, makes the impression of a brilliant, daring, but largely doctrinaire and untrustworthy body of personal dicta. Yet, in spite of all this, Le Bon deserves the credit of having indicated problems and outlined a system; a service which social psychologists will willingly recognize as valuable. The translation is anonymous, and apparently the work of a "hack." To say nothing of awkward English, misplaced clauses, and the like, one or two inexcusable blunders may be noted. The American "War of Succession" (p. xvi) (orig. *sécession*) is, perhaps, not so surprising from an English translator — the work was evidently done in London — but what can we say for this sentence (p. 195): '. .' . . a few Arab tribes, unified by the thought of Mahomet, conquered in a few years nations *who ignored their very names* . . . ." (orig. ' qûi ignoraient jusqu'à leurs noms ")?

George E. Vincent.

The Criminal Insane in the United States and in Foreign Countries. Report by S. J. Barrows. Washington, 1898.

This Senate document has been prepared by one of the most competent men in the nation. It deserves the careful attention of all who are interested in humane treatment of irresponsible persons, and in the protection of society against those who are dangerous. This work should quicken the movement to provide in all states special asylums for criminals of unsound mind. It is a wrong to the ordinary insane to compel them to associate with lawbreakers in the state hospitals.

C. R. H.

NOTES AND ABSTRACTS.

Agricultural Occupation for Convicts in Austria and Germany. (*Blätter für Gefängnisskunde*, 32. Band, 3. u. 4. Heft, 1898. Article by ANTON MARCOVICH; chief director of the prison in Marburg a. D. (Austria).)— Labor is one of the most essential factors of education in the correctional process. The convict should work in order that he may not forget the art he has learned in freedom, that he may form better habits of continuous industry, and that he may not by idleness during the period of punishment become a spiritual and physical cripple.

There are many difficulties in the way of the ordinary prison industries. In some cases convicts are employed with work which has no educational value to them, and which produces very little toward their support. Tailoring, shoemaking, cabinet work, locksmithing, are about the only industries which can be carried on with profit, and these, owing to the danger of competition with outside shops, are confined to the narrow field of production for public institutions. Other occupations, such as envelope and paper-bag making, picking wool and horse hair, spinning, and weaving are neither remunerative nor instructive, but merely serve to keep men busy.

More than 50 per cent. of the prisoners are of the class of peasants and agricultural laborers. To give them training in small crafts tends to add them to the miserable city proletariat, and to enfeeble them in body and mind. These facts long since led to experiments with agricultural labor for convicts.

In all states there is much public work waiting to be done in the control of streams, the making and repair of roads and streets, and drainage systems. It is evident that there would be great economic advantage in employing convict labor on such useful tasks, if serious difficulties do not prevent.

The first inquiry as to the effect of labor in the open country relates to health. On this point the testimony of the medical officer of Marburg prison is explicit and favorable.

The second inquiry relates to the economic results. The author is confident that labor on public works, too costly to be carried on by ordinary taxation, has a tendency to remove convict labor out of the sphere of competition with ordinary industry.

The most serious question arises in connection with discipline. American students and practical people will at once think of the lease system which was so severely criticised in the National Conference of Charities in 1883, and elsewhere. The author of this article declares that the men not only worked with vigor and efficiency, but that few escaped — in eight years there were only five cases at Marburg. In one instance the detachment earned honor by assisting in rescuing lives and property in a conflagration. During the years 1890–97 there were 1,983 convicts thus employed from Marburg, the number increasing from 62 to 454 per year; and from Wildbach 878 persons.

The conditions under which convict labor can safely and profitably be employed are such as the following:

The work should be one requiring considerable time and force, and of large public utility. Contracts should be made with local governments providing for subsidy in local improvements on condition that convict labor should be used. The cost of support diminishes with numbers, and the product of labor increases; therefore at least thirty convicts should be worked in a group. The prisoners must be carefully selected; only those who have served for some time in solitary confinement, who have shown reliable qualities, and who are of rural origin and adapted to farm labor being chosen. The director of the prison must, in person or by a competent deputy, provide in advance for suitable quarters and food.

The discipline must be firm and rigorous, as in a military camp. But with humane and steady management, bayonets and bullets are rarely required.

Director Link, of the Lichtenau prison, confirms the views of Marcovich by the results of his own considerable experience. He calls attention to the fact that experiments have been tried with success in Italy, Austria, England, and France. The prisons of Lichtenberg, Insterburg, Düsseldorf, Aachen, Münster i. W., and Zweibrücken are specially mentioned. He urges that the greatest care should be given to secure housing, the food, the clothing, the discipline, the education, and the religious influences.

One group of 36 prisoners worked for three months under 3 officers. In another place 80 men worked on a river dam under 3 officers. On the Elbe river works 75 prisoners labored for two years under the eyes of 3 officers.

It may be added that the experiment should not be tried in America without employing all the precautions mentioned by these Austrian and German directors.

It is a serious question whether such experiments should be tried on any scale whatever in America. The abstract is given without editorial indorsement, as a contribution to discussion. The following comment of Superintendent Brockway may profitably be read in this connection.— C. R. HENDERSON.

"I have your personal note of the 5th with a condensation of the German article, which I have carefully perused.

"The publication of it in your magazine would be well warranted for communicating interesting foreign news as to the kind of attention they are giving over there to this phase of the prison question; but if the influence of the publication should be, or the publication of the article is so intended, that the plan of employing prisoners upon public works or agricultural occupations in this country should be promoted by it, then I think it would be the advocacy of a false system of prison employment, and be injurious, perhaps, to the progress of true prison science. I quite agree with the comment you make, that, if prisoners are to be so employed, they must be carefully selected; only those who have served their time (approaching the period of their final release), who are not of the reckless class, those of rural life previous to their imprisonment, adapted to farm labor, should be chosen. This principle of selection must needs result in the utilizing of a very small percentage of the prisoners of the state in this agricultural or public works employment. The prisoners so employed would belong to the corrigible class whose corrigibility carries with it an obligation of the state to fit them in the best possible way for earning, without painful effort, a sufficiency for their proper subsistence and enjoyments. This last-mentioned principle of employment, taken in connection with your plan of selection, would leave for such service only the prisoners who are to be engaged in agricultural employment or as laborers, plus any mechanics who might be properly and profitably employed in the construction of public buildings. The really difficult problem of prisoners' employment is to find the best engagement to be provided for the prisoners not probably susceptible, for the period of the imprisonment, to confident preparation for legitimate industry and law-abiding behavior after their release. To employ such prisoners in agricultural work and on public works is, I believe, impracticable, that is to say, inconsistent with the purpose for which the state restricts a man's liberty for a period and turns him out again. The whole scheme of employing prisoners in large numbers in this country, in the open, is wrong. In these northern states it will not prove economical. The experiment, at the northern prison of this state, of building roads with convicts shows that the work performed by the prisoners could have been done by free labor at ordinary wages at less cost to the state than the actual cost of it as performed by prisoners. Such employment is also inconsistent with proper discipline. We cannot hold to suitable strict discipline prisoners working in the field, without the barriers preventing escapes and insurrections such as exist in a well-established prison establishment. The experience of the whole world is that the convict gangs employed, as is proposed, are centers of corruption, both of the prisoners themselves so employed, and that a similar influence is disseminated to the locality where they work by their presence and behavior there.

"It may be that where this experiment you refer to was tried, there were few escapes, but in this broad country of ours, without a national police, escapes or attempts to escape will be frequent under any supervision the state will pay for these gangs. Frequent escapes would disintegrate the whole plan, and the necessary 'casualties to the escaping criminals would be repugnant to the public sense of our civilization, and soon result in an outcry against the plan and insistence that they be turned in again within the proper inclosures where prisoners are usually confined. The crime and criminals of a state do in some proper sense constitute 'the skeleton in the closet' of the public family, and ought to be kept in the closet, never unnecessarily exhibited to the public gaze.

"Most of the prisoners in this country, in the densely populated and eastern and middle states at least, come from and will return to the cities. They should be trained to such occupation as will enable them to earn a living where they will probably reside. The teaching of trades, carefully selected according to the adaptation and forecast of circumstances for the prisoner himself, should be carried on completely for every prisoner who may probably be reclaimed. A considerable class of criminals are so defective that they must always belong to the dependent or dangerous classes, and these should be reclused, not for punishment, but for treatment for the public protection by their continued detention, except those that may possibly be restored. The remainder of prisoners will not be a majority of them by any means, and, under the conditions of this country, while a few of them, carefully selected, may be temporarily or occasionally employed on such work as the German writer mentions, the most of this remaining, apparently incorrigible class might be employed best at productive mechanical work, if the state will allow it, at some coarse industries to be acquired by purchase, and to be forever after held as state mechanical work, with which no citizen of the state has a right to interfere; or, as is done in this New York state at present very successfully, they may be employed in the production of useful articles for penal and charitable institutions, and certain supplies for public use of civil divisions of the state. Very truly yours,
Z. R. Brockway."

Disarmament.—The circular of August 24, 1898, addressed to the representatives of the powers, by order of Nicholas II of Russia, marks an important date in history. It is the first time since the era of atrocious butcheries lasting from 1854 to 1871 that one sincere word of peace has been uttered by the chief of a great military state. The circular amounts to a suggestion that in future there be no addition to present existing armaments. The major portion of the laudatory comment it has received has been directed toward the motives of its author rather than toward the practical value of the suggestion itself. The socialist, upon the other hand, is inclined to leave to one side all consideration of motive, and to attend sharply to the probable bearing of the circular upon the trend of events, with special reference to the programme of reform to which socialism stands pledged. He does not befool himself with the abortive hope that governments which are but the sorry masks, or, at most, the pitiful puppets, of a ruling class will meet the proposals of Nicholas II in good faith. National hatreds, quarrels, and bickerings; popular prejudices, hostilities, discussions — these are essential to the maintenance of power by the ruling class of today. That it should joyfully gather about the altar of universal concord is not among the possibilities of a future so startingly immediate as to be unhealthfully exciting. The socialist is wasting little time in pink-hued day-dreams as to how pretty things will be in a few weeks when the powers shall have had time to favorably consider the Czar's proposal. In a Europe of iron and fire such dreamings are perceptibly ill-timed. On the contrary, he sees in the Czar's circular a means of bringing into prominent notice before whole classes of people, who would otherwise have scorned to give it a moment's thought, an important part of the socialist programme, *i. e.*, the abolishment of government by force. He sees in the possible outcome of the deliberations of any commission or convention called to consider the Czar's suggestion a powerful aid to the socialist cause. Should the proposition be favorably received — a most unlikely thing! — the people, freed from the stultifying and debasing power of the barracks — a power whose vile influence does not cease to be felt short of the primary school and the infant's cradle — will be fitted, mentally and economically, for a better understanding of the socialist programme and for a readier acceptance of its practicable implications. Should the proposition fail of consideration, or meet with unfavorable consideration, then, too, will the socialist cause be helped. For once again will have been demonstrated the unwillingness or inability of governments, subservient to class interests and filled with territorial jealousies, to banish the specter of war. The people will then be in a fairer way to perceive that genuine disarmament and the downfall of militarism are logical and immediate consequences of a general triumph of socialist doctrines. The socialist, therefore, has only to wait and to be faithful to his principles. Meanwhile he can afford to justly applaud any real service rendered to the proletariat of two hemispheres—even though that service be rendered by the Czar of all the Russias.— PAUL LOUIS, "Désarmement," *Revue socialiste*, September, 1898.

Disarmament: A Study in International Law.—Law is the refuge of the weak; it is remarkable to see the first military power of the globe coöperate to limit the rule of force. Before attempting this vast reform it would be necessary to obtain the assent of all the powers, including the United States. The first difficulty is that of the maintenance of existing treaties without power to enforce them. Whatever respect we may have for treaties, the changes in the life of nations cause treaties to become obsolete, like private contracts.

The coming conference will have the difficult task of combining disarmament with a fundamental principle of international law, viz., the independence of nations. Independence implies the right of coercive action, *i. e., war*. No one can imagine that the vote of a congress will transform the world. Suppose that shortly after an agreement to disarm the conditions in one of the countries should change; for example, that there should be a civil war or a rebellion in a colony. The nation must continue to exist, even if it has signed such a treaty; and to do so it must arm itself, and that, too, quickly. What would be done with such a nation? It would be necessary to prevent its abruptly breaking its new legal bonds, and to do this a permanent commission would be necessary. The powers of the commission would have to be very broad; for, suppose, by way of example, that an engineer or chemist should invent some new method of destruction capable of taking the place of large armies, would it not be necessary to gain the permission of the commission before any power could use it? The larger the powers of the commission would have to be, the more difficult it would be to establish it. It would have to be invested with the gravest political questions, and at times would have in its hands the fate of empires. Would rulers and parliaments give up to a commission of diplomats the greater part of their power? Impossible. The decisions of the commission would have to have more than a moral force; an international army would be necessary. It would have to be larger than that of any particular country, for it could not be mobilized rapidly and would be composed of heterogeneous elements. The obstacles to disarmament seem insurmountable, but genius overcomes obstacles seemingly insurmountable. The congress ought to assemble. The surest way to reduce a fortress is to take the advance works, which in this case is to codify international law and render certain principles more definite and general.— M. ARTHUR DESJARDINS, *Revue des Deux Mondes*, October, 1898.

Psychology and Art.— Art offers to psychology two groups of problems: First, by what psychical process does the mind create art? Second, by what psychical process does the mind enjoy art? In trying to answer the first, the sociological, biological, and historical methods of psychology are used; the second favors the experimental methods.

The first begins with a biological study of the play of animals and proceeds to a study of primitive art. We learn how climate, political conditions, etc., influence art production.

The second includes a study of phenomena such as tones and beats, harmony, rhythm and its relation to the time sense, rhythm in verse, agreeable and disagreeable combinations of forms and colors.

How far can such studies become productive or suggestive in the teaching of drawing?

A study of the causes that produce art will aid us to understand how to train the æsthetic activities of the pupil. A study of the effects of art suggests the rules and facts that are to be taught. The healthy atmosphere for the taste of a child is harmonious classical beauty; and it is an educational mistake to allow "primitivistic art" in the school.

Nevertheless there is danger in trying to work out technical prescriptions for art. This psychological scheme is one-sided, and our time confronts dangers for its ideal life if triumphant psychology crushes under its feet every idealistic opposition. I cannot forget that this view-point is an artificial one for real, living art.— HUGO MÜNSTERBERG, *Atlantic Monthly*, November, 1898.

Annual Statement Relating to the Operatives and Wage-Earners at Pullman.— A canvass of all the wage-earners at Pullman, completed October 11, 1898, shows that, exclusive of house servants, there were 5,997 persons employed in all our industries and business establishments; 5,730 of them being males and 267 females; 3,425 of these operatives are married, and 2,572 are single; 2,408 are reported as skilled workmen, 1,748 as "fairly skilled," and 1,841 are classed as laborers; 1,406 rented homes in Pullman, and 1,515 boarded here, while 915 owned homes outside of Pullman, and 1,143 rented homes outside of Pullman, and 1,018 boarded outside. A few more than one-half of the whole number neither resided nor boarded in Pullman. The average length of time these operatives have been here or have worked here is six years and nine months. The nativity of these 5,997 working people is exhibited in the following tabular statement.

NATIVITY OF OPERATIVES.

Types	Countries where born	Number born in each country	Totals of types
American	United States	1,921	1,921
Scandinavian	Denmark	57	
	Finland	7	
	Norway	112	
	Sweden	1,155	1,331
British	Australia	7	
	Canada	230	
	England	303	
	Scotland	104	
	Wales	18	632
German	Austria	129	
	Bohemia	23	
	Prussia and other German states	692	844
Irish	Ireland	196	196
Latin	Belgium	9	
	France	5	
	Italy	143	
	Spain	0	
	Switzerland	18	175
Dutch	Holland	640	640
Other countries	Hungary	48	
	Mexico	1	
	Poland	112	
	Russia	51	
	Elsewhere	16	228
Totals		5,997	5,997

PULLMAN, ILL., October 11, 1898.   DUANE DOTY.

BIBLIOGRAPHY.

January—for November-December.

CONDUCTED BY C. H. HASTINGS.

NEW BOOKS AND NOTICES OF BOOKS REVIEWED.

Explanation. *Titles not starred* represent new publications announced in the standard publishers' lists since the last issue of the bibliography. A *star prefixed* to a title indicates that it was taken from a review of the work in the periodical cited after the title. It may or may not be a new announcement. The *arithmetical signs* following the citation to a review indicate the tenor of the review: X, uncertain ; +, favorable ; —, unfavorable ; + —, favorable, but with reservations ; — +, unfavorable, but with commendation ; + +, very favorable ; — — very unfavorable ; + + —, very favorable, but with reservations ; — — +, very unfavorable, but with commendation. Absence of any sign indicates that review has not been read. The *publication date* when not given is understood to be the current year. *Prices quoted* are usually for volumes bound in cloth in the case of American and English books, in paper in the case of all others. *New editions, translations,* and *new periodicals* are bracketed. Abbreviations. *See* at end of Bibliography.

SUBJECT INDEX.

AUTHOR INDEX TO NOTICES OF BOOK REVIEWS.

NEW BOOKS.

1. Anthropology, Ethnology, Archæology.

Curtin, J. Creation myths of primitive America in relation to the religious history & mental development of mankind. B., ?. 12s.

Egypt exploration fund. Archæological report, 1897-8. . . . ed. by T. L. Griffith. L., Frowde. 4to. 2s. 6d.

[Gobineau, Graf. Versuch üb. die Ungleichheit der Menschenracen. Deutsche Ausg. 2. Bd. St., F. Frommaun. 382 pp. 8vo. M. 4.20.]

*Groome, F. H. Gipsy folk tales. L., Hurst & Blackett. 12s. (Academy. D. 3 + + —)

*Haddon, A. C. Study of man. N. Y., G, P. Putnam's Sons. 410 pp. 8vo. $2. (Science ser., V. 1.) (AJS., N. +) (Outlook, O. 22 + +)

Parker, Mrs. K. L. More Australian legendary tales, collected from various tribes. . . . L., Nutt. 128 pp. 8vo. 3s. 6d.

Skinner, C. M. Myths & legends beyond our borders. Phil., J. B. Lippincott, 319 pp. il. 12mo. $1.50.

2. Biology, Evolution, Science.

*Argyll, Duke of. Organic evolution cross-examined; or, some suggestions on the great secret of biology. L., Murray. 208 pp. 8vo. (Outlook, D. 17 X) (Athenæum, N. 5 +) [Reprint of magazine articles.]

Earl, A. The living organism: an intro. to the problems of biology. L., Macmillan Co. 286 pp. 8vo. 6s.

Earl, Pliny, Memoirs, ed. by F. B. Sanborn, with selections from his diaries, letters and writings. Bo,. Damrell & Upham. 409 pp. $2.

Jordan, D. S. Footnotes to evolution: a series of popular addresses on the evolution of life. . . . N. Y., D. Appleton & Co. 392 pp. 12mo. $1.50.

*Mivart, St. G. Groundwork of science: a study of epistemology. L., Murray. 352 pp. 8vo. 6s. (Progressive science ser.) (Athenæum, N. 12 — —)

[Spencer, Herb. Principles of biology. Rev. & enl. ed. 2 v. V. 1. N. Y., D. Appleton & Co. 706 pp. 8vo. $2. (Synthetic philosophy.)

Talbot, E. S. Degeneracy; its causes, signs & results. N. Y., D. Appleton & Co. 388 pp. 12mo. $1.50. (Contemp. sci. ser.)

3. Charities.

Bericht über die Gedenkfeier der inneren Mission u. des 50-jähr. Jubiläum des Centralausschusses f. die innere Mission der deutschen evangel. Kirche . . . . 1898. Wittenberg, P. Munschmann. 121 pp. 8vo. M. 1.20.

Broglie, E. de. Saint Vincent de Paul, trans. by Mildred Partidge. . . . L., Duckworth. 272 pp. 8vo. 3s. (The Saints.)

Chappell, Jennie. Four noble women and their work (Frances Willard. Agnes Weston, Sister Dora and Catharine Booth). Lo., Partridge. 160 pp. 8vo. 1s. 6d.

Erster Jahresbericht der Frauen-Vereinigung f. sociale Hilfsthätigkeit in Wien. 1897. Wien, A. Schulze. 28 pp. 8vo. M. 0.30.

Fletcher, Horace. The last waif; or, social quarantine. C., H. S. Stone & Co. 12mo. $1.50.

Flugschriften des Evangelischen Bundes. Hrsg. vom Vorstand des Ev. Bundes. 155.-157. Hft. B., A. Haack.

Great Britain — Report of the Committee of Council for Eng. & Wales on Schools for the Blind & Deaf. 8vo. 3s. 6d.

Hansult, Mor. Das Patronat in der evangelischen Landeskirche des Grossherzogt. Hessen. Giessen, E. Roth. 95 pp. 8vo. M. 2.

Guida delle instituzioni pubbliche di beneficenza: pubblicazione del Bolletino delle opere pie del regno, Disp. 26-27. Bologna, soc. tip. gia Composatori. pp. 401-32 8vo.

Jahre, 50, innere Mission, Bericht über die Thätigkeit des Central-Ausschusses f. die innere Mission der deutschen evangel. Kirche, 1848-98. B., Central-Ausschuss f. die innere Mission. 185 pp. 8vo. M. 1.60.

Lallemand, Léon. La révolution et les pauvres. P., libr. Picard et fils. 398 pp. 8vo. f. 12.

Leithold, Friederike. Erinnerungen aus meinem Diakonissenleben. Nach ihren Aufzeichngn. bearb von Luise Freifrau v. Ketelbrodt. Lp., A. Deichert. 411 pp. 8vo. M. 5.

[Oertzen, Cl. v. Armenpflege in Deutschland nach Theorie u. Praxis. 2. Aufl. Gotha, F. A. Perthes. 124 pp. 8vo. M. 2.]

Opere (Le) pie di Torino nell' anno 1898: notizie raccolte per cura della congregazione di carita . . . . 4 congresso delle opere pie. Torino, tip. eredi Botta. 217 pp. 4to.

[Paris charitable et prévoyant. Tableau des œuvres et institutions du département de la Seine, publié par les soins de l'Office central des œuvres de bienfaisance. 2e édition. P., Plon, Nourrit & Cie. 648 pp. 8vo.]

Richter, Paul. Die Zukunft der weiblichen Diakonie. . . . Gütersloh, C. Bertelsmann. 29 pp. 8vo. M. 0.50.

Riis, J. A. Out of Mulberry Street. N. Y., Century Co. 269 pp. 16mo. $1.25.

Schabert, O. Die innere Mission u. die ihr verwandten Bestrebungen in Riga. Eine Skizze. Riga, A. Stieda. 34 pp. 8vo. M. 1.20.

Schriften des deutschen Vereins f. Armenpflege u. Wohlthätigkeit. 35.-39. Hft. Lp., Duncker & Humblot. M. 1.60, 2, 1.80, 2, 3.20.

Stanton, Elizabeth Cady. Eighty years and more, 1815-87: reminiscences. 484 pp. 8vo. 7s. 6d.

University & social settlements; ed. by W. Reason. L., Methuen. 208 pp. 8vo. 2s. 6d. (Social questions of today.)

Wanless, W. J. The medical mission, ... Phil., Westminster Press. 96 pp. 16mo. $0.10.

Witts, Florence. Frances E. Willard. . . . N. Y., T. Whittaker. 143 pp. il. 12mo. $0.50.

4. Cities.

Argus guide to municipal London; a poll-book & a year-book combined. Full list of members of city corporation, county council, school board . . . . ed. by F. J. Higginbottom. L., Argus office. 264 pp. 12mo.

[Bender, Herm. Rom u. römisches Leben im Altertum. Mit 10 Vollbildern u. über 150 Abbildgn. im Text, nebst vergleich. Plan des alten u. neuen Rom 2. Aufl. (In 10 Lfg.) 1. Lfg. pp. 1-64. Tübingen 1893.)]

Berlin. Bericht über die Gemeinde-Verwaltung der Stadt Berlin in den J. 1889-95. 1. Thl. B., C. Heymann's Verl. 300 pp. 8vo. M. 5.

Crawford, F. M. Ave Roma immortalis: studies from the chronicles of Rome. L., Macmillan Co. 2 v. 696 pp. 8vo. 21s.

*Einaudi, Luigi. La municipalisation du sol dans les grandes villes. P., Giard & Brière. 60 pp. 8vo. (MA., S. +) [Draws illustrations from Chicago, London, Paris, etc.]

Gomme, G. L. London in the reign of Victoria, 1837-97. 256 pp. 8vo. 2s. 6d. (Victorian era series.)

Great Britain — Water supply of the metropolis — Report, 1898. L., Eyre & Spottiswoode. 6d.

[Greenwell, A., & Curry, W. T. Rural water supply: a practical handbook. Ed. 2, rev. 220 pp. 8vo.]

Hamilton, P. J. Colonial Mobile: an historical study, largely from original sources. Bo., Houghton, Mifflin & Co. 446 pp. (Nation, O. 27 + +)

*James, E. J. Charters of the city of Chicago, Pt. I. The early charters, 1833-37. C., Univ. of Chicago Press. 76 pp. 8vo. $0.50. (MA., S. + +)

Kruse, W. Ueber den Einfluss des städtischen Lebens auf die Volksgesundheit. Vortrag. (Aus Centralblatt f. allg. Gesundheitspfl.) Bonn, E. Strauss. 79 pp. 8vo. M. 1.60.

Lindner, Thdr. Die deutsche Hanse. Ihre Geschichte u. Bedeutg. . . . . Mit Abbildgn. Lp., F. Hirt & Sohn. 215 pp. 8vo. M. 5.

Monographien zur Weltgeschichte. Hrsg. v. Ed. Heyck. 6. Below, Geo. v. Das ältere deutsche Stadtwesen u. Burgetum. 136 pp. 8vo. M. 3.

Powell, L. P., ed. Historic towns of New England. N. Y., G. P. Putnam's Sons. Il. 8vo. $3.50.

Professione, Alf. Siena e la compagnie di ventura nella seconda metà del sec. 14: recerche . . . . Civitanova Marche, Domenico Natalucci. 187 pp. 8vo.

Replier, Agnes. Philadelphia: the place & the people. 392 pp. il. 8vo. $2.50. (Outlook, N. 12 + +)

[Rimmer, A. Our old country towns. New ed. L., Chatto & Wundus. 336 pp. 16mo. 3s. 6d.]

Sarum, The Use of. I. The Sarum customs as set forth in the consuetudinary & customary. Original texts by W. H. Frere. Camb., Camb. Univ. Press. 8vo. 12s.

*Sparling, S. E. Municipal history & present organization of Chicago. (AJS., S., 274 p.) (MA., S. + —)

Urkunden u. Akten der Stadt Strassburg. 1. Abth. Urkundenbuch der Stadt Strassburg. 4. Bd. 1. Hälfte. Nachträge u. Berichtiggn. zu Bd. 1-3. Gesammelt v. Wilh. Wiegand. Register zu Bd. 2-4. Strassburg, K. J. Trübner. 360 pp. 4to. M. 18.

5. Criminology and Penology.

*Annali di statistica. Atti della commissione per la statistica guidiziaria civile e penale. Sessione del decembre 1897. Rome, 359 pp. 8vo. (RIS., N. + +)

[Archiv für Kriminal-Anthropologie u. Kriminal-Statistik. Mit e. Anzahl v. Fachmännern hrsg. v. Dr. Hanns Gross. Lp., F. C. W. Vogel. 1. Bd. 1. Hft. 136 pp. 8vo. M. 10.]

[Berner, A. F. Lehrbuch des deutschen Strafrechts. 18. Aufl. Lp., B. Tauchnitz. 752 pp. 8vo. M. 9.]

Butterworth, A. R. Criminal evidence act, 1898. With intro. chapter & practical notes. 8vo. 5s.

Clemens, Just. Strafrecht u. Politik. Kriminalpolitische Gedanken e. alten Richters. B., O. Liebmann. 103 pp. 8vo. M. 1.60.

Ferri, E. Difese penali e studi di giurisprudenza. Torino, fratelli Bocca. 469 pp. 8vo. L. 9.

George, J. Humanität u. Kriminalstrafen. Eine Zusammenstellg. samtl. Kriminalstrafen vom frühesten Mittelalter bis auf die Gegenwart unter Berüchsicht. aller Staaten Europas. . . . . Jena, H. Costenoble. 383 pp. 8vo. M. 10.

Great Britain — Prisons & convict prisons. Report of the commissioners & directors for 1897-8. Appendices. 8vo. 1s. 11½ d.

*Horsley, J. W. Prisons & prisoners. L., Pearson. 242 pp. 8vo. 3s. 6d. (Academy, N. 26 +) [Popular account of prisons & prison life.]

Jahrbücher der Gefängnis-Gesellschaft f. die Prov.

Sachsen u. das Herzogt, Anhalt. N. F. 3, Bd. (13. Jahr. der alten Folge.) A. u. d. T. Jahr bücher f. Kriminalpolitik u. innere Mission. . . . . Halle, M. Niemeyer. 112 pp. 8vo. M. 2.40.

Orsini, Ant. Criminalita femminile: conferenza tenuta nell' aula consolare di Alessandra . . . . 1898. Orvieto, A. Maglioni. 44 pp. 8vo.

*Saleilles, Raymond. L'individualisation de la peine. P., F. Alcan. 8vo. (RIS., N. + +)

6. Education.

Bagnisky, Adf. Handbuch der Schulhygiene, see 16.

Balfour, G. Educational systems of Great Britain & Ireland. L., Frowde. 356 pp. 8vo. 7s. 6d.

Brebner, Mary. Method of teaching modern languages in Germany; being the report . . . . as Gilchrist traveling scholar. N. Y., Macmillan Co. 71 pp. 12mo. $0.40.

Craik, H. Report on secondary education for the year 1898. Appendix. L., Eyre & Spottiswoode. 1s.

Dexter, T. F. G., & Garlick, A. H. Psychology in the schoolroom. L., Longmans, Green & Co. 422 pp. 8vo, 4s. 6d.

Evans, E. P. Beiträge zur amerikanischen Litteratur- u. Kulturgeschichte. St., J. G. Cotta. 424 pp. 8vo. M. 9.

Feilner, T. J. Beiträge zur Geschichte der Kultur u. Kunst. Philosophische Aphorismen. Braunschweig, R. Sattler. 160 pp. 8vo. M. 2.40.

Gilman, D. C. University problems in the U. S. N. Y., Century Co. 319 pp. 8vo. $2.

Great Britain — Commission on manual & practical instruction in primary schools under it. Bd. of Nat. Educa. in Ireland. Appendices to reports. L., Eyre & Spottiswoode. 4s. 10½ d.

Great Britain — Reformatory & industrial schools. 41st rept. of inspector for 1897. L., Eyre & Spottiswoode. 8vo. 2s. 7d.

Heckel, H. Sur l'organisation de l'enseignement colonial dans-les universités françaises. Marseilles, impr. Barlatier. 11 pp. 8vo.

Leonard, D. L. Story of Oberlin: the institution, the community, the idea, the movement. Bo., Pilgrim Press. 447 pp. 8vo. $1.50.

Matthews, F. H. A dialogue on moral education. L., Swan Sonnenschein. 262 pp. 8vo. 3s. 6d.

*Morgan, C. L. Psychology for teachers. N. Y., Chas. Scribner's Sons. 240 pp. 8vo. (Nation, N. 17 — +)

*Salmon, D. Art of teaching. N. Y., Longmans, Green & Co. 289 pp. 12mo. $1.25. (Athenæum, N. 19 + +)

Zimmern, Alice. Renaissance of girls' education in England: a record of fifty years' progress. L., Innes. 264 pp. 8vo. 5s.

7. Ethics, Philosophy, Psychology.

Alexander, W. Primary convictions. L., Harper & Bros. 360 pp. 8vo. 3s. 6d.

Gomperz, Heinr. Kritik des Hedonismus. Eine psychologisch-eth. Untersuchg. 121 pp. 8vo. M. 2.40.

*Marshall, H. R. Instinct & reason: an essay . . . . with some special study of the nature of religion. N. Y., Macmillan & Co. 574 pp. 8vo. $3.50. (Outlook, D. 17)

Philosophie, e., f. das 20. Jahrh. B. C. Skopnik. 274 pp. 8vo. M. 4.

Siebert, Otto. Geschichte der neueren deutschen Philosophie seit Hegel. Ein Handbuch zur Einführg. in das philosoph. Studium der neuesten Zeit. Göttingen, Vandenhoeck & Ruprecht. 496 pp. 8vo. M. 7.50.

[Sizycki, Paul. Vom Baume der Erkenntnis. Fragmente zur Ethik u. Psychologie aus der Weltlitteratur. 1. Grundprobleme. 2. Aufl. B., F. Dummler's Verl. 800 pp. 8vo. M.7.50.]

Wagner, Frdr. Freiheit u. Gesetzmässigkeit in den menschlichen Willensakten . . . . Tübingen, H. Laupp. 115 pp. 8vo. M. 2.80.
Ziehen, Thdr. Psychophysiologische Erkenntnistheorie. Jena, G. Fischer. 105 pp. 8vo. M. 2.80.

8. Family.

Norway, G. A Roman household; ill. by W. S. Stacey. L., National Society. 224 pp. 8vo 2s. 6d.
Renooz, C. Psychologie comparée de l'homme et de la femme. P., Bib. de la Nouvelle Encyclopédie, 76, rue de Rennes.
Roux, J. Psychologie de l'instinct sexuel. P., J. B. Baillière & fils. 96 pp. 16mo. f. 1.50.
Scott, J. F. Sexual instinct: its use & dangers as affecting heredity & morals. N. Y., E. B. Treat & Co. 436 pp. 12mo. $2.
Wilpert, James v. Der Herr der Schöpfung u. das gefallene Weib. Ein Apell an die Gerechtigkeit. Lp., M. Spohr. 105 pp. 8vo. M. 1.80.

9. Finance, Taxation.

Austria — Mitteilungen des k. k. Finanz-Ministeriums. Red. im Präsidial-Bureau des k. k. Finanz-Ministeriums. 4. Jahrg. 3. Hft. Wien, Hof u. Staatsdruckerei. pp. 431-718. 8vo. M. 3.
Beauré, Aug. Théorie et pratique de la monnaie. Tome 1. Traité théorique de la monnaie et statistique des métaux précieux . . . . B., Puttkammer & Mühlbrecht. 144 pp. M. 3.20.
Bump, O. F. Law & practice in bankruptcy; rev. & adapted to the act of July 1, 1898 . . . . 11th ed. Wash., W. H. Lowdermilk & Co. 923 pp. 8vo. $6.50.
[Cook, W. W. Treatise on the law of corporations having a capital stock. Ed. 4. Chi., Callaghan & Co. 3 v. 8vo. $18.]
Dictionnaire du commerce, de l'industrie et de la banque, publié sous la direction de MM. Yves Guyot et A. Raffalovich. P., Guillaumin & Cie. Livraisons 1-3, pp. 1-480.
France — Annuaire général des finances, publié d'après les documents officiels, sous les auspices du ministère des finances (9e année 1898-99). P., Berger-Levrault & Cie.
[Fuisting, B. Die preussischen direkten Steuern. 1. Bd. Kommentar zum Einkommensteuergesetz. 4. Aufl. B. C. Heymann's Verl. 756 pp. 8vo. M. 12.]
Germany — Report of savings banks in Prussia. L., Eyre & Spottiswoode. 1d.
Grunau, Gust. Inschriften u: Darstellungen römischer Kaisermünzen von Augustus bis Diocletian. Kiel, E. Kuhn. 152 pp. 8vo. M. 3.
King, Moses, ed. Clearing-house of New York city: New York Clearing-House Association, known as the Associated Banks; historical, descriptive, statistical. N. Y., Moses King. 32 pp. il. pors. 12mo. $0.25.
Luzzatti, Giac. Delle moneta ideale ne' suoi rapporti colla moneta reale in circolazione in una paese. Verona, fratelli Drucker. 60 pp. 8vo.
McLeod, F. F. Hist. of fiat money & currency inflation in New England from 1620 to 1789. Phil., Amer. Acad. of Pol. & Soc. Sci. pp. 57-77 8vo. $0.25. (Publications of the society.)
Macleod, H. D. Indian currency. N. Y., Longmans, Green & Co. 55 pp. 8vo. $1.
Magee, H. W. A work on state banks & bank officers, including sections of the constitution & codes of California relating to banks & banking . . . . Los Angeles, C. W. Palm Co. 356 pp. 8vo. $4.
Miller, H. A. Money & bimetalism. N. Y., G. P. Putnam's Sons. 308 pp. 12mo. $1.25.

Mitteilungen aus der Verwaltung der direkten Steuern im preussischen Staate. Nr. 36. Br., R. v. Decker. 84 pp. 8vo. M. $0.95.
Trasi, Ant. Proposta di una tassa unica in surrogazione del dazio consumo. Milano, V. Ruperti. 14 pp. 8vo.

10. History.

Alford, H. S., L., & Sword, W. D. Egyptian Soudan: its loss and recovery . . . . [with] a full account of the Nile expedition, 1897-8. L., Macmillan Co. 352 pp. 10s.
Arangio, Ruiz Gae. Storia constituzionale del regno d'Italia (1848-98). Firenze, G. Civelli. 561 pp. 8vo. L. 10.
Beha ed Din. Life of Saladin. N. Y., New Amsterdam Book Co., 1897. 20 + 420 pp. 8vo. $3.50.
*Blok, P. J. Hist. of the people of the Netherlands, tr. by O. A. Bierstadt & Ruth Putnam. N. Y., G. P. Putnam's Sons. (Outlook, D. 10 + +)
Boulger, Demetrius. History of China. New rev. ed. N. Y., Macmillan Co. 2 v., pors., maps. 8vo. $9.
Burckhardt, Jak, Griechische Kulturgeschichte. Hrsg. v. Jak. Oeri. 2 Bde. B., W. Spemann. 370 u. 443 pp. 8vo. M. 14.
[Channing, Ed. Students' history of the U. S. New ed. enl. N. Y., Macmillan Co. 615 pp. 8vo. il. $1.40.]
Conybeare, F. C. The Dreyfus case; first complete English narrative. . . . N. Y., Dodd, Mead & Co. 12mo. $1.50.
Dana, C. A. Recollections of the civil war . . . . N. Y., D. Appleton & Co. 296 pp. 8vo. $2.
Davis, R. H. Cuban & Porto Rican campaigns. N. Y., Chas. Scribner's Sons. 360 pp. 12mo. $1.50.
Demelitsch, Fred. Metternich u. seine auswärtige Politik. 1. Bd. 692 pp. 8vo. St., J. G. Cotta. 692 pp. 8vo. M. 14.
Dill, S. Roman society in the last century of the Western Empire. N. Y., Macmillan. 402 pp. 8vo. $3.
Dixon, Mrs. Archibald. True history of the Missouri compromise & its repeal. Cin., Robert Clarke Co., 1899. 623 pp. 8vo. $4.
*Duruy, Victor. A general history of the world, from the French, thoroughly revised, with an introduction & a summary of contemp. hist. (1848-98), by E. A. Grosvenor. N. Y., T., Crowell. 744 pp. 12mo. $2. (Outlook, N. 19 + +)
Dyer, T. F. T. Old English social life as told by the parish registers. L., Elliot Stock. 264 pp. 8vo. 6s.
Earle, Mrs. Alice Morse. Home life in colonial days; written in the year 1898. N. Y., Macmillan Co. 470 pp. 12mo. $2.50.
Ehlert, Louis. Römische Tage. Wohlf.- [Titel-] Ausg. B., Behr's Verl. 243 pp. 8vo. M. 3.
Field, Lilian F. An introduction to the study of the Renaissance. N. Y., C. Scribner's Sons. 307 pp. 12mo. $1.50.
Fisher, S. G. The true Benj. Franklin. Phil., J. B. Lippincott Co. 369 pp. 8vo. $2.
Forbes, Archibald. Life of Napolean III. N. Y., Dodd, Mead & Co. 8vo. $3.50.
*Ford, H. J. Rise & growth of Amer. politics: a sketch of constitutional development. N. Y., Macmillan Co. 409 pp. 12mo. $1.50. (Outlook, N. 19 + +)
*Foxcraft, H. C. Life & letters of Sir Geo. Savile, Bart., First Marquis of Halifax. L., Longmans. (Academy, O. 22 + +)
Francke, Kuno, Glimpses of modern German culture. N. Y., Dodd, Mead & Co. 233 pp. 16mo. $1.25.

[Frazer, R. W. British India. Ed. 2. L., T. F. Unwin. 416 pp. 8vo. 5s. (Story of the nations.)]

[Gairdner, James. History of the life & reign of Richard III, to which is added the story of Perkin Warbeck, from original docs. New rev. ed. N. Y., Macmillan Co. 388 pp. 12mo. $2.25.]

Garnett, R. Edward Gibbon Wakefield: the colonisation of South Australia & New Zealand. L., T. F. Unwin. 408 pp. 8vo. 5s. (Builders of Great Britain.)

[Gasquet, F. A. Henry VIII & the English monasteries. L., J. C. Nimmo. Rev. ed. 526 pp. 8vo. 10s. 6d.]

Gibbins, H. de B. English people in the 19th century. N. Y., Macmillan Co. 172 pp. 16mo. $0.90.

Great Britain — Egypt, No. 2. Correspondence with the French gov. respecting the valley of the upper Nile. 3s. No. 3. 1898. Further correspondence [on same]. L., Eyre & Spottiswoode.

Great Britain Historical MSS. Commission. 15th report. App. Pt. 7. MSS. of the Duke of Somerset, Marquis of Arleshwry, & Sir T. H. G. Puleston. 8vo. 1s. 9d.

*Griffis, W. E. Romance of Amer. colonisation: how the foundation stones of our history were laid, etc. B., ? 7s. 6d. (Outlook, N. 12 +)

Henderson, G. F. R. Stonewall Jackson and the Amer. civil war. N. Y., Longmans, Green & Co. 2 v. (550 & 641 pp.) 8vo. $10. (Nation, D. 1 —)

*Hume. M. A. S. The great Lord Burleigh: a study in Elizabethan statecraft. L., Nisbet. 12s. 6d. (Academy, N. 26 + +)

Imbart de la Tour. Les paroisses rurales dans l'ancienne France, du 4e au 11e siècle. (Extrait de la Revue historique, 1896-7.) P., Daupeley-Gouverneur. 198 pp. 8vo.

Johnson, T. Imperial Britain: a comprehensive description of the geography, history, commerce, trade, government, and religion of the British empire. 2 v. maps & ills. V. 1. British empire in Europe. 312 pp. 8vo. 7s. 6d. L., Imperial press.

Kleinschmidt, Arth. Drei Jahrhunderte russischer Geschichte. Ueberblick der russ. Geschichte 1598-1898. B., J. Rade. 505 pp. 8vo. M. 9.

Kraemer, Hans. Das 19. Jahrhundert in Wort u. Bild. Politische u. Kulturgeschichte. 1. Bd. 1795-1840. B., Bong & Co. 504 pp. 4to. M. 12.

*Lacombe, Paul. Introduction à l'histoire littéraire. P., Hachette. 8vo. (RIS., N. + +)

[Langlois, C. V., & Seignobos, Ch. Introduction to the study of history, tr. by G. G. Berry. . . . N. Y., H. Holt & Co. 350 pp. 12mo. $2.25.]

Lepreux, Georges. Nos représentants pendant la Révolution (1789-99). Lille, libr. Leleu. 271 pp. 8vo. f. 10.

Lodge, H. C. Story of the Revolution. N. Y., C. Scribner's Sons. 2 v. (324 & 286 pp.) 8vo. $6.

Milukow, Paul. Skizzen russischer Kulturgeschichte. Deutsch v. E. Davidson. 1. Bd. 240 pp. 8vo. M. 6.

Monroe, James. Writings, including a collection of his public and private correspondence, now for the first time printed. Ed. by S. M. Hamilton. In 6 or 7 v. V. 1, 1778-94. N. Y., G. P. Putnam's Sons. 8vo. half leath. Subs., $5.

Monumenta Germaniæ historica. . . . Gestorum pontificum romanorum. V. 1. Liber pontificalis. Pars 1. Edidit Thdr. Mommsen. B., Weidmann. 295 pp. 4to. M. 15.

*Morris, Chas. The war with Spain: a complete history. Ph., J. B. Lippincott Co. 383 pp. 12mo. $1.50. (Outlook, N. 12 +)

Muirhead, J. F. The land of contrasts: a Briton's view of his Amer. kin. Bo., Samson, Wolffe & Co. 282 pp. 8vo. $1.50.

Müllenhoff, Karl. Deutsche Altertumskunde. 4. Bd. 1. Hälfte. B., Weidmann. 384 pp. 8vo. M. 10.

*O'Brien, R. B. Life of Charles Stewart Parnell. L., Smith, Elder & Co. 2 v. (Athenæum, N. 12 + + —)

*Oman, C. W. C. England & the hundred years' war (1327-1485). N. Y., C. Scribner's Sons. 168 pp. 16mo. $1.50. (Oxford manuals of Eng. hist.) (Athenæum, D. 3 + + —)

Publikationen aus den k. preussischen Staatsarchiven. Veranlasst. u. unterstutzt durch die k. Archivverwaltg. 72. Bd. Briefwechsel Friedrichs des Grossen m. Grumbkow u. Maupertius (1731-51.) Hrsg. v. Rhold. Koser. 64 + 342 pp. 8vo. M. 12.

Ramsay, J. H. Foundations of England; or, twelve centuries of British history (B. C. 55— A. D. 1154). N. Y., Macmillan Co. 2 v. (553 & 509 pp.) 8vo. $7.50.

(The) Reign of Terror: a collection of authentic narratives of the horrors committed by the revolutionary government of France. . . . Written by eye-witnesses. . . . With biographical notices and anecdotes. Ph., J. B. Lippincott. 2 v. (258 & 347 pp.) 8vo. $6.

*Robinson. J. H., & Rolfe, H. W. Petrarch, the first modern scholar & man of letters; a selection from his correspondence with Boccaccio & other friends, designed to illustrate the beginning of the Renaissance. tr. from the original Latin, with historical introduction & notes. N. Y., G. P. Putnam's Sons. 436 pp. 8vo. $2. (Outlook, O. 22 + +)

*Romero, Matias. Mexico & the U. S.; a study of subjects affecting their political, commercial, & social relations. made with a view to their promotion. V. 1. N. Y., G. P. Putnam's Sons. 759 pp. 8vo. $4.50. (Outlook, N. 5 + +)

Rossa, O'Donovan. Rossa's recollections, 1838-98. . . . The Fenian movement. N. Y., P. J. Kenedy. 402 pp. 12mo. $1.

Sanderson, Edgar. Africa in the 19th century. N. Y., imp. by Chas. Scribner's Sons. 420 pp. 8vo. $1.75. (Events of our own time ser.)

Sanderson, E. History of the world, from the earliest historical time to the year 1898. L., Hutchinson. 800 pp. 8vo. 5s.

Schriften des Vereins f. Reformationsgeschichte. Nr. 59-61. Halle, M. Nemeyer in Komm. à M. 1.20.

*Schwill, Ferd. History of modern Europe. (AJS., N., p. 422) (Nation, N. 17 + —)

Sikes, E. W. Transition of North Carolina from colony to commonwealth. Balt., Johns Hopkins Press. 86 pp. 8vo. $0.50. (J. H. U. studies.)

Smith, G. B. Canada: its rise & progress. L., Partridge. 320 pp. 8vo. 2s. 6d. (Romance of civilization.)

Smith, G. Barnett. The romance of colonization. V. 4. Canada. L., S. W. Partridge & Co. 8vo. 2s. 6d. (V. 1, 2, 3. 2s. 6d each.)

Spears, J. R. Our navy in the war with Spain. N. Y., Chas. Scribner's Sons 406 pp. 12mo. $1.50.

Spiegler, S. Der Freiheitskampf der ungarischen Nation (1848-9) kritisch beleuchtet. Lp., W. Friedrich. 148 pp. 8vo. M. 4.

*Stillman. W. J. Union of Italy, 1815-95. N. Y., Macmillan Co. 412 pp. 12mo. $1.75. (Cambridge histor. ser.) (Outlook D. 10 + —)

*Strobel, E. H. Spanish revolution. 1868-75. Bo., Small, Maynard & Co. 293 pp. 12mo. $1.50. (Nation, O. 27 + +)

Sydney, W. C. Early days of the 19th century in England, 1800-20. L., Redway. 524 pp. 8vo, 18s.

Vince, C. A. John Bright. C., H. S. Stone & Co. 12mo. $1.25. (Victorian era ser.)

Watterson, Henry. History of the Spanish-American war. N. Y., W. W. Wilson. 650 pp. 8vo. $2.50.

Wheeler, Jos. Santiago campaign, 1898. Bo., Lamson, Wolffe & Co. 369 pp. 8vo. $3.

Worcester, D. C. Philippine Islands and their people: a record of personal observation and experience; with a short summary of the more important facts in the hist. of the archipelago. N. Y., Macmillan Co. 529 pp. 8vo. $4.

Wright, Marie R. Picturesque Mexico: a comprehensive & authentic account of the present condition of Mexico . . . from data collected under the patronage of the Mexican govt. Ph., J. B. Lippincott. 445 pp. il. 8vo. $7.50.

11. International Law.

[Weiss, A. Manuel de droit international privé. 2ᵉ édition. P., libr. Larose. 694 pp. 8vo.]

12. Labor.

[Die Arbeiterbewegung. Rundschau der wirthschaftl. u. sozialen Vorgänge. Red., Max Koppe. 1. Jahrg. Oktbr.-Dezbr. 1898. 13. Nrn. 4to. (Nr. 1, 8 p.) B., M. Warschauer. M. 1.50.]

France — Office du Travail. Les caisses patronales de retraites des établissements industriels. P., Impr. nationale. 441 pp. 8vo.

Hall, F. S. Sympathetic strikes and sympathetic lockouts. N. Y., Macmillan Co. 118 pp. 8vo. $1. (Columbia Univ. studies. V. 10, no. 1.)

Higgins, A. P. Employer's liability and compensation to workingmen on the continent. L., Stevens & Hall. 8vo 5 s.

[Lynch, H. F. Redress by arbitration: a digest of the law relating to arbitrations & rewards, incorporating the arbitration act of 18 9 . . . . Ed. 3, rev. L., E. Wilson. 112 pp. 8vo. 5s.]

Schloss, D. F. Methods of industrial remuneration. Ed. 3. rev. & enl. L., Williams & Norgate. 7s. 6d.

Senhouse, R. M. M., & Emery, G. F. Accidents to workmen. . . . Employers' liability act, 1880, Lord Campbell's act, workingmen's compensation act, 1897. . . . 430 pp. 8vo. 15s.

Wyckoff, W. A. The workers: an experiment in reality: the West. N. Y., Chas. Scribner's Sons. 378 pp. 12mo. $1.50.

13. Political Economy.

Amer. economic assoc. Publications. General contents & index. V. 1-11. N. Y., Macmillan Co. 52 pp. 8vo.

Avenel, G. d. Histoire économique de la propriété, des salaires, des denrées et de tous les prix en général, depuis l'an 1200 jusqu'à l'an 1800. P., libr. Leroux. T. 3 & 4. 705 & 607 pp. 8vo.

Billeter, Gust. Geschichte des Zinsfusses im griechisch-römischen Altertum bis auf Justinian. Lp., B. G. Teubner. 103 pp. 8vo. M. 3.60.

*Cohn, Gustav. System der Nationalökonomie. (AJS., S., p. 277.) (YR., N. + + —)

[Conrad, J. Grundriss zum Studium der politischen Oekonomie. 2. Tl. Volkswirthschaftspolitik. 2. Aufl. Jena, G. Fischer. 144 pp. 8vo. M. 2.80.]

Devine, E. T. Economics. N. Y., Macmillan Co. 404 pp. 12mo. $1

Jahrbuch der internationalen Vereinigung f. vergleichende Rechtswissenschaft u. Volkswirthschaftslehre zu Berlin, hrsg. v. Prof. Bernhöft

u. Dr. Meyer. IV. Jahrg., 1898. 1. Abtlg. B., K. Hoffmann. 283 pp. 8vo. M. 7.

Münchener volkswirthschaftliche Studien. Hrsg. v. Lujo Brentano u. Walth. Lotz. 27.-29. Stück. 8vo. St., G. Cotta Nachf. M. 3, 3 u. 2.40.

Neymarck, Alfred. Vocabulaire-manuel d'économie politique. P., Colin & Cie. 482 pp. 18mo.

Rodbertus, K. Over-production & crises; tr. by Julia Franklin. L., Swan Sonnenschein. 144 pp. 8vo. 2s. 6d.

Schmoller, Gust. Umrisse u. Untersuchungen zur Verfassungs-, Verwaltungs- u. Wirthschaftsgeschichte, besonders des preussischen Staates im 17. u. 18. Jahrh. Lp., Duncker & Humblot. 686 pp. 8vo. M. 13.

Wiener staatswissenschaftliche Studien. Hrsg. v. Edm. Bernatzik u. Eug. v. Philippovich. 1. Bd. 2. Hft. Fr., J. C. B. Mohr.

14. Political Science.

Baldwin, Simeon E. Modern political institutions. Bo., Little, Brown & Co. 387 pp. 8vo. $2.

Bierling, Rud. Juristische Prinzipienlehre. 2. Bd. Fr., J. C. B. Mohr. 367 pp. 8vo. M. 9.

*Bismarck, Prince. Bismarck the man & the statesman; being the reflections & reminiscences of Otto Prince von Bismarck written & dictated by himself . . . . tr. under the supervision of A. J. Butler. N. Y., Harper, 1899. 2 v. (415 & 362 pp.) 8vo. $7.50. (Athenæum, D. 3 X)

Breley, Ernest. Grandeur et décadence de la guerre. P., Guillaumin & Cie. 16 pp. 8vo.

Cleveland, F. A. Growth of democracy in the U. S.; or the evolution of popular coöperation in govt. & its results. Chi., The Quadrangle Press. 532 pp 12mo. $1.50.

Collier, W. M. Law of bankruptcy & the national bankruptcy act . . . . with citations to all applicable cases decided under the former U. S. bankruptcy acts, many English decisions & extended notes. Albany, Matthew Bender. 586 pp. 8vo. $5.

Contuzzi, F. P. Il codice civile nei rapporti col diritto internazionale privato. V. 1. Napoli, N. Jovene & C. 526 pp. 8vo. L. 10.

Deploge, S. Referendum in Switzerland, tr. by C. P. Trevelyan, ed. by L. Tomm. 8vo. 7s. 6d. (Studies in economics & political sci.)

Dritto (Il) civile italiano secondo la dottrina e la guirisprudenza, esposto dai proff. Bianchi, Caporali, Cuturi [& others], per cura Pasquale Fiore. Disp. 265-76. Napoli, Eugenio Marghieri. pp. 97-758. L. 1 la disp.

[Ducrocq, Th. Cours de droit administratif et de législation française des finances. . . . 7ᵉ édition. T. 3. Principes de droit public. . . . P., libr. Fontemoing. 852 pp. 8vo.]

*Farlie, J. A. Centralization of administration in N. Y. state. N. Y., Columbia Univ. Press. 207 pp. 8vo. $1. (Columbia Univ. studies). (MA., S.+ + —)

Gaulke, Johs. Ueber die Grenzen des Nationalismus u. Internationalismus. B., J. Sassenbach. 30 pp. 8vo. M. 0.20.

*Godkin, E. L. Unforeseen tendencies of democracy. (AJS., S., p. 277) (YR., N.—— +) (AAP., N.X)

Great Britain — Public general acts of 1898. 8vo. 3s. Index, 8vo. 8½d.

Great Britain — Foreign Office. State papers, British & foreign. V. 84. L., Eyre & Spottiswoode. 10s.

*Hamilton, E. H. Mr. Gladstone: a monograph. L., Murray. (Athenæum, N. 19 + + —)

Hess, Willy. Die Reichstagswahlen v. 1898 nach ihren Ergebnissen. Auf Grund amtl. Quellen zusammengestellt. B., S. Cronbach. 37 pp. 8vo. M. 0.75.

Huber, Max. Die Staatensuccession. Völkerrechtliche u. staatsrechtl. Praxis im 19. Jahrh. Lp., Duncker & Humblot. 318 pp. 8vo. M. 7.20.

Indiana — Powers & duties of the county & township officers in the state of Indiana, including a complete treatise on the board of county commissioners. . . . . Ed. 2, rev. Indianapolis, Bowen-Merrill Co. 1206 pp. 8vo. $6.

Kidd, Benjamin. Control of the tropics. L., Macmillan Co. 108 pp. 8vo. 3s.

La Chapelle, S. de. Le suffrage universel . . . . P., libr. Larose. 22 pp. 8vo.

Laughton, J. K. Memoirs of the life & correspondence of Henry Reeve. N. Y., Longmans. 2 v. (404 & 436 pp.) 8vo. $8.

Lely, J. M. Annual statutes of practical utility, passed during 1898, with notes. L., Sweet & Maxwell. 7s. 6d.

*McConachie, L. G. Congressional committees. (AJS., S., 278 pp.) (AJS., N.++)

[Mackenzie, Lord. Studies in Roman law; with comparative views of the laws of France, England, & Scotland; ed. by John Kirkpatrick. 7th ed. L., Blackwood & Son. 522 pp. 8vo.]

Meili, Fr. Institutionen der vergleichenden Rechtswissenschaft. Ein Grundriss. St., F. Enke. 286 pp. 8vo. M. 8.

*Novicow, J. La guerre et ses prétendus bienfaits. P., Armand, Colin & Cie. 198 pp. (AJS., N. +—)

Pepper, G. W., & Lewis, W. D. Digest of decisions & encyclopaedia of Penn. law, 1754–1898. V. 2. (Assumpsit to constables.) Phil., Rees, Welsh & Co. cols. 1629–3386. 8vo. $7.50.

Pilon, Eustache. Essai d'une théorie générale de la représentation dans les obligations (thèse). Caen, impr. Valin. 370 pp. 8vo.

Polen, G. G. Shall our presidents be elected for eight years? N. Y., Fritz Schmidt, Jr. 32 pp. 12mo. $0.20.

Rose, J. H. Rise of democracy. C., H. S. Stone & Co. 12mo. $1.25. (Victorian era ser.)

Siotto Pintor, Manfredi. Sovranita popolare o sovranita degli ottimi? Contributo alla teoria democratica della sovranita. Torino, fratelli Bocca. 219 pp. 8vo.

Testa, Lu. Le voci del servizio diplomatico-consolare italiano e straniero. Firenze, G. Barbera. 533 pp. 16mo. L. 5.

Thompson, H. M. Russian politics. L., T. F. Unwin. 300 pp. 8vo. 3s. 6d.

Trattato (Primo) completo di diritto amministrativo italiano, a cura del prof. V. E. Orlando. Fasc. 33–36. Milano, Società editrice libraria. pp. 289–480. 8vo. L. 1 il fasc.

Tripier, Louis. Les codes français collationnés sur les textes officiels . . . . Ouvrage remanié et tenu au courant de la législation la plus récente . . . . 49e édition. P., libr. Pichon. 2,616 pp. 8vo. f. 20.

Vermont — Revised laws . . . . passed by the General Assembly of the Representatives of the Freeman of the State . . . . 1782. Reprinted in photo-facsim. by Statute Law Book Co. Wash., D. C. 38 pp. 2do. $8.50.

Willoughby, W. W. Rights & duties of American citizenship. N. Y., Amer. Book Co. 336 pp. 12mo. $1.

15. Religion, Churches.

Beaton, D. Selfhood & service: relation of Christian personality to wealth & social redemption. 220 pp. 8vo. 3s. 6d.

Blau, Ludw. Das altjüdische Zauberwesen. Strassburg, K. J. Trubner. 167 pp. 8vo. M. 4.

*Bliss, F. J. Excavations at Jerusalem, 1894–7.

Plans and illus. by A. C. Dickie. L., Palestine Exploration Fund. 390 pp. 8vo. 12s. 6d. (Athenæum, N. 12++)

Bryant, Sophie. Teaching of Christ on life & conduct. L., Swan Sonnenschein. 100 pp. 8vo. 2s. 6d.

Campbell, L. Religion in Greek literature: sketch in outline. 434 pp. 8vo. 15s.

Chabin, R. P. La science de la religion. P., libr. Poussielgue. 442 pp. 8vo.

Clarke, W. N. Outline of Christian theology. L., T. & T. Clark. 498 pp. 8vo. 7s. 6d.

Cutts, E. L. Parish priests & their people in the Middle Ages in England. L., Soc. for promoting Christ. knowledge. 598 pp. 8vo. 7s. 6d.

Elias, R. Tendency of religion. 230 pp. 8vo. 3s. 6d.

Feasey, H. J. Monasticism: what is it? Forgotten chap. in the hist. of labor. L., Sands & Co. 280 pp. 8vo. 6s.

Fielding, H. The soul of a people: a study of Buddhism. N. Y., Macmillan Co. 363 pp. 8vo.

Gehring, Johs. Die Sekten der russischen Kirche (1003–1897). Nach ihrem Ursprunge u. inneren Zusammenhange dargestellt. 240 pp. 8vo. Lp., Fr. Richter. M. 5.

Gilbert, Otto. Griechische Götterlehre, in ihren Grundzügen dargestellt. Lp., E. Avenarius. M. 10.

Hurll, Estelle M. The life of our Lord in art, with some account of the artistic treatment of the life of St. John the Baptist. B., Houghton, Mifflin & Co. 370 pp. 8vo. $3.

Lorimer, G. C. Christianity & the social state. Phil., Am. Baptist Pub. Soc. 488 pp. 8vo. $2.

[Mackennal, A. Seven churches of Asia considered as types of the religious life of today. Ch. Al., L., Elliot Stock. 140 pp. 12mo. 2s.]

Maitland, F. W. Roman canon law in the church of England: 6 essays. L., Methuen. 192 pp. 8vo. 7s. 6d.

Moulton, R. G., & Bruce, A. B. The Bible as literature. L., Service. 394 pp. 8vo. 6s.

[Naumann, Fr. Gotteshilfe. Gesammelte Andachten, 1. Bd. Andachten aus dem J. 1895. 2. Aufl. Göttingen, Vandenhoeck & Ruprecht. 120 pp. 8vo. M. 1.30.]

One hundred years: being a short history of the Church Missionary Society. Church Miss. Soc. 212 pp. 8vo. 1s.

[Pastor, L. Hist. of the popes from the close of the Middle Ages. Drawn from the secret archives of the Vatican & other original sources. From the German, ed. by T. 1. Atrobus. V. 6. L., Paul. 700 pp. 8vo. 12s.]

Pigge Henr. Die religiöse Toleranz Friedrichs des Grossen nach ihrer theoretischen u. praktischen Seite. Auf Grundlage der Quellen dargestellt. Mainz, F. Kirchheim. 419 pp. 8vo. M. 4.

Price, J. M. Story of religions. L., Newnes. 228 pp. 18mo. 1s. (Libr. of useful stories.)

Richard, J. W. Philip Melancthon, the Protestant preceptor of Germany, 1497–1560. N. Y., G. P. Putnam's Sons. 399 pp. 12mo. $1.50. (Heroes of the Reformation ser., no. 2.)

[Robertson, F. W. Sermons preached at Brighton. 3d ser. 324 pp. 12mo. 1s. 6d.]

[Sabatier, Aug. Die Religion u. die moderne Kultur: Vortrag, aus dem Franz. F., J. C. B. Mohr. 52 pp. 8vo. M. 0.80.]

Sayce, A. H. Early Israel & the surrounding nations. L., Service. 338 pp. 8vo. 6s.

Small, C. H. Corner-stones of faith; or, the origin & characteristics of the Christian denominations of the U. S. N. Y., E. B. Treat & Co. 500 pp. 12mo. $2.

Söderblom, Nathan. Die Religion u. die soziale Entwicklung: Vortrag. F., J. C. B. Mohr. 96 pp. 8vo. M. 1.60.

Some features of modern Romanism, with appendix . . . . to 1898. L., Soc. for promoting Christian knowledge. 224 pp. 12mo. 1s. 6d.

Spence, H. D. M. The church of England: a history for the people. V. 4. The Anglican church. L., Cassell. 488 pp. 8vo. 6s.

Streane, A. W. Age of the Maccabees, with special reference to religious literature of the period. L., Eyre & Spottiswoode. 290 pp. 8vo. 6s.

[Tiele, C. P. Geschichte der Religion im Altertum bis auf Alexander den Grossen. Deutsch v. G. Gehrich. II. Bd. Die Religion bei den iran. Völkern. 1. Hälfte. Gotha, F. A. Perthes. 187 pp. 8vo. M. 3.60.]

Wallace, E. S. Jerusalem the holy: a brief history of ancient Jerusalem, with an account of the modern city . . . . N. Y. & Chi., F. H. Revell. 259 pp. 8vo. $1.50.

[Wellhausen, J. Die kleinen Propheten. Übers. u. erklärt. 3. Ausg. B., G. Reimer. 222 pp. 8vo. M. 7.]

Withrow, W. H. Makers of Methodism. N. Y., Eaton & Mains. 310 pp. 12mo. $0.90.

*Yonge, Charlotte M. Patriots of Palestine: a story of the Maccabees, il by W. S. Stacey. N. Y., T. Whittaker. 263 pp. 12mo. (Outlook, O. 22 + +)

16. Sanitary and Domestic Science.

[Baginsky, Adf. Handbuch der Schulhygiene mit Unterstützg. v. Otto Janke. 3. Aufl. 1. Bd. 748 pp. 8vo. M. 16.]

Haig, A. Diet & food; considered in relation to strength & power of endurance, training & athletics. L., Churchill. 94 pp. 8vo. 2s.

Hueppe, Ferd. Handbuch der Hygiene. B., A. Hirschwald. 664 pp. 8vo. m. 210 Abbildgn. M. 13.

Lush, Ethel R. Lessons in domestic science. Pts. 1 & 2. N. Y., Macmillan Co. 88 & 77 pp. 12mo. Each $0.20.

[Mangin, L. Principes d'hygiène. 2e édition. . . . P. Hachette & Cie. 412 pp. 16mo. f. 3.]

Murché, V. T. Object lessons in domestic economy. N. Y., Macmillan Co. 334 pp. 16mo. $0.60.

Parloa, Maria. Home economics: a guide to household management, including the proper treatment of the materials entering into the construction & furnishing of the house. N. Y., Century Co. 378 pp. 12mo. $1.50.

Rideal, S. Disinfection & disinfectants. . . . L., Sanitary Pub. Co. 384 pp. 8vo. 12s. 6d.

Williams, A. W. Domestic hygiene, including some general problems affecting the public health. L., Bell. 184 pp. 8vo.

[Wilson, G. Handbook of hygiene & sanitary science. Ed. 8. L., Churchill. 826 pp. 8vo. 12s. 6d.]

17. Socialism.

Bischoff, Diedr. Echte u. falsche Gerechtigkeit. Ein Wort wider den Socialismus. Lp., H. Hesse. 175 pp. 8vo. M. 2.

Braasch, Aug. Irrtümliche Ideale der Social-demokratie. Lübeck, M. Schmidt in Komm. 36 pp. 8vo. M. 0.50.

[Cathrein, Vic. Der Socialismus. Eine Untersuchg. seiner Grundlagen u. seiner Durchführbarkeit. 7. Aufl.]

[Colajanni, Nap. Il socialismo. 2a ed. Palermo, Remo Sandron. 328 pp. 16mo. L. 4.]

Geschichte, die, des Socialismus in Einzeldarstellungen v. E. Bernstein, C. Hugo, K. Kautsky [& others.] 3. Bd., 2. Tl. St., J. H. W. Dietz. 8vo. M. 5.

Gotthardt, Carl. 15 Jahre Sozialdemokrat! Wahrheitsgetreue Schildergn. des inneren Wesens der Sozialdemokratie. Magdeburg, A. Rathke. 39 pp. 8vo. M. 0.20.

*Gronlund, Lawrence. The new economy : a peaceful solution of the social problem. C., H. S. Stone & Co. 364 pp. 12mo. $1.25. (Outlook, N. 12 ✕)

Hobson, J. A. John Ruskin, social reformer. L., Nisbit. 348 pp. 8vo. 10s. 6d.

Howard, E. To-morrow: a peaceful path to real reform. L., Swan Sonnenschein. 184 pp. 8vo. 2s. 6d.

[Hyndman, H. M. Socialism & slavery; being an answer to Herb. Spencer's "Coming Slavery." Ed. 2, rev. N. Y., Internat. Pub. Co. 26 pp. 12mo. Pap. $0.05.

Lassalle, Ferd. What is capital? freely tr. from chap. 4 of "Herr Bastiat Schultze von Delitsch." N. Y., Internat. Pub. Co. 28 pp. 12mo. Pap. $0.05.

Lassalle, Ferd. Workingman's programme & addresses, tr. by E. Peters. N. Y., Internat. Pub. Co. 62 pp. 12mo. $0.10. (Internat. lib.)

* Lichtenberger, André. Le socialisme utopique. (AJS., S., p. 278) (RIS., O.)

Mehring, Frz. Geschichte der deutschen Socialdemokratie. 35. u. 36. (Schluss-) Heft. St., J. H. W. Dietz. pp. 513-98. 8vo. à M. 0.20.

Mulberger, Arth. B. S. Proudhon. Leben u. Werke. Stuttgart, F. Frommann. 240 pp. 8vo. M. 2.80.

Neumann-Hofer, Adf. Die Entwicklung der Sozialdemokratie bei den Wahlen zum deutschen Reichstage. Statistisch dargestellt. 2. Ausg. B., C. Skopnik. 75 pp. 8vo. M. 1.

Neumann, Jac. Die städtische Arbeitsmittlung als Mittel des Kampfes gegen die Socialdemokratie (Wiener Arbeiter-Bibliothek). Wien, Wiener Volksbuchh. 32 pp. 8vo. M. 0.20.

Produktion u. Konsum. im Sozialstaate v. Atlanticus. (Umschlag: ein Blick in dem Zukunftsstaat.) Mit e. Vorrede v. Karl Kautsky. St., J. H. W. Dietz. 104 pp. 8vo. M. 1.50.

Protokoll über die Verhandlungen des Parteitages der sozialdemokratischen Partei Deutschlands. . . . . 1898. B., Buchh. Vorwärts. 239 pp. 8vo. M. 0.35.

Schaub, Frz. Die Eigentumslehre nach Thomas v. Aquin u. dem modernen Sozialismus m. besond. Berücksicht. der beiderseitigen Weltanschauungen. Gekrönte Preisschrift. Fr., Herder. 446 pp. 8vo. M. 6.

* [Sombart, Werner. Socialism & the social movement in the 19th century, tr. by A. P. Atterbury. N. Y., G. P. Putnam's Sons. 199 pp. 12mo. $1.25. (AJS., N. +)

Sulzer, Geo. Die Zukunft des Sozialismus. Dresden, O. V. Bohmert. 421 pp. 8vo. M. 6.

*Vallance, Aymer. William Morris: his art, his writing & his public life. N. Y., Macmillan Co. 462 pp. 4to. $6.50. (Critic, S. + +)

Woltmann, Ludw. Die Darwinische Theorie u. der Sozialismus. Ein Beitrag zur Naturgeschichte der menschl. Gesellschaft. Düsseldorf, H. Michels. 397 pp. 8vo. M. 5.

18. Sociology.

*Annals de l'Institut international de sociologie. T. 4. (AJS., S., p. 278) (AJS., N. ✕)

*Berenger, Henry. La conscience nationale. P., Armand Colin & Cie. (RIS., N. + +)

Berlin, Israel. Die Haushaltung der Gesellschaft. Eine Abhandlg. über den Bedarf u. die Herstellg. der Existenzmittel. Bern, F. Semminger. 36 pp. 8vo. M. 0.70.

*Bosanquet, Mrs. Bernard. Standard of life (AJS., N., p. 426) (Nation, N. 17 + +) (Outlook, O. 29 + +) (Academy, N. 19 + +)

Donisthorpe, W.   Down the stream of civilization.
L., Newnes. 344 pp. il. 8vo. 6s.
Doring, A, Handbuch der menschlich-natürlichen
Sittenlehre f. Eltern u. Erzieher. . . . St., F.
Frommann. 415 pp. 8vo. M. 5.
[Flerowsky, N. Das A B C der sozialen Wissen-
schaften. Die gegenwärt. west-europ. Zivili-
sation. Die griechisch-röm. Zivilisation, das
Mittelalter, das Aufleben der Wissenschaft.
Uebersetzung des Autors (aus dem Russ.).
Lp., H. Haacke. 614 pp. 8vo. M. 12.]
*Giddings, F. H. Elements of sociology: a text-
book for colleges & schools. N. Y., The Mac-
millan Co. 353 pp. 12mo. $1.10 (Outlook,
N. 5 X)
Gullotta, Salvatore. Studio etico-sociale. Fasc. 1.
Catania, stab. tip. Catania. pp. 1-54. L. 2 il
fasc.
*Henderson, C. R. Social elements. (AJS., S.,
18) (AJS., N. + +)
Jahrhundert, das 19., in kommerzieller, industrieller
u. socialer Beziehung. Als Beitrag zur Lösg.
der dringendsten socialen Fragen v. P. J.
S(chwinges). Aachen, J. Schweitzer. 89 pp.
8vo. M. 1.
Judge, Thomas. Social & political economy. L.,
Simpkin, Marshall & Co. 178 pp. 8vo. 3s. 6d.
*Le Bon, Gustave. Psychology of peoples, its
influence on their evolution. N. Y., Mac-
millan Co. 236 pp. 8vo. $1.50. (Outlook,
N. 19 — —)
*Lilienfeld, Paul de. Zur Vertheidigung der
organischen Methode in Sociologie. (AJS.,
S., p. 279) (RIS., N.)
Mansuetus. Le sens commun et son application
aux sciences. P., libr. Revue socialiste. 391
pp. 8vo. f. 5.
Natorp, Paul. Sozialpädagogik. Theorie der
Willenserziehg. auf der Grundlage der Gemein-
schaft. St., F. Frommann. 352 pp. 8vo.
M. 6.
Scudder, V. D. Socials ideals in English letters.
B., Houghton, Mifflin & Co. 329 pp. 8vo.
$1.75.
Staats- u. socialwissenschaftliche Forschungen.
Hrsg. v. Gustav Schmoller. 16. Bd. 2. Hft.
(Der ganzen Reihe 69. Hft.) Wiedfeldt,
Otto Statistische Studien zur Entwicke-
lungsgeschichte der Berliner Industrie von
1720 bis 1890. Lp., Duncker & Humblot. 411
pp. 8vo. M. 9 60.
* Stein, Ludwig. Wesen u. Aufgabe der Soci-
ologie. (AJS., S., p. 279) (RIS., N.)
* Tarde, G. Les lois sociales. (AJS., S., 279)
(AJS., N. + —) (RIS., O, +)
Verolzheimer, Fritz. Aristo-Plutokratie das poli-
tische System der nächsten Zukunft. Mün-
chen, Th. Ackermann. 32 pp. 8vo. M. 0.50.
[Watson, J. Outline of philosophy, with notes.
. . . . Ed. 2. L., Maclehose. 512 pp. 8vo.
7s. 6d. (Formerly called Comte, Mill &
Spencer.)]

19. Statistics.

Austria—K. k. Ackerbau-Ministerium. Stati-
stisches Jahrbuch, 1897. 1. Hft., u. 2. Hft. 1.
u. 3. Lfg 8vo. Wien, Hof- u. Staatsdruckerei.
M. 5 u. 3.20.
Austria—K. k. statist. Central-Commission. 50.
Bd. 3. Hft., 51. Bd. 1. u. 2. Hft. Wien, C.
Gerold's Sohn in Komm. M. 6 u. 10.
Austria   K. k. statist. Central-Commission.
Oesterreichisches statistisches Handbuch f. die
im Reichsrathe vertretenen Königreiche u.
Länder. . . . 16. Jahrg., 1897. Wien, C.
Gerold's Sohn in Komm. 357 pp. 8vo. M. 6.
Austria—Statist Depart. im k. k. Handelsmini-
sterium. Statistik des auswärtigen Handels
des österreichisch-ungarischen Zollgebiets,

1897. 2. Bd. 8vo. Wien, Hof- u. Staatsdruckerei. 811 pp. 8vo. M. 6.
Bremen—Jahrbuch f. bremische Statistik, Hrsg.
vom Bureau f. Brem. Statistik, 1897. II. Heft.
Zur allgemeine Statistik, 1897. Bremen, G. A.
v. Halem in Komm. M, 7.50
[Bulletin de statistique et de législation comparée.
Table alphabétique des matières contenues
dans les quarante premiers volumes (1877-96).
P., Impr. nationale. 168 pp. 8vo. f. 2.]
Germany—Kaiserl. statist. Amt. Statistik des
deutschen Reichs, 95., 96., 97., 114., 115., 116.,
u. 117. Bd. 4to. B., Puttkammer & Mühlbrecht. M. 10, 5, 6, 5, 5, 5 u. 5.
Great Britain — Statistical Abstract: Foreign
countries, 1886-1895-6. no. 24. L., Eyre &
Spottiswoode. 1s. 5d.
Great Britain—Trade & navigation of the United
Kingdom: Accounts . . . . for each month . . . .
1898. L., Eyre & Spottiswoode. 8s. 8d.
Hubner's, Otto, Geographisch-statistische Tabellen
aller Länder der Erde. hrsg. von Fr. v. Jura-
schek. 47. Ausg., 1898. F., H. Keller. M.
1.20.
Italy—Direzione generale della statistica. Atti
della commissione per la statistica giudeziaria
civile e penale, sess. del dic. 1897. Roma tip.
Nazionale di G. Bertero. 359 pp. 8vo. L.
2.50.
Kopp, Léon. Contribution à l'étude de la morti-
natalité parisienne pendant les années 1891-6
(thèse). P., libr. Bordier Michalon. 55 pp.
8vo.
Munich—Jahres-Mitteilungen. Statistische Daten. 1. Jahrg, 1898. 40 pp. 16mo. München,
Nationale Verlagsanstalt. M. 0.20.
Prussia—K. statist. Bureau. Preussische Statistik.
151., Heft, 2 Thle. 153. u. 154. Heft. B.,
Verlag des k. statist. Bureaus. 4to. M. 17.20,
9, 6 u. 6.60.
Prussia — K. statist. Bureau. Gemeindelexikon f.
das Königr. Preussen. Auf Grund der Mate-
rialen der Volkszählg. vom 1895 u. anderer
amtl. Quellen bearb. 1, Prov. Ostpreussen; 2,
Westpreussen; 5, Posen. B., Verlag des k. statist. Bureaus.
Statistiches Handbuch f. den preussischen Staat.
3. Bd. Lp. Verlag des königl. statist. Bureau.
600 pp. 8vo. M. 5.
Switzerland — Bureau des eidg. Departements des
Innern. 116, 117 u. 118. Lfgn. 4to. Bern,
Art. Institut Orell Füssli in Komm. M. 10.
Württemberg—K. statist. Landesamt. Würtember-
gische Jahrbücher f. Statistik u. Landskunde.
1. Ergänzungsband, 1. Hft. St., W. Kohlhammer in Komm. 305 pp. 8vo. M. 4.

20. Unclassified.

Allan, C. E. Housing of the working classes
acts. L., Butterworth. 263 pp. 8vo. 7s. 6d.
Anarchismus u. seine Heilung, von Emanuel. Lp.,
W. Friedrich. 47 pp. 8vo. M. 0.60.
Arbeiten der deutschen Landwirthschafts-Gesellschaft. 32.-35. Heft. B., P. Parey. à M. 2.
Aubert, E., & A. Lapresté. L'alcoolisme, ses causes,
ses conséquences; moyens de le combattre.
P., libr. André fils. 48 pp. 12mo.
Bailey, S. H. Sketch of the evolution of our native fruits. N. Y., Macmillan Co. 472 pp.
8vo. $2.
Beach, C. F. Treatise on the law of monopolies &
industrial trusts, as administered in Eng. & in
the U. S. St. Louis, Central Law Journal Co.
760 pp. 8vo. $6.
Bernard, François. Principes d'économie rurale
(les systèmes de culture; les spéculations agricoles). P., Masson & Cie. 392 pp. 8vo. f. 4.
Bogart, E. L. Housing of the working people in
Yonkers. N. Y., Macmillan Co. (for Amer.

Econ. Assoc.). pp. 273-348. 12mo. $0.50.
(Economic studies, V. 3, no. 5.)
Bordiga, Oreste. Economia rurale. Partie 1. I
fattori della produzione agraria. Milano,
Francesco Vallardi. 251 pp. 16mo. L. 2.50.
[Bourne, H. R. T. English merchants: memoirs
in illustration of British commerce. New ed.,
ill. L., Chatto & Wundus. 598 pp. 8vo. 3s. 6d.]
Cenni monografici intormo ai singoli servizi dis-
penti dal ministero dei lavori pubblici per
gli anni 1891-7, compilati in occasione della
esposizione nazionale di Torino dell' anno
1898. . . . Roma, tip. dell Unione Cooperativa
editrice. 3 v. 1. Viabilita, tramvie, edilizia.
2. Opere idrauliche. 3. Strade ferrato.
Clough, Emma R. Study of Mary Wollstonecraft
& the rights of woman. N. Y., Longmans,
Green & Co. 234 pp. 8vo. $2.50.
Commercial geography of the United Kingdom of
Great Britain and Ireland. L., I. Pitman. 128
pp. 8vo. 1s.
Congrès international de la presse (Stockholm,
1897). Compte rendu. Bordeaux, impr. Gou-
nouilhou. 115 pp. 8vo.
Coulet, Elie. Le mouvement syndical et cooperatif
dans l'agriculture française: la féderation agri-
cole (these). P., Masson et Cie. 230 pp. 8vo.
Croly, Mrs. Jane Cunningham. History of the
woman's club movement in America, with
introd. by Mrs. Ellen M. Henrotin. N. Y., H.
G. Allen & Co. 1200 pp. il. pors. 4to. $5.
Die Vererbung des landlichen Grundbesitzes im
Königr. Preussen. Im Auftrage des kgl. Mi-
nisteriums f. Landwirthschaft, Domänen. u.
Forsten. Hrsg. v. M. Sering. B., P. Parey.
106 pp. 8vo. M. 3.
Fischer, G. Zustand u. Fortschritte der deutschen
Lebenversicherungs-Anstalten im J. 1897.
Jena, G. Fischer. 67 pp. 8vo. M. 2.40.
Genossenschaftliche Streit- u. Zeitfragen. Hrsg. v.
Ludf. Parisius u. Hans Crüger. 3.1Heft.'8vo.

B., J. Guttentag. 3. Wernicke, Johs. Umsatz-
steuer u. Konsumvereine. 44 pp. M. 0.60.
Gomel, Charles. Les grandes compagnies de chemins de fer français en 1897. P., Guillaumin
et Cie. 43 pp. 8vo.
Gonnard, René. L'assurance sociale contre la
vieillesse et l'invalidité en France. P., libr.
Fontemoing. 16 pp. 8vo.
Great Britain.—Foreign trade competition. Opinions of H. M. diplomatic & consular officers
on British trade methods. L., Eyre & Spottiswoode. 10½ d.
House of Commons. Report from select committee on telephones. L., Eyre & Spottiswoode. 5s. 2d.
Railway companies. General report for 1897 in
regard to share and loan capital, traffic expenditure & net profits. L., Eyre & Spot. 4½ d.
Royal commission on liquor licensing laws. 5th
report. Same. V. 7, Ireland. Evidence, appendices & index. L., Eyre & Spottiswoode.
Humbert, G. Traité des chemins de fer d'intérêt
local (chemins de fer à voie étroite; tramways
. . .). P., Baudry et Cie. 494 pp. 8vo.
[Kraft, Guido. Lehrbuch der Landwirthschaft auf
wissenschaftlicher u. praktischer Grundlage.
4. Bd. Die Betriebslehre. 6. Aufl. B., P. Par-
rey. 250 pp. 8vo. M. 5.]
Lacan, Raymond. Cinq mois chez les collectivistes.
Une déception; la Juiverie. Lille, impr. Du-
coulombier. 32 pp. 8vo.
[Leblanc, René. L'enseignement agricole . . . 3e
édition. P., libr. Larousse. 152 pp. 8vo.]
Phillipps, Mrs., & others. Dictionary of employments open to women, with details of wages,
hours of work, & other information. L., Woman's Institute. 170 pp. 8vo. 1s. 6d.
Wines, F. H., & Koren, John. Liquor problem
in its legislative aspects. New ed., with an
additional chapter. B., Houghton, Mifflin &
Co. 12mo. $1.25.

ARTICLES IN PERIODICALS

[Articles preceded by stars and followed by a reference to a number of the JOURNAL will be found in abstract under the head "Notes and Abstracts" in that number of the JOURNAL. Articles dealing with *Biography*, *Associations*, *Cities*, and *Towns* will be found grouped under those heads.

Æsthetics: Shaler, N. S. The landscape sa a
means of culture, Atlantic, D.
Africa: Roujre, M. La France et l'Angleterre
dans la vallée du Niger, RDM., O. 15.
Agriculture: Coletti. Francisco. Il congresso
degli agricoltori in Torino, GEc., N.
Conrad, J. Die Landwirtschaft im Deutschen
Reiche nach den landwirtschaftlichen Betriebs-
zählung von 14. Juni 1895, JNS., Q.
Grandeau, L. Le mouvement agricole, JEc., N.
Anarchism: L'idée du progrès et l'anarchisme,
HN., N.
Beltrani-Scalia, M. La conferenza internazio-
nale contro l'anarchia ed il riordinamento della
P. S. in Italia, RDC., N.
Nitti, F. S. Italian anarchists, NAR., N.
Zenker, V. E. Der Anarchismus und seine
Bekämpfung, ZS., O. 15.
Anthropology: Morgan, J. de. Stone age in
Egypt.
Arbitration, International: Pierantoni, Au-
guste. La nullité d'un arbitrage international,
RDI., 30:4.
Archæology: Peet, S. D. Great houses & for-
tresses. Amer. Antiqua., D.
Art: *see* Women.
Associations: Gibson, G. H. The Christian
commonwealth, The Commons, O.
Hausonville, Comte de. Entre femmes, RDM.,
D. 1.
Austria: *see* Finances.

Bankruptcy: Hotchkiss, W. H. Bankruptcy
laws, past & present, NAR., N
Biography: Bakounine. L'histoire de ma vie,
ReS., N.
Bayard, T. F., by George F. Parker, CoR., N.
Bismarck & Motley, by J. P. Grund, NAR., N.
Comte & Stuart Mill d'après leur correspondence,
par Lévy Bruhl, RPh., D.
Marx, Karl, GM., D.
Reeve, Henry., by T. H. S. Escott, FR., N.
Rivier. A. P. O., by Ernest Nys, LQR.
Sister Dora, by S. M. Jackson, ChR., N.
Waring, Col. Geo. E., S.
Waring, Col. Geo. E., by Wm. Potts, ChR., D.
Waring, Col. G. E., by Albert Shaw, RRN , D.
California: Hunt, R. D. Legal status of Cali-
fornia, 1846-9, AAP., N.
Jordan, D. S. California & the Californians,
Atlantic, D.
Canada: Porritt, Ed. Dominionian politics in
1898, YR., N.
Porritt, Edward. Canadian plebiscite, NAR., N.
Canals: Abbott, H. L. New Panama canal,
F., N.
Johnson, E. R. The Nicaragua canal & our
commercial interests, RRN., N.
Keasbey, L. M. The Nicaragua canal in the
light of present politics, RRN., N.
Miller, Warner. Nicaragua canal, F., N.
Stadden, C. M. Latest aspects of the Nicaragua
canal project, NAR., D.

Boulger, D. C. Fashoda & the upper Nile, CoR., N.

Decle, Lionel. The Fashoda question, FR., N.

Dehérain, Henri. L'occupation égyptienne du haut Nil, RDM., N. 1.

Deloncle, J. L. La question de Fashoda, RPP., N.

General Gordon's territory, CoR., O.

Spencer-Churchill, Winston. The Fashoda incident, NAR., D.

See also Finance.

Emigration: Olivi, Louis. L'émigration au point de vue juridique international et les délibérations de l'institut de droit international, RDI, 30:4.

Ethics: O'Rell, Max. Studies in cheerfulness, NAR., D.

See also Politics.

Ethnology: Kollmann, J., & Buchly, W. Die Persistenz der Rassen und prähistorischer Schädel, Archiv für Anthropologie, 25:4.

Morse, E. S. Was middle America peopled from Asia? PSM., N.

Ripley, W. Z. Racial geography of Europe, PSM., N.

Siemiradzki, Josef v. Beiträge zur Ethnographie der südamerikanischen Indianer, Mittheil. d. Anthropol. Gesell. in Wien, Ag.

See also Venice.

Evolution: *see* Æsthetics, Sociology.

Family: Wolf, Julius. Das Verhältnis von Eltern und Kindern bei dem Landvolk in Deutschland, ZS., O. 15.

Fashoda: *see* Egypt.

Fiber: Dodge, C. R. Possible fiber industies of the U. S., PSM., N.

Finance: Amery, L. S. Astro-Hungarian financial relations, EcJ., S.

Cuthbertson, Clive. On the depreciation of assignats, EcR , O.

Davis, A. M. Connecticut land : bank of the eighteenth century, QJE., O.

Franconie, J. Le controle financier internationale en Egypte (1876-97), AEL., N.

Giffen, Robert. Indian gold standard problem, EcJ., S.

Greef, G. de. Essais sur la monnaie, le crédit & les banques, HN., N., O.

Häbler, Konrad. Die Stellung der Fugger zum Kirchenstreite des 16. Jahrh., HV., N.

Heckel, Max von. Das Budget Frankreichs für das Jahr 1898, JNS., N.

Helfferich, Karl. Die bevorstehende Erneuerung des deutschen Bankgesetzes, JGV., 22:4.

Lodge, Oliver. Functions of money, EcR., O.

Manchez, Georges. La bourse et les affaires, RPP., N.

Shortt, Adam. Canadian currency & exchange under French rule, JCB., O.

Sumner, W. G. Coin shilling of Massachusetts Bay, YR., N.

Tangorra, V. Le teorie finanziarie di A. G. R. Turgot, GEc., O.

Viallate, Achille. L'établissement et l'échec du bi-métallisme aux Etats-Unis (1782-1861), JEc., N.

Zielinski, Ludwik. Der Rubel jetzt u. vor 100 Jahren, JNS., N.

See also Bankruptcy, Credit.

Fisheries: McGrath, P. T. The Atlantic fisheries question, NAR., D.

Forests: Gannett, Henry. Forest fires, F., D.

France : Donnet, Gaston. The French colonial craze, FR., D.

Guyot, Yves. The Dreyfus affair, F., N.

Lamy, Étienne. La France du Lévant, RDM., N. 15.

Martin, Germain. La grande industrie en France aux 17e & 18e siècles, RIS., N.

See also Africa, Scotland, Shipping.

Gas : Gray, J. H. Gas supply of Boston, QJE., O.

Germany : Caudel, M. Les élections allemandes du 16 Juin 1898 et le nouveau Reichstag, AEL., N.

Katzenstein, Simon. Les élections en Allemagne, HN., O.

La situation commerciale en Allemagne, JEc., N.

Philippson, M. Die innere Entwicklung im Norddeutschen Bunde. Aus Max v. Forckenbecks ungedruckten Briefen, DR., N.

Poinsard, Léon. L'Allemagne contemporaine, SS,. N.

Schäffle, Albert von. Germany and Great Britain, F., N., D.

See also Colonies, Family.

Great Britain : Diezmann, M. Englands Aussenhandel im Jahre 1897, JNS., O.

Faraday, Ethel R. Some economic aspects of the imperial idea, FR., D.

Hurd, A. S. Coal, trade and the empire, NC., N.

See also Africa, China, Colonies, Germany, Legislation.

History : Harrison, Frederic. Historical method of Prof. Freeman, NC., N.

Kralik, Richard von. Zur Philosophie der Geschichte, Leben, O.

Housing : Bogart, E. L. Housing of the working people in Yonkers, Economic Studies. O.

India : Zimmermann, A. Kaiserlicher Konsul in Berlin. Die letzte Hungersnot in Indien, ZS., N.

Indians: Abbott, Lyman. Our Indian problem, NAR., D.

Leupp, F. E. The protest of the Pillager Indians, F., D.

Individualism : Moore, Wentworth. The individualist, FR., D.

Industry : Schwiedland, E. Formen und Begriff der Hausindustrie, JNS., O.

See also Fiber.

Innere Mission : Ein halbes Jahrhundert Innere Mission, MIM., Ag.

See each no. of MIM.

Infanticide : (De)Maurans. Sur une disposition légale pour prévenir l'infanticide, AAC., N.

Inheritance: *see* Property.

Insurance : Bottoni, C. Le casse di Risparmo e i magazzini agricoli di deposito, O.A.

Die stadtkölnische Versicherungskasse gegen Arbeitslosigkeit im Winter 1897-8, JNS., N.

Industrial insurance in America, ChOR., O.

Mazzini, G. M. La funzione economica e sociale dell' assicurazione sulla vita, BRP., S.

Nachweisung der Geschäfts- u. Rechnungsergebnisse der auf Grund des Invaliditäts- u. Altersversicherungsgesetzes errichteten Versicherungsanstalten, 1896, Annalen des Deutschen Reiches, 31:12.

Rochetin, Eugène. La législation des assurances fraternelles aux Etats-Unis, JEc., O.

See also Old Age & each no. of BDL., GEc., LG., RT.

Interest : Stork, T. B. Equitable basis of interest, CM., D.

International Law : Morse, A. P. Rights & duties of belligerents & neutrals from the American point of view, ALR., N.

Takahashi, Sakue. The application of international law during the Chino-Japanese war, LQR., O.

See also Intervention.

Intervention : Denby, Charles. The doctrine of intervention, F., D.

Invention : Paulhan, F. Le développement de l'invention, RPh., D.

Italy : Ouida, & G. D. Vecchio. Impeachment of modern Italy, & a reply, RRN., N.

See also Anarchism.

Sanitary Science: *see also* Biography, National Health.
Saving: Hamilton, J. H. Educational aspect of saving, QJE., O.
Scotland: Stocquart, Émile. L'alliance de la France et de l'Écosse au moyen-âge et son influence juridique, RDI., 30: 4.
Settlements: *see* each no. of The Commons.
Shipping: Dubreucq, H., & R. de la Grasserie. Notre marine marchande, est-elle en décadence? RéfS., D. 1.
Social Movements: *see* each no. of RIS., SS.
Socialism: Eitelberg, M. Fichte u. der Sozialismus, Deutsche Worte, N.
Fournière, Eugène. La cité idéale, ReS., S.
Heath, Richard. The church & social democracy in Germany, CoR., O.
Leroy-Beaulieu, Anatolie. Collectiviste et anarchiste, RDM., O. 15.
Morant, A. C. Evolution du socialisme, HN., N.
Zur Geschichte der deutschen Socialdemokratie, ZS., O. 15.
See also Collectivism, and each no. of ReS., NZ.
Sociology: Baldwin, J. M., & Dewey, J. Social interpretations, RPh., N.
Chiappelli, A. Sul metodo delle scienze sociali, RItS., S.
Deschamps, F. Bismarck et la question sociale, RSC., N.
Goblot, E. Sur la théorie physiologique de l'association, RPh., N.
Heine, Wolfgang. Paul Barth's Geschichtsphilosophie, Deutsche Worte, O.
La Grasserie, R. de. Le duel au point de vue sociologique, RIS., N.
Loncao, E. Guerre e lotte di classe, RItS., S.
Posada, A. Gli studi sociologici in Ispagna, RItS., S.
Richard, G. La philosophie du droit et la sociologie juridique, RPh., D.
Small, A. W. Methodology of the social problem, AJS., N.
Small, A. W. Sanity in social agitation, AJS., N.
Spencer, Herbert. What is social evolution? PSM., N.
Wille, Ulrich. Nicht stehendes Heer, sondern Volkswehr, ZS., O.
See also Venice.
Statistics: Brants, V. Quelques traits de la psychologie des enquêtes, RSC., N.
Digest of recent foreign statistical publications, BDL., S.
See also Census.
Stock Companies: Kuefstein, Franz. Das Actienwesen u. seine Bedeutung im heute herrschenden Wirthschaftssystem, Leben, O.
Street Railways: Freund, E. de. Les chemins de fer d'intérêt local en Europe, AEL., N.
Strikes: Roussel, Félix. La grève générale et le syndicat guérard, RPP., N.
Suffrage: Lacombe, P. Le vote libre, RMM., N.
Sugar: Smith, K. L. Sugar beet industry in America, GM., D.
Tariff: England's future policy, CM., N.
See also Labor.
Taxation: Gomme, G. L. Local taxation in London, Jour. Roy. Statistical Society, S.
Hartung, J. Die direkten Steuern u. die Vermögensentwickelung in Augsburg von der

Mitte des 16. bis zum 18. Jahrhundert, JGV., 22: 4.
Luçay, Comte de. L'impôt peytral sur le revenu et la réforme fiscale des successions, RéfS., D.1.
Malzac, Miranda. L'impôt communal sur le revenu, RPP., N.
Stuart, A. J. C. Progressive taxation in Holland, EcJ., S.
Veber, Adrien. La question de l'octroi à Paris, ReS., N.
Telephones: Donald, Robert. The state & the telephones, CoR., O.
Hastie, A. H. The telephone tangle & the way to untie it, FR., D.
Traditions: *see* each no. of Journal of Am. Folklore & Revue des traditions populaires.
Tin Plate: McVey, F. L. Tin plate industry, YR., N.
Tramps: Berard, Alexandre. Le vagabondage en France, AAC., N.
Trusts: Wells, D. A. Scope & effect of the anti-trust act, YR., N.
Willcox, David. Recent construction of the federal anti-trust act, F., D.
See also Newspapers.
United States: Babcock, J. W. Lessons of the recent election, F., D.
Chamberlain, Joseph. Recent developments of policy in the U. S., D.
Clowes, W. L. American expansion and the inheritance of the race, FR., D.
Colquhoun, A. R. Eastward expansion of the United States, Harpers, N.
Kidd, Benjamin. The United States & the control of the tropics. Atlantic, D.
Leonard, M. H. Revolutionary records of a country town, New England Mag., N.
Low, Sidney. Change in English sentiment toward the U. S., N.
McMaster, J. B. Annexation and universal suffrage, F., D.
Parker, J. H. Our army supply departments, RRN., D.
See also Census, Colonies, Judiciary. Navies.
Vacation Schools: American, Sadie. Movement for vacation schools, AJS., N.
Milliken, O. J. Chicago vacation schools. AJS., N.
Vaccination: Speeches on, S., N.
Venice: Lombroso, Cesare. Sociological & ethnical sources of the greatness of Venice, F., D.
Wages: Hewins, W. A. S. The regulation of wages by the justices of the peace, EcJ., S.
Hopkinson, A., & Bowley, A. L. Bibliography of wage statistics in the United Kingdom in the nineteenth century. EcR., O.
Wages in the U. S. & Europe, 1870-1898, BDL., S.
Water: Nash, Vaughan. The East London water company, CoR., O.
Wheat: Atkinson. Ed. Wheat-growing capacity of the U. S., PSM., D.
Women: Doumic, René. Le féminisme au temps de la renaissance, RDM., O. 15.
Lory, Karl. Die Frau u. die Kunst der Gegenwart, Leben, O.
Sorabji, Cornelia. Legal status of women in India, NC., N.
See also Associations.
Y. M. C. A.: Shaw, Albert. The army & navy "Y. M. C. A.," RRN., N.

ABBREVIATIONS USED IN BIBLIOGRAPHY.

Places of Publication: B., Berlin; Bo., Boston; C., Chicago; Cin., Cincinnati; F., Frankfurt a. M.; Fr., Freiburg i. B.; L., London; Lp., Leipzig; M., Milan; N. Y., New York; P., Paris; Ph., Philadelphia; S., Strassburg; St., Stuttgart; T., Turin; W., Washington. *Prices:* d., pence; f., franc; L., lira; M., mark; s., shilling. *Months:* Ja. F. Mr. Ap. My. Je. Jl. Ag. S. O. N. D. *Periodicals:*

A.	Arena.
AA.	American Anthropologist.
AAC.	Archives d'anthropologie criminelle.
AAE.	Archivo per l'antropologia e la etnologia.
AAP.	Annals of the American Academy of Political and Social Science.
AC.	L'Association catholique.
ACQ.	American Catholic Quarterly Review.
AEL.	Annals d'Ecole libre des sciences politiques.
AGP.	Archiv für Geschichte der Philosophie.
AHR.	American Historical Review.
AIS.	Annals de l'Institute de science sociale.
AJP.	American Journal of Psychology.
AJS.	American Journal of Sociology.
AJT.	American Journal of Theology.
ALR.	American Law Register.
ALRv.	American Law Review.
AMP.	Académie des sciences morales et politiques, Séances.
AOR.	Archiv für öffentliches Recht.
ASA.	American Statistical Association, Publications.
ASAr.	Allgemeine statistisches Archiv.
ASG.	Archive für sociale Gesetzgebung und Statistik.
ASP.	Archiv für systematische Philosophie.
BDL.	Bulletin of the Department of Labor.
BG.	Blätter für Gefängnisskunde.
BML.	Banker's Magazine, London.
BMN.	Banker's Magazine, New York.
BOT.	Bulletin de l'Office du Travail.
BS.	Bibliotheca Sacra.
BSt.	Bulletin de statistique et de législation comparée.
BUI.	Bulletin de l'Union internationale de droit pénale.
C.	Cosmopolis.
ChOR.	Charity Organisation Review.
ChR.	Charities Review.
CoR.	Contemporary Review.
DL.	Deutsche Litteraturzeitung.
DR.	Deutsche Revue.
DRu.	Deutsche Rundschau.
DS.	Devenir social.
DZG.	Deutsche Zeitschrift für Geschichtswissenschaft.
EcJ.	Economic Journal.
EcR.	Economic Review.
EdR.	Educational Review.
EHR.	English Historical Review.
EM.	Engineering Magazine.
F.	Forum.
FR.	Fortnightly Review.
GEc.	Giornale degli economisti.
GM.	Gunton's Magazine.
HLR.	Harvard Law Review.
HN.	Humanité nouvelle.
HR.	Hygienische Rundschau.
HZ.	Historische Zeitschrift.
IAE.	Internationales Archiv für Ethnographie.
IJE.	International Journal of Ethics.
JAI.	Journal of the Anthropological Institute of Great Britain and Ireland.
JCB.	Journal of the Canadian Bankers' Association.
JEc.	Journal des économistes.
JFI.	Journal of the Franklin Institute.
JGV.	Jahrbuch für Gesetzgebung, Verwaltung und Volkswirthschaft.

JHS.	Johns Hopkins University Studies in History and Political Science.
JPE.	Journal of Political Economy.
JNS.	Jahrbücher für National-Oekonomie und Statistik.
LC.	Literarisches Centralblatt.
LG.	Labor Gazette.
LoQR.	London Quarterly Review.
LQR.	Law Quarterly Review.
MHM.	Mansfield House Magazine.
MIM.	Monatsschrift für innere Mission.
MA.	Municipal Affairs.
NA.	Nuova antologia.
NAR.	North American Review.
NC.	Nineteenth Century.
NS.	Natural Science.
NT.	New Time.
NW.	New World.
NZ.	Neue Zeit.
PhR.	Philosophical Review.
PSM.	Popular Science Monthly.
PSQ.	Political Science Quarterly
PsR.	Psychological Review.
QJE.	Quarterly Journal of Economics.
QR.	Quarterly Review.
RBP.	Rivista benificenza publica.
RCS.	Revue de christianisme sociale.
RDC.	Rivista di discipline carcerarie.
RDI.	Revue de droit internationale.
RDM.	Revue des deux mondes.
REA.	Revue mensuelle de l'École d'anthropologie de Paris.
RéfS.	Réforme sociale.
ReS.	Revue socialiste.
RH.	Revue historique.
RHD.	Revue d'histoire diplomatique.
RIF.	Rivista italiana di filosofia.
RIS.	Revue internationale de sociologie.
RiIS.	Rivista italia na di sociologia.
RISS.	Rivista internazionale di scienze sociali;
RMM.	Revue metaphysique et de morale.
RP.	Revue philanthropique.
RPe.	Revue pénitentiaire.
RPh.	Revue philosophique.
RPP.	Revue politique et parliamentaire.
RRL.	Review of Reviews, London.
RRN.	Review of Reviews, New York.
RSC.	Revue sociale catholique.
RSI.	Revista storica italiana.
RSP.	Revue sociale et politique.
RT.	Revue du travail.
S.	Sanitarian.
SR.	School Review.
SS.	Science sociale.
VWP.	Vierteljahrschrift für wissenschaftliche Philosophie.
YR.	Yale Review.
ZE.	Zeitschrift für Ethnologie.
ZGS.	Zeitschrift für die gesammte Staatswissenschaften.
ZPK.	Zeitschrift für Philosophie und philosophische Kritik.
ZPO.	Zeitschrift für das private und öffentliche Recht.
ZPP.	Zeitschrift für Psychologie und Physiologie der Sinnesorgane.
ZS.	Zeitschrift für Socialwissenschaft.
ZVR.	Zeitschrift für vergleichende Rechtswissenschaft.
ZVS.	Zeitschrift für Volkswirthschaft, Socialpolitik und Verwaltung.

[The titles of articles selected from periodicals not in this list will be followed by name of periodical in full.]

THE AMERICAN

JOURNAL OF SOCIOLOGY

VOLUME IV   MARCH, 1899   NUMBER 5

THE WORLD'S FIRST SOCIOLOGICAL LABORATORY.

OLD EDINBURGH was a city set on a hill. From the castle to the palace, the main street of the old city runs along the top of a ridge which was left between two deep grooves caused by glacial action. The location of the city on the ridge was due to the presence of the castle built on the precipitous rocks at its western end. The thoroughfare from the castle on the heights gradually descends to Holyrood Palace, and has been the scene of storied pageants without number. No city in western Europe is richer in historical associations; still the city of Edinburgh is no more remarkable than its topography, and is indeed dependent on the latter.

Professor Geddes, speaking of the permanence of physical characteristics, says: "What was decided among the prehistoric protozoa cannot be annulled by act of Parliament." With equal truth it may be said, the destiny of Edinburgh carved out in the ice age may be aided or retarded, but cannot be obliterated, by the deed of man. The history of its civilization is recorded in the progress from the warlike castle on the rocks, along the descending thoroughfare, to the domestic palace in the peaceful valley at the foot of Salisbury Crags.

> "Even thus, methinks, a city reared should be, ...
> Yea, an imperial city that might hold
> Five times a hundred noble towns in fee . . . .
> Thus should her towers be raised; with vicinage
> Of clear bold hills, that curve her very streets,
> As if to indicate, 'mid choicest seats
> Of Art, abiding Nature's majesty."

If one were to choose a point on the main street near the castle, where he could see the city, old and new, spread out before him, he could read, not merely the chronicle of Edinburgh, but the history of civilization. Such a point has, in fact, been chosen by one of the pioneers in modern sociological investigation and social activity.

As early as 1887 one might walk along the great central artery of Old Edinburgh, and, passing in through a narrow close, enter one of the dingy courts, which give access to the tall buildings that line this ancient street. Ascending three flights of dark stairs, almost feeling one's way, one might knock at the door which admitted to the apartments of Professor and Mrs. Geddes. After the gloomy climb to step within the well-adorned rooms was a pleasure, but to pass to the windows was to enjoy a scene bewildering, both in its surprise and its charm. The ascent of three flights on the southern side of the building had given one an elevation or eight stories on the northern front, on account of the steepness of the hill on which the buildings are located. And the picture framed by this seemingly magic casement was of Princes Gardens immediately before the windows, edged with the splendidness of the famed Princes street, lying on the slope which leads down to the Firth of Forth, beyond whose cool and blue waters rise the proud Scottish highlands. This panorama of natural grandeur and beauty, second only to the scene from the castle, is typical, too, of the commanding intellectual survey which is made possible by the effort of Professor Geddes, who here, in 1887, established a university hall.

The beginning of this social work seems to date from the organization in 1886 of a summer meeting, which included in that year only courses in seaside zoölogy and garden botany. The next year there was added a course in the theory of evolution; the three following years, in the classes held at Granton Marine Station, near Edinburgh, the attendance continually increasing, botany and zoölogy continued to be the chief subjects of instruction. In 1889 and 1890 the application of the idea of evolution to social as well as biological studies consti-

PRINCES GARDENS AND OLD EDINBURGH — BUILDINGS OF THE TOWN AND GOWN ASSOCIATION ON THE RIGHT

tuted a central course of lectures, delivered by Professor Geddes. In 1891 most of the classes were held in Edinburgh, near the first of the residential houses for students with which Professor Geddes inaugurated his university hall project.   From 1893 till 1895 the meeting was held in the Normal School of the Training College, and was assisted in its work by grants of money from the town council.   The number of courses offered has been

THE OUTLOOK TOWER

continually increased, especially in philosophy, sociology, history, and geography.   There have participated in the meetings, among many others, such well-known educators from Great Britain and the continent as J. Arthur Thomson and A. J. Herbertson, of Edinburgh ; J. K. Ingram and A. C. Haddon, of Dublin ; Lloyd Morgan, of Bristol ; Richard G. Moulton, of Chicago ; Ernst Grosse, of Freiburg ; Elisée Reclus, of Belgium ; Edmond Demolins and Paul Desjardins, of Paris ; Henry Dyer, of Glasgow; Professor Rein, of Jena; Professor Wenley, of Ann Arbor. A typical program follows:

A. GENERAL COURSES.

9–10. *Contemporary Social Evolution.* Twenty lectures. Professor Geddes.
10–11. *History and Principles of the Sciences.* Twenty lectures.
(Studios and sloyd workshop open throughout the day.)

B. SECTION OF EDUCATION. SOCIAL SCIENCE, AND HUMANITIES.	B. SECTION OF NATURAL SCIENCE.
10–11.	10–11. *Comparative Psychology.* Ten lectures. Professor Lloyd Morgan (first half). *Hygiene.* Ten lectures. Dr. Louis Irvine (second half).
11–12. *Modern History.* Twenty lectures. Mr. Victor Branford.	11–12. *Biology.* Twenty lectures. Mr. J. Arthur Thomson and Mr. Norman Wyld.
12–1. *La Science Sociale.* Ten lectures by M. Demolins (first half). *La Renaissance Morale de la France au Temps Présent.* Two lectures by M. Desjardins (second half).	12–1.
2–4. *Seminars of Practical Economics* (Professor Geddes); *History* (Mr. Branford); *Education* (Miss Newcomb); and ten lessons in *Elocution* by Miss Etka Glyn.	2–4. *Practical Botany* (including field work). Twenty meetings. Mr. Robert Turnbull. *Field Geology.* Ten excursions. Mr. Wyld (first half). *Practical Zoölogy* (at Marine Station). Twenty meetings. Mr. Thomson.
8–9. Weekly Musical Recitals by Mrs. Kennedy–Fraser and Mrs. Geddes. Several Literary Recitals by Miss Etka Glyn.	8–9. *Edinburgh and Neighborhood.* A regional survey. Twelve lectures.

The curriculum has expanded until it includes the most interesting synthesis of studies to be found anywhere. This year it somewhat changed its character by laying stress on the study of modern languages; next summer the old methods are to be restored, with the modern languages added. The educational purpose may be stated in the words of Professor Geddes:

Starting from the familiar idea of working from the concrete to the abstract, from the senses toward the intellect, it is attempted in each subject of study (1) to freshen the student's mind by a wealth of impressions; (2) to introduce him to the advancing literature of the subject; (3) to supply him with the means of summarizing, arranging, and more clearly thinking out these accumulations of observation and reading. Hence (1) the insistence upon demonstrations, experiment, and field excursions; (2) the introduction in several subjects of the seminar, which, with its guidance to the world of books and activity in using them, is so marked a strength of the German university; (3) the extended use of graphic methods.

The student, though first of all freshened as an observer, is regarded, not as a receptacle for information, but as a possible producer of independent thought. Hence the examination method, everywhere falling into such merited disrepute, is here definitely abandoned; a keener stimulus, even a more satisfactory test of progress, being found in accustoming the student to take part in his own education, by attention first to the increase and systematization of his materials, next to the occasional contribution of his best results to the common stock of class notes and summaries, and thence to fuller collaboration with his teacher.

Passing from the manner to the matter of education, it is attempted not merely (1) to offer a series of special courses, each of adequate thoroughness, but (2) to keep up as far as possible a parallelism of treatment, and (3) to coördinate these courses into a larger whole. Hence the general courses addressed to all students, dealing especially with the history of civilization, the historical development of the sciences, their general principles and mutual relations. The present scheme is, in fact, an attempt to work in theory toward the organization of knowledge and in practice toward the more rational arrangement of curricula of study.

The legitimate claim of the man of science is affirmed by the very existence and method of these courses; yet the corresponding claim of the scholar and humanist that, whatever be the progress of natural science, the study of man must remain supreme, is also recognized — witness that subordination of biology to social science which is a characteristic feature.

Therefore, the work of Professor Geddes has included, not merely a synthesis of studies, but also, and logically, a correlation of activities.

In May, 1887, three small flats housed the first seven students in the first university hall. The absence of dormitories in the Scotch universities was part of the reason for this endeavor, and is one explanation of its growth. Other flats were taken, and still the number of students increased, until it was possible to begin the construction of independent buildings to house the little colony. Year by year the numbers grew, until provision

THE MOUND, OLD EDINBURGH, AND THE CASTLE

has been gradually made, not only for housing a hundred or more students and a little Bohemia of artists, literary and other professional people, but also for the rebuilding of the old town of Edinburgh bit by bit. Over five hundred thousand dollars have been expended in the improvement of nearly forty tenements and closes, with the consequence of both sanitary and æsthetic improvement, and without alteration of the organic character of this historical region. No portion of this sum has been obtained by gift or loan without interest; but a moderate return, averaging 4½ per cent., has uniformly been paid upon the capital invested in Professor Geddes' lands. At length, in 1896, the Town and Gown Association was organized by the initiative of Professor Geddes, and larger schemes are developing. If the philosophy of education, according to Professor Geddes, is to imply the necessary connection of studies and activities, it is also to include the development of studies as the consequence of activities. The crystallization of all this effort in easily visible form is to be seen in the Outlook Tower.

The Outlook Tower was originally a popular observatory. It commands even finer views of Edinburgh than are to be obtained from the castle, and for the best use of these it is surmounted by a *camera obscura*, originally constructed for purely commercial purposes, now the culmination of this new scientific institute. The ascent of the tower provides one with a cyclopædia, the descent, a laboratory.

Although constructed on the scientific method of proceeding from the known to the unknown, the near to the distant, if we begin with the ascent of the tower we should see first the final product of this method, graphic representations of the entire world. So, logically to follow the method, we must start from the top, but in ascending we may glance at the results. Professor Geddes says: "The intellectual tradition of Edinburgh is not only of education, but of publication; not only of abstract philosophy, but also very largely of concrete encyclopædias (Britannica, Chambers', etc.); notably, also, of atlases, maps, and gazetteers. Unusually rich and complete in all the elements of a regional survey, it is also interested in world survey, and, if less proportionately important in the practical world than of old, it has become more widely connected with the old than ever—witness the proverbially wide dispersion of Scotsmen over England and the empire, through America, and, indeed, through the whole world. . . . . This regional Outlook Tower is thus itself a regional product ; although its principle is easily adaptable to every region, as that of an encyclopædia may be used anywhere." We begin, therefore, with our encyclopædia, not, however, in print, but in graphic form, including not simply organized data, but mutually related facts. In the basement we find the results, not only of the processes carried on above, but also classifications of the arts and sciences, from Aristotle or Bacon to Comte and Spencer, and we incidentally have light thrown on the intellectual development of the presiding genius here. Comte is among the intellectual ancestors of Professor Geddes, as are Le Play and others who have attempted a correlation of the facts of life. Here we find an appeal made to students of all the arts and sciences, the floors above being of interest, primarily, to the sociologist. Successive floors give us, in chart, in plan, in photograph and sketch, the whole of Europe, the empire, Scotland, Edinburgh and the immediate neighborhood.

We shall find it more profitable to begin a careful inspection of the tower at the very summit, where is situated the *camera obscura*.

This instrument combines for the sociologist the advantages of the astronomical observatory and the microscopical laboratory. One sees both near and distant things. One has a wider field of view than can be enjoyed by the naked eye, and at the same time finds more beautiful landscape thrown on the table by the elimination of some of the discordant rays of light. One sees at once with the scientist's and the artist's eye. The great purpose of the *camera obscura* is to teach right methods of observation, to unite the æsthetic pleasure and artistic appreciation with which observation begins, and which should be habitual before any scientific analysis is entered upon, with the synthetic attitude to which every analysis should return.   In this little dome, the light admitted only from above, whence by reflection it throws the images of the outer world on the round, white table, we begin a study of Old Edinburgh.   As the table turns, we may see successively the magnificent new group of buildings immediately to the west of the tower, now taken over by the Town and Gown Association ; beyond these, the esplanade, the castle, and portions of the new city, as well as an ancient approach to the old, the Grass Market.   To the south, as the table revolves, we may examine minutely in the foreground Heriot's Hospital, Greyfriars' Church, the Royal Infirmary, and, less and less closely, the Meadows, the public golf links, and the Pentlands beyond. Looking to the east, one sees the rare significance of this location.   The tower is situated on the north side of the great thoroughfare of Old Edinburgh.   One looks down this narrow, high-walled slum street, where history is written in every old residence, in St. Giles' Church, Parliament House, and numberless other historic monuments, until in the distance one sees Holyrood Palace, Salisbury Crags, and Arthur's Seat.   To the north stretches the unique panorama which includes Princes Gardens and Princes street, and, with their public institutions, the Mound and Calton Hill.   Beyond the new town of Edinburgh and its port, Leith, stretches the Firth of Forth ; and, on a clear day, the highlands may be seen.

> " Traced like a map the landscape lies
>   In cultured beauty stretching wide ;
>   There Pentland's green acclivities ;
>   There Ocean with its azure tide ;
>   There Arthur's Seat ; and gleaming through
>   Thy Southern wing, Dunedin blue !
>   While in the Orient Lammer's daughters,
>   A distant giant range, are seen,
>   North Berwick Law with cone of green,
>   And Bass amid the waters."

In this physical environment the sociologist finds every variety of modern life, from the worst of Scotch slums at his feet, under the shadow of a majestic military stronghold, past the seats of ecclesiastical and political authority to the former

A BIT OF UNIVERSITY HALL — ALLAN RAMSAY'S COTTAGE ON THE RIGHT

home of royalty ; or, through such types of modern commercial activity as the railway in Princes Gardens, the shops in Princes street, and the bridge over the Firth of Forth, to the simple shepherds of the uplands. He sees, also, the monuments of modern arts and sciences, from gallery, museum, and observatory, to garden and hospital ; nor can he fail to be impressed with the relation of social conditions to topography. If one can learn to observe accurately in watching these shifting scenes, he should be equipped with the method by which he may study the geography of the world, and, through that, social institutions.

If we descend from the *camera obscura* to the turreted roof of the tower, we may enjoy much of the vision without artificial aid, and with a deeper appreciation because of the significance given to the panorama by its previous concentration on the small table above. We fortify ourselves for our return to earth by a cup of tea in the tower tea rooms, and begin our descent with the story devoted to Edinburgh. Here we find a permanent synthesis of the passing pageant we have just witnessed. The relief model of the city of Edinburgh carries us back to the time antecedent to all the present buildings, and, with the aid of charts and pictures, we have little difficulty in tracing history, beginning with the first castle walls, and continuing to the renewal of Old and the extension of New Edinburgh. Indeed, we find on this floor evidences that the tower is not only scientific, but practical. The plans for rejuvenating the old city, as undertaken by Professor Geddes and his colleagues, are here in evidence. In his words : " The interests of archæology and public health, of æsthetics and finance, of the housing of the people, and of the collegiate beginnings of the academic community, are here, as far as may be, reconciled in actual practice."

The story below is devoted to Scotland. On the floor is a huge map, conforming to the points of the compass, so that one may easily orient himself. The walls also are covered with graphic representations of the topography, the history, and the social conditions of Scotland, from the occupations of the primitive highlander to the great commercial and naval undertakings of the Firth and Clyde ship canal. The possibilities of the labo·

ratory study of sociology may be shown in connection with this department of the Outlook Tower by a passage in which Professor Geddes illustrates the significance of topography in the case of the popular sport we have imported from Scotland:

Everyone has his own ideas about Scotland; has heard, let us say, more or less of the romantic aspect and associations of Edinburgh, or of the industrial intensity and world-wide commerce of Glasgow; he has heard, too, of golf at St. Andrews, of sport in the highlands, and of yachting on the west coast. Shooting on moor and mountain, sailing on the great sea lochs, are obviously intelligible; but taking St. Andrews and golf as a somewhat less obvious example, why should this be so developed? What is the explanation of the preëminence of this little town, and what has enabled it to popularize its characteristic game almost more fully and widely than even Oxford and Cambridge theirs of rowing? What has made its club "royal and ancient" and given it a metropolitan authority excelling that of the Marylebone Cricket Club in its way? Why should this be? There certainly are sand dunes with a grassy margin — links, as they call them. But these links stretch more or less along the eastern coasts of Scotland and England, and from northern France along the shores of the Netherlands and Prussia up to Finland and the innermost Baltic — a long field for St. Andrews! Consider first, why should we find golf on such a soil? Watch first the blowing sand, and see what holds it — the strong blue lyme grass, which rambles with its long creeping stems and tough roots among the sand. But for this, the sand would travel inland indefinitely, destroying whole fields and parishes in its progress; as, for that matter, it does here and there. Upon these half-fixed dunes the wind still blows, and here and there blows out holes large and small which give the famous "bunkers," the main hazards of the game. Over the more fixed surface, however, there soon come the finer grasses eaten by sheep, and so the sheep itself, and with the sheep the shepherd. This fringe of pasture is narrow, else we should have a pastoral civilization; but here in western Europe this can be no more than a broken fringe; no migratory pastoral families, much less a great patriarchal one, is possible; the shepherd remains at the simplest level, scarcely distinct from the ordinary agricultural population. He retains its type, and instead of contemplating indefinitely like the Eastern, he needs something to do. His sheep are not the sole possessors of the pasture; the dry sandy soil and grass are suited admirably also to the rabbit both for its burrow and its pasture. As the shepherd goes along, he knocks now and then a stone into a rabbit hole with his crook. Having put the stone in — it is a white one — he fishes it out again, and drives it on to another hole. He idles away his hour and also invents the game of golf.

We see then the origin of golf and its relation to the links; but why to St. Andrews in particular? Here is a university town, with remote position, and no mountain, river, or other athletic resources. Its whole resources are those of the sea and of golf upon the far-reaching moor. The student, often originally himself a shepherd, takes most naturally to the game, and becomes more expert in it than the working shepherds or others have time to be, and the inventive and mechanical townsman improves both "club" and "ball." He carries on the game through youth and age; at last he writes of it with enthusiasm; in every way he diffuses it, by and by from London as journalist and politician. But for centuries every St. Andrews man has been more or less of a Balfour or an Andrew Lang. (*The Co-operative Wholesale Societies' Annual*, 1895, article on "Education for Economics and Citizenship, and the Place of History and Geography in This," pp. 485–529.)

DESIGNS BY THE OLD EDINBURGH SCHOOL OF ART

Leaving the Scottish division of the tower, we reach the story below Scotland, which is devoted to the empire, and to an alcove for the United States. Here one finds an incipient record of the English-speaking world, and indication of the inclusiveness of the project. The descent of another flight of steps brings us to Europe. Again we may see the combination of the scientific and the practical, in the record of Professor Geddes' recent experiments in Cyprus, which he chose as "a geographical and historic, racial and social microcosm; and as a unique region which, while practically a portion of the colonial empire, at once unites many of the most characteristic developments and problems of the old world, since still, as of old, linking Europe with Asia, and both, through Egypt, even with Africa," and which we may choose as typical of the province of this department of the Outlook Tower. Professor Geddes has not only gathered here some remarkable graphic evidences of conditions in Cyprus, and utilized this material in his lectures and publications, but he has organized (again on business lines, similar to those of the Town and Gown Association) a society for the development of the island, the methods being not those of bounty, nor protection, nor enforced coöperation, but the development of the soil, and the reconstitution of the forests.

There still remains a story devoted to the world, as yet but little developed, waiting for the consummation of the plans of Professor Reclus for the great globe, which was to have been erected for the Paris exhibition of 1900, had time allowed. Not discouraged, Professors Reclus and Geddes are now combining their respective and complementary schemes of globe and tower into that of a complete geographical exhibition, which may be arranged in Paris, in Great Britain, or in America, as circumstances may determine, or if possible reduplicated in all — with smaller regional museums, or outlook towers, for different cities, and with minor outlines adapted to geographical education in colleges and even schools.

The Outlook Tower is not only a museum and laboratory for the Edinburgh summer meeting and the occasional student; it is the center for a school of geography, the Town and Gown Association, the Old Edinburgh School of Art, and a publishing department through which "Patrick Geddes and Colleagues" have issued some beautiful books contributing to the Celtic renascence in literature and art, the significance of which has been explained in one of these publications, *The Evergreen:*

Industrial initiative and artistic life are reappearing, and each where it was most needed, the first amid this ice-pack of frozen culture [Edinburgh], the latter in our western inferno of industry [Glasgow]. Architecture, too, is renascent ; the work of the past dozen years will, on the whole, bear comparison with anything in English or continental cities, in a few cases may even challenge it, and in at least one case, that of the noble Academic Aula of Edinburgh, carry the challenge back to the best days of the Renaissance. The current resuscitation of Old Edinburgh, more unnoticed just because more organic, is hence a still deeper sign. First came the opening up of the cathedral, the rebuilding of the city cross, then of the castle gates and Parliament Hall. Now the old courts and closes from Holyrood to Castlehill are slowly but steadily changing, and amid what was and is the most dense and dire confusion of material and human wreck and misery in Europe, we have every here and there some spark of art, some strenuous beginning of civic sanitation, some group of healthy homes of workman and student, of rich and poor, some slight but daily strengthening reunion of democracy with culture; and this in no parliamentary and abstract sense, but in the civic and concrete one.

The Edinburgh School of Art has been equally successful in reviving old Celtic designs and discovering new Celtic artists, but it is a marvel to the visitor to find how much of their activity is due to the inspiration of the scientist Patrick Geddes. Whether in his own apartments, in the university halls, in the historical procession to be the crowning art work of the castle hill, or in the architectural improvement of the old town, everywhere is seen the hand of the master. The redemption of Cyprus and the teaching of botany at Dundee, the reconstruction of Edinburgh and the printing of books, the teaching of art and the scientific collections of the Outlook Tower, are all reconciled in the personality of the man to whom synthesis is the chief function of contemporary science. He has said: "While our studies are nothing if not historical, they must begin with the present day, and the past be seen by help of the present; while our studies are nothing if not geographical, they must begin at our own doors; and while nothing if not scientific, they must still begin with art!"

The Outlook Tower, at once school, museum, atelier, and observatory, may fitly be called the world's first sociological laboratory.

CHARLES ZUEBLIN.

THE UNIVERSITY OF CHICAGO.

PROFIT-SHARING AND COÖPERATION.

I.

IT is a significant fact that most economists who have dealt with this subject have favored profit-sharing and have been skeptical as to the merits, or at least the possibility, of coöperation; while, on the other hand, sociologists, or those who have taken a more comprehensive view of social and economic relations, have pronounced in favor of the latter, and have viewed profit-sharing, if with any favor at all, as a temporary palliative of very restricted applicability at best. There are those who have taken a middle ground, believing that coöperation was the ultimate ideal to be reached through an extensive development of profit-sharing. No doubt one class has considered too exclusively the economic difficulties of coöperation, and the other too exclusively its social and moral advantages, whereas neither consideration should be overlooked. It is the economic difficulty of selecting and retaining the requisite managerial ability by a group lacking the necessary intelligence, foresight, and self-control that the one class has emphasized; it is the social insufficiency of the principle underlying profit-sharing, the economic difficulties of its universal application, and more than all else the obstacle offered by the defective, or at least unsymmetrical, moral character of those upon whom its introduction and continuance depend, that the other class of students has considered.

John Stuart Mill closes his chapter on the "Probable Future of the Laboring Classes" with the following paragraph on this subject: "The value of this 'organization of industry' for healing the widening and embittering feud between the class of laborers and the class of capitalists must, I think, impress itself by degrees on all who habitually reflect on the condition and tendencies of modern society. I cannot conceive how any such person can persuade himself that the majority of the community will forever, or even for much longer, consent to hew wood and draw water all their lives in the service and for the benefit of others, or can doubt that they will be less and less willing to coöperate as subordinate agents in any work when they have no interest in the result, and that it will be more and more difficult to obtain the best work-people, or the best service of any work-people, except on conditions similar in principle to those of M. Leclaire. Although, therefore, arrangements of this sort are now in their infancy, their multiplication and growth, when once they enter into the general domain of popular discussion, are among the things which may most confidently be expected."[1]

The gravity of the condition here set forth is not overestimated. Nor has it become any less critical since the days when Mill wrote; rather the reverse. And yet the concluding sentence must be classed with the many other unfulfilled prophecies of economics and other social sciences, all illustrative of the extreme unreliability of social prevision in the present stage of social knowledge. Such failures of prophecies do not detract from the motives prompting them, nor from the wisdom of the author, but do emphasize the fact, to which conclusion we must come, that profit-sharing, however commendable in isolated instances, is of very limited applicability under our present industrial system, and offers no adequate means of escape from that system.

A discussion of profit-sharing still earlier than Mr. Mill's is that of Charles Babbage in his *Economy of Manufactures*. By some this is held to be the origin of the idea. The prophetic element of this discussion had a more happy outcome than many such, for there have been many realizations of the system here expounded as ideal.

It has been held that the "academic" influence upon the coöperative movement has been injurious; even the influence of its friends. But the reverse is certainly true of profit-sharing. Most extensively advertised and most highly commended by nearly all the systematic economists since Mill, it owes to them much of its strength, at least its publicity and the general favor in which it is held.

Mr. Mill's opinion is still the general one. General Walker,

[1] J. S. MILL, *Principles of Political Economy*, Book IV, chap. 7.

after an unfavorable discussion of coöperation, says in regard to profit-sharing: "That something of the sort is practicable, with the exercise of no more of patience, pains, and mutual good faith than it is reasonable to expect of many employers and many bodies of workmen, I am greatly disposed to believe. Many experiments, and probably much disappointment and some failures, will be required to develop the possibilities of this scheme and determine its best working shape, yet in the end I see no reason to doubt that such a relation will be introduced extensively with the most beneficial results."[1] General Walker's pronounced views are no doubt due to the great emphasis which he places on the functions of the entrepreneur.

Mr. Cairnes holds "that the condition of any substantial improvement of a permanent kind in the laborer's lot is that the separation of industrial classes into laborers and capitalists which now prevails shall *not* be maintained; that the laborer shall cease to be a laborer — in a word, that profits shall be brought to reinforce the wages fund;"[2] "that he should be, in one way or other, lifted out of the groove in which he at present works, and placed in a position compatible with his becoming a sharer in equal proportion with others in the general advantages from industrial progress."[3] The solution advocated is that the workmen become coöperators, that is, capitalists on a small scale. But the process is not through profit-sharing, as with others, but by means of saving. To this the "chief obstacles in the way are not physical, are not economical, but moral or intellectual. . . . . Coöperation — the contribution by many workmen of their savings toward a common fund which they employ as capital and coöperate in turning to profit — constitutes the one and only solution of our present problem; the sole path by which the laboring classes as a whole, or even in any large number, can emerge from their condition of mere hand-to-mouth living, to share in the gains and honor of advancing civilization."[4]

Professor Jevons takes the other view, and agrees with most

[1] F. A. WALKER, *The Wages Question*, p. 281.
[2] CAIRNES, *Leading Principles of Political Economy*, p. 284.
[3] *Ibid.*, p. 285.　　　　　[4] *Ibid.*, p. 289.

of the economists in favoring profit-sharing. "There can be no doubt," he says, "that the soundest possible solution of the labor question will eventually be found in such a modification of the terms of partnership as shall bind the interests of the employer and workmen more closely together. Under such a system the weekly wages would be regarded merely as subsistence money or advances which the employer would make to enable the laborer and his family to await the completion of the interval between manufacture and sale. The balance of the value would be paid at the end of the year or half year in the form of a dividend or bonus, consisting in a share of all surplus profits realized beyond the necessary charges of interest, wages of superintendence, cost of depreciation of capital, reserve to meet bad debts, and all other expenses of production for which the employer can fairly claim compensation."x Elsewhere he says: "The partnership scheme is, I believe, by far the truest form of coöperation. I do hope very much from coöperation in many forms, but the name of the thing will not be sufficient; the real interest of all employed must be enlisted, if coöperative societies are to prosper and grow. . . . . It is well understood that a successful military leader must be perfectly unfettered in judgment and supreme in executive power; and yet he must manage to earn the confidence and devotion of his men. It is to a position resembling this that the Messrs. Briggs seem to me to have raised themselves by the courageous adoption of a true principle, and I do believe that, when their example is followed, our workshops and factories will become so many united and well-organized regiments of laborers. Good leaders will seek good men, and good men in return will seek good leaders. We shall have an honorable rivalry between one firm and another as to which shall get the best men and pay the best dividends."² The unfortunate failure of the system adopted by the Messrs. Briggs is the most striking comment upon this prediction. It is evident that in this Professor Jevons does not look beyond the present militant organization of industry upon a despotic basis, while Professor Cairnes

---

¹ *The State in Relation to Labor*, p. 142.

² *Methods of Social Reform*, p. 142.

does look forward to a truly democratic organization, though order and system must, of course, still be an essential feature.

Professor Fawcett takes a middle ground, advocating profit-sharing as a transition stage to coöperation. Speaking of the Briggs experiment he says: " In this case it will be again perceived that the portion of profits allotted to workmen does not diminish, but, on the contrary, greatly increases, the gain of the employer. From this circumstance it may confidently be hoped that these copartnerships will so rapidly extend as to fundamentally change the economic relations now existing between employer and employed. . . . . Ultimately it may be hoped that there will be so much moral and social advancement as to enable a perfect union between capital and labor to be established; this is secured when laborers supply all the capital which is required to sustain the industry in which they are engaged. When this is accomplished there is coöperation in its highest form." [1]

Professor Marshall's opinion is substantially the same. There is, he says, "*de facto* some sort of profit- and loss-sharing between almost every business and its employés; and perhaps this is in its very highest form when, without being embodied in a definite contract, the solidarity of interests between those who work together in the same business is recognized with cordial generosity as a result of true brotherly feeling. But such cases are not very common; and, as a rule, the relations between employer and employed are raised to a higher plane both economically and morally by the adoption of the system of profit-sharing, especially when it is regarded as but a step toward the still higher, but much more difficult, level of true coöperation." [2] In another place, speaking of the future of coöperation, the same author writes: "Enough has been said to show that the world is only just beginning to be ready for the higher work of the coöperative movement, and that its many different forms may therefore be reasonably expected to attain a larger success in the future than in the past, and to offer excellent opportunities for work-

---

[1] *Manual of Political Economy*, p. 253.

[2] MARSHALL, *Principles of Economics*, p. 755.

ingmen to practice themselves in the work of business management to grow into the trust and confidence of others, and gradually rise to posts in which their business abilities will find scope." [1]

Most recent economic writers agree in taking this more comprehensive view of their subject, and as a result these judgments are based upon a consideration of social forces other than economic, quite as much as is the case with those who write from the sociological viewpoint. Two further illustrations will suffice.

Professor Clark premises the identity of interests of capitalist and laborer in production, and the antagonism of interests in distribution. The adjustment of these antagonistic interests is first made by competition. But competition, which at first is a fair rivalry, becomes a bitter struggle and finally an open warfare. This is succeeded logically, and is being succeeded in reality, by arbitration. But, while arbitration is a substitution of justice for force, yet attention is concentrated on the terms of division of the joint product. This in time tends in the direction of antagonisms, and also fails to secure the largest product for division. Both competition and arbitration emphasize the element of antagonism. But profit-sharing and coöperation emphasize the element of harmony. Profit-sharing, being the stage intermediate between arbitration and coöperation, has this advantage of coöperation that it blends the two classes, the employer and the workmen; for the workman becomes, in connection with the employer, an entrepreneur, though not a capitalist. Yet the organization and direction of the business retain most of the advantages of the preceding systems. Most of Professor Clark's illustrations are in reality product-sharing; therefore constitute a substitute form for the wage system, really preceding it, and are not a modification of the wage system at all. But profit-sharing, as a modification of the wage system, is favored because it is a means of transition to true coöperation.

The following quotation summarizes this opinion: "In some fields it [profit-sharing] has proved superior to competition at

[1] *Principles of Political Economy*, p. 387.

its best; it will easily excel, in many more fields, the wreck of the old system with which it is now brought into comparison. If a corporation were to adopt the share system in dealing with its employés, and were to pay the amount given to them, in excess of daily wages, in the form of stock, the effect would be to gradually transmute the partial coöperation into the complete form. New establishments started on this plan have, as a rule, perished in their infancy. Experience has shown that the mortality among them is increased by loans of capital made to them either by governments or by philanthropic societies. Such loans strain the enterprises at their weakest point, namely, their general management. Profit-sharing retains the experienced employer as the general director, and enlists the interest of every workman in the oversight of details within his province. Full coöperation, unless established by the gradual method above spoken of, renders a managing committee necessary, and the inexperience of the men selected for this function imperils the enterprise." [1]

Professor Hadley considers some form of collective property necessary to supply the motive to industry and thrift hitherto supplied by the opportunity offered to all workmen to save and become independent producers, and perhaps employers. The possibilities of saving are just as great now as during the past generation, but it takes so much more to become a capitalist that this motive does not work now as then. Thus the great advantage of private property is neutralized and must be supplied by some form of collective property, if there is to be advance out of the present conditions. Stock-holding by employés, profit-sharing, and coöperation are such forms now on trial. However, profit-sharing is disappointing, because the opportunity to increase wages at the expense of the employer is slight, and the extra profit is so small when divided among a large operating force. Both profit-sharing and coöperative production will meet with little success where the laborer already puts forth the maximum of effort, as is quite largely the case in England and the United States. On the continent, both for this

[1] J. B. Clark, *The Philosophy of Wealth*, pp. 187, 188.

reason and because accustomed to paternalism, these schemes will meet with greater success. From certain forms of cousumers' coöperation, especially that of governmental management and control, Professor Hadley seems to hope for better results. At least when there are not opportunities for considerable gain, profit-sharing is to be condemned as only multiplying the occasions for misunderstandings between the employer and his workmen.[1]

Mr. Herbert Spencer affords a fair type of the class of sociological critics. Profit-sharing is merely one variation of many, coöperation being the one among these to be developed by evolutionary forces. Mr. Spencer finds the great obstacle to the success of the present form of coöperation to be the injurious effects of "trade-union" ideas, especially as to piece-work wages. He suggests as a solution of the difficulties industrial coöperation on the basis of piece work ; the rate of remuneration being somewhat lower than that which, at the ordinary speed of production, would give the ordinary wage. The workman then exists in a double capacity, as a unit in the body taking the place of the employer, and as an employé of that body, participating, in both capacities, in the product of his labor. Then can there be no rivalry of interests between the two capacities, and in the one capacity or the other he will receive the full returns upon his labor. In regard to such a system Mr. Spencer concludes : "What would be the character of these arrangements, considered as a stage in industrial evolution ? We have seen that, in common with political regulation and ecclesiastical regulation, the regulation of labor becomes less coercive as society assumes a higher type. Here we reach a form in which the coerciveness has diminished to the smallest degree consistent with combined action. Each member is his own master in respect to the work he does, and is subject only to such rules, established by the majority of the members, as are needful for maintaining order. The transition from the compulsory coöperation of militancy to the voluntary coöperation of industrialism

[1] A. T. HADLEY, *Economics; an Account of the Relations between Private Welfare and Public Property*, chap. 12, " Co-operation."

is completed. Under present arrangements it is incomplete. A wage-earner, while he voluntarily agrees to give so many hours' work for so much pay, does not, during the performance of his work, act in a purely voluntary way : he is coerced by the consciousness that discharge will follow if he idles, and is sometimes, more manifestly, by an overlooker. But under the arrangement described his activity becomes entirely voluntary.

"Otherwise presenting the facts, and using Sir Henry Maine's terms, we see that the transition from *status* to contract reaches its limit. So long as the worker remains a wage-earner, the marks of *status* do not wholly disappear. For so many hours daily he makes over his faculties to a master, or to a coöperative group, for so much money, and for the time is owned by him or it. He is temporarily in the position of a slave, and his overlooker stands in the position of a slave driver. Further, a remnant of the *régime* of *status* is seen in the fact that he and other workers are placed in ranks, receiving different rates of pay. But, under such a mode of coöperation as that above contemplated, the system of contract becomes unqualified. Each member agrees with the body of members to perform certain work for a certain sum, and is free from dictation and authoritative classing. The entire organization is based on contract, and each transaction is based on contract."[1] Such an opinion is not unobjectionable, but our only concern, at present, is Mr. Spencer's view.

But what of the possibility for the realization of these various ideals ? And here the sociologist and economist agree for the most part. The difficulties in the way of realization of either profit-sharing or the higher form of coöperation are not really economic, but moral. Mill, Marshall, Fawcett, Jevons, and Cairnes practically agree, as the latter states, that "the obstacles in the way are not physical, are not even economic, but moral, or intellectual ; or if economic, only in so far as economic results depend on intellectual and moral conditions." And Spencer comes to the conclusion that "the practicability of such a system depends on character." Continuing, he says : "It

[1] Spencer, *Principles of Sociology*, Vol. III, pp. 571, 572.

has been variously shown that higher types of society are made possible only by higher types of nature; and the implication is that the best industrial institutions are possible only with the best men. Judging from the temporary success which has been reached under the ordinary form of coöperative production, it is inferable that permanent success might be reached, were one set of the difficulties removed; leaving only the difficulty of obtaining honest and skillful management. Not in many cases, however, at present." [1]

Such difficulties are found in the nature of both classes engaged in industry : in the case of employers, difficulties growing out of inherent selfishness, intensified by the schooling given by the present industrial system; and on the part of the employés, difficulties founded in the same inherent selfishness, intensified by ignorance. With both classes there exists a prejudice and narrowness of view into which both ignorance and selfishness enter. These difficulties can be removed only by education and the development of character. In the case of coöperation such difficulties seem no greater than with profit-sharing. In fact, they seem more pronounced in the less highly developed system; for selfishness united with intelligence may be more difficult to overcome than the selfishness and prejudice that are the outgrowth of ignorance.

Postponing a further discussion of this phase of the subject, there is a second relation between coöperation and profit-sharing that is deserving of attention.

Paul Monroe.

Teachers College,
    Columbia University.

[1] Spencer, *Principles of Sociology*, Vol. III, pp. 573, 574.

(To be continued.)

THE SIGNIFICANCE OF THE CHURCH TO THE SOCIAL MOVEMENT.

WHATEVER inspiration there may lie in a literature that just now seems swinging from love to theology ; whatever instruction there may be in the researches into religion now being conducted by psychologists ; whatever confirmation of the hope of immortality there may lie in the recent report of the Society for Psychical Research — so far as organized Christianity is concerned, there is nothing comparable in importance with that uprising against social miseries that already amounts to a new crusade, and which, from every point of view, is critical for both the church and society.

What is a church ? The word means today almost every sort of religious organization, from a mission to the Roman Catholic empire ; but the proper meaning of the word is twofold. It is, first, that of a localized social group of men and women more or less organized, composed (at least constructively) of religious persons, who have associated themselves together for the purpose of incorporating the spirit and diffusing the teachings of Jesus. Its second use is that of a general conception which stands for organized Christianity in its universal and historical aspects. Whether such a definition as the first would include all forms of organized Christian activity as well as those popularly termed churches, we need not stop to inquire. It is enough to set forth the definition in broad lines, for such is and has been the expression of the ecclesiastical self-consciousness for centuries.

And what is the social movement ? Without attempting to define all its various phases, it may be said to be the attempt now being made throughout Europe and America to bring greater happiness and possibility to the life of the so-called masses. In its most energetic form it appears as labor agitation, labor organization, philanthropic institutions like social settlements, and, as much as in anything, in socialism.   In such a ubiquitous and varied movement there are many things to condemn, many persons insincere.   Social settlements and "slumming" too often supplant Browning societies as mere diversions of the hour; bescriptured philosophy and crude generalization about the social organism very often masquerade as sociology; but back of all such conscious or unconscious shams there is a determination to obtain social betterment that is not superficial, but sincere, and even passionate.

I.

At first glance it would seem as if there would be coöperation between such a movement and the church as a representative of the social teaching of Jesus, but it must be confessed that the relation of the two, as it actually exists, is one of mutual ignorance and distrust.   On the part of the churches there is, it is true, an increasing effort to understand and to sympathize with the movement among the masses.   Here and there men with the spirit of Maurice and Kingsley have endeavored to capture socialism bodily for the church.   But such efforts have met with only partial success—the difficulty lying quite as much with the clergy as with the labor leaders.   And so it has come to pass that the two great altruistic movements of the century have refused coöperation, mistrusting each other today almost as much as in the past; and, in consequence, each has lost the other's aid.

Earnest and noble as is the movement among the masses, it is suspicious, if not the enemy, of the churches.   It is, in part, the frank expression of this fact that has caused so much ecclesiastical hostility to social leaders, the churches being convinced that no good could come from violent and blasphemous hands.   Yet a closer knowledge of the actual attitude of the masses and their leaders might have led to a better understanding.   The essentials of one age are often the bric-a-brac of its successor.   The spinning-wheels and swords which were to our ancestors the symbols of toil and adventure, and even life itself, fill museums and adorn the walls of reception-rooms.   Their mission is past, and an age which they created, but by which they have been outgrown, regards them with curiosity rather than reverence. Similarly, to many men working at the cost of infinite sacrifice for their less fortunate fellows the churches are pieces of bric-a-brac. Useful in the life of the past, doubtless of the utmost value as agents in the production of the life of today, they are now judged no longer needed. The age is believed to have outgrown them, except as reminders of a less perfect civilization. The teachings of Jesus, it is true, Christian ethics, and to some degree Christian theology, are honored, even though they may be judged impracticable. But a regard for Christian ethics does not imply a regard for Christian churches. Many an honest man, both within and without the ranks of the laboring class, is convinced that the time has come for self-respecting philanthropists to cut loose from the churches and form themselves into more efficient organizations. Charges of hypocrisy are frequently made against the churches by men who are passionate champions of the teaching of Jesus. It is easy to exaggerate, but it certainly seems within the bounds of proba-bility that, wholly apart from a materialistic hostility to super-naturalism, the majority of workingmen and their leaders, of socialists, and of professional sociologists are convinced that the churches at present are composed of the well-to-do fraction of the community; that clergymen as a class have little or no sympathy with economic reform; that political corruption is condoned in the case of wealthy church members; and that it is useless to expect anything more of churches than that they will become religious clubs, limiting their support of social reform to words, to denominational missions, and conventional Sunday morning collections, untrue to the ideals of Jesus, as centers of social convalescence worthless.

But something even more unpleasant must be said. Below this distrust of the church as a social institution is a disregard for religion. The most important factors in the social awakening, socialism and sociology, at least in the past have been predomi-nantly materialistic, and, if not aggressively atheistic, somewhat patronizing in their attitude toward the deity. It may be that at present, as Professor Nash has recently said, "the deeper social-ism of England and America is looking toward, if it has not already entered into, a religious phase," but at the best it has not yet undone its early work. The social movement (of course excepting the social work of Christian organizations) is irreli-gious. The faith of the church to it is other-worldliness, and of the existence of another world it has serious doubts. In the universe of matter it sees only impersonal forces and evolution, and, insisting with a recent writer in the *Westminster Review* that religion is loyalty to truth and goodness, it eliminates a personal God from the universe of morals, and the Jesus whom it honors is but a companion of Socrates and Lassalle.

And here one meets a phenomenon hard for the man reared in the atmosphere of traditional evangelicalism to credit.

Anti-ecclesiastical and even unreligious as the movement among the masses may be, its Messianic hope in the future is the creature of Christianity. Discontent is the child of idealism, and the demand for human betterment springs from a belief in the worth of the individual that is the gift, not of the primitive German, but of the Christian. Human brotherhood already is something more than a rhetorical flourish. And has not organized Christianity, through all its devious and too often unholy ways, held up that ideal? What period in which aristocracy has lifted its head without or within the church but has had also its St. Francis ready to cast home and parents and very garments away in devotion of Christian fraternity? In this light, the hostil-ity of the social movement to the church is an Indian mutiny, in which men trained by imperial masters, in the name of love and justice, are turning their newly acquired discipline against their teachers; and the church of today must do something more than complacently praise its past and optimistically dream of its future, if it would not see too late that its influ-ence and power have passed into other hands, less intelligent perhaps, but quicker to come to the aid of a discontented race.

This is no rhetorical crisis, painted black that presently the certain victory of the church may be the more brilliantly set forth. There are, happily, many churches and clergymen excepted from such distrust, but even with this allowance one cannot say that the situation has been overdrawn. One can still mention a recent disposition among social writers to regard religion itself as a merely temporary basis of ethics; the constant tendency of our churches to follow the line of social cleavage; the decay of country churches; the steady growth of organizations like Salvation Armies, Young People's Societies, Christian Associations. Such facts do not portend the end of Christian morality. The ethical teachings of Jesus must stand and be operative as long as goodness is better than badness, and love more advantageous than hate. Nor is there any likelihood that churches as institutions will disappear. The danger is lest the churches as religious organizations shall cease to be of any social service or significance.

And this brings us to the heart of the matter. Without attempting to justify this criticism or to eulogize or blame the discontent from which it springs, let us put the matter frankly and distinctly: Is such distrust legitimate? Has the Christian church as a social institution any significance for a movement which is preëminently ambitious to elevate the classes that as yet have had comparatively little share in a Christian civilization?

I.I

The conditions of the problem themselves indicate the responsibilities which the church must assume. The church must recognize that its fundamental mission is religious — dynamic, and not regulative. "Sometimes," says Mr. Bryce in his *American Commonwealth*, "standing in the midst of a great American city . . . . one is startled by the thought of what might befall this huge yet delicate fabric of laws and commerce and social institutions were the foundation it has rested on to crumble away. Suppose that all these men ceased to believe there was any power above them, any future before them, anything in heaven or earth but what their senses told them of; . . . . Would men say, 'Let us eat and drink, for tomorrow we die'? Or would custom, and sympathy, and a perception of the advantages which stable government offers to the citizens, as a whole,

and which orderly self-restraint offers to each one, replace supernatural sanctions and hold in check the violence of masses and
the self-indulgent impulses of the individual? History, if she
cannot give a complete answer to this question, tells us that
hitherto civilized society has rested on religion, and that free
government has prospered best among religious peoples."

It would be impossible to deny the truth in this generalization, as will presently appear, but it should be clearly understood that the significance of the church to society is something
more than that of a check upon crime and materialism. Its
mission is not that of a policeman.

Even the authority of tradition, for which the church has
been commonly held to stand, is but regulative and conservative,
too often quick to hold by the form while despising the spirit.
Precedent is the stumbling-block as well as the foundation of
progress. However much one may appreciate the service which
the Roman church rendered civilization in furnishing the immu-
table center about which for centuries the elements of a new
Europe might gather; however much one may honor that devotion
to the persistent elements of religious life that finds its expression in the Anglican's devotion to his prayer-book and bishop;
however much one may honor the steady independence of Nonconformists of all sorts, one must at the same time say that, in
the same proportion as he has preferred to check rather than
create Christian impulses, Catholic, Anglican, and Nonconform-
ist has been untrue to the highest conception of the duty owed
by the church to the society in which he lived. If tradition be
all for which it can stand in society, it will be hard indeed to
prophesy perpetuity for the church. To plead its conservative
capacity is possible only after one has established other and
stronger presumptions in its favor. It cannot be content to
make good citizens. They must make good men. That which
is the salt of the earth is likewise to be its leaven.

However multiform the service the churches may and must
render human society in a Christian age, such service must
be unqualifiedly religious. It must furnish the spiritual material;
the age itself will provide the institutional forms. In the divi-

sion of labor that characterizes society today, the school, the state, the bank has its special duties. In the same way the church, as the plain purport of the words of Paul implies, has but one supreme mission, and that is the religious. However much a church may employ charitable organizations, amusements, employment bureaus, a consciousness of this spiritual mission must be its coördinating and unifying force. It is to the honor of most "institutional churches," so needed in every city and country town, that, even more clearly than many of the older sort, they make religion supreme. But to make a church a religionless mixture of civil-service reform, debating societies, gymnasiums, suppers, concerts, stereopticon lectures, good advice, refined negro minstrel shows, and dramatic entertainments, is to bring it into competition with the variety theater. And when the masses have to choose between that sort of church and its rival, if they have any sense left within their perplexed heads, they will choose the variety theater. That at least is performing its proper social function.

III.

But as a religious organization the church is especially fitted to educate and direct the social impulses, both within itself and within society at large. And in two ways : by enforcing regard for law, and by guaranteeing sanity in reform.

1. It can keep social impulses law-abiding.

Periods of transition, we are repeatedly told, may easily become revolutionary; but quite as dangerous, in some ways more dangerous, to a society than open revolution is the spirit of contempt for law. Our day is marked by a decrease in actual armed revolts, but, none the less, law is still held in too little regard. As it is made with astonishing ease and volume, so is it as easily and universally despised. The governor of Illinois has declared recently that he proposed to prevent by force a mining company's importation of negro workmen into Virden, Illinois, on the ground that it is sometimes necessary for an executive of a state to enforce law in advance of its legislative enactment, while the labor officers maintain that they may resort to bloodshed because the company has no right to import bad negroes as substitutes for strikers. Company, men, negroes, governor, so far as newspaper accounts can be trusted, carry on their struggle as if laws might be enforced or forgotten to suit one's need. In our cities, municipal statutes are ignored and broken by those who have "pulls," while who has not been, wittingly or unwittingly, an accessory to forgery in the use of railroad tickets bought of "scalpers"?

This superiority to the will of society which justifies disobedience whenever disobedience appears desirable is especially characteristic of those persons who are the avowed champions of society. Sometimes, indeed, the individualistic spirit is undisguised, and we have anarchists pure and simple. But men who are not anarchists do not hesitate to hold the will of the individual superior to the will of a community. The very nobility of an avowed end is judged a sufficient excuse for disobeying law. The anti-ecclesiastical spirit of too much effort for social betterment is accompanied by an anti-legal spirit. Having closed its ear to the voice of God, it hears the voice of the people only when it chooses.

To such a spirit the church as a social institution has something better to impart than ethical platitudes. It, too, has suffered from unrighteous laws; it, too, has felt the pressure of its own ideals pushing it toward a disregard of law. Sometimes, perhaps, it has too much yielded to the power of precedent and to God-ordained powers. But its slowness in rising against injustice has been the deliberation of preparation. Not by violence or contempt of law has it been resultful, but by a patience that has linked submission with such transforming power that unjust laws have been repealed or have fallen into desuetude, to be replaced by others breathing mercy and justice. Perishing by the sword, its chief victories have been won by peace and love. The blood of its martyrs has been the seed of new legislation and new government. Nor could it be otherwise. That recognition of the whole of things which is the metaphysical formula for religion does not permit the man who has come within the influence of the church to arrogate to himself discretionary power as to what laws should be obeyed and what may be disobeyed. Authority always is an element in religion. In part it is because of the deep reverence felt by the church for law as the earthly analogue of the will of God that reformers oppose it, slandering it as committed to reaction, because it refuses to join in an orgy of iconoclasm. But who will dare say that in its reverence for law the church is wrong? Better a law-abiding spirit and bad laws than anarchy, however disguised or procrastinating. If there is one lesson above all others that social enthusiasts need to learn, it is that born of the church's experience: a regard for law, even though it be unjust law, is the first guarantee of progress, of legal reform, and of the permanence of the good law that may replace the bad. Besides the church, so far as I can see, there is no institution, state or school, court or prison, capable by history, nature, ideals, and martyrs of enforcing this unpalatable but indispensable truth.

2. The church, better than any other popular institution, can guarantee sanity in reform. To respect law is not to champion passive obedience, but the greatest danger that threatens today's life is not unemployed laborers, but unemployed reformers. From all sides they come. Young women on fire to prevent the abuse of children by cruel and tyrannical parents; college men and women who long to win the submerged tenth to sweetness and light and the appreciation of art by residence in a university settlement during three weeks in the winter after graduation; men with all sorts of social panaceas, from a new method of reading music at sight to tin dinner pails; temperance reformers who tremble for the nation if a war vessel is christened with champagne; diet, drink, clothes, house, school, church, Bible, street-cleaning reformers — all promising millennia, and all taking themselves seriously. Far be it from anyone to disparage the motives of such enthusiasts, but, with the remembrance of the similar altruistic hysteria that preceded the French Revolution of 1789, one cannot help seeing the danger that lies in unregulated and visionary amateur philanthropy. Far more worthy of serious study is the danger attending the fanaticism of professional reformers. Millennial programs are easy to print, but as

difficult as the genius of the *Arabian Nights* to control—if indeed they once miss the broad way leading to the limbo of impracticability. What is worse is that the conservative is not mistaken when he sees in their champions not merely earnest men and women striving for the good of mankind, but possible social firebrands. Agitators are indispensable, but an agitator mad with altruism is as dangerous as any other madman.

Perhaps an acquaintance with such facts should have made surprise impossible, but none the less it is surprising that leaders in the social movement should not have seen how extravagance injures their cause. An admirable evidence of this fact, as well as the efficiency of sane efforts at reform, is to be seen in the history of woman's suffrage. Perhaps a better illustration is to be seen in the history of social democracy in Germany. But the socialist himself can learn lessons in the methodology of social reform from the church. With all its demands, socialism today proposes nothing like the radical change in society as did Jesus when he swept away Mosaism and pointed the way to an ideal social order in which men should be sons of God and brothers of each other; nor does any declaration of the rights of man contain more than a shadow of the equality that bursts out in the words of the apostolic radical of the first century who confronted an age steeped in slavery and inequality with the Magna Charta of a new age: in Christ there is neither Jew nor Greek, male nor female, bond nor free. Yet in Jesus and in Paul radicalism in teaching was tempered by sanity in method. Jesus dared to lay down his life and—what must have been harder—the life of his followers while preventing a revolutionary and unintelligent effort to realize his new social order. Paul sent the converted slave Onesimus back to his Christian master, and counseled women not to let their equality deprive them of veils. The spirit of the church was equally sane, and its sanity quite as much as its love carried its regenerating influence from the upper room in Jerusalem to every corner of the empire. As a social institution, while as earnest as any group of men in the world, the church still can show men that, if individualism is not anarchy, reform is not that virtue of madmen, iconoclasm.

From the days when Paul counseled his Corinthian brethren not to turn their prayer-meetings into bedlams, down through the days of Ambrose agitating and yet restraining the masses of Milan; the mediæval church tempering universal feud by the truce of God; St. Bernard directing the military spirit of empires; Thomas à Becket defying the passions of a hot-headed Englishman; Luther denouncing the extravagances of a Peasants' Revolt; Wesley utilizing the enthusiasms of Methodism; and Moody bridling the impetuosity of college students, the church has said, by word and example: Let reforms come; make reforms come; but let everything be done decently and in order. Until there can be shown some other social institution or movement which can boast an equal record of permanent social reforms — of slavery ended, of life protected, of woman ennobled, of children educated, of homes sanctified, of schools, and missions, and charities, and martyrs — your social reformer had best give himself a course in church history. There he will learn something of the effectiveness that comes to a reform through the sanity bred within the Christian church he affects to regard as outgrown. Contempt is here the sign manual of ignorance and conceit.

IV.

The church can aid the social movement by emphasizing its own method of social regeneration.

Within the region of philosophy there are few questions more delicate or elusive than those which concern the relations of the individual to society. Indeed, one might almost say that the terms themselves are still in search of definition. None the less, two things are increasingly evident: the individual is of worth, and the individual is complete, only as his life is joined with the lives of others. These two considerations are at present claimed as among the chief foundations of the multicolored social philosophy and social propaganda which go under the name of socialism, and it is the earnestness of the socialist's efforts, on the one hand to convince society at large that the proletariat has souls, and on the other to raise society as a unit into a good-natured deity, that gives it much of its efficiency. Now, with economic programs of all sorts a church as an organization, if it be wise, will have nothing to do; but with socialism's demand for economic justice; with its unquenchable determination to secure for all, however humble, the rights and enjoyments of common humanity; with its insistence upon fraternity, a church is profoundly concerned. For—it may well be repeated —the spirit that lies back of this better ambition of socialism is the child of the Christian church—a prodigal, perhaps, strayed far from home and into strange companionship, but none the less a child. But the Christian church has a doctrine of the individual that no hard and fast system of socialism, however noble and ethical, can duplicate, if, indeed, as a matter of self-preservation, accept. The final test of a system's worth lies not so much in what it proposes as in what it presupposes. Socialism and Christianity are alike in that they are both laboring for a new and higher social order, in which all—men, women, and children—shall live better and happier lives; but they are unlike in the position each takes as to the relation of these individuals to society. Although there is untruth in any antithesis, the difference can be roughly stated as this: socialism expects society to make good individuals; Jesus expects good individuals to make a good society. The untruth in such an antithesis lies in its disregard of the fact that socialism does not ignore the need of an ethical basis of social life, and of the other fact that Christianity is oblivious neither of the influence of environment nor of the need of law. But after this common element has been eliminated, the differences in the presuppositions may still be stated in terms of the individual: socialism assuming that the individual must be raised through his connection with a better social order, Christianity assuming that it is impossible to have a good social order composed of bad men. Thus the point of attack, so to speak, is, in the case of socialism, environment, and in the case of Christianity, the individual.

Now, at this point one is likely to be prejudiced, if, like the writer, he is not a socialist. There are, of course, Christians who are socialists, and—what is quite another matter—socialists who are Christians. Indeed, it is not uncommon to hear men identify socialism and Christianity. But after guarding, as best I can, against prejudice, and judging the two from their most significant elements, if words mean anything and there be any distinction between the two, the position of Christianity seems more capable of producing permanent social betterment than does socialism. The church has chosen the slower and more difficult method; for it is always easier to attempt reform by legislation than by the education and conversion of individual lives. It would, indeed, be untrue to facts to say that much good cannot be accomplished by legislation that expresses the sentiments of an intelligent and righteous minority, but a study of such reformatory and prohibitive legislation will convince any man that it succeeds in something like the proportion of influential men in a community who are in sympathy with its objects. There is here not merely a question of regard for law sufficient to lead to its conventional enforcement, but also the question as to whether a good law enforced by a part of a community is ideally so desirable as such an elevation in the personal character of each citizen as makes such a law unnecessary. If it be replied that the social will must always be in advance of a considerable number of individuals, the original question is again presented: granted such must be the case, which is likely to be of more permanent social service, a belief that the chief effort should be made to make the individual good through social environment, or to produce such men and women as will themselves constitute a proper society? It is easy to reply that both are needed, but such an answer leaves the point at issue undecided, and if the alternative be frankly met as it actually exists, the answer seems to favor the philosophy of the church. Its method has one great advantage: to use a printer's term, it does not throw society into "pi" as the first step toward recombinations. Utopias presuppose utopians, and the church undertakes the production of utopians.

And in another particular the social doctrine of the church is superior in its practical bearings upon the individual to that of socialism. I know that the socialist will strenuously deny the

statement, but, do the best it can to avoid the criticism, socialism is essentially an economic system and approaches the individual life with much the same presupposition as did the older
political economy it assails. And that presupposition is the
existence of an "economic man." In a word, socialism says
this: Make the economic man prosperous, and the moral, the
altruistic, the intellectual, the æsthetic, and (as a concession)
the religious man will inevitably be prosperous. Here again
indiscriminate criticism is unwise. No one can deny the influence of economic conditions upon the character of men, and
the Christian who follows the better impulses of his nature will
make common cause with any rational effort at producing
greater economic equality. Indeed, if once socialism as a merely
economic program according to which some or all industries were
to become socialized, were seen to be just and best, there is no
reason why Christians should not accept it. But as homeopathy
as practiced today is one thing, and homeopathy as Hahne-
mann worked it out is another, so socialism as a form of
economic life and socialism as an all-embracing philosophy
of social reform are not to be confounded. Good economic
surroundings, so far as ordinary observation shows, are in no
way the guarantee of good or even contented men, and as a
working theory of life the position of Jesus is not only more
philosophical, but more practicable: "Seek first the fraternity
of the kingdom of God and His righteousness, and food, clothes,
and creature comforts will follow." It may very well be that a
thoroughly Christian civilization will be—at least partially—
socialistic. It is not so clear that a socialistic state would be
Christian.

At the same time it must be granted that, as both are today,
the church has much to learn from socialism. It is hard to say
it, but the church has hardly yet the clear vision which enables
socialism to see the moral aspects of today's economic life.
Yet such a charge must certainly soon be removed. The fact
that it unfortunately is composed of certain strata of society
may retard its action, but it is impossible that the church
should not soon see the inconsistency between its religious

teachings as to the supreme worth of each individual soul in God's sight and any form of oppression, whether ecclesiastical or economic. A Christian man has no excuse for corrupting legislatures or for stealing property, by whatever euphemistic synonym such acts may be described. He cannot be true to the Christ he serves if he wantonly neglects the rights of others, whether competitors or employés.

But to say this is not to give up the church, nor to despair of the salvability or the fundamental justice of a regulated competition. It is simply to say that justice and goodness are superior to business success; it is but to paraphrase the words of Jesus, "Seek first the kingdom of God and His righteousness," "Make friends through the mammon of unrighteousness." It is high time that the historic church already crowned with centuries of beneficence ; which, however slowly, has for centuries been molding economic life to the pattern of its Master; which has produced the only stable material out of which socialism can hope to build a new society, should challenge socialism to say why it arrogates to itself a monopoly of love for the masses, and challenge it again to say whether, instead of the Christian nation of kings and priests, its social regeneration through economic comfort will produce anything better than smug, selfish respectability, a comfortable but heroless mediocrity.

V.

The church can aid all efforts at social betterment by producing religiously regenerate lives. A church does not, it is true, regenerate a man, and were the purpose of this paper theological, it would be necessary to make the language more exact. But, however more exactly it might be expressed, the duty of the church remains. Its office is not that of a school, but of a home into which new sons and daughters are continually being born. It, and it alone, of all social institutions is capable of furnishing the individuals out of which a good society can be built.

The Christian ideal of the individual is social. A man cannot conform to the example of Jesus unless his life be joined consciously to others. The spontaneity with which Christians have always crystallized into the social groups of school and state and church, as well as the social reforms that have always accompanied its religious revivals, abundantly evidence this fact. But the church, except as its zeal for others has too often committed it to a pauperizing charity, has never flattered men into believing that their miseries were simply the result of environment. It has dared to cut deep into the heart of that lie, and to teach that sin is at the bottom of misery. But it does something more—it defines sin as the voluntary withdrawal of a man from his normal life with God and fraternal life with men. Irreligion, it holds, lies behind social iniquities. Then, having clearly in mind the disease, it undertakes the remedy. By the interpretation of God through human love, it shows men the way to that religious environment that is the source of righteousness. By the story of its Christ it inspires men to sacrifice in social service. As sin is selfishness, so righteousness is fraternity. The great ecclesiastical doctrine of regeneration has, therefore, a social application, not by accommodation, but by necessity. Regeneration is nothing more than the change of a man's life from insulation to social union. He is a son of God, and therefore a brother of men. In the Christian sense, therefore, to produce regenerate individuals is inevitably to produce a regenerate society. Goodness in the Christian sense is social, not monastic. To determine the forms in which this social goodness shall express itself does not fall within the power of the church as an institution. Reforms are for church members, not churches. Any economic or political expedient that will best and most effectively express Christian fraternity will be supported by Christian church members if only their heads are as clear as their hearts are warm.

And it is precisely here that evangelical religion is resultful as a social force. We may well thank Unitarianism and ethical societies for their insistence upon morality and rational faith. But with all possible respect for their profound theological influence, with notable exceptions, they cannot be said to have exercised wide influence over the masses. The age today, as never before, knows the right, but needs the power to do the right.

The so-called liberal movement, while justly criticising evangelicalism in the old, crude, popular sense, has confused religion with ethical culture, and, with all its undeniable services as a corrective of a too often irrational orthodoxy, lives institutionally today largely by the adoption of dissatisfied products of evangelicalism. Morality has little power of inspiration in comparison with religion. God is more dynamic than truth, and it is in the religious procreativeness of evangelical churches, notwithstanding the sneer of Matthew Arnold, that the solution of social problems will largely rest. What new sort of humanity the future may have in store one cannot, of course, foresee, but, with all respect for a current belief to the contrary, so long as men continue to resemble the men of the past, it is certain that a churchless society and a religionless morality mean social and moral degeneration. If the social movement has any respect for the results of experience, it will not disregard this fact. At the very least, it must count upon religious men and women as the central force of any reform or reformed social life.

VI.

And thus we arrive at a conclusion which is neither novel nor sensational: the church is not outgrown, for it furnishes its age regenerating social influences in the shape of men and women whose hearts are fraternal because they are religious. But it does more. These men and women, who serve their fellows because they love and fear their God, are not sent forth altogether altruistic dilettantes and untrained enthusiasts. The church is a social institution—or better, each church is a little social group, a microcosm of society itself. To belong to a church that is worthy of the name is to be trained in the art of social, not individualistic, living. A genuinely Christian church member is always material ready at hand for any rational social movement, and if a census were made of those who are effectively connected with social, municipal, and national reforms, it is no very rash statement that the large majority of such persons would be found to have come, either personally or through family example, under the influence of some church. It could not be otherwise. The simple fact is that, while men dream and agitate, the church is creating and organizing altruistic and religious impulses, is training men to live together in mutual recognition of each other's rights, and compelling them to recognize social as well as individual units. In a word, as exemplified in the Christian church, religion breeds and disciplines *corporate enthusiasms.* Can the social movement afford to despise it?

VII.

But a word must be added as to the duty of the church. If it would be as significant as its past and its Founder make possible, it can no longer preach an individualistic salvation. It must educate the social sympathies of its children; it must teach that the question of right and wrong must have its answer from the counting-room as well as from the pulpit; it must train its members to trust their Christian impulse to side with whatever cause is true and beautiful and sane; it must teach that, if there can be no regenerate society without regenerate men, neither can there be regenerate men without a regenerate society. And therefore, for the sake of all, it must fulfill its central duty of throwing into an irreligious but generous age a host of sons and daughters filled with the fraternal enthusiasm of its Founder. This is the evangelicalism that our age needs: not merely the gospel of a man's saving his soul, but the gospel of the kingdom of God. Let men be reborn, not that they may by and by get comfortably into a heaven above the earth, nor yet as a matter of duty or penance perform good deeds on earth; but rather let men be reborn' that, just because of their new natures which draw love from God himself, they may constitute a better social environment and a better humanity here on earth. In a word, through becoming sons, let Christians remember that they have become brothers.

SHAILER MATHEWS.

THE UNIVERSITY OF CHICAGO.

THE WORKINGMAN'S ALIENATION FROM THE CHURCH.

My dear Sir : Will you do me the kindness to give me your aid in trying to solve a vexing problem ? The problem is this : Why are so many intelligent workingmen non-churchgoers ? It may be that the church can be of more service to the men of its community than it is at the present time. Will you please send me an answer, within a few days, to the questions submitted ?

1. What reasons would be given by your associates, who do not attend church, for their absence from the church ?

2. What remedies would you propose to bring your associates into closer touch with the church ?   Sincerely,

H. Francis Perry.

The plan of this research has been to seek, from three classes of men, an answer to two central questions. Accordingly the above letter was sent to —

1. Representative leaders of the wage-earners.

2. Workingmen who are churchgoers.

3. Laboring men who are alienated from the church.

The response has been most cordial and gratifying. Of the three classes from which replies have been invited, I consider Class 1 — the representative leaders of the wage-earners — to be the least important in reflecting the real relation of the working-man to the church, because there is here a possible professional bias.

The replies received were from Mr. Samuel Gompers, president of the American Federation of Labor ; Mr. John B. Lennon, general secretary of the Journeymen Tailors' Union of America; Mr. M. M. Garland, fourth vice-president of the American Federation of Labor; Mr. John F. O'Sullivan, president of the Central Labor Union of Boston ; Rev. Herbert N. Casson, of the Labor Church, Lynn, Mass.; Miss Mary A. Nason, of Haverhill, Mass.; Mr. George H. Paige, treasurer of the H. & P. Engineers.

These replies offer several definite causes for the alienation

in question.   The most general is that the laboring man believes
there is an alliance between the rich man, who oppresses him,
and the church.   Some comments touching this point are worth
noticing :

MR. GOMPERS.— My associates have come to look upon the church and
the ministry as the apologists and defenders of the wrong committed against
the interests of the people, simply because the perpetrators are possessors of
wealth, ... whose real God is the almighty dollar, and who contribute
a few of their idols to suborn the intellect and eloquence of the divines, and
make even their otherwise generous hearts callous to the sufferings of the
poor and struggling workers, so that they may use their exalted positions to
discourage and discountenance all practical efforts of the toilers to lift themselves out of the slough of despondency and despair.

MR. LENNON.— Workmen stay away from the church because their
employers attend and control the church, and in their daily life, in shop and
factory, the workman receives but little of Christian treatment from the
employers.

MR. GARLAND.— Workingmen find much difficulty in reconciling the
religious fervor of the wealthy while at church with their attitude to their
fellows in actual life.

MR. O'SULLIVAN.— Believing, as I do, that employers are not all worth
praying for, and disliking to pray for the prosperity of a " sweater," I do not
go to church, even if I had the time to do so.

REV. HERBERT M. CASSON.— The men who grind them in business are
the ones whom they recognize in the front pews.

MISS NASON.— The churches are not built by them, nor for them, but
with money taken from them to be used against them.

The other causes, with explanatory extracts, follow :

There is plenty of ecclesiasticism in the churches, but there is little
Christianity.

MR. CASSON.— Workingmen are understanding better the teaching of
Christ, and do not see any similarity between Christ and the church.

MISS NASON.— Workingmen understand that Christianity is only another
name for justice, love, and truth, and that churchianity is only another name
for wrong, injustice, oppression, misery, and want.   Then they take the two
apart, and cheer the name of Jesus Christ and hiss the church, separating
Christianity from churchianity ; honoring the one, scouting the other.

The church is wrong in trying to reconcile present industrial
circumstances with a normal and just theory of life :

MISS NASON.— The cornerer, the syndicate, the trust, hold back the
riches of earth, sea, and sky from their fellows who famish and freeze in the

dark . . . . and the effort of the church to reconcile the commercial morals of modern industrialism with the revelation of human law and life in Christ is treason to the kingdom of God in the eyes of most of my associates.

The church does not treat living issues :

MR. CASSON.— The church must base its right to existence on present usefulness, on character, and on living issues, and not on a past revelation and a future life. This we have done in our labor church, and have no trouble in reaching the masses.

The church frowns upon trade unions :

MR. GOMPERS.— The means and methods which my associates have, by experience, learned to be particularly successful in maintaining their rights and securing improved conditions — *i. e.*, organization of the trade unions — have been generally frowned down upon with contempt, treated indifferently, or openly antagonized by the ministers and the apparently staunch supporters of the church.

Pew rents are an objection :

MR. CASSON.— They cannot pay for a front pew, and are too self-respecting to take a back one.

Church services are stale and uninteresting :

MR. PAIGE.— I don't find the average sermon preached in the churches interesting to the union workingmen. They are interested in a shorter working day, more pay for their labor, better homes to live in, and better conditions for their families and children in this world, which the church ignores.

MR. CASSON.— Church services are stale and uninteresting to practical or hungry men.

For these evils, four remedies are suggested :

The ministry must show their sympathy with the great struggling mass of workingmen. Mr. Gompers thinks that there is an honorable exception to the ministers of whom he has previously spoken in

The men who preach from their pulpits and breathe with every word their sympathy with the great struggling masses of humanity ; . . . . these ministers you will find always interesting, and not only interesting, but the churches filled with the workers who go to hear them.

Mr. Lennon testifies that he himself is a churchgoer, and continues :

I believe the church will fill with workers and their families as soon as the church makes manifest its intention to help the masses to secure a better and more comfortable daily life.

Give the workingmen the same rights and privileges which the rich enjoy:

MR. PAIGE.—If the church would let the workingmen have the same rights and privileges that the rich enjoy, the church would be too small to hold them all. Let the church help us fight some of our battles with the rich, and show it is friendly with the working classes.

Preach and study less theology and more social ethics:

MISS NASON.—Set the ministers earnestly to studying, not theology, nor creeds, but social economy and its bearing on morality . . . . until the church repents of its money-worship it is not a fit companion for the common people.

Miss Nason prescribes the last remedy suggested by the labor-leader class. It is a no less radical one than driving the rich out of the church altogether. In Miss Nason's own words she proposes

To drive the money-changers out of the temple.

Rev. Herbert N. Casson returns a reply still more startling. Mr. Casson despairs of any remedy until the church repents and is converted:

The church has nothing to give that we care to receive, and nothing to teach that we care to know. We are very well satisfied to have workingmen out of touch with the church. The church must learn before it can instruct.

The replies from workingmen who are churchgoers strike an entirely different note from the foregoing, as regards both cause and remedy. The causes assigned by this class are four in number:

Viciousness on the part of workingmen. A Christian workingman writes:

In the present shop where I am some devote Sunday to worldly pleasure, and in the case of some it would interfere with vicious ways.

The results of poverty:

Some think they cannot pay for religious privileges, and cannot dress well enough to be present in the church.

The inconsistencies of Christian men. A deacon writes:

All that the majority of my daily associates know about the church is what they see in the lives of us who are Christians. The most frequent reason I receive for non-churchgoing is that there are as good people out of the church as in its membership. In other words, the apparently inconsistent lives of those who profess to love the church is an excuse most difficult to meet.

Indifference :

No real reason ; they are more ready to bluff me when I invite them than to suggest any genuine reason for absence from the church.

The remedies proposed are :

More spiritual life and personal effort for non-churchgoers. Writes one correspondent :

Christians should be more spiritual in heart and life, and so be better fitted for personal effort with all classes.

Show that the church cares for the welfare of the working-man, not as a workingman, but as a man :

There is not much sympathy now between employers and employés ; each is seeking to get the better of the other, and there is an impression that the church does not, as a body, care for workingmen, as distinguished from salaried men. I think if I were preaching I would not say much about classes, but of the pressing need of all men to seek salvation through Christ.

True living by Christians :

We must be sure and serve our earthly employers faithfully, not as eye-servants, but as honest Christians.

We next come to the most interesting and important evidence of all. Here we have neither the possible " professional bias" of the labor representative, nor the different point of view of the workingman within the church, but the alienated workman speaking for himself. We should here, if anywhere, strike the root of the matter.

In the replies received from this class, five causes of alienation appear:

Loss of faith :

Men have grown hard under bitter conditions, and think of God as unjust and unkind, if there be any God.

Childhood training. A bookbinder replies :

Men do not go to church because they had so little training at home when they were children. If the Bible be not taught them at home and in Sunday school, they will not be found in church in later years.

Using Sunday for rest and recreation :

It is the disposition of many to make Sunday a day of recreation.

The churches are opposed to the workingman,

writes one man,

inasmuch as the church opposes Sunday newspapers, Sunday theaters, the Sunday opening of libraries, and every other reform of the kind that would benefit the laboring class.

Too much theology and too little practical preaching:

There is too much theology and not enough plain gospel truth in the sermon. This theology is beyond the comprehension of the workingman. He has no interest in it.

Many men who do not go to church claim that it is because they honestly believe that theology is a scheme gotten up to turn the poor man's thought away from the present life to some dim, mysterious future world, where all his sufferings here will be made up for, and in this way to prevent his trying to better himself and his class by overthrowing the system of slavery which our present method of business entails.

The ministers and churches have but little interest in the workingman:

Wage-earners fail to attend church because the ministers of the various churches fail to visit their homes. The wage-earner has an idea that, while all ministers will be courteous to him, they give all their time to the richer members of the church. They claim that the church is doing nothing positive to help them in their difficulties.

The churches are sustained by rich men who grind their workmen.

We are interested more in the getting of food, raiment, and the paying of our rent than in a future life. We want a heaven on earth instead of a heaven after death. Jesus Christ is with us outside the church, and we shall prevail with God.

Other comments on this point are in a bitterer vein:

The church has, as an organized body, no sympathy with the masses. It is a sort of fashionable club where the rich are entertained and amused, and where most of the ministers are muzzled by their masters and dare not preach the gospel of the carpenter of Nazareth.

The unjust and inequitable manner in which the commercial class, which sustains and supports the churches for its own selfish purposes, has treated them, causes the laboring men to have nothing to do with the churches.

As one of the leaders has expressed it:

The American workingman hates the very shadow that the spire of the village church casts across his pathway.

The church is too fashionable a place for the poor clothing which I must wear,

is the conviction of another.

REMEDIES.

Apply the Sermon on the Mount:

Have courage to apply the Sermon on the Mount to the social order of today.

The ministers of the church must make themselves familiar with the social and economic questions of the day:

Let the ministers study economics. Let them thoroughly inform themselves upon the labor question; then let them talk upon these things and not upon dead issues, such as those concerning Jonah and Lot.

Preach Christianity instead of theology. Preach of a heaven on earth:

Advocate and teach a heaven on earth.

Let the pastor have a personal relation with the needs of labor. Be our champion. Visit the laboring man and study his needs:

Ministers should mingle more freely with the poor and less with the rich. By doing so you can come in contact with the person, and can better judge for yourself of the best way of inducing him to attend church.

Why should I wish to go into a $200,000 church and listen to a minister who gets perhaps $3,000 a year for preaching one sermon a week, denouncing the poor railroad man who is striking that his brother-worker should have $2 per day?

You must have their temporal welfare at heart and understand the great questions that interest them as nothing else can until these are settled.

Let the minister of the gospel visit the homes of the non-churchgoers. I believe many fail to attend church because the ministers fail to visit their homes.

It is interesting to notice here a cry from a laboring man in Newton, Mass., who echoes a sentiment we have already heard from Rev. Herbert N. Casson:

I would propose no remedy, and have no hope of social reform through the church as it exists today.

I have thus far given in detail many of the answers received in my research. None of the bitter things have been suppressed. The submitted declarations are a fair résumé of the opinions received. Five indictments are made against the church:

1. The church is subsidized by the rich. The minister is, consequently, tongue-tied. The rich man's influence is so pow-

erful that anything which would arouse his conscience will never unwisely escape the preacher's lips.

While these charges are doubtless true of a few so-called churches and of a very few preachers, yet we know scores and hundreds of men who would resign a pulpit at once where there was a command, either open or implied, to padlock their lips in the presentation of truth.   It is culpable beyond ordinary cowardice for a preacher of righteousness to sell his conviction for gold, and such a man would be frowned out of the fellowship of the ministers of any community.

2. The ministry discusses themes which are stale and flat. They are not living issues.

This is thoroughly false to the genuine spirit of the church. The pulpit teaches preparation for this world's conflicts and temptations, as well as safety in a future world.   These themes ought not to be stale and flat to the earnest man.

3. The ministry is not well enough informed on economic and social questions.

To this we plead guilty in part.   Social science is a new study, and could not be found in the college curriculum ten or fifteen years ago.   To have studied economics or ethics years ago is not now to be informed in sociology.   To study the labor movement as the ordinary laboring man glances at it would be far from satisfactory.

4. The workingman is not welcome in the churches of the land.

This is a mistake on the part of wage-earners.   Some churches may be icy toward him, but these are the isolated exception, not the rule.

5. The church is not aggressive enough in assisting the workingman to secure his rights.

Grant all the necessary exceptions to the rule, and deduct considerable for sluggishness in the performance of duty, and even then the fact remains that most of those who unselfishly are aiding the causes of humanity are Christian men, and a large proportion of these are ministers.   In considering the causes dear to the wage-earner which are left unaided by the church, the difficulty often is that the postulates of the workingman are so wide of the truth that the church cannot champion them. It is not true that men are in a prison-house and the church is holding the key. The church may be depended upon to lead in securing justice and truth. It must also warn the workingman that his alienation often results from tendencies within himself rather than within the church. The Jesus who is applauded by the average workingman is a minimized Jesus Christ, a fictitious person, not the Christ of the gospels.

H. FRANCIS PERRY.

ENGLEWOOD BAPTIST CHURCH,
Chicago.

CRIMINAL ANTHROPOLOGY IN ITS RELATION TO CRIMINAL JURISPRUDENCE.

II.

THE principal phases of criminal law and procedure to which the criminal anthropologists have directed their attention may be included under two divisions — those relating to procedure and those relating to law. Under the first may be enumerated discussions of the jury system, expert testimony, evidence of accomplices, incriminating evidence, insanity and allied defenses, burden of proof, and appeal; while the second may comprise discussions of habitual criminal acts, indeterminate sentence, public trial, education and qualification of judges, attorneys, and wardens, and carcerial regulations. The criminal anthropologists have not been content merely to recognize existing evils. In submitting these proposed changes, they recognize that, when any system has obtained undisputed possession in a country for many years, it has acquired the prescriptive right, and that, if anyone seeks to alter it or substitute a new one, the innovator is bound to show, not only a probability that the new will succeed and be superior to the old, but that it will save for the government and require no new expenditure; hence the reforms proposed are not revolutionary. The first discussed is that relating to the jury system.

By the United States' and by the various state constitutions it is provided that criminal trials shall be by a jury, which shall consist of twelve citizens, chosen in the district in which the case is to be tried. The verdict must be unanimous, based upon the facts presented in the evidence. The privilege is substantially the same in nearly all of the states. Of the various reforms which have been suggested by thinkers along all lines, that relating to the jury system is best known and has received the strongest criticism. From the point of view of criminal anthropology, the system is not characterized as inherently evil; the criticism applying rather to the degenerate condition into which it has been permitted to lapse. Legislation, while retaining the common-law form, has changed the practice into one of the most fruitful sources of crime. As it now exists, it is inconsistent with any theory of a scientific legal system. Originally jurors testified and decided the issue upon their own knowledge, and were selected from the vicinage where the crime was committed, because of their familiarity with the facts of the crime and with its perpetrator. Now the rule is so far changed that such knowledge is a disqualification, and the method of selection has become a financial burden. The following evils have been especially enumerated, and, unless remedied, the abolishment of the entire system is proposed:

1. The system, as administered, is no longer a trial by a jury of peers, and this is due to these causes: (*a*) disqualifications and exemptions of jurors by statute; (*b*) excuses by the court; (*c*) failure in performance of duty by those who make up the lists, determine the qualifications, and deposit the ballots; (*d*) the public and political apathy of the best elements of the community; (*e*) the impotency of the oath from the decay of religious belief. As an illustration of the exemptions from jury service may be cited the New York law, where the statute provides for the exemption of fifteen classes of persons. A more serious direct cause is the abuse of the power of the court in granting excuses to prominent citizens, and the collusion of those who prepare the lists and those who wish to escape service.

2. The method does not subserve the interests of justice, by reason of delay and heavy financial burden.

3. The rules relating to qualification of jurors are such as to render the most intelligent, trained, and thoughtful men ineligible.

4. The unanimity vote, which is almost universally required, is detrimental to the conviction of criminals. The ratio of convictions to commissions of crime is already too inadequate for the protection of society.

5. The jury is incapable of dealing with criminal trials conducted upon a scientific legal basis. All questions of medical jurisprudence or psychiatry should be tried before a body of men possessing technical training, and they should be authorized not simply to make suggestions and render opinions, but give a real decision or final judgment The right of a judge to demand the decision of science, and also to possess the right and power to disregard such decision, is a manifest contradiction.

6. The system has developed a large class of so-called professional jurors, which is a source of much evil.

The criminal anthropologist believes that in modern times the common sense of the countrymen of early English history would not be capable of grasping and deciding the numerous and intricate questions discussed in criminal as well as civil actions. If a jury is deemed incapable of dealing with the complex questions of admiralty law and has never been called therein, how much more reasonably does the objection apply to criminal trials! It is not an exploded theory or obsolete fact that criminal lawyers appeal more to the sympathy than to the reason of jurors. Sentimentality and sympathy have too long controlled in courts of justice, in charitological and penal institutions, and in the general treatment of defective and delinquent classes. Society is as seriously handicapped by the attitude today as was the criminal by the rigorous system characteristic of early English and Roman law. Absolute justice may seem less humane in individual instances, but the resultant good to society is incalculable.

The question of expert testimony is of equal importance with the jury system. The rule relating to it is almost uniform, *i. e.*, that when, in the discretion of the court, it is a proper case for expert testimony, either party may call qualified persons, who shall give their opinion, which is generally based upon hypothetical questions arising out of the evidence in the case.

In its relation to criminal cases the testimony of such experts is so imperfectly secured as in many cases to negative its value and in others to reduce the value to a minimum. Where expert testimony is introduced by persons selected by the opposing counsel, the result necessarily is a flat contradiction, as each selects only those favorable to his own cause. Where evidence is secured in this manner, a high degree of discrimination is required, which the average juror does not possess.

It is proposed that there shall be a board of examiners which shall be permanent or selected by the court, and which shall not be attached to either party or be remunerated by them. In the United States the jurists are the greatest opponents of the movement that legislation should provide for the creation of these boards and should consider all other expert testimony as opinion evidence, and no exception to the rules governing the latter. It is also proposed that the opinions of this board be not based upon hypothetical questions, but that its members should have a personal knowledge of the criminal and of all matters connected with the crime.

In 1894 the Medical Society of the County of New York appointed a committee to consider the matter. It recommended a law providing for the appointment of a commission of experts by the courts. It suggested that the attorneys should agree to the commission, and that all members of it should have equal facilities for examining the accused, without interference by attorneys, and that no member should make an examination, except in the presence of the other members. No action has resulted from this recommendation. Similar movements have been made by medical associations in other states, but with no better success.

The recent case of the People *vs.* Fleming serves as an excellent illustration of the present difficulties attending expert testimony, and, in commenting upon the case, the *Medico-Legal Journal* says: "Rarely, if ever, have the defects of expert testimony been presented so unmistakably as in this case. A fair estimate of the cost to the defense and the prosecution separately for the expert evidence introduced is $12,000. These eminent and high-priced scientists contradicted each other directly and explicitly, as they always do. These witnesses are not witnesses at all, as they are not called to establish truths, but to support theories, the acceptance of which makes for conviction or acquittal. They are chosen with that end in view and with an eye to nothing save the skill with which they can protect themselves and their contentions in cross-examinations. They are not necessarily dishonest, and some of them are men of high character. But they become under the existing system simply a part of the array of counsel of either side. Every one of them would consider it a disloyalty to omit a scintilla of evidence tending in the least to combat or even confuse the contention for the maintenance of which he is retained. This is a sorry hand-maidenship of science to justice. It disgraces both."

In France, in homicide cases, a medical expert is appointed to serve from the time the crime is committed, and is a close observer from that stage until the end of the trial. It is in the discretion of the judge whether other experts shall be admitted. In New York and a few of the other states it is provided that, where the plea is guilty and insanity is alleged, the accused can be adjudged insane and committed without standing trial, but this only operates where the plea of guilty is entered.

It is a rule of practice, and in some states it is provided by statute, that a prosecuting attorney can accept the evidence of an accomplice, and in return grant him immunity from the punishment for his participation in the crime. This is a survival of the early common-law rule of approvement, where one indicted for a capital offense might confess the fact in order to obtain pardon, and was termed an accuser. The person accused was tried, and, if convicted, a pardon was granted the accuser; but if the accused were not convicted, the accuser was executed. The practice in the United States is that the testimony shall not be used to convict the accomplice, even if the accused is not convicted.

If the object of punishment is protection to the state, it is not quite clear what the gain is when one avowed criminal is turned loose in order that another may be convicted. Not infrequently the greater criminal is released (Lindsey *vs.* People, 63 N. Y., 143), although some of the states have sought to avoid this result (State *vs.* Ray, 1 Gr. Ia., 319). It seems anomalous that to procure the *chance* for the conviction of one whom the law assumes innocent another whose guilt is *unquestioned* is pardoned, and this lest the tender sensibilities of the criminal be wounded by a personal examination, as is permitted in France. A conviction may be had on the uncorroborated testimony of an accomplice, but this is not the general rule in the United States (1 Gr., 316). It exists in the United States as a rule of practice, rather than as a law. In 9 Cowen, 707, the rule is stated that the least guilty morally and least hardened is selected for state's evidence, and it should appear probable that his testimony will secure a conviction, without which it would have been impossible. This is, however, more theoretical than practical. In nearly all states this method is permissible, and its faults are obvious. It is inevitable that one criminal must escape, and it is a reflection upon the ability of the law that it must secure punishment with the aid of the accomplice.

Closely related with this rule is that which provides that a witness is not compelled to incriminate himself, and need not give evidence if he is a party defendant. This is also a modified survival of the earlier English common law. One advance may be said to have been made, in that, if a criminal elects to give evidence, he subjects himself to all the hardships as well as to all the privileges granted to other witnesses, although he cannot be examined as to matters in regard to which he has not testified (People *vs.* O'Brien, 66 Cal., 602 ; State *vs.* Chamberlain, 89 Mo., 129). With one exception (Com. *vs.* Cleaves, 59 Me., 298), no inference can be drawn from the silence of the accused (People *vs.* Tyler, 36 Cal., 522 ; Price *vs.* Com., 77 Va., 593). The rule in some jurisdictions has been so extended that the prisoner need not give evidence which tends merely to disgrace him, and is himself the judge as to whether the testimony will incriminate him. In Austria and France prisoners are interrogated with good success, on the theory that no criminal should be allowed to menace society through his liberty, and that all efforts to prevent this are just. It is true an interrogated criminal will not often answer truthfully, but it would be much more difficult for him to establish his innocence were he not given the *benefit* of his silence. Science has no patience with the safeguards thrown about the criminal, and believes, if he is guilty, it is just that he should not be protected. If he is innocent, his testimony will tend to prove him so. In justice to the state, his silence should be construed against him.

So long as the tendency is to grant greater immunity to the criminal, a decrease in crime is impossible. The certainty or *reasonable assurance* of not being convicted is one of the strongest incentives to crime, and, judging from the present ratio of the convictions to the crimes committed and the number of recidivists, the risk seems well worth assuming.

With the technicalities of legal insanity, involving the numerous questions of degrees, proof, elements constituting insanity, etc., criminal anthropologists have made no leading suggestions, although the inadequacy is recognized. The question whether the test of insanity shall be the legal or medical one is not so much considered as whether one acquitted on the ground of insanity shall be released. Insanity should be no *defense*, although it may be an *explanation*. The insane criminal is as dangerous to society as the sane criminal, and, being equally incorrigible, should be incarcerated. The absolute release of insane criminals has led to an abuse of the plea of insanity, and if crime is to be lessened by the prevention of further acts, and a transmission of defective organisms to descendants, incarceration must be assured. In France, Germany, Belgium, Austria, Hungary, and the United States an insane criminal, when acquitted on the ground of insanity, is withdrawn from all judicial control; but in Denmark, Russia, Spain, Holland, and England the judiciary is empowered to order seclusion in an ordinary or criminal asylum, or to keep the person under police surveillance. Italy, also, by her penal code of 1889 (Art. 46), gives a similar authority to her judges. Ferri, the Italian jurist, has proposed that the following classes be sent to these asylums: prisoners acquitted upon the ground of insanity, or sentenced for a fixed period on preliminary inquiry; convicts who become insane during the term of their sentences; insane persons committing a crime in ordinary asylums; and persons under observation for weak intellect, who have been once on trial.

As a result of the Barberi trial, concluded in New York in 1896, a bill has been introduced providing for the imprisonment of guilty, but acquitted, insane, and this should apply to any defense which questions mental responsibility. From society's point of view it cannot make the slightest difference whether the criminal is sane or insane, for in either case he is equally dangerous.

Kleptomania and intoxication are defenses which are demanding much thought, and legislation relative to them is being urged. In some few jurisdictions the former is admitted as a defense, while the latter is not so held, although it may mitigate the punishment.

In criminal trials the burden of proof is upon the state, to show that the accused is guilty, and there is thus a presumption of innocence. In justice to the state no presumption should exist, as it is as equitable to require one to exculpate himself as to require the state to inculpate him. The whole legal tendency of criminal anthropology is to place the state and the accused upon an equality. The rule as existing makes conviction more difficult by reason of the additional and unnecessary burden upon the state. For this reason it has been suggested that the verdict of "not proven" be restored in cases where the accused was not free from guilt, although not convicted. It is urged also upon the ground that it would avoid the tendency upon the part of jurors to compromise in favor of guilt and lighten the punishment. A committee of the American Bar Association, at the annual meeting of 1890, to which this suggestion was referred, reported unfavorably, and this is the only effort thus far made for its restoration.

The question of appeal is, perhaps, the strongest illustration of the inequality of the administration of justice, as applied to the state and to the criminal. As appeal now exists, a decision against the state is final, unless there be some error in the indictment, or the court has not jurisdiction. There are no other universal grounds common to both state and accused, although there are many technicalities upon which a criminal can secure an appeal.

It is argued, first, that the system of appeal is too elaborate and that one fair trial and one appeal satisfy justice, and much litigation would thereby be avoided. The same ground upon which an appeal is granted the accused should be extended to the state. Because one court acquits, it does not establish the innocence of the accused, especially when the appeal is granted upon a legal technicality and deals only remotely with the question of guilt and innocence.

In the United States the tendency is in favor of the equality rule, and a greater liberty is being granted the state. However, the common-law rule in all its vigor remains in force in many of the states. The law that a person shall not be placed twice in jeopardy for the same offense has been sought to be made a barrier to appeal by the state, but unsuccessfully. This jeopardy is held to begin when the jury is impaneled and sworn to try the case (State *vs.* Bowman, 62 N. W. Rep., 759). In the case of the State *vs.* Lee, 30 Atl., 1110, which arose under the Connecticut statute No. 1637, in which it was provided that a case may be taken from the superior to the supreme court, with permission of the presiding judge, on all questions of law, in the same manner by the state as by the accused, the extent of equal appeal has been reached. The alleged error in the case was the exclusion of certain evidence offered by the state, and it was held that an appeal on this ground, and a reversal for a new trial, did not violate the provision relating to former jeopardy. Other cases holding advanced decisions are People *vs.* Damon, 13 Wend., 351, for misconduct of jurors ; State *vs.* Reed, 26 Conn., 208. The reason for the proposed change is that, if an individual has a right to claim that he shall not be condemned through the mistake or ignorance of his judges, the state also has the right to demand that those whose acquittal is equally the result of mistake or ignorance shall not be allowed to go free. The justice of a sentence rests equally upon a just condemnation or a just acquittal. The extreme rules of former jeopardy, incriminating evidence, public trial, and many others, which grew out of the severity of early common law, are now only a menace to society, and the law governing appeals may also be said to be such. From an economic point of view it is better that one innocent man should be punished than that ten guilty should be liberated, although the sentiments of humanity generally refuse to accept this converse of the ordinary rule.

The accused has a constitutional right to a speedy and public trial. The requirement of this public trial is for the benefit of the accused, that the public may see him not unjustly condemned, and that the presence of spectators may keep his triers alive to their responsibility. This requirement is fairly observed if, without partiality, a reasonable portion of the public is suffered to attend (Cooley's *Constitutional Limitations*, p. 379). Criminal anthropologists demand a greater restriction in public trials and executions, upon the theory of criminal contagion. Public trials, together with the newspaper reports, form an important means of extending this criminal contagion. Any knowledge tending to lower the moral standard of the community does not make the latter more criminal, but does lessen its resistance to criminal influence. This may be illustrated by the many well-known epidemics of crime, which show so admirably humanity's power of imitation, and its susceptibility to contagion.

In the United States so firm is the belief in this relic of mediæval barbaric practice that it is incorporated in nearly all, if not all, state constitutions. There is a discretion vested in the judges, but they have been reluctant to exercise the discretion, possibly because it is not unlimited and has often furnished a ground for reversal (People vs. Hartman, 37 Pac., 153 ; Williamson vs. Lacey, 29 Atl., 943). Cases illustrating a liberal construction of the rule are Grinnette vs. State, 22 Tex. Ap., 36, in which exclusion was held not to be a violation of right, wherever it was necessary to support public morals and protect witnesses, and People vs. Swafford, 65 Cal., 223, where all were excluded except those connected with the case.

Public executions are also a source of the perpetuation rather than of the prevention of crime ; and it has been demonstrated that the publicity does not operate as a deterrent, as was at one time so firmly believed.

We now pass to a consideration of those questions which are more distinctly matters of law, and shall first consider habitual criminal acts.

The greater number of criminals are known to be recidivists, and it is from this class that the greater number of dangerous criminals are recruited. To prevent this growth of crime, special legislation is advocated for habitual offenders. It is the criminal in connection with the crime which should be judged ; and the theory is that for each additional commission of felony there should be an increase of punishment, and that after the third sequestration imprisonment should be indefinite, pending the decision of certain designated officials. By this change a decrease of crime is anticipated in two lines — by cutting short a probable career of crime, and by preventing the birth of a family of paupers or criminals. In connection with the latter may be noted the statute passed by Connecticut in 1895, which provides that no man or woman either of whom is epileptic, imbecile, or feeble-minded shall intermarry while the woman is under forty-five years of age, the penalty being imprisonment for three years. The object is obviously to prevent an increase of defective organisms. In this relation may be mentioned two somewhat radical bills along the line of preventing criminality. In Michigan, in April, 1897, there was introduced a bill[1] providing for the asexualization of the inmates of the state institutions for epileptic and feeble-minded persons convicted of the crime of rape, and those for the third time convicted of felony. This bill did not pass.[2] The other bill was introduced in the Ohio legislature in February, 1898, and provides that it shall be the duty of the probate judge in each county to appoint an examining board of three physicians who shall consider and pass upon all applications for licenses to marry. By the terms of the proposed law, this board shall not be allowed to grant a license to persons contemplating marriage, unless upon examination they are found to be free from true insanity, dipsomania, hereditary insanity, and tuberculosis. An appeal may be taken from this board to a state board. This law contemplates the prevention of crime and disease by limiting the transmission of defective organisms.

In France and England some legislation has been obtained, and also in the United States, but it cannot be said that the test made has been a fair one. The majority of the states still maintain the maximum and minimum penalties, while the discretion of the judge is permitted to run the gamut between them. The states having passed habitual-criminal acts are California (Penal Code, No. 667), Virginia (Penal Code, p. 752), Massachusetts (Stat. 1887, chap. 435, No. 1), Missouri, Illinois (Rev. S., 1895, No. 498), Maine (Rev. S., chap. 135, No. 2), Ohio, and Connecticut. While there is some variance in these statutes, all of them substantially provide that after the commission of two or more felonies there shall be imprisonment for fifteen years and upward, and that the prison officials or boards of pardons shall have power to release on parole or without condition. These statutes have been subjected to various attacks. It has been sought to hold them unconstitutional on the ground of constituting second jeopardy (People vs. Stanley, 87 Cal., 113) ; that they violate the provision that the penalty shall be proportionate to the offense (Kelley vs. People, 115 Ill., 583) ; and that they are cruel and unusual punishments (Sturtevant vs. Com., 33 N. E., 648). In each instance the statute has been sustained. It has been held, however, that the previous offenses must have been felonies in themselves and not made so by the statute (Carson vs. State, 19 S. R., 32 ; Stover vs. Com., 22 S. E., 874).

In the application of habitual-criminal acts the mere seriousness of the crime cannot divide the categories of criminals, and the division

[1] House Bill No. 672, Michigan Legislature.

[2] For arguments favoring asexualization consult H. M. BOISE, *Prisoners and Paupers*.

into born and occasional criminals has been suggested. Born criminals are those who have a tendency to commit crime through heredity or disease, and who inevitably will become recidivists. The occasional criminals are those having no inborn or active tendency to commit crime, but who lapse into it through temptation afforded by personal condition and by physical and social environment, but who do not relapse when these disappear. The second class is more capable of reform, but may become recidivists.

Closely allied and indispensable to the success of habitual-criminal acts is that of indeterminate sentence. Both of these measures were advocated before criminal anthropology approved them. The Swiss Prison Reform Association first advocated the indefinite segregation of habitual offenders in 1867. In the United States by the indeterminate sentence the maximum penalty is retained, but the minimum penalty is removed, the discretion as to time of release being vested in those in control of the institution to which the offender is sent. The reformation of the delinquent, or at least his resignation to social laws and respect for them, is the essence of the theory of conditional liberation. As one can count to a certain extent upon the vitality of the criminal instinct, and upon the persistence of the social conditions which nourish it, it is necessary to prepare for a long incarceration, which may be regarded as the result of incurability on the part of the criminal. The idea is the proportion of the length of the imprisonment to the nature of the delinquent, to the degree of his perversity, and to the danger of his return to society before his evil tendencies are enfeebled or neutralized. This would enable errors in judgment to be more easily corrected, and would protect society from having thrust upon it at the end of a definite time individuals who are unfitted for return. New York, Massachusetts, Ohio, Pennsylvania, Kansas, Maine, Louisiana, and Illinois have passed these acts, and conditional liberation is provided for; but in no state has the maximum penalty been removed, as is suggested. In consequence, the criminal, if his offense be not serious enough, may return to society regardless of his unfitness at the expiration of his sentence. The United States, with the Elmira Reformatory[1] as its most noted exponent, leads in this reform and has ably demonstrated its possibilities. No uniform system exists in any country.

In order that the indeterminate-sentence plan shall he successful, there must be a reorganization of the prison staff, since its efficiency

[1] See A. WINTER, *New York State Reformatory School at Elmira.*

depends largely upon the capability of those individuals who shall have control of the prisoners and shall determine when they are fitted to return. These officials must be removed from the sphere of political influence, and training and qualification made the basis for their appointment. In Italy, France, and Belgium special training schools for prison attendants have been established.

Again, habitual-criminal acts or indeterminate sentence can never operate successfully without a better system of identification than exists in the United States and most of the European countries. The prevailing system of photography has been proved inadequate, and the Bertillon system in use in France is recommended as a substitute. Illinois, in connection with its indeterminate-sentence act, authorized the adoption of the Bertillon or a similar system, and to some extent the former has been used.[1]

In the matter of the education of jurists, judges, and attorneys, criminal anthropologists believe that one of the greatest barriers to reform is the present antagonism between jurisprudence and science, particularly medical science. This condition is more nearly true of the United States than of any European country. To obviate this antagonism there is needed a more extended and systematic study of medical jurisprudence and sociology by criminal lawyers, and the separation of criminal and civil courts. Moreover, the knowledge and training of a criminal judge should not be the same as those of a civil judge. It is obvious that the same studies which qualify one for a civil judge do not necessarily qualify one for a criminal judge. The learned jurists in civil law are, in fact, accustomed by their studies to abstractions of humanity, and look solely to judicial bearings, being ignorant of science and thus not fitted to judge human nature. With the American tendency to consolidate courts, it is seemingly an impossibility to apprehend such a division. It is also advocated that professors and students of criminal law should have a clinical study of criminals, and efforts are being made to introduce these studies. Both the legal and medical fraternities indorse these propositions.

Carcerial regulations and methods have an interest in this study of law and criminal anthropology, because the success of a scientific system of jurisprudence depends largely upon these methods. If repression and prevention of crime are the objects of punishment, carcerial regulations become of the utmost importance, and are also dependent upon

[1] See McClaughry's translation of BERTILLON's *System of Identification* for a detailed account.

legislation for their removal or continuance. The most prominent existing regulations noted as retrogressive are:

1. Legislation restricting or prohibiting labor. This limits the opportunity for becoming proficient in trades, tends to decrease the adaptability of the prisoner to society, and prevents his procuring an honest livelihood upon his release. The prison containing an excellent labor and self-disciplining system is primarily of assistance in decreasing crime. In the United States, in the majority of institutions, labor and the learning of a trade is compulsory, and provision is made for it. In some states, as New York, for political and economic reasons the legislatures have prescribed the variety and amount of labor which shall be done by convicts. This may reduce the competition with outside establishments and manufactories, but the ultimate gain to the state or society is not quite so clear.

2. The indiscriminate incarceration in prisons and jails of youthful and old offenders. This is a well-recognized source of criminal contagion, and is a reform advocated early in the beginning of the present century. This indiscriminate association of criminals has laid the foundation for the assertion that these institutions are "schools of crime" and are the "most potent agents in producing experienced and educated criminals." In the United States a division of sexes is made, but beyond this little thought has been given to the subject by legislators. France has the most complete system in this respect, although many faults remain. It includes five classes of prisons—those for criminals with long sentences, those for criminals having short sentences, correctional establishments, lockups, and depots for convicts sentenced to relegation and hard labor. There are committees which classify the criminals and determine the destination of everyone arrested and convicted. The rule is rigid that first offenders shall be kept separate. Although but limited conversations are permitted in most institutions, many ingenious methods of conversing exist, and many future crimes are planned, or ideas imbibed which will develop into crimes.

3. The cellular system of imprisonment. This is illustrated by the Eastern Penitentiary at Philadelphia, and is much more common in Europe than in the United States. It is condemned upon the ground of being detrimental to reformation. Instead of fitting a convict to reënter society, it makes him less independent and develops only a small degree of self-control, an attribute in which he is already deficient. The absence of association during incarceration is not the

wisest method of creating or developing a greater degree of adaptability to society.

Outside of the main topics enumerated above, many other questions
relating to the judicial system and to legislation are receiving thought
and study, but are not deemed so absolutely essential to a decrease of
crime as those mentioned.

The discussion relating to a public defender is almost entirely confined to the legal members of criminal anthropology, and the arguments
are legal rather than scientific.

The attitude of district attorneys has received some attention, but
may be said to be the result of a condition, rather than a cause needing
legislation. It does not appear that justice is best served by the attitude taken by them, as their intense antagonism is not compatible with
the basis upon which criminal anthropology founds its system. They
are not the simple ministers of justice, but are the attorneys for parties
on the record. Their duty should be as much to save the innocent as
to convict the guilty; but many of them are imbued with the idea that
they *must* convict at all hazards, notwithstanding the presumption of
the law that the prisoner is innocent until proven guilty. In some of
the states the practice of awarding premiums for convictions is authorized. Apart from acknowledging an inherent defect in the legal system,
this practice does not produce a greater number of convictions. These
abuses by attorneys consist largely in opening the case to the jury, in
the argument to the jury, in abuse of the defendant, and serve more
often to influence the jury in favor of the accused. The office is one
which is usually filled by election, the number of convictions being
often used as an argument for reëlection. Under a scientific legal
system a radical change in this respect would be necessary.

The matter of more complete statistics is a question for the United
States more than for any European country, and legislation influences
it to a great extent. No study of crime can be accurate without trustworthy and complete statistics, but the statistical methods existing in the
different states make this almost impossible. Statistics in the United
States are taken as mere matters of record, and not with any view to
the purposes of social science. Aside from the national census report
there are no uniform data for comparative purposes.

Before leaving this discussion of the United States it will be interesting to glance at peculiar conditions which make this country imperatively in need of a better system of jurisprudence. These and other
conditions render it incomparable with European countries, and con-

stitute obstructions to a uniform system of jurisprudence, not existing elsewhere.

1. The form of government is, perhaps, one of the greatest impediments to a uniform system of jurisprudence, and the administration of criminal law forms a strong argument for the centralization of governmental power. Now each state enacts its own laws and penalties, and has its own procedure; and, as a result, all grades of punishment and different methods of procedure exist for the same crime. A serious crime in one state may be only a misdemeanor in another, and the range of penalties in one state may often result in a criminal's receiving a maximum penalty for a crime in one jurisdiction, while in another, under precisely similar conditions, only a minimum penalty would be imposed. This discrepancy is often seen in comparing states. The impossibility of uniform law is well illustrated by the laws of capital punishment. With the exception of four states, it is the penalty for homicide; in less than half the states it is the penalty for both homicide and treason; in nine states arson and rape are added to the above.[1] The various methods of arrest, identification, and of police and judicial systems only add to the hindrances against unification.

2. The negro element of population, which presents such a large class of citizens out of harmony with the advanced civilization existing in the greater part of the United States, is responsible for no small degree of criminality, and has given the United States the preëminence which it enjoys as the exponent of lynch law. The number of negro prisoners—it being remembered that convictions are very disproportionate to the number of crimes committed—is entirely out of proportion to the negro population. In 1890, of the 82,329 convicts 24,277 were negroes, although the negro population was only 7,470,040, or 11.93 per cent.; while the white population, with 87.70 per cent., only furnished 57,310 convicts.[2] The number of executions by lynching was twice as great in 1890 as the number of legal executions. This is a

[1] In this connection it will be gratifying to note the late revision of the federal law relating to capital punishment. The bill was introduced in Congress by General N. M. Curtis, and was passed in January, 1897. At the time of its passage there were sixty offenses punishable by death in the United States statutes. By this bill the number is reduced to some half dozen offenses, and it is provided that in certain cases a verdict of "guilty, but without capital punishment," may be returned. This law is a most important step in the way of securing uniform criminal law and penalties.

[2] Cf. Eleventh Census Report, "Department of Crime, Pauperism, and Benevolence."

condition which must be considered in the discussion of any better administration of criminal law.

3. No small portion of criminality is due to immigration, since a comparatively large proportion of criminals are foreign-born. No country which receives the convicts and outcasts of other countries can expect a decrease of crime by an improved system of law while the influx continues.

The system of electing judges for a short period of time, and the appointment of penitentiary incumbents by political methods, are well-recognized evils, to which reference has been made. Immigration, the negro element, and the errors in the political and judicial system are three elements which must be considered in a study of crime in the United States. The increase of crime, notwithstanding the deficient statistics, is shown by the following table to be worthy of grave consideration :[1]

Year					Prisoners in United States	Ratio to population
1850,	-	-	-	-	6,737	1 in 3,442
1860,	-	-	-	-	19,086	1 in 1,617
1870,	-	-	-	-	32,901	1 in 1,171
1880,	-	-	-	-	58,609	1 in 855
1890,	-	-	-	-	82,329	1 in 757

It is true, an apparent decrease of crime may only mean defective laws, and it is not infrequent that the moral progress of a nation is marked by its increase in criminality; but when this rate of increase is compared with that of other countries, it is seen to be unusually large.

From the preceding statement of the lines of reform upon which criminal anthropologists are engaged it will be seen that the science and the jurisprudence are vitally related, and that the sole purpose of the former is to provide a more accurate, logical basis for the latter, to eradicate many of the existing principles and the system of their administration. It will be seen that only a comparatively small number of isolated attempts have been made in the direction of the "new jurisprudence." These isolated attempts are of but little value, as most of the reforms are closely related or developed out of each other, and, if given a fair test, it should be as part of a system. This can be well illustrated by the operation of the habitual-criminal act in Massachusetts. There is no accurate method of identification, and most of

[1] This table is misleading in its representation of the increase in crime, owing to the inaccuracy of the reports preceding 1870.

the neighboring states have not similar acts, and the effect has been, not to *diminish* the number of criminals, but to drive them into other jurisdictions after the first conviction for crime.

If there is to be any progress, criminal anthropology and criminal jurisprudence must coöperate, or the one must yield to the other, and while there is much to be criticised in the work of the scientists, the judiciary is itself too faulty to be the critic. If the science shall demonstrate that its principles are enduring, its proposed changes sound, and its knowledge not erroneous, it must have a directly beneficial result in its relation to jurisprudence. It remains to be seen whether this will result from coöperation or substitution, or whether the precedent of legal systems shall remain unchanged.

Before closing, it may be of interest to note the strength which the new movement has gathered in the brief period of its existence. This can best be done by a reference to the principal organizations which are studying crime scientifically, and are thereby assisting in the establishment of a new basis for criminal jurisprudence. If criminal anthropologists were the only persons devoted to a study of the delinquent and his relation to society, the movement would not have assumed the importance now accredited to it. There are many minor associations engaged in the various lines of study, but here reference is made only to the most important, in order to dispel the idea that the study is a fad, or has not the attention of the great mass of scientific and legal workers.

First in importance is the International Congress of Criminal Anthropology,[1] which now meets biennially. Four meetings have been held — at Rome, Paris, Brussels, and Geneva. Its members comprise both schools, so that its work is conducted from sociological and psychological, as well as biological, standpoints. Its work consists of papers, discussions, and reports upon the various lines of work, and investigation which its members pursue in the interim. This association is the great center and impetus of the scientific study of crime and the criminal, and its work extends directly into the countries of France, Germany, Italy, Austria, Russia, the United States, and South American republics, and collaterally into many of the minor states. Its members include prominent scientists, jurists, physicians, alienists, and professors, and the field of investigation is correspondingly broad. The work done is continuous, and the congress may be said to be but the biennial report or correlation of the work.

[1] See published reports of International Congress of Criminal Anthropology.

In 1889, in Brussels, the first meeting of the Criminal Law Association was held. The organization was due to Professor von Liszt, of Halle. In 1892 the membership exceeded five hundred persons, and included a number of citizens of the United States. This organization was indirectly the result of criminological agitation, and, while composed largely of jurists, its fundamental principles embody the following propositions, and membership requires adhesion to them :

1. The mission of penal law is to combat criminality regarded as a social phenomenon.

2. Penal science and penal legislation must, therefore, take into consideration the results of anthropological and sociological studies.

3. Punishment is one of the most efficacious means which the state can use against crime. It is not the only means and must not be isolated from the other social remedies, nor lead to the neglect of preventive measures.

4. The distinction between accidental (occasional) and habitual criminals is essential in practice as well as in theory, and must be the foundation of penal law.

5. Repressive tribunals and prisons have the same end in view; and inasmuch as sentences acquire value only by mode of execution, the separation consecrated by our modern laws between court and prison is irrational and harmful.

6. The length of imprisonment should depend upon the material and the moral gravity of the offense, and upon the results obtained by treatment during imprisonment.

7. So far as incorrigible or habitual criminals are concerned, the association holds that, independent of the gravity of the offense, the penal system should aim at placing them for as long as possible under conditions where they can do no injury.

The work of this association is particularly valuable, as its members are almost entirely jurists.

The fourth annual meeting of the International Congress of Psychology, held at Munich in the summer of 1896, is especially notable by reason of its devoting one of its sections to work in pathological psychology. Many prominent psychologists are interested in this field, and papers relating to the bearing of psychology upon criminal law, heredity, and psycho-pathology, criminal suggestion, etc., were read and discussed. The methods of the biological school of criminal anthropology are identical with those of physiological psychology, the same instruments of measurement being used in both. Thus the tendency of psychologists to study the abnormal, in addition to the excellent work being done in the study of the normal, is of especial value in advancing criminal anthropological studies. In many universities the scientific study of crime is being conducted in connection with psychological and sociological courses.

At the last meeting of the International Congress of Demography, held in Budapest in 1894, the study of crime was considered in relation to movements and development of populations. All discussions from a biological point of view were laid aside, the sociological receiving the attention of the congress.

The International Prison Association,[1] which held its last congress in Paris in 1895, is one of the most influential organizations in the development and dissemination of criminal anthropological ideas and aims. This association is of American origin, being due to the efforts of the late Dr. E. C. Wines. Five congresses have been held—at London, Stockholm, Rome, St. Petersburg, and Paris; and at each of these criminal law has received no small amount of consideration and discussion. The work of this association is valuable, because its members are largely engaged in the practical application of law, and in the direct management of the criminal. Its reports are particularly full and reliable, but are to be found only in French.

In America, among the numerous organizations may be mentioned some whose work is especially valuable. The National Prison Association,[2] which meets annually, gives its entire sessions to a consideration of crime, legislation, and prison management. The Medico-Legal Society, which is making strenuous efforts to bring medicine and law into a closer harmony, is a strong organization, and by its publications and meetings is doing much to extend the knowledge of criminal anthropology in the United States. The American Association of Social Science, in its publications and discussions, has given especial attention to the subject under discussion, and its papers are among the most valuable printed in English. The American Statistical Association has contributed some valuable papers in anthropometry and criminal statistics.

FRANCES ALICE KELLOR.

THE UNIVERSITY OF CHICAGO.

[1] See *International Prison Association Reports.*

[2] See *National Prison Association Reports.*

THE SOCIAL AND THE EXTRA-SOCIAL.[1]

§4. *Extra-social Conditions* (Sec. 313*a*).—While considering as we have the two intra-social or psychological forces, which we have now discussed as the only truly social forces, we should not overlook the very important group of influences which condition the sociological movement. These influences are really, so to speak, the banks or barriers which set limits to the social current, and even, by interaction with the strictly social forces, leave their marks within the social body. Their relation to the social forces properly so called is similar to that which the psychologists recognize between the strictly psychological and the physiological. The various states of the body, such as intoxication, fatigue, starvation, and over-nourishment, affect the mind, and so influence the individual's mental development; but we do not call them psychological forces. They are of psychological value only because, through the sorts of stimulation and limitation which they afford, they condition certain uniform results in the psychological organization itself. The analogy thus cited— between the extra-social influences with the effects they bring about in the social whole, and the extra-mental or physiological influences with their influence upon the individual's mental life —is indeed more than an analogy. When we reflect, we find that it is through the connection of mind and body—one term of the analogy—that the extra-social forces—the other term of the analogy—get their value. It becomes, therefore, still more apparent that we cannot call the influences enumerated below social forces; for so far are they from having direct value in the organization of society that they become factors in that organization only by the indirect road of stimulation to the nervous system of individuals. It would be just as appropriate to call blood-changes psychological facts as to call physical changes,

---

[1] The form of this brief article and its allusions are due to its consisting of certain new sections added by the writer in the new editions of his work *Social and Ethical Interpretations.*

649

such as the cutting of the Suez canal, social facts; yet both undoubtedly deserve recognition in a philosophical statement of all the determining conditions in these two branches of knowledge.

The sort of conditions which I mean by the phrase "extra-social" will appear from the enumeration below. It does not claim to be complete, however. Their full discussion does not come within our province, seeing that they are extra-psychological.

1. *Group-selection* (described above, Sec. 120).—In group-selection we have a condition of enormous importance in the development of social aggregations, especially in the instinctive and spontaneous periods; that is, of so-called "companies." It holds, however, for all societies when the conditions are such that groups as groups come into competition. Not only real war, but commercial and social wars of all kinds, illustrate group-selection. The working of the principle is strictly analogous, indeed identical, with that of natural selection in biology, an analogy excellently worked out by Bagehot in his remarkable work, *Physics and Politics*. It is one of the foundation stones also of S. Alexander's work, *Moral Order and Progress*. Bagehot acutely recognizes the distinction, without explicitly drawing it, between group-selection as a condition of evolution in the earlier stages of human aggregation and the operation of the real social force of "discussion" (described above under the heading "generalization") in the higher forms. It is, moreover, an additional proof that group-selection is a condition, and not a social force, that there is this difference between the lower and the higher; for the lower are determined, as we have seen, very largely by biological principles, such as instinct and physical heredity, and do not involve the social progress which the operation of the psychological forces brings in later on. Yet it is just there that group-selection is all-important.[1]

[1] The corresponding truth has often been pointed out (see COPE, *Primary Factors of Evolution*, chap. 7; CATTELL, *Science*, N. S., Vol. III, p. 668; BALDWIN, *Psychological Review*, Vol. IV, 1897, p. 219) that natural selection in biological evolution is not a force or cause, but a condition. Spencer's phrase, "survival of the fittest," itself analyzes natural selection. The fitness is assumed; it is due to earlier

2. *Individual selection*, which is natural selection working upon individuals who are brought into competition with one another for life and death. For instance, let us suppose that a man of genius who has not yet given to the world his invention—his machine which, if produced by him, would have great influence upon the condition of the working classes—that this man meets a burglar in his library and is shot dead. Here is a case of natural selection which determines the course of social evolution in a nation or in the world by the elimination of an individual. Such a case shows that the natural selection of individuals is a condition of importance—when the individuals are important—in social development. But it is not a force even in biology, as we have just seen. It is a negative condition ; a statement—in sociology as in biology—of evolution as it is, rather than as it would have been if the conditions had been other. This again is of especial importance in those stages of sociality in which the direct competition of individuals by physical strength or mental acuteness is in full operation.

3. *The intrusion of the "physiological cycle."*—In an earlier place (Sec. 43) we saw that the "cycle of causation" which psychological and sociological facts, such as beliefs, desires, etc., represent, often intrudes upon the operation of the "physiological cycle" by the personal selection of individuals in marriage. The physical heredity of the individuals is due to the mixed strains of the parents, and is in part, therefore, determined by their mutual choice of each other. The converse is also true : the physiological intrudes upon the sociological, and thus becomes an "extra-social condition" in its determination. This is seen in all cases in which physical heredity works results in individuals or groups which incapacitate them, especially endow them, or modify in any way their social fitness. A tall, manly race of men would have social advantages in winning wives from a higher group, and such marriages would tell at once inside their

real causes; the survival or selection which "natural selection" formulates is an *ex post facto* statement of results. It merely states that no further force of a positive sort is necessary (as against, *e. g.*, "special creation"). The distinction between "forces," which are *intrinsic*, and "conditions," which are *not intrinsic*, to the particular content, might well be traced through the sciences from biology to ethics.

own group. Where social preferment depended upon physical prowess, the inherited clubfoot would be an element of social unfitness. In the fact of what is called physical "presence," probably largely a matter of posture and vitality, we all recognize an easy substitute in many social positions for brains, culture, or oratorical gifts. Yet these things are not in themselves social; nor can they by any manipulation become social. The influence they have is entirely through the psychological states of which they are the conditions. A man with the illusion of a clubfoot would be as helpless as if it were real. And where is the hero so commonplace that his "presence" is not lordly to some love-sick maid?

4. Then there are the much-talked-of *physical conditions*, "the broken earth and the vaulted sky," the canal and the river-course, the mountain and the meadow. These, we are told, determine social development. They do; but by conditioning it, by intrusion upon it, by limiting it, not by being themselves social. That they are never. Let a race of animals that cannot think, nor recognize a social situation, nor know one another as reciprocating and fulfilling social give-and-take, run over the meadows and swim in the rivers, under a sky never so blue — and what effect of a social kind would these physical things have upon them? But given the psychological traits, make them men — and then what would not the human race do even on the levelest plain? Here again we have extra-social conditions. The land and water condition separation and segregation, competition and mutual defense, toleration and alliance, commerce and confederation; but the essentials of social matter and process must be there, and it is they that work under these conditions or those. Again, an illustration from recent biological theory, a case which often turns upon the effects of such physical differences as those mentioned: Isolation has been said to be a biological force, since, when animals are isolated from each other, the race is prevented from having the in-mixture of their hereditary strains, and so the heredity of the race is pre-limited. True, as a fact; but why make an abstraction do justice for a force? Isolation is always accomplished by some real force —

say a whirlwind which blows away the isolated individuals; but the biological forces are the life processes in those which are left. The whirlwind is the condition by which the result has been in a measure negatively determined; but who would say that the whirlwind is a biological force? At the most it is an intrusion of physics into the biological cycle. Just so with all the physical changes considered as influencing social life and development: they are conditions, intrusions from physics; not social forces.

The consideration of these extra-social conditions confirms us, therefore, in our view that only psychological sources of change[1] can be called "social forces," even in the figurative sense in which it is legitimate to use that word at all.[2] Other such conditions may be pointed out, but the examination of them will lead to the same conclusion.

(Sec. 169a.)—The question may very well be asked at this point how the various so-called "self-thoughts" hitherto distinguished are related to each other, and also how they are possible if the mind in all its development is proceeding with what has been called an identical content, in its thought of self. It is desirable, therefore, to make sure that we are not entangling ourselves in the meshes of our own details and distinctions. The matter straightens itself out when we recall to mind certain points already made out in what precedes.

First, we may recall the fact that a mental content may be considered either for itself or with regard to the attitudes, the

---

[1] And these of a particular sort. Inside of psychology the same distinction is to be made between "conditions" and "social forces." Not even all thoughts (as I have been represented as saying), but only certain thoughts (see *Soc. and Eth. Interpretations*, Secs. 325 f.), become social. Beliefs, desires, appetites, etc., are psychological *conditions* of the social.

[2] Figurative, since "force" is a physical conception. It means that which produces a change of rest or motion; and the sorts of forces are those producers of change which manifest themselves under different but constant physical conditions. We speak of mental, sociological, etc., forces in the analogous case of change in phenomena of one of these several orders; and to give the term any intelligible meaning we must keep within the particular order of phenomena as strictly as does the physicist in defining his forces always in terms of motion in space which determines other motion in space. In other words, the force is *intrinsic* or internal to the movement in which it is said to be manifested.

active processes, which accompany it.   We have found, on the
one hand, that the active processes are always functions of the
content; and, on the other hand, that the content is always
largely determined by earlier active processes.   This is a genetic
circle on which we have already remarked.   It follows that the
same content may be present in connection with different attitudes.   When, for example, a self-content, at whatever stage of
its development, is presented, having the additional marks which
determine it to be another person, an alter, then the self-attitude
aroused may be either what has been called "aggressive" or
what has been called "accommodating," according as it, the
attitude, is determining the content, or as the content is, in some
degree, also determining the attitude.   In the former case the
alter is "ejective;" in the latter case it has elements which are
"projective."   What we mean, therefore, by the "self of habit
or aggression," and the "self or accommodation or imitation,"
are not different self-contents.   They have differences, to be sure,
from the presence of an alter requiring one attitude or the other;
but these are not elements of self, not self-marks, so to speak,
until they have been taken over, by accommodation, from the projective and incorporated in the content of self.   The differences
of attitude are the differences of real genetic importance.

Second, the distinction between projective and ejective content turns upon the same requirement that we distinguish
between content and attitude.   When the self-content is accompanied by the aggressive attitude, the alter is never projective,
never considered unfinished; it is then always ejective, thoroughly
understood.   The projective is always the aspect of persons
which excites the accommodating imitative attitude.   Once
accommodated to, however, it becomes self-content, arouses
habitual attitudes, and so goes on to be ejected.

Third, granted, then, that we have a developing self-content
which at any time may be associated either with an aggressive
or with an accommodating attitude, what shall we say of the
"general" and of the "ideal" self?   The general self, like the
general everywhere in mental things, is, I believe, an attitude;
an attitude which is a more or less complex integration of the

partial attitudes aroused in definite concrete cases. The self-content remains one, growing with experience, it is true, but never more than one self-content. The partial attitudes which habitually determine and express it tend to realize themselves severally; but it is the mark of the general that they are in some degree held in the larger issue which constitutes the limit of personal growth up to date. The general self is, therefore, the sense of a system of attitudes which avail, by reason of the relative adequacy of their ejective content, to cope with the varied personal experiences of life.

Fourth, this "general," like all mental attitudes considered with reference to their contents, is itself inadequate to personal situations not yet covered by experience. The attitude called the general is therefore itself different according as the content is determined "ejectively" or "projectively," *i. e.*, according as it determines the content, or the content in part determines it; according, that is, as the person met with, or the personal situation experienced, has new, interesting, instructive features, or, on the other hand, is thoroughly understood, and already successfully acted upon. The former is the "general" as above defined, and as properly designated — the attitude which is not violated in the round of concrete personal experiences; the latter is the "ideal" self. The ideal self, then, is the attitude which looks forward toward a statement of the self-content which is not yet secured, and which no concrete self-experience suffices to fulfill, but which would respond adequately, if we had it, to all possible personal demands. In its actual mechanism this means, I think — what it means also on the lower plane — the readiness or habit of our motor nature to accommodate itself ever more adequately, while at the same time it is becoming general and spontaneous in its expression. We may, indeed, recall here the outcome of the earlier chapter on the ethical self (Sec. 29) to the effect that in the ethical "ought" we have a "habit of violating habits;" a call to accommodate to what is as yet unrealized in actual self-content, and to modify the attitudes which accompany the actual content.

J. MARK BALDWIN.

PRINCETON UNIVERSITY.

PROLEGOMENA TO SOCIAL PSYCHOLOGY.

I.

THE NEED OF THE STUDY OF SOCIAL PSYCHOLOGY.

HERBERT SPENCER begins his *Study of Sociology* with a chapter emphasizing the practical need of it; in like manner, perhaps, there is no better way of entering upon a discussion of the subject of social psychology than by pointing out the theoretical need of such a science. This paper accordingly will be a plea for the study of social psychology, with an attempt to show the necessity of it by a partial inventory of the problems dependent upon a social psychology for their scientific solution. Some sort of social psychology, it is true, has usually been assumed by social science; but the plea of this article is for a systematically worked out and carefully verified social psychology as a condition of complete social knowledge. For, if it be assumed that the phenomena of society are chiefly psychical, a knowledge of the psychical processes which characterize group-life as such is manifestly a most important condition of complete social knowledge.

A few preliminary statements of position may, however, be helpful in rendering our plea more intelligible.

Külpe speaks of social psychology as the science which "treats of the mental phenomena dependent upon a community of individuals."[1] This we may accept as a rough, working definition of the science. Now, the assumption that there are "mental phenomena dependent upon a community of individuals" presupposes psychical processes which are more than *merely* individual, which are *inter*-individual; in last analysis it implies that through the action and reaction of individuals in a group upon one another there arise psychical processes which cannot be explained by reference to any or all of the individuals

[1] See KÜLPE'S *Outlines of Psychology*, translated by Titchener, p. 7; *cf.* also the original.

as such, but only by reference to the group-life considered itself as a unity. Social psychology, then, if somewhat more strictly defined, has as its task to examine and explain the form or mechanism of these group psychical processes. It is an interpretation of the psychical processes manifested in the growth and functioning of a group as a unity. Whatever psychical phenomena may be regarded as *pertaining to group-life as such* are, therefore, the proper subject-matter of social psychology. As such phenomena we may instance, for the sake of provisional illustration, political revolutions, mob action, group action, and organization of all sorts, down even to the psychical adjustments which take place in small groups, such as a family or a committee. Whether these facts are properly classified among those of social psychology or among those of individual psychology we cannot here discuss: the logical delimitation of the facts with which the two sciences respectively deal, and a discussion of the problems therein involved, must be reserved for a later article.

It is here acknowledged, however, that if the abstraction of the individual from the group and of the group from the individual is an unjustifiable abstraction for any purpose whatsoever, as some may assert, then the creation of a separate science of social psychology is also unjustifiable. Again, it is conceded that, if individual psychology can explain all the phenomena of group-life, as some individualists maintain, social psychology as a science has little excuse for existence. But the individualistic hypothesis, it must be added, needs demonstration quite as much as its opposite, and as yet such demonstration seems decidedly wanting. Indeed, it is notorious that psychology has up to the present failed to furnish that aid in the solution of social problems which was expected from it a half century ago. It may be suspected that a reason for this is that psychology has been developed too much on its purely individualistic side, and has neglected the not less real psychical processes of group-life.

Here another possible misunderstanding must be guarded against. In emphasizing the importance of social psychology we do not mean to imply that it can furnish a complete interpretation of society. There are many physical phenomena of land and climate, and many physiological phenomena of race and population, which are not less than psychical facts to be taken into account in a complete interpretation of society, but which social psychology as such cannot consider. Hence an objective as well as a subjective interpretation is essential for the proper understanding of the social life : neither alone will yield complete knowledge of society; both are necessary for the understanding, not only of society as a whole, but of any particular side of societary life. Nor is the subjective or psychological interpretation to be set over against the objective or biological interpretation ; both are parts of a philosophic whole, and each is supplementary to the other.

The objective interpretation of society has been, perhaps, sufficiently developed and emphasized during the present century by such men as Comte, Spencer, Buckle, and their followers. They regarded the physical and objective as fundamental, and brought in the subjective and mental only as modifications of the physical. Hence they treated the science of society logically as a physical science. In this proceeding they were justified, since they all explicitly or implicitly denied that the actions of men are independent phenomena having laws of their own. It is because we question, however, on methodological grounds the rightfulness of such an assumption that we would now shift the emphasis from the objective to the subjective interpretation. We do not question the value of an objective interpretation ; it is absolutely necessary to any complete understanding of the social process; but experience has shown that it is inadequate to explain the principal and characteristic features of that process; that it explains the incidental rather than the essential facts of societary life. We must, therefore, reverse the methodological order of the older sociologists and proceed from man to nature in our interpretation of society, not from nature to man.[1] That is to say, a social psychology is needed to interpret the processes

---

[1] *Cf.* PATTEN'S *Theory of Dynamic Economics,* Introduction. The methodological justification for the above position will appear in a later article.

of social growth and functioning, which are essentially psychical and subjective, before we can proceed to examine intelligently the relations of society to nature.

Now, if sociology be conceived as the complete interpretation of society, as the bringing-to-bear of all knowledge upon the problems of societary growth, structure, and function to effect their solution, it will be a synthesis of the objective with the subjective interpretation of society. In this synthesis the subjective interpretation of the social process, afforded by individual and social psychology, becomes progressively important as we pass from the lower to the higher stages of social development. Thus an objective or biological interpretation of society may seemingly answer very well for its primitive stages, but it is felt to be entirely inadequate for the interpretation of present social life with its preponderance of the psychic factor. Again, as we pass from the lower to the higher stages of society, *social* psychology becomes increasingly important for the interpretation of the social life. As social groups become more highly unified and organized, that is, "individualized," they act more and more as "individuals," and group life-processes become more definite and coherent. Corresponding to these group life-processes are psychical processes, which, though manifested in individuals, may properly be regarded as the expression of group-life. They represent the coördination and organization of the activities of group-life on its inner side. They not only function to secure those inner and outer adjustments necessary to the continuance of group-life, but they embody in themselves all those emotional and volitional attitudes, all those ways of thinking, feeling, and acting, which are favorable to the persistence solidarity, and growth of the group. They hand down in unbroken tradition the ideas, valuations, and methods which have been to the group of life-saving advantage. Thus group psychical processes become the great vehicle of progress; and group or social psychology, rather than individual psychology, must interpret the general method or mechanism of that progress. If this reasoning be substantially correct — and in a later article evidence will be adduced to show that it is correct — the need of the sociologist's studying social psychology is simply the need of developing his own science. Sociology cannot hope to become a well-organized and perfected discipline until it has, for a part of its foundation at least, a fully developed social psychology.

One particular respect may here be pointed out in which social psychology can aid in the construction of a general sociology. When conceived as social philosophy, it is evident that sociology in its genetic aspect may be regarded as the philosophy of history. Now, social psychology in its genetic aspect has also to do with the problem of a philosophy of history on its subjective side. Group psychical processes are the historical processes on their *subjective* side *par excellence*. When the genetic aspect of social psychology is fully worked out, therefore, it should yield a philosophy of history. Without entering upon any discussion of the difficulties of such a discipline, we would merely remark that such a subjective interpretation of historical processes would seem possible, if any interpretation is. If the psychical factor is the unifying, life-preserving, and life-developing factor in the group, it would seem that, if any philosophy of history whatever is attainable, it must be reached through the interpretation of the psychical process of societary development, that is, through the explanation of the process of growth of what we may, for want of a better term, call the "social mind." Such a subjective philosophy of history, however, would undoubtedly need supplementing by reference to those physical facts which constantly affect the process of social growth; and such a supplementing it would be the duty of sociology to furnish in its complete interpretation of the historico-genetic process of societies.

If the study of social psychology may be regarded as necessary to the further development of sociology, it is hardly of less importance for the special social sciences. Even that social science which from its nature is most bound by the facts of the physical world, namely, economics, would be greatly helped by the development of social psychology. Within the last twenty years economic thinkers have come to look more and more to individual psychology for new and deeper interpretations of the economic life. They have done so with some degree of success, both because individual psychology is a factor in all social interpretation, and because of its essential unity with social psychology. Where they have failed, they have failed chiefly because they have lacked a social psychology to complete their view. Take, for instance, the problem of value. The Austrian economists were successful in explaining the phenomenon of economic value in so far as they referred it to a psychological origin ; they were unsuccessful in explaining it in so far as they referred it to a purely individual origin. Economic value is now widely admitted to be a social phenomenon, to be explained only through reference to the social life as a whole, or, at least, to the life of the particular group within which it appears. The last word upon value is, however, far from said, and social psychology may yet throw much light upon this fundamental economic problem. The theory of consumption furnishes another illustration. So long as there was no subjective interpretation of the economic life, consumption occupied no place in the discussions of economic writers. Now, however, the theory of consumption is admitted to be one of the most important parts of economic science, though a satisfactory theory remains yet to be developed. As Professor Patten has pointed out, such a theory can be developed only along socio-psychological lines, since consumption is a matter of social (group) habits, customs, and feelings. It must, in other words, be worked out with the aid of social psychology. In the closely related question of economic crises the necessity of understanding the social psychical processes is even more plainly evident. Hitherto economic science has had almost no serious theory of crises. What has been written concerning them has often been worthless, and often, it is not too much to say, vague, mysterious, and superstitious. To the social psychologist, however, it is evident that economic crises are phenomena that lie wholly within the psychical process of group-life, and that their explanation is to be found in the mechanism of that process. A satisfactory theory of economic crises, if such can ever be given, must be reached through the aid of social psychology. Illustrations of the service which social psychology might render to economic science might be multiplied *ad libitum*. Among the more important questions which must receive, in whole or in part, a socio-psychological solution are those of distribution, of the rise and persistence of economic classes or groups, of the genesis and various expression of the so-called "economic instinct," and of the relation which various economic systems bear to the political, legal, and moral systems with which they are found. But perhaps enough has been said to show that economic science has much to expect from the development of a social psychology, and that its own progress in the future must be in an essentially socio-psychological direction.

In political science the need of the study of social psychology is not less evident. A host of questions concerning the origin and development of legal and political institutions await a socio-psychological settlement. Government and law are two of the most important products, or rather sides, of the social psychic process, and the attempt to understand them without understanding it is like an attempt to understand an organic species without reference to organic evolution as a whole, or to explain attention without reference to the whole process of the mental life. The natural history of government and of the various forms of government, when it comes to be properly written, must seek the help of social psychology to explain the phenomena with which it deals. Monarchy, aristocracy, and democracy, with their variations and "perversions," will be truly explained as phenomena only when they are shown to be expressions of the particular psychical processes which characterize particular stages of social growth, or special social coördinations. The same method of interpretation will have to be applied to the legal systems and institutions which are bound up with government. It will be the further task of political science to show, through the facts of history and ethnography, what forms of government and of law are regularly associated with certain types of social psychic coördination. Thus it is possible that some degree of prevision may be reached as regards the relation between a society and its form of government; but no exact prevision, since, as individual psychology teaches, no two psychical coördinations can ever be exactly alike. On this account a socio-psychological interpretation of political and legal phenomena will, perhaps, be unacceptable to those who, like Comte, long for a rigid science of society, a "social physics," which shall make possible in social life the exact prevision of the mathematical sciences.

Concerning the inner life of the state, as well as concerning political and legal systems, social psychology will have somewhat to say. The problem of political parties, of their rise, growth, and disappearance, lies almost wholly within its territory. Here, too, belongs the explanation of those disturbances of the political life called revolutions. The objective interpretations of revolutions have notoriously failed; none of them have been principles of universal, or almost universal, applicability. If any principle of explanation of universal validity can be found, it must be a socio-psychological principle; for revolutions are matters of social habit, feeling, and belief, that is, of the social psychic process.

The need of social psychology in the judging of social programs for reform may here also be noted. The real objections to the propositions of socialism, for example, are mainly socio-psychological, inasmuch as socialism concerns social organization. A thorough understanding of the psychical life of society will furnish criteria for the just criticism of the propositions of socialism. Through social psychology their consistency or inconsistency with the psychical process of social development can be shown, and a judgment formed as to the probable effect of a socialistic régime upon that process. Not alone the propositions of socialism, but also other programs for social betterment, need the criticism of social psychology. The propositions of the individualist as well as those of the socialist are likely to show the lack of a proper understanding of the psychical life of society. In fact, the proper method of procedure in all attempts at general social betterment can be determined only through social psychology. As individual psychology must underlie the doctrine of individual education, so a full knowledge of social psychology must underlie the doctrine of social transformation; that is, a "social pedagogy" or "teleology" must be developed from a knowledge of the processes of normal social growth, of psychical adjustment and readjustment in society, just as pedagogy is developed from a knowledge of similar processes in the individual. When social psychology has reached the completed stage in which it can yield a doctrine of social betterment, or "social teleology," it is possible that there will be one other person beside the socialist who knows exactly what he wants done for the betterment of society; that person will be the social psychologist. The methods of social improvement which he may propose will perhaps not pretend to be so speedy and cocksure as those of socialism, but they will at least have the merit of resting upon a knowledge of the nature of the social process. We claim, therefore, for the study of social psychology ultimately a practical as well as a theoretical value.

We have already reached in our discussion the territory of ethics. In so far as ethics is a social science, it rests upon the facts of the psychical life of society, and so has much to expect from the development of social psychology. The phenomenon of moral valuation affords an illustration. Moral value, like economic value, has now come to be regarded as a social phenomenon; that is, it is regarded as explicable only through the psychical life of society as a whole, not through the life of the individual. The reason why society regards one act as virtuous and another as wicked, one thing as having moral value and another as not, must, in the last resort, be found in the nature of the social psychic process, and can be understood only through understanding it, that is, through social psychology. The relation of beliefs to the moral life is another problem which illustrates the dependence of ethics upon the development of social psychology. The function of beliefs in the moral life of society, especially of the beliefs in God, in the immortality of the soul, and in moral freedom and responsibility, needs to be made out, and to be embodied by ethics in its discussion of the facts of the moral life. Whether the ethical activities of society can be carried on and ethical progress be possible without these beliefs, that is, whether they are essential economies of the social psychic process or not, is a question which social psychology alone can answer, yet a question of the greatest importance to moral as well as social philosophy.

In this article, intended merely as a plea for the study of social psychology, it is not the place to discuss either the difficulties of the construction of such a science or the methods it should employ. Of these we shall speak later. What we trust we have made clear is the need of such a science in any rational attempt to solve the problems of the social sciences. It is certainly essential to the interpretation of the societary process as a whole. It is needed in economics, political science, and ethics to correct and supplement prevailing theories and to formulate new ones. Finally, it is needed for the criticism of false and for the construction of wise programs for social betterment.

CHARLES A. ELLWOOD.

THE UNIVERSITY OF CHICAGO.

CONTRIBUTIONS TO THE COMPARATIVE STUDY OF ASSOCIATION.[1]

I.

THE various attempts to describe and interpret the phenomena of associate life have left upon the minds of those making such attempts a very definite impression that the problems encountered were far from simple. Human society, as it exists today among civilized races, is a reality which embodies the most complex and highly evolved activities of the most complex and highly evolved organisms known to our intelligence. And since these organisms have an evolution which proceeds, phylogenetically, from primitive protoplasm and recapitulates, ontogenetically, a considerable number of its earlier phases, we need not be surprised, perhaps, that their activities should be difficult, indeed, of adequate analysis and interpretation. Certain it is that these activities are multiplied and various; that they are blended with, and melted into, each other in a manner to render their isolation extremely difficult. Again, they are most bafflingly evanescent, while their sphere of manifestation is so vast as to put a comprehensive survey of its reaches practically beyond the power of the individual investigator. Because of these characteristics the attempts at the systematic observation and analysis of the phenomena of society have been constantly threatened with the danger of attaining, at most, only a qualified success.

Fronting such difficulties, the majority of investigators seem to have been impelled, according to circumstances and type of mind, in one of two general directions. Apparently they have been inclined either toward the ascertainment and exhibition of the laws, principles, elements, etc., of the whole mass of fact conveniently styled "societary," or else to devote their energies

[1] Other papers, dealing with the subject in a more positive way, will appear at convenient intervals. The object of the present article is to present certain general considerations preliminary to a more specific treatment of particular phases of the subject-matter.

solely to the descriptive and analytic consideration of the characteristics of some one phase of the entire phenomenal complex. It is unnecessary to discuss here the relative vulnerability of these two points of attack or to compare at length the merits of the different methods of approach appropriate to each. It is probable that each point of attack is of high significance, and that each method is destined to play a part of great import to the general development of the science of sociology.

Were this a comparative study of sociologies, rather than of the subject-matter of sociology, it would be of interest at this point to make an analysis of the works of the various writers upon subjects social, to the end of determining the motives, particular phases treated, points of attack, methods of procedure, and substantial results of each. After this preliminary step had been taken and each work had been, as it were, "reduced to its elements," it would then be in order to make the further attempt, through a still more searching analysis and comparison, to trace back all these elements to certain fundamental factors, and, having found these factors, to exhibit synthetically the coördination and correlation of the whole about them as it has actually occurred thus far in the process of growth. To be sure, the relation to the entire age environment would have to be kept constantly in view at each step, but when the whole task had been completed, it would be surprising, indeed, were it not discovered that in large degree these different works form parts—widely sundered, possibly—of a developing unity whose symmetries, naturally, can be but vaguely foreshadowed in the early evolution of a comparatively small number of its constituent factors. Such a comprehensive survey of the field, however, would of itself require many pages, and must, therefore, be left to another time and place. It will answer our purpose here to anticipate one of its possible results in calling attention to a trait which, in varying degree, seems to be characteristic of the majority of the works thus far appearing under titles which may be classed as sociological.

Influenced partly by the prevailing trend of thought, which is wont to consider each fact as a term in a genetic series, partly by the force of certain illustrious examples, and in part also by the possible advantages for analysis and explanation to be gained in so doing, sociologists, while dealing with the phenomena of human association, have been in the habit of making use of "analogies" drawn from the phenomena of association as these are found among forms of life lower than man. This habit is so widespread, and in many instances so marked, as to command serious consideration from anyone making a study such as the one alluded to above. It is as though there existed a tacit assumption that, in the task of describing and interpreting human association, help is in some way to be gotten from references to associational phenomena as exhibited by lower forms of life.[1]

That this assumption is not without foundation the writer considers there are good grounds for asserting. *A priori* it seems as reasonable to suppose that the association of the lower forms of life has as much of value to tell us concerning that of the higher forms as has the function of the brain, or of the eye, for example, in the lower organisms to tell of that function in the higher organisms. A given associational form, factor, or center, which, as such, has had a development antecedent to its development among men, may reasonably be expected to have light thrown upon its higher phases by a careful consideration of its lower phases. A form of associational activity, the family for example, may be better studied in its more evolved stage, which we call the human family, if it is first studied in the lower stages of its development, let these be found where they may and be called as we will.

Of course, it is not assumed that the relation to each other of the terms in an evolutional series has been adequately comprehended or explained. Between any pair of terms in any such series there intervenes a lacuna which we have not filled, but have simply ignored as by common consent. The terms of a genetic series are after all but the focal points of one side of a process, the beginning, the end, and the other sides of which we neither see nor are able to picture to ourselves in a satisfactory manner. It is conceiv-

---

[1] This assumption is so greatly in harmony with the spirit of the age that it has gone unquestioned for the most part. Whether this or that particular relation obtains between human association and animal association has been vigorously debated, but that *some* relation exists has seldom been denied.

able that when our knowledge relative to these shall have grown somewhat, the evolutionary hypothesis itself may be found subject to modifications of which we do not now dream.

Again, the anatomist, the physiologist, and the neurologist — the psychologist will presently be counted of this goodly company — in view of the great complexity of the subject-matter presented to each — a complexity the individual factors of which the facilities of no laboratory can possibly enable the investigator to isolate and study under controlled conditions — have found themselves compelled to descend the evolutional series until they encounter in other reaches of nature a simpler condition of things than they must confront among human beings. Learning from this, they reascend the scale step by step, taking careful note of each new factor as it appears, until they stand again before their problem as it presents itself at the level of mankind; but now equipped with a knowledge of its genesis and a familiarity with its component parts which make of it a very much simpler problem indeed, though, to be sure, there are yet left difficulties enough and to spare. If these sciences are advantaged by extending their field of observation downward along the scale of life sufficiently to include the simpler and less evolved stages of their subject-matter, the question at once arises whether sociology would not be similarly advantaged by a similar process. The answer depends to a certain extent upon the nature of the subject-matter of sociology — whether it resembles that of the sciences alluded to above in those particular respects which have made such a proceeding so valuable to them.

Confining ourselves to the briefest and most comprehensive statement as to what, in actuality, has been, and is today, the subject-matter of sociology, we may say that it is *the association of human beings with each other.* The task which sociology has constantly striven to perform is the analysis and interpretation of this plexus of phenomena.[1] Let us see what the performance of this task involves.

[1] Long citations from the works of the various sociological writers in illustration of this would be tedious and superfluous. It is thought that the reader has only to call to mind the general outline of subjects treated and results arrived at in these works to be convinced of the fairness of the statement of the text.

By association[1] we mean, in the most general sense, activity[1] conceived either as incited in, or put forth by, one thing[1] in virtue of the existence of another; activity conceived as the expression,[2] and as the possible occasion, of the apparent constitution,[2] of the relations of one thing with another.

No dogmatic attempt is here made to fix the content of the term "association." It is far too early in the sociologic day for such an attempt to appear other than ill-timed. Usage, guided by the results of further research and by certain practical considerations, will probably determine in the end what this content shall be. But until usage shall have attained years of discretion and authority, it will be allowable for each writer to state for himself what meaning he will attach to the term. In the proper place the reasons will be given which have led the present writer to the use indicated in the text. Since this use is for the larger part one of the latest results, rather than the earliest presupposition, of the work which it is the task of these articles to outline, the end rather than the beginning of the account will manifestly be the most appropriate point at which to mass, and discuss in detail, these reasons. The only excuse for giving, thus early in the study, a tentative definition of the term is that the reader may have from the start a clue to what is meant when the word "association" is used in a given connection.

Now, this association, composed of the activities of the associating beings, is, in part at least, a function of what these beings are, and the complexity of this varies directly as does the complexity of the beings themselves.[3] And if those sciences, some of which were enumerated above, which have as their task the comprehension and interpretation of what man is, are driven by the complexity of their subject-matter to consider what man was, how he evolved, what he was in that evolution, it seems a likely hypothesis that those sciences whose task is the analysis

[1] It is to be noted that "association" is here used in the sense of associa*ting* and that "activity" has a meaning far broader than would be covered by the expression "movement which has, or has had, psychic concomitants." The word "thing" is also used in the most general and inclusive sense.

[2] It is not intended to assert that we first have *unrelated* things which afterward become related in some mysterious manner. Things and their relations grow up together; but the fact of this growth seems to make it necessary to suppose an entering-in to the series of "an element of the new" (whatever that may mean) at appropriate points. To embrace both these facts we allude to the "expression" and to the "apparent constitution" of relations.

[3] See HERBERT SPENCER, *Principles of Biology*, edition of 1884, Vol. I, p. 156.

and interpretation of what the relations, activities, associations of these complex beings are must also be driven to a consideration of what these were; and that accordingly sociology, in order to deal adequately with the association of human beings, must pay most careful and considerate attention to the association of beings lower than those we see fit to call human.[1] In view, therefore, of the characteristics of the phenomena to be dealt with and of the resulting difficulties involved in the attempt to isolate and observe under relatively simple conditions any particular aspect of the same, it seems not improbable that the comparative method, which has yielded such worthy results in other sciences confronted with a similar complexity of subject-matter, may be susceptible of fruitful application in the field of societary phenomena. For it is perhaps not an unwarrantable hypothesis that association has a genetic history corresponding, in large outlines at least, to that of the associating organisms.

It will at once be evident that from the standpoint here implied the distinctions between sociology and other sciences will be based upon considerations varying in their nature with the particular science which at a given time we may be seeking to distinguish from sociology. A ground of distinction which will hold good when certain others fail to do so will be found in what is usually designated by the phrase "point of view." Reference is made to that aspect of point of view under which it appears as the observer's mental attitude toward the phenomena under investigation. This basis of distinction is particularly useful in helping us to differentiate from each other branches of knowledge concerned with the analysis and interpretation of phenomena related to each other in the process of development. An integration of phenomena, which occurs in growth, is of such a nature as to give rise to some curious relations between a science proposing to deal with a given phase or stage of that integration and other sciences dealing with earlier stages or phases of the same. The latter are in a way propædeutic to the former,

---

[1] It is here that the so-called "biological explanation of society"—the oft-heralded demise of which has a rhythmic periodicity deserving the attention of some astute investigator—may one day wreak a poetic vengeance upon those who are so fond of proclaiming its defunct condition.

while the former embodies in its subject-matter and point of view the subject-matter and points of view of the latter in a manner which makes the differentiating from each other of the sciences concerned a matter of less ease than might be supposed.   One or two illustrations may help to make clear what is meant here.   Before a given science (let us say psychology) shall be able to deal to the best advantage with certain phenomena (as those of vision), other sciences (in this case physics, chemistry, anatomy, and physiology) must each in turn have dealt to the fullest of their capabilities with the phenomena in question; and in so doing they will have prepared the phenomena[1] for the psychologist's consideration.   Here the propædeutic relation, sustained by the first four sciences mentioned to psychology, is very plain.   Another instance may better serve us in making more explicit the meaning implied in the reference to the second phase of this relation, made some lines above. Suppose we are bent upon an understanding of a commonplace hand clasp.   We may say roughly that physics would be concerned with it as a group of physical changes; chemistry, as a group of chemical changes ; anatomy, as an assemblage of bodily structures; physiology, with the functioning of these structures. Psychology would consider it in its bearing upon the structure and function of consciousness.

If this were all, the thing might be simple enough ; but, unfortunately, things are not so simple here as they seem.   In the case of the actual hand clasp we get no chemical change without including a physical change also; we get no functioning of the bodily structures without having bound up with it both chemical changes and physical changes; and we get no functioning without appropriate structures.   When the psychologist comes to consider, in its relation to consciousness, this complex of phenomena we call a hand clasp, he must deal with it as an assemblage of bodily structures, as a functioning of these structures, as a group of chemical changes, and as a group of physical changes; and in so dealing with it he must use the light thrown

---

[1] The same thing may be put from the other side by saying, "prepared the psychologist to investigate the phenomena."

upon it by physics, chemistry, anatomy, and physiology. At this stage of the proceedings it becomes greatly desirable to find some mark which will keep one's conception of psychology from incontinently swallowing the conception one may have formed of any one of the other sciences mentioned. It seems to the writer that such a mark is found in that aspect of "point of view" before referred to.[1] While the psychologist, as such, must consider the same aspect of the complex of phenomena as does the physiologist, for example, and from the same standpoint also (*in so far as is implied in seeing as clearly as does the physiologist the hand clasp as the functioning of certain bodily structures*), it yet remains true that while so seeing it he sees it *as centripetal* to a different focus of attention from that toward which the physiologist orients it. The psychologist sees it as centripetal to the one focal point of attention called "consciousness," and he sees it as centrifugal to all else. It is in this point of most intense attention, in this focusing of the facts, in this direction of greatest stress, that we find a characteristic upon which to base a distinction which will serve to differentiate the sciences from each other at times when classifications based upon certain other grounds fail to remain valid.

And with this distinction in mind we may say of the psychologist that he may consider anything in the heavens above or in the earth beneath, and so long as he considers it with reference to the structure and function of consciousness, no man may say him nay, or justly complain that he invades the "fields" of the other sciences.

We return now to the sociologist, who has been purposely left out of account for a time. In his consideration of the hand clasp his attention's focal point will be upon the associating of the persons whose hands so meet, as expressed, or as set up, in the hand clasp. It is in whatever the hand clasp has to tell him of this that the sociologist is interested. But in order to be able to understand what the hand clasp has to tell him—in order to understand its language, if the figure may be allowed—he must

[1] Of course, it must not be inferred from this that the writer is seeking to advance this as a panacea for taxonomic ills.

know what the hand clasp is physiologically, psychologically, ethically, chemically, physically; and in order thus to know what it is, he must be able to see it from the standpoints of the sciences in question.[1] It must be remembered constantly that the sociologist wants to know about the associating, the relating, the reciprocality, of the persons concerned in this hand clasp, as that associating is expressed in, or set up by, the hand clasp. And if he would thoroughly comprehend this, he must avail himself of analyses of this act which sift it to its very ultimates. He must know what it means when seen from the standpoints of those sciences which have made it their task to study it from their own points of view. It may be to them state of consciousness, bodily function, or physical change ; and while it will be to him also state of consciousness, bodily function, and physical change, yet, translating these into terms of association, he will read them as the components or phases — psychical, physiological, physical — of the association of the persons concerned as expressed, or as instituted, in the act named. In other words, while he will see the phenomena as state of consciousness, bodily function, and physical change, and see them in these differing aspects as clearly as does the psychologist, the physiologist, or the physicist, he will none the less see them in every case as centripetal to his attention's focus, *i. e.*, the associating, the relating, the reciprocal functioning, of the persons concerned.

Thus we are brought to a point where we may say of the sociologist, as we have said of the psychologist : Let him consider any fact the relation of which to his task he can make clear, and so long as he considers it as centripetal to his attention's focus — the association of human beings — he cannot justly be complained

---

[1] This does not mean that the sociologist must be ethical philosopher, physiologist, psychologist, chemist, and physicist, in the sense of being a specialist in each, any more than the psychologist dealing with vision must be specialist enough in physics, or physiology, or chemistry, or anatomy, to have discovered and formulated the principles he uses which belong to these respective domains of science. The sociologist need not have elaborated all the data he uses, any more than the biologist needs to have elaborated his microscope. But he must be able to see the meaning of those data from the standpoint of the man who elaborated them, just as clearly as possible, if he proposes to make a proper use of them for his own purposes.

of as an intruder, or as an interloper in fields of research already covered by the investigations of other sciences.

Primarily, then, the focus of the sociologist's attention will be upon the association of human beings ; upon their reciprocality; upon their activities, considered as functional relations and as functional relatings of man to man ; briefly and somewhat figuratively, upon human beings as functions of each other. As sociologist he will see all things else as centripetal to this. To learn in what this association consists, both as a whole and in any given phase ; to analyze it to the last degree ; to learn how it came to be ; to discover its meaning and the laws of its growth : these are tasks to which the sociologist dedicates his energies. But he has not gone far toward the performance of these before he discovers that human association is a thing with a history, and that in order to comprehend it he must study it historically. It represents an evolution, a development, and can be thoroughly understood in its later stages only by being thoroughly understood in its earlier stages. It is a term in a great series, and as such its relations to the other terms demand careful attention. It is also an epitome of a great series, and the nature and growth of that epitomization, together with the relations to each other, and to the whole, of the epitomized parts, must be painstakingly traced out. It is a many-phased and many-factored complex of phenomena, and each phase and factor must be subjected to exhaustive and methodical research. Thus out of the sociologist's primary attempt to describe and interpret human association there grows, as naturally and inevitably as root from seed, the necessity of the further attempt to describe and interpret association as it is found among forms of life less complex than the human form ; just as out of the attempt to understand the human physique there arose the demand for an understanding of the physique of allied, though lower, forms.

It would seem that in response to this necessity a comparative sociology must sooner or later be wrought out. It cannot be produced by one or by any fixed number of investigators. When it assumes its rightful proportions, it will not be a mere addendum to sociology as it is now known, or to some other than a comparative sociology. Quite the contrary. It will be a growing organism into which will be assimilated and integrated the labors of successive workers, each of whom will have devoted himself more or less exclusively to the consideration of some one phase or factor of the whole. It is not impossible that the comparative method in sociology, from being considered at first as a mere method, and later as a method plus certain results, will later still be seen to be the best available symbol of the habits of growth according to which the reality considered has developed and continues to develop; and in accordance with which also the science of that reality has had, and must continue to have, its evolution. For only so can sociology become that which it is an ambition of every science to become eventually, *i. e.*, a perfect account of the actual constitution and behavior of that aspect of reality, the importance of which to human interest has called into being the science in question.

Since the application of the comparative method[1] to a given subject-matter implies that those portions of that subject-matter which it is proposed to compare with each other exhibit some common trait or are susceptible of being viewed from a common standpoint, and since, in accordance with the foregoing, we assume that the subject-matter of sociology is susceptible of having applied to it the comparative method, the question arises at once: What are these common traits, what are these common standpoints, which will serve as fundamentals upon which to base our comparative study of the phenomena of association? For, up to a certain degree, the more numerous and the more constant these may be, the more likely is the application of the comparative method to yield a body of data of sufficient importance to rise to the dignity of a science.

[1] The words "the comparative method" are not unambiguous. The whole process of gaining knowledge is a comparison of one thing with another. *The* comparative method may be roughly characterized as a specialization of this general process applied to data bearing a certain serial relation to each other. This relation is usually that obtaining in the genetic series. Organisms and their activities, structures and their functions, have an evolution. To comprehend them in a given phase of that evolution we study them in other phases, higher and lower, both in ontogenetic and in phylogenetic series. To do this is, generally speaking, to follow the comparative method, as it is commonly received.

That there are certain factors — possibly certain groups of factors — which make their appearance in the earliest and simplest forms of the associational complex, and are distinctly traceable, under such modifications as development may be expected to entail, throughout the whole range of those forms, from that displayed by primitive protoplasm to that displayed by the most highly civilized man, is a hypothesis which, in a more or less clearly recognized way, underlies a large proportion of the sociological work of our time.[1] But the clear demonstration of what these common factors are, and the exhibition of their relation to each other and to the remaining factors, is a task which in large measure yet remains to be performed. The reasons for this are manifest. Its performance is involved in the continuous growth of a science of comparative sociology, and the one cannot be completed short of the completion of the other. From this it may readily enough be seen why the answer to the questions just proposed is one which cannot be given in advance of the actual work of analysis and interpretation of the whole societary complex, for this analysis and interpretation is necessary to the discovery and determination of the existence and nature of these factors. The work is more than the mere tracing out of the interconnections of factors the existence and characteristics of which have previously been well known. We are confronted with a case in which the task of discovery and that of development, or exhibition, are two mutually dependent processes, and the continuance of the one is momentarily conditioned upon the continuance of the other. Highly desirable though it may be to be able at this stage to point out in a perfectly clear and definite manner those factors, the existence of which will afford us a common ground upon which to compare with each other the different terms of the associational series, it is, nevertheless, impossible. We might quite as reasonably expect the explorer of an unknown country to furnish us, in advance of his explorations, with a detailed map of the land he expects to visit. We must content ourselves for the present with the assumption that such common factors do exist, and leave the proof of

[1] See, for example, GIDDINGS, *Principles of Sociology*, pp. 61 ff.

their existence, together with a delineation of their characteristics and affiliations, to the progress of the science.

But, while one may refuse to make the attempt to describe in advance of their exploration the fields of a new science, he might less readily be excused for leaving his readers with no hint as to the general direction his own immediate excursions into those fields may be expected to take. While making no pretense, therefore, to enumerate the common factors which future investigation may find to exist in the different terms of the associational series, some slight attempt will be made to indicate, in a preliminary way, the nature of those common factors, the relations of which to the various forms of the associational complex this series of papers may be expected to consider in due time.

It will be remembered that the subject-matter of sociology was tentatively defined [1] to be the activities of living organisms, *when these activities are considered from a certain focal point of attention;* and that the description and interpretation of these activities, viewed in this orientation, were posited [1] as the most immediate task of sociology.

It is significant that among those characteristics of the activities of things which are earliest to command attention, none is more striking than that of their apparent dependence upon antecedent activities. When the consequent activity is that of living matter, we call it a response to the antecedent activity which is considered to be the stimulus of its consequent. Postponing for the present the consideration of some very important peculiarities of the more intimate nature of this stimulus-organism-response relationship, we have to note here that it obtains generally throughout the whole range of living matter. There is no activity of any organism which can conceivably be without appropriate relations to adequate stimuli. Again, these stimuli are separable into certain great groups and classes. There seems a reasonable possibility, then, that the activities of living matter will themselves be separable into groupings analogous to the groupings of their stimuli ; and, owing to the

[1] See p. 675.

connection of the organism with its own activities, and through these with the stimuli of these activities, it would not be a matter of great surprise if further research should reveal a grouping of organisms corresponding to the groupings of stimuli and activities. Furthermore, we might hope to find a development in the nature of these groupings which shall pro‑ceed *pari passu* with the development of the stimulability of the organism. It would also be a matter of some interest to afford a tentative classification of stimuli based upon the duration of the period during which they are respectively operant upon the organism's evolution. It would be found, of course, that while certain groups of stimuli affect living matter from its earliest to its latest developmental phase, certain other groups are effective during a comparatively limited number of these phases.

These are but hints of a whole series of problems of greater or less interest which are suggested for solution *à propos* of this stimulus-organism-response relationship. For the present we shall address ourselves to the attempt to describe and analyze the associational phenomena incident to the affecting of organic life by certain of the great groups of stimuli.[1]

By way of recapitulating the contents of the foregoing pages we may say :

1. That the subject-matter of sociology, as determined by an inspection of the work thus far done in the science, has been chiefly the activities of human beings, when these activities are considered as oriented toward a certain focal point of attention

2. That the task of sociology, as determined by a similar inspection, has been the analysis and interpretation of these activities as seen in this orientation.

3. That the attempts to perform this task have demonstrated

[1] The value in the associational life of mankind of that group of stimuli we call "sex" is being considered in the pages of this Journal by Professor William I. Thomas. As the work of the present writer is, in a measure, an attempt to carry into the domains of the lower forms of life the methods and type of research used by Professor Thomas among the races of mankind, the reader is referred to the articles in question. See AMERICAN JOURNAL OF SOCIOLOGY, Vol. I, pp. 434–45; Vol. III, pp. 31–63, 754–76; Vol. IV, pp. 474–88. The next paper of the series, "Sex in Primitive Morality," is to appear in the May number of this Journal.

the nature of this subject-matter to be such as to demand that it be studied in the simpler phases of its development, as well as in the more complex phases, if we are to hope to arrive at an adequate understanding of any given phase. It is a corollary of this that, if we are to comprehend perfectly any given type of association as it appears among human beings, we must study it as it appears among beings lower than human, if it be found to have an existence among these lower beings.

4. That this comparison of one phase with another, higher or lower in the genetic series of associational phenomena, means nothing less than the application of the comparative method to the subject-matter of sociology.

5. That, in consideration of the nature of the relations obtaining between the activities of living organisms and certain great groups of stimuli, it appears that these stimulus-complexes afford bases upon which to attempt a comparison of the organism- and the activity-groupings growing up around these complexes.

Ralph G. Kimble.

The University of Chicago.

REVIEWS.

John Ruskin, Social Reformer. By J. A. HOBSON. Boston : Dana, Estes & Co., 1898. Pp. ix + 357.

A BOOK by Mr. Hobson is anticipated with exceptional interest by those who are looking for original contributions to the economic and sociological thought of today. In this book he might seem to have gone into a new field, and yet to have precluded the possibility of contributing anything original. One immediately discovers, however, that the writer is on familiar ground, though leading us in new paths. He has done several things remarkably well. In the first place, as a literary production, the bringing together of scattered and disconnected utterances into a system which should be logical without losing its literary form, is an achievement ; in the second place, the discovery of a philosophy in Mr. Ruskin's writings will be to many people a revelation ; in the third place, the tribute paid to Mr. Ruskin as an economist, though it may seem exaggerated to those who do not know his writings well, appears to be amply supported ; finally, Mr. Hobson's personal contributions, by way of expounding or criticising Mr. Ruskin, are illuminating.

Mr. Hobson points out in the beginning how, in spite of no signs of interest in social movements in Mr. Ruskin's early life, there was a natural progression toward his later views, evidenced even in the first volume of *Modern Painters,* and not attaining full expression until quite late years.

Though incautious and sometimes extravagant in words, John Ruskin was a plodding and careful thinker ; his thoughts had never been directed, by necessary contact with his early interests, to the social and economic structure of societies, and therefore he had never formed any definite convictions relating to them. Never being thrown into the eddying tide of any of the radical movements in politics or philosophy which marked that restless age, he was not impelled by contact with other fervent souls into hasty speculations or cheaply acquired convictions upon the fundamental problems of society.

Even after he had begun to express his social ideas, he suffered from the misfortune of having thought so thoroughly and written so lucidly.

No great writer has shown a more contemptuous disregard for those literary arts of concealment commonly used to secure an appearance of consistency; no one has so freely and loudly proclaimed his repudiation of past pronouncements upon important topics; in no case has this serviceable frankness been treated with such lack of courtesy and understanding. Because Mr. Ruskin has always striven to confer upon the public that greatest service which a thinker can confer, by making everything he writes "part of a great confession;" because he has set down all his thoughts and feelings in their natural order, without exaggeration or extenuation of their form and intensity, many of his critics have chosen to represent him as a loose and reckless thinker, borne along by sudden gusts of sentiment, and void of any stable unity of thought or clear order of development. Now the utter groundlessness of such criticism is demonstrable by anyone who takes the trouble to read his representative books in the order of their publication.

In addition to the influence exerted by Mr. Ruskin's scientific studies, Mr. Hobson points out his obligation to Turner and Carlyle: "Turner made him an art prophet, Carlyle a social reformer." Mr. Hobson shows the growth of Mr. Ruskin's ideas by giving a very admirable chronological summary of the steps by which he advanced from art to social reform, which he sums up in the statement:

Such is the general growth of Mr. Ruskin's thought and labors, from nature to art, through art to human life, in the art of life a growing sense of the demands of eternal law in the making and governance of human society founded on principles of justice and humanity.

Instead of abandoning his proper work as an art teacher in order rashly to embark in political economy, for which he had neither natural aptitude nor the requisite training and knowledge, ... Mr. Ruskin's first qualification is that of being a skilled specialist in the finer qualities of work on the one hand, and of enjoyment or consumption on the other hand. Both from personal practice and from long habits of close observation of the work of skillful men in many places, he obtained a wide and varied knowledge of the handling of different tools and materials for the production of useful and beautiful goods. This experience was by no means confined to painting, sculpture, and the so-called "fine arts," but comprised the practical work of architecture, wood and metal work, pottery, jewelry, weaving, and other handicrafts.

His investigations into agriculture, both on the continent of Europe and in Britain, were minute and painstaking; and though his experiments in reclaiming and draining land were not always sucessful, they indicated close knowledge of the concrete facts.

Moreover, Mr. Ruskin made a lifelong study of animal and vegetable life, and of the structure and composition of the earth, thus gaining an intimate acquaintance with the nature of the raw materials of that wealth which formed the chief subject-matter of commercial economy. He had spent most of his laborious life in patient detailed observation of nature and the works of man. Both from contemporary observation and from study of history, the actual processes by which large classes of goods were produced and consumed were familiar to him. How many of the teachers of political economy who have been so scornful of Mr. Ruskin's claims possessed a tithe of this practical knowledge?

In addition Mr. Ruskin had as qualifications a remarkable mastery of language, fearless honesty, and at least one of "the most analytic" minds in Europe.

His arraignment of current political economy may be formally divided into two parts. Firstly, he accuses the science of commercial wealth of wrongfully assuming the title and function of political economy. Secondly, he impugns the accuracy of many of the fundamental doctrines of this commercial science, and imputes to them an injurious influence upon the happiness and morality of society.

Mr. Hobson seems to make out his case that Mr. Ruskin successfully controverted the claim of the older economists that they could isolate the hypothetical self-seeking man and then make allowance for the disturbing influence of other motives; he is especially successful in demonstrating that the "disturbing elements" are not of the same nature as the other influences. This has certainly led more than any other criticism of the older political economy to a wider interpretation by the later students. What Mr. Ruskin has also demonstrated, and what the newer economist does not always appreciate, is that when the latter

points out how raising the character of civic life will react upon the efficiency of industry, his arguments are so many tacit admissions that the segregation of purely industrial phenomena is not, in fact, the convenient hypothesis for political economy which he averred it was.

Mr. Hobson sums up his chapter which gives Mr. Ruskin's criticisms of current political economy in these words:

Our claim is not that Mr. Ruskin has formed a system of sociology, or that he has advanced far toward such a system, but that he has pointed the way to such a science, and has laid down certain hypotheses of fact and terminology such as are consistent with advances made independently by other scientific men. By insisting upon the reduction of all economic terms, such as value, cost, utility, etc., to terms of "vitality," by insisting upon the organic integrity and unity of all human activities, and the organic nature of the coöperation of the social units, and finally by furnishing a social ideal of reasonable humanity, Mr. Ruskin has amply justified his claim as a pioneer in the theory of social economics.

Mr. Ruskin's "humanizing" of the term "wealth" takes the form of asking with regard to the value of goods: (1) What good human purpose can they serve? (2) What kind of persons will get them? (3) How much will each of these persons get? He also analyzes the problem of cost to correspond with his analysis of value, first inquiring as to the "intrinsic nature of the work in relation to the worker;" and second, "this determination of intrinsic cost requires to be supplemented by consideration of the capacities of the workers;" third, "in estimating the cost as we estimate the utility of a quantity of goods, we require to know how the labor is distributed."

Mr. Hobson does not fail to point out Mr. Ruskin's exaggerations and failure to see some of the merits in modern competitive industry, but he defends him against the charges made of totally ignoring the value of machinery and modern improvements, showing that these criticisms usually arise from a consideration of isolated observations, instead of following Mr. Ruskin's qualifications of his own statements. There is also pointed out Mr. Ruskin's inadequate appreciation of the significance of interest, showing that he fails to see the importance of making money serviceable where most needed. This recognition of Mr. Ruskin's weakness gives all the more force to Mr. Hobson's vigorous defense of Mr. Ruskin's constructive teachings which have seemed to so many chimerical. In spite of Tory politics and an undue confidence in the voluntary devotion of the upper classes to the lower, Mr. Ruskin's state socialism has largely triumphed thus far both over individualism and social democracy. His emphasis of the physiological basis of the social question, his admirable conception of education, his denial of equality while demanding equality of opportunity, his emphasis of the importance of agriculture, and his insistence on the general provision of employment, are obtaining more recognition every day. The strength and weakness of Mr. Ruskin's state socialism give Mr. Hobson an opportunity of, at the same time, criticising him and many current reformers, but show the futility of depending on the voluntary action of the upper classes and the necessity of constantly resorting to democratic action.

Mr. Hobson's closing chapters give a concise account of the industrial experiments which Mr. Ruskin undertook, and a final tribute to his work and influence, concluding with this paragraph:

To clarify the vision, to elevate the aim, to humanize, and so to dignify, the ends of conduct, are the persistent endeavors of John Ruskin's teaching. His hope and his appeal as reformer of society is to those misdirected or ill-directed forces of character which have made us so successful as individuals and as nations in the grosser forms of activity, and which, well economized for nobler purposes, might secure for us a "greatness" measurable neither in miles of territory, millions of population, nor in volume of commerce, but in "the multiplication of human life at its highest standard."

This book will serve as a guide to the writings of Mr. Ruskin which should not only be invaluable to all students of his books, but should lead to a wider reading and appreciation of his work as a whole. It is a piece of work which probably only Mr. Hobson was prepared to do, and seems almost beyond criticism.

CHARLES ZUEBLIN.

Instinct and Reason: An Essay concerning the Relation of Instinct to Reason, with some Special Study of the Nature of Religion. By HENRY RUTGERS MARSHALL, M.A. New York: The Macmillan Co., 1898. Pp. vii + 574. $3.50.

THIS is a large book on an old question, and one is prepared to find an important contribution to psychology in it, or to be somewhat annoyed. It turns out, however, that the volume is not primarily on the relation of instinct to reason, but is a biological plea for religion. Religion is regarded as a part of the machinery of natural selection, and the race has survived because through systems of religion checks have been established on individual conduct to the advantage of the group to which the individual belongs. Three classes of instincts are considered in some detail : (1) those of service to the individual; (2) those of service to the race, that is, relating to the reproduction of the race ; and (3) those of service to the group. Religion, it is claimed, is an instinct, and an instinct of service to the group, its function being the regulation of group conduct. Mr. Marshall makes the very interesting claim, also, that, generally speaking, instinct is a safer guide than reason, reason being the variant principle, and instinct the beaten path. The standpoint naturally throws great stress upon the idea of duty, and the subordination of the individual. "Under my view, what is here called the suppression of our will to a higher will may be expressed in psychological terms as the restraint of individualistic impulses to racial ones ; that such restraint has effect upon the moral character being, of course, granted" (p. 329). ". . . . The function of religion which lies back of its ceremonial is the suppression of the tendency to individualistic, elemental impulses, in favor of those which have a higher significance. . . . . It would appear, then, that in relation to our modern complex and self-conscious intellectual life the function of religion will lie to a great extent in the restraint of reason and its subordination to faith" (pp. 297–8). It is obvious that the general view of the social importance of religion held by Mr. Marshall is very similar to that of Mr. Kidd, but differences of detail are pointed out in a special chapter.

The author is at great pains to make it appear that religion is an instinct, but it is not evident that he has done this. His treatment of instinct on the animal side is very clear, but not new in any important respect, and only preliminary, and interest is whetted in anticipation of a fine bit of work based on child-study and perhaps on ethnological data. But this does not follow; it is not even seriously attempted. The one definite case taken from children is given in a footnote, and relates to a girl, intentionally reared without mention of religious subjects, who at an early age asked her mother if she might not "say a little prayer." But though the mother and the kindergarten teacher had not given the child religious notions, it must be admitted that children get a good deal of information from others than their parents and teachers. This child had learned the word for prayer from some-one, and doubtless had some description of the practice from the same person, and the case seems not one of instinct, but of imitation. Similarly, the use of ethnological facts is scant and chary. This line is so fruitful and so unexplored in connection with instinct and habit that it seems sheer pity that a writer touching on race psychology should merely "look back into the dim past and imagine the conditions which must have existed amongst the ancestors of the human race . . . ." (p. 309). Far better consult the old travelers, unveracious as they often were. So far, then, as proof goes we have no occasion to conclude that religious feeling and practice are not socially rather than instinctively kept up. The importance of this contention appears to be, in the author's scheme, its newness, more than anything else, for he says: "But even if we assume that religious activities are not instinctive, but are entirely due to tradition and to the imitation of the example of others, even then it seems to me that we are compelled to assume that the activities have functional import in the development of the race." This is profoundly true, but it has been a commonplace ever since Spencer and others worked it out. It thus appears that the interesting field of the relation of instinct and habit to religion is not here worked out, and that, on the other hand, it was unnecessary to remind anybody that religion has had a functional value in the development of the race. It must be said, also, that when we compare his incidental interpretation of such phenomena as hallucination, circumcision, and phallic worship with the facts and practices which we may examine in such works as Stoll's *Hypnotismus und Suggestion in der Völkerpsychologie*, Andree's *Ethnographische Parallelen und Vergleiche*, and Payne Knight's *Discourse on the Worship of Priapus*, we wonder whether the construction put upon these matters by the writer could ever have occurred to him if they had not happened to fit conveniently into his general theory. But waiving these and like inadequacies, the book is an important addition to the literature which attempts to interpret social facts from the standpoint of psychology. It is unfortunate, however, that interest in the argument should be hindered by a singularly procrastinating style, to which, indeed, the generous size of the book is really due. There is so much anticipation of what is to be said, and so much revival of what has been said, that the reader is pestered with a lack of certainty that he is ever at any time in the thick of the argument.

W. I. THOMAS.

Labor Copartnership: Notes of a Visit to Co-operative Workshops, Factories, and Farms in Great Britain and Ireland, in which Employer, Employé, and Consumer Share in Ownership, Management, and Results. By HENRY D. LLOYD. New York: Harper & Bros., 1898. Pp. 351.

THIS is the chief book on coöperation since Mrs. Webb's well-known *Co-operative Movement*. Benjamin Jones' *Co-operative Production*, which followed Mrs. Webb's book, was an important account of the work done, especially by the Rochdale system, in establishing workshops, but it followed the principles laid down by Mrs. Webb's book. Mr. Lloyd has given an account of the newer form of coöperation, labor copartnership, which is succeeding in two or three directions in which productive coöperation has hitherto failed, and is at the same time laying down a new principle. The new successes are first in establishing coöperative dairies in Ireland, a most remarkable achievement in view of the previous experiences in Irish industrial reform and the prevalent opinions with regard to possibilities of organizing the Celt. The work of Mr. Plunkett, which is carefully described by Mr. Lloyd, is at once romantic and instructive. The poorest part of Ireland has been invaded by coöperation, and while the organization does not approach that adopted by the labor copartnership societies in England, it is in this direction, and with this as a goal. Mr. Lloyd quotes Mr. Plunkett as saying :

The report of the eight years' work was the history of associations composed almost exclusively of working farmers engaged in the transaction of the daily business of their members — in improving the conditions of their industry — applying to its development the most modern and complex system of commercial organization, with its federation acting as agencies for the sale and distribution of the produce of Irish farms in the large cities of England, including London, where they have to meet the competition of the world. In eight years these societies of frieze-coated farmers, in spite of their small beginnings, have transacted business amounting to close on a million sterling. And I think it would be easy to demonstrate that they have saved over a quarter of a million of profit for themselves.

Some of the interesting phases of coöperation further described are, first, more or less successful (unfortunately almost invariably less successful) experiments in coöperation on the land ; the societies in Woolwich and Glasgow furnish instances of successful coöperative farming in connection with coöperative stores; second, the development of building societies, in connection with coöperative organizations, for the housing of their members ; this is made possible both by the surplus capital owned by the coöperative societies and by the dividends paid by the coöperative societies to their members; third, the development of coöperative stores, productive societies, and building societies, with their attendant educational and recreative institutions, making some towns predominantly coöperative (Mr. Lloyd's description of Kettering and Leicester furnishes remarkable indications of the possibilities of coöperation when widely extended); fourth, the extension of coöperation in such a new direction as the provision of the "Scottish Coöperative Convalescent Seaside Home which has been built by the coöperators' money as a place of rest and recreation for their tired and sick working people on the west hills of Killbride, overlooking the sea, in one of the most beautiful spots on the shore of Scotland ; " fifth, the development of labor copartnership, and the distinction between that and the Rochdale system.

This last subject occupies the bulk of the book, introduces the new coöperative principle, and provides the one controversial subject. Mr.

Lloyd takes issue with the defenders of the Rochdale system who have followed Mrs. Webb in denouncing a bonus to labor as unnecessary and undemocratic. He quotes the statement by one of the Rochdale adherents, which explains their attitude :

The manager of the Wheat Sheaf was outspoken in his condemnation of the labor copartnership idea. It was the "creation," he said, "of an aristocracy of labor." In his opinion, the duty of coöperative manufacturers is to get the goods to the consumer at the cheapest possible price, and they have no right to make this price dearer by paying more than the market rate of wages.

The case is stated much more strongly by Mrs. Webb when she urges that the danger of labor copartnership lies in the undermining of the trade-union standard by a vertical instead of a horizontal cleavage in industry. Mr. Lloyd contends that the labor copartnership organizations have always encouraged trade-unionism, and have merely added to its benefits. He, however, includes in his book a description of the profit-sharing system of the South Metropolitan Gas Company of London, which was really introduced in order to break up trade-unionism, and has not only been successful in that, but

Mr. Livesey has himself made it an argument against municipal ownership of gas works that municipalities having no stock could not admit their employés, as his company has done, to participation in profits and management; and he has repeatedly avowed that he believes that the Employé Shareholder and Workman Director is an institution which will make socialism impossible, because it will give the wage-earner the possession of property.

This is certainly a menace to the large democratic movement of the Rochdale system, but it seems to be obviated in the actual practice of the copartnership system. The new element introduced into the labor copartnership societies is the admission of other bodies than coöperative stores as shareholders. The Christian Socialists and all the older schools of coöperation advocate paying a bonus to workingmen, and this has been the practice of the Scottish Wholesale Society, but the labor copartnership organizations have not only done this, but they often require all workingmen to be shareholders and permit them to be directors, and they admit outside individuals as shareholders. The dividends are then distributed among all the shareholders, whether societies, or individual workers, or outsiders, and in addition to this they pay several kinds of bonus.

A member of a managing committee in a coöperative concern like this gets, first, his wages, if an employé; second, his share of 40 per cent. of the profits, according to his wages; third, an extra payment as member of the committee, which, if there are, as here, nine members, would be one-ninth of 10 per cent.; fourth, his dividend on whatever share capital he may have in; fifth, his interest on whatever loan capital he may have deposited; sixth, his share of the benefits of the provident and educational fund; and last, but not least, his general benefit as a coöperator.

The weakness of this system, which Mr. Lloyd does not clearly see, is the failure to insure the same interest of the consumers as is secured in the Rochdale system. Against this may be set, however, the higher standard of work secured through labor copartnership. It must be recognized that, while the British and Scottish Wholesale Societies, with their remarkable system of stores and factories and farms, form a wonderfully organized industry, and provide an admirable education in democracy, the system has done little to raise the standard of workmanship beyond paying a good rate of wages and avoiding adulteration. It has not viewed the worker, as such, as a necessary object for improvement. It has tended to improve him only incidentally, while striving to satisfy the demands of the consumer.

Mr. Lloyd has performed a great service in calling attention to the significance of this new movement, which represents now an investment of over $5,000,000, annual sales $11,000,000, and dividends of $80,000 paid on wages. It seems evident that the next problem of coöperation is to harmonize these two movements, each of which has a principle indispensable to the extension of democracy in industry. Mr. Lloyd's book ought to be a means of demonstrating the necessity that the older movement should recognize and adopt the principle of the new. There are two or three items which need correction in a subsequent edition, which will doubtless be a necessity, as this movement is growing so rapidly. Mr. Lloyd does not carefully discriminate in his account of the Irish dairies between those which are on a labor copartnership basis and those which are not. He uses the word "capitalist" as a term of reproach when applied to the English Coöperative Wholesale Society, but seems to ignore the capitalistic character of the labor copartnership societies. It must be admitted that the English Wholesale Society is not all that it ought to be, and Mr. Lloyd's criticism would be more effective if there were not this loose use of the term "capitalistic." The experience of the South Metropolitan Gas Company has been given undue prominence. There is only an external appearance of similarity between this and the other labor copartnership organizations. He says on p. 280 :

The feeling of the English Wholesale is so strong against labor copartnership that it will not take part in the exhibitions of the Coöperative Festivals because the Labor Association shows its productions there.

The fact is the Coöperative Festivals only admit the products of labor copartnership, and the English Wholesale Society thus excludes itself. In spite of these slight errors Mr. Lloyd's book is the chief economic contribution of 1898.

CHARLES ZUEBLIN.

The Evolution of the English House. By SIDNEY OLDALL ADDY, M.A. With 42 illustrations. New York: The Macmillan Co., 1898. Pp. xxviii + 223. $1.50.

THIS is one of the " Social England " series edited by Kenelm D. Cotes. The aim of the series, as set forth in the editorial preface of the present number, is noteworthy and praiseworthy: "The 'Social England' series rests upon the conviction that it is possible to make a successful attempt to give an account, not merely of politics and wars, but also of religion, commerce, art, literature, law, science, agriculture, and all that follows from their inclusion, and that without a due knowledge of the last we have no real explanation of any of the number." "The central idea is that the greatness or weakness of a nation does not depend on the greatness or weakness of any one man or body of men, and that the odd millions have always had their part to play. To understand how great that was and is, we must understand the way in which they spent their lives, what they really cared for, what they fought for, and, in a word, what they lived for. To leave out nine-tenths of the national life, and to call the rest a history of the nation, is misleading." The reader is led to expect, with the completion of the series, a scientific analysis by specialists of the many elements — whether found in natural environment, in the heritage from past ages, in innovations from abroad, or in the immediate social environment — which go to make up the English nation and the English society. However successful this particular attempt may prove, it at least indicates the lines upon which all scientific historical and sociological investigation must proceed.

The present number of the series is an interesting study of the development of English architecture, and incidentally illuminates the development of the social and domestic life involved therewith. English architecture may be said to begin in the prehistoric artificial caves with their underground galleries, survivals of which may be found even at the present time. The earliest structure which merits the name of "house" was the round hut, a type still to be found among the modern charcoal burners. The rectangular form of house finds its origin in the tent-like summer shelter of the ancient herdsman, consisting of a pair of "forks," or "crutches," connected at the top by a ridge pole, and covered with branches, mud, or other material. This type of house increased in length by the erection of more "forks," and in breadth by the addition of "outshuts," and the resulting framework became the general plan upon which were constructed houses and barns (which were often combined under one roof), and churches with their central nave and side aisles. The distance between a pair of "forks" in an interesting way became constant, and was taken as a unit of measure—the rod, or perch. A host of other equally interesting facts are demonstrated. The author proceeds to trace step by step the evolution of the town house, the country manor, the castle, the church, emphasizing constantly the points of similarity between the English architecture and that of the continent, especially the Græco-Roman influence wherever apparent.

Aside from its specific purpose, the book gives insight into the evolution of the social structure. Every town house, every manor, every castle, every church, contains crystallized in its walls social influences from the various periods of the past. We are led back, for example, to a time when the church "belfry" was not merely a bell-tower, but it was the "berfrey," or "beffroy"—"a beacon or watchtower." "In the year 1452 a bell was suspended in the tower of the cathedral of Frankfort-on-the-Maine, which was to be rung in times of feudal alarm, and all the watchmen on the steeples were then to blow their horns and hoist their banners." The church was also the courthouse, and the parish rector the fiscal officer of his district.

The survivals of past times found in the architecture of the present have for the most part lost their meaning to the people. Yet this architectural environment, formed by all the social influences expressed in it, reacts potently upon modern life.

ARTHUR W. DUNN.

Étude de Psychologie Sociale. Par G. Tarde. Paris : V. Giard et Brière, 1898. Pp. 326.

This volume is a collection of essays, most of which originally appeared as contributions to periodicals and the proceedings of societies. In many cases one recognizes materials which have been organized into the more comprehensive system of Tarde as presented in his three volumes : *Les lois de l'imitation*, *La logique sociale*, *L'opposition universelle*. The rather miscellaneous character of the contents of this recent book is evident from a glance at the list of essays, which includes :

La sociologie.	La jeunesse criminelle.
Les deux éléments de la socio-	Souvenirs de transports judici-
logie.	aires.
Le transformisme social.	La graphologie.
L'idée de l' "organisme social."	Sympathie et synthèse.
Criminalité et santé sociale.	La sociologie de M. Giddings.
La criminalité professionelle.	Crimes, délits, contraventions.

The first paper, on "Sociology," is a clear account of the various analogies by which social relationships have been interpreted. It is designed to show how the mechanical and organic conceptions have given way to the psychological method of explanation. It can hardly be said that anything new appears in these pages, but the treatment is at once vigorous and attractive.

The second essay, on "The Two Elements of Sociology," is inspired by Durkheim's theory of the objectivity of social phenomena. Tarde attacks this point of view with all the force of his logic and ridicule. He insists that the rôle of consciousness is the chief part in the social drama. He characterizes very cleverly the tendency to explain social phenomena by means of terms which are themselves simply labels for mystery. Thus, he remarks, "there is a fetich, a *deus ex machina*, which the newer sociologists use as an 'open sesame' whenever they are embarrassed, and it is high time to call attention to this abuse, which is really becoming a source of anxiety. This talismanic explanation is *le milieu*. When this word is invoked, all has been said" (p. 78).

The discussion of "Social Evolution" is in reality a review of De Greef's volume. As we should expect, Tarde criticises what he regards as the *doctrinaire* theory of the Belgian professor, whom he declares to be too much dominated by the Comtean tradition.

In the paper on "The Idea of the Social Organism" Tarde finds an opportunity to deal another series of blows at the old organic analogy. He reiterates the familiar "differences" and ingeniously adds to the number. One is convinced, from the reading of this essay, that the fundamental ideas of the organic concept have really been "generalized," as Baldwin would say, and incorporated into the thinking and terminology of the science, while the countless details of similarity and difference have practically been rejected and will be more and more ignored.

Of the other essays little need be said. They deal largely with technical criminal and judicial questions. The American reader is impressed by the serious way in which "Graphology" is treated. There are references to a growing literature, to a scientific terminology, and to other evidences of systematic study of the "physiognomy of handwriting."

The essay on Giddings' system is perhaps chiefly an exchange of compliments with the American sociologist. Tarde treats Giddings' work with great respect. While here and there he makes a mild criticism (*petit reproche*), on the whole the essay may be described as an appreciation. The French apostle of imitation does not, however, seem to be greatly impressed by "consciousness of kind." Indeed, this alliterative phrase loses much of its mystical magic when it is transformed into *conscience d'espèce*.

As a whole, the volume does not, of course, rank with the more systematic works of the same author, but it presents in an attractive form a variety of problems of current interest in several departments of social science.

GEORGE E. VINCENT.

A Study of Mary Wollstonecraft and the Rights of Woman. By EMMA RAUSCHENBUSCH-CLOUGH, PH.D. London: Longmans, Green & Co., 1898. Pp. iv + 234.

WE rather expect on taking up a book with this title by a woman to encounter some extreme views and statements, but we find nothing of the kind in this case. The volume is a very careful and sufficiently exhaustive study of a remarkable and lovable woman, a kindred spirit of Shelley, Byron, Tom Paine, Godwin, and the revolutionists of her day, but one whose impatience of social restraint was tempered with a most striking and consistent display of good sense—so far as her theories are concerned, at any rate : in her practices she was less fortunate.

She was at variance with her times, but at this day the most of us would not hesitate to say that in her points of difference with the world Mary Wollstonecraft was in the main right and the world wrong. For the gist of her quarrel with the world was that the activities of women did not have free play.

The volume treats of: (1) her life; (2) her literary work; (3) her religious and ethical views; (4) the rights of man, and her reply to Edmund Burke; (5) the rights of woman, and her polemics against writers on female education; (6) her investigation of the causes of woman's intellectual inferiority; (7) her discussion of woman's moral inferiority; (8) her demands for the education of woman; (9) her vindication of the civil rights of woman; (10) the relation of her views to those of Godwin and later socialists; (11) the reception of her work in Germany. Her biographer points out in conclusion that many of the conceptions of Mary Wollstonecraft have been adopted by society, but wisely refrains from insisting that the changes are directly traceable to her influence and writings. It is perhaps unfortunate that the title should suggest that the volume treats of the question of woman's rights aside from the relation of Mary Wollstonecraft to this question, for the views of Mrs. Rauschenbusch-Clough are not very elaborately expressed and are so reasonable that they perhaps demand no expression in print.

W. I. THOMAS.

Workingmen's Insurance. By W. F. WILLOUGHBY. New York: I. T. Crowell & Co., 1898. Pp. 386. $1.75.

THE work of Mr. John Graham Brooks on *German Insurance*, prepared for the Department of Labor, was a valuable contribution to the subject and made the German experience accessible to English readers. It is still indispensable. But there was need of a general survey, brought up to date, of the experiments in all modern countries. In the book of Mr. Willoughby we have this survey. The elements of the problem, economic and administrative, are clearly presented. The German and Austrian laws providing for sickness, accidents, and old age are discussed in detail. The forms of the movement seen in France, Belgium, Italy, Switzerland, Scandinavia, England, and the United States are carefully analyzed, and the limitations of each fairly brought to view. The bibliographical notes at the end enable the student to go to the sources.

When we consider the anxiety, the terror, with which the average thoughtful wage-earner regards the possibilities of accident, sickness, and infirmity of age, and when we take into account the grave social unrest which springs from this solicitude about the future, we may well give a large place in our social studies to the modern inventions for distributing the burdens of provision for the emergencies of the workman's life. The essential elements of these inventions may be found in this valuable volume.   C. R. H.

The Principles of the Law of Public Corporations. By CHARLES B. ELLIOTT, PH.D., LL.D. Chicago: Callaghan & Co., 1898. Pp. lxxx + 364.

THE lively interest manifested of late years in city government and the question of its betterment insures a hearty welcome to a book dealing with any phase of the subject. The present volume is from the pen of a district judge of Minnesota, and is an attempt to state the law of public corporations in a manner suited to the needs of students. The attempt is fairly successful. In a volume of less than 400 pages the chief topics of the law are discussed and its salient features made plain. In classification and arrangement the author does not depart radically from the great work of Judge Dillon on *Municipal Corporations.* After an introduction devoted to definition, classification, and history, Bk. I discusses the creation and control of public corporations, Bk. II takes up the powers of public corporations, Bk. III describes the mode and agencies of corporate action, and Bk. IV treats of the liabilities of public corporations. The discussion is logical and clear, and the citation of authorities is ample. The volume is provided with an analytical table of contents, a table of cases, and a copious index. All in all it makes a very serviceable text-book. The publishers are to be criticised for not providing a label which corresponds more nearly with the title page.

                                                     CARL EVANS BOYD.

The City Wilderness. Edited by ROBERT A. WOODS. Boston and New York: Houghton, Mifflin & Co., 1898. Pp. 319.

THE social settlements have borne no better fruit than this remarkable study of urban conditions in a crowded part of South End, Boston. In twelve chapters, written by competent. and trained observers who have resided in the district, we have not merely a revelation of local conditions, but of world-wide tendencies. The maps are beautifully drawn and the materials carefully selected. The descriptive pages present the facts with most intelligent interpretation. Elements of population, conditions of public health, economic status, political activities, criminal tendencies, amusements, church work, educational agencies, charities, philanthropies, and organization of self-help are all admirably treated. The volume should be placed by the side of the "Hull-House Maps and Papers" on the shelves of every student of social life in America.

C. R. HENDERSON.

The Negro in America. By T. J. MORGAN, D.D., LL.D. American Baptist Publication Society. Pp. 203, 12mo. $1.

THE eight papers collected in this little book are the deposit of long matured and careful thinking, after varied and extended personal contact with many aspects of the conditions discussed. We may question the author's perspective sometimes, as, for instance, the implications from the absence of an academy equal to Worcester Academy for black pupils. Does the South possess an academy equal to Worcester Academy for *white* pupils? On the whole, however, the book is candid, moderate, kindly, serious, and stimulating. It deserves respectful attention both north and south.

A. W. S.

NOTES AND ABSTRACTS.

Æsthetic Evolution.—In a previous article it was shown that æsthetic evolution depends upon religious evolution. But religion depends upon man's conception of the fundamental facts of nature. With the formation of this conception science comes to have more and more to do. Theology also is a conception of these facts. The conception furnished by science and that furnished by theology are not infrequently radically opposed to each other; hence a tendency toward opposition between that phase of religion and its corresponding phase of æsthetic, dependent upon that conception of nature furnished by science and the members of the same series furnished by theology. It has generally proven true that, when thus opposed, science and its dependents have come to be generally accepted rather than theology and its dependents. Therefore we are to look to science for the spiritual renovation and regeneration so much needed today, and may confidently trust the scientific religion thus evolved to furnish to art and æsthetic the highest sources of inspiration. The modern scientific conception of the world is not less æsthetic than the false conception of the ancients. It will furnish a sufficient inspiration to the noblest altruism, to the practice of the highest virtues, to the philosophic contemplation of nature, and to the attainment of great moral perfection. It will teach mankind that civilization would retrograde and disappear if human betterment were not insured by science, by art, and by morals.—ÉDMOND GALABERT, "L'évolution esthétique," *Revue internationale de sociologie*, October, 1898.

Religion and Morality.—Religion is a certain relation established between man and the eternal and infinite universe, or with its principle and first cause. It is an answer to the question, "What is the meaning of my life?" Morality is what exhibits and illuminates the activity of man, and which naturally proceeds from his relation with the universe. There are three relations in which man may stand to the universe, and correspondingly three kinds of morality:

The first is primitive, savage, personal morality. It includes all that is based upon the welfare of the individual; for instance, Mohammedan morality; that taught by the Christian church, which seeks individual welfare especially in the other world; utilitarian ethics.

The second is pagan morality, for which the end is the welfare of a group of individuals; as for instance; the official morality of the state, that of the ancient Jews, that of the Greeks and Romans.

The third kind is Christian morality, the essence of which is that man recognizes in himself an instrument for the service of one supreme will whose plans he should realize. It is the source of the most elevated systems man knows, viz., Pythagoreanism, Stoicism, Buddhism, Brahmanism, Taoism, Christian morality in the true sense of the word, which demands the renunciation of all will, of all good, not only of self, but also of family, of society, of the state, and that in the name of the accomplishment of His will who made us live, of that will of which we are conscious when it unveils itself to us. Morality cannot be independent of religion. Hideous abstraction, obscurity, unintelligibility, unthankfulness for life characterize modern pagan ethics. All rules of morality considered from the point of view of non-Christian ethics are only lies and hypocrisy. Some have sought to found Christian morality on pagan science; but no subtlety of thought, no sophism, can prevail against this simple principle, viz.: The theory of evolution is founded upon the survival of the fittest; consequently everyone ought, in his own interest or that of the society of which he is a member, to try to be one of the fittest in order that he or his group might not perish, but instead others less fit for the struggle. It would be desirable to have a moral system free from superstition. But since morality is a certain relation of man to the universe, and since this relation is expressed in terms of superstition, we ought to try to make this expression more reasonable and exact. Above all we ought not to try to construct a non-religious moral system.— LÉON TOLSTOI, *L'Humanité nouvelle*, September, 1898.

The Application of the Collectivist System.— Collectivism, as is well known, consists essentially in the resumption by the state of all means of production, and in the changes and adjustments necessitated by such resumption. That a society founded upon the principles of collectivism would be far preferable to our modern individualistic society is to be inferred from the following considerations: (1) all those now living in idleness, or non-productively employed, or employed in callings which would become useless under the new régime, would be set to work in productive pursuits; (2) all the forces now wasted under individual methods of production would be conserved and utilized; (3) the hours of labor would be reduced, and the labor of women and children would be suppressed, save in rare cases; (4) many of the sources of the abuse of money would be removed, since the money of the collectivist state would have a fixed and unchanging value; (5) the social mobility of the individual would be an assured fact, while under the present system it is only an enticing promise; (6) education, according to fitness and needs, would be guaranteed to every child in the state; (7) each would receive, as a salary, the whole of the value created by his labor. These are not all. Certain reforms in the laws relating to marriage, inheritance, the punishment of crime, etc., might be mentioned in addition as flowing indubitably from an adoption and application of the principles of collectivism. But surely the points enumerated are sufficient to suggest the immeasurable superiority of the collectivist over the individualistic society.—X. . . . ., " L'Application du système collectiviste," *La Revue socialiste*, August, 1898.

Individualism and Social Feeling in England.— Individualism as here used may be defined as the tendency to develop in one's self with the greatest intensity possible, and to make dominate as far as possible one's own personality. In some respects the undisciplined and critical neo-Latin may seem more individualistic than the Anglo Saxon, but really energetic will does not exclude obedience to authority. On the other hand, lack of discipline, fickleness, a tendency to neglect authority, difficulty in obeying steadily and patiently, the habit of depending upon others, do not constitute individualism proper, but rather a kind of negative individualism characterized by lack of will, self-control, and coöperation with others. What are the psychological and ethical sources of English individualism? Ethnic explanations alone are insufficient; so are climatic explanations, though both are important. Insular situation has also been important. The Germanic races are characterized by realism, mixed with a certain mystic idealism; the former reaches its highest development in England, but the latter does not disappear.

The English are also characterized by individualism, together with social subordination. This latter is due to the Normans. The sensibility of the English is less fine and more limited than that of the French or the Italians. This is due to their phlegmatic temperament in harmony with the cold, damp climate of Great Britain. The character of the English has been influenced by the dark, cloudy sky, which inspires melancholy; but race is more important than climate here, for we see the Irish in the same climate keeping something of their Gallic lightness. English sensibility is German sensibility, but, because of a life more active and utilitarian, it is less sentimental and less mystic. Because of its habitual calm and seriousness the English mind has greater power of attention and profound concentration. The English mind is practical; it loves facts. The firm, patient, persevering will is where they most resemble the ancient Germans. They are not prudent, like the French, but earn money that they may spend it, leaving their children to do the same. In morality the Englishman is not governed by any sentiment, like honor or social instinct, but by religious law or humane considerations. But the Englishman has his faults : his independence exposes him to egoism, his spirit of originality to eccentricity, his power and riches to contempt for the weak and poor. His habit of associating for some end has been maintained for centuries. On the continent executive ability was always of capital importance; on the British Isles, where security reigned, as far as neighbors were concerned at least, the people were not obliged to be so continually ready to take up arms, nor were they obliged to contract permanent alliances; executive power, therefore, became subordinate to deliberative power. The three great events in the history of England are : the establishment of constitutional liberty and the parliamentary régime ; colonial expansion ; and the triumph of Protestantism.

Combine the Danish-Saxon tendency and the Celtic, and join to that the Latin influence exercized by France and Italy, and you will understand how the greatest poetry of modern times could be born and develop in England. The individual character was for English individualism the proper object for dramatic poetry.— ALFRED FOUILLÉE, *Revue des Deux Mondes*, October 1, 1898.

Public Service and the Question of Monopolies in the United States.— Monopoly constituted in opposition to the will of cities or states is a purely American phenomenon. The administration of continental Europe offers no examples of it. It results from the peculiar conception which obtained in the United States in the first half of this century concerning the functions of the state, of local government, and of city administration. These functions were reduced to a minimum. Material conditions then permitted it; agriculture was the ruling occupation, and there were few great fortunes. Besides, Anglo-Saxon spirit tended to organize strongly private life and to defend it from all intervention of public powers rather than to assure the development of these latter. But, the habit of treating public affairs as if they were private produced a veritable confusion. Concessions were granted to companies in every case where they could be made. But in place of imposing guarantees upon these companies in ceding to them all or part of their monopoly, the public authorities exercised their ingenuity to put them in competition with one another, thinking that competition would assure cheapness here as in ordinary affairs. Since the public put all its hope in the efficiency of competition, it was very disagreeably surprised to see that here competition did not long persist. The situation was all the more serious because the public found itself disarmed. Monopoly was organized against it and without compensation. The means which people had imagined would prevent it proved an illusion. The companies, often provided with perpetual charters, shut themselves up in their rights. The only resource which remained was to attack them in the name of the common law or by means of laws against trusts, which declared null all combinations which aimed at monopoly. Neither of these means, however, has been very efficacious. While in private industry a conjunction of exceptional circumstances is necessary to create monopoly, in the organization of public services it is the nature of the business which creates the monopoly. Instead of being exceptional, as in ordinary affairs, monopoly is here natural, normal, obligatory, and nothing is efficient against it. The abandonment of a public service without sufficient guarantee is here what has produced the abuse.

There are two principal sorts of trusts in the public service of the United States : those in the municipal service and those in the telegraphic service. Among the most prominent of the former are the gas companies. They obtained their charters at a period when the belief in the sovereign efficacy of competition was still intact. Thus five or six companies were often given charters in the same city. These afterward combined tacitly or openly to form a trust. The most conspicuous of these has been the Chicago Gas Trust. All legislative and legal efforts to kill this trust have been in vain, and it is still in existence. The situation is somewhat different for street railways, elevated roads, and other means of public transport. Inasmuch as street railways are much more recent than the use of gas, the municipalities have lost some faith in the efficacy of competition when it is a matter of public service; and they accordingly grant to transit companies licenses necessary for the construction of their roads. Generally they also exact a compensation. The tendency is to make the compensation greater and to limit the franchises to a shorter period.

The American telegraphs are in the hands of two companies only, the Western Union and the Postal Telegraph Company. These also practically form a trust. They have one tariff for the ordinary public, another for certain large business houses, and especially the press syndicate known as the Associated Press. A comparison of rates with the European systems is difficult to make, and, as usually made, is fallacious. This is at least true of Gunton's comparison. A strict comparison of American rates with those obtaining in continental Europe, both as to distance and as to the number of words, would probably result in favor of the latter. In conclusion, one gains nothing in taking away from or in refusing to public authority a service which is normally relevant to it. It may be well to distrust its encroachments; but if a people trust to private initiative an enterprise which encroaches upon the prerogatives of the state or municipalities, under the pretext of escaping their tyranny, they end simply in creating another tyrant. That is what has happened in the United States in the case of the telegraph system, as in the case of municipal services in a large number of cities. Today it is recognized in the United States that what is necessary is to organize these monopolies in place of prohibiting them, to make use of them in place of letting them play the rôle of robbers. — PAUL DE ROUSIERS, "Les services publics et la question des monopoles aux États-Unis," *Revue politique et parlementaire*, October, 1898.

Anarchism and the Social Movement in Australia. — The social condition of Australia, since its first colonization, has been chiefly determined by these circumstances: the uniform mildness of the climate; the absence of dangerous animals, and of numerous, powerful, and hostile natives; the right of property over the entire soil affirmed by the state before any immigrant population was installed there; the system of colonization by convicts pursued for a half century by the English government; the discovery of gold, and the revolutionary movement of 1848. In these circumstances certain Englishmen, who had conceived the idea of making their fortune in Australia, and of setting up there a landed aristocracy, obtained a law which forbade the sale of the soil below a price high enough to be prohibitive as regards the common people. After the discovery of gold fields, the existence of a new class necessitated rendering more easy the acquisition of arable soil under certain restrictions. But the great mass of the people remained always fatally excluded from property in land. The result has been that the population is concentrated, especially in the great cities, to an incredible degree, while the capitalization of the soil is extreme. There is not a peasant proprietor throughout the continent of Australia. Harvesting and sheep-shearing are the work of nomad laborers, who live, not in the country, but in the cities, and who overrun the pastoral and agricultural districts during the working season. These conditions have been especially favorable to the development of communistic sentiments.

In Victoria the elements are historically different, even to absolute divergence, from those which have operated in the rest of Australia. This part of the country has never known the work of convicts which has elsewhere degraded the proletariat. In the gold fields the conditions of life were necessarily equal, and the population which gathered there was composed principally of emigrants of 1848, who had conceived the hope of founding, on Australian soil, a free and equal community. This moral sentiment has had its baptism of blood. In the first years of the gold fields the miners revolted against the exactions of the government, raising the standard of the Australian republic. Since then the governing classes of Australia have conceived the state as the representation of the social interest, while in the rest of eastern Australia the state has been for the people only the government, the supreme and absolute power over them. Thus in Victoria the socialist idea has always been an element of practical politics. Republican, agrarian, and collectivistic theories have always constituted an integral part of the ideas of the Victorian people. It was from these aspirations, instincts, and thoughts that the anarchistic idea disengaged itself at Melbourne a dozen years ago. An anarchistic club was organized in 1886, and several anarchistic newspapers were established. An agitation, more or less successful, has been conducted often in connection with the socialist agitation. The most noteworthy development has been an attempt at reconciliation between anarchism and socialism. This new movement is called communistic anarchism. It was organized by the writer of this article. As yet, however, an anarchist party can scarcely be said to exist in Australia. It is still merely an agitation. But it has developed both quantitatively and qualitatively during the period of its existence. At first it appealed directly to the spirit of revolution, but today anarchists believe that such agitation might lead to a governmental revolution merely, and that it is better to agitate simply for the logical acceptance of their principles.— J. A. ANDREWS, "L'Anarchisme et le mouvement social en Australie," *L'Humanité nouvelle*, August, 1898.

Proportional Representation.— Even with a just division of electoral districts the votes of electors have not an equal value, and a proportional representation of the different party groups in the electorate is not secured in the popular representation. The cause of disproportional representation is to be sought in the division into election districts as such. Indeed, this division permits no other result than that the popular representation becomes a representation of victorious majorities in single election districts instead of a representation of the whole electorate.

If it be presupposed that an election law is intended to serve the purpose of validating the constitutional principle of the equality of votes, then an election law which cuts up an electorate into many territorial election districts is unjust and impractical. It is unjust, because thereby it engenders great difference in the value of the votes. By this method of election no small number of electors will be sentenced to silence from the beginning, viz., all voters who live in election districts which are already conceded politically to one party or another. The method is impractical, because thereby the popular representation becomes only in a distorted way the representation of the political tendencies among the people. A division into election districts could, nevertheless, be justified if the election districts should present economically and culturally a half-way closed whole ; but the opposite is the case.

There are two methods of securing proportional representation — the quotient method, which is practically applicable only with small constituencies, and the list-competition method, applicable with both large and small constituencies. We shall discuss only the latter. According to this method both large and small parties present through unions of voters, at an official place and at a definite time before the election day, nominations, lists of candidates, with as many names as each party can hope under the most favorable circumstances to elect. On election day the voter polls a double vote. In the first place he votes for a certain candidate. In the case that this candidate does not need his vote, either because he has already enough, or because he does not receive enough to elect him, the voter gives his vote to the remaining candidates upon the list. That is, the voter presents a list of men whom he wishes chosen, under obligatory preference of one among them. This method makes possible a proportional representation of parties. The loss of votes which assumes so great dimensions with the election-district system is here reduced to a minimum.

But it is claimed that this method secures proportional representation at the expense of delocalizing the party and of sacrificing the feeling between voter and candidate. The program takes the place of the person, and wire-pullers rule the political life. Very recently, however, the theory of proportional representation has had a supplementing, the significance of which can hardly be overestimated for the utility of the system. It is concerned with nothing less than the reconciliation of decentralizing local interests with centralizing tendencies. Richard Siegfried. in a book on proportional representation, discusses this new method in connection with the Württemberg electoral system. It is called the method of "connected lists" (*verbundene Listen*). A country is conceived as covered with a network of local committees of the different parties. Every committee nominates its own candidates and hands in its own nominations. But the local committees of one and the same party in the whole country designate their lists of candidates as "connected lists." At the ascertainment of the result of the election, first of all is determined how many votes have fallen to the nominations of the same party; that is, to the local candidates of the several parties. According to this is computed the number of mandates which falls to each body of "connected lists." The further distribution of mandates is then made to the single lists upon the basis of the number of votes which every single list has received. Within these the mandates are further distributed to the candidates according to the number of votes which have fallen to each. The technique of proportional procedure gains through these "connected lists" a great elasticity and is applicable to great constituencies. The weightiest consequence of the possibility of "connected lists" will be decentralization of parties, and therewith an avoidance of all the disadvantages which we have become acquainted with as consequences of a proportional method. The centrifugal and centripetal tendencies are happily equalized.— Dr. Rudolf Einhauser, "Proportionalwahl," in *Zeitschrift für die gesamte Staatswissenschaft*, Viertes Heft, 1898.

Insurance against Non-Employment in St. Gall and Berne. — The chances for the prosperous development of insurance against non-employment in Switzerland have recently materially decreased. Frost has nipped the early buds of plans and projects. It almost looks as if with the extinguishing of the first enthusiasm this once warmly commended remedy for non-employment would also disappear. The difficulties of carrying out this branch of insurance have dampened the ardor of many of its friends. To the considerations and scruples which were recognized as valid from the start is now added, as a weighty argument, the collapse of the bank for the unemployed (*Arbeitslosenkasse*) in St. Gall. The experiences there have been cited, without criticism, against the principle of insurance for non-employment, and have already demonstrated their influence in the grand council of Zurich. This event will doubt-less be cited in Basel also, as an argument against insurance for non-employment, where already a paralyzing standstill has succeeded the first enthusiasm. The fate of the banks for the non-employed of the two cities of Berne and St. Gall has not fulfilled the prophecies made at their founding. The bank at Berne was prophesied a short life, because it rested upon the voluntary principle, while the compulsory insurance against non-employment of St. Gall was regarded as the pioneer of the only right method for this branch of labor insurance. The bank of Berne has existed for more than five years, and has contributed materially to the solution of the problem of the unemployed of that city. But the insurance against non-employment at St. Gall collapsed after two years. The causes of this contradictory phenomenon are many. Along with inner causes inherent in the organization itself, the political conditions and personal qualities of the administrators play an important rôle. Both these banks show a notable agreement in their experiences which is valuable for the solution of technical questions connected with this kind of insurance. To these questions belong especially those of occupation, residence, status, age, and wages of the insured.

I. Insurance against non-employment must take into consideration the risk by means of gradation of premiums. The occupation of the insured is the first means of measuring this risk. Therefore a gradation in the risk according to the groups of occupations must be sought. For example, out of 4,220 insured of the city of St. Gall, 430 men reported themselves in the first year as out of work, according to which the total average of non-employment amounted to 10.2 per cent. But in the irregular occupations an average of 19.6 per cent. was shown, while among thatchers and day laborers non-employment amounted to over 30 per cent. Therefore any system of insurance against non-employment must be based upon statistics of occupation.

II. The question of the origin of the unimployed is very important for the problem of insurance against non-employment. The fear of immigration and of pretended settlement is widespread. Reprisals on the floating element in general, and foreign-ers in particular, have essentially influenced the practical form of this branch of insurance. Therefore it has been proposed either fully to exclude foreigners from insurance or to exclude those merely who are not permanently located. The experi-ence of Berne, however, does not confirm this position. Berne originally limited the right of insurance to laborers of Swiss extraction, but after two years' experience authorized the admission of all laborers settled in the commune. In St. Gall, the first year, out of 430 reported out of work 27.4 per cent. were foreigners; the second year foreigners were represented by 36 per cent. But 72.4 per cent. of the foreign unem-ployed had dwelt six years or more in St. Gall. Therefore this would seem to show that the chief source of the non-employed is not from those fluctuating elements of which people suppose the crowds of unemployed in cities to be composed, but from permanently settled laborers. The conclusion is that a limitation of the right of insurance to the permanently settled laboring element is unnecessary and unjustified.

III. The family status of the non-employed is of significance for this kind of insurance in two respects. First, it makes a difference in capacity for assessment with premiums, while, secondly, it seems to justify a differentiation of benefits. While 27.4 per cent. of the total insured in St. Gall were single men, only 23.9 per cent. of the 430 reported out of work the first year were single. The danger of non-employ-ment seems to be considerably greater with the married than with the single. In St. Gall, of the married insured, 15.9 per cent. were out of work, while of the single, 4.1 per cent. If it is desired to derive advantage for the insurance fund from the unmar-

ried, it may be done through a slight raising of the premium for the unmarried. This can be more lightly borne by the insured than a differentiation in benefits.

IV. The age of the unemployed has concerned insurance against non-employment hitherto chiefly in respect to its minimum limit. This latter varies from fourteen to eighteen years. But for insurance the maximum limit of age is even more important, and it is very remarkable that this has not yet received extended consideration. Capacity for work decreases rapidly with increasing age. To the greater risk of non-employment in the older years of life is added the difficulty of obtaining new positions. The experience of St. Gall shows that of the total non-employed over 28 per cent. were men over fifty years of age. Out of ninety-two men employed in the irregular trades who were over sixty years of age, 36.9 per cent. were out of work, while of those under sixty years of age only 20 per cent. were out of work. For these reasons the establishment of a maximum age limit for admission to insurance seems entirely justified. People who are over sixty years of age occasion for the insurance bank so great a risk that they should be excluded from the right of insurance. Here the question of the duration of membership comes into consideration. Insured who have been members at least four years might be compensated for non-employment of at most thirty days after they have passed their sixtieth year. But insured members of less than four years' standing should lose their right of membership after their sixtieth year.

V. The principle of grading premiums and benefits along with the risk according to wages is fairly well accepted. The opinion was general that the laborer who received a higher wage should contribute a somewhat greater premium. But the expectations of financial gain attached to this plan have shown themselves in St. Gall delusive. The laborers were divided into three classes according as they earned per day three francs or less, three to four fr., and four to five fr. These respectively paid a premium of fifteen centimes per week, twenty centimes, and thirty centimes. But out of 993 men insured in the first class 197 became unemployed, while out of 335 men of the second class sixty-four men became unemployed, and out of the six men of the third class two. Benefits were paid to the first class to the amount of 13,519 fr., to the second class 4,531 fr., to the third class 159 fr. The ratio of benefits in each class was such that no considerable financial gain resulted to the insurance fund. For these reasons Berne has made a good move in establishing unconditionally a single-premium class. This premium amounts monthly to fifty centimes, that is, it is lower than the lowest premium demanded by most other systems of insurance against non-employment. Furthermore, the experience of St. Gall shows that approximately a third of the unemployed had a daily wage not amounting to more than three francs. More, than the half of the unemployed received a wage between three and four francs daily and only 13 per cent. received a daily wage amounting to more than four francs. Therefore, to disencumber the administration and to avoid injustice and friction, the establishment of a single-premium and benefit class is commended. Finally, the administration and management of the insurance fund should give the greatest room to the influence of the insured laborers, because therein lies the best guarantee for the prosperous development of such insurance, as the experience of St. Gall, on the one hand, and the favorable results in Berne, on the other, clearly show.—DR. E. HOF-MANN, "Die Arbeitslosenversicherung in St. Gallen und Bern," *Acrhiv für sociale Gesetzgebung und Statistik*, Band XIII, 1. u. 2. Heft.

BIBLIOGRAPHY.

March—for January-February.

CONDUCTED BY C. H. HASTINGS.

NEW BOOKS AND NOTICES OF BOOKS REVIEWED.

Explanation. *Titles not starred* represent new publications announced in the standard publishers' lists since the last issue of the bibliography. A *star prefixed* to a title indicates that it was taken from a review of the work in the periodical cited after the title. It may or may not be a new announcement. The *arithmetical signs* following the citation to a review indicate the tenor of the review: ×, uncertain ; +, favorable ; −, unfavorable; + −, favorable, but with reservations ; − +, unfavorable, but with commendation ; + +, very favorable ; − −, very unfavorable ; + + −, very favorable, but with reservations ; − − +, very unfavorable, but with commendation. Absence of any sign indicates that review has not been read. The *publication date* when not given is understood to be the current year. *Prices quoted* are usually for volumes bound in cloth in the case of American and English books, in paper in the case of all others. *New editions, translations,* and *new periodicals* are bracketed.
Abbreviations. *See* at end of Bibliography.

SUBJECT INDEX.

[The *figures* refer to the number of the class; *each* of the *letters* following the figures refers to initial of author's surname, or to entering word of title.]

705

AUTHOR INDEX TO NOTICES OF BOOK REVIEWS.

NEW BOOKS.

1. Anthropology, Ethnology.

Castellani, C. Les femmes au Congo. P., libr. Flammarion, 1898. 315 pp. 12mo. f. 3.50.

Curtin, Jeremiah. Creation myths of primitive America in relation to the religious history & mental development of mankind. Bo., Little, Brown & Co., 1898. 532 pp. 8vo. $2.50.

[Dubois, J. A. Hindu manners, customs & ceremonies, tr. from French. Ed. 2. L., Henry Frowde. 766 pp. 8vo. 15s.]

*Frobenius, L. Der Ursprung der Kultur. 1. Bd. Der Ursprung der afrikan. Kulturen . . . B., Gebr. Borntraeger, 1898. 368 pp. (9 Taf. 240 Textillustr. u. s. w.) M. 10. (DL. D. 24)

*Frobinus, L. Die Weltanschauung der Naturvölker. Weimar, E. Felber, 1898. 427 pp. 8vo. (LC., D. 17) (DL., D. 34)

*Gomme, Mrs. A. B. Traditional games. V. 2. L., David Nutt, 1898. 12s. 6d. (Academy, D. 17 +)

Kollman, Paul. Der Nordwesten unserer afrikanischen Kolonie. Eine Beschreibg. v. Land u. Leuten am Victorja-Nyanza nebst Aufzeichngn. einiger daselbst gesprochenen Dialekte. Mit 372 Abbildgn. B., A. Schall. 191 pp. 8vo. M. 7.50.

*[Smirnov, Jean M. Les populations finnoises des bassins de la Volga et de la Kama. Etudes d'ethnographie historique tr. du russe . . . Pt. 1. Groupe de la Volga. 1. Les Tchéremisses. 2. Les Mordves. P., Lerou, 1898. 486 pp. 8vo.] (LC., Ja. 14 + +)

Spencer, Baldwin, & Gillen, F. J. Native tribes of central Australia. N. Y., Macmillan Co. 371 pp. il. 8vo. $6.50.

[Untrodden fields of anthropology: observations on the esoteric manners & customs of semicivilized peoples, being a record of 30 years' experience in Asia, Africa, America & Oceania by a French army surgeon. Ed. 2. 2 v. (343 & 502 pp.) P., Ch. Carrington, 1898.]

2. Biology, Evolution, Science.

*Brooks, W. K. Foundations of zoölogy. N. Y., Macmillan Co. 339 pp. 8vo. $2.50. (Outlook, F. 18 + +)

Haeckel, Ernst. The last link; our present knowledge of the descent of man . . . N. Y., Macmillan Co. 156 pp. 8vo. $1.

Haeckel, Ernst. Ueber unsere gegenwärtige Kenntniss vom Ursprung des Menschen. Vortrag. Mit erläut. Anmerkgn. Bonn, E. Strauss, 1898. 53 pp. 8vo. M. 1.60.

3. Charities.

Associazione di avvocati e procuratori per la gratuita difesa penale dei poveri [in Roma: statuto]. Roma, Paolo Vespasiani, 1898. 15 pp. 16mo.

Ergebnisse, die, der Sommerpflege in Deutschland (Ferienkolonien, Kinderheilstätten, u. s. w.) im J. 1897. Bericht der Centralstelle der Vereinigen. f. Sommerpflege in Deutschland. B., W. Steinmetzstr. 16 (B., Puttkammer & Mühlbrecht), 1898. 59 pp. 8vo. M. 1.20.

Fry, H. Royal guide to the London charities . . . First London annual charity guide. 35th ed. L., Chatto & Wundus, 1898. 344 pp. 8vo. 1s. 6d.

Henderson, C. R. Social settlements. N. Y., Lentilhon & Co. 196 pp. 16mo. $0.50. (Handbooks for practical workers in church & philanthropy.)

La Flize, Docteur. Enfants assistés et protection des enfants du premier âge. Nancy, Berger-Levrault & Cie., 1898. 47 pp. 8vo.

Mahlung, Pastor. Beiträge zur Geschichte der Entwicklung der inneren Mission m. besond. Beziehung auf Hamburg . . . Hamburg, L. Grase. 1898. 237 pp. 8vo. M. 1.

Massaroli, Fr. Vagabondaggio terre incolte, colonie o la questione sociale in Italia. Piacenza, Giacomo Farari, 1898. 20 pp. 8vo. L. 0.20.

Salomon, L. Le pauvre et son médecin devant la loi sur l'assistance medicale gratuité. P., libr. Chamul, 1898. 116 pp. 18mo.

Société philanthropique (1898–99). Rapports et comptes rendus . . . 1897-8. Nemours, impr. Bouloy, 1898. 232 pp. 8vo.

[Die Volksunterhaltung. Zeitschrift f. die gesamten Bestrebgn. auf dem Gebiete der Volksunterhaltg. Hrsg. v. Kaph. Löwenfeld. 1. Jahrg. Oktbr. 1898-Septbr. 1899, 12 Hfte. 1. u. 2. Hft. 16 pp. 8vo. B., F. Dummeler's Verlag, 1898. M. 2.]

Werner, Ant. Die örtlichen Stiftungen f. die Zwecke des Unterrichts u. der Wohlthätigkeit . . . Augsburg, M. Rieger, 1898. 236 pp. 4to. M. 3.60.

Woods, R. A., ed. City wilderness: a settlement study ; by residents & associates of the South End House, Bost. V. 1. Bo., Houghton, Mifflin & Co., 1898. 12mo. $1.50.

4. Cities.

[Bender, Herm. Rom u. römisches Leben im Altertum. 2. Aufl. Tübingen, H. Laupp. 1898. 594 pp. 8vo. M. 7.]

Bippen, Wilh. Geschichte der Stadt Bremen. 6. Lfg. (2. Bd. pp. 241-414.) Bremen, C. E. Müller. M. 1.80; 2. Bd. kplt. geb. M. 6.

Great Britain—Police of the metropolis. Report of the Commissioner for 1897. L., Eyre & Spottiswoode, 1898. 7d.

Grosse, Karl. Geschichte der Stadt Leipzig von der ältesten bis auf die neueste Zeit . . . 2. Bd. 1. Hälfte. Lp., Alvin Schmidt, 1898. 448 pp. 8vo. M. 5.

Laurie, A. L'oncle de Chicago (mœurs scolaires en Amérique). P., Hetzel & Cie., 1898. 307 pp. 8vo. f. 7.

Local government manual for 1899. L., Shaw & Son. 7s.

Pilon, E. Monopoles communaux. Eclairage au gaz et à l'électricité. Distribution d'eau et de force motrice. Omnibus tramways (these). Caen, impr. Valin, 1898. 271 pp. 8vo.

Quellen zur Geschichte der Stadt Wien. II. Abth. Registen aus dem Archive der Stadt. 1. Bd. Verzeichnis der Orig.-Urkunden des städtischen Archives, 1239-1411. Wien, C. Konegen, 1898. 626 pp. 4to. M. 36.

Schriften des Vereins f. die Geschichte Berlins. 35. Hft. B., E. S. Mittler & Sohn. 123 pp. 8vo. M. 2.50.

Statistisches Jahrbuch der Haupt- & Residenzstadt Budapest. II. Jahrg., 1895 u. 1896. Red. u. bearb. v. Gust. Thirring. B., Puttkammer & Mühlbrecht, 1898. 425 pp. 8vo. M. 8.

Whelen, F. London govt. Richards, 1898. 302 pp. 8vo. 3s. 6d.

Wien—(Die) Gemeinde-Verwaltung. Bericht des Bürgermstrs., Dr. Karl Lueger. Wien, W. Braumüller in Komm. 677 pp. 8vo. M. 10.

Woods, R. A. City wilderness (see 3).

[Württemberg, wie es war u. ist. 8. Aufl. 6.-11. Lfg. St., Zeller. à M. 0.40.]

5. Criminology and Penology.

Arnauldt, E. Des incapacités résultant des condamnations pénales (thèse). Angers, libr. Lachèse & Cie., 1898.

[Carrara, Fr. Opuscoli di diritto criminale. Quinta ed. Firenze, fratelli Giachetti, 1898. 3v. (667 656, 659 pp.) 8vo. L. 21.]

Corbellini, P. Sulla funzione della giuria penale nella società. Brescia, Unione tip lit. bresciana, 1898. 21 pp. 8vo.

[Gross, Hanns. Handbuch f. Untersuchungsrichter als System der Kriminalstatistik. 3. Aufl. 1. Hälfte. Graz, Leuschner & Lubensky, 1898. 400 pp. 8vo. M. 6.]

Halton, W. H. Étude sur la procédure criminelle en Angletere et en France. P., impr. de Soye et fils. 200 pp. 8vo.

[Harris, S. F. Principles of the criminal law. Ed. 8. L., Stevens & Hall. 8vo. 20 s.]

Horsley, J. W. Prisons & prisoners. N. Y., M. F. Mansfield & Co. 233 pp. 12mo. $1.25.

Koni, A. F. Doktor Friedrich Haass. Lebensskizze e. deutschen Philantropen in Russland. Zur Gesch. des russ. Gefängniswesens im 19. Jahrh. Aus dem Russ. L., Duncker & Humblot, 1898. 207 pp. 8vo. M. 4.

Labrouche, Jean. Instruction et criminalité. Aire-sur-Adour, impr. Labrouche, 1898. 58 pp. 8vo.

Laroche. A. De la rélegation des récidivistes . . . (thèse). Nancy, impr. Kreis. 284 pp. 8vo.

Liebmann, Justus. Strafrecht u. Politik. Kriminalpolitische Gedanken eines alten Richters. B., Otto Liebmann, 1898. 103 pp. 8vo. M. 1.60.

Normand, A. Texte et commentaire de la loi du 8 décembre 1897 sur la réforme de l'instruction criminelle . . Étude historique et critique. P., libr. Pédone. 89 pp. 8vo. f. 2.50.

Saleilles, R. L'individualisation de la peine (étude de criminalité sociale). P., F. Alcan, 1898. 288 pp. 8vo.

6. Education.

*Balfour, Graham. Educational systems of Great Britain & Ireland. N. Y., Oxford Univ. Press. (Dial, F. 16 ×)

*Chicago.— Educational Commission. C. (Dial, Ja. 16 + +)

Demolins, Edmond. L'éducation nouvelle. L'école des Roches. P., Firman Didot & Cie., 1898. 302 pp. 18mo. f. 3.50.

Ferriani, Lino. Nel mondo dell' infanzia: studi e note di psicologia. Milano, tip. L. F. Cogliati. 173 pp. 16mo. L. 2.50.

Herbart, J. F. Letters and lectures on education. tr. & ed. by Henry M. & Emmie Felkin. L., Swan Sonnenschein. 302 pp. 8vo.

*Holman, H. English national education: a sketch of the rise of public elementary schools. L., Blackie & Son, 1898. 256 pp. 2s. 6d. (EdR., F. + +)

*Natorp, Paul. Herbart, Pestalozzi u. die heutigen Aufgaben der Erziehungslehre. Acht Vorträge. St., Fr. Frommann. 151 pp. 8vo. M. 1.80. (DL., Ja. 7)

Pädagogische Abhandlungen. Neue Folge. Hrsg. v. W. Bartholomäus. 3. Bd., 6. Hft. Ruland, Wilh. Ueber musikalische Erziehung. Bielefeld, A. Helmich, pp. 83-103. M. 0.50.

Renouard, A. Histoire de l'Ecole supérieure de commerce de Paris (1820-98). P., Union amicale des anciens élèves, 79. Av. de la République, 1898. 216 pp. 8vo.

[Riant, A. Hygiène scolaire. Influence de l'école sur la santé des enfants. 8e éd. P,. Hachette & Cie., 1898. 399 pp. f. 3.50.]

Tadd, J. L. New methods of education: art, real manual training, nature study . . . N. Y., Orange Judd Co., 1898. 436 pp. 12mo. $4.

Walker, F. A. Discussions in education, ed. by J. P. Monroe. N. Y., H. Holt & Co. 342 pp. 8vo. $3. (Dial, F. 16 + +)

*Ziehen, Th. Die Ideenassociation der Kindes. 1. Abthg. B., Reuther & Reichard, 1898. 66 pp. 8vo. M. 1.50. (DL., D. 24)

7. Ethics, Philosophy, Psychology.

Berry, Henri. L'avenir de la philosophie: esquisse d'une synthèse des connaissances, fondée sur l'histoire. P., Hachette & Cie. 8vo. f. 7.50.

Chavez, L. E. A. Resumen sintetico de los principios de moral de Herbert Spencer. P., libr. Bouret, 1898. 212 pp. 16mo.

*Crozier, J. B. My inner life: being a chapter in personal evolution & autobiography. N. Y., Longmans, Green & Co. 562 pp. 8vo. $3.50. (Literature, Ja. 10 + +)

Franke, Armin. Die Religion der Menschheit od. die natürl. Schöpfungsgeschichte. Eine neue Weltanschaug. f. alle nach Wahrheit streb. Menschen. Münster, F. C. Mickl. 98 pp. 8vo. M. 1.

Flügel, Otto. Idealismus u. Materialismus der Geschichte. [Aus Ztschr. f. Philosophie u. Pädagogik.] Langensalza, H. Beyer & Söhne, 1898. 221 pp. 8vo. M. 3.

Gilardoni, Camille. Le positivisme. Vitry-le-François. V. Tavernier et fils, 1898. 212 pp. 8vo.

Glossner, M. Savonarola als Apologet u. Philosoph. Eine philosophiegeschichtl. Studie. Paderborn, F. Schöningh, 1898. 124 pp. 8vo. M. 2.

Kaufmann, N. Philosophie naturelle d'Aristote. Etude de la cause finale et son importance au temps présent, tr. de l'allemand. P., F. Alcan, 1898. 155 pp. 16mo. f. 2.50.

Lotz, Rud. Ormuzd u. Ahriman. Die eth. Frage im Lichte der dualistich-idealist. Weltanschuuang. Athen, Barth & von Hirst. 339 pp. 8vo. M. 5.

Marshall, H. R. Instinct & reason: essay concerning relation of instinct to reason, with

study of nature of religion.   L., Macmillan &
Co., 1898. 588 pp. 8vo. 12s. 6d.
Mauroy, V. Le pur esprit, ou le mentalisme ab-
solu & relatif. T. 1er, 719 pp. 18mo. P.,
Bib. artistique et littéraire, 1898. f. 10.
Pajk, Joh. Praktische Philosophie. Wien, C,
Konegen in Komm., 1898, 180 pp. 8vo. M. 3.
Rossi, Pas. L'animo della folla: appunti di psico-
logia colletiva. Consenza, Raffaele Riccio,
1898. 286 pp. 8vo. L. 3.
Stout, G. F. Manual of psychology. V. 1. L.,
Clive, 1898. 252 pp. 8vo. 4s. 6d. (Univ. tut.
ser.)
Sullivan, M. R. W. Morality as a religion: Ex-
position of some first principles. L., Swan
Sonnenschein, 1898. 304 pp. 8vo. 6s.
Vidal, V. Études morales. L'art d'être heureux . . .
P., libr. Lahure, 1898. 379 pp. 16mo. f. 3.50.

8. Family.

[Fleisch, Max. Prostitution u. Frauenkrankheiten.
Hygienische u. volkswirthschaftl. Betrachtgn.
2. Aufl. Mit e. Anh. Bemerkungen üb. die
strafrechtl. Verfolge der Uebertragg. v. Ge-
schlechtskrankheiten in der Sex. F., Heinze,
1898. 76 pp. 8vo. M. 1.80.]
Hagen, Karl v. Worin liegt die Erklärung f. den
Geschlechtsdrang? Eine populär - medizin.
Studie. Lp., Ernst. 60 pp. 8vo. M. 1.
Hanstein, Adb. v. Die Frauen in der Geschichte
des deutschen Geisteslebens des 18. u. 19.
Jahrh. 1. Bd. Lp., Freund & Wittig, 362 pp.
8vo. M. 8.60.
Hassel, Henriette. Geschichte der deutschen Frau-
enwelt in der Culturbewegung der Zeiten bis
zur Gegenwart . . . Braunschweig, Bock &
Co., 1898. 386 pp. 8vo. M. 8.
Hermann, G. Naturgeschichte der Geschlechts-
liebe. 1. Bd. Sexualismus u. Aetiologie. Beiträge zur Sexual-Physiologie. L., A. Strauch,
1898. 116 pp. 8vo. M. 2.50.
Plea for polygamy. P., libr. Charles Carrington.
280 pp. 8vo.
Salari, Docteur. La syphilis au double point de
vue individuel et social. P., libr. Maloine,
1898. 94 pp. 16mo. f. 2.50.
Schulz, C. T. Gefallene Mädchen u. die Frauen-
forderung: "Gleiches moralisches Maas f.
beide Geschlechter." B., Verlagshaus f.
Volksliteratur. 78 pp. 8vo. M. 1.
Starcke, C. N. La famille dans les différentes sociétés. P., Giard & Brière, 1898. 280 pp. 8vo.
f. 5.
Tarnowsky, B. The sexual instinct & its morbid
manifestations, from the double standpoint of
jurisprudence & psychiatry; tr. from Russian.
P., libr. Charles Carrington, 1898. 240 pp.
8vo.
Weisser, Anna. Schleiermacher's 10 Gebote der
Frau. Ein Beitrag zur Frauenfrage. Pyr-
mont, Vereins-Buchdr , 1898. 63 pp. 8vo. M,
0.75.

9. Finance, Taxation.

Austria— K. k. Finanz-Ministerium. Tabellen
zur Währungs-Statistik. 2. Aufl., 7. Hft., 10.
Abschnitt. Creditverkehr. Tabellen 118-172,
pp. 489–596. Fol. Wien, Hof- u. Staatsdruckerei. M. 0.40.
Benner, S. Benner's prophecies of future ups and
downs in prices ; what years to make money
on pig-iron, hogs, corn, and provisions. 12th
ed.. with forecast for 1899. Cin., Robert Clark
& Co. 233 pp. 8vo. $1.
Bryan, A. C. Hist. of state banking in Maryland. Balto., Johns Hopkins Press. 3–144

pp. 8vo. $1, (J. H. U. studies, 17th ser.,
nos. 1, 2, 3.)
[Catalogue général illustré de monnaies françaises.
Les Bourbons (1589–1789). 2e édition. P., Ca-
binet de numismatique, 2, rue Louvois, 1898.
36 pp. 18mo. f. 2.]
Continental-Compass. Jahrbuch f. Finanz-, Versi-
cherungs- u. Verkehrswesen,l Handel u. In-
dustrie . . . hrsg. v. der Red. der " Finanziellen
u. Assecuranz Revue." 2. Jahrg. 1899. Wien,
C. Konegen. 1210 pp. 8vo. M. 16.
Helferich, Karl. Zur Erneuerung des deutschen
Bankgesetzes. Erweiterter Sonderabdr. aus
Schmollers Jahrbuch. Lp., Duncker & Hum-
blot, 1898. 136 pp. 8vo. M. 3.
Highest & lowest prices, 1899. 27th year. L.,
Mathieson, 1898. 46 pp. 4to. 2s. 6d.
*Issaieff, A. A. Zur Politik des russischen
Finanzministeriums seit Mitte der achtziger
Jahre. St., J. H. W. Dietz, 1898. 72 pp.
8vo. (JGV., 23:1)
Ledos de Beaufort, R. L'achèvement et l'appli-
cation de la réforme monétaire de la Russie.
P., Giard & Brière, 1898. 53 pp. 8vo. f. 2.50.
Lorini, E. La réforme monétaire de la Russie, tr.
. . . . P., Giard & Brière, 1898. 247 pp. 8vo.
f. 6.
Miguet, E. Les inégalités fiscales. Les sociétés
religieuses et les sociétés laïques devant l'im-
pôt. Havre, impr. Murer, 1898. 48 pp. 8vo.
Miller, H. A. Money and bimetallism. L., G.
P. Putnam's Sons. 8vo. 5s.
Monete greche. romane e venete (Museo civico
Correr in Venezia). Venezia, tip. Emiliana,
1898. 249 pp. 8vo. L. 5.
Skinner, T. Stock exchange year book for 1899.
25th year of publication. L., Skinner. 1716 pp.
8vo. 25s.

10. History.

Adams, H. B., ed. ared Sparks & Alexis de
Tocqueville. Balto., Johns Hopkins Press,
[1898]. (J. H. U. studies, 16th ser., no. 12.)
pp. 4-61. $0.25.
Addy. S. O. Evolution of the English house. L.,
Swan Sonnenschein. 252 pp. 12mo. 4s. 6d. (So-
cial England ser.)
Alford. H. S. S., & Sword, W. D. The Egyptian
Soudan, its loss & recovery . . . . N. Y.,
Macmillan Co., 1898. 336 pp. 8vo. $4.
Arndt, Ernst Moritz. Ein Lebensbild in Briefen.
Nach ungedruckten u. gedruckten Quellen,
hrsg. v. Heinr. Meisner u. Rob. Geerds. B.,
G. Reimer, 1898. 561 pp. 8vo. M. 7.
Bates, F. G. Rhode Island & the formation of the
Union. N. Y., Macmillan Co., 1898. 3–320
pp. 8vo. $1.50. (Columbian Univ. studies,
V. 10, no. 2.)
Below, G. v. Die neue historische Methode [aus
" Historische Zeitschrift."] München, R.
Oldenburg, 1898. pp. 193-273. 8vo. M. 1.60.
[Blok, P. J. History of the people of the Nether-
lands. Pt. 1. L., G. P. Putnam's Sons. 8vo.
12s. 6d.]
[Blondel, G. L'essor industriel et commercial du
peuple allemand. 2e édition. P., libr. La-
rose, 1898. 404 pp. 18mo. f. 3.50.]
Cadell, R, Sir John Cope & the rebellion of 1745.
L., Blackwood & Sons. 4to. 10s. 6d.
Caro, Geo. Genua u. die Mächte am Mittelmeer
1257-1311. Ein Beitrag zur Gesch. des 13.
Jahrh. 2. Bd. Halle, M. Niemeyer, 1898. 471
pp. 8vo. M. 14.
Carpenter, E. J. America in the Hawaiian islands.
Bo., Small, Maynard & Co. 275 pp. 12mo
$1.50.

Cox, W. V., & Northrup, M. H. Life of Samuel Sullivan Cox & his friend Milton Harlow Northrup. Syracuse, N. Y., M. H. Northrup, 1898. 280 pp. 8vo. $2.

Cunerville, de. Le Canada et les intérêts français. P., libr. André & Cie. 79 pp. 18mo.

Cutts, E. L. Parish priests & their people in the middle ages in England. N. Y., E. & J. B. young & Co., 1898. 596 pp. il. 12mo. $3.

*Dandliker, K. A short history of Switzerland, tr. by E. Salisbury. N. Y., Macmillan Co. 322 pp., maps. 8vo. $2.50. (Outlook, Ja. 28 + +)

Dill, S. Roman society in the last century of the Roman empire. N. Y., Macmillan Co., 1898. 382 pp. 8vo. $4.

Dictionnaire historique et biographique de la Révolution et de l'Empire (1789-1815). Ouvrage rédigé pour l'histoire générale par le docteur Robinet, sous-conservateur à la bibliothèque Carnavalet, pour la partie descriptive et biographique par Adolphe Robert, et pour les matières constitutionnelles et législatives par J. Le Chaplain. T. 1er. A-F. P., libr. historique de Révolution et de l'Empire, 41, rue de Seine.

*Earle, Alice Morse. Home life in colonial days (AJS., Ja., p. 565) (Nation, Ja. 5++) (Literature, ++)

Edgar, J. D. Canada & its capital, with sketches of political & social life at Ottawa. L., Gay, 1898. 10s. 6d.

*Fisher, Herbert. The mediæval empire. N. Y., Macmillan Co. 2 v. 8vo. (Outlook, Ja. 28 + +)

*[Foulke, W. D. Slav or Saxon: a study of the growth & tendencies of Russian civilization. Ed. 2. rev. N. Y., G. P. Putnam's Sons. 141 pp. 8vo. $1.] (Questions of the day ser.) (Outlook, F. 4 X)

Garnett, Rich. Edward Gibbon Wakefield. N. Y., Longmans, Green & Co., 1898. 386 pp. 12mo. $1.50. (Builders of Great Britain ser. no. 4.)

Geschichte der europäischen Staaten. Hrsg. v. A. H. L. Heeren, F. A. Ukert, W. v. Giesebrecht u. K. Lamprecht. 58. Lfg., 2. Abtlg., u. 59. Lfg., 1. Abtlg. Gotha, F. A. Perthes. 496 pp. 8vo. M. 10.

Giacometti, G. L'unità italienne: deuxième partie, 1861-2: aperçus d'histoire politique et diplomatique. P., Plon, Nourrit & Cie., 1898. 459 pp. 18mo. f. 3.50.

[Gordon in Central Africa, 1874-79. With portrait, map of the country . . . . From original letters and documents. Ed. by G. B. Hill. New ed. L., Macmillan & Co. 478 pp. 8vo. 6s.]

Greene, E. B. Provincial governor in the English colonies of No. America. N. Y., Longmans, Green & Co., 1898. 292 pp. 8vo. $1.50. (Harvard historical monographs, no. 7.)

Gregorovius, F. The emperor Hadrian: a picture of the Graeco-Roman world in his time, tr. by Mary E. Robinson. L., Macmillan Co., 1898. 436 pp. 8vo. 12s.

Grisar, H. Geschichte Roms u. d. Päpste im Mittelalter. 2. u. 3. Lfg. F., Herder, 1898. à M. 1.60.

Hagenmeyer, K. Die Revolutionsjahre 1848-9. Schilderung auf Grund eigener Anschaug. u. persönl. Erlebnisse. Karlsruhe, J. J. Reiff, 1898. 192 pp. 8vo. M. 1.50.

Halstead, Murat. Story of the Philippines. N. Y., Western M. Wilson, 1898. 400 pp. 8vo. $2.

Historical Society Transactions. New series. V. 12. L., Longmans, Green & Co., 1898. 8vo. 21s.

[Historische Bibliothek. Hrsg v. der Red. der Historischen Zeitschriften. 1. Bd. Schiemann, Thdr. Heinrich v. Treitschkes Lehr- u. Wan-

derjahre 1834-66. 2. Aufl. München, R. Oldenburg, 1898. 291 pp. 8vo. M. 5.]

Hourst, Lieut. French enterprise in Africa. Personal narrative of his exploration of the Niger, tr. by Mrs. Arthur Bell. L., Chapman & Hall, 1898. 536 pp. 8vo.

Hume, M. A. S. Spain: its greatness & decay (1479-1788). N. Y., Macmillan Co. 470 pp. 8vo.

Janes, L. G. Our nation's peril: social ideals & social progress. Bo., J. H. West Co. 31 pp. 8vo. $0.25. [Against expansion.]

*Jones, R. J. C. British merchant service: hist. of British mercantile marine from earliest times to present day. L., Low, Marston & Co., 1898. (Athenæum, D. 24++)

Jullian, C. Notes sur l'histoire en France au 19e siècle. P., libr. Hachette & Cie., [1898]. 128 pp. 16mo.

Kennan, G. Campaigning in Cuba. N. Y., Century Co. 269 pp. 8vo. $1.50.

Kennedy, J. Story of the West Indies. L., H. Marshall, 1898. 162 pp. 12mo. 1s. 6d. (Story of the empire.)

*Ketterer, J. A. Karl der Grosse u. die Kirche. München, R. Oldenburg, 1898. 279 pp. 8vo. M. 5. (DL., D. 3)

King, Rufus. Life & correspondence of Rufus King. Ed. by his grandson, C. R. King, 1898. In 6 v. V. 5. N. Y., G. P. Putnam's Sons, 1898. $5.

Klacko, Julian. Rome et la Renaissance . . . . Jules II. P., libr. Plon, Nourrit & Cie., 1898. 453 pp. 8vo. f. 10.

*Kuhne, Alfred. Das Herrscheridéal des Mittelalters u. Kaiser Fried. I. [Leipziger Studien aus dem Gebiet der Geschichte, V. 5, 2. Hft.] Lp., Duncker & Humblot, 1898. 63 pp. 8vo. M. 1.60. (DL., D. 24)

Kurth, G. Les origines de la civilisation moderne. P., libr. Retaux, 1898. 2 v. (328 pp. & 358 pp.) 8vo.

Lala, Ramon Reyes. Philippine islands. N. Y., Continental Pub. Co. 342 pp., maps, Q. $2.50.

La Roncière, C. de. Histoire de la marine française. 1. Les origines. P., Plon, Nourrit & Cie. 536 pp. 8vo.

[Lincoln, Abraham, & Douglas, Stephen A. Political debates, 1858 . . . . also the two great speeches . . . . 1859. New ed. Cleveland, Burrows Bros. Co., 1898. 415 pp. 8vo. $3.50.]

Macdonald, G. The Gold Coast, past & present: a short description of the country & its people. N. Y., Longmans, Green & Co., 1898. 352 pp. 12mo. $2.50

*Mayer, Ernst. Deutsche u. französische Verfassungsgeschichte vom 9. bis zum 14. Jahrh. Lp., Deichert. 2 Bde. M. 24, (LC., Ja. 21 + +)

Molinier, E. Histoire générale des arts appliquées à l'industrie du 5e au 18e siècle. T. 3: le mobilier aux 17e et 18e siècles. P., libr. Levy, 1898. 294 pp. 4to.

Molmenti, P. La vie privée à Venise depuis l'origine jusqu'à la chute de la république. Part 2-3. Venise, Ferd. Ongania, 1896-7 [1898]. 2 v. (216 & 166 pp.) 16mo.

[Montesquieu. Considérations sur les causes de la grandeur des Romains et de leur décadence, 2e. éd. P., Hachette & Cie., 1898. f. 1.80.]

Monumenta Germaniae historica . . . . Epistolarum tom V, pars I. Karolini aevi III. (1. Hälfte.) B., Weidmann. 360 pp. 4to. M. 12.

*Ratzel, Friedrich. Deutschland. Lp., F. W. Grunow, 1898. 332 pp. 8vo. M. 2.50. (Globus, 75:4) (DL., Ja. 14)

*Ropes, J. C. Story of the Civil War : a concise account of the war in the U. S. A. between

1861 and 1865. In 4 v. V. 2. Campaigns of 1862. N. Y., G. P. Putnam's Sons. 8vo. $2.50. (Outlook, F. 4 + +)

Sagnac, Ph. La législation civile de la Révolution française (1789-1804). P., Hachette & Cie. 8vo. f. 10.

Schelbicky, C. M. Die Inquisition u. ihre Gegner. Graz, U. Moser, 1898. 78 pp. 16mo, M. 0.16.

Siebert, W. H. The underground railroad from slavery to freedom. N. Y., Macmillan Co., 1898. 478 pp. 8vo. $4. (Dial, F. 16 + +)

Stevens, G. W. With Kitchener to Karthoum. N. Y., Dodd, Mead & Co., 1898. 326 pp. 12mo. $1.50.

*Trevelyan, G. O. American Revolution. Pt. 1, 1766-76. 480 pp. 8vo. 16s. (Outlook, Ja. 28 ×)

*Van Dyke, Paul. Age of the Renaissance. N. Y., Christ. Literature Pub. Co. $1.50. (Outlook. F. 4 + +)

Watson, T. E. Story of France, from the earliest times to the consulate of Napoleon Bonaparte. In 2 v. V. 1, To end of the reign of Louis XV. N. Y., Macmillan Co.

Williams, Helen Maria. Narrative of events in France .... 1815, with an account of the state of society .... New ed. Cleveland, Burrows Bros. Co., 1898. 225 pp. 8vo. $2.50.

[Williams, S. W. Middle kingdom: survey of the geography, government, literature, social life, arts & history of the Chinese empire & its inhabitants. Revised ed. L., W. H. Allen. 2 v., il. (1650 pp.) 8vo. 42s.]

Wolf, Gust. Deutsche Geschichte im Zeitalter der Gegenreformation. 1. Bd. 3. Abtlg. B., O. Seehagen. pp. 509-789. M. 9.

*Worcester, D. C. Philippine islands & their people: record of personal observation & experience; summary of important facts in the hist. of the archipelago. N. Y., Macmillan Co., 1898. 550 pp. 8vo. $4. (Academy, D. 17 + +) (Dial, D. 16 + +) (Critic, Ja. + +) (AA., F + +)

Zévort, E. Histoire de la troisième république. T. 3. La présidence de Jules Grévy. P., F. Alcan, 1898. 550 pp. 8vo. f. 7.

11. International Law.

Dupuis, C. Le droit de la guerre maritime d'après les doctrines anglaises contemporaines. P., libr. Pédone, 1898. 476 pp. 8vo. f. 10.

Holland, T. E. Studies in international law. L., Henry Frowde, 1898. 322 pp. 8vo. 10s. 6d.

Valmigere, P. De l'arbitrage internationale (thèse). P., A. Rousseau. 75 p. 8vo. [1898.]

12. Labor.

[Arbeitsmarkt, der. Monatsschrift der Centralstelle f. Arbeitsmarkt-Berichte. Zugleich Organ des Verbandes deutscher Arbeitsnachweise. Hrsg. J. Jastrow. 2. Jahrg. Oktbr. 1898-Septbr. 1899. 12 Nrn. 8vo. (Nr. 1, 16 pp.) B., H. S. Hermann, 1898. M. 2.]

Arbeitsnachweis-Konferenz zu Leipzig .... 1898. Bericht. Hamburg, Verlagsanstalt u. Druckerei. 107 pp. 8vo. M. 1.50.

[Bellom, J. Les grèves: leurs origines, leur caractère, leur causes, leur conséquences, leur remède. 3e édition. P., l'auteur, 36, rue de Varennes, 1898. 29 pp. 8vo.]

Bertheau, Ch. L'ouvrière. La vie de famille; l'ouvrier logé chez lui; accession à la propriété. P., libr. Chevalier-Marescq, 1898. 293 pp. 8vo.

Brunel, H. De la conciliation, en matière commerciale (thèse). P., libr. Larose. 231 pp. 8vo.

*Crook, J. W. German wage theories: a history of their development. N. Y., Macmillan Co., 1899. 8vo. $1.50. (Columbia Univ. studies, V. 9, no. 2.) (Dial, F. 1 + ?)

Donohoe, T. Popular progress: the cause of agricultural & industrial depression & the remedy. Buffalo, N. Y., T. Donohoe, 1898 (Murray & Dawson). 236 pp. 12mo. $1.

Gardissal, Marcel. Loi du 9 avril 1898 sur les ré-sponsabilités des accidents dont les ouvrières sont victimes dans leur travail. P., A. Rousseau, 1898. 64 pp. 8vo.

Gewerbe-Verzeichnis in systematischer u. alpha-betischer Ordnung nach der Berufs- u. Gewerbe-zählung 1895. Hrsg. v. kaiserl. statist. Amt. B., Puttkammer & Mühlbrecht, 1898. 99 pp. 8vo. M. 1.

Great Britain—Chief Labour Correspondent of the Board of Trade. Strikes & lockouts of 1897. Statistical tables. L., Eyre & Spottiswoode, 1898.

Great Britain—Parliament. Friendly societies, in-dustrial & provident societies & trade unions. Reports for 1897. Part A. Appendices. L., Eyre & Spottiswoode, 1898.

Hauser, H. Ouvriers du temps passé (15e et 16e siècles. P., F. Alcan. 252 pp. f. 6.

Kolisch, R. Die Gewerbeordnung f. das Deutsche Reich m. den Ausführungsbestimmung. 1. Bd. Hannover, Helwing, 1898. 702 pp. 8vo. M. 20.

Legge e regolamento per gli infortuni degli operai sul lavoro. Alessandria, tip. succ. Gazzotti e C., 1898. 47 pp. 8vo.

Législation du travail en Italie. Loi du 17 mars 1898 et règlement du 25 sept. 1898. P., Sécré-tariat du Congrès international des accidents du travail, [1898]. 55 pp. 8vo.

Martin, G. La grande industrie sous le règne de Louis XIV (1660-1715). P., A. Rousseau. 452 pp. 8vo. f. 9.

Piolet, J. B. L'œuvre des jardins ouvriers à Saint-Etienne, a Sedan, en France et à l'étranger. P., libr. Retaux, 1898. 154 pp. 18mo.

Rieu, F. La cooperation ouvrière à travers les âges .... (thèse). P., Chevalier-Marescq & Cie., 272 pp. 18mo. f. 4.

*Robinson, Mrs. Harriet H. Loom & spindle. (AJS., N., p. 424) (Nation, Ja. 5 + —) (Dial, F. 16 +)

Schriften der Centralstelle f. Arbeiter-Wohlfahrts-einrichtungen. Nr. 16. B., C. Heymann's Verl., 1898. 274 pp. 8vo. M. 1.

*Sommerfeld, Th. Handbuch der Gewerbekrank-heiten. I. Bd. B., Coblentz, 1898. 536 pp. 8vo. M. 6. (JGV., 23 : 1).

[Suttner, Bertha v. Das Maschinenzeitalter. Zu-kunftsvorlesungen üb. unsere Zeit. 3. Aufl. Dresden, C. Pierson. 335 pp. 8vo. M. 3.50.]

Violot, Robert. Théorie juridique de la partici-pation aux bénéfices dans le louage de services. P., A. Rousseau, 1898. 267 pp. 8vo.

*Waentig, Heinr. Gewerbliche Mittelstandpolitik. Lp., Duncker & Humblot, 1898. 483 pp. 8vo. M. 9.60. (LC., D. 17).

13. Political Economy.

Amer. Econ. Assoc. President's annual address: Relation between economics & politics, by A. T. Hadley. Report of the committee on cur-rency reform, report of committee on 12th census. N. Y., Macmillan Co. 3-69 pp. 12mo. $0.50. (Economic studies, no. 1.)

Arendt, Ch. Economie politique scientifique: définitions et méthodes. P., libr. Larose, 1898. 130 pp. 8vo. f. 3.

Cossa, Em. Del consumo delle ricchezze . . . .

Pt. 2. Teorio del consumo. Bologna, libr. Treves, 1898. 129 pp. 8vo. L. 2.50.

*Grunzel, J. Handbuch der internationalen Handelspolitik. Mainz, Vienne, 1898. ? (JEc., D. + +)

*Hecht, G. H. Colberts politische u. volkswirthschaftliche Grundanschauungen. Fr., J. C. B. Mohr, 1898. 69 pp. 8vo M. 2. (DL., D. 17)

Hellen, Ed. v. der. Italiens Volkswirtschaft. Ein Vortrag. Fr., J. C. B. Mohr. 40 pp. 8vo. M. 0.80.

Loria, Achille. La costituzione economica odierna. Torino, fratella Bocca. [1899.] 822 pp. 8vo. L. 16

Rambaud, Joseph. Histoire des doctrines économiques. P., libr. Larose, 1898. 516 pp. 8vo. f. 10.

Sayous, A. E. Etude économique et juridique sur les bourses allemandes de valeurs et de commerce. P., A. Rousseau, 1898. 661 pp. 8vo. f. 12.50.

Tessonneau, M. Esquisse d'un tableau raisonné des causes de la production, de la circulation, de la distribution et de la consommation de la richesse. P., Giard & Brière, [1898]. 132 pp. 18mo. f. 2.

*Weichs-Glon, Friedr. Die Brotfrage u. ihre Lösung. Lp., Duncker & Humblot. 1898. 110 pp. 8vo. M. 2.20. (LC., Ja. 14) (DL., D. 24)

14. Political Science.

Adams, C. F. Imperialism & the tracks of our forefathers: a paper read before the Lexington, Mass., Historical Society . . . Bo., Dana, Estes & Co. 37 pp. 8vo. $0.25.

Binding, Karl. Deutsche Staatsgrundgesetze in diplomatisch genauem Abdrucke . . . 2. u. 3. Hft. 8vo. Lp., W. Engelmann. 91 u. 58 pp. 8vo. M. 1 50 u. 1.

Bouvier, J. Encyclopædic dictionary of English & American law. L., Sweet & Maxwell. 2 v. 8vo. 50s.

Brentano, Lujo. Gesammelte Aufsätze. 1. Bd. Erbrechtspolitik, alte u. neue Feudalität St., J. G. Cotta. 1898. 592 pp. 8vo. M. 14.

Constitutional year-book for 1899. 15th year. L., Blackwood & Sons. 454 pp. 8vo. 10s.

Deploge, Simon. Referendum in Switzerland, tr. . . . N. Y., Longmans, Green & Co., 1898.

*Dernberg, Heinr. Das bürgerliche Recht des Deutschen Reichs u. Preussens. III. Bd. Das Sachrecht. Halle a. S., Buchh. d. Waisenhauses, 1898. 792 pp. 8vo. M. 12. (LC., D. 24)

Deutscher Kolonial-Kalender u. statistisches Handbuch f. d. J. 1899. Nach amtl. Quellen bearb. u. hrsg. v. Gust. Meinecke. 11. Jahrg. B., Deutscher Kolonial-Verlag., 1898. 245 pp. 8vo. M. 1.50.

Dilke, C. W. The British empire. L., Chatto & Wundus, 1898. 166 pp. 8vo. 3s. 6d.

Dumont, A. Natalité et démocratie. Conférences faites à l'Ecole d'anthropologie de Paris. P., Sleicher frères, 1898. 231 pp. 16mo.

[Esmen, A. Eléments de droit constitutionnel français et comparé. 2e édition. 1er fasc. P., libr. Larose, 1898. 416 pp. 8vo. f. 10.]

Etienne. Eug. Les compagnies de colonisation. P., libr. Challamel, 1898. 78 pp. 8vo.

Fernald, J. C. The imperial republic. N. Y., Funk & Wagnalls Co. 192 pp., maps, 12mo. $0.75. [Strongly advocates expansion.]

Ford. H. J. Rise & growth of American politics: sketch of constitutional development. N. Y., Macmillan, 1898. 418 pp. 8vo. $1.25.

France—Ministère des affaires étrangères. Documents diplomatiques. Affaires d'Orient.

Evacuation de la Crète. . . . P., Impr. nationale. 53 pp. 4to.

Garland, A. H. Experience in the supreme court of the U. S. with some reflections & suggestions as to that tribunal. Wash., J. Byrne & Co., 1898.

Garufi, C. A. Monete e coni nella storia del dritto siculo dagli Arabi ai Martini. Parte 1, con documenti. . . . Palermo, Alberto Reber, 1898. 174 pp. 8vo. L. 7.

Great Britain—Colonial reports for 1897-8. British Solomon Islands, 1d. Gibraltar, 1d. Gold Coast, 2d. Grenada, 1½d. Leeward Islands, 1½d. Mauritius & Rodriguez, 2½d. L., Eyre & Spottiswoode, 1898.

Hamelin, Maurice. Des concessions coloniales. Etude sur les modes d'alienation de terres domaniales en Algérie et dans les colonies françaises (thèse). P., A. Rousseau, 1898. 432 pp. 8vo.

[Handwörterbuch d. Staatswiss. 2. Aufl. 3. Lfg. Jena, G. Fischer, 1898. M. 5.]

Hassert, Kurt. Deutschlands Kolonien. Erwerbungs- u. Entwickelungsgeschichte, Landes- u. Volkskunde u. wirthschaftl. Bedeutg. unserer Schutzgebiete. Lp., Seele & Co. 332 pp. 8vo. M. 4.50.

Hyslop, J. H. Democracy: a study of government. N. Y., Ch. Scribner's Sons. 300 pp. 8vo. $1.50.

[Jahnke, Herm. Fürst Bismarck. Sein Leben u. seine Zeit. Vaterländisches Ehren- u. Heldenbuch des 19. Jahrh. 2. Aufl. . . . B., P. Kittel. 1080 pp. 8vo. M. 10.]

Japan—Civil code, 1898. Tr. by Dr. Ludwig Lönholm. L., P. S. King & Co., 1898. 190 pp. 8vo. 10s.

Koloniales Jahrbuch. Beiträge u. Mitteilgn. aus dem Gebiete der Kolonialwissenschaft u. Kolonialpraxis. Hrsg. v. Gust. Meinecke. 11. Jahrg. 1898. 11. Hft. 96 pp. 8vo. B., Deutscher Kolonial-Verlag, 1898. M. 6.

Krausse, A. China in decay: Handbook to Far Eastern question. L., Chapman & Hall, 1898. 421 pp. 8vo. 6 maps, 21 ill. 12s.

Kuhlenbeck, Ludw. Von den Pandekten zum bürgerlichen Gesetzbuch. Eine dogmat. Einführg. in das Studium des bürgerl. Rechts. 2. Tl. 1. Hälfte. B., C. Heymann's Verl. 382 pp. 8vo. M. 7.

La Chapelle, S. de. De la vraie représentation politique. . . . P., libr. Pichon, 1898. 373 pp. 18mo.

Laws of England Encyclopædia, ed. by A. Wood Renton. L., Sweet & Maxwell. 12 v. 8vo. £12.

[Mac Adaras. Le salut de la République par la décentralisation et les réformes démocratiques. Nouvelle éd. P., l'auteur, 50, avenue Marceau, 1898. 50 pp. 18mo.]

[Mattiroli, Lu. Instituzioni di diritto giudiziario civile italliano. 2d ed. . . . ampliata. Torion, fratelli Bocca [1899]. 626 pp. 8vo. L. 12.]

*Meier, Ernst. Hannoversche Verfassungs- u. Verwaltungsgeschichte, 1680–1866. 1. Bd. Die Verfassungsgeschichte. Lp., Duncker & Humblot, 1898. 556 pp. 8vo. (JGV., 23:1)

*Meili, Fr. Institutionen der vergleichenden echtswissenschaft. Ein Grundriss. St., F. Enke, 1898. 286 pp. 8vo. M. 8. (LC., Ja. 7)

Morelli, A. Corso di diritto costituzionale: la costituzione italiana. Modena, G. Pizzolotti, 1897-8. 380 pp. 8vo.

*Palmer, Roundell (Earl of Selborne). Memorials. Pt. 2. Personal & political. L., Macmillan Co. 2 v. (Athenæum, D. 10 + +) (Academy, D. 31 + +)

Reichstag-Session (die) 1897-8. 9. Legislatur-
periode. V. Session. Nebst Anh., Die Reichstagswahlen v. 1898. 1. u. 2. Hft. Br., Puttkammer & Mühlbrecht, 1898. M. 2.
Sabbatini, Pio. Corso di scienza dell, amministra-
zione, anno academico 1897-8, Modena, G.
Pizzolotti, 1897-8. 408 pp. 8vo.
[Saillard, F. De l'éducation et du gouvernement de
la démocratie, ou du seul moyen pour mettre
fin à nos divisions et pour fonder l'unité de la
France. Nouvelle éd. P., impr. Motteroz,
1898. 82 pp. 16mo.]
Sammlung nationalökonomischer u. statistischer
Abhandlungen des staatswissenschaftlichen
Seminars zu Halle a. d. S., hrsg. v. Prof. Joh.
Conrad. 19. Bd. Tildsley, J. L. Die Entste-
hung u. die ökonomischen Grundsätze der
Chartistenbewegung. Jena, G. Fischer. 139
pp. 8vo. M. 3.50.
Sciotto Pinto, Manfredi. Sovranita popolare o sovranita degli ottimi. Contributo alla teoria democratica della sovranita. Torino, fratelli Bocca,
1898. 49 pp. 8vo.
Seckel, Emil. Beiträge zur Geschichte beider
Rechte im Mittelalter. (In 3 Bdn.) 1. Bd.
Zur Geschichte der popularen Literatur des
römisch-canon. Rechts. Tübingen, H. Laupp,
1898. 539 pp. 8vo. M. 20.
Société de la législation étrangère. Annuaire de la
législation étrangère, contenant le texte des
principales lois votées dans les pays étrangers
en 1895. (25e année.) P., libr. Pichon. 1063
pp. 8vo. f. 18.
Treitscke, Heinr. v. Politik. Vorlesungen, geh.
an der Universität zu Berlin. 2. (Schluss-) Bd.
Lp., S. Hirzel. 575 pp. 8vo. M. 12.
Weissbuch. Vorgelegt dem Reichstage in der 1.
Sess. der 10. Legislatur-Periode. 19. Tl. B.,
C. Heymann's Verl. 218 pp. 2do. M. 5.

15. Religion, Churches.

*Ayres, S. G., & C. T. Sitterly. History of the
English Bible studied by the library method.
N. Y., W. B. Ketcham. (Outlook, Ja. 14 + +)
Baptist handbook for 1899. L., J. Clarke. 552 pp.
8vo. 3s.
Briggs, C. A. General introduction to the study
of Holy Scripture, containing the principles,
methods, history, & results of its several
departments & of the whole. N. Y., Ch.
Scribner's Sons. 688 pp. 8vo. $3.
Bright, W. Some aspects of primitive church life.
N. Y., Longmans, Green & Co. 268 pp.
12mo. $1.75.
Buttgenbach, Frz. Die kirchliche Kunst in Mono-
graphien, Skizzen u. Kunstbildern. Aachen,
I. Schweitzer, 1898. 204 pp. 8vo. M. 20.
Bygone church life in Scotland, ed. by William
Andrews. L., Andrews, 278 pp. 8vo. 7s. 6d.
Camut, L'abbé. Coup d'œil sur l'état du catholi-
cisme dans le monde à la fin du 19e siècle. P.,
libr. de l'Oeuvre de Saint-Paul, 1898. 144 pp.
8vo.
Carnagie, W. H. Church troubles & common
sense : a plea for reason & responsibility. L.,
L. Murray. 134 pp. 8vo. 2s. 6d.
Catholic directory, ecclesiastical register &
almanac for 1899. 62d year. L., Burns &
Oates. 598 pp. 12mo. 1s. 6d.
Congregational year-book, 1899 containing pro-
ceedings of Congregational Union for 1898
. . . . L., Congregational Union. 634 pp. 8vo.
2s. 6d.
*Copinger, W. A. The Bible & its transmission.
L., H. Sotheran & Co., 1898. (220 copies
printed.) £5, 5s. (Athenæum, D. 17. p.
849)

Cornill, C. H. Geschichte des Volkes Israel von
den ältesten Zeiten bis zur Zerstörung Jeru-
salems durch die Römer. Chicago. Lp., P.
Harrassowitz. 326 pp. 8vo. M. 8.
Creighton, M. Position of the Church of England :
an address. L., Longmans. 24 pp. 8vo. 6d.
[Deutsch-evangelische Jahrbuch f. 1899. Hrsg.
im Auftrag der freien kirchlich sozialen
Konferenz v. Lic. Weber. 1. Jahrg. B., Buchh.
der Berliner Stadt-Mission, 1898. 328 pp.
8vo. M. 3.
Dictionary of the Bible, ed. by James Hastings.
(AJS., N. 1898, p. 425) (Outlook, Ja. 14—)
(AJT., Ja.+ — [A symposium by many
writers])
*Gamble, Eliza Burt. God-idea of the ancients or
sex in religion. N. Y., G. P. Putnam's, 1897.
(Globus, 75 : 4 — —)
*Gehring, Johannes. Die Sekten der russischen
Kirche (1003-1897). Lp., Fr. Richte, 1898.
240 pp. 8vo. M. 5. (DL., Ja. 21)
*Gilbert, G. H. Student's life of Jesus. N. Y.,
Macmillan Co. (Outlook, Ja. 7 + +)
Graham, J. A. Missionary expansion since the
Reformation. N. Y. & C., F. H. Revell
Co. 244 pp. 12mo. $1.25.
Green, S. G. Christian creed & the creeds of
Christendom : 7 lectures. L., Macmillan Co.
368 pp. 8vo. 6s. (Angus lectures, 1898.)
Hall, Newman. Autobiography. Bo., T. Y.
Crowell & Co., [1898]. 391 pp. 8vo. $3.
[Handwörterbuch des biblischen Altertums f.
gebildete Bibelleser. Hrsg. v. E. C. A. Riehm.
2. Aufl. Mit vielen Abbildgn. (In 24 Lfg.)
1.-8. Lfg. (1. Bd.) Bielefeld, Velhagen &
Klasing. 640 pp. M. 1.]
[Harcourt, Sir W. V. Crisis in the church : letters
to the "Times." Enl. ed. L., Thynne. 152 pp.
12mo. 6d.]
Harnack, Adolph. History of dogma, from 3d
German ed. . . . . V. 5. Bo., Little, Brown
& Co. 331 pp. 8vo. $2.50. (Theological
trans. libr., V. 10.)
*Holman, A. J. Comparative self-pronouncing
Sunday-School Teacher's Bible. Phil., A. J.
Holman. (Outlook, Ja. 28 +)
Hore, A. H. Eighteen centuries of the orthodox
Greek church. L., Parker. 714 pp. 8vo. 15s.
*Hubrick, Ed. Die parlamentarische Rede-
freiheit u. Disciplin. Auf der Grundlage von
Rechtsversicherung u. Rechtsgeschichte dar-
gestellt nach deut. Recht. B., C. Heymann's
Verl., 1898. 494 pp. 8vo. M. 9. (LC., Ja. 14)
DL., Ja. 14)
Jaulmes, Edmond. Les Quakers français : étude
historique (thèse). Nimes, impr. Chastanier,
1898. 59 pp. 8vo.
Kalendar of the English church & ecclesiastical
almanac for 1899. L., Church Print. Co.
372 pp. 8vo. 1s. 6d.
Die) katholische Kirche unserer Zeit u. ihre
Diener in Wort u. Bild. Hrsg. v. der Leo-
Gesellschaft in Wien. 1. Bd. Rom. Das Ober-
haupt, die Einrichtg. u. die Verwaltg. der
Gesamtkirche. Bearb. v. Paul Maria Baum-
garten . . . . B., Allgemeine Verlagsgesell-
schaft. 691 pp. (1209 ill.) 4to. M. 36.
La Barre, R. P. de. La vie du dogme catholique.
Autorité; évolution. P., libr. Lethielleux,
[1898]. 292 pp. 16mo.
Langin, Geo. Der Christus der Geschichte u.
sein Christentum. Der Gemeinde dargestellt.
2. Abth. Lp., O. Wigand, 1898. 209 pp.
8vo. M. 2.
Laveleye, E. de. De l'avenir des peuples catho-
liques, avec les opinions de Gladstone,
Michelet, Quenet, Sismondi, d'Hulst et

autres. P., Fischbacher & Cie., 1898. 109 pp. 16mo.
*Lorimer, G. C. Christianity and the social state. Ph., H. J. Rowland, 1898. 12mo. (Outlook, Ja. 14 + +)
Milsand, J. Le catholicisme et le mal de notre époque. P., libr. Fischbacher, 1898. 168 pp. 16mo.
Onclair, A. Le clergé et la question sociale. P., libr. Teque, 1898. 177 pp. 18mo.
Peters, C. King Solomon's Golden Ophir: research into most ancient gold production in history. L., Leadenhall Press. 118 pp. 8vo. 2s. 6d.
Picard, L. Christianity or agnosticism? tr. by J. G. Macleod. L., Sands.
*Resch, Alfred. Die Logia Jesu nach dem griechischen u. hebräischen Text wiederhergestellt. Ein Versuch. Lp., J. C. Hinrichs, 1898. 301 pp. 8vo. M. 10. (DL., D. 3)
[Robertson, F. W. Sermons preached at Oxford, Cheltenham, & Brighton. Pref. by C. B. Robertson. Intro. by Ian Maclaren. 5th series. People's ed. L., Kegan Paul, 1898. 368 pp. 12mo. 1s. 6d.]
Sabatier, Maxime. L'église et le travail manuel. P., Bloud & Barral, 1898. 63 pp. 16mo. (Science et religion.)
*Sayce, A. H. Early Israel & the surrounding nations. (AJS., Ja., p. 568) (Athenæum, Ja. 7 + —)
Smith, G. A. Life of Henry Drummond. N. Y., Doubleday & McClure Co., 1898. 541 pp. 8vo. $3. (Nation, Ja. 12 + +) (Literature, F. 3 + +)
Springer, Jaro. Das Leben Jesu in Bildern alter Meister. Mit kunsthistor. Einleitg. B., Fische & Franke, 1898. 36 Taf. m. 8 pp. Text. Kart. M. 6.
Tissot, J. J. Life of our Lord Jesus Christ. il. Autograph ed. N. Y., Doubleday & McClure Co., 1898. 4 v. 4to. silk. Subs. $150. Edition de grande luxe, 2 v. $500.
Tolstoi, L. Religion et morale, tr. du russe . . . P., impr. Davy. 50 pp. 16mo.
Wallace, W. Lectures & essays on natural theology & ethics. Ed. & biog. intro. by Ed. Caird. L., Henry Frowde. 606 pp. 8vo. 12s. 6d.

16. Sanitary and Domestic Science.

Arbeiten aus dem kaiserl. Gesundheitsamte (Beihefte zu den Veröffentlichgn. des kaiserl. Gesundheitsamtes. 15. Bd.) B., J. Springer. M. 9.
Edwards, W. N. Beverages we drink: popular treatise . . . . L., Ideal Pub. Union. 228 pp. 8vo. 1s.
Encyclopädische Jahrbücher der gesammten Heilkunde. Hrsg. v. Alb. Eulenberg. 3. Jahrg. 2. Hälfte. Wien, Urban & Schwarzenberg. pp. 321–671. 8vo. M. 7.50. (Kplt. geb. M. 17.50.)
[Hanausek, T. F. Lehrbuch der Somatologie u. Hygiene f. Lehrer- u. Lehrerinnenbildungsanstalten. Mit 104 Abbildgn. 2. Aufl. Lp., G. Freytag, 1898. 158 pp. 8vo. M. 2.80.]
Howard, O. O. Fighting for humanity, or camp & quarterdeck. N. Y., F. T. Neeley, 1898. 221 pp. 12mo. $1.25. $0.50.
Luckes, E. C. E. General nursing. L., Kegan Paul, 1898. 366 pp. 8vo. 5s.
Moeller, Dr. Die Hausfrau in ihrem Schalten u. Walten. Ulm, J. Ebner, 1898. 904 pp. 8vo. M. 6.80.
Moore, E. C. S. Sanitary engineering: practical treatise on collection, removal, final disposal of sewage . . . 534 ill. 34 pl. L, Batsford, 1898. 650 pp. 8vo.
Murique, Mme. Economie domestique et hygiène à l'usage des écoles primaires de filles . . . P., Delalain frères, 1898. f. 1.50.
Parloa, Maria. Home economics: guide to house hold management, including the proper treatment of the materials entering into the structure & furnishing of the modern home. N. Y. 7s. 6d.
Peschaud, Marcel. L'intervention de l'Etat en matière d'hygiène publique (thèse). P. Lamulle et Poisson, 1898. 443 pp. 8vo.
*Winthrop, Alice W. Diet in illness & convalescence. N. Y., Harper & Bros. (Outlook Ja. 14 + +)

17. Socialism.

Almanach socialiste illustré pour 1899 (5e année). P., rue Réaumur, 1898. 128 pp. 16mo. f. 0.30.
Baratta, C. M. La libertà dell' operario. Parma, tip. Salesiana, 1898. 134 pp. 8vo. L. 1.
Hamilton, C. G. Dal detto al fatto nel socialismo. Firenze, libr. Raffaele, 1898. 396 pp. 16mo. L. 3.
Le Bon, G. Psychologie du socialisme. P., F. Alcan, 1898. 502 pp. 8vo. f. 7.50. (Bibliothèque de philosophie contemporaine.)
Lichtenberger, A. Le socialisme et la Révolution française. Etude sur les idées socialistes en France de 1789 à 1796. P., F. Alcan, 1898. 320 pp. 8vo. f. 5.
Merlino, S. Formes et essences du socialisme P., Giard & Brière, 1898. 298 pp. 18mo. f. 3.50. (Bibliothèque socialiste internationale.)
Rienzi (H. Van Kal). Socialisme et liberté. P. Giard & Brière, 1898. 272 pp. 18mo. f. 3. (Bibliothèque socialiste internationale.)

18. Sociology.

Bechterew, W. v. Suggestion u. ihre sociale Bedeutung. Rede . . . . Deutsch v. Rich. Weinberg. Lp., A. Georgi, 1898. 84 pp. 8vo. M. 2.
Bertheau, C. Réformes pratiques. P., libr. Chevalier Marescq, 1898. 208 pp. 16mo.
Beukemann, Wilh. Zur Frage der wirtschaftlichen u. sozialen Entwickelung. Nach 2 Vorträgen. Hamburg, L. Friederichsen & Co. 30 pp. 8vo. M. 0.60.
Cohn, Georg. Gemeinderschaft u. Hausgenossenschaft. Vortrag. [Aus Zeitshr. f. vergleich. Rechtswissenschaft.] St., F. Enke, 1898. 128 pp. 8vo. M. 4.
Comte, A. Auguste Comte méconnu. Auguste Comte conservateur. Extraits de son œuvre finale (1851-7). P., libr. Le Soudier. 335 pp. 8vo.
Duprat, G. L. Étude relative aux rapports entre la psychologie et la sociologie. P., Impr. nationale. 20 pp. 8vo. (Extrait du Bulletin des sciences économiques et sociales du comité des travaux historique et scientifique.)
*Espinas, Alfred. La philosophie sociale du 18e siècle et la Révolution. (Monist, Ja. + +)
Ferrari, Celso. La libertà politica e il dritto internazionale: saggio d'interpretazione sociologica della storia. Torino, Roux Frassati e C., 1898. 340 pp. 8vo. L. 4.
Fingerrique f. das Studium der Socialwissenschaften. Vortrag. Aschaffenburg, C. Krebs, 1898. 14 pp. 12mo. M. 0.30.
Fourniere, E. L'idéalisme social. P., F. Alcan. 314 pp. 8vo. f. 6.
Hauriou, Maurice. Leçons sur le mouvement social, données à Toulouse en 1898. P., libr. Larose, 1898. 176 pp. 8vo. f. 4.

Hillemand, Constant. La vie et l'œuvre d'Auguste Comte: discours. P., 10, rue Monsieur le Prince, 1898. 22 pp. 8vo. f. 0.15.

Hobson, J. A. John Ruskin, social reformer. Bo., Dana, Estes & Co., 1898. 357 pp. 8vo. $1.50.

*[Holbach's Sociales System, oder natürliche Principien der Moral u. der Politik, mit einer Untersuchung über den Einfluss der Regierung auf die Sitten. Nach dem Original übersetzt. . . . . 3 Tle. in 1 Bd. Lp., Thomas, 1898. 552 pp. 8vo. M. 5.] (LC., Ja. 14 + +)

*Izoulet, Jean. Les quatre problèmes sociaux. P., Colin & Cie. 31 pp. (JGV., 23 : 1)

Lotz, Rud. Die Philosophie u. der Zweck des Lebens. Athen, Barth u. von Hirst. 73 pp. 8vo. M. 1.20.

Luporini, Ciro, La questione sociale e l'educazione popolare. Palermo, Alberto Reber, 1898. 72 pp. 8vo. L. 1.50.

Massart, Jean, et Emile Vandervelde. Parasitisme organique et parasitisme social. P., libr. Reinwald, 1898. 175 pp. 16mo. f. 2.50. (Bibliothèque internat. des. sci. sociologiques, 2.)

Massow, C. v. Die soziale Frage vom konservativen Standpunkt. St., Ch. Belser. 47 pp. 8vo. M. 0.80. (Zeitfragen des christlichen Volkslebens, 175. Hft.)

Mikalowitch, Nikolai. Die Gottwerdung des Menschen. Ein Beitrag zur Entwicklungsgeschichte der Menschheit. C., Koelling & Klappenbach. 116 pp. 8vo. M. 2.

*Morselli, Emilio. Elementi di sociologia generale. Mailand, Hoepli, 1898. 170 pp. 8vo. M. 1. 50. (Manuali Hoepli, Serie scientifica 271) (LC., D. 10) ,

*Natorp, Paul. Sózialpädagogik. (AJS., Ja., p. 570) (DL., Ja. 7)

Patten, S. N. Development of English thought: a study in the economic interpretation of history. N. Y., Macmillan & Co. 415 pp. 8vo.

Payson, E. P. Suggestions toward an applied science of sociology. N. Y., G. P. Putnam's Sons, 1898. 237 pp. 12mo. $1.25.

Perris, G. H. Life of Count Leo Tolstoï. N. Y., imported by the New Amsterdam Bk. Co., 1898. 8vo. $1.75.

*Ratzenhofer, Gustav. Die sociologische Erkenntnis. (AJS., N., p. 426; Ja., + +) (LC., Ja. 7)

Reichesberg, N. Die Sociologie, die sociale Frage u. der sogen. Rechtssocialismus. Eine Auseinandersetz. von Ludwig Stein, Verf. des Buches: Die soziale Frage im Lichte der Philosophie. Bern, Steiger & Co., 1898. 131 pp. 8vo. M. 2.50.

Stubbs, C. W. Charles Kingsley & the social movement. L., Blackie. 200 pp. 8vo. 2s. 6d. (Victorian era ser.)

Ziegler, Theob. Die geistigen u. socialen Strömungen des 19. Jahrh. B., G. Bondi, 1898. 714 pp. 8vo. M. 10.

19. Statistics.

(Statistics will be brought up to date in the next issue.)

20. Unclassified.

Alcoolisme (l') : sa nature, ses effets, ses remèdes. Notions sommaires. Par les Frères des écoles chrétiennes. P., libr. Poussielgue. 24 pp. 8vo.

Ambrozovics, R. Der ungarische Eisenbahn-Zonentarif u. seine Theorie. . . . Wien, Spielhagen & Schwrick. 44 pp. 8vo. M. 1.20.

Anderlind, O. B. L. Die Landwirthschaft in Aegypten. L., Landwirthschaftl. Schulbuchh., 1898. 97 pp. 8vo. M. 2.

Arbeiten der deutschen Landwirthschafts-Gesellschaft. Hrsg. vom Direktorum, 36. Hft. Br., P. Parey, 1898. 290 pp. 8vo. M. 3. 36. Neuere Erfahrungen auf dem Gebiet des Ackerbaus. 10 Vorträge.

Bailey, L. H., ed. Principles of agriculture: a text-book for schools & rural societies. N. Y., Macmillan Co. 300 pp. 16mo. $1.25. (Rural science ser.)

Bericht üb. Handel u. Industrie der Schweiz im J. 1897. Erstattet vom Vorort des schweizer. Handels- u. Industrie-Vereins. Zürich, Meyer & Zeller, 1898. 211 pp. 4to. M. 4.

Bibliothek f. Socialwissenschaft m. besond. Rücksicht auf sociale Anthropologie u. Pathologie, hrsg. v. Hans Kurella. 13. Bd. Grotjahn, Alfred. Der Alkoholismus nach Wesen, Wirkung u. Verbreitung. Lp., G. W. Wigand, 1898. 412 pp. 8vo. M. 6.

Bigg's General railway acts. Collection of public general acts for regulation of railways . . . . 1830–98. 15th ed. L., Waterlow & Son. 968 pp. 8vo. 25s.

Blondel, Georges. Die landwirthschaftlichen Zustände im Deutschen Reiche. Nach dem Franz. bearb. v. Dr. Alb. Ahn u. Prosper Mullendorff. Köln, A. Ahn. 264 pp. 8vo. M. 4.

*Böhm, Otto. Eine Studie über die Organisation des Getreidenkaufs in Amerika. Indien u. Russland, sowie in einigen deutschen Staaten. St., J. G. Cotta, 1898. 96 pp. 8vo. (Münchener volkswirth. Studien.) (JGV., 23 : 1)

Bonne, Geo. Die Alkoholfrage in ihrer Bedeutung f. (die) ärztliche Praxis . . . Tübingen, Osiander, 1898. 47 pp. 8vo. M. 1.

Case for Sunday closing. Compiled for service of Sunday-closing special campaign. L., Ideal Pub. Union. 198 pp. 8vo. 1s.

Charles-Roux, J. Notre marine marchande. P., Colin & Cie. 410 pp. 16mo. f. 4.

Coulon, H. De la liberté de tester. Exposé des motifs et projet de loi. P., Marchal & Billard, 1898. 81 pp. 8vo.

France—Direction générale des douanes. Tableau générale du commerce et de la navigation, 1897. 2e volume. Navigation internationale. . . . P., Impr. nationale, 1898. 526 pp. 4to.

France—Ministère de l'agriculture. Statistique agricole annuelle, 1897. P., Impr. nationale, 1898. 269 pp. 8vo.

Great Britain—Registrar of Friendly societies. Proceedings of registrars under Building Societies Acts ; abstract of annual accounts. Pt. 2. L., Eyre & Spottiswoode, 1898. 1s. 7d.

Lechler, Paul. Der erste Schritt zur nationalen Wohnungsreform. Vortrag. B., E. Hofmann & Co. 28 pp. 8vo. M. 0.50.

Luzzati, Ippolito. Sul riordinamento del credito agrario. Torino, Unione tipografico-edit., 1898. 202 pp. 8vo. L. 4.

Mathéi de Valfons, H. Les sociétés de secours mutuels en France (these). Poitiers, Blais & Roy 193 pp. 8vo.

Morris, W. Art & beauty of the earth: a lecture delivered . . . . 1881. N. Y., Longmans, Green & Co. 31 pp. 8vo. $1.

Prévost, G. Essai d'une nouvelle esthétique basée sur la physiologie. P., Roger & Chernoviz, 1898. 63 pp. 12mo. f. 1.25.

Pulling. N. Old age pensions: scheme for the establishment of a govt. superannuation fund. L., Chapman & Hall, 1898. 8vo. 1s.

*Rousiers, Paul de. Les industries monopolisées (trusts) aux Etats-Unis. P., libr. Colin & Cie., 1898. 339 pp. 18mo. f. 4. (YR., F. X)

Schlemmer, G., et H. Bonneau. Recueil de documents relatifs à l'histoire parlementaire de

chemins de fer français. Principaux discours aux chambres. . . . P., libr. Dunod, 1898.
Schriften der Centralstelle f. Vorbereitung v. Handelsvertragen. 5. Hft. Brandt, D. M. v.
China u. seine Handelsbeziehungen zum Auslande. m. besond. Berücksicht der deutschen. B., Siemenroth & Troschel. 139 pp. 8vo. M. 3.
Schulte im Hofe, A. Die Ramiefaser u. die wirthschaftliche Bedeutung der Ramiekultur f. die deutschen Kolonien. B., Deutscher Kolonial-Verlag, 1898. 50 pp. 8vo. M. 1.50.
Stewart, Freeman. Shall we grow the sugar that we consume? Some considerations suggested by Secretary Wilson's article in the "Forum." . . . Swarthmore, Pa., R. S. Dare. 32 pp. 16mo. $0.15.
Switzerland—Landwirthschaftsdepartement. Landwirtnschaftliches Jahrbuch der Schweiz. 12. Bd. 1898. Bern, K. J. Wyss, 1898. 386 pp. 8vo. M. 5.

Syndicat de l'Union des marchands de soie de Lyon. Statistique de la production de la soie en France et à l'étranger (1895), 25e année. Lyon, impr. Rey, 1898. 51 pp. 8vo.
Taggart, W. S. Cotton spinning. V. 3. L., Macmillan Co., 1898. 458 pp. 8vo. 10s.
Ueberhorst, Wilh. Amethysta. Ein Versuch zur Lösg. der Alkoholfrage. . . . 87 pp. 8vo. M. 1. (Tages- u. Lebensfragen. Nr. 24.)
United States—Interstate commerce reports. V. 7. Decisions of the Interstate Commerce Commission, Sept., 1896—May, 1898. Rochester, N. Y., Lawyers' Coöp. Pub. Co., 1898.
Verzeichnis der Betriebs- (Fabrik-) Krankenkassen des Deutschen Reiches. Nebst e. alphabet. Register der Ortschaften u. die Fabrikationszweige. B., Verlag der Arbeiter-Versorg., A. Troschel, 1898. 184 pp. 8vo. M. 6.
Volmar, Frdr. Beiträge zur Eisenbahnpolitik der europäischen Staaten. Bern, Steiger & Co., 1898. 45 pp. 8vo. M. 0.80.

ARTICLES IN PERIODICALS.

[Articles preceded by stars and followed by a reference to a number of the JOURNAL will be found in abstract under the head "Notes and Abstracts" in that number of the JOURNAL. Articles dealing with *Biography, Associations, Cities,* and *Towns* will be found grouped under those heads.]

Æsthetics : Dessoir, Max. Beiträge zur Aesthetik, ASP., 5 : 4.
See also Art.
Africa : Baratieri, O. Les Anglais au Soudan et la question d'Abyssinie, RDM., Ja. 15.
Bennett, E. N. After Omdurman, CoR., Ja.
Decle, Lionel. Tanganika railway, FR., Ja.
Agriculture : Kautsky, Karl. Schranken der kapitalistischen Landwirthschaft, ASG., 13 : 4.
Verney, Edmund. Agricultural depression, CoR., Ja.
Anthropology : Ardu Onnis, C. Contributo all' antropologia della Sardegna, AAE., 28 : 2.
Keller, C. Fortschritte auf dem Gebiete der Haustierkunde, Globus, 75 : 4.
Peet, S. D. Social & domestic life of the cliff dwellers, AA., F.
Verhandlungen der Berliner Gesellschaft für Anthropologie, Ethnologie u. Urgeschichte, ZE., 30 : 4.
See also Craniometry, Ethnology, Folk-Lore.
Arbitration, Industrial : Price, L. L. Industrial conciliation : a retrospect, JEc., D.
Army : *see* United States.
Art : Cammerts, E. A propos de l'art et la Révolution, HN., Ja.
Labusquière, John. Le congrès international de l'art public, ReS., Ja.
Robinson, Sir Chas. Reorganization of our national art museums, NC., D.
Associations : Anethran, Jules d'. Une fédération mutualiste, RéfS., Ja. 16.
Calisse, C. Le associazioni in Italia avanti le origini del comune, RISS., D.
Dufourmantelle, Maurice. Les associations coopératives en Allemagne, RéfS., Ja. 1.
Flox, Fournier de. Les associations agricoles allemandes, RéfS., D. 15.
La Société d'économie sociale, RéfS.. Ja. 1.
Austria : *see* Finance, Labor.
Bankruptcy : Demscomb, S. W. Federal bankruptcy law, PSQ., D.
Biography : Aguinaldo : a character sketch, RRN., F.
Brace, Emma. Chas. Loring Brace, ChR., F.
Clarke, Wm. Bismarck, CoR., Ja.
Ford, P. L. Many-sided Franklin, Century, Ja.
Gide, Ch. Un nouveau socialiste chrétien (Prof. Herron), RCS., Ja.
Horton, R. T. Robert William Dale, CoR., Ja.

Le Play, Frédéric, et Jean Reynaud : fragments de correspondence inédits, RéfS., D. 16
Lewis, C. T. Bismarck the man & the statesman, Harper's Magazine, Ja.
Morse, A. E. Politics of John Adams, AHR., Ja.
Simons, Sadie E. Educational value of biography, EdR., Ja.
Biology : Morgan, C. L. Vitalism, Monist, Ja.
Bohemia : Lutzow, Francis. Bohemian question, NC., D.
Canals : Crowninshield, A. S. Advantages of the Nicaragua canal, Century Magazine, Ja.
Hunter, W. H. Amer. isthmus & the interoceanic canal, EM., F.
Hunter, W. H. Equipment, management, & economic influence of the ship canal, EM., D.-Ja.
Census : Report of committee on the 12th census, Economic Studies, F.
Charities : Addams, Jane. Subtle problems of charity, Atlantic, F.
Ayres, Philip. Training for practical philanthropy, RRN., F.
Bosanquet, H. Industrial training of women, ChOR., D.
Münsterberg. Emil. Beiträge zur Gesch. u. Theorie des Armenwesens. Aus dem Nachlass Fr. Reitzensteins, JGV., 23 : 1.
See also Biography, Children, Housing, & each no. of ChR., ChOR., RBP., RP.
Children : Kelsey, Carl. Proposed child saving in Illinois, ChR., Ja.
Vane, Lady. Boarding out under ladies committees. National Review, Ja.
See also Pedagogy.
Child-Study : Sully, Ja. Dollatry, CoR., Ja.
China : Leroy-Beaulieu, Pierre. Le problème chinois, RDM., Ja. 1.
Marco, E. De Viti de. Rivalita internazionali in Cina, GEc., Ja.
Reid, Gilbert. Shall the open door be closed? National Review, D.
Schumacher, Hermann. Die chinesischen Vertragshäfen, ihre wirthschaftliche Stellung u. Bedeutung, JNS., 16 : 6.
Smith, Judson. Awakening of China, NAR., F.
See also Great Britain, Railroads, Russia.
Christianity : Talamo, S. La morale cristiano secondo il socialista moderno, RiISS., Ja.

Evolution: Lloyd, A. H. Evolution evolved, Monist, Ja.

Mantegazza, Paolo. L'evoluzione regressiva, AAE., 28:2.

Expansion: Clinch, B. J. Imperialism as a policy for America, ACQ., Ja.

Clowes, W. L. American expansion & the inheritance of the race, FR., D.

Giddings, F. H. Imperialism, PSQ., D.

Family: Letourneau, Ch. Un fait de psychologie primitive, Bulletins de la Société d'anthropologie de Paris, 9:4.

Schmoller, Gustav. Urgeschichte der Familie, Mutterrecht u. Gentilverfassung, JGV., 23:1.

Feeble-Minded: Johnson, Alex. Concerning a form of degeneracy. II., AJS., Ja.

Finance: Andrew, A. P. What ought to be called money? QJE., Ja.

Carlile, W. W. Transition to gold in England & in India, JPE., D.

Cleveland, F. A. Final report of the monetary commission, AAP., Ja.

Fiamingo, G. M. Measure of the value of money according to European colonies, JPE.

Finances françaises et la budget, RPP., Ja.

Foville, A. de. Spanish currency, JPE., D.

Glauert, O. Börse u. Reichsbank, JNS., 16:6.

Hazell, A. P. Quantity theory of money from the Marxist standpoint, JPE., D.

Helfferich. Le renouvellement du privilège de la Banque de l'Empire, RPP., Ja.

Mitchell, W. C. Resumption of specie pay't in Austria-Hungary, JPE., D.

Northbrook, Earl of. Alternatives before the Indian gov't, National Review, D.

Raffalovich, Arthur. Le marché financier en 1898, JEc., Ja.

Report of committee on currency reform, Economic Studies, F.

Roberts, G. E. Increasing supply of gold, F., F.

Sayous, A. E. Concentration du traffic de banque en Allemagne, JEc., Ja.

Sayous, A. E. Reorganisation der französichen Produkten u. Warenbörsen, JNS., 16:6.

Stroll, Moritz. Ueber das deutsche Geldwesen im Kriegsfall, JGV., 23:1.

Taussig, F. W. United States treasury in 1894-6, QJE., Ja.

Will, T. E. Stable money, JPE., D.

See also each no. of BML., BMN., JCB., Journal of Finance.

Folk-Lore: Dunlop, W. Australian folk-lore stories, JAI., N.

Food: Bache, Rene. What the very poor eat, S., F.

Forests: Wagner, Gustav. Die Regelung der Waldproduktion nach ihren gesamtwirthschaftlichen Nutzleistungen, ZGS., 55:1.

France: Adye, Lieut.-Colonel. Colonial weakness of France, NC., Ja.

Billot, A. Le rapprochement commercial entre la France et l'Italie, souvenirs diplomatiques, RDM., Ja., 1.

Coming social revolution in France, CoR., Ja.

France, Russia, & the Nile, CoR., D.

Guyot, Yves. Dreyfus drama & its significance, NC., Ja.

Hauser, Henri. French reformation & the French people in the 16th century, AHR., Ja.

oly, Henri. Nos grandes institutions nationJales: la magistrature, RéfS., Ja. 16.

McGrath, P. T. France in Newfoundland, NC., Ja.

Robinson, J. H. France today, PSQ., D.

Rouxel. A quoi tient l'infériorité actuelle des Français? JEc., Ja.

See also Africa, Art, Colonies, Finance, Insurance, Italy, Labor, Russia, Socialism, Sociol.

Gambling: Hoyois. Du jeur devant le Parlement Belge, RéfS., Ja. 16.

Germany: Arch-enemy of England, CoR., D.

Blondel, Georges. La politique commerciale de l'Allemagne et son influence sur la situation sociale du pays, RéfS., Ja. 1.

Eucken, Rudolf. Are the Germans still a nation of thinkers? F., Ja.

Valbert, G. L'Allemagne de la fin de ce siècle, RDM., Ja. 1.

See also Colonies, Finance, Great Britain, Labor, United States.

Girls : *see* Housing.

Great Britain : Fashoda & Lord Salisbury's vindication, FR., D.

Lande, Ch. de la. En route vers le particularisme, SS., D.

Rogers, J. G. Liberal collapse, NC., Ja.

Stutfield, H. E. M. The company scandals, National Review, D.

See also Africa, China, Education, Egypt, Finance, Germany, Philosophy, Trade.

Gold : *see* Finance.

Heredity : Le Dantec, F. Les néo-darwiniens et l'hérédité des caractères acquis, RPh., Ja.

History : Cunningham, W. L'utilità della studia della storia economica, RilS., N.

Round, J. H. Historical research, NC., D.

Thompson, Anna B. How to study history, EdR., F.

Housing: Hardy, C. Sur le ogement des classes laborieuses, RéfS., Ja. 16.

Hill, Octavia. Management of houses for the poor, ChOR., Ja.

Leake, Mrs. Percy. A girls' lodging house, NC., D.

Meade, T. de C., & Addie, Peter. Housing of the working classes, S., Ja.

Nerincx, Alfred. Les habitations ouvrieres à Berlin, RéfS., Ja. 1.

Hungary : Matlekovits, A. v. Die wirthschaftliche Entwicklung Ungarns seit 1867, ZVS, 7:4.

Imagination : Giuffrida-Ruggeri, V. L'evoluzione dell' imaginazione, AAE., 28: 2.

Imperialism: *see* Expansion.

India: *see* Finance, Land.

Indians: Grinnell, G. B. The wild Indian, Atlantic, Ja.

Grinnell, G. B. The Indian on the reservation, Atlantic, F.

Industry: Bellet, Daniel. Mouvement scientifique et industriel, JEc., Ja.

Martin, Germain. Buffon et la Fayette manufacturiers, RéfS., Ja. 1.

Institutional Church: *see* Church.

Insurance : Frankenberg, H. v. Reichsgesetzliche Familienversicherung, JGV., 23:1.

Lange, Ernst. Statistik der Krankenversicherung im Deutschen Reich . . . 1896, ASG., 13:4.

Turquan, Victor. Les retraités de l'état, RéfS., D. 16.

See also Associations, Old Age.

Interstate Commerce: *see* Railroads.

Italians: Kelly, Florence. Die Italiener Chicagos, ASG., 13:4.

Italy: Dalla Volta, R. La prima breccia nel dazio consumo dei comuni italiani, GEc., Ja. (?)

Giretti, E. L'accordo commerciale colla Francia, GEc., Ja.

Vitali, V. Elementi etnici e storica del carattere degli italiani, RilS., N.

See also Associations, France.

Japan : Lorini, Eteocle. Commercio e industria del Giappone secondo le statistiche piu recenti, RilS., Ja.

Pathogenese psychosexueller Anomalien, Archiv f. Kriminal-Anthropologie, O.-Ja.
See also Criminology & Penology, Women.
Single Tax: *see* Taxation.
Shipping: Payne, S. E. Our merchant marine, NAR., F.
Slavery: Bugbee, L. G. Slavery in early Texas, PSQ., D.
Socialism: Deville, Gabriel. L'affaire Dreyfus et le parti socialiste, DS., N.
François, G. Socialism in France, JPE., D.
Laterade. La définition du socialisme, ReS., Ja.
Milhaud, Edgard. Le congrès socialiste de Stuttgart, ReS., Ja.
Veber, Adrien. Le sixième congrès de la Fédération des conseillers municipaux socialistes, ReS., Ja.
Sociology: Borrowed foundation; foundation of sociology, PSM., D., F.
Bouet, H. Adam Ferguson et ses idées politiques et sociales, JEc., D.
Cady, G. L. Sentimental sociology, BS., Ja.
Croce, Benedotto. Le livre de M. Stammler, DS., N.
Fages, C. Evolution du Darwinisme sociologique, HN., Ja.
Groppali, A. Roberto Ardigò, la sociologia e il materialismo storico, RiIS., N.
Groppali, Alessandro. La science comme phénomène social, DS., O.
May, R. E. Verhältnis des Verbrauches der Massen zu demjenigen der "kleinen Leute," der Wohlhabenden u. Reichen u. die Marxistische Doktrin, JGV., 23:1.
Rambaud, Joseph. Un jugement sur Le Play et l'école de la réforme sociale, RéfS., Ja. 16.
Rivet, Victor. Science sociale et les français d'aujourd'hui, RCS., N.
Rivalta, Valentino. I problemi sociali e la loro formola ideale, RISS., D.
Schinz, A. Le positivisme est une méthode et non un système, RPh., Ja.
Schubert-Soldern, Richard. Individuum u. Gemeinschaft, ZGS., 55:1.
Small, A. W. Unit in sociology, AAP., Ja.
Solvay, Ernest. Le productivisme sociale, AIS., 4:5.
Tangorra, V. La sociologia e l'economica politica, RiIS., N.
See also Biography, Philosophy.
Street Railways: Crocker, G. G. Passenger traffic of Boston & the subway, New England Magazine, Ja.
Strikes: Grandmaison, Charles le Cour. La grève du batiment, RDM., D. 15.
Sugar: Développement de l'industrie sucrière en Russe, JEc., D.
McVey, F. L. Sugar importations & revenues, JPE.,D.
Tariff: Lang, L. La politique douanière internationale de l'avenir, RPP., Ja.
Taxation: Adams, H. C. Federal taxation of interstate commerce, RRN., F.
Garrison, W. L., & others. Ethics of the single tax, A., Ja.
Inhulsen, C. H. P. Die englischen Nachlasssteuern, JNS., 16:6.
Laurent, Fr. L'impôt du tabac en France: ses origines et son développement, RPP., Ja.
Powers, L. G. Some inequalities in land taxation, AJS., Ja.
Thwing, C. F. Taxation of college property, EdR., F.
Veber, Adrien. La suppression des octrois, ReS., D.

Wells, D. A. Diffusion of taxes, PSM., Ja.-F.
Telegraphs: Ch. Extension of submarine telegraphy in 25 years, EM., D.
Telephones: Hastie, A. H. Telephone tangle & the way to untie it, FR., D.
Trade: Farrer. Lord. Does trade follow the flag? ColR., D.
Lambert, Agnes. Neglecting our customers, NC., D.
Raffalovich, Arthur. Un manuel de la politique commerciale internationale, JEc., D.
Trade Unions: Addams, Jane. Trades unions & public duty, AJS., Ja.
Cummings, Edward. Collectivist philosophy of trade unionism, QJE., Ja.
Hollander, J. H. Study of trade unionism, PSQ., D.
See also Labor.
United States: Adler, Felix. Parting of the ways in the foreign policy of U. S., IJE., O.
Bradford, R. B. Coaling stations for the navy, F., F.
Clarke, G. S. Imperial responsibilities a national gain, NAR., F.
Corbin, H. C. Army of the U. S., F., Ja.
Denby, Charles. Why the treaty should be ratified, F., F.
Dilke, C. W. Future relations of Great Britain & U. S., F., Ja.
Eliot, C. W. Destructive & constructive energies of our gov't compared, Atlantic, Ja.
Hart, A. B. United States as a world power, Harper's Magazine, F.
Hoar, G. F. Four national conventions, Scribner's Magazine, F.
Gilbert, G. A. The Connecticut Loyalists, AHR., Ja.
Kerr, J. H. Recent election & its results, F., F.
Julian, G. W. First Republican national convention, AHR., Ja.
Law, A. M. American affairs, National Review, D.-Ja.
Lowell, A. L. Colonial expansion of the U. S., Atlantic, F.
Mabie, H. W. American literature & American nationality, F., Ja.
Peck, F. W. America & the Paris exposition of 1900, NAR., Ja.
See also Bankruptcy, Biography, Canals, Census, Cuba. Education, Expansion, Finance Indians, Legislation, Negro, Philippines Shipping, Taxation.
Wages: Bowley, A. L. Comparison of the changes in wages in France, the U. S., & the U. K. from 1840 to 1891, JEc., D.
Bowley, A. L. Statistics of wages in the United Kingdom during the last 100 years, Jour. Roy. Statist. Society, D.
War: Hill, D. J. War & extension of civilization, F., F.
Novicow, J. The spirit of conquest, PSM., F.
Water: Lefevre, G. S. London water supply NC., D.
Wealth: Merrill, C. C. Christian conception of wealth, BS.
See also Luxury.
Wheat: Hyde. John. America & the wheat problem, NAR., F.
Women: Braun, Lily. Anfänge der Frauenbewegung, ASG., 13:14.
Thomas, W. I. Sex in primitive industry, AJS. Ja.
Veblen, Thorstein. Barbarian status of women AJS., Ja.
See also Charities, Political Economy.

ABBREVIATIONS USED IN BIBLIOGRAPHY.

Places of Publication: B., Berlin; Bo., Boston; C., Chicago; Cin., Cincinnati; F., Frankfurt a. M.; Fr., Freiburg i. B.; L., London; Lp., Leipzig; M., Milan; N. Y., New York; P., Paris; Ph., Philadelphia; S., Strassburg; St., Stuttgart; T., Turin; W., Washington. *Prices:* d., pence; f., franc; L., lira; M., mark; s., shilling. *Months:* Ja. F. Mr. Ap. My. Je. Jl. Ag. S. O. N. D. *Periodicals:*

A.   Arena.
AA.   American Anthropologist.
AAC.   Archives d'anthropologie criminelle.
AAE.   Archivo per l'antropologia e la etnologia.
AAP.   Annals of the American Academy of Political and Social Science.
AC.   L'Association catholique.
ACQ.   American Catholic Quarterly Review.
AEL.   Annals d'École libre des sciences politiques.
AGP.   Archiv für Geschichte der Philosophie.
AHR.   American Historical Review.
AIS.   Annals de l'Institute de science sociale.
AJP.   American Journal of Psychology.
AJS.   American Journal of Sociology.
AJT.   American Journal of Theology.
ALR.   American Law Register.
ALRv.   American Law Review.
AMP.   Académie des sciences morales et politiques, Séances.
AOR.   Archiv für öffentliches Recht.
ASA.   American Statistical Association, Publications.
ASAr.   Allgemeine statistisches Archiv.
ASG.   Archive für sociale Gesetzgebung und Statistik.
ASP.   Archiv für systematische Philosophie.
BDL.   Bulletin of the Department of Labor.
BG.   Blätter für Gefängnisskunde.
BML.   Banker's Magazine, London.
BMN.   Banker's Magazine, New York.
BOT.   Bulletin de l'Office du Travail.
BS.   Bibliotheca Sacra.
BSt.   Bulletin de statistique et de legislation comparée.
BUI.   Bulletin de l'Union internationale de droit pénale.
C.   Cosmopolis.
ChOR.   Charity Organisation Review.
ChR.   Charities Review.
CoR.   Contemporary Review.
DL.   Deutsche Litteraturzeitung.
DR.   Deutsche Revue.
DRu.   Deutsche Rundschau.
DS.   Devenir social.
DZG.   Deutsche Zeitschrift für Geschichtswissenschaft.
EcJ.   Economic Journal.
EcR.   Economic Review.
EdR.   Educational Review.
EHR.   English Historical Review.
EM.   Engineering Magazine.
F.   Forum.
FR.   Fortnightly Review.
GEc.   Giornale degli economisti.
GM.   Gunton's Magazine.
HLR.   Harvard Law Review.
HN.   Humanité nouvelle.
HR.   Hygienische Rundschau.
HZ.   Historische Zeitschrift.
IAE.   Internationales Archiv für Ethnographie.
IJE.   International Journal of Ethics.
JAI.   Journal of the Anthropological Institute of Great Britain and Ireland.
JCB.   Journal of the Canadian Bankers' Association.
JEc.   Journal des économistes.
JFI.   Journal of the Franklin Institute.
JGV.   Jahrbuch für Gesetzgebung, Verwaltung und Volkswirthschaft.

JHS.   Johns Hopkins University Studies in History and Political Science.
JPE.   Journal of Political Economy.
JNS.   Jahrbücher für National-Oekonomie und Statistik.
LC.   Literarisches Centralblatt.
LG.   Labor Gazette.
LoQR.   London Quarterly Review.
LQR.   Law Quarterly Review.
MHM.   Mansfield House Magazine.
MIM.   Monatsschrift für innere Mission.
MA.   Municipal Affairs.
NA.   Nuova antologia.
NAR.   North American Review.
NC.   Nineteenth Century.
NS.   Natural Science.
NT.   New Time.
NW.   New World.
NZ.   Neue Zeit.
PhR.   Philosophical Review.
PSM.   Popular Science Monthly.
PSQ.   Political Science Quarterly
PsR.   Psychological Review.
QJE.   Quarterly Journal of Economics.
QR.   Quarterly Review.
RBP.   Rivista benificenza publica.
RCS.   Revue de christianisme sociale.
RDC.   Rivista di discipline carcerarie.
RDI.   Revue de droit internationale.
RDM.   Revue des deux mondes.
REA.   Revue mensuelle de l'École d'anthropologie de Paris.
RéfS.   Réforme sociale.
ReS.   Revue socialiste.
RH.   Revue historique.
RHD.   Revue d'histoire diplomatique.
RIF.   Rivista italiana di filosofia.
RIS.   Revue internationale de sociologie.
RiIS.   Rivista italia na di sociologia.
RISS.   Rivista internazionale di scienze sociali
RMM.   Revue metaphysique et de morale.
RP.   Revue philanthropique.
RPe.   Revue pénitentiaire.
RPh.   Revue philosophique.
RPP.   Revue politique et parliamentaire.
RRL.   Review of Reviews, London.
RRN.   Review of Reviews, New York.
RSC.   Revue sociale catholique.
RSI.   Revista storica italiana.
RSP.   Revue sociale et politique.
RT.   Revue du travail.
S.   Sanitarian.
SR.   School Review.
SS.   Science sociale
VWP.   Vierteljahrschrift für wissenschaftliche Philosophie.
YR.   Yale Review.
ZE.   Zeitschrift für Ethnologie.
ZGS.   Zeitschrift für die gesammte Staatswissenschaft.
ZPK.   Zeitschrift für Philosophie und philosophische Kritik.
ZPO.   Zeitschrift für das private und öffentliche Recht.
ZPP.   Zeitschrift für Psychologie und Physiologie der Sinnesorgane.
ZS.   Zeitschrift für Socialwissenschaft.
ZVR.   Zeitschrift für vergleichende Rechtswissenschaft.
ZVS.   Zeitschrift für Volkswirthschaft, Socialpolitik und Verwaltung.

[The titles of articles selected from periodicals not in this list will be followed by name of periodical in full.]

THE AMERICAN

JOURNAL OF SOCIOLOGY

VOLUME IV   MAY, 1899   NUMBER 6

TWO WEEKS IN DEPARTMENT STORES.[1]

It is so common for those who purchase goods to think nothing at all about the clerk in attendance, or the conditions under which the goods were produced, that it seems timely just now, when the Consumers' League[2] has started upon a crusade of educating the public, to give a true picture of some conditions existing in Chicago.

The necessity for a thorough investigation of the work of women and children in the large department stores in the city was apparent, and the difficulties manifold. With a view to ascertaining some things which could be learned only from the inside, the investigation which is to form the subject-matter of this paper was undertaken. It seemed evident that valuable information could be obtained if someone were willing to endure the hardships of the saleswoman's life, and from personal experience be able to pass judgment upon observed conditions. The urgency of the need, coupled with an enthusiastic interest in the

[1] It should be distinctly stated that the two department stores in which the material for this paper was collected are not the establishments which have the best reputation of their class in Chicago.

[2] The Consumers' League of Illinois was organized by the collegiate alumnæ of this city in February, 1897, when a standard was adopted and a provisional constitution drawn up. A permanent organization, with Mrs. Charles Henrotin as president, was effected at a meeting held in Hull-House, November 30, 1898. The league at the present time has about eight hundred members.

work for which the Consumers' League stands, led me to join the ranks of the retail clerks for two weeks during the rush of the holiday trade. It may be urged that just judgments could not be formed at a time when conditions must be abnormal. It is true that conditions were abnormal, but the importance of knowing to what extent cannot be overestimated. The consumer should know how far his Christmas shopping works hardship for the clerks. Moreover, he should concern himself with the question as to whether the abnormal conditions he has helped to create are in part mitigated by adequate payment for the work exacted. The law in Illinois[1] prohibits the employment of children under fourteen years, and limits the working day of those between the ages of fourteen and sixteen to ten hours in manufacturing and mercantile establishments, and it should be a matter of concern to the purchaser if his persistence in late shopping leads the merchant to break, or at least evade, the law. It is admittedly a menace to the social weal to have children and young girls working late at night, and thus exposed to the dangers of city streets at a time when physical and moral safety demand that they be at home. One of the objects of this investigation was to find the amount of overtime exacted, and the compensation, if any, that was given. Employers are always ready to tell the best conditions that exist; it remains to others to find the worst. And the Consumers' League utterly refuses to indorse stores that do not live up to its standard all the time.

And yet some will argue that any effort in behalf of the employés in the great stores is unnecessary. Many objections were urged against factory legislation in the early days of that reform. The champions of the movement in England met with strenuous opposition, but finally their frightful revelations of actual conditions overcame their opponents, and a wave of enthusiastic reform set in. The history in this country is similar. From 1830 to 1874 agitation for the protection of women and children in the factories was kept up, till finally, at the latter date, the Massachusetts Act became a reality. Then other

[1] Child-labor law of Illinois, February, 1897.

states followed the example set, until, at the present time, almost all the states having large manufacturing interests have very good factory laws. Illinois is a notable exception.[1] Such, in a word, has been the history of the factory laws. We are just on the eve of an agitation for the amelioration of the conditions under which a vast army of saleswomen and cash children work. Thoughtful people all over the country have already recognized the necessity for this; but the whole body of the people must be awakened. And to help, in a small way, the educative movement here my labor was undertaken.

The difficulty of finding employment was not so great as might be supposed. Owing to the holiday rush, and the consequent need of large reinforcements to the original help, the employers were not insistent on experience as a requisite for the successful applicant. However, it was not until several visits had been made that I was promised a position at three dollars a week. Work was to begin the following Monday, which would give me just two weeks of the Christmas trade. Employment being promised, it seemed desirous to engage board in some home for working women; for the environment which such a place would provide gave promise of the best results. I was fortunate in finding a most satisfactory place not far from the heart of the city, and there I went as a working-woman. This home is deserving of more than passing mention. It provides board and lodging, together with the use of pleasant parlors and library, to working-women under thirty years of age for two dollars and a half a week, if they are content to occupy a single bed in a dormitory. These dormitories are thoughtfully planned, and accommodate from ten to fifteen each. A large proportion of the sixty-five residents were saleswomen, and they, in the course of conversation, gave me much useful information. All classes of girls were there, and most of them received very low wages. A few entries in the house register are here inserted to show the nature of the records kept, and the way in which the girls fill in the columns.

[1] The supreme court declared the law of 1893 unconstitutional.

Name	Age	Nationality	Occupation	Wages per week
	18	American	Saleslady	$4.00
	27	Virginian	Stenographer	6.00
	24	American	Clerk	4.50
	23	American	Clerk	3.00
	29	German	Cashier	6.50
	23	Irish	Saleswoman	6.00
	28	American	Fur worker	5.00
	20	American	Saleslady	3.00

This, then, was the place from which I started out to work on the appointed Monday morning. The hurried breakfast, the rush out into the street thronged with a lunch-carrying humanity hastening to the down-town district, and the cars packed with pale-faced, sleepy-eyed men and women, made the working world seem very real. Hurrying workers filled the heart of the city; no one else was astir. I reached my destination promptly at eight, the time of opening. Then I had to stand in line at the manager's office awaiting my more definite appointment, which was received in due time. But the manager had changed his mind about wages, and said he would give me two dollars a week plus 5 per cent. commission on sales, instead of the regular salary he had mentioned in our former interview. I was then given a number, and by "424" I was known during my stay there. I was sent to the toy department, where I found sixty-seven others who were to be my companions in toil. The place was a dazzling array of all kinds of toys, from a monkey beating a drum to a doll that said "mamma," and a horse whose motor force was to be a small boy. Our business was first to dust and condense[1] the stock, and then to stand ready for customers. We all served in the double capacity of floorwalkers and clerks, and our business was to see that no one escaped without making a purchase. The confusion can be readily imagined. As soon as the elevators emptied themselves on the floor, there was one mad rush of clerks with a quickly spoken, "What would you like, madam?" or, "Something in toys, sir?" And the responses to these questions were indicative of the characters of the people making

[1] This meant to pile like things together in as small space as possible.

them. The majority were rude, some amused, and a few alarmed at the urgency of the clerks. One young boy, on being assailed by half a dozen at once, threw up his hands in horror, and said : "For God's sake, let me get out of here !" and fled down the stairs, not even waiting for the elevator. The cause of such watchful activity on the part of so many employés was the 5 per cent. commission which was to eke out the two or three dollars a week salary. Those who were experienced received the latter sum. And the extra nickels earned meant so much to many of them. Most of the girls in that department lived at home or with relatives, but in many cases the necessity for money was most urgent.

One of the difficult things at first was keeping track of the prices, for they were frequently changed during the day, and the penalty for selling under price was immediate discharge, while selling above price met with no disapproval.

Every morning there were special sales. Sometimes articles that had sold for one dollar would be reduced to ninety-eight cents, with much blowing of trumpets, while, again, twenty-five cent articles would be offered at a bargain for *forty cents* "today only." But we soon learned what things were to be "leaders" from day to day, and the manager's brief instructions each morning were sufficient to keep us posted on the bargains. The charms of the bargain counter vanish when one has been behind the scenes and learned something of its history. The humor of it seemed to impress the clerks, for often knowing winks would be exchanged when some unwary customer was being victimized.

Oh, the weariness of that first morning! The hours seemed days. "Can I possibly stand up all day?" was the thought uppermost in my mind, for I soon learned from my companions that abusive language was the share of the one who was found sitting down. Later in the week I found this to be true. One of the girls who was well-nigh exhausted sat a moment on a little table that was for sale—there was not a seat of any kind in the room, and the only way one could get a moment's rest was to sit on the children's furniture that was for sale on one part of the floor. The manager came along and found the poor girl resting. The only sympathy he manifested was to call out in rough tones : "Get up out of that, you lazy huzzy, I don't pay you to sit around all day !" Under such circumstances it is small wonder that the stolen rests were few. By night the men as well as the women were limping wearily across the floor, and many sales were made under positive physical agony.

How well I remember my first service there ! The people were slow in coming that morning; in fact, they were every morning. We scarcely ever had any business worth mentioning till eleven o'clock, and the greatest rush came about six. From half-past twelve to two was a busy time also. People seemed determined to shop when we ought to be getting our meals. My first two customers were of a type that abounds. First an angular woman with a business-like expression came to me and in peremptory tones demanded that I show her building blocks. They were dutifully shown, but proved unsatisfactory. Then dolls' buggies, boys' sleds, laundry sets, and skates were examined in slow succession, and I was catechized in a thoroughly pedagogical manner regarding the prices and merits of the same. When the last skate had been critically examined, she fixed a patronizing gaze upon me and said : " I do not intend to buy today ; I merely wished to examine your goods." "Was she a revenue officer?" was the first thought that came to my mind. Oh ,no ! in the language of the shop, she was only a "rubber-neck.'" I afterward estimated the distance walked with her, and found it to be about one-twelfth of a mile, and still I had not a sale on my book. She took half an hour of my time.

The next customer who fell to my lot was a man of vinegary mien who wanted a boy's sled at a cost of one dollar and a half. Now, we had none at that particular price, but we had them at one dollar and thirty-five, and one dollar and sixty-five cents, either of which I thought would suit him. But I was mistaken, for he turned upon me a look of utter scorn, and then proceeded to denounce me for advertising things we did not have in stock. I meekly suggested that I was not responsible for the advertisements which appeared in the morning papers, but he was not at all mollified, and left in high dudgeon. I felt rather blue, but the comforting voice of a little cash girl said : " Don't yer mind him, he's only a cheap skate." Thus reassured I started out on another venture. This time it was a small boy who wanted to buy, and the bright-faced little fellow did me good. He had eighty cents, he said, and he wanted presents for the baby, and Tom, and Freda, and cousin Jack, and several others. I suggested one thing after another, till finally he had spent his money; so I made out my first check and looked at it with pride. It read thus :

X. Y. Z. HOUSE.

SOLD BY			AM'T REC'D
424			.80
1	"Dewey" bank - - - -		05
2	Sets dishes - - - - -	15	30
1	Laundry set - - - -		15
1	Mother Goose ladder - - -		12
1	Rubber ball - - - -		10
2	Bb'ls clothespins - - - -	04	08
			80
CASH NO.			AMOUNT
127			.80
			.80

The boy was happy, and so was I. I looked admiringly at the eighty cents set down on my index sheet. It meant that I had earned four cents. After that the sales came frequently. They were all small, of course, and amounted to only $14.98 for the day. But this was more than I sold any succeeding day. It has often been noticed that new clerks do better at first than they do later. With me, freshness and interest in the novelty helped to banish weariness and invite sales.

My first day ended at half-past six. Through some oversight, a supper ticket was not given to me, and so I was allowed
to go home. I went wearily to the cloak-room and more wearily
to my boarding place. When I arrived there, I could only throw
myself upon my little white cot in the dormitory and wildly
wonder if it would be all right for a working girl to cry. Presently I was dreaming that blows from an iron mallet were falling
fast upon me; and in a little while it was morning, and another
day was begun. Hundreds of clerks in the city were starting
out for work just as weary as I, but with them there was not the
knowledge that labor could be ended at will.

It must be understood that "our house" was open every
evening till about ten o'clock, and the only compensation given
for the extra work was a supper, the market value of which was
about fifteen cents. That, like the lunch, had to be eaten in
great haste. The maximum time allowed, in either case, was
thirty minutes, but our instructions were to "hurry back." That
half an hour was wholly inadequate one can readily imagine. It
sometimes took ten or fifteen minutes to get a simple order filled
in the crowded restaurants near by. The lunch outside meant
from ten to fifteen cents a day out of our small earnings, but the
breath of even the smoky outdoor air was worth that to us.
The air inside was always foul, and the continual noise was fairly
maddening. We were obliged to eat our supper in the store,
where it was provided. The second day I partook of what the
management magnanimously called the "free supper." We were
fed in droves and hurried away before the last mouthful was
swallowed. The menu consisted of a meat dinner and an oyster
stew, the latter of which I always elected with the lingering hope
that it had not been made of scraps left from the regular café
dinner earlier in the day. The said stew consisted of a bowl of
hot milk, in the bottom of which lurked *three* oysters, except on
that memorable day when I found *four.*

The days in the store were much the same, with their endless
fatigue. At times the rush would be great; then again we would
have nothing to do but stand around and talk. Thus we became
surprisingly well acquainted in a short time. We talked about

our wages and compared index sheets on every possible occasion. Some sold very little and at the end of the week had no more than three dollars.[1] The mental anguish of some of the girls when they saw at night how small their sales had been is impossible to describe. One may elect to become a worker, and endure the hardships of the toil, and live the life of the laborer, and receive the same starvation wages, but he can never experience the abject wretchedness of not knowing where to turn when the last dollar is gone. Three dollars a week to a girl alone in the city means starvation or shame.

The fourth day of the week was one I remember well. There had been special sales the day before, and everyone was more tired than usual; consequently those in charge were more than usually harsh and discourteous. One girl was ill. She should not have left home, but she feared losing her place if she remained away. She found after an hour or two that she could not work, so she asked permission to go home. The answer given was that she need not return if she left then. The floorwalker, who had a spark of humanity in his breast, told her that she could go to the toilet-room to lie down, if she would come out to her place once in a while to show that she was there. That poor girl spent the day on the rough, dirty floor, with a cash girl's apron for a pillow. At intervals she dragged herself out to her place in the department, only to crawl back more wretched than before. We wondered sometimes why there was no large chair or couch provided for an emergency case of that kind. There were comforts in the customers' waiting-rooms, but discharge was the fate of the employé who dared go in there.

A shop girl might die on the bare, hard floor, while easy chairs and couches in another room were unoccupied. Surely it would not be unreasonable to require that suitable rest-rooms be provided for the employés. Undue advantage could not well be taken of such a thing, for we could not leave the floor without asking the floorwalker—a man—for a pass, and his injunc-

---

[1] On Saturday night all those whose sales averaged less than five dollars a day were discharged.

tion always was, "Don't stay long." The unpleasantness of
asking for a pass was sometimes overcome by girls slipping
away in the crowd without permission. We thought some
woman might be commissioned to grant such requests. We had
to endure so many unnecessary hardships.

The cloak-, toilet-, and lunch-rooms were the gloomiest and
filthiest it was ever my misfortune to enter. The cobwebs and
dirt-besmeared floors looked "spooky" under the flickering
glare of insufficient gaslight. The only ventilation came through
a foul basement, and there the little girl attendants stayed all
day and late into the night. And that was where the girls who
brought lunches had to eat them. A few rough board tables
and chairs in a more or less advanced state of ruin were provided, and scores of hungry girls sat around and ate lunches
from newspaper parcels and drank coffee from tin cans.[1] It
was not a healthful atmosphere, either physically or morally,
and yet it was typical of the poorer class of stores. The slang
of the streets, interspersed with oaths, formed the staple medium
of communication. A young and innocent newcomer could not
fail to feel shocked at what she heard. But the surroundings
were not conducive of elevated thoughts. Refinement of thought
and speech would soon disappear in such an environment. I
never saw a clean towel in the toilet-room. Several hundred
pairs of hands were wiped on the coarse, filthy piece of crash
each day, and there was no woman in attendance to see that
things were kept in a sanitary condition. Two little girls were
in the cloak-room, but they had nothing to do with the adjoining
places. The rooms were merely narrow hallways. The wretchedness of all these appointments was forced upon me the day
my fellow-worker was so ill. It was so hard to get our wraps at
night, for then all the employés were there pushing their way to
the front. One night a young girl in the line was rather restless, and one of the store officials charged her with crowding,
and jerked her out of line so that she struck against a counter
on the right. He then shoved her back with such force that she
fell against another on the left. She was badly hurt, and the

[1] Coffee was supplied to employés at the rate of two cups for five cents.

uproar which followed was mob-like in its intensity. The boys were going to shoot the offender, they said, but he only smiled, secure in the justness of his attack. The case was afterward reported to the managers, but no reparation was ever made. The girl was unable to work the next day on account of the soreness of her back. In addition to the physical discomfort she had to endure, she lost a day's wages. From that warlike atmosphere we went forth into the night, and many of us had o go alone. That night I felt timid; so I asked if anyone was going my way. A little cash girl of only thirteen years spoke up and said: " I'll go wid yez." She had eight blocks to walk after she left me. The only mitigating circumstance was her total lack of fear. She was used to sights and sounds to which I was a stranger. There were always men on the street corners ready to speak to a girl alone, and one hesitating step meant danger. Almost every morning the girls had some story to tell of encounters with men of that class; and that they were not exaggerating was proved satisfactorily to me by an experience of my own. I stepped from the car one night after midnight, and soon found that I was being followed. The chase continued for two blocks, when I staggered breathless into my doorway, with my pursuer not five feet away. My terror had given me power to outrun him.[1]

I always pitied the cash children. Many of them were too young to be working, but the sin was at their parents' door. They placed on file the required affidavits,[2] and the employer asked no questions. One little girl confessed to me that she was *not quite twelve years old*, but she told me not to tell anyone, because her mother told her to say she was fourteen. This burst of childish confidence came when I was pitying her because she had the toothache. The poor little things always had the toothache. There seems to be something about enforced work that brings on that malady in a child! But their trouble was probably more real than imagined. They often carried

[1] This happened during my second week.

[2] The child-labor law of this state requires all children under sixteen to file affidavits sworn to before a notary public.

some cheap candy in one apron pocket and a little vial of tooth-ache drops in the other, but they thought of no relationship existing between the two. The little girls frequently responded to the cry of, "Cash! Here cash!" with tears streaming down their faces; and the cause was always the one just mentioned, or sore feet. They got tired, of course. They were only chil-dren, and the instinct for play was strong. They would kiss the dolls and trundle the carts they were taking to the wrapping-room. A change of any kind was hailed with delight, as for instance the "running" of a C. O. D. check, which occasioned a trip to another floor. The added labor entailed was not con-sidered. There were a great many extra ones employed at that time, and there was a continual war between the regulars and extras. The latter were engaged every morning at thirty-three cents a day, while the former were paid two dollars a week. The "enunciator," or one who had charge of the others, received two dollars and a half a week. In that particular store the little girls looked down on the boys, of whom there were compara-tively few. The latter were supposed to clear away rubbish from under the counters, and on one occasion, when no boy was in sight, the floorwalker told a girl to carry away some waste papers, and she replied with a toss of her head: "You bloke you, I ain't no cash boy!" Childlike, they had their favorites among the clerks, and the fortunes of those they watched with much interest. One day the manager of the store appeared on our floor, and in ringing tones called out "424!" As I was starting to answer the summons, my young friend threw her arms around me and said: "Don't you mind Tom Jones,[1] he can't hurt you. Tell him you're a new girl, if he scolds you; and if he's ugly, tell him to go to h—." I did not do any of those things, and I got away unhurt. He had no grievance against me, but he had such a rude way of address-ing the clerks that they were all afraid of him.

We had our troubles with the manager and other officials, but they were not all. Some of the customers were so hard to

[1] This was the way the manager was spoken of by everybody. The name here is fictitious.

please and so uncivil; and they made us feel like criminals because of our inability to do what apparently could not be done. Then there was the well-meaning buyer who persisted in asking us how much wages we got. Just why saleswomen should be subjected to such rudeness by seemingly intelligent people is difficult to see. One rather independent girl, on being asked this question for the fifth time one day, replied that she got ten dollars a week, and added: "How much do you get?" The questioner was a gentleman of clerical appearance, and he replied: "My dear young woman, I am afraid your surroundings are corrupting your good manners!" Then he passed on, doubtless feeling very righteous over his reproval.

On the whole, the week there passed quickly, and on Saturday night I decided to leave and try my fortune elsewhere. I thought that one week each in two stores would be better than the whole time spent in one. I told the manager that I wanted my pay because I was going to leave. He was rather abusive and said: "What do you want to leave for? You are making good money; you girls want the earth." I left that night with my two dollars in my pocket; my commission could not be obtained till the following week. Wages are always paid weekly there.

I was "out of a job," and trusted to luck to find another.

Sunday in the home was a quiet day. Everybody was tired and discouraged. There had been extra work, but no extra pay, and there were so many Christmas things to be bought. Sunday had to be the general mending day, and that day many were making little gifts for the friends at home. Most of the girls were sensible about dress, and they guarded their small earnings carefully. I guided my expenditure by theirs and kept an accurate account of my expenses for the week. The items are here presented:

Board for one week - - - - - - -	$2.50
Car fare, 6 days,[1] @ 10c. - - - - -	.60
Lunch, 5 days, @ 15c. - - - - - -	.75
" 1 day, @ 10c. - - - - - -	.10

[1] Many of the girls walked as far as two miles to save car fare.

For charity dinner[1] - - - - - - - - .13
Paper, 3 nights - - - - - - - .06
Postal cards - - - - - - - - .05
Candy[2] - - - - - - - - .10
Stamps - - - - - - - - - .10
Oranges[2] - - - - - - - - .09
Present for table girl - - - - - - - .05
    "   "   matron - - - - - - .10
Laundry - - - - - - - - - .16
                                         ————
    Total expense - - - - - - $4.79

What I earned for the week was as follows :

Wages - - - - - - - - - $2.00
Commission - - - - - - - - 3.25
                                         ————
                                          $5.25
Less fines[3] - - - - - - - - 30
                                         ————
    Total earnings - - - - - - $4.95

Thus I had a balance of sixteen cents after my bills were paid, and that was as much as many had. At that rate it would take a long time to earn enough to buy a pair of boots.

The next week I started out again to look for a place, and I found one where I most wished to work. When I first sought employment I was an unskilled laborer, but the next time I was an experienced saleswoman, and as such I was engaged at a salary of four dollars a week plus 1 per cent. commission on sales. This time my work was selling dolls, and there were four of us at the one counter. I realized at once that this was a much better place than the first one. The managers and floorwalkers were gentlemanly and kind, and the work was carried on in a thoroughly business-like way. I breathed freely when I found that no one would swear at me. There it was no crime to sit down, and behind each counter could be found one or two little boxes which the girls used for seats. They were awkward things,

---

[1] The matron asked for contributions from two cents up. Every girl in the home responded.

[2] These articles were for a " treat."

[3] A fine of ten cents was imposed for each tardiness, unless over half an hour ; then twenty-five cents was charged.

though, and very much in the way when we were moving around, waiting on customers. A hinged seat that could be swung under the counter would be such a boon.

The hours were very long. We worked from eight in the morning till eleven at night, with the exception of Christmas eve, when we worked until twelve. Half an hour was the time allowed for each meal. The only extra pay given was thirty cents each night for supper money. There was a very good cheap restaurant in the store, and there we bought our suppers for from twenty to thirty cents. Many of the clerks ate two cold lunches a day in order to save the money, while others were quite reckless and bought what they considered dainties. One day a girl who had a very bad headache went to lunch with me, and this is what she ordered:

Plum pudding with wine sauce - - - -	$0.10
Swiss cheese sandwiches - - - - - -	.05
Chocolate ice cream - - - - - -	.05
Strong coffee - - - - - - - -	.05

My astonishment was too great for words.

The work in this store was in many ways not so difficult as in the first. Our work was confined to one counter, and then we could sit down for a moment once in a while; but the customers were just as hard to suit and equally regardless of our feelings. And how long the days were! It seemed to me that my thoughts were always centered on my feet! Our arms got tired, too; we had to reach a good deal for stock. A man made me open and take the dolls from nineteen boxes to see if I could not find him one with black eyes and yellow hair. I told him they were all gone, at the price he desired, but he wanted me to verify my statement. As if it would matter to his two-year-old baby whether the doll had black or green eyes! He was evidently buying one for his own delectation. That is only one instance of the many exacting customers we met.

There the sanitary conditions were good, lunch- and cloak-room accommodation ample, and the treatment kind and courteous; but the wages were woefully insufficient. From four to five dollars a week was the average. The commission given was only temporary, and designed to give an extra impetus to the sale of the holiday goods. One girl who had worked there for seven years told me that she had never received more than five dollars a week; and she had to keep up a respectable appearance. It was an openly acknowledged fact among the girls there that the paths of dishonor were traversed to supplement their small incomes. Some of them did not hesitate to advise newcomers of this lucrative employment. They viewed the matter solely from a commercial standpoint, and justified their conduct by the urgency of the need. The girls themselves said that more than a third of them were leading lives of shame. It was common to hear such expressions as this uttered in agonized seriousness: "If I don't get more wages I'll have to go bad. But I'd hate to disgrace my family." Lecherous men were always around ready to offer aid. They came, professedly, to buy, but it was not the wares of the store they wanted. The young and pretty girls yielded most easily. They would weep, sometimes, and say: "Good people look down on us. But they don't know—they don't know. *We have to earn our living.*"

Surely any effort which is being made to bring the saleswoman's wages up to a point where she can live without the wages of sin is worthy of the most respectful consideration. Whatever is done in this direction is manifestly a social good. And, moreover, the best interests of society demand that thinking people should consider this matter seriously. All the hardships of the shop girl's life fade into insignificance before this grave danger she has to face. Adequate support is the first necessity. Improved sanitary conditions and opportunity for rest may well take a second place. They can be secured by legislation; the other must come from united action on the part of the buyers, and the organization of the saleswomen themselves. The trades-union spirit should be fostered, and the working-women taught the power of united effort.

Many merchants in this city do give living wages, but there are others who do not. I know from actual experience, and I know from reliable testimony.

My earnings for the first week have already been presented, and those of the second are here given:

Salary	$4.00
Commission on sales	1.53
Supper money	1.80
Total	$7.33
Less fines[1]	40
Week's wages	$6.93

My expenses for the week were as given below:

Board	$2.50
Car fare, 6 days, @ 10c.	60
Lunch, 4 days, @ 15c.	60
" 2 days, @ 10c.	20
Supper, 6 days, @ 25c.	1.50
Paper, 3 days, @ 2c.	06
Stamps	04
Toy dog for cook's baby	11
Bananas[2]	10
Witch hazel	10
Chewing gum[3]	06
Laundry	18
	$6.05

Thus my balance was eighty-eight cents. One girl at the home had only two cents left when her bills were paid. And she it was who said in answer to someone's expressed wish one night that "tomorrow would be Sunday": "I wish there wouldn't be any tomorrow." So many times they were overcome by the utter hopelessness of the future. They have to grapple with the wages problem in a most practical way.

It is true that the present rate of women's wages has been brought about by forces over which the public has or can have but little control; yet it is equally true that a conscientious investigation of the whole subject in this city could not be value-

[1] These were unavoidable owing to the crowds of employés using the elevators, and the shortness of the time allowed for meals.

[2] For a "treat."

[3] This investment was to enable me to respond affirmatively to the oft-repeated question: "Got any chewin's on you?"

less. While it is impossible to improve matters at once, or perhaps ever, it is yet certainly worthy of an attempt. That women in other vocations may be in dire straits does not preclude the legitimacy of centering public efforts on one occupation.

In the two weeks I was employed I worked one hundred and seventy-five hours and received eleven dollars and eighty-eight cents, or a little more than six cents an hour. Under normal conditions the hours would be about one hundred and twenty for the same length of time. This, of course, would be exclusive of Sunday work, which is required all the year, at least in some stores. A certain number of clerks are needed for two or more hours during the day. In my first place no remuneration of any kind was given for this; in the second, car fare was always given, and lunch if the duties did not end before noon. The cash children in those two stores earned three and one-third cents an hour. When kept overtime, as they were in the first store in which I worked, they earned not quite two and one-third cents an hour. It must be said, however, that the managers did not insist upon children who worked at night being there promptly at eight in the morning. Sometimes they did not go until nine.

I am going to present just here in tabulated form some information I gathered from my fellow-workers regarding themselves. The statements are made for the month of December, and refer only to employés in the big down-town stores. In some cases I have had a dozen or more names followed by identical information, so I have inserted in the table but one to serve as a type. As a rule the working-women object to telling the wages they receive, particularly if they are low. They like to give the impression that they receive much more than they do, and this, I suppose, is not characteristic of any one particular class in society. Any figures based on a canvass made from the outside are almost sure to be misleading. The cases here cited have been carefully examined, and from intimate acquaintance with the individuals I believe them to be correct:

Name	Employment	Hours (A.M.–P.M.)	Overtime	Weekly wage	For extra work	Cost of living per week	Conjugal condition	Health	Remarks
A.....	saleswoman	8:00–6:00	none	$ 6.00		$2.50	single	fair	same place 3 years
B.....	"	8:00–6:30	evenings till 10	3.00		2.50	"	"	
C.....	inspector	8:00–6:00	none	5.00		3.00	"	bad	
D.....	wrapper	8:00–6:30	till 10 or 11 P.M.	3.50		lived home	"	fair	
E.....	buyer	8:00–6:00	till 7 sometimes	4.00		"	"	bad	
F.....	enunciator	8:00–6:00	none	10.00		$4.75	separated	good	
G.....	saleswoman	8:00–6:30	till 10 or 11 "	2.50	supper	lived home	single	fair	
H.....	cashier	8:00–6:30	"	3.50	"	$2.50	married	"	husband and 4 children
I.....	saleswoman	8:00–6:30	till 11	6.50	50c per week	3.00	single	"	one child
J.....	saleswoman	8:00–6:30	till 10	3.00	35c for supper	2.50	married	good	
K.....	saleswoman	8:00–6:00	none	5.00		2.50	widow	"	
L.....	cash girl	9:30–4:30	evenings	3.25	supper	lived home	single	fair	
M.....	saleswoman	8:00–6:30	"	5% commission	"	"	"	"	
N.....	cash girl	8:00–6:30	"	$2.00	"	"	"	good	
O.....	saleswoman	8:00–6:30	"	$2.00+5% com.	cup of coffee	$2.50	"	"	
P.....	saleswoman	8:00–6:30	none	$3.00		2.50	"	"	
Q.....	sewer	8:30–5:30	evenings	6.50	30c for supper	2.50	widow	fair	one child
R.....	saleswoman	8:00–6:00	none	5.00		lived home	single	"	same place 7 years
S.....	cash girl	8:00–6:00	evenings	2.00	30c for supper	"	"	bad	
T.....	inspector	8:00–6:00	none	$4.50+1% com.	"	"	"	fair	
U.....	saleswoman	8:00–6:00	"	4.00+1% com.	supper	$1.50 at home	"	"	mother to help
V.....	"	8:00–6:30	"	2.00+5% com.	"	$2.50	"	bad	
W.....	"	8:00–6:00	none	12½c per doz.		$2.00 at home	"	fair	
X.....	shirt-maker	8:00–6:00	"		supper	lived home	married	bad	husband had no work
Y.....	wrapper-maker	8:00–6:00	"		"	"	"	fair	ill; 2 children
Z.....	saleswoman	8:30–5:30		$7.00		$3.75	single	good	

The organization that is attempting to mitigate the evils connected with life in mercantile establishments has most laudable aims and methods. The ameliorative movement on the part of consumers is a rational one. It is representative of the most enlightened forces in society, and rests on a sound basis. So long as the consumer will patronize bad stores, so long will they exist; so long as people will buy clothing produced under inhuman conditions, so long will they continue to be produced under just those conditions. Has the public no duty in the matter? Women and children are in the industrial world, and it is useless to wrangle over the expediency of their filling the places they do. They are there, and as the weaker members of society they need protection. Inhuman and demoralizing conditions must be removed. Some of the evils here could be speedily remedied by legislation and faithful inspection. Those who have not already considered the matter would do well to peruse carefully the Consumers' standard of a fair house, and ask themselves whether or not they can do something to lessen the hardships of the salespeoples' lives.

CONSUMERS' LEAGUE OF ILLINOIS.

CONSUMERS' STANDARD.

Children.— A standard house is one in which no child is allowed to work after six o'clock in the evening, and the requirements of the child-labor law are all complied with.

Wages.— A standard house is one in which equal pay is given for work of equal value, irrespective of sex. In the departments where women only are employed the minimum wages are $6 per week for adult workers of six months' experience, and fall in few instances below $8.

In which wages are paid weekly or fortnightly.

In which fines, if imposed, are paid into a fund for the benefit of the employés.

In which the minimum wages of cash girls and boys are $2.25 per week, with the same conditions regarding weekly payments and fines.

Hours.— A standard house is one in which the hours from 8 A. M. to 6 P. M. (with not less than three quarters of an hour for lunch) constitute the working day, and a general half holiday is given on one day of each week during the summer months.

In which a vacation of not less than one week is given, with pay, during the summer season to employés of six months' standing.

In which all overtime is compensated for.

Physical conditions.— A standard house is one in which work-, lunch , and retiring rooms are apart from each other and are in good sanitary condition.

In which seats are provided for saleswomen and the use of seats permitted.

Other conditions.— A standard house is one in which humane and considerate behavior toward employés is the rule.

In which fidelity and length of service meet with the consideration which is their due.

It is a comparatively easy matter to enlist the sympathy of intelligent and educated people, and through them reform must be brought about. The great body of buyers who regularly patronize the cheap stores will take no interest in the matter. Some may feel that they have done their duty when they cease buying at stores where evils exist; but that is a dwarfed conception of social obligation. We should not rest until the bad stores improve or go out of business.

ANNIE MARION MacLEAN.

THE UNIVERSITY OF CHICAGO.

THE SINGLE TAX: WHAT AND WHY.

In all ages, men who aspire to a reputation for great wisdom have found much more difficulty in comprehending simple truths than in comprehending complicated ones. Whenever a new theory is brought forward, with a claim on its behalf to far-reaching importance, and yet such a theory appears to be simple, clear, and easy of comprehension, everybody responds with an incredulous: "Is that all?"

Such is the fortune of the single-tax theory. Nothing is more simple or more easily understood; yet many learned men dismiss the subject from their minds, upon the express ground that nobody can understand what the single tax is. Other learned, sincere, and earnest men attempt to define it, and immediately compound such a mixture of abstruse perplexities that they pronounce it an utterly impracticable scheme. Roughly speaking, it may be said that there are only two classes of people who understand what the single tax is; the one being the large and growing class who believe in it, and the other the small but immensely powerful class who know that it would deprive them of the privilege of taxing their fellow-men.

Be it right or wrong, the idea of the single tax is one of the simplest, most straightforward, easily understood, and easily carried into practical execution, within the whole range of political economy. The very idea of a "single tax," that is, of abolishing the present vast multiplicity of taxes, nearly all of which are admitted by everybody to be injurious, and of collecting all public revenue by one tax, is perfectly simple; and, taken by itself, it is so absolutely just and reasonable that nothing can be said against it. Whether it is *practicable* or not is an entirely separate question. But if it is possible to discover one tax which will be just, equal, and practicable, and which will supply all the proper requirements of all governments, one can hardly conceive of any ground of objection to the collection of all government revenue by that tax. Even if there are other taxes just as good, yet the argument in favor of simplicity and unity in the assessment and collection of taxes seems conclusive in favor of a single tax. But if it can be easily demonstrated, not only that there is no other tax just as good, but that all other taxes are positively bad, unjust, unequal, and more or less disastrous to humanity in their operation, the argument in favor of some single form of taxation which is not open to these objections simply admits of no answer whatever, and has never received any. Thus, the central idea of *one tax* is obviously an ideal method of taxation.

But we have to explain what is meant, not merely by *a* single tax, but by *the* single tax. In passing, let it be noted that, in all the history of political economy, nobody has been known to advocate seriously any form of single tax except *the* single tax which we are about to explain. This single tax was first expounded by the illustrious French physician Quesnay, more than one hundred and fifty years ago. The theory was accepted with enthusiasm by the most eminent men of the time. But it was submerged in the tremendous agitation of the French Revolution and the Napoleonic wars; any attempt to teach it in Great Britain was regarded as no better than treason, and if seriously made would have been severely punished; and thus the very idea of the single tax was practically lost to mankind. It has now been revived; and it is slowly making its way in all classes of society, including the rich as well as the poor. It would be a breach of confidence to mention names; otherwise it would be easy to give the names of distinguished men in every department of life : statesmen, college professors, divines, lawyers, editors, merchants, and manufacturers, who, in private, freely express their unqualified acceptance of this doctrine, but who, for good reasons, do not think it expedient to give public expression to their faith. A theory which has commanded such assent as this surely deserves attention and explanation.

The name *impôt unique* was invented by Quesnay, and has simply been translated in English into "the single tax." By this phrase is to be understood the abolition of all existing taxes save one; that one being the tax on ground rent, or, as it is otherwise called, the value of land ; and, of course, the concentration of all public burdens upon ground rent. The single tax, therefore, implies the total abolition of all taxes upon personal property, buildings, and improvements, of all custom tariffs, all excise duties, all stamp duties, all poll taxes, and, in short, every tax of every description, except that which is now levied upon the rent of bare land.

Thus far, the matter would surely seem perfectly simple. No new taxes are to be invented or imposed. All that needs to be done is to abolish all existing taxes except this one. But some explanation of the terms used is necessary. "Ground rent" and the "value of land" are in reality the same thing. Rent is the price which the owner of land either does or can obtain for the privilege of using land ; and what is usually called the value of land, or the price of land, is nothing but the capitalized value of its rent ; or, to use simpler terms, it is the present market value of the landlord's power of collecting rent in future, as compensation for the privilege of using land.

Here, however, is a fertile source of confusion. We are all so accustomed to thinking of land as being necessarily worth a great sum in and of itself that almost everybody beginning the study of this subject is overwhelmed with confusion, when some solemn critic informs him that "land is the least productive of all improvements," because the rent of land usually brings a smaller return upon the investment than the income of any equal investment in other property. Thus, in Great Britain, when the usual rate of interest on good investments was 4 per cent., the average income from investments in land was not more than 3 per cent.; and something of the same proportion has always existed. This seems to multitudes a conclusive proof that the rent of land is very low; whereas there is nothing in the statement, except a clever trick. Land costs nothing to produce ; and it cannot be produced. All other investments are produced by human skill and labor, and cost enormously in production. Rent is not, therefore, measured by the value of land ; but the value of land is always measured by rent. A piece of land for which nobody ever did and nobody ever will pay any rent has no market value whatever. The value of land, therefore, depends entirely upon the amount of rent which is annually collected at present, and which it is believed can be, annually collected in future. Men are willing to give for a piece of land just as much as, and no more than, such a price as in their judgment would, if invested in other perfectly safe securities, produce an annual income equal to the rent which they believe will, on the average, be paid for the use of that land. Suppose the ordinary rate of interest upon a perfectly safe bond to be 4 per cent. Such a 4 per cent. bond would then sell for $100. A piece of land which produced a net rent, after deducting all taxes and all expenses, of $4 every year, and which all men were satisfied would never produce any more or any less, would also sell for $100. This is called "twenty-five years' purchase;" and this is the term constantly used in ascertaining the value of land. It is always estimated at just as many years' purchase of the annual net rent as the capital of perfectly safe investments bears to the current rate of interest on them. When the current rate of interest is 5 per cent., land is worth, on the average, twenty years' purchase of its annual rent. When the rate of interest falls to 4 per cent,. land is worth twenty-five years' purchase. When the rate falls to 3 per cent., land is worth thirty-three years' purchase. Thus the value of land rises and falls with its rent; but the market value of land has no influence whatever on fixing rent.

Again, it must be noted that the value of land may be present or speculative. Most men believe that the rent of land will always continue to rise; and therefore they believe that the market value of land will rise also. This, however, is a matter of speculation, as to which nobody is ever quite correct, and most people are generally very much out of the way. When land speculators make a correct guess, they acquire what is termed "the unearned increment." When they make a mistake, they lose what some philosophers have attempted to call "the unearned decrement." In reality, there is no such thing as a "decrement" in land, unless it is swept away by a flood or otherwise intrinsically injured. Every penny of the value of land is unearned increment; and as the value can never be less than nothing, there is no such thing as decrement. All discussions about increment and decrement are, therefore, mere trifling, and should not be allowed to mislead anyone.

It is of the greatest importance, however, to understand what land is, and in what its value consists — in other words, what rent is paid for. "Land," in a scientific sense, includes everything which does not belong to the animal creation and which has not been made or seriously modified by man. What man has made decays; and therefore it often falls back into the land and becomes an indistinguishable part of land. But so long as it is distinguishable it is not "land," in a scientific sense. For example, man builds a house; and this, although planted in the land, and often perhaps built entirely underneath the surface, is nevertheless not land, but improvement. If abandoned by man, and overgrown, it falls into ruin; it mingles, in its decay, with other fragments of stone and earth; and it becomes land again. So man ploughs and cultivates a field, sowing it perhaps with grass. Grass which grows purely by nature is part of the land; but grass planted by man, and all improvements in the quality of the land, made by human industry, are not, in strict science or in political economy, part of the land. All this is perfectly simple; although it requires many words to make it clear.

The value of land obviously consists in the value of the privilege of using it. No man would ever pay rent for land which he was not permitted to use for any purpose. Accordingly, land which can be used for only a limited number of purposes has a comparatively small value; while land that can be used for every conceivable purpose has very great value. This is especially important to bear in mind when considering what are called franchises. The mere franchise to carry on business as a corporation is not land and has no land value. But the so-called "franchise" of running a railroad or extending a telegraph over land, or of laying gas-pipes or oil-pipes under the surface of land, is, in the light of science, political economy, and common sense, a land value, and nothing else. It is not, in any sense, personal property. It is attached to the land; it is part of the land; and it would therefore be included, first and foremost, among those land values which are subject to the single tax.

The single-tax theory, therefore, proposes to lay all taxation upon the value of the privilege of using land, for any and all purposes, including not merely nor mainly the use of land for farms, but, to a vastly greater extent, the use of land for building purposes in villages, towns, and cities; the use of land for mines and quarries, for railroads, telegraphs, telephones, gas-pipes, water-pipes, electric wires, and any and every other conceivable use to which land can be put. It demands the abolition of all taxes upon earnings, food, furniture, clothing, merchandise, money, buildings; the rails, rolling stock, and depots of railroad companies; the wires, poles, and other articles used for telegraphs; in short, upon anything whatever produced by man. In the case of farms, the single tax would abolish all taxation upon growing crops, planted trees, drains, fences, and structures of any kind, and would not even tax that increased value which is given to land by ploughing, sub-soiling, or otherwise improving it.

This is the single tax. It may be summed up in three sentences: *Tax nothing made by man. Tax everything not made by man. Collect all public revenue out of, and in exact proportion to, the revenue which some men collect from other men, for permission to use that which no man made.*

This is all that is *necessarily* implied in the single tax. But some of its advocates believe in what is called the single tax, limited, and others in what is called the single tax, unlimited. The former class believe that the state should take no more out of the annual rent of land than is required for the just and proper administration of government, year by year. The latter class believe that government should take just as much of the annual rent of land as it can possibly collect, without regard to the necessities of the state, and that it should devise some method of using, for the benefit of the people at large, the revenue thus taken.

The claim that the single tax should not be limited to the necessities of public revenue rests upon an argument which it is not necessary to follow to its full extent here. It has never been more clearly stated than it was by Herbert Spencer, in 1851, in his chapter of *Social Statics*, entitled: "The Right to the Use of the Earth." Although Mr. Spencer, forty years later, suppressed this chapter, in deference to an almost ferocious opposition from the ruling classes of English society, he has never refuted it, nor indeed explicitly retracted it. His original statement was, in substance, that all men have an equal right to the use of the earth, just as truly as all men have an equal right to breathe the air; that no man, and no collection or organization of men, can ever have the right to appropriate the surface of the earth, to the exclusion of the equal right of all other men, any more than they could have the right, if they had the power, to absorb into their own private vaults one-half of all the air surrounding the earth, leaving half mankind to perish from absolute inability to breathe. He showed that this equal right to the use of the earth could not be enforced by a mere equal partition of the surface, according to area, but must be effected by the appropriation of ground rent, for the benefit of the entire community; in other words, that the distribution of land, in order to effect real equality, must be made according to value, and not according to area.

With the exception of those modern philosophers who deny that any man has any rights whatever, no one having the ability to express himself intelligently has ever undertaken to deny that Herbert Spencer's original doctrine was one which ought to have been applied at the origin of society; and the argument against it has been confined solely to its application to the present condition of society; which, under the influence of Roman law, has grown entirely away from this foundation of justice. Mr. George, taking up the subject again, many years after Herbert Spencer had written, but without knowing that anyone had preceded him in the same line of thought, arrived at the same general conclusion; and then, after reading Herbert Spencer, he went one step farther, and maintained that there could be no vested right in a future and continuing wrong, and therefore that no claim for compensation for the loss of future ground rent ought to be recognized, but that all ground rent, for the future, should be taken for the public use. But, as it is our present object to discuss only questions of taxation, we do not feel called upon to go any farther into the discussion of this question of natural right to the use of the earth. In all that we have to say, therefore, it must be understood that we refer, under the name of " single tax," only to a method of collecting all needed government revenue from ground rent alone.

Is the single tax a just method of taxation?

That a tax of *some* amount upon ground rent, or the value of land, is just and right, is conceded by everyone. Universal theory and practice alike agree in recommending such a tax. As no one has ever disputed this, no argument need now be made in support of it. Is there any other tax of which the same thing can be said? If not, then we certainly have a tremendous presumption in favor of making the only just tax the exclusive tax. Here is a tax which can be easily assessed, without asking any questions of the taxpayer, because the value of the thing assessed is known to everybody. Here is an income, which is not earned in any degree by the labor, skill, or effort of the person receiving it. The landlord does not make land or make rent. The moment that we attempt to collect taxes from any other source we find ourselves taking from men a portion of that which they have made by their own labor and skill, by methods which impose heavy burdens upon honesty and put a premium upon fraud, evasion, and falsehood.

Beginning with direct taxes, every tax upon the value or income of personal property inevitably depends for its assessment upon the truthfulness of the taxpayer, since nobody but himself can do more than make a blind guess at what the value of his personal property is. If no sworn returns are required from him, then every assessment is a mere guess, and every taxpayer will pay either far too much or far too little. And as the power of evasion will increase in proportion to the extent and variety of his personal property, it follows that the more personal property any man possesses, the less in proportion is he likely to be taxed. If sworn returns are required, the burden is to some extent shifted from poverty upon honesty. The honest and simple-minded man pays all the taxes; while the very shrewd, or the reckless perjurer, goes free. But even with regard to buildings and other improvements on land, much the same thing is true. The homes of the poor are of such comparatively uniform value that they can be assessed with great precision. But the dwellings and factories of the rich depend for their salable value upon a multitude of considerations, concerning which assessors must be ignorant. Their value is judged entirely from their outside appearance, which is often quite deceptive, and which is systematically made so when the pressure of taxation becomes heavy. And both as to personal property and improvements upon land, taxation operates as a heavy discouragement upon industry and progress, and most especially discourages all that class of improvements which the owner shares with his neighbors. The man who keeps his sidewalk well paved, his front garden green and bright, and the whole exterior of his house a delight to the eye, is heavily punished by taxation; while the man who leaves the outside of his house to decay, although constantly adding to the beauty of the interior, is very lightly taxed.

A vast majority of taxes, everywhere, are, however, indirect. All such taxes must, in the very nature of things, be collected mainly from those who are relatively poor; because every indirect tax is levied in proportion to what a man consumes, and not in proportion to his wealth. The millionaire's family eats very little more food than the family of any hard-working mechanic. They do not wear any more clothes at any one time; although they undoubtedly have a greater assortment of clothing, of a more valuable kind. But, except in rare cases of extravagance, the difference between the value of a rich man's clothing and the value of a comparatively poor man's bears no sort of relation to the difference between their respective wealth. All taxes upon movable goods, therefore, bear with tremendous disproportion upon the poor, to the comparative exemption of the rich. Nor is it possible to avoid this result. The often expressed idea that large taxes can be collected from the luxuries of the rich is

a pure delusion. The number of the rich is always and everywhere small; and their total consumption is therefore small.
There is no country in the world which has ever been able to
raise one-tenth of its income from indirect taxes out of articles
consumed only by the rich.

While indirect taxation thus presses most heavily and
unjustly upon the poor, it also affords continual opportunities for
fraud and evasion. As the special advocates of indirect taxation
are the loudest in their complaints on this score, it cannot be
necessary to give illustrations. The only method by which it is
even pretended that this injustice can be avoided is by the system of so-called specific duties, that is, taxing everything by the
pound, gallon, or yard, without regard to its cost. This method
is largely resorted to, all over the world, with the obvious result
of adding tremendously to the burdens of the poor; since, when
clothing is taxed by the yard, it is obvious that the poor woman's
cloth, costing twenty-five cents a yard, must pay as much as the
rich woman's cloth, costing five dollars.

Thus all methods of indirect taxation resolve themselves into
a choice between allowing governments to rob the poor, or
allowing shrewd taxpayers to rob the government. Of the general demoralization among business men, caused by the enormous premium on fraud which is offered by these methods of taxation, much might be said; but, unhappily, the entire business community is so accustomed to the spectacle, if not to the practice,
of such fraud, that conscience is nearly dead upon the subject.

The income tax is sometimes held up as the ideal method.
But the only income tax concerning which Americans have ever
known anything or are willing to learn anything is one which
offers a premium to fraud, vastly exceeding that of any other
form of taxation. When the income tax expired, in 1872, false
returns had become so general as to make the returns ridiculous. Even in Great Britain, where far more stringent methods
are employed by the government than are possible here, owing
to the concentration of population there, it is officially estimated
that no more than two-thirds of the proper amount of income
tax is collected from those who make sworn returns.

All opponents of the single tax emphatically agree in declaring that all other taxes are unjust, unequal, injurious, and demoralizing. But, they say: "*All* taxes are bad." This, however, none of them will maintain, when brought to close quarters, with respect to a tax on the value of land. Such a tax, they are compelled to acknowledge, can be laid and collected with greater approximation to fairness and equality than any other, provided (they hasten to add) the tax is made very light. But, when further pushed, they are compelled to admit that it makes no difference whether the tax is light or heavy; it cannot be evaded in either case, and cannot be made the means of fraud and inequality, as between the owners of land value. Their only final claim is that it is unjust to select the owners of ground rents as the sole payers of taxes. This, therefore, is all the argument which we need to consider.

We maintain that it is perfectly just to lay all taxes upon ground rent, because it is nothing in the world but a species of private taxation. It is paid by the industrious for the privilege of exerting their industry. It is paid to those who need not be industrious in order to receive it. It is paid by every man, in proportion to the benefit which he derives from being permitted to monopolize some small section of the earth. It is paid to a man who has no more right to that particular section of the earth than has the man who pays him for it. Rent itself is just and inevitable. It is perfectly right that every man should pay rent; because that represents only the value of an advantage which he has upon the earth over his fellow-men, and to which he has no more right than any other man, until he has paid for it. It is paid, however, to men who have no right whatever to receive it, except such as is given by the law of their country; in other words, by the general consent of their fellow-citizens.

Rent, therefore, is paid as the fair price of all the advantages which men gain by occupying a specially advantageous situation. In paying rent, men take into account all the advantages of government, and pay for those, among other things. Indeed, the advantages of human society and of good government are more valuable than all other advantages put together; and, accordingly, rent is higher where these advantages are greatest than it is anywhere else. Fertility of soil, health of climate, brightness of sky, salubrity of air, and all other natural blessings put together will not compare, in rent-producing power, with a situation in the midst of a vast, well-organized and well-ordered community. A fragment of rock or a hole filled up with refuse in the middle of New York city is worth more than 10,000 fertile acres of the best rural land.

The landlord, therefore, collects from his tenants the full market value of all the advantages of society and government. Is it not a matter of simple justice that, having received the price of these blessings, he should pay for their cost? Having received the price, ought he not, in justice, to deliver the goods?

All other taxation than that upon the value of land is double taxation. The landlord, by force of natural competition, collects from his tenants the highest price which any human beings are willing to pay for the privilege of living in the society and under the government of that particular location. To tax the tenants over again, for what it costs to maintain that government, is simple robbery, under the forms of law. They have already paid, under the operation of that law, both natural and artificial, which compels them to pay the full value of those privileges to their landlord, all that they ought to pay; and it is no better than legalized swindling to charge them for these advantages a second time.

It is because of their persistent ignoring of these considerations that nearly all writers on the subject of taxation are compelled to abandon the old and perfectly just theory that taxation should be levied according to benefits received by the taxpayers. There is no system of taxation, other than the tax upon ground rent, under which it is possible to apportion taxation according to benefits. But under that system it is not merely possible to do so; it is impossible to do anything else. Each landlord collects from each tenant a sum, exactly proportioned to the relative benefit which that tenant receives from his particular situation. A tax, and an exclusive tax, upon ground rents, thus collected, would in turn collect from the landlord a sum exactly proportioned.to the benefits which he has received from being permitted to collect from others that for which he toiled not, neither did he spin.   No one can devise an honest method of collecting a single tax on ground rents, which will lay the burden of taxation *otherwise* than in exact proportion to the benefits conferred by government.   Without government, it is obvious that the landlord could not collect a dollar.   And the market value of every improvement in government goes to the direct benefit of the landlord.   The more economically, honestly, and efficiently any government is administered, the higher will be the rents which tenants are glad to pay for the privilege of living under it ; and thus the entire cream of the benefits thus conferred goes directly to the landlord.

It would make this paper too long to show how and why an exclusive tax upon land values would suffice to meet all the requirements of government, and yet leave a very handsome surplus to landlords.

It has been amply demonstrated elsewhere that all taxes together would not absorb half the rent of the land ; and no attempt has ever been made to refute the statistics given.[1]   But even if this could not be proved, that would constitute no reason whatever for not collecting for public revenue as much as possibly could be collected out of ground rent.   It would be time enough to add other taxes, all necessarily unjust and unequal, to this just, simple, and equal tax, when it had been found in practice insufficient.

In Great Britain, where the land is all monopolized in the possession of a few, no one pretends that the poorer classes of the community would suffer by the adoption of the single tax. All sympathy there is expended upon the unfortunate wealthy; who might, by the adoption of such a system, be deprived of some of their purple and fine linen.   In the United States, the eloquence and ingenuity of opponents of the single tax are mostly concentrated in plaintive sympathy for the poor farmers.

The arguments against the single tax, made ostensibly on

[1] *Natural Taxation*, chap. x.

behalf of farmers, are (1) that farmers would be compelled to bear more than half the burden of all taxation under such a system; and (2) that the annual value of bare land in farming districts is never enough to pay even the cost of mere local government.

Every champion of the farmer asserts the truth of both of these propositions. Very little investigation is needed to prove that they cannot both be true, and that both of them are false.

1. As to the claim that the burden upon farmers would be increased, the census of 1890 shows that of the 17,000,000 adult males in the United States there were about 7,700,000 farmers and farm laborers, of whom only 3,100,000 owned any farms. The total value of their farms, including all improvements, was less than \$9,000,000,000, out of a total taxable real estate value of \$46,000,000,000.[1] They, therefore, own less than one-fifth of the real-estate value, and very much less than one-sixth of the value of land, without improvements. Instead of paying half of the taxes under the single-tax method, as is pretended, farmers would not pay so much as one-sixth part of them. At present they pay more than twice as much.

2. It has been demonstrated that the annual value of land in the United States is sufficient to pay all taxes, of every kind, more than twice over.[2] If, then, the farmers really did own more than half of this land value, the claim that out of this they would be unable to pay even their small local taxes out of land values becomes obviously absurd.

More than ten years have now passed since any attempt has been made to attack the soundness of the single-tax theory upon the basis of any general statistics. This has not been because the theory has been neglected and left free from attack. On the contrary, the flow of criticism has been abundant. But, without exception, recent criticisms have either been founded upon mere generalities, or have been supported by carefully selected statistics, from such localities as seemed to furnish the best material for the critics. The reason for this singular form of criticism is that rather more than ten years

[1] *Natural Taxation*, p. 184.   [2] *Ibid.*, p. 147.

ago several writers, almost simultaneously, attempted to refute the single-tax theory by means of statistics, professedly covering the whole of Great Britain. In reply it was shown conclusively that these statistics included the entire taxation for Great Britain and Ireland, while they excluded, in every case, all the land values of the city of London, all railroad and other franchises, and, in some cases, all land values in Scotland and Ireland.[1] When these values were included, it appeared that the ground rents of Great Britain and Ireland amounted to more than double the entire amount of taxation.

The opponents of the single tax have in recent years reversed their methods. They have abandoned all attempts to show that it would not work well in large cities and old communities; and they concentrate their efforts upon arguing that it would be entirely impracticable in rural districts and very new communities. But, obviously, in a *perfectly* new community there is nothing except the value of land to tax. In such a community there are tents, but no houses; there is very little furniture, few tools, no bonds, no banks, and no visible money. In short, there are no taxable improvements or personal property. But instantly upon the formation of any community, land values arise. Accordingly, the history of all new communities, from Ohio to Oklahoma, shows that taxation was at first levied upon the value of land alone; that this source was amply sufficient to provide all needed revenue; and that the growth of each community, under that form of taxation, was more rapid than it ever has been under any other.

A moment's reflection will show how absurd and impossible it would be to adopt, in any strictly new community, the forms of taxation which are so highly commended among us. Would any new settlers on an uninhabited island impose a tariff on imports? Would they think of levying a tax upon money brought into the island? Would they think of taxing the comforts, necessaries, or luxuries of life, either when coming in or after they had been brought in? In short, would they ever dream, during the first year, of imposing any tax upon personal property or upon build-

[1] *Natural Taxation*, p. 137.

ings ? Would they not rather offer a bounty for the introduction of all these necessaries of life ?

It is, in fact, only after a country has become settled, and in some degree wealthy, that its people are seized with the madness of keeping out wealth by taxes upon importations, or of driving out wealth by taxes upon money, tools, machinery, and useful productions in general. It is no wonder that men declare all taxes to be bad. All taxes which in any way tend to diminish wealth, morality, and comfort *are* bad. As every tax, other than the single tax upon ground rent alone, produces precisely these evil results, every tax, except that upon the value of land alone, is irredeemably bad. And as there must be *some* taxation, and heavy taxation too, the single tax, which, to say the very least, does *not* produce any of these bad results, is necessary, just, and righteous.

THOMAS G. SHEARMAN.

NEW YORK.

TAXATION AND THE PHILOSOPHY OF THE STATE.

THE question of the basis and principles of taxation used to be regarded as purely and strictly of an economic character. Today the sociological significance of taxation is very generally recognized, but it may be doubted whether the average writer upon the subject sufficiently realizes the close and vital connection between theories of taxation and conceptions of the nature and province of the state. The animated controversy between determined upholders of the so-called "American" principles of proportionality and uniformity in taxation, and the champions of the progressive or alleged "socialistic" principle, may be profitably reviewed here from a sociological, as distinguished from a politico-economic, point of view.

We know that progressive or graduated taxation has gained considerable ground in the United States, despite strenuous and specious opposition. Ohio and Illinois have passed progressive inheritance- or transfer-tax laws, and these laws have been sustained, not only in the state courts, but in the highest federal court as well. The clear and vigorous decision in the Illinois case rendered by the United States supreme court disposes effectually and finally of the shallow contention that progressive taxation is violative of the constitutional guarantees of "equal protection of the law." State legislatures are now perfectly free to pass graduated income- and inheritance-tax laws, making *amount* of property possessed or inherited the *basis* of classification and discrimination. The federal constitution interposes no obstacle, and the question is properly referred to ethical and sociological principles, to "public policy."

Is progressive taxation unjust, unequal, and dangerous ? Is it to be regarded as an entering wedge for confiscatory and socialistic legislation, and does it involve arbitrary discrimination against the well-to-do ? If so, it is of course to be profoundly regretted that the Fourteenth Amendment, as now interpreted by the supreme court, does not prohibit it, and it becomes the duty of enlightened men to warn state legislatures and Congress against this pernicious principle of taxation. This is precisely what Mr. William D. Guthrie, the able New York lawyer, affirms in his excellent work, just published, on *The Fourteenth Amendment.* To quote Mr. Guthrie :

Expediency or prejudice may hereafter prompt attempts at progressive taxes, or tax laws exempting those of moderate means ; but we shall pay a fearful price if we introduce any such principle into our legislation. Equality of burden, by making every man according to his means a contributor to the expenses of the state, is one of the most wholesome things in our civil institu. tions. . . . If progressive or unequal taxes are permitted, the time cannot be dis. tant when the majority of the voters will confiscate private property under the cloak or pretense of taxation, and the worst follies and crimes of history will be repeated. (P. 140.)

This is strong language, but it is not argument. The reasoning of those who share Mr. Guthrie's views may be thus summarized : "The government is pledged to protect all citizens in the exercise of their freedoms and faculties, and if some, through superior intelligence and industry, earn more than others, it is wrong and short-sighted to punish them for their superior qualifications ; and to tax them at a *higher rate* than others is to discourage intelligence and weaken incentive to labor and thrift." But how is it proposed to prove the injustice, the vice, of progressive taxation ? Question-begging and hard names aside, on what principle is it contended that all persons and all property must be taxed *at the same rate ?*

If those who violently denounce progressive taxation as "socialistic" were logical and unterrified individualists, and consistently followed the doctrine that government is an insurance company for the mere protection of personal and property rights, they could with propriety advocate a system of taxation under which *cost* would determine the premium. It is more expensive and burdensome to a government, regarded as an insurance agency, to protect tangible than intangible forms of property, to protect improvements or land than securities or specie, and those who espouse the Spencerian or strictly individualistic view of the functions and province of government cannot be expected to favor any other basis of taxation than *cost* or pain to

the taxing power.   But the proportional taxationists are not individualists, and they would repudiate with no little warmth and
indignation the charge that they seek to limit the government
to mere police duties.   Many of them are protectionists and
advocates of bounties.   Many of them favor legislation distinctly
socialistic in character.   Most of them certainly believe that it
is the duty of the state to provide free schools and free libraries.
All these beliefs and demands are anything but individualistic,
yet when the subject of taxation is broached we find a strange,
not to say suspicious, and sudden conversion to individualism on
the part of the opponents of progressive taxation!   In point of
fact, the only alternative to the cost principle of the extreme
individualists is the principle of "ability to pay."   John Stuart
Mill, who denies that government has only police functions,
writes as follows on the theory of taxation :

> Government must be regarded as so preëminently a concern of all that
> to determine who are most interested in it is of no real importance.   If a per-
> son, or class of persons, receive so small a share of the benefit as to make it
> necessary to raise the question, there is something else than taxation which
> is amiss, and the thing to be done is to remedy the defect, instead of recog-
> nizing it and making it a ground for demanding less taxes.   As in a case of
> voluntary subscription for a purpose in which all are interested, all are thought
> to have done their part fairly when each has contributed according to his
> means—that is, has made an equal sacrifice for the common object ; in like
> manner should this be the principle of compulsory contributions.

To say that this view is socialistic is only true if all who
support the present political system are socialists.   It is a view
which every non-individualist tacitly adopts whenever he discusses internal improvements, finance, trade, education, and
similar subjects.   It is a view which is never rejected except
when *taxation* is considered.   Accept the theory of government
upon which the overwhelming majority of Americans act, and
all the alleged unfairness of progressive taxation, which is an
application of the "ability-to-pay" principle, disappears at
once.

Most economists and writers on political science have discarded the proportional principle and adopted that of equality of
sacrifice.   They show that it is the proportional system which is

unjust and unequal. The apparent uniformity which deceives the superficial is achieved at the expense of real uniformity. A German economist, K. H. Rau, lays down the following principle : "A given sum of money possesses the higher value for its owner, the greater a proportion of his aggregate disposable goods it constitutes, and the greater a portion it consequently represents of the aggregate enjoyments at his command, especially in case the one who is to be deprived of a given sum will have to stint himself in expenditures for the most necessary articles in order to afford it." This principle, as shown in the recently translated work on *The Science of Finance*, by Professor Gustav Cohn, of the Göttingen university, leads to the progressive basis of taxation. For the smaller the income of a household is, the more will a given sum levied as tax abstract from the means required for pressing necessities, and the tax will fall so much the heavier on the particular household; on the other hand, the larger the income, the more will the tax tend to fall on less pressing or even trivial needs, and will consequently exert but a slight pressure or none at all. This point was once tersely and vigorously expressed by Frederic the Great in an official statement. "A wealthy man," he said, "possessing an income of 5,000 thalers might well be able to spare one-half of it, as he could still live, while a poor man, having an income of 80 thalers, could not spare one-half, as it would leave him nothing to live on. In the case of this latter, he would have done his part if he contributed one thaler."

The "equality-of-sacrifice" or "ability-to-pay" principle rests on another important consideration which the proportional taxationists overlook or deny. It is well stated by Professor Cohn in the following passage :

The enjoyment of peace and civil liberty is unquestionably a privilege of very unequal value to different members of the commonwealth. The fact that these advantages cannot be measured or apportioned by no means prevents the rich and the poor deriving very widely different benefits from them. One who is able to call his own, not merely a bare existence, but also an extensive estate, who may be exposed to the violence of the foreign armies or domestic malefactors, not only in his person, but also in his property, is entitled, or, rather, he is in duty bound, to look upon the institutions which secure him against these dangers as being contrivances of the same kind with those coparcenary dikes which are constructed to protect his own and his neighbors' estates against destructive floods. He is bound to pay in due proportion for this peculiar advantage which accrues to his property above what other, less well-to-do or propertyless, members of the commonwealth enjoy.

It is strangely inconsistent for those who reject the conception of a tax as an insurance premium and who, taking a "broad view of the nature of the state," regard the tax as a direct deduction from the principle of national, organic solidarity, to ask, as some of them do, what would be said of a shopkeeper who asked a different price for the same goods from different customers, according to their ability to pay. To ask this question is to assume a fundamental likeness between the services of the shopkeeper to his patrons and those of the state to its subjects—to assume that in both cases *cost* ought to govern price, to accept implicitly the very insurance conception which has been explicitly repudiated. Besides, while shopkeepers do not ask different prices from different patrons, it is well known that physicians, attorneys, and members of other liberal professions do, to a great extent, regulate their charges by the ability of their patrons to pay. Would not the state be classed with the liberal professions by the proportionalists? There is, in fact, no escape from progressive taxation for those who adopt the organic theory of the state. The proportional basis was a sort of crude application of the "insurance" principle, and it does not satisfy either the individualists, who want a more exact application of the cost theory of the state's functions and services, or the adherents of the broader views of the state, who adopt the doctrine that a tax is a payment made by members of the political community toward its expenses simply in virtue of their being members.

To declare dogmatically that there is anything in or about the "American system" which rigorously excludes progressive taxation is to offend both against fact and reason. In the first place, any tariff which taxes articles of comfort and luxury at a higher rate than articles of necessity is a clear violation of the proportional principle. The federal system of taxation is indirectly progressive. Its tariffs are not horizontal or uniform, and only such tariffs would accord with the proportional principle. To tax the rich at higher rates on the goods imported for their exclusive consumption than on articles of general consumption is to recognize by implication the ability-to-pay principle. No one objects to our tariff laws as un-American. The fact is that there has been a wide departure from the early ideas of government. The Jeffersonian aphorism that "that government is best which governs least" is rightly supposed to sum up the extreme individualistic philosophy of government, but who pretends that our present practice conforms thereto? The Republicans never professed this principle, and the Democrats have abandoned it. Democracy today leans toward socialism rather than toward individualism. It is the Democrats who demand the exclusive supply of paper currency by the government, and it is the Republicans who advocate the "withdrawal of the government from the banking business." The Republicans have taken advanced individualistic ground on several vital questions, while the Democrats have been drifting toward what is called paternalism in the state.

This is said, not with the intention of passing judgment, but solely for the purpose of indicating present social and political tendencies. It lies not in the mouth of any existing party to condemn progressive taxation as revolutionary, because all parties have adopted the philosophy from which such taxation is but a logical corollary. No one can reasonably affirm that progressive taxation is out of harmony with current theory and practice.

Progressive taxation may be oppressive, but the injustice is not in the principle itself in any case. Proportional taxation may be ruinously high, yet no one finds injustice in the principle on that account. It is no doubt easier to enact unfair and confiscatory legislation under a progressive system than under a proportional system, but the possibility of abuse does not affect the theoretical question. Proportionality, as has been ably shown by Controller Roberts of New York, is not proportional in practice. The term is a misnomer and is used without reference to the facts.

The true individualist does not demand proportionality. He

regards the state as an insurance company, and his classification of the subjects of taxation would be based on the cost and burden of protection.   The dominant view of the state cannot escape the logical conclusion from its own premises—namely, that the only equality to be sought in taxation is equality of sacrifice and burden.

V. S. YARROS.

CHICAGO.

THE SOCIAL OBJECTS OF THE NATIONAL-SOCIAL MOVEMENT IN GERMANY.[1]

THE National Socialists constitute the most recent group among the political parties in Germany. The father of this movement was in reality J. H. Wichern, the founder of the German Inner Mission. This Inner Mission is the organization of the practical philanthropy of the German Protestant church, which is, as is doubtless known in America, a truly powerful and beneficent agency. Yet, with all its practical labor, it attains only one object: it mitigates and restricts, but does not remove, distress. Although it momentarily and for a time assists individual sufferers, for the most part it does not permanently stop the sources of misery. It is, however, clear that if this could be attained it would denote a still higher and triumphant evidence of the power of Christianity, the religion of love. But the sources of modern social distress are not in the fault of individual persons, but principally in the structure of the modern economic system. If Christianity is ever to help destroy these evils in their origin, it must venture out upon the sea of social politics and of political action in general.

This course, which Wichern and his contemporaries did not take, was pursued by Dr. Stöcker, formerly Berlin court preacher. He started the Christian Social movement, initiated the Evangelical Social Congress, and his friends established the evangelical workingmen's associations. These three organizations still exist, and, in spite of the decline of social enthusiasm in Germany, labor on faithfully and assiduously, and have an acknowledged record of success in economic science and in practical politics. But they have all come by experience to discover that the social ethics of Christianity can indeed supply a moral basis of a general kind for social work and social politics, but not

[1] The name of Paul Göhre will be recognized as that of the author of *Three Months in a Workshop* and of *Die evangelisch-soziale Bewegung*. The translation of this article is by C. R. Henderson.

765

a precise and firm social principle, nor a compact and original social political program. It is very apparent that individual Christians who accept the general social ethical principles with earnestness and convictions, at the moment when they proceed to realize them by action in practical politics and social politics, are disposed to follow the most diverse paths determined by temperament, education, abilities, and social position. Very properly does Christianity decline to proceed beyond the point where its ethics begin to be made an affair of a particular political and social party. It supplies members of each party with the right spirit and the right disposition, but it does not furnish them a program. Therefore a movement which will draw the ethics of Christianity into the contests of social politics as an influence must derive its principles and the particulars of its program from other sources than Christianity.

Those of the Christian Social tendency who had a clear view of this position joined together in consequence, about two and one-half years since, into a new and directly political party group. The national interest became for them the constitutive principle of their program and of their social efforts, which continued as before to be inspired by the social and ethical spirit of Christianity, and sought to bring this spirit to apprehension and authority. Thus arose in the summer of the year 1896 the National Social party. Its leader is Pastor Frederick Naumann, a man of about thirty-eight years of age. Educated men as well as workingmen are counted among his adherents. The movement is already organized in more than half of the elective districts of the German Reichstag; it has for its organ the weekly paper, *Die Hilfe,* a bimonthly, *Die deutsche Volks-Stimme,* two dailies, and several small local and society papers.

The fundamental thoughts of its program are the following: The development of Germany to even greater power, energy, and welfare must be the first object of all practical politics. This object will be attained primarily by means of an ever-increasing economical and political development of the foreign power of the German empire. Therefore the growth and extension of German industry, of its foreign markets, and of its commercial policy are to be promoted by all means; and by undiminished support of its armed defense, by suitable increase of the German fleet, and by the enlargement of German colonies are to be protected and supported. This growth of German industry, world commerce, and world power, this policy of power abroad, are on the other hand conditions of the possibility of organic social reforms at home. Social reforms for the benefit of the weaker members of the people are never possible in a state whose development has been arrested. Only as the state as a whole moves upward can its lower strata be elevated. And again, power abroad will be maintained permanently when the people and its parts and members, in themselves sound and strong, persistently advance.

In order to maintain such progress, and especially to render the lower classes of the population ever more capable of production, a consistent social reform is likewise necessary. And therefore to the policy of foreign power is connected, as the second fundamental principle, the policy of social reform at home.

How, then, shall this social reform, according to the view of the National Socialists, be carried out? They have on this point placed the following general statement in the fourth paragraph of their program:

We desire an increase of the share which labor, in its different kinds and forms, in city and country, among men and women, enjoys of the total production of German industry; and we expect this, not from the utopias and dogmas of a revolutionary communism of the Marxist type, but from continued political, trades-union, and associated effort, upon the basis of existing relations, whose historical development we wish to influence to the benefit of labor.

From this are deduced the following general ideas: The National Socialists plant themselves on the firm ground of the economical reality of the present, from the moderation born of knowledge. This reality, however, is determined by the economical principle of the free play of forces, the well-known Manchester doctrine. The National Socialists by no means deny the immense economic, social, and political advance which has been gained since this principle has been accepted. But they do not close their eyes to the terrible results which its ascendency has brought with it. These evils, and not the advantages which have been gained, and the permanent good and approved sides of the principles, are to be removed by unwearied work of social reform, and are to be replaced by better arrangements. The fundamental law of gradual organic development must be set in the highest position. From this it follows that the National Socialists are opponents of the crass, extreme doctrine of private capital, as well as of one-sided communism, according to which the proletarians will seize at one stroke the dictatorship, and introduce a communistic society and industrial order. The National Socialists see herein a vicious utopia which even in case of successful realization would mean a certain advance for particular classes, but, through its partiality, would result in many great and unexpected injuries. We have learned that the one-sided private capitalistic theory, when carried unconditionally into practice, actually made mischief, although it was at one·time believed that it would bring all blessing and nothing but blessing. On the other side, however, the National Socialists know that they stand near to Social Democracy when this, as is already often true, strives for a fundamental and gradual upward development of the working class by means of practical social efforts in particular measures, as occasion for them arises. In the main we can accept as the watchword of the National Socialists this cry : Higher development of the German working classes.

Now, in what particular ways do the National Socialists propose to forward this upward development ?

First of all by efforts in and with the trade associations. It is well known that there are in Germany three kinds of trade associations : those of Social Democracy, which are by much the strongest; those of the Ultramontanes, the Catholic Centrum party; and the so-called Hirsch-Duncker trade unions, which subscribe to civic and liberal principles. All three kinds move in particular party courses, one being Social Democratic, the next Ultramontane, and the third German Liberal (*Freisinnig*). The National Socialists see, however, in this partisan character the destruction of the trades unions, or at least a very serious diminution of the power and influence which they might exert. Since, in the first place, a force divided into three parts is never so strong as a united force; secondly, a part of the workingmen who will hear nothing of party politics are thereby frightened away from entrance into trades unions; and, thereby, the connection with the Social Democratic party especially offers the capitalist managers a good excuse for denouncing the trades unions before the German government as purely political, and thus for restricting their freedom of action. All this the National Socialists would remove from the trades unions by impressing on them a non-partisan character, by transforming them into a separate, independent agency which goes its own way and knows no other purpose than securing better wages and conditions for labor in the contest with capitalists. Before the eyes of the National Socialists float as an ideal the splendid English trades unions which have hitherto remained non-partisan, and have been so successful. They purpose to work unceasingly until this ideal is realized. Their labors have already been crowned with partial success. Already this ideal has been discussed fully in Social Democratic trades unions, and with such effect that already a large number of adherents have been won to it.

In addition to the promotion and transformation of trades unions, the National Socialists have undertaken, as the second of their social efforts, an intensive work on behalf of associations (*Genossenschaften*). In Germany there exist at the present time over 20,000 associations of rural handicraftsmen, peasants, and laborers. First among these, the credit associations of the handicraftsmen have attained a high degree of success by the method established more than fifty years ago by their founder, Schulze-Delitsch. On the contrary, this method of administration has not been followed where associations for purchase, sale, and production are concerned. Never have these attained any importance. And the National Socialists find the reason for this failure in their present form of organization. Some of them have given themselves entirely to associated work, and have thus established new associations on modern methods of organization. The beginnings already made justify good hopes, and present a prospect that the master handicraftsmen may join in a form of common production and common sale of their common products, by a method according to which they can enjoy the advantages of the modern great industry and, at the same time, retain at least a part of the advantages of their former complete independence as masters.   Thereby would arise a mixed form of purely individualistic and purely communistic trades, which appears to be a natural step of economic progress.   Frankfort-on-the-Main has shown itself hitherto as an especially favorable field for these experiments.   Still higher than these associations of handicraftsmen do the National Socialists esteem the value of the workingmen's societies of consumers.   In Germany these are still very young and not at all numerous.   The cause of this lies in the fact that formerly Lassalle denounced the thoroughly middle-class associations of Schulze-Delitsch as not at all adapted to the needs of the workingmen.   This view of Lassalle was maintained until lately by the workingmen, who were busy enough with trades unions and political affairs, and only recently have the consumers' societies, favored by the workingmen's party, grown apace among the workingmen themselves.   The industrial kingdom of Saxony seems especially to be a fruitful soil for their growth.   It is one of the chief efforts of the National Socialists to cultivate this movement by all available means, and thus to organize and assist the workingmen, not only as workingmen, but also as consumers.   Here again England, with its powerful consumers' societies, serves as an example for the National Socialists.

Most highly prized of all by the National Socialists are the peasants' associations, which have grown up everywhere in great numbers as agencies for the purchase of fodder, artificial fertilizers, seeds, and agricultural implements and machines; for the marketing of draft oxen, animals for slaughter, horses, butter, milk, fruit, vegetables, seeds, and cereals; for dairy, breeding, herd-book, and distillery purposes; for drainage and irrigation, slaughtering and baking; and for culture of fields and fruits. The National Socialists hope from their development an even greater result for the poorer and medium peasant class than has been attained for the handicraftsmen by means of the new associations of handicraftsmen begun by them : a new, advantageous, half individualistic, half socialistic mode of possession and economy in the country.

Just this last purpose of associations the National Socialists of late hold to be all the earlier and more certainly to be realized, and more easily attained, since a very marked advance in land-property reform has been made. The leaders of their reform are also leaders of the National Socialists, and their organs are those of the National Socialists.   Indeed, the German land reformers have a different character from those of other countries.   They do not swear by one theory and the battle-cry of the single tax, as we hear they do in America.   They have rather learned of recent years, and particularly under the influence of the National Socialists, from Social Democracy and Manchesterism alike, that a particular one-sided theory never by itself causes economic advance.   So they have concluded to saw and split up the entire huge trunk of their land-reform ideal into a number of logs, billets, boards, and beams, which can be used as desired in the many-sided transformation and rebuilding of the social edifice, as may be best adapted to German needs.   One of these demands of reform, both of the land reformers and of the National Socialists, relates to the socialization of mortgage credits on land security, and a second to a systematic state policy in respect to peasant proprietorship.   The first demand is immediately intelligible, while the second is different.   It is well known that in eastern Germany the feudal, usurious, great landlordism has existed from the Middle Ages to the present, and that it is an Alp and plague for modern Germany.   Latterly, however, through various changes in world commerce, these estates have become unprofitable, and they will become even less profitable with time.   One huge estate after another, one country squire after another, falls into ruin.   The question now arises whether these bankrupt estates, as has often occurred in England, shall pass over into the hands of rich urban manufacturers and merchants, and be transformed into forests and pastures, or whether they shall become peasant property and support a peasant population. The National Socialists work for the method of the formation of rented estates; they demand that the state, as the greatest and most non-partisan capitalist, shall make this economical manipulation unselfish; that whenever a new peasant property is established, the state shall retain the first right of purchase, and thereby, as well as through the principle of rent, retain a sort of superior proprietorship. This position would be strengthened if mortgage credit were also socialized by the state, and would be still more strengthened and confirmed, without becoming oppressive, by helping to impress a half individualistic, half socialistic character of the rural form of proprietorship and cultivation on the already extensive association. A third earnest social and political demand of the National Socialists and of the land reformers is the communalization of ground in cities and their surroundings, in order to put a stop to the usury of dwelling owners and to the swindling operations of builders of houses. In this field the success of agitation is already greater than in the others.

In respect to the great industry the National Socialists are more conservative in demands than in respect to the rural landlordism which is doomed to decay. For the great industry is still a relatively new system, is in the line of development, and cannot be so easily as the Social Democrats ordinarily imagine radically changed and transformed. Yet the National Socialists are friendly to the idea of socializing certain particular industries, as those of electricity, mines, ship-building, in the same way as that in which the railroads have been nationalized. They also decidedly favor the taking over by urban administration of the gas and water supply, of street-car transportation, and of similar profitable agencies in cities. In general, they sharply watch the tendency toward combinations of particular industries, since every such combination implies the beginning of the conquest of the existing Manchesteristic, anarchical method of industry, and the beginning of a systematic organization of production, wages, and fixing of prices. Of course, this works at first exclusively to the advantage of the managers. But it would be merely a question of practical, although of fundamental, social reform, at each stage to divide the advantages of these new and gradually established combinations equally between the managers, the workingmen, and the consumers. It may be regarded as a new factor in the social thinking of the National Socialists to influence the development of the great industry, so far as possible, in this direction.

According to what has been said, it is only natural that the National Socialists should first of all make use of, and faithfully coöperate with, every convenient means, however small, of improving the economic condition of all poor people, so long as they are practicable and conform to economic progress. As a matter of course, therefore, they labor for the further extension of the German workingmen's insurance, and for legal protection for workingmen, in which measures there are still many defects ; and they labor for the extension of non-partisan bureaus of employment over the entire empire, and, with this extension, for an organization of employment in general. They support all efforts to ameliorate the dwellings of workingmen ; found associations for building such dwellings, and participate in undertakings for the elevation and education of all half-educated, quarter-educated, and uneducated persons ; and for this task they are especially fitted, and they are under obligation to it, since the majority of all German Protestant teachers are counted among the adherents of their mode of thought. Naturally so new a movement as that of the National Socialists has yet no exhaustive social program. Gradually, piece by piece, one will arise in the course of common effort. The demands which have been described are practically those which have been thus far fixed. At present we are engaged in making a special communal program. Perhaps at a later time it will be permitted and possible in these pages to give news of further social and social-political progress.　　　　　PAUL GÖHRE,

Pfarrer a. D.

LEIPZIG.

SEX IN PRIMITIVE MORALITY.

THE function of morality is to regulate the activities of associated life so that all may have what we call fair play. It is impossible to think of morality aside from expressions of force, primarily physical force. "Thou shalt not kill; thou shalt not steal; thou shalt not bear false witness; thou shalt not commit adultery; thou shalt not remove the ancient landmark;" and all approvals and disapprovals imply that the act in question has affected or will affect the interests of others, or of society at large, for better or for worse. And since morality goes back so directly to forms of activity and their regulation, we may expect to find that the motor male and the more stationary female have had a different relation to the development of a moral code.

As between nutrition and reproduction, in the struggle for life, nutrition plays a larger rôle—in volume, at any rate—in the life history of the individual. A consideration of the causes of the modification of species in nature shows that the changes in morphology and habit of the animal which relate to food-getting are more fundamental and numerous than those which relate to wooing. In a moral code, likewise, whether in an animal or human society, the bulk of morality turns upon food rather than sex relations; and since the male is more active in both these relations, and since, further, morality is the mode of regulating activities in these relations, it is to be expected that morality, and immorality as well, will be found primarily to a greater degree functions of the motor male disposition.

Tribal safety and the preservation and extension of the territory furnishing food demand the organized attention of the group first of all; and the emotional demonstrations and social rewards following modes of behavior which have a protective or provident meaning for the group, and the public disapproval and disallowance of modes of behavior which impair the safety or force capacity, and consequent satisfactions of the group, become in the tribe the most powerful of all stimuli, and stimuli to which the male is peculiarly able to react. This is not like the case of hunger and other physiological stimuli which are conditioned from within, but if the individual acts for the advantage of the group rather than for his personal advantage, the stimulus to this action must be furnished socially. Group preservation being of first-rate importance, no group would survive in which the public showed apathy on this point. Lewis and Clarke say of the Dakota Indians: "What struck us most was an institution peculiar to them and to the Kite Indians, further to the westward, from whom it is said to have been copied. It is an association of the most active and brave young men, who are bound to each other by attachment, secured by a vow never to retreat before any danger, or to give way to their enemies. In war they go forward without sheltering themselves behind trees, or aiding their natural valor by any artifice. . . . . These young men sit, and encamp, and dance together, distinct from the rest of the nation; they are generally about thirty or thirty-five years old; and such is the deference paid to courage that their seats in the council are superior to those of the chiefs, and their persons more respected."[1] The consciousness of the value of male activity is here expressed in an exaggerated degree — in a degree bordering upon the pathological, since the reckless exposure of life to danger is not necessary to success at a given moment, and is unjustifiable from the standpoint of public safety, unless it be on the side of the suggestive effect of intrepid conduct in creating a general standard of intrepidity. Similarly, the Indians in general often failed to get the full benefit of a victory, because of their practice that the scalp of an enemy belonged to him who took it, and their pursuits after a rout were checked by the delay of each to scalp his own.

The pedagogical attempts of primitive society, so far as they are applied to boys, have as an end the encouragement of morality of a motor, not a sentimental, type. The boys are taught war and the chase, and to despise the occupations of women. Thompson says of the Zulu boys: "It is a melancholy fact that

[1] LEWIS AND CLARKE, *Travels to the Source of the Missouri*, ed. 1814, Vol. I, p. 60.

when they have arrived at a very early age, should their mothers attempt to chastise them, such is the law that these lads are at the moment allowed to kill their mothers."[1] Ethnologists often make mention of the fact that the natural races do not generally punish children, and while this is due in part to a less definite sense of responsibility, as well as of less nervousness in parents, non-interference is a part of their system of training: "Instead of teaching the boy civil manners, the father desires him to beat and pelt the strangers who come to the tent; to steal or secret in joke some trifling article belonging to them; and the more saucy and impudent they are, the more troublesome to strangers and all the men of the encampment, the more they are praised as giving indication of a future enterprising and warlike disposition."[2] Theft is also encouraged among boys as a developer of their wits. The Spartan boy and the fox is a classical example; and Diodorus relates that in Egypt the boy who wished to become a thief was required to enroll his name with the captain of the thieves, and to turn over to him all stolen articles. The citizens who were robbed went to the captain of thieves and recovered their property upon payment of one-fourth of its value.[3] Admiration of a lawless deed often foreruns censure of the deed in consciousness today: there are few men who do not admire a particularly daring and successful bank or diamond robbery, though they deprecate the social injury done.

Formally becoming a man is made so much of in early society, because it is on this occasion that fitness for activity is put to the test. Initiatory ceremonies fall at the time of puberty in the candidate, and consist of instruction and trials of fortitude. A certain show of the proceeds of activity is also exacted of young men, especially in connection with marriage, and the youth is not permitted to marry until he has killed certain animals or acquired certain trophies. The attention given to manly practices in connection with marriage is seen in this example

[1] G. THOMPSON, *Travels and Adventures in Southern Africa*, Appendix, p. 286.

[2] J. L. BURCKHARDT, *Notes on the Bedouins and Wahabys*, Vol. I, p. 98.

[3] POST, *Bausteine einer allgemeinen Rechtswissenschaft*, Vol. I, p, 287.

from the Kukis: "When a young man has fixed his affections upon a young woman, either of his own or of some neighboring *Parah*, his father visits her father and demands her in marriage for his son: her father, on this, inquires what are the merits of the young man to entitle him to her favor; and how many can he afford to entertain at the wedding feast; to which the father of the young man replies that his son is a brave warrior, a good hunter, and an expert thief; for that he can produce so many heads of the enemies he has slain and of the game he has killed; that in his house are such and such stolen goods; and that he can feast so many (mentioning the number) at his marriage."[1] Occasionally the ability to take punishment is even made a part of the marriage ceremony. At Arab marriages "there is much feasting, and the unfortunate bridegroom undergoes the ordeal of whipping by the relations of his bride, in order to test his courage. Sometimes this punishment is exceedingly severe, being inflicted with the coorbatch, or whip of hippopotamus hide, which is cracked vigorously about his ribs and back. If the happy husband wishes to be considered a man worth having, he must receive the chastisement with an expression of enjoyment; in which case the crowds of women in admiration again raise their thrilling cry."[2]

A very simple record of successful activity is the bones of animals. McCosh says of the Mishmis of India: "Nor are these hospitable rites allowed to be forgotten; the skull of every animal that has graced the board is hung up as a record in the hall of the entertainer; he who has the best-stocked Golgotha is looked upon as the man of the greatest wealth and liberality, and when he dies the whole smoke-dried collection of many years is piled upon his grave as a monument of his riches and a memorial of his worth."[3] And Grange of the Nagas: "In front of the houses of the greater folks are strung up the bones of the animals with which they have feasted the villagers, whether

[1] MACRAE, "Account of the Kookies or Lunctas," *Asiatic Researches*, Vol. VII, p. 193.

[2] S. W. BAKER, *The Nile Tributaries of Abyssinia*, p. 125.

[3] *Journal Asiatic Society of Bengal*, Vol. V, p. 195.

tigers, elephants, cows, hogs, dogs, or monkeys, or aught else, for it signifies little what comes to their net."[1]

The head-hunting mania of Borneo is also a pathological expression of the desire to get approval of destructive activity from both the living and the dead: "The aged of the people were no longer safe among their kindred, and corpses were secretly disinterred to increase the grizzly store. Superstition soon added its ready impulse to the general movement. The aged warrior could not rest in his grave till his relatives had taken a head in his name; the maiden disdained the weak-hearted suitor whose hand was not yet stained with some cowardly murder."[2]

Class distinctions and the attendant ceremonial observances go immediately back to an appreciation of successful motor activities. It needs only to observe the conduct of weaker animals in the presence of the stronger to appreciate the differences in behavior induced by the presence of superior motor ability. The recognition of this difference, as it is finally expressed in habitual forms of behavior, becomes the sign of the difference, while the difference goes back, in reality, to a difference in capacity. This example from Raffles illustrates the intensity of moral meaning which the appreciation of achievement may take on in the end: "At the court of *Súra-kérta* I recollect that once, when holding a private conference with the *Súsunan* at the residency, it became necessary for the *Rádan adipáti* to be dispatched to the palace for the royal seal: the poor old man was, as usual, squatting, and as the Susunan happened to be seated with his face toward the door, it was fully ten minutes before his minister, after repeated ineffectual attempts, could obtain the opportunity of rising sufficiently to reach the latch without being seen by his royal master. The mission on which he was dispatched was urgent, and the Susunan himself inconvenienced by the delay; but these inconveniences were insignificant compared with the indecorum of being seen out of the *dódok* posture. When it is necessary for an inferior to move, he must still retain

[1] Journal Asiatic Society of Bengal, Vol. VIII, p. 470.

[2] F. BOYLE, *Adventures among the Dyaks of Borneo*, p. 170.

that position, and walk with his hams upon his heels until he is out of his superior's sight."[1] Drury says that a Malagasy chief, on his return from war, "had scarcely seated himself at his door, when his wife came out crawling on her hands and knees until she came to him, and then licked his feet; when she had done, his mother did the same, and all the women in the town saluted their husbands in the same manner."[2]

An examination of the causes of the approval of conduct in early times thus discloses that approvals were based to a large degree on violent and socially advantageous conduct, that the training and rewards of early society were calculated to develop the skill and fortitude essential to such conduct, and that the men were particularly the representatives of conduct of this type. In the past, at any rate, there has been no glory like military glory, and no adulation like military adulation, and in the vulgar estimation still no quality in the individual ranks with the fighting quality.[3]

But checks upon conduct are even more definitely expressed, and more definitely expressible, than approvals of conduct. Approval is expressed in a more general expansive feeling toward the deserving individual, and this may be accompanied with medals for bravery, promotions, and other rewards, but in general the moral side of life gets no such definite notice as the immoral side. Practices which are disliked by all may be forbidden, while there is no equally summary way of dealing with practices approved by all. In consequence, practices which interfere with the activities of others are inhibited, and to the violation of the inhibition is attached a penalty, resulting in a body of law and a system of punishment. An analysis of the following crimes and punishments among the Kaffirs, for instance, indicates that a definite relation between offensive forms of activity and punishments is present at a comparatively

[1] T. S. Raffles, *History of Java*, Vol. I, p. 309,

[2] R. Drury, *Madagascar*, p. 77.

[3] No notice is here taken of the moral content of forms of worship, since forms of worship are to be regarded as reflections of social states of mind, and behavior to gods is of a piece with behavior to men.

early period of development: "Theft: restitution and fine. Injuring cattle: death or fine, according to the circumstances. Causing cattle to abort: heavy fine. Arson: fine. False witness: heavy fine. Maiming: fine. Adultery: fine, sometimes death. Rape: fine, sometimes death. Using love philters: death or fine, according to circumstances. Poisoning, and· practices with an evil intent (termed 'witchcraft'): death and confiscation. Murder: death or fine, according to circumstances. . . . . Treason, as contriving the death of a chief, conveying information to the enemy : death and confiscation. Desertion from the tribe: death and confiscation."x Similarly among the Kukis: "Injuring the property of others, or taking it without payment; using violence ; abusing parents; fraudulently injuring another; giving false evidence; speaking disrespectfully to the aged; marrying an elder brother's wife; putting your foot on, or walking over, a man's body; speaking profanely of religion — are acts of impiety."²

As the vigorous and aggressive activities˙of the male have a very conspicuous value for the group when exercised for the benefit of the group, they become particularly harmful when directed against the safety or interests of the group or the members of the group, and we find that civil and criminal law, and contract, and also conventional morality, are closely connected with the motility of the male. The establishment of moral standards is mediated through the sense of strain — strain to the personal self, and strain to the social self. Whether a man is injured by an assault upon his life or upon his property, he suffers violence, and the first resort of· the injured individual or group is to similar violence ; but this results in a vicious tit-for-tat reaction whereby the stimulus to violence is reinstated by every fresh act of violence. Within the group this vicious action and reaction is broken up by the intervention of public opinion, either in an informal expression of disapproval, or through the headmen. The man who continues to

---

¹ J. SHOOTER, *The Kafirs of Natal and the Zulu Country*, p. 102.

² MAJOR J. BUTLER, *Travels and Adventures in Assam*, p. 88; quoted in SPENCER, *Descriptive Sociology*, Vol. V, p. 33.

kill may be killed in turn, but by order of the council of the tribe, and one of his kinsmen may be appointed to execute him, as under that condition no feud can follow. But there is always a reluctance to banish or take the life of the member of the group, both because no definite machinery is developed for accomplishing either, and because the loss of an able-bodied member of a group is a loss to the group itself. The group does not seek, therefore, immediately to be rid of an offensive member, but to modify his habits, to convert him. Jones says of the Ojibways that there were occasionally bad ones among them, "but the good council of the wise sachems and the mark of disgrace put upon unruly persons had a very desirable influence."[1] The extreme form of punishment in the power of the folk-moot of the Tuschinen is to be excluded from the public feasts, and to be made a spectator while stoned in effigy and cursed.[2] Sending a man to Coventry is in vogue among the Fejir Bedouins: one who kills a friend is so despised that he is never spoken to again, nor allowed to sit in the tent of any member of the tribe.[3] The formulation of sentiment about an act depends also on the repetition of the act. The act is more irritating, and the irritation more widespread, with each repetition, and there is an increase of the penalty for a second offense, and death for a slight offense when frequently repeated: in the Netherlands stealing of linen left in the fields to be bleached led to the death penalty for stealing a pocket handkerchief. And with increasing definiteness of authority there follows increasing definiteness of punishment, and when finally the habit becomes fixed, conformity with it becomes a paramount consideration, and a deed is no longer viewed with reference to its intrinsic import so much as to its conformity or nonconformity with a standard in the law: *summum jus, summa injuria.*

Morality, involving the modification of the conduct of the individual in view of the presence of others, is already highly

[1] JONES, *History of the Ojibway Indians*, p. 57.

[2] VON SEIDLITZ, "Ethnog. Rundschau," *Intern. Archiv f. Ethnographie*, 1890, p. 136.

[3] DOUGHTY, *Travels in Arabia Deserta*, p. 360.

developed in the tribal stage, since the exigencies of life have demanded the most rigorous regulation of behavior in order to secure the organization and the prowess essential to success against all comers.   But the tribe is a unit in hostile coexistence with other similar units, and its morality stops within itself, and applies in no sense to strangers and outsiders.   The North American Indians were theoretically at war with all with whom they had not concluded a treaty of peace.   In Africa the traveler is safe and at an advantage if by a fiction (the rite of blood-brotherhood) he is made a member of the group; and similarly in Arabia and elsewhere.   The old epics and histories are full of the praises of the man who is gentle within the group and furious without it.   The earliest commandments doubtless did not originally apply to mankind at large.   They meant, Thou shalt not kill within the tribe, Thou shalt not commit adultery within the tribe, etc.   Cannibalism furnishes a most interesting example of the prohibition of a practice as applied to the members of the group, while extra-tribal cannibalism continued unabated. And within the tribe there is a continuance of this practice in the forms which do not interfere with the efficiency and cripple the activity of the group.   That is, while cannibalism in general is prohibited, the eating of the decrepit, the aged, of invalids, of deformed children, and of malefactors is still practiced.

But there gradually grew up a set of disapprovals of conduct as such, whether within or without the group.   In the *Odyssey* Pallas Athene says that Odysseus had come from Ephyra from Ilus, son of Mermerus, "For even thither had Odysseus gone on his swift ship to seek a deadly drug, that he might have wherewithal to smear his bronze-shod arrows: but Ilus would in no wise give it him, for he had in awe the everlasting gods."[1] Here is an extension to society in general of a principle which had been first worked out in the group; for poisoning without the group was long allowed after it was disallowed in the group. The case of poisoning is, indeed, a particularly good instance of an unsatisfaction felt in the substitution of clandestine methods for simple motor force in deciding a dispute, and affords a clear

[1] *Odyssey*, i, 260 (translated by LANG AND MEYER).

example of an important relation between moral feeling and physiological functioning. Animal as well as human society has developed strategy alongside of direct motor expressions, but strategy is only an indirect application of the motor principle. Coördination, associative memory, will, judgment, are involved in strategy; it is only a different mode of functioning. On the other hand, there is a peculiar abhorrence of murder by night, poisoning, drowning in a ship's hold, because, while all the physiological machinery for action is on hand, there is no chance to work it. It is a most exasperating thing to die without making a fight for it. The so-called American duel is an abhorrent thing, because life or death is decided by a turn of the dice, not on the racially developed principle of the battle to the strong. When, then, it is observed within the group that this, that, and the other man has died of poison, each interprets this in terms of himself, and no one feels safe. The use of poison is not only a means of checking activities and doing hurt socially, but this form is most foul and unnatural because it involves a death without the possibility of motor resistance (except the inadequate opportunity on the strategic side of taking precautionary measures against poison), and a victory and social reward without a struggle. The group, therefore early adopts very severe methods in this regard. Death is the usual penalty for the use of poison, and even the possession of poison, among tribes not employing it for poisoning weapons, is punished. Among the Karens of India, if a man is found with poison in his possession he is bound and placed for three days in the hot sun, his poison is destroyed, and he is pledged not to obtain any more. If he is suspected of killing anyone, he is executed.[1] Particularly distressing modes of death, and other means of penalizing death by poison more severely than motor modes of killing, were adopted. The Chinese punish the preparation of poisons or capture of poisonous animals with beheading, confiscation, and banishment of wife and children. In Athens insanity caused by poison was punished with death. The

---

[1] F. MASON, "On the Dwellings, Works of Art, Laws, etc., of the Karens," *Journal of the Asiatic Society of Bengal*, 1868, p. 149.

Sachsenspiegel provides death by fire. In the lawbook of the tsar Wachtang a double composition price was exacted for death by poison. And in ancient Wales death and confiscation was the penalty for death by poison, and death or banishment the penalty of the manufacturer of poisons. The same quality of disapproval is expressed in early law of sorcery, and it is unnecessary to give details of this also. But, stated in emotional terms, both poison and sorcery, and other underhand practices, arouse one of the most distressing of the emotions—the emotion of dread, if we understand by this term that form of fear which has no tangible or visible embodiment, which is apprehended but not located, and which in consequence cannot be resisted: the distress, in fact, lying in the inability to function. The organism which has developed structure and function through action is unsatisfied by an un-motor mode of decision. We thus detect in the love of fair play, in the golden rule, and in all moral practices a motor element, and with changing conditions there is progressively a tendency, mediated by natural selection and conscious choice, to select those modes of reaction in which the element of chance is as far as possible eliminated. This preference for functional over chance or quasi-chance forms of decision is expressed first within the group, but is slowly extended, along with increasing commercial communication, treaties of peace, and with supernatural assistance, to neighboring groups. The case of Odysseus is an instance of a moment in the life of the race when a disapproval is becoming of general application.

On our assumption that morality is dependent on strains, and that its development is due to the advantage of regulating these strains, we may readily understand why most of the canons of morality are functions of the katabolic male activity. Theft, arson, rape, murder, burglary, highway robbery, treason, and the like, are natural accompaniments of the more aggressive male disposition; the male is *par excellence* both the hero and the criminal. But on the side of the sex we might expect to find the female disposition setting the standards of morality, since reproduction is even a greater part of her nature than of man's.

But here we find the male standpoint carried over and applied to the reproductive process, and the regulation of sex practices transpiring on the basis of force. In the earliest period of society, under the maternal system, the woman had her own will more with her person; but with the formulation of a system of control, based on male activities, the person of woman was made a point in the application of the male standpoint. "The wife, like any other of the husband's goods and chattels, might be sold or lent."[x] "Even when divorced she was by no means free, as the tribe exercised its jurisdiction in the woman's affairs and the disposal of her person."[2] Forsyth reports of the Gonds that "infidelity in the married state is . . . . said to be very rare; and, when it does occur, is one of the few occasions when the stolid aborigine is roused to the extremity of passion, frequently revenging himself on the guilty pair by cutting off his wife's nose and knocking out the brains of her paramour with his ax."[3] The sacrifice of wives in Africa, India, Fiji, Madagascar, and elsewhere, upon the death of husbands, shows how completely the person of the female had been made a part of the male activity. Where this practice obtained, the failure of the widow to acquiesce in the habit was highly immoral. Williams says of the strangling of widows by the Fijians : " It has been said that most of the women thus destroyed are sacrificed at their own instance. There is truth in this statement, but unless other facts are taken into account it produces an untruthful impression. Many are importunate to be killed, because they know that life would henceforth be to them prolonged insult, neglect, and want. . . . . If the friends of the woman are not the most clamorous for her death, their indifference is construed into disrespect either for her late husband or his friends."[4] Child marriages are another instance of the success of the male in gaining control of the person of the female and of regulating her conduct from his own standpoint. Girls were married or

[1] Bonwick, *Daily Life of the Tasmanians*, p. 75.

[2] *Ibid.*, p. 74.

[3] *Highlands of Central India*, p. 149.

[4] T. Williams, *Fiji and the Fijians*, p. 201.

betrothed before birth, at birth, at two weeks, three months, or seven years of age, and variously often to an adult, and their husbands were thus able to take extraordinary precautions against the violation of their chastity. On the other hand, it frequently happens, especially where marriage by purchase is not developed, that the conduct of the girl is not looked after until she is married; it becomes immoral only when disapproved by her husband. In the Andaman Islands, "after puberty the females have indiscriminate intercourse . . . . until they are chosen or allotted as wives, when they are required to be faithful to their husbands, whom they serve. . . . If any married or single man goes to an unmarried woman, and she declines to have intercourse with him by getting up or going to another part of the circle, he considers himself insulted, and, unless restrained, would kill or wound her."[1] Under these conditions the rightness or wrongness of the sexual conduct of the wife turned upon the attitude of the husband toward the act. Hence a very general practice that the men prostituted their wives for hire, but punished unapproved intercourse. "The chastity of the women does not appear to be held in much estimation. The husband will, for a trifling present, lend his wife to a stranger, and the loan may be protracted by increasing the value of the present. Yet, strange as it may seem, notwithstanding this facility, any connection of this kind not authorized by the husband is considered highly offensive and quite as disgraceful to his character as the same licentiousness in civilized societies."[2]

When woman lost the temporary prestige which she had acquired in the maternal system through her greater tendency to associated life, and particularly when her person came more absolutely into the control of man through the system of marriage by purchase, she also accepted and reflected naïvely the moral standards which were developed for the most part through male activities. Any system of checks and approvals in the group, indeed, which was of advantage to the men would be of advantage to the women also, since these checks and approvals were safe-

---

[1] OWEN, *Transactions Ethnological Society*, New Series, Vol. II, p. 35.

[2] LEWIS AND CLARKE, *loc. cit.*, Vol. I, p. 421.

guards of the group as a whole, and not of the men only. The person and presence of woman in society have stimulated and modified male behavior and male moral standards, and she has been a faithful follower, even a stickler for the prevalent moral standards (the very tenacity of her adhesion is often a sign that she is an imitator) ; but up to date the nature of her activities, the nature, in short, of the strains she has been put to, has not enabled her to set up independently standards of behavior either like or unlike those developed through the peculiar male activities. There is, indeed, a point of difference in the application of standards of morality to men and to women. Morality as applied to man has a larger element of the contractual, representing the adjustment of his activities to those of society at large, or more particularly to the activities of the male members of society; while the morality which we think of in connection with woman shows less of the contractual and more of the personal, representing her adjustment to men, more particularly the adjustment of her person to men. This represents the case as it has been historically, at least, and as it is at present for the most part, but I do not wish to imply that this difference is altogether inherent in the male and female disposition ; it is, in fact, partly a matter of habit and attention. It is now beginning to be true that the energies of women may find expression in forms of activity appropriate to their nature, and this will doubtless, in the long run, favor constructive, as over against destructive, modes of social interaction. The doctrines of the Sermon on the Mount and non-resistance, and the practices of asceticism and chivalry, in so far as they represent the sympathetic and passive side of the association, show something of the female quality ; but we may be sure that a society which has developed a system of approvals and checks based on the fact of strains will not be adequately regulated by any system of approvals and checks based on a non-strain theory, unless human nature is modified more deeply than anthropology gives us grounds to believe possible.

W. I. THOMAS.

THE UNIVERSITY OF CHICAGO.

PROFIT-SHARING AND COÖPERATION.

II.

HAVING considered the relation between profit-sharing and coöperation in theory and in the discussion of economists, let us turn to their relation in practice. And here we find a phase of profit-sharing quite distinct from that previously considered and from that usually considered. Profit-sharing here is not an end in itself, but simply a means for carrying out the coöperative ideal. The economists have usually considered profit-sharing as an intermediate stage between the wage system as it now exists and coöperation as an ideal status; or they have considered it as the best attainable modification of the wage system. This latter subject has been previously considered.[1] But before considering profit-sharing as a transition stage to coöperation, let us consider it as one element of the *modus operandi* of coöperation. This is best illustrated by an account of the experience in Great Britain, where both plans have had many adherents, and where profit-sharing has had many trials in both producers' and consumers' coöperation.

Profit-sharing was an essential part of the original coöperative scheme of Buchez, elaborated during the earlier part of the century. Laborers were to associate and organize, contribute their work and a limited capital, pay the regular rate of wages to themselves, set aside one-half the profits to accumulate a fixed capital, perhaps a portion of it for collective aid, education, or similar purposes, and divide the remainder among themselves in proportion to the labor contributed by each. One school of coöperators, known in Great Britain as the Individualist Coöperators, has maintained this principle as an essential of all forms of coöperation, whether distributive or productive. It is impossible to give exact and exhaustive details and statistics of this phase of profit-sharing, but a general idea of its scope, its success

[1] AMERICAN JOURNAL OF SOCIOLOGY, Vol. II, No. 4.

and failure, the merits and defects urged for and against it, can be presented.

The coöperative movement which originated in France about the time of the revolution of 1830 had this feature as one of its essential elements. So also with the one of 1848, abnormally stimulated by the government.[1] During both periods the societies founded were very numerous; and an enumeration of them would be an enumeration of such institutions practicing this form of profit-sharing—and, it might be added, an enumeration of the failures of this plan. The more recent coöperative movement has been largely distributive coöperation, and profit-sharing has been less uniformly incorporated into the plan. The International Coöperative Alliance, growing out of the International Coöperative Congress held in Paris in 1895, attempted to force the acceptance of this plan upon all coöperators by restricting membership to those who practiced profit-sharing as an essential feature of their system. While this was unanimously supported by the French coöperators, it was not insisted upon, since the great majority of English coöperators would thus have been excluded. The congress, however, did resolve, with practical unanimity, that the true coöperative principle required "all coöperative associations employing labor to assign to their workmen a fair share in the profits."

The situation in England has been a very complicated one. Coöperation in England sprang from two distinct sources. From Robert Owen, through the "Rochdale Pioneers," has come the influence creating the great movement of distributive coöperation which now includes more than a million families, almost one-eighth of the population of Great Britain. On the other hand, the productive coöperative movement was fostered by the Christian Socialists, and was an imported idea, though since then largely developed aside from their influence. Such establishments now number almost two hundred, with more than twenty-five thousand workmen employed. The former, as a rule, reject profit-sharing both in their productive and distributive departments; the latter, as a rule, incorporate it as an essential element,

[1] Three million francs were granted by the government for this purpose.

Mr. Benjamin Jones, speaking of the associations formed at the instigation of the Christian Socialists, says: "In these associations the men employed were supposed to elect the officers and to share the profits in proportion to the amount of their weekly wages or allowances. All these efforts failed. Then those Christian Socialists who had allied themselves to the coöperators strove to convert that steadily growing body to their views on profit-sharing. The coöperators treated the subject in their usual manner. They thought over it, they discussed it, and they experimented with it. The result is that, after forty years, out of more than a million coöperators there are some forty thousand who believe in it as an expedient; but the overwhelming majority have discarded profit-sharing altogether, and reject it, either as being a useless expedient, or as being contrary to the fundamental basis of coöperation. It is true that coöperative congresses have, again and again, passed resolutions in favor of profit-sharing; but in the comparatively few instances where it has been attempted to translate these resolutions into action at the business meetings of their societies, the attempts have been mostly unsuccessful."[1]

The struggle between these two contending factions, growing out of the antagonistic ideas, has been by no means a harmonious one. Nearly all the coöperative associations started by the Christian Socialists in the stormy period marking the middle of the century soon became extinct; while the Rochdale movement has, despite many adversities, continued to prosper and increase. But about 1870 a new impetus was received by the productive coöperative movement, and since that time many such societies have been founded. It is among these that profit-sharing exists. It is popularly supposed that productive coöperation has been a complete failure in Great Britain, but this certainly is a misapprehension. Many coöperative enterprises, both distributive and productive, have failed, and the phenomenal success of distributive coöperation has completely overshadowed the less spectacular development of productive coöperation. Its success, nevertheless, has been quite substantial.

[1] BENJAMIN JONES, *Economic Journal*, Vol. II, pp. 616, 617.

In August, 1897, there were reported 152 of these societies that divided profits with the workmen.[1]

In support of the assertion that this movement has been a failure is the often published list of 224 alleged failures that had been registered between 1850 and 1880. This period would include the greater portion of both coöperative movements. This statement has gone almost unchallenged. But some recent authorities give the following explanation.[2] Of the 224 only twenty-four were copartnership workshops, giving a definite share of the profits to the laborers; some two or three in addition had established some form of philanthropic fund; forty-four had been consumers' workshops, where the labor was employed as under any other industry; the remainder were joint-stock concerns, registered as industrial societies to escape expenses. When the Labor Association, which has for its object the promotion of labor copartnership, as this form of coöperation is called, was formed in 1883, there were only fifteen such societies in existence. There have been many failures since that time, but the ratio of success to failure has been largely increased.

Out of the various coöperative interests grew the Coöperative Union, founded about 1871. It is now a loosely organized body of 1,500 or more coöperative societies, representatives of which meet annually in a coöperative congress. While merely a body for the exchange of ideas, it yet attempts to outline the policy of the general movement. At every one of these congresses the question of profit-sharing has come up for discussion, often quite acrimoniously. Year after year resolutions have been adopted indorsing the copartnership idea, but with no appreciable effect. Miss Potter sums up the results of one of these resolutions and the subsequent investigation, called for by the congress of 1888: "Out of the 1,503 societies only 488 thought fit to reply to the circular of the Central Board, the remainder

---

[1] Of this number, 61 are Irish societies, giving only fragmentary information. A more recent account given in HENRY D. LLOYD's *Labor Co-partnership* increases this number to 228 for 1898, but without giving any further information concerning the profit-sharing feature.

[2] ANUERIN WILLIAMS and HENRY VIVIAN in the *Economic Review*, Vol. IV, p. 310.

being presumably either indifferent or antagonistic to the reso-
lution accepted with fervor by the majority of their delegates.
Of these 274 societies were prepared to 'use their influence' in
favor of profit-sharing, while only 180 societies were willing to
consider the adoption of profit-sharing in their own establishments. . . . . The 180 faithful societies were requested to state,
after the lapse of a year, whether they had embodied the principles of profit-sharing in their rules, or whether they intended
to recommend its immediate adoption. Of these only 35
replied; 14 being associations of producers. Out of the 21
stores, 12 habitually paid a bonus to labor (though this is not
profit- and loss-sharing, still less the creation of a self-governing
workshop), 4 were prepared to recommend a bonus system to
their members, while the remaining 5 refused to consider the
question. The 274 societies willing to 'use their influence'
proved even more refractory: only 19 of these vouchsafed an
answer; 14, while 'fully sympathizing with the idea of profit-
sharing,' deemed themselves incompetent to suggest 'any plan
upon which profit-sharing should be worked in a federal institution;' while the 5 societies with the courage of their convictions
elaborated five mutually exclusive schemes, which they were
prepared to recommend to the federal institutions."[1]   At the
Huddersfield congress in 1895 a similar agreement in theory
resulted quite similarly in practice.

Many coöperators, especially those interested in the larger
societies, are opposed to profit-sharing in principle as well as by
reason of the practical difficulties. At the Woolwich congress
in 1896 the committee on conciliation reported:

1. That the object of coöperation is to utilize the capital of coöperators
by employing it in coöperative industry for the production and distribution
of all the requirements of coöperative societies and the public generally
under equitable conditions as regards labor and remuneration.

2. That in connection with all coöperative enterprises, whether distributive or productive, there should be set apart some portion of the profits as
they arise, for the purpose of making some provision for the workers over
and above such remuneration as they would receive in ordinary competitive
workshops.

[1] BEATRICE POTTER, *The Co-operative Movement in Great Britain*, pp. 178, 179.

3. That such portions of the profits may be used for the benefit of the workers, either (1) by way of increasing their remuneration ; (2) by enabling them to become shareholders ; (3) by providing superannuation or pensions in old age, under such conditions as the society concerned may fix from time to time.

If these recommendations were adopted, we think there would be an elasticity about them which would enable most coöperators to agree, whilst at the same time it would promote the object we have in view, viz., that coöperative industry should be superior to private industry in its treatment of those who have to labor.

The minority, representing the English Wholesale Society, reported that the existing basis of working their society was the most equitable and just to the body of coöperators ; and having once tried (1874–6) the payment of bonus to employés, they had not found it to produce the advantages claimed for it. Even the majority report did not satisfy the profit-sharing party as an expression of principle, and the question is apparently no nearer solution than ever. It is only the second method proposed above that satisfies, namely, a copartnership, a sharing in capital, control, and responsibility. The minority, in the minority only in the congress, but really the great majority in the movement, are termed the Federals, and represent the new movement, as opposed to the old idea fostered by the Christian Socialists. With the Federals, coöperation is carried on by consumers for the benefit of consumers. The entire body of consumers is grouped primarily into district societies. Each district society is to carry on for itself such production as it can, and the federation of district societies, the wholesale societies, are to carry on production in the remaining industries. The actual workers in either case, as also those employed in the stores, are employed, as in any competitive business, for wages only ; and only as consumers do they become members of the society, or derive any benefit from it. The idea of the Federals is that, when the laborers are organized as consumers, the factor of profits is thus eliminated, and the laborers receive as consumers all the advantages desired for them under the profit-sharing plan.

Miss Potter gives the solution thus : "Is it possible for an association of consumers to realize profits ? Profits I imagine

to be the net results of two distinct operations: the act of buying and the act of selling (I include in the act of buying all
payments, such as rent of land, of capital, of ability, as well as
the price of raw material, and the wages of labor). But if I
produce for my own consumption, I buy the raw material, but I
do not sell the product; therefore, I make no profit. And if,
further, I engage an artist to paint my portrait, an architect to
build my house, or a landscape gardener to lay out my grounds
(supplying them with all materials), a bailiff to grow my corn,
a foreman miller to grind it, a cook to bake it, while I and my
household enjoy or consume the whole product, I realize no
'profits.' A steward may supervise all these operations, or I
may be my own housekeeper; the wages I offer may be the
mean, or they may be extravagant; I may pay by the day, or I
may pay by the piece; but whatever remuneration I choose, or
am forced to give, I cannot ask my employés to share in a fund
that does not exist—profits." [1]

So far as the worker himself is concerned, this offers no solution whatever. It is the more equitable division of the results
of production that the laborers are interested in, no matter
whether called profits, dividends on purchases, consumers' saving, or what not. That there is a clear distinction between the
members of the society as employers of labor and as consumers
who profit through dealing with the society is evident. No less
evident is it that, as now organized and managed, there is no
distinction, so far as the laborer is concerned, between his present employment and that in the normal competitive enterprise.
The settling of the difficulty by an elimination of the word
"profits" is a mere evasion. The margin represented by the dividends on purchases is certainly the same element in the transaction that is termed profits under the ordinary arrangement,
perhaps slightly increased through certain peculiar influences,
and slightly decreased through others. It is the element to
which the laborer contributes by his care and exertion, just as
the management of the association does by its foresight; and,
according to the profit-sharing theory, a portion of which is

[1] POTTER, *The Co-operative Movement in Great Britain*, p. 96.

justly due him in addition to his stipulated normal wage   In the sense of the entrepreneur, who takes all the risks and guarantees to both capital and labor a fixed return, and in return reaps a variable profit, there is no "profits." For the entrepreneur, as under any system of coöperation, becomes merely the manager of the first rank, employed on a fixed wage. And that which under the existing system is profits, and under a system of productive coöperation goes as the *raison d'être* of such a system to the laborers engaged in the enterprise, under a system of coöperative distribution exists just the same, whatever name may be appropriate. Avoiding the dilemma, so far as it exists in theory, by a dividend on purchases, or by an increased wage charged to the cost of production, is an elimination of the terms, but not of the logical possibility of the plan. The same merits that are claimed for profit-sharing in the normal capitalistic system of industry are applicable, both in theory and practice, to coöperative distribution and the production carried on under such a régime.

The results of experience justify the statement as to practice. The results in such enterprises have not been any more discouraging to the adherents of a profit-sharing system than have the results in competitive enterprises.

The Individualist Coöperators hold that coöperation, as a solution of the present industrial difficulties, demands that the labor have (1) a share in the profits of the industry, not necessarily the whole of the profits, especially where the industry is carried on by a body of coöperative consumers; (2) a share in the control of the business, not necessarily the whole, as under the above circumstances. They hold this to be true, whether the enterprise is started by outsiders for the benefit of the workmen, by distributive coöperative societies for the benefit of the consumer, or by a group of workmen for their own benefit. And, in truth, as much difficulty has arisen in the latter case as in the former ones. The tendency is for such an organization to become a small joint-stock concern, and for the holders of stock to exclude other workmen from participating in the profits. This does not, then, differ from ordinary business enterprises. The individualists hold that profit-sharing is a necessary element in any such form of coöperation, but only one of two. In this last is found the difference between this form of profit-sharing and profit-sharing as ordinarily considered.

It is impossible to give an accurate and comprehensive account of the experience of this form of profit-sharing in the past. The number of such enterprises is unknown, as is also the length of the experience and the results As previously stated, all those started under the patronage of the Christian Socialists were of this type, and nearly all have ceased to exist. Nearly all the Scottish enterprises were of this plan, but there is no record of the number of failures. Many of the "working class limited" associations adopted this plan, but none at present practice it.[1] Of the seventy-six Oldham cotton mills of this type, Mr. Schloss mentions two that have adopted and later abandoned the plan.[2] Mr. Jones [3] argues from the experience of these societies the insufficiency of profit-sharing. In these "working class limiteds" the interest on capital averages only 4½ per cent., while wages are above the normal, having been increased more than 40 per cent. during the last twenty years. Hence the trades unions and the workmen in general feel that such societies are superior to profit-sharing, for under all profit-sharing schemes the interest and the dividends on capital are far higher, while frequently wages are not up to the normal rate.

In 1897 there were reported 1,845 distributive coöperative societies, or stores. Comparatively few of these give a bonus to labor. The Coöperative Union has made every effort to obtain information upon this point, but with no great success. The inquiry made in 1890 embraced 1,418 societies. The replies were not very numerous, while " about sixty societies state that they share profits with their employés, but to what extent and in what manner it is almost impossible to determine. Many societies, however, state that their employés get the same amount

---

[1] BENJAMIN JONES, *Co-operative Production*, chap. 28.

[2] D. F. SCHLOSS, *Report on Profit Sharing*, p. 14.

[3] *Co-operative Production*, p. 789.

per pound on their wages as is paid to the members on their purchases."[1] This is the usual method with such societies, and such bonuses would average from 5 to 12 per cent. on wages. But this cannot be regarded as an addition to wages in all cases, for in many such cases the wages are below the normal, on account of the bonus given. In addition to this, it is to be noted that in some of these cases the bonus paid is merely a commission on sales, and not a division of profits. To what extent this is true cannot be stated. The last investigation, completed in 1897, included 1,434 distributive societies, of which 235, or about one in six, divided profits.

In reply to a similar inquiry concerning those consumers' societies having productive departments, answers were received from only 199, sixty-one of which had productive departments. Of these only ten claimed to practice profit-sharing. But three of these were really not cases of profit-sharing, but rather of extra wages not depending on profits. The Scottish Wholesale Society is the largest of these, and for a long time has divided profits with the laborers, now numbering about 2,000. The bonus has averaged 3 or 4 per cent. on wages over a long period of years.

As to a dozen or more "supply associations," which are really middle-class joint-stock companies, but one, the Agricultural and Horticultural Association, practices profit-sharing. This it has done since 1874.[2]

Finally, as to the societies of producers: as previously remarked, under the influence of the Labor Association, most of these are profit-sharing. In August, 1897, there were 152 such societies reported.[3] Yet in the minority are included all the great productive enterprises, so far as their financial importance is concerned. No account of the failures is possible, though an explanation of a popular error in this respect has been given. Yet a similar error is apt to be made in regard to the successes. These figures are given from the summaries of the *Labor Co partnership* without any consideration of the wages paid, whether

---

[1] SCHLOSS, *Report on Profit Sharing*, p. 16.

[2] *Ibid.*, pp. 44–6.

[3] *Labor Co-partnership*, August, 1897.

they are below the normal trade-union wage, or whether there are other disadvantages offsetting the extra compensation. The following analysis of the latest report will, however, throw some light on this point: 152 productive societies shared profits; of these, 24 made no report concerning profits, and 42 made no report concerning dividends to laborers; of the 86 reporting a dividend, 4 gave no means of determining the ratio of dividends to wages, half of the remainder gave a dividend of less than 1 per cent. on the wages paid, 20 gave more than 2 per cent., and but 3 gave as much as 7 per cent. This is decidedly better than the previous year, when only 44 out of 155 reported dividends. Of the 114 dealt with by Mr. Schloss in his report, for the year 1892, 55 made no returns; of the remaining 59, there were 27 cases in which no dividend was made, there was 1 which gave a bonus of 16.4 per cent., 15 which gave a bonus of from 4 to 9 per cent., and the remainder gave a bonus of less than 4 per cent. For the entire 59 cases, the average was 2.4 per cent. on wages. A partial explanation of the fragmentary and discouraging reports during the past few years is found in the fact that the increase in the number of the societies consists almost exclusively in Irish creameries, there now being 58 of these out of a total of 152. Very fragmentary reports are received from these; while all of them are reported as dividing profits with labor, only 16 of them really showed a dividend.

A brief consideration of the structure of these productive societies may be of interest. While the type is the same, the details are of the greatest variety. All have limited liability; most of them have shares of one pound or less; nearly all of them adhere to the rule of one individual, one vote, and no proxy voting; all are directed by committees elected at a general meeting, and these control the business through a secretary and usually a manager. They differ chiefly in defining who is eligible to membership and to the committees, and as to the method of division of the profits. In some every member is eligible; in some all committeemen are employés, in some only a certain number, and in some they are excluded altogether. The following is a type of the methods of division of profits:

After providing for depreciation, for 5 per cent. interest on capital, certain per cent. for reserve, and perhaps for propaganda, education, philanthropic works, etc., the remaining profits are divided thus : to workers 40 per cent., to customers 20 per cent., 12 per cent. to officers and committeemen, 10 per cent. to provident fund, 10 per cent. to share capital, 5 per cent. to educational fund, 3 per cent. to special service fund. Yet these details vary without limit, some of the above funds being altogether wanting in many cases.

Since the real purpose here is to discover the application of a principle, and not to give an exhaustive account of its operation, further consideration of this phase of the subject is hardly possible. In no country has the subject received the attention that it has in Great Britain ; coöperation in any form being much more of a rarity, at least as a modification of "capitalistic production." Even in France there were reported only 202 productive coöperative societies for 1897. Not only is this true, but the information concerning their experience is much more fragmentary upon the point under consideration.[1] The only reason for considering this phase of the subject is that in Great Britain producers' coöperation has been developed by insisting on the profit-sharing principle, and that the great development of coöperation, especially that of consumers, does not affect the problem of wages save through profit-sharing. This is not true elsewhere. Any wider investigation of coöperation would lead to the consideration of the agricultural syndicates, popular banks, and other forms of coöperative credit common on the continent and, in one or two special forms, in Great Britain and the

[1] The results of an investigation concerning similar societies in France were published in 1897, the data being for the year 1895. There were then 172 such societies, 165 of them furnishing data for the report. These 165 societies had 9,129 members, had capital amounting to 8,904,000 francs, did a business of 32,220,000 francs, and realized profits to the sum of 1,832,000 francs. The profits of those societies realizing all but about 300,000 francs of the total profits were divided as follows : 154,290 francs to reserve funds ; 912,000 francs to interest and dividends on capital ; 68,760 francs to management ; 218,170 francs to laborers belonging to the associations ; 158,430 francs to laborers not members ; and 50,000 francs to provident funds. In 1896 these societies had increased in number to 202. (ARTHUR FONTAINE, *Les associations ouvrières de production*, Paris, 1897.)

United States. This is the form of consumers' coöperation that is developed especially in Germany and Russia. While there could be given quantitative statements of considerable value, if our interest was primarily in coöperation, their relation to profit-sharing is so remote and indirect, and the information on this subject so fragmentary, that the results are altogether inconclusive and of little value. For example, the one phase of this form of coöperation developed in the United States is the building and loan association. It is evident that it is so remote from profit-sharing that it throws no light upon the subject. This is true of all forms of coöperative credit, and, with the exception noted above, of all forms of consumers' coöperation, since profit-sharing has popular interest and social importance only as a modification of the wage system.[1]

III.

The third phase of the subject is worthy of special attention. While John Stuart Mill's confident expectation in regard to the future of profit-sharing and coöperation has been far from realized, and in truth gives no further promise of realization now than then, yet there are several instances of such evolution. While the vast majority of coöperative enterprises are formed outright by the workmen interested, or, in Great Britain, are developed in connection with the profit-sharing principle as explained above, there are several very prominent instances of the growth of successful profit-sharing enterprises into true coöperative ones. While Mr. Mill had greater hopes of the frequency of such occurrences than other economists, yet there are many, interested in this phase of the social question, who have centered their hopes in this very process. Hence the half dozen or more instances of this character are of more than passing interest.

First of all is the well-known instance of the *Maison Leclaire*, the accredited originator of the system. The system of profit-

[1] The most recent special study of this phase of the coöperative movement is MR. HENRY D. LLOYD's *Labor Co-partnership*, a most excellent and enthusiastic account. The only additional statistical information given is that mentioned in the preceding footnote, giving, however, no further information concerning profit-sharing. A review of Mr. Lloyd's book will be found in the March (1899) number of the JOURNAL.

sharing introduced in 1842 continued in force for the period of a generation, and in 1869, a few months previous to the founder's death, was transformed into a true coöperative association, now known as *Redouly et Cie*. The experience of this firm is so well known that it hardly needs repetition here.

Less well known, but of scarcely less importance, is the firm of *Larouche-Joubert et Cie*, now the coöperative paper works of Angoulème, France. The difficulties in the way of both profit-sharing and coöperation in this industry are very great, for the fixed capital is proportionately very large, and the cost of labor is but a small portion of the total cost of production. But the success is no less marked. Beginning a rudimentary participation the year after Leclaire instituted his profit-sharing scheme, various modifications of the wage system, such as progressive wages, bonus on production, and prizes based on quality, guaranteed high rate of interest on deposits made by laborers toward the purchase of stock, and stock-holding by employés were successively introduced. It is this latter that has become of greatest importance. This firm has adhered to the plan of paying in cash all dividends from profits, and hence some phases of the transition do not appear to as great advantage as in other systems. The employés purchase stock as they are able, exceptional advantages to this end being afforded. The dividends made would, in time, make the purchase, but there is no compulsion. Deposits of from 20 to 5,000 francs were received, drawing 12 per cent. interest, the one provision being that the depositor had worked for the firm for two years. When the deposit amounted to 100 francs, it received a specified share in the profits. The larger deposits are exchanged for shares of stock, so that in time the workmen shall become the owners of the entire establishment. The profit-sharing system was quite complex, being specifically adapted to the several different departments of the business. After paying all fixed charges and expenses, including 5 per cent. interest on stock and salaries of managers, 30 per cent. of the net profit is divided among the six directors, 10 per cent. to the superior employés, 12 per cent. among the customers of the house, much after the manner of the English wholesale coöperative societies, and the remainder is declared as a dividend to capital, the participating depositors, and that portion of the wage-earners which is not included in the distribution of profits in any of the special departments. The founders of the house still retain a large share in the control of the business.

Of still greater reputation is the *Maison Boucicaut*, the *Bon Marché* of Paris, now become *Plassard, Morin, Fillot et Cie*, a true coöperative company, after a substantial growth of twenty-five years. M. Boucicaut introduced a system of profit-sharing in 1876, in the form of a provident fund. After his death Madame Boucicaut took up his work and his plans. In 1880 twenty-six heads of departments and other superior employés were admitted into the firm as sleeping partners. Several of these associates were simply representatives of groups of employés, who were thus enabled to become associated in the business. In this manner 7,500,000 francs, three-eighths of the total capital, were placed in the hands of employés, in shares of 50,000 francs. Madame Boucicaut continued to cede portions of her stock in shares of similar amounts as fast as employés desired to obtain them. Provident funds, retiring funds, percentage on sales, etc., are additional advantages, or, rather, are features of the profit-sharing system, and are specially advantageous to those not associated with the stockholders. However, a five-year service is the only qualification required of stockholders. In 1896 a "Civil Society" was constituted, which was to come into possession of the capital stock held by the head of the firm upon her death. This event occurred the following year. At the same time was founded the retiring fund, out of the private fortune of the benefactress. This fund secures pensions to those employés who have no interest in the business of the house. The Civil Society, when it took charge as a limited stock company, consisted of 373 members; and it remains sole proprietor of the capital stock under the name of Plassard, Morin, Fillot et Cie, these being the three directors selected by Madame Boucicaut previous to her death. In addition to the 373 stockholders, 81 employés have an interest in the total business of the house, and 158 have special interest in the profits of their departments. The remainder of the 3,000 or more employés are benefited by the special funds mentioned.

The best example of such a development is the "Familistère Society of Guise, Coöperative Association of Capital and Labor," formerly the *Maison Godin* of Guise, France. Though some phases of M. Godin's communistic ideas were put in force as early as 1860 in the construction of the first *familistère*, yet the profit-sharing and coöperative plan was contemplated for almost forty years after the business was founded before it was put into practical operation. We have here no interest in the *familistère*, the communistic tenement houses, though this feature has been made of greatest importance, and, in fact, has a greater prominence than the more commendable features of the system. The profit-sharing system was introduced in 1877, and was continued for three years, with an average distribution of 57,000 francs, but in 1880 the profit-sharing scheme was elaborated and combined with a plan ultimately making the enterprise coöperative.

The workmen in the enterprise are divided into five classes, the first three of which are members of the association that now has complete control. These are the *associés*, the *sociétaires*, the *participants*, the *intéressés*, and the *auxiliaires*. The members of the first three groups are the coöperators. An *associé* must be twenty-five years of age, a resident of a *familistère*, and an employé of the society for at least five years, able to read and write, and owner of certificate of stock of the society to the value of 500 francs, and must be admitted by the general assembly as an *associé*. A *sociétaire* must be twenty-one years of age, free from military duty, a resident of a *familistère*, an employé for three years, and must be admitted by the general council. A *participant* must possess similar qualifications, except that only one year's employment is requisite. The *intéressés* are outsiders who have come into possession of certificates of stock, but take no part in the work. The *auxiliaires* are workmen employed by the society when extra help is needed, but who have not fulfilled the requirements of membership. The first three classes numbered 1,041 out of a total of 1,720 employés in 1895. The *associés* have entire control of the management of the enterprise. The transfer to the coöperative basis began in 1880, and was completed in 1894. The total capital stock, based on a careful inventory, was 4,600,000 francs. This was divided into founder's certificates, to be replaced by association certificates as the members of the society came into possession of them. This was done as follows: After expenses of production, including interest on certificates, had been met, the net profits were applied to the purchase of founder's certificates, instead of being divided as cash dividends on wages of the members of the society, as was done from 1877 to 1879, after the manner of most profit-sharing enterprises. The dividends were thus paid to employés as association certificates, and the founder's certificates were canceled as fast as purchased. The last founder's certificates were replaced by association certificates in 1894, and the society came into complete possession of the property. Since then such dividends are paid in cash. A member now receives, in addition to his wages, profits on capital, interest on capital, and profits or dividends earned by his wages; so that with many wages constitute only 70 per cent. of the annual income. The division of profits is as follows: 25 per cent. is allotted to the directors, and the remainder is allotted to labor and capital. The 25 per cent. is divided as follows: 4 per cent. to the general manager, 14 per cent. to the members of the general council, 2 per cent. to the council of audit and control, 2 per cent. in awards to workmen for exceptional service, and 1 per cent. for the advanced education of one or more scholars, these awards being made by the managing council. Out of the 75 per cent. allotted to labor and capital (until 1881 one-third of this was devoted to the formation of a reserve fund equaling 10 per cent. of the capital stock), capital draws a fixed proportion. That is, the earnings of capital amount to 5 per cent. on the capital stock, or 230,000 francs annually. Labor earns a varying amount. The *associés* share in profits on the basis of twice the amount of their earnings, the *sociétaires* on the basis of one and a half times the amount of their earnings, and the *auxiliaires* and *participants* on the exact amount of their earnings. The 75 per cent. of the profits is declared as a dividend upon the above sums and then divided among the members of the groups in accordance with the earnings estimated as above. Space forbids a more detailed account of this most interesting of all such developments. A most accessible as well as complete account is found in the *Bulletin of the Department of Labor*, for September, 1896, by W. F. Willoughby. M. Godin's *Solutions sociales*, published in 1871, is but an earnest of that which has come to pass.

The best-known of English attempts at such a transition is that of Wm. Thompson & Sons, of Huddersfield, manufacturers of woolen goods. The transition was made in 1886. The capital stock is about £6,000 in £1 shares, and about £11,000 loan capital bearing 5 per cent. interest. The latter belongs for the most part to Mr. Thompson. The shares are held by working-class coöperative societies, by trade-union organizations, by 150 employés, by other workmen, and by twenty-six other persons "interested in the movement." Mr. Thompson is president and manager of the society, removable only by a vote of five-sixths of all the members of the association and five-sixths of all votes capable of being given at a general meeting. He also may appoint his successor. The " manager shall control all business carried on by the society, and engage, remove, or discharge all assistant managers, salesmen, or employés of every description, and fix their duties, salaries, or other remuneration at such rates, and require them to give such security, as he may determine, subject to the duty of regularly reporting all such acts to the committee." The committee's functions are mainly advisory.

Profits are divided as follows: (1) to a depreciation fund; (2) in paying 5 per cent. dividend on share capital; (3) in forming a reserve fund; (4) in educational funds; (5) in subscribing to the coöperative union; (6) to an insurance and pension fund; the remainder of the profits are divided into two equal parts, one of which is divided among all persons who have been employed by the society for not less than six months as a bonus on wages, and the other half among the customers of the society. The bonus to employés is applied on the purchase of shares in the society.

A society quite similar to the above is the *Brownfield's Guila Potter Society*, of Cobridge, Staffordshire. This was founded in 1892 from the firm of Wm. Brownfield & Sons. It is in every respect similar to the above, save that the number of employés is considerably larger, about 400, and that some of them do not as yet hold stock.

The only instance of this character found in the United States is that establishment of the N. O. Nelson Co., of St. Louis, which is located at Leclaire, Ill. The failure of a previous attempt to make this transition has been noted.[1] This was in December, 1895. A few months later the transition was made in one of the six departments of the works at that place. To *The Leclaire Coöperative Cabinet Association* were transferred buildings, machinery, and material to the value of $60,000. More than one-half of the workmen in that department subscribed for one share each at $1,000 per share. One-tenth of this was to be paid by deducting 15 per cent. from wages, the remainder to be paid out of profits. Others of the workmen may go in when they choose upon the same terms, and no new men are hired except on these terms. Six per cent. interest is paid the company on the unpaid balance of the purchase price, and to each member on the amount of his paid-up stock. These payments are charged to the expense account before there is any division of profits. One-half of the profits are then divided in proportion to wages and credited on each one's share. Ten per cent. of the profits is devoted to education, and the remainder to public maintenance, pension and old-age funds, to depreciation and surplus funds. It is hoped in time to establish all the departments at Leclaire on this basis, and the same terms are now open for them to accept.

PAUL MONROE.

TEACHERS COLLEGE,
    Columbia University.

[1] AMERICAN JOURNAL OF SOCIOLOGY, May, 1896.

PROLEGOMENA TO SOCIAL PSYCHOLOGY.

II.

THE FUNDAMENTAL FACT IN SOCIAL PSYCHOLOGY.[1]

In spite of the remarkable development which this century has witnessed in the science of psychology from the time of Fechner to the present, most psychologists will admit that the science has as yet contributed little to the development of the social sciences, to the solution of the problems of societary life. A beginning, it is true, has been made in some of the social sciences in applying psychological principles to the solution of their problems. This is the case, for example, in political economy, especially in the attempt which the Austrian school has made to build up a theory of value upon principles furnished by the older individual psychology. But the contributions which psychology has thus far made to social science have been, with a few exceptions, small and insignificant compared with what has been expected from it.

The reasons for this failure of psychology to contribute materially to the solution of social problems have been many. One has already been suggested in the preceding article of this series, namely, the dominance of the individualistic method and point of view in psychological investigation. Another is to be found, perhaps, in the failure to develop a comparative or genetic psychology. The reason, however, which appears to us fundamental and inclusive of the others is that psychology has not been developed from the point of view of *function* or life-process. A mere *structural*[2] psychology of the adult human individual cannot, from its very nature, give an interpretation of life in its broadest phases, much less of the activities of society.

[1] This paper appears slightly out of its logical order in the series. Many of its presuppositions will be found in the paper following.

[2] *Cf.* TITCHENER on "The Postulates of a Structural Psychology," in the *Philosophical Review*, September, 1898.

Though the psychical life of the social group may be roughly analogous to the psychical life of the individual, yet the analogy, if such there be, is wholly on the side of function, not on the side of structure. The whole development of psychology, therefore, which has been represented by such men as Wundt and Külpe, however valuable it may be in other respects, has had no special significance for the development of the social sciences. A functional psychology is what is wanted for the interpretation of society or any section of its activities. The essential principles of such a psychology, we believe, have already been formulated. The credit of having formulated them belongs to Professor John Dewey,[1] a statement of whose point of view is a necessary preliminary to the argument of this paper.

Professor Dewey's psychological point of view may be put somewhat schematically as follows: The fundamental fact in the psychical life, according to him, is not the sensation, but the coördination of the living organism in some activity — the act.[2] We cannot get back of the coördination in psychology. Wherever we begin, we must begin with a living organism *doing something*. The unit of psychical activity, therefore, is the act or coördination. In reality there is only one large coördination — the act of living or the life-process. But within this supreme coördination there arise minor coördinations in the adapting of one part of the organism to another, or of one portion of the life-process to another portion. Or, looking at the process from the opposite standpoint, we may say particular acts are coördinated, unified, into larger coördinations which control the smaller acts; and all are finally unified into, and controlled by, the general life-process of the organism. Thus the psychical life is to be regarded and interpreted as a function of the general life-

[1] The leading ideas of this paper were first suggested to the writer in listening to a course of lectures by Professor Dewey on "Advanced Psychology" in the winter quarter of 1896–7.

[2] See, concerning the problem here involved, PROFESSOR DEWEY's article on "The Reflex Arc Concept in Psychology," in the *Psychological Review* for July, 1896. The coördination (or act) may perhaps be defined as "the bringing to a unity of (objective) aim of minor, unorganized activities." The term "coördination" is preferred to the term "act" merely because it can be given a more definite scientific content.

process. Function, then, rather than organism or environment, is the thing to be considered in psychology. From this point of view all forms of psychical activity can be reduced to two types: coördination and adaptation. All the phenomena of psychical life group themselves about these two fundamental forms — are the outgrowth of them, and are functionally explained by their reference to them. Thus a coördination which has once been successfully established tends to persist, or becomes a habit. The necessity of adjustment, however, arising from some variation in the organism or environment, causes the old coördination or habit to break up, and sensation results. Sensation, then, is the sign of the interruption of a habit, and represents the point at which an activity is reconstructed. The old coördination in breaking up, however, must yield the material for the new coördination; that is, it must be used as means for the construction of a new coördination. The processes of discrimination, attention, and association come in to build up the new coördination. They are all processes which arise only through the transition from one coördination to another. The discriminative process, for example, represents the breakdown of the old coördination, and what we call association represents the building up of the new coördination. Attention represents the conflict of two or more activities involved in the building up of the new coördination; it is the attempt, on the part of the organism, to discover, select, the adequate stimulus for the construction of the new coördination. These illustrations will suffice for our purposes. In the same manner all psychical processes may be interpreted — as referring either to the coördination or to the transition from one coördination to another. The coördination is, therefore, the fundamental and central fact of the psychical life. All other psychical facts are functional expressions of the coördination, or of the relation of one coördination to another within the life-process. Thus the psychical life presents itself as a system of means and ends, whose unity finds expression in the general end of control over the means of existence, that is, over the conditions of survival. Summarizing, then, we may say that Professor Dewey's psychological point of view is that of a life-process, or life-activity, functioning to secure control over its own life-conditions, and thereby its own development. The resulting interpretation of the facts of the psychical life yields a psychology whose chief categories are coördination, adaptation, habit, instinct, selection, evaluation, and the like; in brief, an *evolutionary* psychology.[1]

The value of such a psychology to the social sciences must be evident, even from such a schematic and fragmentary statement as we have given. Such a psychology comes into contact with life at every point and interprets functionally the processes of life; it is no formal, over-abstracted science, but shows us the actual workings of the psychic reality. The question at once suggests itself: Are not these categories, which have been so successfully applied to the interpretation of the psychical life of the individual, also applicable to the interpretation of the life of society on its psychical side? Cannot the fundamental principles of such a functional psychology be transferred at once from the interpretation of the life of the individual to that of society? If it be granted that social groups function, act, as unities, and that therefore they, as well as individual organisms, may be regarded as functional unities, then there would seem to be no logical objection to such a procedure. On the contrary, when both society and the individual are regarded as functional unities, it would seem highly probable that the fundamental principles and categories employed in the interpretation of the psychical life of the one would apply equally in the interpretation of the psychical life of the other. Thus the transference of principles of interpretation from the individual to society may be easily justified as a working hypothesis. Professor Dewey's point of view, if fully stated, would, indeed, be favorable to such an extension of his psychological principles of interpretation to society. He recognizes that the individual life-process is not an isolated fact, but only a differentiated center within a larger life-process of the group. This position implies, not only the possibility of

---

[1] Of course, other psychologists have made use of the evolutionary point of view in their interpretation of the psychical life; but their systems have been incapable of assimilating thoroughly evolutionary concepts and principles, and it is only fair to say that their psychologies have not been distinctively evolutionary in their character.

a group psychology, but also the possibility of applying the same fundamental principles of interpretation in it as in individual psychology. But the real warrant for transferring the principles and categories of a functional psychology of the individual to the interpretation of society must be found in the facts of societary life itself. The question which must be asked, accordingly, is: Are there real processes in the group which correspond to those denoted in the individual by the categories coördination, adaptation, habit, etc.? Is there anything, for example, in group-life answering to the coördination in individual life? If so, does it occupy the same central position in the life of the group as in that of the individual?[1]

In group-life, as in the life of the individual organism, we cannot get back of the group *doing something*. If we go back of that point, we get merely an aggregation of individuals, of which we predicate no group-life. We may explain biologically how the aggregation was primitively formed, but we do not think of the aggregation as a unity until group-action appears. The group-act is the sign of group-life throughout the scale of living organisms, whether among human beings or among the lowest forms. Forms merely dwelling in proximity can hardly be said to have a common group-life until they become functionally related to each other as parts of a functioning whole. In a psychological interpretation of group-life, then, we must begin with the group *acting together* in some particular way; for it is this

[1] The equivocal meaning of many sociological terms is a great hindrance to clearness in sociological discussion. Many terms, for example, have both subjective and objective meanings. An attempt has been made in this series of papers, however, to use terms with approximate consistency. Thus, the word "social," ordinarily used in any one of half a dozen different subjective senses, has been used mainly in an objective sense, implying simply "necessary interdependence of forms *among themselves* in the life-process." It is true that this definition, suggested by Professor George H. Mead, widens the meaning of the term very greatly; but the widening is necessary to the proper understanding of the phenomena to which the term is applied. The word "society" has been used in a sense corresponding with that of "social," though often with human cultural or national groups in mind; while the word "group" has been used in a somewhat looser sense, though always implying some measure of "interdependence of forms among themselves." Where it has seemed desirable to use a colorless term, meaning simply "of society," in order especially to exclude the narrower meanings of the word "social," the word "societary" has often been employed.

which constitutes the group a functional unity. This acting together of the individual organisms in a group evidently corresponds in form exactly to the coördination in the individual. We may call it, therefore, the group or social coördination.[1] It is in group-life what the coördination is in the individual organism — the unit of psychical activity, the fundamental psychical fact about which all other facts of psychical activity group themselves. As in the case of the individual, too, particular social coördinations become unified into a general life-process of the group, which we term the social process. The origin of group-acts or coördinations among primitive forms may be explained on biological grounds; but the group-act or coördination is none the less the first psychic manifestation of group-life. It is accordingly the fact upon which social psychology must be built up, and from which it must proceed in functionally interpreting the life of society. The fundamental fact in social psychology is, therefore, the social coördination.

While the social coördination may be objectively defined as the acting together of the individual organisms of a group in some particular way, subjectively it doubtless always involves, where consciousness exists, a certain psychical attitude of the individual members of the group toward each other. At least in so far as concerns human society, the social coördination may be subjectively defined as the mental attitude which the individuals of a group maintain toward each other. Thus in a family group the mental attitude of its members toward each other is an expression of their common group-life and group-activities, and may be expected to change as those activities change. It is evident that we have here to do with the beginnings of social organization. The acting together of the individual organisms

---

[1] Of course, from one point of view, the group-act, or "social coördination," is but a continuation, an extension, a result, of the acts of the individual members of the group. This point of view is in no way inconsistent with that generally maintained in this paper. We can either look at the group as a whole, or regard it as composed of individual elements. Both points of view are necessary for the full understanding of group-life. The former has been generally maintained by the writer, for the sake of simplicity, though the latter has also occasionally been taken. There is no dualism implied here between the individual and the group; nor elsewhere in the paper, if the argument is properly apprehended.

of a group in some particular way necessitates relationships among the members of the group, varying according to the part which each member plays in the functioning of the whole. These varying relationships subjectively involve varying mental attitudes of the members of the group toward each other. Now, the mental attitude of one member of a group toward another is necessarily that of authority, subordination, equality, or some variation of these three primary "forms of association."[1] Hence the social coördination is the beginning of social organization both on its conscious and unconscious sides. The psychical attitude of the members of a group toward each other is the initial stage of social organization on its conscious side; while from the necessity of functional relationship in a common life-process springs social organization in both its aspects. The organization of any group is accordingly an outcome of its group-coördinations, of its life-process as a group. All social organization, then, is but an expression of social coördination; and it is from this point of view that social organization must be studied if it is to be functionally understood.

It may be objected that "social coördination" is but a new name for the phenomenon of coöperation. The very definitions which have been given of social coördination, it may be urged, validate the objection. The reply is that if by "coöperation" is meant all that we mean by "social coördination," then there is no objection to the use of the term "coöperation." But both popularly and by scientific writers the term "coöperation" has been used in a much more restricted sense. It implies just that element of consciousness on the part of the individuals engaged in group-action which the term "social coördination" is especially designed to exclude. Thus Professor Giddings speaks of coöperation as requiring "unity of purpose and of method on the part of two or more individuals," and says: "There can be no coöperation except among those who are, in good degree, like-minded, and who are so far conscious of their agreement

---

[1] The valuable work of Dr. Simmel, of the university of Berlin, in making out and classifying these "forms of association," or, as we would prefer to call them, "types of social coördination," deserves here to be referred to. It is the most serious and important study of social organization yet attempted.

that they can intelligently plan their common activity."[1]   In another place he says: "There must be . . . . a perception by each of the coöperating individuals that . . . . all have the same interest, and that all are endeavoring to accomplish the same end."[2]   These statements of Professor Giddings involve, we believe, a correct definition of the term "coöperation" in its usual acceptation.   But the large amount of consciousness which they imply on the part of coöperating individuals is just what is often noticeably absent in that acting together of the members of a group which we have called the social coördination.   So far from being conscious of any purpose or end, the individual is usually in group-activities unconscious of the connection of his act either with his own life-process or with that of the group.   He is conscious, if at all, generally only of the gratification or working out of an instinctive impulse.   Especially among lower forms the end which controls the activity cannot be supposed to exist for the consciousness of the form.   Consciousness of the task to be performed, of the end to be reached, in the acting together of members of a group would seem to be the exception rather than the rule, if we take into view the group-life of the whole organic world; while consciousness of the "acting together" as a definite means to an end is a still rarer phenomenon.   The psychical attitude which social coördination involves (where consciousness exists) on the part of the coördinated individuals is not a consciousness of "acting together," or even of a definite task to be performed, but rather a feeling or sense of relationship to one another.   The social coördination, in other words, comes into consciousness only at a relatively late period in mental development, and then only when some new condition necessitates the reconstruction of the coördination.   It is evident, then, that if the term "coöperation" is used to cover all cases of social coördination, it must be used wholly in an objective sense and must be stripped of its usual implication of consciousness.   If used in this sense, there is no objection to saying, as Spencer does, "Social life in its entirety

[1] *Elements of Sociology*, p. 77.

[2] *Ibid.*, p. 78.

is carried on by coöperation;"·and the proposition would be equally true if the limiting adjective were dropped. On account of the narrowed meaning of the word in popular usage, however, it would be better, in our estimation, to borrow a term like "coördination" from a science which in its essentials is one with social psychology, and to retain the word "coöperation" for those cases to which it manifestly applies : namely, the cases of social coördination which have come more or less fully into consciousness.

A social coördination which has once been successfully established, as in the case of the coördination in the individual organism, tends to persist, or becomes a social habit. Social habits are the basis of all activities of group-life. Every new social coördination, every new adaptation in the group-life, is made upon the basis of already existing social habits. Without the fixity or definiteness which social habit gives to the forms of group-activities there could be no group-life, as unity and stability in the group would be lacking. On the other hand, too great fixity of social habit gives rise to many of the abnormal phenomena of societary life. As in the case of the individual, if the social habit does not retain a certain amount of flexibility, enabling the group to adapt its activities to a constantly changing environment, then it becomes of disadvantage to the group in its life-struggle, causing pathologic conditions, and even the disintegration and destruction of the group. Social habits pass insensibly into customs and institutions. The term "custom" is, indeed, almost synonymous with the term "social habit." But customs are usually thought of as peculiar to the group, that is, as the habits which distinguish one group from another. Thus an almost universally prevalent social habit, like the storing up of food products for future consumption, is rarely spoken of as a custom. Institutions are social habits which have received a peculiar social sanction and which have been organized more or less fully into the structure of the group. Forms of marriage, property, government, religion, and the like become such. From the point of view of social psychology, at least, an institution is not an individual invention. It is rather an organized mode of societary activity, a social habit, which has been of such life-saving advantage to the group that the authority and sanction of the group as a whole have been conferred upon it. Laws are formal expressions of social habits which have come into consciousness. They are established by the group for the sake of greater control over the habit. Nearly the same thing may be said of ethical rules which have been approved by the group. Habit, then, is a category which applies to societary as well as to individual life. It is a fundamental category in interpreting the psychical life of society, if that interpretation proceeds from a functional point of view.

With the idea of transition as applied to social life we are already familiar. In the terminology of social psychology a social transition is obviously a transition from one social habit to another, from one social coördination to another. In the face of new life-conditions social habits, like individual habits, must be readjusted. In other words, the old social coördination breaks down and the phenomenon of adaptation, of building up a new social coördination, arises. It is here that some of the most important of societary phenomena come in. Where processes of discrimination, association, and attention in the individual aid in building up a new coördination, processes of discussion, social suggestion, and social selection in the group come in to construct the new social coördination. The process of discussion, which may be called the societary process of discrimination, represents especially the breakdown of the old social coördination, while the processes of social suggestion and social selection particularly represent the building up of the new coördination. In human society, at least, all these processes may arise in the transition from one coördination to another, that is, in the adaptation of the group life-process to some new condition in either the external or the internal environment. Adaptation,[1] then, is a fact of group-life as well as of individual life, and next to coördination the most fundamental and important fact.

Thus in theory the categories and principles of a functional psychology of the individual seem to apply in a subjective inter-

[1] Or accommodation, as Professor Baldwin would prefer to say.

pretation of the social life. Let us now see how they fit into the concrete facts of the social process, and whether or not they will serve at all to interpret that process in its various phases. The case of political revolutions furnishes us a good illustration with which to begin, both because revolutions are such striking facts in the social process, and because from a sociological point of view no satisfactory theory of revolutions has yet been proposed.

The transition from one habit to another is not always an easy thing either for individuals or social groups. Where the habit has become inflexible, where peculiar conditions in the inner or outer environment prevent the normal break-up of the habit, in short, where power of adaptation has for any reason been lost, violent disturbances of the psychical life are apt to take place in the change from one habit to another. Especially is this the case when the habit to be changed is a general one which affects the whole life-process. From a psychological point of view revolutions are such disturbances in the psychical life of society, produced by the breaking down of a social habit under abnormal conditions. Where social habits have for any reason become inflexible—as is so often the case with institutions, bolstered up and exploited as they frequently are by class interest, even though they are opposed to the interest of the society as a whole—in the face of new life-conditions there is apt to be a revolution. Instead of the gradual and peaceful transformation of one social habit into another which ordinarily goes on in society, in a revolution we witness the sudden and violent breakdown of social habits which have long outlived their usefulness to the social process. The breakdown is sudden because the old habit has been sustained until accumulating opposing tendencies have overwhelmed it; it is violent just in proportion as hindrances stand in its way. Instead of the ordinary period of uncertainty and confusion which normally follows the breakdown of a habit both in the individual and in society, in a revolution we have a period of great confusion, at times amounting even to absolute disorganization or anarchy. The confusion and disorganization are, of course, proportionate to the importance of the habit in the societary life-process and to the completeness and suddenness of the breakdown. The recuperative vigor of a society may be such that a new social coördination, adapted to the new life-conditions, will speedily be constructed, which will put an end to the reign of confusion and anarchy. Or, where a society has largely lost its power of adaptation, the effort to build up a new coördination, adapted to the new life-conditions, may repeatedly fail, as it did in the case of the French Revolution. Under such circumstances we have a series of unsuccessful experiments, extending over a longer or shorter period of time, in building up new social coördinations; hence there may be a series of revolutions, each of which may add to the confusion and anarchy already existing. For such a society often the only hope of avoiding disintegration is to find or " select " an individual who, when clothed with sovereign authority, shall be capable of reorganizing and readjusting the societary life in accordance with the new conditions ; hence the tendency to dictatorship which revolution often breeds. The phenomena of revolutions are thus susceptible of interpretation through the application of the categories and principles of a functional psychology. Such a subjective interpretation needs, of course, to be supplemented by an objective interpretation; but the important thing we wish here to be noted is that a social psychology built up upon the facts of coördination and adaptation in social life has a theory of revolutions to offer. That theory is, in summary, that revolutions are caused by the breakdown of social habits under abnormal conditions, such as we have noted above; that, in other words, the phenomena of revolutions are all susceptible of interpretation as phenomena which in principle may arise in any psychical organism in the transition from one habit to another under like abnormal conditions.

It is recognized that the theory of revolutions here proposed is not wholly new, but is implicit in the writings of many historians and social thinkers. Nevertheless, this is the first explicit statement of the theory that we know of. It is introduced here, in a discussion of the principles upon which a social psychology must be built up, as a theory growing out of our point of view and illustrating the application of that point of view to the concrete problems of social life.

In a similar manner the principles of interpretation furnished by a functional psychology may be applied to other social problems. Though we can but roughly apply our principles in most instances, there is, so far as we have been able to discover, no case of change within a society to which such principles of interpretation will not apply, and upon which they will not throw some light, whether the transition be one occupying a few years or a century. Let us now, for the sake of further illustration, take another concrete case in which the transition has been gradual and unattended by violent disturbance in the social process. The semi-patriarchal type of family which prevailed in Christendom up to the present century has been gradually breaking down. It has been unfitted to meet the new conditions of modern life. The old social habit has been going to pieces, and the usual confusion, uncertainty, and disorganization, attendant upon the breakdown of an important habit, have been manifested. Divorces have increased, and irregular forms of union have been, perhaps, more common. But in the meanwhile a new type of family, a new social habit, has been forming. By discussion, continuous social suggestion, social selection of ideas and ideals — processes familiar in every period of transition in human society — a new social coördination is being built up. We have every reason to believe, therefore, that when the process of social selection has been completed, and ideas adequate to the construction of a new social coördination, adapted to the present life-conditions, have been found, there will be a return to comparative fixity in the form of family life. A new type of family, in other words, will have emerged, a new social habit will have been formed. Present disturbances in family life, then, are to be regarded largely as phenomena attendant upon a transitionary stage, when an old social habit has broken down and a new habit has not yet been formed. Thus the principles of a functional social psychology may throw light upon present social phenomena and problems as well as upon those of the past. Hundreds of illustrations of the application of the principles and categories of functional psychology to societary changes might be drawn from industrial, political, and social history, but space permits only the giving of the above two.

The fact must here be noted that the breakdown of a social habit is not always followed by the building up of a new one in its place. The breakdown may be a sign, not of adaptation, but of social degeneration or dissolution; or a social habit may be simply "weeded out," as it were, because it has become of disadvantage to the society in the life-struggle. With societies not degenerate, however, the breakdown of a social habit of any importance or value in the life-process is always followed by the building up of a new social habit. With societies which, though not degenerate, yet contain a large number of degenerate individuals, the building-up process may occupy a period of centuries, and may involve (as it always does *implicitly* involve) a selection of individuals, as well as of psychical stimuli, ideas, etc.; but the new social habit comes in time, if the society survives. Before the church, for example, succeeded in building up a new type of family life, at the beginning of our era, upon the ruins of the patriarchal Roman type, a process of selection involving both individuals and ideas had to go on for centuries; but the Christian type of family of the Middle Ages was finally evolved. In any such case, where certain individuals in a society are hindrances to the building up of a new social habit necessary to the survival or development of the society, the tendency manifestly is to select those individuals whose beliefs, ideals, and general psychical attitude are favorable to the construction of the new social coördination, and to suppress the others.

A word may here, perhaps, appropriately be said in reference to social selection. Professor James and Professor Baldwin are right in emphasizing the importance of social selection in the societary process. But neither has given any adequate reason why one individual or one idea is "selected," rather than another individual or another idea. Both have failed to show the basis upon which society makes its selection from the variations produced by individuals, utilizing some, rejecting others. Both are practically content to state the fact that *society selects*, without inquiring into the causes of the selection. From our point of view it is obvious that social selection is exactly analogous to the selection which goes on in the individual through the process of attention in the building up of a new coördination. Society selects ideas and individuals, in other words, upon the basis of their utility in building up or maintaining its coördinations. It is especially in the building up of new social habits that the process of social selection is manifest. A Napoleon could never have been so acceptable to the French people if the nation as a whole had not been striving to build up new and stable institutions after the repeated failures of its revolutionary governments. If a Napoleon had not been found by the French people, some other, inferior individual would have been selected to perform his task. Concerning Cromwell, or any other great historical personage, essentially the same may be said as concerning Napoleon, namely, that he was "called forth," selected, "by the social needs of the hour," the need being the reconstruction of some societary activity. The social selection of ideas is made upon the same basis as that of individuals. Those ideas, beliefs, ideals, philosophies, psychical attitudes, etc., are selected by a society which aid it in building up new coördinations or maintaining old ones. Ideas survive, not because of any inherent fitness to survive, nor yet because of their "fitness for imitative reproduction,"[1] as some would maintain, but because of their utility[2] in the social life-process. If it be asked why certain ideas arise and permeate entire societies at certain periods, the answer, from the point of view maintained throughout this paper, must be, because such ideas are selected by the social life-process to aid in building up new coördinations. The genesis of the states of the social mind, in other words, is not different from the genesis of the states of the individual mind. Ideas make and unmake the world, not because they are forces outside of the life-process, but because of their connection with that process;

---

[1] BALDWIN, *Social and Ethical Interpretations*, p. 183.

[2] "Utility" must here be taken, of course, in its broadest sense, not as used by the pleasure-pain philosophers, but as simply implying that which favors the constructive process of life.

because they are, as it were, tools forged by it for its own development and perfecting.

We are tempted to follow farther the application of the principles and categories of functional psychology in the interpretation of the phenomena of the social life, but the scope of this paper does not permit. Criticism of theories which do not seem to accord with the point of view of this article must also be left till a later date. In the meanwhile, if this article succeeds in arousing a candid and careful consideration of its chief proposition, namely, that a social psychology can be constructed upon the fundamental principles and categories of a functional psychology of the individual, its main purpose will be accom plished. What we have said has been in the way of illustrating this proposition. It has been an attempt to demonstrate the possibility of constructing, rather than to construct, such a social psychology.

CHARLES A. ELLWOOD.

THE UNIVERSITY OF CHICAGO.

REVIEWS.

The Development of English Thought. By SIMON N. PATTEN.
New York: The Macmillan Co., 1899. Pp. xxvii + 415.

AN EXAMINATION OF PROFESSOR PATTEN'S PSYCHOLOGY.

PSYCHOLOGISTS have of late years observed with appreciative interest the growing tendency among economists and sociologists to build
certain portions of their respective sciences upon psychological foundations.   Mr. Patten's latest work is a striking illustration of this
tendency, and his psychological doctrines are sufficiently heretical to
render them at once interesting and worthy of examination.   It may
contribute to a juster estimate of our discussion of these doctrines, if
at the outset we comment briefly on the general intellectual temper of
the book in which they are presented.

Few writers on social topics have dared to be so elliptical in their
processes of inference as Mr. Patten, and a reader sensitive to the
niceties of argumentation is teased now and again by the suspicion
that all sides of the questions under discussion have not been fully and
fairly dealt with.   Remarkable generalizations are often made as
though their truth were, like that of the multiplication table, obvious
past all necessity for elaboration and defense.

Take, for example, the following diagnosis of English pessimism as
a dermal disorder, the cherished opinions of regiments of philosophers
to the contrary notwithstanding (p. 193): "An unbathed Englishman is a sensualist; a bath turns him into a gentle optimist.   The
bath-tub is the parent of that English optimism of which the last two
centuries have seen so many examples."   What more obvious?   You
wonder how it can have escaped you before, and immediately you
behold in your mind's eye the dark and horrid hordes of pessimism
retreating along with other noxious parasites, before the gentle erosive
influences of the virtuous bath-tub.   On second thought you suspect
this is allegory.   But if so, the author leaves you to discover the fact
unaided.

This quotation will, perhaps, serve to suggest that Mr. Patten is
fertile in generalization and subtle in deduction rather than strenuous
in analysis.   And let it not be supposed that this characteristic is

823

wholly wanting in merit. On the contrary, it results in immensely entertaining reading, in suggestiveness, in stimulation, in a dozen other desirable and admirable consequences ; but it cannot always conjure the forces of serious conviction, and it greatly enhances the difficulties of the reviewer, who desires to confront fairly the warrant for his author's assertions. We shall be obliged, therefore, in examining Mr. Patten's psychology to treat it upon its apparent merits, and without complete assurance of the foundations upon which it rests.x

Sensory ideas, motor ideas, and an environment constitute the chief materials with which the author transacts his psychological business. The sensory ideas represent the information obtained by the struggling organism concerning its environment. The motor ideas represent the utilization by the organism of this information. Certain kinds of environment necessitate for self-preservation a relatively higher development of the sensory ideas, while other kinds demand more imperatively a motor specialization. Significant factors in such differences of environment are the conditions of food supply, the local or cosmopolitan nature of the social relations, the general economic circumstances represented by the civilization, etc. On this basis, and apparently springing from the shifting interplay of these processes, Mr. Patten distinguishes four distinct types or classes of individuals, for which he has selected the picturesque titles of clingers, sensualists, stalwarts, and mugwumps.[2] The clingers and the mugwumps do not lend themselves readily to biographical treatment, the former being apparently too similar to one another and the latter not similar enough for cogent and profitable description. So Mr. Patten abandons them and confines his attention to the less refractory careers of the stalwarts and sensualists.

Mr. Patten's fundamental conception concerning sensory and motor

[1] The genealogy of Mr. Patten's interesting psychological doctrines may be. somewhat more accurately detected in his monograph upon the *Theory of Social Forces*, 1896. He has at least escaped the perverse fate which has so often overtaken economists and sociologists when discussing mental processes, for he shows himself wholly free from the fetishes of the faculty psychology. The present work devotes the opening chapter (fifty-six pages) to an explicit discussion of psychological principles, and the author states definitely in his preface that the remainder of the book is built upon these.

[2] There have been many hard sayings anent the mugwumps, but Mr. Patten's is quite the " most unkindest cut of all." He says (pp. x–xi) : "Such men are vigorous in thought, but weak in action. They cannot act together, but make admirable critics. They are cosmopolitans in their sympathies, advocates of compromise in politics, and agnostics in religion, and may be called mugwumps."

ideas and their relations to the environment will seem to many readers so obvious and reasonable that we shall doubtless encounter but little sympathy in our criticism of this portion of his psychology. This will be especially true in the case of readers familiar (and who is not ?) with the general doctrines advanced by Darwin and Spencer. Not that the position underlying our criticism is necessarily hostile to the principles represented by these writers, but simply that the correct application of these principles involves a psychological formulation somewhat different from the one proposed by Mr. Patten. Men certainly differ vastly from one another in the relative amounts of reflection and muscular action in which they indulge, and one of the important items in determining this relation is undoubtedly the environment, in the broad sense of that term. But reflection cannot be regarded as completely synonymous with the having of sensory ideas, as Mr. Patten seems at times to imply (p. 30), although we frankly confess that we find him difficult to follow on these points; nor can action be exclusively connected with one special class of ideas, such as those Mr. Patten denominates motor. For, in the first place, all sensory processes are implicated with motor consequences; and, in the second place, there are no such things as motor ideas which *as ideas* are not sensory. That *all* consciousness is motor is today a psychological commonplace. Movement as a psychological factor is always represented by sensations, originating sometimes in the part of the body moved and sometimes in sense organs relatively remote from the moving member. But in every case the movement is reported by a group of sensations, and a voluntary repetition of the movement is executed psychologically by a mental anticipation of some of the sensory effects of the movement. Mr. Patten appears, moreover, entirely to overlook the motor accompaniments of sensory activities, as is natural in view of his position. He says, for example (p. 7) that a cosmopolitan environment develops the sensory powers by necessitating nice discrimination, and straightway forgets that every act of sensory analysis involves a definite motor adjustment for its execution, and that modern psychology has shown this motor adjustment to be the very heart of the sensory activity, and consequently a process which must necessarily develop *pari passu* with the sensory action. The fact is that the difference between sensory and motor ideas is, as has recently been pointed out by several writers, one of function and not of content. Our criticism of Mr. Patten at this point may appear to involve a merely ornamental logical refinement upon the common-sense facts of the situations. But to this it may be replied that, if an author indulges himself in psychology, he may fairly be asked to do it correctly, and that, if the distinctions for which we are contending are correct, a neglect of them will ultimately be followed by confusion. We shall find an illustration of the last point in certain of Mr. Patten's other doctrines.

After the considerations advanced in the previous paragraphs it is hardly necessary to say that we cannot assent unhesitatingly to Mr. Patten's assertion that races differ more in their motor reactions than in their sensory ideas. It would be practically impossible to prove this assertion, supposing it were true, and inferentially, on the basis of the grounds just canvassed, we are confident that it is not true. The only warrant for the statement is the fact that we see races acting in different ways. Whether their sensations are alike or not is a matter of sheer speculation. But, unless our notions of the psychological antecedents of movements are intrinsically erroneous, we can feel speculatively assured that races are as diverse in sensory experiences as in any others.

Mr. Patten's doctrine that character depends upon habitual motor response belongs in the same general category with the matters just mentioned, although the author may expect to meet a less extended range of sympathizers upon this point, while to not a few of his readers the proposition will seem to furnish an instructive illustration of putting the cart before the horse.

In order to get his machinery agoing Mr. Patten introduces us to our old psychological friends pleasure and pain, but under the aliases of "pain economies" and "pleasure economies." It appears that a pain economy is the name for a condition in which men are principally engaged in avoiding pain, while a pleasure economy is one in which the chief occupation is seeking pleasure. Primitive conditions are more richly represented under the pain economy, civilized societies tending to monopolize the pleasure economy. It must grieve the pains-taking critics of hedonism, whose contentions are distinctly relevant as against the view here presented, to hear an enlightened man like Mr. Patten setting down these principles as blandly as though no one had ever questioned them. But, anyhow, this is the point at which Mr. Patten begins to make his environment efficacious in the development of classes, the only genuine classifications being, he assures us, based on psychic characteristics. Wealth and social position, which are typical of prevailing classifications, do not represent psychic conditions, and are therefore superficial.

In examining Mr. Patten's classes we shall find our prophecy of logical disaster confirmed by a practical desertion of the genuine sensory and motor distinction. We shall meet with classes whose characteristics are defined in terms of activities, comprising both sensory and motor elements, together with certain other factors previously unmentioned. I do not remember that Mr. Patten anywhere asserts that his classes are deduced from his sensory-motor premises. But it seems reasonably clear that, if his original position was correct, the differentiation into classes should afford the strongest confirmation of it, instead of involving its practical abandonment.

The first class described is that of the clingers, and we are immediately confronted with an account of certain emotional conditions — timidity, shyness, etc. These characteristics are called out in response to an environment with a limited food supply. The people are conservative and stay at home, instead of going out to search for fatter lands, as might seem the more natural procedure. It does not appear that they possess either peculiar proficiencies or defects in their sensory qualities, and their motor activities do not seem to be stunted save in the direction of travel, adventure, and fighting. It is rather their emotional life, which is confessedly both sensory and motor in its constitution, that marks them off from others.

Similarly class two, the sensualists, are described as persons with some dominant passion to be satisfied, and their time is spent exploiting man and nature in its gratification. To the onlooker it must be admitted that a man of this class might seem more definitely motor than the clinger. But it is the direction of his muscular energies which distinguishes him, rather than the sum total of such energy expended, and both of them seem to have emotional characteristics as their most specific marks.

The third type, the stalwarts, manage to combine "a love of dogmas and creeds" with "independence in thought and action." We are now frankly involved with a description in which sensory and motor elements are blended beyond the hope of profitable analysis.

The fourth and last class, the mugwumps, are apparently the only ones legitimately descended from our sensory and motor ideas. They are strong in sensory analysis and weak in action, especially organized action. But again, when one recalls the amount of trouble the mugwumps have caused first and last, it seems incredible that they should be described in terms of inactivity, and we are led to see once more that the only tenable distinction applies to the nature and direction of their action, and not to the presence or absence of action as such.

In short, the description which Mr. Patten offers of his social classes not only enforces our strictly psychological contention regarding the indissoluble connection of sensory and motor processes, but it also suggests that Mr. Patten has worked with a somewhat narrow and arbitrary conception of action. He seems always to have in his mind, when emphasizing motor activities, the more violent, or, at least, the more distinctly manual, forms of occupation. That these involve the larger muscles and a larger expenditure of muscular energy, hardly admits of debate. But if the distinctions at issue are those of motor as against sensory processes (granting the validity of the distinction for the sake of the argument), it will not do to substitute unannounced a distinction resting on the size of the muscles employed, or the violence with which they are exercised, and it is something of this kind to which several of Mr. Patten's differentiations reduce themselves.

To sum up this part of our criticism we may say, then, that the notion of the separate development of certain ideas called sensory and certain ideas called motor is psychologically untenable : that the attempt to apply this notion in the classification of individuals on a psychic basis results, first, in the introduction of emotional characteristics supplementary to the sensory-motor distinction, and, second, in a practical abandonment of the distinction in favor of a classification based on activities in which both sensory and motor elements are equally represented.

The relation of the environment to the organism involves problems which are usually regarded as biological rather than psychological. But there is, of course, also a psychological problem involved here, and we must notice briefly Mr. Patten's mode of handling it. Moreover, it is here that he shows most clearly the school in which his thought has developed. Waiving the frequent passages in which he finds it necessary, as would any writer employing the point of view of common sense, to speak of the individual as producing changes in the environment, his fundamental doctrine, both from the psychological and the historical standpoint, is expressed in the proposition (*cf.* p. 14) that "every marked change in the environment gives rise to a new epoch in thought." He carries this further in the remarkable doctrine, whose validity falls outside the scope of this examination, that the constructive thought of each epoch follows the regular order : economics, æsthetics, morals, and religion, and that the ethical thought of any epoch—to illustrate in a single instance what Mr. Patten postulates of each of

these fields of reflection — springs entirely from its own economic antecedents and not from the ethical thought of preceding epochs.

So far as there is a psychology involved in this conception of the
significance of the environment for the organism, it is the position of
the extreme associationists, the conception of a relatively quiescent
mind bandied about by the forces of its surroundings. Against this
doctrine the apperceptionists have waged a vigorous and generally
successful campaign, emphasizing its decrepitude on the side of both
substantiating facts and coherent theory. I cannot discover that Mr.
Patten examines systematically the warrant for assigning to the economic environment such tremendous intellectual consequences, while
seeming to assume that it is itself in its origin relatively independent
of consciousness. If Mr. Patten means his statements merely as an
account of certain periods in history and chooses to begin with the
appearance of apparently new economic epochs, there is little ground
for questioning his procedure. But this does not seem to be his intention, and we are obliged to protest that his theory is one-sided. No
one doubts that economic conditions have been factors of utmost
moment in the development of reflective consciousness, but the psychological doctrine (leave alone the historical verification of the implications) here advocated (p. 43), in accordance with which these economic conditions are made to appear as the sole real causes of the
trend of reflective thought, can only be established by making the term
"economic" cover all the other fields from which its application has by
implicit definition already been distinguished.

Mr. Patten is, however, better than his theory, and he actually
traces for us, in his exceedingly graphic manner, a number of instances
in which, so far as concerns the individual, the strict validity of his
theory is refuted. Indeed, one of his more important doctrines lends
itself only reluctantly to reconciliation with the conception we have
just discussed. Character, which, it will be remembered, is connected
with motor response, is, he says, enduring, whereas the environment
is constantly undergoing change. This leaves us with the somewhat
perplexing psychological problem on our hands of accounting for a
relatively stable set of motor activities, manifesting considerable independence of changes in the environment, and a highly unstable set of
reflective thought processes, varying with every important alteration
in this environment. Leaving this problem out of consideration, however, the point we wish to emphasize is the absolute dependence of
only part of the processes of consciousness upon the environment, *i. e.*,

those which are reflective, the motor elements possessing on Mr. Patten's showing relative permanence and independence. We are again face to face, therefore, with Mr. Patten's sensory-motor distinction. All that we have previously said upon the subject is necessarily relevant here, and it can hardly be doubted now that Mr. Patten really has separated the two realms as completely as we indicated. From the practical, common-sense point of view we venture to inquire whether the average intelligent reader is ready to admit that the results of ethical and religious thought are as transitory and fleeting as this conception requires, and whether motor activities are in any sense so obstinate against the ravages of time as this theory implies. If not, it may be that the seemingly technical contention which we discussed earlier in the paper in maintaining the fallacy of Mr. Patten's sensory-motor doctrines, had involved in it consequences of real practical moment for the psychological interpreter of history. Either thought and action are more intimately related than Mr. Patten's views admit, or else our psychological and common-sense notions are all wrong.

Mr. Patten advances several other interesting theories, which we cannot examine at this time. His treatment of the transmission of psychological characteristics from generation to generation is one of these. He has also a good deal to say of curves of thought and visualization, although these points strike me as chiefly interesting for the suggestive light they throw upon the author's own thought processes. These matters are mentioned simply to indicate that we have not touched upon the whole of Mr. Patten's psychology.

If our criticism has been almost wholly hostile, it must not be assumed that we regard Mr. Patten's accomplishment as worthless. Quite the contrary. Where we have been obliged to differ with him most sharply, his shortcomings, as we believe them to be, exhibit in the most conclusive manner the really vital uses to which psychology can be put in the service of such inquiries. Too often writers have confined themselves to the mere enunciating of a program. Mr. Patten has made an extremely interesting effort actually to realize such a program, and for this he deserves every credit. Furthermore, psychology has not yet emerged so completely from the limitations of individualism as to render impossible the cherishing of diverse and opposing views. We have attempted to state the merits of the case as between Mr. Patten's views and what we believe to be the facts. The reader must decide the issue for himself.   JAMES ROWLAND ANGELL.

THE UNIVERSITY OF CHICAGO.

AN EXAMINATION OF PROF. PATTEN'S HISTORY AND ECONOMICS.

Every epoch has given to the world its own philosophy of history, or attempt to interpret events of the past and present in the light of the *Zeitgeist*. This interpretation has always been determined by the peculiar circumstances and dominant thought of the period. Consequently, since Josephus the content of the term "philosophy of history" has changed many times. Nor is this strange, for civilization in its triumphant march impresses its character upon all the vital ideas of the race, widening the thoughts of men from age to age. Montesquieu gives the theme for all our modern philosophies of history, upon which there have been many variations in these latter days. For he affirms the authority of law in human events and seeks to connect historical periods through the relations of cause and effect. One of the latest contributions to the field is Barth's *Philosophie der Geschichte als Sociologie*, which seeks to identify the two subjects, philosophy of history and sociology. And now we have before us another achievement along the same line.

Dr. Patten's *Development of English Thought* is an interpretation of history from the economist's standpoint. This we learn from the title: "The Development of English Thought — A Study in the Economic Interpretation of History." And the author, moreover, informs us in the preface that it is his aim to present a theory of history through concrete illustrations. An economic interpretation of history is not new, for we discover it in the writings of St. Simon and Louis Blanc at the beginning of this century, and again in Émile de Laveleye's *Political Economy*, where the following statements appear:

> The power of states is proportional to their population and their wealth. The development of population and wealth depends upon economic causes. These, therefore, are the ultimate source of the great events of history.[1]

Dr. Patten's economic bias is decidedly shown in his treatment of the French Revolution, which he attributes solely to the rise in the price of wheat. According to him, the revolution was a veritable bread riot. The people were not crying for food, but for comfort, for wheat bread had become the standard of comfort in the eighteenth century. The oppressions of the poor, the outrages they were forced to endure at the hands of the nobles, all the woes of the peasants with which we have become familiar through the graphic pen of Taine, would never

---

[1] *The Elements of Political Economy*, translated by ALFRED W. POLLARD, pp. 12 and 13.

of themselves have produced the French Revolution. These ills, more-over, have been woefully exaggerated, says Dr. Patten. No, this great social upheaval was caused alone by the economic change which forced wheat out of France into England.

The central idea of the book is that economic conditions deter-mine the development of civilization and thought in any particular epoch, and the type of man that shall survive. Therefore, new philos-ophies develop out of new economic conditions and not out of old theories. In the end, the philosophies may blend, but this blending is an afterthought, and is not due to the second philosophy having sprung from the first. To the ideas of St. Simon and Louis Blanc, that the two factors which form history are economic desires and eco-nomic progress, he adds a third, that of national character. "The interplay of the character forces in men and the economic forces in their environment causes progress," he tells us on p. 13. We thus see that Dr. Patten gives almost as much weight to the influence of national character on the development of civilization as Le Bon when he says, "The character of a people is the keynote to its destiny. It creates its destiny;" or as Bagehot, when he declares: "By far and out of all question the most important of all circumstances affecting polit-ical problems is *national character*." Le Bon, in his *Lois psychologiques de l'évolution des peuples*, says that the mental constitution or character of a race represents, not only the synthesis of the living beings which compose it, but, above all, that of the ancestors who have contributed to form it. It is not the living but the dead that play the preponder-ating rôle in the existence of a people. They are the creators of its morals and the unconscious motives for its conduct. We find much the same thought in Dr. Patten's careful analysis of national character. For he tells us that the forces generated by the present environment are not the only forces that determine the action of the men who live in it. Past environments still exert force through the modifications they have made in national character. These two forces are always in conflict. The ideas holding over from the past give tone to the civil-ization. The remodeling influences come from conditions set by the immediate environment, and through them the economic forces get their power (p. 13).

Dr. Patten chooses the three epochs of English history since the time of the Reformation for illustration of his theory. England, on account of its isolation, presents the best field for the study of normal thought development, and in the three epochs just mentioned English thought was less influenced by foreign ideas than at any time in its history. Yet we are astonished that a book dealing with the development of English thought should confine itself to periods after Bacon and Shakespeare, and should practically ignore the work of the literary man if expressed in any other than economic or philosophic form. With the exception of Wordsworth and his contemporaries, Dr. Patten ignores the English "littérateur" as a shaper of the thought of his age. The popular writer receives no credit for his influence in the formation of public opinion, in the molding of national character, or in the dissemination of the great truths of science. When we consider the tremendous influence of Tennyson since the middle of the century upon public thought, to say nothing of the effect of the social novel since Dickens' innovation of the same, in creating ideals, we can but conclude that Dr. Patten's treatment of his subject is not as broad as it might have been. We know how responsible the popular writer is for the public sentiment prevailing on any topic of the hour. We must all agree with Mr. Stead, for instance, that Kipling, through his works, is a shaper of the destiny of the race. In the English *Review of Reviews* for March, Mr. Stead comments thus on "The White Man's Burden":

It is an international document of the first importance. It is a direct appeal to the United States to take up the policy of expansion. The poet has idealized and transfigured imperialism. He has shown its essence to be, not lordship, but service. . . . . It will be strange if these seven stanzas do not prove more than a match for all the millions and all the eloquence of anti-expansionists like Mr. Carnegie and Mr. Bryan.

And, again, it seems passing strange that no weight is given to the effect upon English national character of chivalry, that great institution of the Middle Age. Its contributions to thought and character were permanent, for we can trace the ideals of self-sacrifice and self-assertion — two important traits in English character — back to this very period. And these ideals were fixed in English literature for all time by Sir Thomas Malory in his great epic, *Morte Arthure*, at a time when the institution which had produced them was about to yield to other forms of organization for which society, owing to the revolutionizing economic progress of the fifteenth century, was then more fit.

After the psychological preliminaries discussed above by Dr. Angell there follow the statements that the history of thought passes through four stages — the economic, the æsthetic, the moral, and the religious; that the study of any epoch involves, first, the consideration of the prevailing economic conditions, then that of the economic doctrines which flow from them, and next that of the æsthetic, moral, and religious ideas which the epoch produces. But most startling of all, and absolutely at variance with our accepted ideas on the subject of thought development, the author next asserts that the history of æsthetic, moral, or religious thought, each taken independently, is impossible because later epochs do not grow out of older ones, but out of new material. History must be studied in epochs, and each group of ideas should be connected with its roots in the underlying conditions, and not with its antecedents in the same group. The blending of the old with the new of the same group (which fact Dr. Patten must acknowledge) happens after new conditions have exerted their force or have brought out what is most peculiar to them. Here we strike the keynote of the author's theory — new economic conditions form the basis of thought development. The race has passed through a series of temporary environments, each of which has contributed certain characteristics that have become a part of national character. Character is the one enduring, growing element in a civilization where all else is temporary and fleeting. Economic conditions produce the primary motor reactions. Under new environments, where new conditions for survival obtain, these motor reactions respond to abstract instead of concrete phenomena. The concepts created by the motor reactions disappear if they do not harmonize with new conditions. If they do, they become ideals. Motor reactions, once formed, do not readily fall into disuse; they are appropriated by ideals.

Dr. Patten next informs us that there are two classes in society capable of progressive thought — the philosophers and the economists; that the influence of the observers (economists) on the thinkers (philosophers), and of the thinkers on the observers, causes progression in thought. Every transition to a new environment tends to develop a new type of man and remodel the old. From the new arise the economists, from the old the philosophers. The former proceed on an upward curve of thought from facts to theory, the latter on a down curve from theory to facts. English thought divides itself into three epochs. In the first progress is due to Hobbes, Locke, and Newton; in the second Mandeville, Hume, and Adam Smith are the master spirits; and in the last it is the work of Malthus, Mill, and Darwin that influences thought development.

Chapter 2 is devoted to the antecedents of English thought. Following Montesquieu and Buckle, Dr. Patten makes the determining factors in the production of the three types of early civilizations the action of the immediate physical environment on man and man's reaction against nature. Thus, in the cold, wet country, where natural forces act regularly, where man subdues nature, we discover well-knit social groups with a civilization distinctively moral. The German is a type of this development. In the hot, dry country, where natural forces are overpowering, where man yields to nature, hope and humility are developed, and we discover a civilization essentially religious in character. Of this type Semitic civilization is a good instance. The third class is formed by the tribute-takers—the conquerors who live by controlling other people. In this society the concept of citizenship is formed and law is developed. Roman civilization is the type. These three types have together furnished the basis of English thought and character.

The fifteenth century was a period of change and progress for England as well as for the rest of Europe. The invention of printing, the use of gunpowder and the compass, the discovery of America, the introduction of chimneys and glass windows into houses, and beer, sugar, and sweets into diet, revolutionized every phase of society. Family life was now made possible and agreeable. In part, at least, communal life was supplanted, and woman's position became higher. The church of the Middle Age inculcated habits of thought that lay at the basis of social progress.

In the sixteenth century the development of England began to be differentiated from that of the continent. From now on it was more normal.

The next period treated is that dominated by the thoughts of the Calvinists; indeed, the chapter is entitled "The Calvinists." Calvin's scheme was the outgrowth of the economic ideas of the age. Its central thought was the covenant between man and God. The whole scheme was legal rather than moral. Resulting from the sudden change in economic conditions, which clothed the Englishman in wool and placed him before a fire, we have three types of character—the sensualist, the original, unmodified Englishman, who retained the dross of primitive times; the clinger, who wished to keep things as they were, who wanted peace and security, and believed in the divine right of kings; and the stalwart, or concrete Puritan, who soon died of consumption because he did not care for comfort.

The first great thinker of the age was Hobbes. His main thoughts are, that necessity is the only rule of action; that nature is in a state of warfare, to overcome which societies are formed; that the power of the king is supreme. He fails to solve the problem of the age.

Locke next follows with an important contribution. This is the principle of indifference. "There are things in their own nature indifferent," he declares. He thus adds a new group to the old categories of the good and the bad—the indifferent. He attacks superstition on the one hand, and enthusiasm on the other, declaring that all ideas come through sense impressions. There is no expression without impression. Any excess of expression is either superstition or enthusiasm, and therefore bad.

Dr. Patten next speaks of the relation of Locke to deism, and in the following passage seems to contradict part of his theory: "If we follow the development of abstract thought subsequent to Locke, the contributions of the deists cannot be overlooked. But it is more important to look on the practical side of Locke's work and see how the deists are connected with it. Viewed in this way they make a stage in religious development that begins with Locke and ends with Wesley."x Does not this conflict with his statement in chap. 1 that it is impossible to follow the history of thought in any one field independently—that the development of any line of thought does not depend on the antecedent thought in the same field, but on new economic conditions of the later epoch? The deists attack the prevailing notion of God, denying that he delegated his power to anyone, or that he interfered in the affairs of men. Consequently they were antagonists of the current doctrine of the divine right of kings. At this time Newton began his work which resulted in a reconstruction of the theory of the universe. The law of gravitation transformed the old concept of chaos to the new one of cosmos. Dr. Patten tells us that since Locke there has been no development of political thought in England. Progress in the eighteenth century was absolutely independent of political life. Does careful investigation of English political institutions warrant his summary disposal of this most important topic?

To Locke, the deists, and Newton are due the new idea of God as a God of love, the transformation of morality (everything of which the reason can judge is placed in the new category of the indifferent), and the separation of government and law from morals and religion. Two new types of character now arise—the stalwart, who places race ideals above reason, and the mugwump, who places reason first.

The next chapter, on "The Moralists," traces the evolution of

x P. 175.

REVIEWS 837

thought in the eighteenth century. Eighteenth-century thought, Dr. Patten says, was not a continuation of seventeenth-century ideas, but a new movement. In the seventeenth century the city invaded the country and destroyed sensual customs, the survival of communal days, while in the eighteenth the towns were the places that needed reform. One section moved forward in the seventeenth century, another in the eighteenth. The improvement in agriculture and the elevation of family life are the two marked features of social progress in the last century. Mandeville is cited as the first thinker. In his "Fable of the Bees" he states his thesis — that spending makes trade lively, frugality causes industrial stagnation. Therefore the necessities, vices, imperfections of men are the sources of all the arts, trades, and industries. He emphasizes the contrast between the workers and the leisure class, and makes the usefulness of the latter depend upon the need of luxury and vice to maintain trade. This theory was not wholly controverted until Mill proved the usefulness of frugality and the indispensability of capital. Hume, the successor of Mandeville, aims "to give a check to all kinds of superstitious delusions." He asserts that physical conditions have no effect on the human mind, that men owe nothing to air, food, or climate. "If we run over the globe or revolve the annals of history, we shall discover everywhere *signs of a sympathy or contagion of manners*, none of the influence of air or climate," he tells us in his *Essay on National Characters*. Do we not here find a suggestion of Tarde's theory of imitation ? The third great thinker of the epoch makes human nature the controlling element of his doctrine. In his *Wealth of Nations* Adam Smith collects all the economic principles which had previously appeared and applies certain laws of human nature to the discussion of economic problems. He emphasizes the advantages of parsimony and condemns the evils of prodigality. It was due to his efforts that political economy became a recognized science.

The advancement in economic and philosophic thought paved the way to the religious awakening of Methodism. Puritans and plagues had disappeared. Religion needed a reinforcement of its claim. Wesley and Whitefield arose as the leaders of the new movement. The Calvinists visualized long-past events, especially the covenant and the assembled host of Israel at the foot of Mount Sinai. Whitefield visualized the future, laying stress on the picture of the last judgment. The failure of Calvinism was due to the ruling principle of predestination, which is incompatible with social progress, and which implies resignation, the mental attitude characteristic of women. When society is confronted with evils beyond its control, this spirit is reflected in religion. Unavoidable evils foster, even in men, the spirit of resignation; unnecessary evils stir up, even in women, revolt. The environment and economic conditions thus determine what attitude will be dominant in a given society and what type of religion will do most for its elevation.

Just here, Dr. Patten tells us, a new type of man, "the womanly man," was beginning to be a factor in English society. He accounts for the existence of this new type in the following way: With the great industrial change brought about by the discovery of America there came a revolution in social life for which woman was responsible. Now really arises the English home. Men were satisfied with the established order of things. The great change from communal to home life and pleasures was accomplished by woman. It was she who cooked, scrubbed, worked in the fields, spun clothes, taught the children, and took care of the men. She was responsible for the cleanliness of the household, which in the days of the plague was the necessary condition of survival. So the industrial type of woman became dominant. Along with her duties came her power. She became the ruling factor in the home, and the womanly type of man—the man who accepted woman's ideals and standards of purity and resignation—became a fact in English history. A womanly type of man, in the industrial sense, *did* now become dominant, owing to the necessary change in activities brought about by economic development. Men were forced into new employments against their natural bent. Their new life kept them more at home. Consequently they felt the influence of woman in the creation of standards for conduct more strongly than ever before. Thus arose the "womanly man" of Patten. The author's interpretation of the great social changes of the fifteenth century as due to woman's initiative is hardly in accord with our accepted theory of woman's conservatism.

The eighteenth century demanded "manly men," or those vigorous in will-power. As Methodism brought forward this type, it tended to check the growing power of women. It brought to the front men who were too strong to be influenced by women. Hence the more primitive type of women who performed the duties of motherhood better tended to survive. Methodism and economics created a non-moral state of mind, which has remained a characteristic of English civilization. The new ideals made the people less moral, but not less conscientious. The effect of Wesley and Smith on English thought was to inculcate a distrust of general principles, a distaste for foreign innovations, and a dislike of customs and traditions. People became individual, concrete, and local in their habits of thought. This attitude of mind fitted them for the next epoch.

The fifth chapter opens with a discussion of the causes of the decline of France. Our author boldly asserts that the wickedness and vice of the people were in no wise responsible for the decline of the country. He attributes the decay to economic causes—the rise in the price of wheat especially—which produced a constantly increasing deficiency in her economic resources. To the French Revolution he gives a picturesque value only, for he says : " The revolution in commerce, industry, social philosophy, and national ideals would have gone on just the same if France had submitted quietly to the inevitable loss of power and the rule of the Bourbons. She did not alter the course of history by her bold struggle for supremacy, but simply made history more interesting."[1]

This chapter, which is entitled "The Economists," shows how thought in the nineteenth century is dominated by economists and philosophers who believe in social progress through influence as opposed to progress by selection. Thus we find the economic utilitarian and the philosophic utopian making human happiness the end of action. From this point of view Carlyle, Newman, Spencer, and Gladstone may all be classed together. Bentham first appears on the scene with the principle that security, not comfort, is the goal of human society. He gives us a negative idea of pleasure, emphasizing the removal of pain more than the acquisition of pleasure. Society was to be improved by burdening the evil-doer until he ceased to do wrong. Malthus follows with his theory of population, which caused an immediate conflict between the economists and the moralists, as it taught that progress meant poverty. To Ricardo is due the new concept of society which now arises. Smith and Malthus viewed society as an agricultural community. Now emphasis is laid upon the city and all the economic problems and complications which it entails.

John Stuart Mill contributes a new ideal of social progress and a new method of thought. His method was first that of pure induction based on experience. The generalizations thus obtained are then used as premises for deduction, and conclusions reached through this deduction are verified by fresh induction. The study of Wordsworth and the ideas of Sterling and St. Simon had great influence on Mill's own development. Comte also was one of the important factors in shaping

[1] P. 278.

Mill's views.   It was the study of Comte that led him to place great emphasis on the new sciences of ethology and sociology, which fact Professor Patten regrets in the following words : " The fact is that Mill's diversion from the natural trend of his development by Comte so weakened the credit of social studies that they have not yet recovered, nor can they recover their standing until the crude analogies derived from physical science are discarded.   The bias of physical study hinders everyone who goes from physical to social science.   The method of social science must be determined from its own problems."x Mill tried to establish a general law of causation by simple enumeration for the social sciences.   Patten declares that no law of causation is needed to establish the position of social science, and then proceeds to give us his own social theory, with which we are all familiar—that the laws of pleasure and pain are the laws of social science, that the field of pleasure and pain is the field of social science.

With Darwin we have the completion of one epoch and the beginning of a new one.   Darwin's argument may be divided into two parts—the economic, which may be summed up as the economy of food and its effect on the organism, and the biologic, which may be stated as the mutability of species and the idea of common ancestors. His four propositions are (1) the limitations of food supply, (2) the rapid increase of each species, (3) variability of descendants, and (4) evolution through pressure of numbers.

From the beginning of the nineteenth century we notice a change in the ideals of activity, of pleasure, and of God.   The poets and the Oxford movement had much to do with this transformation.   Through the poet nature became an animated personality—God was seen in everything.   The Oxford movement created the ideal of a united church and gave an impetus to the service of praise that has influenced all denominations.

In the last chapter Dr. Patten sums up the conclusions of his study and offers a few predictions.   He tells us that the cause of development during the three epochs in English history just reviewed was the opposition between communal and home interests and pleasures, and that the great result has been the reconciliation of religion and economics.   The stock ideals of the race *were* religious, they have *now* become economic.   Religious concepts have become utilitarian. The capitalistic tendency which leads men to put confidence in remote results develops faith in the unseen.   In English civilization, the local

¹ P. 332.

and peculiar has been subordinated to the general and national. The unity of the older race was sensory. Men were held together by common environment. The unity of the English race is not environmental, but psychic. The race is held together by race ideals and social standards. The success of these means the success of the race. Our progress and ascendency depend upon decisions which have already been made. The types of man that will ultimately prevail, Dr. Patten tells us, are the stalwart and the mugwump. The sensualists and the clingers are fast disappearing. There has been very little growth in national literature and art, we are told, owing to the fact that these fields have been dominated by the steriles or racial suicides, who can have no permanent influence on the race. So long as æsthetic feelings are a useless variation, unconnected with vital activities, progress will be impossible. Can we agree with Dr. Patten that a literature which has produced a Shakespeare, a Milton, a Wordsworth, a Tennyson, a Browning, and a Kipling is undeveloped ? Though the author tells us that a psychic change is taking place in the men of the race rather than a physical one in the women — making the men more and more subservient, willing to give, and the women less and less economic, eager to receive — we cannot accept this conclusion in the face of the facts of today which seem to prove the direct contrary. For when has woman been more economic, more capable of standing alone in the struggle for advancement than she now is ?

To gain that higher civilization for which the laws of economics discover the necessary qualities demanded by the conditions of environment, men must become active, hopeful, and altruistic, full of confidence in the future and in the unseen. The effect of present economic conditions on character is to cause the sacrifice of the higher for the lower which is incarnation, just as the sacrifice of the lower for the higher is evolution.

Dr. Patten concludes with the statement that the adjustment of the race is about half finished. Literature and art have failed to become national except in the first part of this century. Philosophy and education still adhere to foreign models, and there has been little development in law and politics.

We have already called attention to the fact that the vital parts of Dr. Patten's theory — that new philosophies develop out of new economic conditions and not out of old theories — is opposed to the best historical and sociological views of our age. Take but a single instance. I quote from Topinard in the *Monist* for October, 1898.

" Bacon, Hobbes, and Locke are the inaugurators of the English school [of philosophy]. . . . It led to Adam Smith, who discovers the sanction of morality in altruism or public approbation ; to Bentham, who sees it in interest rationally understood ; to Hume and the Scottish school, and finally to the existing school of J. S. Mill, Darwin, and Herbert Spencer."[1]   This is but a typical instance of the historical interpretation of thought in every field today.

Moreover, we cannot agree with many of Dr. Patten's conclusions —statements which are utterly at variance with our accepted beliefs. Perhaps the most startling of these is his decision regarding English political development.   The claim of the English that they have a peculiar aptitude for the development of political institutions is, he tells us, without basis.   Since Locke there has been no development of political thought.   The English have been too conservative to develop institutional life beyond the needs of primitive society.   For the past two centuries there has been no dominant class, and so the race has prospered under conditions that would otherwise have demanded a development of its institutions.   The peace and security which have prevailed far more in England than in any other European country, he declares, are due, not to Anglo-American institutions, but to instincts inculcated during the supremacy of the church, favorable economic conditions, and the spirit of compromise from opposing types.   Given these conditions, and any institution would be successful.   Quite a different valuation does Andrew D. White give to the influence of political institutions on the progress of civilization.   In his preface to Müller's *Political History of Modern Times* he recommends the work "to all who desire a clear idea of that political development in modern Europe which has brought on the amazing events of these latter years."

Nor can we accept Dr. Patten's unique explanation of the transformations of social life in England from communal to domestic as due mainly to woman's initiative.   Nor yet his statement that women are becoming more and more domestic and less and less economic.   And, again, we are sure that loud cries of dissent will greet his assertion that there has been little or no literary development in England.   Who will not resent as a reflection upon our culture the following: "Fathers and mothers have not yet become artistic and are too active to indulge much in novel-reading.   The taste of the average mother seldom rises

[1] P. TOPINARD, "Man as a Member of Society," translated by T. J. McCORMACK, the *Monist*, October, 1898, p. 68.

above the level of bric-à-brac and chromos, while the father is quite content with his newspaper."[1]

Also, Dr. Patten's failure to recognize the splendid work that is being done in the field of sociology today, and his lack of appreciation of the achievements of his brother-scientists along lines so near to those of his own interest, are much to be regretted. Speaking of the emphasis Mill placed on the new sciences of ethology and sociology, he takes occasion to say: "The new sciences were yet to be made, and, unfortunately for Mill's reputation as a prophet, are still to be made." Mill let ethology drop, and no one has since taken it up. "Nor has sociology fared much better," he continues. "Until recently it was made up of a few analogies derived from biology, and even now it is not far enough advanced to obtain general recognition nor to have its method well defined."[2]

Thus, while we cannot agree with all that Dr. Patten says, while we must feel that there are important omissions in his book, while we must admit the biased attitude of the author, yet we are glad to welcome *The Development of English Thought* as an original, strong, and suggestive contribution to the economic and philosophic literature of the day.   SADIE E. SIMONS.

CENTRAL HIGH SCHOOL,
Washington, D. C.

Problems of Modern Industry. By SIDNEY AND BEATRICE WEBB. London: Longmans, Green & Co., 1898. Pp. 286. $2.50.

THESE gifted writers have collected a number of papers into an interesting volume of studies of English industrial conditions. "The Diary of an Investigator" shows a shrewd observer in contact with the life of the London sewing women. "The Jews of East London" introduces us to a world little known, perhaps, to wealthy members of the same race. Two chapters are given to questions of women workers, their wages, and the factory acts which aim to protect them. The latter part of the book is an interpretation of the socialistic program from the Fabian point of view. The relationship between coöperation and trade-unionism is the subject of an important chapter. The poor law is studied in connection with the general movement for enlarging the functions of the state.

[1] P. 385.   [2] P. 332.

Since we cannot reproduce or discuss a tithe of the vital problems presented, we may select a few of the most important conclusions, typical of all. "This competitive wage we Socialists seek to replace by an allowance for maintenance deliberately settled according to the needs of the occupation and the means at the nation's command. We already see official salaries regulated, not according to the state of the labor market, but by consideration of the cost of living. This principle we seek to extend to the whole industrial world." And as to ground rents: "A socialist state or municipality will charge the full economic rent for the use of its land and dwellings, and apply that rent to the common purposes of the community."

The discussion of poor-law reform and pensions for the aged ought to be thoroughly discussed in the United States. It will soon be for us, as it is in England, a theme of practical politics.

C. R. HENDERSON.

The Federal Census: Critical Essays by Members of the American Economic Association. Collected and edited by a Special Committee. (Publications of the American Economic Association, New Series, No. 2, March, 1899.) New York: The Macmillan Co. Pp. 4+516, 8vo. $2.

IT is a well-known fact that the United States government spends more money for the collection and compiling of census statistics than any other nation. The cost of the previous censuses has been in round numbers, according to official figures, as follows: 1790, $44,000; 1800, $67,000; 1810, $178,500; 1820, $208,500; 1830, $378,500; 1840, $833,500; 1850, $1,329,000; 1860, $2,000,000; 1870, $3,500,000; 1880, $6,000,000; 1890, $11,000,000.

That the accuracy of the 1890 census and of previous censuses is not all that could be desired, those who have followed the articles by Mr. Bliss in this and the previous volume of the Journal will be convinced.

In view of the enormous and increasing cost and the undoubted shortcomings of our census work, all will agree that the American Economic Association has done excellent service in arranging for and publishing this volume of papers by authorities on the department of statistics of which they treat.

The following are the divisions: "Report of the Committee on the Scope and Method of the Twelfth Census": "Area, Population," etc., by W. F. Wilcox; "Colored Population of African Descent," by W. Z. Ripley; "Census of the North American Indians," by Franz Boas; "Age, Sex, Dwellings and Families, and Urban Population," by G. K. Holmes; "Educational Statistics," by D. R. Dewey; "Statistics of Occupations," by Richmond Mayo-Smith; "Mortality Statistics," by C. L. Wilbur and Irving Fisher; "Statistics of Crime," by R. P. Faulkner; "Pauperism and Benevolence," by S. M. Lindsay; "Agriculture," by N. I. Stone; "Farm and Home Proprietorship," by David Kinley; "Transportation," by E. R. Johnston and W. E. Weyl; "Manufactures," by S. N. D. North, W. M. Stewart, and W. C. Ford; "Wages," by C. J. Bullock; "Valuation and Taxation," by C. C. Plehn; "Municipal Finance," by H. B. Gardner; "Scope and Method of the Twelfth Census," by W. C. Hunt; "Extracts from Letters;" appendix: "Provisions of the Census Laws of 1889 and 1899;" index.

The papers are designed to be in the main critical studies of the leading divisions of the eleventh census. But they are also very valuable for comparative estimates and information on all the previous censuses and contain considerable constructive work.

It is unfortunate that the publication could not have appeared a couple of years sooner, so that it could have been used in its entirety, as a testimony to the need of reform in our census methods before the taking of the twelfth census.

The law for the census of 1900, given in the appendix, does show that Congress is not utterly lost to reason; for it asks for returns on somewhat fewer and simpler heads, and provides for more expert help than did the census of 1890. But the short time allowed for organizing the force, the refusal to place it under civil-service rules, and the failure to provide for a permanent census bureau show that the publication under review may yet do royal service as a tract to be circulated among members of Congress. C. H. Hastings.

NOTES AND ABSTRACTS.

Criminality in France in 1895.—The official statistics for 1895 show an important decrease in crime in France. For a number of years there has been a diminution of crime, coincident with the development of instruction and the progress of civilization. This diminution is not always apparent from the crude figures of statistics. But those who believe crime is increasing overlook the fact that population has increased, that the law now specifies as crime many things that formerly existed unchecked, that the police is more effective in bringing crime to light, and that public opinion is more sensitive. But in 1895 even the crude figures show the diminution. Thus, in 1894 there were 1451 indictments and 1704 accused of crimes against persons, and 1402 indictments and 2271 accused of crimes against property, while in 1895 there were only 1302 indictments and 1562 accusations for crimes against persons, and 1124 indictments and 1991 accusations for crimes against property. Up to 1892 indictments for crimes against property exceeded those for crimes against persons, while the reverse was the case in 1893, 1894, 1895. The total number of indictments for crimes against persons and property from 1886 to 1895 was successively: 3252, 3164, 3126, 2950, 2982, 2939, 2949, 3035, 2853, 2526. The total number of accused for the same years was: 4397, 4298, 4258, 4113, 4078, 4207, 4096, 4269, 3975, 3553.

The statistics for homicide, extending over fifty years (1845–95), also show a decrease, though not so marked. Assassination and murder together show an increase in 1895 over the years 1845, 1855, 1865, and 1875, but a diminution from the years 1885, 1893, and 1894; the increase of these crimes for the fifty years is proportionally more than the increase of population. But there is a decrease in the number of cases of poisoning and of parricide during the same period, which compensates for the increase of murder and assassination, so that the proportion of homicides to the total population was, in 1895, 1.30 per 100,000 inhabitants, as against 1.50 per 100,000 in 1845, and 1.47 in 1893. This proportion places France below England (0.48) and Germany (0.85), but in advance of Belgium (2.41), Spain (4.17), Italy (6.45), and the United States (11 to 12).

Homicide is most frequent in Corsica (22 per 100,000) and in the southeastern departments, where the passionate Italian element is strong. Then follows the department of the Seine, including Paris (2.44). The smallest proportion is found in the Jura, the most advanced department from the cultural point of view (0.29). No rule is apparent in the distribution of homicides: industrial and rural, northern and southern, eastern and western departments are mingled in confusion in the classification. Yet, aside from the southeastern districts and Paris, homicides are most numerous in the rural departments.

With respect to sex, women commit 15 per cent. of the homicides in France, as against 21 per cent. in England, and 5 per cent. in the United States. If infanticide is included, the proportion rises to 37 per cent.

The number of those accused of rape against adults decreased between the years 1875 and 1895 from 186 to 87, and against children, from 831 to 519. The rural departments show the greatest number of assaults upon children.

The number of indictments for theft decreased from 1238 in 1875 to 975 in 1890 and 707 in 1895. Prosecutions for arson have decreased regularly for many years, the record for the five years ending with 1895 being 215, 196, 190, 168, 157.

Until 1894 there had been a constant and rapid increase of crime among minors from sixteen to twenty-one years of age. But in 1895 there was a sudden fall—30,763, as against 32,317 in 1894. This improvement is especially shown with reference to theft.

This decrease in criminality is the more striking as it coincides with a general current of indulgence indicated by the correctional prosecutions of 1895, as compared with those of 1894. There were condemned :

	1894	1895
To imprisonment for more than a year - - - -	4,032	3,795
" " " a year or less - - - -	133,751	122,615
" fines - - - - - - - - -	93,718	94,824
Acquitted - - - - - - - - -	12,398	11,798
Granted suspension of sentence - - - - -	21,377	23,388

The number of accused recidivists decreased from 1590 in 1894 to 1380 in 1895. The number of recidivists (before trial) has also been reduced from 104,644 in 1894 to 99,434 in 1895.

The official report attributes this general amelioration to the Bérenger law. "The menace of punishment, in the present state of our penitentiary régime, seems to be more efficacious than its execution, at least with respect to first offenders." This explanation, however, is hardly convincing. It would seem to be due not so much to legislation as to the intellectual progress of the nation.—A. BÉRARD, "La criminalité en France en 1895," in *Archives d'Anthropologie criminelle*, January, 1898.

The Evolution of Punishment.—I. *The essence of punishment.*—Events produce impressions upon men in societies which call forth reactions. An immoral act arouses moral disapprobation, expressed, perhaps, merely by coolness on the part of the other members of society toward the offender. If the act is harmful to the society, it becomes a crime and provokes a stronger reaction, which is in a measure of the same kind as the offense. The immoral act and the crime on the one hand, and the blame and the punishment on the other hand, are essentially identical. In uncivilized communities the criminal nature of an act can only be determined by the nature of the reaction against it. In civilized communities a reaction is a punishment only when it is inscribed in the penal code of the state. The stigmatizing reaction becomes penal when the character of publicity, of exteriority, and of universality is attached to it. The purpose of the stigmatizing reaction and of the penal reaction is the infliction of an evil upon the individual who acts contrary to the interests of society. The social reaction is inherent in the nature of society, in the psychology of the masses, in the natural desire for vengeance which may be overcome by the great soul, but never by a considerable group of men who consider an anti-social act as bad and loathsome. There has been a flux and reflux of sentiment with respect to the social reaction against crime, at one time a sentimentalism in the administration of justice and an aversion to the death penalty appearing, followed by a current of social selection which considers the death penalty as an infallible means of purifying the atmosphere. The function of the penal reaction is still to indicate in a more precise manner the element of evil which ought to be inflicted upon the individual ; it ought also to increase this element to a much higher degree than is done by the stigmatizing reaction. This is forgotten by the theorists who have exclusively in view the correction or the cure of the delinquent, and who make no distinction between the reaction against crime and the reaction against mental alienation. The reaction against crime is, and always will be, "*malum passionis quod infligitur propter malum actionis.*"

II. *Punishment has not its origin in personal vengeance.*—The number of laws which restrict the struggle for life within the group and the crimes which result from it is in direct relation to the degree of civilization. In spite of restrictions imposed by society, it is always possible for individual forces to come into conflict. Society is indifferent to these conflicts so long as they do not attack *its* true interests. In a slight degree of development the number of crimes is inconsiderable : society, having few interests to protect, has few laws to make. In such a society he who has been injured at once satisfies his desire for vengeance. If he cannot reach his enemy, he takes vengeance upon any object whatever. The spirit of vengeance is not to destroy the offender, and thus to prevent further offense, but it is especially to satisfy wounded pride. It makes no difference whether the vengeance is just, or whether it exceeds the gravity of the aggression. Families sometimes assume the quarrels of one of their members, giving rise to hereditary vengeance.

The principle of retaliation is a modification of vengeance. "An eye for an eye," etc., expresses an attempt to equalize the offense and its repression. The fundamental idea is always the same, viz., that the individual is independent of the community and secures justice for himself.

Yet it is a mistake to think that anarchy reigns in such communities, or that crimes and punishments as such are unknown. Every such society punishes offenses which menace the *public safety*, although it is indifferent to injuries done to individuals. Thus murder may go unpunished except by private vengeance, while sorcery, which is a menace to all persons and things, is punished by death. It is only later that society interests itself in acts harmful to individuals. The first step is to take vengeance under its control: the injured person must satisfy certain conditions imposed by society before he is at liberty to avenge himself. But society goes farther than this: it *aids* the avenger. In case of resistance on the part of the offender, the whole community (as in Polynesia) assists the avenger in securing justice. *At this point* private vengeance becomes *equivalent* to punishment, or to a *social* reaction; the injured person becomes the executor of the punishment which is recognized and *guaranteed* by the state. Another step is taken when there are included in the things harmful to society actions which are not directly aimed against its existence. The murderer, for example, is delivered by the law into the hands of the victim's relatives. In the course of time the state monopolizes the judicial authority and establishes an organ of reaction, the executioner. The right of the offended family to vengeance then gradually disappears.

Private vengeance may also be supplanted by the payment of indemnity. This form of development is in relation with the development of private property, for here cupidity, a passion as strong as revenge, appears. Society is indifferent to these contracts, except that in some cases it makes the right of vengeance depend upon the non-payment of indemnity, and forbids the acceptance of a ransom where vengeance plays the rôle of an equivalent of punishment.

The amount of indemnity was originally determined by the people in assembly, but their action was gradually reduced to a minimum, the chief or some specially appointed persons acting in their stead. But in any case certain rules determined the amount. The need felt for a definitive establishment of this customary law gave rise to written "laws," like the Salic law, which consisted chiefly of a tariff of prices of human flesh. These systems of payment are not the penal law of the country; they are only an enumeration of *delicta privata* for which society has established compensations to the profit of the injured man. Behind these laws there exists the penal law, properly speaking, including the social reaction. The right of society to punish crime does not arise from a system of composition. Besides the composition, which has a juridico-private character, and which represents only in a slight degree a social reaction, we find in every society a distinct penal law which deals with crimes not remissible, crimes against the public welfare. Composition is only one of several means which arose to suppress personal vengeance.

The fact that composition has played a greater rôle in the settlement of conflicts than other means may be attributed, first, to the fact that it filled better than other means the two essential ends, viz., compensation for the wrong and the termination of the difference; and, second, to the fact that it was preceded by another institution which developed in an identical manner, viz., the purchase of women, a purchase which was originally nothing else than a money penalty inflicted upon the author of a rape.

III. *Social reaction.* — Social reaction may take three forms: (1) public, social, and instinctive vengeance; (2) paternal authority, giving rise to family and tribal jurisdiction; (3) sacerdotal jurisdiction.

1. Social vengeance. — The instinctive reaction of society against a violator of its laws has for a basis the same desire for vengeance that marks the individual reaction against wrong. Mass-vengeance is not limited to primitive societies, as lynch law in America testifies. A crowd is a collective individual. Social vengeance, like all vengeance, aims at the destruction of the offender. Exclusion from the community is equivalent to death in primitive societies. Death and exile are therefore two forms of social vengeance. The participation of the people in the execution of the death sentence (as among the Hebrews) is a reminiscence of public vengeance. Legally and

sociologically public vengeance differs from private vengeance, but psychologically they are identical. Public vengeance passes through the same phases of development as private vengeance. It is first a right, and then becomes obligatory. It passes through the phase of retaliation or compensation. Prevention of a repetition of an offense was accomplished by depriving the offender of the means of repeating it, as by cutting off the hand, etc.; or by public humiliation. Public vengeance, like private vengeance, is replaced by composition. Amends are paid to the society, or to its representative, the king. The state is the injured party. Yet there are some crimes which provoke an implacable reaction on the part of society.

2. Patriarchal punishments. — The most natural process of development makes an autocrat of the head of the family. Among savages the patriarch is the chief of the tribe; all the others are chiefly his children, grandchildren, and wives. Later appear adopted and conquered members. The father had the right to judge and to punish. Every transgression was an offense against him. Later this reaction, which was purely instinctive, was considered as the execution of the will of the gods. The administration of patriarchal justice was the beginning or model of the despotic juris-diction of the chief of the tribe. The supreme power becomes an unlimited authority. The punishments inflicted by a despot emanate from a social reaction. In the first phase of human development the chief is the executor of the general will; if he for-gets it, he is assassinated or exiled. In the modern state it is ultimately the general interest which decides. A people has not only the government that it deserves, but also the governmental form that the majority wishes to have.

3. The sacred factor. — At the epoch when the crime constitutes an offense against deity, the reaction contains a religious element, but does not lose its essence. The malefactor may be sacrificed by *any* member of the community; or the commu-nity as a whole may rise against him to testify before the gods to their displeasure in his act; or certain men may be set apart as the avengers, viz., the priests. Human sacrifice is identified with punishment by death. When a people has the custom of making periodic sacrifices, criminals are used for the purpose. Besides the priests, there exist everywhere secret societies, bound up with religious ceremonial, whose purpose is to execute the sacred reaction.

The reaction of the state is a natural consequence of the primitive reaction of the *people*. In the punishment inflicted by the state we see a social reaction, which long ago was transferred under some form to a monarch, who, in turn, gave over the execu-tion to judges. Then appeared the idea of the state, and the judicial attributes of the sovereign have largely disappeared. Though punishments are inflicted in his name, society itself is the source of the reaction. — Juliusz Macarewicz, " Évolution de la peine," in *Archives d'Anthropologie criminelle*, March, 1898.

Questions upon the Method of Sociology. — Every science ought to con-form to the rules upon which the existence of scientific thought depends in its essence; but besides there are special rules which are the consequence of the aim and subject-matter which characterize the science itself. The method of a science cannot be constructed *a priori;* it does not precede the science itself, it follows it. Method is always the result of a practice, of an experience of ways leading to incontestable conclusions. The four methods of empirical research formulated by John Stuart Mill are only abstract formularies of diverse inductive conclusions. The inductive sciences had long practiced these methods instinctively. Sociology must conform to these methodic rules. It will never become a science if social phenomena are of too com-plex a nature to observe and analyze them exactly. When the physical sciences began their conquests, many felt overwhelmed by the variety of phenomena and regarded with skepticism the possibility of reaching valid results. The varied and complex character of phenomena is never an obstacle for science; it can hinder only the application in practice of its results. The physicist cannot predict where each stone of a tumbling house will fall, the complexity of the determining forces being too great for observation and combination. He lets alone such too complex phenomena, limiting himself to observing elementary facts in which the forces are placed under determinable conditions.

Sociology must take the same course. Although the practical and useful end consists in the prediction of concrete social states, the immediate task of sociological science must be the investigation of elements out of which every social state is composed. The preliminary question which sociology must set before itself is what phenomena outside of the reach of existing sciences it is going to study. We can easily define what life in society is. It is the life which is formed by the common life of men. But, if the elements of society are individuals, there would seem to be no good reason for separating sociology from biology and psychology. This consequence cannot be avoided by saying that society is not the simple sum of its individual members. The developed organism is also not the simple sum of its cells. Nevertheless no one wishes to regard the theory of the developed organism as an independent science alongside of the science of the cells. We cannot see the reasons which will establish sociology as an independent science alongside of biology and psychology, if the individual is the element of society.

Psychology explains to us the formation of social feelings in the individual. When we foresee the actions of a man, his political opinions, his moral ideas, etc., we are only psychologists. But can the psychologist foresee anything of the actions of a people? We do not believe it. The psychology of the people is a new science; it is sociology. The conditions of the victory of an idea, or of a tendency, are not the same for societies as for the individual. The individual becomes a member of society and participates in its life by bio-psychological processes; but the conditions of the development of society are rather its preceding states than the psychological dispositions of individuals. As biology is independent in respect to chemistry, because it presents the phenomena of life in their dependence upon the antecedent states of the organism, so sociology will be independent in respect to psychology and biology. It is independent as over against them in so far as it examines, not human actions which are explained by the life in common, but collective human actions which are explained by preceding collectivity. The origin of society, then, is not a problem of sociology, but of biology; the sociological problem will be the development of society.

History, in the widest sense, furnishes sociology its necessary materials. History does not become in itself sociology, because it does not give us general laws of all societies, but only the form of the special development of a single people. Comparative history aims, however, so much at the establishment of general laws that its differentiation from sociology will be superficial. While all sociologists make use of comparative history, some think that it suffices to solve all problems, and others say not. This divergence is, however, of a secondary importance. That the compilation and systematization of materials does not suffice, goes without saying. Analysis of facts has never founded a science. The synthesis, the hypothesis, is indispensable. Comparative history gives the materials which suggest ideas to the ingenious mind. We find the method of our science in the analysis of complex societies, for the purpose of discovering the small elementary societies of which they are composed. The question of sociology in itself is: Through what causes do these groups become more and more organized and differentiated? Sociology is composed of three sorts of investigations: (1) the analysis of societies in order to discover the small elementary social groups; (2) the study of the ideas which act as motives of the individual in entering and remaining in the group; (3) the study of the laws and forces which determine the organization, evolution, and differentiation of these groups.— C. N. STARCKE, "Quelques questions sur la méthode de la sociologie," in *Revue internationale de sociologie*, January, 1899.

The Individual and Society.— Men do not enter into society (*Gemeinschaft*) through the fact that they live in neighborhood with one another, nor through the fact that their bodies touch each other. In the external world alone there is no bond which could unite them. Were men bound into bundles, they would be merely bundles of men, not societies. For society there is required a relationship of internal worlds to one another. But the simple, mutual knowledge of inner life is not yet community of life, not even if mutual sympathy is added. If, however, through mutual knowledge of their feelings there arises also the effort mutually to influence them, then there is at once either enmity or sociality (*Gemeinschaft*) — enmity in so far as their feelings are in conflict, and so call forth the endeavor to counteract each other; sociality in so far as their feelings agree and call forth effort toward a mutual furtherance. But in order to call forth such a mutual furtherance, knowledge of the agreement of feelings does not suffice; there must still enter the insight that such mutual furtherance of feelings can take place through external actions. So long as the common coöperation is left to chance or instinct, so long there are no common ends and no society in the human sense. Common purpose must yet be added, and this can proceed only from common insight into the advantageousness of coöperation. In other words, mutually recognized and pursued ends make a human society out of the animal world.

If a narrower society becomes a part of a wider society (voluntarily or through force), some ends (*Ziele*) must remain to the narrower society, otherwise it ceases to be a society and is entirely swallowed up in the wider society. Only in so far as every society possesses its own ends can it be a society distinct from others.

There is no entity, society, which possesses its own ideas, feelings, or will, or leads an independent life over and above its individuals; society has no separate body. It is not a visible but an ideal community. For this reason it can have no ends apart from the ends of its individuals. By this I do not mean to deny that the human organism and society can be placed in justifiable analogy. But this view is very different from that which ascribes to society a soul which is superior to individuals, guides and governs them, has and pursues its own ends. The existence of such a soul not only can never be established, it even contradicts the analogy between the human body and the state or the nation. No physiologist explains the functions of the body from a soul guiding and moving it; from his standpoint he dare not assume such a soul as the ground of explanation, for the object of his observation is only the body itself, and his ideal must be to derive the function of the body from the function of its cells. For him the brain cells are what set the body in motion, guide it and lead it to definite ends. So, too, what leads a nation is not a soul, but individuals.

Society as such not only cannot think, feel, will, it also cannot act, for it possesses no body of its own. Every expression of a common thought can only occur individually. No single action can be executed by a society, but only a *system* or *sum* of actions. In the first case different actions of individuals harmonize in a common end; in the second case all the actions are of the same sort, and the result is only a sum of the results of the single actions.

No society lives with agreement among all its members; every society hides oppositions within itself, without which it could not come to a consciousness nor to a further development of itself. If every member of a society were in exact agreement with all the other members, such a society would be automatic. A society which shows no individual varieties would also almost entirely lose its capacity for adaptation to new circumstances. A species which shows no varieties would be changed through external circumstances much more slowly and with more difficulty than a variable species. The case is the same with human societies: the more numerous the oppositions among their members, the easier they are able to adapt themselves to new circumstances, if the oppositions are not so great as to make impossible common thinking, willing, and acting.

Because society is no independent entity, it can experience no welfare of its own. Its welfare must be sought in the welfare of the individual. The general welfare cannot be separated from the welfare of individuals, but nevertheless is not identical with it, because well-being cannot be distributed, but only the means to well-being.— RICHARD VON SCHUBERT-SOLDERN, "Individuum und Gemeinschaft," in *Zeitschrift für die gesamte Staatswissenschaft*, I, 1899.

Among Women.—The number of men in France belonging to societies for mutual aid number 1,142,000; of women, only 418,000. One reason for this disproportion is that the small salaries of women do not permit them to add to their expenses that of the payment of dues. Societies for mutual aid are divided by law into three groups: (1) those recognized to be of public utility, comprising but a small number; (2) those whose statutes are submitted to the minister of the interior; (3) those authorized by the local prefect of police. I have to do in this article only with the second class. There are 5,326 such societies for men, 2,143 for men and women, and 227 for women only. Their expenses are of two sorts: (1) those imposed upon them by their statutes, *e. g.*, medical expenses, indemnity in case of sickness, funeral expenses; (2) optional expenses which are occasioned by certain other advantages offered by some societies. The assessments of the members do not pay the expenses of these societies; they are all supported in part by charity. I will treat in detail three typical societies, composed chiefly of women engaged in work connected with dressmaking and the toilet. There are many difficulties in such a life for a young girl of eighteen recently arrived from the country and without friends. Such girls often pass gradually into prostitution, and end in the street or in the hospital. I will first speak of the *Parisienne.* It demands of its members a franc and a half monthly. It excludes from its membership those suffering from chronic diseases. To married women, who, in sickness, are taken care of at home, it pays a franc a day. In case of child-birth it pays a franc a day for twenty days. Unmarried members are cared for at the house of the Sisters of Marie Auxiliatrice, where many of the members live permanently for forty francs per month. A savings department has recently been created. The amount deposited is not at the disposition of the depositor, but is returned only in case of marriage, establishment of a household, or business of one's own, or of entry into religion. After twenty years it pays an annuity.

The *Courturière* pays every member who gives birth to a child fifty francs on condition that she does no work for a month, and twenty-five francs more if she nurses the child herself. The *Mutualité maternelle* does the same. It has reduced the infant death-rate among its members 10 per cent. It used to be as high as 35 or 40 per cent. It makes no distinction between married women and unmarried women who give birth to a child; only about 5 per cent. are unmarried. Women already pregnant are admitted, but receive a smaller benefit. The membership of these three societies is about 3,200. There are no other societies for mutual aid for women at Paris, at least in the ranks of laboring women, properly so called. In the industries above spoken of alone there are 303,000 women employed. It can therefore be seen how small a proportion of the working people take advantage of the benefits of mutuality. This is not due wholly to the smallness of women's salary. Some leave the society because, when out of work, it could not find them a new place on the moment; another because a bottle of soda-water was not given her daily; another because her comrade was not given a pair of glasses, etc. Many having been well for a year or two trust that they never will be sick.

There is also a society for loaning money to persons temporarily in need of it. Loans are limited to six months, and are proportional to the salary of the borrower. There is another way to make societies of mutual aid appeal to young women, that of affording a place of meeting where they can stay Sundays and evenings. To associate charity with mutual aid is a fruitful idea. Without charity mutuality among women could not live.—HAUSSONVILLE, *Revue des deux Mondes,* December 1, 1898.

The Telephone Tangle and the Way to Untie It.— In a comparatively poor state like Norway or Switzerland it is possible to speak upon the telephone from almost any farmhouse or hotel to almost any other farmhouse or hotel in the country. In England it is only with difficulty and delay that it is possible for a subscriber to telephone from one principal town to another. I propose to show how, with great profit to the government, a thoroughly efficient service can be established over the United Kingdom. I propose to show (1) that it is impossible to have the best service over the whole of the United Kingdom, unless it is entirely in one hand and under one control; (2) that, after acquiring the existing system at a fair price, it will prove an enormously remunerative enterprise. Under the present system, when telephoning from one city to another, it is impossible to find who is responsible for delays. A subscriber in London who constantly reports any unreasonable delay can generally connect with any other subscriber in London in fifty seconds. Any subscriber in the United Kingdom who cannot communicate with any other subscriber in the same area in three or, at the outside, five minutes has a grievance that ought to be inquired into. Mr. Preece, of the general post-office, has committed himself to the deliberate statement, "there is no reason why the time occupied in trunk working should be more than that occupied in local telephoning." We know that town service is very remunerative, and that every wide-awake corporation (Glasgow, the London county council, etc.) is most anxious to get hold of such a gold mine. The trunk-line service is a monopoly that would have been eagerly seized upon in a dozen places subject to any possible conditions as to a speedy service. I do not believe that the telegraph service will lose anything at all by the taking over of the telephones, for a written message has its own very great advantages in all business transactions. It is probable that the capital of the National Telephone Company has been watered 400 per cent. If the government purchased on the lines indicated, borrowing the money at 2½ per cent. interest, it would make an annual profit of £178,612. It will make a further great profit on this transaction because it has very valuable rights in regard to wayleaves which the National Telephone Company has not. Personally, however, I would prefer to deal with a public company which can be talked to at its half-yearly meetings, and sued in the courts, rather than with a government department which is amenable neither to public opinion nor to the law of the land. At present rates money laid out in the future will pay 20 per cent. A message could be sent from any call office for 3d.— A. H. HATHE, *Fortnightly Review*, December, 1898.

Determinism and Responsibility: A Criticism of M. Hamon.—After having criticised M. Hamon I will now briefly set forth my own ideas. I agree with him that the present system of criminal jurisprudence is altogether bad. The impossibility of finding a legal or scientific criterion for responsibility, individual variations of the notion of responsibility, etc., expose the judge to grave errors. According to my opinion the judge and jury ought to acquit or condemn, and apply the penalties according to the law, without hearing physicians on the mental condition of the prisoner. The hearing of medical specialists in court is harmful; it troubles the minds of judge and jury, and makes them acquit here and condemn there according to the ideas of the medical specialist, or the way he expresses them. The impression of the moment, and not justice, brings the verdict. Often the prisoner is judged irresponsible and returned to society; he will be so much the more dangerous because the legal decision regarding his mental condition renders him free to recommence his lawlessness.

Only when the work of the magistrate is finished ought that of the medical specialist to begin. The condemned man can then be examined at leisure without his being excited, without the influence of a bad and mobile public opinion, and without the disturbing influence of pseudo-science. Then the physicians should decide whether he should be sent to prison or the hospital. *Separate the rôle of the magistrate and the physician, that is my thesis.*—DR. LAUPTS, *L'Humanité nouvelle*, December, 1898.

BIBLIOGRAPHY.

May—for March-April.

CONDUCTED BY C. H. HASTINGS.

NEW BOOKS AND NOTICES OF BOOKS REVIEWED.

Explanation. *Titles not starred* represent new publications announced in the standard publishers' lists since the last issue of the bibliography. A *star prefixed* to a title indicates that it was taken from a review of the work in the periodical cited after the title. It may or may not be a new announcement. The *arithmetical signs* following the citation to a review indicate the tenor of the review: X, uncertain ; +, favorable ; —, unfavorable ; +—, favorable, but with reservations ; — +, unfavorable, but with commendation ; + +, very favorable ; — — very unfavorable ; + + —, very favorable, but with reservations ; — — +, very unfavorable, but with commendation. Absence of any sign indicates that review has not been read. The *publication date* when not given is understood to be the current year. *Prices quoted* are usually for volumes bound in cloth in the case of American and English books, in paper in the case of all others. *New editions, translations,* and *new periodicals* are bracketed.

Abbreviations. *See* at end of Bibliography.

N. B.—For Index to Bibliography see general Index to this volume.

NEW BOOKS.

1. Anthropology, Ethnology.

Hagen, B, Anthropologischer Atlas östasiatischer & melanesischer Völker. Mit Aufnahmeprotokollen, Messungstabellen u. e. Atlas v. 101 Taf. . . . Wiesbaden, C. W. Kriedel. 113 pp. 4to. M. 100.

2. Biology, Evolution, Science.

Cornish, C. J. Animals of to-day: their life & conversation. N. Y., New Amsterdam Bk. Co. 8vo. $1.25.

3. Charities.

*Boston.—Associated Charities. Directory of the charitable & beneficent organizations of Boston. . . . Bo., Damrell & Upham. 475 pp. 12mo. $1. (ChR., Mr. +)
*Brown, M, W. Development of thrift. N. Y., Macmillan Co. 222 pp. 16mo. $1. (Literature, Mr. 24 — +)
Charitas-Schriften. 1. Hft. Das deutsche Armenrecht. . . . F., Geschäftstelle des Charitasverbandes f. das kathol. Deutschland. 91 pp. 8vo. M. o.80.
Oesterreich's Wohlfahrts-Einrichtungen, 1848-98. Festschrift zu Ehren des 50-jähr. Regierungs-Jubiläums . . . . Kaisers Franz Joseph I. Hrsg. v. der Commission der öster. Wohlfahrtsausstellg. (In 4 Bdn.) 1. Armenpflege u. Wohlthätigkeit in Oesterreich, red. v. Ernst Mischler. Wien, M. Perles. 479 pp. 8vo. Subskr.-Pr. (1-4) M. 40.
Richmond, Mary E. Friendly visiting among the poor: a handbook for charity workers. N. Y., Macmillan Co., 1899. 225 pp. 16mo. $1. (ChR., Mr. — + +)
Verein f. Armenpflege u. Wohlthätigkeit. Schriften. 40. Hft. Lp., Duncker & Humblot. 143 pp. 8vo. M. 3.60.

4. Cities.

Alongi, G. Manuale di polizia scientifica, ad uso di medici, periti, avvocati, magistrati . . . . studenti . . . . Milano, tip. Sonzogno, 1898. 359 pp. 8vo. L. 4.

Bemis, E. W. Municipal monopolies: a collection of papers by Amer. economists & specialists. N. Y., T. Y. Crowell. 691 pp. 12mo. $2. (Library of economics & politics, no. 16.)
Bruns, F. Verfassungsgeschichte des Lübeckischen Freistaates, 1848-98. Lübeck, Lubcke & Hartmann. 185 pp. 4to. M. 4.
Cole, W. H. Light railways at home & abroad. L., Griffin, 352 pp. 8vo. 16s.
County councils, municipal corporations, urban district, rural district, & parish councils companion, magisterial directory, poor law authorities & local govt. year-book for 1899, 23d year. 1220 pp. 8vo. 10s. 6d.
Dejean, A. Etude économique et juridique sur les chemins de fer d'intérêt local (thèse). P., libr. Larose. 190 pp. 8vo.
Eheberg, Th. Verfassungs-, Verwaltungs- u. Wirthschaftsgeschichte der Stadt Strassburg bis 1681. Hrsg. m. Unterstützg. der Stadtverwaltg. 1. Bd. Urkunden u. Akten. Strassburg, J. H. E. Heitz. 771 pp. 8vo. M. 15.
Leslie's history of Greater New York. N. Y., Arbell Pub. Co. 1500 pp. il. 4to. $25.
Municipal year-book of the United Kingdom for 1899, ed. by Robert Donald. 494 pp. 8vo. 2s. 6d.
Norden, Hans. Wiens Gegenwart u. Zukunft. Breslau, Honsch & Tiesler. 44 pp. 8vo. M. x.
Shadwell, A. London water supply. L., Longmans, Green & Co. 282 pp. 8vo. 5s.
Sisley, R. The London water supply: a retrospect & a survey. 204 pp. 4to. 21s.

5. Criminology and Penology.

Annecchino, Raimondo. La stampa e la psicosi suicida e criminale. Roma, fratelli Capaccini, 1898. 32 pp. 16mo. L. 0.30.
Chonez, M. De la réhabilitation des condamnés en matière criminelle, correctionnelle et disciplinaire (thèse). P., Impr. d'ouvriers sourde-muets, 1898. 192 pp. 8vo.
Corsi, Car. Nel mondo del delitto: divagazioni di psicologia criminale. Firenze, Giovanni Fratani. 32 pp, 8vo.
Perrieri, Lino. Delinquenti che scrivono: studio di psicologia criminale. Como, Vittorio Omarini. 342 pp. 8vo. L. 4.

Fleury, M. de. L'âme du criminel. P., F. Alcan. 192.pp. 18mo.
[Gross, Hanns. Handbuch f. Untersuchungsrichter als System der Kriminalistik. 3. Aufl. 2. Hälfte. Graz, Leuschner & Lubensky. Pp. 401–813. 8vo. M. 6.
Korn. A. Ist die Deportation unter den heutigen Verhältnissen als Strafmittel praktisch verwendbar? (Veröffentlichung der Holtzendorf Stiftg.) B., J. Guttentag. 259 pp. 8vo. M. 4.50.
Laschi, Rod. La delinquenza bancaria nella sociologia criminale, nella storia e nel diritto. Torino, fratelli Bocca. 180 pp. L. 3.

6. Education.

Kant on education (Ueber Pädagogik), tr. by Annette Churton. L., Kegan Paul. 146 pp. 8vo.
Luchaire, A. L'Université de Paris sous Philippe Auguste. P., Chevalier-Marescq & Cie. 59 pp. 8vo. f. 2. (Bibliothèque internat. de l'enseignement supérieur.)
McMurry, C A. Elements of general method. Bloomington, Ill., Public School Pub. Co., 1898. 12mo. $0.75.
Mark, H. T. Outline of hist. of educational theories in England. L., Swan Sonnenschein. 152 pp. 8vo. 3s.
Page, D. P. Theory & practice of teaching; or, motives & methods of good school keeping, ed. by E. C. Branson. N. Y., Amer. Bk. Co. 382 pp. 12mo. $1.
Russell, J. E. German higher schools: the history, organization, & methods of secondary education in Germany. N. Y., Longmans, Green & Co. 455 pp. 12mo. $2.25.
Thomas, Grace Power. Where to educate, 1898-99; a guide to the best private schools, higher institutions of learning, etc., in the U. S. Bo., Brown & Co., 1898. 382 pp. 8vo. $3.
[Zeitschrift f. pädagogische Psychologie. Hrsg. v. F. Kemsies. 1. Jahrg. 1899. 6 Hfte. (1. Hft. 56 pp.) B., H. Walther. M. 8.]

7. Ethics, Philosophy, Psychology.

Gomme, Alice Bertha, ed. Traditional games of England, Scotland, & Ireland, with tunes, singing rhymes & methods of playing according to the variants extant & recorded in different parts of the kingdom. In 2 v. V. 2. N. Y., imported by C. Scribner's Sons. $5.
Groos, Karl. Die Spiele der Menschen. Jena, G. Fischer. 538 pp. 8vo. M. 10.
Heinrich, W. Zur Prinzipienfrage der Psychologie. Zürich, E. Speidel. 74 pp. 8vo. M. 1.40.
Lipps, T. Die ethischen Grundfragen. 10 Vorträge. Hamburg, L. Voss. 308 pp. 8vo. M. 5.
Spielberg, Otto. Die Moral der freien Mannesart. Zürich, E. Speidel. 316 pp. 12mo. M. 3.20.
Weir, Jr. The dawn of reason; or, mental traits in the lower animals. N. Y., Macmillan Co. 234 pp. 16mo. $1.25.

8. Family.

Deck, L. Syphilis et réglementation de la prostitution en Angleterre et aux Indies (étude de statistique médicale 1866–96) (thèse). P., libr. Carré et Naud. 94 pp. 8vo.
Gunther, C. Das Recht der Frau auf Arbeit, e. soziolog. Betrachtg. B., G. Wattenbach. 14 pp. 8vo. M. 1.
Heinzen. K. The rights of women & the sexual relations. . . . C., C. H. Kerr & Co. 385 pp. 18mo. $0.50. (Library of progress, No. 29.)
Schrank, J. Die amtlichen Vorschriften betr. die Prostitution in Wien, in ihrer administrativen

sanitären u. strafgerichtlichen Anwendung. Wien, J. Safar. 126 pp. 8vo. M. 3.60.

9. Finance, Taxation.

Arendt, Otto. Die Ursache der Silberentwerthung. An die rechtlich Denkenden aller Parteien. . . . B., H. Walther. 215 pp. 8vo. M. 2.
Austria – K. k. Finanz-Ministerium. Mitteilungen. 4. Jahrg. 4. Hft. Wien, Hof- u. Staatsdruckerei. Pp. 716–1031 8vo. M. 3.
Austria — K. k. Finanz-Ministerium. Tabellen zur Währungs-Statistik. 2. Ausg. 9. Hft. Nachtrag zum 6. Abschnitt. Industrielle Verwendig. 1895. 1896 u. 1897. Pp. 657–770. 2do. Wien, Hof- u. Staatsdruckerei. M. 1.
France—Ministère des finances. Compte définitif des dépenses pour l'exercice 1897. Session de 1899. 209 pp. 4to. P., Impr. nationale.
Gondinet, P. Les impôts sur les valeurs mobilières au point de vue économique et fiscal (thèse). P., A. Rousseau. 175 pp. 8vo.
Italy—Annuario dei ministeri delle finanze e del tesoro del regno d'Italia, anno 37 (1898–9). Roma, tip. Adelaide Ked. Pateras, 1898. 756 pp. 8vo.
Noyes, A. D., comp. The Evening Post's handbook of Amer. finance, comprising high & low records in banking returns, treasury exhibits & trade statistics, with comparative tables. N.Y., Evening Post Pub. Co. 27 pp. 16mo. $0.10.
Steinacker, Edm. Zur Börsenreform in Ungarn. Auszug aus den stenog. Protokollen der vom königl. ungar. Handelsministerium veranstalteten Enquête u. Materialiensammlg. zu deren Vorbereitg. Wien, A. Holder. 287 pp. 8vo. M. 5.40.
Viti de Marco, A de. Saggi di economia e finanza. Roma, Giornali degli economisti, 1898. 188 pp. 8vo. L. 4.

10. History.

Adams, G. B. European history: an outline of its development. N. Y., Macmillan Co., 1899. 577 pp. 8vo. $1.40.
Ali, Ameer Syed. Short hist. of the Saracens: rise & decline of Saracenic power & economic, social & intellectual development of the Arab nation from earliest times to destruction of Bagdad & expulsion of the Moors from Spain. 662 pp. 8vo. 7s. 6d.
Amico, Carl. Die Republik San Marino. Eine Studie. Augsburg, M. Rieger. 159 pp. 8vo. M. 1.50.
Arbuthnot, A. J. Lord Clive: the foundation of British rule in India. N. Y., Longmans, Green & Co. 318 pp. 12mo. $1.50. (Builders of greater Britain ser., no. 5.)
Armée (l') à travers les âges. Conférences faites en 1898, à l'Ecole spéciale militaire de Saint-Cyr. par MM. Lavisse, Guiraud, Langlois, Gebhart, Lehugeur, Sorel, Vandal et Boutroux. P., libr. Chapelot & Cie. 283 pp. 18mo.
Belloc, H. Danton: a study. N. Y., C. Scribner's Sons. 440 pp. 8vo. $2.50.
Bennett, E. N. Downfall of the dervishes. N. Y., New Amsterdam Book Co. 8vo. $1.40.
Bluddemann, M. Der Krieg um Cuba. Nach zuverläss. Quellen dargestellt. Mit zahlreichen Abbildgn. 2. Lfg. B., E. S. Mittler & Sohn. Pp. 81–258. M. 3.40.
Bonsal, Stephen. The fight for Santiago: the story of the soldier in the Cuban campaign from Tampa to its surrender. N. Y., Doubleday & McClure Co. 543 pp. 8vo. $2.50.
*Burleigh, K. Karthoum campaign, 1898, or reconquest of the Soudan. L., Chapman & Hall. 352 pp. 8vo. 12s. (Literature, Mr. 24 + —)

Chaillu, P. B du. Land of the midnight sun: summer & winter journeys through Sweden, Norway, Lapland, and northern Finland. Description of inner life of the people, manners, customs, primitive antiquities. L., Newness. 766 pp. 8vo.

[Cuday, Eug. Die Geschichte der Ungarn. 2. Aufl. übers. v. M. Darvai. 2 Bde. B., A. Bodenburg. 509 u. 575 pp. 8vo. M. 15.]

Dahn, F. Die Könige der Germanen. Das Wesen des ältesten Königthums der german. Stamme u. seine Geschichte bis zur Auflösg. des karoling. Reiches. 8. Bd. Die Frauen unter den Karolingen. 2. Abth. Lp., Breitkopf & Hartel. 266 pp. 8vo. M. 8.

Fischer, D. Italien u. die Italiener am Schlusse des 19. Jahrh. . . . B., J. Springer. 467 pp. 8vo. M. 9.

Fiske, A. K. The West Indies. N. Y., G. P. Putnam's Sons. 414 pp. 8vo. $1.50. (Story of the nations ser.)

Gériolles, A de. Choses des Philippines. P., libr. Taffin-Lefort. 155 pp. 8vo.

Guénin, E. La nouvelle France. P., libr. Fourneau, 1898. 475 pp. 18mo. f. 3.50. (Histoire de la colonisation française.)

Hawthorne, Julian. History of the United States from the landing of Columbus to the signing of the peace protocol with Spain. N. Y., Péter Fenelon Collier. 3 v. 8vo. $5.

Hill, G. B. Gordon in central Africa, 1874-79, from original letters & documents. N. Y., Macmillan Co. 456 pp. 8vo. $1.75.

History of South America from its discovery to the present time, by an American. Tr. from the Spanish by A. D. Jones. L., Swan Sonnenschein. 354 pp. 8vo. 10s. 6d.

Hunter, W. W. History of British India. V. 1. To the overthrow of the English in the Spice archipelago. N. Y., Longmans, Green & Co. 475 pp. 8vo. $5.

*Inama-Sternigg, K. T, Deutsche Wirthschaftsgeschichte in den letzten Jahrhunderten des Mittelalters. 1. Tl. Lp., Duncker & Humblot. 455 pp. 8vo. M. 12. (LC., Mr. 4)

Johnston, H. H. A. History of the colonization of Africa by alien races. N. Y., Macmillan Co. 319 pp. 12mo. $1.50. (Cambridge hist. ser.)

King, W. N. The story of the war of 1898, with introds. by O. O. Howard & Robley D. Evans. N. Y., P. F. Collier. il. ports. 2do. $15.

La Gorce, P. de. Histoire du second empire. T. 4. P., Plon, Nourrit & Cie. 617 pp. 8vo.

*Lamprecht, Karl. Die historische Methode des Herrn v. Below. Eine Kritik. B., R. Gaertner. 50 pp. 8vo. M. 1. (LC., F, 25)

McCarthy, Justin. Story of the people of England in the 19th century. Pt. 1, 1800-1835. N. Y., G. P. Putnam's Sons. 12mo. $1.50. (Story of the nations ser., no. 57.)

Monod, G. Études critiques sur les sources de l'histoire carolingienne. 1e partie. Introduction. . . . Des origines à 829. P., libr. Bouillon. 179 pp. 8vo.

Noble, F. P. The redemption of Africa: a story of civilization, with bibliography & statistical tables. N. Y., F. H. Revell Co. 2 v. (450 & 450 pp.) 8vo. $4.

Peck, C. H. The Jacksonian epoch. N. Y., Harper. 472 pp. 8vo. $2.50.

Publikationen aus den k. preussischen Staatsarchiven. Veranlasst u. unterstützt durch die k. Archivverwaltg. 73. Bd. Lp., S. Hirzel. M. 20.

Russell, H. B., Proctor, Readfield, & Thurston, J. M. An illustrated history of our war with Spain. . . . Hartford, A. D. Worthington & Co. 780 pp., il., maps. 8vo. $3.25.

Saltus, Edgar. Battles of all nations from the earliest times to the present day. N. Y., P. F. Collier. 2 v. 12mo. $3.

Warner, G. T. Landmarks of English industrial history. L., Blackie. 376 pp. 8vo. 5s.

Whitman, S., & M'Ilrath, J. R. Austria. N. Y., G. P. Putnam's Sons. 428 pp. 8vo. $1.50.

Wolff, Emil. Grundriss der preussisch-deutschen socialpolitischen u. Volkswirtschafts-Geschichte (1640-1898). B., Weidmann. 232 pp. 8vo. M. 3.60.

11. International Law.

Chomette, H. De l'amnestie, specialement dans ses effets au point de vue pénal et au point de vue civil (thèse). P., A. Rousseau (1898). 162 pp. 8vo.

Coste, A. De l'indemnité d'expropriation (thèse). P., libr. Pédone. 180 pp. 8vo.

Kauffmann, W. Die Rechtskraft des internationalen Rechtes u. das Verhältnis der Staatsgesetzgebung u. der Staatsorgane zu demselben. Stuttgart, F. Enke. 126 pp. 8vo. M. 4.

Manlion, P. Des mesures destinées à prévenir et à réprimer les collisions en mer . . . (thèse). Rennes, impr. Simon. 191 pp. 8vo.

12. Labor.

Boueil, F. La communauté des marchands de bois à œuvre (1415-1898), ses origines, ses développements, son état actuel. P., 38 quai de la Râpée (siège de la communauté). 151 pp. 8vo.

Bouloc, E. A propos du procès de Toulouse. Les grèves et le droit commun . . . P., Guillaumin & Cie. 96 pp. 8vo. f. 1.50.

Brentano, L. Schutz der Arbeitswilligen. (See Volkswirthschaftliche in 13.)

Children's labour question. Repr. from Daily News. L., Daily News office. 156 pp. 8vo. 6d.

Dufour, J. Étude historique sur les théories du droit au travail (thèse.) P., libr. Larose. 118 pp, 8vo.

Du Mesnil et Mangeot. Étude d'hygiène et d'économie sociale. Enquête sur les logements, professions, salaries et budgets . . . P., libr. Chaix. 168 pp. 8vo.

Great Britain—Labour Dept. Report . . . on trade unions in 1897; comparative statistics for 1882-96. L., Eyre & Spottiswoode. 8vo. 1s. 4½d.

Halstead, W. R. Christ in the industries. Cin., Curtis & Jennings.

Hitze, F. Die Arbeiterfrage u. die Bestrebungen zu ihrer Lösung. Nebst Anlage: Die Arbeiterfrage im Lichte der Statistik. B., Germania in Komm. 146 pp. 8vo. M. 2.

Italy—Legge concernente gli infortunati sul, lavoro, 1898. Torino, G. Sacerdote, 1898. 14 pp. 16mo. L. 0,10.

Kropotkin, P. A. Fields, factories & workshops . . . B., Houghton, Mifflin & Co. 8vo. $3.

Lohmann, F. Die amtliche Handelsstatistik Englands u. Frankreichs im 18. Jahrh. B., G. Reimer in Komm. 34 pp. 8vo. M. 2. (Aus Sitzungsber. d. preuss. Akad. d. Wiss.)

Zacher, R. Die Arbeiter-Versicherung im Auslande. 5. Hft.: Die Arbeiterversicherung in England. B., L. Simon. 99 pp. 8vo. M. 1.50.

13. Political Economy.

Beckmann, J. Was ist uns Geld? Eine Studie über die kapitalist. Wirtschaft der Gegenwart. Wien, Selbstverlag (VII., 2, Lerchenfelderstr. 15). M. 1.

Cohn, H. Die subjektive Natur des Werthes. B., J. Guttentag. 38 pp. 8vo. M. 1.

Conrad, J. Grundriss zum Studium der politischen Oekonomie. 3. Tl. Finanzwissenschaft. Jena, G. Fischer. 176 pp. 8vo. M. 3.50.

Loria, A. Economic foundations of society, tr. from 2d French ed. by L. M. Klashey. L., Swan Sonnenschein. 402 pp. 8vo. 3s. 6d.

Macfarlane, C. W. Value, price & distribution: an historical, critical & constructive study in economic theory . . . Phil., J. B. Lippincott Co., 1898. 300 pp. 8vo. $2.50.

Mallner, W. Wahrer Werth aller im Wiener Coursblatte notirten Lose f. d. J. 1899, berechnet zu den Coursen vom 28. IX. 1898. 16. Jahrg. Wien, Huber & Lahme. 24 pp. 8vo. M. 0.80.

Root, E. T. "The profit of the many": the biblical doctrine & ethics of wealth. N. Y., F. H. Revell. 321 pp. 12mo. $1.25.

Veblen, Thorstein. Theory of the leisure class: an economic study in the evolution of institutions. N. Y., Macmillan Co. 400 pp. 8vo. $2.

Virgilii, F., e Garibaldi, C. Introduzione alla economia matematica. Milano, Ulrico Hoepli. 210 pp. 16mo.

Volkswirthschaftliche Mitteilungen aus Ungarn. Red. v. J. Szterenyi. Jahrg. 1899. 4 Hfte. Wien, A. Holder. 349 pp. 8vo. M. 20.

Volkswirthschaftliche Zeitfragen. Vorträge u. Abhandlgn., hrsg. v. der volkswirthschaftl. Gesellschaft in Berlin. 159. Hft. 20. Jahrg. 7. Hft. Brentano, L. Der Schutz der Arbeitswilligen . . . B., L. Simon. 35 pp. 8vo. M. 1.

14. Political Science.

Bacou, A. De l'influence du fédéralisme sur l'institution des chambres hautes (thèse). Toulouse, libr. Rivière. 203 pp. 8vo.

Billiard, A. Politique et organisation coloniales (principes généraux). P., Giard & Brière. 300 pp. 8vo. f. 5.

Blanchard, G. Formation & constitution politique de l'Etat indépendant du Congo (thèse.) P., libr. Pedone. 399 pp. 8vo.

Blumbach, E. Der bürgerliche Stand in Russland, seine Rechte u. Pflichten. Riga, Ernst Plates. 64 pp. 8vo. M. 1.50.

Bradford, Gamiel. The lesson of a popular govt. N. Y., Macmillan Co. 2 v. (526 & 590 pp.) 8vo. $4.

Brunelli, Ign. Teorico della sovranita. Ferrara, Antonio Soati, 1898. 301 pp. 8vo.

Chenilliard, G. Les colonies anglaises. P., libr. Challamel. 415 pp. 8vo.

Debrett's House of Commons & the judicial bench, 1899, 33d year. L., Dean. 470 pp. 8vo. 7s. 6d.

Démaret, E. Organisation coloniale et fédération. Une fédération de la France et de ses colonies (thèse). P., impr. Noblet. 208 pp. 8vo.

Deutsche Kolonial-Gesellschaft. Verhandlungen. Berlin-Charlottenburg, 1898-99. 2. u. 3. Hft. B., D. Reimer. M. 0.60 u. 1.

Dod's Parliamentary companion (67th year). L., Whittaker. 408 pp. 32mo. 4s. 6d.

Entscheidungen des königl. preussischen Oberverwaltungsgerichts, hrsg. v. Freytag, Techow, Schultzenstein, Reichmann. 33. Bd. B., C. Heymann. 497 pp. 8vo. M. 7.

Fauran, R. De l'élection du président de la République (étude de législation comparée) (thèse). Toulouse, impr. Passeman & Alquier. 301 pp. 8vo.

Gorham, G. C. Life & public services of E. M. Stanton. Bo., Houghton, Mifflin & Co. 2 v. (456 & 502 pp.) 8vo. $6.

Guide annuaire illustré de la Cochinchine. P., au bureau de la Revue des colonies, 63 bvd. St. Michel. 688 pp. 8vo. M. 5.

Handbuch f. das Deutsche Reich auf d. J. 1899. Bearb. im Reichsamt des Innern. 24. Jahrg. B., C. Heymann. 570 pp. 8vo. M. 5.

Handbuch f. d. preussischen Haus der Abgeordneten. Ausg. Jan. 1899. L., B. M. Moser in Komm. 355 pp. 12mo. M. 4.50.

Hof- u. Staats-Handbuch der österreichisch-ungarischen Monarchie f. 1899. Wien, Hof- u. Staatsdruckerei. 1335 pp. 8vo. M. 10.

Jahrbuch d. k. u. k. auswärtigen Dienstes 1899, . . . 3. Jahrg. Wien, Hof- u. Staatsdruckerei. 460 pp. 8vo. M. 10.

[Jennings, G. H. Anecdotal hist. of British parliament for earliest period, with notices of men & examples of oratory. 4th ed. L., H. Cox. 734 pp. 8vo. 7s. 6d.]

Journal of the Society of comparative legislation, ed. by J. Macdonal & E. Manson. L., John Murray. 8vo. 5s.

MacCabe, J., & Darien, G. Can we disarm? L., Heinemann. 160 pp. 8vo. 2s. 6d.

Maitland, F. W. Canon law in England. N. Y., New Amsterdam Bk. Co., 1899. 8vo. $3.

Michon, L. L'initiative parlementaire et la réforme du travail législatif. P., Chevalier, Maresco & Cie. 352 pp. 8vo. f. 5.

Muirhead, J. A. Historical introduction to the private law of Rome. Ed. 2, rev. & ed. by H. Goudy. N. Y., Macmillan Co. 457 pp. 8vo. $5.

*Peel, Sir Robert. From his private papers, ed. for his trustees by C. S. Parker. 3 v. V. 2 & 3. (1300 pp.) 8vo. 32s. (Athenæum, F. 11++)

Pensavale, Fr. Evoluzione storica del concetto di stato nel periodico genetico . . . Catania, tip. C. Galàtola, 1898. 247 pp. 8vo. L. 6.

Politisches Jahrbuch der Schweizerischen Eidgenossenschaft. Hrsg. v. C. Hilty. 12. Jahrg. 1898. Bern, K. J. Wyss. 746 pp. 8vo. M. 9.

Prinz, J. Die Kolonie der Brüdergemeinde. Ein Beitrag zur Geschichte d. deut. Kolonien Südrusslands. Odessa, E. Berndt. 164 pp. 8vo. M. 4.

Prussia — Haus der Abgeord. 18. Legislatur-Periode. 5. Session. Uebersicht über die Geschäftsthätigkeit. B., M. Moser. 817, 339 u. 172 pp. M. 25.

Schiappoli, Dom. La politica ecclesiastica del conte di Cavour e la libera chiesa in libero stato: discorso inaugurale . . . Macerata, tip. Bianchini. 46 pp. 8vo.

Scrive, J. Expansion commerciale et coloniale. Mise en valeur des colonies. Rapports et notes. Lille, impr. Danel. 74 pp. 8vo.

Stead, W. T. United States of Europe on the eve of the Parliament of Peace. L., Review of Reviews office. 216 pp. 4to. 1s. (Review of Reviews annual.)

Untersuchungen zur deutschen Staats- u. Rechtsgeschichte, hrsg. v. Otto Gierke. 56. Hft. Halban, A. Das römische Recht in den germanischen Volksstaaten . . . Breslau, H. & H. Marcus. 312 pp. 8vo. M. 10.

Virchow, R. Die Bevölkerung der Philippinen. 2. Mitthlg. B., G. Reimer in Komm. 13 pp. 8vo. M. 0.50.

15. Religion, Churches.

Bruce, A. B. The epistle to the Hebrews; the first apology for Christianity: an exegetical study. N. Y., C. Scribner's Sons. 451 pp. 8vo. $2.50.

Controversies religieuses du temps présent, L'Américanisme; les religeuses enseignements; la démocratie chrétienne. . . . P., libr. Victorion. 112 pp. 18mo.

Elliott, Walter. Father Hecker, founder of the Paulists. . . . N. Y., Catholic Book Exchange. 444 pp. 12mo. $1.

Fairbairn, A. M. Catholicism, Roman & Angli-
can. N. Y., C. Scribner's Sons. 481 pp. 8vo.
$2.
Hale, E. E. Works. (In 10 v.) V. 2. In his
name & Christmas stories. B., Little, Brown
& Co. 12mo. $1.50.
Harcourt, W. V. Lawlessness in the national
church. L., Macmillan Co. 164 pp. 8vo. 1s.
Hodges, G. The battles of peace. N. Y., T.
Whittaker. 273 pp. 12mo. $1.
Orr, Ja. Neglected factors in the study of the early
progress of Christianity. N. Y., A. C. Armstrong & Son, 1899. 235 pp. 12mo. $1.50.
Raboisson, Abbé. Judith; la veracité du livre de
ce nom devant les documents cunéiformes et les
Histoires d'Hérodote. Rome, impr. Poly-
glotte de la s. c. de propaganza fide. 396 pp.
8vo. L. 12.
Richard, J. W. Philip Melanchthon, the Protestant
preceptor of Germany, 1497–1560. L., Putnam. 416 pp. 8vo. 6s. (Heroes of the Reformation.)
Smith, H. P. Critical & exegetical commentary
on the books of Samuel. N. Y., C. Scribner's
Sons. 421 pp. 8vo. $3. (International crit-
ical commentary.)
Tiele, C. P. Elements of the science of religion,
being the Gifford lectures delivered before the
Univ. of Edinburgh in 1896. V. 2. Ontological.
N. Y., imp. by C. Scribner's Sons. 286 pp.
12mo. $2.
Ulhorn, F. Der gegenwärtige Zustand der evangel.
Kirche u. ihre Ausgestaltung f. die Zukunft.
Vortrag. Hameln, Th. Fuendeling. 32 pp.
8vo. M. 0.50.

16. Sanitary and Domestic Science.

Baratier, A. Hygiène générale. L'école de village au point de vue de l'hygiène publique et
privée. P., impr. Maurin. 40 pp. 8vo.
Le Bèle, J. L'hygiène pratique et la vie chrétienne. Notions élémentaires sur les moyens
de conserver la santé du corps et de l'âme . . . .
2e ed. P., libr. Retaux. 760 pp. 18mo.
Nursing profession: how & where to train. Particulars of nurse training schools in the United
Kingdom & abroad, & outline of principal
laws affecting nurses, etc., ed. by Sir H. Burdett. L., Scientific Press 374 pp. 8vo.

17. Socialism.

Fischer, Ernst. Im Kampfm. den Führern der So-
zialdemokratie. Ein offenes Wort. B., H.
Walther. 48 pp. 8vo. M. 0.20.
Goldstein, F. Unchristentum u. Sozialdemokratie.
Zürich, C. Schmidt. 191 pp. 8vo. M. 3.
Jentsch, Karl. Rodbertus. Stuttgart, F. From-
mann. 259 pp. 8vo. M. 3.80.
Kampffmeyer, Paul. Mehr Macht. Kritische
Streiflichter auf das Erfurter Programm der
deut. Sozialdemokratie. B., Verlag der
sozialist. Monatshefte. 39 pp. 8vo. M. 0.30.
Kautsky, Karl. Die Agrarfrage. Eine Uebersicht
über die Tendenzen der modernen Landwirth-
schaft u. die Agrarpolitik der Sozialdemokratie.
St., J. H. W. Dietz. 451 pp. 8vo. M. 5.
Tucker, B. R. State socialism & anarchism, how
far they agree and wherein they differ. N. Y.,
B. R. Tucker. 33 pp. 16mo. $0.05.

18. Sociology.

Barbagallo, Corrado. Pel materialismo storico.
Roma, Ermanno Laescher e C. 115 pp. 8vo.
L. 1.50.
Barolin, J. Entlastung der Gemeinden. Lösung
der socialen Frage durch Schaffg. des socialen
Staats im freien Staate. . . . Wien, Selbstverlag.
15 pp. 8vo. M. 0.40.

Bloch, J. v. Der Krieg. Uebersetz. des russ.
Werkes des Autors: Der zukünft. Krieg, in
seiner techn., volkswirthschaftl. u. polit. Be-
deutg. (In 8 Bdn.) 1. u. 6. Bd. M. 8 u. 4.
Chironi, G. P. L'individualismo e la funzione
sociale: discorso inaugurale. Torino, fratelli
Bocca. 19 pp. 8vo. L. 1.
Gumplowicz. Soziologische Essays. Innsbruck,
Wagner. 174 pp. 8vo. M. 2.
Inaugurazione dell' anno scolastico 1898-99 nel r.
istituto di scienze sociali Cesare Alfieri in
Firenze. Firenze, Salvadore Landi, 1899. 25
pp. 8vo.
La Grasserie, R. de. Mémoire sur les rapports
entre la psychologie et la sociologie. P.,
impr. nationale. 24 pp. 8vo.
Loria, Achille. L'antropologia sociale. Firenze,
tip. Cooperativa, 1898. 13 pp. 8vo. (Estr.
La Rivista moderna, 1898.)
Mackenzie, H. Scotland's share in civilizing the
world. N. Y. & Chi., F. H. Revell. 190 pp.
12mo. $1.
Reinhardt, L. Die einheitliche Lebensauffassung
als Grundlage f. die soziale Neugeburt.
Strassburg, L. Beust. 424 pp. 8vo. M. 3.60.
Rendsa, Carl. Die wichtigsten Fragen des Volks-
wahls. Zur Belehrg. f. Jedermann. Ein
Beitrag zur Besserg. unserer wirthschaftl. u.
sozialen Verhältnisse. Lp., W. Friedrich.
50 pp. 8vo. M. 0.80.
Rommel, O. Das Recht zu leben od. der Völker-
frühling. Soziale Betrachtung üb. Krieg,
menschl. Elend, Duelle, Todesstrafe u. Tötgn.
in Nötwehr u. Notstand. Ein Beitrag zur
Lösg. der sozialen Frage. München, A.
Schupp. 94 pp. 8vo. M. 1.
Sacher, Ed. Die Gesellschaftskunde als Natur-
wissenschaft. Dresden, E. Pierson. 358 pp.
8vo. M. 4.
Walter, F. Socialpolitik u. Moral. Eine Dar-
stellg. ihres Verhältnisses m. besond. Bezug-
nahme auf die v. Prof. Werner Sombart neue-
stens geförderte Unabhängigkeit der Socialpolitik v. der Moral. F., Herder. 346 pp. 8vo.
M. 3.60.

19. Statistics.

Austria — Statist. Depart. im k. k. Handelsministerium. 69. Bd. 1. u. 2. Hft. Statistik
des österreichischen Post- u. Telegraphen-
wesens im J. 1897. Mit e. statist. Uebersicht
üb. die Post u. den Telegraphen in Europa.
1898. 334 pp. 8vo. M. 5.
*Blenck, E. Das königliche statistische Bureau
während der Jahre 1885-96. B., Königl.
statist. Bureau, 1898. 180 pp. 8vo. M. 2.80.
(DL., Ja. 7)
Budapest — Statist. Bureau. Publikationen.
XXV, 3, u. XXVI-XXVIII. B., Puttkammer
& Mühlbrecht, 1898, 8vo. M. 5, 6 u. 1.50.
Faulkner, R. P. Development of the census.
Ph., Am. Acad. Pol. & Soc. Sci., 1898. pp.
34-62. 8vo. $0.25. (Publications of the
society, no. 240)
France — Ministère des colonies. Résumé des
statistiques coloniales pour les années, 1892-5.
P., Impr. nationale, 1898. 465 pp. 8vo.
France — Ministère du commerce. Statistique an-
nuelle. Année 1896. P., Impr. nationale.
225 pp. 8vo.
Germany — Kaiserl. statist. Amt. Statistik des
Deutschen Reichs. Neue Folge. 113. Bd.
Berufs- u. Gewerbezählung von 1895. Ge-
werbestatistik f. das Reich im Ganzen. 543 pp.
4to. M. 6.
Germany — Kaiserl. statist. Amt. Vierteljahrshefte zur Statistik des Deutschen Reichs.
Jahrg. 1898. Ergänzung zum 3. Hft. Statistik
der Reichstagswahlen, 1898. Ergänzung zum

4. Hft. Die deutsche Handels-Statistik nach ihrem gegenwärt. Gam-Ein- u. Ausfuhr, 1889-97. B., Puttkammer & Mühlbrecht. 78 u. 45 pp. 4to. M, 1 u. 1.
Great Britain — Parliament. Judicial statistics of England & Wales, 1897. Pt. 1. Criminal statistics. . . . L., Eyte & Spottiswoode. 1s. 10½ d.
Great Britain — Parliament. Trade & navigation for Oct., 1898. L., Eyre & Spottiswoode, 1898. 8vo. 8½ d.
Hartleben's statistiches Taschenbuch üb. alle Länder der Erde. 6. Jahrg. 1899. Nach den neuesten Angaben. . . . Wien, H. Hartleben. 96 pp. 16mo. M. 1.50.
Körösy, Jos. v. Einfluss der Confession, Wohlstandes u. der Beschäft. auf die Todesursachen. [Aus Publikation Nr. 26 des statist. Bureau . . . Budapest.] B., Puttkammer & Mühlbrecht, 1898. 97 pp. 8vo. M. 2.
Prussia — Königl. statist. Bureau. Gemeindelexikon f. das Königr. Preussen. Auf Grund der Materialien der Volkszählgn. vom . . . 1895. Generalregister, 2 Bde. (Bd., A–K. 597 pp. 8vo. M. 16.40.
Statistical abstract for the several colonial & other possessions of the United Kingdom in each year from 1883–97. L., Eyre & Spottiswoode. 8vo. 1s. 6d.
Statistisches Jahrbuch der Stadt Berlin. 23. Jahrg. Statistik des J. 1896 nebst den weiteren Ergebnissen der beiden Volkszählgn. vom J. 1895. Hrsg. v. R. Boekh. B., P. Stankiewicz. 613 pp. 8vo. M. 10.
Statistisches Jahrbuch deutscher Städte. Hrsg. v. M. Neefe. 7. Jahrg. Breslau, W. G. Korn. 416 pp. 8vo. M. 12.60.
Théry, E. Europe et Etats-Unis d'Amérique. Statistique d'ensemble. " Maritimimisme ;" Populations ; Dépenses budgetaires, dettes publiques; Chemins de fer, Commerce, etc. P., libr. Flammarion. 352 pp. 8vo. f. 3.50.
Zeitschrift f. die schweizerische Statistik. Journal de statistique suisse. Hrsg. v. der Centralkommission der schweizer. statist. Gesellschaft . . . 35. Jahrg. 1899. Bern, Schmid & Francke in Komm. 260 pp. 8vo. M. 4.

20. Unclassified.

Annuaire-Almanach du commerce, de l'industrie, de la magistrature et de l'administration, ou Almanach des 1,500,000 adresses de Paris, des departements, des colonies et des pays étrangers. 3 v. in 4to. 2 to 4 pp each. P., 54 rue Jacob.
Brown, Mary W. Development of thrift. N. Y., Macmillan Co. 222 pp. 16mo. $1.
Dangers (les) de l'alcool et de l'alcoolisme. Petit manuel à l'usage de l'armée. Extrait des

brochures et conférences de M. le docteur Laborde. 13e éd. P., libr. Ch. Lavauzelle. 35 pp. 32mo.
Dow, Neal. Reminiscences. Portland, Me., *Evening Express* Pub. Co. 781 pp. 8vo. $2.50.
Ducroquet, P. Une nouvelle institution sociale : la Société de prévoyance des functionaires et employés tunisiens. 44 pp. 8vo. Amiens, impr. Jeunet.
Gordon, F. G. R. The govt. ownership of railways. C., C. H. Kerr & Co. 32 pp. 16mo. $0.10.
Great Britain — Royal Commission on liquor licensing laws. V. 8. Minutes of evidence. V. 9. Summary of reports of commissions . . . . since 1800. L., Eyre & Spottiswoode. 3s. 6d. & 1s. 7d.
Herron, G. D. Between Cæsar & Jesus. N. Y., T. Y. Crowell & Co. 278 pp. 12mo. $0.75.
Koppe, Hugo. Die Thatsachen üb. den Alkohol . . . . Mit zahlreichen statist. Tabellen. Dresden, O. V. Bohmert. 168 pp. 8vo. M. 3.60.
[Landwirthschaftliches Jahrbuch. Zeitschrift f. wissenschaftl. Landwirthschaft u Archiv des königl. preuss. Landes-Oekonomie-Kollegiums. Hrsg. v. H. Thiel. 27. Bd. 1898. 4. u. 5. Ergänzungsbd. B., P. Parez. M 18 u. 13.]
Newcomb, H. T. Railway economics. Phil., Railway World Pub. Co., 1898. 152 pp. 12mo. $1.
Sekon, G. A. Evolution of the steam locomotive, 1803-98. 336 pp. 8vo. 5s.
Shipping world year-book, 1899 : a desk manual in trade, commerce & navigation, ed. by E. R. Jones. L., *Shipping World* office. 1144 pp. 8vo. 5s.
Systematische Zusammenstellung der Zolltarife des In- u. Auslandes. B. Industrie der Metalle, Stein u. Erden. Hrsg. im Reichsamt des Innern. B., E. S. Mittler & Sohn. 475 pp. 4to. M. 3.
Trueblood, B. F. The federation of the world. Bo., Houghton, Mifflin & Co. 162 pp. 8vo. $1.
•Waxweiler, Emile. Participation aux bénéfices. P., A. Rousseau. 320 pp. 8vo. (YR., F. +—)
Webersik, Glieb. Weltpost-Statistik. Telegraphen- u. Telephonverkehr, Postsparkassenwesen. Wien, G. Freytag & Berndt. 27 pp. 12mo. M. 2.
Wilkinson, F. The story of the cotton plant. N. Y., Appleton. 191 pp. 16mo. $0.40.
Wilson, W. B. Hist. of the Pennsylvania railroad company, with plan of organization, portraits of officials & biographical sketches. Phil., H. T. Coates & Co. 2 v. (418 & 323 pp.) 8vo. $5.

ARTICLES IN PERIODICALS.

[Articles preceded by stars and followed by a reference to a number of the JOURNAL will be found in abstract under the head " Notes and Abstracts" in that number of the JOURNAL. Articles dealing with *Biography, Associations, Cities,* and *Towns* will be found grouped under those heads.]

Æsthetics: Galabert, E. Les fondements de l'esthétique scientifique, RIS., Ja.
Marschner, Franz. Grundfragen der Aesthetik im Lichte der immanenten Philosophie, Zeit. f. immanenten Philosophie, 4:1.
See also Art, Landscape Gardening.
Africa: Roberts, Morley. War game in South Africa, FR., F.
Wills, J. T. "The Cape to Cairo," CoR., F.
Wirtschaftliche Erschliessung Deutsch-Südwest-Afrikas, Globus, F. 25.
Agriculture: Kurs, Victor. Abgabenfreiheit

der deutschen Ströme u. die deutsche Landwirthschaft, JNS., 77 : 2.
See also Italy, Political Economy.
Anarchism: Bloch, J. Les théories anarchistes et leur rapports avec le communisme, HN., Mr.
Animals: see Psychology.
Anthropology: Closson, C. C. Further data of anthropo-sociology, JPE., Mr.
Onnis, E. A. Contributo all'antropologia della Sardegna, RAE., 28 : 2.

Cuba: Porter, R. Future of Cuba, NAR., Ap.
Wolf, Julius. Die Eroberung Kubas durch die Vereinigten Staaten und die Zukunft der europäischen Zuckerindustrie, ZS., F.
Democracy: *see* Labor.
Divorce: The Holy Scriptures & divorce, BS., Ap.
Education: Collins, J. C. A university for the people, NC., Mr.
Demolins, E. L'avenir de l'éducation nouvelle—Conférence faite à la Sorbonne, SS., Mr.
Garmo, C. de. Scientific vs. poetic study of 'education. EdR., Mr.
Hanus, P. H. Secondary education. EdR., Ap.
Hawthorne, Julian. Public schools and parents' duties. NAR., Ap.
Hyde, W. D. President Eliot as an educational reformer, Atlantic, Mr.
Joly, H. L'université, RéfS., Mr. 16.
Milner, Florence. School management from the side of social life, School Review, Ap.
(The) Sirdar's College at Khartoum, CoR., F.
Report of the Chicago Educational Commission, EdR., Mr.
Robinson, C. M. Vacation schools, EdR., Mr.
Russell, J. E. Training teachers for secondary schools, EdR., Ap.
Stimson, H. Evolution of the college president, RRN., Ap.
Tetlow, J. The high-school principal, EdR., Mr.
Thwing, C. Pecuniary aid for poor and able students. F., Ap.
See also Science.
Elections: *see* Political Science.
Ethics: Cantoni, C. Sulla morale, RIF., N.-D.
Fisk, John. Mystery of evil, Atlantic, Ap.
Fowler, T. Ethics of intellectual life and work, IJE., Ap.
Lefevre, A. Significance of Butler's view of human nature, PhR., Mr.
See also Modesty, Sociology.
Ethnology: Ripley, W. The peoples of the Balkan peninsula. PSM., Mr.
Zemmrich, J. Deutsches und französisches Volkstum in der Schweiz, Globus. Mr. 4.
Evolution: Cunningham, J. T. Professor Weldon's evidence of the operation of natural selection, NS., Ja.
Mantegazza, Paolo. L'evoluzione regressiva, AAL., 28: 2.
Expansion: *see* Imperialism.
Finance: American booms and bungling, Journal of Finance, F.
Badiani, A. G. Il problema monetario latino e la questione dell'argento, RISS., Mr.
Bynum, W. Needed reforms in our monetary system, F., Mr.
Conant, C. A. Development of credit, JPE., Mr.
De Greef, G., et. Dénis, H. Banque nationale de Belgique, AISS., 5: 1-2.
Dingley, N. Service of national revenue. NAR., Mr.
Greef, G. de. Essais sur la monnaie, le crédit et les banques, ReS., Mr.
Lambrechts, Hector. Le crédit urbain, RSC., Mr.
Lévy, R. G. Finances égyptiennes, RDM., F. 1.
Lévy, R. G. Taux actuel de l'intérêt et de ses rapports avec la production des métaux précieux et les autres phénomènes économiques, JEc., Mr.
Lubbock, Sir John. The Indian currency, CoR., F.
Marx, K. L'argent ou la circulation simple, HN., Mr.
Neumann, F. J. Geschichte der Lehre von der

Gravitation der Löhne nach gewissen Kostenbeträgen, JNS., 77:2.
Reuton, D. Investment of surplus revenue, EcJ., Mr.
Van Oss, S. Malthusian view of wealth, Journal of Finance, F.
See also Gold, Saving.
France: Blondel, G. Les ennemis de notre progrès économique, RéfS., Ap. 1.
Brunetière, F. Les ennemis de l'âme française, RéfS., Ap. 1.
Coubertin, P. France since 1814, FR., F.
Drumont & others. Zola, the Dreyfus case & the anti-Jewish crusade in France, RRN., Mr.
Lacombe, P. La question cruelle, RMM., Mr.
Maeterlinck. Le 18 Brumaire, CoR., F.
See also Judiciary.
Germany: Industrial boom in Germany, Journal of Finance, Mr.
See also Colonies.
Gold: Outerbridge, A. Marvelous increase in production of gold, PSM., Mr.
Great Britain: Pressense, Frances de. England & France, CoR., F.
Young, J. Menace to England's commercial supremacy, F., Ap.
See also Colonies.
Heredity: Alden, S. P. Environment versus heredity, ChR., Ap.
History: Lamprecht, Karl. Wandlungen in der Auffassung der Aufgaben der Geschichtswissenschaft, ZS., F.
New Haven meeting of the Amer. Hist. Assoc., AHR., Ap.
Immigration: Ottolenghi, C. Le migrazioni del lavoro agli Stati Uniti d'America, GEc., Mr.
Imperialism: Louis, P. L'imperialisme Anglo-Saxon, ReS., F.
Our right to acquire and hold foreign territory, ALRv., Mr., Ap.
Potter, H. National bigness or greatness—which?, NAR., Ap.
Teichmueller, H. Expansion and the constitution, ALRv., Mr.
Thayer, J. B. Our new possessions, HLR., Mr.
Walton, J. Lawson. Imperialism, CoR., Mr.
India: Jones, J. British rule in India, NAR., Mr.
Muller, F. A prime minister and a child-wife, FR., F.
See also Finance.
Industry: *see* Russia.
Insane: Stedman, H. R. The after care of the insane, ChR., Mr.
Interest: *see* Finance.
International Law: Gilson, J. Le caractère international du droit romain, RDI., Mr.
Interstate Commerce: *see* Railroads.
Invention: Escher, R. Erfinden & Erfinder, ZS., Mr.
Italy: Dehou. La crise agricole et l'action catholique en Italie, AC., Ja.
Gatti, G. Les partis politiques et l'agriculture en Italie, ReS., Mr.
Ward, W. &, Ouida. Italy, FR., Mr.
Japan: Lettre du Japon, JEc., Mr.
Toru-Terao. Les relations entre l'Europe et le Japon, RHD., 13: 1.
Jews: Passy, Frédéric. La vraie solution de la question juive, JEc., F.
Judiciary: Calonne, Comte de. French judicial system, NC., Mr.
Korea: Hulbert, Homer. Korea and the Koreans, F., Ap.
Labor: Carrington, Earl. The land & the laborers. NC., Mr.
Gannett, W. C. Béni soit le joug du travail quotidien, RCS., Mr.

Solomons. L. M. Alleged proof of parallelism from the conservation of energy, PhR., Mr.
See also Sociology.
Seal Question: Clark, A. Scientific experts & the Bering Sea controversy, PSM., Mr.
Sexes: Oliphant, J. Relations of the sexes, IJE., Ap.
Shipping: Dunell, G. R. The prospective expansion of American ship-building, EM., Ap.
Socialism: Ingegnieros, J. Le socialisme en Argentine, HN., F.
Justinien, Laurent. Catholicisme social et démocratie chrétienne, AC., F.
Pascal, G. de. Conceptions philosophiques et historiques du socialisme allemand, AC., Mr.
Rossignoli, Giovanni. Democrazia cristiana e diritto divino, RISS., F.
Sorel, G. Y a-t-il de l'utopie dans le marxisme? RMM., Mr.
See also Sociology.
Sociology: Achelis, T. Die Philosophie in ihrer Erneuerung durch Sociologie und Psychologie, ZS., Mr.
Ammon, O. Some social applications of the doctrine of probability, JPE., Mr.
Araujo, Oscar d'. L'hyperpositivisme de M. de Roberty, HN., Mr.
Asturio. A. La scienza morale e la sociologia generale, RiIS., Ja.
Baldwin, J. M. The social & the extra-social, AJS., Mr.
Barth, P. Die Frage des sittlichen Fortschritts der Menschheit, VWP., 23: 1.
Benini, R. Gerarchie sociali.—Contributo alla teoria qualitativa della popolazione, RiIS., Ja.
Delbet, E. Les bases sociales d'après Auguste Comte, RISS., Ja.
Duprat, G. L. Morphologie des faits sociaux, RIS., F.
Elwood, C. A. Prolegomena to social psychology, AJS., Mr.
Fouillée, Alfred. L'idée de justice sociale d'après les écoles contemporaines, RDM., Mr. 1.
Groppali, A. Discussion avec M. le professeur Ardigo sur la sociologie et le matérialisme historique, RIS., Ja.
Groppali, A. La science comme phénomène social, DS., D.
Kimble, R. G. Contributions to the comparative study of association, AJS., Mr.
Lerda, G. Consequenze sociologiche di recenti teorie sull' eredità, RiIS., Ja.
Limousin. Delbet et Tarde. Bases sociales. RIS., F.
Sorel, G. Marxismo e scienza sociale, RiIS., Ja.
Starcke, C. N. Quelques questions sur la méthode de la sociologie, RIS., Ja.
Tolman, W. League for social service, A., Ap.
ard, L. F. Sociology & economics, AAP., WMr.
Zueblin, C. World's first sociological laboratory, AJS., Mr.
See also Anthropology, Churches, United States.
Spain: Clarke, H. Spanish government vs. the nation, F., Ap.

Spanish-American War: Lodge, H. C. Spanish-American war, Harper's, Mr.-Ap.
Speculation: Emery, H. Futures in the grain market, EcJ., Mr.
Street Railways: Garcke, Emile. Commercial aspects of electric traction in Great Britain, EM., Ap.
Monge, F. de. Une question délicate, RSC., Mr.
Streets: *see* Cities.
Strikes: *see* Coöperation.
Suffrage: *see* Negro.
Sugar: Crampton, C. Opportunity of the sugar-cane industry, NAR., Mr.
Sunday: Byles, C. E. Sunday in London, New Century Review, Ap.
Tariff: Reeves, W. Protective tariff in Australia & New Zealand, EcJ., Mr.
Taxation: Guillot, P. La suppression des octrois, RPP., Mr.
Inhülsen, C. H. P. Einkommensteuer in Grossbrittanien und Irland, JNS., 72: 3.'
Manchez, G. L'impôt général sur le revenue, RPP., Mr.
Meyer, R. Die ersten Ergebnisse der Personaleinkommensteuer in Oesterreich, ZVS., 8: 1.
Sanger, C. Is the English system of taxation fair? EcJ., Mr.
Wells, D. Best methods of taxation, PSM., Ap.
Telephone: Hemming, A. Telephonwesen Schwedens, JNS., 77: 2.
Theology: King, H. C. Reconstruction in theology, AJT., Ap.
Trade: Adams., B., & Taylor, B. The commercial future, FR., F.
Magee, Louis J. America & Germany as export competitors & customers, EM., Mr.
Trade Unions: *see* Labor.
Tramps: Lambert, A. Un étrange délit; le vagabondage, RP., F.
Trusts: The future of trusts, BS., Ap.
Macrosty, H. W. The growth of monopoly in British industry, CoR., Mr.
Morgan, F. W. Great problems in organization, Cosmopolitan, Ap.
See also Capital.
United States: Frost, W. G. Our contemporary ancestors in the southern mountains, Atlantic, Mr.
Grasso, G. Nouveaux freins dans les institutions politiques américaines, RPP., Mr.
See also Army, Cuba, Imperialism, Mail, Navies, Philippines, Railroads, Trade, War.
Vacant-Lot Cultivation: Chastaud, G. Choses à faire: les jardins ouvriers, RCS., Mr.
Vacant-lot cultivation, ChR., Mr., p. 5.
Vacation Schools: *see* Education.
War: Rowe, L. Influence of the war on our public life, F., Mr.
Wyatt, H. F. War as the supreme test of national value, NC., F.
Wealth: Powers, H. H. Wealth and welfare, AAP., Mr.
Wheat: Atkinson, Edward. Wheat problem again, PSM., Ap.
Block, M. Le commerce des céréales en Amérique et en Europe, RPP., RPP., F.
Wolf, Julius. Die Getreidekonjunktur, ZS., Mr.

ABBREVIATIONS USED IN BIBLIOGRAPHY.

A.	Arena.	JHS.	Johns Hopkins University Studies in History and Political Science.
AA.	American Anthropologist.		
AAC.	Archives d'anthropologie criminelle.	JPE.	Journal of Political Economy.
AAE.	Archivio per l'antropologia e la etnologia.	JNS.	Jahrbücher für National-Oekonomie und Statistik.
AAP.	Annals of the American Academy of Political and Social Science.	LC.	Literarisches Centralblatt.
		LG.	Labor Gazette.
AC.	L'Association catholique.	LoQR.	London Quarterly Review.
ACQ.	American Catholic Quarterly Review.	LQR.	Law Quarterly Review.
AEL.	Annals d'École libre des sciences politiques.	MHM.	Mansfield House Magazine.
		MIM.	Monatsschrift für innere Mission.
AGP.	Archiv für Geschichte der Philosophie.	MA.	Municipal Affairs.
AHR.	American Historical Review.	NA.	Nuova antologia.
AIS.	Annals de l'Institute de science sociale.	NAR.	North American Review.
AJP.	American Journal of Psychology.	NC.	Nineteenth Century.
AJS.	American Journal of Sociology.	NS.	Natural Science.
AJT.	American Journal of Theology.	NT.	New Time.
ALR.	American Law Register.	NW.	New World.
ALRv.	American Law Review.	NZ.	Neue Zeit.
AMP.	Académie des sciences morales et politiques, Séances.	PhR.	Philosophical Review.
		PSM.	Popular Science Monthly.
AOR.	Archiv für öffentliches Recht.	PSQ.	Political Science Quarterly.
ASA.	American Statistical Association, Publications.	PsR.	Psychological Review.
		QJE.	Quarterly Journal of Economics.
ASAr.	Allgemeine statistisches Archiv.	QR.	Quarterly Review.
ASG.	Archive für sociale Gesetzgebung und Statistik.	RBP.	Rivista benificenza publica.
		RCS.	Revue de christianisme sociale.
ASP.	Archiv für systematische Philosophie.	RDC.	Rivista di discipline carcerarie.
BDL.	Bulletin of the Department of Labor.	RDI.	Revue de droit internationale.
BG.	Blätter für Gefängnisskunde.	RDM.	Revue des deux mondes.
BML.	Banker's Magazine, London.	REA.	Revue mensuelle de l'École d'anthropologie de Paris.
BMN.	Banker's Magazine, New York.		
BOT.	Bulletin de l'Office du Travail.	RéfS.	Réforme sociale.
BS.	Bibliotheca Sacra.	ReS.	Revue socialiste.
BSt.	Bulletin de statistique et de legislation comparée.	RH.	Revue historique.
		RHD.	Revue d'histoire diplomatique.
BUI.	Bulletin de l'Union internationale de droit pénale.	RIF.	Rivista italiana di filosofia.
		RIS.	Revue internationale de sociologie.
C.	Cosmopolis.	RiIS.	Rivista italia na di sociologia.
ChOR.	Charity Organisation Review.	RISS.	Rivista internazionale di scienze sociali
ChR.	Charities Review.	RMM.	Revue metaphysique et de morale.
CoR.	Contemporary Review.	RP.	Revue philanthropique.
DL.	Deutsche Litteraturzeitung.	RPe.	Revue pénitentiaire.
DR.	Deutsche Revue.	RPh.	Revue philosophique.
DRu.	Deutsche Rundschau.	RPP.	Revue politique et parliamentaire.
DS.	Devenir social.	RRL.	Review of Reviews, London.
DZG.	Deutsche Zeitschrift für Geschichtswissenschaft.	RRN.	Review of Reviews, New York.
		RSC.	Revue sociale catholique.
EcJ.	Economic Journal.	RSI.	Revista storica italiana.
EcR.	Economic Review.	RSP.	Revue sociale et politique.
EdR.	Educational Review.	RT.	Revue du travail.
EHR.	English Historical Review.	S.	Sanitarian.
EM.	Engineering Magazine.	SR.	School Review.
F.	Forum.	SS.	Science sociale.
FR.	Fortnightly Review.	VWP.	Vierteljahrschrift für wissenschaftliche Philosophie.
GEc.	Giornale degli economisti.		
GM.	Gunton's Magazine.	YR.	Yale Review.
HLR.	Harvard Law Review.	ZE.	Zeitschrift für Ethnologie.
HN.	Humanité nouvelle.	ZGS.	Zeitschrift für die gesammte Staatswissenschaften.
HR.	Hygienische Rundschau.		
HZ.	Historische Zeitschrift.	ZPK.	Zeitschrift für Philosophie und philosophische Kritik.
IAE.	Internationales Archiv für Ethnographie.		
IJE.	International Journal of Ethics.	ZPO.	Zeitschrift für das private und öffentliche Recht.
JAI.	Journal of the Anthropological Institute of Great Britain and Ireland.	ZPP.	Zeitschrift für Psychologie und Physiologie der Sinnesorgane.
JCB.	Journal of the Canadian Bankers' Association.		
		ZS.	Zeitschrift für Socialwissenschaft.
JEc.	Journal des économistes.	ZVR.	Zeitschrift für vergleichende Rechtswissenschaft.
JFI.	Journal of the Franklin Institute.		
JGV.	Jahrbuch für Gesetzgebung, Verwaltung und Volkswirthschaft.	ZVS.	Zeitschrift für Volkswirthschaft, Socialpolitik und Verwaltung.

[The titles of articles selected from periodicals not in this list will be followed by name of periodical in full.]

INDEX.

Lightning Source UK Ltd.
Milton Keynes UK
UKHW031834290119
336364UK00006B/226/P

9 780483 502963